Discovering Psychology

Survival Guide #1 (collage, 24" x 48", 1995)

Phoebe Beasley, an American artist and lithographer created the collages that appear on the cover and chapter-opening pages of this book. She has been named Woman of the Year by the Los Angeles *Sentinel* and Black Woman of Achievement by the NAACP Legal Defense and Education Fund. Ms. Beasley's luminous collages bring the viewer face to face with all kinds of people and their unique, yet universal, stories. Similarly, psychologists study a variety of experiences—love, hate, sexuality, growing up and growing old, dreaming—looking for general patterns underlying human individuality. The personal narratives portrayed in Ms. Beasley's work, like those in the chapter prologues, reflect common experiences and help us in our quest to understand humankind.

Discovering Psychology

Don H. Hockenbury

Tulsa Community College

Sandra E. Hockenbury

WORTH PUBLISHERS

Discovering Psychology

Copyright © 1998 by Worth Publishers, Inc.

All rights reserved

Manufactured in the United States of America

Library of Congress Catalog Card Number: 97–062139

ISBN: 1–57259–415–2

  1–57259–556–6 (complimentary copy)

Printing: 2 3 4 5   01 00 99 98

Executive Editor: Catherine Woods

Development Editor: Cecilia Gardner

Design: Malcolm Grear Designers

Art Director: George Touloumes

Production Editor: Timothy Prairie

Production Manager: Patricia Lawson

Picture Editor: June Lundborg Whitworth

Graphic Arts Manager: Demetrios Zangos

Line Art: Monotype Composition Company, Inc.

Illustrations: J/B Woolsey Associates

Cover and Chapter Opener Art: Phoebe Beasley

Composition and Prepress: Monotype Composition Company, Inc.

Printing and Binding: R. R. Donnelley and Sons

Illustration credits begin on page IC-1 and constitute an extension of the copyright page.

Value Pack bundled items with corresponding ISBN numbers:

Hockenbury and Hockenbury: **Discovering Psychology** & Rea: **Study Guide** (1–57259–662–7)

Hockenbury and Hockenbury: **Discovering Psychology** & Rea: **Study Guide** & Ludwig: **PsychQuest** CD-ROM (1–57259–667–8)

Hockenbury and Hockenbury: **Discovering Psychology** & Rea: **Study Guide** & Ludwig: **PsychSim 4.0** (Windows version) (1–57259–668–6)

Hockenbury and Hockenbury: **Discovering Psychology** & Rea: **Study Guide** & Ludwig: **PsychSim 4.0** (Macintosh version) (1–57259–669–4)

Hockenbury and Hockenbury: **Discovering Psychology** & Rea: **Study Guide** & Ludwig: **PsychSim 4.0** (CD-ROM version) (1–57259–670–8)

Worth Publishers

33 Irving Place

New York, NY 10003

**To Erv and Fern,
with love**

About the Authors

Don and Sandra E. Hockenbury are the authors of *Psychology,* published in 1997. As an author team, they bring their unique talents and abilities to the teaching of introductory psychology.

Don H. Hockenbury is an Assistant Professor of Psychology at Tulsa Community College, where he has taught undergraduate psychology courses since 1978. Don received his B.S. in psychology and his M.A. in clinical psychology from The University of Tulsa. Before he began his teaching career, Don worked in psychiatric facilities and in private practice. With twenty years of experience in teaching introductory psychology, Don appreciates the challenges of engaging the diverse students of today's college classrooms and of showing them the scientific nature and the personal relevance of psychology. Before co-authoring *Psychology* and *Discovering Psychology,* Don served as a reviewer and supplements author for several psychology textbooks. Don is an associate member of the American Psychological Association and a member of the American Psychological Society.

Sandra E. Hockenbury is a science writer who specializes in psychology. Sandy received her B.A. from Shimer College and her M.A. from the University of Chicago, where she was also a Research Associate at the Institute of Social and Behavioral Pathology. Prior to co-authoring *Psychology* and *Discovering Psychology,* Sandy worked for several years as a psychology editor in both academic and college textbook publishing. Sandy's particular areas of interest are cross-cultural psychology, comparative cognition, and nonconscious processes. Sandy has also taught as an adjunct faculty member at Tulsa Community College. She is a member of the American Psychological Society.

Don and Sandy have a delightfully energetic seven-year-old daughter named Laura, a calorically challenged tail-less cat named Nubbin, and a house in the woods outside of Tulsa, Oklahoma. They are still happily married, despite having co-written two books and numerous other publications.

New Concept Training Center

Certified Prometric Testing Center

136-87 Roosevelt Ave. 3rd Floor

Flushing, NY 11354

CERTIFICATE OF ACHIEVEMENT

This certificate is presented to

Badar Chaudhry

Has satisfactorily completed

Advance Java Developer

(JBuilder, Servlets, JSP, RMI, JDBC, SQL Server)

In witness whereof, We have caused this Certificate to be signed this from February 3rd , 2001 to March 10th , 2001

Susan Wang

Authorized Signature

Contents in Brief

Contents

CHAPTER 1

Introducing Psychology

CHAPTER 2

The Biological Foundations of Behavior

CHAPTER 3

Sensation and Perception

CHAPTER 4

Consciousness and Its Variations

CHAPTER 5

Learning

CHAPTER 6

Memory

CHAPTER 7

Thinking, Language, and Intelligence

CHAPTER 8

Motivation and Emotion

CHAPTER 9

Lifespan Development

CHAPTER 10

Personality

Prologue: The Secret Twin **359**

CHAPTER 11

Social Psychology

Prologue: The "Homeless" Man **399**

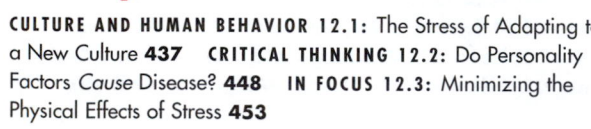

To the Instructor

The publication of *Psychology* in 1997 represented the culmination of many years of intensive research and writing for us. Following its publication, we had the opportunity to meet and exchange views with psychology faculty at teaching conferences and on visits to college campuses. As we talked with other professors, we became aware of the many different kinds of teaching situations faced by psychology faculty at other institutions. Recognizing that many psychology faculty find a concise text more suitable for their goals in teaching introductory psychology, we created *Discovering Psychology.*

Although *Discovering Psychology* is a new text, it shares many features with its predecessor and parent text, *Psychology. Discovering Psychology* continues to reflect our determination to remain true to the goals that have guided us, as teachers and textbook authors, over the past several years. Indeed, we invite you to explore every element of *Discovering Psychology* so that you can see firsthand how we:

- Communicate the scientific rigor and personal relevance of psychology

- Show how classic psychological studies set the stage for today's research

- Clearly explain psychological concepts and how they are linked

- Encourage and model critical thinking

- Expand student awareness of cultural and gender influences

- Actively engage diverse students, including adult learners

- Create a warm, personal learning environment

- Provide an effective pedagogical system to help students test for retention *and* help them learn how to learn.

On the surface, the obvious challenge was to accomplish these goals in a new text that was almost 200 pages shorter than *Psychology.* But for us as authors, the real challenge was to meet our goals in a way that created a concise introductory text with its own identity and integrity. Thus, we obsessively scrutinized every topic, feature, and illustration. We reorganized many discussions to retain the emphasis on important ideas and concepts. And, we rewrote many sections to condense information without losing the clarity of explanations.

Features of *Discovering Psychology*

Every feature and element in this text was carefully developed and serves a specific purpose. From comprehensive surveys, reviewers, and our many discussions with faculty and students, we learned what elements people wanted in a text and why they thought those features were important tools that enhanced the learning process. Armed with that information, we surveyed the research literature on text comprehension, student learning, and memory. We acquired many valuable insights from the work of cognitive and educational psychologists. Described below are the features that we decided to incorporate into *Discovering Psychology* and how those features enhance the learning process.

The Narrative Approach

As you'll quickly discover, our book has a distinctive voice. From the very first page of this text, the reader comes to know us as people and teachers through carefully selected stories and anecdotes. Many of our friends and relatives also graciously allowed us to tell stories about their lives. The stories are quite varied—some are funny, others are dramatic, and some are deeply personal. All of them are true.

The stories we tell reflect one of the most effective teaching methods— the **narrative approach.** In addition to engaging the reader, each story serves as a pedagogical springboard to illustrate important concepts and ideas. Every story is used to connect new ideas, terms, and ways of looking at behavior to information with which the student is already familiar.

Associate the new with the old in some natural and telling way, so that the interest, being shed along from point to point, finally suffuses the entire system of objects. . . . Anecdotes and reminiscences [should] abound in [your] talk; and the shuttle of interest will shoot backward and forward, weaving the new and the old together in a lively and entertaining way.

William James *Talks to Teachers* (1899)

Prologues

As part of the narrative approach, every chapter begins with a **Prologue,** a true story about ordinary people with whom students can readily identify. Each Prologue effectively introduces the chapter's themes and lays the groundwork for explaining why the topics treated by the chapter are important. The Prologue establishes a link between familiar experiences and new information—a key ingredient in facilitating learning. Later in the chapter, we return to the people and stories introduced in the Prologue, further reinforcing the link between familiar experiences and new ways of conceptualizing them.

Logical Organization, Continuity, and Clarity

As you read the chapters in *Discovering Psychology,* you'll see that each one tells the story of a major topic in psychology in a logical way that flows continuously from beginning to end. Themes are clearly established in the first pages of the chapter. Throughout the chapter, we come back to those themes as we present subtopics and specific research studies. Chapters are very thoughtfully organized so that students can easily see how ideas are connected. The writing is carefully paced to maximize student interest and comprehension. Rather than simply mentioning terms and findings, we explain concepts clearly. And we use analogies and everyday examples, rather than metaphors, to help students grasp abstract concepts and ideas.

Paradoxically, one of the ways that we maintain narrative continuity throughout each chapter is through the use of in-text boxes. The boxes provide an opportunity to explore a particular topic in depth without losing the narrative thread of the chapter. The **In Focus boxes** do just that—they focus on interesting topics in more depth than the chapter's organization would allow. These boxes highlight interesting research, answer questions that students commonly ask, or show students how psychological research can be applied in their own lives. *Discovering Psychology* includes the following In Focus boxes:

- Questions About the Use of Animals in Psychology Research (p. 29)
- Do Pheromones Influence Human Sexual Behavior? (p. 94)
- What You *Really* Want to Know About Sleep (p. 128)
- What You *Really* Want to Know About Dreams (p. 136)
- Watson, Classical Conditioning, and Advertising (p. 165)
- Changing the Behavior of Others: Alternatives to Punishment (p. 170)
- Biological Preparedness and Conditioned Fears: What Gives You the Creeps? (p. 187)
- Does a High IQ Score Predict Success in Life? (p. 253)
- Everything You Wanted to Know About Sexual Fantasies (p. 292)
- Explaining Those Amazing Identical Twin Similarities (p. 388)
- Minimizing the Physical Effects of Stress (p. 453)
- Self-Help Groups: Helping Yourself by Helping Others (p. 515)

Scientific Emphasis

Many first-time psychology students walk into the classroom operating on the assumption that psychology is nothing more than common sense or a matter of opinion. Clearly, students need to come away from an introductory psychology course with a solid understanding of the scientific nature of the discipline. To help you achieve that goal, we show students in every chapter how the scientific method has been applied to help answer different kinds of questions about behavior and mental processes.

Because we carefully guide students through the details of specific experiments and studies, students develop a solid understanding of how scientific evidence is gathered and the interplay between theory and research. And, because we rely on original rather than secondary sources, students get an accurate presentation of both classic and contemporary psychological studies.

One unique way that we highlight the scientific method in *Discovering Psychology* is with **Science Versus Pseudoscience boxes.** In these boxes, students see the importance of subjecting various claims to standards of scientific evidence. These boxes focus on topics that students frequently ask about in class. *Discovering Psychology* includes the following Science Versus Pseudoscience boxes:

- Iridology (p. 82)
- Biorhythms Versus Circadian Rhythms (p. 123)

- Remembering Past Lives (p. 213)
- Subliminal Self-Help Tapes: Effortless Motivation? (p. 297)
- Is Your Personality Written in the Stars? (p. 393)

Critical Thinking Emphasis

Another important goal of *Discovering Psychology* is to encourage the development of critical thinking skills. To that end, we do not present psychology as a series of terms, definitions, and facts to be skimmed and memorized. Rather, we try to give students an understanding of how particular topics evolved. In doing so, we also demonstrate the process of challenging preconceptions, evaluating evidence, and revising theories based on new evidence. In short, every chapter shows the process of psychological research—and the important role played by critical thinking in that enterprise.

Because we do not shrink from discussing the implications of psychological findings, students come to understand that many important issues in contemporary psychology are far from being settled. Even when research results are consistent, how to interpret those results can be the subject of considerable debate. In encouraging students to join these debates, we often challenge them to be aware of how their own preconceptions and opinions can shape their evaluation of the evidence.

Beyond discussions in the text proper, virtually every chapter includes one or more **Critical Thinking boxes.** These boxes are carefully designed to encourage students to think about the broader implications of psychological research—to strengthen and refine their critical thinking skills by developing their own position on questions and issues that don't always have simple answers. Often, we leave the students with specific issues to think about, or questions that you can use in classroom discussions. The Critical Thinking boxes in *Discovering Psychology* include:

- What Is Critical Thinking? (p. 14)
- "His" and "Her" Brains? (p. 63)
- ESP: Can Perception Occur Without Sensation? (p. 99)
- Hypnosis: A Special State of Consciousness? (p. 142)
- Is Human Freedom Just an Illusion? (p. 172)
- Recovering "Repressed" Memories of Childhood Sexual Abuse (pp. 219–220)
- The Persistence of Unwarranted Beliefs (p. 245)
- The Effects of Child Care on Attachment and Development (p. 327)
- Freud Versus Rogers on Human Nature (p. 376)
- Freud Versus Bandura on Human Aggression (p. 381)
- The Ethics of Milgram's Obedience Experiments (p. 420)
- Do Personality Factors *Cause* Disease? (p. 448)
- Media Images of Mental Illness (p. 464)
- Is DID a Real Psychological Disorder? (p. 484)
- Prozac: Better Living Through Chemistry? (p. 525)

Cultural Coverage

As you can see in Table 1, we weave cultural coverage throughout many discussions in the text. But because students are usually unfamiliar wth cross-cultural psychology, we also highlight specific topics in **Culture and Human Behavior boxes.** These boxes increase student awareness of the importance of culture in many areas of human experience. They are unique in that they go beyond simply describing cultural differences in behavior. Instead, they show students how cultural influences shape behavior and attitudes, including the student's own behavior and attitudes. *Discovering Psychology* has the following Culture and Human Behavior boxes:

- What Is Cross-Cultural Psychology? (p. 10)
- Culture and Visual Illusions (p. 110)
- Do Cultural Beliefs Affect Memory in Old Age? (p. 227)
- The Effect of Language on Perception (p. 247)
- Who's More Emotional—Men or Women? (p. 301)
- Where Does the Baby Sleep? (p. 326)
- Attributional Biases in Collectivistic Versus Individualistic Cultures (p. 406)
- The Stress of Adapting to a New Culture (p. 437)
- From Cannibals to Computer Games (p. 487)
- Cultural Values and Psychotherapy (pp. 518–519)

TABLE 1 Integrated Cultural Coverage

Page(s)	Topic	Page(s)	Topic
9–11	Cross-cultural perspective in contemporary psychology	262	Changes in IQ scores in different nations
96	Use of acupuncture in traditional Chinese medicine for pain relief	263–264	Cross-cultural studies of group discrimination and IQ
135	Dream themes in different cultures	264	Role of culture in tests and test-taking behavior
143	Meditation in different cultures	277	Culture's effect on food preferences and eating behavior
149	Use of the stimulant drugs caffeine and nicotine in different cultures	282–283	Standards of female beauty in different cultures
150	Peyote use in religious ceremonies in other cultures	283	Cultural influences on eating disorders
172	Clash of B. F. Skinner's philosophy with American cultural ideals	296	Culture and achievement motivation
		300	Culture and the classification of emotions
201	Seven-item limit of short-term memory in non-Western cultures	301	Cross-cultural studies of physiological arousal associated with emotions
246–248	Properties of language that are common to all cultures	303	Universal facial expressions
252	Historical misuse of IQ tests to evaluate immigrants	304	Cultural display rules in emotional expression
254	Wechsler's consideration of culture in developing intelligence tests	326	Child-rearing practices in other cultures
		328–329	Culture and language development
257	Role of culture in Gardner's and Sternberg's theories of intelligence	328	Cross-cultural research on infant-directed speech
		328	Culture and patterns of language development
260–261	IQ and cross-cultural comparison of educational differences	336–337	Influence of culture on cognitive development
		344	Culture and moral reasoning

(cont.)

TABLE 1 Integrated Cultural Coverage (continued)

Page(s)	Topic	Page(s)	Topic
349	Culture and images of aging	465	Cultural considerations in defining a psychological disorder
370–371	Jung on archetypal images, including mandalas, in different cultures	471	*Taijin kyofusho,* a culture-specific disorder related to social phobia
376	Rogers on cultural factors in the development of antisocial behavior	474	Cultural influences in obsessions and compulsions
		481–482	Role of culture in dissociative experiences
410–414	Culture, stereotyping, and prejudice	484	Screening for dissociative symptoms in different cultures
412	Ethnocentrism	487	Effect of culture on the content of delusions and hallucinations
416	Influence of cultural norms on conformity		
421	Cross-cultural comparisons of destructive social influence	489	Prevalence of schizophrenia in different cultures
436	Cultural differences as source of stress	517	Impact of cultural differences on effectiveness of psychotherapy
455–456	Effect of culture on coping strategies		
463	Role of culture in distinguishing between normal and abnormal behavior	520	Reserpine in traditional medicine in India to treat psychotic symptoms

Gender Coverage

Gender influences and gender differences are also described in many chapter discussions. Table 2 shows the coverage of gender-related issues and topics in *Discovering Psychology,* as well as the coverage of sexuality issues. Also, to highlight the contributions made by female researchers, the full names of researchers are provided in the References section at the end of the text. When researchers are identified using initials instead of first names (as APA style requires), many students automatically assume that the researchers are male.

Chapter Applications

Among all the sciences, psychology is unique in the degree to which it speaks to our daily lives and applies to everyday problems and concerns. The **Application** at the end of each chapter provides an opportunity to present the findings from psychological research that address a wide variety of problems and concerns. In every Application, we present research-based information in a form that students can use to enhance everyday functioning. As you can see in the following list, topics range from improving self-control to overcoming gender differences in handling interpersonal conflict.

- Thinking Critically About Psychology and the Media (p. 30)
- Pumping Neurons: Keeping Your Brain in Shape (pp. 69–70)
- Controlling Pain (p. 112)
- Improving Sleep and Mental Alertness (p. 152)
- Using Learning Principles to Improve Self-Control (pp. 190–191)
- How to Make Those Memories Last (p. 228)
- A Workshop on Creativity (pp. 266–267)
- Bridging the Gender Gap During Emotional Conflict (pp. 310–311)

TABLE 2 Integrated Gender Coverage

Page(s)	Topic	Page(s)	Topic
5–6	Contributions of Mary Whiton Calkins to psychology	319–320	Sex differences in genetic transmission of recessive characteristics
51–52	Endocrine system and effects of sex hormones	330–332	Development of gender identity and gender roles
63	Sex differences in brain structure	338–339	Gender differences in the onset of secondary sex characteristics and sexual behavior
86	Gender differences in color blindness	343–344	Gilligan's research on gender and moral development
94	Pheromones and the menstrual cycle	345–346	Gender differences in friendship patterns and age of first marriage
145	Gender influence on drug effects		
147	Gender and rate of metabolism of alcohol	348	Gender differences in parenting responsibility and stress
248–249	Language, gender stereotypes, and gender bias	367–369	Gender in Freud's theory of psychosexual development
264	Impact of gender stereotypes on test-taking; stereotype threat theory	371	Gender constructs (anima, animus) in Jung's personality theory
280	Sex differences in metabolism rate	371–372	Horney's critique of Freud's view of female psychosexual development
282–283	Standards of female beauty in different cultures		
282–283	Gender and sex differences in rate of eating disorders	374	Critique of sexism in Freud's theory
284–285	Sexual motivation and sexual behavior	411	Gender stereotypes
285–286	Sex differences in the pattern of human sexual response	450–451	Gender differences in social support
287–289	Sexual orientation	466	Gender differences in the prevalence of psychological disorders
289–291	Gender differences in adult sexual behavior and attitudes	470	Gender differences in prevalence of phobias
292	Gender differences in sexual fantasies	477	Gender differences in prevalence of major depression
300–301	Gender differences in emotional experience and expression	477	Gender differences in prevalence of seasonal affective disorder
304	Gender differences in cultural display rules and emotional expression	478	Lack of gender differences in prevalence of bipolar disorder
310–311	Overcoming gender differences during interpersonal conflict	504–505	Contributions of Mary Cover Jones to behavioral therapy

- Raising Psychologically Healthy Children (pp. 353–354)
- Possible Selves: Imagine the Possibilities (pp. 394–395)
- The Persuasion Game (pp. 426–427)
- Providing Effective Social Support (p. 456)
- Understanding and Helping Prevent Suicide (p. 493)
- What to Expect in Psychotherapy (p. 527)

The Pedagogical System

The pedagogical system in *Discovering Psychology* was carefully designed to help students identify important information, test for retention, and learn how to learn. It is easily adaptable to an SQ3R approach, for those instructors who have had success with that technique. The pedagogical system has two key components—Advance Organizers and Concept Reviews—and several supporting features.

We designed the unique **Advance Organizers** several years ago. Major sections are introduced by an Advance Organizer that consists of a one-sentence summary or definition followed by three or four focus questions. The Advance Organizer mentally primes the student for the important information that is to follow and does so in a way that encourages active learning. Students often struggle with trying to determine what's important to learn in a particular section or chapter. As a pedagogical technique, the Advance Organizer provides a guide that directs the reader toward the most important ideas, concepts, and information in the section. It helps students identify main ideas and distinguish them from supporting evidence and examples.

The **Concept Reviews** encourage students to review and check their learning at appropriate points in the chapter. As you look through the text, you'll see that the Concept Reviews vary in format. They include multiple choice, matching, short answer, and true/false questions. Many of the Concept Reviews are interactive exercises that help students transfer their learning to new situations or examples.

Supporting the Advance Organizers and Concept Reviews are several other pedagogical aids. Every chapter begins with a **Chapter Outline** that provides an overall view of topics and organization. Within the chapter, **Key Terms** are set in boldface type and defined in the margin. **Pronunciation guides** are included for difficult or unfamiliar words. Because students often have trouble identifying the most important theorists and researchers, names of **Key People** are set in boldface type within the chapter. We provide a brief biography of each key person at the end of each chapter, mentioning again why the person is important. A comprehensive **Chapter Summary** includes key points bulleted under each major section heading. We also provide a **page-referenced list of Key Terms** at the end of each chapter.

Taken together, the different elements of this text form a pedagogical system that is very student-friendly, straightforward, *and* effective. We've found that it appeals to diverse students with varying academic and study skills, enhancing the learning process without being gimmicky or condescending. The complete pedagogical system, and how to make the most of it, is described for students in the special section entitled **To the Student: Learning from *Discovering Psychology*** on pages xxxi to xxxiii.

The Supplements Package

A comprehensive teaching package accompanies this textbook. The supplements have been designed to help you save time and teach more effectively. Many elements of the supplements package will be particularly helpful to the adjunct or part-time instructor. This superb teaching package includes the following elements:

- **Student Study Guide,** prepared by Cornelius Rea, Douglas College, New Westminster, British Columbia, Canada. The Study Guide has been carefully designed to help students understand text information and prepare for exams. It includes note-taking exercises for each chapter and progress tests.

- **Instructor's Resource Manual,** prepared by Wayne Hall, San Jacinto College Central, and Granville Sydnor, San Jacinto College North, Pasadena, Texas. The Instructor's Resource Manual includes an abundance of materials to aid instructors in planning their course, including detailed chapter outlines, lecture guides highlighting common student problems, classroom demonstrations, student exercises, advice on teaching the nontraditional student, and "Psychology in the News" topics.

- **Activities Book,** prepared by Wayne Hall and Tom Kellow of San Jacinto College Central, Pasadena, Texas. The activities book is a collection of more than 50 student and instructor activities and demonstrations, organized by topic.

- **Test Bank,** prepared by text authors Don and Sandra Hockenbury and Study Guide author Cornelius Rea, Douglas College, includes more than 2,500 multiple-choice and true-false test questions. The test questions have been classroom tested and include a mix of conceptual, applied, and factual questions. Each question is page-referenced to the textbook.

- A **Computerized Test Bank** is available for Macintosh and Windows platforms. The software program allows instructors to edit, add, or scramble questions.

- **Full-color transparencies** with more than 200 illustrations from the textbook including tables, photographs, and artwork.

- **Scientific American Frontiers Video Collection for Introductory Psychology** is a collection of 26 video segments, 8 to 13 minutes in length. The collection is an excellent resource to stimulate class discussion and interest on a variety of topics.

- **Second edition of *The Brain* Teaching Modules videocassettes.** Along with new modules from the acclaimed PBS series, the second edition of *The Brain* package includes a guide for faculty that links the modules to specific topics in the textbook.

- ***The Mind* videocassettes** contain 38 short modules that dramatically enhance and illustrate important points in a lecture.

- **PsychQuest** is the award-winning student CD-ROM by Thomas Ludwig, Hope College. This interactive tool allows students to explore various psychological research topics, participate in experiments and simulations, quiz themselves on content, and link to the World Wide Web for additional information and quizzes. Topics include depth perception in sports, psychoactive drugs, memory, weight regulation, depression, chronic stress, stereotyping, and mate selection.

- **PsychSim Interactive Computer Simulations 4.0,** by Thomas Ludwig, Hope College, contains 19 programs in Macintosh or Windows format. These programs place the student in the role of the experimenter or the subject in simulated research, or provide dynamic demonstrations illustrating fundamental psychology principles.

- **The Psychology Videodisc** brings a library of still images and brief, exciting video clips to your classroom presentation. The videodisc is accompanied by a detailed Instructor's Guide by Martin Bolt, Calvin College, and Richard O. Straub, University of Michigan-Dearborn. The guide includes bar codes, a descriptive listing of all items on the videodisc, lecture suggestions, and a subject index, to aid cross-referencing of all items by major topic or concept.

- **The Critical Thinking Companion for Introductory Psychology,** by Jane Halonen, Alverno College, is a handbook for the student that includes critical thinking exercises that are keyed to main topics in introductory psychology.

- **Web companion** (available Spring/Summer 1998) is a Web site that accompanies *Discovering Psychology* and can be accessed at:

  http://www.worthpublishers.com/discoveringpsych

  Features include an automated quiz for each chapter, Web exercises, and links to other psychology-related Web sites.

- **Syllabus+** (available Fall 1998) combines the audio-visual quality, interactive precision, and delivery speed of CD-ROM with the currency, immediacy, and go-anywhere spontaneity of the Web. In a simple browserlike environment, it offers a wealth of documents, images, videos, Web links, and study and teaching aids, all carefully coordinated with the textbook's table of contents. Syllabus+ is an instructor- and student-friendly interactive multimedia product that adds unprecedented range, depth, and effectiveness to classroom, study, and review time.

These teaching aids are available to all qualified adopters of this text. For more information, or to examine any of these supplements, contact your regional Worth sales representative.

Acknowledgments

Many talented people contributed to this project. First, we would like to acknowledge the efforts of our supplements team. Our thanks to: Cornelius Rea, of Douglas College in British Columbia, Canada, for writing a very effective Student Study Guide and contributing to the Test Bank; Wayne Hall of San Jacinto College Central, for preparing a comprehensive Instructor's Resource Manual; and Tom Kellow, also of San Jacinto College Central, who co-authored a new Activities Book with Wayne Hall. We would also like to thank Marie Thomas at California State University, San Marcos, for providing a student-friendly statistics appendix. As colleagues who care as much as we do about teaching, they have our gratitude for their hard work and commitment to excellence.

We are indebted to our many colleagues in the United States and Canada who acted as reviewers in the development of *Discovering Psychology* and its parent text, *Psychology.* Their suggestions and advice helped us craft a text that was comprehensive, balanced, and accurate. Their enthusiastic response to our approach intensified our commitment to the goals we had set for ourselves. To each and every reviewer, thank you for generously sharing your time and candid thoughts with us:

Lynn Haller Augsbach, Morehead State University

Susan J. Bartzak-Graham, Roxbury Community College

Brian R. Bate, Cuyahoga Community College, Western Campus

Michael G. Bergmire, Jefferson College

Connie Bosworth, El Paso Community College

Saundra K. Ciccarelli, Gulf Coast Community College

Marie G. Cisneros-Solis, Austin Community College

John M Clark, Macomb Community College

Lorry Cology, Owens Community College

Dana H. Davidson, University of Hawaii, Manoa

Kaye K. Diefenderfer, Seminole Community College

George J. Downing, Gloucester County College

Gilles O. Einstein, Furman University

Linda L. Faldetta, Fernald School

Michael K. Garza, Brookhaven College

Larry Goff, El Centro College

Peter Gram, Pensacola Junior College

Eddie M. Griggs, Abraham Baldwin Agricultural College

Phyllis Grilikhes-Maxwell, City College of San Francisco

Jim Hail, McLennan Community College

Wayne W. Hall, San Jacinto College Central

Jane S. Halonen, Alverno College

William Hampes, Black Hawk College

Joseph J. Hanak, Corning Community College

William T. Hardy, Sierra College

Hope Hartman, City University of New York, City College

Matthew Hogben, State University of New York, Albany

Teri Hudson, Diablo Valley College

Richard A. Hughes, Laredo Community College

Doris Ivie, Pellissippi State Technical Community College

Andrew Kinney, Mohawk Valley Community College

Richard J. Klimek, Montgomery College

Gloria J. Lawrence, Wayne State College

Thomas W. Lombardo, The University of Mississippi

Joan Lovensheimer, Butler County Community College

Robert F. Massey, Saint Peter's College

Douglas G. Mook, University of Virginia, Charlottesville

Edward R. Mosley, Passaic County Community College

Melinda L. Myers-Johnson, College of the Redwoods, Humboldt State University

William C. Owen, Virginia Western Community College

Elizabeth Weiss Ozorak, Allegheny College

Gregory Pezzetti, Rancho Santiago College

Peter H. Platenius, Queens University

Christopher Potter, Harrisburg Area Community College

Sandra Prince-Madison, Delgado Community College

Cornelius P. Rea, Douglas College

Theresa J. Reis, Eastern Washington University

Valda Robinson, Hillsborough Community College

Paul Rosenfeld, Navy Personnel Research and Development Center

Marcia J. Rossi, Tuskegee University

Alan M. Schultz, Prince George's Community College

Richard Seefeldt, University of Wisconsin, River Falls

Betty Sunerton, Dawson College

Margaret Johnson Thornburg, Henry Ford Community College

Mary Trahan, Randolph-Macon College

M. Lisa Valentino, Seminole Community College

Wayne Van Zomeran, Northwest Missouri State University

John Vitkus, Case Western Reserve University

Scott D. Wright, University of Utah

Cecelia K. Yoder, Oklahoma City Community College

Matthew J. Zagumny, Tennessee Technological University

We would also like to thank the following faculty members for their thoughtful comments and suggestions, which proved invaluable in the early stages of developing *Discovering Psychology:*

Edward Brady, Belleville Area College

Phillip Compton, Ohio Northern University

Eugene Galindro, El Paso Community College

Patricia Goldentyer, Community College of Philadelphia

Peter Gram, Pensacola Junior College

Andrew Kinney, Mohawk Valley Community College

Laura Madson, New Mexico State University

Gary Nickell, Morehead State University

Teri Nicoll-Johnson, Modesto Junior College

John Nield, Utah Valley State College

Keith W. Pannell, El Paso Community College

Ralph Roberts, University of Denver

Christina Sinisi, Charleston Southern University

Tom Smith, Vincennes University

Helen Taylor, Bellevue Community College

Phyllis Walrad, Macomb Community College

Ann L. Weber, University of North Carolina at Asheville

Randall Wight, Ouachita Baptist University

The remarkable people who make up Worth Publishers have a reputation for producing college textbooks of the highest quality. From the earliest stages of the editorial process to the last stages of the production process, their attention to every detail of this project never wavered. Each one of them played a critical role in helping us produce the best possible book.

From the inception of *Discovering Psychology,* Susan Driscoll, the president of Worth Publishers, has enthusiastically supported our project. Catherine Woods, the executive editor for psychology, skillfully and patiently guided us through the writing and production processes. At every stage in the development of this project, Catherine was a reliable source of encouragement, insight, and friendship. Kate Steinbacher, marketing manager for psychology, kept us well-supplied with ideas about how to make *Discovering Psychology* accessible to the widest possible range of instructors and students. Cecilia Gardner, our developmental editor, analyzed reviewer and survey feedback and provided numerous helpful suggestions for restructuring chapter discussions.

Working quietly behind the scenes, managing editor Suzanne Thibodeau solved problems before we knew they even existed, always with grace and a smile. Production editor Tim Prairie never lost his sense of humor (or anything else) throughout the sometimes nerve-wracking production schedule. Tim's conscientious attention to getting every last detail right made our task much easier.

The visual appeal of *Discovering Psychology* reflects the talent and creativity of several people. Every page of this book is a testament to the extraordinary abilities of art director George Touloumes, artist Demetrios Zangos, and designer Pat Appleton of Malcolm Grear Designers.

The wonderful photographs throughout this text are due to the hard work and admirable eye of June Lundborg Whitworth, who served as our photo researcher, and of Cindy Joyce, director of photo research. The innovative illustrations by John Woolsey and his colleagues at J/B Woolsey Associates help teach psychological concepts better than any art we've seen in a college textbook. And, we thank award-winning artist Phoebe Beasley for embracing the goals of our book and graciously allowing us to use her stunning collages for our cover and chapter opening images.

Production manager Patricia Lawson coordinated a bewildering array of technical details, maintaining quality right up until the last page came off the press. Proofreader Laura Rubin and bibliographer Beverly Wehrli chased down the gremlins that seem to haunt publishing companies at night and managed to catch just about every one of them. Supplements editor, Penny Bice, expertly coordinated the development of the diverse elements of the supplements package.

Finally, a few personal acknowledgments are in order. Many friends and family members kindly allowed us to share their stories with you, the reader. Sandy's parents, Fern and Erv, who recently celebrated their 50th wedding anniversary, deserve particular thanks for their constant support and never-ending supply of funny stories. We also thank Judy and Dean, Janeen and Marty, and all the other members of our extended family for their support and encouragement—and for putting up with our absences from family gatherings over the past eight years. We thank our good friends Paul and Asha, Marcia and Bill, Marie and David, and Warren for allowing us to tell stories about them in the pages of our book. And, special thanks to our good friend Tom Gay, for his wisdom, sage advice, and wonderful sense of humor.

Last but not least, our daughter Laura has lived with our psychology books since their inception and her conception, as the two events very nearly coincided. Over the years, Laura has become accustomed to postponing many simple pleasures of childhood "until the chapter is done." Now seven years old and an exuberant second-grader, Laura has been a source of joy and happiness, laughter and love throughout the writing process.

An Invitation

We hope that you will let us know how you and your students like *Discovering Psychology*. We welcome your thoughts, suggestions, and comments! You can write to us in care of Worth Publishers, 33 Irving Place, New York, NY 10003, or contact us via e-mail at:

psychology@aol.com

Above all, we hope that your semester is an enjoyable and successful one as you introduce your students to the most fascinating and personally relevant science that exists.

With best wishes,

To the Student: Learning from *Discovering Psychology*

Welcome to psychology! Our names are Don and Sandy Hockenbury, and we're the authors of your textbook. Every semester we teach several sections of introductory psychology, and we wrote this text to help you succeed in the class you are taking. We carefully designed every aspect of this book to help you get the most out of your introductory psychology course. Before you begin your reading, you will find it well worth your time to take a few minutes to familiarize yourself with the special features and learning aids.

First, take a look at the **Chapter Outline** at the very beginning of each chapter. The Chapter Outline shows you the progression of topics and subtopics that will be covered in the chapter. You might also want to flip through the chapter and browse a bit so you have an idea of what's to come.

Next, read the chapter **Prologue,** which is a true story about real people. Some of the stories are humorous, some dramatic. We think you will enjoy this special feature, but it will also help you to understand the material in the chapter, and why the topics are important. The Prologue will help you relate the new information in this book to experiences that are already familiar to you. In each chapter, we return to the people and stories introduced in the Prologue to help illustrate important concepts and ideas.

As you begin reading the chapter, you will notice several special elements. Major sections begin with an **Advance Organizer**—a short section preview that looks like this one:

> *Social support refers to the resources provided by other people. How does social support benefit health? How can social support sometimes increase stress? What gender differences have been found in social support?*

The first sentence of the Advance Organizer provides a definition or summary statement of the material in the section that follows. This summary statement is followed by focus questions. Read the questions and try to keep them in mind as you read the section. They will help you identify important points being discussed in each section. When you finish a section, look again at the Advance Organizer. Make sure that you can comfortably answer each question before you go on to the next section. Ideally, you should answer each question in an Advance Organizer in writing. You can also use the questions in the Advance Organizer to aid you in taking notes or outlining chapter sections.

You will also notice that some terms in the chapter are printed in **boldface,** or darker, type. Some of these **Key Terms** may already be familiar to you, but most will be new. The dark type signals that the term has a specialized meaning in psychology. Each Key Term is formally defined within a sentence or two of being introduced. The Key Terms are also defined in the margins, usually on the page upon which they appear. Some Key Terms include a **pronunciation guide** to help you say the word correctly. Occasionally, we also print words in *italic type* to signal either that they are boldfaced terms in another chapter or that they are specialized terms in psychology.

Certain names also appear in boldface type. These are the **Key People**—the researchers or theorists who are especially important within a given area of psychological study. Typically, Key People are the psychologists or other researchers whose names your instructor will expect you to know.

A **Concept Review** appears several times in every chapter. The Concept Reviews contain exercises that allow you to test yourself to make certain that you understand and remember important information. Write out your answers by filling in the blanks before you check your answers against the correct ones that are provided at the end of the chapter.

Each chapter in *Discovering Psychology* has up to four boxes that focus on different kinds of topics. Take the time to read the boxes, because they are an integral part of each chapter. They also present important information that you may be expected to know for class discussion or tests. There are four types of boxes:

- **Critical Thinking boxes** ask you to stretch your mind a bit, by presenting issues that are provocative or controversial. They will help you actively question the implications of the material that you are learning.

- **Science Versus Pseudoscience boxes** examine the evidence for various popular pseudosciences—from astrology to subliminal motivation tapes. In addition to being interesting in themselves, these boxes will help teach you how to critically evaluate evidence.

- **Culture and Human Behavior boxes** are a special feature of this text. Many students are unaware of the importance of cross-cultural research in contemporary psychology. These boxes highlight cultural differences in thinking and behavior, and they will also sensitize you to the ways in which people's behavior, including your own, has been influenced by cultural factors.

- **In Focus boxes** present interesting information or research. Think of them as sidebar discussions. They deal with topics as diverse as sexual fantasies, whether animals dream, and why snakes give so many people the creeps.

We think you'll find the **Application** section at the end of each chapter particularly helpful. Each Application provides concrete suggestions to help you deal with a real-life problem or issue. These suggestions are based upon psychological research, rather than opinions, anecdotes, or self-help philosophies. The Applications show you how psychology can be applied to a wide variety of everyday concerns. We hope that the Applications make a difference in your life. Because the Applications for Chapters 5 and 6 deal with study skills, motivation, and enhancing memory, you may want to skip ahead and read those after you finish this section.

Several elements are placed at the end of the chapter to help you review what you've learned. The **Chapter Summary** provides a concise overview of the main points of the chapter. All of the chapter's **Key Terms** are listed, along with the pages on which they appear and are defined. You can check your knowledge of these terms by going down the list and defining each term in your own words, then comparing it to information on the page where it is discussed. Brief biographical sketches of the chapter's **Key People** appear at the end of each chapter, which will help you remember why they are important.

Beyond the study aids contained in each chapter of *Discovering Psychology,* there is an appendix at the back of the text entitled **Statistics: Understanding Data.** This appendix discusses how psychologists use statistics to summarize and draw conclusions from the data they have gathered. Your instructor may assign this appendix, or you may want to read it on your own.

Also at the back of this text is an alphabetical **Glossary** containing the definitions for all Key Terms in the book. You can use the **Subject Index** to locate discussions of particular topics.

We also highly recommend the excellent **Student Study Guide** that accompanies this text. The Study Guide was written by our colleague, Cornelius Rea, at Douglas College in New Westminster, British Columbia, Canada. Your bookstore should have copies available or will be happy to order it.

Finally, many colleges and universities have computer centers that provide students with access to the World Wide Web. You can access the home page for *Discovering Psychology* at the following URL or Web address:

http://www.worthpublishers.com/discoveringpsych

Once there, you'll have access to a practice quiz for each chapter, Web links to other psychology-related sites, and other great resources.

That's it! We hope you enjoy reading and learning from *Discovering Psychology.* If you want to share your thoughts or suggestions for the next edition of this book, you can write to us at the following address:

Don & Sandy Hockenbury
c/o Worth Publishers
33 Irving Place
New York, NY 10003

If you have access to e-mail, our e-mail address is easy to remember:

psychology@aol.com

Discovering Psychology

Case Studies

Surveys

Correlational Studies

Ethics in Psychological Research

APPLICATION: Thinking Critically
About Psychology and the Media

Chapter

Introducing Psychology

Prologue: April 19, 1995: Oklahoma City

It was a little after 10:30 a.m. when the phone rang in your author Sandy's office. It was Fern, Sandy's mother, calling from Chicago. Fern's usually cheery voice was shaking. "Are you all right? Where's Laura? Is she OK? Where's Don?"

"I'm fine, Mom. Laura's at day care. She's *fine*. And Don's at the college. What's wrong, Mom?"

"Don't you know what happened?" Fern blurted out, her voice frantic. "Aren't you listening to the news? Turn on your TV! Somebody blew up a big office building in Oklahoma!" Fern started to cry. "They bombed a day-care center! They killed *children* and *babies*."

Like millions of other Americans, we later watched in horror as the aftermath of the Oklahoma City bombing unfolded on television. Oklahoma City was not much more than an hour's drive from our home in Tulsa. Psychologically, it felt much closer on that day. Too close. Was some deranged person targeting day-care centers in Oklahoma? Was our four-year-old daughter safe?

Sandy immediately called Laura's school. Everything was fine, but like other schools and day-care centers in Oklahoma, our daughter's school had received telephoned bomb threats within hours of the blast. All the doors were locked and two armed guards were patrolling the grounds. When we picked Laura up early that afternoon, every car was stopped at the entrance to the parking lot and checked by the guards.

Why Do People Risk Their Lives to Help Others? From all over the country, rescue workers volunteered to come to Oklahoma City to help in the search for survivors buried in the rubble. Working around the clock, these men and women risked their lives to help complete strangers. What motivated their behavior? And why is it that in other situations, people will ignore people who clearly need help? This is just one of the many issues about human behavior that we will explore in this text.

The Aftereffects of Trauma What will be the long-term effects of the Oklahoma City bombing on the survivors, rescue workers, and those who lost family members, friends, and co-workers? How can they best be helped in dealing with the aftereffects of this tragedy? These are just some of the kinds of questions that psychologists study.

The immediate response to the tragedy was as dramatic as the bomb blast itself. Rescue teams, doctors, nurses, and trauma specialists, including psychologists, flew in from all over the country. In Tulsa, people stood in line for hours to donate blood to the Red Cross. Churches, schools, and businesses collected money, food, clothing, and medical supplies to help the victims and rescue workers.

Thunderstorms hit Oklahoma City that night, yet the rescue workers continued their efforts around the clock. Working under massive floodlights, they refused to sleep, risking their own lives in the unstable building in a desperate attempt to find and rescue survivors. And in their efforts to save others, some died. Rebecca Anderson, a nurse who came to the Murrah Building to help survivors, was killed when she was hit by falling debris (Irving, 1995). One of our students told us the story of her uncle, Michael Loudenslager. Loudenslager survived the initial blast. But rather than leaving the unsafe building immediately, he helped free some of his co-workers from the rubble, and then headed toward the area where the day-care center had been. As he tried to make his way toward the trapped children, he was crushed by a heavy concrete block.

Amid the outpouring of public support, rumors ran rampant. At first, many people believed that the bombing was the result of an international terrorist attack of some sort, like the World Trade Center bombing in New York City. Arab-Americans living in and near Oklahoma City, including college students, were afraid to leave their homes. Some had their windows shot out. Some Muslim organizations received bomb threats.

After the initial shock came the questions: What kind of a person would do such a thing? And why? Beyond the inevitable questions about the bomber's identity and motives came a host of others: How will the survivors cope with the tragedy? How can they be helped? More than 200 children had lost a parent. Thirty children had lost *both* parents. Will those children be psychologically scarred for life? How will their future relationships and emotional development be affected?

Broader questions were also raised. Why would people travel across the country to risk their lives to help complete strangers? Why were Arab-Americans threatened even though they had been members of the community for years?

You probably have your own personal story to tell of the day that Oklahoma City was bombed—your emotions, thoughts, and attempts to explain what happened. As you'll see, the kinds of questions and issues that the Oklahoma City bombing raises are often studied by psychologists. Throughout this text, we'll explore what psychologists have learned about human behavior, both in crisis situations such as the Oklahoma City bombing and in more commonplace circumstances.

Introduction

What Is Psychology?

Psychology is now defined as the science of behavior and mental processes, but the definition has changed throughout psychology's short history. How did philosophy and physiology influence the evolution of psychology? What roles did Wilhelm Wundt and William James play in the founding of psychology?

Psychology is now formally defined as *the science of behavior and mental processes*. However, the definition of psychology has changed radically over the past century. Indeed, the history of psychology is the history of a field struggling to define itself as a separate and unique scientific discipline (Hilgard, 1987).

We begin this introductory chapter with a brief overview of psychology's history. Why is the history of psychology important? Students and others are often surprised at the wide range of topics studied by psychologists. As you'll see later in this chapter, psychology's subject area is extremely broad. It ranges from the behavior of a single brain cell to the behavior of people in groups. The topics that fall within psychology today, the emphasis that is given to particular areas, and the diverse methods that psychologists use to study these different areas are all the result of the shifting concerns of psychologists over the past century.

The Early History of Psychology

Psychology has always focused on the scientific study of human experience. However, the definition of *which* areas of human experience should be studied, and *how* they should be studied, has changed and evolved. What is the proper subject matter of psychology? What methods should psychologists use? What should the nature of psychology be? As you'll see in the next few sections, the first psychologists struggled with these questions.

The beginnings of psychology can be traced back several centuries to the writings of the great philosophers. Three centuries before the birth of Christ, the Greek philosopher Aristotle wrote extensively about topics like sleep, dreams, the senses, and memory (Watson & Evans, 1991). Hundreds of years later, French philosopher René Descartes (1596–1650) proposed that mind and brain were separate entities, an issue that is still discussed in psychology today. In later centuries, philosophers asked whether human character and knowledge are inborn or the results of environmental influences—an issue that today is called the *nature-nurture* debate (Fancher, 1996).

Such philosophical discussions influenced the topics that would be considered in psychology. But the early philosophers could only advance the understanding of human behavior to a certain point. Their methods were limited to intuition, observation, and logic.

The eventual emergence of psychology as a science hinged on advances in other sciences, particularly physiology (Fancher, 1996). *Physiology* is a branch of biology that studies the functions and parts of living organisms, including humans. In the 1600s, physiologists were becoming interested in the human brain and its relation to behavior. By the early 1700s, it was discovered that damage to one side of the brain produced a loss of function in the opposite side of the body.

Nature or Nurture? Both mother and daughter are clearly enjoying the experience of painting together. Is the child's interest in painting an expression of her natural tendencies, or is it the result of her mother's encouragement and teaching? Parental influence is just one of many environmental factors that can nurture the developing child's talents, interests, and motives. Are such environmental factors more important than the child's inborn abilities? Originally posed by philosophers hundreds of years ago, such questions continue to interest psychologists today.

psychology
The scientific study of behavior and mental processes.

By the early 1800s, the idea that different brain areas were related to different behavioral functions was being vigorously debated. Collectively, the early scientific discoveries made by physiologists were establishing the foundation for an idea that was to prove critical to the development of psychology: that scientific methods could be applied to issues of human behavior and thinking.

Wundt, Titchener, and Structuralism

By the late 1800s, the stage was set for the emergence of psychology as a separate scientific discipline. The leading proponent of this idea was a German physiologist named **Wilhelm Wundt.** Wundt applied experimental methods to the study of fundamental psychological processes, such as mental reaction times in response to visual or auditory stimuli. For example, Wundt tried to measure precisely how long it took to consciously detect the sight and sound of a bell being struck.

In 1874, Wundt published the first bona fide psychology textbook, *Principles of Physiological Psychology*, in which he outlined the connections between physiology and psychology. In his book he promoted his belief that psychology should be established as a separate scientific discipline, one that would use experimental methods to study mental processes. Wundt also opened the first working research laboratory in the new field at the University of Leipzig in March 1879, which is regarded by many as the formal beginning of psychology as a science (Fancher, 1996).

It was Wundt's most devoted student, Edward B. Titchener (1867–1927), who established structuralism, the first major approach, or "school," in psychology. **Structuralism** held that even our most complex conscious experiences can be broken down into elemental *structures*, or component parts, of sensations and feelings. To identify these structures of conscious thought, Wundt and Titchener trained subjects in a procedure called *introspection*. The subjects would view a simple stimulus, such as an apple, then try to reconstruct their sensations and feelings immediately after viewing it (Hilgard, 1987). They might first report on the colors they saw, then the smells, and so on, to create a total description of their experience.

Along with being the first school of thought in early psychology, structuralism also holds the dubious distinction of being the first school to disappear. The structuralists relied heavily on the method of introspection, but introspection had many limitations. First, even a subject who was well trained in introspection varied in his responses to the same stimulus from trial to trial. And different subjects often provided very different introspective reports about the same stimulus. Thus, introspection did not seem to be a very reliable method of investigation.

Second, introspection could not be used to study children or animals. And third, complex topics such as learning, development, mental disorders, and personality did not lend themselves to be investigated using introspection. Thus, structuralism was simply too limited to accommodate the rapidly expanding field of psychology.

James and Functionalism

Psychology may have officially begun in Germany in 1879, but it was already well on its way to being established in the United States through the efforts of Harvard professor **William James.** James began teaching a physiology and anatomy class at Harvard University in the 1870s. He was an intense, enthusiastic teacher who actively engaged his students in the quest for new knowledge. James was also prone to changing the subject matter of his classes as his own interests changed (B. Ross, 1991).

Wilhelm Wundt (1832–1920) German physiologist Wilhelm Wundt is generally credited as being the founder of the new science of psychology. In 1879, he established the first psychology research laboratory in Leipzig, Germany. Wundt's student, Edward Titchener, founded the first major school or approach in psychology, called structuralism.

structuralism
Early school of psychology that emphasized studying the most basic components, or structures, of conscious experiences.

functionalism
Early school of psychology that emphasized studying the purpose, or function, of behavior and mental experiences.

William James (1842–1910) Harvard professor William James was instrumental in establishing psychology in the United States. In 1890, James published a highly influential text, *Principles of Psychology*. James's ideas became the basis of another early school of psychology called functionalism, which stressed studying the adaptive and practical functions of human behavior.

G. Stanley Hall (1844–1924) G. Stanley Hall helped organize psychology in the United States. Among his achievements, Hall established the first psychology research laboratory in the United States, started publishing the *American Journal of Psychology*, and founded the American Psychological Association.

Gradually, his lectures came to focus more on psychology than physiology. By the late 1870s, James was teaching classes devoted exclusively to the topic of psychology (Fancher, 1996). Around this time, James also began writing a comprehensive textbook of psychology, a task that would take him over a decade to complete. Finally published as two volumes in 1890, it was entitled *Principles of Psychology* and was over 1,400 pages long! Despite its length, James's *Principles of Psychology* quickly became the leading psychology textbook and had an enormous impact on the development of psychology in the United States (B. Ross, 1991).

James's ideas became the basis for functionalism, an approach to psychology that differed from structuralism. **Functionalism** stressed the importance of how behavior *functions* to allow people and animals to adapt to their environment. The functionalists did not limit their methods to introspection. They expanded the scope of psychology research to include direct observation of living creatures in natural settings. Functionalists also examined how psychology could be applied to areas such as education, child rearing, and the work environment.

Like the structuralists, the functionalists thought that psychology should focus on conscious experiences. But rather than trying to identify the fundamental "structures" of consciousness, William James saw consciousness as an ongoing "stream" of mental activity. As James wrote in *Talks to Teachers* in 1899:

> *Now the* immediate *fact which psychology, the science of mind, has to study is also the most general fact. It is the fact that in each of us, when awake (and often when asleep),* some kind of consciousness is always going on. *There is a stream, a succession of states, or waves, or fields (or whatever you please to call them), of knowledge, of feeling, of desire, of deliberation, etc., that constantly pass and repass, and that constitute our inner life. The existence of this is the primal fact, [and] the nature and origin of it form the essential problem, of our science.*

Thus, both the functionalists and the structuralists saw the study of consciousness as a fundamental goal of the new science of psychology. However, they had very different ideas about how and why consciousness should be studied.

Like structuralism, functionalism no longer exists as a school of thought in contemporary psychology. Nevertheless, functionalism's twin themes of (1) the importance of the adaptive role of behavior and (2) the emphasis upon applying psychology to enhancing human behavior continue to be evident in many areas of modern psychology (D. N. Robinson, 1993).

William James and His Students James also profoundly influenced American psychology through his students, many of whom became prominent American psychologists. Two of James's most notable students were G. Stanley Hall and Mary Whiton Calkins.

In 1878 **G. Stanley Hall** received the first Ph.D. in psychology to be awarded in America. In the mid-1880s, Hall founded the first psychology research laboratory in the United States. He also began publishing the *American Journal of Psychology*, the first U.S. journal devoted to psychology. Most important, in 1892, Hall founded the American Psychological Association (Street, 1994). Today, the American Psychological Association is one of the world's leading professional organizations of psychologists, with over 140,000 members.

In 1890 **Mary Whiton Calkins** was assigned the task of teaching experimental psychology at a new women's college—Wellesley College. Calkins studied with James at nearby Harvard University. She completed all the requirements for a Ph.D. in psychology. However, Harvard refused to officially grant her the Ph.D. degree because she was a woman. At the time, Harvard was not coeducational (Brennan, 1991).

Mary Whiton Calkins (1863–1930) Under the direction of William James, Mary Whiton Calkins completed all the requirements for a Ph.D. in psychology. Calkins had a distinguished professional career, establishing a psychology laboratory at Wellesley College and becoming the first woman president of the American Psychological Association.

Despite the fact that she was never formally awarded the degree she had earned, Calkins went on to make several notable contributions to psychology (Stevens & Gardner, 1982). She conducted research in many areas, including dreams, memory, and personality. In 1891 she established a psychological laboratory at Wellesley College, one of the first in the United States. At the turn of the century, she wrote a well-received textbook herself, titled *Introduction to Psychology*. In 1905 Mary Whiton Calkins was elected president of the American Psychological Association—the first woman, but not the last, to hold that position (Street, 1994).

Twentieth-Century Leaders in Psychology

Behaviorism dominated American psychology until the 1960s, but psychology was also influenced by psychoanalysis, Gestalt psychology, and humanistic psychology. What were the key ideas stressed by each approach? Who were the key proponents of each approach?

Beginning in the early 1900s, new approaches emerged that challenged the principles of structuralism and functionalism. In this section, we will focus on four of these approaches: behaviorism, psychoanalysis, Gestalt psychology, and humanistic psychology.

Ivan Pavlov

John B. Watson

B. F. Skinner

Three Key Figures in the Development of Behaviorism Based on the pioneering research of Russian physiologist Ivan Pavlov (1849–1936), American psychologist John B. Watson (1878–1958) founded the school of behaviorism. Behaviorism advocated that psychology should study observable behaviors, not mental processes. Following Watson, B. F. Skinner (1904–1990) continued to champion the ideas of behaviorism and became one of the most influential psychologists of the twentieth century. Like Watson, Skinner strongly advocated the study of observable behaviors rather than mental processes.

behaviorism
School of psychology and theoretical viewpoint that emphasizes the study of observable behaviors, especially as they pertain to the process of learning.

Watson and Behaviorism

The course of psychology changed dramatically in the early 1900s, when an approach called **behaviorism** emerged as a dominating force. Behaviorism rejected the emphasis on consciousness promoted by the structuralists and the functionalists. Instead, behaviorism contended that psychology should focus its scientific investigations on observable behavior that could be objectively measured and verified.

Behaviorism grew out of the pioneering work of a Russian physiologist named **Ivan Pavlov.** Pavlov demonstrated that dogs could learn to associate a neutral stimulus, such as the sound of a bell, with an automatic behavior, such as salivating to food. Once the association was formed, the sound of the bell alone would make the dog salivate. Pavlov optimistically believed he had discovered the mechanism by which all behaviors were learned.

In the United States, Pavlov's enthusiasm was shared by a young, dynamic psychologist named **John Watson.** Watson championed behaviorism as a new school, or approach to psychology. Behaviorism rejected both introspection as a method and the idea that consciousness or mental processes should be studied by psychology. As Watson wrote in his classic 1924 book entitled *Behaviorism*:

Behaviorism, on the contrary, holds that the subject matter of human psychology is the behavior of the human being. Behaviorism claims that consciousness is neither a definite nor a usable concept. The behaviorist, who has been trained always as an experimentalist, holds, further, that belief in the existence of consciousness goes back to the ancient days of superstition and magic.

Instead of mental processes, the early behaviorists focused exclusively on overt behavior. Their goal was to discover the fundamental principles of *learning*—how behavior is acquired and modified in response to environmental influences. For the most part, the behaviorists studied animal behavior under carefully controlled laboratory conditions. In Chapter 5, on learning, we'll look at the contributions of Pavlov, Watson, and Skinner in greater detail.

The influence of behaviorism on American psychology was enormous. Although Watson left academic psychology in the early 1920s, behaviorism was later championed by an equally forceful proponent—the famous American psychologist **B. F. Skinner.** Between Watson and Skinner, behaviorism largely dominated American psychology for almost half a century. During that time, the study of conscious experiences was virtually ignored as a topic in psychology (Hilgard, 1992; Leahey, 1992).

Freud and Psychoanalysis

While Watson and others studied directly observable behaviors, across the Atlantic Ocean an Austrian physician named **Sigmund Freud** focused on uncovering causes of behavior that were *unconscious*—that is, hidden from the person's conscious awareness. Freud's school of psychological thought was called **psychoanalysis,** and it emphasized the role of unconscious conflicts in determining behavior and personality.

Freud's theories about personality and behavior were based largely on his work with his patients and on insights derived from self-analysis. Freud believed that human behavior was motivated by unconscious conflicts that were almost always sexual or aggressive in nature. Past experiences, especially childhood experiences, were thought to be critical in the formation of adult personality and behavior. According to Freud (1904), glimpses of these unconscious impulses are revealed in everyday life in dreams, memory blocks, slips of the tongue, and spontaneous humor. Freud believed that when unconscious conflicts become extreme, psychological disorders can be the result.

Many of the basic ideas of psychoanalysis continue to influence psychologists and other professionals in the mental health field. Along with being a form of psychotherapy, Freud's psychoanalysis also provided a landmark theory of personality. In Chapter 10, on personality, and Chapter 14, on psychotherapy, we'll explore Freud's ideas in more detail.

Sigmund Freud (1856–1939) Sigmund Freud began his career as a neurologist and physician in Vienna, Austria. Freud's probing of the unconscious conflicts of his patients led him to the formulation of psychoanalysis, his influential theory of personality and psychotherapy.

Wertheimer and Gestalt Psychology

Another early influence on American psychology was the school of Gestalt psychology. Founded by German psychologist **Max Wertheimer** in the early 1900s, **Gestalt psychology** emphasized the perception of whole figures rather than the individual elements of conscious experiences stressed by the structuralists (Leahey, 1992). After Wertheimer and other Gestalt psychologists immigrated to the United States during the rise of the Nazis in Germany in the 1930s, Gestalt psychology helped advance the study of perception and problem solving in American psychology. Unlike behaviorism, Gestalt psychology assigned an important role to mental activities in organizing sensations into meaningful perceptions (Hilgard, 1987). In Chapter 3, on sensation and perception, we'll encounter some of the contributions of the Gestalt psychologists.

psychoanalysis
Personality theory and form of psychotherapy that emphasizes the role of unconscious factors in personality and behavior.

Gestalt psychology
(Guess-TALT) School of psychology that emphasized the perception of whole figures rather than the individual elements of conscious experiences.

humanistic psychology
School of psychology and theoretical viewpoint that emphasizes each person's unique potential for psychological growth and self-direction.

Carl Rogers (1902–1987)

Two Key Figures in the Development of Humanistic Psychology Carl Rogers and Abraham Maslow were key figures in establishing humanistic psychology. Humanistic psychology emphasized the importance of self-determination, free will, and human potential. The ideas of Carl Rogers have been particularly influential in modern psychotherapy. Abraham Maslow's theory of motivation emphasized the importance of psychological growth.

Rogers, Maslow, and Humanistic Psychology

In combination, behaviorism and psychoanalysis dominated research and practice in American psychology for several decades. However, in the 1950s a new school of thought emerged, called **humanistic psychology.** Because humanistic psychology was distinctly different from both psychoanalysis and behaviorism, it was sometimes referred to as the "third force" in American psychology (Maslow, 1970).

Humanistic psychology was largely founded by American psychologist **Carl Rogers.** Like Freud, Rogers was heavily influenced by his experiences with his psychotherapy clients. However, rather than emphasizing unconscious conflicts and causes of behavior, Rogers emphasized the *conscious* experiences of his patients, including each person's unique potential for psychological growth and self-direction. In contrast to the behaviorists, who saw human behavior as being determined solely by environmental influences, Rogers emphasized *self*-determination, free will, and the importance of choice in human behavior (Leahey, 1992).

Abraham Maslow (1908–1970)

Abraham Maslow, another humanistic psychologist, developed a theory of motivation that emphasized psychological growth, which we discuss in Chapter 8. Like psychoanalysis, humanistic psychology included both influential theories of personality and a form of psychotherapy, which we'll discuss in later chapters.

The history of psychology has included considerable debate about the proper course that the new science should follow. Each of the schools that we've briefly described helped shape the focus of psychology in the first half of the twentieth century. And, as you'll see throughout this textbook, psychological research has been strongly influenced by the changing perspectives in psychology.

CONCEPT REVIEW 1.1

Major Schools in Psychology

Identify the school or approach *and* the founder associated with each of the following statements.

1. Psychology should study how behavior and mental processes allow organisms to adapt to their environments.
School/Approach _____
Founder _____

2. Psychology should emphasize each person's unique potential for psychological growth and self-directedness.
School/Approach _____
Founder _____

3. Psychology should focus on the elements of conscious experiences, using the method of introspection.
School/Approach _____
Founder _____

4. Human behavior is strongly influenced by unconscious sexual and aggressive conflicts.
School/Approach _____
Founder _____

5. Psychology should scientifically investigate observable behaviors that can be measured objectively, and should not study consciousness or mental processes.
School/Approach _____
Founder _____

6. Rather than studying the individual elements of conscious experience, psychology should emphasize the role of active mental processes in organizing sensations into meaningful perceptions.
School/Approach _____
Founder _____

Psychology Today

Psychology today is a very diverse field. What important influences have helped shape psychology in the last few decades? What are the major perspectives in psychology, and what are some of psychology's important specialty areas?

Since the 1960s, several approaches have emerged as important influences on contemporary psychology, including biological, cognitive, and cross-cultural psychology.

Contemporary Trends in Psychology

Biological psychology emphasizes studying the physical bases of human and animal behavior. Several factors have contributed to the growth of biological psychology in the last few decades. For example, during the late 1950s and early 1960s, drugs were developed that helped control the symptoms of serious psychological disorders. The relative success of these new drugs led psychologists to focus on the important interaction between biological factors and human behavior. Equally important were later technological advances that allowed psychologists and other researchers to study the structures of the intact brain such as the CAT scan, PET scan, and MRI. Gradually, the complex functions of the brain were beginning to be unraveled, producing new understandings about the biological bases of memory, learning, emotions, mental disorders, and other aspects of human behavior.

The 1960s also witnessed a return to the study of mental processes and their influence on behavior, a development that is often called "the cognitive revolution" because it represented a break from traditional behaviorism. The new field of *cognitive psychology* focused once again on the important role of mental processes in how people process information, develop language, solve problems, and think (Anderson, 1995).

One important factor in the cognitive revolution was the development of the first computers in the 1950s (Ellis & Hunt, 1992). Computers gave psychologists a new model for conceptualizing human mental processes. Like a computer, human thinking, memory, and perception could be understood in terms of an "information processing" model.

More recently, psychologists began to take a closer look at how cultural factors influence patterns of behavior. By the late 1980s, *cross-cultural psychology* had emerged in full force as large numbers of psychologists began studying the diversity of human behavior in different cultural settings and countries (Triandis, 1996). In the process, some well-established psychological findings that were thought to be universal turned out not to be so.

For example, one well-established psychological finding was that people will exert more effort on a task when working alone than when working as part of a group, a phenomenon called *social loafing*. Social loafing was originally demonstrated during the 1970s, and it has been a common finding in many psychological studies conducted with American and European subjects. But when similar studies were conducted with Chinese participants in Taiwan during the 1980s, the exact *opposite* was found to be true (see Moghaddam & others, 1993). Chinese participants worked harder on a task when they were part of a group than when they were working alone.

As it turned out, such findings were just the tip of the iceberg. Today, psychologists have become very sensitive to the influence of cultural and ethnic factors on behavior. We have included "Culture and Human Behavior" boxes throughout this textbook to help sensitize you, as well, to the influence of culture on behavior—including your own.

CULTURE AND HUMAN BEHAVIOR 1.1

What Is Cross-Cultural Psychology?

Culture is a broad term that refers to the attitudes, values, beliefs, and behaviors shared by a group of people and communicated from one generation to another (Matsumoto, 1994). A person's sense of *cultural identity* is influenced by such factors as ethnic background, nationality, race, religion, and language. When this broad definition is applied to people throughout the world, about 4,000 different cultures can be said to exist. Studying the differences between those cultures as well as the more general issue of how culture influences behavior are the fundamental goals of *cross-cultural psychology* (Betancourt & López, 1993).

On the one hand, people around the globe share many attributes: we all eat, sleep, form families, seek happiness, and mourn losses. After all, we are all members of the same species. On the other hand, the way we learn to express our human qualities can vary considerably from one culture to the next. What we eat, where we sleep, how we form families, define happiness, and express sadness can take very different forms in different cultures.

As we grow up within a given culture, we learn our culture's *norms,* or rules of behavior. Once those cultural norms are understood and internalized, people tend to act in accordance with

their cultural norms without too much thought.

Most people share a natural tendency to accept their own cultural rules as defining what's "normal". The tendency to use your own culture as the standard for judging other cultures is called **ethnocentrism** (Triandis, 1994). Ethnocentrism can lead to the inability to separate ourselves from our own cultural backgrounds and biases so that we can understand the behaviors of others (Matsumoto, 1994). Ethnocentrism may also prevent you from being aware of how your behavior has been shaped by your own culture.

Some degree of ethnocentrism is probably inevitable, but extreme ethnocentrism can lead to intolerance for other cultures (Moghaddam & others, 1993). If you believe that your way of seeing things or behaving is the only proper one, other ways of behaving and thinking may seem not only foreign but ridiculous, wrong, or immoral.

Along with influencing how we behave, culture also affects the way we define our sense of personal identity (Kitayama & others, 1997; Markus & Kitayama, 1991). For the most part, the dominant cultures of North America, Australia, New Zealand, and Europe can be described as individualistic cultures (Brislin, 1993). **Individualistic**

All cultures are simultaneously very similar and very different.

Harry Triandis (1994)

cultures emphasize the needs and goals of the individual over the needs and goals of the group (Triandis, 1996). In such cultures, the self is seen as *independent,* autonomous, and distinctive. Much of a person's identity is defined by his or her individual achievements, abilities, and occupation.

In contrast, **collectivistic cultures** emphasize the needs and goals of the group over the needs and goals of the individual. The cultures of Asia, Africa, and Central and South America tend to be collectivistic (Brislin, 1993). In a collectivistic culture, the self is seen as being much more *interdependent* with others (Kitayama & others, 1997; Simon & others, 1995). A person's relationships with others and his or her identification with a larger group, such as the family or tribe, are key components of his or her personal identity (Triandis, 1996).

Like all psychologists, cross-cultural psychologists look for consistent patterns in human behavior. Cross-cultural psychologists make generalizations about the behaviors and attitudes of people in different cultures. However, they also recognize that there is a great deal of individual variation among the members of *every* culture.

The Culture and Human Behavior boxes that we have included in this book will help you learn about human behavior in other cultures. They will also help you understand how culture affects *your* behavior, beliefs, attitudes, and values as well. We hope you find this feature to be both interesting and enlightening!

Cultural Differences in Subway Norms
Like thousands of commuters in major cities in the United States, commuters in Tokyo take the subway to work each day. In Japan, however, commuters line up politely behind white lines on the subway platform and patiently wait their turn to board the train. White-gloved conductors obligingly "assist" passengers in boarding by shoving them in from behind, cramming as many people into the subway car as possible. Clearly, the norms that govern "subway-riding behavior" are very different in American and Japanese cultures.

Perspectives and Specialty Areas in Psychology

TABLE 1.1 Perspectives in Psychology

Perspective	Emphasis
Biological	Physical bases of behavior
Behaviorial	Environmental influences on behavior
Psychoanalytic	Unconscious influences on behavior and personality
Humanistic	Psychological growth and personal potential
Cognitive	Mental processes
Cross-cultural	Influence of culture on behavior

In the last few decades, the scope of topics in psychology has become progressively more diverse. And, as psychology's knowledge base has increased, psychology itself has become more specialized (Bower, 1993). Rather than being dominated by a particular school of thought, today's psychologists tend to characterize themselves according to (1) the *perspective* they emphasize in investigating psychological topics and (2) the *specialty area* in which they practice.

Any given topic in contemporary psychology can be approached from a variety of perspectives. Traditionally, five major perspectives have been identified in psychology: *biological, behavioral, psychoanalytic, humanistic,* and *cognitive.* Because of the increasing importance of cross-cultural research in psychology, the *cross-cultural perspective* has also become influential. As you can see in Table 1.1, each perspective reflects a particular emphasis in studying a given topic or issue.

Let's illustrate how the different perspectives might approach studying the developmental period that spans the first two years of life—infancy.

- From a *biological perspective,* a psychologist might investigate brain development during infancy, sensory abilities, or the influence of genetics.

- Taking a *behavioral perspective,* a psychologist might focus on how the infant's behavior is influenced by facial expressions and other responses of the caregiver.

- From a *psychoanalytic perspective,* a psychologist might study the impact of the infant's emotional relationship with his mother or father on his developing personality.

- From a *humanistic perspective,* a psychologist might be interested in how different parenting practices promote or restrict a child's striving to reach her potential.

- From the *cognitive perspective,* a psychologist would study how the infant processes, stores, and remembers information. She might investigate when the infant understands that objects continue to exist even if he can't see them, or how the infant gradually acquires an understanding of language.

- From a *cross-cultural perspective,* a psychologist might study the influence of culturally specific child-rearing practices, such as being raised in a kibbutz, a collective community in Israel.

Listed below are some of the important specialty areas in contemporary psychology, which reflect the enormous diversity of psychology today. Figure 1.1 on page 12 shows the approximate percentage of U.S. psychologists working in different specialty areas.

- **Biological psychology** focuses on the relationship between behavior and the body's physical systems, including the brain and the rest of the nervous system, the endocrine system, the immune system, and genetics.

- **Cognitive psychology** investigates mental processes, including reasoning and thinking, problem solving, memory, perception, mental imagery, and language.

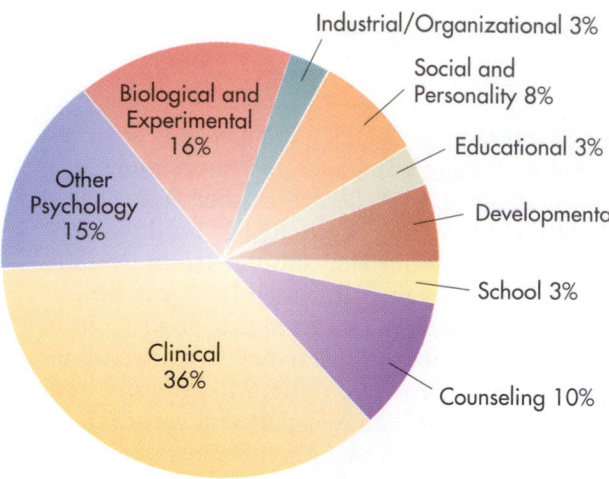

Industrial/Organizational 3%
Social and Personality 8%
Educational 3%
Developmental 6%
School 3%
Counseling 10%
Clinical 36%
Other Psychology 15%
Biological and Experimental 16%

FIGURE 1.1 Percentages of Psychologists Working in Various Specialty Areas
The approximate percentage of psychologists in each of the major specialty areas is shown here. Psychologists can be found working in private practice, universities and colleges, business and industry, and federal, state, and local government offices. (Adapted from Thurgood & Clarke, 1995, and APA Research Office, 1995)

● **Experimental psychology** focuses on research in basic topics like sensory processes, principles of learning, emotion, and motivation. However, note that experiments are used by psychologists in every area of psychology.

● **Developmental psychology** studies the physical, social, and psychological changes that occur at different ages and stages over the lifespan, from conception to old age.

● **Social psychology** explores how people are affected by their social environments, including how people think about and influence others. Topics as varied as conformity, obedience, persuasion, interpersonal attraction, helping behavior, prejudice, and aggression are studied by social psychologists.

● **Personality psychology** examines individual differences and the characteristics that make each person unique, including how those characteristics originated and developed.

● **Health psychology** focuses on the role of psychological factors in the development, prevention, and treatment of illness. Health psychology includes areas like stress and coping, the relationship between psychological factors and health, patient/doctor relationships, and ways of promoting health-enhancing behaviors.

● **Educational psychology** studies how people of all ages learn. Educational psychologists help develop the instructional methods and materials used to train people in both educational and work settings. A related field, *school psychology,* focuses on designing programs that promote the intellectual, social, and emotional development of children, including those with special needs.

● **Industrial/organizational psychology** is concerned with the relationship between people and work. This specialty includes such topics as worker productivity and job satisfaction, personnel selection and training, consumer reactions to a company's products or services, and the interaction between people and equipment.

● **Clinical psychology** studies the causes, treatment, and prevention of different types of psychological disorders, such as debilitating anxiety or depression, eating disorders, and chronic substance abuse. A related specialty area is *counseling psychology,* which aims to improve everyday functioning by helping people solve problems in daily living and cope more effectively with challenging situations.

Clinical Psychologists Clinical psychologists have a doctorate in psychology along with extensive training in psychological disorders, psychotherapy techniques, and psychological testing. Unlike *psychiatrists,* clinical psychologists do not have a medical degree and cannot prescribe medications or perform medical procedures. Clinical psychologists may conduct psychotherapy with individuals, married couples, families, or groups of people.

Despite diverse work settings and interests, psychologists share the methods by which they investigate facets of human behavior and mental processes. In the next section, we'll look at how psychologists are guided by the scientific method in their efforts to understand behavior and mental processes.

Major Perspectives and Specialty Areas in Psychology

1. Dr. Chan conducts research on specialized cells in the brain and nervous system. Which perspective in psychology does Dr. Chan's research best represent?
- **a.** biological
- **b.** behavioral
- **c.** cognitive
- **d.** cross-cultural

2. A Canadian researcher found that when workers were part of a group, they were less productive than when working alone. However, researchers in Taiwan reported the opposite finding. These contradictory findings emphasize the importance of the _____ perspective in psychological research.
- **a.** cognitive
- **b.** cross-cultural
- **c.** behavioral
- **d.** humanistic

3. Dr. Webb focuses her research on the use of mental images in problem solving and memory. Dr. Webb is most likely a _____ psychologist.
- **a.** biological
- **b.** behavioral
- **c.** humanistic
- **d.** cognitive

4. Recently David has begun to feel so tense, anxious, and depressed that he sometimes spends the whole day in bed and can no longer study or work. It would be most beneficial for David to be examined by a(n) _____ psychologist.
- **a.** experimental
- **b.** developmental
- **c.** social
- **d.** clinical

The Scientific Method

The scientific method is a set of assumptions, attitudes, and procedures that guide scientists as they conduct research. What are the four goals of psychology? What assumptions and attitudes are held by psychologists? What characterizes each step of the scientific method?

The four basic goals of psychology are to (1) describe, (2) explain, (3) predict, and (4) control or influence behavior and mental processes. In trying to achieve these four goals, psychologists rely on the scientific method. The **scientific method** refers to a set of assumptions, attitudes, and procedures that guide researchers in creating questions to investigate, generating evidence, and drawing conclusions (Heiman, 1995).

Like all scientists, psychologists are guided by the basic scientific assumption that *events are lawful* (American Association for the Advancement of Science, 1989). When this scientific assumption is applied to psychology, it means that *psychologists assume that behavior and mental processes follow consistent patterns.*

In striving to discover and understand consistent patterns of behavior, psychologists are *open-minded.* They are willing to consider new explanations of behavior and mental processes. However, their open-minded attitude is tempered by a healthy sense of *scientific skepticism.* That is, psychologists *critically evaluate the evidence* for new findings, especially those that seem contrary to established knowledge. And in promoting new ideas and findings, psychologists are *cautious* in the claims they make.

Ideally, you should assume the same set of attitudes as you approach the study of psychology. To learn how to be a better critical thinker, see Critical Thinking Box 1.2.

scientific method
A set of assumptions, attitudes, and procedures that guide researchers in creating questions to investigate, generating evidence, and drawing conclusions.

CRITICAL THINKING 1.2

What Is Critical Thinking?

As you'll see throughout this text, many issues in contemporary psychology are far from being settled. Many important questions have no clear-cut answer. And although research findings may have been arrived at in a very objective manner, the *interpretation* of what findings mean and how they should be applied can be a matter of considerable debate. In short, there is a subjective side to *any* science, including psychology.

As you look at the evidence that psychology has to offer on many topics, we want to encourage you to engage in critical thinking. Just exactly what does *critical thinking* mean? There are many definitions of critical thinking (e.g., Halpern & Nummedal, 1995; Halonen, 1995). However, some common themes have emerged.

In general, *critical thinking* refers to *actively questioning* statements rather than blindly accepting them. More precisely, we define **critical thinking** as the active process of:

- Trying to minimize the influence of preconceptions and biases while rationally evaluating evidence;

- Determining the conclusions that can be drawn from the evidence;

- Considering alternative explanations for the evidence.

The following list summarizes some of the key attitudes and mental skills that characterize critical thinking.

1. The critical thinker can assume other perspectives. Critical thinkers are not imprisoned by their own point of view. Nor are they limited in their capacity to imagine life experiences and perspectives that are fundamentally different from their own.

Rather, the critical thinker strives to understand and evaluate issues from many different angles.

2. The critical thinker is aware of biases and assumptions. In evaluating evidence and ideas, critical thinkers strive to identify the biases and assumptions that are inherent in any argument. Critical thinkers also try to identify and minimize the influence of their *own* biases.

3. The critical thinker is flexible, yet maintains an attitude of healthy skepticism. Critical thinkers are open to new information, ideas, and claims. They genuinely consider alternative explanations and possibilities. However, this open-mindedness is tempered by a healthy sense of skepticism as the critical thinker consistently asks, "What evidence supports that claim?"

BIZARRO

CAPRICORN: TODAY IS A GOOD DAY TO MAKE IMPORTANT DECISIONS ABOUT YOUR LIFE BASED ON ARBITRARY NONSENSE WRITTEN BY AN ANONYMOUS STRANGER IN A NEWSPAPER.

4. The critical thinker engages in reflective thinking. Critical thinkers avoid knee-jerk responses. Instead, critical thinkers are *reflective*. Most complex issues are unlikely to have a simple resolution. Therefore, critical thinkers resist the temptation to sidestep complexity by boiling an issue down to an either/or, yes/no kind of proposition. Instead, the critical thinker *expects* and *accepts* complexity.

5. The critical thinker scrutinizes the evidence before drawing conclusions. Critical thinkers strive to weigh all the available evidence *before* they arrive at conclusions. And, in evaluating evidence, the critical thinker distinguishes between *empirical evidence* and *opinions* based on feelings or personal experience.

As you can see, critical thinking is a *set* of attitudes and thinking skills that you can actively apply in logically evaluating the pros and cons of arguments. As is true with any set of skills, you can get better at critical thinking with practice. That's one of the reasons that we've included Critical Thinking boxes in every chapter of this text.

You'll discover that these Critical Thinking boxes are very diverse. Some will challenge your preconceptions on certain topics. Some will invite you to take sides in the debates of some of the most important contributors to modern psychology. And other Critical Thinking boxes will help you critically evaluate the evidence for a variety of phenomena—from biorhythms to repressed memories. In each case, our goal is to encourage you to actively use your critical thinking skills.

We hope you enjoy this feature!

The Steps in the Scientific Method

Like any science, psychology is based on *empirical evidence,* or evidence that is the result of observation, measurement, and experimentation. As part of the overall process of producing empirical evidence, psychologists follow the steps of the scientific method. In a nutshell, these steps are: (1) creating testable questions, (2) designing a study to collect data, (3) analyzing the data to arrive at conclusions, and (4) reporting the results. While not foolproof, the basic guidelines of the scientific method help minimize the chance for error and faulty conclusions. Let's look at some of the key concepts associated with each step of the scientific method.

Formulating a Hypothesis Hypotheses are often generated from casual observations. For example, do you think this accomplished young musician mentally processes music differently from someone who is just beginning to learn to play a musical instrument? How could a psychologist investigate this question? What variables would need to be operationally defined?

Step 1. Formulate a Hypothesis That Can Be Tested Empirically

Once a researcher has identified a question or an issue that he or she wishes to investigate, it must be posed in the form of a hypothesis that can be tested empirically. Formally, a **hypothesis** is a tentative statement that describes the relationship between two or more variables. A hypothesis is often posed in terms of a specific prediction that can be empirically tested, such as the hypothesis "mental distraction increases pain tolerance." (We discuss this particular hypothesis in Chapter 3.)

The **variables** contained in any given hypothesis are simply the factors that can vary, or change. These changes must be capable of being observed, measured, and verified. In describing the variables to be investigated, the psychologist must provide an operational definition of each variable. An **operational definition** defines the variable in terms of how the factor is to be measured or manipulated.

Operational definitions are critical because many of the concepts that psychologists investigate—like memory, happiness, or stress—can be measured in more than one way. In providing operational definitions of the variables in the study, the researcher spells out in very concrete and precise terms how the variables will be manipulated or measured. This allows other researchers to understand exactly how the variables were measured or manipulated in a particular study.

For example, consider the hypothesis that "negativity reduces marital stability" (see Karney & Bradbury, 1995). To test this hypothesis, you would need to operationally define each variable. How could you operationally define "negativity" and "marital stability"? What could you measure?

You could operationally define "negativity" in many different ways. For example, you might operationally define "negativity" as the number of arguments the couple has per month. In a similar way, you would have to devise an operational definition for "marital stability," such as the number of times the couple discussed getting divorced or the number of times the couple separated.

Step 2. Design the Study and Collect the Data

This step involves deciding which research method will be used for collecting data. There are two basic categories of research methods—*experimental* and *descriptive*. Each research method answers different kinds of questions and provides different kinds of evidence.

The *experimental method* is used to show that one variable *causes* change in a second variable. In an experiment, the researcher deliberately and systematically varies one factor, then measures the changes produced in a second factor. For example, to study the effect of the number of bystanders on a person's willingness to help a stranger, the researcher would deliberately vary the number of bystanders (Latané & Darley, 1970). Then, he would measure how the willingness to help a stranger was affected by the change in the number of bystanders.

Ideally, all experimental conditions are kept as constant as possible except for the factor that is deliberately changed. Then, if changes occur in the second factor, those changes can be attributed to the variations in the first factor. In the next main section, we'll take a detailed look at how the experimental

hypothesis
(high-POTH-eh-sis) A tentative statement about the relationship between two or more variables.

variable
A factor that can vary, or change, in ways that can be observed, measured, and verified.

operational definition
A precise description of how the variables in a study will be manipulated or measured.

method provides evidence of a *cause-and-effect relationship* between two variables.

In contrast to the experimental method, *descriptive methods* are research strategies for *observing and describing behavior,* including identifying the factors that seem to be associated with a particular phenomenon. Descriptive methods answer the *who, what, where,* and *when* kinds of questions about behavior. Who engages in a particular behavior? What factors or events seem to be associated with the behavior? Where does the behavior occur? When does the behavior occur? How often? In a later section, we'll discuss commonly used descriptive methods, which include *naturalistic observation, surveys, case studies,* and *correlational studies.*

Step 3. Analyze the Data and Draw Conclusions

Once the observations and measurements have been collected, the "raw" data need to be summarized and analyzed in a way that allows overall conclusions to be drawn. To do so, researchers rely on **statistics,** which are mathematical methods that are used to summarize, analyze, and draw conclusions about data.

Researchers use statistics to determine if the results support the hypothesis. Statistics are also used to determine whether the findings are statistically significant. If the finding is **statistically significant,** it means the results are not very likely to have occurred by chance (Grimm, 1993). As a rule, statistically significant results confirm the hypothesis. If you're interested in the use of statistics in the scientific method, we provide an introduction to the basic principles of statistics in the Statistics Appendix at the back of the book.

Keep in mind, statistical significance and practical significance are not necessarily the same (Scarr, 1997). If a study involves a large number of participants, even small differences among groups of subjects may result in a statistically significant finding. But the actual average differences may be so small that they have little practical significance or importance. So remember that a statistically significant result is simply one that is not very likely to have occurred by chance. Whether the finding is significant in the everyday sense is another matter altogether.

A statistical technique called **meta-analysis** is increasingly being used in psychology to analyze the results of many research studies on a specific topic (Rosenthal, 1994; Schmidt, 1992). Meta-analysis is also useful when a large number of studies have produced inconsistent or contradictory results. Basically, meta-analysis involves pooling the results of several studies into a single analysis. By creating one large pool of data to be analyzed, meta-analysis can sometimes reveal overall trends that are not evident in individual studies.

Step 4. Report the Findings

For advances to be made in any scientific discipline, researchers must publish or share their findings with other scientists. Along with reporting their results, psychologists provide a detailed explanation of the exact methods and procedures that were used. Describing the methods in detail makes it possible for other investigators to **replicate,** or repeat, the study. Replication is an important part of the scientific process. When a study is replicated and the same basic results occur again, it increases scientific *confidence* that the results are accurate. And, obviously, if the replication of a study fails to produce the same basic findings, it reduces confidence in the original findings.

One way that psychologists report their findings is by formally presenting their research at a professional conference. Researchers can also report their findings by writing a paper summarizing the study and submitting it

statistics
Mathematical methods used to summarize data and draw conclusions based on the data.

statistical significance
A mathematical indication that research results are not very likely to have occurred by chance.

meta-analysis
A statistical technique that involves combining and analyzing the results of many research studies on a specific topic in order to identify overall trends.

replicate
To repeat or duplicate a scientific study in order to increase confidence in the validity of the original findings.

for publication in one of the many psychology journals. Most of these scientific journals have the research reviewed by other psychologists before accepting it for publication. Reviewers critically evaluate different aspects of a study, including how the results were analyzed. If the study conforms to the principles of sound scientific research and contributes to the existing knowledge base, it is accepted for publication.

Throughout this text, you'll see citations like the one at the end of this sentence (Leichtman & Ceci, 1995). These citations identify the sources of the research and ideas that we discuss. The citation tells you the author or authors of the published study (Leichtman & Ceci) and the year (1995) in which the study was published. Using this information, you can go to the alphabetized References section at the back of this text and find the complete reference, which lists the authors' full names, the article title, and the journal or book in which it was published. In Figure 1.2, you can see how to interpret the different parts of a typical journal reference.

Year study published   Authors   Title of study

Leichtman, Michelle D., & Ceci, Stephen J.

(1995). The effects of stereotypes and suggestions

on preschoolers' reports.

Developmental Psychology,   31 (4), 568–578.

Title of scientific journal   Volume number   Issue number   Page numbers

FIGURE 1.2 How to Read a Journal Reference
Using the references section at the back of this text, you can find the complete source for each citation that appears in a chapter. The figure above shows what the different components of a typical journal reference mean. In the chapter itself, the citation for this particular reference would read "(Leichtman & Ceci, 1995)."

theory
A tentative explanation that tries to integrate and account for the relationship among various findings and observations.

experimental method
A method of investigation used to demonstrate cause-and-effect relationships by purposely manipulating a factor thought to produce change in a second factor.

independent variable
The purposely manipulated factor thought to produce change in an experiment.

Building Theories

As research findings accumulate from individual studies, eventually theories develop. A **theory,** or *model,* is a tentative explanation that tries to account for diverse findings on the same topic. Note that theories are *not* the same as hypotheses. As we said earlier, a hypothesis is a specific question or prediction to be tested. A theory, in contrast, integrates and summarizes a large number of findings and observations. Along with explaining existing results, a good theory generates *new* hypotheses to be tested by further research.

As you encounter different theories, try to remember that theories are *tools* for explaining behavior and mental processes, not statements of absolute fact. A theory's usefulness is judged by how much it furthers understanding of behavior and stimulates new research. Often more than one theory is useful in understanding a particular area of behavior or mental processes.

Theories evolve and change as new findings are reported. When new research results challenge the established way of thinking about a phenomenon, theories are expanded, modified, and even replaced. Put simply, the knowledge base of psychology is constantly evolving.

In the next section, we'll look at the scientific method in action as we describe the experimental method and descriptive methods in more detail.

The Experimental Method

The experimental method is used to demonstrate a cause-and-effect relationship between two variables. What are the hypothesis, independent variable, and dependent variable in the Sam Stone experiment? What are the roles of random assignment, the control group, and the experimental groups?

The **experimental method** is a research method that is used to demonstrate a cause-and-effect relationship between changes in one variable and the effects on another. Essentially, conducting an experiment involves *deliberately varying* one factor, which is called the **independent variable,** then *measuring* the effects on another factor, called the **dependent variable.** The dependent variable is so named because it "depends" on the changes in the independent variable. Assuming that all other conditions in the experiment have been held constant, any changes that occur in the dependent variable can be attributed to the changes in the independent variable. That's how an experiment can demonstrate a cause-and-effect relationship between the independent and dependent variables.

To help you understand important aspects of the experimental method, we will look at an ingenious experiment recently conducted by psychologists Michelle Leichtman and Stephen Ceci. They were interested in the reliability of young children's memories in court cases.

Leichtman and Ceci (1995) found that like adult witnesses, children are often repeatedly questioned over the course of several weeks by people involved in the case, such as police officers, social workers, psychotherapists, lawyers, and family members. Sometimes, interviewers use *suggestive questioning.* That is, they may word their questions in such a way that the questions suggest to the child what the interviewer thinks happened. Leichtman and Ceci were interested in whether suggestive questioning, especially when it takes place on several occasions, could influence a preschooler's later memory of an event.

In some court cases, children are repeatedly exposed to negative information about a person that can potentially distort a young child's interpretations of actual events (Ceci & Bruck, 1993). For example, in custody court battles, children often hear one parent openly criticizing the other parent. In turn, this negative pre-information can influence how the child perceives the subsequent actions of the parent who has been criticized. So, Leichtman and Ceci were also interested in whether negative pre-information could influence a young child's memory of a later event.

Leichtman and Ceci's experiment was designed to realistically create both these conditions—suggestive questioning and exposure to pre-information—and then measure their effect on the accuracy of young children's memories of a neutral event. They refer to their experiment as the "Sam Stone study" because the event in question involved the visit of a stranger called Sam Stone.

The Sam Stone Study

The 176 preschoolers who participated in the study were enrolled in private day-care centers. All the children experienced the visit of a stranger named Sam Stone to their day-care classroom. Here is how psychologists Michelle Leichtman and Stephen Ceci (1995) describe Sam Stone's visit:

> *First, he entered the classroom and said hello to a teacher or aide who sat amidst the assembled children during a story-telling session, and he was introduced by the teacher or aide to the children [as Sam Stone]. Next, he commented on the story that was being read to the children by the teacher or aide ("I know that story; it's one of my favorites!") and strolled around the perimeter of the classroom. Finally, he departed, waving goodbye to the children. In each case, the entire event was timed and lasted approximately 2 minutes.*

Random Assignment

Collectively, the preschoolers represented a wide range of social and ethnic groups. The researchers used a process called *random assignment* to assign each class of preschoolers to one of the four different experimental conditions. **Random assignment** means that all subjects have an equal chance of being assigned to any of the experimental conditions.

dependent variable
The factor that is observed and measured for change in an experiment; thought to be influenced by the independent variable.

random assignment
Assigning subjects to experimental conditions in such a way that all subjects have an equal chance of being assigned to any of the conditions or groups in the study.

FIGURE 1.3 The Experimental Design of the "Sam Stone" Study

The diagram shows the basic design of the "Sam Stone" study. Two independent variables were manipulated: (1) whether the children received information about Sam Stone before his visit; and (2) whether suggestive questioning of the children occurred after Sam Stone's visit. This created four experimental conditions, the control group and three experimental groups, as shown here.

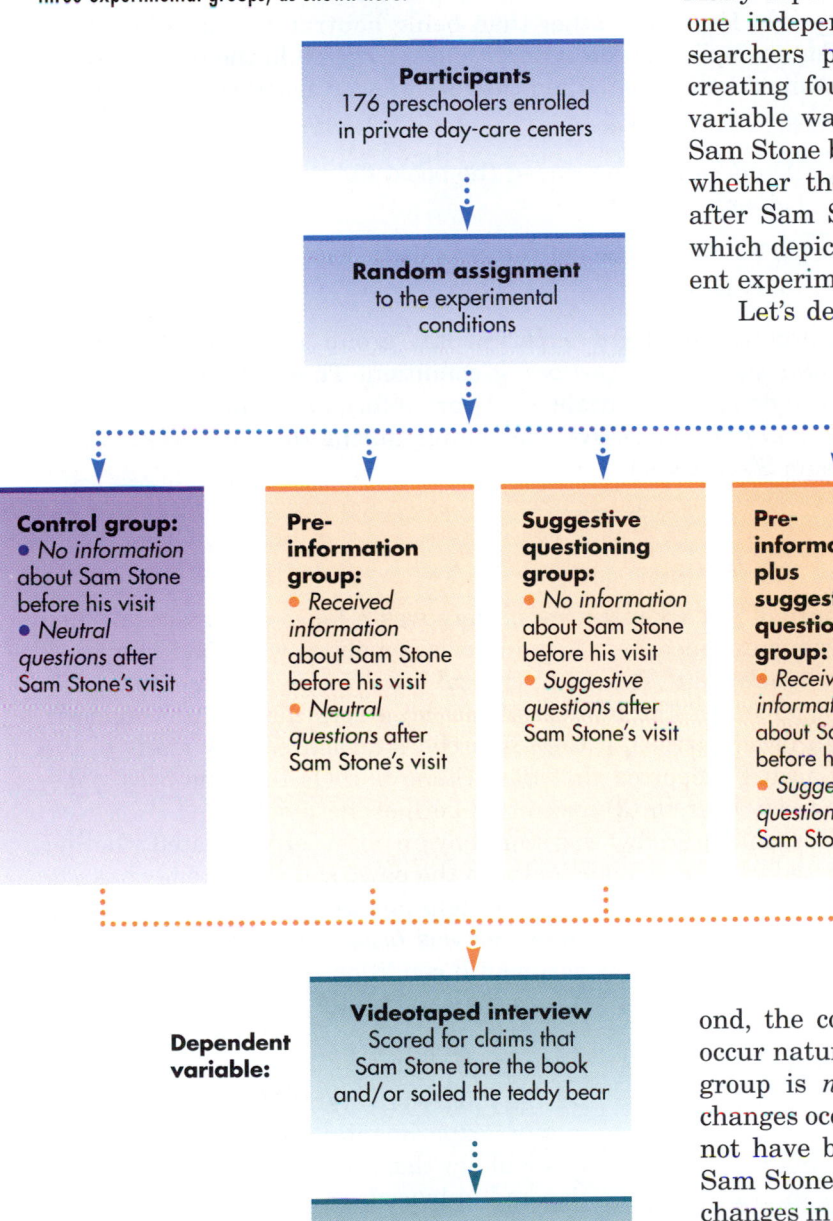

Participants
176 preschoolers enrolled in private day-care centers

Random assignment
to the experimental conditions

Control group:
• *No information* about Sam Stone before his visit
• *Neutral questions* after Sam Stone's visit

Pre-information group:
• *Received information* about Sam Stone before his visit
• *Neutral questions* after Sam Stone's visit

Suggestive questioning group:
• *No information* about Sam Stone before his visit
• *Suggestive questions* after Sam Stone's visit

Pre-information plus suggestive questioning group:
• *Received information* about Sam Stone before his visit
• *Suggestive questions* after Sam Stone's visit

Dependent variable:

Videotaped interview
Scored for claims that Sam Stone tore the book and/or soiled the teddy bear

Groups compared

control group
The group of subjects who are exposed to all experimental conditions, except the independent variable.

experimental group
The group of subjects who are exposed to all experimental conditions, including the independent variable.

Random assignment is an important element of good experimental design. First, randomly assigning subjects ensures that differences among the subjects are spread out across all experimental conditions. And second, because the same criteria are used to assign all subjects to the experimental conditions, random assignment helps ensure that the assignment of subjects is done in an unbiased manner.

The Experimental Conditions

Many experiments involve deliberately manipulating more than one independent variable. In the Sam Stone study, the researchers purposely manipulated two independent variables, creating four experimental conditions. The first independent variable was whether the children received *information* about Sam Stone before his visit. The second independent variable was whether the children were exposed to *suggestive questioning* after Sam Stone's visit. Take a moment to look at Figure 1.3, which depicts the study's design and summarizes the four different experimental conditions.

Let's describe the four experimental conditions in more detail. The children randomly assigned to the **control group** did *not* experience either of the independent variables. In other words, the children in the control group received *no* information about Sam Stone before his visit. Following Sam Stone's visit, the control-group children were individually questioned once per week for four weeks with simple, neutral questions about what Sam Stone had done during his visit. During this neutral questioning, *no* suggestions were given to the control-group children about how Sam Stone behaved during his visit.

In any experiment, the control group serves several important functions. First, it serves as a *baseline* to which changes in the other experimental groups can be compared. Second, the control group can be used to check for changes that occur naturally or spontaneously over time. Because the control group is *not* exposed to the independent variable, whatever changes occur in the dependent variable in the control group cannot have been caused by the independent variable. So, in the Sam Stone study, the control group was used as a way to detect changes in the memories of preschoolers who were *not* exposed to information or suggestive questioning.

In addition to the control group, there were three **experimental groups** in the Sam Stone study. Each experimental group was exposed to one or both of the independent variables. The children assigned to the first experimental group represented the *pre-information group*. These children were repeatedly told stories about Sam Stone before his visit to their classroom. Each week during the month before Sam Stone's visit, a research assistant told the children a different, carefully scripted story. Each story depicted Sam Stone as a kind and well-meaning, but very clumsy and bumbling, person.

The children in the pre-information group were also individually interviewed every week during the month following Sam Stone's visit. Like the children in the control group, the children in the information group were asked neutral questions about what Sam Stone had done during his visit to their classroom. The interviewers made no suggestions about what Sam Stone had done.

The second experimental group represented the *suggestive questioning condition*. The preschoolers assigned to this condition did *not* receive any information about Sam Stone before his visit. After Sam Stone's visit, the children in the suggestive questioning group were also interviewed once per week for a month. However, rather than being neutral, the questions were *suggestive*. For example, the interviewer showed the child the torn page of a book and a stained teddy bear. Then the interviewer asked suggestive questions like these:

- When Sam Stone ripped the book, did he do it alone or with a helper?
- When Sam Stone got the bear dirty, was he wearing long or short pants?

The children in the third experimental group represented the *pre-information-plus-suggestive-questioning* condition. These children were exposed to both independent variables: (1) pre-information about Sam Stone before his visit *and* (2) suggestive questioning during the four weekly interviews after Sam Stone's visit.

The Dependent Variable

After the month of weekly interviews, there was a lapse of six weeks. Then each child was questioned by a new interviewer about what had happened during Sam Stone's visit. This fifth, critical interview was videotaped. The dependent variable was the number of factual errors the children made in the fifth interview. Specifically, the researchers measured how many of the children erroneously reported that Sam Stone had (1) torn the book page, (2) soiled the teddy bear, or (3) committed both of these acts.

Each videotaped interview was scored by an observer who rated whether the child claimed that Sam Stone had torn the page, soiled the teddy bear, or both. To help ensure the rater's objectivity, the rater was *blind,* or unaware of the experimental condition to which the child had been assigned. If the rater knew a participant's experimental condition, it could inadvertently influence the rating. Thus, having judges or raters "blind" to the participants' experimental condition makes it more likely that evaluations will be objective and unbiased.

The Results of the Sam Stone Study

The results of the Sam Stone study are shown in Figure 1.4. As you can see, the young children were clearly influenced by both pre-information and suggestive questioning. In comparison to the control group, the most dramatic effect was for the chil-

FIGURE 1.4 The Results of the Sam Stone Study

In the Sam Stone study, the results were analyzed separately for the youngest preschoolers in the 3-to-4 age range and for older preschoolers in the 5-to-6 age range. Below, you can see the results for the youngest preschoolers. Clearly, the greatest effect can be seen with those preschoolers who were exposed to both pre-information about Sam Stone and suggestive questioning. In general, the older preschoolers were about half as likely as the youngest preschoolers in each condition to claim that Sam Stone had committed the acts.

(Adapted from Leichtman & Ceci, 1995)

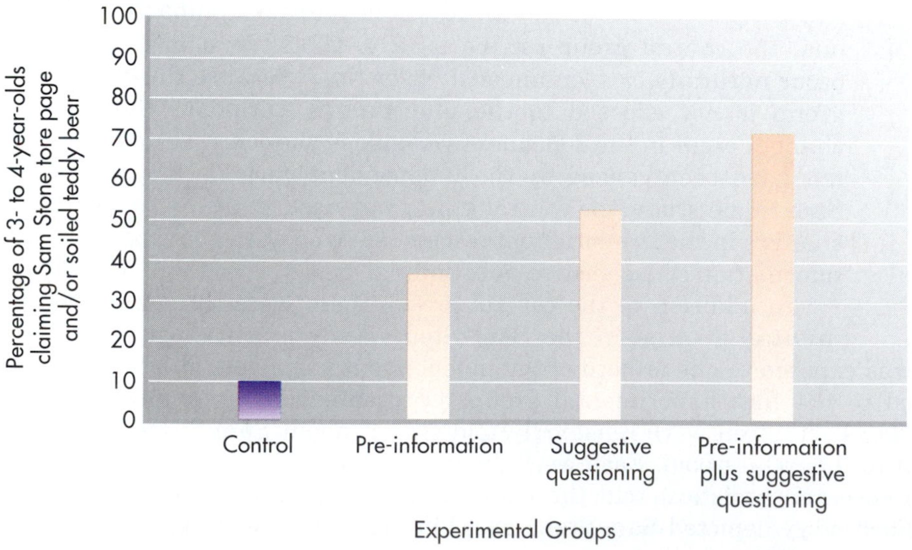

dren in the pre-information-plus-suggestive-questioning group: 72 percent of them claimed that Sam Stone had torn the book page or soiled the teddy bear (Leichtman & Ceci, 1995). Keep in mind that *neither* of these events occurred during Sam Stone's visit to their classroom.

Leichtman and Ceci (1995) note several implications of their findings. First, the study replicates, or repeats, the findings of earlier studies showing that young children's memories can be influenced by the suggestions of an adult. Second, the low rate of errors made by children in the control group demonstrates that even young children can accurately report an event if the situation remains free of added information and suggestive or leading questions.

Variations in Experimental Design

Experimental designs can vary, depending on the question to be investigated. What is a placebo control group, and when is it likely to be used? What is the expectancy effect? Why do researchers use the double-blind technique? What are some limitations of the experimental method?

Depending on the research question, experimental designs can vary. For example, experiments designed to assess the effectiveness of a treatment, such as a particular drug, often involve the use of a **placebo control group.** The participants assigned to this experimental condition receive a *placebo,* which is a fake treatment or a substance with no known effects. However, the subjects don't know whether they are receiving the actual or fake treatment.

Why is a placebo control group important in experiments designed to assess the effectiveness of a treatment? A placebo control group helps check for **expectancy effects,** which refer to changes that may occur simply because subjects expect change to occur. Thus, researchers can compare the effects of the actual treatment versus the expectancy effects, if any, that are demonstrated by the placebo control group.

In such studies, researchers often use a double-blind technique. A *double-blind* study is one in which neither the participants nor the researcher who interacts with them is aware of which experimental condition each participant has been assigned to. For example, in a study with a placebo control group, the researcher who interacted with the subjects would not know which subjects got the placebo and which subjects received the actual treatment. The researchers who *do* know which participants have been assigned to each experimental condition do not interact with or evaluate the participants. In contrast, a *single-blind study* is one in which the researcher, but not the subjects, is aware of critical information.

The purpose of the double-blind technique is to guard against the possibility that the researcher will inadvertently display *demand characteristics,* which are subtle cues or signals that communicate what is expected of particular subjects (Kihlstrom, 1995). A behavior as subtle as the researcher smiling when dealing with certain participants, but not others, could bias the outcome of a study.

placebo control group
(pluh-SEE-bo) An experimental control group in which subjects are exposed to a fake independent variable.

expectancy effect
Change in a subject's behavior produced by the subject's belief that change should happen.

Limitations of Experiments

The strength of a well-designed experiment is that it can provide convincing evidence of a cause-and-effect relationship between the independent and dependent variables. However, experiments are not without their limitations. Because experiments are often conducted in highly controlled laboratory situations, they are frequently criticized for having little to do with actual behavior. That is, the artificial conditions of some experiments may produce results that do not *generalize* well, or apply to real situations or to a more general population beyond the participants in the study.

In order to make experimental conditions less artificial, sometimes experiments are conducted in a natural setting rather than in a laboratory. This strategy was used in the Sam Stone study: all experimental manipulations and measurements were conducted at the children's preschools. The researchers also tried to create conditions that realistically reflected those faced by young children in the judicial process. However, experiments conducted in natural settings have their own disadvantages, such as a decrease in experimental control. For example, in the Sam Stone study, it was impossible to control for what the preschoolers might have said to one another between the interviews.

Another limitation of the experimental method is that it's not always feasible to study a particular issue experimentally. For example, if participants would be harmed by being exposed to a variable or experimental condition, the experiment could not ethically be performed. Later in the chapter we'll discuss ethics in psychological research in more detail.

Finally, it may be impossible to create experimentally the kinds of conditions that researchers want to study. For example, in the prologue to this chapter we described the aftereffects of the Oklahoma City bombing. The effects of that disaster on the lives of those directly and indirectly affected will be the subject of psychological study for many years to come. Obviously, the conditions involved in the Oklahoma City bombing could not be experimentally manipulated. Thus, psychologists must also rely on other research methods to advance the understanding of human behavior. We'll look at these alternative research methods, called *descriptive methods,* in the next section.

CONCEPT REVIEW 1.3

The Experimental Method

Identify each component of the Sam Stone study. Choose from the following terms:

(A) independent variable(s)
(B) control group
(C) dependent variable(s)
(D) experimental group
(E) replicate
(F) hypothesis
(G) operational definition

_____ **1.** Leichtman and Ceci believed that suggestive questioning and negative pre-information might influence the accuracy of preschoolers' memories of a neutral event.

_____ **2.** Number of factual errors made in the final interview.

_____ **3.** Children who received no pre-information about Sam Stone before his visit and were exposed to neutral, not suggestive, questions after his visit.

_____ **4.** The Sam Stone study duplicated findings previously reported by other researchers.

_____ **5.** Children who receive pre-information before Sam Stone's visit and/or are exposed to suggestive questioning after his visit.

_____ **6.** Negative pre-information and suggestive questions about Sam Stone.

_____ **7.** "Accuracy of memory" is measured by the number of errors made in the final interview.

descriptive methods
Scientific procedures that involve systematically observing behavior in order to describe the relationships among behaviors and events.

naturalistic observation
The systematic observation and recording of behaviors as they occur in their natural setting.

Descriptive Methods

Descriptive methods are research methods used to observe and describe behavior. How is naturalistic observation usually conducted? What are case studies, and when are case studies typically used?

The **descriptive methods** do *not* involve deliberately manipulating the variables to which subjects are exposed. Rather, they are research strategies for observing and describing behavior. Using descriptive methods, researchers can answer important questions, such as when certain behaviors take place, how often they occur, and whether they are related to other factors, such as a person's age, race, and educational level. As you'll see, descriptive methods can provide a wealth of information about behavior, especially behaviors that would be difficult or impossible to study experimentally.

Naturalistic Observation

When psychologists systematically observe and record behaviors as they occur in their natural settings, they are using the descriptive method called **naturalistic observation.** Naturalistic observation can be used to study many different kinds of behavior and subjects. Usually, the researcher tries to avoid being detected by the subjects, whether they are people or animals. The basic goal of naturalistic observation is to detect the behavior patterns that exist naturally—patterns that might not be apparent in a laboratory or if the subjects knew they were being watched.

As you might expect, psychologists very carefully define the behaviors that they will observe and measure before they begin their research. Often, two or more observers are used to increase the accuracy of the observations. In some studies, the observations are videotaped or audiotaped, so that the researchers can record and carefully analyze the details of the behavior they are studying.

One advantage of naturalistic observation is that it can allow researchers to study human behaviors that could not be ethically manipulated in an experiment. For example, suppose a psychologist wanted to study bullying behavior in children. It would be completely unethical to deliberately create a prolonged situation in which one child is aggressively bullied by another child. However, psychologists *could* ethically study bullying by observing aggressive behavior in children on crowded school playgrounds.

Psychologists Debra Pepler and Wendy Craig (1995) did just that. From their vantage point on the second floor of a school, they used a camcorder with a telephoto lens and small, wireless microphones to observe the spontaneous interactions of schoolchildren. Using this naturalistic observation strategy, they discovered that physical and verbal aggressive incidents are far from rare. Even among children whom teachers regarded as nonaggressive, instances of physical aggression occurred about once every 11 minutes, and verbal aggression about once every 5 minutes. And, contrary to what many people assume, Pepler and Craig found that girls bully other children at the same rate as boys do.

Naturalistic Observation Since 1960, Jane Goodall has been observing the behavior of chimpanzees in the wild. Goodall, shown here in an early photograph, made many discoveries about chimpanzee behavior through the use of naturalistic observation. For example, she discovered that chimpanzees, like humans, use objects as tools. Most psychologists engaged in naturalistic observation would never get this close to their subjects. Ideally, the observer tries to avoid disturbing or interfering with the natural behavior pattern that she is investigating.

case study
A highly detailed description of a single individual or event.

survey
A questionnaire or interview designed to investigate the opinions, behaviors, or characteristics of a particular group.

As a research tool, naturalistic observation can be used virtually anywhere that patterns of behavior can be openly observed—from the jungles of Tanzania to fast-food restaurants, college campuses, or singles bars. Because the observations occur in the natural setting, the results of naturalistic observation studies can often be generalized more confidently to real-life situations than can the results of studies using artificially manipulated or staged situations (see Pepler & Craig, 1995).

Case Studies

A **case study** is an intensive, in-depth investigation of an individual. Case studies are most often used to investigate rare, unusual, or extreme conditions. Nevertheless, case studies often provide psychologists with information that can be used to help understand normal behavior (Adler, 1993).

Case studies involve compiling a great deal of information, often from a variety of different sources, to construct a detailed picture of a single subject. For example, the subject may be intensively interviewed, and his or her friends, family, and co-workers may be interviewed as well. Psychological records, medical records, and even school records may be examined. Other sources of information can include extensive psychological testing and observations of the person's behavior.

Surveys

> Surveys, questionnaires, and interviews are descriptive methods that involve directly asking people about their behavior. Why is random selection important in choosing a sample? What does it mean to say that a sample is representative of a larger population, and why is it important?

A direct way to find out about the behavior, attitudes, and opinions of people is simply to ask them. **Surveys** and questionnaires typically involve a paper-and-pencil format in which the subjects respond to a structured set of questions about their experiences, beliefs, behavior, or attitudes. One key advantage offered by survey research is that researchers are able to gather information from a much larger group of people than could be obtained through other research methods.

Surveys can also be conducted in person, with the interviewer recording the person's responses. As with surveys and questionnaires, the interviewer usually asks a structured set of questions in a predetermined order.

CALVIN AND HOBBES

Surveys, questionnaires, and interviews are seldom administered to everyone within the particular group or population under investigation. Instead, the researchers usually select a **sample**—a segment of the larger group or population. Selecting a sample that is representative of the larger group is the key to getting accurate survey results. A **representative sample** very closely parallels, or matches, the larger group on relevant characteristics, such as age, sex, race, marital status, and educational level.

How do researchers select the participants for the sample so that they end up with a sample that is representative of the larger group? The most common strategy is to randomly select the sample participants. *Random selection* means that every member of the larger group has an equal chance of being selected for inclusion in the sample.

One potential problem with surveys and questionnaires is that people do not always answer honestly. Subjects can misrepresent their personal characteristics or lie in their responses. This problem can be addressed in a well-designed survey. For example, the same basic question can be asked at different points in the survey or during the interview and can be posed in slightly different ways. The researchers can then compare the two responses to make sure that the participant was responding honestly and consistently.

Correlational Studies

Correlational studies show how strongly two factors are related to one another. What is a correlation coefficient? What is the difference between a positive correlation and a negative correlation? Why can't correlational studies be used to demonstrate cause-and-effect relationships?

Along with answering who, what, where, and when, the data gathered by descriptive research techniques can be analyzed to show how various factors are related. A **correlational study** examines how strongly two variables are related to, or associated with, each other. Probably the best way to develop an appreciation of correlational studies, including their limitations, is to look at a simple example.

Many people believe that there is a relationship between stress and susceptibility to colds—that the more stress you're under, the more likely you are to catch a cold. How could we investigate the relationship between stress and colds? First, we could survey people on the number of stressful events they've experienced in the last six months, such as financial troubles, relationship problems, job-related pressures, and so on. Second, we could ask them how many colds and respiratory infections they've had during the same time period.

With these data in hand, we could use a statistical procedure to calculate a figure called a correlation coefficient. A *correlation coefficient* is a numerical indicator of how strongly related two factors seem to be. A correlation coefficient always falls in a range from –1.00 to + 1.00. There are two parts to any correlation coefficient—the number and the sign. The number tells us about the *strength* of the relationship and the sign indicates the *direction* of the relationship between the two variables.

More specifically, the closer a correlation coefficient is to 1.00, whether it is positive or negative, the stronger the correlation or association between two factors. Hence, a correlation coefficient of +.80 or −.80 would represent a strong association, while a correlation of +.20 or −.20 would represent a weak correlation.

sample
A selected segment of the population used to represent the group that is being studied.

representative sample
A selected segment that very closely parallels the larger population being studied on relevant characteristics.

correlational study
A research strategy that allows the precise calculation of how strongly related two factors are to one another.

Notice that correlation coefficients do not function like the algebraic number line. A correlation of −.80 represents a stronger relationship than a correlation of +.20. That's because the plus or minus sign in a correlation coefficient simply tells you the direction of the relationship between the two variables. A **positive correlation,** like a +.60, is one in which the two factors vary in the same direction. That is, the two factors increase or decrease together. For example, there's a positive correlation between years of education and average annual earnings. As years of education increase, average yearly earnings also increase.

In contrast, a **negative correlation** is one in which the two variables move in *opposite* directions. For example, a negative correlation exists between marital satisfaction and rate of divorce. As the degree of reported marital satisfaction *increases,* the rate of divorce *decreases* (Karney & Bradbury, 1995). Thus, when two factors are negatively correlated, the two factors vary in opposite directions.

Given the basics of correlation coefficients, let's go back to our example. After crunching the data, let's assume that we found a very strong, positive correlation of +.90 between the number of stressful events that people have experienced and the number of colds people have. That is, people who experienced a high number of stressful events also have a higher number of colds than people who experienced a lower number of stressful events. Now, here's the critical question: Can we conclude that stress *causes* susceptibility to colds?

Not necessarily. Even if stressful life events and colds are very strongly correlated, it's completely possible that some other factor is involved. For example, it may be that people who are under a great deal of stress have more contact with other people and thus are more frequently exposed to cold germs. Or it could be that people who are under a great deal of stress engage in more unhealthy behaviors, such as smoking, eating a poor diet, or getting inadequate sleep. Rather than stress, it may be that unhealthy behaviors increase vulnerability to colds.

The critical point here is that even if two factors are very strongly correlated, *correlation does not necessarily indicate causality.* All a correlation tells you is that two factors seem to be related or co-vary in a systematic way. Although two factors may be very strongly correlated, different evidence is required to demonstrate a true cause-and-effect relationship. As we discussed earlier in the chapter, experimental evidence is required to demonstrate a cause-and-effect relationship between two variables.

Even though you can't draw conclusions about causality with correlational research, correlational research is still very valuable for two reasons. First, correlational research can be used to rule out some factors and identify others that merit more intensive study. For example, correlational research has been used to identify which factors contribute the most to episodes of depression (Kendler & others, 1993a).

Second, the results of correlational research can allow you to make meaningful predictions. As you'll see in Chapter 12 on stress, health, and coping, there is compelling evidence demonstrating a strong positive correlation between stress and susceptibility to colds and infections (e.g., Cohen & others, 1993). Thus, how much stress you are under *is* a good predictor of susceptibility to colds and infections.

Even though all the descriptive methods are limited by the fact that they don't provide evidence of causality, they can provide important information about when behavior happens, how often it happens, and if other factors or events are related to the behavior being studied. Finally, if you want to know more about correlation coefficients, they are discussed in greater detail in the Statistical Appendix.

positive correlation
A finding that two factors vary systematically in the same direction, increasing or decreasing together.

negative correlation
A finding that two factors vary systematically in opposite directions, one increasing as the other decreases.

Descriptive Methods and Correlational Studies

Fill in each blank with one of these terms: naturalistic observation, the case study method, correlational research, positive correlation, negative correlation.

1. A psychologist discovers that as negative life events increase, episodes of depression also increase. He concludes that there is a _____ between negative life events and episodes of depression.

2. A psychologist is interested in what hospital staff members say about their patients in public. His research assistants spend four hours riding elevators in various hospitals and unobtrusively recording the public conversations. This psychologist is using _____.

3. A psychologist is using police reports and weather reports to determine whether there is any relationship between the frequency of arrests for aggressive behavior and the temperature. She is using _____ to study this relationship.

4. Researchers have found that the more credit cards people have, the less money they tend to have in their savings accounts. These researchers have discovered a _____ between the number of credit cards and the amount of savings.

5. Dr. Romano conducts in-depth interviews and gives extensive psychological tests to individuals who claim to have been abducted by aliens. Dr. Romano is using _____ in his investigations of alien abductees.

Ethics in Psychological Research

All psychological research is subject to ethical guidelines developed by the American Psychological Association. What are five key provisions of the APA guidelines for research involving humans? Why do psychologists sometimes conduct research with animal subjects?

What might happen if you were to volunteer to participate in a psychology experiment or study? Are psychologists allowed to manipulate or control you without your knowledge or consent? Could a psychologist force you to reveal your innermost secrets? Could he or she administer electric shocks? Trick you into doing something weird against your will?

The answer to all these questions is "No." The American Psychological Association has developed a strict code of ethics for conducting research with both human and animal subjects. This code is contained in a document called *Ethical Principles of Psychologists and Code of Conduct* (APA, 1992a).

In general, psychologists must respect the fundamental rights, dignity, and welfare of all subjects. Psychologists cannot expose research participants to dangerous or harmful conditions that might cause either physical or emotional harm. And, any psychological research using human or animal subjects must be approved by an ethics panel at the institution where the study is to be conducted.

Here are five of the key provisions in the most recent version of the APA ethical guidelines regulating research with human participants:

- **Informed consent and voluntary participation.** In reasonably understandable language, the psychologist must inform the participants of the nature of the research, including significant factors that might influence a person's willingness to participate in the study, such as physical risks, discomfort, or unpleasant emotional experiences. The psychologist must also explain to the participants that they are free to decline to participate or to withdraw from the research at any time.

- **Students as research participants.** When research participation is a course requirement or an opportunity for extra credit, the student must be given the choice of an alternative activity to fulfill the course requirement or earn extra credit.

- **The use of deception.** Psychologists can use deceptive techniques as part of the study only when two conditions have been met: (1) when it is not feasible to use alternatives that do not involve deception; (2) when the potential findings justify the use of deception because of their scientific, educational, or applied value.

- **Confidentiality of records.** Psychologists do not publicly disclose personally identifiable information about research participants.

- **Information about the study and debriefing.** All participants are provided with the opportunity to obtain information about the nature, results, and conclusions of the research. Psychologists are also obligated to *debrief* the participants—that is, to correct any misconceptions that participants may have had about the research.

Who makes sure that these ethical guidelines are followed? First, the institution or organization where psychological research is conducted has usually established an ethics committee that must review and approve research proposals. Second, the APA has established the Committee on Scientific and Professional Ethics, which investigates all complaints it receives. If a psychologist is found to be in violation of the ethics code, that person may be suspended or expelled from the APA.

Not surprisingly, the ethical guidelines for research with human and animal subjects are somewhat different. However, the use of animals in psychological research is also governed by specific ethical guidelines (APA, 1992b). These guidelines, as well as other issues, are discussed in Box 1.3.

IN FOCUS 1.3

Questions About the Use of Animals in Psychological Research

The use of animal subjects in psychological and other research is based on the premise that human life is intrinsically more valuable than animal life. Not everyone agrees with this position (see Rowan, 1997; Mukerjee, 1997).

The American Psychological Association (1992b) condones the use of animals in psychological research—but only under certain conditions. First, research using animal subjects must have an *acceptable scientific purpose.* Second, there must be a reasonable expectation that the research will (a) increase knowledge about behavior; (b) increase understanding of the species under study; or (c) produce results that benefit the health or welfare of humans or other animals.

How many animal subjects are used in psychological research?

The vast majority of psychological research involves human subjects, not animals. Animals are used in only about 7 to 8 percent of psychological studies conducted in a given year. Most psychological research with animal subjects does *not* involve pain, suffering, or deprivation (APA, 1995b; Shapiro, 1991; Coile & Miller, 1984).

In the most recent survey conducted by the APA, the total number of animals used by psychology departments throughout the United States was about 200,000. Of these, about 170,000 were rats, mice, or other rodents. There were approximately 1,200 primates, 800 dogs, and about 600 cats. The rest of the total was made up of a variety of creatures, from bats to sea snails (APA, 1986). In comparison, over *20 million* dogs and cats are destroyed in pounds every year.

Why are animals used in psychological research?

Here are a few of the key reasons that psychologists might use animal subjects rather than human subjects in research:

1. *Many psychologists are interested in the study of animal behavior for its own sake.* The branch of psychology that focuses on the study of the behavior of different species is called *comparative psychology.* Some psychologists also do research in the area called *animal cognition,* which is the study of animal learning, memory, thinking, and language.

Animal research is also pursued for its potential benefit to animals themselves (Azar, 1994b). For example, information gained from psychological research on animal behavior has been used to improve the quality of life and survival of animals in zoos and to increase the likelihood of survival of endangered species in the wild.

2. *Research on animal subjects is sometimes conducted that would not be feasible or possible to conduct on human subjects.* For example, there are many similarities between human and animal behavior, but animal behavior tends to be much less complex. Thus, it is sometimes easier to identify basic principles of behavior by studying animals. Psychologists can also observe animals throughout their entire lifespan, from the prenatal stage to old age. To track such changes in humans would take many decades of research. Finally, psychologists can exercise much greater control over animal subjects than human subjects. Researchers can control every aspect of the animal subjects' environment and even their genetic background.

In what areas of psychology has research using animals produced significant and valuable information?

Psychological research with animal subjects has made essential contributions to virtually every area of psychology (Domjan & Purdy, 1995). Along with contributing to knowledge of the workings of the human brain, animal research has contributed to psychological knowledge in the areas of learning, memory, cognition, psychological disorders, therapies, and stress. Research with animals has produced significant gains in the treatment of many human conditions, from premature infants to people who suffer from chronic migraines, hypertension, or insomnia. Significant gains have also been made in helping animals, including the successful breeding and preservation of endangered species, improvements in the care of zoo animals, and the prevention of animal diseases (APA, 1995b; Miller, 1985).

Psychologists Helping Animals Psychologist Benjamin Beck directs a program that has successfully reintroduced over 100 Golden-Lion Tamarins, an endangered species, to the wild. The tamarin is a small, tree-dwelling monkey that is native to Central and South America. Here, Beck is shown weighing a Golden-Lion Tamarin in Brazil.

Thinking Critically About Psychology and the Media

Given all the attention to psychology and psychology-related topics in the popular press, how can you determine if the information being presented has any credibility? There are several ways to be a more informed consumer of psychology-related information in the mass media. The guidelines that follow will help you critically evaluate the claims and information you may encounter in the media.

1. Be especially skeptical of sensationalistic findings or claims. Headlines proclaiming "discoveries" or "breakthroughs" in psychological research are designed to grab your attention. Almost always, if you listen or read further, you'll encounter a much more conservative tone in the statements of the researchers themselves. As scientists, psychologists tend to be conservative in stating their research results, their purpose being not to mislead the public. Reporters, on the other hand, are sometimes more interested in attracting readers or viewers than they are in accurately portraying scientific results (Connor-Greene, 1993; McCall, 1988).

2. Consider the motivations of the researchers. It's difficult to put much stock in research that was funded by a company or agency whose motive is to convince you to buy some product, service, or device.

3. Separate opinions from data. Testimonials, isolated cases, and conjecture are not the same as scientifically gathered data. The essence of any science is objective data gathering that supports or refutes the ideas being tested. It's difficult for individuals to be objective about events with which they are directly connected. Emotions, attitudes, past history, and culture can all play a part in the misinterpretation of events.

4. Look for the original source of professional publication. When the study has been conducted by a reputable researcher, whether it's reported in print or on television, the original source of professional publication is almost always noted. Usually, psychological research is first published in a professional psychology journal before it is shared with the general public. Even so, reporters may add their own interpretation to those of the researchers, thereby distorting or misrepresenting the actual findings (Connor-Greene, 1993; McCall, 1988).

5. Consider the methods and operational definitions used. At this point you should understand the importance of such elements as control groups in experiments, operational definitions of key variables, the use of multiple observers in descriptive research, random assignment of subjects, and the use of a sample that is representative of the population being studied. Look for these elements in the description of the study to increase your confidence in the research findings.

6. Remember the difference between correlation and causality. Many of the research results reported in the mass media are correlational studies. Yet the reports often imply that a cause-and-effect relationship has been discovered (Connor-Greene, 1993). From our earlier discussion, you now understand that just because two factors are correlated, one does not necessarily cause the other. It is entirely possible that a third factor is responsible for the behavior in question. As a general rule, whenever the words *link, tie, connection, association,* and *rela-*

tionship are used in describing psychological findings, the research being described is correlational.

7. Be especially cautious of pseudoscientific claims. A **pseudoscience** is a fake or a false science. Often, a pseudoscience displays all the trappings of the stereotype that many people have about a "real" science, such as sophisticated technical jargon, researchers with impressive-sounding credentials, striking statistical graphs, and elaborate theories (Hines, 1988). In reality, a pseudoscience has little or no scientific basis, and its proponents are often unwilling to submit their claims to scientific scrutiny (Jacobson & others, 1995). Examples of popular pseudosciences include graphology, astrology, numerology, palmistry, and biorhythms (Hines, 1988).

8. Skepticism is the rule, not the exception, in science. It seems as if it is basic to human nature to look for easy answers to life's dilemmas—whether it's increasing motivation and self-discipline, improving your memory, combating stress, or enhancing relationships. As you'll see in these Application sections at the end of each chapter, psychological research has much to say about these and other practical topics. But achieving these goals is rarely as simple as is portrayed in the popular press. Therefore, remember one final axiom: If it sounds too good to be true, it probably is!

GEECH®

Summary

Introducing Psychology

What Is Psychology?

■ Psychology is now defined as the science of behavior and mental processes. However, the definition of psychology has evolved over time.

■ Early philosophers, such as Aristotle and Descartes, used observation, logic, and intuition to understand psychological topics. In later centuries, the discoveries of physiologists demonstrated that scientific methods could be applied to psychological topics.

■ Wilhelm Wundt, a German physiologist, is credited with formally founding the science of psychology. Wundt's student, Edward B. Titchener, established structuralism, the first school of psychology. The structuralists focused on studying the "structure" of conscious experience; their primary research method was introspection.

■ William James was the founder of psychology in the United States. James established functionalism, a school of psychology that emphasized the adaptive role of behavior. James's students, G. Stanley Hall and Mary Whiton Calkins, were two important early figures in American psychology.

■ Behaviorism emerged in the early 1900s, based on Ivan Pavlov's research. Behaviorism was first championed by John Watson and further developed by B. F. Skinner. Behaviorism rejected the study of mental processes and emphasized the study of observable behavior, especially the principles of learning.

■ Other influences on psychology during the first half of the twentieth century were Sigmund Freud and psychoanalysis; Max Wertheimer and Gestalt psychology; and Carl Rogers and Abraham Maslow and humanistic psychology.

Psychology Today

■ Advances in drug treatments and technology increased the influence of biological psychology, the study of the physical bases of behavior.

■ The "cognitive revolution" represented a break with behaviorism and a renewed focus on the role of mental processes in behavior.

■ The insights of cross-cultural psychology revealed that psychological findings cannot always be universally applied and emphasized the importance of human diversity and cultural influences in psychology.

■ Psychology today is very diverse. Topics can be approached from different perspectives. These include the biological, behavioral, psychoanalytic, humanistic, cognitive, and cross-cultural perspectives.

The Scientific Method

■ The four goals of psychology are to describe, explain, predict, and influence human behavior and mental processes.

■ Psychology is based on empirical evidence. The four steps of the scientific method are as follows: generate a hypothesis that can be tested empirically; design the study and collect the data; analyze the data and draw conclusions; and report the findings. The variables must be operationally defined as to how they will be measured or manipulated.

■ Research methods include the experimental method and descriptive methods. Statistics are used to analyze the data and to determine whether findings are statistically significant. Meta-analysis can be used to combine and analyze multiple studies on a single topic. Reporting the results of a study in a professional publication allows other researchers to replicate the study.

■ As research findings accumulate from individual studies, theories or models develop to explain the different findings on a related topic. Theories are tools for understanding and explaining behavior and mental processes. Theories evolve and change as new evidence emerges.

The Experimental Method

■ The experimental method is a research method that demonstrates a cause-and-effect relationship between one variable and another. Experiments involve manipulating the independent variable and measuring the effects of the manipulation on the dependent variable. A model experiment is the Sam Stone study by Leichtman & Ceci (1995).

■ A well-designed experiment includes the following characteristics: random assignment of subjects to experimental conditions; experimental groups compared to a control group; systematic manipulation of the independent variable; and objective measurement of the dependent variable.

■ There are many variations in experimental design. A placebo control group is included to check for expectancy effects. The double-blind technique helps ensure objectivity. Although experiments can provide evidence of causality, they do have certain limitations. Not all questions can be studied experimentally.

Descriptive Methods

■ Descriptive methods are research strategies to observe and describe behavior. Descriptive methods include naturalistic observation, case studies, surveys, and correlational studies.

■ Surveys, questionnaires, and interviews are administered to a sample of the larger group to be investigated. For results to be generalizable to the larger population, the sample must be representative. Participants are usually chosen through random selection.

■ Correlational studies investigate how strongly two factors are related to each other, and the relationship is expressed in terms of a correlation coefficient. A positive correlation indicates that two factors vary in the same direction, while a negative correlation indicates that two factors vary in opposite directions.

■ Even when two factors are strongly related, conclusions cannot be drawn about causality; a third factor may actually be responsible for the association. However, correlational evidence can be used to identify important relationships and to make meaningful predictions.

Ethics in Psychological Research

■ All psychological research is subject to regulations contained in an ethical code developed by the American Psychological Association. For research with human subjects, the ethical code requires that: informed consent and voluntary participation must be ensured; student subjects must be given alternatives to participating in research; deceptive techniques can be used only under specific conditions; records are kept confidential; participants are to be debriefed and given the opportunity to learn more about the study.

■ Research with animal subjects is also governed by an ethical code developed by the American Psychological Association.

Key Terms

psychology (p. 3)

structuralism (p. 4)

functionalism (p. 5)

behaviorism (p. 6)

psychoanalysis (p. 7)

Gestalt psychology (p. 7)

humanistic psychology (p. 8)

culture (p. 10)

ethnocentrism (p. 10)

individualistic cultures (p. 10)

collectivistic cultures (p. 10)

scientific method (p. 13)

critical thinking (p. 14)

hypothesis (p. 15)

variable (p. 15)

operational definition (p. 15)

statistics (p. 16)

statistical significance (p. 16)

meta-analysis (p. 16)

replicate (p. 16)

theory (p. 17)

experimental method (p. 17)

independent variable (p. 17)

dependent variable (p. 18)

random assignment (p. 18)

control group (p. 19)

experimental group (p. 19)

placebo control group (p. 21)

expectancy effect (p. 21)

descriptive methods (p. 23)

naturalistic observation (p. 23)

case study (p. 24)

survey (p. 24)

sample (p. 25)

representative sample (p. 25)

correlational study (p. 25)

positive correlation (p. 26)

negative correlation (p. 26)

pseudoscience (p. 30)

Key People

Mary Whiton Calkins (1863–1930) American psychologist who conducted research on memory, personality, and dreams; established one of the first U.S. psychology research laboratories; first woman president of the American Psychological Association.

Sigmund Freud (1856–1939) Austrian physician and founder of psychoanalysis.

G. Stanley Hall (1844–1924) American psychologist who established the first psychology research laboratory in the United States; founded the American Psychological Association.

William James (1842–1910) American philosopher and psychologist who founded psychology in the United States and established the psychological school called functionalism.

Abraham Maslow (1908–1970) American humanistic psychologist who developed an influential theory of motivation.

Ivan Pavlov (1849–1936) Russian physiologist whose pioneering research on learning contributed to the development of behaviorism; discovered the basic learning process that is now called classical conditioning.

Carl Rogers (1902–1987) American psychologist who founded the school of humanistic psychology.

B. F. Skinner (1904–1990) American psychologist and leading proponent of behaviorism; developed a model of learning called operant conditioning; emphasized studying the relationship between environmental factors and observable behavior.

John B. Watson (1878–1958) American psychologist who founded behaviorism, emphasizing the study of observable behavior and rejecting the study of mental processes.

Max Wertheimer (1880–1943) German psychologist who founded the school of Gestalt psychology.

Wilhelm Wundt (1832–1920) German physiologist who founded psychology as a formal science; opened first psychology research laboratory in 1879 in Leipzig, Germany.

CONCEPT REVIEW 1.1 Page 8

1. functionalism; William James
2. humanistic psychology; Carl Rogers
3. structuralism; Edward Titchener
4. psychoanalysis; Sigmund Freud
5. behaviorism; John Watson
6. Gestalt psychology; Max Wertheimer

CONCEPT REVIEW 1.2 Page 13

1. a
2. b
3. d
4. d

CONCEPT REVIEW 1.3 Page 22

1. F
2. C
3. B
4. E
5. D
6. A
7. G

CONCEPT REVIEW 1.4 Page 27

1. positive correlation
2. naturalistic observation
3. correlational research
4. negative correlation
5. the case study method

34

Chapter

2

The Biological Foundations of Behavior

Prologue: Asha's Story

The headaches began without warning. A pounding, intense pain just over Asha's left temple. Our friend Asha, a healthy, active 32-year-old, chalked up her constant headache and fatigue to stress and exhaustion. After all, she *was* under considerable stress. The end of her demanding first semester of teaching and research at a major university was drawing near. Still, Asha had always been extremely healthy and usually tolerated stress well. She didn't drink or smoke or take any kind of drugs. And no matter how late she stayed up working on her lectures and research proposals, she still got up at 5:30 every morning to work out at the university gym.

There were other signs that something was wrong. Asha's husband, Paul, noticed that she had been behaving rather oddly in recent weeks. For example, at Thanksgiving dinner, Asha picked up a knife by the wrong end and tried to cut her turkey with the handle instead of the blade. A few hours later, Asha made the same mistake in trying to use a scissors: she held the blades and tried to cut with the handle.

Asha laughed these incidents off, and for that matter, so did Paul. They both thought she was simply under too much stress. And when Asha occasionally got her words mixed up, neither Paul nor anyone else was terribly surprised. Asha was born in India, and her first language was Tulu. Although Asha was extremely fluent in English, she often got English phrases slightly wrong—like the time she said that it was "storming cats and birds" instead of "raining cats and dogs."

There were other odd lapses in language. "I would say something thinking it was correct," Asha recalled, "and people would say to me: 'What are you saying?' I wouldn't realize I was saying something wrong. I would open my mouth and just nonsense would come out. But it made perfect sense to me. At other times, the word was on the tip of my tongue—I knew I knew the word, but I couldn't find it. I would fumble for words but it would come out wrong. Sometimes I would slur words, like I'd try to say Saturday, only it would come out 'salad-day.'"

A few weeks later, on Christmas morning, Paul and Asha were opening presents with Paul's family. Asha walked over to Paul's father to look at the pool cue he had received as a gift. As she bent down, she fell forward onto her father-in-law. At first, everyone thought Asha was just joking around. But then she fell to the floor, her body stiff. Seconds later, it was apparent that Asha had lost consciousness and was having a seizure.

Asha remembers nothing of the seizure or of being taken by ambulance to the hospital intensive care unit. She floated in and out of consciousness for the first day and night. Tests were run. A CAT scan showed some sort of blockage in her brain. An MRI scan showed a large white spot on the left side of Asha's brain. At only 32 years of age, Asha had suffered a stroke.

She remained in the hospital for twelve days. It was only after she was transferred out of intensive care that both Asha and Paul began to realize just how serious the repercussions of the stroke were. Asha couldn't read or write and had difficulty comprehending what was being said. Although she could speak, she couldn't name even simple objects, such as a tree or a clock.

In this chapter, you will discover why the brain damage that Asha experienced impaired her ability to perform simple behaviors like naming common objects. In the process, you'll gain a better understanding of the biological bases of your own behavior. Indeed, one important way to make sense out of your experiences is to understand the physical structures and processes that are responsible for them.

Introduction

Biological Psychology

Biological psychology is the study of the internal physical events and processes that correspond with our experiences and behavior. It may surprise you to learn that psychology is so closely related to biology. But if you think about it, the "psychological you" is really inseparable from the "biological you." Psychological processes are closely linked to biological processes, and biological processes can profoundly influence human behavior.

Throughout this text you'll see that biological psychology has contributed important insights about many different dimensions of human behavior. This area of research reflects the contributions of psychologists as well as other kinds of scientists, including biologists, chemists, neurologists, and psychiatrists.

In this chapter, we'll lay an important foundation for the rest of this book by helping you develop a broad appreciation of the *nervous system*—the body's most important communication network. We'll start by looking at the most important cells of the nervous system, called *neurons*. We'll also consider the organization of the nervous system and another important communication network—the *endocrine system*. We'll then move on to a guided tour of the brain. We'll look at how certain areas in the brain are specialized to handle different functions, like language and vision. In the chapter's Application, we discuss how the brain responds to environmental stimulation by literally altering its structure. And at several points, we'll return to Asha's story and tell you how she fared after her stroke.

The Scope of Biological Psychology Maintaining your balance on a bicycle, smiling, talking with a friend, avoiding other vehicles—all of our behaviors involve the complex integration of many physical processes working in harmony. For that matter, so does your ability to perceive and recognize the image in this photograph.

The Neuron: The Basic Unit of Communication

Information in the nervous system is transmitted by the neuron, a type of cell that is specialized for communication. What are glial cells, and what is their role in the nervous system? What are the three main types of neurons? What are the basic components of the neuron, and what are their functions?

Communication throughout the nervous system takes place via **neurons**—cells which are highly specialized to receive and transmit information from one part of the body to another. The number of neurons in the nervous system is astronomical. The human brain is estimated to have 100 billion neurons (Fischbach, 1992). To help put this in perspective, if you could count neurons at the rate of 100 per second, it would take over 30 years to count the neurons in a human brain!

For the record, no one has actually counted all of the neurons in the nervous system because most neurons are extremely small, especially many of those in the compact area that the brain occupies. Special magnifying equipment, like the electron microscope, is often needed to study them.

Fortunately for neuroscientists, there are often striking similarities between the workings of the human nervous system and the nervous systems of many other animals. For example, sea snails and squids tend to have larger neurons and simpler nervous systems than humans. Neuroscientists have been able to observe the actions and reactions of a single neuron by studying the nervous systems of such simple animals.

Along with neurons, the human nervous system is made up of another type of specialized cell, called **glial cells.** Glial cells outnumber neurons by about ten to one, but are much smaller than neurons. *Glia* is Greek for "glue," and at one time it was believed that glial cells were the "glue" that held the neurons of the brain together. While they don't actually glue neurons together, glial cells do provide structural support for neurons. Glial cells also help neurons by providing nutrition, enhancing the speed of communication between neurons, and removing waste products, including neurons that have died or been damaged (Kandel, 1995a; Lees, 1993).

Although individual neurons can vary greatly in size and shape, there are three basic types of neurons, each communicating different kinds of information. **Sensory neurons** convey information about the environment, such as light or sound, from specialized receptor cells in the sense organs to the brain. Sensory neurons also carry information from the skin and internal organs to the brain. **Motor neurons** communicate information to the muscles and glands of the body. Simply blinking your eyes activates thousands of motor neurons. Finally, **interneurons** communicate information *between* neurons. By far, most of the neurons in the human nervous system are interneurons, and many interneurons connect to other interneurons.

Characteristics of the Neuron

Most neurons have three basic components: a *cell body, dendrites,* and an *axon* (see Figure 2.1 on the next page). The **cell body** contains the nucleus, which provides energy for the neuron to carry out its functions. The cell body also contains genetic material and other structures that are found in virtually all the cells in the body.

Extending out from the cell body are many short, branching fibers, called **dendrites.** The term *dendrite* comes from a Greek word meaning "tree," and

biological psychology
Specialized branch of psychology that studies the relationship between behavior and body processes and systems.

neuron
Highly specialized cell that communicates information in electrical and chemical form; a nerve cell.

glial cells
(GLEE-ull) Support cells that assist neurons by providing structural support, nutrition, and removal of cell wastes; manufacture myelin.

sensory neuron
Type of neuron that conveys information to the brain from specialized receptor cells in sense organs and internal organs.

motor neuron
Type of neuron that signals muscles to relax or contract.

interneuron
Type of neuron that communicates information from one neuron to the next.

cell body
The part of a neuron that contains the nucleus.

dendrites
Multiple short fibers that extend from the neuron's cell body and receive information from other neurons or sensory receptor cells.

FIGURE 2.1 The Parts of a Neuron

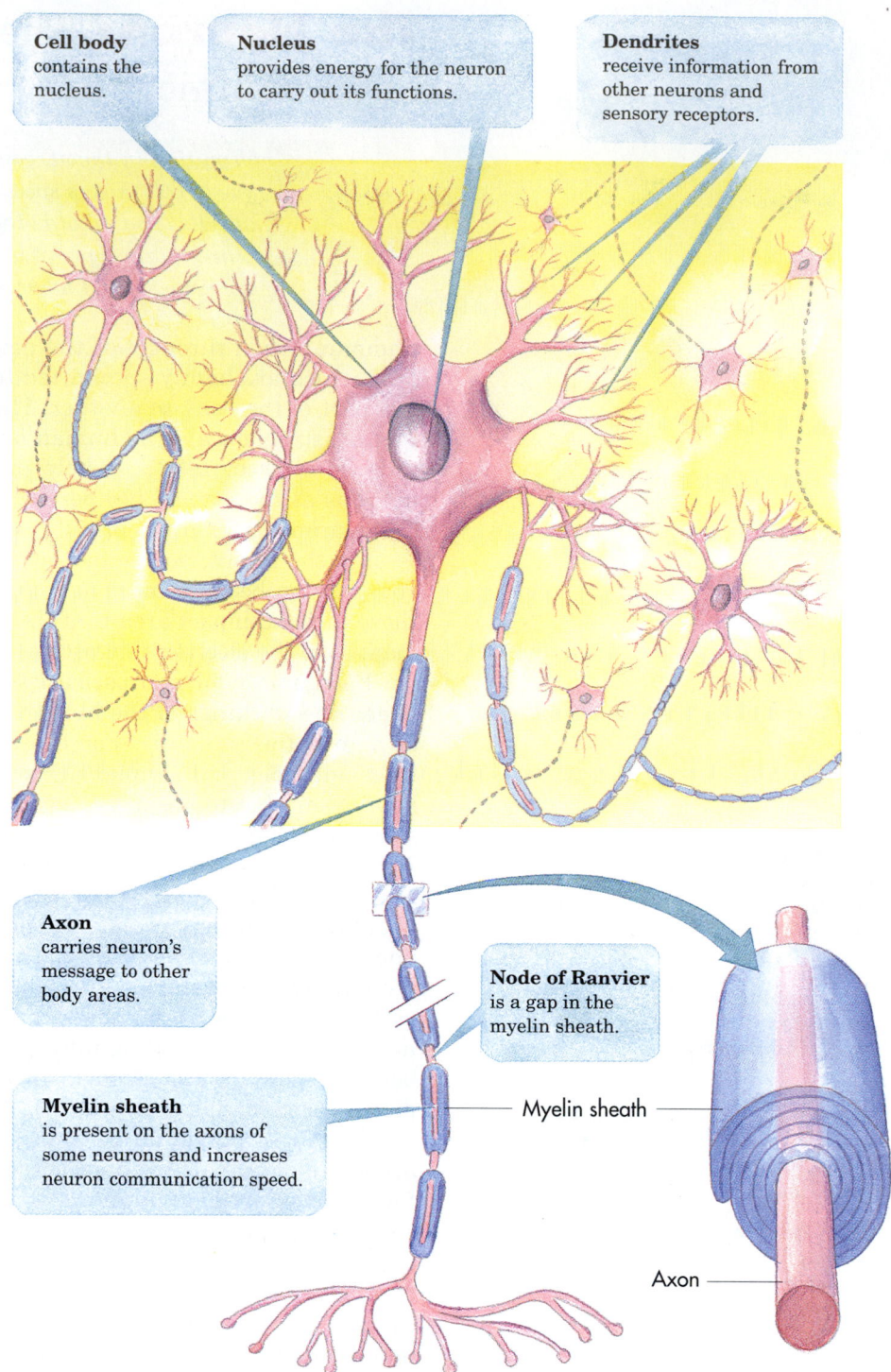

Cell body contains the nucleus.

Nucleus provides energy for the neuron to carry out its functions.

Dendrites receive information from other neurons and sensory receptors.

Axon carries neuron's message to other body areas.

Node of Ranvier is a gap in the myelin sheath.

Myelin sheath is present on the axons of some neurons and increases neuron communication speed.

Myelin sheath

Axon

the intricate branching of the dendrites does often resemble the branches of a tree or bush. Dendrites *receive* messages from other neurons or specialized cells (Johnston & others, 1996). Dendrites with many branches have a greater surface area, which increases the amount of information that the neuron can receive. Some neurons have thousands of dendrites.

The **axon** is a single, elongated tube that extends from the cell body in most, though not all, neurons. (Some neurons do not have axons.) Axons carry information *from* the neuron *to* other cells in the body, including other neurons, glands, and muscles. In contrast to the potentially large number of dendrites, a neuron has no more than one axon exiting from the cell body.

axon
The long, fluid-filled tube that carries a neuron's messages to other body areas.

However, many axons have branches near their tips that allow the neuron to communicate information to more than one target (Kandel, 1995a).

Axons can vary enormously in length. Most axons are very small; some are no more than a few thousandths of an inch long. Other axons, however, are quite long. For example, the longest axon in your body is that of the motor neuron that controls your big toe. This neuron extends from the base of your spine into your foot. If you happen to be a seven-foot-tall basketball player, this axon could be four feet long! For most of us, of course, this axon is closer to three feet in length.

The axons of many, though not all, neurons are surrounded by the **myelin sheath.** The myelin sheath is a white, fatty covering manufactured by special glial cells. In much the same way that you can bundle together electrical wires if they are each insulated with plastic, myelin helps insulate one axon from the axons of other neurons. Rather than being a continuous coating of the axon, the myelin sheath occurs in segments that are separated by small gaps where the myelin is missing. The small gaps are called the *nodes of Ranvier* or simply *nodes* (see Figure 2.1). Neurons wrapped in myelin communicate their messages up to twenty times faster than unmyelinated neurons (Schwartz, 1995b).

Communication Within the Neuron:

The All-or-None Action Potential

Neurons communicate information in the form of brief electrical impulses called action potentials. How is the action potential produced, and how does it "travel" down the axon? What factors affect the speed at which the nerve impulse travels?

The function of neurons is to transmit information throughout the nervous system. But exactly *how* do neurons transmit information? What form does this information take? In this section, we'll consider the nature of communication *within* a neuron, and in the following section we'll describe communication *between* neurons. As you'll see, communication in and between neurons is an electrochemical process.

In general, messages are gathered by the dendrites and cell body and then transmitted along the axon in the form of a brief electrical impulse called an **action potential** (Fischbach, 1992). The action potential is produced by the movement of electrically charged particles, called *ions,* across the membrane of the axon. Some ions are negatively charged, others positively charged.

Think of the axon membrane as a gatekeeper that carefully controls the balance of positive and negative ions on the interior and exterior of the axon. As the gatekeeper, the axon membrane opens and closes *ion channels* that allow ions to flow in and out of the axon (Koester & Siegelbaum, 1995a).

Each neuron requires a minimum level of stimulation from other neurons or sensory receptors to activate it. This minimum level of stimulation is called the neuron's **stimulus threshold.** While waiting for sufficient stimulation to activate it, the neuron is said to be *polarized.* This means that the axon's interior is more negatively charged than the exterior fluid surrounding the axon. And how much electricity are we discussing? About −70 millivolts (or thousandths of a volt). The −70 millivolts is referred to as the neuron's **resting potential** (Koester, 1995a).

This polarized, negative-inside/positive-outside condition is primarily due to the different concentrations of two particular ions: sodium and potassium. The fluid surrounding the axon contains a larger concentration of sodium ions

myelin sheath
(MY-eh-linn) A white, fatty covering wrapped around the axons of some neurons that increases their communication speed.

action potential
A brief electrical impulse by which information is transmitted along the axon of a neuron.

stimulus threshold
The minimum level of stimulation required to activate a particular neuron.

resting potential
State in which a neuron is prepared to activate and communicate its message if it receives sufficient stimulation.

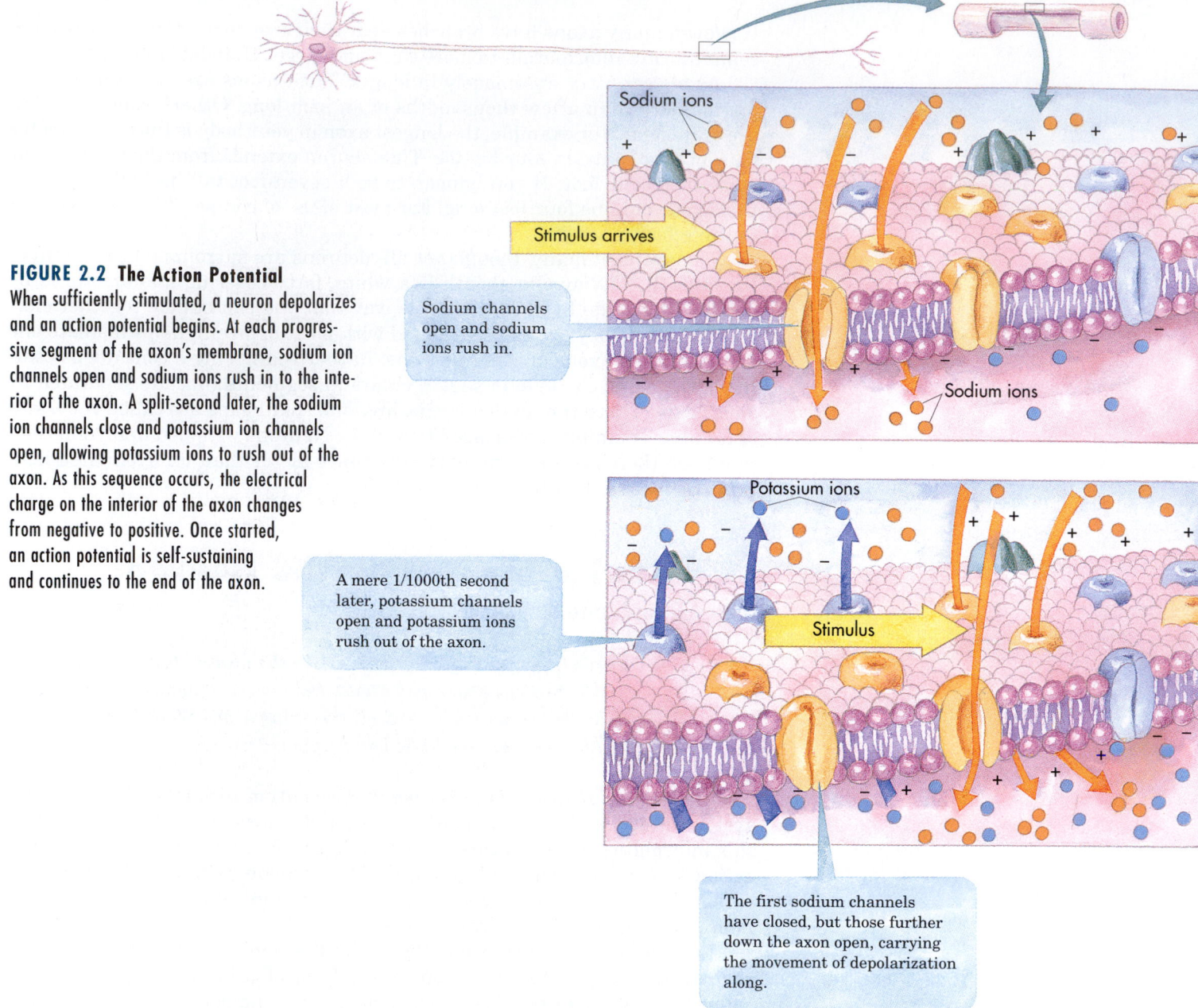

FIGURE 2.2 The Action Potential
When sufficiently stimulated, a neuron depolarizes and an action potential begins. At each progressive segment of the axon's membrane, sodium ion channels open and sodium ions rush in to the interior of the axon. A split-second later, the sodium ion channels close and potassium ion channels open, allowing potassium ions to rush out of the axon. As this sequence occurs, the electrical charge on the interior of the axon changes from negative to positive. Once started, an action potential is self-sustaining and continues to the end of the axon.

than the fluid within the axon. The fluid within the axon contains a larger concentration of potassium ions than the fluid outside the axon.

When sufficiently stimulated by other neurons or sensory receptors, the neuron *depolarizes,* beginning the action potential. At each successive axon segment, sodium ion channels open for a mere 1/1000 of a second. The sodium ions rush to the axon interior from the surrounding fluid, and then the sodium ion channels close. Less than a thousandth of a second later, the potassium ion channels open, allowing potassium to rush out of the axon and into the fluid surrounding it. Then the potassium ion channels close (see Figure 2.2). This sequence of depolarization and ion movement continues in a self-sustaining fashion down the entire length of the axon (Koester, 1995a, 1995b).

As sodium ions penetrate the axon membrane and potassium ions exit, the electrical charge on the inside of the axon momentarily changes to a positive electrical charge of about +30 millivolts. The result is a brief positive electrical impulse that progressively occurs at each segment down the axon—the action potential.

all-or-none law
The principle that either a neuron is sufficiently stimulated and an action potential occurs or a neuron is not sufficiently stimulated and an action potential does not occur.

synapse
(SIN-aps) The point of communication between two neurons.

synaptic gap
(sin-AP-tick) The tiny space between the axon terminal of one neuron and the dendrite of an adjoining neuron.

Keep a couple of things in mind. First, although it's tempting to think of the action potential as being conducted in much the same way that electricity is conducted through a wire, that's *not* what takes place in the neuron. The axon is actually a poor conductor of electricity. At each successive segment of the axon, the action potential is *regenerated* in the same way that it was generated in the previous segment—by depolarization and the movement of ions (Kalat, 1995).

Second, once the action potential is started, it is self-sustaining and continues to the end of the axon. In other words, there is no such thing as a partial action potential. Either the neuron is sufficiently stimulated and an action potential occurs, or the neuron is not sufficiently stimulated and an action potential does not occur. This principle is referred to as the **all-or-none law.**

Following the action potential, a *refractory period* occurs during which the neuron is unable to fire. This refractory period lasts for a mere 1/1000 of a second or less. During the refractory period, the neuron *repolarizes* and reestablishes the negative-inside/positive-outside condition. Like depolarization, repolarization occurs progressively at each segment down the axon. This process of "pumping" sodium ions out and drawing potassium ions back in reestablishes the resting potential conditions so that the neuron is capable of firing again (Carlson, 1994).

Remember, action potentials are generated in mere thousandths of a second. Thus, a single neuron can generate hundreds of neural impulses per second. Given these incredibly small increments of time, just how fast do neural impulses zip around the body?

The fastest neurons in your body communicate at speeds of up to 270 miles per hour. In the slowest neurons, messages creep along at about 2 miles per hour. This variation in communication speed is due to two factors: the axon diameter and the myelin sheath. The greater the axon's diameter, the faster the axon conducts action potentials. And, as we said earlier, myelinated neurons communicate faster than unmyelinated neurons. In myelinated neurons, the sodium ion channels are concentrated at each of the nodes of Ranvier where the myelin is missing. So in myelinated neurons the action potential "jumps" from node to node rather than progressing down the entire length of the axon (Koester & Siegelbaum, 1995b).

Communication Between Neurons:
Bridging the Gap

Communication between neurons takes place at the synapse, the junction between two adjoining neurons. How is information communicated at the synapse? What is a neurotransmitter, and what is its role in synaptic transmission?

The point of communication between two neurons is called the **synapse.** At this communication junction, the message-*sending* neuron is referred to as the *presynaptic neuron.* The message-*receiving* neuron is called the *postsynaptic neuron.* For cells that are specialized to communicate information, neurons have a surprising characteristic: they don't touch each other. The presynaptic and postsynaptic neurons are separated by a tiny fluid-filled space, called the **synaptic gap,** which is only about *five-millionths* of an inch wide.

The transmission of information between two neurons occurs in one of two ways: electrically or chemically. When communication is electrical, the synaptic gap is extremely narrow, and special ion channels serve as a bridge

The Brain Capturing a Thought In the brain, as in the rest of the nervous system, information is transmitted by electrical impulses (red area) that speed from one neuron to the next.

(a) Path of a Neural Impulse

1. Action potential travels along axon of sending neuron.

FIGURE 2.3 Communication Between Neurons: The Process of Synaptic Transmission

Axon terminals of sending neuron

Dendrites of receiving neuron

2. Synaptic transmission occurs when action potential reaches a synapse and causes neurotransmitters to be released by the synaptic vesicles in the axon terminals.

(b) Enlarged View of a Synapse

Axon terminal of presynaptic neuron

Dendrite of receiving neuron

Synaptic vesicles

Synaptic gap between presynaptic neuron and postsynaptic neuron

3. The neurotransmitters cross the synaptic gap and "search" for the correctly shaped receptor sites on the receiving neuron.

(c) Synaptic Transmission

Neurotransmitters

4. The neurotransmitter must fit perfectly into the receptor site.

Na^+

Receptor sites on the dendrite of the receiving neuron

Na^+ (sodium ions)

This neurotransmitter does not fit into the receptor site.

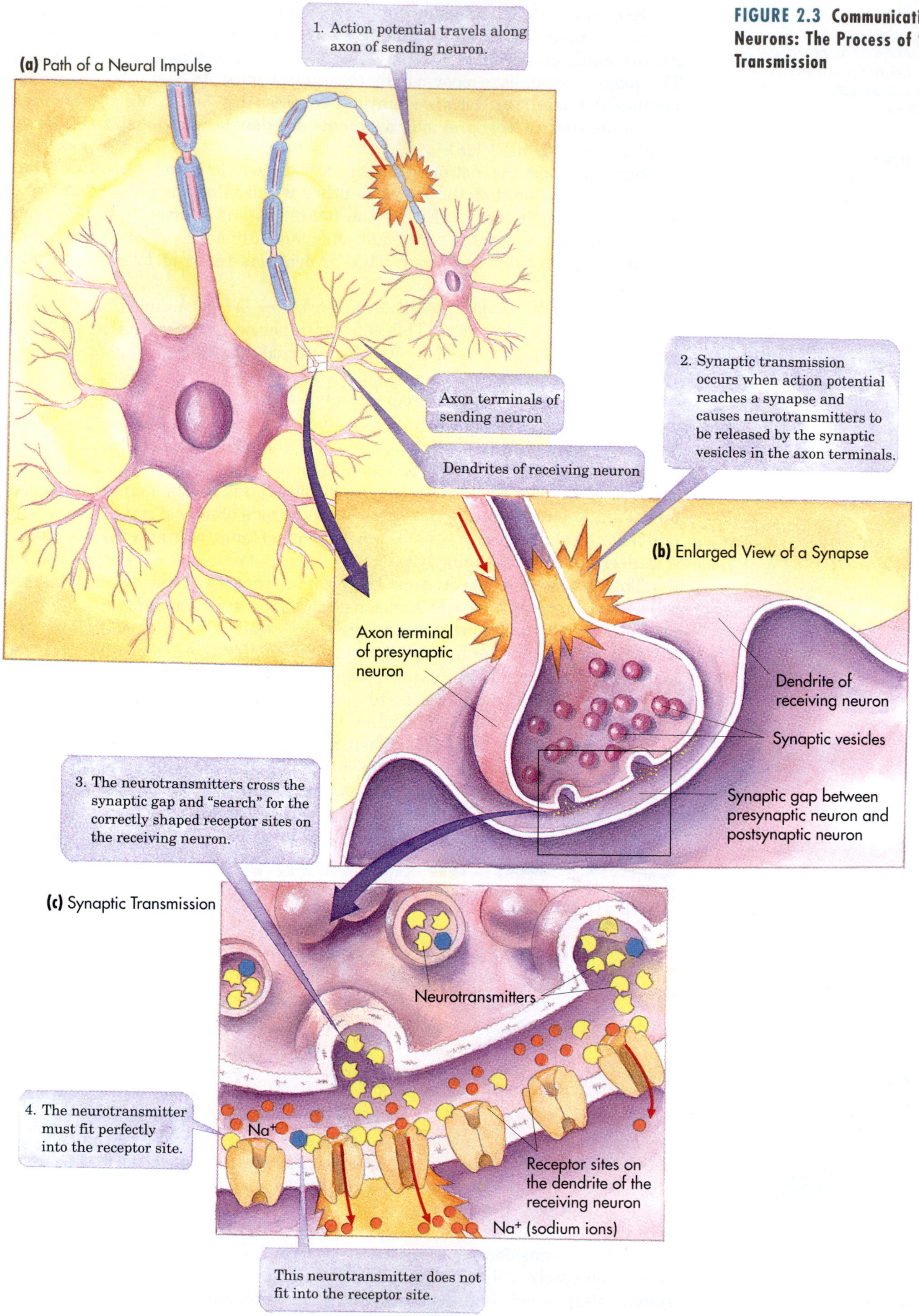

axon terminals
Branches at the end of the axon that contain tiny pouches or sacs called synaptic vesicles.

synaptic vesicles
(sin-AP-tick VESS-ick-ulls) Tiny pouches or sacs in the axon terminals that contain chemicals called neuro-transmitters.

neurotransmitter
Chemical messenger manufactured by a neuron.

synaptic transmission
(sin-AP-tick) The process in which neurotransmitters are released by one neuron, cross the synaptic gap, and affect adjoining neurons.

reuptake
The process by which neurotransmitter molecules detach from a postsynaptic neuron and are reabsorbed by a presynaptic neuron so they can be recycled and used again.

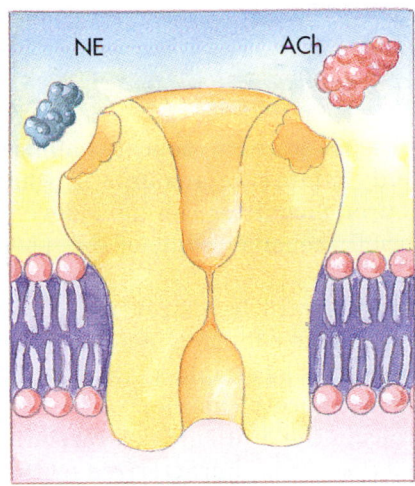

FIGURE 2.4 Neurotransmitter and Receptor Site Shapes
NE is the abbreviation for the neurotransmitter norepinephrine and ACh is the abbreviation for acetylcholine. Each neurotransmitter has a chemically distinct shape. Like a key in a lock, a neurotransmitter must fit the receptor site on the receiving neuron perfectly for its message to be communicated.

between the neurons. Electrical communication between the two neurons is virtually instantaneous (Kandel & Siegelbaum, 1995).

Although some neurons communicate electrically in the human nervous system, the most common form of communication between neurons is chemical. Chemical communication occurs when the presynaptic neuron creates a chemical substance that diffuses across the synaptic gap and is detected by the postsynaptic neuron. This one-way communication process has many important implications for human behavior.

More specifically, here's how chemical communication takes place between neurons: As we've seen, when the presynaptic neuron is activated, it generates an action potential that travels to the end of the axon. At the end of the axon are several small branches called **axon terminals.** Floating in the interior fluid of the axon terminals are tiny sacs called **synaptic vesicles** (see Figure 2.3 on the facing page). The synaptic vesicles hold special chemical messengers manufactured by the neuron, called **neurotransmitters.**

When the action potential reaches the axon terminals, some of the synaptic vesicles "dock" on the axon terminal membrane, then release their neurotransmitters into the synaptic gap (Kandel, 1995c). These chemical messengers cross the synaptic gap. Then they attach to receptor sites on the dendrites of the surrounding neurons. This neurotransmitter "journey" across the synaptic gap takes less than 10 millionths of a second. This entire process of transmitting information at the synapse is called **synaptic transmission.**

What happens to the neurotransmitter molecules after they've attached to the receptor sites of the postsynaptic neuron? Most commonly, they detach from the receptor and are reabsorbed by the presynaptic neuron so they can be recycled and used again. This process is called **reuptake.** Reuptake also occurs with many of the neurotransmitters that failed to attach to a receptor and are left floating in the synaptic gap. Neurotransmitter molecules that are not reabsorbed or that remain attached to the receptor site are broken down or destroyed by enzymes (Schwartz, 1995a). As you'll see in the next section, certain drugs can interfere with both of these processes, prolonging the presence of the neurotransmitter in the synaptic gap.

The number of neurotransmitters that a neuron can manufacture varies. Some neurons produce only one type of neurotransmitter, while others manufacture three or more. Although estimates vary, scientists have identified about fifty neurotransmitters thus far, and expect to find many more.

Each type of neurotransmitter has a chemically distinct, different shape. When released by the presynaptic neuron, neurotransmitters "search" for the correctly shaped receptor sites on the dendrites of the postsynaptic neurons. Like a key in a lock, a neurotransmitter's shape must precisely match that of receptor sites on the postsynaptic neuron's dendrites for the neurotransmitter to affect that neuron. Keep in mind that the postsynaptic neuron can have many differently shaped receptor sites on its dendrites, thereby accommodating several different neurotransmitters (see Figure 2.4).

A given neurotransmitter can communicate either an excitatory or an inhibitory message to a postsynaptic neuron. An *excitatory message* increases the likelihood that the postsynaptic neuron will activate and generate an action potential. Conversely, an *inhibitory message* decreases the likelihood that the postsynaptic neuron will activate. If a postsynaptic neuron simultaneously received an excitatory and inhibitory message, the two messages would cancel each other out (see Kandel, 1995b).

Thus, depending on the number and kind of neurotransmitter chemicals that are taken up by the dendrites of the adjoining neurons, the postsynaptic neurons are more or less likely to activate. If the net result is a sufficient number of excitatory messages, the postsynaptic neuron depolarizes, generates an action potential, and releases its own neurotransmitters.

When released by a presynaptic neuron, neurotransmitter chemicals cross hundreds, even thousands, of synaptic gaps and affect the intertwined dendrites of adjacent neurons. Because the receiving neuron can have thousands of dendrites that intertwine with the axon terminals of many presynaptic neurons, the number of potential synaptic interconnections between neurons is mind-boggling. In your brain alone, there are up to 100 *trillion* synaptic interconnections (Kandel & Siegelbaum, 1995; Koester, 1995b). To help put this in perspective, look up at the sky on a clear, dark night. There are nearly a thousand times more synaptic connections in your brain than there are stars in our entire galaxy.

CONCEPT REVIEW 2.1

The Neuron

Match the part of the neuron in the list with its function in neural communication.

a. action potential   **b.** myelin sheath
c. axon   **d.** neurotransmitters
e. synapse   **f.** dendrite

1. _____ A fluid-filled tube that carries information to other neurons, glands, and muscles

2. _____ Receives information from other neurons

3. _____ Brief electrical charge that communicates information within the neuron

4. _____ Fluid-filled space between sending and receiving neurons

5. _____ Chemical messengers manufactured by a neuron

6. _____ White, fatty covering surrounding an axon that increases speed of neural communication

Neurotransmitters and Their Effects

Neurotransmitters are involved in every thought, action, and emotion. What are the general functions of some common neurotransmitters? How can drugs affect synaptic transmission?

Your ability to think, feel, perceive, and move depends on the delicate balance of neurotransmitters. They are present in only minuscule amounts in your body, but too much or too little of a given neurotransmitter can have devastating effects. To illustrate this point, let's briefly consider some of the most common neurotransmitters.

Acetylcholine was the first neurotransmitter to be discovered. It is found in all motor neurons and stimulates muscles to contract, including the heart and stomach muscles. Whether a movement is as simple as the flick of an eyelash or as complex as a back flip, it involves acetylcholine.

Acetylcholine is also found in many neurons in the brain and is especially important in Alzheimer's disease. *Alzheimer's disease* is characterized by the progressive loss of memory and deterioration of intellectual functioning. Although the exact cause of Alzheimer's disease has yet to be identified, it is known that the neurons in the brain that produce acetylcholine degenerate into tangled clumps. The result is that brain levels of acetylcholine are greatly reduced in Alzheimer's disease. This deficiency is thought to be responsible for many of the disease's symptoms.

The neurotransmitter called **dopamine** is involved in movement, attention, learning, and pleasurable or rewarding sensations (Nader & others, 1997; Schultz & others, 1997). Evidence also suggests that the addictiveness of some drugs, including cocaine and nicotine, is related to their dopamine-increasing properties (Volkow & others, 1997; Wise, 1996).

acetylcholine
(uh-*seet*-ull-KO-leen) Neurotransmitter that produces muscle contractions and is involved in memory functions.

dopamine
(DOPE-uh-meen) Neurotransmitter that is involved in the regulation of bodily movements, thought processes, and rewarding sensations.

TABLE 2.1 Summary of Important Neurotransmitters

Neurotransmitter	Primary Roles	Associated Disorders
Acetylcholine	Muscle contractions Memory	Alzheimer's disease
Dopamine	Movement Thought processes Rewarding sensations	Parkinson's disease Schizophrenia Drug addiction
Serotonin	Sleep Emotional states	Depression
Norepinephrine	Physical arousal Learning Memory	Depression
GABA	Inhibits brain activity	Anxiety disorders
Endorphins	Pain perception Positive emotions	None

The degeneration of the neurons that produce dopamine in one brain area causes Parkinson's disease. *Parkinson's disease* is characterized by rigidity, muscle tremors, poor balance, and difficulty in initiating movements. These movement disruptions are the result of the diminished dopamine production in that brain area. Symptoms can be alleviated by a drug called *L-dopa*, which converts to dopamine in the brain (Youdim & Riederer, 1997).

Interestingly, excessive brain levels of dopamine are sometimes involved in the hallucinations and perceptual distortions that characterize the severe mental disorder called *schizophrenia*. Antipsychotic drugs that relieve schizophrenic symptoms work by blocking dopamine receptors and reducing dopamine activity in the brain (Julien, 1995). In the chapters on psychological disorders (Chapter 13) and therapies (Chapter 14), we'll discuss schizophrenia, dopamine, and antipsychotic drugs in detail.

The neurotransmitters called serotonin and norepinephrine are found in many different brain areas. **Serotonin** is involved in sleep, moods, and emotional states, including depression. Antidepressant drugs like *Prozac* increase the availability of serotonin in certain brain regions. **Norepinephrine** is implicated in the activation of neurons throughout the brain and helps the body "gear up" in the face of danger or threat. Norepinephrine also seems to be a key player in learning and memory retrieval. Like serotonin and dopamine, norepinephrine dysfunction is implicated in some mental disorders, especially depression.

GABA is the abbreviation for **gamma-aminobutyric acid,** a neurotransmitter found primarily in the brain. GABA usually communicates an inhibitory message to other neurons, helping to balance and offset excitatory messages. Alcohol makes people feel relaxed and less inhibited partly by increasing GABA activity, which reduces brain activity. Antianxiety medications like Valium and Xanax also work by increasing GABA activity, which inhibits action potentials and slows brain activity.

Interestingly, GABA seems to play a dual role in the brain area that regulates daily sleep/wake cycles. During the day, GABA communicates an excitatory message to other neurons in this brain area. But at night, GABA communicates an inhibitory message to the exact same neurons (Wagner & others, 1997).

The **endorphins** play a key role in the perception of pain. Chemically, the endorphins are very similar to morphine. Morphine is one of the *opiates,* a group of addictive drugs that relieve pain and produce euphoria. The opiates are discussed in Chapter 4. Along with pain perception, the endorphins are also associated with positive moods. For example, endorphins are involved in the "runner's high" that can occur with aerobic exercise. In marathon runners, endorphin levels can increase to as much as four times their normal levels.

While researchers have linked abnormal levels of specific neurotransmitters to various physical and behavioral problems, the connection between specific neurotransmitters and specific behaviors is seldom a simple one-to-one relationship. In other words, the action of neurotransmitters is very complex. The effect of any neurotransmitter usually depends on the particular receptor to which it binds (Kandel & Siegelbaum, 1995).

Thus, it is possible for the same neurotransmitter to have an inhibitory effect on one neuron and an excitatory effect on another neuron. In the case of GABA, the time of day seems to influence whether GABA communicates an excitatory or inhibitory message to the same neurons in the brain area that regulates sleep/wake cycles (Wagner & others, 1997).

serotonin
(ser-ah-TONE-in) Neurotransmitter that is involved in sleep and emotions.

norepinephrine
(nor-ep-in-EF-rin) Neurotransmitter involved in learning and memory; also a hormone manufactured by the adrenal glands.

GABA (gamma-aminobutyric acid)
Neurotransmitter that usually communicates an inhibitory message.

endorphins
(en-DORF-ins) Neurotransmitters that regulate pain perception.

How Drugs Can Affect Synaptic Transmission

Much of what is known about different neurotransmitters has come from observing the effects of drugs and other substances. Many drugs, especially those that affect moods or behavior, work by interfering with the normal functioning of neurotransmitters in the synapse (Julien, 1995).

As Figure 2.5 illustrates, some drugs increase or decrease the amount of neurotransmitter released by neurons. For example, the venom of a black widow spider bite causes acetylcholine to be released continuously by motor neurons, causing severe muscle spasms. Drugs may also affect the length of time that the neurotransmitter remains in the synaptic gap, either increasing or decreasing the amount available to the postsynaptic receptor.

One way that drugs can prolong the effects of the neurotransmitter is by blocking the reuptake of the neurotransmitter back into the sending neuron. For example, as we noted earlier, Prozac works by inhibiting the reuptake of serotonin, increasing the availability of serotonin in the brain. The illegal drug cocaine produces its exhilarating "rush" by interfering with the reuptake of dopamine (Volkow & others, 1997).

Drugs can also *mimic* specific neurotransmitters. When a drug is chemically similar to a specific neurotransmitter, it may produce the same effect as the neurotransmitter. That's partly how nicotine works as a stimulant. Nicotine is chemically similar to acetylcholine and can occupy acetylcholine receptor sites, stimulating skeletal muscles and causing the heart to beat more rapidly.

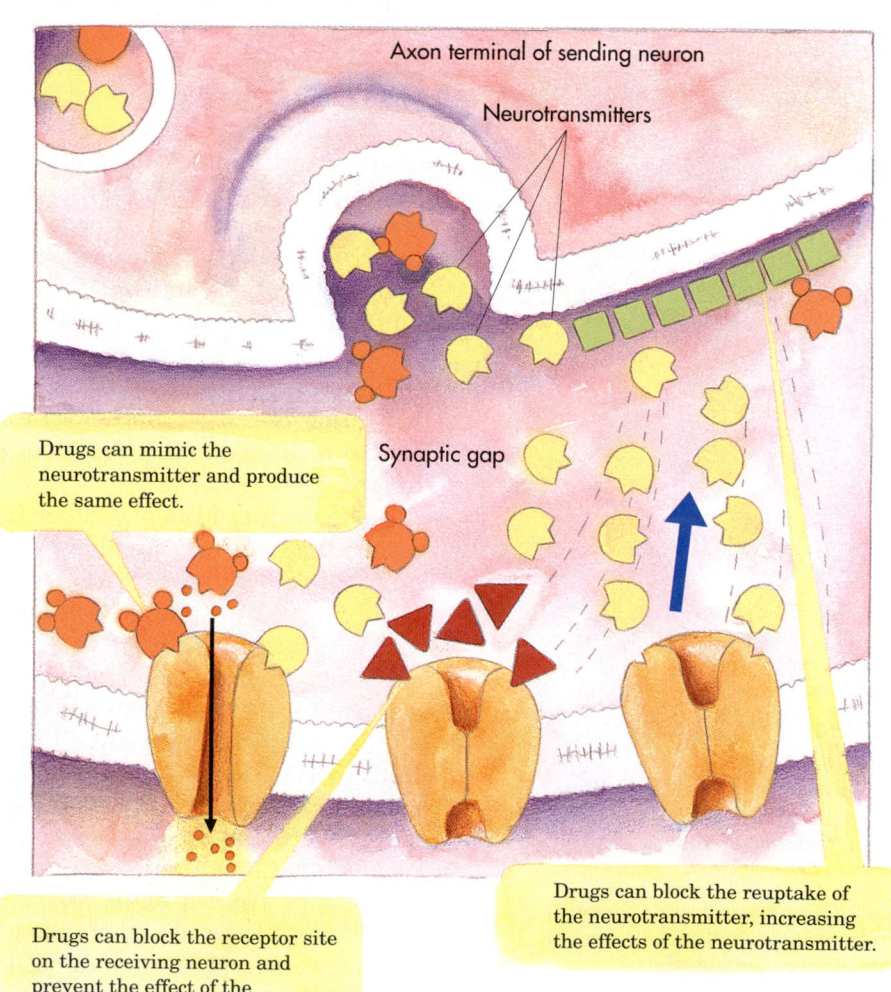

Axon terminal of sending neuron

Neurotransmitters

Drugs can mimic the neurotransmitter and produce the same effect.

Synaptic gap

Drugs can block the reuptake of the neurotransmitter, increasing the effects of the neurotransmitter.

Drugs can block the receptor site on the receiving neuron and prevent the effect of the neurotransmitter.

FIGURE 2.5 How Drugs Can Affect Synaptic Transmission

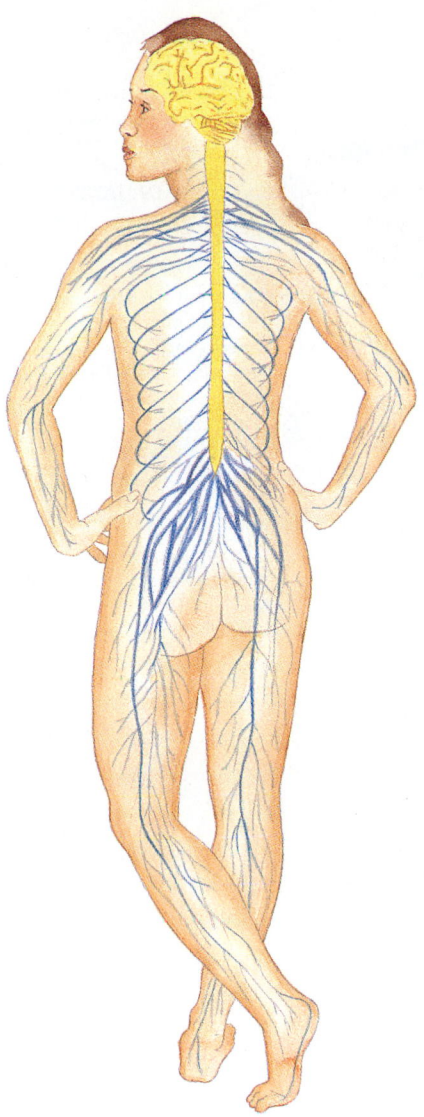

■ Central nervous system

■ Peripheral nervous system

FIGURE 2.6 The Nervous System
The nervous system is a complex organized communication network that is divided into two main divisions: the central nervous system (shown in yellow) and the peripheral nervous system (shown in blue).

nervous system
The primary internal communication network of the body; divided into the central nervous system and the peripheral nervous system.

nerve
Bundle of neuron axons that carries information in the peripheral nervous system.

central nervous system
Division of the nervous system that consists of the brain and spinal cord.

spinal reflexes
Simple, automatic behaviors that are processed in the spinal cord.

Or, a drug can mimic and *block* the effect of a neurotransmitter by fitting into receptor sites and preventing the neurotransmitter from acting. For example, the drug *curare* mimics acetylcholine and blocks acetylcholine receptor sites, causing almost instantaneous paralysis. The brain sends signals to the motor neurons, but the muscles can't respond because the motor neuron receptor sites are blocked by the curare.

In coming chapters, we'll continue to look at the role that neurotransmitters play in a variety of psychological and behavioral processes.

The Nervous System and the Endocrine System: Communication Throughout the Body

> *The nervous system includes the central and peripheral nervous systems. What are the spinal cord's functions? What are the key divisions of the peripheral nervous system, and what are their functions?*

Specialized for communication, up to one *trillion* neurons are linked throughout your body in a complex communication network called the **nervous system.** The human nervous system is divided into two main divisions: the *central nervous system* and the *peripheral nervous system* (see Figure 2.6). For even simple behaviors to occur, such as curling your toes or scratching your nose, these two divisions must function as a single, integrated unit. Yet each of these divisions is highly specialized, performing different tasks.

The neuron is the most important transmitter of messages in the central nervous system. In the peripheral nervous system, communication occurs along **nerves.** Nerves and neurons are not the same thing. Nerves are made up of large bundles of neuron axons. Unlike neurons, many nerves are large enough to be seen easily with the unaided eye.

The Central Nervous System

The **central nervous system** includes the brain and the spinal cord. Every action, thought, feeling, and sensation you experience is processed through the central nervous system. The central nervous system is so critical to your ability to function that it is entirely protected by bone—the brain by your skull, and the spinal cord by your spinal column. As an added measure of protection, the brain and spinal cord are suspended in *cerebrospinal fluid* to protect them from being jarred.

Think of the spinal cord as a very busy telephone switchboard, handling both incoming and outgoing messages. Sensory receptors send messages along sensory nerves to the spinal cord, then up to the brain. To activate muscles, the brain sends signals down the spinal cord, which are relayed out along motor nerves to the muscles.

Most behaviors are controlled by your brain. However, the spinal cord can produce **spinal reflexes**—simple, automatic behaviors that occur without any brain involvement. One of the simplest spinal reflexes involves a three-neuron loop of rapid communication—a *sensory neuron* that communicates sensation to the spinal cord, an *interneuron* that relays information within the spinal cord, and a *motor neuron* leading from the spinal cord that signals muscles to react (see Figure 2.7 on the next page).

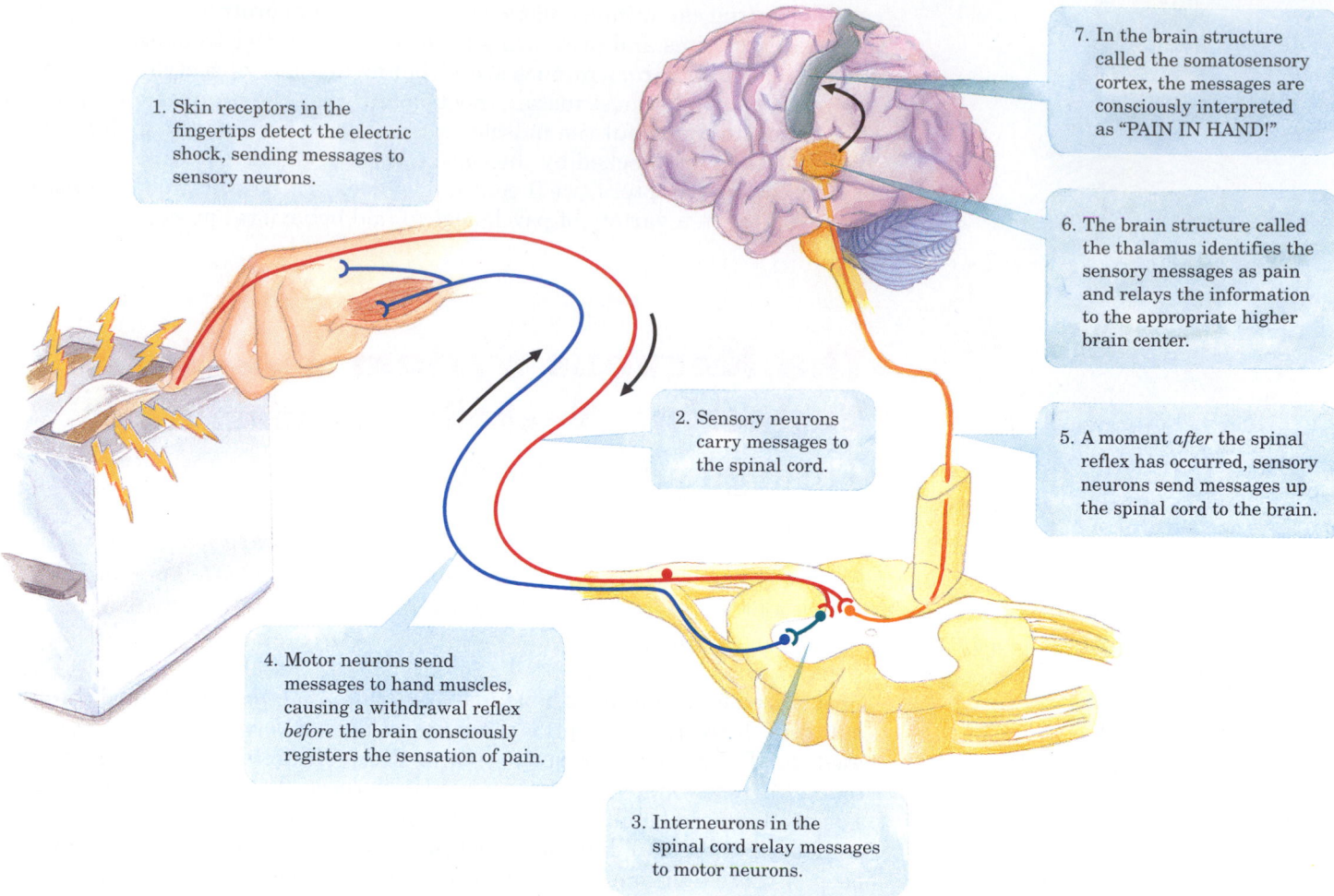

1. Skin receptors in the fingertips detect the electric shock, sending messages to sensory neurons.

2. Sensory neurons carry messages to the spinal cord.

3. Interneurons in the spinal cord relay messages to motor neurons.

4. Motor neurons send messages to hand muscles, causing a withdrawal reflex *before* the brain consciously registers the sensation of pain.

5. A moment *after* the spinal reflex has occurred, sensory neurons send messages up the spinal cord to the brain.

6. The brain structure called the thalamus identifies the sensory messages as pain and relays the information to the appropriate higher brain center.

7. In the brain structure called the somatosensory cortex, the messages are consciously interpreted as "PAIN IN HAND!"

FIGURE 2.7 A Spinal Reflex Arc
A spinal reflex is a simple, involuntary behavior that is processed in the spinal cord without brain involvement. As you follow the sequence shown here, you can see that the withdrawal reflex occurs before the brain processes the conscious perception of pain.

Spinal reflexes are crucial to your survival. The additional few seconds that it would take you to consciously process sensations and decide how to react could result in serious injury. Spinal reflexes are also important as indicators that the neural connections and pathways in your spinal cord are working correctly. That's why physicians test spinal reflexes during neurological examinations by tapping just below your kneecap for the knee-jerk spinal reflex, or scratching the sole of your foot for the toe-curl spinal reflex.

The Peripheral Nervous System

The **peripheral nervous system** is the other major division of your nervous system (see Figure 2.8). The word *peripheral* means "lying at the outer edges." Thus, the peripheral nervous system comprises all the nerves outside the central nervous system that extend to the outermost borders of your body, including your skin. The communication functions of the peripheral nervous system are handled by its two subdivisions: the *somatic nervous system* and the *autonomic nervous system*.

The **somatic nervous system** takes its name from the Latin word *soma*, which means "body." It plays a key role in communication throughout the entire body. First, the somatic nervous system communicates sensory information received by sensory receptors along sensory nerves *to* the central nervous system. And second, it carries messages *from* the central nervous

peripheral nervous system
(per-IF-er-ull) Division of the nervous system that includes all the nerves lying outside the central nervous system.

somatic nervous system
Subdivision of the peripheral nervous system that communicates sensory information to the central nervous system and carries messages from the central nervous system to the muscles.

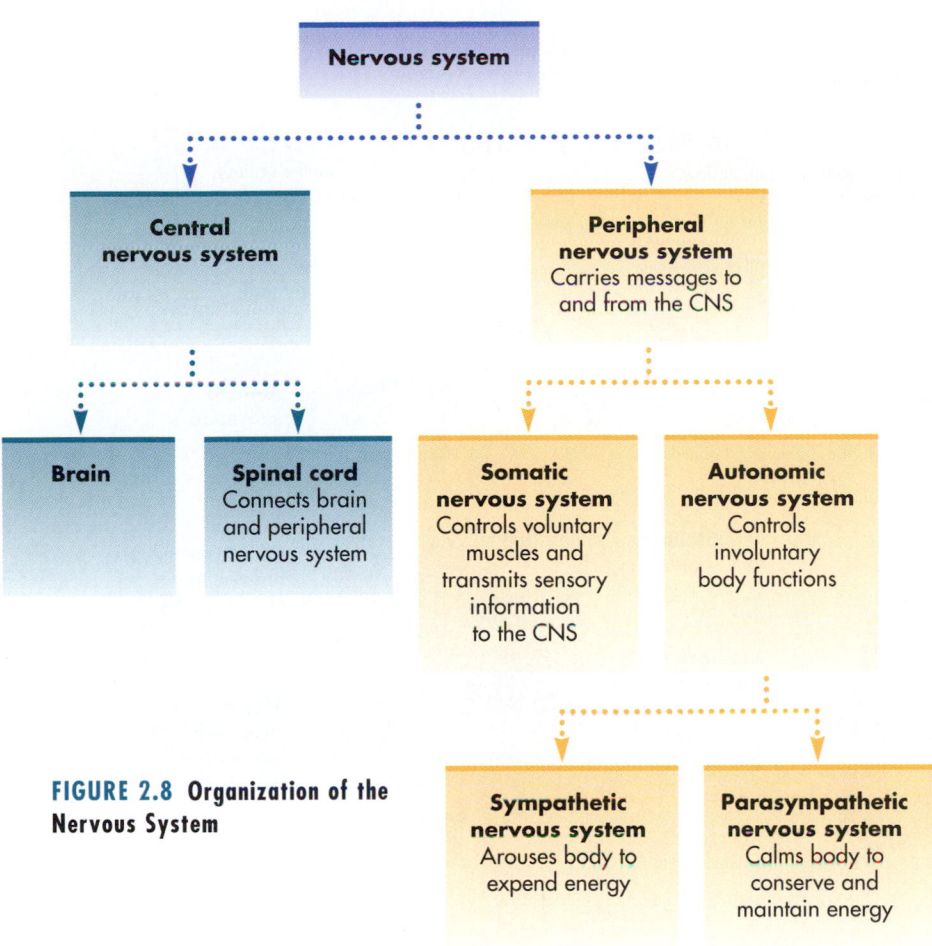

FIGURE 2.8 Organization of the Nervous System

system along motor nerves to perform voluntary muscle movements. All the different sensations that you're experiencing right now are being communicated by your somatic nervous system to your spinal cord and on to your brain. When you perform a voluntary action, such as turning a page of this book, messages from the brain are communicated down the spinal cord, then out to the muscles via the somatic nervous system.

The other subdivision of the peripheral nervous system is the **autonomic nervous system.** The word *autonomic* means "self-governing." Thus, the autonomic nervous system regulates *involuntary* functions, such as heartbeat, blood pressure, breathing, and digestion. These processes occur with little or no conscious involvement. This is fortunate, because if you had to mentally command your heart to beat or your stomach to digest the pizza you had for lunch, it would be difficult to focus your attention on anything else.

However, the autonomic nervous system is not completely self-regulating. By engaging in physical activity or purposely tensing or relaxing your muscles, you can increase or decrease autonomic activity. You can also influence your autonomic nervous system with mental imagery. Vividly imagining a situation that makes you feel angry, frightened, or even sexually aroused can dramatically increase heartbeat and blood pressure. A peaceful mental image can lower many autonomic functions.

The involuntary functions regulated by the autonomic nervous system are controlled by two different branches: the *sympathetic* and *parasympathetic nervous systems.* These two systems control many of the same organs in your body, but cause them to respond in opposite ways (see Figure 2.9). In general, the sympathetic nervous system arouses the body to expend energy, while the parasympathetic nervous system helps the body conserve energy.

The **sympathetic nervous system** is the body's emergency system, rapidly activating body systems to meet threats or emergencies. When you are frightened, your breathing accelerates, your heart beats faster, digestion stops, and the bronchial tubes in your lungs expand. All these physiological responses increase the amount of oxygen available to your brain and muscles. Your pupils dilate to increase your field of vision, and your mouth becomes dry, because salivation stops. You begin to sweat in response to your body's expenditure of greater energy and heat. These bodily changes collectively represent the *fight-or-flight response*—they physically prepare you to fight or flee from a perceived danger (Cannon, 1932).

As a short-term response, the fight-or-flight response helps you cope with an emergency situation. However, if this heightened physiological arousal continues, such as during times of prolonged stress, you can suffer from mental and physical deterioration or exhaustion (Stein & Miller, 1993). We'll discuss the fight-or-flight response in greater detail in later chapters on emotion (Chapter 8) and stress (Chapter 12).

autonomic nervous system
(aw-toe-NOM-ick) Subdivision of the peripheral nervous system that regulates involuntary functions.

sympathetic nervous system
Branch of the autonomic nervous system that produces rapid physical arousal in response to perceived emergencies or threats.

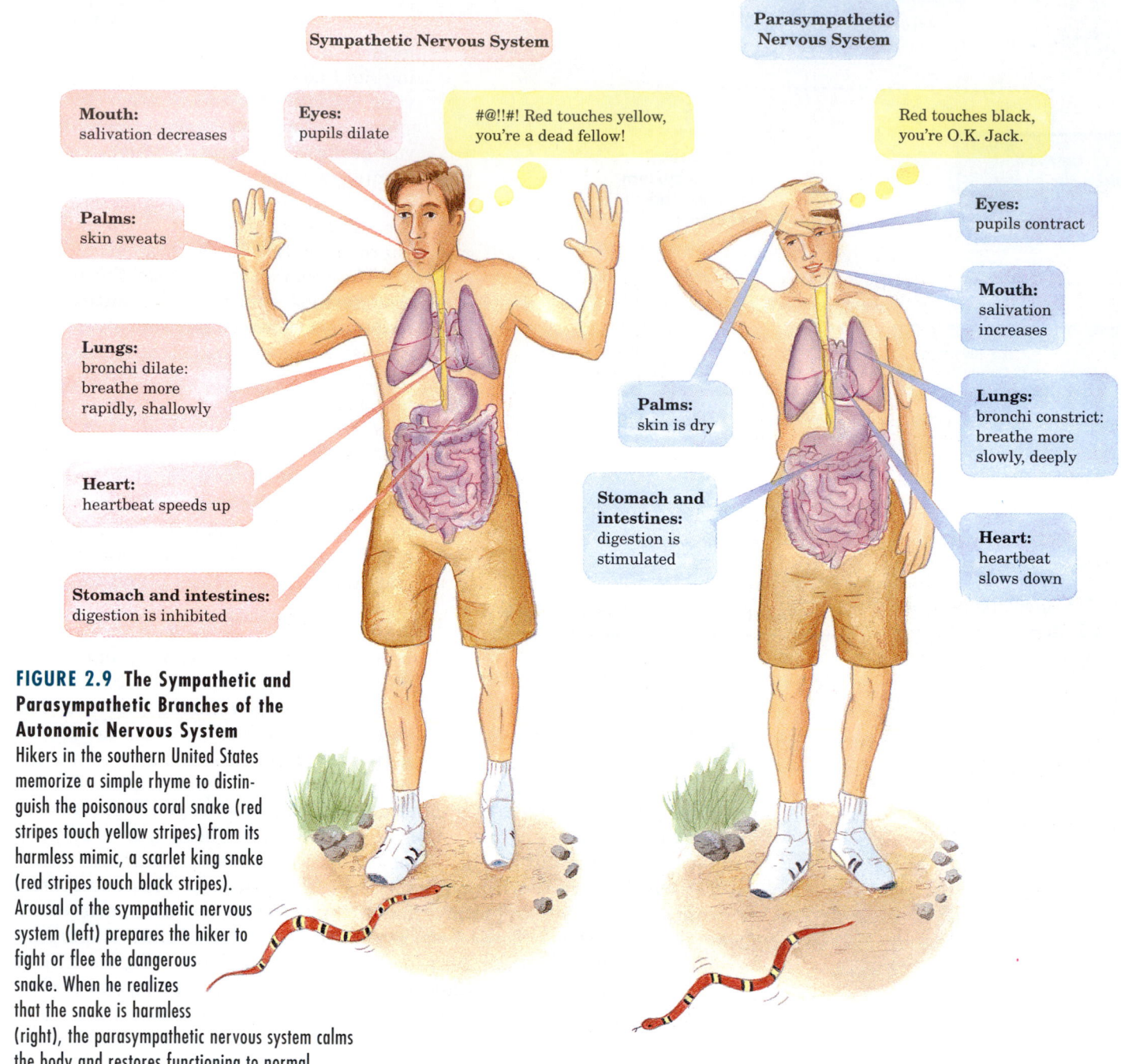

Sympathetic Nervous System

Parasympathetic Nervous System

Mouth: salivation decreases

Eyes: pupils dilate

#@!!#! Red touches yellow, you're a dead fellow!

Red touches black, you're O.K. Jack.

Palms: skin sweats

Lungs: bronchi dilate: breathe more rapidly, shallowly

Heart: heartbeat speeds up

Stomach and intestines: digestion is inhibited

Eyes: pupils contract

Mouth: salivation increases

Palms: skin is dry

Lungs: bronchi constrict: breathe more slowly, deeply

Stomach and intestines: digestion is stimulated

Heart: heartbeat slows down

FIGURE 2.9 **The Sympathetic and Parasympathetic Branches of the Autonomic Nervous System** Hikers in the southern United States memorize a simple rhyme to distinguish the poisonous coral snake (red stripes touch yellow stripes) from its harmless mimic, a scarlet king snake (red stripes touch black stripes). Arousal of the sympathetic nervous system (left) prepares the hiker to fight or flee the dangerous snake. When he realizes that the snake is harmless (right), the parasympathetic nervous system calms the body and restores functioning to normal.

parasympathetic nervous system Branch of the autonomic nervous system that maintains normal body functions and conserves the body's physical resources.

endocrine system (EN-doe-krin) A communication system composed of glands located thoughout the body that secrete hormones into the bloodstream.

hormones Chemical messengers secreted into the bloodstream by endocrine glands.

While the sympathetic nervous system mobilizes your body's physical resources, the **parasympathetic nervous system** conserves and maintains your physical resources. It calms you down after an emergency. Acting much more slowly than the sympathetic nervous system, the parasympathetic nervous system gradually returns body systems to normal. Heartbeat, breathing, and blood pressure level out. Pupils constrict back to their normal size. Saliva returns, and the digestive system begins operating again. Although the sympathetic and parasympathetic nervous systems produce opposite effects, they act together, keeping the nervous system in balance.

Although each division of the nervous system handles different functions, the nervous system as a whole works in unison so that both automatic and voluntary behaviors are carried out smoothly. In the next section, we'll look at the second major communication system in the body: the endocrine system.

The Endocrine System

The endocrine system is made up of glands that transmit information via chemical messengers called hormones. How does information transmission in the endocrine system differ from that in the nervous system? What roles are played by the pituitary gland, the hypothalamus, the gonads, and the adrenal glands?

The **endocrine system** is made up of glands that are located throughout the body (see Figure 2.10). Like the nervous system, the endocrine system involves the use of chemical messengers to transmit information from one part of the body to another. Endocrine glands communicate by secreting messenger chemicals called **hormones** into the bloodstream. The hormones circulate throughout the bloodstream until they reach specific hormone receptors on target organs or tissue. By interacting with the nervous system and affecting internal organs and body tissues, hormones regulate physical processes and influence behavior in a variety of ways. Metabolism, growth rate, digestion, blood pressure, and sexual development and reproduction are just some of the processes that are regulated by the endocrine hormones. Hormones are also involved in emotional response and the response to stress (Thompson, 1993).

Endocrine hormones are also closely linked to the workings of the nervous system. For example, the release of hormones may be stimulated or inhibited by certain parts of the nervous system. In turn, hormones can promote or inhibit the generation of nerve impulses. Finally, some hormones and neurotransmitters are chemically identical. That is, the same molecule can act as a hormone in some locations and act as a neurotransmitter in the nervous system.

In contrast to the rapid speed of information transmission in the nervous system, communication in the endocrine system takes place much more slowly. Because hormones rely upon the circulation of the blood to deliver their chemical message to target organs, it may take a few seconds or longer for the hormone to reach its target organ once it is secreted by the originating gland.

FIGURE 2.10 The Endocrine System
The endocrine system and the nervous system are directly linked by the hypothalamus in the brain, which controls the pituitary gland. The location and main functions of several important endocrine glands are shown here.

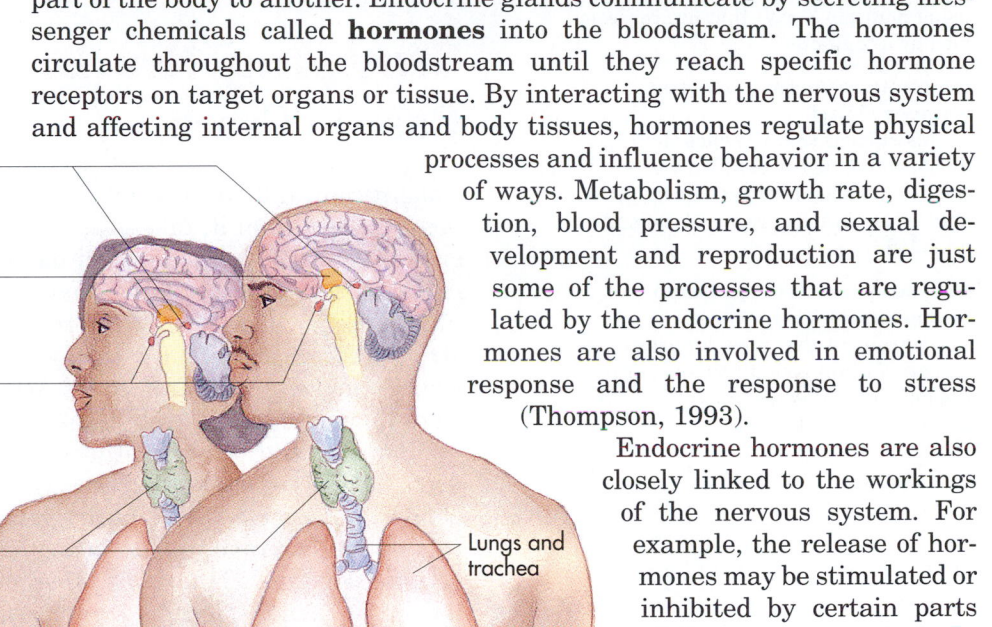

Pineal gland
produces *melatonin,* which helps regulate sleep/wake cycles

Hypothalamus
brain structure that controls the pituitary gland; links nervous system and endocrine system

Pituitary gland
regulates activities of several other glands; produces *growth hormone*; also produces *prolactin* and *oxytocin,* which stimulate milk production in nursing mothers

Thyroid gland
controls body metabolism rate

Adrenal glands
produce *epinephrine* (adrenaline) and *norepinephrine,* which cause physical arousal in response to danger, fear, anger, stress, and other strong emotions

Pancreas
regulates blood sugar and insulin levels; involved in hunger

Ovaries
secrete *estrogen* and *progesterone,* which regulate female sexual development, reproduction, and sexual behavior

Testes
secrete *testosterone,* which regulates male sexual development, reproduction, and sexual behavior

Lungs and trachea

Uterus

Kidneys

pituitary gland
(pi-TOO-ih-tare-ee) Endocrine gland attached to the base of the brain that secretes hormones that affect the function of other glands as well as hormones that act directly on physical processes.

electroencephalograph
An instrument that uses electrodes placed on the scalp to record the brain's electrical activity.

CAT scan (computerized axial tomography)
An instrument that produces two-dimensional pictures of brain structures using multiple X-rays that are reassembled by a computer.

magnetic resonance imaging scanner (MRI)
An instrument that provides three-dimensional, highly detailed views of the brain using electrical signals generated by the brain in response to magnetic fields.

PET scan (positron emission tomography)
An instrument that provides color-coded images of brain activity by measuring the amount of glucose or oxygen used in different brain regions.

The signals that trigger the secretion of hormones are regulated by the brain, primarily by a brain structure called the *hypothalamus.* (You'll learn more about the hypothalamus later in the chapter.) The hypothalamus serves as the main link between the endocrine system and the nervous system. The hypothalamus directly regulates the release of hormones by the **pituitary gland,** a small, pea-sized gland just under the brain. The pituitary's hormones, in turn, regulate the production of other hormones by many of the glands in the endocrine system. Thus, under the direction of the hypothalamus, the pituitary gland directly controls hormone production in other endocrine glands.

Studying the Brain: The Toughest Case to Crack

Imagine how difficult it would be to figure out how something works without being able to open it, take it apart, or watch it operate. Because the brain is entirely encased by bone, such has long been the challenge faced by scientists. Another obstacle is the complexity of the brain itself—complex not only in its enormous number of interconnected neurons, but also in the intricate structures, regions, and pathways formed by those neurons. But scientists are not an easily discouraged lot. When direct methods of studying the brain were unavailable, indirect methods were found.

Some of the oldest methods of studying the brain are still commonly used. Using the *case study,* researchers systematically observe and record the behavior of people whose brains have been damaged by illness or injury. A related method involves producing *lesions*—surgically altering or destroying specific portions of the brain, then observing the subsequent effects on behavior. In humans, lesions are sometimes produced for medical reasons, such as when part of the brain is surgically altered or removed to relieve uncontrollable seizures. To experimentally investigate the effects of brain lesions on different aspects of behavior, animals are used.

Researchers have also studied the behavioral effects of electrically stimulating specific brain areas with small electrified discs or wires called *electrodes* (e.g., Penfield & Perot, 1963; Delgado, 1969). Although each of these techniques has limitations, they have produced valuable insights into the brain's role in such diverse functions as memory, speech, emotion, personality, and sleep.

As technology has become more advanced, so have the tools that can be used to study the brain. The **electroencephalograph** records the brain's electrical activity through the use of electrodes placed harmlessly on a person's scalp. The graphic record of the brain's electrical activity that this instrument produces is called an *electroencephalogram,* abbreviated *EEG.* Modern electroencephalographs provide sophisticated computerized analyses of the brain's electrical activity, recording the electrical activity of the brain from millisecond to millisecond (see Azar, 1994a).

Computerized axial tomography, commonly called a **CAT scan,** produces an image of the brain's structure. CAT scans work by taking multiple X-rays of the brain from different angles. These multiple images are reassembled by computer. Researchers can look at a picture of the brain from any angle, viewing a "slice" of the brain. CAT scans can detect brain abnormalities and are widely used in medicine and in research.

Another advanced instrument for viewing the brain's structure is the **magnetic resonance imaging scanner,** or **MRI.** While a person lies mo-

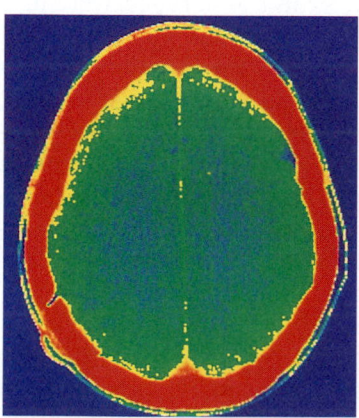

CAT Scan of a Normal Brain

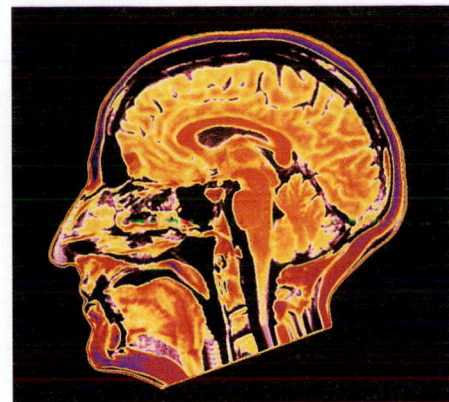

MRI Scan of a Normal Brain

Where Chess Players Think PET scans can identify the specific brain areas that are activated by different tasks. For example, researchers have used PET scans to identify the brain areas involved in the complex mental activities during a chess game (Nichelli & others, 1994). In **(a),** areas at the back of the brain, where visual information is processed, are most active when a player distinguishes between black and white chess pieces. In **(b),** the lower middle region of the brain is more active when a player is determining if a particular chess piece can capture another piece.

tionless in a long, magnetic tube, his brain is bombarded with harmless magnetic fields. In response to these magnetic fields, the molecules of the brain generate electromagnetic signals that are analyzed by computer to create highly detailed images of the brain. Like the CAT scan, MRI is a harmless, noninvasive technique that can be used to study brain structures and to detect abnormalities.

Unlike MRI and CAT scans, which provide pictures of the brain's structure, **positron emission tomography,** or **PET, scans,** generate images of the brain's *activity.* The PET scan tracks the brain's use of glucose, a type of sugar that is the brain's main source of energy. Brain regions use more glucose when they are actively functioning than when they are inactive. The PET scan measures the amount of radioactively tagged glucose or oxygen used in thousands of different brain areas while the subject reads, talks, or engages in other kinds of mental activity. This information is analyzed by computer to create dramatic color-coded images showing the brain areas that are active during different tasks, such as those of chess players in the photographs below.

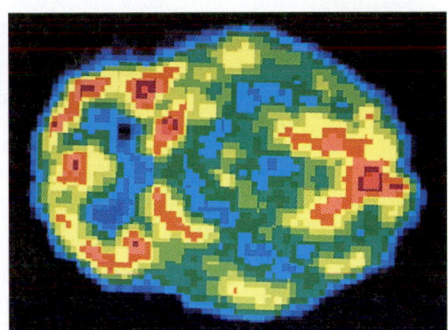

PET Scan of a Normal Brain

The use of PET scans has had a tremendous impact on the field of neuroscience. Recently, a new technique has become available that holds even greater promise than the PET technology. *Functional MRI* refers to a new kind of MRI that can, like a PET scan, reveal the activity of the working brain (Naeye, 1994). One key difference is that in functional MRI, researchers take a rapid series of brain images. When put together by computer, these images create a sort of "movie" of brain activity. Because MRI scanners are less costly and more widely available than PET scanners, many researchers believe that functional MRI will be the dominant brain-mapping technique in years to come (Azar, 1994a). Functional MRI also produces a much sharper picture than PET scans and can be used to image much smaller brain structures.

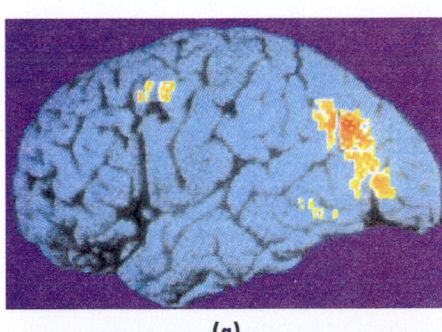

(a)

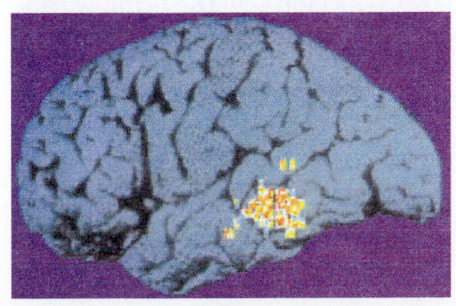

(b)

Sophisticated techniques for imaging the brain continue to be developed. With the availability of ever more precise and sophisticated instruments to study the living brain, neuroscientists believe that a new era in brain research has begun. But even the most sophisticated technological device is simple in comparison to the phenomenal complexity of the brain itself.

CONCEPT REVIEW 2.2

Brain Imaging Techniques

Match each of the following terms with the correct description: EEG, CAT, PET, MRI.

1. A technique that provides color-coded images of brain activity by measuring the amount of glucose used in different regions of the brain. _____

2. A technique that creates three-dimensional, detailed views of the brain using electrical sig-

nals generated by the brain in response to magnetic fields. _____

3. An instrument that uses electrodes placed on the scalp to record the brain's electrical activity. _____

4. A technique that uses a computer to create two-dimensional pictures of brain structures from multiple X-rays. _____

A Guided Tour of the Brain

Although particular areas of the brain correspond with particular functions, multiple brain areas are involved in most behaviors. What are neural pathways? What do we mean when we say that the brain is an integrated system? How does the brain develop?

Forget all the hype about the Internet. The *real* information superhighway is the human brain. In fact, the most complex mass of matter known to exist sits right between your two ears: your brain.

Neuroscientists have made enormous advances in the past decades in understanding the brain structures and neural pathways involved in behavior. New discoveries are made so frequently that even experts find it hard to keep up with the explosion of research on the brain. All the same, a great deal remains to be explained about how the brain processes information and translates neural impulses into complex behavior (Bullock, 1993).

In this section, we'll take you on a guided tour of the human brain. As your tour guides, our goal is to familiarize you with the basic organization and structures of the brain. In later chapters, we'll add to your knowledge of the brain as we discuss the brain's involvement in specific psychological processes. Our second goal is to give you a general sense for *how* the brain works.

At the beginning of this tour, it's important to note that the brain generally does not lend itself to simple explanations. As we describe the different areas of the brain, we'll identify important centers where particular functions seem to be localized. Nevertheless, bear in mind that specific functions seldom correspond neatly to a single, specific brain site (Farah, 1994).

Think of the brain as an *integrated system*. Many psychological processes, particularly complex ones, involve multiple brain structures and regions. Even simple tasks—such as carrying on a conversation or walking down the

brainstem
A region of the brain made up of the hindbrain and the midbrain.

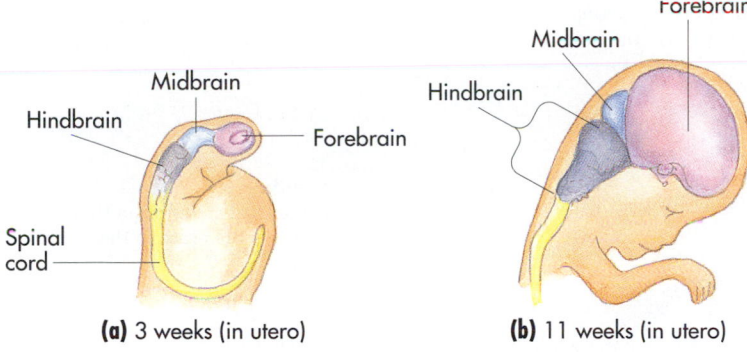

(a) 3 weeks (in utero)

(b) 11 weeks (in utero)

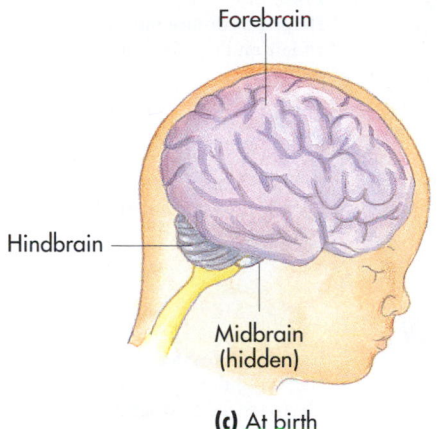

(c) At birth

FIGURE 2.11 The Sequence of Fetal Brain Development
The human brain begins its development as a fluid-filled tube at about two weeks after conception. The hindbrain structures are the first to develop, followed by midbrain structures. The forebrain structures develop last, eventually coming to envelop and surround the hindbrain and midbrain structures.

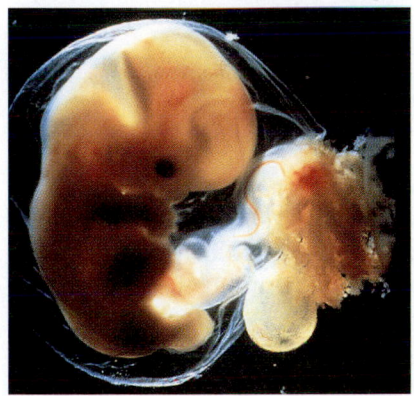

Human Embryo at Six Weeks Though the embryo is less than an inch long, the prominent structures of the hindbrain and the beginnings of the forebrain can clearly be seen at this early stage of prenatal development.

street—involve the smoothly coordinated synthesis of information among many different areas of your brain.

How is information communicated and shared among these multiple brain regions? Many brain functions involve the activation of neural pathways that link different brain structures. *Neural pathways* are formed by groups of neuron cell bodies in one area of the brain that project their axons to other brain areas. Like the transcontinental telephone system that links different parts of the world, these neural pathways form communication networks and circuits that link different brain areas. As a result, damage to one area of the brain may disrupt many neural pathways and affect many different functions.

Our guided tour will follow the same general sequence that the brain follows in its development before birth. The human brain begins as a fluid-filled tube that forms about two weeks after conception. Gradually, the tube expands and develops into separate fluid-filled cavities called *ventricles,* which are at the core of the fully developed brain. *Cerebrospinal fluid* is manufactured in the ventricles. We noted previously that cerebrospinal fluid acts as a shock absorber for the central nervous system and cushions the brain.

As the human fetus develops, brain cells multiply, differentiate, and migrate to their final locations (Jessell, 1995a). Between conception and birth, the number of neurons is increasing in the developing person by an average of 250,000 neurons per *minute* (Thompson, 1993). During this phase, there is an overabundance of neurons, which compete to form synaptic connections (Rakic, 1995). Neurons that fail to form connections are eliminated. Progressively, the three major divisions of the brain develop—the *hindbrain,* the *midbrain,* and the *forebrain.* As you can see in Figure 2.11, during the course of fetal brain development, the forebrain structures eventually surround and envelop the midbrain and hindbrain structures.

At birth, the infant's brain weighs less than a pound. Virtually all the neurons that a person will ever have are present at birth, but the newborn brain is only about one-fourth the size of an adult brain. The number of neurons does not increase after birth; rather, the neurons grow in size. The neurons continue to develop new dendrites (Johnston & others, 1996). Axons also grow longer, and the branching at the ends of axons becomes more dense (Shatz, 1992). By adulthood, the fully mature human brain weighs about three pounds.

The Brainstem:

Hindbrain and Midbrain Structures

The brainstem includes the hindbrain and midbrain. Why does damage to one side of the brain affect the opposite side of the body? What functions are associated with each hindbrain and midbrain structure?

The major regions of the brain are illustrated in Figure 2.12 on the next page, which can serve as a map to keep you oriented during our tour. At the base of the brain lie the hindbrain and, directly above it, the midbrain. Combined, the structures of the hindbrain and midbrain are called the **brainstem.**

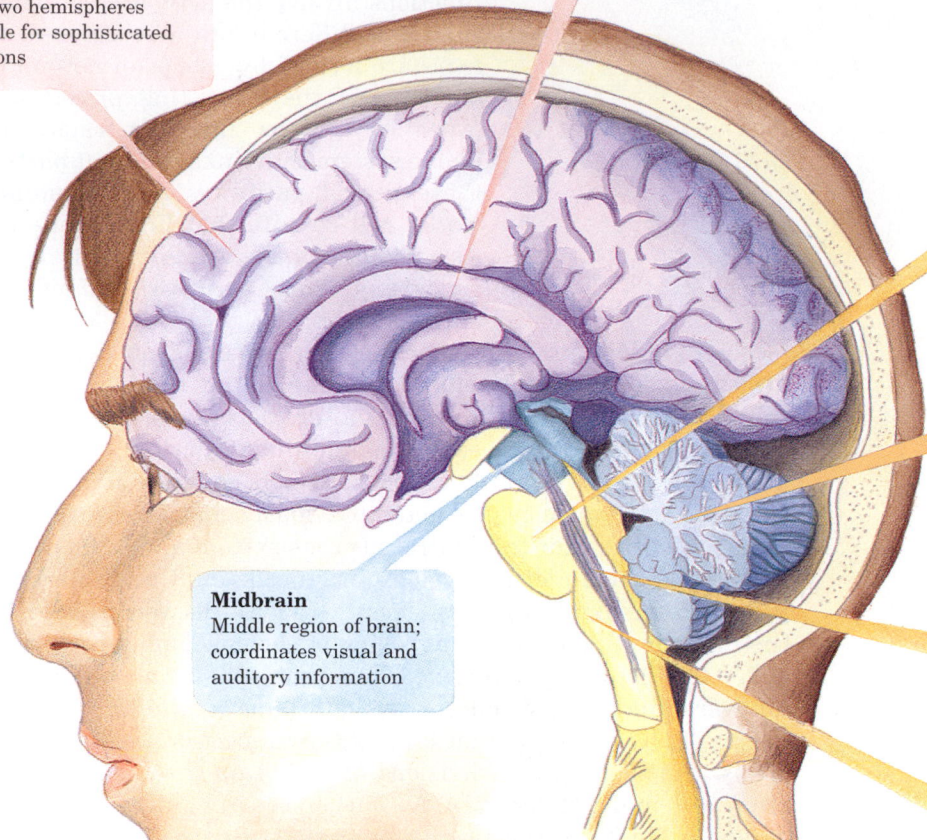

Forebrain
Uppermost and largest brain region composed of several structures, the most prominent being the cerebral cortex

Corpus callosum
Thick band of axons connecting the two hemispheres of the cerebral cortex

Cerebral cortex
Divided into two hemispheres and responsible for sophisticated mental functions

Hindbrain
Region at base of brain that connects the brain to the spinal cord

Pons
Helps coordinate movements on left and right sides of body

Cerebellum
Coordinates movement, balance, and posture

Reticular formation
Helps regulate attention, alertness, and incoming sensory information

Midbrain
Middle region of brain; coordinates visual and auditory information

Medulla
Controls breathing, heartbeat, and other vital life functions

FIGURE 2.12 Major Regions of the Brain
This cross section of the human brain shows the primary structures that make up the hindbrain region (yellow), the midbrain region (blue), and the forebrain region (pink). The hindbrain and midbrain regulate many basic life functions, while the forebrain is involved in more sophisticated behaviors and mental processes.

hindbrain
A region at the base of the brain that contains several structures that regulate basic life functions.

The Hindbrain

The **hindbrain** connects the spinal cord with the rest of the brain. It is through the hindbrain that sensory and motor pathways pass to and from regions that are situated higher up in the brain. Sensory information coming in from one side of the body crosses over at the hindbrain level, projecting to the opposite side of the brain. And outgoing motor messages from one side of the brain also cross over at the hindbrain level, controlling movement and other motor functions on the opposite side of the body

That's why people who suffer strokes on one side of their brain experience muscle weakness or paralysis on the opposite side of their body. Our friend Asha, for example, suffered only minor damage to motor control areas in her brain. However, because the stroke occurred on the *left* side of her brain, what muscle weakness she did experience was localized on the *right* side of her body, primarily in her right hand.

Three structures make up the hindbrain—the medulla, pons, and cerebellum. The **medulla** lies directly above the spinal cord and contains centers involved in the control of such vital autonomic functions as breathing, heart rate, and digestion. Because the medulla is involved in such critical life functions, damage to the medulla can result in death. The medulla also controls a number of vital reflexes, such as swallowing, coughing, vomiting, and sneezing.

Above the medulla is a swelling of tissue called the **pons,** which represents the uppermost level of the hindbrain. Bulging out behind the pons is the large **cerebellum.** On each side of the pons, a large bundle of axons connects the pons to the cerebellum. The word *pons* means "bridge," and the pons is a bridge of sorts: Information from various other brain regions located higher up in the brain is relayed to the cerebellum via the pons.

The cerebellum functions in the control of balance, muscle tone, and coordinated muscle movements. It's also involved in the learning of habitual or automatic movements and motor skills, such as typing, writing, or gracefully backhanding a tennis ball.

Jerky, uncoordinated movements can result from damage to the cerebellum. Simple movements such as walking or standing upright may become difficult or impossible. The cerebellum is also one of the brain areas that is affected by alcohol consumption. That's why a person "under the influence" may stagger and find it impossible to walk a straight line or stand on one foot. (That's also why a police officer will ask a suspected drunk driver to execute these normally effortless movements.)

At the core of the medulla and the pons is a network of neurons called the **reticular formation,** or the *reticular activating system*. The reticular formation is composed of many groups of specialized neurons that project up to higher brain regions and down to the spinal cord. The reticular formation plays an important role in regulating attention and sleep.

In regulating attention, the reticular formation helps screen the flood of sensory information picked up by sensory receptors and directed to the midbrain and forebrain regions. Although the neural pathways involved are far from thoroughly understood, the reticular formation seems to help filter out unimportant sensory information. However, when you deliberately, *consciously* focus your attention on specific aspects of your environment, other brain areas come into play, particularly forebrain regions (Hillyard & others, 1995).

The Midbrain

The **midbrain** is an important relay station, where auditory and visual information is integrated. Auditory sensations from the left and right ears are coordinated in the midbrain, allowing you to detect the direction of a sound. The midbrain also coordinates visual information, including eye movements, helping you to locate objects and track their movement. Once coordinated at the midbrain level, auditory and visual information is relayed to sensory processing centers farther up in the forebrain region.

A midbrain area called the **substantia nigra** is involved in motor control and contains a large concentration of dopamine-producing neurons. *Substantia nigra* means "dark substance," and as the name suggests, this area is darkly pigmented. The substantia nigra is part of a larger neural pathway that is involved in preparing other brain regions to initiate organized movements or actions (Kalat, 1995). In the section on neurotransmitters, we noted that Parkinson's disease involves symptoms of abnormal movement. Many of those movement-related symptoms are associated with the degeneration of dopamine-producing neurons in the substantia nigra.

medulla
(meh-DULL-uh) A hindbrain structure that controls vital life functions such as breathing, circulation, and muscle tone.

pons
A hindbrain structure that connects the medulla to the two sides of the cerebellum; helps coordinate and integrate movements on each side of the body.

cerebellum
(sare-uh-BELL-um) A large, two-sided hindbrain structure at the back of the brain responsible for muscle coordination, fine motor movements, and maintaining posture and equilibrium.

reticular formation
(reh-TICK-you-ler) A network of nerve fibers located in the center of the medulla that helps regulate attention, arousal, and sleep.

midbrain
The smallest brain region, which helps coordinate auditory and visual sensations.

substantia nigra
(sub-STANCE-ee-uh NEE-gruh) An area of the midbrain that is involved in motor control and contains a large concentration of dopamine-producing neurons.

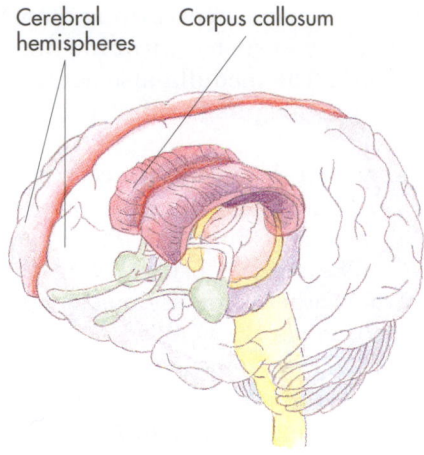

Cerebral
hemispheres   Corpus callosum

FIGURE 2.13 The Cerebral Hemispheres and the Corpus Callosum
This transparent view of the brain shows the corpus callosum, the C-shaped bundle of axons that links the left and right hemispheres of the cerebral cortex.

forebrain
The largest and most complex brain region, which contains centers for complex behaviors and mental processes.

cerebral cortex
(suh-REE-brull or SARE-uh-brull) The wrinkled outer portion of the forebrain, which contains the most sophisticated brain centers.

cerebral hemisphere
The nearly symmetrical left and right halves of the cerebral cortex.

corpus callosum
A thick band of nerve fibers that connects the two cerebral hemispheres and acts as a communication link between them.

temporal lobe
An area on each hemisphere of the cerebral cortex near the temples that is the primary receiving area for auditory information.

occipital lobe
(ock-SIP-it-ull) An area at the back of each cerebral cortex hemisphere that is the primary receiving area for visual information.

parietal lobe
(puh-RYE-et-ull) An area on each hemisphere of the cerebral cortex located above the temporal lobe that processes somatic sensations.

The Forebrain

The forebrain includes the cerebral cortex and the limbic system structures. What are the four lobes of the cerebral cortex, and what functions have been identified with each lobe? What is the limbic system? What functions are associated with the thalamus, hypothalamus, hippocampus, and amygdala?

Situated above the midbrain is the largest region of the brain: the **forebrain.** In humans, the forebrain represents about 90 percent of the brain. Many important structures are found in the forebrain. We'll start by describing the forebrain's most prominent structure.

The Cerebral Cortex

The outer portion of the forebrain is called the **cerebral cortex,** which is divided into two **cerebral hemispheres.** The word *cortex* means "bark," and much like the bark of a tree, the cerebral cortex is the outer covering of the forebrain. A thick bundle of axons called the **corpus callosum** connects the two cerebral hemispheres, as shown in Figure 2.13. The corpus callosum serves as the primary communication link between the left and right cerebral hemispheres (Hoptman & Davidson, 1994).

The cerebral cortex is only about a quarter of an inch thick. It is mainly composed of glial cells and neuron cell bodies and axons, giving it a grayish appearance—which is why the cerebral cortex is sometimes described as being composed of *gray matter.* Extending inward from the cerebral cortex are white myelinated axons that are sometimes referred to as *white matter.* These myelinated axons connect the cerebral cortex to other brain regions.

Numerous folds, grooves, and bulges characterize the human cerebral cortex. The purpose of these ridges and valleys is easy to illustrate. Imagine a flat, three-foot by three-foot piece of paper. You can compact the surface area of this piece of paper by scrunching it up into a wad. In much the same way, the grooves and bulges of the cerebral cortex allow about three square feet of surface area to be packed into the small space of the human skull.

Lobes of the Cerebral Cortex

Each cerebral hemisphere can be roughly divided into four regions, or *lobes:* the *temporal, occipital, parietal,* and *frontal* lobes (see Figure 2.14). Each lobe is associated with distinct functions. Located near your temples, the **temporal lobe** contains the *primary auditory cortex,* which receives auditory information. At the very back of the brain is the **occipital lobe.** The occipital lobe includes the *primary visual cortex,* where visual information is received.

The **parietal lobe** is involved in processing bodily or *somatosensory information,* including touch, temperature, pressure, and information from sense receptors in the muscles and joints. A band of tissue on the parietal lobe, called the *somatosensory cortex,* receives information from touch receptors in different parts of the body.

Each part of the body is represented on the somatosensory cortex, but this representation is not equally distributed. Instead, body parts are represented in proportion to their sensitivity to somatic sensations. For example, your hands and face, which are very responsive to touch, have much greater representation on the somatosensory cortex than the backs of your legs, which are far less sensitive to touch. If body areas were actually proportional to the amount of representation on the somatosensory cortex, humans would resemble the misshapen character on the right side of Figure 2.15 on page 60.

FIGURE 2.14 Lobes of the Cerebral Cortex
Each hemisphere of the cerebral cortex can be divided into four regions or *lobes,* as shown. Each lobe is associated with distinct functions. The association areas, shaded in purple, make up most of the cerebral cortex.

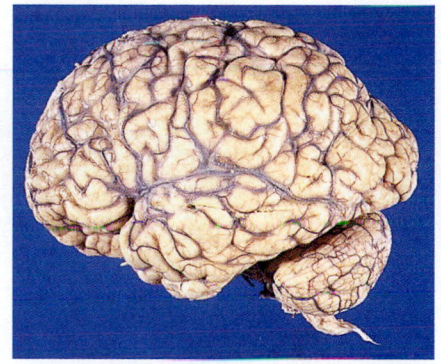

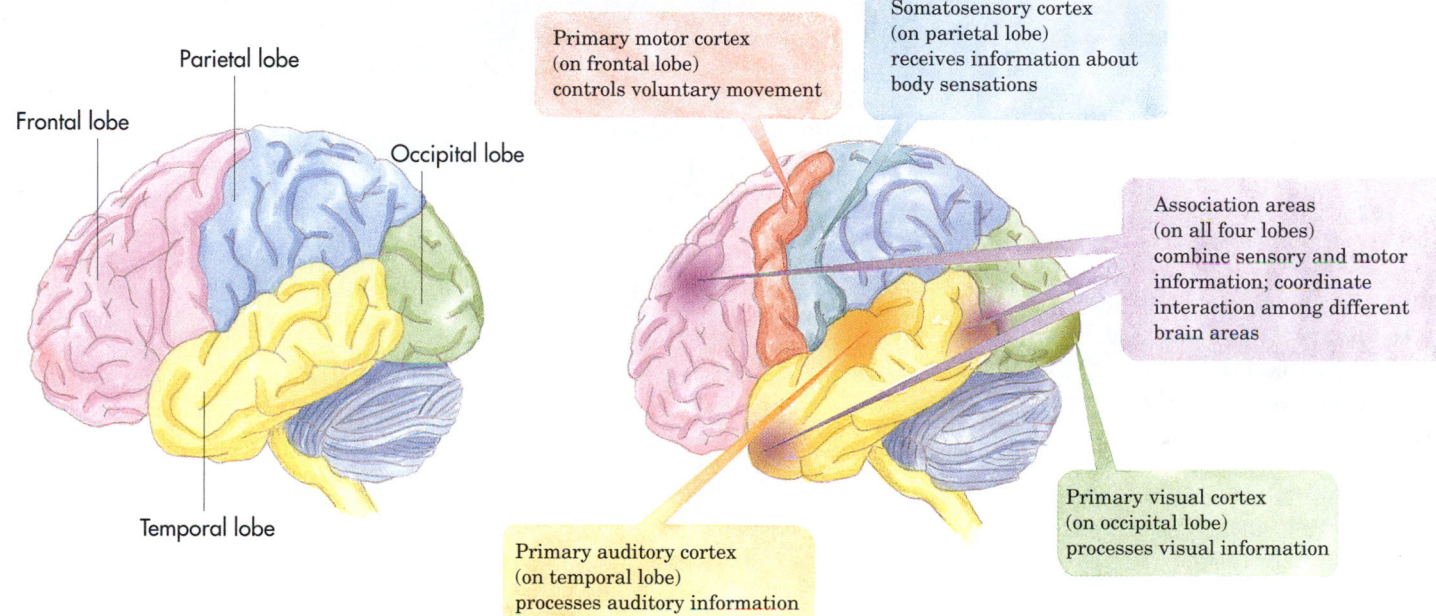

Primary motor cortex (on frontal lobe) controls voluntary movement

Somatosensory cortex (on parietal lobe) receives information about body sensations

Association areas (on all four lobes) combine sensory and motor information; coordinate interaction among different brain areas

Primary visual cortex (on occipital lobe) processes visual information

Primary auditory cortex (on temporal lobe) processes auditory information

Parietal lobe

Frontal lobe

Occipital lobe

Temporal lobe

The largest lobe of the cerebral cortex is called the **frontal lobe.** The frontal lobe is involved in planning, initiating, and executing voluntary movements. The movements of different body parts are represented in a band of tissue on the frontal lobe called the *primary motor cortex.* The degree of representation on the primary motor cortex for a particular body part reflects the diversity and precision of its potential movements, as shown on the left side of Figure 2.15 on the next page. Thus, it's not surprising that almost one-third of the primary motor cortex is devoted to the hands and another third is devoted to facial muscles. The disproportionate representation of these two body areas on the primary motor cortex is reflected in the human capacity to produce an extremely wide range of hand movements and facial expressions.

The primary sensory and motor areas found on the different lobes represent just a small portion of the cerebral cortex. The remaining bulk of the cerebral cortex consists mostly of three large **association areas.** These areas are generally thought to be involved in processing and integrating sensory and motor information (see Jessell, 1995b). For example, the *prefrontal association cortex,* situated in front of the primary motor cortex, is involved in the planning of voluntary movements. Another association area includes parts of the temporal, parietal, and occipital lobes, and is involved in the integration of perceptions and memories.

frontal lobe
The largest lobe of the cerebral cortex; processes voluntary muscle movements and is involved in thinking, planning, and emotional expression and control.

association areas
Areas of the cerebral cortex where information from different brain centers is combined and integrated.

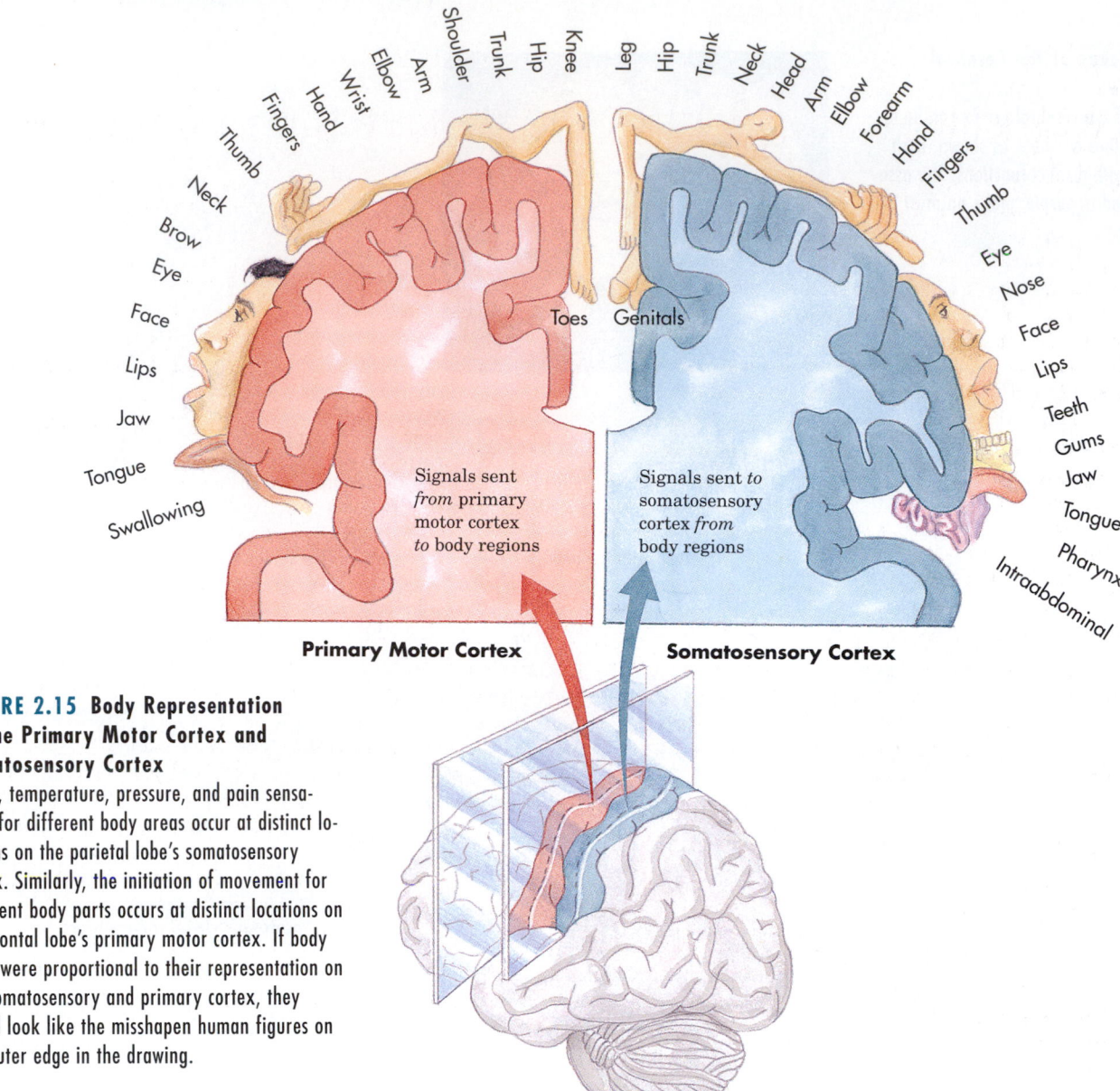

Primary Motor Cortex

Signals sent *from* primary motor cortex *to* body regions

Somatosensory Cortex

Signals sent *to* somatosensory cortex *from* body regions

Toes   Genitals

FIGURE 2.15 Body Representation on the Primary Motor Cortex and Somatosensory Cortex
Touch, temperature, pressure, and pain sensations for different body areas occur at distinct locations on the parietal lobe's somatosensory cortex. Similarly, the initiation of movement for different body parts occurs at distinct locations on the frontal lobe's primary motor cortex. If body parts were proportional to their representation on the somatosensory and primary cortex, they would look like the misshapen human figures on the outer edge in the drawing.

The Limbic System

Beneath the cerebral cortex are several other important forebrain structures, which are components of the **limbic system.** The word *limbic* means "border," and as you can see in Figure 2.16, the structures that make up the limbic system form a border of sorts around the brainstem. In various combinations, the limbic system structures form complex neural circuits that play critical roles in learning, memory, and emotional control (Squire & Knowlton, 1995; Kupfermann & Kandel, 1995).

One interesting aspect of the limbic system is its involvement in pleasurable or rewarding sensations. In the 1950s, neuropsychologist James Olds (1958, 1962) discovered that rats could be trained to perform a task, such as pressing a bar, in order to receive electrical stimulation to certain regions in the limbic system. In their early work, Olds and other researchers found that the rats seemed to prefer brain stimulation to food, even when the rats were extremely hungry.

limbic system
A group of forebrain structures that form a border around the brainstem and that are involved in emotion, motivation, learning, and memory.

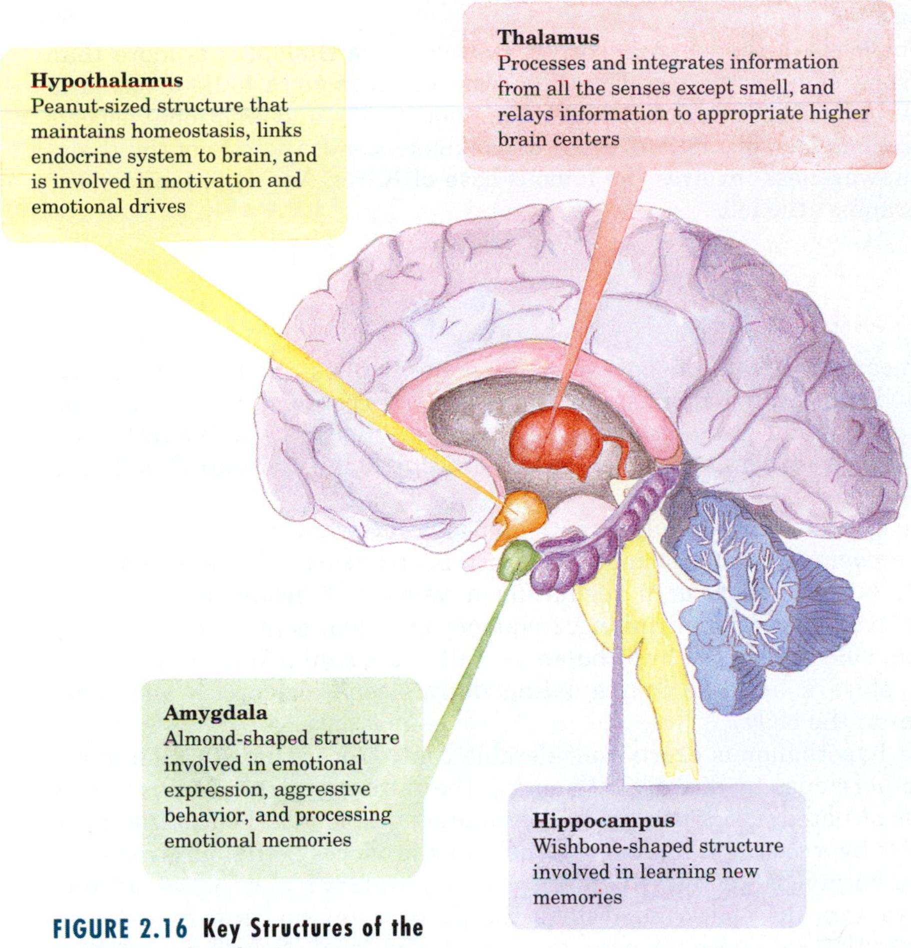

Hypothalamus
Peanut-sized structure that maintains homeostasis, links endocrine system to brain, and is involved in motivation and emotional drives

Thalamus
Processes and integrates information from all the senses except smell, and relays information to appropriate higher brain centers

Amygdala
Almond-shaped structure involved in emotional expression, aggressive behavior, and processing emotional memories

Hippocampus
Wishbone-shaped structure involved in learning new memories

FIGURE 2.16 Key Structures of the Forebrain and Limbic System
In the cross-sectional view shown here, you can see the locations and functions of four important subcortical brain structures. In combination, these structures make up the *limbic system*, which regulates emotional control, learning, and memory.

This finding led researchers to speculate that there might be some sort of "pleasure center" located in the limbic system. Since the initial discovery, the existence of such pleasure centers has also been demonstrated in other animals, including rabbits, cats, dogs, monkeys, and even goldfish.

Today, it's known that electrical stimulation of *many* different parts of the brain can produce similar effects (Olds & Fobes, 1981). Exactly how electrical stimulation can produce rewarding sensations is still not completely understood, but neural pathways involving the neurotransmitter dopamine seem to play a prominent role (Schultz & others, 1997; Wise, 1996).

Let's briefly consider some of the key limbic system structures and the roles they play in behavior.

The Thalamus

The word *thalamus* comes from a Greek word meaning "inner chamber." And indeed, the **thalamus** is a rounded mass of cell bodies located within each cerebral hemisphere. The thalamus processes and distributes almost all of the sensory and motor information going to and from the cerebral cortex (Jessell, 1995a). Figure 2.17 depicts some of the neural pathways going from the thalamus to the

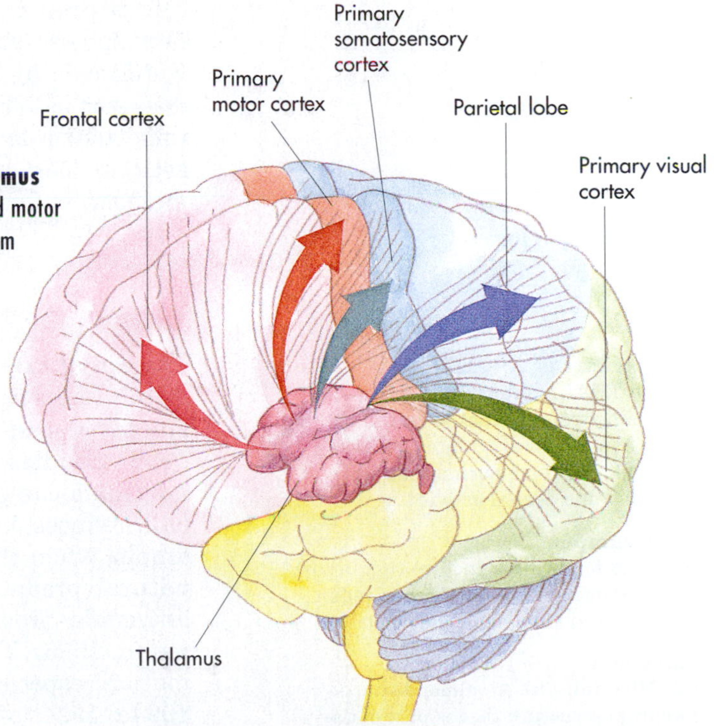

FIGURE 2.17 The Thalamus
Almost all of the sensory and motor information going to and from the cerebral cortex is processed through the thalamus. This figure depicts some of the neural pathways from different thalamus regions to specific lobes of the cerebral cortex.

Frontal cortex
Primary motor cortex
Primary somatosensory cortex
Parietal lobe
Primary visual cortex
Thalamus

thalamus
(THAL-uh-muss) A forebrain structure that processes sensory information for all senses, except smell, and relays it to the cerebral cortex.

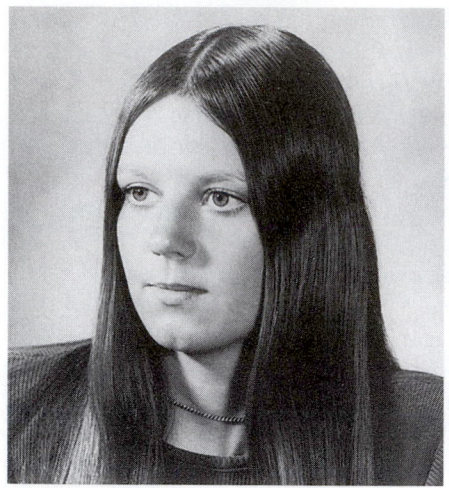

Karen Ann Quinlan After ingesting liquor, Darvon, and Valium, Karen Ann Quinlan lapsed into a permanent coma that lasted for many years. After her death, Quinlan's brain was examined. Although her cerebral cortex was relatively intact, her thalamus was badly damaged. This and other evidence suggests that the thalamus plays a key role in regulating human awareness (Fackelmann, 1994).

different lobes of the cerebral cortex. However, the thalamus is more than just a sensory relay station. The thalamus is also thought to be involved in regulating levels of awareness, attention, motivation, and emotional aspects of sensations (Jessell, 1995a). Some of the evidence for the role of the thalamus in awareness involves the famous case of Karen Ann Quinlan (see the photograph at the left).

The Hypothalamus

Hypo means "beneath" or "below." As its name implies, the **hypothalamus** is located below the thalamus. Although it is only about the size of a peanut, the hypothalamus contains many neural connections. These neural pathways ascend to other forebrain areas and descend to the midbrain, hindbrain, and spinal cord.

The hypothalamus regulates both divisions of the autonomic nervous system, increasing and decreasing such functions as heartbeat and blood pressure. It is also involved in regulating a variety of behaviors related to survival, such as eating, drinking, frequency of sexual activity, fear, and aggression. One area of the hypothalamus, called the *suprachiasmatic nucleus* (SCN), plays a key role in regulating daily sleep/wake cycles and other rhythms of the body.

The hypothalamus exerts considerable control over the secretion of endocrine hormones by directly influencing the pituitary gland. The *pituitary gland* is situated just below the hypothalamus and is attached to the hypothalamus by a short stalk. The hypothalamus produces both neurotransmitters and hormones that directly influence the pituitary gland. As we noted in the section on the endocrine system, the pituitary gland, in turn, releases hormones that influence the activity of other glands.

The Hippocampus

The **hippocampus** is located beneath the temporal lobe in each cerebral hemisphere (see Figure 2.16). The word *hippocampus* comes from a Latin word meaning "seahorse." If you have a vivid imagination, the hippocampus does sort of look like the curved tail of a seahorse. The hippocampus plays an important role in the ability to form new memories. In Chapter 6, we'll take a closer look at the role of the hippocampus and other brain structures in memory.

The Amygdala

The **amygdala** is an almond-shaped clump of neuron cell bodies at the base of the temporal lobe. The amygdala is involved in controlling a variety of emotional response patterns, including fear, anger, and disgust (Aggleton, 1992). Studies with animals have shown that electrical stimulation of the amygdala can produce these emotions. In contrast, destruction of the amygdala reduces or disrupts behaviors that are linked to fear and rage. For example, when the amygdala is destroyed in monkeys, they lose their fear of natural predators, like snakes. In humans, electrical stimulation of the amygdala produces feelings of fear and apprehension (Kandel & Kupfermann, 1995). The amygdala is also involved in learning and in memory formation, especially memories with a strong emotional component (LeDoux, 1994a, 1994b).

hypothalamus
(hi-poe-THAL-uh-muss) A peanut-sized forebrain structure that is part of the limbic system and regulates behaviors related to survival, such as eating, drinking, and sexual activity.

hippocampus
A curved forebrain structure that is part of the limbic system and is involved in learning and forming new memories.

amygdala
(uh-MIG-dull-uh) An almond-shaped forebrain structure that is part of the limbic system and is involved in emotion and memory.

CRITICAL THINKING 2.1

"His" and "Her" Brains?

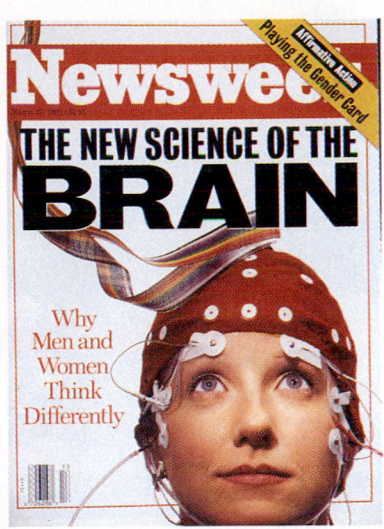

Sex Differences and the Brain Subtle gender differences in brain function and structure make headlines. This headline implies that new discoveries about the brain will explain "why men and women think differently." How valid is this conclusion?

The mass media have seized upon the notion of sex differences in the human brain. The *Newsweek* cover reproduced here is just one example of the attention this topic has received from the popular press. Are there consistent and significant differences between male and female brain structure? Do such differences explain why "men and women think differently," as the headlines proclaim?

Before you swallow the headlines hook, line, and sinker, a more critical examination of the evidence is in order. Here are several points that are usually *not* emphasized in mass media reports of gender differences in brain structure.

Point 1. Studies showing anatomical and functional differences are typically based on very small samples. One widely reported study found that men and women used different parts of their brain when they read nonsense words and determined whether or not they rhymed (Shaywitz & others, 1995). That study, however, involved just 19 men and 19 women.

Perhaps the small sample sizes contribute to the inconsistent and contradictory findings in studies comparing male and female brains. For example, the most consistently reported sex difference is the number or shape of neuronal fibers making up the corpus callosum. However, as psychologist Marc Breedlove (1994) notes, "The literature concerning the corpus callosum and possible sex differences in the corpus callosum in humans is filled with contradictory findings."

Point 2. There is far more similarity than difference between male and female brains. Even when sex differences are found, there is often a great deal of overlap between men and women. In the rhyming task study, 8 out of the 19 women displayed the "male" pattern of brain function rather than the "female" pattern.

Point 3. There is considerable individual variation in brain structure and function. Some average differences have been consistently found. For example, following comparable injuries to the left cerebral hemisphere, men are more likely than women to experience disruptions in speech and language (Kimura, 1992). To explain this result, some researchers have suggested that the cerebral hemispheres are more symmetrical in women and that women are less dependent on the left hemisphere for processing speech and language (Collaer & Hines, 1995).

However, it's important to remember that the average range of difference *within* each sex is larger than average difference *between* sexes. In other words, differences *among* individual women are often greater than the average differences *between* men and women. Some individual females are found to resemble the average male pattern more closely than the average female pattern. And some individual men resemble the average female pattern more closely than the average male pattern.

Point 4. Other than a slight difference in average weight, no sex differences in brain structure have been detected at birth or prenatally (Breedlove, 1994). As you'll see in the chapter Application, brain structures *can* change in response to environmental experiences. Therefore, it is entirely possible that any male/female brain differences could be due to different environmental and learning experiences.

Point 5. Sex differences grab headlines. Differences in male and female brains are much more likely to receive media attention than similarities. The same conclusion holds true even in scientific journals (Unger & Crawford, 1996).

Finally, just for the sake of argument, let's assume that the corpus callosum is found to be consistently larger in one sex than the other. What exactly does this mean? No one knows what the functional significance of such subtle differences in the corpus callosum or any other brain structure might be. The organization of the human brain is incredibly complex and is only beginning to be understood. Even in animals whose brains have been studied for many years, researchers are still uncertain about the exact function of many brain areas (Gorski, 1995). In other words, "explaining" behavioral differences by pointing to subtle structural differences in the brain is simply speculation.

Undoubtedly, future studies will suggest other differences between male and female brains. As you encounter headlines proclaiming sex differences in the brain, remember these key points: First, even the best-substantiated differences are small and inconsistent. Second, their meaning and practical significance are unclear. And third, the results are open to many different interpretations.

However, one thing *is* known with certainty: Male and female brains are much more alike than they are dissimilar. Given that, how well-justified is the conclusion that subtle brain differences prove that "men and women think differently"? In what other ways could differences in male and female behavior be explained?

Specialization in the Cerebral Hemispheres

Over a hundred years ago, Broca and Wernicke provided the first evidence that the left hemisphere is specialized for language functions. What are Broca's and Wernicke's areas? How did clinical findings on aphasia contribute to our knowledge of the brain?

Although the two cerebral hemispheres appear to be symmetrical, they are *not* symmetrical in their functioning. Each cerebral hemisphere is specialized for certain abilities. Here's a rough analogy: Imagine two computers that are linked through a network. One computer is optimized for handling word processing, the other for handling graphic design. Although specialized for different functions, the two computers actively share information and can "talk" to each other across the network. In this analogy, the computers correspond to the left and right hemispheres, and the network that links them is the corpus callosum.

The first discoveries about the dramatic differences between the two hemispheres of the brain were made more than a hundred years ago by two important pioneers in brain research, Pierre Broca and Karl Wernicke.

Language and the Left Hemisphere:
The Early Work of Broca and Wernicke

In the 1860s, a French surgeon and neuroanatomist named **Pierre Paul Broca** (1824–1880) treated a series of patients who had great difficulty speaking but could comprehend written or spoken language. Subsequent autopsies of these patients revealed a consistent finding—brain damage to an area on the lower *left frontal lobe*. Today, this area on the left hemisphere is referred to as *Broca's area*, and it is known to play a crucial role in speech production (see Figure 2.18).

About a decade after Broca's discovery, a young German neurologist named **Karl Wernicke** (1848–1905) discovered another left hemisphere area that, when damaged, produced a different type of language disturbance. Un-

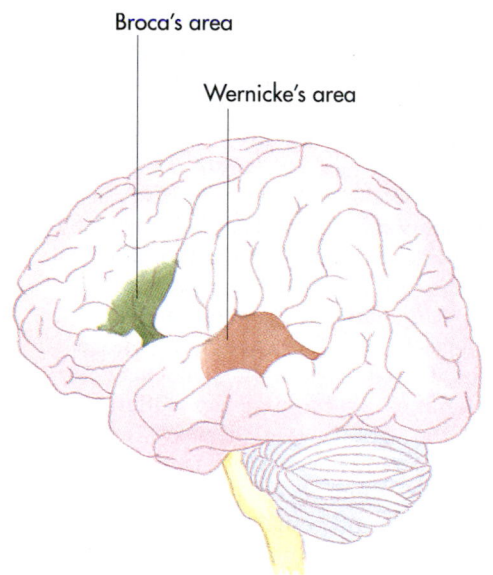

Broca's area

Wernicke's area

FIGURE 2.18 Broca's and Wernicke's Areas of the Cerebral Cortex
Broca's area, located in the lower frontal lobe, is involved in the production of speech. Wernicke's area, found in the temporal lobe, is important in the comprehension of written or spoken language. Damage to either of these areas will produce different types of speech disturbances or aphasia. In most people, both of these areas are found on the left hemisphere.

like Broca's patients, Wernicke's patients could not understand spoken or written communications. They could speak quickly and easily, but their speech sometimes made no sense. Their sentences seemed to be grammatical, but the patients would use meaningless words or even nonsense syllables (Fancher, 1990). If asked how he was feeling, the patient might respond by saying something like, "Don't glow glover. Yes, uh, ummm, bick, bo chipickers the dallydoe mick more work mittle." Autopsies of these patients' brains revealed consistent damage to an area on the *left temporal lobe* that today is called *Wernicke's area* (see Figure 2.18).

The discoveries of Broca and Wernicke provided the first compelling clinical evidence showing the specialized language abilities of the left hemisphere. If damage occurs in the exact same locations on the *right* hemisphere, language and speech functions are *not* affected. The pattern of language abilities in the left hemisphere is typical for virtually all right-handed individuals.

What about left-handed people? About 70 percent of left-handers show the same pattern as right-handers, with the left hemisphere dominant for language. But about 15 percent of left-handed individuals show the opposite pattern, with language functions localized in their right hemisphere. The remaining 15 percent of left-handed individuals process language in both hemispheres (Springer & Deutsch, 1993; Damasio & Damasio, 1992).

The language disruptions that Broca and Wernicke's patients demonstrated represent different types of aphasia. **Aphasia** refers to the partial or complete inability to articulate ideas or understand spoken or written language due to brain injury or damage. There are many different types of aphasia. Victims of *Broca's aphasia* find it difficult or impossible to produce speech, but their comprehension of verbal or written words is unaffected. Victims of *Wernicke's aphasia* can speak, but they often have trouble finding the right words and have great difficulty comprehending written or spoken communication. In more severe cases of Wernicke's aphasia, speech can be characterized by nonsensical, meaningless, incoherent words, as in the example given above.

At the beginning of this chapter, we described the symptoms experienced by our friend Asha following a stroke that damaged her left temporal lobe. Asha experienced many symptoms of Wernicke's aphasia. Talking was difficult, not because Asha couldn't speak, but because she had to stop frequently to search for the right words. Asha was unable to name even simple objects, like the cup on her dinner tray at the hospital or her doctor's necktie. She "recognized" the objects but was unable to say what they were. Asha also had a great deal of difficulty following a normal conversation or understanding speech, whether it was in English or her native language, Tulu. Telephone conversations were virtually impossible.

When we visited Asha in the hospital, we brought her a Christmas present: a portable cassette tape player with headphones and some tapes of relaxing instrumental music. Little did we realize how helpful the music would be for Asha. One tape was a recording of Native American flute music called *Sky of Dreams*. The music was very beautiful and rather unusual, with intricate melodies and unexpected, complex harmonies. Although it was very difficult for Asha to follow normal speech, listening to *Sky of Dreams* was an entirely different experience. As Asha explains:

I tried cranking up the music very high and it soothed me. I could sleep. At the time, the flute music seemed to be just perfectly timed with the way my brain was working. It was tuning out all the other noises so I could focus on just one thing and sleep. So I would play the music over and over again at a very high level. I did that for a long time because my mind was so active and jumbled that I couldn't think.

aphasia
(uh-FAZE-yuh) The partial or complete inability to articulate ideas or understand spoken or written language due to brain injury or damage.

split-brain operation
A surgical procedure that involves cutting the corpus callosum.

Asha's language functions were severely disrupted. Yet she was able to listen to and appreciate instrumental music, even very complex music. Why? At the end of the next section, we'll offer a possible explanation for what seems to have been a disparity in Asha's cognitive abilities after her stroke.

Cutting the Corpus Callosum:
The Split Brain

In the split-brain operation, the corpus callosum is cut. How were split-brain patients tested to reveal differences in the abilities of the two hemispheres? How do the left and right hemispheres differ?

Since the discoveries by Broca and Wernicke, the most dramatic evidence illustrating the independent functions of the two cerebral hemispheres has come from a surgical procedure called the **split-brain operation.** This operation is used to stop or reduce recurring seizures in severe cases of epilepsy that can't be treated in any other fashion. The procedure involves surgically cutting the corpus callosum, the thick band of axons that connects the two hemispheres.

What was the logic behind cutting the corpus callosum? An epileptic seizure typically occurs when neurons begin firing in a disorganized fashion in one region of the brain. The disorganized neuronal firing quickly spreads from one hemisphere to the other via the corpus callosum. If the corpus callosum is cut, seizures should be contained in just one hemisphere, reducing their severity or eliminating them altogether. This is exactly what happened when the split-brain operation was first tried in this country in the 1940s (Springer & Deutsch, 1993).

Surprisingly, cutting the corpus callosum initially seemed to produce no noticeable effect on the patients, other than to reduce their epileptic seizures. Their ability to engage in routine conversations and tasks seemed to be unaffected. On the basis of these early observations, some brain researchers speculated that the corpus callosum served no function whatsoever (see Gazzaniga, 1995). One famous psychologist, Karl Lashley, joked that its primary function seemed to be to keep the two hemispheres from sagging (Hoptman & Davidson, 1994).

In the 1960s, however, psychologist and neuroscientist **Roger Sperry** (1913–1994) and his colleagues began unraveling the puzzle of the left and right hemispheres. Sperry and his colleagues used the apparatus shown in Figure 2.19 to test the abilities of split-brain patients. They would direct a split-brain subject to focus on a point in the middle of a screen, while briefly flashing a word or picture to the left or right of the midpoint.

In this procedure, visual information to the right of the midpoint is projected to the person's *left* hemisphere, and visual information to the left of the midpoint is projected to the *right* hemisphere. Behind the screen were several objects that were hidden from the split-brain subjects. The split-brain subject could reach under a partition below the screen to pick up the concealed objects, but could not see them (Sperry, 1982).

In a typical experiment, Sperry projected the image of an object concealed behind the screen, such as a hammer, to the left of the midpoint. Thus, the image of the hammer was sent to the right, nonverbal hemisphere. If a split-brain subject was asked to *verbally* identify the image flashed on the screen, he could not do so, and often denied that anything had appeared on the screen. Why? Because his verbal left hemisphere had no way of knowing the information that had been sent to his right hemisphere. However, if a

Roger Sperry (1913–1994) For his pioneering research using split-brain patients to investigate the relationship between brain and behavior, Sperry received the 1981 Nobel Prize in Physiology or Medicine.

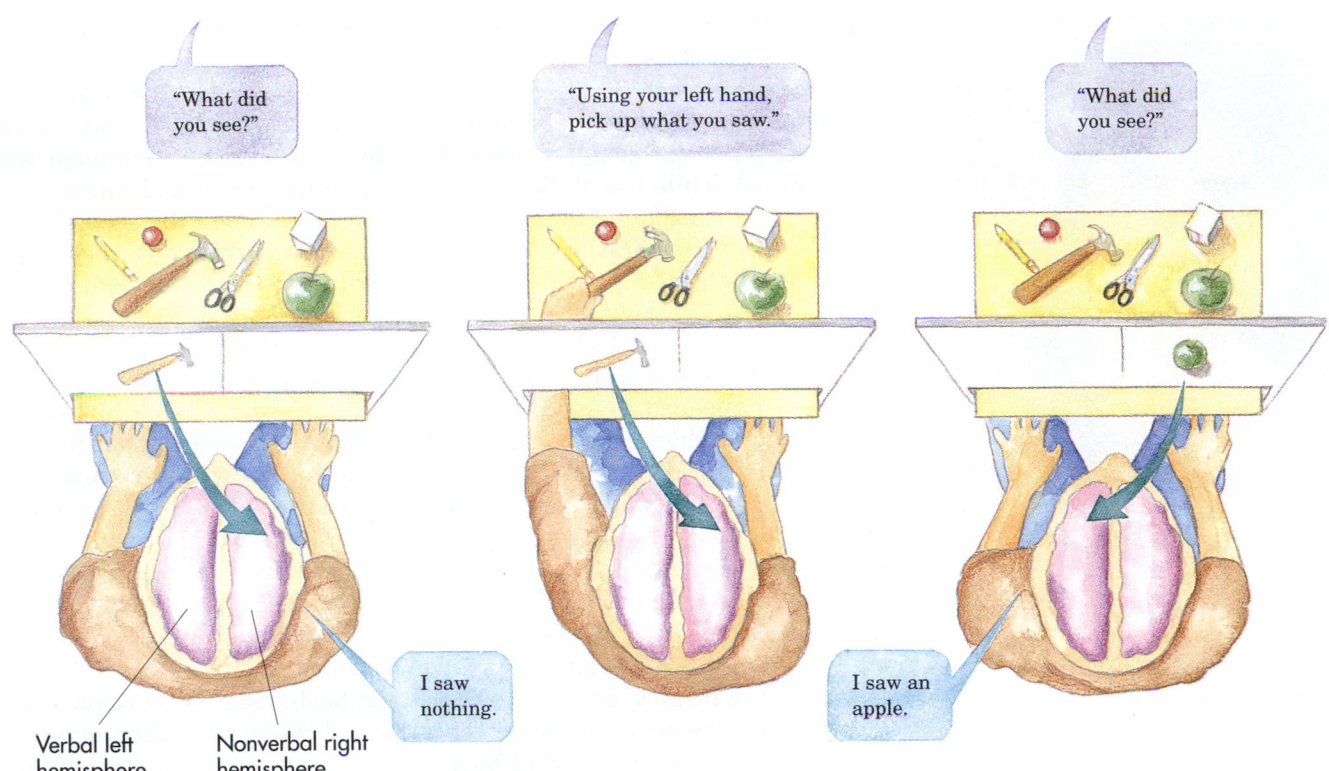

Verbal left hemisphere   Nonverbal right hemisphere

FIGURE 2.19 The Experimental Setup in Split-Brain Research
In a typical split-brain experiment, as shown here, the participant focuses his attention on the midpoint of the screen. Notice that he is unable to verbally identify the picture that is flashed to his nonverbal right hemisphere, but he is able to grasp the hammer with his left hand. In contrast, when the image of the apple is flashed to his verbal left hemisphere, he can easily name it.

split-brain subject was asked to use his left hand to reach under the partition for the object that had been displayed, he would correctly pick up the hammer. This was because his left hand was controlled by the same right hemisphere that saw the image of the hammer.

Sperry's experiments reconfirmed the specialized language abilities of the left hemisphere that Broca and Wernicke had discovered over a hundred years earlier. But notice, even though the split-brain subject's right hemisphere could not express itself verbally, it still processed information and expressed itself *nonverbally*—the subject was able to pick up the correct object.

On the basis of this and other evidence, researchers have concluded that in most people the left hemisphere is superior at language abilities, speech, and writing. The right hemisphere is superior at nonverbal emotional expression and visual perception tasks that involve deciphering visual clues, such as completing a puzzle or manipulating blocks to match a particular design (Gazzaniga, 1995). The right hemisphere also excels at other visual perception tasks such as face recognition, reading maps, copying designs, and drawing. Finally, the right hemisphere shows a higher degree of specialization for musical and artistic appreciation or responsiveness—but not necessarily for musical or artistic ability, which often involves the use of the left hemisphere as well.

The different "talents" of the two hemispheres are summarized in Table 2.2. More than three decades of research have confirmed that similar

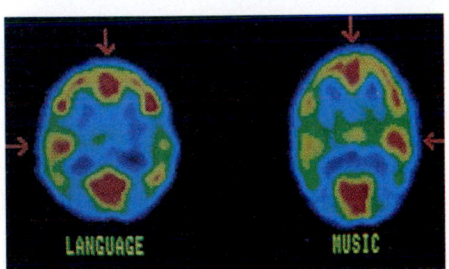

The Specialized Abilities of the Left and Right Hemispheres The red arrow at the top of each PET scan is pointing to the front of the brain. The red and yellow colors show the areas of greatest brain activity. Listening to speech involves the language processing functions of the left hemisphere, while listening to music activates the nonverbal functions of the right hemisphere.

TABLE 2.2 The Specialized Abilities of the Two Hemispheres

Left Hemisphere Superiority	Right Hemisphere Superiority
Language abilities	Visual perception tasks
Speech	Nonverbal emotional expression
Writing	Artistic and musical appreciation

Asha Today

patterns of specialization exist in individuals whose corpus callosum has *not* been cut (see Gazzaniga, 1995).

Given the basic findings of the split-brain research, can you speculate why Asha was unable to read or follow a simple conversation, but could easily concentrate on a complex piece of music? Why were her language abilities so disrupted, while her ability to appreciate music remained intact?

A plausible explanation has to do with the location of the stroke's damage on Asha's left temporal lobe. Because the left hemisphere is specialized for language, the stroke produced serious disruptions in Asha's language abilities. However, her *right* cerebral hemisphere sustained no detectable damage. Because one of the right hemisphere's abilities is the appreciation of musical sounds, Asha retained the ability to understand and appreciate music.

What happened to Asha? Fortunately, Asha's story has a happy ending. After being discharged from the hospital, she began several months of intensive speech therapy. She set a very high goal for herself: to return to teaching at the university by the fall semester. With the help of her husband, Paul, and her mother, who traveled from India to stay with her for four months, Asha made remarkable gains. Her speech therapist assigned a great deal of "homework" that consisted of repetitiously pairing pictures with words, objects with words, and words with objects. Especially at first, it was frustrating for Asha. But gradually, she made significant gains.

Asha reached the goal that she had set for herself. With remarkable determination, she returned to her teaching and research at the university the following fall semester. Today, more than two years after her stroke, you would be unable to detect any signs of impairment indicating that Asha had sustained significant brain damage.

What Asha's story illustrates is that the brain has an incredible ability to gradually shift functions from damaged to undamaged areas, a phenomenon called *functional plasticity*. Even more astonishing, the uninjured brain also has the ability to change and grow throughout life. As researchers have discovered, the brain can literally change its structure in response to the quality of environmental stimulation. In the chapter Application, we'll look at how researchers have documented the remarkable *structural plasticity* of which the brain is capable. And you'll learn how research findings on brain plasticity can be used to enhance your dendritic potential!

Specialization in the Cerebral Hemispheres

Match the following terms to the correct statement below: Broca's area, Wernicke's area, left hemisphere, right hemisphere, corpus callosum.

1. This area is superior at visual perception tasks and at musical and artistic appreciation.

2. Damage to this specific area disrupts the ability to understand spoken or written communication.

3. This area is surgically cut in the split-brain operation.

4. Damage to this specific area disrupts the ability to speak but not the ability to understand spoken or written communication.

5. This area is superior at language tasks.

Pumping Neurons:
Keeping Your Brain in Shape

The Flexible Brain: Structural Plasticity

Researchers once believed that by early adulthood the brain's physical structure was "hard-wired" for life. It's now known that exposure to stimulating or unstimulating environmental conditions actually causes some *brain structures to physically change* throughout the lifespan. Called **structural plasticity,** this phenomenon was first demonstrated in the early 1960s in studies with rats (Rosenzweig, 1996).

The basic experimental procedure was relatively simple. Rats were systematically exposed to either an "enriched" or an "impoverished" environment at different ages and for varying lengths of time. As the accompanying photograph shows, the "enriched" environment is spacious, houses several rats, and has assorted wheels, ladders, tunnels, and objects to explore, which are regularly changed to add further variety. In the "impoverished" environment, a solitary rat lives alone in a small laboratory cage with only a water bottle and food tray to keep it company.

Using this basic design, researchers found that enrichment increases the number and length of dendrites, enlarging the size of neurons and increasing the number of potential connections with other neurons (Johnston & others, 1996). Enrichment also increases the number of glial cells, which manufacture the myelin sheath that increases communication speed between neurons (Diamond, 1988).

In simple terms, enrichment produces *more synaptic connections* between brain neurons; impoverishment decreases synaptic connections. With more synapses, the brain has a greater capacity to integrate and process information, and to do so more quickly. The cerebral cortex, where sophisticated mental functions occur, is the area most strongly affected by enrichment or impoverishment. Structures below the cerebral cortex, such as those in the limbic system, apparently change very little in response to environmental enrichment or impoverishment.

Even the aged brain can change in response to environmental stimulation. In fact, no matter what age of rats was studied, environmental enrichment or impoverishment had a significant impact on brain structure (Diamond, 1993, 1988). As psychologist William Greenough (1993) summarizes, "What we know from animals suggests that the harder you use your brain, the more in shape it's going to be."

From Animal Studies to Humans

Can the conclusions drawn from studies on rats and other mammals be applied to human brains? Psychologists and other researchers have amassed an impressive array of correlational evidence showing that the human brain also seems to benefit from enriched, stimulating environments (Rosenzweig, 1996).

For example, autopsy studies have compared the brains of university graduates versus high school dropouts. The brains of university graduates had up to 40 percent more synaptic connections than those of high school dropouts (Jacobs & others, 1993). According to UCLA neuroscientist Bob Jacobs (1993), "This is the human equivalent of the animals exposed to enriched environments having smarter brains. As you go up the educational ladder there is a dramatic increase in dendritic material."

However, the key is not just getting a higher education. University graduates who lead mentally unstimulating lives had fewer dendritic connections than did those who remained mentally active throughout their lives. According to Jacobs (1993), "The bottom line is that you have to use it or you lose it."

Other research has shown that environmental stimulation of the brain is critical for normal development, even from the first day of life (Stromswold, 1995; Shatz, 1992). Infants and children should be exposed to a wide variety of experiences to enhance brain connections and intellectual development (Greenough & others, 1987).

Over the lifespan, the degree to which a person remains mentally active can act as an insulator against intellectual decline. Since 1956, psychologist K. Warner Schaie and his colleagues have followed some 5,000 people as they have aged to learn what happens to intellectual abilities. Schaie found

Rats in an Enriched Environment
Compared to rats raised in solitary lab cages, rats raised in an enriched environment, like the one shown here, show significant increases in brain growth and synaptic interconnections.

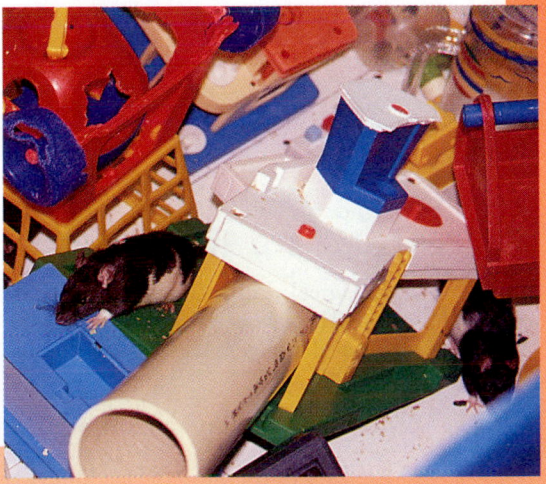

that intellectual decline is not an inevitable result of aging. Rather, intellectual decline depends to a large degree on whether a person is a mental athlete—or a cerebral couch potato. Among the factors that can help protect a person from intellectual decline is being involved in a complex and stimulating environment, including being married to a smart spouse (Schaie, 1995a, 1994).

Pumping Neurons: Keeping Your Brain Fit

The bottom line? Your brain is never too old to learn and change in response to new and mentally stimulating experiences. According to neuroscientist Arnold Scheibel (1994), "The important thing is to be actively involved in areas unfamiliar to you. Anything that's intellectually challenging can probably serve as a kind of stimulus for dendritic growth, which means it adds to the computational reserves in your brain." In short, keep your brain active and flexible. On a regular basis, try the new and unfamiliar. Here are just a few of the possible ways you can exercise and stimulate your own brain:

- Learn to play a musical instrument.

- If you are a "number" or "word" person, sign up for an art class.

- If you are an "art" person, start a personal journal or take a creative writing class.

- Listen to different radio stations.

- Buy a newspaper or magazine you've never read before.

- Read books with new ideas that challenge your opinions or beliefs.

- Talk to people of a different ethnic or religious background about their upbringing or family holidays.

- Take up a new hobby.

- Try to fix something.

- Attend a play or a performance of the symphony.

- Try all kinds of puzzles—word, visual, matching, and maze puzzles.

- Go to the library and browse until you find at least three books that spark your interest, then check them out and read them.

Never Too Old to Learn
At 102 years of age, Gemisto Villani returned to school to complete his education. Intellectual decline is not an inevitable consequence of aging, especially if your environment is mentally challenging.

Summary
The Biological Foundations of Behavior

Biological Psychology

- Psychological and biological processes are closely linked. Biological psychologists investigate the physical processes that underlie psychological experience and behavior.

The Neuron: The Basic Unit of Communication

- Information in the nervous system is transmitted via cells specialized for communication, called neurons. Glial cells help neurons by providing nutrition, removing waste products, and producing the myelin sheath.

- Most neurons have three basic components. The neuron's cell body provides energy and directs the neuron's activity. Dendrites receive information from other neurons or sensory receptors. And the axon carries the information away from the neuron's cell body toward other locations. The axons of some neurons are wrapped in a myelin sheath, which speeds the rate at which neural messages are sent.

- Within the neuron, information is communicated in the form of brief electrical messages called action potentials. When prepared to activate, the neuron carries a slight negative electrical charge, which is referred to as the resting potential. If sufficiently stimulated, the neuron activates and depolarizes. Electrically charged ions rush into and out of the axon, changing the electrical charge of the neuron from negative to positive. After a brief pause, the neuron reestablishes the resting potential so that it can activate again.

The point of communication between two neurons is called the synapse. Neurons communicate information to other neurons either electrically or chemically. The most common process is chemical communication involving neurotransmitters, which cross the fluid-filled space and affect neighboring neurons. There are many different kinds of neurotransmitters, each capable of sending either an excitatory or inhibitory message to the receiving neuron. Certain drugs can influence behavior and mental processes by mimicking neurotransmitters, by occupying receptor sites, or by blocking the reuptake of neurotransmitters.

The Nervous System and the Endocrine System: Communication Throughout the Body

The nervous system is divided into two main divisions, the central nervous system and the peripheral nervous system. The central nervous system is composed of the brain and the spinal cord. Some simple forms of behavior, such as spinal reflexes, occur in the spinal cord without brain involvement.

The peripheral nervous system consists of all the nerves outside the central nervous system. The two main subdivisions of the peripheral nervous system are the somatic nervous system, which communicates sensory and motor information, and the autonomic nervous system, which regulates involuntary functions like heartbeat and respiration. The autonomic nervous system is divided into the sympathetic nervous system, which arouses the body to meet threats or emergencies, and the parasympathetic nervous system, which maintains normal functions and conserves physical energy.

The endocrine system is composed of glands that secrete hormones into the bloodstream, regulating a diverse range of body functions including physical growth, stress responses, and sexual development. The endocrine system is regulated by the hypothalamus in the brain. The hypothalamus produces neurotransmitters and hormones that influence the pituitary gland. In turn, the pituitary gland releases hormones that influence the other endocrine glands.

Studying the Brain: The Toughest Case to Crack

Because the brain is encased by bone, it has been especially challenging for scientists to study. Among the first techniques were case studies of people with brain damage or disease. In animal studies, researchers would produce lesions in a particular brain area, then observe the behavioral effects. Researchers have also used electrodes to electrically stimulate specific areas of the brain.

Technological advances have produced a variety of techniques to image the brain's structures and activity. The electroencephalograph records the brain's electrical activity. CAT scans use X-rays to make images of the brain's structures. MRI scanners use magnetic signals to produce highly detailed images of the brain's structures. PET scans use radioactive oxygen or glucose to produce color-coded images of the brain's activity. Functional MRI scans take rapid, multiple MRI images that are computer-assembled to create a "movie" of brain activity.

A Guided Tour of the Brain

Most psychological processes involve the integrated processing of information via neural pathways in multiple brain structures and regions. During the earliest stages of prenatal development, the human brain begins as a fluid-filled tube, which ultimately forms the three key brain regions: the hindbrain, midbrain, and forebrain.

Combined, the hindbrain and midbrain structures constitute the brainstem. Sensory and motor pathways cross over in the hindbrain so that each side of the body is controlled by the opposite side of the brain. The key structures of the hindbrain are the medulla, which helps control autonomic functions such as breathing and digestion; the cerebellum, which is involved in muscle movements and balance; and the pons, which relays information from higher brain regions to the cerebellum. Located in the core of the medulla and the pons is the reticular formation, which is involved in attention and filtering incoming sensory information.

The midbrain contains areas where auditory and visual information is integrated and coordinated. A darkly pigmented area called the substantia nigra contains a concentration of neurons that produce the neurotransmitter called dopamine.

The outer portion of the forebrain is called the cerebral cortex, which is divided into two cerebral hemispheres. Each hemisphere is roughly divided into four lobes. The temporal lobe contains the primary auditory cortex, where auditory information is received. The occipital lobe contains the primary visual cortex, where visual information is received. The parietal lobe contains the somatosensory cortex, where body sensations are registered. And the frontal lobe contains the primary motor cortex, where voluntary muscle movements originate. The remainder of the cerebral cortex is composed of association areas, which are thought to be involved in processing and integrating sensory and motor information.

Beneath the cerebral cortex are several important structures. The thalamus distributes sensory and motor information going to and from the cerebral cortex, and is involved in regulating attention, awareness, motivation, and emotional aspects of sensations. The hypothalamus regulates the autonomic nervous system and the endocrine system, and is involved in behaviors related to survival, including hunger, fear, and aggression. The hippocampus is involved in the ability to form new memories.

The amygdala helps control emotional response patterns involving fear, anger, or disgust. Combined, these structures along with regions of the frontal cortex, form the limbic system. The limbic system structures form neural circuits that play critical roles in learning, memory, and emotional control.

Specialization in the Cerebral Hemispheres

■ The first clinical evidence for the specialized abilities of the two cerebral hemispheres occurred in the mid-1800s, when it was discovered that damage to the left hemisphere produced different forms of aphasia, such as Broca's aphasia and Wernicke's aphasia.

■ More evidence for the specialized abilities of the two hemispheres has resulted from the split-brain operation, in which the corpus callosum connecting the two hemispheres is cut to reduce epileptic seizures. Using special testing procedures that directed information to just one hemisphere, Roger Sperry and his colleagues demonstrated the different strengths of each hemisphere. The left hemisphere is specialized for language tasks, while the right hemisphere is superior at visual-spatial tasks.

Key Terms

biological psychology (p. 36)

neuron (p. 37)

glial cells (p. 37)

sensory neuron (p. 37)

motor neuron (p. 37)

interneuron (p. 37)

cell body (p. 37)

dendrites (p. 37)

axon (p. 38)

myelin sheath (p. 39)

action potential (p. 39)

stimulus threshold (p. 39)

resting potential (p. 39)

all-or-none law (p. 41)

synapse (p. 41)

synaptic gap (p. 41)

axon terminals (p. 43)

synaptic vesicles (p. 43)

neurotransmitter (p. 43)

synaptic transmission (p. 43)

reuptake (p. 43)

acetylcholine (p. 44)

dopamine (p. 44)

serotonin (p. 45)

norepinephrine (p. 45)

GABA (gamma-aminobutyric acid) (p. 45)

endorphins (p. 45)

nervous system (p. 47)

nerve (p. 47)

central nervous system (p. 47)

spinal reflexes (p. 47)

peripheral nervous system (p. 48)

somatic nervous system (p. 48)

autonomic nervous system (p. 49)

sympathetic nervous system (p. 49)

parasympathetic nervous system (p. 50)

endocrine system (p. 51)

hormones (p. 51)

pituitary gland (p. 52)

electroencephalograph (p. 52)

CAT scan (computerized axial tomography) (p. 52)

magnetic resonance imaging scanner (MRI) (p. 52)

PET scan (positron emission tomography) (p. 53)

brainstem (p. 55)

hindbrain (p. 56)

medulla (p. 57)

pons (p. 57)

cerebellum (p. 57)

reticular formation (p. 57)

midbrain (p. 57)

substantia nigra (p. 57)

forebrain (p. 58)

cerebral cortex (p. 58)

cerebral hemispheres (p. 58)

corpus callosum (p. 58)

temporal lobe (p. 58)

occipital lobe (p. 58)

parietal lobe (p. 58)

frontal lobe (p. 59)

association areas (p. 59)

limbic system (p. 60)

thalamus (p. 61)

hypothalamus (p. 62)

hippocampus (p. 62)

amygdala (p. 62)

aphasia (p. 65)

split-brain operation (p. 66)

structural plasticity (p. 69)

Key People

Pierre Paul Broca (1824–1880) French surgeon and neuroanatomist who in 1861 discovered an area on the lower left frontal lobe of the cerebral cortex that, when damaged, produces speech disturbances but no loss of comprehension.

Roger Sperry (1913–1994) American psychologist who received the Nobel Prize in 1981 for his pioneering research on brain specialization in split-brain patients.

Karl Wernicke (1848–1905) German neurologist who in 1874 discovered an area on the left temporal lobe of the cerebral cortex that, when damaged, produces meaningless or nonsensical speech and difficulties in verbal or written comprehension.

CONCEPT REVIEW 2.1 Page 44

1. c
2. f
3. a
4. e
5. d
6. b

CONCEPT REVIEW 2.2 Page 54

1. PET
2. MRI
3. EEG
4. CAT

CONCEPT REVIEW 2.3   Page 64

1. hindbrain; midbrain; forebrain
2. cerebellum
3. corpus callosum
4. temporal
5. primary motor cortex; frontal
6. hippocampus
7. limbic system

CONCEPT REVIEW 2.4   Page 68

1. right hemisphere
2. Wernicke's area
3. corpus callosum
4. Broca's area
5. left hemisphere

Chapter

3

Sensation and Perception

Prologue: Don't Ask These Guys to Stop and Smell the Roses

We have two good friends, quite dissimilar in most ways, who share one common characteristic—they have no sense of smell. Paul is an electrical engineer in his late twenties; Warren is a well-known professor of psychology some twenty years older. Although you might guess this condition to be extremely rare, the inability to smell (called *anosmia*) is relatively common, occurring in about 1 in 500 people (Engen, 1991).

Paul was born without a sense of smell, a fact he was completely unaware of until he was about ten years old. Paul's mother asked him to smell an arrangement of freshly cut flowers, but the puzzled child couldn't detect a thing.

Because Paul has never experienced smell, it's impossible for him even to imagine what a smell smells like. Friends have tried to describe the aroma of garlic, flowers, burning leaves, and so forth. But, like trying to describe the color red to someone who's been blind since birth, it's almost impossible to describe one smell without relating it to another. Try it and you'll see what we mean. How would you describe the smell of steaks barbecuing? a new car? a locker room? sour milk?

As you'll discover in this chapter, the senses of taste and smell are closely related, and the flavor of a food is strongly tied to its aroma. That's part of the reason that food often tastes bland or "cardboardy" when you have a bad head cold. What does food taste like for Paul? Just as it's hard for us to describe odors to Paul, it's hard for Paul to describe the way he experiences food.

Paul is married to Asha, whom you met in Chapter 2. Asha cooks some wonderfully spicy Indian meals. When she tries out different Indian dishes on Paul, Asha has discovered that Paul bases many of his food preferences on the *texture* of foods instead of on their flavor. For example, Paul dislikes noodles because their texture seems "slimy" to him. He also dislikes the sensation of certain textures combined, like nuts in ice cream or brownies. Other foods, like chocolate, have no taste at all.

Unlike Paul, Warren knows what he's missing. Warren was born with a normal sense of smell, but as a young man he underwent major surgery to repair an artery at the front of his brain. To get to the artery, the surgeon had to cut through the sensory nerves for smell, destroying Warren's sense of smell.

For several days following the surgery, Warren's eyes were swollen shut. Deprived of both visual and odor cues, he was unable to identify many of the foods he was fed. For example, he couldn't tell the difference among strawberry, chocolate, and vanilla pudding—they all tasted the same to him. And like Paul, Warren found that the texture of different foods became much more significant. For example, peanut butter now tasted like "oily sand" to Warren.

At first, the experience of taste was very different for Warren than it had been before the surgery. He experimented with familiar as well as new and unusual foods to see how they would taste. However, in the years following his surgery, Warren learned to compensate for the missing sense of smell, at least for its role in taste. Now, many years later, Warren has become accustomed to the way things taste, despite the lack of odor cues.

In this chapter, we'll explore how we sense the world around us and how the brain integrates and interprets those sensory signals to form meaningful perceptions. As we go along, we'll tell you more about our friends Paul and Warren.

Introduction

Sensation and Perception

Glance around you. Notice the incredible variety of colors, shades, shadows, and images. Listen carefully to the diversity of sounds, loud and soft, near and far. Focus on everything that's touching you—your clothes, your shoes, the chair you're sitting on. Now, inhale deeply through your nose and identify the aromas in the air.

With these simple observations you have exercised four of your senses: vision, hearing, touch, and smell. As we saw in Chapter 2, the primary function of the nervous system is communication—the transmission of information from one part of the body to the other. Where does that information come from? Put simply, your senses are the gateway through which your brain receives all its information about the environment. It's a process that is so natural and automatic that we typically take it for granted until something happens, as it did to Paul and Warren. As Paul and Warren demonstrate, people with one nonfunctional sense are amazingly adaptive. Other senses may compensate for the missing environmental information.

In this chapter, we will explore the overlapping processes of *sensation* and *perception*. **Sensation** refers to the sensory processes—the detection and basic sensory experience of environmental stimuli, such as sounds, objects, and odors. **Perception** occurs when we integrate, organize, and interpret sensory information in a way that is meaningful (Matlin & Foley, 1992). Here's a simple example to contrast the two terms. Your eye's physical response to light, splotches of color, and lines reflects *sensation*. Integrating

sensation
The process of detecting a physical stimulus, such as light, sound, heat, or pressure.

perception
The process of integrating, organizing, and interpreting sensations.

and organizing those sensations so that we interpret the light, splotches of color, and lines as a painting, a flag, or some other object reflects *perception*.

Where does the process of sensation leave off and the process of perception begin? There is no clear boundary line between the two processes as we actually experience them. In fact, many researchers in this area of psychology regard sensation and perception as a single process.

Although the two processes overlap, in this chapter we will present sensation and perception as separate discussions. In the first half we'll discuss the basics of *sensation*—how our sensory receptors respond to stimulation and transmit that information in usable form to the brain. In the second half of the chapter, we'll explore *perception*—how the brain actively organizes and interprets the signals sent from our sensory receptors.

Some Basic Principles of Sensation

Sensation is the result of stimulation of sensory receptors by some form of physical energy, which is converted into neural impulses and transmitted to the brain. What are the two types of sensory thresholds? How do Weber's Law and sensory adaptation demonstrate that the experience of sensation is relative?

We're accustomed to thinking of the senses as being quite different. However, all of our senses involve some common processes. All sensation is a result of the stimulation of specialized cells called **sensory receptors** by some form of *energy*.

Imagine biting into a crisp red apple. Your experience of hearing the apple crunching is a response to the physical energy of vibrations in the air, or *sound waves*. The sweet taste of the apple is a response to the physical energy of *dissolvable chemicals* in your mouth, just as the distinctive sharp aroma of the apple is a response to *airborne chemical molecules* that you inhale through your nose. The smooth feel of the apple's skin is a response to the *pressure* of the apple against your hand. And the red color is a response to the physical energy of *light waves* reflecting from the irregularly shaped object that you've just bitten into.

Sensory receptors convert the different forms of physical energy into electrical impulses that are then transmitted via neurons to the brain. The process by which a form of physical energy is converted into a coded neural signal that can be processed by the nervous system is called **transduction.** These neural signals are sent to the brain, where the perceptual processes of organizing and interpreting the coded messages occur. In Figure 3.1 on the next page, you can see the basic steps involved in sensation and perception.

We are constantly being bombarded by many different forms of energy. For instance, at this very moment radio and television waves are bouncing around the atmosphere and passing through your body. However, sensory receptors are so highly specialized that they are only sensitive to very specific types of energy (which is lucky, or you might be seeing *I Love Lucy* reruns in your brain right now). So, for any type of stimulation to be sensed, the stimulus energy must first be in a form that can be detected by our sensory receptor cells. Otherwise, transduction cannot occur.

Experiencing the World Through Our Senses Imagine biting into a crisp, red apple. All of your senses are involved in your experience—vision, smell, taste, hearing, and touch. Although we're accustomed to thinking of our different senses as being quite distinct, all forms of sensation involve the stimulation of specialized cells called sensory receptors.

sensory receptors
Specialized cells unique to each sense organ that respond to a particular form of sensory stimulation.

transduction
The process by which a form of physical energy is converted into a coded neural signal that can be processed by the nervous system.

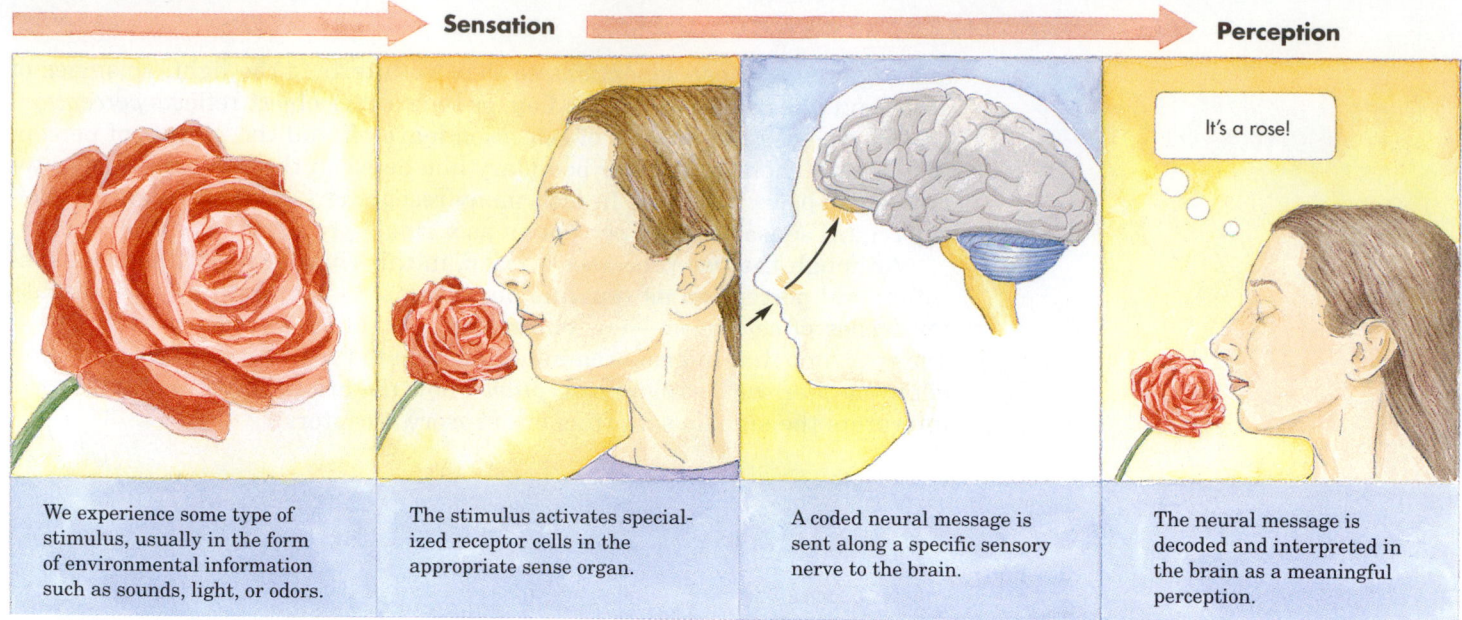

Sensation → **Perception**

| We experience some type of stimulus, usually in the form of environmental information such as sounds, light, or odors. | The stimulus activates specialized receptor cells in the appropriate sense organ. | A coded neural message is sent along a specific sensory nerve to the brain. | The neural message is decoded and interpreted in the brain as a meaningful perception. |

FIGURE 3.1 How We Sense and Perceive the World

For all of our senses, moving from sensation to perception is a continuous process that involves four basic steps.

TABLE 3.1 Absolute Thresholds

Sense	Absolute Threshold
Vision	A candle flame seen from thirty miles away on a clear, dark night
Hearing	The tick of a watch at twenty feet
Taste	One teaspoon of sugar in two gallons of water
Smell	One drop of perfume throughout a three-room apartment
Touch	A bee's wing falling on your cheek from a height of about half an inch

Psychologist Eugene Galanter (1962) has provided these examples of the absolute thresholds for our senses. In each case, people are able to sense these faint stimuli at least half the time.

Sensory Thresholds

Along with being specialized as to the types of energy that can be detected, our senses are specialized in other ways as well. We do not have an infinite capacity to detect all levels of energy. If we did, you would probably find it hard to concentrate on studying because you might hear not just your next-door neighbor's stereo but also the hum of her computer and the sound of her breathing. To be sensed, a stimulus must first be strong enough to be detected—loud enough to be heard, concentrated enough to be smelled, bright enough to be seen. The point at which a stimulus is strong enough to be detected by activating a sensory receptor cell is called a **sensory threshold.** There are two general kinds of sensory thresholds for each sense—the absolute threshold and the difference threshold.

The **absolute threshold** refers to the smallest possible strength of a stimulus that can be detected half the time. Why just half the time? Because the minimum level of stimulation that can be detected varies from person to person and from trial to trial. Because of such human variability, researchers have arbitrarily set the limit as the minimum level of stimulation that can be detected half the time. Under ideal conditions (which rarely occur in normal daily life), our sensory abilities are far more sensitive than you might think. Table 3.1 provides examples of the absolute thresholds for our senses.

While absolute thresholds describe the minimum levels of stimuli that we can detect, another important threshold involves detecting the *difference* between two stimuli. The **difference threshold** is the smallest possible difference between two stimuli that can be detected half the time. Another term for difference threshold is **just noticeable difference,** which is abbreviated **jnd.**

The just noticeable difference will *vary* depending on its relation to the original stimulus. This principle of sensation is called **Weber's Law.** It holds that for each sense, the size of a just noticeable difference is a constant proportion of the size of the initial stimulus. So, whether or not we can detect a change in the strength of a stimulus depends on the intensity of the *original* stimulus. For example, if you are holding a pebble (the original stimulus), you will notice an increase in weight if a second pebble is placed in your hand. But if you start off holding a very heavy rock (the original stimulus), you probably won't detect an increase in weight when the same pebble is balanced on it.

What Weber's Law underscores is that our psychological experience of sensation is *relative*. There is no simple one-to-one correspondence between

sensory threshold
The level at which a stimulus is strong enough to be detected by activating sensory receptors.

absolute threshold
The smallest possible strength of a stimulus that can be detected half the time.

difference threshold
The smallest possible difference between two stimuli that can be detected half the time. Also called **just noticeable difference.**

just noticeable difference (jnd)
The smallest possible difference between two stimuli that can be detected half the time. Also called **difference threshold.**

Weber's Law
A principle of sensation that holds that the size of the just noticeable difference will vary depending on its relation to the strength of the original stimulus.

sensory adaptation
The decline in sensitivity to a constant stimulus.

the objective characteristics of a physical stimulus, such as the weight of a pebble, and our psychological experience of it.

Sensory Adaptation

Suppose your best friend has invited you over for a spaghetti dinner. As you walk in the front door, you're almost overwhelmed by the odor of onions and garlic cooking on the stove. However, after just a few moments, you no longer notice the smell. This example demonstrates another characteristic of our senses. After being exposed to a steady stimulus for a time, we become less aware of it. Why? Because our sensory receptor cells become less responsive to a constant stimulus. This gradual decline in sensitivity to a constant stimulus is called **sensory adaptation.** Once again, this illustrates that our experience of sensation is relative—in this case, relative to the *duration of exposure.*

Because of sensory adaptation, we become accustomed to constant stimuli. This allows us to quickly notice new or changing stimuli. This makes sense: if we were continually aware of *all* incoming stimuli, we'd be so overwhelmed with sensory information that we wouldn't be able to focus our attention. Thus, once we manage to land our posterior on the sofa, we don't need to be constantly reminded that the sofa is beneath us.

CONCEPT REVIEW 3.1

Principles of Sensation

1. Sensation is to perception as _____ is to _____.
   a. detection; interpretation
   b. interpretation; organization
   c. integration; interpretation
   d. adaptation; transduction

2. When a researcher presented many sounds at very low levels of intensity, Natalie could detect them less than 50 percent of the time. These sounds were below Natalie's
   a. difference threshold
   b. just noticeable difference level
   c. sensory adaptation level
   d. absolute threshold

3. Which of the following is an example of sensory adaptation?
   a. not noticing how cold the water is after you have been in the pool for a while
   b. increased reliance on hearing when you are blindfolded
   c. exiting the building immediately when you hear the fire alarm
   d. covering your ears at an extremely loud rock concert

4. Sensory receptors convert different forms of physical energy into neural signals through the process of
   a. sensory adaptation   c. transduction
   b. accommodation   d. Weber's Law

Vision: From Light to Sight

The eye contains the visual receptor cells, which are sensitive to the physical energy of light. What is the visible spectrum? What are the key structures of the eye? What are the functions of the rods and cones of the retina?

A lone caterpillar on the screen door, the pile of dirty laundry in the corner of the closet, a spectacular autumn sunset, the bowl of multicolored Sugar

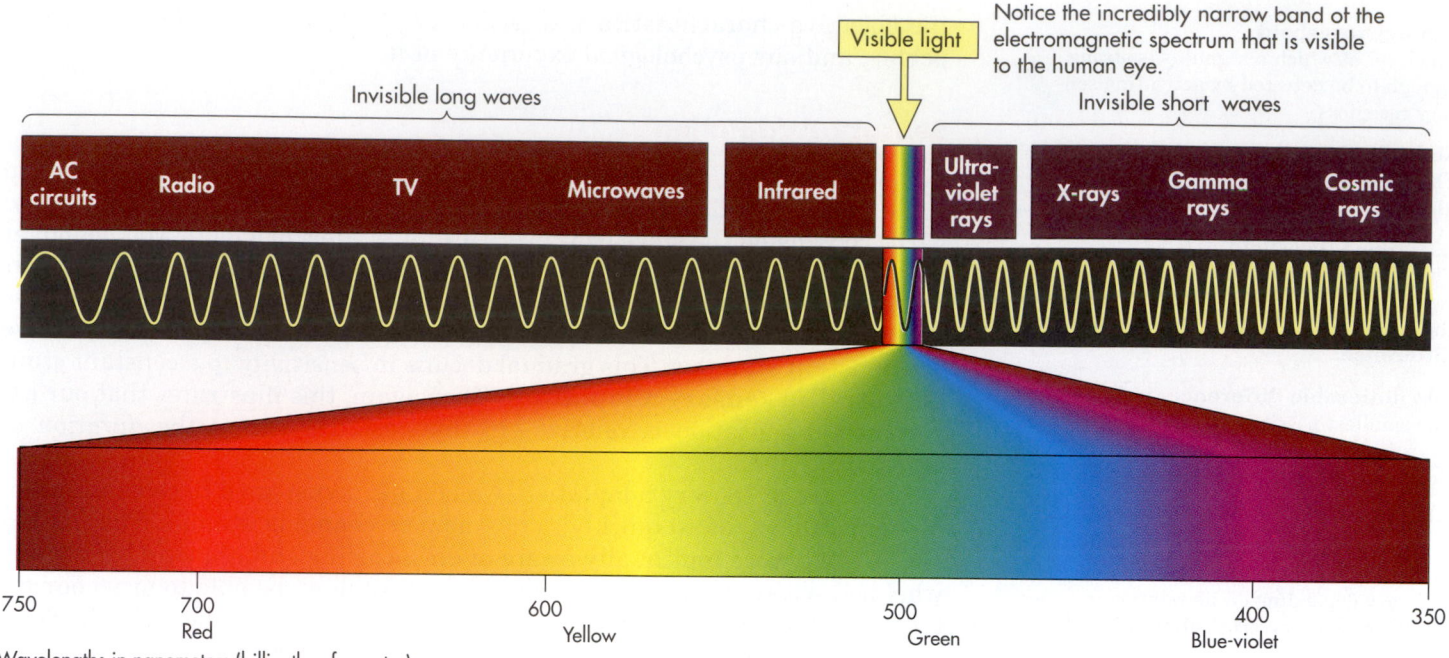

Visible light

Notice the incredibly narrow band of the electromagnetic spectrum that is visible to the human eye.

Invisible long waves

Invisible short waves

| AC circuits | Radio | TV | Microwaves | Infrared | | Ultra-violet rays | X-rays | Gamma rays | Cosmic rays |

750   700   600   500   400   350
Red   Yellow   Green   Blue-violet

Wavelengths in nanometers (billionths of a meter)

FIGURE 3.2 The Electromagnetic Spectrum
We are surrounded by different kinds of electromagnetic energy waves, yet we are able to see only a tiny portion of the entire spectrum of electromagnetic energy. Electronic instruments, like radio and television, are specialized receivers that detect a specific wavelength range. In a similar fashion, the human eye is sensitive to only a very narrow range of wavelengths. Many species of insects and birds can detect ultraviolet light, which is invisible to humans.

Bombs in front of you at breakfast. You glance at the Sunday comics or examine the intricate play of color, light, and texture in a painting by Monet. All these sensations involve vision; but what is vision and how does it occur?

The sense organ for vision is the eye, which contains receptor cells that are sensitive to the physical energy of *light*. Before we can talk about how the eye functions, we need to discuss briefly some characteristics of light as the visual stimulus.

What We See:
The Nature of Light

Light is just one of many different kinds of electromagnetic energy that travel in the form of waves. Other forms of electromagnetic energy include X-rays, the microwaves you use to bake a potato, and the ultraviolet rays that give you a sunburn. These different types of electromagnetic energy differ in terms of their **wavelength,** which is the distance from one wave peak to another. Figure 3.2 shows the spectrum of different forms of electromagnetic energy.

Humans are capable of visually detecting only a minuscule portion of the electromagnetic energy range. In Figure 3.2, notice that the *visible* portion of the electromagnetic energy spectrum can be further divided into different wavelengths. As we'll discuss in more detail later, the different wavelengths of visible light correspond to our psychological perception of different colors.

How a Pit Viper Sees a Mouse at Night
Does the world look different to other species? In many cases, yes. Each species has evolved a unique set of sensory capabilities. Pit vipers "see" infrared light, which we sense only as warmth. In the photo, the mouse has been photographed through an infrared viewer. The image shows how a pit viper uses its infrared "vision" to detect warm-blooded prey at night (Gould & Gould, 1994).

How We See:
The Human Visual System

Suppose you're watching your neighbor's yellow and white tabby cat sun himself on the front steps. How do you "see" the cat? Seeing even a simple image involves a complex chain of events (see Figure 3.3).

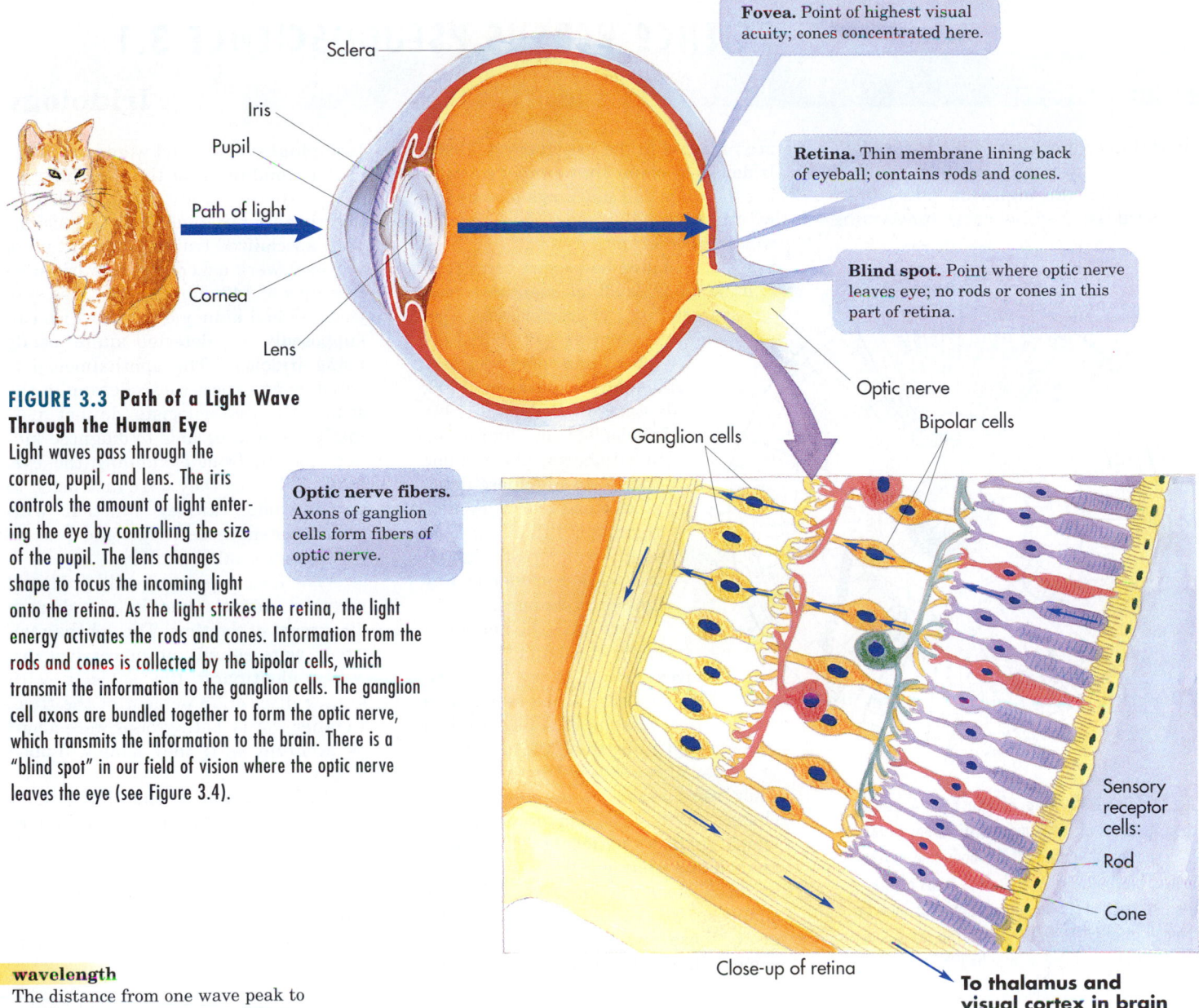

Sclera

Iris

Pupil

Path of light

Cornea

Lens

Fovea. Point of highest visual acuity; cones concentrated here.

Retina. Thin membrane lining back of eyeball; contains rods and cones.

Blind spot. Point where optic nerve leaves eye; no rods or cones in this part of retina.

Optic nerve

Ganglion cells

Bipolar cells

Optic nerve fibers. Axons of ganglion cells form fibers of optic nerve.

Sensory receptor cells:

Rod

Cone

Close-up of retina

To thalamus and visual cortex in brain

FIGURE 3.3 Path of a Light Wave Through the Human Eye
Light waves pass through the cornea, pupil, and lens. The iris controls the amount of light entering the eye by controlling the size of the pupil. The lens changes shape to focus the incoming light onto the retina. As the light strikes the retina, the light energy activates the rods and cones. Information from the rods and cones is collected by the bipolar cells, which transmit the information to the ganglion cells. The ganglion cell axons are bundled together to form the optic nerve, which transmits the information to the brain. There is a "blind spot" in our field of vision where the optic nerve leaves the eye (see Figure 3.4).

wavelength
The distance from one wave peak to another.

cornea
(CORE-nee-uh) A clear membrane covering the visible part of the eye that helps gather and direct incoming light.

pupil
The opening in the middle of the iris that changes size to let in different amounts of light.

iris
(EYE-riss) The colored part of the eye, which is the muscle that controls the size of the pupil.

lens
A transparent structure located behind the pupil that actively focuses, or bends, light as it enters the eye.

accommodation
The process by which the lens changes shape to focus incoming light so that it falls on the retina.

First, lightwaves reflected from the cat enter the eye, passing through the *cornea, pupil,* and *lens.* The **cornea** is a clear membrane that covers the eye and that helps gather and direct incoming light. The **pupil** is the black opening in the middle of your eye. The pupil is surrounded by the **iris,** the colored structure that we refer to when we say that someone has brown or blue eyes. The iris is actually a ring of muscles that contracts or expands to precisely control the size of the pupil, and thus the amount of light entering the eye. In dim light, the iris widens the pupil to let light in; in bright light, the iris narrows the pupil.

Behind the pupil is the **lens,** another transparent structure. In a process called **accommodation,** the lens thins or thickens in order to bend or focus the incoming light so that the light falls on the retina. If the eyeball is abnormally shaped, the lens may not properly focus the incoming light on the retina; the result is a visual disorder, such as *nearsightedness, farsightedness,* or *astigmatism.*

SCIENCE VERSUS PSEUDOSCIENCE 3.1

Iridology

Iridology (pronounced EYE-ruh-*doll*-uh-jee) is a popular pseudoscience that is based on the unproven notion that physical and psychological functioning are reflected in the iris (Barrett, 1996). Iridologists claim that simply examining the color and markings of your iris with a magnifying glass can reveal a wealth of information about you. Supposedly, a skilled iridologist can determine your level of mental stress, personality characteristics, genetic tendencies, nutritional deficiencies, and past diseases and injuries (Jackson, 1993; Jensen & Bodeen, 1992).

Iridologists use highly detailed charts, like the one shown, to "diagnose" such characteristics. They also recommend that you have your eyes "read" about once a year to detect any significant changes.

How have the notions of iridology stood up to scientific investigation? In one study, iridologists were asked to evaluate iris photographs of subjects taken before and after they had developed an acute disease (see Worrall, 1986). They were asked to state whether a change in the iris had occurred and which organ was affected. The iridologists found that one before-and-after set of photographs indicated clear-cut changes. Unfortunately for the iridologists, those two photographs of the same individual had been taken only two minutes apart and were part of the control conditions for the experiment.

In another study, three iridologists and three ophthalmologists (physicians with specialized training in diseases of the eye) were asked to judge iris photographs of 143 subjects. Of these subjects, 48 had kidney disease, which can supposedly be detected quite easily using iridology. The ophthalmologists acted as an expert control group in the study. Ophthalmologists do not normally claim to be able to diagnose kidney disease from examining the eye, but in this case they were instructed to try to judge kidney function with "whatever methods they could best do so" (Simon & others, 1979).

The iridologists correctly predicted whether subjects had kidney disease 49 percent of the time. The ophthalmologists were equally unimpressive, correctly identifying the subjects with kidney disease 53 percent of the time. In other words, both groups were about as accurate as if they simply flipped a coin.

Such controlled scientific studies have failed to confirm the extraordinary claims of iridology. In fact, since iridology was founded over a hundred years ago, advocates of iridology have failed to publish even one well-documented study to support their claims (Worrall, 1986).

An Iridologist's Map of the Eye According to proponents of iridology, specific areas of the iris correspond to areas of the body and psychological functions. Using elaborate maps of the iris like the one shown here, iridologists look for irregularities in the flecks of color in the iris to evaluate physical and mental health.

---

retina

(RET-in-uh) A thin, light-sensitive membrane located at the back of the eye that contains the sensory receptors for vision.

rods

The long, thin, blunt sensory receptors of the eye that are highly sensitive to light but not color and are primarily responsible for peripheral vision and night vision.

cones

The short, thick, pointed sensory receptors of the eye that detect color and are responsible for color vision and visual acuity.

The **retina** is a thin, light-sensitive membrane that lies at the back of the eye, covering most of its inner surface (see Figure 3.3). The retina contains the two kinds of sensory receptors for light: the **rods** and **cones.** When exposed to light, the rods and cones undergo a chemical reaction that results in a neural signal. The rods and cones play an extremely important role in vision, so we'll describe them in some detail.

Rods and Cones

Rods and cones differ in many ways. First, as their names imply, rods and cones are shaped differently. Rods are long and thin, with blunt ends; cones are shorter and fatter, with one end that tapers to a point. The eye contains far more rods than cones. It is estimated that each eye contains about 7 million cones and about *125 million* rods!

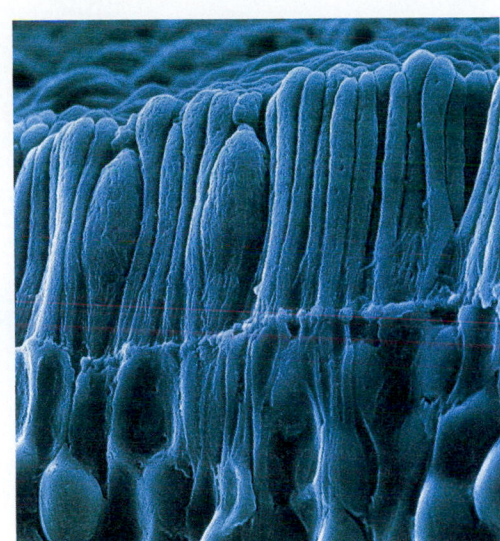

Slim Rods and Fat Cones The rods and cones in the retina are the sensory receptors for vision, converting light into electrical impulses that are transmitted, ultimately, to the brain. This photograph shows the rods and cones magnified about 45,000 times. The rods are long and thin; the cones are shorter, fatter, and tapered at one end. As you can see, the rods and cones are densely packed in the retina, with many rods surrounding a single cone or pair of cones.

Rods and cones are also specialized for different visual functions. Although both rods and cones are light receptors, rods are much more sensitive to light than cones are. Once the rods are fully adapted to the dark, they are about a thousand times better at detecting weak visual stimuli than cones are (Uttal, 1981). Thus, we rely primarily on rods for our vision in dim light and at night.

Rods and cones also react differently to *changes* in the amount of light. Rods adapt relatively slowly, reaching maximum sensitivity to light in about 30 minutes. In contrast, the cones adapt quickly to bright light, reaching maximum sensitivity to the available light in about 5 minutes. That's why it takes several minutes for your eyes to adapt to the dim light of a darkened room, but only a few moments to adapt to the brightness when you switch on the lights.

You may have noticed that it is difficult or impossible to distinguish colors in very dim light. That's because cones require much more light than rods to function effectively, and only the cones are sensitive to the different wavelengths that produce the sensation of color. In addition, the cones are specialized for seeing fine details and for vision in bright light.

Rods are most prevalent in the *periphery*, or outlying areas, of the retina. When you see something "out of the corner of your eye," you are using your peripheral vision and relying primarily on your rods. However, there are a few cones in the peripheral areas of the retina. That's why the world doesn't suddenly become black and white on the edges of your visual field.

Most of the cones are concentrated in the **fovea,** which is a region in the very center of the retina. Cones are scattered throughout the rest of the retina, but they become less and less common as you move toward the periphery of the retina. There are *no* rods in the fovea. Images that do not fall on the fovea tend to be perceived as blurry or indistinct.

Processing Visual Information

Signals from the rods and cones undergo preliminary processing in the bipolar and ganglion cells of the retina before being transmitted to the brain. How are signals processed in the bipolar and ganglion cells? How does information travel from the retina to the brain?

Visual information is mostly processed in the brain. However, before the visual information is sent to the brain, it undergoes some preliminary processing in the retina (see Figure 3.3). Information from the sensory receptors, the rods and cones, is collected by specialized neurons called *bipolar cells.* The bipolar cells, in turn, funnel the information to other specialized neurons called *ganglion cells.* The signals from the rods and the cones are combined and integrated in the bipolar and ganglion cells of the retina before they are sent to the brain. This preliminary processing of visual data in the cells of the retina is possible because the retina actually developed from a bit of brain tissue that "migrated" to the eye during fetal development (see Hubel, 1995).

When the number of rods and cones are combined, there are over 130 million receptor cells. However, there are only about one million ganglion cells. How do just one million ganglion cells transmit messages from 130 million visual receptor cells?

The answer has to do with an important difference in the way that signals from rods and cones are processed in the bipolar and ganglion cells. For the most part, a single ganglion cell receives information from only one or

fovea
(FOH-vee-uh) A small area in the center of the retina that is composed entirely of cones where visual information is most sharply focused.

optic nerve
The thick nerve that exits from the back of the eye and carries visual information to the visual cortex in the brain.

blind spot
The point where the optic nerve leaves the eye, producing a small gap in the field of vision.

two cones. However, a single ganglion cell might well receive information from a *hundred* or more rods. Because the messages from many different rods are combined in the retina before being sent on to the brain, the visual information transmitted by the rods is far less specific. The cones can send messages of much greater visual detail to the brain.

As an analogy to how rod information is processed, imagine a hundred people trying to talk at once over the same telephone line. You would hear the sound of many people talking, but individual voices would be blurred. With cone vision, imagine the voice of a single individual being transmitted across the same telephone line. Every syllable and sound would be clear and distinct. In much the same way, cones use the ganglion cells to provide the brain with much more specific visual information than do rods.

Because of this difference in the way information is processed, the cones are especially important in *visual acuity,* which refers to the ability to see fine details. Visual acuity is strongest when images are focused on the fovea because of the high concentration of cones there.

From Eye to Brain

How does information travel from the retina to the brain? The axons of the ganglion cells are bundled together to form the **optic nerve,** a thick nerve that exits from the back of the eye and extends to the brain. About the diameter of a pencil, the optic nerve transmits messages from the rods and cones to the thalamus in the brain. From the thalamus, the signals are sent to the visual cortex, where they are decoded and interpreted. Most of the receiving neurons in the visual cortex of the brain are highly specialized (Logothetis & Sheinberg, 1996). Each responds to a particular type of visual stimulation, such as angles, edges, lines, and other forms, and even to the movement and distance of objects (Hubel, 1995; Livingstone & Hubel, 1988).

Interestingly, there are no rods and cones in the area where the optic nerve leaves the eye. Consequently, there is a tiny hole or **blind spot** in your field of vision. To experience the blind spot, try the demonstration in Figure 3.4.

Why don't we notice this "hole" in our visual images? Some researchers have suggested that we simply don't notice that any information is missing because the blind spot is located in an area where there are few receptors. Another explanation is that the brain actually "fills in" the missing information (Ramachandran, 1992a, 1992b). In effect, the brain "paves over" the blind spot with the colors and patterns of the surrounding visual information.

FIGURE 3.4 Demonstration of the Blind Spot
Hold the book a few feet in front of you. Close your right eye and stare at the insect spray can with your left eye. Slowly bring the book toward your face. At some point the spider will disappear, because you have focused it onto the part of your retina where the blind spot is. Notice, however, that you still perceive the spiderweb. That's because information has been "filled in" from the surrounding area.

color
The perceptual experience of different wavelengths of light, involving hue, saturation (purity), and brightness (intensity).

hue
The property of wavelengths of light known as color, with different wavelengths corresponding to our subjective experience of different colors.

saturation
The property of color that corresponds to the purity of the light wave.

brightness
The perceived intensity of a color that corresponds to the amplitude of the light wave.

Color Vision

Different wavelengths of light correspond to our perceptual experience of different colors. What properties of light determine the color that is perceived? How is color vision explained by the trichromatic theory and the opponent-process theory?

We see images of an apple, a banana, and an orange because these objects reflect light waves. But why do we perceive the apple to be red and the banana to be yellow? What makes an orange orange?

The Experience of Color

To explain the nature of color, we must go back to the visual stimulus—light. Our experience of **color** involves three properties of the light wave. First, what we usually refer to as color is a property more accurately termed **hue.** Hue varies with the wavelength of light. Look again at Figure 3.2. *Different wavelengths correspond to our subjective experience of different colors.* Wavelengths of about 400 nanometers are perceived as violet; wavelengths of about 700 nanometers are perceived as red. In between are orange, yellow, green, and blue.

Second, the **saturation,** or *purity,* of the color corresponds to the purity of the light wave. Pure red, for example, produced by a single wavelength, would be more *saturated* than pink, which is produced by a combination of wavelengths (red plus white light). In everyday language, saturation refers to the richness of a color. A highly saturated color is vivid and rich, while a less saturated color is faded and washed out.

The third aspect of color is its **brightness** or its perceived intensity. Brightness corresponds to the amplitude of the light wave. These three properties of color—hue, saturation, and brightness—are responsible for the amazing range of colors we experience.

Many people mistakenly believe that white light contains no color. White light actually contains *all wavelengths,* and thus *all colors*, of the visible part of the electromagnetic spectrum. A glass prism placed in sunlight creates a rainbow because it separates sunlight into all the colors of the visible light spectrum.

So we're back to the question: Why is an orange orange? Common sense tells us that the color of an object is an inseparable property of the object (unless we paint it, dye it, or spill spaghetti sauce on it). But actually, *the color of any object is determined by the wavelength of light that the object reflects.* If your T-shirt is red, it's red because the cloth is *reflecting* only the wavelength of light that corresponds to the red portion of the spectrum. The T-shirt is *absorbing* the wavelengths that correspond to all other colors. An object appears white because it *reflects* all the wavelengths of visible light and absorbs none. An object appears black, on the other hand, when it *absorbs* all the wavelengths of visible light and reflects none.

How We See Color

Color vision has interested scientists for hundreds of years. The first scientific theory of color vision was proposed by Hermann von Helmholz (1821–1894) in the mid-1800s and was called the *trichromatic theory.* A rival theory, the *opponent-process theory,* was proposed in the late 1800s. Each

When Red + Blue + Green = White
When light waves of different wavelengths are combined, the wavelengths are added together, producing the perception of a different color. Thus, when green light is combined with red light, yellow light is produced. When the wavelengths of red, green, and blue light are added together, we perceive the blended light as being white.

trichromatic theory of color vision
The theory that the sensation of color is due to cones in the retina that are especially sensitive to red light (long wavelengths), green light (medium wavelengths), or blue light (short wavelengths).

color blindness
One of several inherited forms of color deficiency or weakness in which an individual cannot distinguish between certain colors.

afterimage
A visual experience that occurs after the original source of stimulation is no longer present.

opponent-process theory of color vision
The theory that color vision is the product of opposing pairs of color receptors, red/green, blue/yellow, and black/white; when one member of a color pair is stimulated, the other member is inhibited.

theory was capable of explaining some aspects of color vision, but neither theory could explain all aspects of color vision. Technological advances in the last few decades allowed researchers to gather direct physiological evidence to test both theories. That research evidence showed that *both* theories of color vision are accurate; each theory simply describes color vision at a different stage of visual processing (Hubel, 1995).

The Trichromatic Theory   As you'll recall, only the cones are involved in color vision. According to the **trichromatic theory of color vision,** cones come in three varieties. Each variety of cone is especially sensitive to red light (long wavelengths), green light (medium wavelengths), or blue light (short wavelengths). For the sake of simplicity we will refer to red-sensitive, green-sensitive, and blue-sensitive cones, but keep in mind that there is some overlap in the wavelengths that each cone is sensitive to (Abramov & Gordon, 1994). A given cone will be *very* sensitive to one of the three colors and only slightly responsive to the other two.

When a color other than one of these three strikes the retina, it stimulates a *combination* of cones. For example, if yellow light strikes the retina, both the red-sensitive and green-sensitive cones are stimulated; purple light evokes strong reactions from red-sensitive and blue-sensitive cones. The trichromatic theory of color vision received compelling research support in 1964, when George Wald was able to show that different cones were indeed activated by red, blue, and green light. Wald later received the Nobel Prize for his work.

The trichromatic theory provides a good explanation for the most common form of **color blindness,** which is red-green color blindness. People with this deficiency cannot discriminate between red and green. That's because they have normal blue-sensitive cones, but their other cones are *either* red-sensitive or green-sensitive. Thus, red and green look the same to them. Because red-green color blindness is so common, vertical stoplights are designed so that the red light is always on top. Color-blind individuals can thus interpret traffic signals by the location of the light rather than the color.

The Most Common Form of Color Blindness   To someone with red-green color blindness, these two photographs look almost exactly the same. People with this form of color blindness have normal blue-sensitive cones, but their other cones are sensitive to either red or green. Because of the way red-green color blindness is genetically transmitted, it is much more common in men than in women. People who are completely color-blind and see the world only in shades of black, white, and gray are extremely rare: roughly one in a million people suffers from this disorder (Hurvich, 1981).

The Opponent-Process Theory   The trichromatic theory cannot explain all aspects of color vision. One important phenomenon that it cannot account for is the afterimage. An **afterimage** is a visual experience that occurs after the original source of stimulation is no longer present. To experience an afterimage firsthand, follow the instructions in Figure 3.5. What do you see?

Afterimages can be explained by the opponent-process theory of color vision, which proposes a mechanism of color detection entirely different from the one set forth in the trichromatic theory. According to the **opponent-process theory of color vision,** there are four basic colors, which are divided into two pairs of color-sensitive neurons: red-green and blue-yellow. The members of each pair *oppose* each other. If red is stimulated, green is inhibited. If green is stimulated, red is inhibited. Green and red cannot both be stimulated simultaneously. The same is true for the blue-yellow pair. In addition, black and white act as an opposing pair. Color, then, is sensed and encoded in terms of its proportion of red OR green, and blue OR yellow.

FIGURE 3.5 **Demonstration of Afterimage** Stare at the white dot in the center of this oddly colored flag for about 30 seconds, then look at a white wall or white sheet of paper. What do you see?

For example, red light would evoke a response of RED–YES • GREEN–NO in the red-green opponent pair. Yellow light would evoke a response of BLUE–NO • YELLOW–YES. Colors other than red, green, blue, and yellow activate one member of each of these pairs to differing degrees. Purple stimulates the *red* of the red-green pair *plus* the *blue* of the blue-yellow pair. Orange activates *red* in the red-green pair and *yellow* in the blue-yellow pair.

Afterimages can easily be explained when the opponent process theory is combined with the general principle of sensory adaptation (Jameson & Hurvich, 1989). If you stare continuously at one color, sensory adaptation occurs and your visual receptors become less sensitive to that color. What happens when you subsequently stare at a white surface?

If you remember that white light is made up of the wavelengths for *all* colors, you may be able to predict the result. The receptors for the original color have adapted to the constant stimulation and are temporarily "off duty." Thus, they do not respond to that color. Instead, only the receptors for the opposing color will be activated, and you perceive the wavelength of only the *opposing* color. For example, if you stare at a patch of green, your green receptors eventually become "tired." The wavelengths for both green and red light are reflected by the white surface, but since the green receptors are "off," only the red receptors are activated. This is exactly what occurred in Figure 3.5, when staring at a green, black, and yellow flag produced an afterimage of opposing colors—in the form of a red, white, and blue American flag.

An Integrated Explanation of Color Vision At the beginning of this section we said that current research has shown that *both* the trichromatic theory and the opponent-process theory of color vision are accurate. How can both theories be right? It turns out that each theory correctly describes color vision at a *different level* of visual processing.

As described by the *trichromatic* theory, the cones of the retina do indeed respond to and encode color in terms of red, green, and blue. But recall that signals from the cones and rods are partially processed in the ganglion cells before being transmitted along the optic nerve to the brain. Researchers now believe that an additional level of color processing takes place in the ganglion cells.

As described by the *opponent-process* theory, the ganglion cells respond to and encode color in terms of opposing pairs (De Valois & De Valois, 1975). In the brain, the thalamus and visual cortex also encode color in terms of opponent pairs (Boynton, 1988). Consequently, both theories contribute to our understanding of the process of color vision. Each theory simply describes color vision at a different stage of visual processing (Hubel, 1995).

Vision and Color Vision

Fill in the blanks using the correct term.

1. The sensory receptors for vision are contained in the _____.

2. When a red pen was displayed in Barry's peripheral vision, he correctly identified the object but was unable to name its color. The explanation for this is that there are very few _____ in the periphery of the retina.

3. Information travels from the retina to the brain via the _____.

4. All the wavelengths of the visible part of the electromagnetic spectrum are contained in _____ light.

5. According to the _____ theory of color vision, the person with red-green color blindness has normal blue-sensitive cones.

6. When people stare at a blue circle and then shift their eyes to a white surface, the afterimage of the circle appears _____. This phenomenon can best be explained by the _____ theory of color vision.

Hearing: From Vibration to Sound

Sound waves are the physical stimuli that produce the sensation of sound. What properties of a sound wave correspond to our perception of sound?

We have hiked in a desert area that was so quiet we could hear the whir of a single grasshopper's wings in the distance. And we have waited on a subway platform where the screech of metal against metal forced us to cover our ears. The sense of hearing, or **audition,** is capable of responding to a wide range of sounds, from very soft to very loud, simple to complex, harmonious to discordant. The ability to sense and perceive very subtle differences in sound is important to physical survival, social interactions, and language development. Most of the time, all of us are bathed in sound—so much so that moments of near-silence, like our experience in the desert, can seem almost eerie.

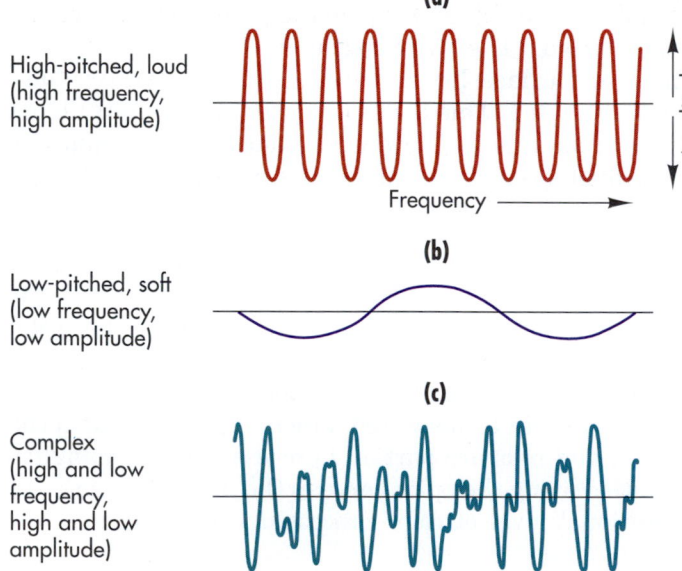

FIGURE 3.6 Characteristics of Sound Waves
The length of a wave, its height, and its complexity determine the loudness, pitch, and timbre that we hear. In (a) the sound would be high-pitched and loud. In (b) the sound would be soft and low. The sound in (c) is complex, like the sounds we usually experience in the natural world.

What We Hear:

The Nature of Sound

Whether it's the ear-splitting screech of metal on metal or the subtle whir of a grasshopper's wings, *sound waves* are the physical stimuli that produce our sensory experience of sound. Usually, sound waves are produced by the rhythmic vibration of air molecules, but sound waves can be transmitted through other media too, such as water. Our perception of sound is directly related to the physical properties of sound waves (see Figure 3.6).

One of the first things that we notice about a sound is how loud it is. **Loudness** is determined by the intensity, or **amplitude,** of a sound wave, and is measured in units called **decibels.** Zero decibels represents the loudness of the softest sound that humans can hear, or the

TABLE 3.2 Decibel Level of Some Common Noises

Decibels	Examples	Exposure Danger
180	Rocket launching pad	Hearing loss inevitable
140	Shotgun blast, jet plane	Any exposure is dangerous
120	Speakers at rock concert, sandblasting, thunderclap	Immediate danger
100	Chain saw, pneumatic drill	2 hours
90	Truck traffic, noisy home appliances, lawn mower	Less than 8 hours
80	Subway, heavy city traffic, alarm clock at 2 feet	More than 8 hours
70	Busy traffic, noisy restaurant	Critical level begins with constant exposure
60	Air conditioner at 20 feet, conversation, sewing machine	
50	Light traffic at a distance, refrigerator	
40	Quiet office, living room	
30	Quiet library, soft whisper	
0	Lowest sound audible to human ear	

audition
The technical term for the sense of hearing.

loudness
The intensity (or amplitude) of a sound wave, measured in decibels.

amplitude
The intensity or amount of energy of a wave, reflected in the height of the wave; the amplitude of a sound wave determines a sound's loudness.

decibel
(DESS-uh-bell) The unit of measurement for loudness.

pitch
The relative highness or lowness of a sound, determined by the frequency of a sound wave.

frequency
The rate of vibration, or the number of sound waves per second.

timbre
(TAM-ber) The distinctive quality of a sound, determined by the complexity of the sound wave.

absolute threshold for hearing. As decibels increase, perceived loudness increases (see Table 3.2).

Pitch refers to the relative "highness" or "lowness" of a sound. Pitch is determined by the frequency of a sound wave. **Frequency** refers to the rate of vibration, or number of waves per second, and is measured in units called *hertz*. Hertz simply refers to the number of wave peaks per second. The faster the vibration, the higher the frequency, the closer together the waves are—and the higher is the tone produced. If you pluck the high E and the low E strings on a guitar, you'll notice that the low E vibrates far fewer times per second than the high E.

Most of the sounds we experience do not consist of a single frequency but are *complex*, consisting of several sound-wave frequencies. This combination of frequencies produces the distinctive quality, or **timbre**, of a sound, enabling you to easily distinguish among the same note played on a saxophone, piano, or guitar. Every human voice has its own distinctive timbre, which is why you can immediately identify a friend's voice on the telephone from just a few words, even if you haven't talked to each other for years.

How We Hear:
The Path of Sound

Sound waves are collected in the outer ear, amplified in the middle ear, and converted to neural messages in the inner ear. What are key structures involved in hearing, and what is their function? How do place theory and frequency theory explain pitch?

The human ear is made up of the outer ear, the middle ear, and the inner ear. In general, sound waves are *collected* in the outer ear, *amplified* in the middle ear, and *transduced* or *transformed into neural messages* in the inner ear. You can trace the path taken by sound waves through the ear in Figure 3.7.

FIGURE 3.7 (a) The Path of Sound Through the Human Ear A complex chain of events leads to the perception of sound. Sound waves are caught by the outer ear, funneled down the ear canal, and ultimately stimulate the hair cells, the sensory receptors in the cochlea (see inset). **(b) The Hair Cells** Magnified thousands of times, this photograph shows the hair cells, embedded in the basilar membrane in the cochlea. As the basilar membrane ripples, the hair cells bend, stimulating the auditory nerve, which transmits neural messages to the auditory cortex of the brain.

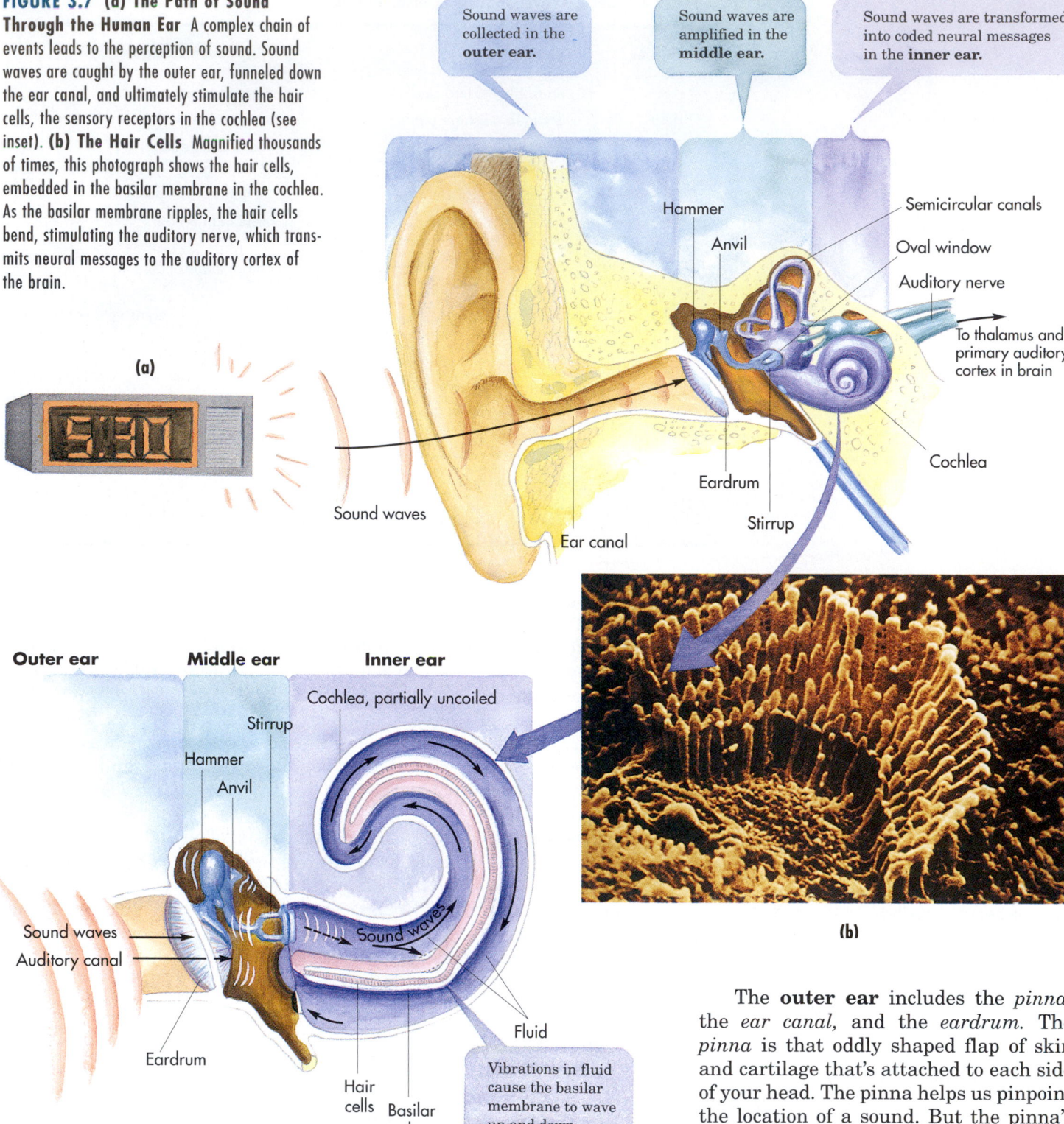

Sound waves are collected in the **outer ear.**

Sound waves are amplified in the **middle ear.**

Sound waves are transformed into coded neural messages in the **inner ear.**

Hammer

Anvil

Semicircular canals

Oval window

Auditory nerve

To thalamus and primary auditory cortex in brain

Cochlea

Eardrum

Stirrup

Ear canal

Sound waves

(a)

Outer ear   **Middle ear**   **Inner ear**

Cochlea, partially uncoiled

Stirrup

Hammer

Anvil

Sound waves

Auditory canal

Sound waves

Eardrum

Fluid

Hair cells   Basilar membrane

Vibrations in fluid cause the basilar membrane to wave up and down.

(b)

The **outer ear** includes the *pinna,* the *ear canal,* and the *eardrum.* The *pinna* is that oddly shaped flap of skin and cartilage that's attached to each side of your head. The pinna helps us pinpoint the location of a sound. But the pinna's primary role is to catch sound waves and funnel them into the *ear canal.* The sound wave travels down the ear canal, then bounces into the **eardrum,** a tightly stretched membrane. When sound waves hit the eardrum, it vibrates, matching the vibrations of the sound wave in both intensity and frequency.

As you can see in Figure 3.7, the eardrum separates the outer ear from the middle ear. As the eardrum vibrates, the vibration is transferred to the **middle ear,** which contains three tiny bones—the *hammer,* the *anvil,* and the *stirrup,* named after the objects they resemble. Each bone sets the next bone in motion. The joint action of these three bones almost doubles the amplification of the sound. The innermost bone, the stirrup, transmits the amplified vibration to the *oval window.* If the tiny bones of the middle ear are damaged or become brittle, as they do in old age, *conduction deafness* may result. Conduction deafness can be helped by a hearing aid, which amplifies sounds.

Like the eardrum, the oval window is a membrane, but it is many times smaller than the eardrum. The oval window separates the middle ear from the **inner ear.** As the oval window vibrates, the vibration is next relayed to an inner structure called the **cochlea,** a fluid-filled tube that's coiled in a spiral. The word "cochlea" comes from the Greek word for "snail," and the spiral shape of the cochlea does resemble a snail's shell. Although the cochlea is a very complex structure, it is quite tiny—no larger than a pea.

As the fluid in the cochlea ripples, the vibration in turn is transmitted to the **basilar membrane.** The basilar membrane runs the length of the coiled cochlea. Embedded in the basilar membrane are the sensory receptors for sound, called **hair cells,** which have tiny, projecting fibers that look like hairs. The hair cells bend as the basilar membrane ripples. It is here that transduction finally takes place: the physical vibration of the sound wave is converted into neural impulses. As the hair cells bend, they stimulate the cells of the auditory nerve, which carries the neural information to the brain. Damage to the hair cells or auditory nerve can result in *nerve deafness,* which cannot be helped by a hearing aid.

Distinguishing Pitch

How do we distinguish between the low-pitched throb of a bass guitar and the high-pitched tones of a flute? Remember, pitch is determined by the *frequency* of a sound wave. The basilar membrane is a key structure involved in our discrimination of pitch. Two complementary theories describe the role of the basilar membrane in the transmission of differently pitched sounds.

According to **frequency theory,** the basilar membrane vibrates at the *same* frequency as the sound wave. Thus, a sound wave of about 100 hertz would excite each hair cell along the basilar membrane to vibrate 100 times per second, and neural impulses would be sent to the brain at the same rate. However, there's a limit to how fast neurons can fire: individual neurons cannot fire faster than about 1,000 times per second. But we can sense sounds with frequencies that are many times higher than 1,000 hertz. A child, for example, can typically hear pitches ranging from about 20 to 20,000 hertz. Frequency theory explains how *low*-frequency sounds are transmitted to the brain, but cannot explain the transmission of higher-frequency sounds.

So how *do* we distinguish higher-pitched sounds? According to **place theory,** different frequencies cause larger vibrations at different *locations* along the basilar membrane. High-frequency sounds, for example, cause maximum vibration near the stirrup end of the basilar membrane. Lower-frequency sounds cause maximum vibration at the opposite end. Thus, different pitches excite different hair cells along the basilar membrane. Higher-pitched sounds are interpreted according to the *place* where the hair cells are most active.

Thus, *both* frequency theory and place theory are involved in explaining our discrimination of pitch. Frequency theory helps explain our discrimination of frequencies lower than 500 hertz. Place theory helps explain our discrimination of higher-pitched sounds. And for intermediate frequencies or mid-range pitches, both place and frequency are involved.

outer ear
The part of the ear that collects sound waves and consists of the pinna, the ear canal, and the eardrum.

eardrum
A tightly stretched membrane at the end of the ear canal that vibrates when sound waves hit it.

middle ear
The part of the ear that amplifies sound waves and consists of three small bones, the hammer, the anvil, and the stirrup.

inner ear
The part of the ear where sound is transduced into neural impulses; consists of the cochlea and semicircular canals.

cochlea
(COKE-lee-uh) The coiled, fluid-filled inner-ear structure that contains the sensory receptors for sound.

basilar membrane
(BASE-uh-ler) The membrane within the cochlea of the ear that contains the hair cells.

hair cells
The hairlike sensory receptors for sound, found in the basilar membrane of the cochlea.

frequency theory
The view that the basilar membrane vibrates at the same frequency as the sound wave.

place theory
The view that different frequencies cause larger vibrations at different locations along the basilar membrane.

Hearing

Complete the following sentences using the correct term from this list: loudness, amplitude, basilar, frequency, pitch, place, cochlea, middle ear.

1. Frequency is to _____ as amplitude is to _____ .

2. The sensory receptors for hearing are embedded in the _____ membrane in the _____ .

3. The _____ theory of hearing best explains how we hear the low-frequency sound of thunder rumbling.

4. Neurons cannot fire faster than about 1,000 times per second, yet humans can sense high-pitched sounds up to 20,000 hertz. The _____ theory of hearing explains how people hear high-pitched sounds.

The Chemical and Body Senses:
Smell, Taste, Touch, and Position

> *Smell and taste receptors are specialized to respond to different types of chemical stimulation. How do airborne molecules result in the sensation of an odor?*

Remember Paul and Warren, who both lack a sense of smell? As Paul and Warren are well aware, the senses of smell and taste are closely linked. If you've ever temporarily lost your sense of smell because of a bad cold, you've probably noticed that your sense of taste was also disrupted. Even a hot fudge sundae tastes bland.

Smell and taste are linked in other ways, too. Unlike vision and hearing, which involve sensitivity to different forms of energy, the sensory receptors for taste and smell are specialized to respond to different types of *chemical* substances. That's why smell, or *olfaction,* and taste, or *gustation,* are sometimes referred to as "the chemical senses" (Bartoshuk & Beauchamp, 1994).

As the cases of Paul and Warren illustrate, people can get along quite well without a sense of smell. In fact, a surprisingly large number of people completely lack a sense of smell or are unable to smell specific odors. Although humans gather most of their information about the world through

CALVIN AND HOBBES

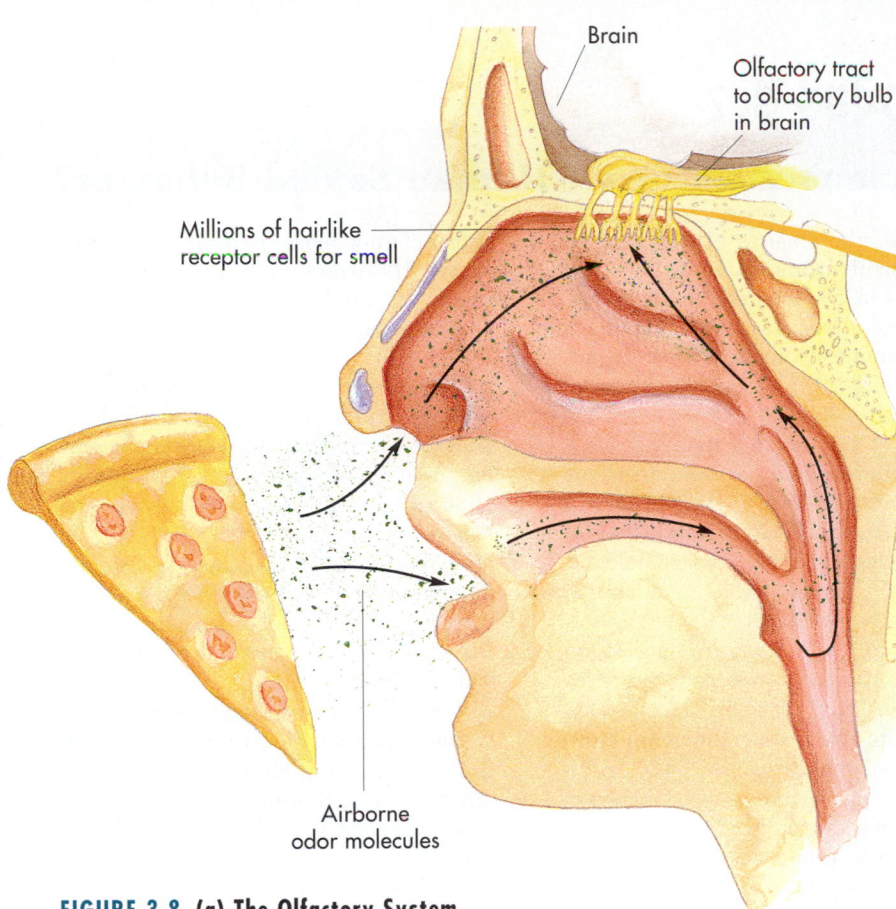

Brain

Olfactory tract
to olfactory bulb
in brain

Millions of hairlike
receptor cells for smell

Airborne
odor molecules

(b)

(a)

FIGURE 3.8 (a) The Olfactory System
Inhaled through the nose or the mouth, airborne
molecules travel to the top of the nasal cavity
and stimulate the olfactory receptors. When stimulated, these receptor cells communicate neural
messages to the olfactory bulb, which is part of
the olfactory cortex of the brain, where the sense
of smell is registered. **(b) The Olfactory Receptor Cells** More than five million olfactory
neurons make up a moist, mucus-bathed tissue at
the back of the nose. Projecting from the olfactory
neurons are the fiberlike olfactory hairs, which
can be clearly seen in this photograph. Olfactory
neurons are replaced every month or two.

olfactory bulb
(ole-FACK-toe-ree) The enlarged ending
of the olfactory cortex at the front of the
brain where the sensation of smell is
registered.

hearing and vision, many animal species, such
as moles, depend on chemical signals as their
primary source of information (Agosta, 1992).

However, even for humans, smell and taste
can provide important information about
the environment. Tastes help us determine
whether a particular substance is to be sa-
vored or spit out. Smells alert us to potential
dangers, such as the odor of a smoldering fire,
leaking gas, or spoiled food.

How We Smell (Don't Answer That!)

What do we smell when we smell a smell? The sensory stimuli that produce
our sensation of an odor are *molecules in the air*. These airborne molecules
are emitted by the substance we are smelling. We inhale them through the
nose and through the opening in the palate at the back of the throat. In the
nose, the molecules encounter millions of olfactory receptor cells located high
in the nasal cavity.

Unlike the sensory receptors for hearing and vision, the olfactory neurons are constantly being replaced, each lasting for only about 30 to 60 days.
In 1991, neuroscientists Linda Buck and Richard Axel identified the odor receptors that are present on the hairlike fibers of the olfactory neurons. Like
synaptic receptors, each odor receptor seems to be specialized to respond to
molecules of a different chemical structure. When these receptor cells are
stimulated by the airborne molecules, the stimulation is converted into
neural messages that travel down the axons that make up the *olfactory nerve*
(Buck 1996).

So far, hundreds of different odor receptors have been identified. We probably don't have a separate receptor for each of the estimated 10,000 different
odors that we can identify, however. Rather, it seems that a given smell activates a *group* of different receptors. Specific odors are identified by the brain
as it interprets the pattern of receptors that are stimulated (Buck, 1996).

The olfactory nerve directly connects to the **olfactory bulb** in the brain,
which is actually the enlarged ending of the *olfactory cortex* at the front of the
brain (see Figure 3.8). It's here that smells are perceived in the brain. Warren
lost his sense of smell because the surgeon cut through the nerves leading to
his olfactory bulb. Axons from the olfactory bulb also project to structures in
the limbic system of the brain (Angier, 1995).

IN FOCUS 3.2

Do Pheromones Influence Human Sexual Behavior?

Many animals communicate by producing **pheromones,** chemical scents that linger in the air. Pheromones are used to mark territories and serve as warning signals to other members of the same species (Agosta, 1992). They are also extremely important in regulating mating and reproductive behavior in many animals. The male cabbage moth, for example, can detect pheromones released from a sexually receptive female cabbage moth that is several miles away (Lerner & others, 1990).

Do humans, like other animals, produce pheromones that serve as sexual signals? A popular notion among some teenage males is that the aroma of male sweat is sexually exciting to women, but this has never been substantiated scientifically. The human sexual response is much more complex than that of other animals, and it is un-

likely that pheromones alone could be the powerful stimulus that they are elsewhere in the animal kingdom. So, until researchers do discover human sex pheromones, your best bet is to just go ahead and throw those sweaty socks in the washer.

This is *not* to say, however, that human pheromones do not exist, or that chemical signals do not affect human behavior. For example, while still a college student, neurobiologist Martha McClintock (1971) set out to scientifically investigate the folk notion that women who lived in the same dorm eventually developed synchronized menstrual periods. McClintock was able to show that the more time the women spent together, the more likely their cycles were to be in sync. She also discovered that women who spent more time with *males* had

shorter and more regular menstrual cycles. It turned out that the women's sense of smell was related to both phenomena.

Research later showed that smelling an unknown chemical substance in underarm sweat from female donors was responsible for synchronizing menstrual cycles (Preti & others, 1986). And smelling an unknown chemical substance in underarm sweat from *male* donors was responsible for producing shorter and more regular menstrual cycles (Cutler & others, 1986). So, even though no one has been able to isolate human sex pheromones that will make you irresistible to members of the preferred sex, there is substantial evidence that chemical signals can affect the functioning of the human reproductive system (McClintock, 1992).

The direct connection of receptor cells to the cortex and limbic system is unique to our sense of smell. As discussed in Chapter 2, all other body sensations are first processed in the thalamus before being relayed to the higher brain centers in the cortex. Olfactory neurons are unique in another way, too. They are the only neurons that *directly* link the brain and the outside world (Axel, 1995). The axons of the sensory neurons that are located in your nose extend directly into your brain!

As with the other senses, we experience sensory adaptation to odors when exposed to them for a period of time. Perhaps you've visited a friend in an industrial section of town and commented on the strong smell of air pollution, while your friend had no idea what you were talking about. In general, we reach maximum adaptation to an odor in less than a minute. We continue to smell the odor, but we have become about 70 percent less sensitive to it. Keep that reassuring thought in mind the next time you squeeze onto a crowded bus in the middle of a heat wave!

Taste:

This Bud's For You!

Taste results from the stimulation of specialized receptors in the the taste buds. What are the primary tastes? How do we perceive tastes?

Our sense of taste, or *gustation,* results from the stimulation of special receptors in the mouth. The stimuli that produce the sensation of taste are chemical substances in whatever you eat or drink. These substances are dissolved by saliva, which allows the chemicals to activate the **taste buds,** which contain the specialized receptors for taste.

The surface of the tongue is covered with thousands of little bumps that have grooves between them (see Figure 3.9). These grooves are lined with the taste buds. Taste buds are also located on the insides of your cheeks, on the roof of your mouth, and in your throat (Oakley, 1986). When activated, special receptor cells in the taste buds send neural messages along neural pathways to the thalamus in the brain. In turn, the thalamus directs the information to several regions in the cortex.

There are four primary taste qualities: sweet, salty, sour, and bitter. All other tastes are actually a combination of the four primary taste qualities. Each taste bud shows maximum sensitivity to one particular taste quality and lesser degrees of sensitivity to the other three taste qualities (Arvidson & Friberg, 1980). More complex tastes are a result of the activation of different combinations of these four types of receptors (Martin & Jessell, 1995).

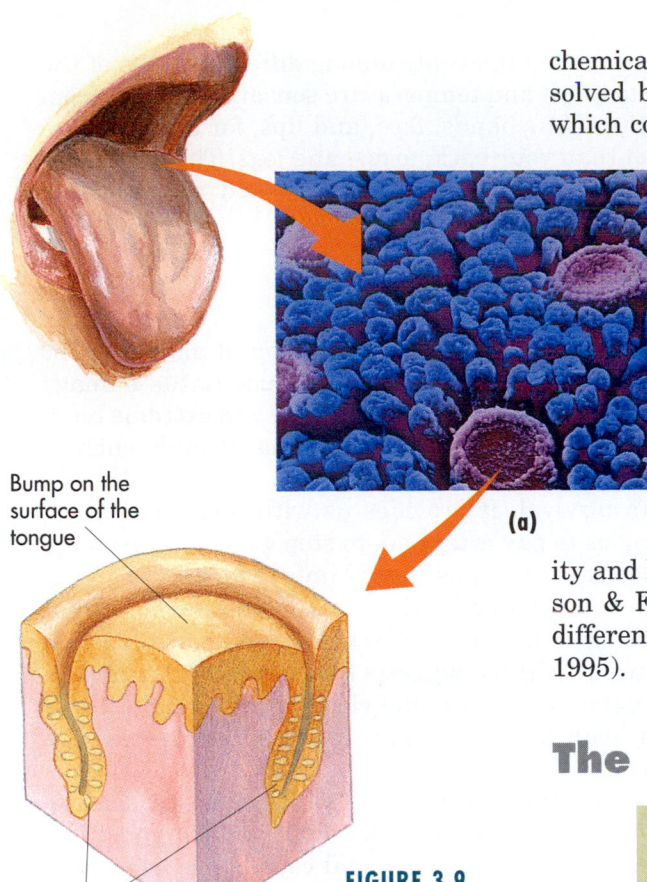

Bump on the surface of the tongue

Taste buds

(b)

FIGURE 3.9
Taste Buds (a)
The photograph shows the surface of the tongue magnified hundreds of times. Taste buds are located in the grooves of the bumps on the surface of the tongue. **(b)** Embedded in the surface of the tongue are thousands of taste buds, the sensory receptor organs for taste. Each taste bud contains an average of fifty taste receptor cells. When activated, the taste receptor cells send messages to adjoining sensory neurons, which relay the information to the brain. Taste buds, like the olfactory neurons, are constantly being replaced. The life expectancy of a particular taste bud is only about 10 days.

(a)

The Skin and Body Senses

The skin senses include touch and pain, whereas the body senses include movement, position, and balance. What is the gate-control theory of pain, and how do psychological factors affect the pain experience? What role is played by the kinesthetic and vestibular senses, and where are their receptors located?

While vision, hearing, smell, and taste provide you with important information about your environment, another group of senses provide you with information that comes from a source much closer to home: your own body. Without looking, can you tell where your left knee is right now? Are you sitting up straight or lying down? Are you wearing shoes? These questions may sound silly, but think about how difficult life would be if you were unable to answer them. In this section, we'll first consider the *skin senses,* which provide essential information about your physical status and your physical interaction with objects in your environment. We'll next consider the *body senses,* which keep you informed as to your position and orientation in space.

Touch

We usually don't think of our skin as a sense organ. But in fact the skin is the largest and heaviest sense organ. The skin of an average adult covers about 20 square feet of surface area and weighs about 6 pounds.

There are many different kinds of sensory receptors in the skin. Some of these sensory receptors are specialized to respond to just one kind of stimulus, such as pressure, warmth, or cold. Other skin receptors respond to more than one type of stimulus.

One important receptor involved with the sense of touch is called the *Pacinian corpuscle,* which is located beneath the skin. When stimulated by pressure, the Pacinian corpuscle converts the stimulation into a neural message that is relayed to the brain. If a pressure is constant, sensory adaptation takes place. The Pacinian corpuscle either reduces the number of signals sent or quits responding altogether (which is fortunate, or you'd be unable to forget the fact that you're wearing underwear).

taste buds
The specialized sensory receptors for taste that are located on the tongue and inside the mouth and throat.

pain

The unpleasant sensation of physical discomfort or suffering that can occur in varying degrees of intensity.

gate-control theory

The theory that pain is a product of both physiological and psychological factors that cause spinal "gates" to open and relay patterns of intense stimulation to the brain, which perceives them as pain.

substance P

A neurotransmitter that is involved in the transmission of pain messages to the brain.

Sensory receptors are distributed unevenly among different areas of the body. That's why sensitivity to touch and temperature sensations varies from one area of the body to another. Your hands, face, and lips, for example, are much more sensitive to touch than your back, arms, and legs. That's because your hands, face, and lips are much more densely packed with sensory receptors.

Pain

A wide variety of stimuli can produce **pain**—the sensation of discomfort or suffering. Virtually any external stimulus that can produce tissue damage can cause pain, including certain chemicals, electric shock, and extreme heat, cold, pressure, or noise. Pain can also be caused by internal stimuli, such as disease, infection, or deterioration of body functions.

Pain is important to our survival. It provides us with important information about our body, telling us to pay attention, to stop what we are doing, or to pull away from some object or stimulus that is injuring us.

The most influential theory explaining pain is called the **gate-control theory,** developed by psychologist Ronald Melzack and anatomist Patrick Wall (1983, 1965). The gate-control theory suggests that the sensation of pain is controlled by a series of "gates" that open and close in the spinal cord. If the spinal "gates" are open, pain is experienced. If the spinal "gates" are closed, no pain is experienced.

Pain begins when an intense stimulus activates small-diameter sensory fibers, called *free nerve endings,* in the skin, muscles, or internal organs. The free nerve endings carry their messages to the spinal cord, releasing a neurotransmitter called **substance P.** In the spinal cord, substance P causes other neurons to become activated, sending their messages through open spinal gates to the *thalamus* in the brain (Turk & Nash, 1993).

When the sensory pain signals reach the brain, the sensory information is integrated with psychological information. Depending on how the brain interprets the pain experience, it regulates pain by sending signals down the spinal cord that either "open" or "close" the gates. If, because of psychological factors, the brain signals the gates to open, pain is experienced or intensified. If the brain signals the gates to close, pain is reduced.

Anxiety, fear, and a sense of helplessness are some of the psychological factors that can intensify the experience of pain. Positive emotions, laughter, distraction, and a sense of control can reduce the perception of pain. The experience of pain is also influenced by social and cultural learning experiences about the meaning of pain and how people should react to pain (Turk, 1994; Turk & Rudy, 1992).

Psychological factors can also influence the release of *endorphins,* the body's natural painkillers that are produced in many parts of the brain and the body (see Chapter 2). Endorphins are released as part of the brain's overall response to physical pain or stress. In the brain, endorphins can inhibit the transmission of pain signals. And in the spinal cord, endorphins inhibit the release of substance P.

Finally, a person's mental or emotional state can influence other bodily processes that affect the experience of pain. Muscle tension, blood flow, physiological arousal, and heart rate can all produce or intensify pain (Turk & Nash, 1993).

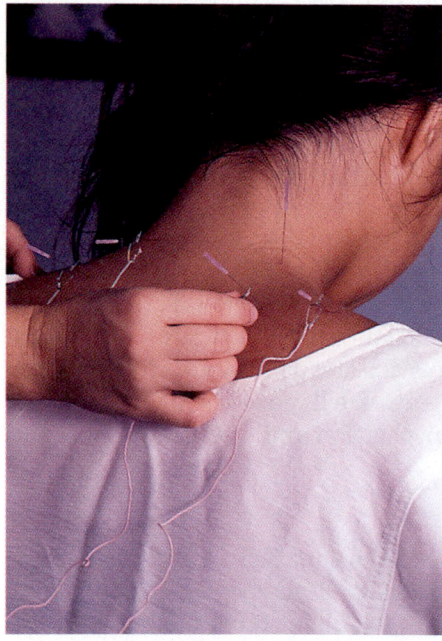

Pain Relief Through Acupuncture Acupuncture is a pain-relieving technique that has been used in traditional Chinese medicine for thousands of years. Acupuncture involves inserting tiny needles at specific points in the body. The needles are then twirled, heated, or, as is shown here, stimulated with a mild electrical current. Although it is not yet understood exactly how acupuncture interrupts the transmission of pain signals, it is known that acupuncture stimulates the release of endorphins.

TABLE 3.3 The Body's Most and Least Sensitive Areas to Pain

Body areas MOST SENSITIVE to pain:

Back of the knee
Neck region
Bend of the elbow

Body areas LEAST SENSITIVE to pain:

Tip of the nose
Sole of the foot
Ball of the thumb

SOURCE: Based on Geldard, 1972.

kinesthetic sense
(*kin*-ess-THET-ick) The technical name for the sense of location and position of body parts in relation to one another.

vestibular sense
(vess-TIB-you-ler) The technical name for the sense of balance, or equilibrium.

Today, a variety of techniques and procedures can effectively eliminate or reduce pain. These techniques are explored in the chapter Application, entitled "Controlling Pain."

Movement, Position, and Balance

The phone rings. Without looking up from your textbook, you reach for the receiver, pick it up, and guide it to the side of your head. You have just demonstrated your **kinesthetic sense**—the sense that involves the location and position of body parts in relation to one another. The word "kinesthetics" literally means "feelings of motion."

The kinesthetic sense involves specialized sensory neurons, called *proprioceptors,* that are located in your muscles and joints. The proprioceptors constantly communicate information to the brain about changes in your body position and muscle tension.

The kinesthetic sense helps you keep track of the position and movement of different parts of your body. Closely related is the **vestibular sense,** which provides a sense of balance or equilibrium by responding to changes in gravity, motion, and body position.

There are two sources of vestibular sensory information, which are both located in the ear: the *semicircular canals* and the *vestibular sacs* (see Figure 3.10). These structures are filled with fluid and lined with hairlike receptor cells that shift in response to motion, changes in body position, or changes in gravity. When you experience environmental motion, like the rocking of a boat in choppy water, the fluids in the vestibular canals and the vestibular sac are affected. Changes in your body position, such as falling backward in a heroic attempt to return a volleyball serve, also affect the fluids. Your vestibular sense supplies the critical information that allows you to compensate for such changes and quickly reestablish your sense of balance.

Maintaining our equilibrium also involves information from other senses, particularly vision. Under normal circumstances, this works to our advantage. However, when information from the eyes conflicts with information from the vestibular system, the result can be dizziness, disorientation, and nausea. These are the symptoms that are commonly experienced in motion sickness, the bane of many travelers, whether they are in cars, on planes, on boats, or even in space. One strategy to combat motion sickness is to minimize sensory conflicts by focusing on a distant point or an object that is fixed, such as the horizon.

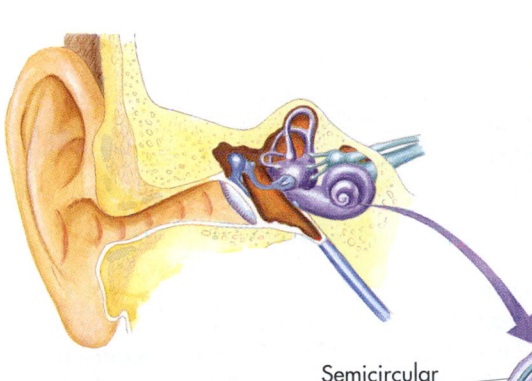

Semicircular canals

Vestibular sacs

(a)

FIGURE 3.10 (a) The Vestibular Sense
The vestibular sense provides our sense of balance, or equilibrium. Shown here are the two sources of vestibular sensory information, both located in the ear: the semicircular canals and the vestibular sacs. Both structures are filled with fluids that shift in response to changes in body position or gravity, and motion. **(b) A Balancing Act** These talented circus acrobats at Montreal's famous *Cirque du Soleil* (Circus of the Sun) are performing a difficult four-person tower—a feat that pushes the sense of balance to its limits. Maintaining equilibrium involves the kinesthetic sense, the vestibular sense, and vision. Signals from the proprioceptors in the muscles and joints (the kinesthetic sense), the fluids in the semicircular canals and the vestibular sacs (the vestibular sense), and visual information must all be integrated to keep the human tower from toppling.

(b)

The Chemical and Body Senses

Fill in the blanks using the correct term from this list: gate-control, olfactory bulb, kinesthetic, taste, touch, olfactory nerve, vestibular, substance P.

1. Because of your _____ sense, you can touch your chin with your index finger even when your eyes are closed.

2. Charmagne felt dizzy and disoriented during a roller coaster ride. Her loss of balance and equilibrium was a function of her _____ sense.

3. Olfactory receptors transmit information via the _____ to the brain structure called the _____.

4. The neurotransmitter called _____ plays an important role in the processing of pain signals.

Perception

> *Perception refers to the process of integrating, organizing, and interpreting sensory information in a way that is meaningful. As we move about the world, what three basic perceptual questions must we routinely answer? Who were the Gestalt psychologists?*

As we've seen, our various senses are constantly registering a diverse range of stimuli from the environment and transmitting that information to the brain. But as we interact with our environment, we don't experience isolated bits and pieces of sensory data. Early in this chapter, we defined *perception* as the process of integrating, organizing, and interpreting sensory information in a way that is meaningful. Thus, we perceive a meaningful environment: objects, people, events. How do you arrive at these perceptual conclusions?

Cognitive processes, such as learning and memory, are involved in determining the "meaning" of an object (Logothetis & Sheinberg, 1996). Our learning experiences create a knowledge base from which we can identify and interpret many objects, including those in the photograph at left. But now take a look at the gizmo pictured at the bottom of this page. Even if you have no idea what the object is, the simple fact remains that you perceive it as an object, not as random bits and pieces of sensory information. How do we accomplish these perceptual feats?

A useful way to think about the process of perception is to consider the basic perceptual questions that we must answer in order to survive. We exist in an ever-changing environment that is filled with objects that may be standing still or moving, just like ourselves. Whether it's a brown bear or a bowling ball, we need to be able to identify objects, locate objects in space, and, if they are moving, track their motion. Thus, our perceptual processes must help us organize our sensations to answer three important questions: (1) How far away is the object? (2) Where is it going? and (3) What is it?

Organizing Sensations into Meaningful Perceptions With virtually no conscious effort, the psychological process of perception allows you to integrate, organize, and interpret the lines, colors, and contours in this image as meaningful objects—a laughing child holding a black cat in front of a Christmas tree. How did you reach those perceptual conclusions?

What Is This?

CRITICAL THINKING 3.3

ESP: Can Perception Occur Without Sensation?

ESP, or **extrasensory perception,** is based on the idea that sensory information can be detected by some means other than through the normal processes of sensation. Forms of ESP supposedly include:

- *Telepathy*—direct communication from one mind to another.

- *Clairvoyance*—the perception of a remote object or event.

- *Psychokinesis*—the ability to influence a physical object, process, or event without touching it.

- *Precognition*—the ability to predict future events.

The general term for such unusual abilities is *paranormal phenomena*, meaning that they are "outside the range of normal experience" and thus unexplainable using known laws of science and nature. **Parapsychology** refers to the scientific investigation of claims of various paranormal phenomena. Only a small percentage of psychologists are parapsychologists.

Have you ever felt as if you had just experienced ESP? Consider the following two examples:

- Your sister was supposed to stop by around 7 p.m. It's now 7:15 and you "sense" that something has happened to her. Shortly after 8 o'clock she calls, informing you that she's been involved in a fender-bender. Did you experience clairvoyance?

- Your author Sandy had a vivid dream that our cat Nubbin got lost. The next morning, Nubbin sneaked out the back door, went for an unauthorized stroll in the woods, and was gone for three days. Did Sandy have a precognitive dream?

Such common experiences may be used to "prove" that ESP exists. However, there are two less extraordinary concepts that can explain both occurrences: coincidence and the fallacy of positive instances.

Coincidence is the term that describes an event that occurs simply by chance. For example, you have over a thousand dreams per year, most of which are about familiar people and situations. By mere chance alone, *some* aspect of *some* dream will occasionally correspond with reality.

The *fallacy of positive instances* is our tendency to remember coincidental events that seem to *confirm* our belief about unusual phenomena, but forget all the instances that do not. For example, think of the number of times you've thought something happened to someone but nothing did. Such situations are far more common that their opposite, but we quickly forget about the hunches that are not confirmed

Why do people attribute chance events to ESP? Research has shown that believers in ESP are less likely to accurately estimate the probability of an event occurring by chance alone. Nonbelievers tend to be more realistic about the probability of events being due to a simple coincidence or chance (Blackmore, 1985).

Parapsychologists attempt to study ESP in the laboratory under controlled conditions. Many initially convincing demonstrations of ESP are later shown to be the result of research design problems or the researchers' unintentional cueing of the subject. Occasionally, outright fraud is involved on the part of either the ESP subject or experimenter (Randi, 1982, 1980).

A second problem involves *replication*. To be considered valid, experimental results must be demonstrations that can be replicated or repeated by other scientists under identical laboratory conditions. ESP experiments have been particularly problematic in this regard. To date, replication has not been achieved for *any* parapsychology experiment that claims to show evidence of the existence of ESP (Hyman, 1994; Hansel, 1991; Hoppe, 1988).

However, keep in mind the history of science is filled with examples of phenomena that were initially scoffed at and later found to be real. For example, the pain-relieving effects of acupuncture were initially dismissed by Western scientists as mere "superstition" or the power of "suggestion" (Zusne & Jones, 1989).

So keep an open mind about ESP, but also maintain a healthy sense of scientific skepticism (Kurtz, 1994). It is entirely possible that someday convincing experimental evidence will demonstrate the existence of ESP abilities (see Bem & Honorton, 1994; Hyman, 1994; Bem, 1994). In the final analysis, all psychologists, including those who accept the possibility of ESP, recognize the need for evidence that meets the requirements of the scientific method.

Gestalt psychology
(geh-SHTALT) A school of psychology founded in Germany in the early 1900s that maintained that our sensations are actively processed according to consistent perceptual rules that result in meaningful whole perceptions, or *gestalts*.

In the next few sections, we will look at what psychologists have learned about how we perceptually answer those three questions. Much of our discussion reflects the work of the early **Gestalt psychologists,** a group of German psychologists who investigated the basic rules of perceptual organization in the early 1900s (see Chapter 1). Roughly translated, the German word *Gestalt* means a unified whole. The Gestalt psychologists emphasized that we perceive whole objects or figures (*gestalts*) rather than isolated bits and pieces of sensory information. As you'll see, their pioneering work established many of the basic principles of perception.

Depth Perception:

"How Far Away Is It?"

> *Depth perception refers to the ability to perceive the distance of objects. What are monocular cues and binocular cues, and how do they differ? How is binocular disparity involved in our ability to see three-dimensional images in stereograms?*

You can easily perceive that some objects are close to you and some farther away. The ability to perceive the distance of an object as well as the three-dimensional characteristics of an object is called **depth perception.** We use a variety of different cues to judge the distance of objects.

Monocular Cues

The first visual cues we'll discuss require the use of only one eye. Thus, they are called **monocular cues** ("mono" means "one"). After you've become familiar with these cues, look again at the photograph of the girl with the cat on page 98. Try to identify the monocular cues you used to determine the distance of each object in that photograph.

1. *Relative size.* If two or more objects are assumed to be similar in size, the object that appears larger is perceived as being closer.

2. *Overlap.* When one object partially blocks or obscures the view of another object, the partially blocked object is perceived as being farther away.

3. *Aerial perspective.* Faraway objects often appear hazy or slightly blurred by the atmosphere.

4. *Texture gradient.* As a surface with a distinct texture, such as a gravel road or a carpet, extends into the distance, the details of the surface texture gradually become fuzzy and less clearly defined.

5. *Linear perspective.* Parallel lines seem to meet in the distance. If you stand in the middle of a railroad track and look down the rails, you'll notice that the parallel rails seem to meet in the distance. The closer together the lines appear to be, the greater the perception of distance.

6. *Motion parallax.* When you are moving, you use the speed of passing objects to estimate the distance of the objects. Nearby objects seem to zip by faster than distant objects. While you are riding in a commuter train, for example, houses and parked cars along the tracks seem to whiz by, while the distant downtown skyline seems to move very slowly.

When any of these same cues are used by artists to create the perception of distance or depth in paintings, they are referred to as *pictorial cues.* If you look at the cover of this book, you can see how artist Phoebe Beasley used pictorial cues, like overlap and relative size, to create the perception of depth in her artwork.

Another monocular cue is called *accommodation.* Accommodation utilizes information about changes in the shape of the lens of the eye to help us estimate distance. When you focus on a distant object, the lens is flat. But focusing on a nearby object causes the lens to thicken. The information provided by the muscles controlling the shape of the lens helps us judge

Texture Gradient, Overlap, and Aerial Perspective When you look at a photograph, you rely on monocular cues to gauge the distance of objects depicted. The details of the tall grass are crisp in the foreground, fuzzy in the background, an example of texture gradient. The bushes are perceived as closer than the house they overlap. Finally, the haze of the low hanging cloud blurs the foothills, contributing to the perception of even greater distance. Linear perspective is also evident in the parallel wheel tracks in the grass that seem to converge.

depth perception
The use of visual cues to perceive the distance or three-dimensional characteristics of objects.

monocular cues
(moe-NOCK-you-ler) Distance or depth cues that can be processed by either eye alone.

binocular cues
(by-NOCK-you-ler) Distance or depth cues that require the use of both eyes.

Relative Size and Linear Perspective Several monocular depth cues operate in this photograph, especially relative size. The very small image of the jogger and the decreasing size of the street lamps contribute to the perception of distance. Linear perspective is evident in the apparent convergence of the walkway railings. And aerial perspective contributes to the perception of depth from the hazy background.

Motion Parallax This photograph of waiters passing a tray from one train car to the next captures the visual flavor of motion parallax. Objects that whiz by faster are perceptually judged as being closer, as in the case here of the blurred ground and bushes. Objects that pass by more slowly are judged as being farther away, as conveyed by the clearer details of buildings and more distant objects.

depth. In general, however, we rely more on pictorial cues than on accommodation for depth perception.

Binocular Cues

In contrast to the monocular cues, **binocular cues** for distance or depth perception require information from both eyes. One binocular cue is *convergence*—the degree to which muscles rotate your eyes to focus on an object. The more the eyes converge, or rotate inward, to focus on an object, the greater the strength of the muscle signals, and the closer the object is perceived to be. For example, if you hold a dime about six inches in front of your nose, you'll notice the slight strain on your eye muscles as your eyes converge to focus on the coin. If you hold the dime at arm's length, less convergence is needed. Perceptually, the information provided by these signals from your eye muscles is used to judge the distance of an object.

Another binocular distance cue is *binocular disparity*. Because our eyes are set a couple of inches apart, a slightly different image of an object is cast on the retina of each eye. When the two retinal images are very different, we perceptually interpret the object as being close to us. When the two retinal images are more nearly identical, the object is perceived as being farther away.

Here's a simple example that illustrates how we use binocular disparity to perceive distance. Hold a pencil just in front of your nose. Close your left eye, then your right. These images are quite different—that is, there is a great deal of binocular disparity between them. Thus, we perceive the pencil as being very close. Now focus on another object across the room and look at it with first one eye closed, then the other. These images are much more similar. Because there is less binocular disparity between the two images, the object is perceived as being farther away. Finally, notice that with both eyes open, the two images are fused into one.

A *stereogram* is a picture that uses the principle of binocular disparity to create the perception of a three-dimensional image (Kunoh & Takaoki, 1994). Look at the stereogram shown below. When you first look at the picture, you perceive a two-dimensional picture of leaves. But if you follow the directions in the caption, a hidden, three-dimensional image should appear.

Binocular Disparity and the Perception of Depth in Stereograms This stereogram, *Rustling Hares,* was created by artist Hiroshi Kunoh (1994). To see the three-dimensional image, first hold the picture close to your face. Focus your eyes as though you are looking at an object that is beyond the book and farther away. Without changing your focus, slowly extend your arms and move the picture away from you. The image of the leaves will initially be blurry, then details will come into focus and you should see three rabbits. The three-dimensional images that can be perceived in stereograms occur because of binocular disparity—each eye is presented with slightly different visual information.

The object on page 98 is a liquid fabric softener dispenser for a washing machine.

A stereogram is actually composed of repeating columns of carefully arranged visual information. If you focus as though you were looking at some object that is farther away than the stereogram, the repeating columns of information present a slightly different image to each eye. This disparate visual information then fuses into a single image, enabling you to perceive a three-dimensional image—three rabbits.

The Perception of Motion:
"Where Is It Going?"

The perception of motion involves the integration of information from several sources. What are key sources of information in perceiving movement? What is induced motion? What is stroboscopic motion? How do we use auditory cues to perceive distance and location?

Along with perceiving the distance of stationary objects, we also need to be able to gauge the path of moving objects, whether it's a baseball whizzing through the air, a falling tree branch, or the egg about to roll off the kitchen counter. How do we perceive movement?

As we follow a moving object with our gaze, the image of the object moves across the retina. Our eye muscles make micro-fine movements to keep the object in focus. We also compare the moving object to the background, which is usually stationary. Complex neural pathways in the brain combine information about eye-muscle activity, the changing retinal image, and the contrast of the moving object with its stationary background (Livingstone & Hubel, 1988; Wallach, 1987). The end result? We perceive the object as moving.

Beyond this basic explanation, researchers are still not completely certain how the brain's visual system processes movement (Chun & Cavanagh, 1997). It's known, for example, that some neurons are highly specialized to detect motion in one direction but not the opposite direction. Other neurons are specialized to detect motion at one particular speed, but not faster or slower. Research also shows that different neural pathways in the cerebral cortex process information about the depth of objects, movement, form, and color (see Livingstone & Hubel, 1988).

Psychologically, we tend to make certain assumptions when we perceive movement. For example, we typically assume that the *object* moves while the background or frame remains stationary (see Rock, 1995). Thus, as you visually follow a billiard ball ricocheting around a pool table, you perceive the ball as moving and not the table, which serves as the background.

Because we have a strong tendency to assume that the background is stationary, we sometimes experience an illusion of motion called *induced motion*. Induced motion was first studied by Gestalt psychologist Karl Duncker in the 1920s. Duncker (1929) had subjects sit in a darkened room and look at a luminous dot that was surrounded by a larger luminous rectangular frame. When the *frame* slowly moved to the right, the subjects perceived the *dot* as moving to the left. The dot, of course, had not moved.

Why did subjects perceive the dot as moving? Perceptually, Duncker's subjects expected to see the smaller dot move within the larger rectangular frame, not the other way around. Or perhaps you've had an experience similar to the one we had recently: We were sitting in a plane that was parked at the gate. As we waited for the plane to leave the gate, a large delivery truck just outside our plane window began slowly backing up. Because of the phenomenon of induced motion, we perceived the *plane* to be moving, rather than the delivery truck.

Stroboscopic Motion and Movies The perception of smooth movements in a motion picture is due to stroboscopic motion. Much like this series of still photographs of a gymnast performing a front flip, a motion picture is actually a series of static photographs that are projected on the screen at the rate of 24 frames per second, producing the illusion of smooth motion.

Another illusion of motion is called *stroboscopic motion*. First studied by Gestalt psychologist Max Wertheimer in the early 1900s, stroboscopic motion creates a compelling illusion of movement with two carefully timed flashing lights (Wertheimer, 1912). A light briefly flashes at one location, followed about a tenth of second later by another light briefly flashing at a second location. If the time interval and distance between the two flashing lights are just right, a very compelling illusion of movement is created.

What causes the perception of stroboscopic motion? Although different theories have been proposed, researchers aren't completely sure (Henderson, 1997). The perception of motion typically involves the movement of an image across the retina. However, during stroboscopic motion the image does *not* move across the surface of the retina. Rather, the two different flashing lights are detected at two different points on the surface of the retina. Somehow the brain's visual system combines this rapid sequence of visual information to arrive at the perceptual conclusion of motion, even though no movement has actually occurred.

We also use *auditory* information to judge distance and direction. Much as we can use information from one or both eyes in perceiving the distance of an object, we can use information from one or both ears to detect the distance of a sound. If you use only one ear, the louder the sound, the closer it is perceived to be.

Using both ears allows us to more accurately locate the direction as well as the distance of a sound (Konishi, 1993). When a sound is directly to your left, the sound wave reaches your left ear a few thousandths of a second before it reaches your right ear. Because your left ear is closer to the source, the sound it detects is also slightly louder. Your brain calculates these differences in time lag and loudness, quickly perceiving that the source of the sound is to your left (Phillips & Brugge, 1985).

The Perception of Shape:
"What Is It?"

> To identify an object, we rely primarily on its shape. What is the figure–ground relationship? What perceptual principles do we follow when we group different visual elements together?

We rely primarily on an object's *shape* to identify it. This tendency is evident at a very early age and becomes even more pronounced as we get older (Landau & Jackendoff, 1993).

A clever series of experiments demonstrated the importance of shape in object identification (see Landau, 1994; Landau & Jackendoff, 1993). Three-year-olds were shown a blue, wooden object like the one depicted in Figure 3.11a. The experimenter told the children that the object was a "dax." Then the children were shown a variety of other objects, like the ones depicted in

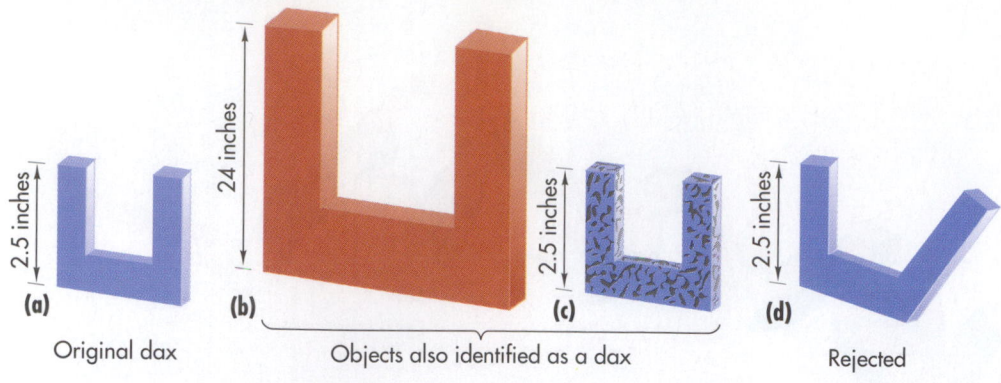

(a) Original dax

(b) **(c)** Objects also identified as a dax

(d) Rejected

FIGURE 3.11 The "Dax" Experiment

Figure 3.11b, c, and d. Some objects had the same shape as the dax, but were made of different materials or were a different color or size. Other objects were identical to the original dax in every way except that they were shaped a little differently. The experimenter asked the children which of these objects was a dax. It turned out that as long as the object had the same *shape* as the original dax, the children identified it as a dax.

FIGURE 3.12 **A Classic Example of Figure–Ground Reversal**
Figure–ground reversals illustrate the psychological nature of our ability to perceptually sort a scene into the main element and the background. With a little psychological effort, it is possible to perceive either the faces or the vase as the main element.

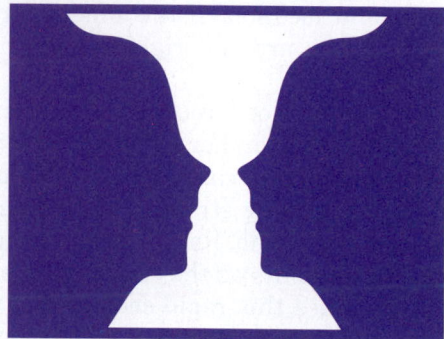

Figure–Ground Relationship

Whether we focus on a "dax," a duck, or some other object, how do we organize our perceptions so that we see the object as separate from other objects? The early Gestalt psychologists established an important perceptual principle called the **figure–ground relationship.** This term refers to the fact that when we view a scene, we automatically separate the elements of that scene into the *figure*, which is the main element of the scene, and the *ground,* which is its background. Usually the "figure" has a definite shape, tends to stand out clearly, and is perceptually meaningful in some way. In contrast, the "ground" tends to be less clearly defined, even fuzzy, and it usually appears to be behind and farther away than the figure.

The separation of a scene into figure and ground is not really a property of the actual elements of the scene we're looking at. Rather, our ability to separate a scene into figure and ground is a psychological accomplishment. To illustrate, look at the classic example shown in Figure 3.12. Depending upon whether you see the dark area or the white area as the "figure," you'll either perceive faces or a vase. The perception of an image in two different ways like this is called a *figure–ground reversal.*

figure–ground relationship
A Gestalt principle of perceptual organization that states that we automatically separate the elements of a perception into the feature that clearly stands out (the figure) and its less distinct background (the ground).

Figure–Ground Reversal in Art The Dutch artist M. C. Escher (1898–1972) is perhaps best known for creating complex visual puzzles. In *Winged Lion,* Escher uses figure–ground reversal to create a compelling image. Even if you look carefully at the picture, it is difficult to perceive the black and gold lions simultaneously. Escher was fascinated by the "psychological tension" created by such images (Schattschneider, 1990).

(a) The Law of Similarity

(b) The Law of Closure

(c) The Law of Good Continuation

(d) The Law of Proximity

FIGURE 3.13 The Gestalt Principles of Organization

The Gestalt psychologists formulated several basic principles of perceptual organization, which are illustrated above. We tend to follow these principles in grouping elements together to arrive at the perception of shapes, forms, and figures. **(a)** The Law of Similarity is the tendency to perceive objects of similar size, shape, or color as a unit or a figure. Thus, you perceive four horizontal rows of holiday cookies rather than six vertical columns of cookies. **(b)** The Law of Closure is the tendency to fill in the gaps or contours in an incomplete image. Thus, you perceive the two circles on the face of the clock as smooth, continuous circles, even though the curved lines are actually interrupted by the hands of the clock, the hands of the person, and the edge of the photograph. **(c)** The Law of Good Continuation is the tendency to group elements that appear to follow in the same direction as a single unit or figure. In this image, good continuation is reflected in the strong tendency to perceptually identify the straight sections of highway as continuous units, and the curved sections of highway as continuous units. **(d)** The Law of Proximity is the tendency to perceive objects that are close to one another as a unit or a figure. Thus, you perceive these six people as two groups of three.

The Perceptual Urge to Organize As you scan this image, you'll experience firsthand the strong psychological tendency to organize visual elements to arrive at the perception of whole figures, forms, and shapes. Notice that as you shift your gaze across the pattern, you momentarily perceive circles, squares, and other geometric forms.

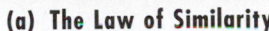

Perceptual Grouping

Many of the forms that we perceive are composed of a number of different elements that seem to "go together" (Prinzmetal, 1995). It would be more accurate to say that we actively organize the elements to try to produce the stable perception of well-defined, whole objects. This is what perceptual psychologist Stanley Coren (Coren & others, 1994) refers to as "the urge to organize." What sort of principles do we follow when we try to organize visual elements?

The Gestalt psychologists studied how the perception of visual elements becomes organized into patterns, shapes, and forms. They identified several "laws" or principles that we tend to follow in grouping elements together to arrive at the perception of forms, shapes, and figures. Examples of these perceptual laws are shown in Figure 3.13.

The Gestalt psychologists also formulated a general principle called the *law of Prägnanz,* or the *law of simplicity.* This law states that when several perceptual organizations of an assortment of visual elements are possible, the perceptual interpretation that will occur will be the one that produces the "best, simplest, and most stable shape" (Koffka, 1935). To illustrate, consider Figure 3.14. If you are following the law of Prägnanz, you perceptually organized the elements in the most cognitively efficient and simple way, perceiving them as three overlapping squares.

FIGURE 3.14 What Do You See?

The law of simplicity is our tendency to efficiently organize the visual elements of a scene in a way that produces the simplest and most stable forms or objects. You probably perceived the image as that of three overlapping squares rather than as two six-sided objects and one four-sided object.

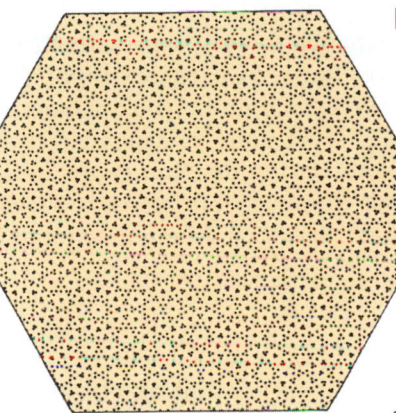

The law of Prägnanz encompasses all the other Gestalt principles, including the figure–ground relationship. The implication of the law of Prägnanz is that our perceptual system works in an economical way to promote the interpretation of stable and consistent forms. The ability to efficiently organize elements into stable objects helps us to perceive the world accurately. In effect, we actively and automatically construct a perception that reveals "the essence of something," which is roughly what the German word *Prägnanz* means (Coren & others, 1994).

Perceptual Constancies

Perceptual constancy refers to the tendency to perceive objects as unchanging despite changes in sensory input. What principles guide our perceptions of size constancy? What are shape constancy and brightness constancy?

Consider this scenario. As you're driving on a flat stretch of highway, a red van zips past you and speeds far ahead. As the distance between you and the van grows, its image becomes progressively smaller until the van is no more than a dot on the horizon. Yet, even though the image of the van on our retinas has become progressively smaller, we don't perceive the van as shrinking or changing color. Instead, we perceive its shape, size, and brightness to be unchanged.

This tendency to perceive objects, especially familiar objects, as constant and unchanging despite changes in sensory input is called **perceptual constancy.** Without this perceptual ability, our perception of reality would be in a constant state of flux. If we simply responded to retinal images, our perceptions of objects would continually change as lighting, viewing angle, and distance from the object changed from moment to moment. Instead, the various forms of perceptual constancy promote a stable view of the world.

Size Constancy

Size constancy is the perception that an object remains the same size despite its changing image on the retina. When our distance from an object changes, the image of the object that is cast on the retinas of our eyes also changes, yet we still perceive it to be the same size. The red van example reflects the perception of size constancy. As the distance between you and the red van increased, the van's retinal image gets progressively smaller. But your brain automatically adjusts your perception of an object's size by combining information about retinal image size and distance.

An important principle of size constancy is that if the retinal image of an object does *not* change but the perception of its distance *increases,* we will perceive an object as larger. That's not as complicated as it sounds. It's also easy to demonstrate. Stare at a 75-watt lightbulb for about ten seconds. Then focus on a bright, distant wall. You should see an afterimage of the lightbulb on the wall that will look several times larger than the original lightbulb. Why? When you looked at the wall, the lingering afterimage of the lightbulb on your retina remained constant but your perception of distance increased. When your brain combined and interpreted this information, your perception of the lightbulb's size increased. Remember this demonstration, as we'll mention it again when we explain how some perceptual illusions occur.

perceptual constancy
The tendency to perceive objects, especially familiar objects, as constant and unchanging despite changes in sensory input.

size constancy
The perception of an object as maintaining the same size despite changing images on the retina.

shape constancy
The perception of a familiar object as maintaining the same shape regardless of the image produced on the retina.

brightness constancy
The perception that the brightness of an object remains the same even though the lighting conditions change.

perceptual set
The influence of prior assumptions and expectations on perceptual interpretations.

Shape Constancy Each door in the photograph is positioned at a different angle and thus produces a differently shaped image on your retinas. Nevertheless, because of the perceptual principle of shape constancy, you easily identify all five objects as rectangular doors.

Shape and Brightness Constancy

Shape constancy is the tendency to perceive familiar objects as having a fixed shape regardless of the image they cast on our retinas. You can easily demonstrate shape constancy by viewing any familiar object, such as a table or a compact disc, from different angles. Your perception of the object's shape, whether it is rectangular or round, remains constant despite changes in your viewing orientation.

Another kind of perceptual constancy is **brightness constancy,** in which the perceived brightness of an object seems to stay the same even though the lighting conditions change. The white sheet on a bed is perceived as equally bright whether seen in full sunlight or in the dim light of a night light. The perception of brightness constancy occurs because objects always reflect the same *proportion* of available light, even if the lighting conditions change dramatically.

Factors That Influence Perceptual Interpretations

> *Perceptions can be influenced by experience, learning, expectations, and culture. What is perceptual set? What is a perceptual illusion? How can the Müller-Lyer illusion and the moon illusion be explained?*

Our perceptual processes are largely automatic and unconscious. On the one hand, this arrangement is very mentally efficient. With a minimum of cognitive effort, we decipher our surroundings, answering important perceptual questions and making sense of the environment. On the other hand, because perceptual processing is largely automatic, we can inadvertently arrive at the wrong perceptual conclusion.

Perceptual Set

In the broadest sense, our educational, cultural, and life experiences shape what we perceive. Past experience often predisposes us to perceive a situation in a particular way, even though other perceptions are possible. Consider the recent experience of one of our students. As he was driving home late at night, he stopped at a convenience store to buy a pack of cigarettes. Standing at the counter and rummaging through his wallet for some cash, he requested "a pack of Nows." When he looked up, the young female clerk had put a copy of *Penthouse* on the counter. Obviously, the clerk perceived what she had expected to hear.

Visitors From Another Planet? Perceptual set may lead the avid believer in UFOs to see this photograph of unusual cloud formations as evidence for the existence of flying saucers. Then again, take another look at the photo on page 98. Your perceptual set might also lead you to believe that these white shapes were really fabric softener dispensers flying through the air.

This example illustrates the notion of **perceptual set**—the expectancies and predispositions that the observer brings to a perceptual situation. We're often mentally primed to interpret a particular perception a particular way. Our perceptual sets are, of course, influenced by our prior learning experiences. To use an example discussed in an earlier section, an oddly shaped piece of wood might be a "dax" to one child and simply an oddly shaped piece of wood to another child.

perceptual illusion
The misperception of the true characteristics of an object or an image.

Müller-Lyer illusion
A famous visual illusion involving the misperception of the identical length of two lines, one with arrows pointed inward, one with arrows pointed outward.

FIGURE 3.15   The Müller-Lyer Illusion
Compare the two photographs. Which corner line is longer? Now compare the two line drawings. Which center line is longer? In reality, the center lines in the photographs and the line drawings are all exactly the same length, which you can prove to yourself with a ruler.

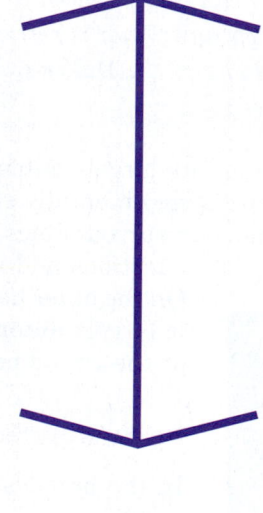

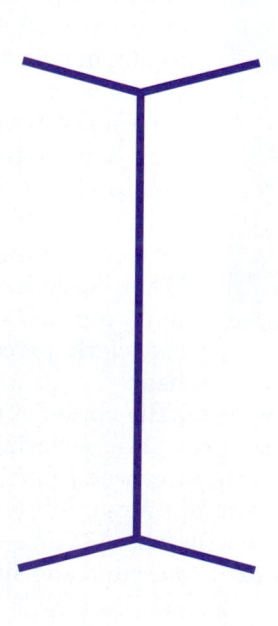

Perceptual sets can exert a strong influence on the perceptual conclusions we reach. Our perceptual sets usually lead us to reasonably accurate conclusions. If they didn't, we would develop new perceptual sets that were more accurate. But sometimes a perceptual set can lead us astray. For example, when the partially decomposed body of a large, hairy creature was discovered in upper New York state, it generated much excitement because the remains were perceived by several people as proof of the existence of "Bigfoot" (Hines, 1988). Scientists operating with a different perceptual set examined the dead creature and duly proclaimed it for what it was—the remains of a brown bear.

Similar examples of erroneous perceptual set have occurred with supposed "sightings" of UFOs, the Loch Ness monster, mermaids, and ghosts. In each case, observers interpreted ambiguous stimuli in terms of the perceptual set they held in that situation and saw what their expectations led them to see.

Perceptual Illusions

The largely automatic nature of perceptual processing can also lead to another kind of misperception. A **perceptual illusion** can occur when we misperceive the true characteristics or properties of an illusion. The visual contradictions of perceptual illusions are fascinating, but they also shed light on how normal perceptual processes guide us to perceptual conclusions. Given the basics of perception that we've covered thus far, you're in a good position to understand two of the most famous perceptual illusions: the Müller-Lyer illusion and the moon illusion.

The Müller-Lyer Illusion   Look at the center line in each of the two photographs in Figure 3.15. Which line is longer? If you said the one in the bottom photo, then you just experienced the **Müller-Lyer illusion.** In fact, the two center lines are the same length, even though they *appear* very different in length. If you measure the corner line in each photograph, you'll confirm that they are the same length. The same illusion occurs when you look at a simple drawing of the Müller-Lyer illusion, which is also shown in Figure 3.15.

Part of what contributes to the Müller-Lyer illusion are the arrows, which are visual depth cues that promote the perception that the bottom line is *farther* from us (Rock, 1995; Gregory, 1968). When you look at the bottom photograph, the center line is that of a wall jutting away from you. When you look at the bottom part of the drawing of the Müller-Lyer illusion, the outward-pointing arrows create much the same visual effect—a corner jutting away from you. In the top photograph and line drawing, visual depth cues promote the perception of *lesser* distance—a corner that is jutting toward you. Try covering the arrows with paper, and you'll see that the illusion evaporates.

Size constancy also seems to play an important role in the Müller-Lyer illusion (see Coren & others, 1994). Because they are the same length, the center lines pro-

moon illusion
A visual illusion involving the misperception that the moon is larger when it is on the horizon than when it is directly overhead.

duce retinal images that are the same size. However, we noted in our earlier discussion of size constancy that if the retinal size of an object stays the same but the perception of its distance increases, we will perceive the object as larger. Previously, we demonstrated this with the afterimage of a lightbulb that seemed much larger when viewed against a distant wall.

The same basic principle seems to occur with the Müller-Lyer illusion. Although the two corner lines produce retinal images that are the same size, the bottom corner line is embedded in visual depth cues that make us perceive it as farther away. Hence, we perceive the bottom corner line as longer, just as you perceived the afterimage of the lightbulb as larger when viewed on a distant wall.

The Moon Illusion Another famous illusion is one that you've probably experienced firsthand: the **moon illusion,** shown in Figure 3.16. When a full moon is rising on a clear dark night, it appears much larger when viewed on the horizon against buildings and trees than it does in the night sky overhead. But the moon, of course, doesn't shrink as it rises. The fact of the matter is that *the retinal size of the full moon is the same in all positions*. Still, if you've ever watched the moon rise from the horizon to the night sky, it does *appear* to shrink in size. What causes this illusion?

Part of the explanation has to do with how far away we perceive objects to be at different locations in the sky (see Rock, 1995; Kaufman & Rock, 1989). Put simply, researchers have found that people perceive objects on the horizon as farther away than objects that are directly overhead in the sky. The horizon contains many familiar distance cues, such as faraway buildings, trees, and the "smoothing" of the texture of the landscape as it fades into the distance. Of course, the moon on the horizon is perceived as being *behind* these depth cues. The depth-perception cue of overlap adds to the perception that the moon on the horizon is farther away.

The moon illusion also involves the misapplication of size constancy, much like the explanation for our perception of the afterimage of a glowing lightbulb as larger when it is viewed against a distant wall. Remember, the retinal image of the moon is the *same* in all locations, just like the afterimage of the lightbulb. Thus, even though the retinal image of the moon remains constant, we perceive the moon as larger because it seems farther away on the horizon.

FIGURE 3.16 The Moon Illusion When viewed on the horizon, the moon appears considerably larger than when it is viewed higher in the sky. Why does the moon illusion occur?

If you look at a full moon on the horizon through a cardboard tube, you'll remove the distance cues provided by the horizon. When you do this, the size of the moon on the horizon will rapidly shrink—and look the same size as it does when directly overhead.

Perceptual illusions like the moon illusion and the Müller-Lyer illusion underscore the fact that what we see is *not* merely a simple reflection of the world, but rather our subjective perceptual interpretation of it. Suppose you showed the Müller-Lyer illusion to a friend or relative. Do you think they would perceive the illusion in the same way as you do—that one line is significantly longer than the other? Do you think people from *any* culture would be equally susceptible to the Müller-Lyer illusion? These questions reflect a longstanding debate on whether perceptual principles are universal or vary from one culture to the next (see Culture and Human Behavior Box 3.4).

We actively construct perceptual conclusions about the information detected through our senses. In arriving at those perceptual conclusions, we are guided by well-established perceptual principles, such as the cues that typically indicate distance, movement, and form.

The illusions, photographs, and other perceptual demonstrations we've looked at in the second half of this chapter clearly illustrate the fundamental difference between sensation and perception. Through our senses we detect different forms of energy—light waves, sound waves, airborne chemicals, pressure, and so on. But it is the brain that integrates and interprets that information, giving it a meaning that is a reasonably accurate reflection of the physical world.

CONCEPT REVIEW 3.5

Perceptual Principles

Fill in the blanks using the correct terms from this list: perceptual set; closure; similarity; figure; shape constancy; ground; size constancy; proximity; stroboscopic motion; brightness constancy; good continuation.

1. When Jenny was flying to the South Pacific she saw several lush green islands that stood out in a sea of bright blue. In this example the islands are the _____ and the sea is the _____ .

2. As you watch four-year-year Jason cling to his horse on a turning Merry-Go-Round, you perceive Jason's form as being continuous and unchanging despite the different images that are cast on the retinas of your eyes. This perceptual tendency is called _____ .

3. As the football is hurtling toward you, it creates a progressively larger image on your retina, and the angle of the ball is constantly changing. Despite these drastic changes in sensory input, the joint phenomena of _____ and _____ enable you to continue to perceive the object as a football.

4. •••• •••• •••• If you followed the law of _____ , you perceived this arrangement as three groups of four dots.

5. ○○○○•••○○○○••• If you followed the law of _____ , you perceived this arrangement as two groups of four circles and two groups of four dots.

6. Hundreds of people flocked to an Indiana town when it was reported that the face of a religious figure appeared in a rust stain on the side of a water tower. This perception was probably an example of _____ .

CULTURE AND HUMAN BEHAVIOR 3.4

Culture and Visual Illusions

The Gestalt psychologists believed that the rules of perception reflected the way the human perceptual system was "hard-wired" in the brain (see Segall, 1994; Hilgard, 1987). This view is called the *nativist* position, because it argues that perceptual processes are inborn. According to the nativists, people everywhere, whatever their background, "see" the world in the same way because they share the same perceptual rules.

On the other side of the debate were psychologists and others who advocated the *empiricist* position. The empiricists believed that perception is strongly influenced by experience, including cultural experience. According to this perspective, people actively construct their perceptions, drawing on their prior learning experiences to arrive at perceptual conclusions. As cross-cultural psychologist Marshall Segall (1994) summarizes this view, "Every perception is the result of an interaction between a stimulus and a perceiver shaped by prior experience." Thus, people from very different backgrounds might well perceive the world differently.

Because visual illusions are ambiguous figures that can be interpreted in more than one way, psychologists believed that illusions could be useful in investigating whether perceptual principles are universal or culture-specific. According to the nativists, the response to illusions should be universal. According to the empiricists, cross-cultural differences might influence susceptibility to specific illusions.

Of all the illusions, the Müller-Lyer has been studied most extensively (see Figure 3.15). Since the early 1900s, it has been known that people in industrialized societies are far more susceptible to the Müller-Lyer illusion than people in some nonindustrialized societies (see Matsumoto, 1994). Segall and his colleagues (1963, 1966) proposed

that this difference might be due to different perceptual experiences.

More specifically, Segall proposed *the carpentered-world hypothesis*: the idea that people living in urban, industrialized environments have a great deal of perceptual experience in judging lines, corners, edges, and other rectangular, manufactured objects. Thus, people in "carpentered" cultures would be more susceptible to the Müller-Lyer illusion. (Remember, the Müller-Lyer illusion seems to occur because the arrows mimic a corner that is jutting toward or away from the perceiver.)

In contrast, people who live in very "*non*-carpentered" cultures more frequently encounter natural objects. In these cultures, perceptual experiences with straight lines and right angles are relatively rare. In these cultures, Segall predicted, people would be less susceptible to the Müller-Lyer illusion.

To test this idea, Segall and his colleagues (1963, 1966) compared the responses of people in "carpentered" societies, such as Evanston, Illinois, with those of people living in "non-carpentered" societies, such as African tribes living in remote areas. The results confirmed their hypothesis. The Müller-Lyer illusion was stronger for those living in carpentered than non-carpentered societies. The findings provided strong support for the idea that culture could influence perception.

However, the nativists were quick to suggest that Segall's results might be due to racial differences rather than cultural differences. After all, they pointed out, the non-Western subjects in Segall's research were mostly Africans, and racial differences in eye pigmentation had been shown to affect the ability to visually detect contours (see Segall, 1994). Could the difference in illusion susceptibility be due to some sort of physiological difference rather than a cultural difference?

To address that issue, psychologist V. M. Stewart (1973) compared groups of African-American and white schoolchildren living in the "carpentered" society of Evanston, Illinois. Stewart found that, regardless of their race, the Evanston children were equally susceptible to the Müller-Lyer illusion. She then compared groups of black African children in five different areas of Zambia—ranging from the very "carpentered" capital city of Lusaka to very rural, "non-carpentered" areas of the country.

The results of this second comparison? The African children living in the "carpentered" society of Lusaka were just as susceptible to the illusion as the white and African-American children in Evanston. And the children living in the rural, non-carpentered countryside were far less susceptible. In other words, the children's race made *no* difference at all. What mattered was the children's experience, or lack of experience, with a carpentered environment.

The Müller-Lyer illusion has played a key role in the debate about whether perceptual processes are universal and inborn or are influenced by learning experiences. Clearly, the evidence supports the latter conclusion, emphasizing once again the important role of culture and learning.

APPLICATION

Controlling Pain

Pain is the body's way of indicating that something is wrong. Fortunately, there are several strategies for controlling pain. Each of the following simple self-administered techniques can be useful for dealing with the everyday pain of a headache, an injury, or a trip to the dentist. Of course the techniques described here are *not* a substitute for seeking appropriate medical attention, especially when pain is severe, recurring, or of unknown origins.

1. Distraction. By actively focusing your attention on some nonpainful stimulus, you can often reduce pain (Turk & Nash, 1993; Fernandez, 1986). For example, you can mentally count backward by 7s from 901; multiply pairs of two-digit numbers, such as 14×23; mentally draw different geometric figures, such as a circle with a triangle in it; count ceiling tiles; or sing "The Star Spangled Banner." You can also stare at the details of a picture or another object, or intently listen to music.

2. Imagery. One form of distraction is *imagery.* Creating a vivid mental image can help control pain or other unpleasant physical symptoms (Rossman, 1993). Usually people create a pleasant and progressive scenario, such as walking along the beach, hiking in the mountains, or enjoying a gathering of friends. Aggressive or arousing imagery can also be useful, such as imagining a heated argument, fighting off an enemy, or driving a race car at high speeds (Lyles & others, 1982). Whatever imaginary scenario you use, try to visualize all the different sensations involved, including the sights, sounds, aromas, touches, and tastes. The goal is to become so absorbed in your fantasy that you distract yourself from the pain sensations.

3. Positive Self-Talk. This strategy involves making positive coping statements, either silently or out loud, during a painful episode or procedure (Cioffi & Holloway, 1993; Fernandez, 1986). Examples of positive self-talk include statements such as "It hurts but I'm okay, I'm in control"; "I'm uncomfortable, but I can handle it"; "The pain is uncomfortable but not unbearable"; and "I can tolerate anything for five minutes."

Such self-talk can also include *redefining the pain.* By using realistic and constructive thoughts about the pain experience in place of threatening or harmful thoughts, you can minimize pain (McCaul & Malott, 1984). For example, an athlete in training might say, "The pain means my muscles are getting stronger." Someone wearing orthodontic braces might tell himself that the pain means that his teeth are moving into place; a woman during childbirth might redefine the painful contractions of labor as work or effort.

4. Counter-irritation. The technique of counter-irritation has been used for centuries. *Counter-irritation* involves decreasing pain by creating a strong, competing sensation that's mildly stimulating or irritating (Sarafino, 1994). People often do this naturally, as when they vigorously rub an injury or bite their lip during an injection. How does rubbing the area where an injury has occurred reduce pain? The intense sensations of pain and the normal sensations of touch are processed through different nerve fibers going to the spinal cord. Increasing normal sensations of touch interferes with the transmission of high-intensity pain signals (Coren & others, 1994).

Other possible counter-irritation strategies include scratching, massaging, or applying very cold water, ice packs, or heat. While undergoing a painful procedure, you can create and control a competing discomfort by pressing your thumbnail into your index finger. Focusing your attention on the competing discomfort may lessen your overall experience of pain.

5. Relaxation. Deep relaxation can be a very effective strategy for deterring pain sensations (Turk & Nash, 1993; Benson, 1993). Relaxation procedures can be used in a particular situation or repeatedly practiced during prolonged pain. One simple strategy to achieve relaxation is *deep breathing:* inhale deeply, then exhale very slowly and completely, releasing tension throughout your body, especially in your neck, shoulders, and chest. As you exhale, consciously note the feelings of relaxation and warmth you've produced in your body (Turk & others, 1983).

Beyond these self-administered strategies, pain specialists use a variety of techniques to control pain, including painkilling drugs and hypnosis. Both of these topics will be discussed in the next chapter. Another strategy is biofeedback. *Biofeedback* is a process of learning voluntary control over largely automatic body functions such as heartbeat, blood pressure, and muscle tension. Using sensitive equipment that signals subtle changes in a specific body function, an individual can learn to become more aware of body signals and exercise conscious control over a particular body process. For example, an individual who experiences chronic tension headaches might use biofeedback to learn to relax shoulder, neck, and facial muscles. Biofeedback has proven to be effective in helping many people who experience tension headaches, migraine headaches, jaw pain, and back pain (M.S. Schwartz & N.M. Schwartz, 1993).

Summary

Sensation and Perception

Sensation and Perception

- *Sensation* refers to the response of sensory receptors in the sense organs to stimulation and the transmission of that information to the brain.

- *Perception* refers to the process through which the brain organizes and interprets sensory information.

- Sensation is the result of the stimulation of sensory receptors by some form of energy. Through the process of transduction, this energy is converted and coded into neural impulses, and then sent to the brain.

- Each sense is specialized in terms of the form of energy to which it will respond. The senses are also responsive only to particular levels of stimulation, called sensory thresholds. Two types of sensory thresholds are the absolute threshold and the difference threshold, or just noticeable difference (jnd). Weber's Law states that the just noticeable difference will vary depending on the strength of the original stimulus.

- Sensory adaptation takes place when the sensory receptor cells gradually decline in sensitivity to a constant stimulus.

Vision: From Light to Sight

- The sensory receptors for vision respond to light waves. Visible light is only a tiny part of the electromagnetic energy spectrum, which is described in terms of wavelength.

- Light waves enter the eye and pass through the cornea, pupil, and lens, which focuses the light on the retina. The retina contains the sensory receptors for vision, the rods and cones.

- Rods are specialized for vision in dim light; cones for color vision and for vision in bright light. Cones adapt quickly to bright light, while rods adapt slowly to dim light. We rely on the rods for peripheral vision and on the cones for seeing fine detail.

- The rods and cones send information to the bipolar and ganglion cells, where it undergoes preliminary processing before being sent to the brain via the optic nerve. There is a much smaller ratio of cones than rods to ganglion cells; thus, cones are important to visual acuity. Cones are concentrated in the fovea. The optic nerve transmits information to the thalamus. From the thalamus, information is sent to the visual cortex. There are no rods or cones in the blind spot, which is where the optic nerve exits the eye.

- Color is the psychological experience of different wavelengths of light and involves hue, brightness, and saturation. White light contains all the wavelengths of the visible spectrum. The color of an object is determined by the light wave it reflects.

- In combination, the trichromatic theory and the opponent-process theory explain color vision. Trichromatic theory explains red-green color blindness and color processing in the retina; opponent-process theory explains afterimages and color processing in the ganglion cells and the brain.

Hearing: From Vibration to Sound

- Sound waves are the physical stimuli that produce the sensation of sound. The amplitude, frequency, and complexity of a sound wave determine the loudness, pitch, and timbre of the sound that we hear.

- Sound waves are collected in the outer ear, amplified in the middle ear, and transduced in the inner ear. The sensory receptors for hearing are the hair cells, which are located on the basilar membrane in the cochlea. In combination, frequency theory and place theory explain the sensation of pitch.

The Chemical and Body Senses: Smell, Taste, Touch, and Position

- The sensory receptors for smell and taste are specialized to respond to chemical substances. The sensation of smell is caused by airborne molecules stimulating odor receptors that are located on the olfactory receptor cells in the lining of the nose; information is transmitted directly to the olfactory bulb in the brain via the olfactory nerve.

- Taste results from the stimulation of sensory receptors in the taste buds, which are located on the tongue and the inside of the mouth. When activated by chemical substances dissolved in saliva, the taste buds send neural messages to the thalamus in the brain. There are four primary tastes: sweet, salty, sour, and bitter.

- The skin and body senses provide important information about the body and include the senses of touch, temperature, pain, movement, position, and balance.

- The skin includes several kinds of sensory receptors, which are unevenly distributed among the parts of the body. The Pacinian corpuscle is the skin receptor that is sensitive to pressure.

- Pain sensation is partly explained by the gate-control theory. Pain sensations also result from the release of a neurotransmitter called substance P. Psychological factors are involved in the experience of pain. The transmission of pain signals is inhibited by the release of endorphins, which can also be influenced by psychological factors.

- The kinesthetic sense involves the location and position of body parts in relation to one another. The sensory receptors for the kinesthetic sense are the proprioceptors, which are located in the muscles and joints. The sense of balance, equilibrium, and orientation is due to the vestibular sense. The vestibular sensory receptors are located in the semicircular canals and the vestibular sacs in the inner ear.

Perception

▪ Perception refers to the process of integrating, organizing, and interpreting sensory information in a meaningful way. Our perceptual processes help us answer important questions about objects in the environment. The Gestalt psychologists studied perception in the early twentieth century, emphasizing the perception of *gestalts,* or whole forms.

▪ Depth perception refers to the perception of the distance of an object or its three-dimensional characteristics. Monocular depth cues include relative size, overlap, aerial perspective, texture gradient, linear perspective, motion parallax, and accommodation. Binocular depth cues include convergence and binocular disparity.

▪ The perception of movement involves integrating information from the eye muscles, the retina, and the environment. The illusion of induced motion is a result of our assumption that the background is stationary. The perception of stroboscopic motion results from images being rapidly registered on the retina. We also use auditory cues to judge the distance and direction of an object.

▪ We rely primarily on shape to identify an object. Figure–ground relationships are important in distinguishing an object from its background.

▪ We actively organize visual information and group different visual elements together. The Gestalt principles of organization include proximity, similarity, closure, good continuation, and the law of Prägnanz.

▪ Perceptual constancy refers to the tendency to perceive objects as unchanging despite changes in sensory input and retinal image. Size constancy, shape constancy, and brightness constancy are three important forms of perceptual constancy. Size constancy results from the combination of information about the size of the retinal image and about the distance of the object. When the retinal image does not change but the perception of distance increases, the object is perceived as larger.

▪ Perception can be influenced by learning experiences. *Perceptual set* refers to the expectations that people bring to a situation, which can affect their interpretation of the situation.

▪ Perceptual illusions can be used to study perceptual principles. The Müller-Lyer illusion involves the principles of depth cues and size constancy. The moon illusion results from the principles of overlap and depth cues.

Key Terms

sensation (p. 76)

perception (p. 76)

sensory receptors (p. 77)

transduction (p. 77)

sensory threshold (p. 78)

absolute threshold (p. 78)

difference threshold (p. 78)

just noticeable difference (jnd) (p. 78)

Weber's Law (p. 78)

sensory adaptation (p. 79)

wavelength (p. 80)

cornea (p. 81)

pupil (p. 81)

iris (p. 81)

lens (p. 81)

accommodation (p. 81)

iridology (p. 82)

retina (p. 82)

rods (p. 82)

cones (p. 82)

fovea (p. 83)

optic nerve (p. 84)

blind spot (p. 84)

color (p. 85)

hue (p. 85)

saturation (p. 85)

brightness (p. 85)

trichromatic theory of color vision (p. 86)

color blindness (p. 86)

afterimage (p. 86)

opponent-process theory of color vision (p. 86)

audition (p. 88)

loudness (p. 88)

amplitude (p. 88)

decibel (p. 88)

pitch (p. 89)

frequency (p. 89)

timbre (p. 89)

outer ear (p. 90)

eardrum (p. 90)

middle ear (p. 90)

inner ear (p. 91)

cochlea (p. 91)

basilar membrane (p. 91)

hair cells (p. 91)

frequency theory (p. 91)

place theory (p. 91)

olfactory bulb (p. 93)

pheromones (p. 94)

taste buds (p. 95)

pain (p. 96)

gate-control theory (p. 96)

substance P (p. 96)

kinesthetic sense (p. 97)

vestibular sense (p. 97)

Gestalt psychology (p. 99)

ESP (extrasensory perception) (p. 99)

parapsychology (p. 99)

depth perception (p. 100)

monocular cues (p. 100)

binocular cues (p. 101)

figure–ground relationship (p. 104)

perceptual constancy (p. 106)

size constancy (p. 106)

shape constancy (p. 107)

brightness constancy (p. 107)

perceptual set (p. 107)

perceptual illusion (p. 108)

Müller-Lyer illusion (p. 108)

moon illusion (p. 109)

CONCEPT REVIEW 3.1 Page 79

1. a
2. d
3. a
4. c

CONCEPT REVIEW 3.2 Page 88

1. retina
2. cones
3. optic nerve
4. white
5. trichromatic
6. yellow; opponent-process

CONCEPT REVIEW 3.3 Page 92

1. pitch; loudness
2. basilar; cochlea
3. frequency
4. place

CONCEPT REVIEW 3.4 Page 98

1. kinesthetic
2. vestibular
3. olfactory nerve; olfactory bulb
4. substance P

CONCEPT REVIEW 3.5 Page 110

1. figure; ground
2. shape constancy
3. size constancy; shape constancy
4. proximity
5. similarity
6. perceptual set

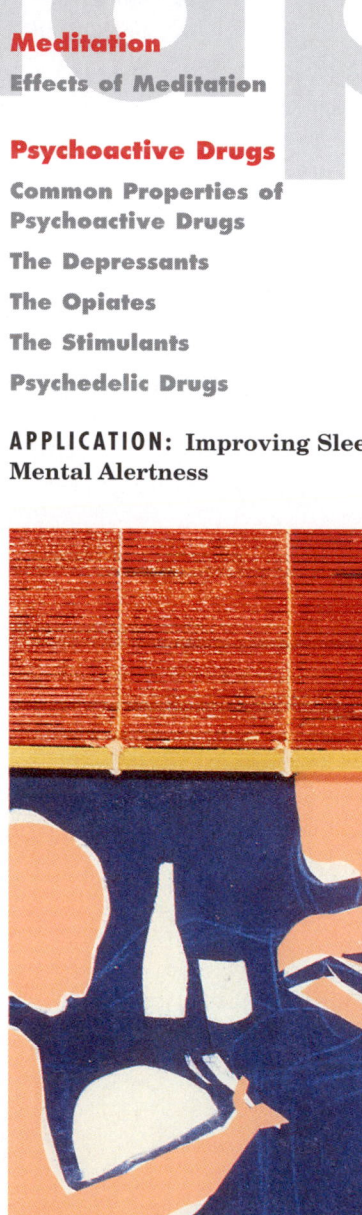

Prologue: Glimpses of the Mind at Night

4

Consciousness and Its Variations

Prologue: Glimpses of the Mind at Night

Still half asleep, we could hear them upstairs, talking and giggling as they traded stories of dreams they remembered. Of course, our four-year-old daughter did not have so long a legacy of dream memories to draw from as did Grandma Fern, Sandy's mom. Downstairs, the brain fog was still pretty thick, but your author Don dragged himself out of the lumpy sleeper sofa, pulled on some clothes, and trudged upstairs in search of a potent antidote to morning brain fog—Fern's strong coffee.

Grandma Fern and Laura were, of course, disgustingly alert as Don joined them at the small kitchen table. Fern mentioned that she had heard Laura calling out in her sleep during the night. Laura had awakened during a bad dream. Right on cue, Laura excitedly retold the details of her dream:

> There was a big monster chasing me and Nubbin the Cat! And we jumped on a golden horse but the monster kept chasing us! Then Nubbin jumped off and started to eat the monster. And then my Mommy came and saved me! And then Daddy took a sword and killed the monster! And then me and Mommy and Nubbin rode the horse into the clouds.

As for most children, nightmares could be frighteningly real to Laura. But even though she was just barely four years old, Laura already had a good grasp of the difference between dreams and actual events—at least once she completely woke up. And, fortunately, the recognition of that difference provides considerable comfort to her when she has an occasional bad dream.

A short while later Sandy trudged upstairs, still in her bathrobe, also in search of Fern's coffee. As Grandma Fern and Laura continued to chatter about monsters and golden horses and other imaginary creatures, Sandy described the dream she had been having shortly before she woke up:

> I was back in high school. The building was huge and old and dark and gloomy. I went to my locker but I couldn't remember the locker combination and I couldn't find my books or my shoes. Then I couldn't find my classroom. The hallways were dark and had very high ceilings. I would turn a corner and keep getting lost. Once I finally got to class, I tried to sneak in the back because I was so late. Then I realized that I hadn't come to class for weeks! And everybody was supposed to turn in a term paper that day—but I didn't even know what the topic was! I slumped at my desk, trying to hide. Then the teacher, who was very stern and wore glasses and a crewcut, announced that we were having an essay exam. In my dream, I was trying to figure out how to get out of this mess and I think I just got up and bolted out the door. Then I woke up—intensely relieved to discover that I was no longer in high school!

The experience of dreams is, of course, a universal one. Although everybody dreams, some people are like Don, who seldom remembers his dreams. Perhaps you're like Sandy and Laura, who vividly recall several dreams a week.

In this chapter, we'll consider the naturally occurring variations in the everyday experience of consciousness, including sleep and dreaming. We'll tackle such issues as the nature of sleep, the significance of dreams, and sleep disorders. Beyond sleep and dreaming, we'll also look at variations in consciousness that are deliberately induced: hypnosis, meditation, and the effects of drugs. In the chapter Application, we'll provide some practical suggestions for dealing with "morning brain fog" and improving the quality of your sleep.

Introduction

Consciousness: Experiencing the "Private I"

Consciousness refers to your immediate awareness of internal and external stimuli. What did William James mean by the phrase "stream of consciousness"? Why was psychological research on consciousness abandoned for a time, and why did research on consciousness regain legitimacy?

Your immediate awareness of thoughts, sensations, memories, and the world around you represents the experience of **consciousness.** That the experience of consciousness varies enormously from moment to moment is easy to illustrate. Imagine that we could videotape three one-minute segments of your conscious activities at different times while your psychology instructor lectures in class. What might those three one-minute segments of consciousness reveal? Here are just a few of the possibilities:

- Focused concentration on your instructor's words and gestures.

consciousness
Personal awareness of mental activities, internal sensations, and the external environment.

- Mental drifting from one fleeting thought, memory, or image to another.

- Awareness of physical sensations, such as the beginnings of a headache or the sharp pain of a paper cut.

- Active mental problem solving, as you try to think of a topic for your humanities term paper.

- Sexual fantasies.

- Mental rehearsal of what you'll say and how you'll act when you meet a friend later in the day.

- Replaying of an emotionally charged conversation.

- Wishful, grandiose daydreams of a future that is fundamentally different from your current situation.

Most likely, the three video clips would reveal very different scenes, dialogues, and content as your consciousness changed from one minute to the next. If we could examine your conscious awareness an hour or two later, the focus of your awareness might be completely different. However, even though your conscious experience is constantly changing, you don't experience your personal consciousness as disjointed. Rather, the subjective experience of consciousness has a sense of continuity. One stream of conscious mental activity seems to effortlessly, and seamlessly, blend into another.

It was this characteristic of consciousness that led the influential American psychologist **William James** (1892) to describe consciousness as a "river" or "stream." Although always changing, consciousness is perceived as unified and unbroken, much like a stream. Despite the changing focus of our awareness, our experience of consciousness as unbroken helps provide us with a sense of personal identity that has continuity from one day to the next.

The nature of human consciousness was one of the first topics to be tackled by the fledgling science of psychology in the late 1800s (Schneider, 1993). In Chapter 1, we discussed how the first psychologists tried to determine the nature of the human mind through *introspection*—verbal self-reports that tried to capture the "structure" of conscious experiences (see page 4). But because such self-reports were not objectively verifiable, many of the leading psychologists at the turn of the century rejected the study of consciousness. Instead, they emphasized the scientific study of *behavior,* which could be directly observed, measured, and verified.

In the second half of this century, many psychologists once again turned their attention to the study of consciousness (Schacter, 1995a; Hilgard, 1992). This occurred for a couple of reasons. First, it was becoming abundantly clear that a complete understanding of behavior was *not* possible for psychologists unless they considered the role of conscious mental processes in behavior.

Second, although the experience of consciousness is personal and subjective, psychologists devised more objective ways to study conscious experiences. For example, psychologists often *infer* the conscious experience that seems to be occurring by carefully observing behavior. Technological advances in studying brain activity were also producing intriguing correlations between brain activity and different states of consciousness, some of which we'll consider in this chapter.

Today, the scientific study of consciousness is incredibly diverse. Working from a variety of perspectives, psychologists and other researchers are piecing together a picture of consciousness that takes into account the role of psychological, physiological, social, and cultural influences (Schacter, 1995a; Farber & Churchland, 1995; Horgan, 1994).

Consciousness, then, does not appear to itself chopped up in bits . . . It is nothing jointed; it flows. A "river" or a "stream" are the metaphors by which it is most naturally described. In talking of it hereafter, let us call it the stream of thought, or consciousness, of subjective life.

William James *Principles of Psychology, Briefer Course* (1892)

The Biological and Environmental "Clocks" Regulating Consciousness

Circadian rhythms are biological processes that systematically vary over a 24-hour period. What roles do the suprachiasmatic nucleus, sunlight, and melatonin play in regulating circadian rhythms? How do "free-running" conditions affect circadian rhythms?

Throughout the course of the day there is a natural ebb and flow to consciousness. The most obvious variation in consciousness that we experience is the daily sleep/wake cycle. But conscious states also change in more subtle ways.

For example, you've probably noticed that your mental alertness varies throughout the day in a relatively consistent way. Most people experience two distinct peaks of mental alertness: one in the morning, usually around 9:00 or 10:00 a.m., and one in the evening, around 8:00 or 9:00 p.m. In between these two peaks, most people experience a slump in mental alertness at about three o'clock in the afternoon. And, should you manage to stay awake, your mental alertness will probably reach its *lowest* point at about three o'clock in the morning.

Mental alertness and the sleep/wake cycle are just two examples of the daily highs and lows you experience in a wide variety of bodily processes. These daily cycles are called **circadian rhythms.** The word *circadian* combines the Latin words for "about" and "day." So, the term *circadian rhythms* refers to biological processes that systematically vary over a period of about 24 hours (Thorpy & Yager, 1991).

You actually experience many different circadian rhythms that ebb and flow over the course of any given 24-hour period (see Table 4.1). In fact, researchers have discovered over 100 bodily processes that rhythmically peak and dip each day, including blood pressure, the secretion of different hormones, and pain sensitivity. Normally, your circadian rhythms are closely synchronized with one another. For example, the circadian rhythm for the

TABLE 4.1 Examples of Human Circadian Rhythms

Function	Typical Circadian Rhythm
Peak mental alertness and memory functions	Two daily peaks: around 9:00 a.m. and 9:00 p.m.
Lowest body temperature	About 97° around 3:00 a.m. to 4:00 a.m.
Highest body temperature	About 99° around 5:00 p.m. to 6:00 p.m.
Peak physical strength	Two daily peaks: around 11:00 a.m. and 7:00 p.m.
Peak hearing, visual, taste, and smell sensitivity	Two daily peaks: around 3:00 a.m. and 6:00 p.m.
Lowest sensitivity to pain	Around 3:00 p.m. to 5:00 p.m.
Peak sensitivity to pain	Around 3:00 a.m. to 5:00 a.m.
Peak degree of sleepiness	Two daily peaks: around 3:00 a.m. and 3:00 p.m.
Peak allergic sensitivity to pollen and dust	Between 11:00 p.m. and 1:00 a.m.

SOURCES: Mitler, 1994; Dinges & Broughton, 1989; and Rose, 1988.

circadian rhythm

(ser-KADE-ee-en) A cycle or rhythm that is roughly 24 hours long; refers to daily fluctuations in many biological and psychological processes.

suprachiasmatic nucleus (SCN)
(soup-rah-*kye*-az-MAT-ick) A cluster of neurons in the hypothalamus in the brain that governs the timing of circadian rhythms.

melatonin
(mel-uh-TONE-in) A hormone manufactured by the pineal gland that produces sleepiness.

release of growth hormone is synchronized with the sleep/wake circadian rhythm, so that growth hormone is released only during sleep.

The Suprachiasmatic Nucleus:
The Body's "Clock"

Your many circadian rhythms are controlled by a master "biological clock"—a tiny cluster of neurons in the hypothalamus in the brain. This cluster of neurons is called the **suprachiasmatic nucleus,** abbreviated **SCN.** Put simply, the SCN is the internal pacemaker that governs the timing of circadian rhythms, including the sleep/wake cycle and the mental alertness cycle (Klein & others, 1991).

Keeping the circadian rhythms synchronized to one another and on a 24-hour schedule also involves environmental time cues. The most important of these environmental cues is bright light, especially sunlight. In people, light detected by special photoreceptors in the eye is communicated via the visual system to the SCN in the hypothalamus (Foster, 1993; Card & Moore, 1991).

How does sunlight help regulate the sleep/wake cycle and other circadian rhythms? In somewhat simplified terms, the connection works like this: As the sun sets each day, the decrease in available light is detected by the SCN through its connections with the visual system. In turn, the SCN triggers an increase in the production of a hormone called **melatonin.** Melatonin is manufactured by the *pineal gland,* an endocrine gland located in the brain (Zoltoski & Gillin, 1994; Illnerová, 1991).

Increased blood levels of melatonin make you sleepy and reduce activity levels. At night, blood levels of melatonin rise, peaking between 1:00 and 3:00 a.m. Shortly before sunrise, the pineal gland all but stops producing melatonin, and you soon wake up. As the sun rises, exposure to sunlight and other bright light suppresses melatonin levels, and they remain very low throughout the day (G. Brown, 1994; Boivin & others, 1994; Lewy & others, 1990). Thus, sunlight *entrains,* or sets, the SCN so that it keeps circadian cycles synchronized and operating on a 24-hour schedule.

Life Without a Sundial:
"Free-Running" Circadian Rhythms

Given that sunlight is responsible for "setting" the internal clock, what would happen to the timing of circadian rhythms if they were allowed to "run free" in the absence of environmental time cues like sunlight and clocks? To create *free-running conditions,* researchers have constructed rooms in underground caves. Volunteers live in these underground bunkers for weeks or months at a time, deprived of all environmental time cues (Kronauer, 1994).

In the absence of normal light/darkness and other time cues, people tend to drift to the natural rhythm of the suprachiasmatic nucleus. What's intriguing is that the SCN naturally tends toward roughly a *25-hour* day, not a 24-hour day. Thus, people in a free-running condition go to sleep about an hour later each day (Campbell, 1997). Exactly why the human sleep/wake cycle gravitates toward a 25-hour cycle rather than a 24-hour cycle remains a mystery (Thompson, 1993).

What happens when people leave the free-running condition and are once again exposed to normal daylight and darkness cues? Within days, sunlight "resets" the biological clock, which resumes operating on a 24-hour cycle rather than a 25-hour cycle (Lewy & Sack, 1987).

Circadian Rhythms and Sunlight:

Some Practical Implications

When environmental time cues are out of sync with our internal biological clock, symptoms of jet lag can result. What situations can produce jet-lag symptoms? How is melatonin involved in jet-lag symptoms?

The close tie between our internal biological clock and environmental time cues has some very important practical applications. For example, imagine that you leave Denver at 2 o'clock in the afternoon on a 10-hour flight to London. When you arrive in London, it's 7:00 a.m. and the sun is shining. However, your body is still on Denver time. As far as your internal biological clock is concerned, it's midnight.

The result? Your circadian rhythms are drastically out of synchronization with daylight/darkness cues. The psychological and physiological effects of this disruption in circadian rhythms can be severe. Thinking, concentration, and memory get fuzzy. You experience physical and mental fatigue, depression or irritability, and disrupted sleep (Zammit, 1997). Collectively, these symptoms are called *jet lag*.

Although numerous physiological variables are involved in jet lag, the circadian cycle of the hormone melatonin seems to play a key role. When it's 10:00 a.m. in London, it's 3:00 a.m. in Denver. Since your body is still operating on Denver time, your melatonin production is peaking. Rather than feeling awake, you feel very sleepy, sluggish, and groggy. For many people, it can take a week or longer to adjust to such an extreme time change (Moore-Ede, 1993).

You don't need to travel across multiple time zones to experience symptoms of jet lag. People who work night shifts or rotating shifts often suffer from jet-lag symptoms because their circadian rhythms are out of sync with daylight/darkness time cues (Monk, 1997; Scott, 1994). Nurses, doctors, and other medical personnel often have to work night shifts or rotating shifts. So do people working in law enforcement and the military, broadcasting and weather services, and other businesses that operate around the clock.

For the night worker, the problem of being out of sync with the environmental clock is compounded every morning when she returns home in the bright morning light. Exposure to the bright morning light is a potent stimulus that can reset the person's body clock to a day schedule (Shanahan & Czeisler, 1991). And unless the person can completely darken her bedroom, even traces of sunlight through curtains can prevent her body clock from staying in sync with the night work schedule (Czeisler & others, 1989). Because sunlight time cues exert such a powerful influence on circadian rhythms, many night-shift workers never fully adjust to a nighttime work schedule (Harma, 1993; Empson, 1993).

Jet Lag and the Direction of Travel
Most people find it is easier to adjust to the time changes when flying westward than eastward. Why? Flying westward adds hours to a traveler's day, which corresponds with the natural tendency of your internal body clock to drift toward longer days. As a general rule, it takes considerably longer to resynchronize your circadian rhythms to a new time zone when you fly eastward, which shortens your day.

SCIENCE VERSUS PSEUDOSCIENCE 4.1

Biorhythms Versus Circadian Rhythms

Biorhythms is a pseudoscience based on the unproven notion that from birth onward, three rigidly fixed "natural biorhythms" reflect high, low, and critical periods of a person's physical, emotional, and intellectual functioning. The timing of these biorhythms is presumably determined by your date of birth. Physical functioning supposedly follows a 23-day cycle; emotional, a 28-day cycle; and intellectual, a 33-day cycle (Lester, 1990).

As in other pseudosciences, biorhythms practitioners use scientific-looking charts, like the one shown at the right, to plot an individual's three cycles. If a particular cycle is above the horizontal midline on a given day, it's a good day to engage in behaviors related to that particular cycle; below the midline is a bad indicator. "Critical days" supposedly occur when a cycle crosses the midpoint. If two cycles cross the midpoint simultaneously, it's a double critical day; when all three cross the midpoint, it's a triple critical day.

To underscore the seriousness of critical days, biorhythms proponents cite examples of airplane crashes, athletic losses, deaths of famous people, space travel mishaps, industrial accidents, and so forth (Hines, 1996). Along with causing disasters, biorhythms cycles also purportedly influence your mental health, marital compatibility, the day on which a woman gives birth, and the sex of the offspring!

Although "biorhythms" and "biological rhythms" *sound* very similar, they have about as much in common as mold and gold. The legitimate scientific study of *biological rhythms* examines the consistent but potentially varying cycles of living organisms over time, including plants, animals, insects, and humans (Webb, 1994; Wheeler, 1990).

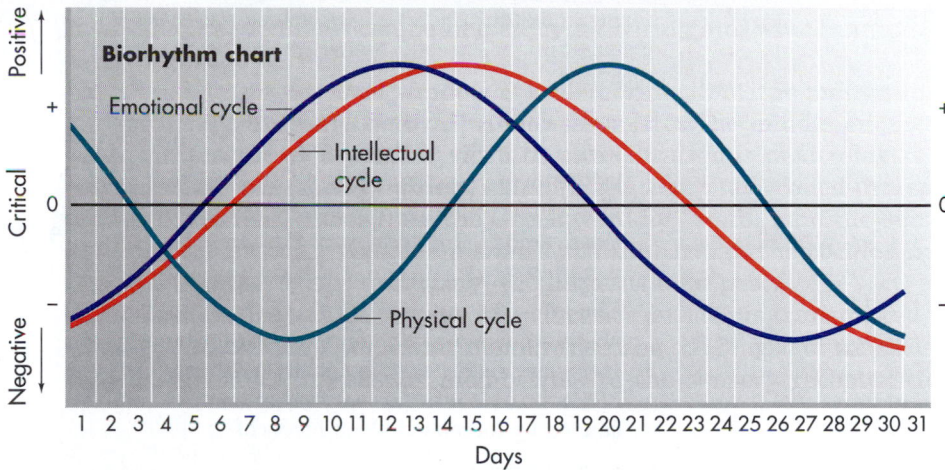

A Sample Biorhythm Chart

The green line represents the 23-day physical cycle, the purple line represents the 28-day emotional cycle, and the red line represents the 33-day intellectual cycle. Performance is presumably better than average on positive days and worse than average on negative days. Performance is supposed to be particularly poor on "critical days," when the cycle crosses the midline. Biorhythm proponents predict that accidents and other mishaps are especially likely on critical days. Are such predictions accurate?

Circadian rhythms are an example of scientifically verified biological rhythms that are highly consistent but certainly not rigidly fixed like the supposed 23-, 28-, and 33-day cycles of biorhythms.

To avoid confusion between the science and the pseudoscience, many psychologists, biologists, and other scientists now use the term *chronobiology* to refer to the scientific study of biological rhythms over time (Thorpy & Yager, 1991).

Scientific investigations of biorhythms are certainly not in short supply (Hines, 1996). Psychologist Terence Hines (1988) has summarized over thirty scientific investigations evaluating the effects of biorhythms. Researchers have studied the relationship between biorhythms and: automobile, aircraft, and industrial accidents; sports, academic, and intelligence test performance; the timing of births, deaths, and suicides; and the sex of newborn babies. Each of these scientific investigations found no relationship between biorhythms and any of these events.

The Biological and Environmental "Clocks" Regulating Consciousness

Complete the sentences below using the following terms: melatonin, jet lag, suprachiasmatic nucleus, sunlight, circadian rhythm, 24, 25, growth hormone.

1. Mark notices that he consistently feels awake and alert in his 9:00 a.m. algebra class, mentally sluggish in his 2:00 p.m. philosophy class, and wide awake again when he studies later in the evening. This consistent daily pattern is an example of a _____.

2. Sheila works the night shift. Despite getting adequate sleep before going to work, Sheila feels very sleepy and physically tired at about 3:00 a.m. Her fatigue at 3:00 a.m. is most likely caused by increased blood levels of _____.

3. As a research volunteer, Keith has agreed to live in an underground bunker for two months. The underground environment contains everything he needs except any means to tell the time. Over the first few weeks, his _____ will naturally drift to a _____-hour cycle, and his circadian rhythms may become desynchronized.

4. When the study concludes, Keith leaves the underground bunker. Within days, exposure to _____ resets his circadian rhythms so they become synchronized and operate on a _____-hour cycle.

Sleep

The invention of the electroencephalograph and the discovery of REM sleep marked the beginning of modern sleep research. What was the significance of these two discoveries? What are the two basic types of sleep? What are hypnagogic hallucinations?

Monitoring Sleep Using electrodes that are attached harmlessly to the face and scalp, the electroencephalograph records the brain's electrical activity throughout the night. Although the electrodes may look uncomfortable and cumbersome, people generally sleep just fine with all the wires attached.

From Aristotle to Shakespeare to Freud, history is filled with examples of scholars, writers, and scientists who have been fascinated by sleep and dreams (Thorpy, 1991). But prior to the twentieth century, there was no objective way to study the internal processes that might be occurring during sleep. So, traditionally, sleep was largely viewed as a period of restful inactivity in which dreams sometimes occurred.

The Beginnings of Modern Sleep Research:

Measuring Sleep

The invention of the **electroencephalograph** by German psychiatrist Hans Berger in the 1920s gave sleep researchers an important tool for measuring the rhythmic electrical activity of the brain. These rhythmical patterns of electrical activity are referred to as *brain waves*. The electroencephalograph produces a graphic record called an **EEG,** or *electroencephalogram*. By studying EEGs, sleep researchers firmly established that brain-wave activity systematically changes throughout sleep.

electroencephalograph

(electro-en-SEFF-uh-low-graph) An instrument that uses electrodes placed on the scalp to measure and record the brain's electrical activity.

EEG

The graphic record of brain activity produced by an electroencephalograph.

REM sleep

Type of sleep during which rapid eye movements and dreaming occur.

NREM sleep

Nondreaming quiet sleep, which is divided into four stages.

beta brain waves

Brain wave pattern associated with alert wakefulness.

alpha brain waves

Brain wave pattern associated with relaxed wakefulness and drowsiness.

hypnagogic hallucinations

(hip-nah-GO-jick) Vivid sensory phenomena that can occur during the onset of sleep.

Along with brain activity, today's sleep researchers monitor a variety of other physical functions during sleep. Eye movements, muscle movements, breathing rate, air flow, pulse, blood pressure, amount of exhaled carbon dioxide, body temperature, and breathing sounds are just some of the body functions that are measured in contemporary sleep research (Cooper & Bradbury, 1994).

The next milestone in sleep research occurred in the early 1950s. Eugene Aserinsky, a graduate student at the University of Chicago, was working in the laboratory of renowned sleep researcher Nathaniel Kleitman (Hobson, 1988). Using his ten-year-old son as a subject, Aserinsky discovered that particular EEG patterns during sleep were often associated with rapid movements of the sleeper's eyes. Moreover, these periods of rapid eye movement were highly correlated with the subject's reports of dreaming. In 1953, Aserinsky and Kleitman published their findings, heralding the discovery of *rapid eye movement sleep,* usually abbreviated *REM sleep.*

Today, sleep researchers distinguish between two basic types of sleep. **REM sleep** is often called *active sleep* or *paradoxical sleep* because it is associated with heightened body and brain activity during which dreaming consistently occurs. **NREM sleep,** or *non-rapid-eye-movement sleep,* is often referred to as *quiet sleep* because the body's physiological functions and brain activity slow down during this period of slumber. NREM sleep is further divided into four stages, as we'll describe shortly.

The Onset of Sleep and Hypnagogic Hallucinations

Awake and reasonably alert as you prepare for bed, your brain generates small, fast brain waves, called **beta brain waves.** After your head hits the pillow and you close your eyes, your muscles relax. Your brain's electrical activity gradually gears down, generating slightly larger and slower **alpha brain waves.** As drowsiness sets in, your thoughts may wander and become less logical.

During this drowsy, presleep phase, you may experience odd but vividly realistic sensations. You may hear your name called or a loud crash, feel as if you're falling or floating, smell something burning, or see kaleidoscopic patterns or an unfolding landscape. These vivid sensory phenomena that occasionally occur during the transition from wakefulness to light sleep are called **hypnagogic hallucinations** (Mavromatis, 1987). Although most tend to be rather ordinary, hynagogic hallucinations can sometimes be so vivid or startling that they cause a sudden awakening (Thorpy & Yager, 1991).

Probably the most common hypnagogic hallucination is the vivid sensation of falling. The sensation of falling is often accompanied by a *myoclonic jerk*—an involuntary muscle spasm of the whole body that jolts the person completely awake (Cooper, 1994; Empson, 1993). Although this experience can seem really weird (or embarrassing) when it occurs, you can rest assured that it's not abnormal. Most people occasionally experience the hypnagogic hallucination of falling combined with a myoclonic jerk. In general, you're more likely to experience a myoclonic jerk when you're very tired or under stress (Mavromatis, 1987).

GARFIELD

sleep spindles
Short bursts of brain activity that characterize stage 2 NREM sleep.

The First 90 Minutes of Sleep and Beyond

During the first 90 minutes of sleep, the sleeper progresses through the four stages of NREM and then enters REM sleep. What are the characteristics of NREM and REM sleep stages? How do sleep cycles vary throughout the remainder of the night? How do sleep patterns change over the lifespan?

The course of a normal night's sleep follows a relatively consistent cyclical pattern. As the person drifts off to sleep, she initially enters NREM sleep and begins a progression through the four NREM sleep stages (see Figure 4.1). In general, the progression through each NREM sleep stage is characterized by corresponding decreases in brain and body activity. For example, during NREM sleep, the sleeper is virtually motionless. On the average, the progression through the first four stages of NREM sleep occupies the first 50 to 70 minutes of sleep (Cooper, 1994). We'll briefly describe the characteristics of each stage of NREM sleep.

Stage 1 NREM

As the alpha brain waves of drowsiness are replaced by even slower *theta brain waves,* you enter the first stage of sleep. Lasting only a few minutes, stage 1 is a transitional stage during which you gradually disengage from the sensations of the world around you. Familiar sounds, such as the hum of the refrigerator or the sound of traffic, gradually fade from conscious awareness. Although hypnagogic experiences can also occur in stage 1, less vivid mental imagery is common, such as imagining yourself engaged in some everyday activity. While dreamlike, these images lack the unfolding, sometimes bizarre, details of a true dream (Hobson, 1988).

Stage 2 NREM

Stage 2 represents the onset of true sleep. Stage 2 sleep is marked by the appearance of **sleep spindles,** which are bursts of brain activity that last a second or two (see Figure 4.1). Other than these occasional sleep spindles,

FIGURE 4.1 The First 90 Minutes of Sleep
From wakefulness to the deepest sleep of stage 4 NREM, the brain's activity, measured by EEG recordings, progressively diminishes, as demonstrated by larger and slower brain waves. The four slow-wave NREM stages occupy the first 50 to 70 minutes of sleep. Then, in a matter of minutes, the brain cycles back to smaller, faster brain waves, and the sleeper experiences the night's first episode of dreaming REM sleep, which lasts 5 to 15 minutes. During the rest of the night, the sleeper continues to experience 90-minute cycles of alternating NREM and REM sleep.

(Based on Hobson, 1989.)

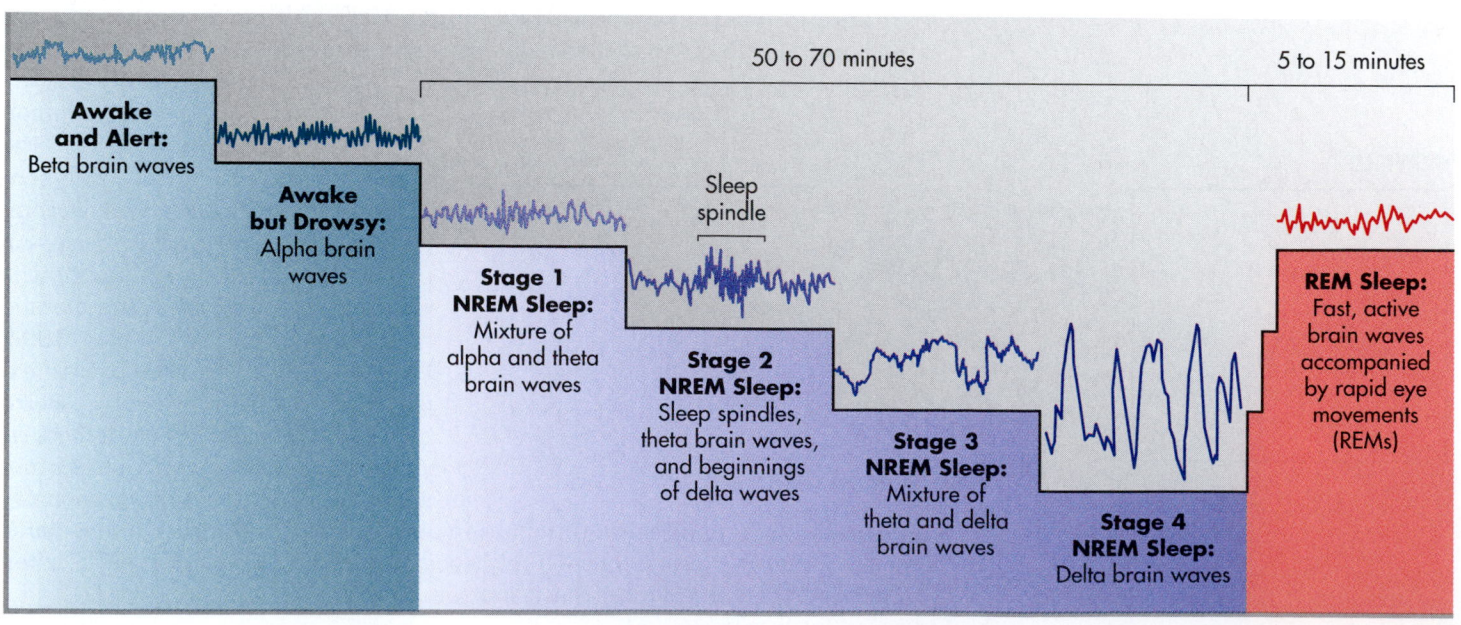

50 to 70 minutes   5 to 15 minutes

Awake and Alert: Beta brain waves

Awake but Drowsy: Alpha brain waves

Sleep spindle

Stage 1 NREM Sleep: Mixture of alpha and theta brain waves

Stage 2 NREM Sleep: Sleep spindles, theta brain waves, and beginnings of delta waves

Stage 3 NREM Sleep: Mixture of theta and delta brain waves

Stage 4 NREM Sleep: Delta brain waves

REM Sleep: Fast, active brain waves accompanied by rapid eye movements (REMs)

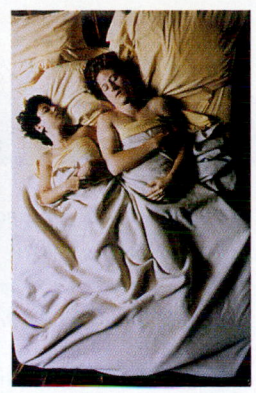

Synchronized Sleepers As these time-lapse photographs show, couples who regularly sleep in the same bed tend to have synchronized sleep cycles. Since bed partners fall asleep at about the same time, they are likely to have similarly timed NREM/REM sleep cycles. The body movements of this couple are also synchronized: Both sleepers shift position just before and after episodes of REM sleep.

brain activity continues to slow down considerably. Breathing becomes rhythmical. Slight muscle twitches may occur. Theta waves are predominant in stage 2, but large, slow brain waves called *delta brain waves* also begin to emerge. During the 15 to 20 minutes initially spent in stage 2, the amount of delta brain waves gradually increases.

Stage 3 and Stage 4 NREM

Stages 3 and 4 of NREM are physiologically very similar. Both stages are defined by the amount of delta brain wave activity. Thus, in combination, stages 3 and 4 are sometimes referred to as *slow-wave sleep* (Thorpy & Yager, 1991). When delta brain waves represent more than 20 percent of total brain activity, the sleeper is said to be in stage 3 NREM. When delta brain waves exceed 50 percent of total brain activity, the sleeper is said to be in stage 4 NREM (Cooper, 1994).

During the 20 to 40 minutes spent in the night's first episode of stage 4 NREM, delta waves eventually come to represent 100 percent of brain activity. At that point, the sleeper's heart rate, blood pressure, and breathing rate drop to their lowest levels. Not surprisingly, the sleeper in stage 4 NREM is virtually oblivious to the world; noises as loud as 90 decibels often fail to wake the sleeper (Empson, 1993). However, the sleeper's muscles are still capable of movement. For example, sleepwalking occurs during stage 4 NREM sleep (see Box 4.2).

It can easily take 15 minutes or longer to regain full waking consciousness from stage 4. It's even possible to answer a ringing phone, carry on a conversation for several minutes, and hang up without ever leaving stage 4 sleep—and without remembering it the next day. When people are briefly awakened by sleep researchers during stage 4 NREM and asked to perform some simple task, they often don't remember it the next morning (see Goodenough, 1991; Dinges, 1990).

Thus far in our description, the sleeper is approximately 70 minutes into a typical night's sleep and immersed in deeply relaxed stage 4 NREM sleep. At this point, the sequence reverses. In a matter of minutes the sleeper cycles back from stage 4 to stage 3 to stage 2, and enters a dramatic new phase: the night's first episode of REM sleep.

REM Sleep

During REM sleep, the brain becomes more active, generating smaller and faster brain waves. Visual and motor neurons in the sleeper's brain fire repeatedly, just as they do during wakefulness. Dreams usually occur during REM sleep. Although the brain is very active, voluntary muscle activity is suppressed, which prevents the dreaming sleeper from acting out her dreams (Cooper, 1994).

IN FOCUS 4.2

What You *Really* Want to Know About Sleep

Is it true that there are some people who never sleep?

No. There are people who *claim* to never sleep (usually on talk shows to promote the book they've written while supposedly awake all night). Such people seldom volunteer for study in sleep labs. When they do, of course, they eventually fall asleep.

Sometimes in the morning when I first wake up, I can't move. I'm literally paralyzed! Is this normal?

REM sleep is characterized by paralysis of the voluntary muscles, which keeps you from acting out your dreams. In a relatively common phenomenon called *sleep paralysis,* the paralysis of REM sleep carries over to the waking state for up to 10 minutes. If preceded by an unpleasant dream or hypnagogic experience, this sensation can be frightening. Sleep paralysis can also occur as you're falling asleep. In either case, the sleep paralysis lasts only for a few minutes. So, if this happens to you, re-lax: voluntary muscle control will soon return.

If I tape-record my chemistry class notes and play them while I sleep, can I learn the material without studying?

Not a chance. Although some perceptual processing can occur during sleep, the ability to learn and recall information requires wakefulness.

Do deaf people who use sign language sometimes "sleep sign" during sleep?

Yes.

Do the things that people say when they're sleeptalking make any sense? Can you get them to answer questions?

There are many anecdotes of spouses who have supposedly engaged their sleeptalking mates in extended conversations, but sleep researchers have been unsuccessful in having extended dialogues with chronic sleeptalkers. As far as the truthfulness of the sleeptalker's utterances go, they're reasonably accurate insofar as they reflect whatever the sleeptalker is responding to while asleep. By the way, not only do people sleeptalk, they can also sleep-*sing*! In one case we know of, a little boy sleep-sang "Frosty the Snowman."

Is it dangerous to wake a sleepwalker?

It's not dangerous to wake a sleepwalker; it's just difficult, because they are in deep sleep. Sleepwalkers will usually respond to verbal suggestions, so it's relatively easy to guide them back to bed.

Sleepwalking may be genetically determined. Identical twins are much more likely to share this characteristic than are nontwin siblings. One college student confided to sleep researcher Jacob Empson (1993) that her whole family sleepwalked. She reported that on one occasion her entire family woke up in the early-morning hours seated around the kitchen table, where they had all gathered in their sleep!

SOURCES: Rothenberg, 1997; Ozbayrak & Berlin, 1995; Empson, 1993; Takeuchi & others, 1992; Ishihara & others, 1992; Arkin, 1991, 1981; Larson & others, 1991; Lugaresi & Montagna, 1990.

REM sleep is accompanied by considerable physiological arousal. The sleeper's eyes dart back and forth behind closed eyelids. Heart rate, blood pressure, and respirations can fluctuate up and down, sometimes extremely. Muscle twitches occur. Both males and females often show signs of sexual arousal during REM sleep, which is not necessarily related to dream content (Hobson, 1989).

This first REM episode tends to be brief—about 5 to 15 minutes. From the beginning of stage 1 NREM sleep through the completion of the first episode of REM sleep, about 90 minutes have elapsed.

Beyond the First 90 Minutes

Throughout the rest of the night, the sleeper cycles between NREM and REM sleep. Each cycle lasts about 90 minutes on the average, but the duration of cycles may vary from 70 to 120 minutes (Morin, 1993). Usually, four more 90-minute cycles of NREM and REM sleep occur during the night. Just before and after REM periods, the sleeper shifts position (Hobson, 1989).

The progression of a typical night's sleep cycles is depicted in Figure 4.2. Stages 3 and 4 NREM slow-wave sleep usually occur only during the first two 90-minute cycles. As the night progresses, episodes of REM sleep become increasingly longer, and less time is spent in NREM. During the last two 90-minute sleep cycles before awakening, periods of REM sleep can last as long as 40 minutes, and NREM sleep is composed primarily of stage 2 sleep.

FIGURE 4.2 The 90-Minute Cycles of Sleep
During a typical night, you experience five 90-minute cycles of alternating NREM and REM sleep. The deepest stages of NREM sleep, stages 3 and 4, occur during the first two 90-minute cycles. Dreaming REM sleep episodes become progressively longer as the night goes on. Sleep position shifts, indicated by the dots, usually occur immediately before and after REM episodes.

(Based on Hobson, 1989.)

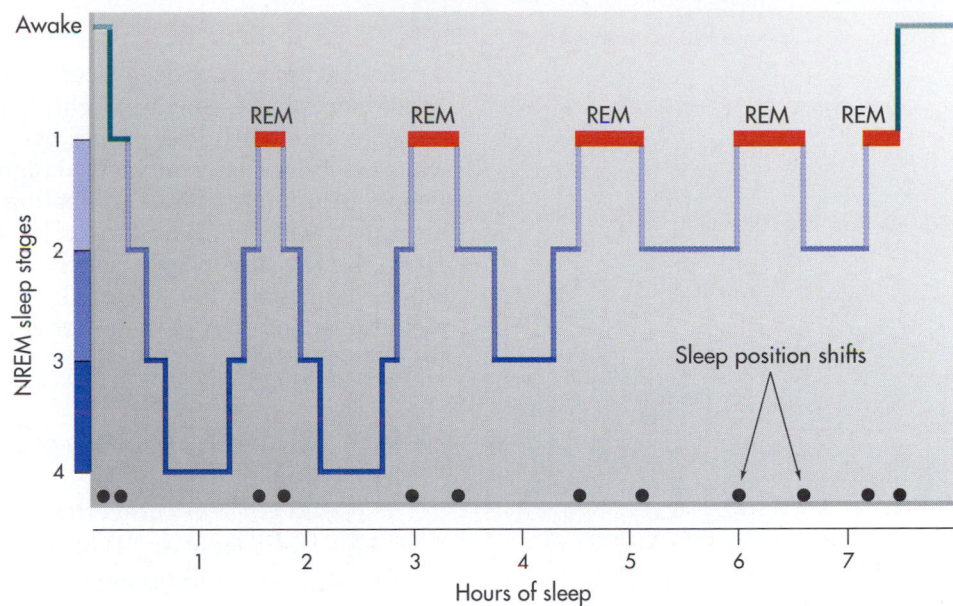

The Beginnings of REM Sleep By studying premature infants and using ultrasound to create images of the developing fetus in utero, researchers have documented the beginnings of REM sleep and rapid eye movements several weeks before birth.

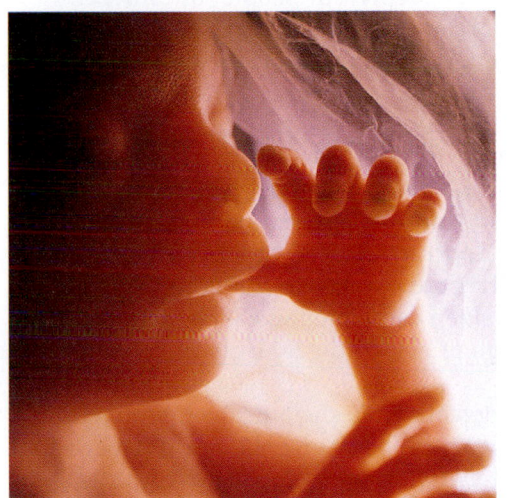

FIGURE 4.3 Changes in REM and NREM Sleep over the Lifespan
Both the quality and quantity of sleep change over the lifespan. Even before birth, the cycles of REM and NREM sleep are evident. A newborn infant sleeps about 16 to 17 hours per day, with about 50 percent of sleep time devoted to REM. From birth onward, total sleep time, REM sleep, and NREM sleep slowly decrease. The amount of time spent in stages 3 and 4, the deepest stages of NREM, also decreases over the lifespan.

(Based on Hobson, 1989.)

Changes in Sleep over the Lifespan

Over the course of our lives the quantity and quality of sleep change considerably. REM sleep begins long before birth, as scientists have discovered by using ultrasound to document fetal eye movements and by studying the sleep of premature infants. Four months before birth, REM sleep seems to constitute virtually all of fetal life (see Figure 4.3). By one month before birth, the fetus demonstrates distinct wake/sleep cycles, spending around 12 hours each day in REM sleep (Mindell, 1997).

At birth, a newborn sleeps about 16 hours a day, about 50 percent of which is REM sleep. By the end of the first year of life, total sleep time drops to around 13 hours a day, a third of which is spent in REM sleep.

In general, from birth onward the average amount of time spent sleeping each day gradually decreases (see Figure 4.3). The amount of time devoted to REM sleep and slow-wave NREM sleep each night also gradually decreases over the lifespan (Bliwise, 1997). Young children can easily spend two hours or more each night in the deep sleep of stages 3 and 4 NREM. By early adulthood, about an hour is spent in deep sleep each night. But by late adulthood, only about 20 minutes of a night's sleep is spent in stages 3 and 4 NREM sleep (Williams & others, 1994).

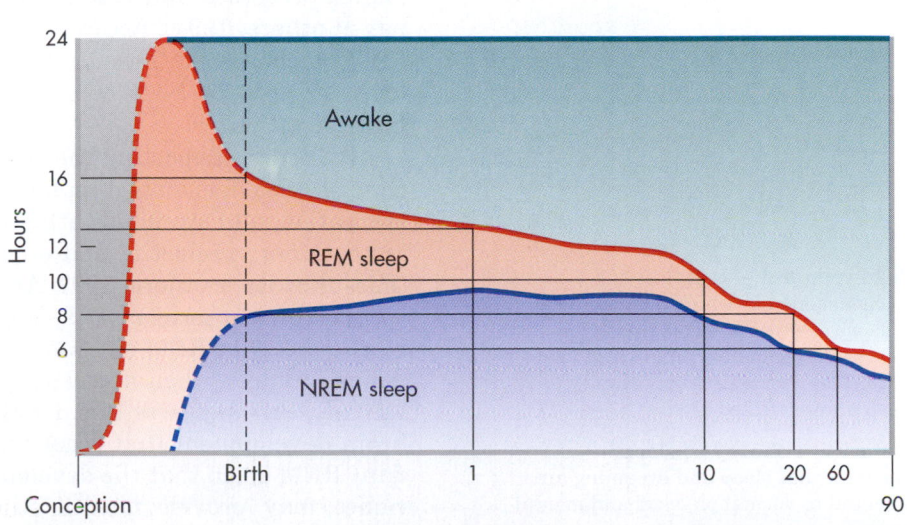

As the amount of deep sleep and REM sleep decreases throughout adulthood, more time is spent in lighter, stage 2 NREM sleep. Consequently, sleep becomes more fitful as people get older. Beginning in their forties, people wake up more easily during the night, and sleep tends to feel less satisfying. People also tend to wake up feeling less rested and find it harder to regain alertness and get their brains in gear each morning (Williams & others, 1994). By the time people reach their sixties, total sleep time averages about 6 hours per night, and the quality of sleep is much more shallow. Older people often spend part of the night simply resting with their eyes closed rather than sleeping (Morin, 1993).

Why Do We Sleep?

Sleep deprivation studies demonstrate that we have a biological need for sleep. What is REM and NREM rebound? What is the restorative theory of sleep? How does the adaptive theory of sleep account for the varied patterns of sleep observed in different animals?

That we have a biological need for sleep is clearly demonstrated by *sleep deprivation studies.* After as little as one day's sleep deprivation, research subjects develop *microsleeps,* which are episodes of sleep lasting only a few seconds that occur during wakefulness. People who go without sleep for a day or more also experience disruptions in mood, mental abilities, reaction time, perceptual skills, and complex motor skills (Gökcebay & others, 1994).

Sleep researchers have also selectively deprived people of different *components* of normal sleep. For example, to study the effects of REM deprivation, researchers wake the subject whenever the monitoring instruments indicate that he is entering REM sleep. After several nights of being selectively deprived of REM sleep, the subject is allowed to sleep uninterrupted. What happens? The first time the subject is allowed to sleep without interruption, he experiences **REM rebound**—the amount of time spent in REM sleep increases by as much as 50 percent (Ellman & others, 1991). The same effect occurs when people are selectively deprived of NREM stages 3 and 4.

The phenomena of REM and NREM rebound seem to indicate that the brain needs to "make up" for the missing sleep components. Clearly, we need to both sleep and experience the full range of sleep stages. But what particular functions does sleep serve?

The **restorative theory of sleep** suggests that sleep promotes physiological processes that restore and rejuvenate the body and the mind (Gökcebay & others, 1994). According to the restorative theory of sleep, NREM and REM sleep serve different purposes. NREM sleep is thought to be important for restoring the body, while REM sleep is thought to restore mental and brain functions.

Evidence supporting the role of NREM sleep in body restoration comes from studies demonstrating increased deep sleep following sleep deprivation, starvation, and strenuous athletic activity. The secretion of growth hormone, testosterone, prolactin, and other hormones increases during NREM sleep (Hirshkowitz & others, 1997; Anch & others, 1988).

The importance of REM sleep in mental and brain functions is suggested by the fact that REM sleep is abundant in the developing fetus, infants, and young children, then decreases throughout adulthood (see Figure 4.3). Tentatively, this suggests that REM sleep plays some role in the high rates of brain development that occur in the early stages of the lifespan. The abundant REM sleep that the developing fetus, infants, and young children experience may provide needed stimulation for brain development (Empson, 1993; Hobson, 1989).

REM rebound
A phenomenon in which a person who is deprived of REM sleep greatly increases the amount of time spent in REM sleep at the first opportunity to sleep uninterrupted.

restorative theory of sleep
The view that sleep and dreaming are essential to normal physical and mental functioning.

Nap, Anyone? From anteaters to zebras, virtually all animals share the need for rest and periodic sleep. Sleep patterns vary greatly from one species to another. According to the adaptive theory of sleep, animals with few predators, like this lion and polar bear, can enjoy the luxury of sleeping unprotected in broad daylight. Animals who are vulnerable to predators, like giraffes and shrews, sleep only fitfully, or in well-protected nests.

As its name implies, the **adaptive theory of sleep** suggests that the sleep patterns exhibited by different animals, including humans, are the result of evolutionary adaptation (Webb, 1975). The basic idea is that different sleep patterns evolved as way of preventing a particular species from interacting with the environment when doing so is most hazardous. Animals with few natural predators, such as gorillas and lions, sleep as much as 15 hours a day. In contrast, grazing animals, such as cattle and horses, tend to sleep in short bursts that total only about four hours per day. Hibernation patterns of animals like bears and gophers also coincide with periods during which environmental conditions pose the greatest threat to survival.

There is evidence to support both the restorative and the adaptive theories of sleep. Sleep does seem to restore the body, but exactly how it does so remains uncertain. And the variations in sleep patterns exhibited by different animals seem to reflect an adaptive process that promotes survival. Researchers still aren't sure exactly what physiological functions are served by sleep. Sleep may well fulfill multiple purposes (Gökcebay & others, 1994).

CONCEPT REVIEW 4.2

The Stages of Sleep

Fill in the blanks using the proper terms from this list: REM, myoclonic jerk, stage 2 NREM, stage 4 NREM, dreaming, hypnagogic hallucination.

1. You have been asleep for about 10 minutes and are experiencing bursts of brain activity, called sleep spindles, which last a few seconds. It is likely that you are in _____ sleep.

2. Joe is just drifting off to sleep when he experiences a sudden sensation of falling and an involuntary muscle spasm that jolts him awake. Joe has experienced the _____ of falling combined with a _____.

3. Marsha has been asleep for well over an hour. Her eyes start to dart back and forth beneath her closed eyelids. Her heart rate and blood pressure fluctuate up and down, yet her voluntary muscle activity is suppressed. Most likely, Marsha is experiencing _____ sleep, and _____ is occurring.

4. You have volunteered to be a subject in a sleep research lab. At some point during your first night's sleep, you answer the phone and have a brief conversation with the research assistant but remember nothing about this incident the next morning. The phone conversation most likely occurred during _____ sleep.

Sleep Disorders:

Troubled Sleep

adaptive theory of sleep
The view that the unique sleep patterns of different animals evolved over time to help promote survival and environmental adaptation.

sleep disorders
Serious disturbances in the normal sleep pattern that interfere with daytime functioning and cause subjective distress.

Sleep disorders are serious disturbances in normal sleep patterns that interfere with daytime functioning and cause subjective distress. How is insomnia defined? What characterizes sleepwalking, night terrors, REM sleep behavior disorder, sleep apnea, and narcolepsy?

Sleep disorders are serious disturbances in the normal sleep pattern that interfere with daytime functioning and cause subjective distress (American Psychiatric Association, 1994). Virtually everyone is seriously troubled by the quality or quantity of their sleep at some point. For example, a 1991 survey sponsored by the National Sleep Foundation found that 36 percent of Americans suffer from some type of sleep problem (Gallup Organization, 1991). Similar surveys have found that better than 25 percent of children, including preschoolers, suffer from sleep disruptions (Mindell, 1997; Chambers, 1995).

Insomnia

By far the most common sleep complaint among adults is insomnia. Insomnia is not defined solely on the basis of amount of time spent sleeping. Put simply, people vary in how much sleep they need to feel refreshed. Rather, people are said to suffer from **insomnia** when they repeatedly complain about the quality or duration of their sleep, have difficulty going to sleep or staying asleep, or wake before it is time to get up (Morin, 1993).

Over the course of any given year, about a third of the adult population is troubled by a bout of insomnia (Mellinger & others, 1985). Not surprisingly, such sleeping difficulties can often be traced to stressful life events, such as job or school difficulties, troubled relationships, the death of a loved one, or financial problems. Concerns about sleeping can add to whatever waking anxieties the person may already be experiencing. This can create a vicious cycle—worrying about the inability to sleep makes troubled sleep even more likely, further intensifying anxiety (Roemer & Borkovec, 1993; Spielman & Glovinsky, 1991).

Sleep disorder specialists use a variety of behavioral and psychological techniques to treat insomnia and help people develop better sleep habits. Educating people on sleep "hygiene" is often part of the successful treatment of insomnia. For example, many people troubled by insomnia use alcohol or over-the-counter sleep medications to induce sleep. Although such remedies may help people sleep in the short run, they can disrupt normal sleep cycles, including REM sleep. Even the sleep-inducing medications sometimes prescribed by physicians must be carefully managed to avoid drug dependence (Bootzin & Rider, 1997; Dement, 1992a).

Sleepwalking and Night Terrors

Unlike insomnia, *sleepwalking* and *night terrors* are sleep disturbances that are much more common in children than in adults (Lask, 1995; Mindell, 1993). These sleep disturbances occur during the deepest stages of NREM sleep, stages 3 and 4. As noted previously, young children spend considerably more time each night in deep sleep than adolescents or adults (Whyte & Schaefer, 1995).

About 25 percent of all children have at least one episode of **sleepwalking,** also known as *somnambulism.* Sleepwalking typically occurs during the first three hours after the child has gone to sleep. After sitting up and getting out of bed, the child moves about in a slow, poorly coordinated, automatic manner, usually with a blank, staring look on his face. Surprisingly, the sleepwalking child is able to navigate around objects without much difficulty. However, the sleepwalker's general lack of awareness of his surroundings is evident: he may try to dress, eat, or go to the bathroom in the wrong location (Ozbayrak & Berlin, 1995).

Night terrors, or *sleep terrors,* also typically occur during stage 3 or 4 NREM sleep in the first few hours of sleep. Physiologically, a night terror is much more intense than a run-of-the-mill nightmare. The first sign of a night terror is sharply increased physiological arousal—restlessness, sweating, and a racing heart. Typically, the child abruptly sits up in bed and lets out a

insomnia
A condition in which a person regularly experiences the inability to fall asleep, stay asleep, or feel adequately rested by sleep.

sleepwalking
A sleep disturbance characterized by an episode of walking or performing other actions during stage 3 or stage 4 NREM sleep; also called *somnambulism.*

night terrors
A sleep disturbance characterized by an episode of increased physiological arousal, intense fear and panic, frightening hallucinations, and no recall of the episode the next morning; typically occurs during stage 3 or stage 4 NREM sleep; also called *sleep terror.*

Terror in the Night French artist Jean Ignace Gerard created this print, entitled "The Nightmare." However, the image of a monster lowering a weight on the sleeper's chest suggests instead the frightening experience of a night terror. Night terrors occur during NREM sleep and are almost always accompanied by sensations of being crushed or smothered.

panic-stricken scream or cry for help as she thrashes about in bed or even sleepwalks. Terrified and disoriented, the child may struggle with a parent who tries to calm her down (Lask, 1995).

Night terrors tend to be brief, usually lasting only a matter of seconds (Ferber, 1994). Amazingly, the child almost immediately goes back to quiet sleep and wakes in the morning with no recollection of the incident (Lask, 1995). Unlike the unfolding dream story of a nightmare, night terrors are usually accompanied by a single but terrifying sensation, such as being crushed or falling. Often, the child imagines that she is choking or that a frightening figure is present, such as a threatening animal or "monster" (Kahn & others, 1991). Though dramatic, night terrors are not regarded as a true sleep disorder or psychological problem unless they occur regularly (Wiedemann, 1987). For the vast majority of children who experience regular night terrors, the problem resolves itself by early adolescence (Lask, 1995).

REM Sleep Behavior Disorder

A more serious sleep disorder that has only recently been recognized by sleep researchers is called **REM sleep behavior disorder** (Mahowald & Schenck, 1990). This sleep disturbance typically affects males over the age of 60 and is characterized by the brain's failure to suppress muscle movements during REM sleep. The dreamer acts out his dreams, sometimes leaping out of bed, running across the bedroom, lashing out at imagined intruders, or tackling a chest of drawers. Such behavior might seem quite comical if the potential for serious injury to the sleeper or the sleeper's bed partner weren't so great. Evidence suggests that the cause of REM sleep behavior disorder is deterioration or damage in lower brain centers that control physical and mental arousal during sleep (Zoltoski & Gillin, 1994; Chase & Morales, 1990).

Sleep Apnea

In **sleep apnea,** the sleeper repeatedly stops breathing during the night (Orr, 1997). Carbon dioxide builds up in the blood, causing a momentary awakening during which the sleeper snorts or gulps in air. Breathing may stop for as little as 10 seconds or for so long that the sleeper's skin turns blue before he wakes up. During a single night, over 300 sleep apnea attacks can occur. Often the person has no recollection of the repeated awakenings, but feels sleepy throughout the following day.

Like REM sleep behavior disorder, sleep apnea is more common in older men, especially those with a weight problem. Special mouthpieces, weight loss, and surgical intervention have been effectively used to treat sleep apnea. For people who suffer sleep apnea only when they sleep on their backs, treatment is sometimes as simple as sewing a tennis ball to the back of their pajama tops, which forces them to sleep on their sides (Saskin, 1997).

Narcolepsy

Unlike the sleep disorders discussed so far, the symptoms of **narcolepsy** are experienced during the day. The most common symptom of narcolepsy is excessive daytime sleepiness and brief lapses into sleep throughout the day,

REM sleep behavior disorder
A sleep disorder in which the sleeper acts out his dreams.

sleep apnea
(APP-nee-uh) A sleep disorder in which the person repeatedly stops breathing during sleep.

narcolepsy
A sleep disorder characterized by excessive daytime sleepiness and brief lapses into sleep throughout the day.

usually lasting an hour or less. However, some narcoleptics experience dramatic, sudden daytime "sleep attacks" that last up to several minutes. Laughter, anger, surprise, and other forms of emotional arousal, including sexual arousal, can trigger the sleep attacks. During sleep attacks, narcoleptics instantly enter REM sleep and experience *sleep paralysis*—their muscles go limp and they collapse. Vivid and sometimes terrifying hypnagogic hallucinations are common during sleep attacks.

The onset of narcolepsy typically occurs during adolescence and is considered a chronic, lifelong condition. Genetics seems to play an important role, as the disorder tends to run in families. Although narcolepsy cannot be cured, scheduled daytime naps increase alertness for narcoleptics. Stimulants and other psychoactive drugs can also help minimize narcoleptic symptoms (Gibbons & Kotagal, 1995; Broughton, 1990).

Dreams and Mental Activity During Sleep

A dream is an unfolding episode of mental images that occurs during REM sleep. What are the characteristics of dreams? What do people dream about, and what factors influence whether a dream is remembered?

On the average, about 25 percent of a night's sleep is spent dreaming, or almost two hours every night. So, assuming you live to a ripe old age, you'll devote more than 50,000 hours, or about six years of your life, just to dreaming.

Although dreams may be the most spectacular brain productions during sleep, they are not the most common mental activity during sleep. More prevalent is **sleep thinking,** which occurs during NREM sleep and consists of vague, uncreative, bland, and thoughtlike ruminations about real-life events (Hobson & Stickgold, 1995; Schatzman & Fenwick, 1994; Hobson, 1988). For example, just before an important exam, students may review terms and concepts during NREM sleep.

In contrast to sleep thinking, a **dream** is an unfolding episode of mental images that is storylike, involving characters and events. According to sleep researcher Allan Hobson (1988), dreams have five basic characteristics:

- Emotions can be intense.
- Content and organization are usually illogical.
- Sensations are sometimes bizarre.
- Even bizarre details are uncritically accepted.
- The dream images are difficult to remember.

Usually, dreams occur during REM sleep, but dreams can also occasionally occur during NREM sleep (Schatzman & Fenwick, 1994). When people are awakened during REM sleep, up to 90 percent of the time they will report a dream—even people who claim that they never dream. In fact, you usually have four or five episodes of dreaming each night, even if you don't remember the dreams. Early-morning dreams, which can last as long as 40 minutes, are the dreams that you're most likely to remember. Contrary to popular belief, dreams happen in real time, not split seconds. In fact, dreamers tend to be quite accurate in estimating how long they've been dreaming (Empson, 1993).

sleep thinking
Repetitive, bland, and uncreative ruminations about real-life events during sleep.

dream
A storylike episode of unfolding mental imagery during sleep.

TABLE 4.2 Common Dream Themes Across Cultures

Although thousands of miles apart and immersed in two very different cultures, American and Japanese college students share many dream themes, as shown in these survey results.

Have you ever dreamed of . . . ?	Percentage Saying Yes	
	Ameri-can	Japan-ese
1. being attacked or pursued	77	91
2. falling	83	74
3. trying again and again to do something	71	87
4. school, teachers, studying	71	86
5. being frozen with fright	58	87
6. sexual experiences	66	68
7. arriving too late, e.g., missing train	64	49
8. dead people as though alive	46	57
9. loved person being dead	57	42
10. being on verge of falling	47	45
11. failing an examination	39	41
12. flying or soaring through air	34	46
13. being smothered, unable to breathe	44	33
14. seeing self as dead	33	35
15. being nude	43	17

SOURCE: Adapted from data reported in Empson, 1993.

What Do We Dream About?

Although nearly everyone can remember an unusually bizarre dream, most dreams are a reflection of everyday life, including people we know and familiar settings (Weinstein & others, 1991). Remember Sandy's "high school" dream, described in the prologue to this chapter? Before she went to sleep that night, Sandy had been talking with her parents about some old friends from high school. The dark hallways, high ceilings, and gloomy classrooms, while somewhat exaggerated in her dream, were a fairly accurate depiction of the public high school she attended in Chicago years ago.

Dream researcher Calvin Hall collected and analyzed over 10,000 dreams from hundreds of people. He found that a dream's themes often reflect the daily concerns of the dreamer (Hall & Van de Castle, 1966). Worries about exams, money, health, or troubled relationships are all likely to be reflected in our dreams. And as you can see in Table 4.2, certain themes, such as falling or being chased or attacked, are surprisingly common across cultures.

Sleep researchers can successfully influence dream content *during* dreaming. In sleep labs, researchers have played recordings of a rooster crowing, a bugle playing reveille, and a dog barking, and have even sprayed water on sleeping research subjects. Depending on the stimulus, up to half of the dreamers incorporated the external stimulation into their dream content (Dement, 1992b, 1978; Arkin & Antrobus, 1991).

Why Don't We Remember Our Dreams?

Even in the best dream recallers, the vast majority of dreams are forgotten—at least 95 percent, by one estimate (Hobson, 1989). Why are dreams so much more difficult to remember than waking experiences? Several theories have been proposed, each with at least some evidence to support them, but the bottom line is that no clear answer has yet emerged from sleep research.

Even so, several generalizations are possible (Goodenough, 1991). First, you're much more likely to recall a dream if you wake up during it. When subjects are intentionally awakened during REM sleep, they usually recall the dream content. There are also individual differences in dream recall. Some people, like your author Sandy, frequently remember their dreams in vivid detail. Other people, like your author Don, hardly ever remember their dreams.

Second, the more vivid, bizarre, or emotionally intense a dream is, the more likely it is to be recalled the following morning. Vivid dreams are also more likely to be remembered days or weeks after the dream has occurred. In many respects, this is very similar to waking experiences: whether we're awake or asleep, mundane and routine experiences are most likely to be forgotten.

Third, distractions upon awakening interfere with our ability to recall dreams. This fact was noted by psychologist Mary Calkins (1893) over a century ago:

> To recall a dream requires usually extreme and immediate attention to the content of the dream. Sometimes the slight movement of reaching for paper and pencil or of lighting one's candle seems to dissipate the dream-memory, and one is left with the tantalizing consciousness of having lived through an interesting dream-experience of which one has not the faintest memory.

IN FOCUS 4.3

What You *Really* Want to Know About Dreams

If I fall off a cliff in my dreams and don't wake up before I hit the bottom, will I die?

The first obvious problem with this bit of folklore is that if you did die, how would anyone know what you'd been dreaming about? Beyond that basic contradiction, studies have shown that about a third of dreamers can recall a dream in which they died or were killed. And such dream sensations as falling, soaring through the air, and being paralyzed seem to be universal.

When my dog yips, twitches his nose, and moves his paws as if he's running while he's asleep, is he dreaming?

Virtually all mammals experience sleep cycles in which REM sleep alternates with slow-wave NREM sleep. Animals clearly demonstrate perception and memory. They also communicate using vocalizations, facial expressions, posture, and gestures to show territoriality and sexual receptiveness. Thus, it's quite reasonable to conclude that the

brain and other physiological changes that occur during animal REM sleep are coupled with mental images. One bit of anecdotal evidence supporting this idea involved a gorilla that had been taught basic sign language to communicate. The gorilla signed "sleep pictures," presumably referring to REM dream activity while it slept.

What do people who have been blind all their lives "see" when they dream?

People who become totally blind before the age of five typically do not have visual dreams as adults. Even so, their dreams are just as complex and vivid as sighted people's; they just involve other sensations, especially sound and touch.

Is it possible to control your dreams?

Yes, if you have lucid dreams. A *lucid dream* is one in which you become aware that you are dreaming while you are still asleep. About half of all people can recall at least one lucid dream, and

some people frequently have lucid dreams. The dreamer can often consciously guide the course of a lucid dream, including backing it up and making it go in a different direction.

Can you predict the future with your dreams?

History is filled with stories of dream prophecies. Over the course of your life, you will have over 100,000 dreams. Simply by chance, it's not surprising that every now and then a dream contains elements that coincide with future events.

Are dreams in color or black and white?

Up to 80 percent of our dreams contain color. When dreamers are awakened and asked to match dream colors to standard color charts, soft pastel colors are frequently chosen.

SOURCES: Halliday, 1995; Green & McCreery, 1994; Schatzman & Fenwick, 1994; Empson, 1993; Weinstein & others, 1991; Hobson, 1989, 1988; Anch & others, 1988.

Finally, it's difficult to remember *any* experience during sleep, not just dreams. Sleep researchers have also found that subjects who are briefly awakened during the night to give reports or perform simple tasks frequently do not remember the incident the next morning (Goodenough, 1991).

It seems clear, then, that the brain is largely "programmed" to forget not only the vast majority of dream experiences but other experiences during sleep as well. As we'll discuss in more detail in the memory chapter (Chapter 6), memory requires that information be processed and stored in such a way that it can be retrieved at a later time. Possibly, the fundamental changes in brain chemistry and functioning that occur during sleep fail to support such information processing and storage, except when dreams are especially vivid. One theory is that the neurotransmitters needed to create new memories are not available during sleep (Hobson & Stickgold, 1995; Hobson, 1990).

Nightmares

An unpleasant anxiety dream that occurs during REM sleep is called a **nightmare.** Nightmares often produce spontaneous awakenings, during which the vivid and frightening dream content is immediately recalled (Thorpy & Yager, 1991). Nightmares are especially common in young children (Halliday, 1995). The general theme of nightmares is of being helpless or powerless in the face of great danger or destruction. Like Laura's dream, described in the prologue, children often have nightmares in which they are attacked by an animal or "monster."

nightmare
A frightening or unpleasant anxiety dream that occurs during REM sleep.

In dealing with a child who has experienced a nightmare, simple reassurance is a good first step, followed by an attempt to help the child understand the difference between an imaginary dream and a real waking experience (Halliday, 1995; Josephs, 1987). In adults, an occasional nightmare is a natural and relatively common experience (Wood & Bootzin, 1990). Nightmares are not considered to be indicative of a psychological or sleep disorder unless they frequently cause personal distress.

The Significance of Dreams

Dreams have been thought to be meaningful for centuries. What was Sigmund Freud's explanation for dreams? How does the activation-synthesis model explain dreaming?

Just as sleep researchers aren't exactly sure why we sleep, they also do not know why we dream every night. However, the idea that dreams are meaningful has a long history. For thousands of years and throughout many cultures, dreams have been thought to contain highly significant, cryptic messages that must be interpreted. In this final section on dreaming, we will look at two theories that try to account for the purpose of dreaming, starting with the most famous one.

Sigmund Freud: Dreams as Fulfilled Wishes

In the chapters on personality and psychotherapy (Chapters 10 and 14), we'll look in detail at the ideas of **Sigmund Freud** (1856–1939), the founder of psychoanalysis. As we discussed in Chapter 1, Freud believed that sexual and aggressive instincts are the motivating forces that dictate human behavior. But because these instinctual urges are consciously unacceptable, sexual and aggressive thoughts, feelings, and wishes are pushed into the unconscious, or *repressed*. However, Freud believed that these repressed urges and wishes could surface in dreams.

In his landmark work, *The Interpretation of Dreams* (1900), Freud wrote that dreams are the "disguised fulfillments of repressed wishes" and provide "the royal road to a knowledge of the unconscious mind." Freud also believed that dreams function as a sort of psychological "safety valve" for the release of unconscious and unacceptable urges.

Freud (1904) proposed that dreams have two components: the *manifest content,* or the dream images themselves, and the *latent content,* which is the disguised psychological meaning of the dream. Like a detective searching for clues, Freud carefully analyzed the dreams of his patients, looking for symbolic expressions of repressed urges and wishes. For example, Freud (1911) believed that dream images of sticks, swords, and other elongated objects are phallic symbols, representing the penis. Dream images of cupboards, boxes, and ovens supposedly symbolize the vagina.

Freud's notions are certainly intriguing and consistent with the ancient belief that dream symbols must be interpreted to reveal the dream's meaning. In many types of psychotherapy today, especially those that follow Freud's ideas, dreams are still seen as an important source of information about psychological conflicts. That said, let's consider a very different view of the meaning of dreams.

Hobson & McCarley: The Activation-Synthesis Model of Dreaming

Armed with an array of evidence that dreaming involves the activation of different brain areas during REM sleep, researchers **J. Allan Hobson** and

FIGURE 4.4 The Activation-Synthesis Model of Dreaming

According to the activation-synthesis model, dreaming sleep is due to the activation of brainstem circuits that arouse more sophisticated areas of the brain, such as visual and auditory centers. These internally generated signals result in the dream images and sensations that the activated brain combines, or "synthesizes." The dreaming person imposes a personal meaning on the dream story.
(Hobson, 1989.)

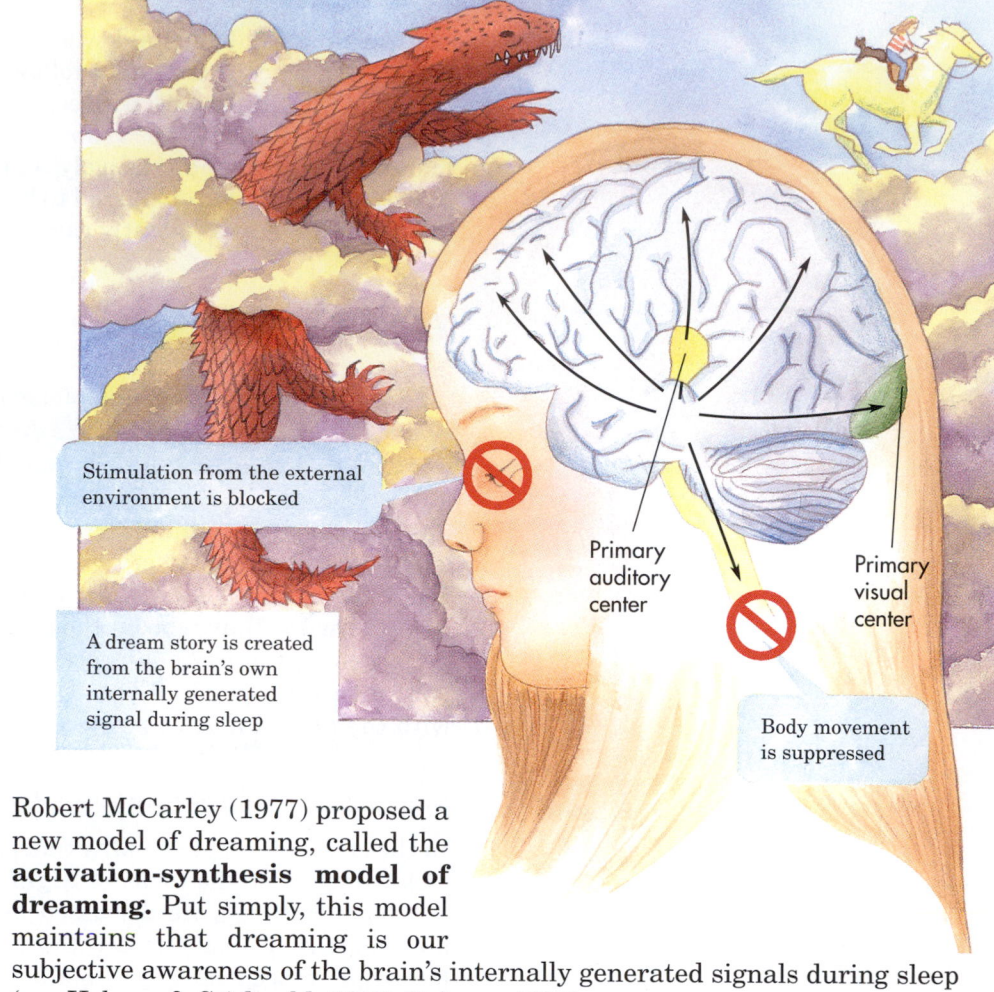

Stimulation from the external environment is blocked

A dream story is created from the brain's own internally generated signal during sleep

Primary auditory center

Primary visual center

Body movement is suppressed

activation-synthesis model of dreaming
The theory that brain activity during sleep produces dream images (*activation*), which are combined by the brain into a dream story (*synthesis*).

Robert McCarley (1977) proposed a new model of dreaming, called the **activation-synthesis model of dreaming.** Put simply, this model maintains that dreaming is our subjective awareness of the brain's internally generated signals during sleep (see Hobson & Stickgold, 1995; Hobson, 1990).

More specifically, the activation-synthesis model maintains that the experience of dreaming sleep is due to the automatic activation of brainstem circuits at the base of the brain (see Figure 4.4). These brainstem circuits arouse more sophisticated brain areas, such as visual centers, that normally register stimuli from the external world. But rather than responding to stimulation from the external environment, the dreaming brain is actually responding to its own internally generated signals.

Different elements of dreams correspond to the activation of particular brain areas. For example, the activation of emotion centers in the brain is reflected in emotionally intense dreams; visual dream elements are due to activation of the brain's visual centers; and so forth.

In the absence of external sensory input, the activated brain combines, or "synthesizes," these internally generated sensory signals and imposes meaning on them. The dream story itself is derived from a hodgepodge of memories and sensations that are triggered by the brain's activation and chemical changes during sleep. According to this model, then, dreaming is nothing more than the brain synthesizing and integrating memory fragments and sensations that are internally triggered (Hobson & Stickgold, 1995).

However, the activation-synthesis theory does *not* state that dreams are completely meaningless (Hobson & Stickgold, 1995). As Hobson (1989) observes, "For all their nonsense, dreams have a clear import and a deeply personal one." But, if there is a meaning to dreams, that meaning lies in the deeply personal way in which the images are organized or "synthesized." In other words, the meaning is to be found not by "decoding" the dream symbols, but by analyzing the way the dreamer makes sense out of the chaos of dream images.

Dreams

1. Lisa is asleep and is having a very frightening dream in which she is being chased by a large dog with big fangs. Lisa is most likely in _____ sleep and experiencing a _____.
  a. stage 4 NREM; night terror
  b. stage 1 NREM; hypnogogic hallucination
  c. REM; nightmare
  d. REM; night terror

2. Jeff enjoys his dreams very much and claims he can often guide the course of his dreams even while he is asleep and experiencing the dream. Jeff is _____.
  a. suffering from narcolepsy
  b. a lucid dreamer
  c. probably using hallucinogenic drugs
  d. lying

3. Mark's psychotherapist suggests that the images in Mark's dreams are actually symbolic of significant people and events in his life. As part of Mark's therapy, his therapist tries to uncover the hidden meaning, or _____ content, of the dream images.
  a. lucid   **c.** manifest
  b. latent   **d.** restorative

4. The night before an important job interview, Marjorie doesn't sleep well and repeatedly awakens for brief periods throughout the night. Each time she briefly awakens, the vague, thoughtlike imagery filling her mind is that of rehearsing details she wants to remember to say during the interview. These ruminations during sleep about the next day's events represent _____.
  a. dreams
  b. nightmares
  c. lucid dreams
  d. sleep thinking

Hypnosis

Hypnosis refers to an unusual state of awareness in which a person responds to suggestions with changes in perception, memory, and behavior. Who can be hypnotized? What are the primary effects of hypnosis? How has hypnosis been explained?

Hypnosis is an unusual and controversial state of awareness that has been the focus of a great deal of scientific research. **Hypnosis** can be defined as a cooperative social interaction in which one person, the subject, responds to suggestions by another person, the hypnotist, which produce changes in perception, memory, and behavior (Kihlstrom, 1987). Hypnosis can also be self-induced.

Hypnosis is characterized by highly focused attention, increased responsiveness to suggestions, vivid images and fantasies, and a willingness to accept distortions of logic or reality. During hypnosis, the subject temporarily suspends his or her sense of initiative, voluntarily accepting and following the hypnotist's instructions (Hilgard, 1986a).

People vary in their susceptibility to hypnosis. Psychologists have found that about 15 percent of adults are highly susceptible to hypnosis, 10 percent are difficult or impossible to hypnotize, and most adults are somewhere in between (Hilgard, 1982). Children tend to be more responsive to hypnosis than adults, and children as young as five years old can be hypnotized (L. Cooper, 1979). Some evidence suggests that the degree of hypnotic susceptibility tends to run in families (Wallace & Persanyi, 1989).

The best candidates for hypnosis are individuals who approach the hypnotic experience with positive, receptive attitudes (Spanos & others, 1987). The subject's expectations of being responsive to hypnosis also plays an important role (Spanos & others, 1993; Silva & Kirsch, 1992). Most important,

hypnosis
(hip-NO-sis) A cooperative social interaction in which a person responds to suggestions with changes in perception, memory, and behavior.

highly susceptible people have the ability to become deeply absorbed in fantasy and imaginary experience. They easily become absorbed in reading fiction, watching movies, and listening to music (Nadon & others, 1991; Roche & McConkey, 1990).

Effects of Hypnosis

Deeply hypnotized subjects sometimes experience profound changes in their subjective experience of consciousness. They may report feelings of detachment from their bodies, profound relaxation, or sensations of timelessness (Tart, 1979). More often, hypnotized people converse normally and remain fully aware of their surroundings.

Sensory and Perceptual Changes

Some of the most dramatic effects that can be produced with hypnosis are alterations in sensation and perception. Sensory changes that can be induced through hypnosis include temporary blindness, deafness, or a complete loss of sensation in some part of the body (Hilgard, 1986a). When the suggestion is made to a highly responsive subject that her arm is numb and cannot feel pain, for example, she will not consciously experience the pain of a pinprick or the pain of having her arm immersed in ice water. This property of hypnosis has led to its use as a technique in pain control. Painful dental and medical procedures, including surgery, have been successfully performed with hypnosis as the only anesthesia (Hilgard & Hilgard, 1983).

People can also experience hallucinations under hypnosis (Kihlstrom, 1985). A highly responsive hypnotic subject can be told that his closest friend is sitting in a chair on the other side of the room. Not only will the hypnotic subject report seeing his friend in vivid detail, he will walk over and "touch" the other person. Under hypnosis, people can also *not* perceive something that *is* there. For example, if the suggestion is made that a jar of rotten eggs has no smell, a highly suggestible subject will not consciously perceive any odor.

Posthypnotic Suggestions

Hypnosis can also influence behavior *outside* of the hypnotic state. When a **posthypnotic suggestion** is made during hypnosis, the subject will carry out that specific suggestion after the hypnotic session is over. For example, under hypnosis, a subject was given the posthypnotic suggestion that the number 5 no longer existed. He was brought out of hypnosis and then asked to count his fingers. The subject counted 11 fingers! Counting again, the baffled subject was at a loss to explain his results.

Most posthypnotic suggestions last only a few hours or days before they wear off, although some posthypnotic suggestions have been reported to last over a year (Kihlstrom, 1984). So, even if the hypnotist does not include some posthypnotic signal to trigger rediscovery of the number 5, the subject will eventually recall that the number 5 exists.

Hypnosis and Memory

Memory can be significantly affected by hypnosis. In **posthypnotic amnesia,** a subject is unable to recall specific information or events that occurred before or during hypnosis (Kihlstrom, 1984). Posthypnotic amnesia is produced by a hypnotic suggestion that suppresses the memory of specific information, such as the subject's street address. The effects of posthypnotic amnesia are usually temporary, disappearing either spontaneously or when a posthypnotic signal is suggested by the hypnotist (Kihlstrom, 1983). When the signal is given, the information floods back into the subject's mind.

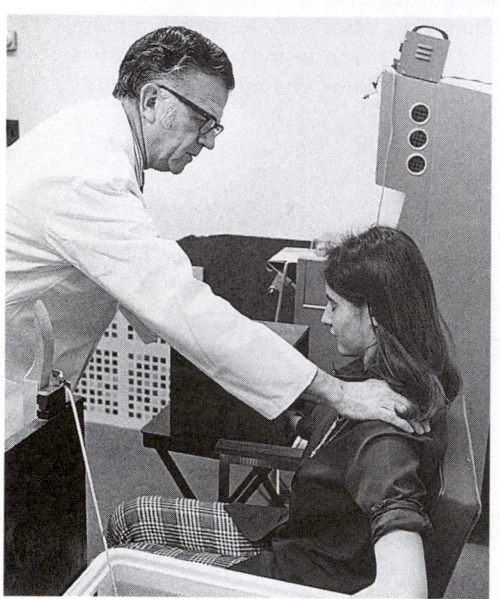

Hypnotic Suppression of Pain After inducing hypnosis in this young woman, Ernest Hilgard instructs her that she will feel no pain in her arm. The subject's arm is then immersed in circulating ice water for several minutes, and she reports that she does not experience any pain. In contrast, a non-hypnotized subject perceives the same experience as being extremely painful and can keep his arm in the ice water for no more than a few seconds.

posthypnotic suggestion
A suggestion made during hypnosis that the person carry out a specific instruction following the hypnotic session.

posthypnotic amnesia
A hypnotic suggestion that suppresses the ability to recall specific information.

Hypnosis and Memory Many people believe that hypnosis can be used to enhance recall, particularly of upsetting or traumatic events. However, research has shown that hypnosis is no more effective than other types of memory-enhancing methods. Simply looking at a family photograph album can provide potent cues to help retrieve once-forgotten memories.

The opposite hypnotic effect is called **hypermnesia,** which is enhancement of memory for past events (Kihlstrom, 1985). Police investigators sometimes use hypnosis in an attempt to enhance the memories of crime victims and witnesses. Despite the common belief that you can "zoom in" on briefly seen crime details under hypnosis, such claims are extremely exaggerated (M. Smith, 1983). When compared to regular police interview methods, hypnosis does not significantly enhance memory or improve the accuracy of memories (Sloane, 1981).

Many studies have shown that efforts to enhance memories hypnotically can lead to distortions and inaccuracies. In fact, hypnosis can greatly increase confidence in memories that are actually incorrect (Kihlstrom & Barnhardt, 1993). False memories, also called *pseudomemories,* can be inadvertently created when hypnosis is used to aid recall (Yapko, 1994a; Lynn & Nash, 1994).

For example, in one study it was suggested to hypnotized subjects that they had been awakened one night during the previous week by loud noises (Laurence & Perry, 1983). Following hypnosis, almost half of the subjects claimed that loud noises had disturbed their sleep during the previous week. Even *after* the subjects were told the loud noises had been hypnotically suggested, several subjects persisted in the belief that the disturbance had actually taken place.

Although the effects of hypnosis can be dramatic, there are limits to the behaviors that can be influenced by hypnosis. First, contrary to popular belief, a person cannot be hypnotized against his or her will. Second, hypnosis cannot make you stronger than your physical capabilities or induce talents that are not already present (Bowers, 1976). However, hypnosis *can* enhance physical skills or athletic ability by increasing motivation and concentration, or by reducing anxiety (LeUnes & Nation, 1989; Stanton, 1989). Third, hypnosis cannot make you perform behaviors that are contrary to your morals and values. Thus, you're very unlikely to commit criminal or immoral acts under the influence of hypnosis—unless, of course, you find such actions acceptable (Hilgard, 1986b).

Explaining Hypnosis:
Consciousness Divided?

According to psychologist **Ernest Hilgard** (1992, 1991, 1986a), the hypnotized person experiences **dissociation**—the splitting of consciousness into two or more simultaneous streams of mental activity. While hypnotized, a person consciously experiences one stream of mental activity that is responding to the hypnotist's suggestions. But a second, dissociated stream of mental activity is also operating, processing information that is unavailable to the consciousness of the hypnotized subject. Hilgard refers to this second, dissociated stream of mental activity as the **hidden observer.** (The phrase "hidden observer" does *not* mean that the hypnotized person has multiple personalities.)

Hilgard accidentally discovered the "hidden observer" while conducting a classroom demonstration (see Hilgard, 1992, 1986a). Hilgard hypnotized the student and induced hypnotic deafness. Seated before the class, the student was completely unresponsive to very loud, sudden sounds, such as the sound of a starter pistol firing or of wooden blocks being banged together.

Another student, observing the demonstration, asked Hilgard if "some part" of the hypnotized subject was actually aware of the sounds. Hilgard instructed the hypnotized student to raise his right index finger if some part of him could still hear. To Hilgard's surprise, the hypnotized student's right index finger rose! When brought out of hypnosis, the student had no recall of any sounds during hypnotically induced deafness, *including* Hilgard's suggestion to raise his index finger. Hypnosis, it seemed, had produced a split in

hypermnesia
(high-perm-NEES-zha) A hypnotic suggestion to enhance a person's memory for past events.

dissociation
The splitting of consciousness into two or more simultaneous streams of mental activity.

hidden observer
Hilgard's term for the hidden, or dissociated, stream of mental activity during hypnosis.

TABLE 4.3 Help Through Hypnosis

Trained professionals have successfully used hypnosis to:

- Reduce the pain and discomfort of cancer treatments in children
- Remove warts
- Reduce stress in secretaries
- Reduce use of narcotics to relieve postoperative pain
- Improve the concentration and motivation of athletes
- Diminish anxiety and fear in the terminally ill
- Lessen maternal depression after childbirth
- Modify behavior in eating disorders
- Eliminate recurring nightmares
- Help insomniacs fall asleep faster
- Lessen the severity and frequency of asthma attacks
- Decrease the intensity and frequency of headaches
- Eliminate or reduce stuttering
- Suppress the gag reflex during dental procedures

consciousness. A conscious segment complied with the hypnotic suggestion of deafness, but a separate, dissociated segment unavailable to consciousness continued to process information. This was the "hidden observer."

Not all psychologists agree that hypnotic phenomena are due to dissociation, divided consciousness, or a "hidden observer" (see Baker, 1996; Kirsch & others, 1995; Fellows, 1990). Rather, some researchers believe that hypnotic phenomena can be understood in terms of social factors. In Critical Thinking Box 4.4, we examine this controversy more fully.

Regardless of how hypnotic phenomena are ultimately explained, the fact remains that hypnosis works. As research has more clearly defined the effects and limits of hypnotic suggestions, the use of hypnosis in medicine, dentistry, and psychotherapy has become more common. Hypnosis has also been used in sports and business to improve performance and enhance motivation. Table 4.3 lists just a few of the situations in which hypnosis has been successfully used to help people.

CRITICAL THINKING 4.4

Hypnosis: A Special State of Consciousness?

Some psychologists, such as Nicholas Spanos (1994, 1989, 1986), have contended that hypnotically produced changes can be explained using well-established concepts in *social psychology,* a branch of psychology that investigates how people influence, think about, and relate to one another.

Because hypnosis involves a voluntary social interaction between two people, Spanos (1994) argued that hypnotic subjects are simply responding to *social demands.* They are motivated to be "good" subjects and to cooperate with the hypnotic suggestions. Thus, they act the way that they think good hypnotic subjects are supposed to act, conforming to the expectations of the hypnotist, their own expectations, and situational cues.

As you'll see in the chapter on social psychology (Chapter 11), there is ample evidence that people will obey an authority figure to a surprising extent, sometimes performing very uncharacteristic and extreme behaviors. Under enough social pressure, people will alter, distort, or lie about their perceptions of objective events to conform to the majority view. When these findings are extrapolated and applied to hypnotic phenomena, social-psychological influences seem to provide a simpler and more logical explanation of hypnotic phenomena than notions like a "dissociation in consciousness" and the "hidden observer."

To back up their social-psychological interpretation of hypnotic phenomena, Spanos (1994, 1989) and his colleagues have amassed an impressive array of evidence showing that highly motivated people often perform just as well as hypnotized subjects in demonstrating pain reduction, amnesia, age regression, and hallucinations. Studies of people pretending to be hypnotized have shown similar results.

Are hypnotic effects the result of social-psychological influences that motivate people to conform, role-play, or act in ways that fulfill the expectations inherent in the situation? Or is hypnosis a special state of consciousness that involves a dissociative "split" in awareness?

Both positions are supported by experimental evidence. Psychologist John Kihlstrom (1986) has argued that a comprehensive understanding of hypnotic phenomena requires a combination of *both* explanations. The importance of social influences is recognized by many hypnosis researchers. However, as Kihlstrom points out, social influences alone seem inadequate to account for the extraordinary phenomena sometimes demonstrated under hypnosis.

What do you think? Research has shown that highly motivated subjects can mimic the effects of hypnosis, but does that invalidate the notion that hypnotic effects are the result of a dissociation in consciousness? What kinds of evidence would prove or disprove the notion that hypnotic effects involve a special dissociative state of consciousness?

meditation

Any one of a number of sustained concentration techniques that focus attention and heighten awareness.

Meditation

Meditation refers to techniques used to control or retrain attention so as to induce an altered state of focused attention and awareness. What are two general types of meditation? What are the effects of meditation?

Meditation refers to a group of techniques that induce an altered state of focused attention and heightened awareness. Meditation takes many forms and has been used for thousands of years as part of religious practices throughout the world. Virtually every major form of religion has a rich tradition of meditative practices—whether Hindu, Taoist, Buddhist, Jewish, Christian, or Muslim. However, many people practice meditation independent of any religious tradition or spiritual context. Some forms of psychotherapy also include meditative practice as a component of the overall therapy (Epstein, 1995).

Common to all forms of meditation is the goal of controlling or retraining attention. Although meditation techniques vary a great deal, they can be divided into two general categories (West, 1987). *Concentration techniques* involve focusing awareness on a visual image, your breathing, a word, or a phrase. When a sound is used, it is typically a short word or a religious phrase, called a *mantra,* that is mentally repeated. *Opening-up techniques* involve a present-centered awareness of the passing moment without mental judgment (see Tart, 1994). Rather than concentrating on an object, sound, or activity, the meditator engages in quiet awareness of the "here and now" without distracting thoughts (West, 1987).

Meditation in Different Cultures Meditation is an important part of many cultures. Above, a group of women are practicing tai chi in a public park in Hong Kong. Tai chi is a form of meditation that involves a structured series of slow, steady movements. Throughout China, many people begin their day with tai chi, often meeting in parks and other public places. Below, a holy man in Katmandu, Nepal, sits motionless, practicing solitary meditation in a Buddhist temple garden.

Effects of Meditation

One meditation technique that has been widely used in research is called *transcendental meditation,* or *TM.* TM is a form of concentrative meditation that can be quickly mastered, follows a simple format, and does not require any changes in lifestyle or beliefs (Wallace, 1987). Meditators sit quietly with eyes closed and mentally repeat the mantra they have been given. Rather than struggling to clear the mind of thoughts, the meditator is taught to allow distracting thoughts to simply "fall away."

Numerous studies have shown that even beginning meditators practicing TM experience a state of lowered physiological arousal, including decreased blood pressure, heart rate, and changes in brain waves (Dillbeck & Orme-Johnson, 1987). Advocates of TM have claimed that such physical changes produce a unique state of consciousness with a wide variety of benefits, including stress reduction. However, in terms of simply reducing physiological arousal, TM appears to be no more effective than merely resting with your eyes closed (Holmes, 1987, 1984). Does this mean that simple rest or relaxation is the *same* as transcendental meditation? Not necessarily.

Like other forms of meditation, TM has diverse effects. Meditators show EEG patterns that are dominated by alpha brain-wave activity, which is similar to the state of drowsiness that precedes stage 1 sleep (Fenwick, 1987). However, experienced meditators tend to describe meditation in very different

subjective terms than drowsiness (Pekala, 1987). Often, meditation is described as producing both relaxation *and* a state of wakeful alertness. In contrast, people who practice mental relaxation with their eyes closed often describe the experience as relaxing but boring (Alexander & others, 1989). Regardless, many studies have shown that regular meditation can enhance physical and psychological functioning (Orne-Johnson, 1987; Jedrczak, 1986). If you would like to try a simple meditative technique, follow the instructions in Table 4.4.

Meditation and hypnosis are similar in that both involve the deliberate use of mental techniques to change the experience of consciousness. In the final section of this chapter, we'll consider one of the oldest strategies for deliberately altering conscious awareness—psychoactive drugs.

TABLE 4.4 How to Meditate

Here is a simple but effective meditation technique that was developed by British psychologist and meditation researcher Michael A. West. Practice the technique for 15 to 20 minutes twice a day, and continue to do so for at least two weeks.

1. Sit quietly in an upright position in a room where you are not likely to be disturbed.
2. Close your eyes and relax your body. Sit quietly for about half a minute.
3. Begin to easily repeat the word "one" silently to yourself. Or choose some other simple word, like "peace" or "calm."
4. Don't concentrate too hard on the sound. The word need only be a faint idea at times—you don't have to keep repeating it clearly.
5. Think the word easily. It may change by getting louder or softer, longer or shorter, or it may not change at all. In every case, just take it as it comes.
6. Remember, the word has no special meaning or special significance. It is a simple device which helps in meditation.
7. Continue the meditation in this way for about 15 minutes. Don't worry about achieving a deep level of meditation or about whether you are concentrating on the sound.
8. Don't try to control thoughts. If thoughts come during meditation, don't worry about it. When you become aware that you have slipped into a train of thought, just go very easily back to the sound. Don't make great efforts to exclude thoughts—just favor the sound.
9. If you become aware of outside noises or other distracting sounds, go easily back to the word; don't fight to exclude those distractions. Do the same as you would with thoughts. Accept them but favor the sound.
10. Above all, you are meant to enjoy the meditation, so don't try too hard, just take it easily as it comes.

SOURCE: West, 1987.

CONCEPT REVIEW 4.4

Hypnosis and Meditation

1. Jill is very responsive to hypnotic suggestions. Jill probably _____.
   a. has a very vivid imagination and a rich fantasy life
   b. has a very negative attitude toward hypnosis
   c. is easily distracted
   d. can be easily hypnotized against her will

2. While Glenda is under hypnosis, the hypnotist tells her that she remembers being lost in a shopping mall as a young child. After being brought out of hypnosis, Glenda is completely convinced that the event occurred. She describes being found by a mall security guard and other details of the event. The hypnotist has successfully created _____.
   a. an age regression   c. hypermnesia
   b. posthypnotic amnesia d. a pseudomemory

3. Dr. Kildare used hypnosis instead of an anesthetic when setting a patient's broken toe. The patient insisted that she felt no pain, but when instructed to raise her right index finger if some part of her felt any pain, she raised her finger. This example best illustrates the notion of _____.
   a. age regression
   b. posthypnotic suggestion
   c. the hidden observer
   d. transcendental meditation

4. Dean's meditation consists of focusing his awareness on mentally repeating the word "peace." Dean is using a(n) _____ technique of meditation.
   a. concentration   c. opening-up
   b. mindfulness   d. Zen

Psychoactive Drugs

Psychoactive drugs alter consciousness by changing arousal, mood, thinking, sensation, and perception. What are the common properties of psychoactive drugs? What factors influence the effects of drugs?

Psychoactive drugs are chemical substances that can alter arousal, mood, thinking, sensation, and perception. In this section, we will look at the characteristics of four broad categories of psychoactive drugs:

1. *Depressants*—drugs that *depress,* or inhibit, brain activity.
2. *Opiates*—drugs that are chemically similar to morphine and that relieve pain and produce euphoria.
3. *Stimulants*—drugs that *stimulate,* or excite, brain activity.
4. *Psychedelic drugs*—drugs that distort sensory perceptions.

Common Properties of Psychoactive Drugs

Addiction is a broad term that refers to a condition in which a person feels psychologically and physically compelled to take a specific drug. When an individual experiences **physical dependence,** his body and brain chemistry have physically adapted to the drug (Berridge & Robinson, 1995). Many physically addictive drugs gradually produce **tolerance,** which means that increasing amounts of the drug are needed to gain the original, desired effect.

When a person is physically dependent on a drug, abstaining from the drug produces withdrawal symptoms. **Withdrawal symptoms** are unpleasant physical reactions to the lack of the drug plus an intense craving for it. Withdrawal symptoms are alleviated by taking the drug again. Often, the withdrawal symptoms are opposite to the drug's action, a phenomenon called the **drug rebound effect.** For example, withdrawing from stimulating drugs, like the caffeine in coffee, may produce depression and fatigue. Withdrawal from depressant drugs, like alcohol, may produce excitability.

Biological Effects of Drugs

Each psychoactive drug has a distinct biological effect. Psychoactive drugs may influence many different body systems, but their consciousness-altering effects are primarily due to their effect on the brain. Typically, these drugs influence brain activity by altering synaptic transmission among neurons (see Julien, 1995). As we discussed in Chapter 2, drugs can affect synaptic transmission by blocking, mimicking, increasing, or decreasing neurotransmitters (see Figure 2.5 on page 46).

The biological effects of a given drug can also vary somewhat from one person to another. The drugtaker's size, gender, and age may influence the intensity of the drug's effects. So can individual metabolism, and whether the person is taking the drug on a full or empty stomach or in combination with other drugs.

Psychological and Environmental Influences

Along with biological factors, psychological and environmental factors influence the effects of a drug. The response to a drug can be significantly affected

psychoactive drug
A drug that alters normal consciousness, perception, mood, and behavior.

physical dependence
A condition in which a person has physically adapted to a drug so that he must take the drug regularly in order to avoid withdrawal symptoms.

tolerance
A condition in which increasing amounts of a physically addictive drug are needed to produce the original, desired effect.

withdrawal symptoms
Unpleasant physical reactions, combined with intense drug cravings, that occur when a person abstains from a drug on which she is physically dependent.

drug rebound effect
Withdrawal symptoms that are the opposite of a physically addictive drug's action.

by the drugtaker's personality characteristics, mood, expectations, experience with the drug, and the setting in which the drug is taken (see Marlatt & others, 1988; Stacy & others, 1990). For example, what kind of effect do you think three drinks would have on each of the following individuals?

- A college student at an end-of-semester bash the night final exams are over.
- A father toasting his youngest daughter at her bat mitzvah.
- A man having an escalating argument with his wife on a hot summer night.

Even though the physiological effect of alcohol is essentially the same for each individual, the behavioral and psychological response would clearly be different. One drinker feels joyously uninhibited; another is feeling sentimental and proud; and the third may be close to committing homicide. Although alcohol may provide the most familiar example, individual responses to other psychoactive drugs are also subject to psychological and environmental influences.

The Depressants

Depressants inhibit central nervous system activity. How does alcohol affect the body and psychological functioning? What are the effects of barbiturates and tranquilizers?

The **depressants** are a class of drugs that depress or inhibit central nervous system activity. In general, depressants produce drowsiness, sedation, or sleep. Depressants also relieve anxiety and lower inhibitions. All the depressant drugs are potentially physically addictive. Finally, the effects of depressant drugs are *additive*. That is, the sedative effects are increased when depressants are combined.

Alcohol

Alcohol provides a good example of the potential for a psychoactive drug to be misused. Used in small amounts, alcohol reduces tension and anxiety. Evidence even exists that light drinking reduces the risk of heart disease, probably because of its beneficial effects on cholesterol levels (Rimm & others, 1991; Gordon & Doyle, 1987). Weddings, parties, and other social gatherings often include alcohol, a tribute to its relaxing and "social lubricating" properties. Yet consider these points:

- Drug experts believe that alcohol abuse has the highest social cost of all drug addictions (Marlatt & others, 1988).
- Every year, alcohol is implicated in over 25,000 fatal automobile accidents and 12,000 murders in the United States.
- Approximately two-thirds of all cases of spouse abuse and violent child abuse involve alcohol use (Steele & Josephs, 1990).
- Drinking by pregnant women is the third leading cause of birth defects producing mental retardation—and the only preventable one (Julien, 1995).

depressants
A category of psychoactive drugs that depress or inhibit brain activity.

Thus, even though alcohol is a legal and readily available drug for adults, it's also a dangerous drug with a high potential for abuse.

The Social and Personal Costs of Alcohol Abuse The family and friends of those killed by a drunk driver can attest to the high costs associated with alcohol abuse. Seven million Americans are *alcoholics*—they are physically addicted to alcohol. Another seven million drink excessively on a regular basis and suffer social, occupational, and health problems as a result of drinking (Rosenberg, 1993). An intoxicated driver has impaired judgment and perceptions, delayed reaction time, and poor coordination. This deadly combination results in more than 25,000 traffic deaths each year.

How Does Alcohol Affect the Body?

Generally, it takes about one hour to metabolize the alcohol in one drink, which is defined as the amount of alcohol in one ounce of 80-proof whiskey, four ounces of wine, or 12 ounces of beer. All three drinks contain the same amount of alcohol; it's simply more diluted in beer than in hard liquor.

Factors such as body weight, gender, food consumption, and the rate of alcohol consumption also affect blood alcohol levels. A slender person who quickly consumes three drinks on an empty stomach will become more than twice as intoxicated as a heavier person who consumes three drinks with food. Women metabolize alcohol more slowly than men. If a man and a woman of equal weight consume the same number of drinks, the woman will become more intoxicated.

Alcohol depresses the activity of neurons throughout the brain. Alcohol impairs cognitive abilities such as concentration, memory, and speech, and physical abilities such as muscle coordination and balance (Julien, 1995). As blood levels of alcohol rise, more brain activity is impaired, until the person loses consciousness. If blood alcohol levels continue to rise, death can occur because the brain's respiratory center can no longer function. This is why drinking "contests" are potentially lethal.

Because alcohol is physically addictive, the alcoholic who stops drinking may suffer from physical withdrawal symptoms. The severity of the withdrawal symptoms depends on the level of physical dependence. With a low level of dependence, withdrawal may involve disrupted sleep, anxiety, and mild tremors ("the shakes"). At higher levels of physical dependence on alcohol, withdrawal may involve confusion, hallucinations, and severe tremors or seizures. Collectively, these severe symptoms are sometimes called the *delirium tremens,* or *DTs*. Alcohol withdrawal causes rebound hyperexcitability in the brain. In cases of extreme physical dependence, withdrawal can cause seizures, convulsions, and even death in the absence of medical supervision (Julien, 1995).

What Are Alcohol's Psychological Effects?

People are often surprised that alcohol is classified as a depressant. Initially, alcohol produces mild euphoria, talkativeness, and feelings of good humor and friendliness, leading many people to think of alcohol as a stimulant. But these subjective experiences occur because alcohol *lessens inhibitions* by depressing the brain centers responsible for judgment and self-control. Reduced inhibitions and self-control are involved in the aggressive and violent behavior sometimes associated with alcohol abuse (Steele, 1986; Steele & Josephs, 1990). But the individual effects of the loss of inhibitions are unpredictable and depend on the person's environment and his expectations regarding alcohol's effects (Bushman, 1993; Marlatt & Rohsenow; 1980).

Barbiturates and Tranquilizers

Barbiturates are powerful depressant drugs that reduce anxiety and promote sleep, which is why they are sometimes called "downers." Barbiturates depress activity in the brain centers that control arousal, wakefulness, and alertness (Julien, 1995; Barondes, 1993). Barbiturates also depress the brain's respiratory centers.

barbiturates
(barb-ITCH-yer-ets) A category of depressant drugs that reduce anxiety and produce sleepiness.

tranquilizers
Depressant drugs that relieve anxiety.

opiates
(OH-pee-ets) A category of psychoactive drugs that are chemically similar to morphine and have strong pain-relieving properties.

stimulants
A category of psychoactive drugs that increase brain activity, arouse behavior, and increase mental alertness.

Heroin Cough Syrup Opium and its derivatives, including heroin, morphine, and codeine, were legal in the United States until 1914. In the late nineteenth and early twentieth century, opiates were commonly used in over-the-counter medications for a variety of ailments, from sleeplessness to "female problems" (Musto, 1991). This ad for "Glyco-Heroin" cough syrup appeared in 1904. Codeine is still used in some prescription cough syrups.

Like alcohol, barbiturates at low doses cause relaxation, mild euphoria, and reduced inhibitions. Larger doses produce a loss of coordination, impaired mental functioning, and depression. High doses can produce unconsciousness, coma, and death. Barbiturates also produce a very deep but abnormal sleep; REM sleep is greatly reduced. Because of the additive effect of depressants, barbiturates combined with alcohol are particularly dangerous.

Common barbiturates include the prescription sedatives *Seconal* and *Nembutal.* The illegal drug *methaqualone* (street name *Quaalude*) is almost identical chemically to barbiturates and has similar effects.

Barbiturates produce both physical and psychological dependence. Withdrawal from low doses of barbiturates produces irritability and REM rebound nightmares. Withdrawal from high doses of barbiturates can produce hallucinations, disorientation, restlessness, and life-threatening convulsions.

Tranquilizers are depressants that are prescribed to relieve anxiety. Common tranquilizers include Xanax, Valium, Librium, and Ativan. We will discuss these drugs in more detail in Chapter 14, on therapies. Chemically different from barbiturates, tranquilizers produce similar, although less powerful, effects.

The Opiates

The opiates are a group of addictive drugs that relieve pain and produce euphoria. How do opiates affect the brain and relieve pain?

Often called *narcotics,* the **opiates** refer to a group of addictive drugs that relieve pain and produce feelings of euphoria. Natural opiates include: *opium,* which is derived from the opium poppy; *morphine,* the active ingredient in opium; and *codeine,* which can be derived from either opium or morphine. Synthetic and semisynthetic opiates include *heroin, methadone,* and the prescription painkillers *Percodan* and *Demerol.*

Opiates produce their powerful effects by mimicking the brain's own natural painkillers, called *endorphins,* which we discussed in Chapter 2. Opiates occupy endorphin receptor sites in the brain (Snyder, 1986). The word *endorphins* literally means "the morphine within."

When used medically, opiates alter an individual's reaction to pain not by acting at the pain site, but by reducing the brain's perception of pain. Many people recovering from surgery experience a wave of pain relief after receiving narcotics such as morphine, Demerol, or Percodan. People who take opiates in such circumstances rarely develop drug tolerance or dependence (Jacox & others, 1994).

The most frequently abused opiate is heroin. When injected into a vein, heroin reaches the brain in seconds, creating an intense "rush" of euphoria that is followed by feelings of contentment, peacefulness, and warmth. Withdrawing from heroin is not life-threatening, but it does produce unpleasant drug rebound symptoms. Withdrawal symptoms include an intense craving for heroin, fever, chills, muscle cramps, and gastrointestinal problems.

The Stimulants

Stimulant drugs increase brain activity. What are the effects of caffeine and nicotine? How does nicotine affect the brain? What are the effects of amphetamines and cocaine?

Stimulants vary in the strength of their effects, legal status, and the way they are taken. All stimulant drugs, however, are at least mildly addicting, and all tend to increase brain activity. We'll first look at the most widely used and legal stimulants, caffeine and nicotine. Then we'll examine much more potent stimulants, cocaine and the amphetamines.

Caffeine and Nicotine

Caffeine is found in coffee, tea, cola drinks, chocolate, and many over-the-counter medications. Most Americans consume caffeine in some form every day (DeAngelis, 1994a). In fact, caffeine is the most widely used psychoactive drug in the world.

Caffeine stimulates the cerebral cortex in the brain, resulting in an increase in mental alertness and wakefulness (Julien, 1995). Even a single cup of coffee has a noticeable effect on the cerebral cortex.

Yes, coffee drinkers, caffeine *is* physically addictive. Regular coffee, tea, or cola drinkers will experience withdrawal symptoms if they abruptly stop their caffeine intake: headaches, irritability, drowsiness, and fatigue may last up to a week (Goldstein, 1994; Griffiths, 1994). At high doses, caffeine can produce anxiety, restlessness, insomnia, and increased heart rate—symptoms that are collectively called "coffee nerves."

Nicotine is another widely used, legal, and extremely addictive stimulant. Nicotine is found in all tobacco products, including pipe tobacco, cigars, cigarettes, and smokeless tobacco. Like coffee, nicotine increases mental alertness and reduces fatigue or drowsiness. About 25 percent of American adults use tobacco regularly. The proportion of smokers is much higher in Japan, many European countries, and developing countries (Bartecchi & others, 1995).

When cigarette smoke is inhaled, nicotine reaches the brain in seconds. But within 30 minutes or so, nicotine has left the brain (Ashton & Stepney, 1983). Thus, the addicted "pack-a-day" smoker will light a cigarette every thirty to forty minutes to maintain a relatively constant nicotine level in the brain. Over the course of a year, that averages out to 70,000 "hits" of nicotine (Carroll, 1993).

TABLE 4.5 Common Sources of Caffeine

Item	Caffeine Content (Average, in mg)
Coffee (5-ounce cup)	100
Tea (5-ounce cup)	50
Cocoa (5-ounce cup)	5
Chocolate (semisweet, baking) (1 ounce)	25
Chocolate milk (1 ounce)	5
Cola drink (12 ounces)	40
Over-the-counter stimulants (No Doz, Vivarin)	100+
Over-the-counter analgesics (Excedrin, Anacin, Midol, Vanquish)	65
	33
Over-the-counter cold remedies (Coryban-D, Triaminicin)	30

SOURCE: Julien, 1995.

Caffeine and Conversation Caffeine is the most widely used psychoactive drug in the world and is commonly consumed in social settings. These French college students are enjoying a cup of espresso at an outdoor cafe.

Amphetamines and Cocaine

Like caffeine and nicotine, amphetamines and cocaine stimulate brain activity, increasing mental alertness and reducing fatigue. However, amphetamines and cocaine also elevate mood and produce a sense of euphoria (Snyder, 1986). When abused, they can produce severe psychological and physical problems.

Common amphetamines are the prescription drugs *Benzedrine* and *Dexedrine*. Sometimes called "speed" or "uppers," **amphetamines** suppress appetite and were once widely prescribed as diet pills. Tolerance to the appetite-suppressant effects occurs quickly, so progressive increases in amphetamine dosage are required to maintain the effect. Consequently, amphetamines are rarely prescribed today for weight control.

caffeine
(kaff-EEN) A stimulant drug found in coffee, tea, cola drinks, chocolate, and many over-the-counter medications.

nicotine
A stimulant drug found in tobacco products.

amphetamines
(am-FET-uh-meens) A class of stimulant drugs that arouse the central nervous system and suppress appetite.

Cocaine Toothache Drops? Prior to 1914, cocaine was legal in the United States and, like the opiates, was widely used as an ingredient in over-the-counter medicines. From this 1885 advertisement for "Cocaine Toothache Drops," it's clear that cocaine was used in treating children as well as adults. Cocaine derivatives are still used medically as anesthetics, such as Novocain and Lidocaine. Cocaine was also part of Coca-Cola's original formula in 1888. It was replaced in 1903 with another stimulant, caffeine. Coca leaves, with the cocaine extracted for medical purposes, are still used for flavoring cola drinks.

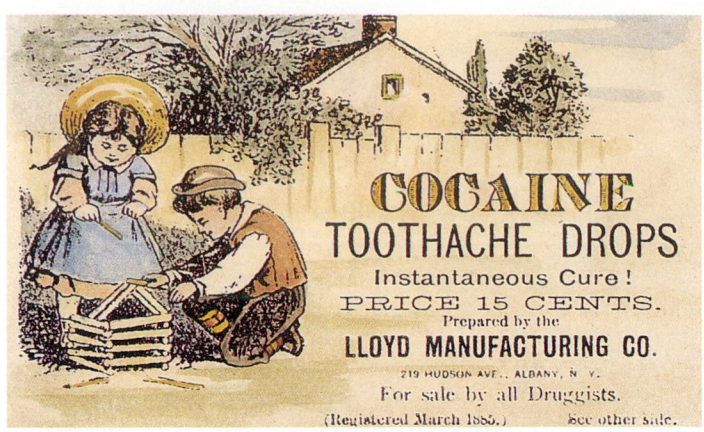

Cocaine is an illegal stimulant that is derived from the leaves of the coca tree, found in South America. (The coca plant is not the source of cocoa or chocolate, which are made from the beans of the *cacao* plant.) When "snorted" in purified, powdered form, cocaine reaches the brain within a few minutes. Inhaling cocaine provides intense euphoria, mental alertness, and self-confidence, which lasts for several minutes. A more concentrated form of cocaine called *crack* is smoked rather than inhaled.

Psychedelic Drugs

The psychedelic drugs create perceptual distortions, alter mood, and affect thinking. What are the effects of mescaline, LSD, and marijuana?

The term **psychedelic** was coined in the 1950s to describe a group of drugs that create profound perceptual distortions, alter mood, and affect thinking. *Psychedelic* literally means "mind-manifesting" (Tart, 1990).

Peyote-Inspired Visions The Huichol Indians of Mexico have used peyote in religious ceremonies for hundreds of years. Huichol yarn paintings, like the one shown here, are flat pieces of wood inlaid with designs made with colored yarn. The yarn paintings often depict imagery and scenes inspired by traditional peyote visions, which resemble the geometric shapes and radiating patterns of hallucinations induced by psychedelic drugs.

Mescaline and LSD

Naturally occurring psychedelic drugs have been used for thousands of years. **Mescaline,** which is derived from the peyote cactus, has been used for centuries in the religious ceremonies of Mexican Indians. Another psychedelic drug called *psilocybin* is derived from the psilocybe mushroom. Sometimes called "magic mushrooms," psilocybin has been used since 500 B.C. in religious rites in Mexico and Central America (Snyder, 1986).

In contrast to these naturally occurring psychedelics, **LSD** (or *lysergic acid diethylamide*) is a powerful psychedelic drug that was first synthesized in the late 1930s. LSD is far more potent than mescaline or psilocybin. Just 25 micrograms, or one-millionth of an ounce, of LSD can produce profound psychological effects with relatively few physiological changes (Julien, 1995).

LSD and psilocybin are very similar chemically to the neurotransmitter *serotonin,* which is involved in regulating moods and sensations (see Chapter 2). LSD and psilocybin mimic serotonin in the brain, stimulating serotonin receptor sites (Aghajanian, 1994; Jacobs, 1987).

The effects of a psychedelic experience vary greatly, depending on an individual's personality, current emotional

cocaine
A stimulant drug derived from the coca tree.

psychedelic drugs
A category of psychoactive drugs that create sensory and perceptual distortions, alter mood, and affect judgment.

mescaline
A psychedelic drug derived from the peyote cactus.

LSD
A synthetic psychedelic drug.

marijuana
A psychoactive drug derived from the hemp plant.

state, surroundings, and the other people present (Smith & Seymour, 1994). A "bad trip" can produce anxiety, panic, and even psychotic episodes.

Tolerance to psychedelic drugs may occur after heavy use. However, even heavy users of LSD do not develop physical dependence, nor do they experience withdrawal symptoms if the drug is not taken. Adverse reactions to LSD include "flashbacks" (recurrences of the drug's effects), depression, long-term psychological instability, and prolonged psychotic reactions (Smith & Seymour, 1994). In a psychologically unstable or susceptible person, even a single dose of LSD can precipitate a severe psychotic reaction.

Marijuana

The common hemp plant, *Cannabis sativa,* is used to make rope and cloth. But when its leaves, stems, flowers, and seeds are dried and crushed, the mixture is called **marijuana,** one of the most widely used illegal drugs. Marijuana's active ingredient is the chemical *THC.* When marijuana is smoked, THC reaches the brain in less than 30 seconds. One potent form of marijuana, *hashish,* is made from the resin of the hemp plant. Hashish is sometimes eaten.

To lump marijuana with the highly psychedelic drugs mescaline and LSD is somewhat misleading. At high doses, marijuana can sometimes produce sensory distortions that resemble a mild psychedelic experience. Low to moderate doses of THC produce a sense of well-being, mild euphoria, and a dreamy state of relaxation. Senses become more attuned and vivid. Taste, touch, and smell may be enhanced; time perception may be altered.

Most marijuana users do not develop tolerance or physical dependence. Chronic users of extremely high doses *can* develop some tolerance to THC and may experience withdrawal symptoms when its use is discontinued (de Fonseca & others, 1997). Such symptoms include irritability, restlessness, insomnia, tremors, and decreased appetite.

Marijuana and its active ingredient, THC, have been shown to be helpful in the treatment of pain, epilepsy, hypertension, nausea, glaucoma, and asthma (Snyder, 1990). In cancer patients, it can prevent the nausea and vomiting caused by chemotherapy. However, at the present time, the medical use of marijuana is extremely limited and politically controversial.

On the negative side, marijuana interferes with muscle coordination and perception and may impair driving ability. When combined with alcohol, marijuana's effects are intensified—a dangerous combination for drivers. Marijuana has also been shown to interfere with learning, memory, cognitive functioning, and reproductive processes (see Julien, 1995; Goldstein, 1994).

CONCEPT REVIEW 4.5

Psychoactive Drugs

For each of the following descriptions, name the drug class and give two (or more) examples.

	Drug Class	Examples
1. Drugs that create perceptual distortions, alter mood, and affect thinking.	_____	_____
2. Drugs that inhibit central nervous system activity; produce drowsiness, sedation, or sleep; and may reduce anxiety and lower inhibitions.	_____	_____
3. Addictive drugs that mimic endorphins and can relieve pain and produce euphoria.	_____	_____
4. Drugs that increase brain activity, are at least mildly addictive, increase mental alertness, and reduce fatigue.	_____	_____

Improving Sleep and Mental Alertness

In this Application we'll give you some research-based, practical suggestions to help you wake up in the morning, improve the quality of your sleep, and minimize the mental and physical disruptions that can occur when your body clock is out of sync with environmental time cues.

Dealing with Morning Brain Fog

There is surprisingly little research on how to deal with **sleep inertia**—sleepiness upon awakening that interferes with your ability to perform mental or physical tasks (Hobson & Stickgold, 1995). For some people, "morning brain fog" can last half an hour or more before they feel fully alert (Little, 1993; Dinges, 1989).

People who have trouble getting up in the morning tend to stay in bed until the last possible moment. This strategy, of course, only intensifies their disorientation because they are forced to hustle out the door before they are fully awake.

The simplest antidote for sleep inertia seems to be the passage of time. So, if you suffer from sleep inertia, try setting your alarm clock (and possibly a second one in the next room) to wake you 15 minutes *earlier* than usual. Resolve to hit the floor when the alarm goes off. The extra 15 minutes will help give your mind time to clear.

During that 15 minutes, sip a cup of coffee or tea. It will take you approximately half an hour to feel the full effects of the caffeine (Julien, 1995). If the sun is up, sit near a window; if it's not, turn on the lights. Bright light, especially sunlight, helps brain fog dissipate by reducing blood levels of the hormone melatonin (Brown, 1994).

Improving the Quality of Your Sleep

Sleep researchers have identified a variety of ways to improve the quality of your sleep.

■ Timing is more important than you probably realize. In the early evening hours, usually between 8:00 and 10:00 p.m., we normally experience a daily period of *increased* wakefulness that occurs prior to sleepiness. Sleep researchers call this presleep burst of wakefulness the "forbidden zone for sleep" (Lavie, 1989). So to avoid suddenly feeling wide awake in bed, you should go to bed *after* the forbidden zone, when your brain has begun to gear down to sleepiness.

■ Going to bed very hungry or very full will disrupt sleep, but a light snack will help reduce nighttime restlessness and increase total sleep time (Empson, 1993).

■ Moderate exercise during the day seems to promote deep sleep, but exercise in the evening or shortly before going to bed may rev you up and keep you awake.

■ Soaking in a very warm bath shortly before retiring promotes deep sleep by raising your core body temperature (Empson, 1993).

■ A consistent bedtime routine and familiar surroundings enhance the quality of sleep. Try to go to bed at about the same time each night and get up at approximately the same time every morning so that you stay in sync with your own pattern of circadian rhythms.

■ Depressant drugs, such as alcohol and barbiturates, may produce drowsiness but they also reduce REM sleep, disrupting the quality of your sleep. Hence, they should be avoided.

Finally, you may be pleased to discover that sex promotes sleep. For example, rabbits tend to sleep very little—with the exception of quickly nodding off into REM sleep after some amorous activity in the old rabbit hutch. The same phenomenon also seems to occur in humans, which may be why sleep so often follows sexual interaction. As sleep researcher J. Allan Hobson (1989) put it, sex "not only leads to muscle relaxation, but also clears the cerebral circuits of tedious humdrum."

Coping with the Night Shift

People vary in the ease with which they develop tolerance for working the night shift or rotating shifts (Harma, 1993). Here are some suggestions for minimizing the negative effects that night work can produce:

■ If you have a choice in your work schedule, the longer you can stay with one shift, the better. Frequent shift changes, such as every other week, increase jet-lag symptoms (Wilkinson, 1992).

■ If you work rotating shifts, try to make your schedule changes more compatible with circadian rhythms (Czeisler & others, 1982). Because of our natural tendency to drift toward longer days, it is easier to lengthen our days than to shorten them artificially. Therefore, try to arrange your shift changes to progress from the morning to evening to night shifts, rather than the other way around (Gallo & Eastman, 1993).

■ If you work the midnight to 8:00 a.m. shift, bright lights in the workplace, especially during the early part of the shift, will help you and your co-workers' circadian cycles adjust to the night schedule (Dawson & Campbell, 1991; Czeisler & others, 1990).

■ To promote sleep during the daytime, ask your doctor about the pros and cons of taking supplemental melatonin. Some researchers have found that melatonin supplements can help induce daytime sleep, improving mental alertness during night shifts (Dawson, 1995; Folkard & others, 1993).

Summary

Consciousness and Its Variations

Consciousness: Experiencing the "Private I"

- Consciousness refers to the immediate awareness of internal and external stimuli. Early psychologists studied consciousness, but the behaviorists believed that consciousness was not an appropriate topic for psychology. Today, consciousness is regarded as an important subject for psychological research.

The Biological and Environmental "Clocks" Regulating Consciousness

- We experience a variety of circadian rhythms, which are regulated by the suprachiasmatic nucleus (SCN), the "master clock" located in the hypothalamus of the brain. In response to light detected by visual receptors, the SCN reduces the production of melatonin by the pineal gland. Increased melatonin makes you sleepy.

- Under free-running conditions, human circadian rhythms seem to drift toward a 25-hour day. Circadian rhythms become disrupted when environmental time cues are out of sync with the body clock. Symptoms of jet lag can be produced by travel across time zones or rotating-shift work.

Sleep

- The traditional view of sleep as a period of inactivity was changed by the invention of the electroencephalograph and the discovery of rapid eye movements (REM). The two basic types of sleep are REM sleep and NREM sleep.

- As people fall asleep, brain activity slows down. The first 90 minutes of sleep include four different stages of NREM sleep followed by a brief episode of REM sleep. As the night progresses, episodes of REM sleep become longer and NREM episodes become shorter.

- As people age, periods of REM sleep and deep sleep generally become shorter and more time is spent in stage 2 NREM.

- Sleep deprivation studies have demonstrated that people have a biological need to sleep. The restorative theory of sleep proposes that sleep promotes physiological processes that restore the body and mind. NREM seems particularly important in physical restoration, and REM seems important in brain development. The adaptive theory of sleep suggests that the varying sleep patterns of different animals evolved as a means of promoting survival and adapting to environmental conditions.

- Sleep disorders are serious disturbances in the normal sleep pattern that interfere with daytime functioning and cause subjective distress.

- The most common sleep disorder is insomnia. Children are most likely to experience sleepwalking and night terrors.

Other sleep disorders include REM sleep behavior disorder, sleep apnea, and narcolepsy.

Dreams and Mental Activity During Sleep

- Sleep thinking occurs during NREM sleep. A dream is a storylike unfolding episode of mental images. Dreams are characterized by intense emotions, illogical content and organization, bizarre sensations, and outlandish details that are uncritically accepted. Dreams are also difficult to remember.

- Most dreams reflect everyday concerns and include familiar people and settings. There are individual differences in dream recall. Several factors contribute to our general lack of ability to recall dreams, including changes in brain chemistry and functioning that occur during sleep.

- Sigmund Freud believed that dream symbols represent, in disguised form, the expression of repressed, unconscious wishes. The activation-synthesis model of dreaming proposes that dreams reflect our subjective awareness of brain activation during sleep. The activated brain combines internally generated sensory signals and imposes meaning on them.

Hypnosis

- Hypnosis is an unusual state of awareness, defined as a cooperative social interaction in which one person responds to suggestions made by another person (the hypnotist). Changes in perception, memory, and behavior may be produced. People vary in their susceptibility to hypnosis.

- Under hypnosis, profound sensory and perceptual changes may be experienced, including hallucinations. Hypnosis has been used in pain control. Posthypnotic suggestions influence behavior outside of the hypnotic state.

- Memory effects include posthypnotic amnesia. However, hypermnesia has not been substantiated as an effect of hypnosis. Hypnosis does not increase the accuracy of memories, but it does increase confidence in memories, even when they are demonstrated to be false. Hypnosis cannot be used to make people perform behaviors that are contrary to their morals or values.

- Ernest Hilgard explained hypnosis as involving dissociation and the "hidden observer." Not all psychologists agree that hypnosis is a special state of consciousness or awareness.

Meditation

- Meditation refers to techniques used to control attention so as to induce an altered state of focused attention and awareness.

■ Research on the effects of transcendental meditation suggests that regular meditation enhances physical and psychological functioning. Some researchers believe that meditation is no more effective than simple rest.

Psychoactive Drugs

■ Psychoactive drugs can alter arousal, mood, thinking, sensation, and perception. Many psychoactive drugs are addictive, producing physical dependence and tolerance. The physically dependent person who stops taking a drug experiences withdrawal symptoms, which often include the drug rebound effect.

■ Biologically, psychoactive drugs disrupt brain activity by interfering with synaptic transmission. Drug effects can be influenced by the person's size, gender, metabolism, and whether the drug is taken alone or in combination with other drugs. Personality characteristics, mood, expectations, experience with the drug, and the setting in which the drug is taken can also affect the drug response.

■ The depressants inhibit central nervous system activity. Depressants include alcohol, barbiturates, and tranquilizers.

■ The physical effects of alcohol depend on the level of alcohol in the blood. Psychologically, alcohol lessens inhibitions. Psychological effects depend on the person's environment and expectations.

■ Barbiturates produce relaxation and reduce inhibitions. These drugs are physically addictive.

■ The opiates are a group of addictive drugs that relieve pain and produce feelings of euphoria. The opiates include opium, morphine, codeine, heroin, methadone, and the prescription painkillers Demerol and Percodan. Opiates relieve pain by mimicking the effect of endorphins in the brain.

■ The stimulants include caffeine, nicotine, amphetamines, and cocaine. The stimulants increase brain activity, and all stimulants are addictive to some degree.

■ The psychedelic drugs include mescaline, LSD, and marijuana. The psychedelics create perceptual distortions, alter mood, and affect thinking. While the psychedelic drugs are not physically addictive, they can cause a variety of harmful effects.

Key Terms

consciousness (p. 118)

circadian rhythm (p. 120)

suprachiasmatic nucleus (SCN) (p. 121)

melatonin (p. 121)

electroencephalograph (p. 124)

EEG (p. 124)

REM sleep (p.125)

NREM sleep (p. 125)

beta brain waves (p. 125)

alpha brain waves (p. 125)

hypnagogic hallucinations (p. 125)

sleep spindles (p. 126)

REM rebound (p. 130)

restorative theory of sleep (p. 130)

adaptive theory of sleep (p. 131)

sleep disorders (p. 131)

insomnia (p. 132)

sleepwalking (p. 132)

night terrors (p. 132)

REM sleep behavior disorder (p. 133)

sleep apnea (p. 133)

narcolepsy (p. 133)

sleep thinking (p. 134)

dream (p. 134)

nightmare (p. 136)

activation-synthesis model of dreaming (p. 138)

hypnosis (p. 139)

posthypnotic suggestion (p. 140)

posthypnotic amnesia (p. 140)

hypermnesia (p. 141)

dissociation (p. 141)

hidden observer (p. 141)

meditation (p. 143)

psychoactive drug (p. 145)

physical dependence (p. 145)

tolerance (p. 145)

withdrawal symptoms (p. 145)

drug rebound effect (p. 145)

depressants (p. 146)

barbiturates (p. 147)

tranquilizers (p. 148)

opiates (p. 148)

stimulants (p. 148)

caffeine (p. 149)

nicotine (p. 149)

amphetamines (p. 149)

cocaine (p. 150)

psychedelic drugs (p. 150)

mescaline (p. 150)

LSD (p. 150)

marijuana (p. 151)

sleep inertia (p. 152)

Key People

Sigmund Freud (1856–1939) Founder of psychoanalysis, who proposed that dream images are disguised and symbolic expressions of unconscious wishes and urges (see Chapter 10).

Ernest R. Hilgard (b. 1904) Contemporary American psychologist who extensively studied hypnosis and advanced the dissociation theory of hypnosis.

J. Allan Hobson (b. 1933) Contemporary American psychiatrist and neurobiologist who extensively researched sleep and dreaming; proposed the *activation-synthesis model* of dreaming with co-researcher Robert W. McCarley.

William James (1842–1910) American psychologist and philosopher who proposed that the subjective experience of consciousness is an ongoing "stream" of mental activity (see Chapter 1).

CONCEPT REVIEW 4.1 Page 124

1. circadian rhythm
2. melatonin
3. suprachiasmatic nucleus; 25
4. sunlight; 24

CONCEPT REVIEW 4.2 Page 131

1. stage 2 NREM
2. hypnagogic hallucination; myoclonic jerk
3. REM; dreaming
4. stage 4 NREM

CONCEPT REVIEW 4.3 Page 139

1. c
2. b
3. b
4. d

CONCEPT REVIEW 4.4 Page 144

1. a
2. d
3. c
4. a

CONCEPT REVIEW 4.5 Page 151

1. Psychedelic drugs: LSD, mescaline, marijuana
2. Depressants: alcohol, barbiturates, tranquilizers
3. Opiates: opium, morphine, heroin, methadone, Demerol, Percodan
4. Stimulants: caffeine, nicotine, amphetamines, cocaine

Chapter

5 Learning

Prologue: The Killer Attic

Sandy's parents, Erv and Fern, recently celebrated their fiftieth wedding anniversary. Sometimes it seems truly amazing that they've managed to survive so long together, as you'll see from this true story.

It was a warm summer morning in Chicago. Erv and Fern drank their coffee and made plans for the day. The lawn needed mowing, the garage needed cleaning, and someone had to go to the post office to buy stamps. Fern, who doesn't like driving, said that she would mow the lawn if Erv would go to the post office. Erv, who doesn't like yard work, readily agreed to the deal.

As Erv left for the post office, Fern started cutting the grass in the back yard. When Erv returned, he parked the car around the corner under some large shade trees so that the car would stay cool while he puttered around in the garage. He walked through the front door to drop off the stamps and noticed that the attic fan was squeaking loudly. Switching it off, Erv decided to oil the fan before he tackled the garage. Fetching the stepladder and oil from the basement, he propped the ladder under the attic trap door, climbed up, and gingerly crawled through the trap door, leaving it open.

Meanwhile, Fern was getting thirsty. As she walked past the garage on the way into the house, she noticed that the car was still gone. "Why isn't he back yet? Erv must have stopped somewhere on the way back from the post office," she thought. As she got a glass of water, she noticed the stepladder and the open attic door. Muttering that Erv never put anything back, Fern latched the attic trap door shut and dragged the ladder back down to the basement.

Erv, who had crawled to the other side of the attic to oil the fan, never heard the attic trap door shut. It was very hot in the well-insulated, airless attic, so he tried to work fast. After oiling the fan, he crawled back to the attic door—only to discover that it was latched shut from the outside! "Fern," he hollered, "open the door!" But Fern was already back outside, mowing away, and couldn't hear Erv over the noise of the lawn mower. Erv, dripping with sweat, kept yelling and pounding on the trap door.

Outside, Fern was getting hot too. She stopped to talk to a neighbor, leaving the lawn mower idling. He offered Fern a cold beer, and the two of them leaned over the fence, laughing and talking. From a small, sealed attic window, Erv watched the whole scene. Jealousy was now added to his list of discomforts. He was also seriously beginning to think that he might sweat to death in the attic heat. He could already see the tabloid headlines in the supermarket checkout line: LAUGHING WIFE DRINKS BEER WHILE HUSBAND COOKS IN ATTIC!

Finally, Fern went back to mowing, wondering what in the world had happened to Erv. Meanwhile, up in the attic, Erv promised God he'd never complain about Chicago winters again. At last, Fern finished the lawn and walked back to the house. Hearing the back door open, Erv began to yell and pound on the trap door again.

"Hey, Fern! Fern! Let me out!"

Fern froze in her tracks. "Erv! Is that you? Where are you?" she called, looking around.

"I'm in the attic! Let me out!"

"What are you doing in the attic? I thought you were at the store!"

"What do you *think* I'm doing? Let me out of here!"

Once Fern was reassured that Erv had suffered no ill effects from his experience, she burst out laughing. Later that day, still grumbling about Fern's harebrained sense of humor, Erv removed the latch from the attic door. Ever since, whenever Erv goes up in the attic, he posts a sign on the ladder that reads MAN IN THE ATTIC! And, even today, Erv breaks into a sweat whenever he has to go up in the attic.

For her part, Fern is careful to check on Erv's whereabouts before she closes the attic door. But she still laughs when she tells the story of the "killer attic"—which she does frequently, as it never fails to crack up her listeners. Luckily, Erv is a good sport and is used to Fern's sense of humor.

Erv and Fern have both learned from their experience, as is reflected in the changes in their behavior. As you'll see, learning can take place in many ways, but it almost always helps us to adapt to changing circumstances.

Introduction

What Is Learning?

> *Learning refers to a relatively permanent change in behavior as a result of experience. What is conditioning? What are the different psychological perspectives in learning research?*

Psychologists define **learning** as a relatively permanent change in behavior that is due to past experience. Erv has learned to feel anxious and uncomfortable whenever he has to work in the attic. He's also learned to take simple precautions, like posting his MAN IN THE ATTIC sign, to avoid getting locked in the attic again. As Erv's behavior demonstrates, the learning of new behavior often reflects some kind of *adaptation to the environment*. On the basis of experience, we acquire new behaviors or modify old behaviors so as to better cope with our surroundings.

learning
A relatively permanent change in behavior as a result of past experience.

behavioral perspective
In learning theory, a general explanation of learning that emphasizes the relationship between outwardly observable behaviors and environmental events, rather than mental processes.

When students first encounter the topic of "learning" in psychology, they sometimes think that it will focus on formal classroom methods of acquiring new knowledge or skills. Classroom methods reflect learning in the everyday sense of the word. This chapter, however, will focus on a more basic form of learning, referred to as *conditioning*. Conditioning is the process of learning associations between environmental events and behavioral responses. This description may sound as if it has only limited application to your life. But conditioning is reflected in most of your everyday behavior, from simple habits to emotional reactions and complex skills.

Earlier in this century, psychologists distinguished between two forms of conditioning: classical conditioning and operant conditioning (Skinner, 1935, 1938; Hilgard & Marquis, 1940). As you'll see in the next section, *classical conditioning* can help explain why climbing into the attic makes Erv anxious. And, as you'll see in a later section, *operant conditioning* will help us understand why Erv now puts up a sign whenever he feels the urge to rummage around in the attic.

We'll structure our discussion of classical and operant conditioning around three key perspectives in the scientific study of learning: the *behavioral,* the *cognitive,* and the *ecological perspectives*. Each of these perspectives emphasizes different aspects of learning, and each has added to our understanding of the factors involved in classical and operant conditioning (Hollis, 1997).

The Behavioral Perspective

The behavioral perspective defines learning in terms of an observable change in behavior. Who founded behaviorism? What are the basic assumptions and beliefs of the behavioral perspective?

As we discussed in Chapter 1, the **behavioral perspective** is a broad approach to the study of learning that emphasizes changes in outwardly observable behaviors. The roots of this perspective can be traced to one of the earliest schools of psychology, called *behaviorism*.

Behaviorism was founded in the early 1900s by the American psychologist **John B. Watson** (1878–1958). Watson (1913) strongly opposed the views of the earliest psychologists, who believed that psychology should study conscious experiences, such as perception and thought processes. Watson—and the behaviorists who followed him—believed that internal mental processes were far too subjective to be included in a scientific study of behavior. He maintained that thoughts, feelings, and other conscious experiences were not appropriate subject matter for the young science of psychology. Instead, Watson (1924/1970) wrote, "Let us limit ourselves to things that can be observed, and formulate laws concerning only those things. Now what can we observe? We can observe *behavior—what the organism does or says.*"

Watson, along with other behaviorists, believed that virtually *all* human behavior is a result of learning—that is, due to past experience and environmental influences. He claimed that neither talent, personality, nor intelligence was inherited. In a characteristically bold (and famous) statement, Watson (1930) boasted:

I should like to go one step further now and say, "Give me a dozen healthy infants, well-formed, and my own specified world to bring them up in and I'll guarantee to take any one at random and train

John Broadus Watson (1878–1958)
Watson founded behaviorism in the early 1900s, emphasizing the scientific study of observable behaviors rather than subjective mental processes. His influence spread far beyond the academic world. He wrote many books and articles for the general public on child-rearing and other topics, popularizing the findings of the new science of psychology.

him to become any type of specialist I might select—doctor, lawyer, artist, merchant-chief and yes, even beggar-man and thief, regardless of his talents, penchants, tendencies, abilities, vocations, and race of his ancestors." I am going beyond my facts and I admit it, but so have the advocates of the contrary and they have been doing it for many thousands of years.

Needless to say, Watson never actually carried out such an experiment. Nevertheless, Watson's influence on psychology cannot be overemphasized: Behaviorism dominated American psychology for more than fifty years. Watson's ideas, however, were based on the earlier work of another scientist. The origins of behaviorism can be traced to a physiologist studying the digestive system of dogs in turn-of-the-century Russia—which is where our story now turns.

Classical Conditioning:
Associating Stimuli

Classical conditioning describes a process of learning associations between stimuli. Who discovered classical conditioning, and how did he investigate it? How does classical conditioning occur? How can classically conditioned responses be weakened or eliminated?

One of the major contributors to modern psychology was not a psychologist, but a Russian physiologist who was awarded a Nobel Prize for his work on digestion. **Ivan Pavlov** (1849–1936) was a brilliant scientist who directed several research laboratories in St. Petersburg, Russia, at the turn of the century (Windholz, 1997). Pavlov's involvement with psychology began as a result of an observation he made while investigating the role of saliva in digestion, using dogs as his experimental subjects.

In order to get a dog to produce saliva, Pavlov (1904/1965) would put food on the dog's tongue. After he had worked with the same dog for several days in a row, Pavlov noticed something curious. The dog would begin salivating *before* Pavlov put the food on his tongue. In fact, the dogs would begin salivating when Pavlov entered the room, or even at the sound of his approaching footsteps. But salivating is a *reflex*—a largely involuntary, automatic response to an external stimulus. The dogs should salivate only *after* the food was presented, not before. Why would the reflex occur before the stimulus was presented? What was causing this unexpected behavior?

Pavlov recognized the important implications of what had at first seemed a problem—a reflex (salivation) occurring *before* the appropriate stimulus (food) was presented (Todes, 1997). Pavlov (1928) abandoned his research on digestion and spent the remaining thirty years of his life systematically investigating this phenomenon.

Principles of Classical Conditioning

The process of conditioning that Pavlov discovered was the first model of learning to be extensively studied in psychology. Thus, it's called **classical conditioning** (Hilgard & Marquis, 1940). Classical conditioning deals with behaviors that are elicited automatically by some stimulus. *Elicit* means

Ivan Pavlov (1849–1936) In his laboratory, Pavlov was known for his meticulous organization, keen memory, and attention to details (Windholz, 1990). But outside his lab, Pavlov was absent-minded, forgetful, and impractical, especially regarding money. He often forgot to pick up his paycheck, and when he did, he sometimes loaned money to people with hard luck stories who couldn't possibly pay him back (Fancher, 1990). On a trip to New York City, Pavlov carried his money so carelessly that he had his pocket picked in the subway, and his American hosts had to take up a collection to pay for his expenses.

classical conditioning
The basic learning process that involves repeatedly pairing a neutral stimulus with a response-producing stimulus until the neutral stimulus elicits the same response.

draw out or bring forth. That is, the stimulus doesn't produce a "new" behavior, but rather *causes an existing behavior to occur.*

Classical conditioning often involves reflexive behaviors. Remember, a reflex is a relatively simple unlearned behavior, governed by the nervous system, that occurs *automatically* when the appropriate stimulus is presented. In Pavlov's (1904) original studies of digestion, the dogs salivated reflexively when food was placed on their tongues. But when the dogs began salivating in response to the sight of Pavlov or to the sound of an experimenter's footsteps, a new, *learned* stimulus elicited the salivary response. Thus, in classical conditioning, a *new* stimulus–response sequence is learned.

How does this kind of learning take place? Essentially, classical conditioning is a process of learning an *association between two stimuli.* Classical conditioning involves pairing a *neutral* stimulus (the sight of Pavlov) with an *unlearned, natural* stimulus (food in the mouth) that automatically elicits a reflexive response (the dog salivates). If the two stimuli (Pavlov + food) are repeatedly paired, eventually the neutral stimulus (Pavlov) elicits the same reflexive response as the natural stimulus (food)—even in the absence of the natural stimulus. So, when the dog in the laboratory started salivating at the sight of Pavlov *before* the food was placed on its tongue, it was because the dog had formed a new, *learned association* between the sight of Pavlov and the food.

The classical conditioning model of learning uses special terms to describe each element of the conditioning process. The natural stimulus that reflexively produces a response without the necessity of prior learning is called the **unconditioned stimulus** (abbreviated **UCS**). In this example, the unconditioned stimulus is the food in the dog's mouth. The unlearned, reflexive response is called the **unconditioned response** (or **UCR**). The unconditioned response is the dog's salivation.

To learn more about his discovery, Pavlov (1927/1960) controlled the stimuli that preceded the appearance of food. For example, in one set of experiments, he used a bell as a neutral stimulus—neutral because dogs don't normally salivate to the sound of a bell ringing. Pavlov would first ring the bell and then give the dog food. After this procedure was repeated several times, the dog would begin to salivate when the bell was rung, before the food was put in its mouth. At that point, the dog was *classically conditioned* to salivate to the sound of a bell alone. That is, the dog had learned a new association between the sound of the bell and the presentation of food.

Pavlov called the sound of the bell the **conditioned stimulus** (or **CS**). The conditioned stimulus is the stimulus that is originally neutral but comes to elicit a reflexive response. He called the dog's salivation to the sound of the bell the **conditioned response** (or **CR**), which is the *learned* reflexive response to a previously neutral stimulus. The steps of Pavlov's conditioning process are outlined in Figure 5.1 on the next page.

Classical conditioning terminology can be confusing. You may find it helpful to think of the word "conditioned" as meaning the same as "learned." Thus, the "conditioned stimulus" would be the "learned stimulus," the "unconditioned response" would be the "unlearned response," and so forth.

It's also important to note that the unconditioned response and the conditioned response describe virtually the same behavior—the dog salivating. Which label is applied depends on which stimulus elicits the response. If the dog is salivating in response to a *natural* stimulus that it had not acquired through learning, it is an *unconditioned* response. If, however, the dog has learned to salivate to a *neutral* stimulus that doesn't normally produce the automatic response, it is a *conditioned* response.

unconditioned stimulus (UCS)
The natural stimulus that elicits a reflexive response without the necessity of prior learning.

unconditioned response (UCR)
The unlearned, reflexive response that is elicited by an unconditioned stimulus.

conditioned stimulus (CS)
A formerly neutral stimulus that acquires the capacity to elicit a reflexive response.

conditioned response (CR)
The learned, reflexive response to a conditioned stimulus.

FIGURE 5.1 The Process of Classical Conditioning
The diagram shows Pavlov's classical conditioning procedure. As you can see, classical conditioning involves the learning of an association between a neutral stimulus (the ringing bell) and a natural stimulus (food).

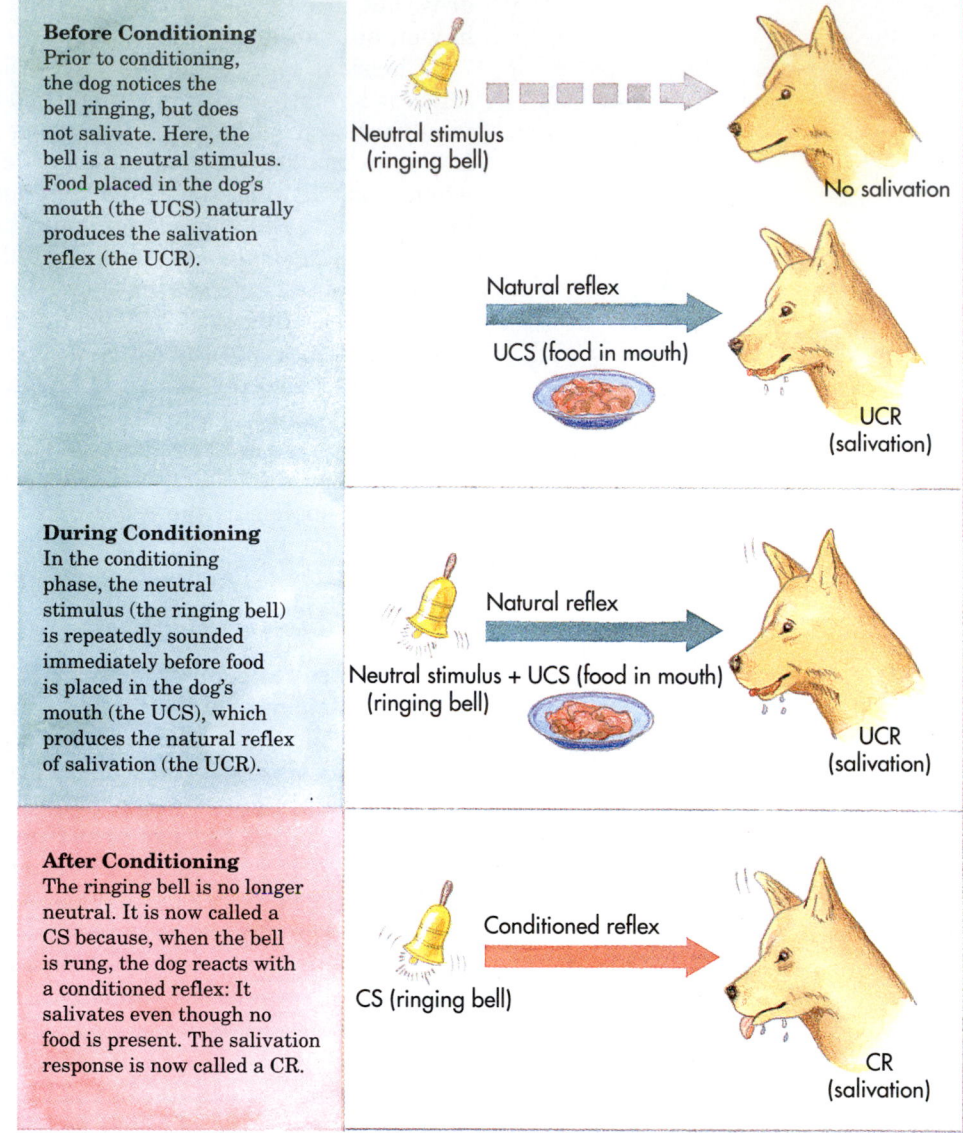

Before Conditioning
Prior to conditioning, the dog notices the bell ringing, but does not salivate. Here, the bell is a neutral stimulus. Food placed in the dog's mouth (the UCS) naturally produces the salivation reflex (the UCR).

Neutral stimulus (ringing bell) — No salivation

Natural reflex
UCS (food in mouth) — UCR (salivation)

During Conditioning
In the conditioning phase, the neutral stimulus (the ringing bell) is repeatedly sounded immediately before food is placed in the dog's mouth (the UCS), which produces the natural reflex of salivation (the UCR).

Natural reflex
Neutral stimulus + UCS (food in mouth) (ringing bell) — UCR (salivation)

After Conditioning
The ringing bell is no longer neutral. It is now called a CS because, when the bell is rung, the dog reacts with a conditioned reflex: It salivates even though no food is present. The salivation response is now called a CR.

Conditioned reflex
CS (ringing bell) — CR (salivation)

CONCEPT REVIEW 5.1

Identifying Elements of Classical Conditioning

Identify the UCS, the UCR, the CS, and the CR in each of the following examples.

1. Before each of his chemotherapy sessions, Allen, a young cancer patient, eats a bowl of ice cream. The chemotherapy makes Allen nauseated. Now just seeing the bowl of ice cream makes him feel queasy.

UCS: _____   UCR: _____.

CS: _____   CR: _____.

2. After swimming in a lake near his home one day, Frank discovered two slimy, blood-sucking leeches attached to his leg. He was revolted by the experience of touching the slimy bodies and pulling them off his leg. Now every time he drives by the lake, he shudders in disgust.

UCS: _____   UCR: _____.

CS: _____   CR: _____.

3. On Halloween night, two-year-old Jodie answered the doorbell and encountered a scary monster with ten flashing eyes. Jodie screamed in fear and ran away. For the next year Jodie screamed and hid in the corner of her bedroom whenever the doorbell rang.

UCS: _____   UCR: _____.

CS: _____   CR: _____.

Factors That Affect Conditioning

Over the three decades that Pavlov (1928) spent studying classical conditioning, he discovered many factors that could affect the strength of the conditioned response. For example, he discovered that the more frequently the conditioned stimulus and the unconditioned stimulus are paired, the stronger the association between the two.

Pavlov also discovered that the *timing* of stimulus presentations affected the strength of the conditioned response. He found that conditioning is most effective when the conditioned stimulus is presented immediately *before* the unconditioned stimulus. In his early studies, Pavlov found that a half-second was the optimal time interval between the onset of the conditioned stimulus and the beginning of the unconditioned stimulus. Later, Pavlov and other researchers found that the optimal time interval could vary in different conditioning situations, but was never more than a few seconds.

Pavlov (1927/1960) also noticed that once a dog was conditioned to salivate to a particular stimulus, new stimuli that were similar to the original conditioned stimulus could also elicit the conditioned salivary response. For example, Pavlov conditioned a dog to salivate to a low-pitched tone. When he sounded a slightly higher-pitched tone, the conditioned salivary response would also be elicited. Pavlov called this phenomenon **stimulus generalization.** Stimulus generalization occurs when stimuli that are similar to the original conditioned stimulus also elicit the conditioned response, even though they have never been paired with the unconditioned stimulus.

Just as a dog can learn to respond to similar stimuli, so it can learn the opposite—to *distinguish* between similar stimuli. For example, Pavlov repeatedly gave a dog some food following a high-pitched tone, but did not give the dog any food after a low-pitched tone. The dog learned to distinguish between the two tones, salivating to the high-pitched tone but not to the low-pitched tone. This phenomenon, **stimulus discrimination,** occurs when a particular conditioned response is made to one stimulus but not to other, similar stimuli.

Once learned, can conditioned responses be eliminated? Pavlov (1928) found that conditioned responses could be gradually weakened. If the conditioned stimulus, like the ringing bell, was repeatedly presented *without* being paired with the unconditioned stimulus (the food), the conditioned response seemed to gradually disappear. Pavlov called this process of decline and eventual disappearance of the conditioned response **extinction.**

But Pavlov also found that a dog does not simply return to its unconditioned state following extinction. If an animal is allowed a period of rest (such as a few hours) after a response has been extinguished, the conditioned response will reappear when the conditioned stimulus is again presented. This reappearance of a previously extinguished conditioned response after a period of time without exposure to the conditioned stimulus is called **spontaneous recovery.**

Applications of Classical Conditioning

Classical conditioning can explain many aspects of human behavior. What was the "Little Albert" study, and why was it important?

Classical conditioning always involves the learning of some type of relatively automatic stimulus–response sequence. This may sound like a fairly limited type of learning. But classical conditioning has wide application beyond training dogs to drool on command (Wolpe & Plaud, 1997). In this section, we'll explore some of the ways that classical conditioning has been used to both explain and influence human behavior.

stimulus generalization
The occurrence of a learned response not only to the original stimulus but to other, similar stimuli as well.

stimulus discrimination
The occurrence of a learned response to a specific stimulus but not to other, similar stimuli.

extinction
The gradual weakening and disappearance of conditioned behavior. In classical conditioning, extinction occurs when the conditioned stimulus is repeatedly presented without the unconditioned stimulus.

spontaneous recovery
The reappearance of a previously extinguished conditioned response after a period of time without exposure to the conditioned stimulus.

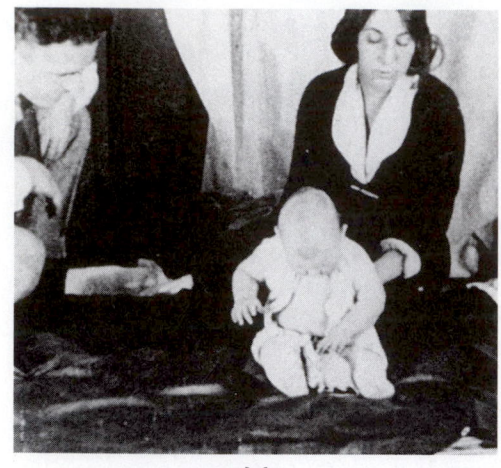

(a)

Conditioned Emotional Reactions

One of the most famous experiments in the history of psychology was conducted in 1920 by behaviorist John B. Watson and his graduate student, Rosalie Rayner. Watson and Rayner (1920) demonstrated that classical conditioning could be used to deliberately establish a conditioned emotional response in a human subject. Their subject was a baby whom they called "Albert B.," but who is now more popularly known as "Little Albert."

Watson and Rayner first assessed Little Albert when he was only nine months old. Little Albert was a healthy, unusually calm baby who showed no fear when presented with a tame white rat, a rabbit, a dog, and a monkey. He was also unafraid of cotton, masks, and even burning newspapers! However, Watson and Rayner did discover one stimulus that made Little Albert fearful: loudly clanging a steel bar behind his head. Here, the clanging noise is the unconditioned stimulus, and the unconditioned response is fear.

Two months after their initial assessment, Watson and Rayner attempted to condition Little Albert to fear the white rat (the conditioned stimulus). Watson stood behind Little Albert. Whenever Little Albert reached toward the rat, Watson clanged the steel bar with a hammer. Just as before, of course, the loud CLANG! (the unconditioned stimulus) scared the daylights out of Little Albert (the unconditioned response).

During this first conditioning session, Little Albert experienced two pairings of the white rat with the loud clanging sound. A week later, he experienced five more pairings of the two stimuli. After only these seven pairings of the loud noise and the white rat, the white rat alone made Little Albert display extreme fear (the conditioned response). Little Albert had developed a classically conditioned fear response to the white rat (see Figure 5.2).

Watson and Rayner found, too, that stimulus generalization had taken place: Little Albert was also afraid of other furry animals, a dog and a rabbit. He had even developed a classically conditioned fear response to a variety of fuzzy objects—a sealskin coat, cotton, Watson's hair, and a white-bearded Santa Claus mask!

Although the Little Albert study has achieved legendary status in psychology, there were a number of problems with it (Paul & Blumenthal, 1989; Harris, 1979). One criticism is that the experiment was not carefully designed or conducted. For example, Albert's "fear and distress" were not objectively measured, but were subjectively evaluated by Watson and Rayner.

The experiment is also open to criticism on ethical grounds. Watson and Rayner did not extinguish Little Albert's fear of furry animals and objects, even though they believed that such conditioned emotional responses would "persist and modify personality throughout life" (Watson & Rayner, 1920). Whether they had intended to do so is not completely clear (see Paul & Blumenthal, 1989). Little Albert left the hospital shortly after the completion of the experiment. Watson (1930) later wrote that he and Rayner could not try to eliminate Albert's fear response because the infant had been adopted by a family in another city shortly after their experiment had concluded. Today, such an experiment could not be ethically conducted under *any* circumstances.

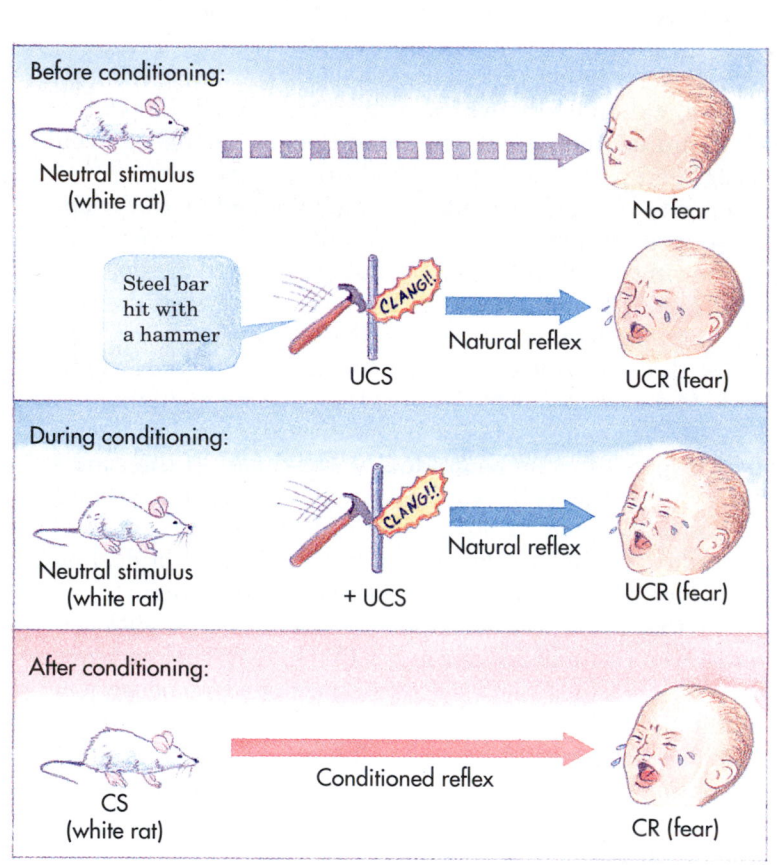

(b)

FIGURE 5.2 A Classically Conditioned Fear Response
(a) In the photograph, Rosalie Rayner holds Little Albert as John Watson looks on. Little Albert is petting the white rat, clearly not afraid of it. **(b)** By repeatedly pairing the white rat with the UCS (a loud noise), the white rat becomes a CS. After conditioning, Little Albert is frightened of the rat and other furry objects.

IN FOCUS 5.1

Watson, Classical Conditioning, and Advertising

From cars to colas, advertising campaigns often use sexy models to promote their products. Today, we take this phenomenon for granted. But it's actually yet another example of Watson's influence.

Shortly after the Little Albert experiment, Watson's wife discovered that he was having an affair with his graduate student Rosalie Rayner. Following a scandalous and highly publicized divorce, Watson was fired from his academic position. Despite his international fame as a scientist, no other university would hire him. Banned from academia, Watson married Rayner and

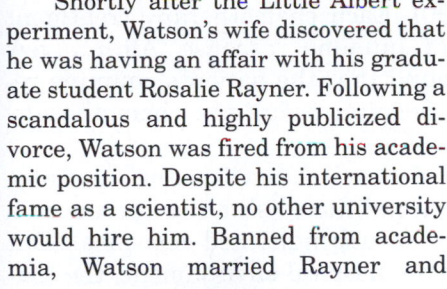

joined the J. Walter Thompson advertising agency (Buckley, 1989).

Watson was a pioneer in the application of classical conditioning principles to advertising. "To make your consumer react," Watson told his colleagues at the ad agency, "tell him something that will tie up with fear, something that will stir up a mild rage, that will call out an affectionate or love response, or strike at a deep psychological or habit need" (quoted in Buckley, 1982).

Watson applied this technique in ad campaigns he worked on in the 1920s for Johnson & Johnson Baby Powder and Pebeco toothpaste. For the baby powder ad, Watson intentionally tried to stimulate an anxiety response in young mothers by creating doubts about their ability to care for their infants.

The Pebeco toothpaste ad campaign targeted the newly independent young woman who smoked. The ad raised the fear that attractiveness might be diminished by the effects of smoking—and Pebeco toothpaste was promoted as a way of increasing one's sexual attractiveness. One ad read, "Girls! Don't worry any more about smoke-stained teeth or tobacco-tainted breath. You can smoke and still be lovely if you'll just use Pebeco twice a day."

While Watson may have pioneered the strategy of associating products

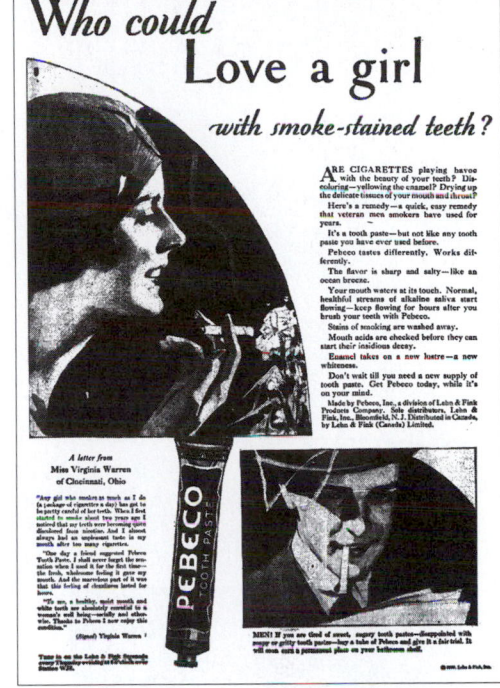

with "sex appeal," modern advertising has taken this technique to an extreme. Similarly, some ad campaigns pair products with images of adorable babies, happy families, or other "natural" stimuli that elicit warm, emotional responses. If classical conditioning occurs, the advertisers hope, the product by itself will also elicit a warm emotional response.

A situation, a particular word, a smell, or even a location can evoke a classically conditioned fear. For example, one of our students told us that whenever he drove past a certain intersection where he had experienced a serious auto accident, his heart would begin to race and his hands would tremble. In the chapter prologue, Erv became classically conditioned to feel anxious whenever he entered the attic.

Other emotional responses can also become classically conditioned. When feelings of happiness, sadness, or sexual arousal are repeatedly paired with a neutral stimulus like a song or the scent of a particular cologne, the stimulus alone may come to evoke the emotional response. Advertisers frequently try to take advantage of this phenomenon by pairing their product (the neutral stimulus) with a sexy, romantic, or exciting image (see In Focus Box 5.1).

Conditioned Physiological Responses

Classical conditioning can also influence physiological responses. For example, many people begin to feel more alert after just a few sips of their morning cup of coffee. Since it takes about 30 to 40 minutes for the caffeine in coffee to reach significant levels in the bloodstream, the sense of increased alertness may be a classically conditioned response.

Researchers have been able to classically condition a drop in immune response in rats and mice (see Ader & Cohen, 1993). Human subjects can also display classically conditioned decreases in immune response. One study involved a group of cancer patients who had undergone a series of chemotherapy treatments (Bovbjerg & others, 1990). Each chemotherapy treatment temporarily lowered the cancer patients' immune response. After a few chemotherapy treatments, researchers found that the patients' immune response dropped when measured in the hospital *before* the chemotherapy treatment was administered.

How can this be explained in terms of classical conditioning? Initially, only the chemotherapy treatments (the unconditioned stimulus) produced a drop in the patients' immune response (the unconditioned response). But with repeated treatments, cues related to the hospital environment (the conditioned stimulus) became associated with the chemotherapy treatments. Now, the conditioned stimulus alone—the hospital environment—produced a conditioned response of reduced immune functioning. Similarly, many chemotherapy patients experience nausea and vomiting—common side-effects of the treatments—simply at the sight of the hospital clinic, the sound of the nurse's voice, or other hospital-related cues (see Ader & Cohen, 1993).

Operant Conditioning: Associating Behaviors and Consequences

> *Operant conditioning deals with the learning of active, non-reflexive behaviors. What were B. F. Skinner's key assumptions?*

Classical conditioning plays a role in a wide range of emotional and physiological responses. However, it cannot account for all learned behaviors, especially the nonreflexive, or voluntary, actions often exhibited by humans and animals. In this section we'll look at another form of learning that describes how we acquire and maintain active, voluntary behaviors.

B. F. Skinner and the Search for "Order in Behavior"

From the time he was a graduate student in psychology until his death, the famous American psychologist **B. F. Skinner** (1904–1990) searched for the "lawful processes" that would explain "order in behavior" (Skinner, 1956, 1967). Skinner was a staunch behaviorist. Like Watson, Skinner believed that psychology should restrict itself to studying only phenomena that could be objectively measured and verified—outwardly observable behavior. Skinner acknowledged the existence of "internal factors" such as thoughts, expectations, and perceptions (Skinner, 1974; Delprato & Midgley, 1992). But "private events" like thoughts and feelings defy direct scientific observation. Thus, Skinner believed that such subjective factors should not be included in an objective, scientific explanation of behavior (Baum & Heath, 1992).

B. F. Skinner (1904–1990) As a young adult, Skinner had hoped to become a writer. When he graduated from college, he set up a study in the attic of his parents' home and waited for inspiration to strike. After a year of "frittering" away his time, he decided that there were other ways to learn about human nature. As Skinner (1967) later wrote, "A writer might portray human behavior accurately, but he did not understand it. I was to remain interested in human behavior, but the literary method had failed me; I would turn to the scientific. . . . The relevant science appeared to be psychology, though I had only the vaguest idea of what that meant."

The practice of looking inside the organism for an explanation of behavior has tended to obscure the variables which are immediately available for a scientific analysis. These variables lie outside the organism, in its immediate environment and in its environmental history.

B. F. Skinner *Science and Human Behavior,* 1953

Skinner acknowledged that classical conditioning could explain the learned association of stimuli in certain reflexive responses (Iversen, 1992). But classical conditioning was limited to existing behaviors that are reflexively elicited. Skinner was interested in a different category of behavior. To Skinner, the most important form of learning was demonstrated by *new* behaviors that were actively *emitted* by the organism.

To study active behaviors, Skinner drew upon the earlier work of an American psychologist, Edward L. Thorndike. Thorndike (1898, 1911) had studied how animals learn new, complex behaviors, such as navigating a maze or escaping from a cage. On the basis of his study of animal learning, Thorndike had proposed the *Law of Effect*. Simply stated, Thorndike's Law of Effect held that behaviors that were followed by a satisfying effect were more likely to be repeated, whereas behaviors that were followed by an unsatisfactory effect were less likely to be repeated.

Skinner coined the term **operant** to describe active behaviors that "operate upon the environment to generate consequences." In everyday language, Skinner's operant conditioning model of learning explains how we acquire the wide range of *voluntary* behaviors we perform in daily life. As a staunch behaviorist, Skinner avoided the term "voluntary," because it would imply that behavior was due to a conscious choice or intention.

As Skinner developed his operant conditioning model, he defined concepts in very objective terms. He emphasized outward behavior that could be observed and measured, and he avoided references to subjective mental states. In our explanation of operant conditioning, we'll try to stay close to Skinner's original terminology and definitions.

Reinforcement:
Increasing Future Behavior

> *The basic premise of operant conditioning is that behavior is shaped and maintained by its consequences. What is reinforcement, and what effect does it produce? How are positive and negative reinforcement similar, and how are they different?*

In a nutshell, Skinner's **operant conditioning** model explains learning as a process in which behavior is shaped and maintained by its consequences. One possible consequence of a behavior is reinforcement. **Reinforcement** is a stimulus or an event that follows an operant and increases the likelihood of the operant being repeated. Notice that reinforcement is defined by the effect that it produces—increasing or strengthening the occurrence of a behavior in the future. In everyday language, a reinforcing stimulus is typically something desirable, satisfying, or pleasant. Skinner, of course, wouldn't use those terms, because they reflect subjective emotional states.

operant
Skinner's term for an actively emitted (or voluntary) behavior that operates on the environment to produce consequences.

operant conditioning
The basic learning process that involves changing the probability of a response being repeated by manipulating the consequences of that response.

reinforcement
The occurrence of a stimulus or event following a response that increases the likelihood of the response being repeated.

positive reinforcement
A situation in which a response is followed by the addition of a reinforcing stimulus, increasing the likelihood of the response being repeated in similar situations.

Positive and Negative Reinforcement

Reinforcement can take two forms: positive reinforcement and negative reinforcement. Both forms of reinforcement increase future behavior, but they do so in different ways. **Positive reinforcement** involves following an operant with the *addition of a reinforcing stimulus*. For example, suppose you study with a friend for your psychology midterm (the operant), which is followed by your receiving an A on the exam (the reinforcing stimulus). If the addition of this consequence makes you more likely to study with a friend in the future, then positive reinforcement has occurred.

negative reinforcement
A situation in which a response results in the removal, avoidance, or escape of a punishing stimulus, increasing the likelihood of the response being repeated in similar situations.

primary reinforcer
A stimulus or event that is naturally or inherently reinforcing for a given species, such as food, water, or other biological necessities.

conditioned reinforcer
A stimulus or event that has acquired reinforcing value by being associated with a primary reinforcer; also called a *secondary reinforcer.*

Negative reinforcement involves the *removal of an unpleasant or aversive stimulus* from a situation, thereby strengthening future occurrences of the behavior that brings about this removal. Like positive reinforcement, negative reinforcement *increases* the likelihood of a behavior being repeated (see Figure 5.3). For example, you take two aspirin (the operant) to remove a headache (the aversive stimulus). Are you more likely to take aspirin to deal with pain in the future? If you are, then negative reinforcement has occurred.

Aversive stimuli typically involve physical or psychological discomfort that an organism seeks to avoid or escape. Consequently, behaviors are said to be negatively reinforced when

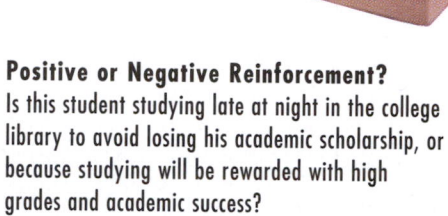

Positive or Negative Reinforcement?
Is this student studying late at night in the college library to avoid losing his academic scholarship, or because studying will be rewarded with high grades and academic success?

they let you either (1) *escape* aversive stimuli that are already present or (2) *avoid* aversive stimuli before they occur. That is, we're more likely to repeat the same avoidance or escape behaviors in similar situations in the future. The headache example illustrates the negative reinforcement of *escape behavior.* By taking two aspirin, you "escaped" the headache. Returning your library books on time to avoid an overdue fine illustrates the negative reinforcement of *avoidance behavior.*

Process	Operant	Consequence	Effect on Behavior
Positive reinforcement	Studying to make dean's list	Make dean's list	Increase studying in the future
Negative reinforcement	Studying to avoid losing academic scholarship	Avoid loss of academic scholarship	Increase studying in the future

FIGURE 5.3 Comparing Positive and Negative Reinforcement
Both positive and negative reinforcement increase the likelihood of a behavior being repeated. Positive reinforcement involves a behavior that leads to a reinforcing or rewarding event. In contrast, negative reinforcement involves behavior that leads to the avoidance or escape of an aversive or punishing event. Ultimately, both positive and negative reinforcement involve outcomes that strengthen future behavior.

Primary and Conditioned Reinforcers

Skinner also distinguished between reinforcing stimuli that were primary and conditioned. A **primary reinforcer** is one that is *naturally* reinforcing for a given species. Even if the species had no prior experience with the stimulus, the stimulus or event would still have reinforcing properties. For example, food, water, adequate warmth, and sexual contact are primary reinforcers for most animals, including humans.

A **conditioned reinforcer,** also called a *secondary reinforcer,* is one that has acquired reinforcing value by being associated with a primary reinforcer. The classic example of a conditioned reinforcer is money, which is reinforcing because we've learned that we can use it to acquire primary reinforcers and other conditioned reinforcers. Conditioned reinforcers can also be more subtle, such as a smile, a nod of agreement, or even eye contact.

Primary and Conditioned Reinforcers
Primary reinforcers, like hugs, are naturally reinforcing; they don't need to be learned. In contrast, conditioned reinforcers acquire their reinforcing value through being associated with primary reinforcers.

Sometimes there are many links in the association between a conditioned reinforcer and a primary reinforcer. You can't plunk your college degree down on the counter to purchase a loaf of bread at the grocery store, but your college degree can lead to a job that provides you with money to exchange for the primary reinforcer of food.

Punishment:
Using Aversive Consequences to Decrease Behavior

> Punishment is a process that decreases the occurrence of a behavior. What factors influence the effectiveness of punishment? What negative effects are associated with the use of punishment, and why is punishment not the best method for changing behavior?

Positive and negative reinforcement are processes that *strengthen* future behavior. The opposite effect is produced by punishment. **Punishment** refers to the presentation of an event or stimulus following a behavior that acts to *decrease* the likelihood of the behavior being repeated. Many people confuse punishment and negative reinforcement, but these two processes produce entirely different effects on behavior (see Figure 5.4). Negative reinforcement *always increases* the likelihood that an operant will be repeated. Punishment *always decreases* the future performance of an operant. Remember that, like reinforcement, punishment is defined by the effect it produces.

Aversive consequences, however, don't always function as effective punishments. That is, they don't always eliminate the behaviors that are targeted. Several factors influence the effectiveness of punishment (Axelrod & Apsche, 1983). For example, punishments are more effective if they immediately follow a response than if they are delayed. Punishment is also more effective if it consistently, rather than occasionally, follows a response. Thus, aversive consequences like speeding tickets and prison sentences are often ineffective. Though commonly referred to as punishments, these aversive consequences are inconsistently applied and often administered only after a long delay.

Even when punishment does decrease the incidence of a particular behavior, its use has several drawbacks. First, punishment doesn't teach or promote a more appropriate response to replace the undesirable response. Second, intense punishment often produces undesirable results, such as complete passivity, fear, anxiety, or hostility (Skinner, 1974). Finally, the effects of punishment are likely to be temporary (Skinner, 1938; Estes & Skinner, 1941). A child who is sent to her room for teasing her little brother may well repeat the behavior when her mother's back is turned. As Skinner (1971) wrote, "Punished behavior is likely to reappear after the punitive consequences are withdrawn."

Throughout his life, Skinner remained strongly opposed to the use of punishment. Instead, he advocated the greater use of positive reinforcement to strengthen desirable behaviors). For some suggestions on changing behavior without applying punishing stimuli, see In Focus Box 5.2 on the next page.

Process	Operant	Consequence	Effect on Behavior
Punishment	Using radar detector	Receive ticket and fine for illegal use of radar detector	Decrease use of radar detector in the future
Negative reinforcement	Using radar detector	Avoid speeding ticket and fine	Increase use of radar detector in the future

FIGURE 5.4 Comparing Punishment and Negative Reinforcement
Punishment and negative reinforcement are two different processes that produce *opposite* effects on a given behavior. Punishment *decreases* the future performance of the behavior, while negative reinforcement *increases* it.

punishment
The presentation of a stimulus or event following a behavior that acts to decrease the likelihood of the behavior being repeated.

IN FOCUS 5.2

Changing the Behavior of Others: Alternatives to Punishment

We'd often like to change the behavior of others. Sometimes we respond to an undesirable behavior with a punishing stimulus, such as criticism, but punishment only suppresses a behavior. It doesn't promote more desirable or appropriate behaviors. We'll briefly describe some alternative ways to reduce undesirable behaviors and to increase the occurrence of desirable behaviors.

Stop Reinforcing the Problem Behavior

Technically, this strategy is called *extinction*. The first step in effectively applying extinction is to observe the behavior as carefully and objectively as you can, and try to identify exactly what reinforcer is maintaining the behavior. If the reinforcer is one that can be easily controlled, eliminate it.

For example, suppose a co-worker is wasting your time with gossip. You want to extinguish his behavior of interrupting your work with needless chitchat. In the past, trying to be polite, you've responded to his behavior by acting interested (a reinforcer). You could eliminate the reinforcer by responding to his interruptions as noncommittally as possible and continuing to work while he talked.

It's important to note that when the extinction process is initiated, the problem behavior often *temporarily* increases, especially if the problem behavior has been only occasionally reinforced in the past. Thus, once begun, it's critical that nonreinforcement of the problem behavior be consistent (see Lawton & others, 1991).

For example, if parents decide to extinguish their young child's emotional outbursts at bedtime, they should initially expect the child to wail longer and louder to get their attention. But if the parents remain consistent in *not* reinforcing the child's outbursts with parental attention, the problem behavior will eventually decrease.

Remove the Opportunity to Obtain Positive Reinforcement

It's not always possible to identify and eliminate all the reinforcers that maintain a behavior. For example, a child's obnoxious behavior might be reinforced by the laughter and social attention he gets from siblings or classmates.

In a procedure called *time-out from positive reinforcement,* the child is removed from the reinforcing situation for a short time, so that the access to reinforcers is eliminated. When the undesirable behavior occurs, the child is immediately sent to a time-out area, such as a chair in a remote corner. The time-out area should be free of distractions, activities, and social contact. The time-out period begins when the child's behavior is under control—for example, once he is sitting quietly. For children, a good rule of thumb is one minute of time-out per year of age.

Reinforce the Nonoccurrence of the Problem Behavior

This strategy involves setting a specific time period after which the individual is reinforced if the unwanted behavior has *not* occurred. For example, if you're trying to reduce bickering between your children, set an appropriate time limit, and then provide positive reinforcement if they have *not* squabbled during that interval.

At first, reinforce the nonoccurrence of the behavior after a relatively short time, and use a highly valued reinforcer. With success, you can gradually increase the time span required for reinforcement, and scale back the reinforcer. This strategy requires closely monitoring the individual to ensure that a positive reinforcer is delivered only after the behavior has not occurred.

Reinforce an Incompatible Behavior

The best method to reduce a problem behavior is to reinforce an *alternative* behavior that is both constructive and incompatible with the problem behavior (Reese, 1986). For example, if you're trying to decrease a child's whining, respond to her requests (the reinforcer) only when she talks in a normal tone of voice. If the goal is to increase cooperative play, reinforce sharing and taking turns rather than quarreling and bullying. As with the other strategies, this procedure works best when it is used very consistently and potent positive reinforcers are initially used.

Enhancing the Effectiveness of Positive Reinforcement

Often, these four strategies are used in combination (see Burgio & Sinnott, 1990; Babbitt & Parrish, 1991). However, remember the most important behavioral principle: *Positively reinforce the behaviors that you want to increase.* There are several ways you can enhance the effectiveness of positive reinforcement.

First, make sure that the reinforcer is strongly reinforcing to the individual whose behavior you're trying to modify. Second, the positive reinforcer should ideally be delivered *immediately* after the preferred behavior occurs. Third, the positive reinforcer should initially be given *every* time the preferred behavior occurs. When the desired behavior becomes well established, *gradually reduce the frequency of reinforcement.*

Fourth, try to use a *variety* of positive reinforcers, such as tangible items, praise, special privileges, recognition, and so on. Keep in mind that you can use a more preferred activity (watercoloring) to reinforce a less preferred activity (picking up one's toys). Finally, encourage the individual to engage in *self-reinforcement* in the form of pride, a sense of accomplishment, and feelings of self-control.

discriminative stimulus
A specific stimulus in the presence of which a particular response is more likely to be reinforced, and in the absence of which a particular response is not reinforced.

Discriminative Stimuli:
Setting the Occasion for Responding

Discriminative stimuli refer to environmental cues in the presence of which a particular response is likely to be reinforced. What important role do discriminative stimuli play in operant conditioning? What is shaping?

The third component of the operant conditioning model of learning is what Skinner called the **discriminative stimulus**—the specific stimulus in the presence of which a particular operant is more likely to be reinforced. From experience, we learn to associate certain environmental cues or signals with particular operant responses, and we learn that we're more likely to be reinforced for performing an operant response when we do so in the presence of the discriminative stimulus. For example, you've learned that you're more likely to be reinforced for screaming at the top of your lungs at a football game (one discriminative stimulus) than in the middle of class (a different discriminative stimulus).

In this way, according to Skinner (1974), behavior is determined and controlled by the stimuli that are present in a given situation. In Skinner's view, an individual's behavior is not determined by a personal "choice" or a conscious "decision." Instead, individual behavior is determined by environmental stimuli and the person's reinforcement history in that environment. Skinner's views on this point have some very controversial implications (see Critical Thinking Box 5.3: "Is Human Freedom Just an Illusion?").

We now have all the fundamental components of the operant conditioning model (see Figure 5.5). Basically, it works like this: In the presence of a specific environmental stimulus (the discriminative stimulus), we emit a particular behavior (the operant), which is followed by a consequence (reinforcement or punishment). If the consequence is either positive or negative reinforcement, we are *more* likely to repeat the operant when we encounter the same or similar discriminative stimuli in the future. If the consequence is some form of punishment, we are *less* likely to repeat the operant when we encounter the same or similar discriminative stimuli in the future.

Next, we'll build on the basic operant conditioning model by considering how Skinner explained the acquisition of complex behaviors.

FIGURE 5.5 The Operant Conditioning Model of Learning

The examples given here illustrate the three key components involved in the operant conditioning model of learning. The basic operant conditioning process works like this: In the presence of a specific discriminative stimulus, an operant response is emitted, which is followed by a consequence. Depending on the consequence, we are more or less likely to repeat the operant when we encounter the same or similar discriminative stimuli in the future.

	Discriminative Stimulus	Operant Response	Consequence	Effect on Future Behavior
Definition	The environmental stimulus that precedes an operant response	The actively emitted or voluntary behavior	The environmental stimulus or event that follows the operant response	Reinforcement increases the likelihood of operant being repeated; punishment or lack of reinforcement decreases the likelihood of operant being repeated.
Examples	Neighbor passes by	Talk to neighbor	Pleasant conversation	Positive reinforcement: More likely to talk to neighbor in the future.
	Red oil light	Shut off car engine	Avoid engine damage	Negative reinforcement: More likely to shut off car in the future when red oil light is present.
	Poison ivy plant	Touch plant	Painful, itchy rash on hand	Punishment: Less likely to touch poison ivy plant in the future.

CRITICAL THINKING 5.3

Is Human Freedom Just an Illusion?

Had B. F. Skinner been content to confine his observations to pigeon or rat behavior, his career might have been relatively uncontroversial. But Skinner was intensely interested in human behavior and social problems. He believed that operant conditioning principles could, and *should,* be applied on a broad scale to help solve society's problems.

Skinner's most radical—and controversial—stance involved his belief that ideas like free will, self-determination, and individual choice are just an illusion. Skinner (1971) argued that behavior is not simply influenced by the environment, but is *determined* by it. Control the environment, he said, and you will control human behavior. As he bluntly asserted in his controversial best seller, *Beyond Freedom and Dignity* (1971), "A person does not act upon the world, the world acts upon him."

Skinner's ideas clashed with traditional American ideals of personal responsibility, individual freedom, and self-determination. Such ideals are based on the assumption that behavior arises from causes that are *within* the individual. All individuals are held responsible for their conduct and given credit for their achievements. Skinner labeled such notions the "traditional prescientific view" of human behavior.

Skinner advocated an entirely different philosophy, one based on scientific evidence. As he put it, "A scientific analysis [of behavior] shifts both the responsibility and the achievement to the environment." Applying his ideas to social problems such as alcoholism and crime, Skinner (1971) wrote, "It is the environment which is 'responsible' for objectionable behavior, and it is the environment, not some attribute of the individual, which must be changed."

To understand Skinner's point of view, it helps if you can think of society as being a massive, sophisticated Skinner box. From the moment of birth, the environment shapes and determines your behavior through reinforcing or punishing consequences. Taking this view, you are no more personally responsible for your behavior than a rat in a Skinner box. Just like a rat, your behavior is simply a response to the unique patterns of environmental consequences to which you have been exposed.

Skinner (1971) proposed that "a technology of behavior" be developed, one based on a scientific analysis of behavior. He believed that society could be redesigned using operant conditioning principles to produce more socially desirable behaviors—and happier citizens. He described such an ideal, utopian society in *Walden Two,* a novel he published in 1948. Critics of Skinner charged him with advocating a totalitarian state. They asked who would determine which behaviors were shaped and maintained (see Todd & Morris, 1992).

As Skinner pointed out, however, human behavior is *already* controlled by various authorities: parents, teachers, politicians, religious leaders, employers, and so forth. Such authorities regularly use reinforcing and punishing consequences to shape and control the behavior of others. Skinner insisted that it is better to control behavior in a rational, humane fashion than to leave the control of behavior to the whims and often selfish aims of those in power. Skinner himself was adamantly opposed to the use of punishment and other aversive stimuli to control behavior. Instead, he repeatedly advocated the greater use of positive reinforcement (Dinsmoor, 1992).

On the one hand, it may seem convenient to "blame" your history of environmental consequences for your failures and misdeeds. On the other hand, that means you can't take any credit for your accomplishments and good deeds either! Given this summary of Skinner's ideas, what do you think? Is your behavior determined by the environment? Are human freedom and personal responsibility just illusions? Or is human behavior fundamentally different from a rat's behavior in a Skinner box? Think about it carefully. After all, exactly *why* are you reading this box?

NON SEQUITER

Recognizing Components of Operant Conditioning: Reinforcement and Punishment

1. Josh studies to avoid the aversive or unpleasant consequence of bad grades. His studying behavior is maintained by:
   a. positive reinforcement
   b. negative reinforcement
   c. punishment
   d. primary reinforcement

2. Katie's room is a mess. Her parents agree to increase her allowance by $5 each week if she cleans her room every Tuesday.
   a. positive reinforcement
   b. negative reinforcement
   c. punishment by application
   d. punishment by removal

3. Judy's dog, Murphy, will roll over, beg, and do other tricks for a food reward. However, when offered a $10 bill, he won't do any of these tricks. It appears that Murphy is more responsive to _____ than to _____.
   a. positive reinforcers; negative reinforcers
   b. bribery; corruption

   c. primary reinforcers; conditioned reinforcers
   d. punishment; positive reinforcement

4. Zachary works on a cattle ranch. When the chuck wagon comes around, the cook rings a big metal bell to signal that the food is ready. Whenever Zak and the other cowhands hear the sound of the bell, they head straight for the chuck wagon. In this example, the sound of the bell is a(n):
   a. primary reinforcer
   b. negative reinforcer
   c. unconditioned stimulus
   d. discriminative stimulus

5. Seeing a stranded motorist, Dean stopped to see if he could help. The stranded motorist robbed Dean and stole his car. Dean no longer stops to help strangers. This is an example of:
   a. positive reinforcement
   b. primary reinforcement
   c. punishment
   d. negative reinforcement

Shaping Behavior:
Getting Closer All the Time

To scientifically study the relationship between behavior and its consequences in the laboratory, Skinner invented the *operant chamber,* more popularly known as a **Skinner box.** A Skinner box is a small glass cage with a food dispenser. Attached to the cage is a device that automatically records the number of operants made by an experimental animal, usually a rat or pigeon. For a rat, the typical operant is to press a bar; a pigeon usually pecks at a small disk. Food pellets are used for positive reinforcement. Often, a light in the cage functions as a discriminative stimulus: When the light is on, pressing the bar or pecking the disk will be reinforced with a food pellet; when the light is off, responses will not result in reinforcement.

When a rat is first placed in a Skinner box, it typically will explore its new environment, occasionally nudging or pressing the bar in the process.

Skinner box

The popular name for an *operant chamber,* the experimental apparatus invented by B. F. Skinner to study the relationship between environmental events and active behaviors.

Shaping Operant Behavior Shaping is often used to train animals to perform impressive tricks, like this dolphin jumping through a hoop high above the water. To shape this behavior, the dolphin was first reinforced for swimming through the hoop underwater. Progressively, the hoop is raised until it is above the water. As the shaping process continues, reinforcement is delivered only for behaviors that become closer to the ultimate goal behavior.

The researcher can hasten the rat's bar-pressing behavior by using a process called shaping. **Shaping** involves reinforcing successively closer approximations of a behavior until the correct behavior is displayed. For example, a researcher might first reinforce the rat with a food pellet whenever it moved to the half of the Skinner box in which the bar was located; other responses would be ignored. Once that response had been learned, reinforcement would be withheld until the rat moved even closer to the bar. Then the rat might be reinforced only when it touched the bar. Step by step, the rat is reinforced for behaviors that correspond ever more closely to the final goal behavior: pressing the bar.

Skinner believed that shaping could explain how people acquire a wide variety of abilities and skills—everything from tying your shoes to operating sophisticated computer programs. Indeed, athletic coaches, teachers, parents, and child-care workers all use shaping techniques. Psychologist Judith Mathews and her colleagues (1992) used shaping to teach visually impaired children as young as two years of age to wear contact lenses. Toys, bubbles, and stars were used as reinforcers. First, the children were positively reinforced for allowing their faces to be touched. Then the children were reinforced for pulling open an eyelid, having an adult's finger approach their eyes, touching the contact lens, and so forth. By the end of the study, the children were wearing their contact lenses every day, and it took an average of only two minutes for an adult to insert or remove the children's contact lenses.

Maintaining Behavior:
The Schedules of Reinforcement

> *Once acquired, behaviors are maintained through different schedules or patterns of reinforcement. What is the partial reinforcement effect? What are the four basic schedules of reinforcement, and what pattern of responses does each schedule produce?*

shaping
The operant conditioning procedure of selectively reinforcing successively closer approximations of a goal behavior until the goal behavior is displayed.

continuous reinforcement
A schedule of reinforcement in which every occurrence of a particular response is reinforced.

partial reinforcement
A situation in which the occurrence of a particular response is only sometimes followed by a reinforcer.

extinction
The gradual weakening and disappearance of conditioned behavior. In operant conditioning, extinction occurs when an emitted behavior is no longer followed by a reinforcer.

Once a rat had acquired a bar-pressing behavior, Skinner found that the most efficient way to strengthen the response was to immediately reinforce *every* occurrence of bar pressing. This pattern of reinforcement is called **continuous reinforcement.** In everyday life, of course, it's common for responses to be reinforced only sometimes—a pattern called **partial reinforcement.** For example, practicing your basketball skills isn't followed by putting the ball through the hoop on every free throw. Sometimes you're reinforced by making a basket, and sometimes you're not.

Now suppose that despite all your hard work, your basketball skills were dismal. If practicing free throws was *never* reinforced by making a basket, what would you do? You'd probably eventually quit playing basketball. This is an example of **extinction:** In operant conditioning, when a learned response no longer results in reinforcement, the likelihood of the behavior being repeated gradually declines.

The Partial Reinforcement Effect:
Building Resistance to Extinction

Skinner (1956) first noticed the effects of partial reinforcement when he began running low on food pellets one day. Rather than reinforcing every bar press, Skinner tried to stretch out his food pellet supply by rewarding responses only *periodically*. He found that the rats not only continued to respond, but actually increased their rate of bar pressing.

One important consequence of partially reinforcing behavior is that such behaviors tend to be more resistant to extinction than behaviors conditioned using continuous reinforcement. This phenomenon is called the **partial reinforcement effect.** For example, when Skinner shut off the food-dispensing mechanism, a pigeon conditioned using *continuous reinforcement* would continue pecking at the disk 100 times or so before the behavior decreased significantly, indicating extinction. In contrast, a pigeon conditioned with *partial reinforcement* continued to peck at the disk thousands of times! If you think about it, this is not surprising. When pigeons, rats, or humans have experienced partial reinforcement, they've learned that reinforcement may yet occur, despite delays and nonreinforced responses, if persistent responses are made.

In everyday life, the partial reinforcement effect is reflected in behaviors that persist despite the lack of reinforcement. For example, parents who *occasionally* give in to their child's whining are inadvertently strengthening the behavior by putting it on a partial reinforcement schedule. If the parents then try to extinguish the behavior by consistently refusing to reinforce it, the whining will persist for a longer period of time than if they had previously reinforced *every* instance of whining.

Superstitious Behavior Professional athletes sometimes develop quirky superstitious rituals, such as these New York Mets baseball players balancing baseballs on their caps. How can this behavior be explained by accidental reinforcement?

partial reinforcement effect
The phenomenon by which behaviors that are conditioned using partial reinforcement are more resistant to extinction than behaviors that are conditioned using continuous reinforcement.

Accidental Reinforcement: Superstitious Pigeons?

Sometimes it only *appears* as if a particular response has resulted in reinforcement, when in reality, the consequence is just a coincidence—the result of *accidental reinforcement*. One of Skinner's (1948/1992) most clever demonstrations was to show how accidental reinforcement could lead to superstitious behaviors. Placing a pigeon in a Skinner box, he set a timer so that every 15 seconds a food reinforcer was automatically dispensed. The pigeon's behavior and the delivery of the food reinforcer were completely independent of each other.

Just as the basic principles of operant conditioning would predict, whatever behavior happened to be occurring when the food pellet was dispensed became strengthened and more likely to be repeated. Over time, several pigeons developed what Skinner called "a sort of superstition." One bird hopped sideways from one foot to the other. Another turned in counterclockwise circles.

The resemblance to the development of human superstitions should be obvious. A few "accidental connections" between a superstitious ritual and favorable consequences may be enough to maintain the behavior, even though the behavior is often *not* reinforced. So the good luck that seems to follow when you eat black-eyed peas on New Year's Day, although simply a coincidence, may "reinforce" the behavior, leading you to repeat it.

Accidental reinforcement is yet another example of partial reinforcement. Thus, superstitious behaviors can be extremely resistant to extinction —as Skinner's superstitious pigeons demonstrated. After Skinner turned off the food dispenser, one pigeon continued to perform its side-to-side hop over 10,000 times! The partial reinforcement effect may help explain the

schedule of reinforcement
The delivery of a reinforcer according to a preset pattern based on the number of responses or the time interval between responses.

fixed-ratio (FR) schedule
A reinforcement schedule in which a reinforcer is delivered after a fixed number of responses has occurred.

variable-ratio (VR) schedule
A reinforcement schedule in which a reinforcer is delivered after an average number of responses that varies unpredictably from trial to trial.

fixed-interval (FI) schedule
A reinforcement schedule in which a reinforcer is delivered for the first response that occurs after a fixed time interval has elapsed.

persistence of various superstitious beliefs and ritualistic practices in many cultures, including our own.

Schedules of Reinforcement

Skinner (1956) found that specific preset arrangements of partial reinforcement produce different patterns and rates of responding. Collectively, these different reinforcement arrangements are called **schedules of reinforcement.** As we describe the four basic schedules of reinforcement, you'll find it helpful to refer to Figures 5.6 and 5.7.

Fixed-Ratio Schedule   With a **fixed-ratio (FR) schedule,** reinforcement occurs after a fixed number of responses. For example, a rat might be on a 25-to-1 fixed-ratio (abbreviated FR-25), meaning it has to press the bar 25 times in order to receive one food pellet. It usually requires shaping to get a rat to press the bar 25 times in order to get one food pellet, but once the behavior is shaped, the ratio of reinforcements to responses is fixed and predictable.

Fixed-ratio schedules typically produce a high rate of responding that follows a burst-pause-burst pattern. The rat displays a burst of bar pressing, receives a pellet of food, pauses briefly, then displays another burst of responding (see Figure 5.6). In everyday life, the fixed-ratio schedule is reflected in any activity that requires a precise number of responses in order to obtain reinforcement. Piecework—being paid for producing a specific number of items, such as being paid $1 for every 100 envelopes you stuff—is an example of an FR-100 schedule. On this sort of schedule, you might work steadily until you'd stuffed 100 envelopes, and then take a short break before you began working again (Mazur, 1994).

Variable-Ratio Schedule   With a **variable-ratio (VR) schedule,** reinforcement occurs after an *average* number of responses that *varies* from trial to trial. For example, a rat on a variable-ratio-20 schedule (abbreviated VR-20) would be reinforced after an average of 20 responses. But the rat might have to press the bar 25 times on the first trial before being reinforced and only 15 times on the second trial before reinforcement. While the number of responses required on any specific trial is *unpredictable,* over repeated trials the ratio of responses to reinforcers works out to the predetermined average.

As you can see in Figure 5.6, variable-ratio schedules of reinforcement produce high, steady rates of responding with hardly any pausing between trials or after reinforcement. Why do variable-ratio schedules produce such persistent responses? One explanation is that it's impossible to predict *which* response will result in reinforcement, but the more responses that are made, the greater the likelihood of reinforcement. The combination of these two factors can make some behaviors, such as gambling, "addictive" for some people (Mazur, 1994). Gambling is the classic example of a variable-ratio schedule in real life. Each spin of the roulette wheel, toss of the dice, or purchase of a lottery ticket could be the big one, and the more you gamble, the greater your chances to win. (And lose, as casino owners are well aware.)

Fixed-Interval Schedule   With a **fixed-interval (FI) schedule,** a reinforcer is delivered for the first response emitted *after* the preset time interval has elapsed. A rat on a two-minute fixed-interval schedule (abbreviated

FIGURE 5.6 Fixed-Ratio and Variable-Ratio Schedules of Reinforcement
The predictable nature of fixed-ratio schedules produces a high rate of responding with a pause after the reinforcer is delivered. In contrast, the unpredictable nature of variable-ratio schedules produces high, steady rates of responding with hardly any pausing between reinforcers.
(Based on Skinner, 1961.)

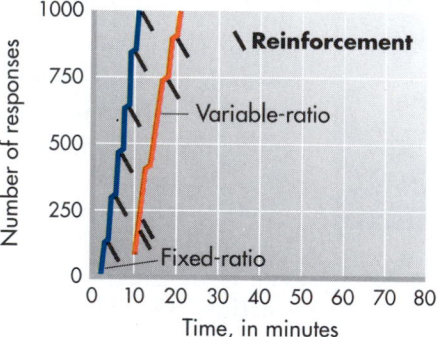

variable-interval (VI) schedule
A reinforcement schedule in which a reinforcer is delivered for the first response that occurs after an average time interval that varies unpredictably from trial to trial.

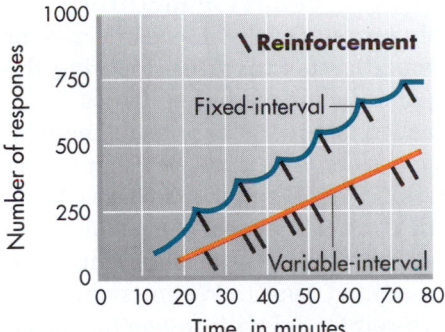

FIGURE 5.7 Fixed-Interval and Variable-Interval Schedules of Reinforcement
The predictable nature of fixed-interval schedules produces a scallop-shaped pattern of responding. As the end of the interval draws near, the rate of responding steadily increases until a reinforcer is delivered; then comes a sharp decrease in responding until the end of the interval draws near again. In contrast, the unpredictable nature of variable-interval schedules produces a moderate but steady rate of responding.
(Based on Skinner, 1961.)

FI-2 minutes) would receive no food pellets for any bar presses made during the first two minutes, whether it pressed the bar twice or 100 times. But the first bar press *after* the two-minute interval had elapsed would be reinforced.

Fixed-interval schedules typically produce a pattern of responding in which the number of responses tends to increase as the time for the next reinforcer draws near. As you can see in Figure 5.7, this produces a scallop-shaped pattern of responses. Long pauses in responding after reinforcement are especially common when the fixed interval is large. For example, a rat conditioned to an FI-10 minutes schedule may go for several minutes without pressing the bar. But as the end of the 10-minute interval draws near, bar pressing steadily increases until reinforcement occurs.

Daily life contains examples of reinforcement that follow a very similar pattern to the laboratory example of fixed-interval reinforcement. For instance, if your instructor gives you a test every four weeks, studying behavior would probably follow the same scallop-shaped pattern of responding as the rat's bar-pressing behavior. As the end of the four-week interval draws near, studying behavior increases. After the test, studying drops off until the end of the next four-week interval draws near.

Variable-Interval Schedule On a **variable-interval (VI) schedule,** reinforcement occurs for the first response emitted after an *average* amount of time has elapsed, but the interval varies from trial to trial. In other words, the length of time that must pass before a particular reinforcement is delivered is unpredictable—but over a *series* of trials, it works out to a predetermined average. A rat on a VI-30 seconds schedule might be reinforced on trial 1 for the first bar press after only 10 seconds have elapsed, for the first bar press after 50 seconds have elapsed on trial 2, and for the first bar press after 30 seconds have elapsed on trial 3. This works out to an average of one reinforcer every 30 seconds.

Generally, the unpredictable nature of variable-interval schedules tends to produce moderate but steady rates of responding, especially when the average interval is relatively short (see Figure 5.7). In daily life, variable-interval schedules are reflected in situations where we must wait for events that follow an approximate, not a precise, schedule.

On a variable-interval schedule, reinforcement depends on the passage of time, rather than on the number of responses. Dramatically increasing the number of responses probably won't result in increased reinforcement. But reinforcement is unpredictable, and *might* occur at any time. Thus, a moderately steady rate of responses will pay off in the long run.

Recognizing Schedules of Reinforcement in Operant Conditioning
Indicate which schedule of reinforcement is being used in the following examples:

Variable interval (VI)
Fixed interval (FI)
Variable ratio (VR)
Fixed ratio (FR)

1. _____ A keypunch clerk is paid $1 for every 100 correct accounting entries made on the computer.

2. _____ At the beginning of the new term, your instructor announces that there will be five surprise quizzes over the course of the semester.

3. _____ At the beginning of the semester, your instructor announces that there will be a test every two weeks.

4. _____ On the average, the campus shuttle bus passes the library about every hour.

5. _____ Michael loves to play the slot machines, and, occasionally, he wins.

6. _____ Miguel gets paid every Friday afternoon.

behavior modification
The application of learning principles to help people develop more effective or adaptive behaviors.

Applications of Operant Conditioning

Applications of operant conditioning principles include behavior modification and animal training. What is behavior modification, and how has it been used to change human behavior?

In a previous section, we described how operant conditioning principles have been applied to help visually impaired children wear contact lenses. We also described several techniques that can reduce problem behaviors without resorting to punishment. These examples illustrate **behavior modification,** the application of learning principles to help people develop more effective or adaptive behaviors. Most often, behavior modification involves applying the principles of operant conditioning to bring about changes in behavior.

Behavior modification has been used in such diverse situations as increasing social skills in schoolchildren, promoting sleep at night, and increasing automobile seatbelt use (Martens & others, 1992; Kamps & others, 1992; Lilie & Rosenberg, 1990). Behavior modification has even been used to reduce "goofing off" by competitive athletes during practice sessions (Hume & Crossman, 1992). When swimmers were reinforced with music for focusing on practicing their skills, productive behavior increased dramatically. In each of these situations, the systematic use of reinforcement and shaping has resulted in the increased occurrence of desirable behaviors.

Using Operant Conditioning An organization called "Helping Hands," founded by behavioral psychologist Mary Joan Willard, trains capuchin monkeys to help people who are paralyzed or otherwise disabled. During the training phase, operant conditioning is used to teach the monkey a wide range of helping skills, such as feeding a person, turning lights on and off, and so forth. The training process may take up to four years before a monkey is placed with a disabled person.

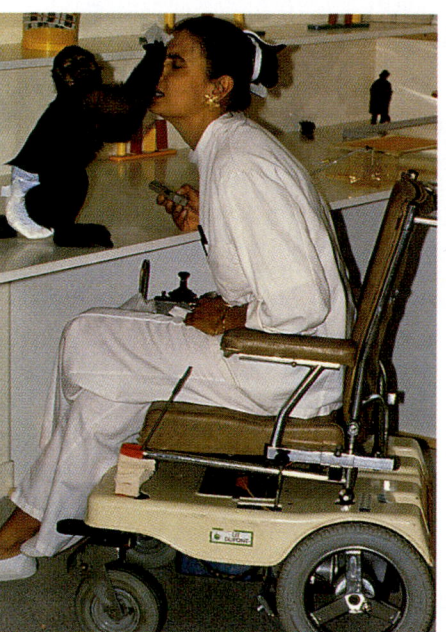

The principles of operant conditioning have also been used in the specialized training of animals to help people who are physically challenged in some way. Seeing-eye dogs for the blind and dogs who assist people who are deaf are just a few examples.

Before you go on to the next section, take a few minutes to review Table 5.1, and make sure you understand the differences between classical and operant conditioning.

TABLE 5.1 Comparing Classical and Operant Conditioning

	Classical Conditioning	**Operant Conditioning**
Type of behavior	Reflexive, involuntary behaviors	Nonreflexive, voluntary behaviors
Source of behavior	Elicited by stimulus	Emitted by organism
Basis of learning	Associating two stimuli	Associating a response and the consequence that follows it
Responses conditioned	Physiological and emotional responses	Active behaviors that lead to reinforcers
Extinction process	Conditioned response decreases when conditioned stimulus is repeatedly presented alone	Responding decreases with elimination of reinforcing consequences

The Cognitive Perspective

According to the cognitive perspective, learning involves mental processes. What kinds of cognitive processes seem to be involved in classical conditioning, and how have they been demonstrated experimentally? What is meant by the phrase, "The animal behaves like a scientist" in classical conditioning?

In our discussion of the behavioral perspective, we noted that the behaviorists saw no need to resort to mental processes or "internal causes" to explain behavior (Skinner, 1987; Blumberg & Wasserman, 1995). From the behavioral perspective, classical conditioning results from a simple association of the conditioned stimulus and the unconditioned stimulus. In operant conditioning, learning results from the association of an operant and its consequence. Hence, the behavioral perspective maintains that learning is accomplished in both classical and operant conditioning without the involvement of mental or cognitive processes.

However, not all psychologists were convinced that mental processes were uninvolved in learning. Some wondered whether conditioning procedures do more than simply change how an organism responds. Could conditioning procedures change what the organism *knows* as well as what it *does*? According to the **cognitive perspective,** mental processes as well as external events are important components of learning. In this section, we'll look first at the role cognitive processes seem to play in classical and operant conditioning. Then we'll consider how cognitive processes are involved in learning through the observation and imitation of the behaviors of others.

Cognitive Aspects of Classical Conditioning:
Reliable Predictors

According to Pavlov, classical conditioning occurs simply because two stimuli are associated closely in time: the conditioned stimulus (the bell) precedes the unconditioned stimulus (the food) by no more than a few seconds. But is it possible that Pavlov's dogs were learning more than the mere association of two stimuli that occurred very close together in time?

To answer that question, let's begin with an analogy. Suppose that on your way to class you had to go through a railroad crossing. Every time a train approaches the crossing, warning lights flash. Being rather intelligent for your species, after a few weeks you conclude that the flashing lights will be quickly followed by a freight train barreling down the railroad tracks. You've learned an association between the flashing lights and an oncoming train, because the lights are a *reliable predictor* of the train.

Now imagine that a friend of yours also has to cross train tracks, but at a different location. The railroad has had nothing but problems with the warning lights at that crossing. Sometimes the warning lights flash before a train roars through, but sometimes they don't. And sometimes they flash when no train is coming. Does your friend learn an association between the flashing lights and oncoming trains? No, because here the flashing lights are an *unreliable predictor;* they seem to have no relationship to a train's arrival.

Psychologist **Robert A. Rescorla** (b. 1940) demonstrated that much like you and your friend at different railroad crossings, classically conditioned rats also assess the reliability of predictors. In Rescorla's 1968 experiment, one group of rats heard a tone (the conditioned stimulus) that was paired

cognitive perspective
In learning theory, a general approach to the study of learning that stresses the role of expectations, mental representation, and other mental processes in learning.

Group 1

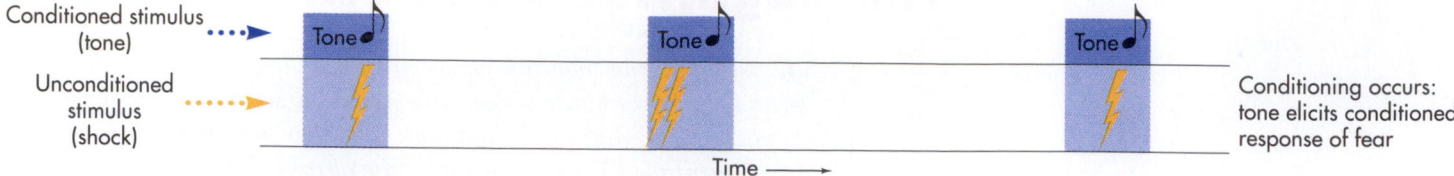

Conditioning occurs: tone elicits conditioned response of fear

Group 2

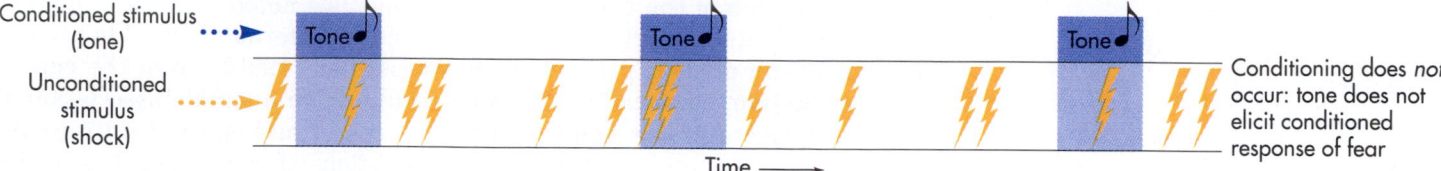

Conditioning does *not* occur: tone does not elicit conditioned response of fear

FIGURE 5.8 Reliable and Unreliable Predictors

In Rescorla's experiment, both groups of rats experienced the same number of shock–tone pairings. However, the rats in group 1 received a shock only when the tone was sounded, while the rats in group 2 experienced additional shocks that were not paired with the tone. Subsequently, the rats in group 1 displayed a conditioned fear response to the tone, while the rats in group 2 did not. Why did only the rats in group 1 become conditioned to display fear when they heard the tone?

(Based on Rescorla, 1988, Figure 1, p. 153.)

twenty times with a brief shock (the unconditioned stimulus). A second group of rats experienced the *same* number of tone–shock pairings, but they also experienced an *additional* twenty shocks with *no* tone (see Figure 5.8).

Then Rescorla tested for the conditioned fear response by presenting the tone alone to each group of rats. According to the traditional classical conditioning model, both groups of rats should have displayed the same levels of conditioned fear. After all, each group had received twenty tone–shock pairings. However, this is not what Rescorla found. The rats in the first group displayed a much stronger fear response to the tone than did the rats in the second group. Why?

According to Rescorla (1988), classical conditioning depends on the *information* the conditioned stimulus provides about the unconditioned stimulus. For learning to occur, the conditioned stimulus must be a *reliable predictor* of the unconditioned stimulus. For the first group of rats, that was certainly the situation: every time the tone sounded, a shock followed. But for the second group, the tone was an unreliable predictor: sometimes the tone preceded the shock, and sometimes the shock occurred without warning.

Rescorla concluded that the rats in both groups were *actively processing information* about the reliability of the signals they encountered. Rather than merely associating two closely paired stimuli, as Pavlov suggested, the animal assesses the *predictive value* of stimuli (Hollis, 1997). Applying this interpretation to classical conditioning, we can conclude that Pavlov's dogs learned that the bell *reliably predicted* food would follow.

According to this view, animals use cognitive processes to draw inferences about the signals they encounter in their environment. To Rescorla (1988), classical conditioning "is not a stupid process by which the organism willy-nilly forms associations between any two stimuli that happen to co-occur." Rather, his research suggests that "the animal behaves like a scientist, detecting causal relations among events and using a range of information about those events to make the relevant inferences" (Rescorla, 1980).

Because of studies by Rescorla and other researchers, today's understanding of how learning occurs in classical conditioning is very different from the explanations offered by Pavlov and Watson. Simply pairing events in time may not be enough for classical conditioning to occur. Instead, a conditioned stimulus must *reliably signal* that the unconditioned stimulus will follow. Put simply, classical conditioning seems to involve *learning the relations between events* (see Rescorla, 1988; Klein & Mowrer, 1989).

Cognitive Aspects of Operant Conditioning:
Rats! I Thought *You* Had the Map!

> *According to the cognitive perspective, operant conditioning involves forming a mental representation of the relationship between a behavior and its consequence. What is a cognitive map? What is latent learning, and how was it demonstrated?*

If cognitive processes are involved in classically conditioned behaviors, what about operant behaviors? Many early behaviorists believed that complex, active behaviors were no more than a chain of stimulus–response connections that had been "stamped in" by their effects. But one early learning researcher, **Edward C. Tolman** (1898–1956), had a different view of learning. Tolman believed that, even in the lowly rat, cognitive processes were involved in the learning of complex behaviors. According to Tolman, although such cognitive processes could not be observed directly, they could still be experimentally verified and inferred by careful observation of outward behavior (Tolman, 1932).

Much of Tolman's research involved rats in mazes. When Tolman began his research in the 1920s, many studies of rats in mazes had been done. In a typical experiment, a rat would be placed in the "start" box, and a food reward would be put in the "goal" box at the end of the maze. The rat would initially make many mistakes in running the maze. After several trials, it would eventually learn to run the maze quickly and with very few errors.

But what had the rats learned? According to traditional behaviorists, the rats had learned a *sequence of responses,* such as "first corner—turn left; second corner—turn left; third corner—turn right," and so on. Each response was associated with the "stimulus" of the rat's position in the maze. And the entire sequence of responses was "stamped in" by the food reward at the end of the maze.

Tolman (1948) disagreed with that view. He noted that several investigators had reported as incidental findings that their maze-running rats had occasionally taken their own shortcuts to the food box. In one case, an enterprising rat had knocked the cover off the maze, climbed over the maze wall and out of the maze, and scampered directly to the food box (Lashley, 1929; Tolman & others, 1946/1992). To Tolman, such reports indicated that the rats had learned more than simply the sequence of responses required to get to the food. Instead, Tolman believed that the rat eventually builds up, through experience, a **cognitive map** of the maze—a mental representation of its layout.

As an analogy, think of the route that you typically take to get to your psychology classroom. If a hallway along the way were blocked off for repairs, you would use your "cognitive map" of the building to come up with an alternative route to class. Tolman showed experimentally that rats, like people, seem to form cognitive maps (Tolman, 1948). And, like us, rats can use their cognitive maps to come up with an alternate route to a goal when the customary route is blocked (Tolman & Honzik, 1930a).

Tolman challenged the prevailing behaviorist model on another important point. According to Thorndike, for example, learning would not occur unless the behavior was "strengthened" or "stamped in" by a rewarding consequence. But Tolman showed that this is not necessarily the case. In a classic experiment, three groups of rats were put in the same maze once a day for several days (Tolman & Honzik, 1930b). For group 1, a food reward awaited the rats at the end of the maze. Their performance in the maze steadily improved; the number of errors and the time it took the rats to reach the goal box showed a steady decline with each trial. The rats in group 2 were placed

Edward Chace Tolman (1898–1956)
Although he looks rather solemn, Tolman was known for his openness to new ideas, energetic teaching style, and playful sense of humor. During an important speech, he showed a film of a rat in a maze with a short clip from a Mickey Mouse cartoon spliced in at the end (Gleitman, 1991). Tolman's research demonstrated that cognitive processes are an important part of learning, even in the rat.

cognitive map
Tolman's term to describe the mental representation of the layout of a familiar environment.

FIGURE 5.9 Latent Learning

Beginning with day 1, the rats in group 1 received a food reward at the end of the maze, and the number of errors they made steadily decreased each day. The rats in group 2 never received a food reward; they made many errors as they wandered about in the maze. Beginning on day 11, the rats in group 3 received a food reward at the end of the maze. Notice the sharp decrease in errors on day 12 and thereafter. According to Tolman, the rats in group 3 had formed a cognitive map of the maze during the first 11 days of the experiment. Learning had taken place, but this learning was not demonstrated until reinforcement was present—a phenomenon that Tolman called latent learning.

(Tolman & Honzik, 1930b.)

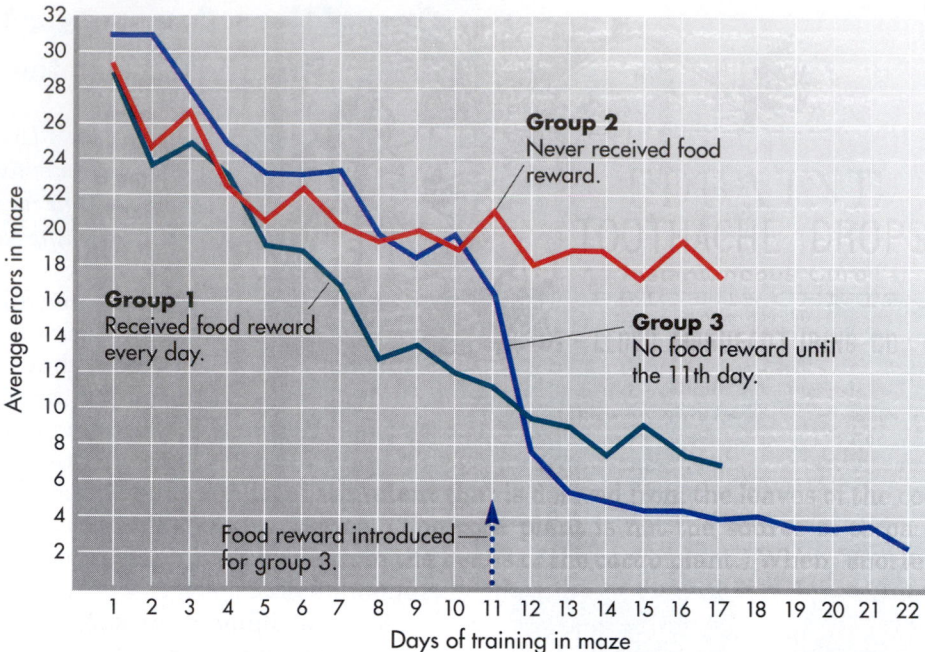

in the maze each day with *no* food reward. They consistently made many errors, and their performance showed only slight improvement. The performance of the rats in groups 1 and 2 is exactly what the traditional behaviorist model would have predicted.

Now consider the behavior of the rats in group 3. These rats were placed in the maze with no food reward for the first ten days of the experiment. Like the rats in group 2, they made many errors as they wandered about the maze. But, *beginning on day 11*, they received a food reward at the end of the maze. As you can see in Figure 5.9, there was a dramatic improvement in group 3's performance between day 11 and day 12. Once the rats had discovered that food awaited them at the end of the maze, they made a beeline for the goal. On day 12, the rats in group 3 ran the maze with very few errors, improving their performance to the level of the rats in group 1 that had been rewarded on every trial!

Tolman concluded that *reward*—or reinforcement—is *not necessary* for learning to take place (Tolman & Honzik, 1930b). The rats in group 3 had learned the layout of the maze, and formed a cognitive map of the maze, simply by exploring it for ten days. However, they had not been motivated to *demonstrate* that learning until a reward was introduced. Rewards, then, seem to affect *performance* of what has been learned rather than learning itself. To describe learning that is not immediately demonstrated in overt behavior, Tolman used the term **latent learning.**

From these and other experiments, Tolman concluded that learning involves the acquisition of knowledge rather than simply changes in outward behavior. According to Tolman (1932), an organism essentially learns "what leads to what." It learns to "expect" that a certain behavior will lead to a particular outcome in a specific situation.

Tolman is now recognized as an important forerunner of modern cognitive theories of learning (Olton, 1992; Gleitman, 1991). Many contemporary cognitive learning theorists follow Tolman in their belief that operant conditioning involves the *cognitive representation* of the relationship between a behavior and its consequence. Today, operant conditioning is seen as involving the cognitive *expectancy* that a given consequence will follow a given behavior (Hollis, 1997; Dickinson, 1989; Bolles, 1972).

latent learning

Tolman's term to describe learning that occurs in the absence of reinforcement but is not behaviorally demonstrated until a reinforcer becomes available.

Observational Learning:

Imitating the Actions of Others

In observational learning, we learn by watching others. What does Bandura's theory have in common with Tolman's ideas? What four mental processes are involved in observational learning? How has observational learning been applied?

Classical conditioning and operant conditioning emphasize the role of direct experiences in learning, such as directly experiencing a reward following a particular behavior. But much human learning occurs *indirectly* by watching what others do, then imitating it. In **observational learning,** learning takes place through observing the actions of others.

Humans develop the capacity to learn through observation at a very early age. Studies of twenty-one-day-old infants have shown that they will imitate a variety of actions, including opening their mouths, sticking out their tongues, and making other facial expressions (Meltzoff & Moore, 1977, 1983; Field & others, 1982).

Albert Bandura (b. 1925) is the psychologist most strongly identified with observational learning. Bandura (1974) believes that observational learning is the result of cognitive processes that are "actively judgmental and constructive," not merely "mechanical copying." To illustrate his theory, let's consider a famous Bandura (1965) experiment involving the imitation of aggressive behaviors. In the experiment, four-year-old children separately watched a short film showing an adult playing aggressively with a Bobo doll. A Bobo doll is a large, inflated balloon doll that stands upright because it has sand in the bottom. In the film, each child observed the adult hit, kick, and punch the Bobo doll.

Albert Bandura (b. 1925) Bandura contends that most human behavior is acquired through observational learning rather than trial and error or directly experiencing the consequences of our actions. Watching and processing information about the actions of others, including the consequences that occur, influences the likelihood that behavior will be imitated.

However, different versions of the film had different endings. Some of the children saw the adult *reinforced* with soft drinks, candy, and snacks after performing the aggressive actions. Other children saw a version in which the aggressive adult was *punished* for the actions with a scolding and a spanking by another adult. Finally, some children watched a version of the film in which *no consequences* occurred to the aggressive adult.

After seeing the film, each child was allowed to play alone in a room with several toys, including a Bobo doll. The playroom was equipped with a one-way window so that the child's behavior could be observed. Can you predict how the children behaved?

As you've probably already anticipated, the consequences the children observed in the film made a difference. Children who watched the film in which the adult was punished were much less likely to imitate the aggressive behaviors than children who watched either of the other two film endings. So far, these results aren't especially surprising.

observational learning
Learning that occurs through observing the actions of others.

TABLE 5.2 Factors That Increase the Likelihood of Imitation

You're more likely to imitate . . .

- People who are rewarded for their behavior.
- Warm, nurturant people.
- People who have control over you or have the power to influence your life.
- People who are similar to you in terms of age, sex, and interests.
- People you perceive as having higher social status.
- When the task to be imitated is not extremely easy or difficult.
- If you lack confidence in your own abilities in a particular situation.
- If the situation is unfamiliar or ambiguous.
- If you've been rewarded for imitating the same behavior in the past.

SOURCE: Based on research summarized in Mazur, 1994; Bandura, 1986, 1977.

The Classic Bobo Doll Experiment Bandura demonstrated the powerful influence of observational learning in a series of experiments conducted in the early 1960s. Children watched a film showing an adult playing aggressively with an inflated Bobo doll. If they saw the adult experience no consequences or rewarded with candy for the aggressive behavior, the children were much more likely to imitate the behavior than if they saw the adult punished for the aggressive behavior (Bandura & others, 1963; Bandura, 1965).

But then Bandura added an interesting twist to the experiment. Each child was asked to show the experimenter what the adult did in the film. For every behavior they could imitate, the child was rewarded with snacks and stickers. Now, virtually *all* of the children imitated the adult's behaviors that they had observed in the film, including the aggressive behaviors. Which version of the film the child had seen made no difference.

Bandura (1965) explained these results in much the same way that Tolman explained latent learning: Reinforcement is *not* essential for learning to occur. Rather, the *expectation of reinforcement* affects the *performance* of what has been learned.

Bandura (1986) suggests that four cognitive processes interact to determine whether imitation will occur. First, you must pay *attention* to the other person's behavior. Second, you must *remember* the other person's behavior so that you can perform it at a later time. That is, you must form and store a mental representation of the behavior to be imitated. Third, you must be able to transform this mental representation into *actions you are capable of reproducing.* These three factors—attention, memory, and motor skills—are necessary for learning to take place through observation.

Fourth, there must be some *motivation* to imitate the behavior. This factor is crucial to the actual performance of the learned behavior. An individual is more likely to imitate a behavior if there is some expectation that doing so will produce reinforcement or reward. Thus, all the children were capable of imitating the adult's aggressive behavior. But the children who saw the aggressive adult being rewarded were much more likely to imitate his behavior than the children who saw him punished. Table 5.2 summarizes other factors that increase the likelihood of imitation.

Like classical and operant conditioning, observational learning has been applied in a variety of settings, including education, vocational and job training, psychotherapy, and counseling. For example, observational learning has been used to help people develop more effective interpersonal skills (see Gambrill, 1995b). Training for nurses, electricians, pilots, and police officers routinely involves watching an experienced professional correctly perform a particular task, then imitating it. Clearly, this is advantageous. After all, would you want to be operated on by a surgeon who was learning strictly by trial and error?

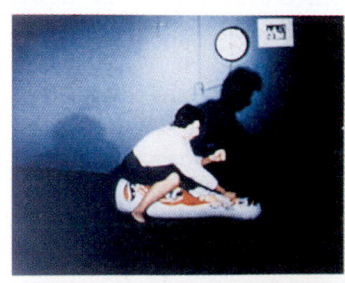

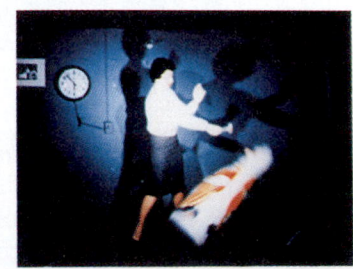

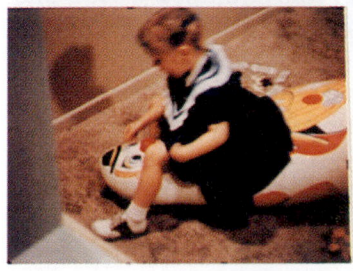

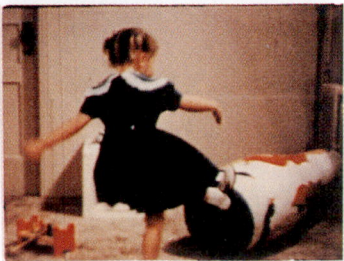

The Ecological Perspective:
Biological Predispositions to Learn

According to the ecological perspective, an animal's natural behavior patterns and other unique characteristics influence what it is able to learn. How do taste aversions challenge the principles of classical conditioning? How does biological preparedness explain taste aversions?

The traditional behaviorist view maintains that the general principles of learning apply to virtually all species and all learning situations. By studying drooling dogs, pecking pigeons, or bar-pressing rats, the behaviorists believed that they could discover these general principles of learning. Once discovered, these principles could supposedly be applied with equal validity to pigs, hummingbirds, whales, and other species, including humans. As B. F. Skinner (1956) wrote:

Pigeon, rat, monkey, which is which? It doesn't matter. Of course, these species have behavioral repertoires which are as different as their anatomies. But once you have allowed for differences in the ways in which they make contact with the environment, and in the ways in which they act upon the environment, what remains of their behavior shows astonishingly similar properties.

Skinner's contention that the particular species studied "doesn't matter" began to be challenged in the 1960s when researchers first reported "exceptions" to the well-established learning principles. As more exceptions were reported, some psychologists began to question just how general the general principles of learning really were (Lockard, 1971; Seligman, 1970).

In this section, we'll consider some findings that challenge the generality of learning principles involving classical and operant conditioning. These findings helped give rise to the ecological perspective (Hollis, 1997). The **ecological perspective** stresses that the study of learning must consider the unique behavior patterns and capabilities of different species. As the result of evolution, animals have developed unique forms of behavior to adapt to their natural environment, or *ecology*. Thus, according to the ecological perspective, an animal's natural behavior patterns and unique characteristics can influence what it is capable of learning (Bolles, 1985).

Ecological Aspects of Classical Conditioning:
Spaghetti? No, Thank You!

Some time back, Sandy made a pot of super spaghetti, with lots of mushrooms, herbs, spices, and some extra-spicy sausage. Being very fond of Sandy's spaghetti, Don ate a few platefuls. Several hours later, in the middle of the night, Don came down with a nasty case of stomach flu. Predictably, Sandy's super spaghetti came up—a colorful spectacle, to say the least. As a result, Don has developed a *taste aversion*—he now avoids eating spaghetti and feels "queasy" whenever Sandy suggests spaghetti for dinner. He cannot abide the taste, the smell, or even the thought of spaghetti.

Such learned taste aversions are relatively common. Our students have told us about episodes of motion sickness, morning sickness, or illness that resulted in taste aversions to foods as varied as cotton candy, strawberries, and chicken soup. At first glance, it seems as if taste aversions can be explained by classical conditioning. In Don's case, a neutral stimulus (spaghetti sauce) was paired with an unconditioned stimulus (a stomach

ecological perspective
In learning theory, a general approach that emphasizes that the study of learning must consider the unique behavior patterns of different species that have evolved in relation to the species' natural environment.

John Garcia (b. 1917) Garcia was one of the first researchers to experimentally demonstrate the existence of taste aversions and other "exceptions" to the general laws of classical conditioning.

Conditioning Taste Aversions in Coyotes
To control coyote predation without killing the coyotes, sheep carcasses are injected with a drug that produces extreme nausea and left where coyotes can find and eat them. In one study, captive coyotes were fed such poisoned rabbit and sheep carcasses. When placed in a pen with live rabbits and sheep, the coyotes avoided them rather than attack them. In fact, some of the coyotes threw up at the sight of a live rabbit (Gustavson & others, 1976).

virus) which produced an unconditioned response (nausea). Now a conditioned stimulus, the spaghetti sauce by itself elicits the conditioned response of nausea.

But notice that this explanation seems to violate two basic principles of classical conditioning. First, conditioning did not require repeated pairings. Conditioning occurred in *a single pairing* of the conditioned stimulus and the unconditioned stimulus. Second, the time span between these two stimuli was *several hours*—not a matter of seconds. Is this possible? The anecdotal reports of people who develop specific taste aversions seem to suggest that it is. But such reports lack the objectivity and systematic control that a scientific explanation of behavior requires.

Enter psychologist **John Garcia** (b. 1917), who demonstrated that taste aversions could be produced in laboratory rats under controlled conditions (Garcia & others, 1966). Garcia's procedure was straightforward: Rats first drank saccharine-flavored water (the neutral stimulus) and then, hours later, were injected with a drug (the unconditioned stimulus) that produced gastrointestinal distress (the unconditioned response). When the rats recovered from their illness, they refused to drink the flavored water. The rats had developed a taste aversion to the flavored water—which had become a conditioned stimulus.

At first, many psychologists were very skeptical of Garcia's findings because they seemed to violate the basic principles of classical conditioning. Several leading psychological journals refused to publish Garcia's research, saying the results were impossible (Garcia, 1981). But Garcia's results have been replicated many times. In fact, later research showed that taste aversions could develop even when a full 24 hours separated the presentation of the flavored water and the drug that produced illness (Etscorn & Stephens, 1973). Clearly, the phenomenon of taste aversions challenges some basic tenets of classical conditioning.

Conditioned taste aversions also challenge the traditional behaviorist notion that associations can be learned between virtually any stimulus and any response. As Pavlov (1928) wrote, "Any natural phenomenon chosen at will may be converted into a conditioned stimulus . . . any visual stimulus, any desired sound, any odor, and the stimulation of any part of the skin." After all, Pavlov had demonstrated that dogs could be classically conditioned to salivate to a ringing bell, a ticking metronome, and even the sight of geometric figures.

But if this is the case, then why didn't Don develop an aversion to other stimuli he encountered between the time he ate the spaghetti and when he got sick? Why was it that only the spaghetti sauce became a conditioned stimulus that triggered nausea, rather than the dinner table, the silverware—or even Sandy, for that matter?

Contrary to what Pavlov suggested, Garcia and his colleagues demonstrated that the conditioned stimulus that is used *does* make a difference in classical conditioning (Garcia & Koelling, 1966). In another

IN FOCUS 5.4

Biological Preparedness and Conditioned Fears: What Gives You the Creeps?

Does this photos give you the creeps? Even if you're not phobic of snakes, you may find this writhing ball of reptiles a bit disturbing. Why?

Does this photograph make you uncomfortable?

A *phobia* is an extreme, irrational fear of a specific object, animal, or situation. It was once believed that all phobias were acquired through classical conditioning, like Little Albert's fear of white rats. But many people develop phobias without having experienced a traumatic event in association with the object of their fear (Merckelbach & others, 1992). Obviously, other forms of learning, such as observational learning, are involved in the development of some fears.

When people do develop conditioned fears as a result of traumatic events, they are more likely to associate fear with certain stimuli rather than others. Erv, not surprisingly, has acquired a conditioned fear response to the "killer attic." But why doesn't Erv shudder every time he hears a lawn mower or sees a ladder, the clothes he was wearing when he got trapped, or his can of oil?

Psychologist Martin Seligman (1971) noticed that phobias seem to be quite selective. Extreme, irrational fears of snakes, spiders, heights, and small enclosed places (like Erv and Fern's attic) are relatively common. But very few people are phobic of stairs, ladders, electrical outlets or appliances, or sharp objects, even though these things are far more likely to be associated with traumatic experiences or accidents.

Seligman has proposed that humans are biologically prepared to develop fears of objects or situations—like snakes, spiders, and heights—that may have once posed a threat to humans' evolutionary ancestors. As Seligman (1971) puts it, "The great majority of phobias are about objects of natural importance to the survival of the species." According to Seligman, people don't commonly develop phobias of knives, stoves, or cars because they're not biologically prepared to do so.

Support for this view is provided by early studies that tried to replicate Watson's Little Albert research. Elsie Bregman (1934) was unable to produce a conditioned fear response to wooden blocks and curtains, although she followed Watson's procedure carefully. And Horace English (1929) was unable to produce a conditioned fear of a wooden duck. Perhaps we're more biologically prepared to learn a fear of furry animals than wooden ducks, blocks, or curtains!

series of experiments, Garcia found that rats did *not* learn to associate a taste with a painful event, like a shock. Nor did they learn to associate a flashing light and noise with illness. Instead, rats were much more likely to associate a *painful stimulus* like a shock with *external stimuli*—flashing lights and noise. And, rats were much more likely to associate a *taste* stimulus with *internal stimuli*—the physical discomfort of illness. Garcia and Koelling (1966) humorously suggested that a sick rat, like a sick person, speculates, "It must have been something I ate."

Why is it that certain stimuli are more easy to associate than others? One explanation is **biological preparedness**—the idea that an organism is innately predisposed to form associations between certain stimuli and responses. If the particular stimulus and response combination is not one that an animal is biologically prepared to associate, then the association may not occur or may occur only with great difficulty.

biological preparedness
In learning theory, the idea that an organism is innately predisposed to form associations between certain stimuli and responses.

When this concept is applied to taste aversions, rats (and people) seem to be biologically prepared to associate an illness with a taste rather than with a location or an object. Hence, Don developed an aversion to the spaghetti sauce and not to the fork he used to eat it. And, because humans and rats are biologically prepared to learn taste aversions, it's not surprising that taste aversions can be classically conditioned more readily than more arbitrary associations, such as that between a ringing bell and a plate of food.

Associations that are easily learned may reflect the evolutionary history and survival mechanisms of the particular animal species. For example, rats in the wild eat a wide variety of foods. If a rat eats a new food and gets sick several hours later, it's likely to survive longer if it learns from this experience to avoid that food in the future (Kalat, 1985; Seligman, 1970).

That different species form some associations more easily than others also probably reflects the unique sensory capabilities and feeding habits that have evolved as a matter of environmental adaptation. Bobwhite quail, for instance, rely primarily on vision for identifying potential meals. In contrast, rats have relatively poor eyesight and rely primarily on taste and odor cues to identify food. Given these species differences, it shouldn't surprise you that quail, but not rats, could easily be conditioned to develop a taste aversion to blue-colored water—a *visual* stimulus. On the other hand, rats learn more readily than quail to associate illness with sour water—a *taste* stimulus (Wilcoxon & others, 1971). In effect, quail are more biologically prepared than rats to associate visual cues with illness. And rats are more biologically prepared than quail to associate taste cues with illness.

Ecological Aspects of Operant Conditioning:
Misbehaving Raccoons

Operant conditioning can be influenced by an animal's natural behavior patterns. What is instinctive drift, and how does it challenge the behavioral view of operant conditioning? What general conclusions can we draw about the validity of the principles of classical and operant conditioning?

Psychologists studying operant conditioning also found that an animal's natural behavior patterns can interfere with the learning of new behaviors. Consider the experiences of Keller and Marian Breland, two of B. F. Skinner's students. The Brelands established a successful business training animals for television commercials, trade shows, fairs, and even displays in department stores (Breland & Breland, 1961; Bailey & Bailey, 1993). The Brelands used operant conditioning to train thousands of animals of many different species to perform all sorts of complex tricks.

But the Brelands weren't always successful in training particular animals. For example, the Brelands tried to train a raccoon to pick up two coins and deposit them in a metal box. The raccoon easily learned to pick up the coins, but seemed to resist putting them into the box. Like a furry little miser, it would rub the coins together. And rather than dropping the coins in the box, it would dip the coins in the box and take them out again. As time went on, this behavior became more persistent, despite the fact that the raccoon was not being reinforced for it. In fact, the raccoon's "misbehavior" was actually *preventing* it from getting reinforced for correct behavior.

The Brelands noted that such nonreinforced behaviors seemed to reflect innate, instinctive responses. Raccoons in the wild instinctively clean and

instinctive drift
The tendency of an animal to revert to instinctive behaviors that can interfere with the performance of an operantly conditioned response.

moisten their food by dipping it in streams or rubbing it between their forepaws. These natural behaviors interfered with the operant behaviors the Brelands were attempting to condition—a phenomenon called **instinctive drift.**

The biological predisposition to perform such natural behaviors was strong enough to overcome the lack of reinforcement. These instinctual behaviors also prevented the animals from engaging in the learned behaviors that would result in reinforcement. Clearly, reinforcement is not the sole determinant of behavior. And, inborn or instinctive behavior patterns can interfere with the operant conditioning of arbitrary responses.

Exploring the Cognitive and Ecological Perspectives

For each of the situations described below, name the process involved (latent learning, observational learning, taste aversions, or instinctive drift) and the psychologist(s) associated with it.

1. Lisa transfers to a new college and spends her first few days on campus getting oriented. At the beginning of her second week, she decides to have lunch at the cafeteria. Although she has never eaten there before, she has no problem finding the cafeteria.

2. Jordan's first job as an animal trainer was to train a pig to pick up a coin and deposit it in a "piggy bank." Through shaping and reinforcement with food, Jordan had some initial success, but soon the pig was more interested in pushing the coin along the ground with its snout than in putting it in the bank.

3. Roger took his girlfriend to an expensive Indian restaurant, even though he was experi-

CONCEPT REVIEW 5.4

encing some symptoms of the flu. After the meal Roger got quite sick. Now even the smell of curry makes him feel nauseated.

4. Keesha wanted to begin weaning her one-year-old baby from drinking out of a bottle to drinking from a cup. The first time she handed her baby a cup of milk, he raised the cup to his lips.

Process	Psychologist(s)
1. _____	_____
2. _____	_____
3. _____	_____
4. _____	_____

The Learning Perspectives in Perspective

Researchers who take the ecological perspective focus on natural behavior patterns of various species, especially as those behaviors occur in their natural environment, or ecology. Equipped by their distinct biological heritage, different species have evolved unique abilities to find food, attract mates, avoid predators, and survive in their natural habitat. To fully understand the process of learning, the ecological perspective maintains that you must consider the innate behavior patterns that have evolved in relation to a species' natural environment (Johnston, 1985). When learning is viewed in this context, miserly raccoons and bobwhite quail who develop taste aversions to blue-colored water begin to make sense.

Do the exceptions and conditioning "failures" that gave rise to the ecological perspective invalidate the principles of classical and operant conditioning? Not at all. Thousands of laboratory experiments have shown that behavior can be reliably and predictably influenced by classical and operant conditioning procedures. By and large, the general principles of classical and operant conditioning hold up quite well. However, a particular species may have evolved specialized behavior patterns and other characteristics that make it biologically prepared to learn certain types of associations or responses more easily than others. So the general principles of learning are just that—general, not absolute.

The fact that the basic principles of classical and operant conditioning hold up quite well is not necessarily a contradiction of the ecological perspective. After all, the general principles of learning are adaptive in almost any conceivable environment. Clearly, there are survival advantages in being able to learn that a neutral stimulus can signal an important upcoming event, as in classical conditioning (Hollis, 1997). An organism also enhances its odds of survival by being responsive to the positive and negative consequences of its actions, as in operant conditioning. Thus, it is probably because these abilities are so useful in so many environments that the basic principles of learning are demonstrated with such consistency across so many species (Staddon, 1988; Beecher, 1988).

In the final analysis, the most important consequence of learning may be that it promotes the adaptation of many different species, including humans, to their unique environments. Were it not for the adaptive nature of learning, Erv would probably get trapped in the attic again!

APPLICATION

Using Learning Principles to Improve Self-Control

Self-control often involves choosing between a *short-term reinforcer* that provides immediate gratification and a *long-term reinforcer* that will provide gratification at some point in the future. Objectively, the benefits of the long-term reinforcer far outweigh the benefits associated with the short-term, immediate reinforcer. Yet despite our commitment to the long-term goal, sometimes we choose a short-term reinforcer that conflicts with it. Why?

The Shifting Value of Reinforcers

The key is that *the relative value of reinforcers can shift over time* (Rachlin, 1974; Ainslie, 1975). Let's use an example to illustrate this principle. Suppose you sign up for an 8:00 a.m. class that meets every Tuesday morning. On Monday night, you set your alarm clock for 6:00 a.m. But when the alarm goes off on Tuesday morning, instead of getting up, you hit the snooze button a few times and eventually go back to sleep—and miss the class.

The explanation? On Monday night, the short-term reinforcer (getting extra sleep on Tuesday morning) and the long-term reinforcer (getting a good course grade at the end of the semester) were both in the future, and the value of making a good grade easily outweighed the value of getting extra sleep on Tuesday morning. So, you virtuously set your alarm for 6:00 a.m.

However, as the availability of a reinforcer gets closer, the subjective value of the reinforcer increases. Consequently, when your alarm goes off on Tuesday morning, the short-term reinforcer is now immediately available: staying in that warm, comfy bed and going back to sleep. Compared to Mon-

day night when you set the alarm, the subjective value of extra sleep has increased significantly. While making a good grade in the course is still important to you, its subjective value has *not* increased on Tuesday morning. After all, that long-term reinforcer is still in the distant future.

At the moment you make your decision, you will choose whichever reinforcer has the greatest subjective value to you. At that moment, if the subjective value of the short-term reinforcer outweighs that of the long-term reinforcer, you're very likely to choose the short-term reinforcer (Ainslie, 1975; Rachlin, 1974). In other words, you'll probably stay in bed.

When you understand how the subjective values of reinforcers shift over time, the tendency to cave in to available short-term reinforcers starts to make more sense. The availability of an immediate, short-term reinforcer can temporarily outweigh the subjective value of a long-term reinforcer in the distant future. How can you counteract these momentary surges in the subjective value of short-term reinforcers? Here are a few suggestions to help you overcome the temptation of short-term reinforcers and improve self-control.

1. Precommitment

Precommitment involves making an advance commitment to your long-term goal, one that will be difficult to change when a conflicting reinforcer becomes available. In the case of getting to class on time, a precommitment could involve setting multiple alarms, or asking an early-rising friend to call you on the phone and make sure you're awake.

2. Self-Reinforcement

Sometimes long-term goals seem so far away that your sense of potential future reinforcement seems weak compared to immediate reinforcers. One strategy to increase the subjective value of the long-term reinforcer is to use *self-reinforcement,* rewarding yourself for current behaviors related to your long-term goal.

It's important, however, to reward yourself only *after* you perform the desired behavior. If you say to yourself, "Rather than study tonight, I'll go to this party and make up for it by studying tomorrow," you've just reinforced yourself for *not* studying! This would be like trying to increase bar-pressing behavior in a rat by giving the rat a pellet of food *before* it pressed the bar. Remember, the basic principle of positive reinforcement is that behavior is *followed by* the reinforcing stimulus.

3. Stimulus Control

Environmental stimuli can act as discriminative stimuli that "set the occasion" for a particular response. In effect, the environmental cues that precede a behavior can acquire some control over future occurrences of that behavior. So be aware of the environmental cues that are likely to trigger unwanted behaviors, such as studying in the kitchen (a cue for eating) or in front of the TV set (a cue for watching television). Then replace those cues with others that will help you achieve your long-term goals.

4. Focus on the Delayed Reinforcer

The cognitive aspects of learning also play a role in choosing behaviors associated with long-term reinforcers (Mischel, 1983, 1981). When faced with a choice between an immediate and a delayed reinforcer, selectively focus your thoughts on the delayed reinforcer. By mentally bridging the gap between the present and the ultimate attainment of your future goal, you'll be less likely to impulsively choose the short-term reinforcer (Ainslie, 1975; Watson & Tharp, 1985).

5. Observe Good Role Models

Observational learning is another strategy you can use to improve self-control. Psychologist Walter Mischel (1966) found that children who observed others choose a delayed reinforcer over an immediate reinforcer were more likely to choose the delayed reinforcer themselves. So look for good role models. Observing others who are currently behaving in ways that will ultimately help them realize their long-term goals can make it easier for you to do the same.

Summary Learning

What Is Learning?

■ *Learning* is defined as a relatively permanent change in behavior that is due to past experience. Learning often reflects adaptation to the environment. Three perspectives on learning are the behavioral perspective, the cognitive perspective, and the ecological perspective.

The Behavioral Perspective

■ The behavioral perspective emphasizes changes in observable behaviors and was founded by John B. Watson. According to the behavioral perspective, all human behavior is a result of learning.

Classical Conditioning: Associating Stimuli

■ Ivan Pavlov, a Russian physiologist, discovered the principles of classical conditioning while studying the digestive system in dogs.

■ Classical conditioning deals with reflexive behaviors that are elicited by a stimulus and results from learning an association between two stimuli. A neutral stimulus is repeatedly paired with an unlearned, natural stimulus (the unconditioned stimulus), producing a reflexive response (the unconditioned response). Eventually, the neutral stimulus (or conditioned stimulus) elicits the same reflexive response (the conditioned response) as the natural stimulus.

■ Factors that affect the strength of the conditioned response include the frequency with which the unconditioned and conditioned stimuli are paired and the timing of the stimulus presentations.

■ When a new stimulus that is similar to the conditioned stimulus produces the conditioned response, stimulus generalization has occurred. In stimulus discrimination, one stimulus elicits the conditioned response but another, similar stimulus does not.

■ In classical conditioning, extinction occurs when the conditioned stimulus no longer elicits the conditioned response. However, spontaneous recovery of the conditioned response may occur.

■ Applications of classical conditioning include conditioned emotional reactions and advertising. Physiological responses can also be classically conditioned.

Operant Conditioning: Associating Behaviors and Consequences

■ B. F. Skinner developed the operant conditioning model of learning to explain how voluntary, active behaviors are acquired.

■ Operant conditioning is a model of learning that explains learning as a process in which behavior is shaped and modified by its consequences. Reinforcement increases the likelihood of an operant being repeated. Two forms of reinforcement are positive reinforcement and negative reinforcement. Reinforcers may be either primary or conditioned reinforcers.

■ Punishment decreases the likelihood of an operant being repeated. Aversive consequences do not always function as effective punishments. As a method of controlling behavior, punishment has many limitations and drawbacks.

■ The discriminative stimulus is the stimulus in the presence of which a particular operant is likely to be reinforced; it sets the occasion for a particular response.

■ New behaviors can be acquired through the process of shaping. A Skinner box is often used to study the acquisition of new behaviors by laboratory animals. Shaping is frequently used in everyday life to teach new behaviors.

■ Once acquired, behaviors are maintained through different schedules of reinforcement. Behaviors on a partial reinforcement schedule are more resistant to extinction than are behaviors on a continuous reinforcement schedule, as demonstrated by the partial reinforcement effect. When behavior is accidentally reinforced, superstitious behavior may result. Schedules of reinforcement include the fixed-ratio, variable-ratio, fixed-interval, and variable-interval schedules.

■ In behavior modification, the principles of operant conditioning are applied to help people develop more adaptive behaviors.

The Cognitive Perspective

■ According to the cognitive perspective, mental processes are involved in learning.

■ Robert Rescorla has demonstrated that classical conditioning involves learning the reliability of predictors rather than simply associating two stimuli.

■ Edward Tolman demonstrated that the learning of active behaviors also involves cognitive processes, such as forming cognitive maps and latent learning.

■ Albert Bandura demonstrated that new behaviors can be learned through observational learning. Observational learning involves the cognitive processes of attention, memory, motor skills, and motivation.

The Ecological Perspective: Biological Predispositions to Learn

■ According to the ecological perspective, natural behavior patterns influence conditioning and the learning of new behaviors.

■ Taste aversions violate key principles of classical conditioning. As John Garcia demonstrated, classical conditioning is affected by biological preparedness: some stimuli are more readily associated with conditioned responses than others.

■ Operant conditioning can also be affected by natural behavior patterns, as shown by the phenomenon of instinctive drift.

Key Terms

learning (p. 158)

behavioral perspective (p. 159)

classical conditioning (p. 160)

unconditioned stimulus (UCS) (p. 161)

unconditioned response (UCR) (p. 161)

conditioned stimulus (CS) (p. 161)

conditioned response (CR) (p. 161)

stimulus generalization (p. 163)

stimulus discrimination (p. 163)

extinction (in classical conditioning) (p. 163)

spontaneous recovery (p. 163)

operant (p. 167)

operant conditioning (p. 167)

reinforcement (p. 167)

positive reinforcement (p. 167)

negative reinforcement (p. 168)

primary reinforcer (p. 168)

conditioned reinforcer (p. 168)

punishment (p. 169)

discriminative stimulus (p. 171)

Skinner box (p. 173)

shaping (p. 174)

continuous reinforcement (p. 174)

partial reinforcement (p. 174)

extinction (in operant conditioning) (p. 174)

partial reinforcement effect (p. 175)

schedule of reinforcement (p. 176)

fixed-ratio (FR) schedule (p. 176)

variable-ratio (VR) schedule (p. 176)

fixed-interval (FI) schedule (p. 176)

variable-interval (VI) schedule (p. 177)

behavior modification (p. 178)

cognitive perspective (p. 179)

cognitive map (p. 181)

latent learning (p. 182)

observational learning (p. 183)

ecological perspective (p. 185)

biological preparedness (p. 187)

instinctive drift (p. 189)

Key People

Albert Bandura (b. 1925) American psychologist who experimentally investigated observational learning, emphasizing the role of cognitive factors.

John Garcia (b. 1917) American psychologist who experimentally demonstrated the learning of taste aversions in animals, a finding that challenged several of the basic assumptions of classical conditioning.

Ivan Pavlov (1849–1936) Russian physiologist who first described the basic learning process of associating stimuli that is now called *classical conditioning*.

Robert A. Rescorla (b. 1940) American psychologist who experimentally demonstrated the involvement of cognitive processes in classical conditioning.

B. F. Skinner (1904–1990) American psychologist who developed the operant conditioning model of learning and emphasized studying the relationship between environmental factors and observable actions, not mental processes, in trying to achieve a scientific explanation of behavior.

Edward C. Tolman (1898-1956) American psychologist who used the terms *cognitive map* and *latent learning* to describe experimental findings that strongly suggested that cognitive factors play a role in animal learning.

John B. Watson (1878-1958) American psychologist who founded behaviorism in the early 1900s, an approach which emphasized the scientific study of outwardly observable behavior rather than subjective mental states.

CONCEPT REVIEW 5.1   Page 162

1. chemotherapy; nausea; ice cream; nausea
2. slimy leeches; disgust; the lake; disgust
3. scary monster; fear; doorbell; fear

CONCEPT REVIEW 5.2   Page 173

1. b
2. a
3. c
4. d
5. c

CONCEPT REVIEW 5.3   Page 177

1. Fixed ratio
2. Variable interval
3. Fixed interval
4. Variable interval
5. Variable ratio
6. Fixed interval

CONCEPT REVIEW 5.4   Page 189

1. latent learning; Tolman
2. instinctive drift; Brelands
3. taste aversion; Garcia
4. observational learning; Bandura

6 Memory

Prologue: The Drowning

Elizabeth was only fourteen years old when her mother drowned. Although Elizabeth remembers many things about visiting her Uncle Joe's home in Pennsylvania that summer, her memory of the details surrounding her mother's death had always been hazy. As she explains:

> In my mind I've returned to that scene many times, and each time the memory gains weight and substance. I can see the cool pine trees, smell their fresh tarry breath, feel the lake's algae-green water on my skin, taste Uncle Joe's iced tea with fresh-squeezed lemon. But the death itself was always vague and unfocused. I never saw my mother's body, and I could not imagine her dead. The last memory I have of my mother was her tiptoed visit the evening before her death, the quick hug, the whispered, "I love you."

It was some thirty years later that Elizabeth began to remember the details surrounding her mother's death. While at her Uncle Joe's ninetieth birthday party, Elizabeth learned from a relative that she had been the one to discover her mother's body in Uncle Joe's swimming pool. With this realization, memories that had eluded Elizabeth for decades began to come back.

> The memories began to drift back, slow and unpredictable, like the crisp piney smoke from the evening campfires. I could see myself, a thin, dark-haired girl, looking into the flickering blue-and-white pool. My mother, dressed in her nightgown, is floating face down. "Mom? Mom?" I ask the question several times, my voice rising in terror. I start screaming. I remember the police cars, their lights flashing, and the stretcher with the clean, white blanket tucked in around the edges of the body. The memory had been there all along, but I just couldn't reach it.

As the memory crystallized, it suddenly made sense to Elizabeth why she had always felt haunted by her vague memories of the circumstances surrounding her mother's death. And it also seemed to partly explain why she had always been so fascinated by the topic of memory.

However, several days later, Elizabeth learned that the relative had been wrong—it was *not* Elizabeth who discovered her mother's body, but her Aunt Pearl. Other relatives confirmed that Aunt Pearl had been the one who found Elizabeth's mother in the swimming pool. Yet Elizabeth's memory had seemed so real.

The Elizabeth in this true story is none other than Elizabeth Loftus, a psychologist who is nationally recognized as the leading expert on the distortions that can occur in the memories of eyewitnesses. Loftus shares this personal story in her book *The Myth of Repressed Memory: False Memories and Allegations of Sexual Abuse,* which she co-wrote with science writer Katherine Ketcham in 1994.

Even though Loftus is an expert on memory distortions and false memories, she wasn't immune to the phenomenon herself. Loftus experienced firsthand just how convincing a false memory can be. In retrospect, Loftus can see how she actively created information in her own mind that corresponded to the inaccurate information that she had been the one to discover her mother's body. As she later wrote, "That elaborate but completely fabricated memory confronted me with its detail and precision, its utter lack of ambiguity" (Loftus & Ketcham, 1994).

In this chapter, we'll consider the psychological and biological processes that underlie how memories are formed and forgotten. As you'll see, memory distortions like the one that Elizabeth Loftus experienced are not uncommon. By the end of this chapter, you'll have a much better understanding of the memory process, including the reason Elizabeth's "memory" of finding her mother's body could seem so real.

Introduction

Memory Processes and Stages

> Memory is a group of related mental processes that enable us to acquire, retain, and retrieve information. What are encoding, storage, and retrieval? What is the three-stage model of memory? How do the stages differ, and how do they interact?

memory
The mental processes that enable us to retain and use information over time.

encoding
The process of transforming information into a form that can be entered into and retained by the memory system.

storage
The process of retaining information in memory so that it can be used at a later time.

retrieval
The process of recovering information stored in memory so that we are consciously aware of it.

Let's begin with an overview of some of the basic terms and concepts we'll be discussing throughout this chapter. **Memory** refers to the mental processes that enable us to acquire, retain, and retrieve information. Rather than being a single process, memory involves three fundamental processes: *encoding, storage,* and *retrieval.*

Encoding refers to the process of transforming information into a form that can be entered and retained by the memory system. For example, if you were trying to memorize the definition of a key term that appears on a text page, you would visually *encode* the patterns of lines and dots on the page as meaningful words that can be retained by your memory. **Storage** is the process of retaining information in memory so that it can be used at a later time. **Retrieval** involves recovering the stored information so that we are consciously aware of it (Butters & Delis, 1995).

The Stage Model of Memory

Researchers have yet to settle on any one model that seems to capture exactly how human memory works (Anderson, 1995). However, one very influential model, called the **stage model of memory,** continues to be useful in explaining the basic workings of memory. In this model, memory involves three distinct stages: *sensory memory, short-term memory,* and *long-term memory* (Atkinson & Shiffrin, 1968). As shown in Figure 6.1, the stage model is based on the idea that information is *transferred* from one memory stage to another. Each memory stage is thought to differ in terms of the following:

- *Capacity:* how much information can be stored
- *Duration:* how long the information can be stored
- *Function:* what is done with the stored information

The first stage of memory is called *sensory memory*. **Sensory memory** registers a great deal of information from the environment and holds it for a very brief period of time. After a few seconds or less, the information fades. Think of your sensory memory as an internal camera that continuously takes "snapshots" of your surroundings. With each snapshot, you momentarily focus your attention on specific details. Almost instantly, the snapshot fades, only to be replaced by another.

Sensory Memory
- Environmental information is registered.
- Large capacity for information
- Duration: 1/4 second to 3 seconds

Attention →

Short-Term (Working) Memory
- New information is transferred from sensory memory.
- Old information is retrieved from long-term memory.
- Limited capacity for information
- Duration: approx. 30 seconds

Encoding and Storage →

← Retrieval

Long-Term Memory
- Information that has been encoded in short-term memory is stored.
- Unlimited capacity for information
- Duration: potentially permanent

FIGURE 6.1 Overview of the Stage Model of Memory

During the very brief time that the information is held in sensory memory, you "select," or pay *attention* to, just a few aspects of all the environmental information that's being registered. While studying, for example, you focus your attention on one page of your textbook, ignoring other environmental stimuli. The information that you select from sensory memory to pay attention to is important, because it is this information that is transferred to the second stage of memory, *short-term memory*.

Short-term memory refers to the active, working memory system (Cowan & others, 1994). Your short-term memory temporarily holds all the information that you are currently thinking about or consciously aware of. Information is stored briefly in short-term memory—for up to about 30 seconds (Cowan, 1994). Because you use your short-term memory to actively process conscious information in a variety of ways, today short-term memory is often referred to as **working memory** (Baddeley, 1995, 1990). Imagining, remembering, and problem solving all take place in short-term memory.

Over the course of any given day, vast amounts of information are temporarily held in your short-term memory. Most of this information quickly fades and is forgotten in a matter of seconds. However, some of the information that is actively processed in short-term memory may be encoded for storage in long-term memory.

stage model of memory
A model describing memory as consisting of three distinct stages: sensory memory, short-term memory, and long-term memory.

sensory memory
The stage of memory that registers information from the environment and holds it for a very brief period of time.

short-term memory (working memory)
The active stage of memory in which information is stored for about 30 seconds.

The Interaction of Memory Stages in Everyday Life Imagine driving on a busy street in a pouring rain. How might each of your memory stages be involved in successfully navigating the wet streets? What kinds of information would be transferred from sensory memory and retrieved from long-term memory?

Long-term memory is the third memory stage, and it represents what most people typically think of as memory—the long-term storage of information, potentially for a lifetime. It's important to note that the transfer of information between short-term and long-term memory is a two-way street. Not only does information flow from short-term memory to long-term memory, but much information also flows in the other direction—from long-term memory to short-term memory (Shiffrin & Nosofsky, 1994).

If you think about it, this makes a great deal of sense. Consider a routine cognitive task like carrying on a conversation. Such tasks involve processing current sensory data and the retrieval of stored information relevant to the task at hand, such as the meaning of individual words (Goldman-Rakic, 1992).

In the next few sections, we'll describe each of the stages of memory in more detail.

Sensory Memory: Fleeting Impressions of Reality

> *The first stage of memory, called sensory memory, holds sensory information from the environment for a few seconds or less. How did Sperling's experiment establish the duration of visual sensory memory? What are the functions of sensory memory?*

Has something like this ever happened to you? You're engrossed in a movie on television. From another room, a family member calls out, "Where'd you put the phone book?" You respond with, "What?" Then, a split second later, the question registers in your mind. Before the other person can repeat the question, you respond, "It's on the kitchen counter."

You were able to answer the question because your *sensory memory* registered and preserved the other person's words for a few fleeting seconds—just long enough for you to recall what had been said to you while your attention was focused on the movie. Sensory memory stores a detailed record of a sensory experience, but only for a few seconds at the most (Crowder, 1992).

The Duration of Sensory Memory:
It Was There Just a Split Second Ago!

It was largely through the research of psychologist **George Sperling** (b. 1934) in 1960 that the characteristics of visual sensory memory were first identified. Sperling would flash the image of twelve letters on a screen for one-twentieth of a second. The letters were arranged in four rows of three letters each. Subjects would focus their attention on the screen and, immediately after the screen went blank, report as many letters as they could remember.

On the average, the subjects could report only four or five of the twelve letters. However, several subjects claimed that they had actually seen *all* the letters. But the complete image faded from their memory as they spoke, disappearing before they could verbally report more than four or five letters.

long-term memory
The stage of memory that represents the long-term storage of information.

With this clue, Sperling tried a simple variation on the original experiment (see Figure 6.2). He arranged the twelve letters in three rows of four letters each. Then, immediately *after* the screen went blank, he sounded a high-pitched, medium-pitched, or low-pitched tone. If the subjects heard the high-pitched tone, they were to report the letters in the top row. The medium-pitched tone signaled the middle row, and the low-pitched tone signaled the bottom row. If the subjects actually did see all the letters, Sperling reasoned, then they should be able to report the letters in a given row by focusing their attention on the indicated row *before* their visual sensory memory faded.

This is exactly what Sperling found. If the tone followed the letter display within less than one-third of a second, subjects could accurately report about three of the four letters in whichever row was indicated by the tone. Sperling found that if the interval between the screen going blank and the sound of the tone was more than one-third of a second, the accuracy of the subjects decreased dramatically. By one second, the afterimage in their visual sensory memory had already faded beyond recall.

Sperling's classic experiment demonstrated that our *visual sensory memory* holds a great deal of information very briefly—for about half a second. This information is available just long enough for us to select and pay attention to specific elements that are significant to us at that moment. It is this meaningful information that is transferred from the very brief storage of sensory memory to the somewhat longer storage of short-term memory.

1. Letters are displayed on a screen for 1/20 of a second

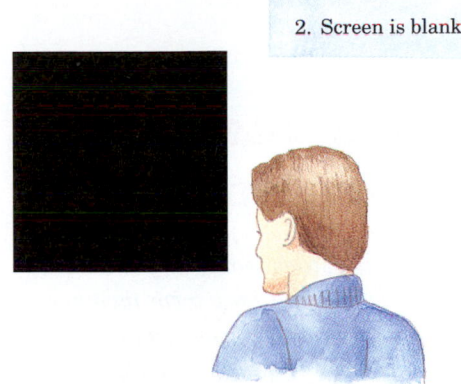

2. Screen is blank

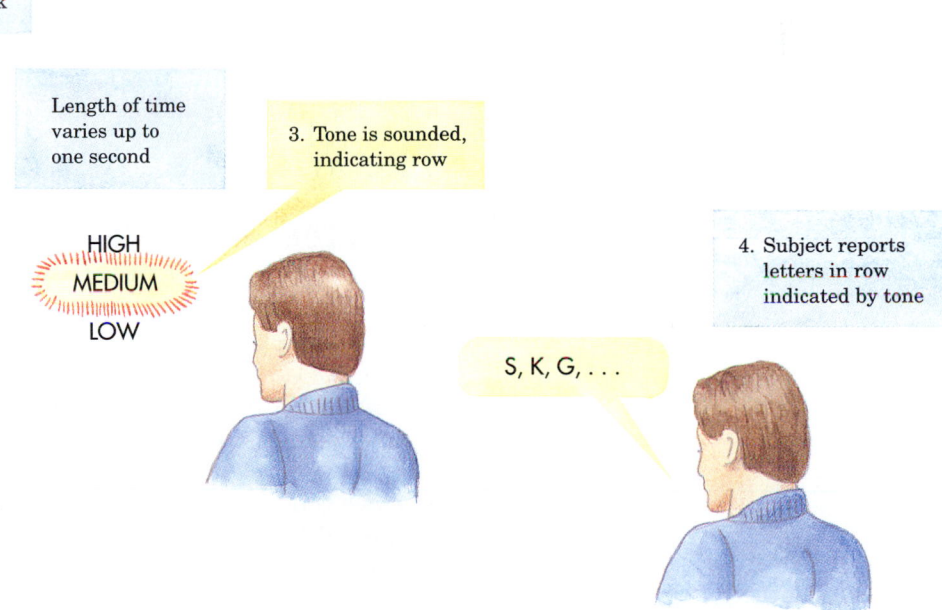

Length of time varies up to one second

3. Tone is sounded, indicating row

HIGH
MEDIUM
LOW

4. Subject reports letters in row indicated by tone

S, K, G, . . .

FIGURE 6.2 Sperling's Experiment Demonstrating the Duration of Sensory Memory
In George Sperling's (1960) classic experiment, subjects stared at a screen on which rows of letters were projected for just one-twentieth of a second (1). The screen then went blank (2). After intervals varying up to one second, a tone was sounded that indicated the row of letters the subject should report (3). If the tone was sounded within about one-third of a second, subjects were able to report the letters in the indicated row (4), because the image of *all* the letters was still in sensory memory.

Types of Sensory Memory:
Pick a Sense, Any Sense!

Memory researchers believe there is a separate sensory memory for each sense—vision, hearing, touch, smell, and so on (Crowder, 1992). Of the different senses, however, visual and auditory sensory memories have been the most thoroughly studied. *Visual sensory memory* is sometimes referred to as *iconic memory*, because it is the brief memory of an image, or *icon*. *Auditory sensory memory* is sometimes referred to as *echoic memory*, meaning a brief memory that is like an *echo*.

Perceiving Sensory Memory Traces A bolt of lightning is actually three or more separate bolts of electricity. Why do we see a continuous lightning bolt streaking across the sky instead of a series of separated flashes? Because our visual sensory memory holds information for a fraction of a second, the separate flashes overlap and we perceive a single bolt of lightning.

Researchers have found slight differences in the duration of sensory memory for visual and auditory information. Your visual sensory memory typically holds an afterimage of your environment for about one-quarter to one-half second before it is replaced by yet another overlapping "snapshot." This is easy to demonstrate. Quickly wave a pencil back and forth in front of your face. Do you see the fading image of the pencil trailing behind it? That's your visual sensory memory at work. It momentarily holds the "snapshot" of the environmental image you see before it is almost instantly replaced by another overlapping image.

Your auditory sensory memory holds sound information a little longer—up to a few seconds (Crowder, 1992). This brief auditory sensory trace for sound allows us to hear speech as continuous words, or a series of musical notes as a melody, rather than as disjointed sounds. That's also why you are able to "remember" something that you momentarily don't "hear," as in our example of the family member asking you where the phone book was.

An important function of sensory memory is to very briefly store our sensory impressions so that they overlap slightly with one another. Thus, we perceive the world around us as continuous, rather than as a series of disconnected visual images or disjointed sounds (Ashcraft, 1994).

Short-Term, Working Memory:
The Workshop of Consciousness

> *Short-term, or working, memory provides temporary storage for information transferred from sensory and long-term memory. What is the duration and capacity of short-term memory? How do we overcome the limitations of short-term memory?*

You can think of *short-term memory,* or *working memory,* as the "workshop" of consciousness. It is the stage of memory in which information transferred from sensory memory *and* information retrieved from long-term memory becomes conscious (Ericsson & Kintsch, 1995). When you recall a past event or mentally add two numbers, the information is temporarily held and processed in your short-term memory. Your short-term memory also allows you to make sense out of this sentence by holding the beginning of the sentence in active memory while you read the rest of the sentence. So an important function of working memory is that it provides temporary storage for information that is currently being used in some conscious cognitive activity (Baddeley, 1995, 1992).

The Duration of Short-Term Memory:
Going, Going, Gone!

maintenance rehearsal
The mental or verbal repetition of information in order to maintain it beyond the usual 30-second duration of short-term memory.

At best, you can hold most types of information in short-term memory up to about 30 seconds before it's forgotten (Cowan, 1994). However, information can be maintained in short-term memory longer than 30 seconds if it is *rehearsed,* or repeated, over and over again. Because consciously rehearsing information will maintain it in short-term memory, this process is called **maintenance rehearsal.** For example, when you look up an office number on a building directory, you use maintenance rehearsal to maintain it in short-term memory until you reach the office. Another example is repeating an unfamiliar phone number until you dial it.

Information that is not actively rehearsed quickly fades, or *decays,* from short-term memory (Cowan, 1994). That's why you sometimes forget an important point that comes to mind while you wait for a talkative friend to pause. Your idea quickly faded from your short-term memory, because listening to your friend's comments prevented you from rehearsing—and remembering—the point you wanted to make.

The Capacity of Short-Term Memory:
So That's Why There Were Seven Dwarfs!

Along with having a relatively short duration, short-term memory also has a relatively limited capacity. This is easy to demonstrate. Look at Figure 6.3. If you've got a friend handy who's willing to serve as your research subject, simply read the numbers out loud to her, one row at a time, and ask her to repeat them back in the same order. Try to read the numbers at a steady rate—about one per second. Note each row that she correctly remembers.

How many numbers could your friend repeat accurately? Most likely, she could correctly repeat between five and nine numbers. That's what psychologist George Miller (1956/1994) described as the limits of short-term memory in a classic paper entitled "The Magical Number Seven, Plus or Minus Two." Miller found that the capacity of short-term memory is limited to about seven items, or bits of information, at one time. So it's no accident that local telephone numbers are seven digits long. And had Snow White met more than seven dwarfs, it would be even more difficult to remember all their names.

This seven-item limit to short-term memory also seems to be the case in other cultures. For example, it's been demonstrated in non-Western cultures in studies using Chinese characters instead of English-language materials (Yu & others, 1985).

So what happens when your short-term memory store is filled to capacity? New information will *displace,* or bump out, currently held information. Maintenance rehearsal is one way to avoid the loss of information from short-term memory. By consciously repeating the information you want to remember, you keep it active in short-term memory and prevent it from being displaced by new information (Cowan & others, 1994).

Although the capacity of your short-term memory is limited, there are ways to increase the amount of information that you can hold in short-term memory at any given moment. To illustrate this point, let's try another short-term memory demonstration. Read the following sequence of letters, then close your eyes and try to repeat the letters out loud in the same order:

U V A F C I C R B S A I

How many letters were you able to remember? Unless you have an exceptional short-term memory (or watch "Wheel of Fortune" too much), you probably could not repeat the whole sequence correctly. Now try this sequence:

V C R F B I U S A C I A

You probably managed the second sequence with no trouble at all, even though it is made up of exactly the same letters as the first sequence. The ease with which you handled the second sequence demonstrates **chunking**—the grouping of related items together into a single unit. The first letter sequence was perceived as twelve separate items and probably exceeded your short-term memory's capacity. But the second letter sequence was perceived as only four "chunks" of information, which you easily remembered: VCR, FBI, USA, and CIA. Thus, chunking can increase the amount of information

Row 1 — 8 7 4 6
Row 2 — 3 4 9 6 2
Row 3 — 4 2 7 7 1 6
Row 4 — 5 1 4 0 8 1 3
Row 5 — 1 8 3 9 5 5 2 1
Row 6 — 2 1 4 9 7 5 2 4 8
Row 7 — 9 3 7 1 0 4 2 8 9 7
Row 8 — 7 1 9 0 4 2 6 0 4 1 8

FIGURE 6.3 Demonstration of Short-Term Memory Capacity

chunking
Increasing the amount of information that can be held in short-term memory by grouping related items together into a single unit, or "chunk."

elaborative rehearsal
Rehearsal that involves focusing on the meaning of information to help encode and transfer it to long-term memory.

held in short-term memory. But to do so, chunking also often involves the retrieval of meaningful information from *long-term memory,* such as the meaning of the initials FBI (Ericsson & Kintsch, 1995).

The basic principle of chunking is incorporated into many important numbers that we need to remember. Long strings of identification numbers, such as social security numbers or bank account numbers, are usually broken up by hyphens so that you can chunk them easily. Notice, however, that short-term memory is still limited to seven chunks. It's as if short-term memory has about seven mental slots for information. Each slot can hold a simple message or a complex message, but only about seven slots are available.

Long-Term Memory

When information is encoded, it is stored in long-term memory over time. What factors increase the efficiency of encoding? What kinds of information are stored in long-term memory, and how is that information organized?

Long-term memory refers to the storage of information over extended periods of time. Technically, any information stored longer than the roughly 30-second duration of short-term memory is considered to be stored in long-term memory. Thus, a long-term memory can be recalling what you were doing five minutes ago or ten years ago. In terms of maximum duration, some long-term memories can last a lifetime.

The amount of information that can be held in long-term memory is limitless. Granted, it doesn't always feel limitless, but consider this: Every day, you effortlessly remember the directions to your college, the names of your instructors, and the faces of your fellow students. You remember how to tie your shoes, zip up your coat, and lock your front door. And simply to read this chapter, you will have retrieved the meaning of thousands of words from your long-term memory. These examples illustrate not only the range and quantity of information stored in long-term memory, but also the fact that retrieving information from long-term memory happens quickly and with little effort—most of the time.

Long-term Memories Can Involve All Your Senses
The information that is stored in long-term memory can include sensations as well as names, dates, and facts. Think back to a particularly memorable experience from your high school years. Can you conjure up vivid memories of smells, tastes, sounds, or emotions associated with that experience? In the years to come, these teenagers may remember many sensory details associated with this impromptu football game on a crisp autumn afternoon.

Encoding Long-Term Memories

How does information get "into" long-term memory? One very important function that takes place in short-term memory is *encoding,* or transforming the new information into a form that can be retrieved later. As a student, you may have tried to memorize dates, facts, or definitions by simply repeating them to yourself over and over again. This strategy reflects an attempt to use maintenance rehearsal to encode material into long-term memory. However, maintenance rehearsal is *not* a very effective strategy for encoding information into long-term memory.

A much more effective encoding strategy is **elaborative rehearsal,** which involves focusing on the *meaning* of information to help encode and transfer it to long-term memory (Ashcraft, 1994). Elaborative rehearsal involves relating the information to other information that you already know (Ellis & Hunt, 1993). Rather than simply repeating the information over and over to yourself, you *elaborate* on the new information in some meaningful way.

procedural information
Long-term memory of how to perform different skills, operations, and actions.

episodic information
Long-term memory of personally experienced events; also called *autobiographical memory.*

semantic information
General knowledge of facts, names, and concepts stored in long-term memory.

Elaborative rehearsal significantly improves memory for new material (Solso, 1991). This point is especially important for students, because elaborative rehearsal is a helpful study strategy. Here's an example of how you might use elaborative rehearsal to improve your memory for new information: In Chapter 2 we discussed three brain structures that are part of the limbic system: the *hypothalamus,* the *hippocampus,* and the *amygdala.* If you tried to memorize the definitions of these structures by reciting them over and over to yourself, you engaged in the not-so-effective memory strategy of maintenance rehearsal.

But if you elaborated on the information in some meaningful way, you would be more likely to recall it. For example, you could think about the limbic system's involvement in emotions, memory, and motivation by constructing a simple story: "I knew it was lunchtime because my hypothalamus told me I was *h*ungry, *th*irsty, and cold. My hippocampus helped me remember a new restaurant that opened on *campus,* but when I got there I had to wait in line and my amygdala reacted with *anger.*" The story may be a bit silly, but many studies have shown that elaborative rehearsal leads to better retention (Lockhart & Craik, 1990).

Creating this simple story to help you remember the limbic system illustrates two additional factors that enhance encoding (Lockhart, 1992). First, applying information to yourself, called the *self-reference effect,* improves your memory for information (Rogers & others, 1977). And second, the use of *visual imagery,* especially vivid images, also enhances encoding (Paivio, 1986; Marschark, 1992).

Types of Information in Long-Term Memory

There are three major categories of information stored in long-term memory (Tulving, 1995, 1985). **Procedural information** refers to the long-term memory of how to perform different skills, operations, and actions. Typing, riding a bike, running, and making scrambled eggs are all examples of procedural information stored in long-term memory. We begin forming procedural memories early in life when we learn to walk, talk, feed ourselves, and so on.

Often, we can't recall exactly when or how we learned procedural information. And usually, it's difficult to describe procedural memories in words. For example, try to describe *precisely* and *exactly* what you do when you blow-dry your hair, play the guitar, or ride a bicycle. You'll find that it's not as easy as you might think. A particular skill may be easy to demonstrate, but very difficult to describe. Partly, this is because well-rehearsed skills become *automatic.* We're so accustomed to riding a bike or drying our hair that we no longer have to think consciously about how to perform the action.

Episodic information refers to your long-term memory of events or episodes in your life, such as when you registered to take this class or when you attended a friend's wedding (Squire & others, 1993). Also called *autobiographical memory,* such information is usually stored along with knowledge about when and where the event occurred (K. Nelson, 1993).

The third kind of information stored in long-term memory is **semantic information**—general knowledge that includes facts, names, definitions, concepts, and ideas. Semantic information represents your personal encyclopedia of accumulated data and trivia that is stored in your long-term memory. Typically, you store semantic information in long-term memory *without* remembering when or where you originally stored the information. For example, can you remember when or where you learned that there are different time zones across the United States? How about when or where you learned the difference in the meanings of *there, their,* and *they're*? Probably not.

Types of Information Stored in Long-Term Memory Playing ping-pong involves all three types of information stored in long-term memory. Examples of *procedural information* might be how to hold the paddles and hit the ball. Remembering the rules of the game would be an example of *semantic information.* And, your vivid recollection of the time you beat your brother-in-law in a close game at a Fourth of July picnic would be an example of *episodic information.*

clustering
Organizing items into related groups during recall from long-term memory.

semantic network model
A model that describes units of information in long-term memory as being organized in a complex network of associations.

retrieval
The process of accessing stored information.

retrieval cue
A clue, prompt, or hint that helps trigger recall of a given piece of information stored in long-term memory.

FIGURE 6.4 Clustering Demonstration
Study the words on this list for one minute. Then count backwards by threes from 108 to 0. When you've completed that task, write down as many of the words from the list as you can remember.

The Organization of Information in Long-Term Memory

You can probably recite the days of the week in about three or four seconds. Now try timing how long it takes you to recite the weekdays in alphabetical order. Probably a minute or more, right? This simple demonstration illustrates that information in long-term memory is organized in some way. Exactly *how* information is organized is not completely understood by memory researchers (Ashcraft, 1994). Nonetheless, memory researchers know that information in long-term memory is *clustered* and *associated*.

chair	apple
boat	car
footstool	airplane
orange	lamp
pear	banana
peach	dresser
bed	sofa
bus	bookcase
train	truck
plum	table
grapes	strawberry
motorcycle	bicycle

Clustering means organizing items into related groups, or *clusters,* during recall. You can experience clustering firsthand by trying the demonstration in Figure 6.4. Even though the words are presented in random order, you probably recalled groups of vehicles, fruits, and furniture. In other words, you organized the bits of information by clustering them into related categories.

Different bits and pieces of information in long-term memory are also logically linked, or associated. For example, what's the first word that comes to your mind in response to the word *red*? When we asked our students that same question, their top five responses were *blue, apple, color, green,* and *rose.* Even if you didn't answer with one of the same associations, your response was based on some kind of logical association that you could explain if asked. Some of the less common but still logical associations that our students made to the word *red* were *hair, coat, hot, flag, tag, wine, alert, embarrassment,* and *ink.*

On the basis of the finding that items stored in long-term memory are both organized and associated, memory researchers have developed several models to show how information is organized in long-term memory (Ratclif & McKoon, 1994). One of the best-known models is called the **semantic network model** (Collins & Loftus, 1975).

A semantic network works like this: There are many kinds of associations we can make between concepts. For example, we can associate an object with its characteristics (ball → round), a location with an activity (library → study), or an activity with an emotion (dancing → excitement). All these associations can in turn be linked with additional associations in a massive network in long-term memory. However, some concepts in the network are more strongly linked than others.

When one concept is activated in the semantic network, it can *spread* in any number of directions, *activating* other associations in the semantic network. For example, the word *red* might activate *blue* (another color), *apple* or *fire truck* (objects that are red), or *alert* (as in the phrase, "red alert").

Figure 6.5 illustrates the potential associations in a greatly simplified semantic network. Each oval represents a piece of information stored in long-term memory. The lines connecting the ovals represent a network of possible associations. The length of the lines between the ovals indicates the strength of the association between two concepts. The shorter the line, the stronger the association and the less time it takes to make that association. Thus, in the semantic network shown in Figure 6.5, if the concept *red* is activated in long-term memory, it's more likely to activate an association with the concepts *apple* or *blue* than with the concepts *fire truck* or *flag.*

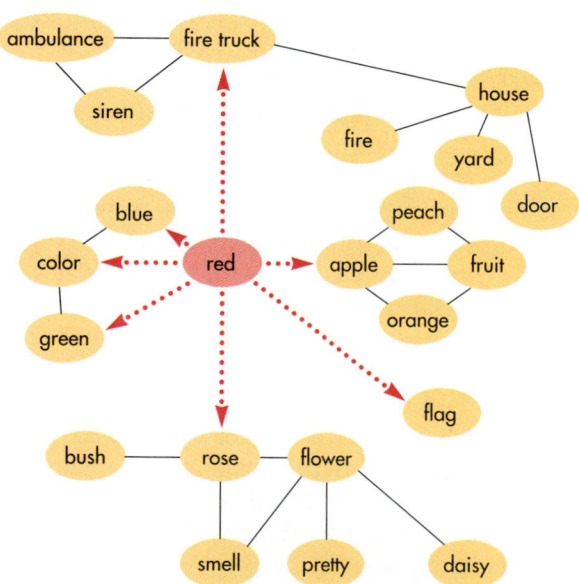

FIGURE 6.5 A Semantic Network Model
The semantic network is one model that has been proposed to show how information in long-term memory is organized through associations and clustering. Activating one concept can trigger a variety of other concepts, which, in turn, can spread throughout the network.
(Based on Collins & Loftus, 1975.)

Comparing the Three Stages of Memory

Identify each of the following descriptions as characteristic of sensory memory (SM), short-term memory (STM), or long-term memory (LTM).

Function

1. Information is stored for later retrieval _____

2. Brief storage of sensory impressions _____

3. Temporary storage of new information; interaction with stored information _____

Duration

4. Potentially permanent _____

5. Approximately 20 to 30 seconds _____

6. Approximately ½ to 3 seconds _____

Capacity

7. Limited capacity of about 7 items _____

8. Large but fleeting capacity _____

9. Unlimited capacity _____

Retrieval: Getting Information from Long-Term Memory

Retrieval refers to the process of retrieving or accessing stored information from long-term memory. What does the TOT experience tell us about the nature of memory? What is the serial position effect? What forms can the encoding specificity principle take?

Before you read any further, try the demonstration in Figure 6.6(a) and (b). Part (a) of the demonstration is on this page. After completing it, go on to part (b) on the next page. We'll refer to this demonstration throughout this section, so please take a shot at it. After you've completed both parts of the demonstration, continue reading.

FIGURE 6.6a
Demonstration of Retrieval Cues

Instructions: Spend 3 to 5 seconds reading each of the following sentences, and read through the list only once. As soon as you are finished, cover the list and write down as many of the sentences as you can remember (you need not write "can be used" each time). Please begin now.

A brick can be used as a doorstop.
A ladder can be used as a bookshelf.
A wine bottle can be used as a candleholder.
A pan can be used as a drum.
A record can be used to serve potato chips.
A guitar can be used as a canoe paddle.
A leaf can be used as a bookmark.
An orange can be used to play catch.
A newspaper can be used to swat flies.
A TV antenna can be used as a clothes rack.
A sheet can be used as a sail.
A boat can be used as a shelter.
A bathtub can be used as a punch bowl.

A flashlight can be used to hold water.
A rock can be used as a paperweight.
A knife can be used to stir paint.
A pen can be used as an arrow.
A barrel can be used as a chair.
A rug can be used as a bedspread.
A telephone can be used as an alarm clock.
A scissors can be used to cut grass.
A board can be used as a ruler.
A balloon can be used as a pillow.
A shoe can be used to pound nails.
A dime can be used as a screwdriver.
A lampshade can be used as a hat.

Now that you've recalled as many sentences as you can, turn to Figure 6.6b on page 206.

(From Bransford & Stein, 1984.)

The Importance of Retrieval Cues

Retrieval refers to the process of accessing, or *retrieving*, stored information. There's a vast difference between what is stored in our long-term memory and what we can actually access. In many instances, our ability to retrieve stored memories hinges on having an appropriate retrieval cue. A **retrieval cue** is a clue, prompt, or hint that can help trigger recall of a stored memory. If your performance on the demonstration experiment in Figure 6.6 was like ours, the importance of retrieval cues should have been vividly illustrated.

FIGURE 6.6b Demonstration of Retrieval Cues (Continued)

Instructions: *Do not* look back at the list of sentences in Figure 6.6a. Use the following list as retrieval cues, and now write as many sentences as you can. Be sure to keep track of how many you can write down.

flashlight	lampshade
sheet	shoe
rock	guitar
telephone	scissors
boat	leaf
dime	brick
wine bottle	knife
board	newspaper
pen	pan
balloon	barrel
ladder	rug
record	orange
TV antenna	bathtub

(From Bransford & Stein, 1984.)

Let's compare results. How did you do on the first part of the demonstration in Figure 6.6(a)? Don remembered 12 pairs of items. Sandy blew Don out of the water on the first part—she remembered 19 pairs of items. Like us, you undoubtedly reached a point at which you were unable to remember any more pairs. At that point, you experienced **retrieval cue failure,** which refers to the inability to recall long-term memories because of inadequate or missing retrieval cues.

Your authors both did much better on the demonstration in Figure 6.6(b), and you probably did, too. (Sandy got 24 out of 26 words, and Don got 26 out of 26 words, except that he remembered *clothes rack* as *clothes line*.) Why the improvement? Because you were presented with retrieval cues that helped you access your stored memories.

Notice, many of the items on the list that you could not recall in Figure 6.6(a) were not forgotten. They were simply inaccessible—until you had a retrieval cue to work with. This illustrates that many memories only *appear* to be forgotten. As Figure 6.6(b) demonstrated, with the right retrieval cue, you can often access stored information that seemed to be completely unavailable.

Retrieval Glitches in Daily Life: The Tip-of-the-Tongue Experience

One of the most common, and most frustrating, experiences of retrieval failure is called the **tip-of-the-tongue (TOT) experience.** The TOT experience refers to the inability to get at a bit of information that you're absolutely certain is stored in your memory. Subjectively, it feels as though the information is very close, but just out of reach—or on the tip of your tongue (Koriat, 1993).

When experiencing this sort of retrieval failure, people can almost always dredge up partial responses or related bits of information from their memory. About half the time, people can accurately identify the first letter of the target word and the number of syllables in it. They can also often produce words with similar meanings or sounds (A. S. Brown, 1991). While momentarily frustrating, most TOT experiences are quickly resolved, sometimes within a few minutes. In one study, more than half of the blocked words spontaneously came to participants' minds within two days (D. M. Burke & others, 1991).

Tip-of-the-tongue experiences illustrate that retrieving information is not an all-or-nothing process. Often, we remember bits and pieces of what we want to remember. In many instances, information is stored in memory but not accessible without the right retrieval cues. TOT experiences also emphasize a point that we made earlier: Information stored in memory is *organized* and connected in relatively logical ways. As you mentally struggle to retrieve the blocked information, logically connected bits of information are frequently triggered. In many instances, these related tidbits of information act as additional retrieval cues, helping you access the desired memory.

Testing Retrieval: Recall, Cued Recall, and Recognition

The first part of the demonstration in Figure 6.6 illustrated the use of recall as a strategy to measure memory. **Recall** (also called *free recall*) involves producing information in the absence of retrieval cues. This is the memory measure that's used on essay tests. Other than the questions themselves, an essay test provides no retrieval cues to help jog your memory.

retrieval cue failure
The inability to recall long-term memories because of inadequate or missing retrieval cues.

tip-of-the-tongue (TOT) experience
A memory phenomenon that involves the sensation of knowing that specific information is stored in long-term memory but being temporarily unable to retrieve it.

recall
A test of long-term memory that involves retrieving information without the aid of retrieval cues.

The second part of the demonstration used a different memory measurement called **cued recall.** Cued recall involves remembering an item of information in response to a retrieval cue. Fill-in-the-blank and matching questions are examples of cued-recall tests.

A third memory measurement is **recognition,** which involves identifying the correct information out of several possible choices. Multiple-choice tests involve recognition as a measure of long-term memory. The multiple-choice question provides you with one correct answer and several wrong answers. If the information is committed to long-term memory, you should be able to recognize the correct answer.

From a student's perspective, cued-recall and recognition tests are clearly to your advantage. Because these kinds of tests provide retrieval cues, the likelihood that you will be able to access stored information is increased.

The Serial Position

Notice that the first part of the demonstration in Figure 6.6 did not ask you to recall the sentences in any particular order. Instead, the demonstration tested *free recall*—you could recall the items in any order. Take another look at your answers to Figure 6.6(a). Do you notice any sort of pattern to the items that you did recall?

Both of your authors were least likely to recall items from the middle of the list. This pattern of responses is called the **serial position effect,** which refers to the tendency to retrieve information more easily from the beginning and the end of a list than from the middle. The tendency to recall the first items in a list is called the *primacy effect,* while the tendency to recall the final items in a list is called the *recency effect.* The serial position effect is especially prominent when you have to engage in *serial recall*—that is, when you need to remember a list of items in their original order. Remembering speeches, ordered lists, and directions are a few examples of serial recall.

The Encoding Specificity Principle

One of the best ways to increase access to information in memory is to recreate the original learning conditions. That simple idea is formally called the **encoding specificity principle** (Tulving, 1983). As a general rule, the more closely retrieval cues match the original learning conditions, the more likely it is that retrieval will occur. The encoding specificity principle can take several forms. Examples include the context effect, state-dependent retrieval, mood-dependent retrieval, and mood congruence.

The Context Effect

Ever had the experience where you can't remember some bit of information during a test but immediately recall it as you walk into the library where you normally study. One form of the encoding specificity principle can help explain this common experience.

The explanation? When you intentionally try to remember some bit of information, such as the definition of a particular key term, you often encode into memory much more than just that isolated bit of information. As you study in the library, for example, at some level you're aware of all kinds of environmental cues. These cues might include the sights, sounds, and aromas within that particular situation. *The environmental cues in a particular context can become encoded as part of the unique memories you form while in that context.* Later, these same environmental cues can act as retrieval cues to help you access the memories that were formed in that context. This particular

cued recall
A test of long-term memory that involves remembering an item of information in response to a retrieval cue.

recognition
A test of long-term memory that involves identifying correct information out of several possible choices.

serial position effect
The tendency to remember items at the beginning and end of a list better than items in the middle.

encoding specificity principle
The principle that when the conditions of information retrieval are similar to the conditions of information encoding, retrieval is more likely to be successful.

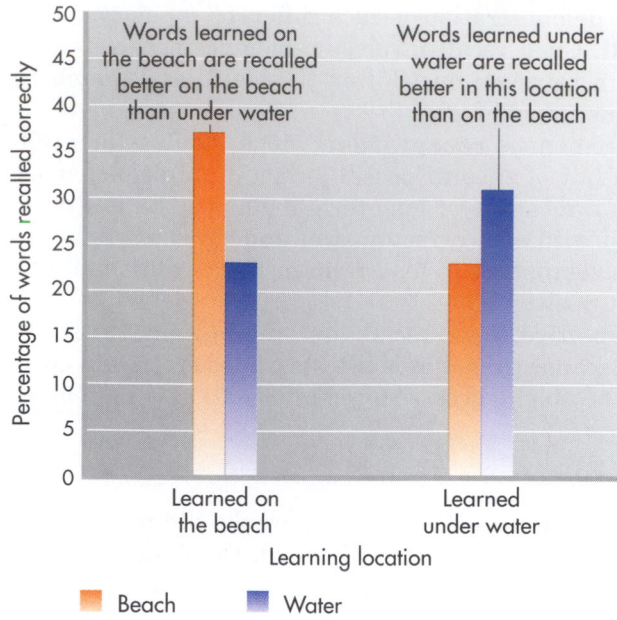

Words learned on the beach are recalled better on the beach than under water

Words learned under water are recalled better in this location than on the beach

FIGURE 6.7 The Context Effect

The influence of the context effect was seen in a clever study in which subjects learned lists of words either while on the beach or while submerged under 15 feet of water. In this graph, you see that when the conditions of learning and retrieval matched, subjects were able to remember more words.

(From Godden & Baddeley, 1975.)

form of encoding specificity is called the context effect. The **context effect** is the tendency to remember information more easily when the retrieval occurs in the same setting in which you originally learned the information (see Figure 6.7).

Thus, environmental cues in the library where you normally study act as additional retrieval cues that helped jog your memory. Of course, it's too late to help your test score, but the memory *was* there. Just for the record, studies have confirmed that when students are tested in the same room where they learned the material, they perform better (e.g., Saufley & others, 1985).

State-Dependent Retrieval

Taking a drug can produce an internal state with unique psychological and physiological characteristics, aspects of which can become encoded with new memories. At a later point, the same intoxicated state can provide additional retrieval cues. Thus, **state-dependent retrieval** involves better recall of information when the pharmacological states of learning and retrieval match (Roediger, 1992).

Studies have shown that when subjects learn information while under the influence of alcohol or marijuana, they recall the information better when they are under the influence of the drugs than when they are sober (Roediger, 1992). Similar effects have been shown with caffeine, nicotine, and other drugs (Horton & Mills, 1984; Peters & McGee, 1982).

Does this mean that drugs such as alcohol or marijuana improve memory? Absolutely not. As we noted in Chapter 4, on consciousness, these drugs tend to *impair* memory. It's also important to note that state-dependent effects are very weak and limited to free-recall tasks. On cued-recall or recognition memory tasks, performance is superior when a person is in a *sober* state, even if the information was encoded in an *intoxicated* state. That's because the strong retrieval cues of recognition or cued-recall tasks easily outweigh the very weak state-dependent retrieval effect (Eich, 1989).

Mood-Dependent Retrieval

Mood-dependent retrieval occurs when information encoded in a certain emotional state is most retrievable when in the same emotional state (Eich & others, 1994). If you're very happy when you encode a particular memory, retrieval of that memory is more likely when you're in a very happy mood.

Overall, findings on mood-dependent retrieval have been mixed. Still, several experiments have successfully demonstrated that when moods match at the time of encoding and retrieval, recall is somewhat better than when they don't match (see Eich, 1995; Blaney, 1986). However, like state-dependent retrieval, the effect is most pronounced on free-recall tasks rather than recognition or cued-recall tasks.

Mood and Memory Your emotional state tends to evoke memories that are consistent with the mood you are experiencing. When you're in a good mood, happy memories more easily come to mind. When you're feeling despondent, you're more likely to recall sad memories.

context effect

The tendency to recover information more easily when the retrieval occurs in the same setting as the original learning of the information.

state-dependent retrieval

An encoding specificity phenomenon in which information that is learned in a particular drug state is more likely to be recalled while the person is in the same drug state.

mood-dependent retrieval

An encoding specificity phenomenon in which information encoded in a certain emotional state is most retrievable when the person is in the same emotional state.

mood congruence

An encoding specificity phenomenon in which a given mood tends to evoke memories that are consistent with that mood.

flashbulb memory

The recall of very specific images or details surrounding a vivid, rare, or significant personal event.

Flashbulb Memories Can you remember where you were when you heard about the death of Princess Diana? The verdict in the O. J. Simpson trial? Significant events can trigger flashbulb memories. Along with public events and national tragedies, meaningful personal events like your wedding day or your high school graduation can also produce flashbulb memories. But are flashbulb memories more accurate than ordinary memories?

Mood Congruence

The idea that a given mood tends to evoke memories that are consistent with that mood is refered to as **mood congruence.** In contrast to the mixed research results on mood-dependent effects, research has consistently shown that your current mood does influence the kinds of memories you recall (Eich & others, 1994; Blaney, 1986). A particular emotional state can act as a retrieval cue that evokes memories of events involving the same emotion. So when you're in a positive mood, you're more likely to recall positive memories. When you're feeling blue, you're more likely to recall negative or unpleasant memories.

Flashbulb Memories:
Vivid Events, Accurate Memories?

If you simply rummage around your own memories, you'll quickly discover that highly unusual, surprising, or even bizarre experiences are easier to retrieve from memory than routine events (Ellis & Hunt, 1993). Such memories are said to be characterized by a high degree of *distinctiveness*. That is, the encoded information represents a unique, different, or unusual memory. In the retrieval cue demonstration in Figure 6.6, if you were more likely to remember the unusual combinations than the ordinary combinations, distinctiveness probably played a role.

Significant events in a person's life can create vivid, distinctive memories that are sometimes referred to as *flashbulb memories*. Just as a camera flash captures the specific details of a scene on film, a **flashbulb memory** is

thought to involve the recall of very precise details and images surrounding a significant, rare, or personally meaningful event (Brown & Kulik, 1982). Do flashbulb memories literally capture specific details, like the details of a photograph, that are unaffected by the passage of time?

National tragedies have provided psychologists with a unique opportunity to study the accuracy of flashbulb memories. When the space shuttle *Challenger* exploded in January 1986, psychologists Ulric Neisser and Nicole Harsch asked college students to write down how they had heard the news (Neisser & Harsch, 1992). Three years later, the same students were asked to recall the episode.

The results? Most of the students were very confident of their recollections, but fully one-third of them were wrong in what they remembered. Over a span of three years, some of the details of their memories had changed. When the students were shown their own handwritten accounts from the day after the explosion, many were so confident that their inaccurate memories were correct that they claimed that their own *original* accounts were wrong (Neisser & Harsch, 1992). Clearly, confidence in a memory, even a vivid one, is no guarantee of accuracy (Weaver, 1993).

Recognizing Factors That Affect Retrieval

1. Janice rushed to the supermarket but forgot her shopping list. When she got home, she discovered that she had remembered most of the items at the beginning and the end of the list but had forgotten most of the items in the middle. Her pattern of remembering is
a. due to state-dependent retrieval.
b. the result of mood-dependent retrieval.
c. referred to as the serial position effect.
d. called tip-of-the-tongue recall.

2. Juan did all his studying for the final exam in the library and was surprised when he had difficulty remembering some information during the exam, which was held in the gym. His problem in retrieval is most likely due to
a. context effects.
b. state-dependent retrieval.

c. mood-dependent retrieval.
e. mood congruence.

3. The more depressed Jody feels, the easier it is for her to remember sad and unhappy events in her life. This best illustrates
a. context effects.
b. state-dependent retrieval.
c. mood congruence.
d. tip-of-the-tongue retrieval.

4. An eyewitness to a bank robbery is asked to identify the suspects in a police lineup. Which type of memory test is being used?
a. free recall
b. serial position test
c. cued recall
d. recognition

Reconstructing Memories:
Sources of Potential Errors

Because retrieval involves the active reconstruction of memories, details of memories can change. What are schemas, and how can they contribute to memory distortions? What is source confusion, and how can it produce false memories? What factors can reduce the accuracy of eyewitness testimony?

For the most part, you remember the general gist of what you see or hear. But the specific details that you remember can change over time. Unintentionally and without your awareness, details can get added, subtracted, exaggerated, or downplayed in your memories (Loftus & Ketcham, 1994).

How do errors and distortions creep into your memories? First, you need to understand that every new memory you form is not simply recorded, but *actively constructed*. To form a new memory, you actively organize and encode information. When you later attempt to retrieve those details from memory, you *actively reconstruct*, or rebuild, the memory (Barclay, 1986). In the process of constructing and reconstructing a memory, two general factors can contribute to errors and distortions: (1) the information you have stored *before* the memory occurs and (2) the information you acquire *after* the memory occurs (Ashcraft, 1994). Let's look at how each of these factors can contribute to memory errors and distortions.

Schemas and Memory Distortions

Since very early in life, you have been actively forming **schemas**—organized clusters of knowledge and information about particular topics (Ashcraft,

schema
(SKEE-muh) An organized cluster of information about a particular topic.

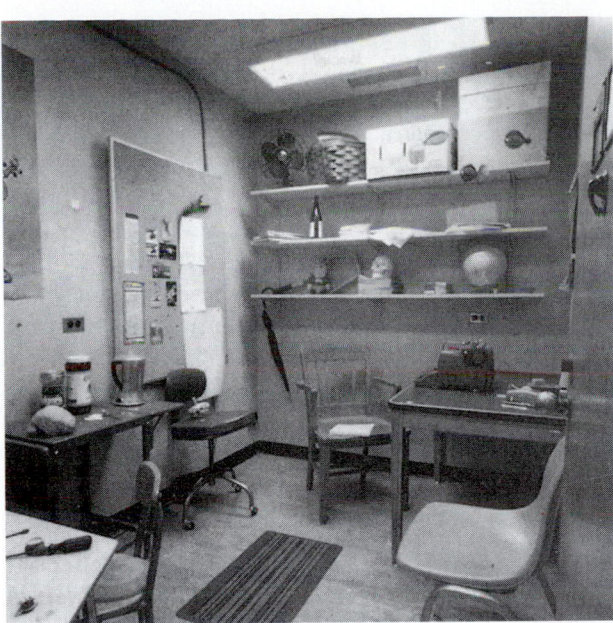

The Psychology Professor's Office in the Brewer and Treyens (1981) Study Take a few moments to "look around" the office, then continue reading.

1994). The topic can be almost anything, such as a particular event, an object, a situation, or a concept. For example, consider the schema you have for a typical kitchen. It probably includes food, a refrigerator, stove, sink, cabinets, pots, pans, silverware, and so forth. You started forming your kitchen schema early in life by gradually identifying the common elements first in your own kitchen, then in other people's. Over time, these common elements became associated and organized into a cluster of knowledge, producing the working schema you have for a kitchen.

On the one hand, schemas are useful in forming new memories. Using the schemas you already have stored in long-term memory allows you to quickly integrate new experiences into your knowledge base (Ellis & Hunt, 1993). On the other hand, schemas can also contribute to memory distortions. To illustrate this point, let's try to recreate some of the conditions in an ingenious study by William Brewer and James Treyens (1981). Imagine that you've signed up to participate in a psychology experiment. When you show up at the psychology professor's office for the study, the professor asks you to wait briefly in his office. Take a few moments to "glance around" the office, which is depicted in the accompanying photograph.

The professor comes back and escorts you to a different room. After you sit down, you are told the real purpose of the study: to test your memory of the details of the professor's office. Without looking at the photograph again, close your book and take out a piece of paper and write down as many details as you can remember about the office, then continue reading.

Did you remember that the office contained books, a filing cabinet, a telephone, a lamp, pens, pencils, and a coffee cup? That's what many of the participants in this study remembered. But *none* of these items were in the professor's office. Compare what you remembered with what is actually shown in the photograph. How accurate was *your* memory?

Why did the participants in this study erroneously "remember" items that weren't there? When the participants reconstructed their memories of the office, they remembered objects that were not in the room but that *did* fit their schema of a professor's office.

Schemas can also contribute to memory distortions when we learn new information that is inconsistent with previously learned information. When we try to account for or incorporate the new information, memories can become distorted to resolve the inconsistencies.

In one clever study, subjects read a brief story about "Bob" and "Margie," a happy, compatible couple who were engaged to be married (Spiro, 1980). Just before the subjects left the experiment, however, the experimenter "casually" mentioned that Bob and Margie broke up and never did get married. When the subjects were later tested for their recall of the written story, they introduced new, inaccurate details to make the story more consistent with the experimenter's remark. For example, one subject recalled that there were problems with Bob's or Margie's parents, and that these troubles led to the breakup. Unknowingly, the subjects fabricated or distorted details of the story to make it consistent with the experimenter's remark and with their own schemas about relationships and marriage.

In combination, the office study and the Bob and Margie study underscore several important points. First, they show how the schemas we already hold can influence what we remember. Second, they demonstrate that once a memory is formed, it has the potential to be changed by new information. And third, they demonstrate how easily memories can become distorted. Notice that neither of these studies involved elaborate efforts to get subjects to distort the memories being formed or remembered.

source confusion
A memory distortion that occurs when the true source of the memory is forgotten.

Source Confusion and False Memories

Memory distortions can also occur because of **source confusion,** which arises when the true source of the memory is forgotten (Johnson & others, 1993; Leichtman & Ceci, 1995). That's because one of the most easily forgotten parts of a memory is its source—how, when, or where you acquired it (Goleman, 1994). Elizabeth's story in the prologue demonstrated how confusion about the source of a memory can give rise to an extremely vivid, but inaccurate, recollection. Vivid and accurate memories of her uncle's home, like the smell of the pine trees and the feel of the lake water, became blended with her fantasy of finding her mother's body. The result was a *false memory*—a distorted or inaccurate memory that feels completely real and is often accompanied by all the emotional impact of a real memory.

Confusion about the source of a memory is a common cause of false memories. Such false memories can arise when you confuse something that you've only heard about, read about, or seen in a film with something that really happened to you (Johnson & others, 1993). In Science Versus Pseudoscience Box 6.1, "Remembering Past Lives," we discuss some unusual examples of false memories that seem to involve source confusion.

Do These Men Look Alike? Seven eyewitnesses identified Father Pagano (top photo) as the armed robber that the press dubbed the "Gentleman Bandit." But Robert Clouser (lower photo) confessed to the crimes during Pagano's trial. How could seven eyewitnesses confuse these two men?

Distortions in Eyewitness Testimony

Given the fallibility of human memory, it's understandable that precautions are often taken when specific details may be critically important. For example, a voice and flight recorder in the cockpit of every commercial airplane documents the details of a flight. If you dial 911, your emergency report and the dispatcher's response are recorded. In these situations and others, steps have been taken to guard against memory distortions *before* a crucial event or dialogue occurs.

One important area where it's often impossible to take such precautions is eyewitness testimony. The guilt or innocence of people in criminal and civil cases often hinges on the accuracy of witnesses' memories. Researchers are well aware of how easily memories can be distorted in the laboratory. If such distortions also occur in real life, they could have serious implications.

As a case in point, consider the differences in appearance between the two men in the accompanying photographs. The older, bald man in the top picture is Father Bernard Pagano, a Roman Catholic priest who was arrested and charged with six armed robberies (Beck & Borger, 1979). It was dubbed the trial of the "Gentleman Bandit" because the robber was very polite and courteous to his victims. At Father Pagano's trial, *seven* eyewitnesses positively identified the priest as the robber.

Now look at the lower picture. That man is Ronald Clouser, who actually committed the robberies. Had Clouser not confessed to the robberies during Father Pagano's trial, Pagano would probably have been convicted of the crimes. But Clouser reported specific details of the robberies that were known only by the police, so there was no doubt that he was the real crook.

How could seven eyewitnesses positively identify Father Pagano as the robber? Before we answer that question, we need to consider some of the research investigating how the memory of eyewitnesses can become distorted. Psychologist **Elizabeth Loftus** (b. 1944), whose story we told in the prologue, is one of the most widely recognized authorities on eyewitness testimony. Loftus not only has conducted extensive research in this area, but has also testified as an expert witness in many high-profile cases (Loftus & Ketcham, 1991).

SCIENCE VERSUS PSEUDOSCIENCE 6.1

Remembering Past Lives

While under hypnosis, people sometimes recover memories of past lives (Baker, 1992; Spanos, 1987–1988). When such memories surface, individuals may report very specific details about the time period of their previously remembered life. Current events, buildings, local customs, people's names, and even previously spoken languages are sometimes recalled. Consider the following cases:

Case #1. Under hypnosis, a Colorado housewife named Virginia Tighe recalled her previous life in Ireland in the 1800s (Rogo, 1985). Speaking with an Irish accent, Tighe remembered many details of her past life as Bridey Murphy, including her marriage to a Brian Joseph McCarthy.

Case #2. Jane Evans, a Welsh housewife, recalled several previous lives (Hines, 1988). In one past life, Evans was a fifteenth-century maid to the wealthy Frenchman Jacques Coeur. Evans recalled very specific details of Coeur's magnificent home, such as carvings over the fireplace. She also remembered that the Frenchman was unmarried and had no children.

Past-life memories like these are frequently offered as evidence of reincarnation. Whether or not you believe in reincarnation, consider the most basic evidence that any reasonably objective person would need to regard such memories as credible.

First, the reincarnation memory must contain information that could not be obtained through relatively ordinary means, such as books, conversations, movies, and newspaper articles. Second, it should not be possible to attribute the demonstration of a complex skill, such as recalling a foreign language, to learning acquired in the person's current life.

Third, the individual reporting the reincarnation memory should be able to provide ordinary information that virtually anyone living at that time would know. So if a person reports that he was a Japanese fighter pilot during World War II, he could reasonably be expected to know who the emperor of Japan was at the time.

Fourth, most of the information in a previous-life memory should mesh with valid historical records. If an individual reports a previous life as the composer Wolfgang Amadeus Mozart living in England in the 1400s, there are some credibility problems, because Mozart was born in 1756 and lived most of his life in Vienna, Austria. Given these basic criteria, let's look at each reincarnation case again.

Case #1 Reconsidered. In the Virginia Tighe case, historical searches failed to uncover evidence for many details of her past-life memories, including any records of either Bridey Murphy or her husband (Rogo, 1985). But investigators learned that while Virginia Tighe was growing up, she lived across the street from an Irish woman who told her stories about Ireland. The neighbor's name? Bridie Murphy. It also turns out that in high school, Virginia Tighe had been involved in theater and had performed several Irish monologues, complete with Irish accent (Alcock, 1978–1979).

Case #2 Reconsidered. Jane Evans's reincarnation memories seem pretty convincing, especially to those of us who have never heard of the fifteenth-century Frenchman Jacques Coeur. But as it turns out, Coeur's home still exists today and is one of France's most photographed homes. The other problem with Evans's recollections of her life as Coeur's maid is that they are incorrect. For instance, Coeur was married and had five children. Jane Evans's memories do, however, mesh very nicely with a detailed novel about Coeur's life entitled *The Moneyman* by Thomas B. Costain—which makes no mention of Coeur's wife or five children (Hines, 1988).

So how are we to explain these memories of past lives? There is good reason to believe that many reincarnation memories are examples of cryptomnesia, which literally means "hidden memories" (Baker, 1992). **Cryptomnesia** is a memory distortion in which a seemingly "new" or "original" memory is actually based on an unrecalled previous memory. In the two cases we've described, existing information seems to form the basis for what the person believes is a genuine reincarnation memory.

Notice that this explanation doesn't necessarily rule out the possibility of reincarnation, which is a religious belief held by many people. It just means that pseudoscientific claims of "proof" for reincarnation are often made with little or no objective consideration of the evidence. In many cases, common psychological processes, such as cryptomnesia, seem to provide simpler and more likely explanations of the phenomenon. So beware. The past life that you remember just might be your own.

MY NAME IS EUNICE. I HAVE LIVED MANY PAST LIVES, MOST OF THEM IN TRENTON, NEW JERSEY....

CHANNELLING ON THE CHEAP

Drawing by M. Stevens; © 1987 The New Yorker Magazine, Inc.

FIGURE 6.8 Estimated Speeds

Word Used in Question	Average Speed Estimate
smashed	41 m.p.h.
collided	39 m.p.h.
bumped	38 m.p.h.
hit	34 m.p.h.
contacted	32 m.p.h.

(After Loftus & Palmer, 1974.)

Misleading information can turn a lie into memory's truth. It can cause people to believe that they saw things that never really existed, or that they saw things differently from the way things actually were. It can make people confident about these false memories and also, apparently, impair earlier recollections. Once adopted, the newly created memories can be believed as strongly as genuine memories.

Elizabeth Loftus, 1992

misinformation effect
A memory-distortion phenomenon in which people's existing memories can be altered by exposing them to misleading information.

To illustrate how eyewitness testimony can become distorted, let's consider a Loftus study that has become a classic piece of research (Loftus & Palmer, 1974). Loftus had subjects watch a film of an automobile accident, write a description of what they saw, and then answer a series of questions. There was one critical question in the series: "About how fast were the cars going when they contacted each other?" Different subjects got different versions of that question. For some subjects, the word *contacted* was replaced with *hit,* while other subjects were given *bumped, collided,* or *smashed.*

Depending on the specific word used in the question, subjects gave very different estimates of the speed at which the cars in the film were traveling. As shown in Figure 6.8, the subjects who gave the highest speed estimates got *smashed* (so to speak). Clearly, how a question is asked can influence what is remembered.

A week after seeing the film, the subjects were asked another series of questions. This time, the critical question was, "Did you see any broken glass?" Although no broken glass was shown in the film, the majority of the subjects whose question had used the word *smashed* a week earlier said yes. Once again, this demonstrates that following the initial memory (the film of the automobile accident), new information (the word *smashed*) can distort the reconstruction of the memory (remembering broken glass that wasn't really there).

More recently, Loftus and her colleagues have demonstrated that subjects can intentionally be led to make inaccurate reports after being exposed to misleading information (Loftus, 1997; Loftus & others, 1989). This **misinformation effect** is relatively easy to produce. In one study, subjects watched a series of slides about a burglary in which a screwdriver was a key element. The subjects then read a written account of the event. However, the written account contained misleading information: it referred to a hammer instead of a screwdriver. The subjects were then tested for their memory of the event.

The results? After exposure to the misleading information, about 60 percent of the subjects quickly and confidently said that a hammer, rather than a screwdriver, had been used in the burglary. In fact, subjects were as confident about their fabricated memories as they were about their genuine memories of other details of the original event. Many other studies have confirmed that misleading questions, misinformation, and other factors can distort eyewitness memories (see Pendergrast, 1995; Loftus & Ketcham, 1991; Wells, 1993; Baker, 1992).

Now we can begin to make sense of Father Pagano's experience. Remember, seven eyewitnesses *confidently,* but *mistakenly,* identified him as the armed robber. As you consider the following additional bits of information that led to his arrest, notice the roles played by schemas and misinformation:

- After the victims experienced the robberies (the original memories), the local media showed a composite sketch of the robber (potentially inaccurate information) based on details remembered by the victims.

- A former member of Father Pagano's parish "recognized" the priest from the sketch and notified the police (Beck & Borger, 1979).

- The behavior of the "Gentleman Bandit" fit the schema of a priest: the robber was very courteous and even apologetic when robbing people, saying he needed the money (schema distortion).

- When police investigators interviewed the witnesses, the officers mentioned that the robber *might* be a priest (misleading information; source confusion).

- *After* witnesses saw news photos of the priest being arrested (more misleading information), they were shown photographs of possible suspects. Only *one* photograph showed a suspect wearing a clerical collar—the picture of Father Pagano.

In combination, these factors contributed to the memory distortions of the seven eyewitnesses. Is the case of Father Pagano an isolated example of eyewitnesses mistakenly identifying the wrong person? Not at all. Psychologist Gary Wells (1993) notes that in more than 1,000 convictions of people who turned out to be innocent, the single largest factor leading to those false convictions was eyewitness error.

Finally, we don't want to leave you with the impression that it's astonishing that anybody remembers *anything* accurately. In reality, people's memories tend to be quite accurate for overall details. When memory distortions occur, they usually involve limited bits of information. In all the examples we've discussed in this section, the general memories were accurate even though some specific details were wrong.

Still, the surprising ease with which bits of memory can become distorted is unnerving. The distorted memories can ring true in our minds and feel just as "real" as accurate memories. In the chapter prologue, you saw how easily Elizabeth Loftus created a false memory. You also saw how quickly she became convinced of the false memory's authenticity and the strong emotional impact it had on her. Rather than being set in stone, human memories are more like clay: they can change shape with just a little bit of pressure.

The Accuracy of Memory Will these people accurately remember the details of this day? Despite the potential for errors in the recall of specific details, our memories are usually accurate for overall themes and general information.

Forgetting: You *Forgot* the Plane Tickets?!

Forgetting is common, and can also be adaptive. Many factors contribute to forgetting. What was Ebbinghaus's contribution to the study of forgetting? What roles do encoding failure, interference theory, motivated forgetting, and decay play in forgetting?

Forgetting is the inability to recall information that was previously available. Forgetting is so common that our lives are filled with automatic reminders to safeguard against forgetting important information. Cars are equipped with buzzers so you don't forget to put on your seatbelt or turn off your lights. News announcements remind you to reset your clocks as Daylight Savings Time begins or ends. Dentists thoughtfully send brightly colored postcards so that your appointment doesn't slip your mind.

Sometimes, of course, we *want* to forget. From the standpoint of a person's psychological well-being, it's probably just as well that we tend to forget the details of unpleasant memories, such as past failures, social embarrassments, and unhappy relationships. Even more generally, it's easy to argue that our minds would be cluttered with mountains of useless information if we remembered every television program, magazine article, billboard, or conversation we've ever experienced. So forgetting *does* have some adaptive value.

forgetting
The inability to recall information that was previously available.

Herman Ebbinghaus:

The Forgetting Curve

German psychologist **Herman Ebbinghaus** (1850–1909) began the scientific study of forgetting over a century ago. Because there was a seven-year gap between his completion of college and his first university teaching position, Ebbinghaus couldn't use university students for experimental subjects (Fancher, 1990). So to study forgetting, Ebbinghaus had to rely on the only available research subject: himself.

Ebbinghaus's goal was to determine how much information was forgotten after different lengths of time. But he wanted to make sure that he was studying the memory and forgetting of completely new material, rather than information that had pre-existing associations in his memory. To solve this problem, Ebbinghaus (1885/1987) created new material to memorize: thousands of nonsense syllables. A *nonsense syllable* is a three-letter combination, made up of two consonants and a vowel, like WIB or MEP. It almost sounds like a word, but is meaningless.

Ebbinghaus carefully noted how many times he had to repeat a list of thirteen nonsense syllables before he could recall the list perfectly. To give you a feeling for this task, here's a typical list:

ROH, LEZ, SUW, QOV, XAR, KUF, WEP, BIW, CUL, TIX, QAP, WEJ, ZOD

Once the nonsense syllables were learned, Ebbinghaus tested his recall of them after varying amounts of time, ranging from 20 minutes to 31 days. He plotted his results in the now-famous Ebbinghaus *forgetting curve,* shown in Figure 6.9.

The Ebbinghaus forgetting curve reveals two distinct patterns in the relationship between forgetting and the passage of time. First, much of what we forget is lost relatively soon after we originally learn it. How quickly we forget material depends on several factors, such as how well the material was encoded in the first place and how often it was rehearsed.

In general, if you learn something in a matter of minutes on just one occasion, most forgetting will occur very soon after the original learning—also in a matter of minutes. However, if you spend many sessions over weeks or months encoding new information into memory, the period of most rapid forgetting will be the first several months after such learning.

Second, the Ebbinghaus forgetting curve shows that the amount of forgetting eventually levels off. As you can see in Figure 6.9, there's very little difference between how much Ebbinghaus forgot eight hours later and a month later. The information that is *not* quickly forgotten seems to be remarkably stable in memory over long periods of time.

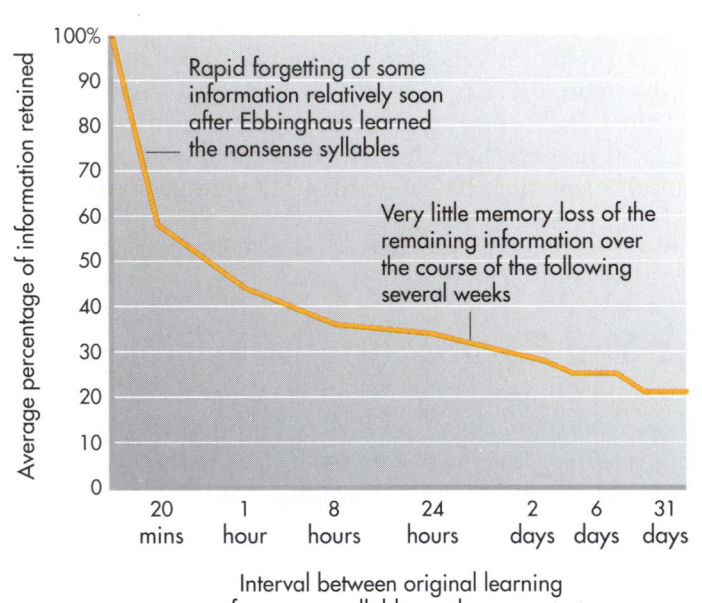

FIGURE 6.9 The Famous Ebbinghaus Forgetting Curve

Ebbinghaus's research demonstrated the basic pattern of forgetting: relatively rapid loss of some information, followed by stable memories of the remaining information.

(Adapted from Ebbinghaus, 1885/1987.)

Factors That Influence Forgetting

Why do we forget? Research on forgetting, both in the laboratory and in everyday life, has identified four potential causes of forgetting: encoding failure, interference, motivated forgetting, and decay. Let's consider how each of these causes can help explain instances of forgetting.

Encoding Failure: It Never Got to Long-Term Memory

Without rummaging through your loose change, look at each drawing in Figure 6.10, then circle the one that accurately depicts the details of a penny. Now, check your answer against a real penny. Was your answer correct?

When this task was presented to subjects in one study, less than half of them picked the correct drawing (Nickerson & Adams, 1982). The explanation: Unless you're a coin collector, you've probably never really looked carefully at a penny. Even though you've handled thousands of pennies, you've only encoded a penny's essential characteristics—like its color, size, and texture—into your long-term memory.

As this simple demonstration illustrates, one of the most common reasons for forgetting is that we never encoded the information into long-term memory in the first place. This phenomenon is called **encoding failure.** Encoding failure explains why you forget where you put your car keys or a person's name five minutes after meeting him. The information momentarily entered your short-term memory, but it was never encoded into long-term memory. As we discussed earlier, information that is not transferred from short-term memory to long-term memory lasts up to about 30 seconds, then evaporates. (You *do* remember that, don't you?) Although we may notice important details, the memory of those details will be fleeting if we don't quickly make a conscious effort to store it.

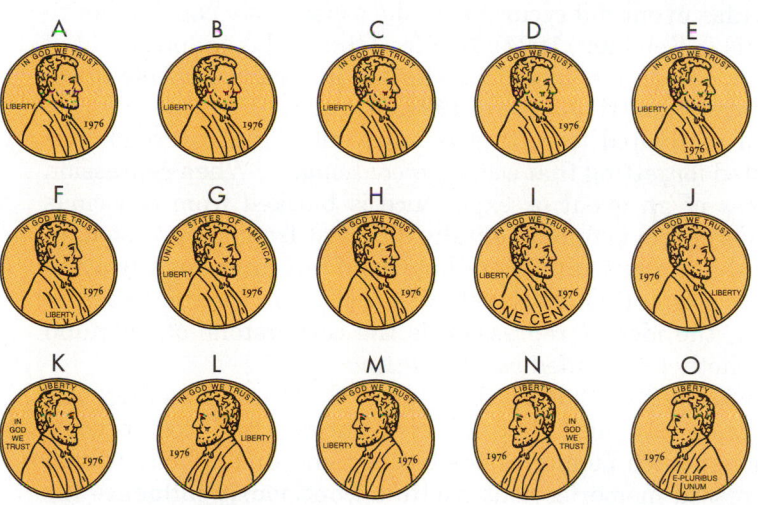

FIGURE 6.10 Test for Memory of Details of a Common Object
Which of these drawings is an accurate picture of a real penny?

Interference Theory: Memories Interfering with Memories

A second reason for forgetting is that memories can interfere with one another. According to the **interference theory** of forgetting, forgetting is caused by one memory competing with or replacing another memory. The most critical influence on whether one memory will create interference with another memory is the similarity of the information. The more similar the information is in two memories, the more likely it is that interference will be produced (Ashcraft, 1994).

There are two basic types of interference. **Retroactive interference** occurs when a *new* memory (your new phone number) interferes with remembering an *old* memory (your old phone number). Retroactive interference can also help explain how misinformation can contribute to the distortions that sometimes occur in eyewitness memories. After the original memory (being robbed), the witness is given inaccurate information that forms a new memory (the robber might be a priest). The new memory then interferes with the old memory, causing the forgetting of details or distortions of the old memory (Riccio & others, 1994). Thus, the misinformation effect that we discussed earlier can be a form of retroactive interference.

Proactive interference is the opposite of retroactive interference. It occurs when an *old* memory interferes with a *new* memory. This is a relatively common experience. For example, proactive interference can occur when you get a new car or borrow someone else's car. You want to switch on the headlights, but you keep turning on the windshield wipers. The old memory (the switch's location in your car) interferes with the more recent memory (the switch's location in the new car). A rather embarrassing example of proactive interference occurs when you refer to your current partner by a previous partner's name. Such momentary memory glitches seem to occur spontaneously, often in the thralls of passion or anger.

encoding failure
The inability to recall specific information because of insufficient encoding for storage in long-term memory.

interference theory
The theory that forgetting is caused by one memory competing with or replacing another.

retroactive interference
Forgetting in which a new memory interferes with remembering an old memory.

proactive interference
Forgetting in which an old memory interferes with remembering a new memory.

motivated forgetting
The theory that forgetting occurs because an undesired memory is held back from awareness.

suppression
Motivated forgetting that occurs consciously.

repression
Motivated forgetting that occurs unconsciously.

Motivated Forgetting

Motivated forgetting refers to the idea that we forget because we are motivated to forget, usually because a memory is unpleasant or disturbing. In one form of motivated forgetting, called **suppression,** a person makes a deliberate, conscious effort to forget information. Although the person remains aware that a particular event did occur, he or she consciously chooses not to think about it (Loftus & Ketcham, 1994). In effect, the goal is to "put it out of your mind." However, research is mixed on whether it's really possible to deliberately forget information (H. Johnson, 1994; Wegner, 1989).

Another form of motivated forgetting is much more controversial. **Repression** is motivated forgetting that occurs *unconsciously*. When repression occurs, all awareness of an event or experience is blocked from conscious awareness. Thus, repression is fundamentally different from suppression, in which people know that a particular event happened but intentionally avoid thinking about it (Ceci & Loftus, 1994). As we'll discuss in greater detail in Chapters 10 and 14, the idea of repression is the cornerstone of Sigmund Freud's famous psychotherapy called *psychoanalysis*.

Freud (1904/1965) believed that psychologically threatening feelings and traumatic events, especially ones that occurred during childhood, become repressed. Even though such memories are blocked and unavailable to consciousness, the repressed memories continue to unconsciously influence the person's behavior and personality, often in maladaptive or unhealthy ways.

Among clinical psychologists who work with psychologically troubled people, the notion that a person's behavior can be influenced by repressed memories is widely, but certainly not universally, accepted (Yapko, 1994a, 1994b). Among the general public, many people believe that we are capable of repressing memories of unpleasant events (Loftus & others, 1994). However, trying to scientifically study the influence of memories that a person does *not* remember is tricky, if not impossible (Loftus, 1993b).

Today, much remains unknown about repression, and the topic is very controversial (Yapko, 1994b; Erdelyi, 1993). At one extreme are many psychologists who do not believe that true repression ever occurs (Holmes, 1990). At the other extreme are psychologists who are convinced that repressed memories are at the root of many psychological problems, particularly repressed memories of childhood sexual abuse (Briere & Conte, 1993). In the middle are memory researchers who agree that extreme emotion can disrupt memory, yet believe that the evidence for repression is far from conclusive (see Baddeley, 1990; Loftus, 1993b; Yapko, 1994b).

In the past several years, a type of psychotherapy that focuses on the recovery of repressed memories of sexual abuse has become widespread (Pendergrast, 1995). This therapy has led to a heated controversy: Are the "recovered" memories true memories, or have they been inadvertently created by the therapist's suggestions? In Critical Thinking Box 6.2, "Recovering 'Repressed' Memories of Childhood Sexual Abuse," we explore this controversy.

DOONESBURY

CRITICAL THINKING 6.2

Recovering "Repressed" Memories of Childhood Sexual Abuse

Sexual abuse of children is a serious problem in our society. It is estimated that approximately 25 percent of all girls and about 10 percent of all boys have been sexually abused (Zgourides, 1996). Sexually abusive acts range from inappropriate touching to vaginal, oral, or anal penetration. Every year, approximately 45,000 cases of childhood sexual abuse are reported to the authorities (Nevid & others, 1995). However, that number may only be the tip of the iceberg. Of adults who remember being sexually abused as a child, only about one out of eight reported the incident to authorities (Janus & Janus, 1993). Without question, the physical and sexual abuse of children can contribute to psychological problems in adulthood (Wenar, 1994; Brewin & others, 1993).

In recent years, many psychotherapists, counselors, social workers, and other mental health workers have embraced a new form of treatment, called *recovery therapy, trauma therapy,* or *repressed memory therapy.* Recovery therapy assumes that most adult "survivors" of childhood sexual abuse have completely repressed all memories of the sexual abuse, although it may have gone on for years and involved multiple family members. Because they are "in denial," these adults consciously remember their childhood as being relatively uneventful—until they enter therapy.

Although all memories of the abuse are blocked, recovery therapists claim that the repressed memories cause a wide range of psychological problems. Symptoms of repressed childhood sexual abuse range from eating disorders, substance abuse, and sexual problems to headaches, anxiety, lack of motivation, relationship problems, and career problems (see Pendergrast, 1995).

The goal of repressed memory therapy is to help adults "recover" their memories of childhood sexual abuse that have presumably been repressed from conscious awareness. As they do so, they can begin "the healing process" of working through the anger and other intense emotions that are related to these repressed memories (Bass & Davis, 1994).

The Controversy: Methods Used to "Recover" Repressed Memories

Repressed memory therapy is at the center of what has become a highly publicized and emotionally charged controversy. At the heart of this controversy are the methods that are used to help people "unblock" or "recover" repressed memories. Repressed memory therapists routinely use hypnosis, automatic writing, guided imagery visualization, and other highly suggestive techniques (Pendergrast, 1995; Yapko, 1994b). For example, recovery therapist Wendy Maltz (1991) advises patients who are unable to remember being sexually abused during childhood to do the following:

> . . . *Spend time imagining that you were sexually abused, without worrying about accuracy, proving anything, or having your ideas make sense. As you give rein to your imagination, let your intuition guide your thoughts.*

Through the use of hypnosis and other highly suggestive techniques, vivid memories of childhood sexual abuse can supposedly be recovered and brought to conscious awareness. In extreme cases, patients have even recovered repressed memories of years of ritual satanic abuse involving secret cults practicing infanticide (the murder of babies), torture, and ritual murder (Sakheim & Devine, 1992).

Repressed memory therapists insist that the recovered memories, however farfetched, are authentic (see Pendergrast, 1995; Loftus & Ketcham, 1994). As evidence of the credibility of the memories, they cite the intense emotional pain experienced by patients, the vividness of the recall, and the fact that thousands of survivors describe similar stories of hidden, repeated abuse going on for years while their families outwardly led normal lives (Bass & Davis, 1994). No one, the repressed memory therapists claim, could invent such vivid, emotional stories.

When patients become convinced of the validity of their memories, they may confront their parents and other family members with detailed accusations of the abuse. When the accusations are vehemently denied, extreme ruptures in family relationships often result. Families are shattered, and sometimes legal action is taken against the accused family members (Pendergrast, 1995). To date, hundreds of civil and criminal cases have been filed based on the retrieved memories of child abuse. And some of the accused have been sentenced to prison solely on the basis of the evidence of recovered memories (Ofshe & Watters, 1994).

The Critical Issue: Recovered Memories or False Memories?

Many psychologists, including many psychotherapists, are very skeptical of the techniques used in repressed memory therapy. These critics contend that many of the supposedly "recovered" memories are actually *false memories* produced by the suggestions of well-intentioned but misguided therapists (Ofshe & Watters, 1994).

Critics note that in documented cases of trauma, most survivors are troubled by the *opposite* problem—they cannot forget their traumatic memories (Pendergrast, 1995; Yapko, 1994b). Rather than being unable to remember the traumatic experiences, the person suffers from recurring flashbacks, intrusive thoughts and memories of the trauma, and nightmares (Loftus & Ketcham, 1994; Loftus, 1993b).

The issue of repression in general is also controversial. Although psychologists generally accept the notion that repression can occur, there are important qualifications to that statement (Schacter, 1995b). For example, it is relatively common for a person to be unable to remember *some* of the specific details of a traumatic event (Ofshe & Watters, 1994; Loftus, 1993b). The person who is injured in an automobile accident may be unable to remember the actual collision. The woman who is brutally raped may remember the events leading up to and following the attack, but not specific details of the rape itself.

Thus, people might experience amnesia for a single traumatic incident or the events surrounding the incident (Schacter, 1995b). However, memory researchers as a whole are extremely

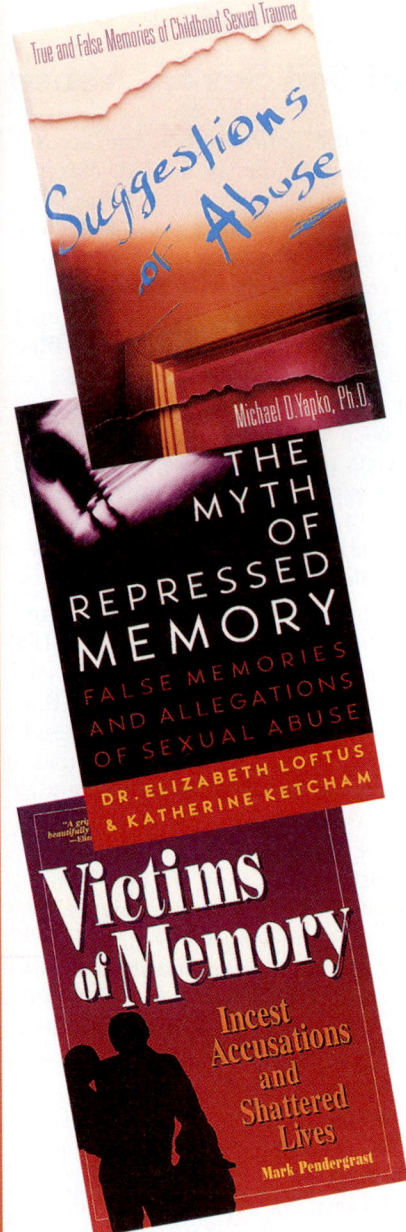

As we've seen in this chapter, compelling evidence exists to support the power of suggestion and misinformation in the creation of vivid but false memories (Loftus, 1997). An experiment by memory researchers Maryanne Garry and Elizabeth Loftus (1994) demonstrated how easily false memories of a mildly traumatic childhood event could be created in some adults.

Each volunteer suggested to another family member that he or she had been lost in a shopping mall at the age of five. The critical issue was whether the other family member would create false memories to support this inaccurate information. The results? Vivid false memories of being lost in a shopping mall were confidently "remembered" by 24 men and women, ages eighteen to sixty-three (Garry & Loftus, 1994).

Advocates of repressed memory therapy have been quick to respond to the results of the shopping mall study. In particular, they stress that there is little parallel between being lost in a shopping mall and the extreme trauma that can accompany childhood sexual abuse (see Bass & Davis, 1994; Loftus & Ketcham, 1994).

What Conclusions Can Be Drawn?

There is no question that physical and sexual abuse of children occurs, and that it can contribute to psychological problems in adulthood (Wenar, 1994). And many psychologists believe it is possible for childhood memories of abuse to become repressed, only to surface many years later in adulthood (see Yapko, 1994a). Nevertheless, it's clear that repressed memories that have been recovered in psychotherapy need to be regarded with caution. Here are some key points to remember in weighing such claims:

First, having confidence in a memory is no guarantee that a memory is accurate. False or fabricated memories can seem just as detailed, vivid, and real as accurate ones. As you've seen in this chapter, the ease with which the details of memories can be distorted is disturbing. Consequently, the use of highly suggestive techniques to "recover" abuse memories raises serious concerns about the accuracy of such memories.

Second, keep in mind that every act of remembering involves reconstructing a memory. The human memory system does not function like a video camera, perfectly preserving the details of an experience. Remembering an experience is not like popping a videotape into your VCR. As we saw when we looked at flashbulb memories, memories can change over time. Without our awareness, memories grow and evolve, sometimes in unexpected ways.

In the last few years, three major books have been published that describe the problems inherent in repressed memory therapy (see the accompanying photographs). Many articles criticizing repressed memory therapy have also appeared in both professional journals and the popular media. These critical attacks have helped sensitize many therapists to the possibility of inadvertently creating false memories. Psychotherapists are also developing guidelines to help mental health professionals avoid inadvertently creating false memories (Byrd, 1994; Gold & others, 1994; Morokoff, 1994). Finally, some leaders of the incest-survivor recovery movement have significantly toned down their more extreme claims.

Clinical psychologist Michael Yapko (1994b) has eloquently summarized the concerns of many mental health professionals about this issue:

> I am deeply concerned that therapy clients will be led to believe destructive things that are untrue, to recall memories of terrible things that never actually happened, to jump to conclusions that are not warranted, and to destroy the lives of innocent people—including their own—in the process.
>
> I am all too aware that the abuse of children is a huge problem growing to ever more sickening proportions. I am also aware that people can be led to believe things that are not true. Abuse happens, but so do false accusations.
>
> The important task of mental health professionals is to sort out which is which with a considerably greater degree of responsibility than we have demonstrated thus far. I hope we are up to the challenge, because the integrity of families and individuals rests on the outcome.

skeptical that anyone could repress all memories of *repeated* incidents of abuse, especially when they stretch over a period of several years (see Pendergrast, 1995; Loftus & Ketcham, 1994).

Memory experts also have many objections to the use of hypnosis and other highly suggestive techniques to "recover" repressed memories. As discussed in Chapter 4, hypnosis has not been shown to increase the accuracy of memories (Kihlstrom & Barnhardt, 1993; Nash, 1987). However, hypnosis does increase a person's *confidence* in the memories that are recalled.

decay theory
The view that forgetting is due to normal metabolic processes that occur in the brain over time.

Decay Theory

Earlier in the chapter we noted that information in sensory memory and short-term memory quickly fades, or *decays,* if it is not transferred to long-term memory. Can the same thing happen with information that *is* stored in long-term memory?

According to **decay theory,** we forget memories because we don't use them and they fade away over time as a matter of normal brain processes. The idea is that when a new memory is formed, it creates a *memory trace*—a distinct change in brain structure or chemistry. Through disuse over time, the normal metabolic processes of the brain are thought to erode the memory trace. The gradual fading of memories, then, would be similar to the fading of letters on billboards or newsprint exposed to environmental elements, like sunlight.

Like motivated forgetting, decay theory makes a good deal of sense intuitively. However, most memory researchers today do not think that long-term memories simply fade or "decay" from disuse (Ellis & Hunt, 1993; Solso, 1991). Why? Because too much evidence contradicts the basic assumptions of decay theory.

For example, many studies have shown that information can be remembered for decades after it was originally learned, even though it has not been rehearsed or recalled since the original memory was formed (Bahrick & Hall, 1991; Bahrick & Phelps, 1987). As we discussed earlier, the ability to access memories is strongly influenced by the kinds of retrieval cues that are provided when memory is tested (Slamecka, 1992). If the memory trace simply decayed over time, the presentation of potent retrieval cues should have no effect on the retrieval of information or events experienced long ago—but, in fact, they do.

Although researchers have not been able to muster compelling evidence for decay theory, there has been enormous interest in trying to explain the physiological basis of memory and forgetting. In the final section of this chapter, we'll look at how memories seem to be created and stored in the brain.

CONCEPT REVIEW 6.3

Identifying Influences on Forgetting

Pick one of the following explanations for each of the examples of forgetting given below: A = encoding failure, B = suppression, C = repression, D = retroactive interference, E = proactive interference.

1. After studying chemistry all afternoon, Brittany is having trouble remembering details of the biology lecture she heard that morning. _____

2. At Drew's ten-year high school reunion, some of his old high school buddies were laughing about an embarrassing incident that happened to Drew at the senior prom. Drew could not remember the incident. _____

3. When asked, you are not able to say which letter of the alphabet is missing from your telephone keyboard. _____

4. Professor Ivanovich has many vivid memories of her students from last semester and can recall most of their names. As a result, she is having problems remembering her new students' names this semester. _____

5. Alayna did very poorly on her statistics midterm exam; now, while she is studying for the final, she makes a deliberate effort not to even think about her low midterm score. _____

The Search for the Biological Basis of Memory

Early researchers believed that memory is associated with physical changes in the brain, but these changes have only recently begun to be discovered. How are memories both "localized" and "distributed"? How do neurons change when a memory is formed? What brain areas are involved in processing memories?

Does the name *Ivan Pavlov* ring a bell? We hope so. As you should recall from Chapter 5, Pavlov was the Russian physiologist who classically conditioned dogs to salivate to the sound of a bell and other neutral stimuli. Without question, learning and memory are intimately connected. Learning an adaptive response depends on our ability to form new memories in which we associate environmental stimuli, behaviors, and consequences.

Pavlov (1927/1960) believed that the memory involved in learning a classically conditioned response would ultimately be explained as a matter of changes in the brain. However, Pavlov only speculated about the kinds of brain changes that would produce the memories needed for classical conditioning to occur. Other researchers would take up the search for the physical changes that were associated with learning and memory. In this section, we look at some of the key discoveries that have been made in trying to understand the biological basis of memory.

The Search for the Elusive Memory Trace

It was an American physiological psychologist named **Karl Lashley** (1890–1958) who set out to find evidence for Pavlov's speculations (Thompson, 1994). Beginning in the 1920s, Lashley began the search for the **memory trace,** or *engram*—the brain changes associated with the formation of a long-term memory. Guiding Lashley's research was his belief that memory is *localized,* meaning that a particular memory is stored in a specific brain area.

Lashley searched for the specific location of the memory that a rat forms for running a maze. Lashley (1929) suspected that the specific memory was localized at a specific site in the *cerebral cortex,* the outermost covering of the brain that contains the most sophisticated brain areas. Once a rat had learned to run the maze, Lashley surgically removed tiny portions of the rat's cortex. After the rat recovered, Lashley tested the rat in the maze again. Obviously, if the rat could still run the maze, then the portion of the brain removed did not contain the memory.

Over the course of thirty years, Lashley systematically removed different sections of the cortex in trained rats. The result of Lashley's painstaking research? No matter which part of the cortex he removed, the rats were still able to run the maze (Lashley, 1929, 1950). At the end of his professional career, Karl Lashley concluded that memories are not localized in specific locations, but instead are *distributed,* or stored throughout the brain.

Lashley was wrong, but not completely wrong. Some memories *do* seem to be localized at specific spots in the brain. Some twenty years after Lashley's death, psychologist **Richard F. Thompson** (b. 1930) and his colleagues resumed the search for the location of the memory trace that would confirm Pavlov's speculations. Thompson classically conditioned rabbits to perform a very simple behavior—an eyeblink. By pairing a tone with a puff of air to the rabbit's eye, he classically conditioned the rabbit to blink reflexively in response to the tone alone (Thompson, 1994, 1993).

memory trace
The brain changes associated with a particular stored memory.

Thompson discovered that after a rabbit learned this simple behavior, there was a change in the brain activity in a small area of the rabbit's *cerebellum,* a lower brain structure involved in physical movements. When this tiny area of the cerebellum was removed, the rabbit's memory of the learned response disappeared. It no longer blinked at the sound of the tone. However, the puff of air still caused the rabbit to blink reflexively, so the reflex itself had not been destroyed.

Thompson and his colleagues had confirmed Pavlov's speculations: The long-term memory trace of the classically conditioned eyeblink was formed and stored in a very localized region of the cerebellum. So why had Karl Lashley failed? Unlike Thompson, Lashley was working with a relatively complex behavior. Running a maze involves the use of several senses, including vision, smell, and touch. In comparison, Thompson's rabbits learned a very simple reflexive behavior—a classically conditioned eyeblink.

Thus, part of the reason Lashley failed to find a specific location for a rat's memory of a maze was that the memory was not a single memory. Instead, the rat had developed a complex set of *interrelated memories* involving information from multiple senses. These interrelated memories were processed and stored in different brain areas. The result was that the rat's memories were *distributed* and stored across multiple brain locations. Hence, no matter which small brain area Lashley removed, the rat could still run the maze. So Lashley seems to have been right in suggesting that some memories are distributed throughout the brain.

When you combine the findings of Lashley and Thompson, they suggest that memories have the potential to be *both localized and distributed* (Squire, 1987). Very simple memories may be localized in a specific area, while more complex memories seem to be distributed throughout the brain. A complex memory involves clusters of information, and each part of the memory may be stored in the brain area that originally processed the information (Squire & Butters, 1992).

More recently, researchers have used PET scans to confirm that many kinds of memories are distributed in the human brain. As you can see in the accompanying photograph, when we are performing a relatively complex memory task, multiple brain regions are activated—evidence of the distribution of memories involved in complex tasks (Squire & others, 1992).

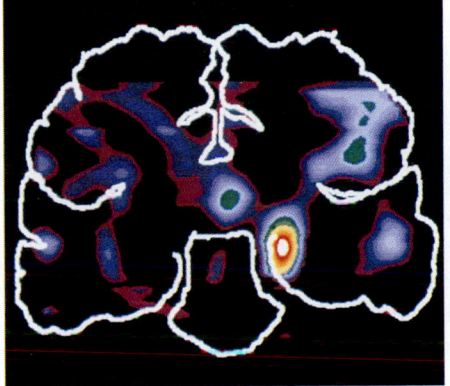

Brain Activity During a Memory Task This PET scan shows a left-to-right cross section of the brain. During a memory task, multiple brain areas are activated. The greatest activity occurs in the hippocampus, the white area that is ringed in red, yellow, green, and blue.

The Role of Neurons in Long-Term Memory

What exactly is it that is localized or distributed? Memories don't just float around in your brain. The notion of a memory trace suggests that some change must occur in the workings of the brain when a new long-term memory is stored. Logically, two possible changes could occur. First, the *functioning* of the neurons in the brain could somehow change. Second, the *structure* of the neurons could somehow change.

Given those two possibilities, the challenge for memory researchers has been to identify the specific neurons involved in a given memory, a task that is virtually impossible with the human brain because of its enormous complexity. What would be required is a creature with a limited number of neurons that is also capable of learning new memories.

Enter *Aplysia,* a gentle, seaweed-munching sea snail that resides off the California coast. The study of *Aplysia* in the last thirty years has given memory researchers important clues to the brain changes involved in memory (Kandel & Hawkins, 1993; Bailey, 1992). *Aplysia* has only about 20,000 good-sized neurons. Thus, memory researchers like Eric Kandel (1995d) at Columbia University have been able to study the neuronal changes that occur

***Aplysia,* the Super-Snail of Memory Research** Eric Kandel holds *Aplysia,* the sea snail that is used to study how neurons change when simple behaviors are learned and remembered.

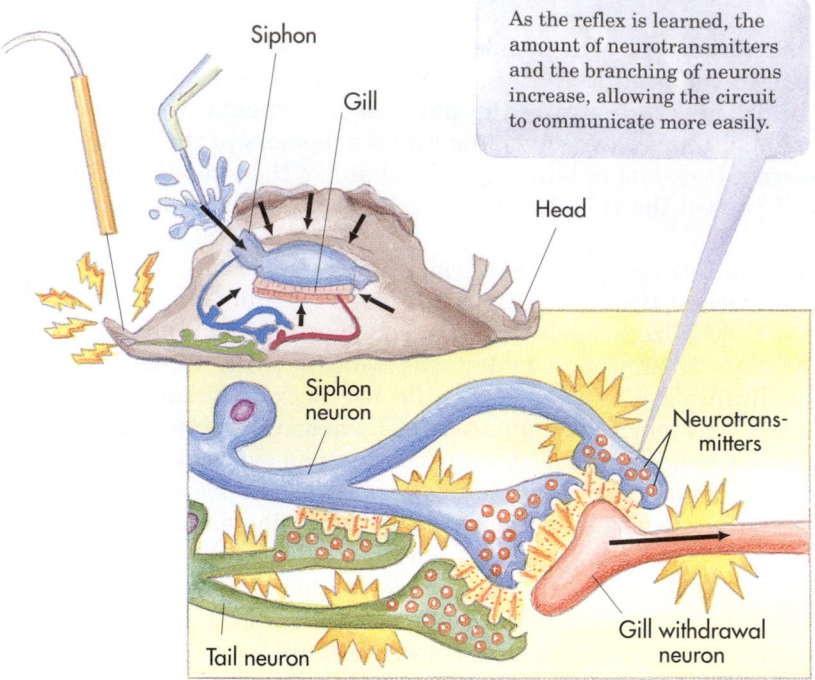

Siphon

Gill

Head

> As the reflex is learned, the amount of neurotransmitters and the branching of neurons increase, allowing the circuit to communicate more easily.

Siphon neuron

Neurotransmitters

Tail neuron

Gill withdrawal neuron

FIGURE 6.11 **How Neurons Change as** *Aplysia* **Forms a New Memory**
When *Aplysia* is repeatedly squirted with water, and each squirt is followed by a mild shock to its tail, the snail learns to withdraw its gill flap if squirted with the water alone. Conditioning leads to structural and functional changes in the three neurons involved in the memory circuit.

when *Aplysia* forms a new memory for a simple classically conditioned response.

If you give *Aplysia* a gentle squirt with a Water-Pik, followed by a mild electric shock to its tail, the snail reflexively withdraws its gill flap. When the process is repeated several times, *Aplysia* wises up and acquires a new memory of a classically conditioned response—it withdraws its gill when squirted with the WaterPik alone. This learned gill withdrawal reflex seems to involve a circuit of just three neurons: one that detects the water squirt, one that detects the tail shock, and one that signals the gill withdrawal reflex (see Figure 6.11).

When *Aplysia* acquires this new memory through repeated training trials, significant changes occur in the three-neuron circuit (Kandel, 1995d). First, the *function* of the neurons is altered; there is an increase in the amount of the neurotransmitters produced by the neurons. Second, the *structure* of the snail's neurons changes. The number of interconnecting branches between the neurons increases, along with the number of synapses or communication points on each branch. These changes allow the neurons involved in the particular memory circuit to communicate more easily.

The same kinds of brain changes have been observed in more sophisticated mammals. Chicks, rats, and rabbits also show structural and functional neuron changes associated with new learning experiences and memories (Rosenzweig, 1996; Greenough, 1992). And, as you may recall from the Chapter 2 Application, "Pumping Neurons: Keeping Your Brain in Shape," there is indirect evidence that the same kinds of changes also occur in humans.

In terms of our understanding of the memory trace, what do these findings suggest? Although there are vast differences between a simple creature such as *Aplysia* and the enormous complexity of the human brain, some tentative generalizations are possible. Forming a memory seems to produce distinct functional and structural changes in specific neurons. These changes create a memory circuit. Each time the memory is recalled, the neurons in this circuit are activated. As the structural and functional changes in the neurons strengthen the communication links in this circuit, the memory becomes established as a long-term memory (Rose, 1993; Lynch, 1986).

CONCEPT REVIEW 6.4

Remembering Famous Names

Match each of the following names with one of the descriptions below: Herman Ebbinghaus, Richard F. Thompson, George Sperling, Elizabeth Loftus, Karl Lashley.

1. The psychologist who identified the duration of visual sensory memory _____

2. One of the most widely recognized experts on memory distortions, eyewitness testimony, and false memories _____

3. The psychologist who was one of the first people to scientifically study memory and forgetting _____

4. The physiological psychologist who tried but failed to find the specific location of individual memories in the brain _____

5. The physiological psychologist who succeeded in identifying the specific brain location of a simple classically conditioned response _____

Processing Memories in the Brain:

Clues from Amnesia

The complexity and inaccessibility of the human brain has made it virtually impossible to study the role of individual neurons in human memory. However, memory researchers have been able to study the role of specific brain structures in processing memories. Much of this research has involved studying individuals who have sustained brain injury or had part of their brain surgically removed for medical reasons. Often, such individuals experience **amnesia,** or severe memory loss (Butters & Delis, 1995). By relating the type and extent of amnesia to the specific brain areas that have been damaged, researchers have uncovered clues as to how the human brain processes memories.

Retrograde Amnesia: The Consolidation of Memories

One type of amnesia is **retrograde amnesia.** People who suffer from retrograde amnesia are unable to remember some or all of their past, especially episodic memories for recent events. Retrograde amnesia often results from a blow to the head. Boxers sometimes suffer such memory losses after years of fighting. Head injuries from automobile and motorcycle accidents are another common cause of retrograde amnesia. Typically, memories of the events that immediately preceded the injury are completely lost, as in the case of accident victims who cannot remember details about what led up to the accident.

Apparently, establishing a long-term memory is like creating a cement wall—it needs time to "set" before it becomes permanent. This process of "setting" a new memory permanently in the brain is called memory consolidation. More specifically, **memory consolidation** is the gradual, physical process of converting new long-term memories to stable, enduring memory codes. If memory consolidation is disrupted before the process is complete, a long-term memory is vulnerable and may be lost. In humans, memory consolidation can be disrupted by brain trauma, such as a sudden blow, concussion, electric shock, or encephalitis (Squire & Butters, 1992; Squire, 1987).

Anterograde Amnesia: The Case of H.M.

Another form of amnesia is **anterograde amnesia**—the inability to form new memories. The most famous case of anterograde amnesia involves a man who is known only by the initials H.M. to protect his identity. In 1953, H.M. was twenty-seven years old and had a history of untreatable epileptic seizures. H.M.'s doctors located the brain area where the seizures seemed to originate. In desperation, they surgically removed portions of the temporal lobe on each side of H.M.'s brain, including the brain structure called the *hippocampus* (Ogden & Corkin, 1991).

After the surgery the frequency and severity of H.M.'s seizures were greatly reduced. However, it was quickly discovered that the surgery had produced another effect: the destruction of H.M.'s ability to form new memories of events and information. Although intended to treat H.M.'s seizures, the surgery dramatically revealed the role of the hippocampus in forming new memories.

Canadian psychologist Brenda Milner (1965, 1970) has studied H.M. extensively over the last forty years. If you were to meet H.M. today, you could carry on a conversation with him and he would appear normal enough. H.M. has a good vocabulary, normal language skills, and above-average intelligence. But he lives in the eternal present. If you left his room and returned five minutes later, he wouldn't remember having seen you before. In fact, he must be reintroduced to his doctors each time he sees them, even though some of them have been treating him for years (Ogden & Corkin, 1991).

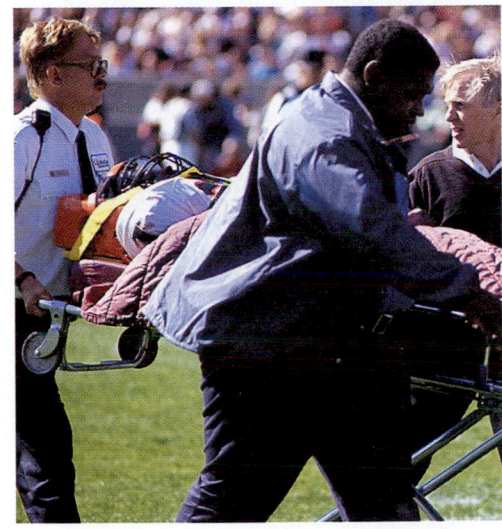

Disrupting the Consolidation of Memories Head injuries are common in football and many other sports. In one study, football players who were questioned immediately after a concussion or other head injury could remember how they were injured and the name of the play just performed. But if questioned thirty minutes later for the same information, they could not. Because the head injury had disrupted the memory consolidation process, the memories were permanently lost (Yarnell & Lynch, 1970).

amnesia
(am-NEE-zha) Severe memory loss.

retrograde amnesia
Loss of memory, especially for episodic information.

memory consolidation
The gradual, physical process of converting new long-term memories to stable, enduring long-term memory codes.

anterograde amnesia
Loss of memory caused by the inability to store new memories.

For the most part, H.M.'s short-term memory seems to work just fine. If he actively repeats or rehearses information in short-term memory, he can hold information in short-term memory for an hour or more. However, he forgets the information if he switches his attention to something else and stops rehearsing it (Ogden & Corkin, 1991). H.M.'s long-term memory is also relatively intact. He can retrieve long-term memories from before the time he was sixteen years old, when the severe epileptic seizures began.

H.M.'s case suggests that the hippocampus is not involved in most short-term memory tasks or in the storage and retrieval of long-term memories. The critical role played by the hippocampus seems to be the *encoding* of new memories for events and information and the *transfer* of them from short-term to long-term memory (Squire & Knowlton, 1995). When the same brain sections are surgically removed in monkeys, they show the same kinds of massive anterograde amnesia that H.M. displays (Zola-Morgan & Squire, 1993).

However, H.M. can form new long-term *procedural* memories, such as the procedural memories involved in learning a new skill. For example, when H.M. was given the same logical puzzle to solve several days in a row, he was able to solve it in less time each day, showing that he remembered the procedures involved in some way. But, of course, he could not consciously remember having learned how to do it or having solved the puzzle before (Cohen, 1984). What this shows is that the hippocampus is critical in forming new episodic memories, but not new procedural memories (Zola-Morgan & Squire, 1993).

Another brain structure involved in processing memories is the *amygdala,* which is situated very close to the hippocampus (see Figure 6.12). The amygdala seems to be responsible for associating memories that involve different senses (Aggleton, 1992). For example, when the amygdala is removed, monkeys seem to lose their ability to link different sensory memories associated with a familiar object. When they see a banana, they behave as if they can't recall how it smells or tastes.

The amygdala also seems to encode the emotional qualities associated with particular memories, such as fear or anger (LeDoux, 1994b; Davis, 1992). Normally, monkeys are afraid of snakes. But if the amygdala is damaged, a monkey loses its fear of snakes and other natural predators.

Although we've simplified many details, this brief section on the biological basis of memory gives you some idea of the promising leads that are currently being pursued by psychologists and other neuroscientists. Neuroscientists are far from a comprehensive understanding of the brain mechanisms involved in memory. Nevertheless, enormous strides have been made in the last thirty years. Clearly, certain brain structures, most notably the hippocampus, are involved in the initial processing of episodic memories (Squire & Knowlton, 1995). Distinct structural and functional changes in circuits of

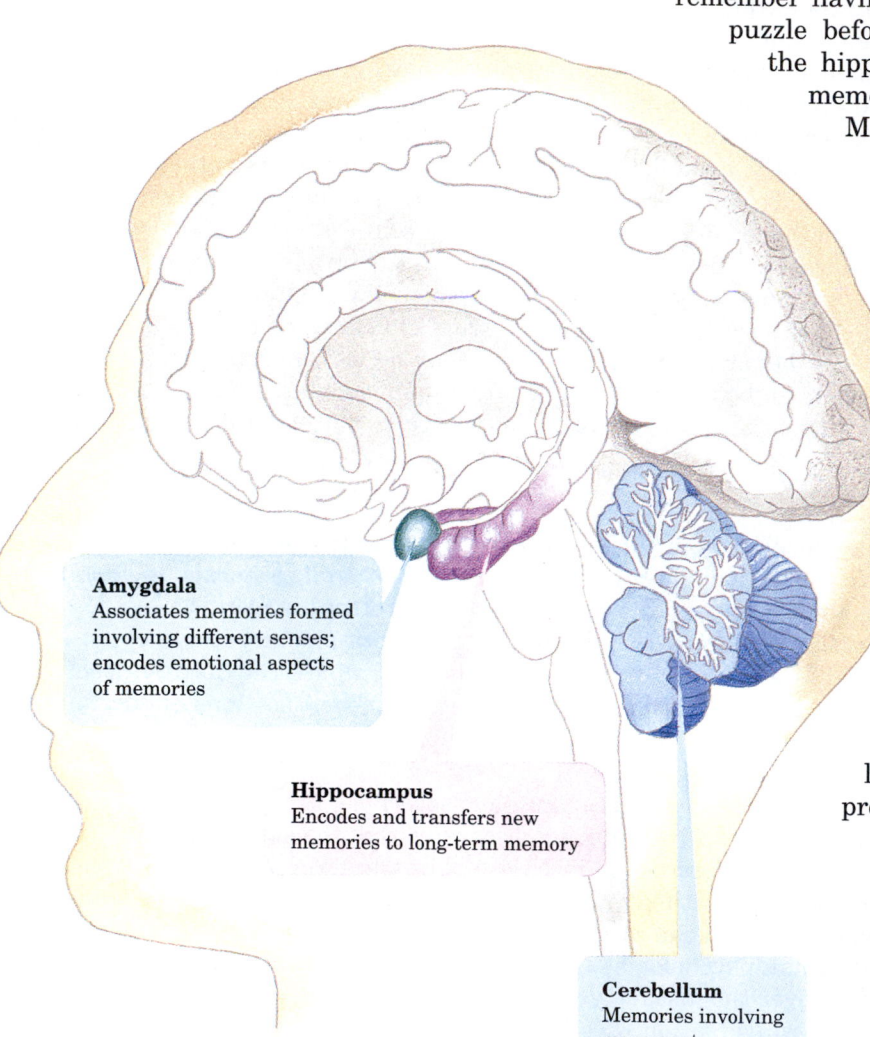

Amygdala
Associates memories formed involving different senses; encodes emotional aspects of memories

Hippocampus
Encodes and transfers new memories to long-term memory

Cerebellum
Memories involving movement

FIGURE 6.12 Brain Structures Involved in Human Memory
In this midline cross-sectional view of the brain, you can see some of the key brain structures involved in encoding and storing memories.

neurons seem to be associated with enduring memories (Bailey, 1992; Greenough, 1992). Researchers are also beginning to understand which neurotransmitters seem to be most involved in the memory process (Baudry & Davis, 1992).

The overall goal of such research is far from being purely academic. For example, progressive memory loss is the hallmark of *Alzheimer's disease. Dementia* is another condition that is characterized by numerous cognitive deficits, of which amnesia is the primary symptom. The prevalence of each of these conditions increases with advancing age (Butters & Delis, 1995). Through the efforts of memory researchers, combined with advances in technology, it may one day be possible to treat these conditions or at least minimize the devastating loss of human memory that accompanies them.

CULTURE AND HUMAN BEHAVIOR 6.3

Do Cultural Beliefs Affect Memory in Old Age?

Many researchers believe that declines in memory ability are part of the natural, biological aging process (Craik, 1994; Salthouse, 1993). However, psychologists Becca Levy and Ellen Langer have offered a very different explanation. They believe that cultural expectations about aging can affect memory abilities in the elderly.

While most Americans believe that memory loss inevitably accompanies old age (Ryan, 1992), Levy and Langer point out that this belief is far from universal. In many cultures, the elderly are accorded high status and revered for their wisdom and accumulated knowledge.

To test the notion that cultural stereotypes of the elderly can influence memory ability, Levy and Langer (1994) first identified two cultural groups that hold a very positive view of aging. One cultural group was people living in mainland China. The other cultural group consisted of hearing-impaired Americans who used American Sign Language and strongly identified with the Deaf culture.

Next, Levy and Langer recruited three groups of subjects: (1) residents of Beijing, China; (2) American members of the Deaf culture who communicated with American Sign Language; and (3) Americans who were part of the main-stream hearing culture. Half of each group consisted of younger people, aged fifteen to thirty; the other half consisted of older adults, aged fifty-nine to ninety-one. Participants in all groups were tested on four different memory tasks. In addition, their attitudes toward old age were measured.

On the memory tasks, Levy and Langer found no significant difference among all three groups of younger adults. But while the younger adults in the three cultural groups performed very similarly, the older adults did not. The older American hearing participants had the *lowest* memory test scores. The elderly Deaf participants had the next-highest memory test scores. And the elderly Chinese subjects had the *highest* scores of all the older adults. In fact, the elderly Chinese subjects performed so well on the memory tests that their scores did not differ from the scores of the young Chinese subjects.

Levy and Langer note that the pattern of memory test scores was directly correlated with each group's view of aging. The more positive each group's view of aging, the better was their performance on actual memory tasks. The Chinese reported the most positive view of aging, and the older Chinese participants scored the highest on the memory tasks. The hearing Americans reported the *least* positive view of aging, and the elderly members of this group scored the lowest on the memory tasks of the three cultures studied. The Deaf participants' views about aging fell between the Chinese and the American hearing group, and their scores on the memory tests were also in the middle of the other two groups.

How can we interpret these findings? Levy and Langer point out that the Chinese and Deaf cultures have little in common other than their esteem for old age. If biological processes were responsible for memory loss in old age, the Chinese and Deaf participants should not have outperformed the older American hearing participants on all four memory tasks.

Levy and Langer (1994) conclude that cultural beliefs about aging may well play an important role in determining the degree of memory loss that people experience in old age. They suggest that the negative stereotypes about aging that are common in main-stream American culture may function as a self-fulfilling prophecy for many older Americans.

How to Make Those Memories Last

None of us are immune to the pitfalls of forgetting. Fortunately, there are several very effective strategies to boost your memory for important information, whether it's textbook material or the location of that extra set of house keys. Based on the memory research, we've compiled ten effective techniques to enhance your memory.

1. Focus Your Attention

Problems in absorbing new information arise when distracting thoughts, background noise, and other interruptions sidetrack your attention. Television is one common culprit. Rather than studying in front of the tube, locate a quiet study space that's free from distractions so you can focus your attention. If distracting thoughts are competing for your attention, start your study session by reading aloud part of what you need to study (Hertel & Rude, 1991).

2. Commit the Necessary Time

The more time you spend learning material, the better you will understand it, and the longer you will remember it. So don't rely on skimming material the night before a test. Budget enough time to carefully read the assigned material. If you read material faster than you can comprehend it, you not only won't understand the material, you also won't remember it.

3. Space Your Study Sessions

Distributed practice means that you learn information over several sessions, which gives you time to mentally process and incorporate the information. Students who take the distributed-practice approach to learning retain significantly more information than students who use cramming, or *massed practice*. It's also been shown that sleep, particularly REM or dreaming sleep, helps consolidate new memories (Karni & others, 1994; Smith & Lapp, 1991). All-night cram sessions just before an exam are one of the *least* effective ways to learn new material.

4. Organize the Information

We have a strong natural tendency to organize information in long-term memory into categories. You can capitalize on this tendency by actively organizing information you want to remember. One way to accomplish this is by outlining chapters or your lecture notes. Use the chapter headings and subheadings as categories or, better yet, create your own categories. Under each category, list and describe the relevant terms, concepts, and ideas. This strategy can double the amount of information you can recall.

5. Elaborate the Material

You've probably noticed that virtually every term or concept in this text is formally defined in just a sentence or two. But we also spend a paragraph or more explaining what the concept means. In order to remember the information you read, you have to do the same thing—engage in elaborative rehearsal and actively process the information for meaning.

How can you actively process information for meaning? Actively question new information and think about its implications. Form memory associations by relating the material to what you already know. Try to come up with examples that relate to your own life. React to what you read by writing your comments or questions in the margin of the textbook. Create sentences that accurately use the concept or term.

6. Use Visual Imagery

Two memory codes are better than one (Paivio, 1986). Rather than just encoding the information verbally, use mental imagery. Much of the information in this text easily lends itself to visual imagery. Use the text photographs and other illustrations to help you form visual memories of the information. A simple way to make text information visually distinct is by using different-colored highlighters for different concepts.

7. Explain It to a Friend

Memory research clearly supports the benefits of explaining new material out loud (Muth & others, 1988). After you read a section of material, stop. Summarize what you have read in your mind. When you think you understand it, try to verbally explain the information to a friend or a family member.

8. Reduce Interference Within a Topic

If you occasionally confuse related terms and concepts, it may be because you're experiencing *interference* in your memories for similar information. To minimize memory interference for related information, first break the chapter into manageable sections, then learn the key information one section at a time. As you encounter new concepts, contrast them with previously learned concepts, looking for differences and similarities. By building distinct memories for important information as you progress through a topic, you're more likely to distinguish between concepts so they don't get confused in your memory.

9. Counteract the Serial Position Effect

The serial position effect is our tendency to remember information at the beginning and end of a sequence. To counteract it, spend extra time with the information that falls in the middle. Once you've initially mastered a sequence of material, start at a different point each time you review the information.

10. Use Contextual Cues to Jog Memories

Ideally, study in the setting where you're going to be tested. If that's not possible, when you're taking a test and a specific memory gets blocked, imagine that your books and notes are in front of you and that you're sitting where you normally study. Simply imagining the surroundings where you learned the material can help jog those memories (S. M. Smith & others, 1978).

Summary

Memory

Memory Processes and Stages

■ Memory refers to the mental processes that enable us to acquire, retain, and retrieve information. Key memory processes are encoding, storage, and retrieval.

■ The stage model of memory describes human memory as the process of transferring information from one memory stage to another. The three stages of memory are sensory memory, short-term memory, and long-term memory. These stages differ in terms of capacity, duration, and function. Short-term memory is also referred to as working memory.

Sensory Memory: Fleeting Impressions of Reality

■ Sensory memory stores information about the environment for a very brief period. Information that we pay attention to is transferred from sensory memory to short-term memory; other information fades quickly.

■ George Sperling discovered that visual sensory memory holds information for about half a second before the information fades.

■ Although there is a separate sensory memory for each sense, visual and auditory sensory memory are the most thoroughly studied. Auditory sensory memory lasts slightly longer than visual sensory memory—up to a few seconds.

Short-Term, Working Memory: The Workshop of Consciousness

■ Short-term memory provides temporary storage for information transferred from sensory memory and long-term memory that we are currently using in some conscious cognitive activity. Most information fades from short-term memory within about 30 seconds. Maintenance rehearsal can be used to keep information active in short-term memory.

■ The capacity of short-term memory is limited to about seven items, plus or minus two. When the capacity of short-term memory is reached, new information will displace existing information. Chunking can be used to increase the amount of information held in short-term memory.

Long-Term Memory

■ Long-term memory stores a limitless amount of information for extended periods of time.

■ Encoding transforms information into a form that can be stored and retrieved later. The most effective encoding strategies involve elaborative rehearsal.

■ Long-term memory includes procedural, episodic, and semantic information. Information in long-term memory is both clustered and associated; thus, long-term memory is organized. The semantic network model is one description of how information is organized in long-term memory.

Retrieval: Getting Information from Long-Term Memory

■ Retrieval refers to the process of accessing information stored in long-term memory.

■ Retrieval cues are hints that help us retrieve stored memories. Sometimes, stored memories cannot be retrieved because of retrieval cue failure. Tip-of-the-tongue experiences are everyday examples of retrieval failure.

■ Retrieval can be tested using recall, cued recall, and recognition measures. The serial position effect is our tendency to remember best the first and last items in a series.

■ According to the encoding specificity principle, recreating aspects of the original learning conditions is one way to increase retrieval effectiveness. There are several different forms of the encoding specificity principle, including the context effect, state-dependent retrieval, mood-dependent retrieval, and mood congruence.

■ Memories that are highly unusual tend to be easier to retrieve from long-term memory. Although flashbulb memories can be extremely vivid, they seem to function like normal memories and are not always accurate.

Reconstructing Memories: Sources of Potential Errors

■ Because retrieval involves the reconstruction of memories, memory details can change. Memories can be distorted by schemas and other preexisting information that we have stored before acquiring a new memory. Schemas can also contribute to memory distortions when we learn new information that is inconsistent with previously learned information. Source confusion occurs when we either don't remember or misidentify the source of a memory.

■ There are many potential causes of inaccuracies in eyewitness testimony, including the misinformation effect, schema distortion, and source confusion.

■ Despite the potential for memories to become distorted, memory tends to be fairly accurate for the general gist of experiences. Meaningful or important details are least likely to be forgotten. Distorted or false memories can be just as vivid as accurate memories.

Forgetting: You *Forgot* the Plane Tickets?!

- Forgetting refers to the inability to recall information that was previously available. The general pattern of forgetting is reflected in the forgetting curve, which is based on the research of Herman Ebbinghaus.

- Several factors can contribute to forgetting. Encoding failure is one important cause. According to interference theory, forgetting results from retroactive and proactive interference with other information. Motivated forgetting is the result of suppression and repression. Research support for repression is mixed. Decay theory is another explanation for forgetting, but it is contradicted by some of the findings of memory research.

The Search for the Biological Basis of Memory

- Pavlov believed that learning and memory are associated with physical changes in the brain. Karl Lashley conducted extensive research searching for the memory trace, but finally concluded that memories are distributed rather than localized. Richard Thompson showed the physical changes that are associated with a simple conditioned reflex in rabbits. Today it is believed that memories are both localized and distributed. Complex memories involve interrelated changes among many different brain areas.

- Research with the sea snail *Aplysia* has shown that acquiring a new conditioned reflex results in functional and structural changes in the neurons involved. These changes in the neurons create a memory circuit. Many researchers believe that similar changes occur in the human brain when memories are formed.

- Case studies of people with amnesia have provided important insights into the brain structures involved in normal human memory. Retrograde amnesia results when the consolidation of memories is disrupted. When the hippocampus is damaged or removed, anterograde amnesia results, as in the case of H.M. The hippocampus is involved in the processing of new episodic memories, and the amygdala seems to be involved in encoding the emotional qualities of memories.

Key Terms

memory (p. 196)

encoding (p. 196)

storage (p. 196)

retrieval (p. 196)

stage model of memory (p. 197)

sensory memory (p. 197)

short-term memory (working memory) (p. 197)

long-term memory (p. 198)

maintenance rehearsal (p. 200)

chunking (p. 201)

elaborative rehearsal (p. 202)

procedural information (p. 203)

episodic information (p. 203)

semantic information (p. 203)

clustering (p. 204)

semantic network model (p. 204)

retrieval (p. 205)

retrieval cue (p. 205)

retrieval cue failure (p. 206)

tip-of-the-tongue (TOT) experience (p. 206)

recall (p. 206)

cued recall (p. 207)

recognition (p. 207)

serial position effect (p. 207)

encoding specificity principle (p. 207)

context effect (p. 208)

state-dependent retrieval (p. 208)

mood-dependent retrieval (p. 208)

mood congruence (p. 209)

flashbulb memory (p. 209)

schema (p. 210)

source confusion (p. 212)

cryptomnesia (p. 213)

misinformation effect (p. 214)

forgetting (p. 215)

encoding failure (p. 217)

interference theory (p. 217)

retroactive interference (p. 217)

proactive interference (p. 217)

motivated forgetting (p. 218)

suppression (p. 218)

repression (p. 218)

decay theory (p. 221)

memory trace (p. 222)

amnesia (p. 225)

retrograde amnesia (p. 225)

memory consolidation (p. 225)

anterograde amnesia (p. 225)

Key People

Herman Ebbinghaus (1850–1909) German psychologist who originated the scientific study of forgetting; plotted the first "forgetting curve," which describes the basic pattern of forgetting learned information over time.

Karl Lashley (1890–1958) American physiological psychologist who attempted to find the specific brain location of particular memories.

Elizabeth F. Loftus (b. 1944) American psychologist who has conducted extensive research on the memory distortions that can occur in eyewitness testimony.

George Sperling (b. 1934) American psychologist who identified the duration of visual sensory memory in a series of classic experiments in 1960.

Richard F. Thompson (b. 1930) American psychologist and neuroscientist who has conducted extensive research on the neurobiological foundations of learning and memory.

CONCEPT REVIEW 6.1 Page 205

1. LTM
2. SM
3. STM
4. LTM
5. STM
6. SM
7. STM
8. SM
9. LTM

CONCEPT REVIEW 6.2 Page 210

1. c
2. a
3. c
4. d

CONCEPT REVIEW 6.3 Page 221

1. D
2. C
3. A
4. E
5. B

CONCEPT REVIEW 6.4 Page 224

1. George Sperling
2. Elizabeth Loftus
3. Herman Ebbinghaus
4. Karl Lashley
5. Richard F. Thompson

Thinking, Language, and Intelligence

Prologue: Mr. and Ms. Fix-It

"I found it! The rubber gasket between the sink and faucet is leaking!" Don yelled from under the kitchen sink.

"The *basket* is leaking!" our three-year old daughter, Laura, who was holding the flashlight, enthusiastically relayed to Sandy.

"The *basket* is leaking?" Sandy asked. "What basket?"

"No, it's called a *gasket*, not a basket, honey," Don explained to Laura.

"Can you fix it?" Sandy asked.

"Piece of cake," Don replied as he crawled out from under the sink. "Laura and I will run down to the hardware store and buy a new gasket."

Of course, the solution would *not* be that simple. "They don't sell *just* the gasket," the man at the hardware store explained. "You gotta buy a whole new faucet."

"What's that going to run me?"

"Kitchen faucets start at $39.95 plus tax," the hardware guy smiled. "Then you'll need some replacement tubing for when you weld the new faucet in place. You got a welding torch, don't you? If you don't, a plumber probably wouldn't charge more than $150 or so to install it, not including the cost of the parts."

"Let me think about it," Don replied, frowning.

"Why didn't we buy a new basket?" Laura asked as she and Don walked out of the hardware store.

"It's called a *gasket*, sweetie," Don explained. "It's just a piece of rubber that fits between two pieces of metal. It keeps the water that splashes around the faucet from dripping under the sink. Does that make sense?"

"I think so," Laura said thoughtfully. "Why didn't we buy one?"

"Because they want too much money for it," Don answered as he buckled Laura into her car seat.

As Laura chattered away on the drive home, Don mulled over calling a plumber. *A couple hundred bucks to replace a lousy piece of rubber. That's ridiculous.*

"We'll make one!" Don suddenly exclaimed.

"Make what, Daddy?" Laura responded, slightly startled.

"A new gasket! And best of all, Laura, it won't cost a cent!"

Less than five minutes later, Don and Laura were at a General Tire store. "Help yourself," the manager replied when Don asked if he could have a discarded inner tube. An hour later, the new "gasket" was in place—a piece of black rubber inner tube that Don had cut to the same shape as the original gasket. It worked like a charm. No drips.

"You missed your calling in life," Sandy quipped as Don stood basking in the glory of the moment.

"Hey, you just have to think creatively," Don smiled back.

Unfortunately, creative thinking is not always the answer. A few weeks later, when the upstairs toilet wouldn't flush properly, Mr. Fix-It spent almost two hours dismantling and lifting the entire toilet off the floor drain in search of the cause.

"You're sure you didn't flush one of your toys down the toilet?" Don asked Laura again.

"No, Daddy," Laura said solemnly, shaking her head, as she peered down the ominous-looking drain in the floor with her Barney flashlight.

"Well, I don't know what the hell is wrong with it," Don announced in frustration, wiping the sweat from his brow.

Sitting on the floor in the corner of the bathroom, Sandy flipped through the pages of a book called *The Complete Home Fix-It-Yourself Manual*. "Did you look at this book? There's a troubleshooting guide for toilets on this page."

"No, I did *not* look at it," Don huffed cynically. "I *know* how to unblock a toilet. First, you try a plunger. If that doesn't work, then you take the toilet off to find whatever is blocking the drain."

"That's what it lists to try *third* in this book," Sandy pointed out calmly. "What was the water level inside the tank?"

"It was a couple inches down from the fill line," Don answered.

"Well, it says here that if the water level is too low, the toilet bowl will drain sluggishly," Sandy explained matter-of-factly, then glanced up. "Did you try raising the water level to the fill line *before* you took the toilet apart?"

Silence loomed in the bathroom.

It was well over an hour later that Laura excitedly called downstairs to Sandy: "Momma! Momma! Come see! Daddy fixed the toilet!"

"What was wrong with it?" Sandy innocently asked as she watched the toilet flush perfectly.

"The water level was just too low," Don replied, then cleared his throat.

"You're kidding!" Sandy feigned disbelief. "That must have been why it was listed as the *first* thing to check in that troubleshooting guide."

"I think you missed your calling in life," Don muttered.

"Well, you know what I always say: 'When in doubt, look it up!'" Sandy smiled.

All of us rely on a variety of cognitive processes to imagine, think, make decisions, and solve problems in daily life. In this chapter, we'll look at the broad issue of how we think, including how we solve problems, make decisions, and occasionally arrive at creative solutions. In the process, we'll come back to this story of Mr. and Ms. Fix-It to illustrate several important concepts and ideas.

Introduction

Thinking, Language, and Intelligence

Thinking typically involves the manipulation of mental images and concepts. What are some of the basic characteristics of mental images, and how do we manipulate them? What are concepts, and how are they formed?

cognition
The mental activities involved in acquiring, retaining, and using knowledge.

thinking
The manipulation of mental representations of information in order to draw inferences and conclusions.

mental image
A mental representation of objects or events that are not physically present.

Cognition is a general term that refers to the mental activities involved in acquiring, retaining, and using knowledge (Matlin, 1989). In previous chapters, we've looked at fundamental cognitive processes like perception, learning, and memory. These processes are critical in order for us to acquire and retain new knowledge.

In this chapter we will focus on how we *use* that knowledge to think, solve problems, make decisions, and use language. As you'll see, such cognitive abilities are widely regarded as key dimensions of *intelligence*—a concept that we will also explore.

The Building Blocks of Thought:

Mental Imagery and Concepts

In the most general sense, *thinking* is involved in all conscious mental activity, whether we are acquiring new knowledge, remembering, planning ahead, or daydreaming (Holyoak & Spellman, 1993). More narrowly, we can say that **thinking** involves manipulating mental representations of information in order to draw inferences and conclusions (Kosslyn, 1995). Thinking, then, involves active mental processes and is often directed toward some goal, purpose, or conclusion.

What exactly is it that we think *with*? Thinking often involves the manipulation of two forms of mental representations: *mental images* and *concepts*. We'll look first at mental images.

A Flower for Your Thoughts? What types of cognitive activities might be involved in growing an elaborate flower garden? Planning, forming mental images, making decisions, and problem solving are some of the mental activities involved.

Mental Images

When you read the chapter's prologue, did you see a mental picture of a little girl peering down a cavernous floor drain with her Barney the dinosaur flashlight? Or Sandy sitting in the corner of the bathroom, looking at the home repair manual? The stories we tell in our prologues typically lend themselves to the creation of a mental image. Formally, a **mental image** is a mental representation of objects or events that are not physically present.

We often rely on mental images to accomplish some cognitive task (Farah, 1995). For example, try reciting the letters of the alphabet that only include curved lines. To accomplish this task, you have to mentally visualize and then inspect an image of each letter of the alphabet.

Note that mental imagery is not strictly limited to visual "pictures." Most people are able to form images that involve senses other than vision (McKellar, 1972). For example, you can probably easily create a mental representation for the taste and texture of a chocolate milkshake, or the feel of wet clothing sticking to your skin. All the same, most research on mental images has involved how we manipulate visual images (Ochsner & Kosslyn, 1994). Thus, we'll focus on visual images in our discussion.

Do people manipulate mental images in the same way that they manipulate their visual images of actual objects? Suppose we gave you a map of the United States and asked you to visually locate San Francisco. Then suppose we asked you to fix your gaze on another city. If the other city was far away from San Francisco (like New York), it would take you longer to visually locate it than if it was located close by (like Los Angeles). If you were scanning a *mental* image rather than a visual image of an actual map, would it also take you longer to scan across a greater distance?

Participants in a classic study by Stephen Kosslyn and his colleagues (1978) first memorized a map of a fictitious island with distinct locations, like a lake, a hut, and grass (see Figure 7.1). After the map was removed, subjects were asked to imagine a specific location on the island, such as the sandy beach. Then a second location, such as the rock, was named. The participants mentally scanned across their mental image of the map and pushed a button when they reached the rock.

The researchers found that the amount of time it took to mentally scan to the new location was directly related to the distance between the two points. The greater the distance between the two points, the longer it took to scan the mental image of the map (Kosslyn & others, 1978).

It seems, then, that we tend to scan a mental image in much the same way that we visually scan an actual image (Ochsner & Kosslyn, 1994). However, we don't just look at mental images in our minds. Sometimes thinking involves the *manipulation* of mental images before we can arrive at an answer. For example, try the problem in Figure 7.2.

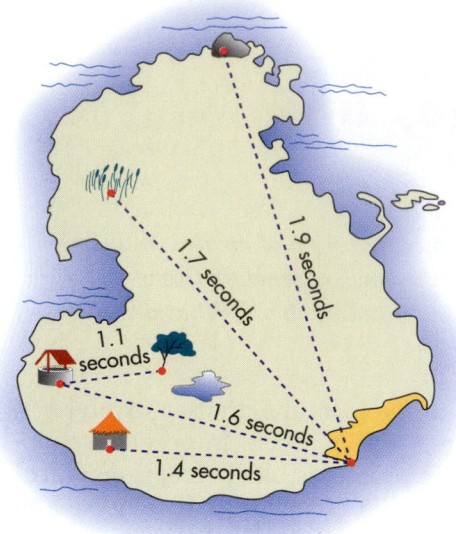

FIGURE 7.1 Mentally Scanning Images
This is a reduced version of the map used by Stephen Kosslyn and his colleagues (1978) to study the scanning of mental images. After subjects memorized the map, the map was removed. Subjects then mentally scanned from one location to another. As you can see from the average scanning times, it took subjects longer to scan greater distances on their mental images of the map, just as it takes longer to visually scan greater distances on an actual map.

FIGURE 7.2 Manipulating Mental Images
Two of these threes are backward. Which ones?

It probably took you longer to determine that the *3* in the middle was backward than to determine that the *3* on the far left was backward. Determining which of the *3*'s were backward required you to mentally *rotate* each one to an upright position. Just as it takes time to rotate a physical object, it takes time to mentally rotate an image. Furthermore, the greater the degree of rotation required, the longer it takes you to rotate the image mentally (Stillings & others, 1987). Thus, it probably took you longer to mentally rotate the *3* in the middle, which you had to rotate 180 degrees, than it did to mentally rotate the *3* on the far left, which you only had to rotate 60 degrees.

Collectively, such research seems to indicate that we manipulate mental images in much the same way that we manipulate the actual objects they represent (Kosslyn & Sussman, 1995). However, mental images are not perfect duplicates of our actual sensory experience. The mental images that we use in thinking have some features in common with actual visual images, but they are not like photographs. Instead, they are *memories* of visual images. And, like memories, visual images are actively constructed and subject to error (Reisberg & Chambers, 1991).

concepts
The mental categories of objects or ideas based on properties that they share.

formal concept
A mental category that is formed by learning the rules or features that define it.

natural concept
A mental category that is formed as a result of everyday experience.

prototype
The most typical instance of a particular concept.

Concepts

Along with mental images, thinking also involves the use of concepts. A **concept** is a mental category we have formed to group objects, events, or situations that share similar features or characteristics. Concepts provide a kind of mental shorthand, economizing the cognitive effort required for thinking and communication.

Using concepts makes it easier to communicate with others, remember information, and learn new information. For example, the concept *food* might include anything from a sardine to a fresh rutabaga. Although very different, we can still group rutabagas and sardines together because they share the central feature of being edible. If someone introduces us to a new delicacy and tells us it is *food,* we immediately know that it is something to eat—even if it is something we've never seen before.

Adding to the efficiency of our thinking is our tendency to organize the concepts we hold into orderly hierarchies composed of main categories and subcategories. Thus a very general concept, like *furniture,* can be mentally divided into a variety of subcategories: *tables, chairs, lamps,* and so forth. As we learn the key properties that define general concepts, we also learn how members of the concept are related to one another (Reed, 1996).

How are concepts formed? When you form a concept by learning the *rules* or *features* that define the particular concept, it is called a **formal concept.** Children are taught the specific rules or features that define many simple formal concepts, such as geometric shapes. These defining rules or features can be either simple or complex. In either case, the rules are logical but rigid. If the defining features or *attributes* are present, then the object is included as a member or example of that concept. For some formal concepts this rigid all-or-nothing categorization procedure works well. For example, a substance can be categorized as a *solid, liquid,* or *gas.* The rules defining these formal concepts are very clear-cut.

However, as psychologist Eleanor Rosch (1973) pointed out, the features that define categories of natural objects and events in everyday life are seldom as clear-cut as the features that define formal concepts. A **natural concept** is one that is formed as a result of everyday experience rather than by logically determining whether an object or event fits a specific set of rules. Rosch suggested that, unlike formal concepts, natural concepts have "fuzzy boundaries." That is, the rules or attributes that define the natural concept are not always sharply defined.

Because natural concepts have fuzzy boundaries, it's often easier to classify some members of natural concepts than others (Rosch & Mervis, 1975). To illustrate this point, think about the defining features or rules that you usually associate with the natural concept of *vehicle.* With virtually no hesitation, you can say that *car, truck,* and *bus* are all examples of this natural concept. How about *sled? wheelbarrow? raft? elevator?* It probably took you a few seconds to determine whether these objects are also *vehicles.* Why are some members of natural concepts easier to classify than others?

According to Rosch (1978), some members are better representatives of a natural concept than others. The "best," or most typical, instance of a particular concept is called a **prototype** (Mervis & Rosch, 1981; Rosch, 1978). We tend to determine whether an object is an instance of a natural concept by comparing it to the prototype, rather than by logically evaluating whether the defining features are present.

The more closely an item matches the prototype, the more quickly we can identify it as being an example of that concept. For example, it usually takes us longer to identify an *olive* or a *coconut* as being a *fruit* because they are so dissimilar from the prototypes we typically think of as fruit, like apples and oranges (Rosch, 1975). (See Table 7.1.)

TABLE 7.1 From Prototypes to Atypical Examples

Vehicles	Fruit
car	orange
truck	apple
bus	banana
motorcycle	peach
train	pear
trolley car	apricot
bicycle	plum
airplane	grape
boat	strawberry
tractor	grapefruit
cart	pineapple
wheelchair	blueberry
tank	lemon
raft	watermelon
sled	honeydew
horse	pomegranate
blimp	date
skates	coconut
wheelbarrow	tomato
elevator	olive

SOURCE: Rosch & Mervis, 1975.

The first items listed under each general concept are the ones that most people tend to think of as the prototype examples of that concept. As you move farther down the list, the items become progressively more dissimilar from the prototype examples.

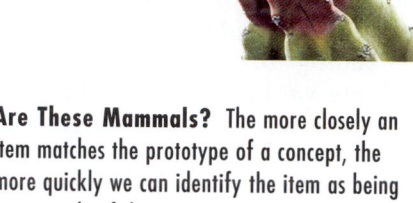

Mental images and concepts help us impose order on the phenomena we encounter and think about. We often rely on this knowledge when we engage in complex cognitive tasks, such as solving problems and making decisions, which we'll consider next.

Are These Mammals? The more closely an item matches the prototype of a concept, the more quickly we can identify the item as being an example of that concept. You would probably identify a dog or a cow as a "mammal" more quickly than a bat or dolphin.

Identifying the Building Blocks of Thought

For each of the following, decide which term best applies. Choose from: formal concept, natural concept, prototype, or mental image.

1. You are asked how many windows you have in your home. To answer this question, you probably rely on a _____.

2. In question 1, the word *home* is used to describe the place where you usually sleep, eat, and keep your belongings. *Home* is an example of a _____.

3. When Mary is asked what object comes to mind in response to the word *furniture*, she immediately says, "Chair." For Mary, *chair* is a _____.

4. In his geometry class, Karl has learned the rules and features that define a parallelogram. Karl has learned a _____.

Solving Problems and Making Decisions

Problem solving refers to thinking and behavior directed toward attaining a goal that is not readily available. What are advantages and disadvantages of each problem-solving strategy? How can functional fixedness and mental set interfere with problem solving?

problem solving
Thinking and behavior directed toward attaining a goal that is not readily available.

Problem solving refers to thinking and behavior directed toward attaining a goal that is not readily available. From fixing flat tires to figuring out how to pay for college classes, we engage in the cognitive task of problem solving so routinely that we often don't even notice the processes we follow.

Problem-Solving Strategies

As a general rule, people tend to attack a problem in an organized or systematic way. Usually, the strategy we select is influenced by the nature of the problem and the amount of time we're willing to invest in solving it. In this section, we'll look at some of the common strategies used in problem solving.

Trial and Error

The strategy of **trial and error** involves actually trying a variety of solutions and eliminating those that don't work. When there is a limited range of possible solutions, trial and error can be a useful problem-solving strategy. If you were trying to develop a new spaghetti recipe, for example, you might use trial and error to fine-tune the seasonings.

When the range of possible answers or solutions is large, however, trial and error can be very time-consuming. For example, our friend Thomas typically learns new computer programs by trial and error. Rather than read the manual, he'll spend hours trying different menu commands to see if he can make the software do what it's supposed to do.

DRABBLE

Algorithms

Unlike trial and error, an **algorithm** is a procedure or method that, when followed step by step, always produces the correct solution. Mathematical formulas are an example of algorithms, like the formula used to convert temperatures from Celsius to Fahrenheit (multiply C by nine-fifths, then add 32).

Even though an algorithm may be guaranteed to eventually produce a solution, using an algorithm is not always practical. For example, imagine that you find a combination lock with no combination attached. Using an algorithm will eventually produce the correct combination. You can start with 0–0–0, then try 0–0–1, followed by 0–0–2, and so forth, and systematically work your way through combinations to 36–36–36. But this solution would take a while, because there are 46,656 potential combinations to try. So while using an algorithm to generate the correct combination for the combination lock is guaranteed to work eventually, it's not a very practical approach to solving this particular problem.

Heuristics

In contrast to algorithms, a **heuristic** is a general rule-of-thumb strategy that may or may not work. Although heuristic strategies are not guaranteed to solve a given problem, they tend to simplify problem solving because they let you reduce the number of possible solutions. With a more limited range of solutions, you can use trial and error to arrive eventually at the correct one.

trial and error
A problem-solving strategy that involves attempting different solutions and eliminating those that do not work.

algorithm
A problem-solving strategy that involves following a specific rule, procedure, or method that inevitably produces the correct solution.

heuristic
A problem-solving strategy that involves following a general rule of thumb to reduce the number of possible solutions.

GARFIELD®

Here's an example: Creating footnotes is described somewhere in the manual for a word-processing computer program. If you use the algorithm of reading every page of the manual, you're guaranteed to solve the problem eventually. But you can greatly simplify your task by using the heuristic of looking up footnotes in the index. This strategy does not guarantee success, because the procedure may not be listed in the index.

The prologue contained a couple of examples of heuristics. For example, to solve the problem of the malfunctioning toilet, Sandy relied on her favorite heuristic: she looked for a solution in a book on the subject. Of course, this particular heuristic will work only when there's a book available that describes how to solve a specific problem.

One common heuristic is to break a problem into a series of *subgoals* (Reed, 1996). This strategy is often used in writing a term paper. Choosing a topic, locating information about the topic, and so on becomes a series of subproblems. As you solve each subproblem, you move closer to solving the larger problem.

Another useful heuristic involves *working backward* from the goal. Starting with the end point, you determine the steps necessary to reach your final goal. For example, when making a budget, people often start off with the goal of spending no more than a certain total each month, then work backward to determine how much of the target amount they will allot for each category of expenses.

FIGURE 7.3 A Demonstration of Insightful Solutions

The solution to each of the following problems is often characterized by sudden flashes of insight. See if you have the "That's it!" experience in solving the following problems without looking at the solutions on page 242.

(Problem 1 adapted from Ashcraft, 1994. Problem 2 adapted from Sternberg, 1986.)

Problem 1 Six drinking glasses are lined up in a row. The first three are full of water, the last three are empty. By handling and moving only one glass, change the arrangement so that no full glass is next to another full one, and no empty glass is next to another empty one.

Problem 2 A man who lived in a small town married twenty different women in that same town. All of them are still living, and he never divorced any of them. Yet he broke no laws. How could he do this?

Insight and Intuition

The solution to some problems seems to arrive in a sudden realization, or flash of **insight,** that happens after you mull a problem over (Kaplan & Simon, 1990). Sometimes an insight will occur when you recognize how the problem is similar to a previously solved problem. Or an insight can involve the sudden realization that an object can be used in a novel way, such as Don's realization that he could make an inexpensive replacement gasket for the kitchen sink from a discarded inner tube. Try solving the problems in Figure 7.3.

Insights rarely occur through the conscious manipulation of concepts or information (Schooler & others, 1993). In fact, we're usually not aware of the thought processes that led to an insight. Increasingly, cognitive psychologists and neuroscientists are investigating nonconscious processes, including unconscious problem solving, insight, and intuition (Bechara & others, 1997; Underwood, 1996). **Intuition** refers to coming to a conclusion or making a judgment without conscious awareness of the thought processes involved.

Canadian psychologist Kenneth Bowers and his colleagues (1990) have proposed a two-stage model of intuition. In the first stage, called the *guiding stage,* you perceive a pattern in the information you're considering, but not consciously. The perception of such patterns is based on your expertise in a given area and your memories of related information.

intuition
Coming to a conclusion or making a judgment without conscious awareness of the thought processes involved.

insight
The sudden realization of how a problem can be solved.

In the second stage, the *integrative stage,* a representation of the pattern becomes conscious, usually in the form of a hunch or hypothesis. At this point, conscious, analytic thought processes take over. You systematically attempt to prove or disprove the hypothesis. For example, an experienced doctor might integrate both obvious and subtle cues to recognize a pattern in a patient's symptoms, a pattern which takes the form of a hunch or educated guess. Once the hunch is consciously formulated, she might order lab tests to confirm or disprove her tentative diagnosis.

An intuitive hunch, then, is a new idea that integrates new information with existing knowledge stored in long-term memory. Such hunches are likely to be accurate only in contexts in which you already have a broad base of knowledge and experience (Benderly, 1989).

Obstacles to Solving Problems:

Functional Fixedness and Mental Sets

When we view objects as functioning only in the usual or customary way, we're engaging in a tendency called **functional fixedness.** Functional fixedness often prevents us from seeing the full range of ways in which an object can be used. (See Figure 7.4.)

Here's an example of functional fixedness. When pilots fly through clouds, they watch an instrument called an "artificial horizon," which shows an outline of an airplane against a horizontal line that represents the horizon. By watching the movement of the outline, they can tell if the aircraft is tilting up or down, or banking to the left or right.

When Don was first learning to fly, he was publicly chastised by a salty old flight instructor for failing to wear a St. Christopher's medal around his neck when flying. Since St. Christopher is the patron saint of travelers, Don assumed that the flight instructor was a bit superstitious. Don's functional fixedness kept him from thinking of any other reason for a pilot to wear a St. Christopher's medal. Finally, Don asked the instructor.

It turned out that a St. Christopher's medal or any other object on a chain can be used to create a makeshift artificial horizon if the flight instrument should fail. You simply drape the chain over the throttle stick. If the aircraft starts pointing down, the medal swings forward; if the aircraft starts pointing upward, the medal swings back. When the aircraft banks, the medal swings to one side or the other. This novel use of an object could literally save the lives of the people in the plane.

Another common obstacle to problem solving is **mental set**—the tendency to persist in solving problems with solutions that have worked in the past. Obviously, if a solution has worked in the past, there's good reason to consider using it again. However, if we approach a problem with a rigid mental set, we may not see other possible solutions. For example, Don's initial attempt to fix the toilet reflected his mental set that when the water in a toilet doesn't drain properly, the drain is probably clogged. Since using a plunger had solved such problems in the past, it made sense to try that solution again.

Mental sets can sometimes suggest a useful heuristic. But they can also prevent us from coming up with new, and possibly simpler or more effective, solutions. If we try to be flexible in our thinking and overcome the tendency toward mental sets, we can often identify simpler solutions to many common problems. Because Sandy did not have any particular mental sets about malfunctioning toilets, she was able to search for and identify an alternative solution that not only worked but was also much simpler than Don's attempt to solve the problem.

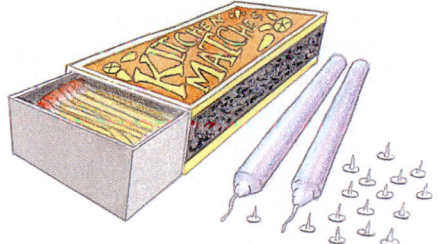

FIGURE 7.4 Overcoming Functional Fixedness

Here's a problem for you to solve: You are given two candles, some thumbtacks, and a box of matches. Using just these objects, try to figure out how to mount the candles on a wall. (Solution is on p. 242.)

(Adapted from Duncker, 1945.)

functional fixedness
The tendency to view objects as functioning only in their usual or customary way.

mental set
The tendency to persist in solving problems with solutions that have worked in the past.

| Problem 1 | Pour the water in glass number 2 into glass number 5. |
| Problem 2 | The man is a minister. |

Solutions to the Problems in Figure 7.3

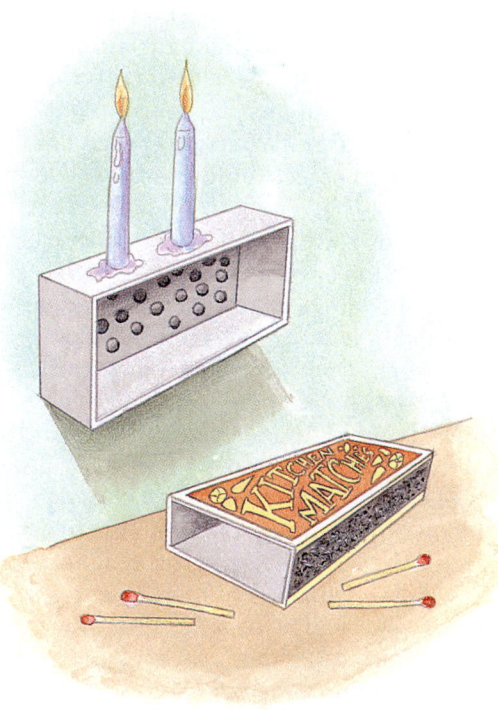

Solution to Figure 7.4

Decisions, Decisions, Decisions

We use a variety of cognitive strategies to make decisions. What are the single-feature model, the additive model, and the elimination by aspects model of decision making? Under what conditions is each strategy most appropriate?

Who hasn't felt like flipping a coin when faced with a complicated decision? Most of the decisions we make in everyday life are relatively minor, but occasionally we have to make a decision where much more is at stake. When a decision is important or complex, we're more likely to invest time, effort, and other resources in considering different options. Doing so can increase our chances of making a correct decision. But how do we make decisions?

Decision-Making Strategies

The decision-making process becomes complicated when each option involves the consideration of several features. What do you do when each option has pros and cons?

The Single-Feature Model One decision-making strategy is called the *single-feature model*. In order to simplify the choice among many alternatives, you base your decision on a single feature (Reed, 1996). When the decision is a minor one, the single-feature model can be a good decision-making strategy. For example, you could simplify your decision among an entire aisle of laundry detergents by deciding to buy the cheapest brand. When a decision is important or complex, however, making decisions on the basis of a single feature can increase the riskiness of the decision.

The Additive Model A better strategy for complex decisions is to systematically evaluate the important features of each option. One such decision-making model is called the *additive model* (Reed, 1996). In this model, you first generate a list of the factors that are most important to you. Then, you rate each option on each factor using an arbitrary scale, such as –5 to +5. Finally, you add up the ratings for each option. This strategy can often reveal the best overall choice. If some factors are more important than others, you can emphasize the more important factors by multiplying the rating by 2.

Taking the time to apply the additive model to important decisions can greatly improve your decision making because it provides a logical strategy for identifying the most acceptable choice among a range of possible decisions. Although we seldom formally calculate the subjective value of individual features for different options, we often informally use the additive model by comparing two choices feature by feature (Reed, 1996). The alternative with the "best" collection of features is then selected.

The Elimination by Aspects Model Psychologist Amos Tversky (1972) proposed another decision-making model called the *elimination by aspects model*. Using this model, we evaluate all the alternatives on one characteristic at a time, typically starting with the feature we consider most important. If a particular alternative fails to meet that criterion, we scratch it off our list of possible choices even if it possesses other desirable attributes. As the range of possible choices is narrowed down, we continue to compare the remaining alternatives, one feature at a time, until just one alternative is left.

For example, suppose you wanted to buy a new computer. You might initially eliminate all the models that were incompatible with your existing software, then the models that were outside your budget, and so forth. Continuing in this fashion, you progressively narrow down the range of possible choices to the one choice that satisfies all your criteria.

availability heuristic
A strategy in which the likelihood of an event is estimated on the basis of how easily other instances of the event are available in memory.

Good decision makers adapt their strategy to the demands of the specific situation (Payne & others, 1993). If there are just a few choices and features to compare, we tend to use the additive method, at least informally. However, when the decision is complex, involving the comparison of many choices that have multiple features, people often use *both* strategies (Reed, 1996). That is, we usually begin by focusing on the critical features, using the elimination by aspects strategy to quickly narrow down the range of acceptable choices. Once we have narrowed the list of choices down to a more manageable "short list," we tend to use the additive model to make a final decision.

Decisions Involving Uncertainty:
Estimating the Probability of Events

Some decisions must be made under conditions of uncertainty, in which we must estimate the probability of a particular event's occurring. How do we use the availability and representativeness heuristics to help us estimate the likelihood of an event?

Some decisions involve a high degree of uncertainty. In these cases, you need to make a decision, but you are unable to predict with certainty that a given event will occur. Instead, you have to estimate the probability of an event's occurring. But how do you actually make that estimation?

For example, imagine that you're running late for a very important appointment. You may be faced with this decision: Should I risk a speeding ticket to get to the appointment on time? In this case, you would have to estimate the probability of a particular event's occurring—getting pulled over for speeding.

In such instances, we often estimate the likelihood that certain events will occur, then gamble. In deciding what the odds are that a particular gamble will go our way, we tend to rely on two rule-of-thumb heuristics to help us estimate the likelihood of events (Tversky & Kahneman, 1982). These two heuristics are the *availability heuristic* and the *representativeness heuristic*.

The Availability Heuristic

When we use the **availability heuristic,** we estimate the likelihood of an event on the basis of how easily other instances of the event are available in our memory. When instances of an event are easily recalled, we tend to consider the event as being more likely to occur. So we're less likely to exceed the speed limit if we can easily remember recent occurrences of other drivers getting speeding tickets, such as having heard that a friend got a speeding ticket.

However, when a rare event makes a vivid impression on us, we may overestimate its likelihood (Tversky & Kahneman, 1982). This is why companies like Publisher's Clearinghouse and American Family Publishers run so many TV commercials showing that lucky person who won the $10 million sweepstakes prize. A vivid memory is created, which leads viewers to an inaccurate estimate of the likelihood that the event will happen to them.

The key point here is that the less accurately our memory of an event reflects the actual frequency of the event, the less accurate our estimate of the event's likelihood will be. That's why the sweepstakes commercials don't show the other 50 million people staring dejectedly at their mailboxes because they did *not* win the $10 million.

Vivid Images and the Availability Heuristic More than a hundred people died when this jet broke up while landing in Sioux City, Iowa. After media coverage of a plane crash, we may exaggerate the dangers of air travel, overestimating the likelihood that the plane we're traveling in might crash. How does the availability heuristic explain this phenomenon?

representativeness heuristic
A strategy in which the likelihood of an event is estimated by comparing how similar it is to the typical prototype of the event.

The Representativeness Heuristic

The other heuristic we often use to make estimates is called the **representativeness heuristic** (Kahneman & Tversky, 1982). Here, we estimate an event's likelihood by comparing how similar its essential features are to our prototype of the event. (Remember, a *prototype* is the most typical example of an object or an event.)

To go back to our example of deciding whether to speed, we are more likely to risk speeding if we think that we're somehow significantly different from the prototype of the driver who gets a speeding ticket. If our prototype is a teenager driving a flashy, high-performance car, and we're an adult driving a minivan with a baby seat, then we will probably estimate the likelihood of our getting a speeding ticket as low.

Like the availability heuristic, the representativeness heuristic can lead to inaccurate judgments. Consider the following description:

> *Maria is a perceptive, sensitive, introspective woman. She is very articulate, but measures her words carefully. Once she's certain she knows what she wants to say, she expresses herself easily and confidently. She has a strong preference to work alone.*

Given the above description, which is more likely: that Maria is a successful fiction writer, or that Maria is a nurse? Most people guess that she is a successful fiction writer. Why? Because the description seems to mesh with what many people think of as the typical characteristics of a writer.

However, when you compare the number of nurses (which is very large) to the number of successful female fiction writers (which is very small), it's actually much more likely that Maria is a nurse. Thus, the representativeness heuristic can produce faulty estimates if (1) we fail to consider possible variations from the prototype or (2) we fail to consider the approximate number of prototypes that actually exist.

Box 7.1, "The Persistence of Unwarranted Beliefs," discusses some of the other psychological factors that can influence the way we evaluate evidence, make decisions, and draw conclusions.

CONCEPT REVIEW 7.2

Problem-Solving and Decision-Making Strategies

Identify the strategy used in each of the following examples. Choose from: (A) trial and error, (B) algorithm, (C) heuristic, (D) insight, (E) representativeness heuristic, (F) availability heuristic, (G) single-feature model.

_____ **1.** As you try to spell the word *deceive,* you recite "*i* before *e* except after *c*."

_____ **2.** You are asked to complete the following sequence: O, T, T, F, F, ____ , ____ , ____ , ____ , ____ . You suddenly realize that the answer is obvious: S,S,E,N,T.

_____ **3.** One by one, Professor Goldstein tries each key on the keychain until she finds the one that opens her new filing cabinet.

_____ **4.** A scientist tests thousands of different chemical combinations, trying to find the one that will work best as a nonpolluting fuel.

_____ **5.** After seeing news reports about a teenager being killed in a freak accident on a roller coaster, Angela refuses to allow her son to go to an amusement park with his friends.

_____ **6.** Jacob decided to rent an apartment at the apartment complex that was the closest to his college campus.

CRITICAL THINKING 7.1

The Persistence of Unwarranted Beliefs

Throughout this text, we've shown how many pseudoscientific claims have been scientifically investigated and disproven. However, once a belief in a pseudoscience or paranormal phenomenon is established, the presentation of contradictory evidence often has little impact.

Several psychological studies have explored how people deal with evidence—specifically, evidence that contradicts their beliefs (see Zusne & Jones, 1989; Ross & Anderson, 1982). The four obstacles to logical thinking described below can account for much of the persistence of unwarranted beliefs in pseudosciences.

The Belief-Bias Effect

The *belief-bias effect* occurs when people accept only the evidence that conforms to their belief, rejecting or ignoring any evidence that doesn't (Matlin, 1989). For example, in a study conducted by Warren Jones and Dan Russell (1980), ESP-believers and ESP-disbelievers watched two attempts at telepathic communication. In each attempt, a "receiver" tried to indicate what card the "sender" was holding.

In reality, both attempts were rigged. One attempt was designed to appear to be a successful demonstration of telepathy, with a significant number of accurate responses. The other attempt was designed to convincingly demonstrate failure. In this case, the number of accurate guesses was no more than chance and could be produced by simple random guessing.

Following the demonstration, the subjects were asked what they believed had taken place. Both believers and disbelievers indicated that ESP had occurred in the successful attempt. But only the believers said that ESP had *also* taken place in the clearly *unsuccessful* attempt. In other words, the ESP-believers ignored the evidence in the failed attempt. This is the essence of the belief-bias effect.

Confirmation Bias

Confirmation bias is the strong tendency to search for information or evidence that confirms a belief, while making little or no effort to search for information that might disprove the belief (Gilovich, 1997). For example, we tend to read the newpaper and magazine columns of editorial writers who interpret events from our perspective and to avoid the columns of writers who don't see things our way.

The Fallacy of Positive Instances

The *fallacy of positive instances* is the tendency to remember uncommon events that seem to confirm our beliefs, while forgetting events that disconfirm our beliefs. Often, the occurrence is really nothing more than coincidence. For example, you find yourself thinking of an old friend. A few moments later, the phone rings and it's him. You remember this seemingly telepathic event, but forget all the times that you've thought of your old friend and he did *not* call. In other words, you remember the positive instance but fail to notice the negative instances when the anticipated event did not occur (Gilovich,1997).

The Overestimation Effect

The tendency to overestimate the rarity of events is referred to as the *overestimation effect*. Suppose a "psychic" comes to your class, which consists of 23 students. Using his psychic abilities, he "senses" that two people in the class were born on the same day. A quick survey finds that, indeed, two people share the same month and day of birth. This is pretty impressive evidence of clairvoyance, right? After all, what are the odds that two people in a class of 23 would have the same birthday?

When we perform this "psychic" demonstration in class, our students usually estimate that it is very unlikely that 2 people in a class of 23 will share a birthday. In reality, the odds are *1 out of 2,* or 50-50 (Cole, 1995; Alcock, 1981). Our students' overestimation of the rarity of this event is an example of the *overestimation effect*.

Thinking Critically About the Evidence

On the one hand, it is important to keep an open mind. Simply dismissing an idea as "impossible" shuts out the consideration of evidence for new ideas or phenomena. At one time, for example, scientists thought it impossible that rocks could fall from the sky (Hines, 1988).

On the other hand, the critical thinking skills we described in Chapter 1 are useful in evaluating all claims, including pseudoscientific or paranormal claims. In particular, it's important to stress again that good critical thinkers strive to evaluate *all* the available evidence before reaching a conclusion, not just the evidence that supports what they want to believe.

language
A system for combining arbitrary symbols to produce an infinite number of meaningful statements.

Language and Thought

Language is a system for combining arbitrary symbols to produce an infinite number of meaningful statements. What are five characteristics of language? How does language affect thinking? Can animals use language?

The human capacity for language is surely one of the most remarkable of all our cognitive abilities. With little effort, you produce hundreds of new sentences every day. And you're able to understand the vast majority of the thousands of words contained in this chapter without consulting a dictionary.

The primary function of language is, of course, to communicate. Human language has many special qualities—qualities that make it flexible, versatile, and complex. **Language** can be formally defined as a system for combining arbitrary symbols to produce an infinite number of meaningful statements. We'll begin our discussion of language and thought by describing these special characteristics of language. In Chapter 9, we'll discuss language development.

The Characteristics of Language

The purpose of language is to communicate—to express meaningful information in a way that can be understood by others. To do so, language requires the use of *symbols*. These symbols may be sounds, written words, or, as in American Sign Language, formalized gestures.

A few symbols may be similar in form to the meaning that they signify, such as the English words *boom* or *pop*. However, for the vast majority of words, the connection between the symbol and the meaning is completely *arbitrary* (Pinker, 1995). For example, *ton* is a small word that stands for a vast quantity, while *millimicron* is a large word that stands for a very small quantity. Because the relationship between the symbol and its meaning is arbitrary, language is tremendously flexible (Ashcraft, 1994). New words can be invented, and the meanings of words can change and evolve (Pinker, 1994).

The word duck does not look like a duck, walk like a duck, or quack like a duck, but refers to a duck all the same, because the members of a language community, as children, all memorized the pairing [between a sound and a meaning.]

Steven Pinker (1995)

A second important characteristic of language is that the meaning of these symbols is *shared* by others who speak the same language. That is, speakers of the same language agree on the connection between the sound and what it symbolizes. Consequently, a foreign language sounds like a stream of meaningless sounds because we do not share the memory of the connection between the arbitrary sounds and the concrete meanings they symbolize.

Third, language is a highly structured system that follows specific rules. Every language has its own unique *syntax,* or rules for combining words. Although you're usually unaware of these rules as you're speaking or writing, you immediately notice when a rule has been violated.

The rules of language help determine the meaning that is being communicated. For example, word-order rules are very important in determining the meaning of an English phrase. "The boy ate the giant pumpkin" has an entirely different meaning than "The giant pumpkin ate the boy." In other languages, meaning may be conveyed by different rule-based distinctions, such as the particular pronouns, the class or category of word, or word endings (Hunt & Agnoli, 1991).

A fourth important characteristic of language is that it is creative, or *generative*. That is, you can generate an infinite number of new and different phrases and sentences (Anderson, 1995).

American Sign Language American Sign Language, used by the hearing impaired, meets all the formal requirements for language, including syntax, displacement, and generativity.

A final important characteristic of human language is called *displacement:* you can communicate meaningfully about ideas, objects, and activities that are not physically present. You can refer to activities that will take place in the future, that took place in the past, or that will take place only if certain conditions are met ("If you get that promotion, maybe we can afford a new car."). You can also carry on a vivid conversation about abstract ideas ("What is justice?") or strictly imaginary topics ("If you were going to spend a year in a space station orbiting Mars, what would you bring along?").

How Language Influences Thinking

All your cognitive abilities are involved in understanding and producing language. You interpret the words you hear or read (or see, in the case of American Sign Language) through the use of perception. Using learning and memory, you acquire and remember the meaning of words. You use language to help you reason, represent and solve problems, and make decisions (Polk & Newell, 1995).

Language can influence thinking in several ways (Matlin, 1985). In this section, we'll consider just a few of the ways in which language affects cognitive processes, including memory and our perception of other people.

Language and Memory

Language can affect our thoughts by influencing what we remember. As a demonstration, spend a few moments looking at the ten patterns of typing symbols in the margin. Then, without looking back, reproduce as many of the patterns as you can on a separate sheet of paper.

You probably found it difficult to reproduce the patterns exactly. Now look at the solution printed at the bottom of the page, which tells you what each pattern means. These combinations of typing symbols are called "smilies" or "emoticons." They are used to represent facial expressions, gestures, and emotions when people communicate by computer in on-line conversations or via electronic mail. In effect, these symbols function as emotional signposts in on-line conversations (A. Nelson, 1995). Once you learn the distinctive name for each pattern, you should find them easier to remember—and reproduce. The same is true of other patterns (Ellis & Hunt, 1993).

1.	:-D	**6.**	:-)
2.	:-(O)	**7.**	:-P
3.	:-(	**8.**	:-&
4.	;-)	**9.**	=:-o
5.	[ ]	**10.**	:-x

1. laughing; 2. yelling; 3. frown; 4. wink; 5. hug; 6. smile; 7. sticking out tongue; 8. tongue-tied; 9. EEK!; 10. My lips are sealed.

Language and Social Perception

Another important way in which language can influence thought has to do with our social perceptions of others. Consider the different images produced in your mind by these pairs of terms:

ambulance chaser	vs.	personal injury lawyer
statuesque brunette	vs.	tall, dark-haired woman
grease monkey	vs.	automotive technician

The nuances of words influence our social perceptions of others, reinforcing or minimizing negative stereotypes. Language that promotes stereotypical thinking can encourage discrimination against women, the elderly, and minorities or members of ethnic groups. In Chapter 11, we'll discuss the effects of stereotypes in more detail.

CULTURE AND HUMAN BEHAVIOR 7.2

The Effect of Language on Perception

Professionally, Benjamin Whorf was an insurance company inspector. But his passion was the study of languages, particularly Native American languages. In the 1950s, Whorf proposed an intriguing theory that became known as the *Whorfian hypothesis.*

Whorf (1956) believed that a person's language determines the very structure of his or her thought and perception. Your language, he claimed, determines how you perceive and "carve up" the phenomena of your world. He argued that people who speak very different languages have completely different world views. More formally, the Whorfian hypothesis is called the **linguistic relativity hypothesis**—the notion that differences among languages cause differences in the thoughts of their speakers (Pinker, 1994).

To illustrate his hypothesis, Whorf contended that the Eskimos had many different words for "snow." Each of these words supposedly described a specific type of snow—falling snow, drifting snow, snow you can use to make an igloo, and so forth. But English, he pointed out, has only the word *snow.* According to Whorf (1956):

We have the same word for falling snow, snow on the ground, snow packed hard like ice, slushy snow, wind-driven flying snow—whatever the situation may be. To an Eskimo, this all-inclusive word would be almost unthinkable; he would say that falling snow, slushy snow, and so on, are sensuously and operationally different, different things to contend with; he uses different words for them and for other kinds of snow.

Whorf's example would be compelling except for one problem: the Eskimos do *not* have dozens of different words for snow. Rather, they have just a few words for snow (Martin, 1986; Pullum, 1991). Beyond that minor sticking point, think carefully about Whorf's example. Is it really true that English-speaking people have only a limited capacity to describe snow? Or that English-speaking people do not discriminate between different types of snow? The English language includes *snowflake, snowfall, slush, sleet, flurry, blizzard,* and *avalanche.* Avid skiers have many additional words to describe snow, from *powder* to *mogul* to *hard-pack.*

More generally, people with expertise in a particular area tend to perceive and make finer distinctions than nonexperts do. This is true regardless of the language spoken. Experts are also more likely to have names for those different distinctions (Pinker, 1994). To the knowledgeable bird-watcher, for example, there are distinct differences between a cedar waxwing and a bohemian waxwing. To the non-expert, they're just two brownish birds with yellow tail feathers.

Despite expert/nonexpert differences in noticing and naming details, we don't claim that the expert "sees" a different reality than a nonexpert. In other words, our perceptions and thought processes influence the language we use to describe those perceptions (Rosch, 1987). Notice that this conclusion is the exact *opposite* of the linguistic relativity hypothesis.

Whorf also pointed out that many languages have different color naming systems. English has names for eleven basic colors: *black, white, red, green, yellow, blue, brown, purple, pink, orange,* and *gray.* However, some languages have only a few color terms. Navajo, for example, has only one word to describe both blue and green, but two different words for black (Fishman, 1960/1974). Would people who had just a few words for colors "carve up" and perceive the electromagnetic spectrum differently?

Eleanor Rosch set out to answer this question ([Rosch] Heider & Olivier, 1972). The people of New Guinea who speak a language called Dani have words for only two colors. *Mili* is used for the dark, cool colors of black, green, and blue. *Mola* is used for light, warm colors, such as white, red, and yellow. According to the Whorfian hypothesis, the people of New Guinea, with names for only two classes of colors, should perceive color differently than English-speaking people, with names for eleven basic colors.

Rosch's procedure was simple: she tested the Dani speakers' ability to recognize and remember colors. She showed Dani speakers a brightly colored chip and then, 30 seconds later, asked them to pick out the color they had seen from an array of other colors. Her results? The Dani-speaking people perceived colors in much the same way as English-speaking people. For example, even though both red and yellow were called *mola,* the Dani could distinguish between them. Despite their lack of a specific word for the color they were shown, the Dani could remember and identify the color from a range of other colors as readily as English-speaking Americans given the same test.

Whorf's strong contention that language *determines* perception and the structure of thought has not been supported. Rather than *determining* perception and thought, language can *influence* perception and thought (see Hunt & Agnoli, 1991). And, it seems more accurate to say that, rather than determining cultural differences, language *reflects* cultural differences (Pinker, 1994; Rosch, 1987).

Language and Gender Bias

When you hear about a course titled, "Man and His Environment," what image comes to mind? Do you visualize a group of men tromping through the forest, or do you imagine a mixed group of males and females?

Technically, the word *man* or the pronoun *he* can refer to either a male or a female in English. That's because there is no gender-neutral pronoun in English. So, according to the rules of the English language, the course title "Man and His Environment" refers to both men and women, just as the sentence, "As man evolved, he developed language" does not apply to men alone, but rather to the entire human race.

However, what do people actually understand by this style of language? Several studies have shown that using the masculine pronoun tends to produce images of males and exclude females (Foertsch & Gernsbacher, 1997; Gastil, 1990). In a study by Nancy Henley (1989), participants were given identical sentence fragments to complete. Examples included "If a writer expects to get a book published . . ." and "If an employee wants a raise . . ." Participants in the first group were given the masculine generic *he* to use in finishing the sentences. Participants in the second group were given either *they* or *he or she* to use in completing the sentences.

After completing the sentences, the subjects were asked to describe their mental imagery for each sentence and to provide a first name for the person they visualized. When the word *he* was used, subjects were much more likely to produce a male image and first name than a female image and name. When the phrase *he or she* was used, subjects were only slightly more likely to use a male rather than a female image or name.

Using the masculine generic pronoun influences people to visualize a male, even when they "know" that *he* supposedly includes both men and women (Hamilton, 1991, 1988). Thus, using *he* to refer to both men and women in speech and writing tends to increase male bias.

Vervet Monkeys Vervet monkeys sound different alarm calls for different kinds of predators. The "leopard" call sends the troop into the trees to avoid leopards and other ground predators. In response to the "eagle" call, the monkeys look up and take cover in bushes to hide from aerial predators.

Animal Communication:

Can Animals Learn Language?

Without question, animals communicate. Chimpanzees "chutter" to warn of snakes, "rraup" to warn of an eagle, and "chirp" to let the others know that a leopard is nearby (Marler, 1967). Each of the warning calls of the vervet monkey of East Africa triggers specific behaviors for a particular danger, such as scurrying for cover in the bushes when the warning for an airborne predator is sounded (Cheney & Seyfarth, 1990).

Clearly, then, animals communicate with one another, but are they capable of mastering language? Some of the most promising results have come from the research of psychologists Sue Savage-Rumbaugh, Duane Rumbaugh, and their co-workers. These researchers are working with a rare chimpanzee species called the *bonobo*. In the mid-1980s, they taught a female bonobo named Matata to press symbols on a computer keyboard. While Matata did not learn many symbols, her infant son, Kanzi, appeared to learn how to use the keyboard simply from watching his mother and her caretakers (Savage-Rumbaugh & Lewin, 1994).

Although Kanzi never received formal training, he quickly learned many symbols. Altogether, Kanzi understands more than 150 spoken English words. Kanzi can respond to new, complex spoken commands like "Go to the refrigerator and get out a tomato" (Savage-Rumbaugh, 1993). These spoken commands are made by an assistant out of Kanzi's view, so he cannot be responding to nonverbal cues.

Kanzi also seems to demonstrate an elementary understanding of syntax. He is able to respond correctly to commands whose meaning is determined by word order. For example, using a toy dog and toy snake, he responds appropriately to commands like "Make the dog bite the snake" and "Make the snake bite the dog" (Savage-Rumbaugh, 1993). Kanzi seems to demonstrate a level of language comprehension that is roughly equivalent to that of a two-and-a-half-year-old human child.

Sue Savage-Rumbaugh with Kanzi
Kanzi, a bonobo, communicates by pressing symbols on a computer keyboard.

Research with other species has produced evidence that nonprimates can also acquire limited aspects of language. Louis Herman and his co-workers (1993) have trained bottle-nosed dolphins to respond to sounds and gestures, each of which stands for a word. The artificial languages taught to the dolphins incorporate rules governing syntax, or word order.

Finally, consider Alex, an African gray parrot. Trained by Irene Pepperberg (1993), Alex can answer spoken questions with spoken words. After about ten years of training, Alex has about a seventy-word vocabulary, which includes the words for objects, names, shapes, numbers, and simple phrases, like "come here," "how many," and "want to go." Alex can answer questions about the color and number of objects and even seems to comprehend certain simple concepts, such as size and color (Gould & Gould, 1994).

Irene Pepperberg with Alex Along with his language abilities, Alex seems to understand some simple concepts. For example, when shown a blue key and a blue cork and asked, "What's the same?" Alex responds, "Color." Here, in response to Pepperberg's request, Alex correctly selects the object that is "blue." Alex does just as well with new objects as he does with familiar objects. This implies that he understands the concepts of color and size and is not just responding to conditioning cues.

When the animal language research first began in the 1960s and 1970s, some critics contended that primates were simply producing learned responses to their trainers' nonverbal cues rather than demonstrating true language skills (Terrace, 1985). In the last decade, however, studies conducted under more carefully controlled conditions have produced some compelling demonstrations of animal language learning. Nevertheless, even the performance of primate superstars like Kanzi pales in comparison with the language learning demonstrated by a three-year-old child (Pinker, 1994).

Collectively, the animal language research reflects an active area of psychological research that is referred to as *animal cognition* or *comparative cognition*. While the results of these studies are fascinating, a great deal remains to be discovered about the limitations and potential of different species of animals to communicate, produce language, and solve problems (Wasserman, 1993; Povinelli, 1993). Many psychologists caution against jumping to the conclusion that animals can "think" or that they possess self-awareness, because such conclusions are far from proven (Blumberg & Wasserman, 1995).

intelligence
The global capacity to think rationally, act purposefully, and deal effectively with the environment.

mental age
A measurement of intelligence in which an individual's mental level is expressed in terms of the average abilities of a given age group.

Measuring Intelligence

Intelligence can be defined as the global capacity to think rationally, act purposefully, and deal effectively with the environment. What roles did Binet, Terman, and Wechsler play in the development of intelligence tests? How did Binet, Terman, and Wechsler differ in their beliefs about intelligence and its measurement?

Up to this point, we have talked about a broad range of cognitive abilities—the use of mental images and concepts, problem solving and decision making, and the use of language. All these mental abilities are aspects of what we commonly call *intelligence*.

What exactly is intelligence? We will rely on a formal definition developed by psychologist David Wechsler. Wechsler (1977, 1944) defined **intelligence** as the global capacity to think rationally, act purposefully, and deal effectively with the environment. Although many people commonly equate intelligence with "book smarts," notice that Wechsler's definition is much broader. To Wechsler, intelligence is reflected in effective, rational, and goal-directed behavior.

The Development of Intelligence Tests

Can intelligence be measured? If so, how? Intelligence tests attempt to measure general mental abilities, rather than accumulated knowledge or aptitude for a specific subject or area. In the next several sections, we will describe the evolution of intelligence tests, including the qualities that make any psychological test scientifically acceptable.

Alfred Binet: Identifying Students Who Needed Special Help

In the early 1900s, the French government passed a law requiring all children to attend school. Faced with the need to educate children from a wide variety of backgrounds, the French government commissioned psychologist **Alfred Binet** (1857–1911) to develop procedures to identify students who might require special help.

With French psychiatrist Théodore Simon, Binet devised a series of tests to measure different kinds of mental abilities. Binet deliberately did not test abilities like reading or mathematics that the students might have already been taught. Instead, he focused on elementary mental abilities like memory, attention, and the ability to understand similarities and differences.

Binet arranged the questions on his test in order of difficulty, with the simplest tasks first. He found that brighter children performed like older children. That is, a bright seven-year-old might be able to answer the same number of questions as an average nine-year-old, while a less capable seven-year-old might only do as well as an average five-year-old.

This observation led Binet to the idea of a mental level or **mental age** that was different from a child's chronological age. An "advanced" seven-year-old might have a mental age of nine, while a "slow" seven-year-old might demonstrate a mental age of five.

It is somewhat ironic that Binet's early tests became the basis for modern intelligence tests. First, Binet did *not* believe that he was measuring an inborn or permanent level of "intelligence" (Kamin, 1995). Rather, he believed that his tests could help identify "slow" children who could benefit from special help.

To judge well, to comprehend well, to reason well, these are the essential activities of intelligence.

Alfred Binet and Théodore Simon (1905)

Alfred Binet French psychologist Alfred Binet is shown here with an unidentified child. Although Binet developed the first systematic intelligence tests, he did not believe that he was measuring innate ability. Instead, he believed that his tests could identify schoolchildren who could benefit from special help.

intelligence quotient (IQ)
A global measure of intelligence derived by comparing an individual's score to that of others in the same age group.

Second, Binet believed that intelligence was too complex a quality to describe with a single number (Siegler, 1992). He steadfastly refused to rank "normal" children on the basis of their scores, believing that such rankings would be unfair. He recognized that many individual factors, such as a child's level of motivation, might affect the child's score. Finally, Binet noted that an individual's score could vary from time to time (Gould, 1993; Fancher, 1996).

Lewis Terman and the Stanford-Binet Intelligence Test

There was enormous interest in Binet's test in the United States. Binet's test was translated and adapted by Stanford University psychologist **Lewis Terman** (1877–1956). Terman's revision was called the *Stanford-Binet Intelligence Scale*. First published in 1916, the Stanford-Binet was for many years the standard for intelligence tests in the United States.

Terman adopted the suggestion of a German psychologist that scores on the Stanford-Binet test be expressed in terms of a single number, called the **intelligence quotient,** or **IQ.** This number was derived by dividing the individual's mental age by the chronological age and multiplying the result by 100. Thus, a child of average intelligence, whose mental age and chronological age were the same, would have an IQ score of 100. A bright ten-year-old child with a mental age of thirteen would have an IQ of 130 (13/10 × 100). A slow child with a chronological age of ten and a mental age of seven would have an IQ of 70 (7/10 × 100). It was Terman's use of the intelligence quotient that resulted in the popularization of the phrase "IQ test."

World War I and Group Intelligence Testing

When the United States entered World War I in 1917, the U.S. military was faced with the need to screen 2 million army recruits (Anastasi, 1988). Using a group intelligence test devised by one of Terman's students, army psychologists developed two group intelligence tests. The *Army Alpha* test was administered in writing, and the *Army Beta* test was administered orally to recruits and draftees who could not read.

After World War I ended, the Army Alpha and Army Beta group intelligence tests were adapted for civilian use. The result was a tremendous surge in the intelligence testing movement. Group intelligence tests were designed to test virtually all ages and types of people, including preschool children, prisoners, and newly arriving immigrants (Kamin, 1995; Anastasi, 1988). However, the indiscriminate use of the tests also resulted in skepticism and hostility.

For example, newly arriving immigrants were screened as they arrived at Ellis Island. The result was sweeping generalizations about the intelligence of different nationalities and races. During the 1920s, a few intelligence testing experts even urged the U.S. Congress to severely limit the immigration of certain nationalities to keep the country from being "overrun with a horde of the unfit" (see Kamin, 1995).

Despite concerns about the misuse of the so-called IQ tests, the tests quickly became very popular. Lost was Binet's belief that intelligence tests were useful only to identify those who might benefit from special educational help. And, contrary to Binet's contention, it soon came to be believed that the IQ score was a fixed, inborn characteristic resistant to change (Gould, 1993).

Terman and other American psychologists also believed that a high IQ predicted more than success in school. To in-

Testing Immigrants at Ellis Island This photograph, taken in 1917, shows an examiner administering a mental test to a newly arrived immigrant at Ellis Island. According to one intelligence "expert" of the time, 80 percent of the Hungarians, 79 percent of the Italians, and 87 percent of the Russians were "feeble-minded" (see Kamin, 1995). The new science of "mental testing" was used to argue that immigration be restricted.

IN FOCUS 7.3

Does a High IQ Score Predict Success in Life?

Starting in 1921, Lewis M. Terman set out to investigate the common notion that genius-level intelligence is related to social and personal maladjustment, physical weakness, and mental instability. Terman identified 1,500 California children between the ages of eight and twelve who had IQs above 140, the minimum IQ score for genius-level intelligence. The average IQ of the children was 150, and eighty children had scores above 170. Terman's goal was to track these children by conducting periodic surveys and interviews to see how genius-level intelligence would affect the course of their lives.

Within a few years, Terman (1926) showed that the highly intelligent children were far from being socially and physically inept. In fact, his findings indicated just the opposite. The children tended to be socially well-adjusted. They were also taller, stronger, and healthier than average children, with fewer illnesses and accidents. And as a group, not surprisingly, these children performed exceptionally well in school.

> *With the exception of moral character, there is nothing as significant for a child's future as his grade of intelligence.*
>
> **Lewis M. Terman** (1916)

Since Terman's death in 1956, the study has been continued by other psychologists, most notably Melita Oden, Robert Sears, and Pauline Sears. These collaborators in Terman's study kept track of the subjects, who were now well into adulthood. Today, more than seventy years after the study began, psychologists continue to assess the professional and personal accomplishments of the surviving original subjects (Holahan & Sears, 1995).

How did Terman's "gifted" children fare in the real world as adults? As a group, they showed an astonishing range of accomplishments (Terman & Oden, 1959, 1947). In 1955, when the average income was $5,000 a year, the average income for the group was $33,000. Two-thirds had graduated from college, and a sizable proportion had gone on to earn advanced academic or professional degrees. There were no "creative geniuses"—no Picassos, Einsteins, or Mozarts—but there were many doctors, lawyers, scientists, university professors, business executives, and other professionals in the group. Collectively, the gifted group had produced 2,200 scientific articles, 92 books, 235 patents, and 38 novels (Goleman, 1980). One individual had become a famous science fiction writer, and another was an Oscar-winning movie director.

However, not all of Terman's subjects were so successful. To find out why, Terman's colleague Melita Oden compared the 100 most successful men (the "A" group) and the 100 least successful men (the "C" group) in Terman's sample. Despite their high IQ scores, only a handful of the C group were professionals, and none was doing exceptionally well. Whereas the C's were

earning slightly above the national average income, the A's were earning almost five times the national income and better than three times the average C-group income. In terms of their personal lives, the C's were less healthy, had higher rates of alcoholism, and were three times as likely to be divorced as the A's (Terman & Oden, 1959).

Given that the IQ scores of the A and C groups were essentially the same, what accounted for the difference in their level of accomplishment? As children, the A's were much more likely to display "prudence and forethought, will power, perseverance, and the desire to excel." As adults, the A's were rated differently from the C's on only three traits: they were more goal-oriented, had greater perseverance, and had greater self-confidence. Overall, the A's seemed to have greater ambition and a greater drive to achieve. In other words, *personality factors* seemed to account for the differences in level of accomplishment between the A group and the C group (Terman & Oden, 1959).

As the general success of Terman's gifted children demonstrates, high intelligence can certainly contribute to success in life. But intelligence alone is not enough. Although IQ scores do reliably predict academic success, success in school is no guarantee of success beyond school. Many different personality factors are involved in achieving success, such as motivation, emotional maturity, commitment to goals, creativity, and—perhaps most important—a willingness to work hard (Goleman, 1995; Sternberg, 1985, 1982; Renzulli, 1986). None of these attributes are measured by traditional IQ tests.

vestigate the relationship between IQ and success in life, Terman (1926) identified 1,500 California schoolchildren with "genius" IQ scores. He set up a longitudinal research study to follow their careers throughout their lives. Some of the findings of this landmark study are described in Box 7.3, "Does a High IQ Score Predict Success in Life?"

David Wechsler Born in Romania in 1896, David Wechsler emigrated with his family to New York when he was six years old. Like Binet, Wechsler believed that intelligence involved a variety of mental abilities. He also strongly believed that IQ scores could be influenced by personality, motivation, and cultural factors (Matarazzo, 1981).

David Wechsler and the Wechsler Intelligence Scales

The next major advance in intelligence testing came as a result of a young psychologist's dissatisfaction with the Stanford-Binet and other intelligence tests in widespread use. **David Wechsler** (1896–1981) was in charge of testing adults of widely varying cultural and socioeconomic backgrounds and ages at a large hospital in New York City. He designed a new intelligence test called the *Wechsler Adult Intelligence Scale (WAIS)*, which was first published in 1955.

The WAIS had two advantages over the Stanford-Binet. First, the WAIS was specifically designed for adults rather than children. Second, Wechsler's test provided scores on eleven subtests measuring different abilities. The subtest scores were grouped to provide an overall "verbal score" and "performance score." The *verbal score* represented scores on subtests of vocabulary, comprehension, knowledge of general information, and other verbal tasks. The *performance score* reflected scores on largely nonverbal subtests, such as identifying the missing part in incomplete pictures, arranging pictures to tell a story, or arranging blocks to match a given pattern.

The design of the WAIS reflected Wechsler's belief that intelligence involves a variety of mental abilities. Because the WAIS provided an individualized profile of the subject's strengths and weaknesses on specific tasks, it marked a return to the attitudes and goals of Alfred Binet (Sternberg, 1990; Fancher, 1996).

The subtest scores on the WAIS also proved to have practical and clinical value. A pattern of low scores on some subtests combined with high scores on other subtests might indicate a specific learning disability (Kaufman, 1990). Or, someone who did well on the performance subtests but poorly on the verbal subtests might be unfamiliar with the culture rather than deficient in these skills (Aiken, 1994). That's because many items included on the verbal subtests draw on cultural knowledge.

Wechsler's test also provided a global IQ score, but he changed the way that the IQ score was calculated. On the Stanford-Binet and other early tests, the IQ represented the "mental age" divided by the "chronological age." But this approach makes little sense when applied to adult subjects.

Instead, Wechsler calculated the IQ by comparing an individual's score to the scores of others in the same general age group, such as young adults. The average score for a particular age group was statistically fixed at 100. The range of scores is statistically defined so that two-thirds of all scores fall between 85 and 115—the range that is considered to indicate "normal" or "average" intelligence. This procedure proved so successful that it was adopted by the administrators of other tests, including the current version of the Stanford-Binet. Today, IQ scores continue to be calculated by this method.

The WAIS was revised in 1981, so that today it is known as the WAIS-R. Since the 1960s, the WAIS has remained the most commonly administered intelligence test. Wechsler also developed two tests for children: the *Wechsler Intelligence Scale for Children* (WISC) and the *Wechsler Preschool and Primary Scale of Intelligence* (WPPSI).

The Wechsler Intelligence Scale for Children (WISC) Revised and updated in 1991, the WISC-III is designed to assess the intelligence of children in the six to sixteen age range. This psychologist is administering the WISC-III picture completion subtest to a six-year-old girl. Other WISC-III subtests include vocabulary, arithmetic, arranging blocks to match a design, and arranging pictures so that they correctly tell a story.

Principles of Test Construction:
What Makes a Good Test?

Psychological tests must meet the requirements of standardization, reliability, and validity. What is the role of norms in standardization, and what is the normal curve? How are reliability and validity defined, and how are they determined?

FIGURE 7.5 The Normal Curve of Distribution of IQ Scores
The distribution of IQ scores on the WAIS-R in the general population tends to follow a bell-shaped normal curve, with the average score defined as 100. Notice that 68 percent of the scores fall within the "normal" IQ range of 85 to 115. Ninety-five percent of the general population scores between 70 and 130, while only one-tenth of one percent scores lower than 55 or higher than 145.

There are many kinds of psychological tests that measure various aspects of intelligence or mental ability. *Achievement tests* are designed to measure a person's level of knowledge, skill, or accomplishment in a particular area, such as mathematics or a foreign language (Aiken, 1994). In contrast, *aptitude tests* are designed to assess a person's capacity to benefit from education or training. The overall goal of an aptitude test is to predict your ability to learn certain types of information or perform certain skills.

To be considered scientifically acceptable, any psychological test must fulfill certain requirements. The three basic requirements of good test design are standardization, reliability, and validity.

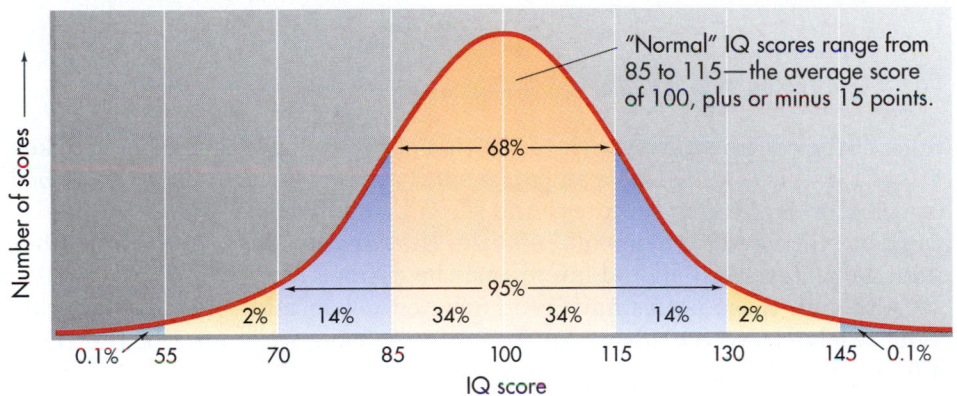

"Normal" IQ scores range from 85 to 115—the average score of 100, plus or minus 15 points.

68%

95%

0.1% 55   70   85   100   115   130   145 0.1%

2% 14% 34% 34% 14% 2%

Number of scores

IQ score

Standardization

If you answer 75 out of 100 questions correctly, what does that score mean? Is it high, low, or average? In order to interpret an individual's test score, it has to be compared against some sort of standard of performance.

Standardization means that the test is given to a large number of subjects who are representative of the group of people for whom the test is designed. All the subjects take the same version of the test under uniform conditions. The scores of this group establish the *norms,* or the standards against which an individual score is compared and interpreted.

For IQ tests, such norms closely follow a pattern of individual differences called the **normal curve,** or **normal distribution.** In this bell-shaped pattern, most scores cluster around the average score (see Figure 7.5). As scores become more extreme, fewer instances of the scores occur.

Reliability

A good test must also have **reliability.** This means that the test must consistently produce similar scores on different occasions. How do psychologists determine if a psychological test is reliable? One way is to give two similar but not identical versions of the test at different times. Another procedure is to compare the scores on one half of the test to the scores on the other half of the test. A test is considered to be reliable if the test and retest scores are highly similar when such strategies are used.

Validity

Finally, a good test must demonstrate **validity,** which means that the test measures what it is supposed to measure. One way to establish the validity of a test is by demonstrating its predictive value. For example, if a test is

standardization
The administration of a test to a large, representative sample of people under uniform conditions for the purpose of establishing norms.

normal curve (normal distribution)
A bell-shaped distribution of individual differences in a normal population in which most scores cluster around the average score.

reliability
The ability of a test to produce consistent results when administered on repeated occasions under similar conditions.

validity
The ability of a test to measure what it is intended to measure.

designed to measure mechanical aptitude, people who received high scores should ultimately prove more successful in mechanical jobs than people who received low scores.

The Nature of Intelligence

Debate over the nature of intelligence centers on two key issues: (1) whether intelligence is a single factor and (2) how narrowly intelligence should be defined. How do Spearman, Thurstone, Gardner, and Sternberg differ in their views of intelligence?

The Wechsler Adult Intelligence Scale and the Stanford-Binet Intelligence Scale are standardized, reliable, and valid. But do they adequately measure intelligence? Psychologists do not agree on the answer to this question. Put simply, there is considerable disagreement about the nature of intelligence, including how intelligence should best be defined (Neisser & others, 1996).

Theories of Intelligence

Much of the controversy over the definition of intelligence centers on two key issues. First, is intelligence a single, general ability? Or is it better described as a cluster of different abilities? And second, should the definition of intelligence be restricted to the mental abilities that are measured by IQ and other intelligence tests? Or should intelligence be defined more broadly?

Although these issues have been debated for decades, they are far from being resolved (see Sternberg, 1995). In this section, we'll describe the views of four influential psychologists on both issues.

Charles Spearman: Intelligence Is a General Ability

Some psychologists believe that a common factor, or general mental capacity, is at the core of different mental abilities. This approach originated with British psychologist **Charles Spearman** (1863–1945). Spearman found that an individual's scores on tests of different mental abilities tended to be similar.

Spearman (1904) believed that a factor he called **general intelligence,** or the **g factor,** was responsible for overall performance on mental ability tests. Psychologists who follow this approach today think that intelligence can be described as a single measure of general cognitive ability, or *g* factor. Lewis Terman's approach to measuring and defining intelligence as a single, overall IQ score was in the tradition of Charles Spearman.

Louis L. Thurstone: Intelligence Is a Cluster of Abilities

Psychologist **Louis L. Thurstone** (1887–1955) flatly disagreed with Spearman's notion that intelligence is a single general mental capacity. Instead, Thurstone believed that there were seven different "primary mental abilities," each a relatively independent element of intelligence. Abilities such as verbal comprehension, numerical ability, reasoning, and perceptual speed are examples that Thurstone gave of independent "primary mental abilities."

***g* factor (general intelligence)**
The notion of a general intelligence factor that is responsible for a person's overall performance on tests of mental ability.

triarchic theory of intelligence
Sternberg's theory that there are three forms of intelligence: componential, experiential, and contextual.

Examples of Gardner's Theory of Multiple Intelligences Gardner points out that many forms of mental ability are not adequately measured by traditional intelligence tests. Examples are the exceptional designs of this Navajo weaver (spatial intelligence), gifted jazz musician Wynton Marsalis (musical intelligence), and the poetic and storytelling genius of Maya Angelou (linguistic intelligence).

FIGURE 7.6 Gardner's "Multiple Intelligences"

To Thurstone, the so-called *g* factor was simply an overall average score of such independent abilities, and consequently was less important than an individual's specific *pattern* of mental abilities (Thurstone, 1937). David Wechsler's approach to measuring and defining intelligence as a pattern of different abilities was very similar to Thurstone's approach.

Howard Gardner: "Multiple Intelligences"

Like Thurstone, **Howard Gardner** (b. 1943) believes that mental abilities are independent and distinct and cannot be accurately reflected in a single measure of intelligence like an IQ score. After studying the kinds of skills and products that are highly valued in different cultures, Gardner (1985, 1993a) has also stretched the traditional definition of intelligence.

Gardner believes that there are "multiple intelligences." He defines an "intelligence" as the ability to solve problems or to create products that are valued within one or more cultural settings. Gardner's multiple intelligences are summarized in Figure 7.6.

Some of Gardner's intelligences, like linguistic intelligence, might be tapped by a standard intelligence test. However, other abilities, like bodily-kinesthetic intelligence, cannot be measured by an IQ test. Nevertheless, Gardner points out, such abilities are recognized and valued in many different cultures.

Robert Sternberg: Three Forms of Intelligence

Robert Sternberg (b. 1949) agrees with Gardner that intelligence is a much broader quality than the narrow range of mental abilities tested by a conventional IQ test. However, Sternberg (1995, 1988a) believes that some of Gardner's "intelligences" would more accurately be described as specialized "talents." To Sternberg, intelligence is a more general quality.

Sternberg's **triarchic theory of intelligence** emphasizes both the universal aspects of intelligent behavior and the importance of adapting to a particular social and cultural environment. More specifically, Sternberg (1997, 1988a) contends that there are three forms of intelligence: componential, experiential, and contextual.

Componential, or *analytic, intelligence* refers to the mental processes used in learning how to solve problems, picking a problem-solving strategy, and solving problems. *Experiential,* or *creative, intelligence* is the ability to deal with novel situations by drawing on existing skills and knowledge.

Linguistic intelligence	Adept at use of language: poet, writer, public speaker, native storyteller
Logical-mathematical intelligence	Logical, mathematical, and scientific intelligence: scientist, mathematician, navigator, surveyor
Musical intelligence	Musician, composer, singer
Spatial intelligence	Excels in ability to mentally visualize the relationships of objects or movements: sculptor, painter, expert chess player, architect
Bodily-kinesthetic intelligence	Control of bodily motions and capacity to handle objects skillfully: athlete, dancer, craftsperson
Interpersonal intelligence	Understanding other people's emotions, motives, intentions: politician, salesperson, clinical psychologist
Intrapersonal intelligence	Understanding one's own emotions, motives, and intentions: essayist, philosopher

Finally, *contextual intelligence,* also called *practical intelligence,* involves the ability to adapt to the particular environment, culture, or situation. "Street smarts" is one way of describing contextual intelligence. Sternberg notes that what is required to adapt successfully in one particular situation or culture may be very different in another situation or culture. He stresses that the behaviors that reflect contextual intelligence can vary depending on the particular situation, environment, or culture. A person who is high in contextual intelligence functions effectively within a given cultural context.

Although intelligence theorists disagree about the exact definition of intelligence, some general conclusions can be drawn. Most psychologists agree that mental abilities such as abstract thinking, problem solving, and the ability to acquire knowledge are important elements of intelligence. These aspects of intelligence are typically assessed in standard intelligence tests like the WAIS and the Stanford-Binet. But many intelligence experts believe that there are other important aspects of intelligence, like creativity and the ability to adapt to your environment, which are *not* measured by conventional intelligence tests (Snyderman & Rothman, 1987, 1988).

The exact nature of intelligence will no doubt be debated for some time. However, the intensity of this debate pales in comparison to the next issue we consider: the origins of intelligence.

CONCEPT REVIEW 7.3

Identifying Major Contributors to the Intelligence Debate

Identify the psychologist who is described. Choose from: Binet, Terman, Wechsler, Spearman, Thurstone, Gardner, Sternberg.

_____ **1.** Contemporary American psychologist who believes that intelligence has three forms: componential, experiential, and contextual.

_____ **2.** French psychologist who is credited with developing the first practical intelligence test.

_____ **3.** American psychologist whose widely used intelligence test provides both a global IQ score and scores on verbal and performance tests.

_____ **4.** British psychologist who advanced the theory that overall intellectual ability is a func-

tion of a general intelligence factor, called the *g factor.*

_____ **5.** Contemporary American psychologist who proposed that there are multiple independent intelligences, and that an intelligence is an ability that is valued within a particular cultural setting.

_____ **6.** American psychologist who believed that there are seven different primary mental abilities rather than a single *g factor.*

_____ **7.** American psychologist who translated and adapted Binet's intelligence test for use in the United States.

The Roles of Genetics and Environment in Determining Intelligence

Both genes and environment contribute to intelligence, but the relationship is complex. How are twin studies used to measure genetic and environmental influences? What is a heritability estimate, and why can't heritability estimates be used to explain differences between groups?

Given that psychologists do not agree on the definition or nature of intelligence, it probably won't surprise you that psychologists also do not agree on the *origin* of intelligence. On the surface, the debate comes down to this: Do we essentially *inherit* our intellectual potential from our parents, grandparents, and great-grandparents? Or is our intellectual potential primarily determined by our *environment* and upbringing?

The simple answer to both these questions is yes. In a nutshell, virtually all psychologists agree that *both* heredity and environment are important in determining intelligence level. Where psychologists disagree is in identifying how much of intelligence is determined by heredity, how much by environment. The implications of this debate have provoked some of the most heated arguments in the history of psychology. In this section, we'll try to clarify some of the critical issues involved in this ongoing controversy.

We will discuss the biological underpinnings of genetics and heredity in more detail in Chapter 9. To make sense out of the IQ controversy, however, a brief discussion of the interaction of environment and genes is required here.

Let's start with some simple examples illustrating the role of heredity and environment. Your eye color is completely genetically determined. If you were born with blue eyes, no level of environmental intervention will change your eyes to brown (colored contact lenses don't count).

Your height is also genetically determined, but to a different degree: you inherit a potential *range* for height, rather than an absolute number of inches. Thus, unlike eye color, your height can be affected by your environmental circumstances. If you are healthy and well-nourished, you may reach the maximum of your genetic height potential. But if you are poorly nourished and unhealthy, you probably won't.

To underscore the interplay between heredity and environment, consider the fact that in the last fifty years, the average height of Americans has increased by several inches. The explanation for this increase is that nutritional and health standards have steadily improved, not that the genetic heritage of Americans has fundamentally changed. However, heredity does play a role in establishing some limits on height. If you're born with "short" genes (like your authors), you're unlikely to reach six foot four, no matter how good your nutrition.

The roles of heredity and environment in determining intelligence and personality factors are much more complex than the simple examples of height or eye color (Plomin & others, 1994). However narrowly intelligence is defined, the genetic range of intellectual potential is influenced by *many* genes, not by just one single gene (Gottesman, 1997; Rose, 1995). No one knows how many genes might be involved. Given the complexity of genetic and environmental influences, how do scientists estimate how much of intelligence is due to genetics, how much to environment?

Twin Studies: Sorting Out the Influence of Genetics Versus Environment

One way this issue has been explored is by comparing the IQ scores of individuals who are genetically related, but to different degrees. *Identical twins* share exactly the same genes, because they developed from a single fertilized egg that split into two. Hence, any dissimilarities between them must be due to environmental factors rather than hereditary differences. *Fraternal twins* are like any other pair of siblings, because they develop from two different fertilized eggs.

As you can see from Figure 7.7 on the next page, comparing IQ scores in this way shows the effects of both heredity and environment. Identical twins raised together have very similar IQ scores, while fraternal twins raised together have IQs that are less similar than those of identical twins (McClearn & others, 1997).

However, notice that identical twins raised in separate homes have IQs that are slightly less similar, indicating the effect of different environments.

Genetics or Environment? These identical twins have a lot in common—including a beautiful smile. How do researchers determine the relative contributions of heredity and environment to personality and other characteristics?

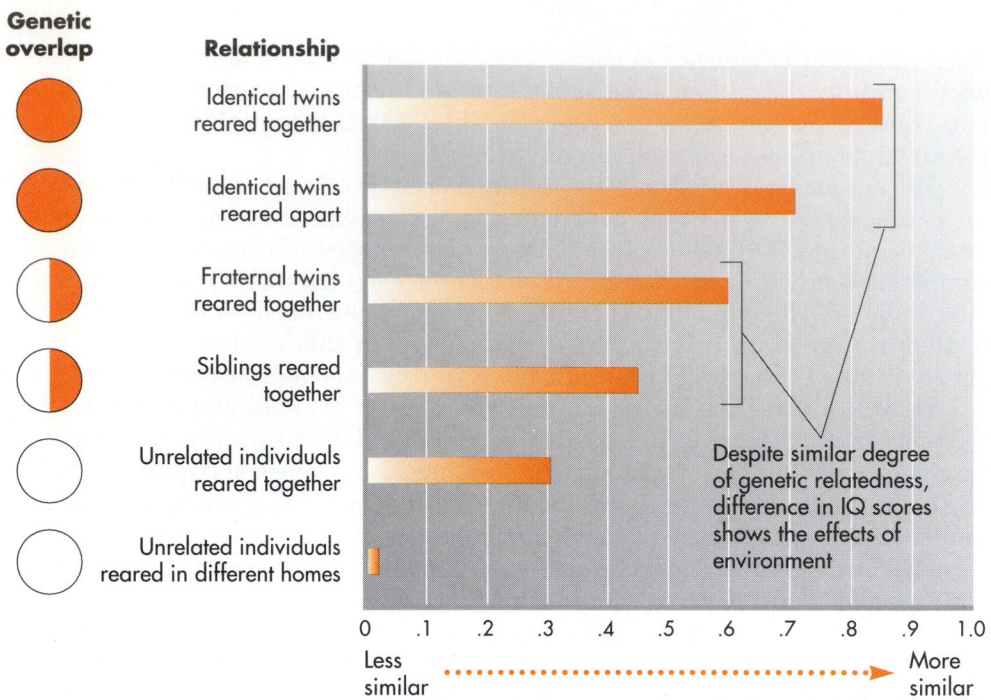

Genetic overlap

Relationship

Identical twins reared together

Identical twins reared apart

Fraternal twins reared together

Siblings reared together

Unrelated individuals reared together

Unrelated individuals reared in different homes

Despite similar degree of genetic relatedness, difference in IQ scores shows the effects of environment

0 .1 .2 .3 .4 .5 .6 .7 .8 .9 1.0

Less similar ---------> More similar

FIGURE 7.7 Genetics, Environment, and IQ Scores

Comparing the IQ scores of individuals who are genetically related to differing degrees shows the effects of both heredity and environment. The more closely two individuals are related genetically, the more similar are their IQ scores. However, the environment also has an effect.

(Adapted from Bouchard & McGue, 1981.)

And, although fraternal twins raised together are *less* similar in IQ scores than identical twins, they show *more* similarity in IQs than nontwin siblings. Recall that the degree of genetic relatedness between fraternal twins and nontwin siblings is essentially the same. But because fraternal twins are the same age, their environmental experiences are likely to be more similar than that of siblings who are of different ages.

Thus, *both* genetic and environmental influences are important (Plomin & others, 1997). Genetic influence is shown by the fact that the closer the genetic relationship, the more similar the IQ scores. Environmental influences are demonstrated by two findings: Two people who are genetically identical but who are raised in different homes have different IQ scores. And two people who are genetically unrelated but who are raised in the same home have IQs that are much more similar than those of unrelated people from randomly selected homes.

Using studies based on degree of genetic relatedness, researchers have scientifically estimated **heritability**—the percentage of variation within a given population that is due to heredity. Using sophisticated statistical techniques to analyze such data, the currently accepted *heritability estimate* is about 50 percent for the general population (Plomin & others, 1994).

In other words, approximately 50 percent of the difference among IQ scores *within* a given population is due to genetic factors. But there is disagreement even over this figure, depending on the statistical techniques and data sources used. Some researchers estimate the heritability of IQ as high as 65 percent (Bouchard & others, 1990a).

It is important to stress that the 50 percent figure does *not* apply to a single individual's IQ score. If Mike's IQ is 120, it does not mean that 60 IQ points are due to Mike's environment and 60 points are genetically inherited. Instead, the 50 percent heritability estimate means that approximately 50 percent of the difference among IQ scores *within a specific group of people* is due to differences in their genetic makeup. More on this key point shortly.

Group Differences in IQ Scores

If the contributions of heredity and environment are roughly equal, why all the fuss? Much of the controversy over the role of heredity in intelligence is due to attempts to explain the differences in average IQ scores for different racial groups.

In comparing the *average IQ* for various racial groups, several studies have shown differences. For example, Japanese and Chinese schoolchildren tend to score above white American children on intelligence and achievement tests, especially in math (Lynn, 1987; Stevenson & Lee, 1990). Are Japanese and Chinese children genetically more intelligent than American children?

Consider this finding: In early childhood, there are *no* significant differences in IQ among American, Japanese, and Chinese schoolchildren. The three groups are essentially the same (Stevenson & Sigler, 1992). The gap begins to appear only after the children start school, and it increases with every

heritability
The percentage of variation within a given population that is due to heredity.

Culture and Educational Achievement
These children attend kindergarten in Kawasaki, Japan. Children in Japan attend school six days a week. Along with spending more time in school each year than American children, Japanese children grow up in a culture that places a strong emphasis on academic success as the key to occupational success.

year of school attended. By middle school, Asian students tend to score much higher than American students on both math and reading tests.

Why the increasing gap when Asian and American students start school? Japanese and Chinese students spend more time in school, more time doing homework, and experience more pressure and support from their parents to achieve academically. Moreover, the Japanese and Chinese cultures place a high value on academic achievement (Gardner, 1995). Clearly, the difference between American and Asian students is due not to genetics, but to the educational system.

In the United States, the most controversy has been caused by the differences in average IQ scores between black and white Americans. *As a group*, black Americans once scored about 15 points lower than white Americans *as a group* (MacKenzie, 1984). However, this gap has narrowed over the past few decades to 10 points or less (Neisser & others, 1996; Nisbett, 1995b).

Once again, it is important to note that such group differences do not predict *individual* differences in IQ scores. Many individual black Americans receive higher IQ scores than many individual white Americans. Also, the range and degree of IQ variation *within* each group—the variation of IQs among individual blacks or among individual whites—is much greater than the 10-point average difference *between* the two groups.

Differences *Within* Groups Versus Differences *Between* Groups

Nonetheless, some group differences in average IQ scores do exist. But heritability cannot be used to explain group differences. Although it is possible to estimate the degree of difference *within* a specific group that is due to genetics, it makes no sense to apply this estimate to the differences between groups (Rutter, 1997). Why? An analogy provided by geneticist Richard Lewontin (1970) may help you understand this important point.

Although it is possible to estimate the degree of difference *within* a specific group that is due to genetics, it makes no sense to apply this estimate to the differences *between* groups. Why? An analogy provided by geneticist Richard Lewontin (1970) may help you understand this point.

Suppose that you have a 50-pound bag of corn seeds and two pots. A handful of the seeds is scooped out and planted in pot A, which has rich, well-fertilized soil. A second handful is scooped out and planted in pot B, which has poor soil with few nutrients (see Figure 7.8 on page 262).

Because the seeds are not genetically identical, the plants *within group A* will vary in height. So will the plants *within group B*. Given that the environment (the soil) is the same for all the plants in each pot, this variation within each group of seeds is *completely* due to heredity—because nothing differs but the plants' genes.

However, when we compare the average height of the corn plants in the two pots, pot A's plants have a higher average height than pot B's. Can the difference in these average heights be explained in terms of overall genetic differences between the seeds in each pot? No. The overall differences can be attributed to the two different environments, the good soil and the poor soil. In fact, because the environments are so different, it is impossible to estimate what the overall genetic differences are between the two groups of seeds.

FIGURE 7.8 Sorting Out the Effects of Genetics and Environment in Intelligence: The Two Pots Analogy

Because the two environments are very different, no conclusions can be drawn about possible overall genetic differences between the plants in pot A and pot B.

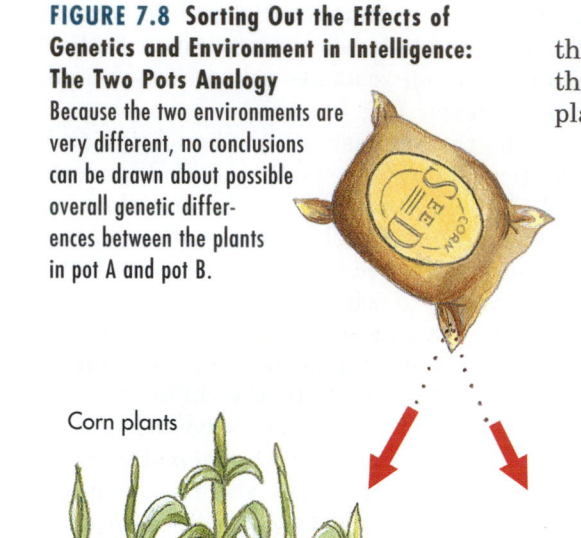

Corn plants

Individual differences in height *within* the group are due to genetics because environment is the same

Pot A
Rich soil, many nutrients

Pot B
Poor soil, few nutrients

Difference in average height *between* groups is due to environment

We need to appreciate that all human behavior is based on biology and, hence, will involve some degree of genetic influence. But, equally, all social behavior is bound to be affected by social context and, hence, will involve an important environmental influence.

Michael R. Rutter (1997)

Note also that even though, on the average, the plants in pot A are taller than the plants in pot B, some of the plants in pot B are taller than some of the plants in pot A. In other words, the average differences *within a group* of plants tell us nothing about whether an *individual* member of that group is likely to be tall or short.

The same point can be extended to the issue of average IQ differences between racial groups. Unless the environmental conditions of two racial groups are virtually identical, it is impossible to estimate the overall genetic differences between the two groups. Even if intelligence were *primarily* determined by heredity, which does not appear to be the case, IQ differences between groups could still be due entirely to the environment.

In the United States, black children, like members of many other minority groups, are more likely than white children to be raised in poverty and to have fewer educational opportunities. Environmental factors associated with poverty, such as poor nutrition and lack of prenatal care, can have a negative impact on intelligence. And, even when their socioeconomic status is roughly equal to that of white Americans, black Americans experience many forms of overt and subtle social discrimination (Steele & Aronson, 1995).

An important study by psychologists Sandra Scarr and Richard Weinberg (1976) explored the relationship between racial IQ differences and the environment in which children are raised. Scarr and Weinberg looked at the IQ scores of black children who had been adopted by white families that were highly educated and above average in occupational status and income. When tested, the black children's IQ scores were several points higher than the average scores of both blacks and whites.

Scarr and Weinberg concluded that IQ differences are due not to race, but rather to the socioeconomic conditions and cultural values to which children are exposed. According to Weinberg (1989), the adopted black children performed well above average because they were provided with home environments in which the children were taught the vocabulary and cognitive skills that IQ and achievement tests reward. A follow-up study of the children a decade later demonstrated the "persisting beneficial effects [on IQ scores] of being reared in the culture of the school and tests" (Weinberg & others, 1992; Waldman & others, 1994).

Other evidence for the importance of the environment in determining IQ scores comes from the improvement in average IQ scores that has occurred in other cultures and countries during the last few generations (see Neisser & others, 1996). For example, average Japanese IQ scores have risen dramatically since World War II (Flynn, 1987).

In a survey of intelligence test scores around the world, 14 nations were found to have shown significant gains in average IQ scores in just one generation (Flynn, 1987). The average IQ in the United States has also steadily increased over the past century (see Kaufman, 1990). Such changes in a population can be accounted for only by environmental changes, because the amount of time is far too short for genetically influenced changes to have occurred.

The Buraku Protest Centuries of Discrimination Members of the Burakumin Emancipation Alliance protest discrimination in a peaceful demonstration in Tokyo. Their vests proclaim their demand for basic human rights for the Buraku. Today, the Burakumin are the poorest group in Japan. Compared to the general population of Japan, only about half as many Burakumin graduate from high school or attend college.

Cross-Cultural Studies of Group Discrimination and IQ Differences

The effect of social discrimination on intelligence test scores has been shown in numerous cross-cultural studies (see Ogbu, 1986). In many different societies, average IQ is lower for members of a discriminated-against minority group, even when that group is not racially different from the dominant group.

Take the case of the Buraku people of Japan. Americans typically think of Japan as being a relatively homogeneous culture, and indeed the Burakumin are not racially different from other Japanese. They look the same and speak the same language. However, the Burakumin are the descendants of an outcast group that for generations worked as tanners and butchers. Because they handled dead bodies and killed animals, the Burakumin were long considered to be unclean and unfit for social contact. For centuries, the Burakumin were forced to live in isolated enclaves, apart from the rest of Japanese society (De Vos & Wagatsuma, 1967).

Today, there are about 3 million Burakumin in Japan. Although the Buraku were legally emancipated from their outcast status many years ago, substantial social discrimination against them persists (Payton, 1992). Because there is no way to tell if a Japanese citizen is of Buraku descent, there are dozens of private detective agencies in Tokyo and other Japanese cities that openly specialize in tracking Burakumin who are trying to "pass" and hide their background. Corporations in Japan routinely consult computer databanks to identify Burakumin who apply for jobs, as do individuals who wish to investigate the ancestral background of prospective marriage partners.

The Buraku are the poorest people in Japan. They are only half as likely to graduate from high school or attend college as other Japanese. Although there are no racial differences between the Burakumin and other Japanese, the average IQ scores of the Burakumin in Japan are well below those of other Japanese, as shown in Table 7.2. However, when Buraku families immigrate to the United States, they are treated like any other Japanese. The children do just as well in school—and on IQ tests—as any other Japanese-Americans (Ogbu, 1986).

Of course, Japan is not the only society that discriminates against a particular social group, whether racially similar or dissimilar. Many societies discriminate against specific minority groups, such as the Harijans in India (formerly called the Untouchables), West Indians in Great Britain, the Maoris in New Zealand, and Oriental Jews in Israel.

TABLE 7.2 The Effects of Discrimination on IQ Scores in Japan

Range of IQ Scores	Percentage of Children Scoring in a Given Range	
	Non-Buraku	Buraku
Above 125	23.3	2.6
124–109	31.8	19.5
108–93	23.3	22.1
92–77	11.7	18.2
Below 76	9.9	37.6

SOURCE: Adapted from De Vos & Wagatsuma, 1967, Table 2, p. 261.

The Buraku people of Japan are not racially different from other Japanese, but they have suffered from generations of discrimination. Their average IQ scores are about 10 to 15 points below those of mainstream Japanese (Ogbu, 1986). In many other cultures, a similar gap in IQ scores exists between the discriminated-against minority and the dominant group.

The children of each of these minority groups score 10 to 15 points lower on intelligence tests than the dominant group's children in their society. Children of the minority groups are often one or two years behind dominant-group children in basic reading skills and mathematical skills. Minority-group children are overrepresented in remedial programs and in the number of school dropouts. They are also underrepresented among students in higher education. The impact of discrimination on group differences in IQ remains even when the minority-group and dominant-group members are of similar socioeconomic backgrounds (Ogbu, 1986). In many ways, the educational experiences of these minority groups seem to parallel those of black Americans, providing a cross-cultural perspective on the consistent effects of discrimination in many different societies.

Are IQ Tests Culturally Biased?

Another approach to explaining group differences in IQ scores has been to look at cultural bias in the tests themselves. If standardized intelligence tests reflect white, middle-class cultural knowledge and values, minority-group members might do poorly on the tests not because of lower intelligence, but because of unfamiliarity with the white, middle-class culture.

Researchers have attempted to create tests that were "culture-fair" or "culture-free." However, it is now generally recognized that it is virtually impossible to design a test that is completely culture-free, because intelligence itself is not free of cultural influences (Sternberg, 1991). Quite simply, a test will tend to favor the people from the culture in which it was developed (Anastasi, 1988).

Cultural differences may also be involved in *test-taking behavior* (Sternberg, 1995). People from different cultural backgrounds may use strategies in solving problems or organizing information that are different from those required on standard intelligence tests (Miller-Jones, 1989). In addition, factors like motivation, attitudes toward test taking, and previous experiences with tests are all cultural factors that can affect performance and test scores.

And, as psychologist Claude Steele (1997) has discovered, simply being aware that you are not expected to do well on a particular test has the effect of lowering your score—whether you are black or white, Native American or Latino, male or female. Steele calls this situation *stereotype threat*—a psychological predicament in which members of a particular group fear that they will be evaluated in terms of a negative stereotype about their group. Students' anxiety and apprehension over being evaluated when they feel that they are expected to perform poorly can lower both the speed and the accuracy of responses to standardized test questions (Steele, 1997; Steele & Aronson, 1995). Steele's research has shown how expectations, attitudes, and social identity can adversely affect an individual's performance, even on objective tests. In this way, members of stigmatized groups may consistently perform below their true potential on intelligence tests and other standardized tests.

Psychologist Claude Steele Stanford University professor Claude Steele (1997) has found that being aware that you're expected to do poorly on a particular test can lower a person's score. His findings are providing new insights that help explain group differences in intelligence and achievement tests.

Some Concluding Thoughts

On the basis of our discussion about the influences of heredity and environment on intelligence, we can draw three broad conclusions about the debate surrounding intelligence and race.

First, it's clear that the IQ of any given individual, regardless of what racial group he or she may belong to, is the result of the complex interaction of hereditary and environmental factors. Second, as far as the IQ differences between racial groups are concerned, environmental factors are much more likely to account for such differences than genetics (Neisser & others, 1996). Third, within any given racial group, the differences among people are due at least as much to environmental influences as they are to genetic influences (Plomin & others, 1994).

IQ scores measure only the selected aspects of intelligence they are designed to measure. We draw upon many different types of mental abilities to solve problems, adapt to our environment, and communicate with others. As the story of Mr. and Ms. Fix-It in the prologue illustrated, solving even the most mundane problems of life often involves creative and flexible thinking. In the Application section, we provide a variety of suggestions that you can use to enhance your creativity.

CONCEPT REVIEW 7.4

Recognizing Important Determinants of Intelligence

1. Most intelligence experts agree that observed differences in average IQ scores between racial groups are due to
   a. genetic factors.
   b. environmental factors.
   c. the deliberate construction of biased tests.
   d. the use of culture-free tests.

2. A researcher tests a group of identical twins raised together and a different group of identical twins who were separated at birth and raised in different environments. She finds that the IQ scores of each pair of twins in the first group are more similar than the IQ scores of each pair of twins in the second group. This difference is the result of
   a. genetic influences.
   b. environmental influences.
   c. neither environmental nor genetic influences.
   d. an equal degree of environmental and genetic influences.

3. One scoop of seeds is planted in a plot of farmland with rich soil and adequate rainfall. Another scoop of seeds from the same batch is planted in a back yard with poor soil that is never watered or fertilized. On the average, the seeds in the rich soil grow taller than the seeds in the poor soil. The difference between the average height of the plants in the rich soil and that of the plants in the poor soil is best accounted for by:
   a. genetic factors.
   b. environmental factors.
   c. 30 percent genetics and 70 percent environment.
   d. 70 percent genetics and 30 percent environment.

4. In question 3, the plants in the rich farmland vary in height: some are taller than others. The same is true of the plants in the back yard. The difference among the heights of the plants in the same plot of soil is best accounted for by:
   a. genetics.
   b. environment.
   c. 30 percent genetics and 70 percent environment.
   d. 70 percent genetics and 30 percent environment.

APPLICATION

A Workshop on Creativity

Creativity can be defined as a group of cognitive processes used to generate useful, original, and novel ideas or solutions to problems (Amabile & Tighe, 1993; Ochse, 1990). Creativity experts generally agree that everyone can learn to be more creative. Here are several suggestions that can enhance your ability to think creatively.

1. Choose the Goal of Creativity

Psychologists have found that virtually everyone possesses the intelligence and cognitive processes needed to be creative (Weisberg, 1993, 1988). But the creative individual values creativity as a personal goal (Hennessey & Amabile, 1988). Without the personal goal of creativity, the likelihood of doing something creative is slim.

2. Reinforce Intrinsic Motivation

People will be most creative when they are motivated by their own interest, the enjoyment of a challenge, and a personal sense of satisfaction and fulfillment. This is called *intrinsic motivation.* In contrast, when people are motivated by external rewards, such as money or grades, they are displaying *extrinsic motivation* (Amabile, 1989, 1983; Hennessey & Amabile, 1988).

If you are driven by extrinsic rather than intrinsic motivation, then you're motivated by the factors that are *least* likely to produce creativity. Instead, the goal of creative expression should be the creative act itself.

3. Engage in Problem Finding

In many cases the real creative leap involves recognizing that a problem exists. This is referred to as *problem finding* (Brown, 1989; Getzels & Csikszentmihalyi, 1976). We often overlook creative opportunities by dismissing trivial annoyances rather than recognizing them as potential problems to be solved (Hayes, 1989).

For example, consider the minor annoyance experienced by a man named Art Fry. Fry, a researcher for 3M Corporation, regularly sang in his church choir. In order to locate the hymns quickly during the Sunday service, Fry would use little scraps of paper to mark their places. But the scraps of paper would sometimes fall out when Fry stood up to sing, and he'd have to fumble to find the right page (Kaplan, 1990).

While sitting in church, Fry recognized the "problem" and came up with a relatively simple solution. If you put a substance that is sticky, but not *too* sticky, on the scraps of paper, they'll stay on the page and you can take them off when they are not needed anymore.

If you haven't already guessed, Art Fry invented Post-It Notes. The formula for the adhesive had been discovered years earlier at 3M, but nobody could imagine a use for a glue that did not bond permanently. The mental set of the 3M researchers was to find *stronger* glues, not weaker ones.

Fry's story demonstrates the creative value of recognizing problems instead of simply dismissing them. One useful strategy to identify potential problems is *bug listing* (Adams, 1979). Bug listing involves creating a list of things that annoy or irritate you. Such everyday annoyances are problems in need of creative solutions.

4. Acquire Relevant Knowledge

Creativity requires a good deal of preparation (Weisberg, 1993). Acquiring a solid knowledge base increases your potential for recognizing how to creatively extend your knowledge or apply it in a new way. As the famous French chemist Louis Pasteur said, "Chance favors the prepared mind."

5. Try Different Approaches

Creative people are flexible in their thinking. They step back from problems, turn them over, and mentally play with possibilities. By being flexible and imaginative, people seeking creative solutions generate many different responses. This is called *divergent thinking,* because it involves moving away (or diverging) from the problem and considering it from a variety of perspectives (Baer, 1993).

Looking for analogies is one technique to encourage divergent thinking. In problem solving, an *analogy* is the recognition of some similarity or parallel between two objects or events that are not usually compared. Similarities can be drawn in terms of the objects' operation, function, purpose, materials, or other characteristics.

For example, Gay Balfour of Colorado recognized a problem—the need to remove prairie dogs from an area without killing them ("New Prairie Dog Vacuum," 1992). When trying to come up with a way to get the prairie dogs out of their burrows, Balfour was struck by the analogy between a vacuum cleaner and the suction devices used to clean out septic tanks. Balfour devised a machine that sucks the critters out of the ground without harming them so they can be relocated. On one occasion, he vacuumed up 53 prairie dogs in a little over an hour.

6. Exert Effort and Expect Setbacks

Flashes of insight or "inspiration" can play a role in creativity, but they usually occur only after a great deal of work. Whether you're trying to write a brilliant term paper or design the next Beanie Baby, creativity requires effort and persistence.

Finally, the creative process is typically filled with obstacles and setbacks. The best-selling novelist Stephen King endured years of rejec-

CALVIN AND HOBBES

tion of his manuscripts before his first book was published. Thomas Edison tried thousands of filaments before he created the first working lightbulb.

To summarize our workshop on creativity, we'll use the letters of the word *create* as an acronym. Thus, the basic ingredients of creativity are:

- **C**hoose the goal of creativity.
- **R**einforce intrinsic motivation.
- **E**ngage in problem finding.
- **A**cquire relevant knowledge.
- **T**ry different approaches.
- **E**xert effort and expect setbacks.

The Prairie Dog Vacuum Balfour's invention harmlessly sucks prairie dogs out of their burrows and deposits them into a holding tank in his truck so that they can be relocated. According to Balfour, "It's quite a ride but the prairie dogs are not too disturbed about it."

Summary
Thinking, Language, and Intelligence

Thinking, Language, and Intelligence

- Thinking involves manipulating internal, mental representations of information in order to draw inferences and conclusions. Thinking often involves the manipulation of two kinds of mental representations: mental images and concepts.

- Most research has been done on visual mental images. We seem to treat mental images much as we do actual visual images or physical objects.

- Thinking also involves the use of concepts. Formal concepts are defined by logical rules. Natural concepts are likely to have fuzzy rather than rigid boundaries. We determine membership in natural concepts by comparing an object to our prototype for the natural concept. The more similar an item is to the prototype, the more quickly and easily we can determine whether it is an instance of the concept.

Solving Problems and Making Decisions

- Problem solving refers to thinking and behavior directed toward attaining a goal that is not readily available.

- Strategies that are commonly used in problem solving include trial and error, algorithms, and heuristics. Heuristics include breaking a problem into a series of subgoals and working backward from the goal. Sometimes problems are resolved through insight or intuition.

- Functional fixedness and mental set are two common obstacles to problem solving.

- Decision-making models include the single-feature model, the additive model, and the elimination by aspects model. Different strategies may be most helpful in different situations.

- When making risky decisions, we often use the availability heuristic and the representativeness heuristic to help us estimate the likelihood of events.

Language and Thought

- Language is a system for combining arbitrary symbols to produce an infinite number of meaningful statements.

- Language has the following characteristics: meaning is conveyed by arbitrary symbols; meaning is shared by speakers of the same language; language is a rule-based system; language is generative; and language involves displacement.

- Language influences thinking by affecting what we remember and our perceptions of others.

- Animals communicate with members of their own species, sometimes in a complex fashion. They can also be taught to communicate with humans. Bonobos and dolphins seem to have demonstrated an elementary grasp of the rules of syntax.

Measuring Intelligence

- Intelligence can be defined as the global capacity to think rationally, act purposefully, and deal effectively with the environment. Intelligence tests are designed to measure general mental abilities.

- Alfred Binet developed the first widely accepted intelligence test, which incorporated the idea of a mental age that was different from chronological age. Binet did not believe that intelligence was inborn or fixed, or that it could be described in a single number.

- Lewis Terman adapted Binet's test for use in the United States and developed the concept of the intelligence quotient, or IQ score. Terman believed that success in life was primarily determined by IQ.

- Group intelligence tests were developed for screening military recruits during World War I.

- David Wechsler developed the Wechsler Adult Intelligence Scale (WAIS), which included scores on subtests that measured different mental abilities. Wechsler also changed the way that overall IQ scores were calculated.

- Psychological tests must meet the requirements of standardization, reliability, and validity. The norms, or standards, for intelligence tests follow the normal curve, or normal distribution of scores.

The Nature of Intelligence

- Debate over the nature of intelligence centers on two key issues: (1) whether intelligence is a single factor or a cluster of different abilities; and (2) how narrowly intelligence should be defined.

- Charles Spearman believed that intelligence could be described as a single factor called general intelligence, or the g factor.

- Louis L. Thurstone believed that there were seven primary mental abilities.

- Howard Gardner believes that there are "multiple intelligences." He defines intelligence as the ability to solve problems or create products that are valued within a cultural setting.

- Robert Sternberg's triarchic theory of intelligence emphasizes both the universal aspects of intelligence and the importance of adapting to a particular cultural environment. He identifies three forms of intelligence: componential, experiential, and contextual intelligence.

- Despite continuing controversy, psychologists generally agree that abstract thinking, problem solving, and capacity to acquire knowledge are important aspects of intelligence and are measurable by intelligence tests. However,

other important aspects of intelligence, like creativity, are not measured by intelligence tests.

- The IQ of any individual is the result of a complex interaction between heredity and environment. Intelligence is not determined by a single gene but by the interaction of multiple genes.

- Twin studies are used to determine the degree to which genetics contribute to complex characteristics like intelligence. Heritability refers to the percentage of variation within a given population that is due to heredity. Within a given racial group, the effects of environment and genetics are roughly equal.

- There are differences in the average IQ scores for different racial groups. However, there is more variation within a particular group than there is between groups.

- While it is possible to calculate the differences within a given group that are due to heredity, it is not possible to calculate the differences between groups that are due to heredity. Unless the environments are identical, no comparisons can be drawn. Rather than genetic factors, environmental factors are more likely to be the cause of average IQ differences among groups.

- Cross-cultural studies have demonstrated that the average IQ scores of groups who suffer social discrimination are frequently lower than the average IQ scores of the dominant social group, even when the groups are not racially different.

- Intelligence tests can be culturally biased. All intelligence tests reflect the culture in which they are developed. Cultural factors may also influence test-taking behavior and individual performance. IQ scores reflect only selected aspects of intelligence.

Key Terms

cognition (p. 235)

thinking (p. 235)

mental image (p. 235)

concepts (p. 237)

formal concept (p. 237)

natural concept (p. 237)

prototype (p. 237)

problem solving (p. 238)

trial and error (p. 239)

algorithm (p. 239)

heuristic (p. 239)

insight (p. 240)

intuition (p. 240)

functional fixedness (p. 241)

mental set (p. 241)

availability heuristic (p. 243)

representativeness heuristic (p. 244)

language (p. 246)

linguistic relativity hypothesis (p. 248)

intelligence (p. 251)

mental age (p. 251)

intelligence quotient (IQ) (p. 252)

standardization (p. 255)

normal curve (normal distribution) (p. 255)

reliability (p. 255)

validity (p. 255)

g factor (general intelligence) (p. 256)

triarchic theory of intelligence (p. 257)

heritability (p. 260)

creativity (p. 266)

Key People

Alfred Binet (1857–1911) A French psychologist who, along with French psychiatrist Théodore Simon, developed the first widely used intelligence test.

Howard Gardner (b. 1943) A contemporary American psychologist whose theory of intelligence states that there is not one intelligence but multiple intelligences, the importance of each being determined by cultural values.

Charles Spearman (1863–1945) A British psychologist who advanced the theory that a general intelligence factor, called the *g factor,* is responsible for overall intellectual functioning.

Robert Sternberg (b. 1949) A contemporary American psychologist whose *triarchic theory of intelligence* includes three forms of intelligence (componential, contextual, and experiential).

Lewis Terman (1877–1956) An American psychologist who translated and adapted the Binet-Simon intelligence test for use in the United States; he also began, in 1921, a major longitudinal study of the lives of intellectually gifted children.

Louis L. Thurstone (1887–1955) An American psychologist who advanced the theory that intelligence is composed of several primary mental abilities, and cannot be accurately described by an overall general, or *g* factor, measure.

David Wechsler (1896–1981) An American psychologist who developed the Wechsler Adult Intelligence Scale, the most widely used intelligence test.

CONCEPT REVIEW 7.1   Page 238

1. mental image
2. natural concept
3. prototype
4. formal concept

CONCEPT REVIEW 7.2   Page 244

1. (C) heuristic
2. (D) insight (*O* = One, *T* = Two, etc.)
3. (B) algorithm
4. (A) trial and error
5. (F) availability heuristic
6. (G) single-feature model

CONCEPT REVIEW 7.3.   Page 258

1. Sternberg
2. Binet
3. Wechsler
4. Spearman
5. Gardner
6. Thurstone
7. Terman

CONCEPT REVIEW 7.4.   Page 265

1. b
2. b
3. b
4. a

Chapter

8

Motivation and Emotion

Prologue: Soaring with Angels

Richard and I had been best friends since our paths first crossed in high school. Even then, Richard was extraordinary. He was good-looking and liked by everyone. He was a highly motivated student who maintained an almost straight-A average in his classes. In our senior year, he was elected student body president. (To be perfectly honest, he beat me in the race for student body president.) And Richard was highly motivated as an athlete. He spent countless hours in the swimming pool, perfecting his dives from the three-meter board. Coming from a family of very modest means, Richard hoped for an athletic scholarship to attend college. He got one: The University of Arkansas awarded him a four-year athletic scholarship.

Richard met Becky when they were both freshmen at the University of Arkansas. They seemed like a good match. Becky was smart, pretty, athletic, and had a wonderful sense of humor. They were also both Catholic, which greatly pleased Becky's parents. So, it came as no surprise when Richard and Becky announced their plans to marry after graduating. But I can't help thinking in retrospect that Richard's timing was deliberate when he asked me, in front of Becky, to be the best man.

"You're *sure* you want to marry this guy?" I half-jokingly asked Becky.

"Only if he takes nationals on the three-meter board," Becky quipped. As it turned out, Richard did place third on the three-meter board the following spring at the national collegiate swimming competition.

Three months before their wedding, Richard and I had the only argument we've ever had. At the time we had the argument, the word *gay* meant lighthearted and cheerful, so the word never came up in our heated exchange.

"What do you mean, you haven't told her!?"

"I don't need to tell her about the past," Richard insisted.

"That's bull, Richard," I shouted. "This woman loves you and if you don't tell her about your homosexual urges, then you are marrying her under false pretenses."

"I do *not* have those feelings anymore!" Richard yelled back.

"If that's true, then tell her!" I demanded.

But it wasn't true, of course. Although Richard would not admit it to himself, he had only become adept at suppressing his sexual attraction to other men. At the time we had that argument, I was still the only person who knew that Richard harbored what he called "homosexual urges." Richard had first told me when we were juniors in high school. I was stunned. But Richard was also adamant that he did not want to feel the way he did. In fact, he felt ashamed and guilty. Back then, homosexuality carried more of a social stigma than it does today.

So when Richard and I were still in high school, we scraped up enough money to secretly send him to a psychologist for a few sessions. Despite our naive hopes for a quick "cure," Richard's troubling feelings remained. When he got to the University of Arkansas, Richard saw a counselor on a regular basis. After months of counseling, Richard believed he was capable of leading a heterosexual life.

Richard and Becky's wedding was magnificent. And, yes, I was the best man. After the wedding, they decided to stay in Fayetteville so Richard could start graduate school. The inevitable happened less than a year later. Becky called me.

"I'm driving to Tulsa tonight. Don, you've *got* to tell me what's going on," she said, her voice strained, shaking. And I did, as gently as I could.

Richard and Becky's marriage was annulled. In time, Becky recovered psychologically, remarried, and had two children. Her bitterness toward Richard softened over the years. The last time I talked with her, she seemed genuinely forgiving of Richard.

For his part, Richard gave up trying to be something he was not. Instead, he came to grips with his sexual orientation, moved to San Francisco, and became a co-owner of two health clubs. True to form, Richard quickly became a respected and well-liked member of San Francisco's large gay community. He eventually met John, an accountant, with whom he formed a long-term relationship. But after Richard's move to San Francisco, our friendship faded.

It was our twenty-year high school reunion that triggered Richard's unexpected call. When I told Richard I simply did not have the time to go to Sioux City, he suggested stopping in Tulsa on his way to the reunion to see me again and to meet Sandy and our daughter, Laura.

So on a warm May evening, Richard, Sandy, and I drank some margaritas, ate Chinese carry-out, and talked until midnight. Just as I expected, Sandy was quite taken with Richard. Indeed, Richard *was* a wonderful man—smart, funny, thoughtful, and sensitive. And, just as I expected, Laura, who was not quite two years old, was also enchanted by Richard. My only regret about that evening is that I did not take a picture of Richard sitting on the deck as Laura brought him first one toy, then another, then another. As it turned out, it would be the last time I saw Richard.

About a year after he visited us in Tulsa, Richard was killed in a hang-gliding accident. As he was soaring over the rocky California coast, Richard swerved to miss an inexperienced flyer who crossed his path in the air. Richard lost control of his hang-glider and was killed on impact when he plummeted into the rocky coastline.

A week later, more than 300 people crowded into St. Mary's Catholic Church in Sioux City, where Richard had been an altar boy in his youth. The outpouring of love and respect for Richard at the memorial service was a testament to the remarkable man he was.

What Richard's story illustrates is that who we are in this life—our identity—is not determined by any single characteristic or quality. Richard was gay, but that's not all Richard was, any more than your sexual orientation is the only characteristic that defines you or motivates your behavior. In this chapter, we'll look at a variety of factors that motivate our behavior, including sexuality, striving to achieve, and the emotions we experience. In the process, we'll come back to Richard's story.

Introduction

The Study of Motivation

Theories of motivation have historically included instinct, drive, incentive, and humanistic theories. How does each theory explain motivation, and what are the limitations of each theory? What characterizes the study of motivation today?

If you think about it, "something" triggered your behavior to get out of bed this morning, such as getting to work or class on time. That "something" is what the topic of **motivation** is about—the forces that act on or within an organism to initiate and direct behavior (Petri, 1996).

In everyday conversations, people often use the word *motivation* when they try to understand or explain the behavior of others. "And what motivated you to take up hang gliding?" "She seems highly motivated to finish school." Such statements reflect three of the basic characteristics commonly associated with motivation: activation, persistence, and intensity (Geen, 1995).

Activation is demonstrated by the initiation or production of behavior, such as the motivated student who initiates going to the library to finish a term paper. *Persistence* is demonstrated by continued efforts or the determination to achieve a particular goal, often in the face of obstacles. Finally, *intensity* is seen in the greater vigor of responding that usually accompanies motivated behavior, such as the highly motivated student who studies harder than her classmates.

In the early days of psychology, motivation theorists tried to create a single unified model that explained the motivation of *all* behaviors. Over the last century, several models of motivation have been proposed. Each model eventually proved to be inadequate, unable to explain certain aspects of motivation. However, key ideas from each model remained essential to a complete understanding of motivation and were incorporated into the new models. As you'll see in this section, the study of motivation has progressively become more diverse and multifaceted.

Motivation: What Makes Them Run?
Motivation researchers study the "why" of human behavior—the forces that motivate an individual to act.

Instinct Theories:

Is There a Diving Instinct?

In the late 1800s, the newly founded science of psychology initially embraced instinct theories to explain motivation. According to **instinct theories,** people are motivated to engage in certain behaviors because of genetic programming. Just as animals display instinctive behavior patterns, like migration or mating behaviors, human behavior was also thought to be motivated by inborn instincts.

motivation
The forces that act on or within an organism to initiate and direct behavior.

instinct theories
The view that some motives are innate and due to genetic programming.

TABLE 8.1 Some Examples of Instincts Proposed by Instinct Theorists

rivalry	combativeness
sympathy	hunting
fear	acquisitiveness
constructiveness	play
curiosity	sociability
shyness	secretiveness
cleanliness	modesty
jealousy	parental love
self-assertion	submission
food-seeking	repulsion
escape	mating

SOURCE: Based on Petri, 1996, pp. 30–31.

drive theories
The view that behavior is motivated by the desire to reduce internal tension caused by unmet biological needs.

homeostasis
(home-ee-oh-STAY-sis) The notion that the body monitors and maintains internal states, such as body temperature and energy supplies, at relatively constant levels.

drive
An impulse that activates behavior to reduce a need and restore homeostasis.

Drawing inspiration from the work of Charles Darwin and his scientifically based theory of evolution, psychologists devised lengthy lists of instincts to account for every conceivable human behavior (see Table 8.1). The behavior of a neat and tidy person, for example, was thought to be motivated by the "cleanliness instinct."

By the early 1900s, thousands of instincts had been proposed in one expert's list or another. (The early instinct theorists were, no doubt, motivated by a "listing" instinct.) But what does it tell you to say that an assertive person has a "self-assertion instinct"? The obvious problem with the early instinct theories was that such theories merely described and labeled behaviors, rather than actually explaining them (Petri, 1996).

By the 1920s and 1930s, instinct theories fell out of favor, primarily because of their lack of explanatory power. But the more general idea that some human behaviors are innate and genetically programmed remained an important element in the overall understanding of motivation.

Drive Theories:
Biological Needs as Motivators

Instinct theories were replaced during the 1940s and 1950s by drive theories. In general, **drive theories** assert that behavior is motivated by the desire to reduce internal tension caused by unmet biological needs, such as hunger or thirst. The basic idea is that these unmet biological needs "drive" or "push" us to behave in certain ways, leading to a reduction in the drive. When a particular behavior successfully reduces a drive, the behavior becomes more likely to be repeated when the same need state arises again.

Leading drive theorists, like psychologists Clark Hull (1943, 1952) and Robert Woodworth (1958), believed that drives are triggered by the internal mechanisms of homeostasis. The principle of **homeostasis** states that the body monitors and maintains relatively constant levels of internal states, such as body temperature, fluid levels, and energy supplies. According to drive theorists, when an internal imbalance is detected by homeostatic mechanisms, a **drive** to restore balance is produced. The drive activates behavior to reduce the need and to reestablish the balance of internal conditions.

For example, after you have not eaten anything for several hours, the internal pangs of hunger signal an imbalance in your body's energy level. According to the drive theorists, this unmet biological need creates a drive state—hunger—that motivates or energizes your behavior. And how might the drive of hunger energize you to behave? You might gravitate to the kitchen and forage in the refrigerator for some leftover guacamole dip or chocolate cake.

Today, the drive concept remains useful in the explanation of some motivated behaviors that have biological components, like hunger, thirst, and sexuality. However, the drive theories also have some limitations. Let's consider hunger again. Is the motivation of eating behavior strictly a matter of physiological need? Obviously not. Often, people eat when they're not hungry, and don't eat when they are.

Beyond that observation, drive theories proved inadequate for other reasons. Rather than a reduction of tension, many behaviors seem to be directed toward *increasing* tension and physiological arousal. For example, how could drive theories account for such behaviors as buying a lottery ticket, running a marathon, or playing competitive tennis? It seems apparent that the motivation of such behaviors has to be explained in some other way.

Incentive Motivation:
Goal Objects as Motivators

Building on the base established by drive theories, incentive theories emerged in the 1950s. **Incentive theories** proposed that behavior is motivated by the "pull" of external goals, such as rewards. Indeed, it's easy to think of many situations in which a particular goal, such as good grades or a promotion at work, can serve as an external incentive that helps activate particular behaviors.

Incentive theories of motivation drew heavily from well-established learning principles, such as reinforcement, and the work of influential learning theorists, such as Pavlov, Watson, Skinner, and Tolman (see Chapter 5). Of particular note, Edward Tolman (1932) stressed the importance of cognitive factors in learning and motivation, especially the *expectation* that a particular behavior will lead to a particular goal.

When combined, drive and incentive theories seemed to account for a broad range of the "pushes" and "pulls" motivating many behaviors. Even in combination with drive theories, however, incentive explanations of motivation still had limitations. The most obvious shortcoming was the inability to explain behaviors that are not primarily motivated by any kind of external incentive—such as mastering a new task, helping others for no apparent gain, or simply trying to satisfy curiosity.

Psychological Motives:
Striving to Reach Our Potential

In the late 1950s, humanistic theories of motivation emerged. While not discounting the role of biological and external motivators, humanistic theories stressed the idea that we are innately motivated to strive for a positive self-concept and the realization of our personal potential (see Franken, 1994).

Humanistic motivational theories emphasized the importance of psychological and cognitive components in human motivation. Motivation was thought to be affected by how we perceive the world, how we think about ourselves and others, and our beliefs about our abilities and skills (Rogers, 1977, 1961). Although the motivation to strive for a positive self-concept and personal potential was thought to be inborn, humanistic theories also recognized the importance of the environment (Maslow, 1970). Without a supportive and encouraging environment—personal, social, and cultural—the motivation to strive toward one's highest potential could be jeopardized.

The most famous humanistic model of motivation is the **hierarchy of needs,** developed by **Abraham Maslow** (1908–1970) and summarized in Figure 8.1. In a nutshell, Maslow (1970, 1968) believed that people are motivated to satisfy the needs at each level of the hierarchy before moving up to the next level. People progressively move up the hierarchy, striving to eventually reach *self-actualization.*

FIGURE 8.1 Maslow's Hierarchy of Needs
Abraham Maslow believed that people are innately motivated to satisfy a progression of needs, beginning with the most basic physiological needs. Once the needs at a particular level are satisfied, the individual is motivated to satisfy the needs at the next level, steadily progressing upward. The ultimate goal is self-actualization, the realization of personal potential.
(Based on Maslow, 1970.)

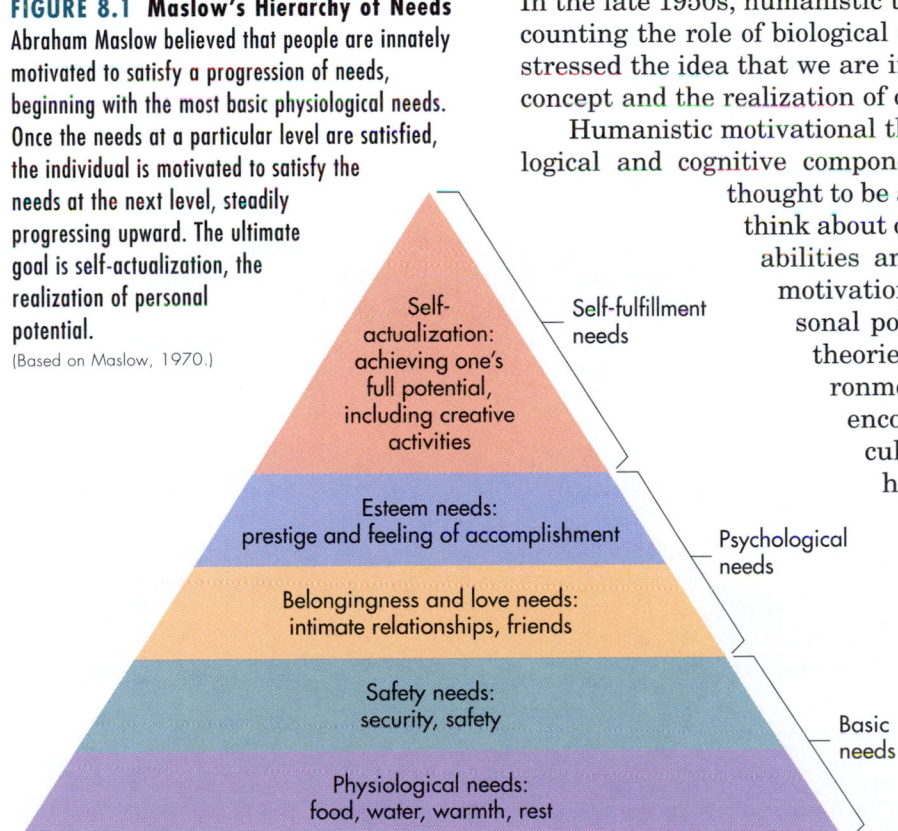

Notice that the lowest levels of Maslow's hierarchy emphasize fundamental biological, safety, and social needs. At the highest levels, the needs become more individualized and growth-oriented.

What exactly is self-actualization? Maslow (1970) himself had trouble defining the term, saying that self-actualization is "a difficult syndrome to describe accurately." Nonetheless, Maslow defined **self-actualization** in the following way:

> It may be loosely described as the full use and exploitation of talents, capacities, potentialities, etc. Such people seem to be fulfilling themselves and to be doing the best that they are capable of doing. . . . They are people who have developed or are developing to the full stature of which they are capable.

Beyond that general description, Maslow's research identified several characteristics that self-actualized people seem to possess. Some of these qualities are summarized in Table 8.2.

Not surprisingly, humanistic models of motivation also have limitations. First, concepts like self-actualization are extremely vague and almost impossible to define in a way that would allow them to be tested scientifically. And Maslow's initial studies on self-actualization were based on limited samples with questionable reliability. For example, Maslow (1970) often relied on the life stories of acquaintances whose identities were never revealed. He also studied the biographies and autobiographies of famous historical figures who he believed had achieved self-actualization, such as Eleanor Roosevelt, Abraham Lincoln, and Albert Einstein.

A more important criticism is that the majority of people do not experience or achieve self-actualization, despite the claim that this is an inborn goal toward which all people supposedly strive. Maslow (1970) himself wrote that self-actualization "can seem like a miracle, so improbable an event as to be awe-inspiring." Maslow explained this basic contradiction in a number of different ways. For instance, he suggested that few people experience the supportive environment that is required for self-actualization.

TABLE 8.2 Maslow's Characteristics of Self-Actualized People

Realism and acceptance	Self-actualized people have accurate perceptions of themselves, others, and external reality. They easily accept themselves and others as they are.
Spontaneity	Self-actualized people are spontaneous, natural, and open in their behavior and thoughts. However, they can easily conform to conventional rules and expectations when situations demand such behavior.
Problem centering	Self-actualized people focus on problems outside themselves. They often dedicate themselves to a larger purpose in life, which is based on ethics or a sense of personal responsibility.
Autonomy	Although they accept and enjoy other people, self-actualized individuals have a strong need for privacy and independence. They focus on their own potential and development rather than the opinions of others.
Continued freshness of appreciation	Self-actualized people continue to appreciate the simple pleasures of life with awe and wonder.
Peak experiences	Self-actualized people commonly have *peak experiences,* or moments of intense ecstasy, wonder, and awe during which their sense of self is lost or transcended. The self-actualized person may feel transformed and strengthened by these peak experiences.

SOURCE: Based on Maslow, 1970.

self-actualization
Defined by Maslow as "the full use and exploitation of talents, capacities, and potentialities."

Although Maslow's theory continues to generate research (e.g., Sumerlin & Norman, 1992; Neher, 1991), the humanistic model of motivation is not as influential as it once was. Nonetheless, Maslow's theory helped establish the important role played by psychological and cognitive factors in human motivation.

Rather than focusing on a single "grand" theory of motivation, today's researchers study specific types of motivated behavior, such as eating, sexuality, curiosity, and achievement. In doing so, they assume that *the motivation of any behavior is determined by multiple factors.* Such factors can include biological, behavioral, cognitive, and social components. Exactly how these different factors interact to energize and motivate specific types of behavior is still the subject of much research, as you'll see in the next several sections.

The Motivation to Eat

The motivation to eat is influenced by psychological, biological, social, and cultural factors. How do oral signals, stomach signals, CCK, insulin, and the hypothalamus seem to influence hunger and eating behavior?

On the surface, it seems simple: you eat because you're hungry. But it's not that simple. What, when, and how much you eat are influenced by diverse psychological, biological, social, and cultural factors.

For example, think about what you ate yesterday. Now contrast your choices with food preferences in other cultures. A typical diet for the Dusan of northern Borneo in Southeast Asia includes anteater, gibbon (a small ape), snake, mouse, and rat meat. After these meats have spoiled to the point of being liquified, the Dusan consume them with rice. South American Indians consume head lice, bees, iguanas, and monkeys. The Guiana of South America eat pebbles as a regular part of their diet, while the Vedda of Sri Lanka like rotted wood (Fieldhouse, 1986).

Psychologically, eating can be related to emotional states, such as depression, anxiety, or stress (Greeno & Wing, 1994). Interpersonally, eating is often used to foster relationships, as when you have friends over for dinner or take a potential customer to lunch. In describing others, we often rely on food-related adjectives, such as saying someone has a "sweet" or "sour" personality. Without question, the themes of food and eating permeate many different dimensions of our lives.

For psychologists, the study of eating behavior has focused on several critical issues. The most fundamental issue has been trying to understand what motivates us to eat on a day-to-day basis. What causes hunger? And how do we sense that we've eaten enough?

Delicious or Disgusting? The need to eat is a universal human motive. However, culture heavily influences *what* we eat, *when* we eat, and *how* we eat. This Chinese woman is clearly enjoying her meal of fried caterpillars and scorpions—a delicacy in her province.

What Causes Us to Start and Stop Eating?

For most of this century, researchers have been searching for the source of the signals that trigger hunger and satiation. (*Satiation* is the feeling of fullness and diminished desire to eat.) For example, it's long been known that the oral sensations involved in tasting and chewing food contribute greatly to the subjective pleasure and satisfaction of eating. However, oral sensations do *not* seem to be what causes us to start or stop eating. Instead, oral signals seem to help maintain or slow down eating behavior once it has begun (Bray, 1991).

Stomach Signals: Stretching It to the Limit

One common-sense explanation of hunger is that we start eating when our stomach "feels empty" and stop eating when we "feel full." In fact, the stomach has sensory neurons that detect the stretching of the stomach muscles. As the stomach stretches to accommodate food, signals from these neurons are relayed to the brain, helping to trigger feelings of satiation (Geliebter & others, 1987).

A hormone called **cholecystokinin,** thankfully abbreviated **CCK,** also seems to play a role in signaling satiation. As food moves from the stomach to the intestines, CCK is secreted into the bloodstream and conveyed to the brain, where CCK acts as a neurotransmitter (Kalat, 1995; Zhang & others, 1986). CCK seems to magnify the satiety-producing effects of food in the stomach by slowing the rate at which the stomach empties and by heightening the sensitivity of "stretch receptors" in the stomach (Bray, 1991; McHugh & Moran, 1985).

Still, even if stretch signals from the stomach provide an important signal to stop eating, other signals must be involved. Why? Because it's long been known that people continue to experience hunger and satiation even after their stomachs have been removed for medical reasons (Wangensteen & Carlson, 1931).

The Role of Insulin:
Does the *Thought* of a Candy Bar Make You Hungry?

Insulin is a hormone secreted by the pancreas that helps regulate the metabolism of carbohydrates, fats, and starches in the body. Psychologist Judith Rodin has assembled an impressive array of evidence demonstrating that higher insulin levels lead us to experience more hunger and eat more food. Normally, insulin levels begin to rise shortly *after* we start eating. But Rodin has shown that we can become classically conditioned to produce increased insulin levels *before* consuming food.

Just as Pavlov's dogs became classically conditioned to salivate to the sound of a bell that had been repeatedly paired with food (see Chapter 5), people can become classically conditioned to associate environmental stimuli with eating. Stimuli such as the sight or smell of appealing food, other people eating, or even just the thought of food can trigger a surge of insulin in our bodies. Once such learned reflexes become firmly entrenched, we can experience increased insulin production and enhanced feelings of hunger before we've taken a single bite (Lucas & others, 1987).

In her studies, Rodin (1981, 1985) found that people vary in their responsiveness to environmental stimuli associated with food. She refers to people who are highly responsive to food-related stimuli as *externals,* while people who are less responsive to food cues are called *nonexternals.* When externals are exposed to an environmental stimulus that they've learned to associate with food, they produce significantly more insulin in anticipation of eating than nonexternals do.

The Brain and Eating Behavior: No Simple Answers

The *hypothalamus,* a small structure buried deep within the brain, was first implicated in the regulation of eating behavior in the 1940s. Researchers found that when a particular area called the *ventromedial hypothalamus* (VMH) was damaged, an experimental animal would eat until it became obese (Hetherington & Ranson, 1940). The photograph on page 279 shows a rat with VMH damage.

A decade later, it was discovered that damage to another area, called the *lateral hypothalamus* (LH), caused an animal to stop eating (Anand & Brobeck, 1951). With the LH damaged, a rat will starve to death if left to its

Is Your Mouth Watering? Researcher Judith Rodin has shown that the sight or thought of appetizing food can trigger a surge of insulin. That's why just looking at this photograph (assuming you like chocolate chip cookies) might make you feel hungry.

cholecystokinin (CCK)
(*kole*-eh-*sist*-oh-KINE-in) A hormone that seems to play a role in signaling satiation, or fullness.

Rat with a Damaged VMH When a particular section of the hypothalamus called the ventromedial hypothalamus is destroyed, rats will eat until they become obese—but only if the food is appetizing. This particular rat tipped the scales at 1,080 grams, or almost two-and-a-half pounds! (The pointer has gone completely around the dial and registers an additional 80 grams.)

own devices. If it is force-fed, the rat will eventually resume eating, but its body weight will drop to a much lower level.

On the basis of these initial findings, it became widely believed that the hypothalamus contained the "start eating" and "stop eating" centers. Though the simplicity of this model is appealing, later research cast serious doubts on its accuracy.

For example, it stands to reason that if the VMH alone provided the signal to stop eating, then rats with a destroyed VMH should eat everything in sight because there would be no "stop eating" signal. In reality, such rats do not eat until they explode. Instead, they become finicky and picky about their food (Ferguson & Keesey, 1975). The quality of diet seems to be the critical factor. If the food is appealing, the rats make pigs of themselves (so to speak), blimp up, and eventually stabilize as very obese rats. But if the food is blah, at least as far as a rat is concerned, they maintain their normal weight or even lose weight. Thus, whether or not damage to the VMH produces obesity is strongly related to the appeal of the food (Keesey & Powley, 1986).

Other research cast doubt on the role of the lateral hypothalamus as the "start eating" center. As it turns out, damage to the LH not only reduces the drive to eat, it also reduces general arousal and other behaviors (Marshall & Teitelbaum, 1974). In other words, damage to the LH seems to reduce a wide variety of behaviors and drives, eating behavior among them.

While it seems reasonable to conclude that the hypothalamus and its surrounding regions play an important role in regulating eating behavior, the exact nature of that role remains unclear. It does seem clear, though, that the earlier notion that the hypothalamus contains specific "start eating" and "stop eating" centers is largely inaccurate.

So what conclusions can we draw about the factors that regulate eating behavior? First, multiple signals appear to be involved, each providing some form of feedback to the brain. Oral signals, such as taste and chewing, seem to play a role in maintaining eating behavior. Stretch receptors and other sensory receptors in the stomach seem to play some role in signaling satiation (see Pennisi, 1994). Chemical signals involving the hormones CCK and insulin also seem to play pivotal roles (Bray, 1991). Second, it appears that the hypothalamus and its surrounding regions detect these varied signals and, in turn, initiate or suppress eating behavior. And third, our psychological response to external signals—such as the smell of freshly popped popcorn—may trigger physiological changes in responsive individuals, such as increased insulin production, that lead to increased feelings of hunger.

While there's no question that physiological mechanisms are involved in regulating eating behavior, a simple fact remains. The decision to start or stop eating is ultimately made consciously, in the brain's most sophisticated centers, despite hunger or satiation signals from the stomach or hypothalamus. Your body may be signaling, "Full! Full! Enough, already!!" but you can still reach for another piece of pumpkin pie after a scrumptious Thanksgiving feast. Likewise, even when you're very hungry, you may deliberately postpone or restrict eating, at least for a short period of time. Thus, what motivates you to eat at a particular moment is governed by a complex system involving the *interaction* of physiological, behavioral, cognitive, and environmental factors.

basal metabolic rate (BMR)
The rate at which the body uses energy for vital body functions when at rest.

The Regulation of Body Weight

People vary in the rate at which body energy is used for vital life functions. What role does basal metabolic rate play in weight regulation? How does set-point theory account for the regulation of body weight? How do obese individuals differ from nonobese individuals in their response to food? What characterizes anorexia and bulimia?

FIGURE 8.2 Age and Sex Differences in Metabolism From birth through adolescence, there is a steep decline in the rate at which your body uses energy for vital functions, such as heartbeat, breathing, and body heat. From early adulthood until old age, your basal metabolic rate continues to decrease, only more slowly. Females generally have a lower metabolic rate than males throughout the lifespan.

(Stuart & Davis, 1972, p. 166.)

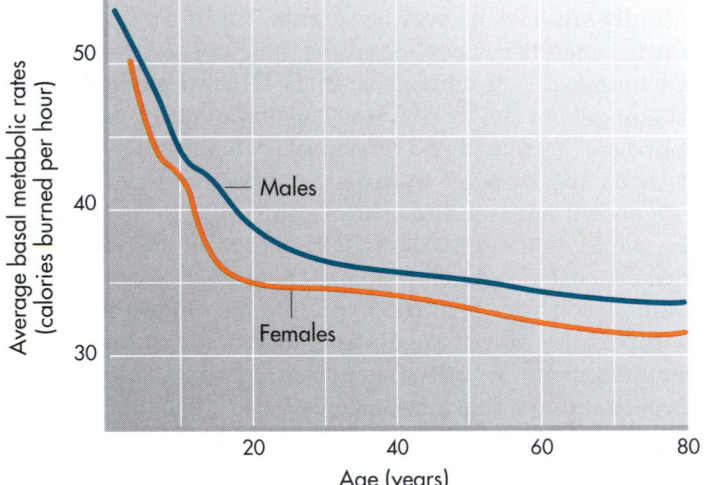

About one-third of your body's energy is used for routine physical activities, such as sitting, walking, and standing in line at the grocery store. The remaining two-thirds is used for continuous body functions that are essential to life, such as respiration, heartbeat, brain activity, and the production of body heat. The rate at which your body uses energy for vital body functions when at rest is referred to as your **basal metabolic rate,** which we abbreviate as **BMR.**

People vary greatly in their basal metabolic rate. In a classic study, investigators tracked the food intake of pairs of same-sex subjects who were carefully matched for weight, age, height, and daily levels of activity (Rose & Williams, 1961). Over the course of several weeks, all subjects maintained their normal weight. Yet, in many cases, one member of the matched pairs was eating *twice as much* as the other member! This finding demonstrates that a constant body weight depends on the critical balance between food intake and BMR.

A variety of factors influence a person's basal metabolic rate. On the average, women have a lower metabolic rate than men. How much a person weighs also influences metabolism. Contrary to popular belief, heavy people typically have a *higher* metabolic rate than slender people (Franken, 1994). Basically, this is because a heavy person's body has to work harder to maintain vital body functions.

Metabolism also decreases with age. Between infancy and your early twenties, body metabolism declines steeply (see Figure 8.2). Consequently, it's not surprising that many people, upon reaching adulthood, suddenly must begin to watch how much they eat. As your BMR decreases with age, less food is required to meet your energy needs. If, as a young adult, you continue to eat as much as you did during your adolescence, it's almost a sure bet that you'll gain weight unless you increase your activity level. After your early twenties, your BMR continues to decline, but more gradually.

Genetics also seems to play a role in determining a person's BMR. For example, the adult weight of adopted individuals is strongly correlated with the adult weights of their biological parents, not their adoptive parents (Stunkard & others, 1986). Usually, a child's approximate adult weight can be reliably predicted from the adult weights of his or her biological parents.

TABLE 8.3 Factors That Influence Basal Metabolic Rate (BMR)

Age	BMR slows down with increased age, especially during the first two decades of life.
Sex	Males generally have higher metabolic rates than females.
Body size	Heavier people have higher metabolic rates than slender people.
Genetics	Evidence strongly suggests that BMR is influenced by heredity.
Diet	Restricted food intake lowers BMR; excess food intake increases BMR.

Set-Point Theory: Are We "Set" to Maintain a Particular Weight?

Anyone who has ever tried to lose weight by dieting or to gain weight by eating more has experienced the body's "resistance" to establishing a new "standard" weight, whether it's lower or higher. According to Richard Keesey and Terry

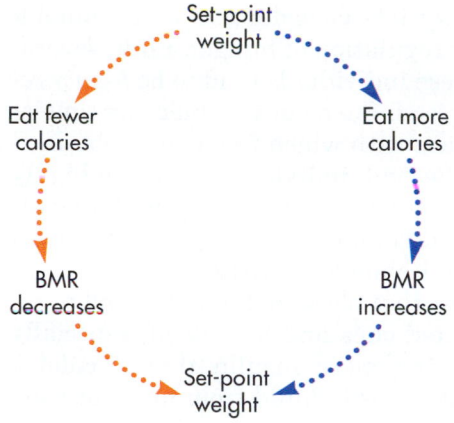

FIGURE 8.3 Set-Point Theory

Powley (1986), this happens because each of us has a **set-point weight**—a particular weight that the body is naturally set to maintain by increasing or decreasing BMR (see Figure 8.3).

For example, assume that you've consistently weighed about 140 pounds for the past several years. This would be your set-point weight. Assume further that you've committed yourself to a New Year's resolution to go on a diet and lose 10 pounds by spring. After you have significantly reduced your normal food intake for a few weeks, your body weight begins to drop below your natural set-point weight.

At this point, your body initiates actions to "defend" and reestablish its set-point weight. Specifically, your body's regulatory mechanisms compensate by reducing your BMR and triggering feelings of hunger. With your body's energy requirements reduced, it becomes easier to return to your set-point weight *even though you're still eating less food than usual*. It's as though your body is programmed to monitor your weight and keep it within a predetermined range.

The opposite effect occurs if you try to gain weight. When you *increase* food consumption and your weight begins to rise above your set-point weight, your body *increases* its expenditure of energy (BMR), and feelings of hunger are reduced. Both actions function to reestablish your set-point weight. Once your set-point weight is reestablished, your BMR returns to its normal level if your food consumption returns to normal.

Set-point theory is based on the well-established principle of homeostasis, discussed earlier. In support of set-point theory, many studies with both animals and humans have demonstrated that increases or decreases in body weight are followed by corresponding changes in the body's basal metabolic rate (Keesey & Powley, 1986).

What exactly does your body monitor to maintain your particular set-point weight? Several lines of research suggest that it's the number and size of fat cells (Faust & others, 1976, 1977a). Both human and animal studies have demonstrated that the number and size of fat cells are established very early in life—by about the age of two (Knittle, 1975; Faust & others, 1977b). These studies suggest that both the number and size of fat cells are at least partly determined by genetic factors.

However, environmental factors, such as what and how much you eat, also play an important role in the amount of fat stored. At any age, if you consistently consume more food than is required to meet your body's energy needs, the excess becomes stored as fat. At first, overeating produces an increase in the *size* of fat cells. However, if overeating continues, fat cells start increasing in *number* (Macedonio, 1984).

Unfortunately, acquiring new fat cells is a one-way street. Once acquired, fat cells are with you for life (Salens, 1984). If you acquire more fat cells, your body essentially becomes programmed to maintain a higher set-point weight (Keesey & Powley, 1986). If you reduce your weight, even dramatically, the *number* of fat cells you have does not decrease—they simply decrease in *size*.

Although set-point theory can help us understand many aspects of body weight regulation, it is not without limitations. One criticism is that set-point theory merely describes what occurs rather than explaining the underlying mechanisms.

When the Regulation of Body Weight Fails: Obesity

Approximately 30 million Americans are **obese**—their weight is 20 percent or more above their optimal weight for their age, sex, and body type (Brownell & Rodin, 1994). For about 5 percent of obese individuals, some specific cause is responsible for the excessive weight, such as a brain tumor or a hereditary disease (Salens, 1984; Rodin, 1982). But for the vast majority of the obese, a specific cause cannot be identified.

set-point weight
The particular weight that is set and maintained by increases or decreases in basal metabolic rate.

obese
Weighing 20 percent or more above one's "ideal" body weight.

Sex Symbols in Other Cultures
Throughout North America and Europe, thinness represents the cultural ideal of beauty and sex appeal. Little wonder, then, that some fifty million Americans are trying to shed pounds to achieve the socially desirable goal of thinness. Now consider the woman shown on this Cairo billboard. Although she's shaped more like a pear than a Barbie Doll, Laila Alwi is Egypt's hottest film star and biggest sex symbol. Egyptian men delight in Alwi's "full, natural, healthy" look and scoff at the "sickly" slenderness prized by Western supermodels (Shadid, 1997). Like other behaviors and social attitudes, ideals of beauty and sexual attractiveness are the product of cultural conditioning.

anorexia nervosa
An eating disorder in which the individual refuses to maintain a minimally normal body weight, is extremely afraid of gaining weight or becoming fat, and has a distorted perception about the size of his or her body.

bulimia nervosa
An eating disorder in which a person engages in binge eating and then purges the excessive food consumption by self-induced vomiting or, less often, by taking laxatives or enemas.

To get a better understanding of obesity, let's consider how obese individuals differ from the nonobese in the daily regulation of hunger. First, several studies have demonstrated that many obese individuals tend to be *highly responsive to external cues* associated with food. Such cues include the time of day, how appetizing the food is, and the ease with which food can be obtained (Schachter, 1971a, 1971b; Rodin, 1981). Second, individuals who are highly responsive to food-related stimuli tend to *react physiologically with greater insulin production*. And third, obese individuals generally operate with *higher body levels of insulin* (Rodin, 1985; Rabinowitz, 1970).

Collectively, these three points suggest that obese individuals tend to respond with greater intensity to food-related cues and food itself, especially highly appetizing foods. Unfortunately, the more insulin that circulates throughout a person's body, the faster fat deposits build from food not used for energy requirements. The more fat deposits a person acquires, the more weight is gained, and the easier it becomes to gain additional weight. As psychologist Judith Rodin (1982) put it, "Our metabolic machinery is devised in such a way that the fatter we are, the fatter we are primed to become."

So what happens when an obese person restricts food intake, sometimes severely, to lose weight? As predicted by set-point theory, the body vigorously defends against the loss by sharply reducing the rate of metabolism. Within as little as two weeks after beginning a diet, an obese person's metabolic rate may drop by 20 percent or more (see Macedonio, 1984). Far fewer calories are now needed to maintain the obese weight because the body's expenditure of energy is sharply reduced. And fat requires less energy to maintain than lean body tissue does (Rodin, 1981).

Also critical is the finding that the metabolic rate *remains* decreased for as long as the person's body weight remains below the obese set-point weight. In one study of obese individuals who maintained their weight loss, their metabolic rate was still reduced *six years* later (Leibel & Hirsch, 1984).

The implications of all these findings are less than encouraging to obese individuals. Regardless of how an individual initially becomes obese, once obesity occurs it seems to be maintained by a complex system of environmental, psychological, and biological factors (Rodin, 1985). The obese person's body becomes primed to maintain and increase fat stores. When obese people diet to lose weight, they are often fighting their own uncooperative bodies. If they are successful in reducing their fat stores and body weight, they've only won the battle, not the war. To maintain their lower weight, people must permanently modify their eating patterns and follow a regular exercise program.

When the Regulation of Eating Behavior Fails: Anorexia and Bulimia

Another disruption of normal weight lies at the opposite end of the spectrum from obesity. **Anorexia nervosa** is a potentially life-threatening disorder that involves near self-starvation. This disorder has three key symptoms: the individual refuses to maintain a minimally normal body weight, is extremely afraid of gaining weight or becoming fat, and has a distorted perception about the size of his or her body. Approximately 90 percent of cases of anorexia nervosa occur in adolescent or young adult females (American Psychiatric Association, 1994). The characteristics of anorexia nervosa are very similar for males and females, but anorexia is much less common among males (Olivardia & others, 1995).

It's rare that a person with anorexia completely loses her appetite. Rather, she places herself on a very restricted diet that may be limited to just a few foods. Weight loss is also often accomplished by excessive exercise, fasting,

Barbie, the American Ideal? If a normal-sized woman (left) was proportioned like a Barbie doll, she would look like the photograph on the right. Yale psychologist Kelly Brownell calculated that if a woman's hips stayed the same size, she would have to gain nearly a foot in height, add four inches to her chest, and lose five inches from her waist to meet the impossible standard set by Barbie. Many psychologists believe that such unrealistic standards contribute to the incidence of eating disorders in Western cultures.

self-induced vomiting, or the misuse of laxatives. By reducing total food intake, individuals with anorexia drop 15 percent or more below their ideal body weight. Depression, social withdrawal, insomnia, and, in women, failure to menstruate frequently accompany the disorder.

A hallmark of anorexia is distorted self-perception. Despite her emaciated appearance, the person with anorexia looks in the mirror and sees herself as being overweight. Or she expresses displeasure with certain parts of her body, such as an abdomen or thighs, that are "too fat." Weight loss is viewed with pride and regarded as an act of extraordinary self-discipline. Approximately 10 percent of people with anorexia nervosa die from starvation, suicide, or physical complications accompanying extreme weight loss (American Psychiatric Association, 1994).

In contrast, people suffering from **bulimia nervosa** are within their normal weight range and may even be slightly overweight. Bulimic people engage in binge eating and then purge themselves of the excessive food consumption by self-induced vomiting. Less often, they may use laxatives or enemas to purge themselves of the food.

People suffering from bulimia usually conceal their eating problems from others. Episodes of binge eating typically occur in secrecy. When a binge occurs, it usually includes the consumption of high-caloric, sweet foods that can be swallowed quickly, such as ice cream, cake, and candy. Once they begin eating, they often feel as if they cannot control their food intake. Sometimes consuming as much as 50,000 calories at one time, they eat until they are uncomfortably, even painfully, full (American Psychiatric Association, 1994; Johnson & others, 1982).

Diverse cultural, psychological, social, and genetic factors seem to be involved in both anorexia and bulimia nervosa (Steinhausen, 1994; North & others, 1995). For example, there is strong cultural pressure, especially for young women, to achieve the thinness ideal. Psychologically, there is often faulty thinking about food intake, distorted body perceptions, and a tendency toward perfectionism (Steinhausen & Vollrath, 1993; Steinhausen & Seidel, 1993).

Genetic factors also seem to play a role in eating disorders. Among female identical twins, when one develops anorexia, better than 50 percent of the time the other twin also develops anorexia. With nonidentical twins, the rate of co-occurrence of anorexia is only 5 percent (Holland & others, 1988).

CONCEPT REVIEW 8.1

The Motivation of Eating Behavior

Indicate whether each of the following statements is true or false.

___ **1.** Higher insulin levels may lead you to eat more.

___ **2.** All your fat cells are acquired by the age of two.

___ **3.** Your basal metabolic rate decreases with age.

___ **4.** Obese people typically have a lower basal metabolic rate than thin people.

___ **5.** Physiological mechanisms control when you eat and how much you eat.

___ **6.** The ventromedial hypothalamus is the brain area that provides the "start eating" signal.

Sexual Motivation and Behavior

Multiple factors are involved in the motivation of sexual behavior. How does sexual motivation differ for lower and higher animals? What biological factors are involved in sexual motivation? What are the four stages of the human sexual response? What factors have been associated with sexual orientation?

Psychologists consider the drive to have sex a basic human motive. But what exactly motivates that drive? Obviously, there are differences between sex and other basic motives, such as hunger. Engaging in sexual intercourse is essential to the survival of the human species, but it is not essential to the survival of any specific person. In other words, you'll die if you don't eat, but you won't die if you don't have sex (you may just *think* that you will).

In most animals, sexual behavior is biologically determined and triggered by hormonal changes in the female. During the cyclical period known as *estrus,* a female animal is fertile and receptive to male sexual advances. Roughly translated, the Greek word *estrus* means "frantic desire." Indeed, the female animal will often actively signal her willingness to engage in sexual activity—as the owner of any unneutered female cat or dog that's "in heat" can testify. In many species, but not all, sexual activity takes place only when the female is in estrus (Rissman, 1995).

As you go up the evolutionary scale, moving from relatively simple to more sophisticated animals, sexual behavior becomes less biologically determined and more subject to learning and environmental influences (Mook, 1996). Sexual behavior also becomes less limited to the goal of reproduction. For example, in some primate species, such as monkeys and apes, sexual activity can occur at any time, not just when the female is fertile. In these species, sexual interaction serves important social functions, defining and cementing relationships among the members of the primate group (Feder, 1984).

One rare species of chimplike apes, the bonobos of the African country of Zaire, exhibits a surprising variety of sexual behaviors (de Waal, 1995). While most animals copulate, or have sex, with the male mounting the female from behind, bonobos often copulate face-to-face. Bonobos also engage in oral sex and intense tongue kissing. And bonobos seem to like variety. Along with having frequent heterosexual activity, whether the female is fertile or not, bonobos also engage in homosexual and group sex.

The Bonobo of Zaire Bonobos demonstrate a wide variety of sexual interactions, including face-to-face copulation, kissing, and sexual interaction among same-sex pairs. Sexual behavior is not limited to reproduction, but seems to play an important role in maintaining peaceful relations among members of the bonobo group. As Frans de Waal (1995) writes, "For these animals, sexual behavior is indistinguishable from social behavior."

Emory University psychology professor Frans de Waal (1995), who has extensively studied bonobos, observes that their frequent and varied sexual behavior seems to serve important social functions. Sexual behavior is not limited to fulfilling the purpose of reproduction. Among the bonobo, sexual interaction is used to increase group cohesion, avoid conflict, and decrease tension that might be caused by competition for food. According to de Waal (1995), the bonobos' motto seems to be "Make love, not war."

In humans, of course, sexual behavior is not limited to a female's fertile period. Nor is the motivational goal of sex limited to reproduction. While a woman's fertility is regulated by monthly hormonal cycles, these hormonal changes seem to have little or no effect on a female's sexual motivation (Davidson & Myers, 1988). Even when a woman's ovaries, which produce the female sex hormone *estrogen,* are surgically removed or stop functioning during menopause, there is little or no drop in sexual interest. In many nonhuman female mammals, however, removal of the ovaries results in a complete loss of interest in sexual activity. If injections of estrogen and other female sex hormones are given, the female animal's sexual interest returns (Feder, 1984).

In male animals, removal of the testes (castration) typically causes a steep drop in sexual activity and interest, although the decline is more gradual in sexually experienced animals. Castration causes a significant decrease in levels of *testosterone,* the hormone responsible for male sexual development. When human males experience lowered levels of testosterone due to illness or castration, a similar drop in sexual interest tends to occur, although the effects vary among individuals. Some men continue to lead a normal sex life, while others quickly lose all interest in sexual activity (Feder, 1984). In castrated men who experience a loss of sexual interest, injections of testosterone restore the sexual drive.

Testosterone is also involved in female sexual motivation. Most of the testosterone in a woman's body is produced by her adrenal glands. If these glands are removed or malfunction, causing testosterone levels to become abnormally low, sexual interest often wanes (Gray & Gorzalka, 1980). When supplemental testosterone is administered, the woman's sex drive returns (Feder, 1984). Thus, in *both* men and women, sexual motivation is biologically influenced by body levels of the hormone testosterone.

The Stages of Human Sexual Response

The human sexual response cycle was first mapped by sex research pioneers **William Masters** (b. 1915) and **Virginia Johnson** (b. 1925) during the 1950s and 1960s. Up until the 1950s, information about sexual response had been gathered by observing the behavior of different animal species. However, Masters and Johnson felt that a more direct approach was needed to further the understanding of human sexual anatomy and physiology. Thus, in the name of science, Masters and Johnson observed hundreds of people engage in more than 10,000 episodes of sexual activity in their laboratory. Their findings, published in 1966, indicated that the human sexual response can be described as a cycle with four stages.

As you read the descriptions of these stages, keep in mind that the transitions between stages are not as precise or abrupt as the descriptions might lead you to believe. Moreover, the duration of time spent in any particular stage can vary on different occasions of sexual interaction.

Stage 1: Excitement

The *excitement phase* marks the beginning of sexual arousal. Sexual arousal can occur in response to sexual fantasies or other sexually arousing stimuli,

Pioneers of Sex Research: William Masters and Virginia Johnson Masters and Johnson broke new ground with their scientific study of sexual behavior in the 1960s. Along with documenting and describing the human sexual response, they also developed many innovative techniques that are still used in sex therapy.

physical contact with another person, or masturbation. In both sexes, the excitement stage is accompanied by a variety of bodily changes in anticipation of sexual interaction. There is a rapid rise in pulse rate and blood pressure. The rate of breathing increases. Blood shifts to the genitals, producing an erect penis in the male and swelling of the clitoris in the female. The female's vaginal lips expand and open up, and her vagina becomes lubricated in preparation for intercourse. Her nipples and breasts may also become enlarged, and the nipples become erect and more sensitive.

Stage 2: Plateau

In the second, *plateau phase,* physical arousal builds as pulse and breathing rates continue to increase. The penis becomes fully erect and sometimes secretes a few drops of fluid (which may contain active sperm). The testes increase in size. The clitoris withdraws under the clitoral hood, but remains very sensitive to stimulation. The vaginal entrance tightens, putting pressure on the penis during intercourse. Vaginal lubrication continues. During the excitement and plateau stages, the degree of arousal may fluctuate up and down (Masters & others, 1995). During the plateau stage, the firmness of the male's erection may increase and decrease, and so may the female's degree of vaginal lubrication.

Stage 3: Orgasm

Orgasm is the third and shortest phase of the sexual response cycle. During orgasm, blood pressure and heart rate reach their peak. The muscles in the vaginal walls and the uterus contract rhythmically, as do the muscles in and around the penis as the male ejaculates. Other muscles may contract as well, such as those in the face, arms, and legs. Both men and women describe the subjective experience of orgasm in similar—and very positive—terms (see Masters & others, 1995).

The vast majority of men experience one intense orgasm. But many women are capable of experiencing multiple orgasms. If sexual stimulation continues following orgasm, women may experience additional orgasms within a short period of time.

Stage 4: Resolution

Following orgasm, both sexes tend to experience a warm physical "glow" and a sense of well-being. Arousal slowly subsides and returns to normal levels in the *resolution phase.* The male experiences a *refractory period,* during which he is incapable of having another erection or orgasm. The length of the refractory period varies; for one man it may last a matter of minutes, for another several hours. As men become older, the length of the refractory period tends to increase.

So, there you have it—the clinical, scientific description of the physiological changes that occur before, during, and after orgasm. Although it is simplified somewhat, Figure 8.4 depicts the basic pattern of sexual response for men and women. Somehow it lacks the lusty appeal of an erotic passage from a Danielle Steele best seller or D. H. Lawrence's (1928) classic novel, *Lady Chatterley's Lover.* Nonetheless, the early work of Masters and Johnson remains a landmark in the study of human sexuality.

Female Sexual Responses: Three Basic Variations

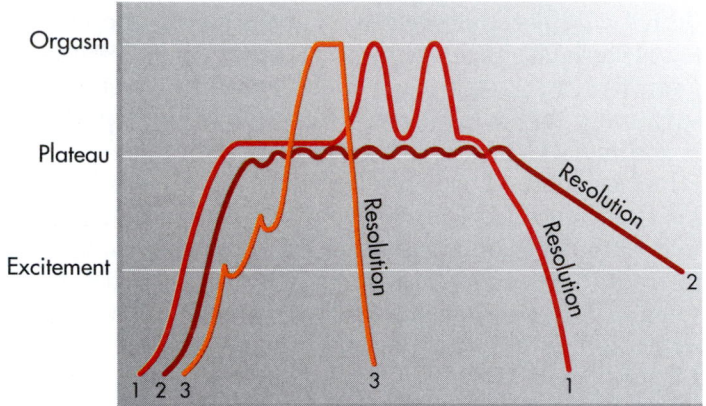

Typical Male Sexual Response

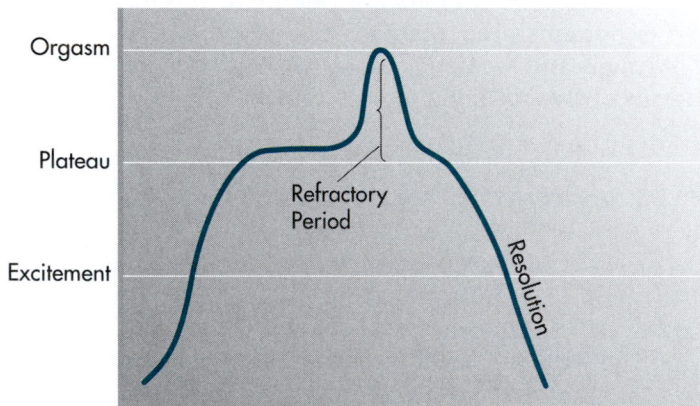

FIGURE 8.4 The Male and Female Sexual Response Cycle
The top figure depicts the three basic variations of the female sexual response. Pattern 1 shows multiple orgasms. Pattern 2 shows sexual arousal that reaches the plateau stage but not orgasm, followed by a slow resolution. Pattern 3 depicts brief reductions in arousal during the excitement stage, followed by rapid orgasm and resolution. The bottom figure depicts the most typical male sexual response, in which orgasm is followed by a refractory period.
(Masters & Johnson, 1966.)

Sexual Orientation:

The Elusive Search for an Explanation

Biological factors play an important role in motivating sexual desire and behavior. Thus, it only seems reasonable to ask if biological factors also play a role in **sexual orientation**—whether a person is sexually aroused by members of the same sex, the opposite sex, or both sexes (Bailey & Zucker, 1995). A *heterosexual* is sexually attracted toward individuals of the other sex, a *homosexual* toward individuals of the same sex, and a *bisexual* toward individuals of both sexes. Technically, the term *homosexual* can be applied to either males or females. However, female homosexuals are usually called *lesbians*. Male homosexuals typically use the term *gay* to describe their sexual orientation. Although estimates vary, approximately 7 million to 15 million American men and women are gay or lesbian (Patterson, 1995a).

Sexual orientation is not nearly as cut and dried as many people believe. Some people *are* exclusively heterosexual or homosexual, but others are less easy to categorize. Many people who consider themselves to be heterosexual have had a homosexual experience at some point in their lives (Seidman & Rieder, 1994). The opposite is also true. Many people, like our friend Richard in the chapter's prologue, consider themselves to be homosexual but have had heterosexual relationships. The key point here is that there is not always a perfect correspondence between a particular person's sexual identity, sexual desires, and sexual behaviors (Laumann & others, 1994).

Despite considerable research on sexual orientation, psychologists and other researchers cannot say with certainty why people become homosexual or bisexual. For that matter, psychologists don't know exactly why people become *heterosexual* either. Still, research on sexual orientation has pointed toward several general conclusions, especially with regard to homosexuality.

Evidence from twin studies suggests that genetics plays a role in determining a homosexual orientation (Gladue, 1994; LeVay & Hamer, 1994). For example, psychologists Michael Bailey and Richard Pillard (1991) compared the incidence of male homosexuality among pairs of identical twins (who have identical genes), fraternal twins (who are genetically as similar as any two nontwin siblings), and adoptive brothers (who have no common genetic heritage but shared the same upbringing). The researchers found that the closer the degree of genetic relationship, the more likely it was that both brothers would be homosexual. Specifically, both brothers were homosexual in 52 percent of the identical twins, 22 percent of the fraternal twins, and 11 percent of the adoptive brothers.

Bailey and his colleagues (1993) discovered very similar results in twin studies of lesbians. In 48 percent of identical twins and 16 percent of fraternal twins, both sisters were lesbian, as compared to only 6 percent of adoptive sisters. While intriguing, such genetic studies are subject to criticisms about methodology and other issues (see Byne, 1994; Byne & Parsons, 1993). Furthermore, since only half of the identical twins were both homosexual, it's clear that genetic predisposition alone cannot explain sexual orientation. Nevertheless, these studies and others support the notion that sexual orientation is at least partly influenced by genetics (Gladue, 1994).

Another biological factor that has been investigated is differences in brain structure between heterosexuals and homosexuals (LeVay & Hamer, 1994). Neurobiologist Simon LeVay (1991) discovered a small but significant difference between male heterosexuals and homosexuals in a tiny cluster of neurons in the *hypothalamus,* which is known to be involved in sexual behavior. In male homosexuals and heterosexual women, the cluster was only half the size as in heterosexual men.

sexual orientation
The direction of a person's emotional and erotic attraction, whether toward members of the opposite sex, the same sex, or both sexes.

U.S. Congressman Barney Frank and His Companion Herb Moses Frank and Moses have shared a home since 1987. Frank realized he was gay in early adolescence. Was heterosexuality ever an option for him? As Frank (1996) explains, "I wished it was. But it wasn't. I can't imagine that anybody believes that a 13-year-old in 1953 thinks, 'Boy, it would really be great to be part of this minority that everybody hates and to have a really restricted life.' You can't make yourself a different person. I am who I am. I have no idea why."

LeVay speculates that this tiny structure may be involved in determining sexual orientation (LeVay & Hamer, 1994). However, LeVay also carefully points out that there is no way of knowing if this difference in brain structure *causes* homosexual behavior in men. Conceivably, it might be the other way around—homosexual behavior might cause the difference in brain structure.

In general, the only conclusion we can draw from these studies is that some biological factors are *correlated* with a homosexual orientation (Byne, 1994). As we've stressed, correlation does not necessarily indicate causality, only that two factors *seem* to occur together. So stronger conclusions about the role of genetic and biological factors in determining sexual orientation await more definitive research findings (Baumrind, 1995; Gladue, 1994).

What about early life experiences? Is homosexuality due to abnormal parenting or early homosexual experiences? Alan Bell and his colleagues (1981) conducted a comprehensive study investigating these and other popular beliefs regarding the causes of homosexual orientation. On the basis of in-depth interviews of almost 1,000 homosexual men and women, and a comparison group of about 500 heterosexual men and women, they came to the following conclusions:

- Homosexuality is *not* due to an unpleasant early heterosexual experience, such as being sexually abused during childhood by a member of the opposite sex.

- Homosexuals are *not* more likely than heterosexuals to report a first sexual encounter with a member of the same sex, such as being seduced by an older member of the same sex.

- Homosexuality is *not* the result of an abnormal relationship between the parents and the child, such as having a father who is an inadequate male role model or having an overly dominant mother.

In short, Bell and his colleagues found *no* consistent differences between homosexual and heterosexual adults in their patterns of early experiences. It seems very unlikely, therefore, that homosexuality is caused by certain parenting styles, an unpleasant early heterosexual experience, or a pleasant early homosexual experience.

Bell and his colleagues (1981) also found that sexual orientation was determined before adolescence and long before the beginning of sexual activity. Gay men and lesbians typically became aware of homosexual feelings about three years before they engaged in any such sexual activity. In this regard, the pattern was very similar to that of heterosexual children, in whom heterosexual feelings are aroused long before the child expresses them in some form of sexual behavior.

Some researchers now believe that sexual orientation is established as early as age six (Strickland, 1995; Melton, 1989). Once sexual orientation is established, whether heterosexual or homosexual, it is highly resistant to change (American Psychiatric Association, 1994). The vast majority of homosexuals would be unable to change their orientation even if they wished to do so, just as the majority of heterosexuals would be unable to change their orientation even if *they* wished to do so. Thus, it's a mistake to assume that homosexuals have deliberately "chosen" their sexual orientation, any more than heterosexuals have. Indeed, when Richard was in high school and college, he would gladly have "chosen" to be heterosexual if the matter had been that simple.

It seems clear that no single factor determines whether people identify themselves as homosexual, heterosexual, or bisexual (Golombok & Tasker, 1996). As psychologist Bonnie Strickland (1995) points out, "Sexual identity and orientation appears to be shaped by a complexity of biological, psycho-

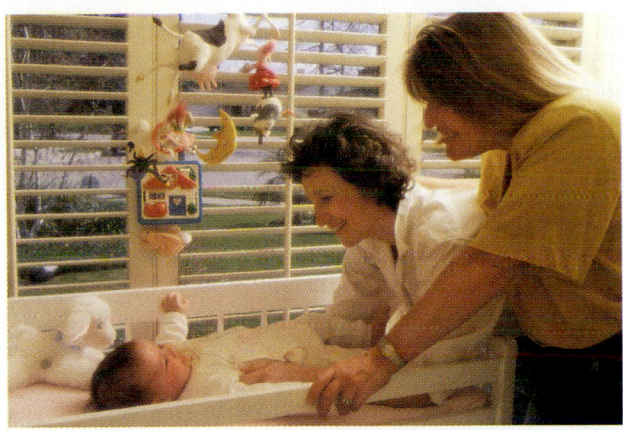

Lesbian Parents Are the children of gay or lesbian parents likely to become homosexual themselves? Apparently the children of homosexual parents are no more likely to be gay or lesbian in adulthood than children raised by heterosexual parents (Bailey & others, 1995; Golombok & Tasker, 1996). In fact, research studies to date show few differences among the children of gay, lesbian, or heterosexual parents (Strickland, 1995).

logical, and social events. Gender identity and sexual orientation, at least for most people, especially gay men, occur early, are relatively fixed, and are difficult to change." As Richard eventually acknowledged, changing his sexual orientation was simply not possible.

Homosexuality in itself is no longer considered a sexual disorder by clinical psychologists or psychiatrists (American Psychiatric Association, 1994). Many research studies have also found that homosexuals who are comfortable with their sexual orientation are just as well adjusted as heterosexuals (see Strickland, 1995).

Like heterosexuals, gays and lesbians can be found in every occupation and at every socioeconomic level in our society. And, like heterosexuals, many gays and lesbians are involved in long-term, committed, and caring relationships (Kurdek, 1995; Patterson, 1995b). Children who are raised by gay or lesbian parents are as well adjusted as children who are raised by heterosexual parents (Flaks & others, 1995; Patterson, 1995c, 1992). Furthermore, children who are raised by gay or lesbian parents are no more likely to be gay or lesbian in adulthood than are children who are raised by heterosexual parents (Golombok & Tasker, 1996; Bailey & others, 1995).

Sexual Behavior in Adulthood

The National Health and Social Life Survey (NHSLS) investigated the sexual behavior of American adults. What characterizes the sexual behavior patterns of adults? What sexual activities do most adults find appealing and unappealing? What are the most common sexual fantasies that people have?

Perhaps because sexual behavior tends to be a private matter, it's understandable that people (psychologists included) are curious about what other people do (and don't do) sexually. Of course, there are always the media images of what people are supposedly doing. If you believe the not-so-subtle media messages, everyone (except you) has such an active, steamy, and varied sex life that you can't help wondering how anyone (except you) ever finds the time to get the laundry done. Are the media images of sex in America accurate?

Researchers Robert T. Michael, Edward O. Laumann, and their colleagues at the University of Chicago will help answer that and other questions about adult sexual behavior in this section. They are the authors of the *National Health and Social Life Survey* (NHSLS)—a state-of-the-art, scientifically constructed national survey of adult sexual behavior in America. Published in 1994, this landmark survey will help us accurately answer the "Who's doing what, when, how often, and with whom" questions about human sexuality.

How Many Sex Partners Do People Have?

The notion that people today, especially younger people, have more sex partners than people did twenty or thirty years ago is fundamentally accurate. Among people aged thirty to fifty, about half have had five or more sexual partners. In contrast, only about a third of those over age fifty have had five or more sexual partners (Laumann & others, 1994).

Why the difference between age groups in the number of sexual partners? The vast majority of adults in the fifty to fifty-nine age range had their first sexual experience in the context of marriage. In contrast, only about a

	Number of Sex Partners in Past Twelve Months			
	0	1	2 to 4	5+
Total	12%	71%	14%	3%
By Gender				
Men	10	67	18	5
Women	14	75	10	2
By Age				
18–24	11	57	24	9
25–29	6	72	17	6
30–34	9	73	16	2
35–39	10	77	11	2
40–44	11	75	13	1
45–49	15	75	9	1
50–54	15	79	5	0
55–59	32	65	4	0

FIGURE 8.5 Number of Sex Partners During the Previous Year
In this chart, you can see that regardless of age or gender, about 80 percent of the respondents in the NHSLS survey reported having had one or no sexual partners during the previous year.

(Adapted from data in Michael & others, 1994, Table 6, pp. 102–103.)

third of today's young adults had their first sexual experience in the context of marriage (Michael & others, 1994). Young adults today tend to become sexually active at an earlier age and are marrying at a later average age. Hence, younger people today tend to have more sexual partners than members of older generations.

Now consider a slightly different issue: the number of sexual partners in the past year. The vast majority of people—about 80 percent—had either *one* sexual partner or *none* in the previous year (see Figure 8.5). Why so few sexual partners in the last year? In a word, marriage. Marriage continues to be a cornerstone of American society as well as a major developmental milestone for most people on the trek through adulthood. As people become adults, they experience considerable social pressure to find a partner and marry. Doing so confers numerous benefits, not the least of which is the social, legal, and moral acceptance of the sexual partnership.

By the age of thirty, about 90 percent of Americans have married. Regardless of age or number of previous partners, once most couples marry or start cohabiting, they feel strongly committed to being faithful to each other. As Michael and his colleagues (1994) explain:

> Marriage regulates sexual behavior with remarkable precision. No matter what they did before they wed, no matter how many partners they had, the sexual lives of married people are similar. Despite the popular myth that there is a great deal of adultery in marriage, our data and other reliable studies do not find it. Instead, the vast majority are faithful while the marriage is intact.

How Often Do People Have Sex?

Perhaps the widest disparity between the media images and the NHSLS results involves the issue of how often people have sex. Put simply, the media images that frequent, frolicking sex is "normal" do not reflect what is going on in America's bedrooms.

Here's what the NHSLS found: One-third of American adults have sex with a partner two or more times per week; one-third have sex a few times per month; and one-third have sex a few times a year or not at all (Michael & others, 1994). When the data are combined for all adults between eighteen and fifty-nine, men have sex an average of about seven times per month, while women have sex an average of about six times per month (Laumann & others, 1994). So any way you look at it, the most frequent activity in America's bedrooms is sleep, not sex.

Which Americans have the most active sex lives? Those young, attractive, footloose, swinging singles, right? Wrong. The fact is that married or cohabiting couples have the most active sex lives (Michael & others, 1994). If you think about it, this finding makes sense. Sexual activity is strongly regulated by the availability of a sex partner. Being a member of a stable couple is the social arrangement most likely to produce a readily accessible sexual partner.

Are people happy with their sex lives? The vast majority of the NHSLS respondents—about 85 percent—reported that they were physically and emotionally satisfied with their sexual relationships (Laumann & others, 1994). Part of the explanation for this high percentage is that in today's society there is considerably less social pressure to endure an unhappy marriage "until death do you part." Hence, those who are sexually dissatisfied with their relationship are likely to separate or get di-

Intimacy, Love, and Sexuality in Adulthood Forming a long-term, committed relationship with another person is a key task of early adulthood. For many couples, the bonds of love and intimacy established in early adulthood last a lifetime.

vorced—and try again with someone else. The net result is that most Americans are happily married or cohabiting.

What Do People *Actually* Do When They Have Sex?

Vaginal intercourse is nearly universal as the most practiced sexual activity among heterosexual couples. What about other practices? More than two-thirds of Americans have either given or received *oral sex* at some point in their lives. Fewer men (26 percent) and women (20 percent) have ever engaged in *anal sex* (that is, a penis inserted in the partner's anus) (Laumann & others, 1994).

What Would People *Like* To Do Sexually?

Given that most Americans seem to be having pretty traditional sex, you may be wondering whether they'd like to be a little more adventurous. After all, researchers have found that people do have sexual fantasies about a wide range of activities (see In Focus Box 8.1). So what do most people find appealing, and is that any different from what they actually do?

Although the list of potential sexual practices is varied, people prefer to stick with the tried and true. The most preferred sexual activities, in descending order for both sexes, are as follows: (1) having vaginal intercourse; (2) watching the partner undress; (3) receiving oral sex; and (4) giving oral sex.

In some ways, the flip side of the coin is more revealing. What do people find *un*appealing? Regardless of age, at least 90 percent of women found no appeal in the following sexual practices: (1) being forced to do something sexual; (2) forcing someone to do something sexual, (3) receiving anal intercourse; (4) having a same-gender sex partner; and (5) having sex with a stranger. With the exception of sex with a stranger, at least 90 percent of men also found these sexual practices unappealing. Other sexual practices that the majority of people do not find appealing include having group sex, using a vibrator or dildo (an object used as a substitute for an erect penis), and watching other people engage in sexual activity (Michael & others, 1994).

The picture that emerges of adult sexuality is *not* one that seems to match the typical media images. The vast majority of Americans follow very traditional patterns of sexual behavior. Rather than hopping from bed to bed, most people spend almost all their adult years involved in a stable sexual relationship with one partner. Compared to single people, married or cohabiting couples have more active sex lives.

For the most part, Americans are fundamentally happy with the relationship they have with their sexual partner. And, as this section has made clear, most American adults are *not* inclined toward kinky or unusual sexual practices. In fact, Americans tend to be rather conservative and traditional in their sexual practices and preferences.

In real life, the unheralded, seldom discussed world of married sex is actually the one that satisfies people the most. It may not be an exciting picture of sex in America, but if we look at the social forces that push us toward married life, it is an understandable, if not predicted, picture.

Robert T. Michael, 1994

Media Images of Sex and Sexuality Sexual themes and images are often used to sell products and movies and to boost TV ratings. How accurate are media images of human sexuality?

IN FOCUS 8.1

Everything You Wanted to Know About Sexual Fantasies

The brain is the most erotic organ in the human body. After all, the brain plays a pivotal role in the expression of human sexuality. What people think about and imagine influences how they behave sexually. And, in turn, people's sexual behavior can influence the content of their *sexual fantasies*—erotic or sexually arousing mental images (Leitenberg & Henning, 1995). In the realm of human sexuality, the mind–body connection is definitely a two-way street.

We experience sexual fantasies in the private theater of our own minds, but psychologists have discovered that sexual fantasies are a nearly universal human phenomenon. Using checklists and questionnaires, researchers have been able to answer various questions about people's sexual fantasies. In this box, with the help of an excellent research summary by University of Vermont psychologists Harold Leitenberg and Kris Henning (1995), we tackle some of the most intriguing questions about this private human experience.

When and How Often Do People Have Sexual Fantasies?

Sexual fantasies tend to begin during the adolescent years, and almost all adult men and women (95 percent) report having had sexual daydreams. It is very common for both men and women occasionally to engage in sexual fantasies during intercourse. But compared to women, men report a higher incidence of sexual fantasies during masturbation and nonsexual activities. In short, men tend to think about sex more often than women.

What Do People Have Sexual Fantasies About?

If you accept the notion that any fantasy, sexual or not, is based to some degree on life experiences, the three most common types of sexual fantasies that men and women have won't surprise you. They are: (1) reliving an exciting sexual experience; (2) imagining that you are having sex with your current partner; and (3) imagining that you are having sex with a different partner.

Do Male and Female Sexual Fantasies Differ?

There are some well-substantiated differences. First, men tend to fantasize themselves in active roles—that is, doing something sexual to their partner. In contrast, women tend to imagine themselves in sexually passive roles—that is, having something sexual done to them.

Second, men tend to have sexual fantasies with more explicit imagery, often involving specific sexual positions or anatomical details. Women are more likely to imagine romantic themes, including warm, loving feelings about their partner and details about the romantic ambiance of the scene.

Third, guys are more likely to imagine having sex with multiple partners. As Leitenberg and Henning (1995) put it, "Fantasizing about having sex with multiple partners at the same time appears to be more consonant with the male stereotype of being a 'superstud' than with the female stereotype of wanting a close, loving, monogamous relationship."

Are Sexual Fantasies Psychologically Unhealthy? Are They a Sign of Sexual Frustration or Dissatisfaction?

In a word, no. Neither of these notions has been supported by the research. In fact, the research has led to just the opposite conclusion: The people who engage in sexual fantasies the most often are those who exhibit the *least* number of sexual problems and the *least* sexual dissatisfaction.

Nonetheless, some people are troubled by their sexual fantasies. About 25 percent of people experience some degree of guilt over having sexual fantasies. The essence of this guilt is often the belief that sexual fantasies are immoral, will harm the relationship with their partner, or indicate that something is wrong with the person.

What About "Dominance" and "Submission" Sexual Fantasies?

Men are more likely to fantasize dominance themes (forcing someone to do something sexual) while women are more likely to report submission themes (being forced to do something sexual). However, it's important to stress that the fact that a woman might find submission fantasies sexually arousing does *not* indicate a desire to

actually be forced into sexual submission, much less assaulted or raped (see Bond & Mosher, 1986; Kanin, 1982). As we note in the chapter, almost no women or men find appealing the idea of actually being forced to do something sexual or actually forcing someone to do something sexual (Michael & others, 1994).

Isn't This a Contradiction?

Not really. First, any kind of fantasy, whether it's sexual or not, allows us to imagine possibilities that may have little probability of occurring. Fantasy provides you with your own internal, private improvisational theater. As the lead character, director, and set designer, you control the plot, action, and dialogue without taking any *real* risks.

Given that, let's go back to the issue of female submission fantasies. The typical female submission fantasy is *not* one of being brutally forced to do something against the woman's will. Instead, as researchers Susan Bond and Donald Mosher (1986) point out, the typical female submission fantasy is one of an attractive man being overwhelmed by the woman's irresistible charms. Does this fantasy sound the least bit familiar? It should. It is a standard sexual fantasy that has been played out in many romantic novels and movies. Such fantasies have *nothing* in common with mental or actual scenes of brutal rape or nonconsensual sex.

Sexual Motivation

On the basis of the research findings described in the text, indicate whether each of the following statements is true or false.

_____ **1.** Single people aged twenty to twenty-five have the most active and satisfying sex lives.

_____ **2.** Although vaginal intercourse was reported as the most common sexual activity, most people secretly preferred other forms of sexual expression.

_____ **3.** With the exception of humans, the sexual behavior of all animal species is governed by hormonal changes in the female and is limited to the goal of reproduction.

_____ **4.** Almost half of all married people in the United States are dissatisfied with their sex lives.

_____ **5.** According to sex researchers Masters and Johnson, the correct order of stages of the human sexual response is excitement, orgasm, plateau, and resolution.

Arousal Motives: Curiosity and Sensation Seeking

> *According to arousal theory, people are motivated to maintain an optimal level of arousal. What factors influence curiosity and exploratory behavior? How does arousal theory help explain the pacing of curious behavior? What is sensation seeking?*

Arousal theory is based on the observation that people find both very high levels of arousal and very low levels of arousal quite unpleasant. When arousal is too low, we experience boredom and try to *increase* arousal by seeking out stimulating experiences. But when arousal is too high, we seek to *reduce* arousal in a less stimulating environment. Thus, according to this theory, people are motivated to maintain an *optimal* level of arousal, one that is neither too high nor too low (Hebb, 1955; see Petri, 1996). The optimal, or "just right," level of arousal can vary from person to person, from time to time, and from one situation to another.

According to psychologist Daniel Berlyne (1960, 1971), when arousal is unpleasantly low, one way that people and other animals increase arousal is by seeking out novel stimuli and situations. Thus, arousal theory can help explain the next motive that we consider—curiosity.

Curiosity and Exploratory Behavior

Curiosity is a motive that has a strong influence on human behavior at all stages of the life cycle (Loewenstein, 1994). Almost immediately after birth, human infants begin visually exploring the environment, their attention captured by the new, the different. Though only a few hours old, an infant will have its curiosity aroused by the sight of objects with relatively complex shapes, patterns, and contours (Fantz, 1963, 1965; Milewski, 1976).

arousal theory
The view that people are motivated to maintain an optimal level of arousal that is neither too high nor too low.

Whoa! What's in Here? The joy of curiosity and discovery is evident in eleven-month-old Laura's face as she explores the fascinating contents of the kitchen pantry. Throughout the life-span, curiosity is a compelling motive that helps us understand our environment.

At My Own Pace, Please! At any age, people "pace" their exposure to new stimuli. For many young children, the prospect of a face-to-face encounter with Santa may be more novelty than they can handle comfortably.

We don't explore the world haphazardly. One purpose of curiosity and exploratory behavior is to become familiar with and understand our world (Loewenstein, 1994). In pursuit of this goal, we "pace" the rate at which we expose ourselves to increasing complexity and novelty (Dember & Earl, 1957). As we become familiar with a stimulus, we *gradually* move toward stimuli that are slightly more complex (Arkes & Boykin, 1971; May, 1963). This pacing produces the optimal level of physical and cognitive arousal that helps motivate curiosity (Berlyne, 1960, 1971).

If the pace of exposure to a complex stimulus is too fast, uncomfortable levels of physical or cognitive arousal can occur. When that happens, the curiosity drive becomes inhibited, and we withdraw from the stimulus. Intense anxiety and fear can even be triggered (Spielberger & Starr, 1994).

An example of this pattern often occurs during the holiday season, when a well-intentioned parent tries to prod his young child to sit on Santa's lap so the photographer can snap a picture. At a safe distance, the young child's pace of curiosity remains comfortable. After all, the odd-looking, bearded guy in the red and white outfit with the black boots *is* a fascinating, novel stimulus to the young child.

To the parent, however, the situation is neither complex nor novel. So, in the interest of speeding things up, the parent lovingly carries Munchkin up to be deposited on the bearded guy's lap. Because the situation is moving faster than the child's exploratory pace, the child's physical and cognitive arousal accelerates exponentially. Curiosity rapidly gives way to extreme fear and the instinctual "flight" response. As the child's screams echo throughout the mall, the photographer captures this magical moment of childhood terror on film forever.

Beyond illustrating the importance of pacing in curiosity, the Santa example underscores a few other important points. First, regardless of a person's age, what's considered "novel" or "complex" is relative to each individual's life experiences. As an individual becomes more familiar with his environment through exploratory behavior, the complexity or novelty of the objects or situations that inspire his curiosity progressively increases (Spielberger & Starr, 1994).

Second, the Santa example illustrates that the tendency to approach or withdraw from new situations varies from one person to another. Not all young children, of course, respond with terror to being placed on Santa's lap. As you'll see in Chapter 9, some children respond positively to novel stimuli and easily adjust to changes in their environment, while other children do not. These temperamental differences seem to be based on genetic predispositions and are often remarkably consistent throughout a person's life (Thomas & Chess, 1977, 1980).

Motivated to an Extreme
They are aptly called "extreme sports" and they include such diverse activities as hang gliding, ice climbing, white-water kayaking, bungee jumping, and parachuting from mountain cliffs and radio towers. Like our friend Richard in the chapter prologue, millions of Americans are motivated to engage in such high-risk activities. For them, the rush of adrenaline that they experience when they push the outer limit is an exhilarating and rewarding experience.

Sensation Seeking

Psychologist Marvin Zuckerman (1994) has extensively studied people who are highly motivated to try risky or exciting activities, whom he refers to as *sensation seekers*. People who are high in **sensation seeking** are motivated to experience the high levels of arousal that are associated with varied and novel activities that often involve some degree of physical or social risk. According to Zuckerman (1983), the tendency toward sensation seeking is an inborn personality trait.

On the surface, it would seem that sensation seekers are drawn to danger. But sensation seekers do not seem to be attracted to danger per se. Instead, they like novel experiences for their own sake and are not about to let a little danger stand in their way.

Sensation seekers tend to view themselves as independent, openminded, and unconventional. They like feeling uninhibited, especially in relaxed social situations. They tend to be flexible in their style of thinking, are tolerant of uncertainty, and enjoy the discovery of new knowledge. When they make decisions, they often give more consideration to their own sentiments than to the feelings of others. This characteristic, coupled with their tendency toward unconventional behavior, can sometimes put them in conflict with authority figures (see Franken, 1994). However, sensation seekers are not more likely than other people to commit antisocial acts or crimes (Levenson & others, 1995).

Competence and Achievement Motivation

> *Competence motivation is striving to be capable, whereas achievement motivation is striving to excel or outperform others. How is achievement motivation measured? How does culture affect achievement motivation? What is self-efficacy?*

When you strive to use your cognitive, social, and behavioral skills to be capable and exercise control in a situation, you are displaying **competence motivation** (R. White, 1959). It is competence motivation that provides much of the "push" to prove to yourself that you can successfully tackle new challenges. Enrolling in this course, mastering algebra, or becoming proficient at a new computer program all reflect competence motivation.

A step beyond competence motivation is **achievement motivation**—the drive to excel, succeed, or outperform others at some task. In the chapter prologue, Richard clearly displayed a high level of achievement motivation. Running for student body president, competing as a diver at the national level of collegiate competition, and striving to maintain a straight-A average are all examples of Richard's drive to achieve.

sensation seeking
The degree to which an individual is motivated to experience high levels of arousal associated with varied and novel activities.

competence motivation
Motivated behavior directed toward demonstrating competence and exercising control in a situation.

achievement motivation
Motivated behavior directed toward excelling, succeeding, or outperforming others at some task.

Extraordinary Achievement Motivation
Gymnast Kerri Strug thrilled onlookers with her vault during the 1996 summer Olympics. Despite a badly sprained ankle, she flawlessly performed a difficult vault, believing that it was necessary for the U.S. team to win a gold medal. Strug's ankle was so badly injured that she had to be carried to the platform by her coach to receive her gold medal.

Henry Murray (1938) first defined the "need to achieve" as the tendency to "overcome obstacles, to exercise power, to strive to do something difficult as well and as quickly as possible." Since the 1950s, David McClelland (1985, 1984; McClelland & others, 1953) has been the leading researcher on the topic of achievement motivation.

Achievement motivation has been most commonly measured by a test called the *Thematic Apperception Test,* abbreviated *TAT.* Originally developed by Christiana Morgan and Henry Murray (1935), the TAT consists of a series of ambiguous pictures. The person being tested is asked to make up a story about each picture, and the story is then coded in terms of its achievement themes and imagery. (In Chapter 10, we discuss the TAT and similar tests in more detail.)

Several studies have shown that TAT measures of achievement do generally correlate well with various measures of success, such as school grades, job success, and performance in laboratory tests (Spangler, 1992). For example, even simple arithmetic tasks are performed more rapidly by people with a high need to achieve than people with a low need to achieve (McClelland, 1985).

Achievement Motivation and Culture

When it is broadly defined as the "desire for excellence," achievement motivation is found in many, if not all, cultures. In individualistic cultures, like those that characterize North American and European countries, the need to achieve emphasizes personal, individual success rather than the success of the group. In these cultures, achievement motivation is also closely linked with succeeding on competitive tasks (Markus & Kitayama, 1991).

In collectivistic cultures, like those of many Asian countries, achievement motivation tends to have a different focus. Instead of being individually oriented, achievement orientation is more *socially* oriented (Bond, 1986). The person strives to achieve not in order to promote himself or herself, but to promote the status or well-being of other members of the relevant social group, such as family members (Matsumoto & others, 1994). Individuals may persevere or aspire to do well in order to fulfill the expectations of family members and to fit into the larger group.

For example, the Japanese student who strives to do well academically is typically not motivated by the desire for personal recognition. Rather, the student's behavior is more likely to be motivated by the desire to enhance the social standing of his or her family by gaining admission to a top university (Hawkins, 1994).

SCIENCE VERSUS PSEUDOSCIENCE 8.2

Subliminal Self-Help Tapes: Effortless Motivation?

A typical subliminal self-help tape contains the sounds of ocean waves or relaxing music. "Subliminal messages," or messages that are below one's level of subjective awareness, are supposedly embedded in the sounds (Merikle, 1988).

The notion that simply listening to a subliminal self-help tape will quickly and easily produce changes in our motivation, behavior, and attitudes is very appealing. Who doesn't want to have "effortless weight control," "peak performance in work, studies, the arts, or sports," and the ability to "conquer habits like smoking, alcohol, and drugs without struggle," to quote a few claims we read in a recent advertisement.

As with many pseudoscientific claims, the illusion of scientific credibility in selling subliminal self-help tapes is often promoted by the use of phrases that certainly *sound* scientific, like "technological breakthrough," "scientific research," and the testimony of "leading authorities." And, in fact, people spend millions of dollars each year on subliminal self-help tapes on the basis of the unsubstantiated claims contained in such ads (Dillingham, 1987). In the last few years, college bookstores have also begun selling subliminal motivation tapes. Our students often ask us about the effectiveness of such tapes and if they should buy them.

How do subliminal self-help tapes stand up to scientific scrutiny? Consider a carefully controlled study involving 79 college students who were enrolled in a career development class (Russell & others, 1991). The students were randomly assigned to one of three groups. The experimental group listened to two subliminal self-help tapes, one on improving study habits and the other on passing exams. The placebo control group listened to what they *thought* were subliminal self-help tapes. In reality, the placebo tapes contained no subliminal messages, just the sound of ocean waves. The real and fake subliminal tapes were provided by the largest manufacturer of subliminal tapes in the United States. The third group was a no-treatment control group that didn't listen to any tapes.

According to the subliminal-tape manufacturer, an individual should listen to the tapes for 20 to 25 hours before expecting significant results. Over ten weeks of the semester, the students listened to the tapes for an average of *120* hours. Some students listened to the tapes for more than 250 hours. At the end of the semester, the final-examination scores of the students in the three experimental groups were compared. The researchers also compared the three groups in terms of their semester grade point average.

The result? There were *no* significant differences among the three groups in their final examination scores or their semester grade point average. In other words, the tapes produced none of the effects that the manufacturer claimed they produced. This finding is consistent with other research that also found no evidence to support the claim that subliminal self-help tapes can influence motivation or complex behaviors (Greenwald & others, 1991; McConnell, 1989).

The moral? Don't be fooled by the advertising claims for subliminal self-help tapes. Their not-so-subliminal claims are designed to get you to spend your money by promising easy answers to life's difficulties. If you absolutely feel compelled to spend your money on something that will help you do better in your classes, buy a fluorescent highlighting pen to use when reading your textbooks. Plus, if you hold the pen's cap up to your ear, you can hear ocean waves. Honest!

Self-Efficacy

Competence and achievement motivation are closely linked to self-efficacy. Albert Bandura (1997) defines **self-efficacy** as the degree to which you are subjectively convinced of your ability to effectively meet the demands of a particular situation. If you have strong beliefs of self-efficacy, you will exert greater motivational effort in trying to master a situation and will persist longer in the face of obstacles (Bandura, 1988). For example, if you believe strongly in your memory capabilities, you will invest more effort in trying to complete memory-related tasks, increasing the likelihood of success (Bandura, 1989b).

Not surprisingly, people who see themselves as competent and capable tend to strive for higher personal goals. In choosing a career, for example, a person with strong self-efficacy will consider a wider range of options and prepare herself better educationally (Wood & Bandura, 1991).

self-efficacy
The degree to which a person is subjectively convinced of his or her ability to effectively meet the demands of a situation.

At virtually any age, we tend to avoid challenging situations or tasks that we *believe* exceed our capabilities (Bandura, 1989a, 1989b). The motivational effort of an individual with self-doubts quickly dwindles. Rather than persisting in trying to master a situation, the self-doubter will often settle for a half-baked solution that doesn't fully reflect his capabilities, or may abandon his efforts altogether. Even though he possesses the necessary skills, he may fail to perform up to his ability (Bandura, 1991a).

CONCEPT REVIEW 8.3

Identifying Arousal Motives

Identify the motive that is demonstrated in each of the following situations. Choose from: curiosity, optimal arousal, sensation seeking, achievement motivation, or self-efficacy.

_____ **1.** Amani was bored, so she called a friend and went to a movie.

_____ **2.** Because Matthew had experience as a paramedic, he felt confident when he entered medical school.

_____ **3.** Ross can't dance, but he went to the prom just to see what it was like.

_____ **4.** Once Alexa perfected her cartwheel, she decided she would learn to do a back handspring within two weeks.

_____ **5.** Although they are mild-mannered English majors during the week, Catherine, Suzanne, and Cele spend every weekend skydiving with other members of the Manhattan Skydiving Club.

Emotion

Emotions serve many functions in human behavior and relationships. What are the three components of emotion? What are basic emotions? How do culture and individual differences influence emotional experience?

Emotions are closely tied to motivational processes. Put simply, we are motivated to seek out experiences that produce pleasurable emotions, such as happiness and pride. And we are motivated to avoid experiences that produce unpleasant emotions, such as anger or fear (Ekman & Davidson, 1994).

More generally, emotions give meaning to our daily experience (Izard, 1989). In fact, emotions are so important to human experience that it's hard to imagine a life without them. Even the thoroughly rational Vulcan, Mr. Spock, occasionally lost his cool on "Star Trek" (no doubt a result of his half-human parentage). Unlike Vulcans, humans seem to be born with a tendency to experience certain emotions, although the conditions that give rise to those emotions vary greatly from person to person.

How are emotions different from moods? Although *emotions* and *moods* are clearly related, psychologists draw a distinction between the two states. **Emotion** can be formally defined as a psychological state involving three distinct components: subjective experience, physical arousal, and a behavioral or expressive response. Generally, emotions are intense but rather short-lived. Emotions are also more likely to

The Many Functions of Emotion Emotions play an important role in relationships and social communication. If a friend tells you that she is thrilled, happy, or proud, you immediately understand her internal emotional state.

emotion
A distinct psychological state that involves subjective experience, physical arousal, and a behavioral expression or response.

have a specific cause, to be directed toward some particular object, and to motivate a person to take some sort of action (Frijda, 1994). In contrast, a *mood* involves a milder emotional state that is more general and pervasive, such as gloominess or contentment, that lasts for a few hours or days (Watson & Clark, 1994).

The Subjective Experience of Emotion:
Classifying Emotions

Given the central role that emotions play in our psychological experience, it may surprise you that considerable disagreement exists among psychologists regarding the definition and classification of emotions (LeDoux, 1995; Ekman & Davidson, 1994). Some psychologists assert that there are a limited number of universal, basic emotions. According to this view, the *basic emotions* are universal, and they are biologically determined products of evolution (Ekman, 1992). Anger, happiness, sadness, and fear are most commonly cited as the basic emotions. To this list, other researchers add disgust, surprise, anxiety, shame, and interest (Turner & Ortony, 1992).

According to some emotion theorists, more complex emotions are produced by various combinations of basic emotions. For example, combining anger and disgust yields contempt; sadness plus surprise equal disappointment; and love is the result of combining joy and acceptance (Plutchik, 1984). Other theorists, however, reject the idea of basic emotions. Instead, they believe that a large number of qualitatively different emotions exist (Ortony & Turner, 1990).

People often experience a *blend* of emotions, rather than a "pure" form of any single given emotion. Thus, you might simultaneously feel unhappy, worried, and gloomy about a test that you have to take tomorrow. In more complex situations, we may experience *mixed emotions,* in which very different emotions are experienced simultaneously or in rapid succession. For example, ending a relationship might involve a bittersweet combination of anger, jealousy, sadness, nostalgia, and relief.

Emotions can be classified in an orderly way. When emotions are compared, they tend to be arranged along two dimensions: how pleasant or unpleasant the emotion is, and how much arousal is present (Russell, 1980). For example, how would you distinguish between the positive emotions of *contentment* and *joy*? Or the negative emotions of *rage* and *resentment*? Although each pair of emotions is alike in terms of being pleasant or unpleasant, they differ in terms of the intensity of the arousal experienced. Joy and rage involve high levels of arousal or intensity, while contentment and resentment involve relatively low levels of arousal. Other emotions can be arranged along the same dimensions (see Figure 8.6).

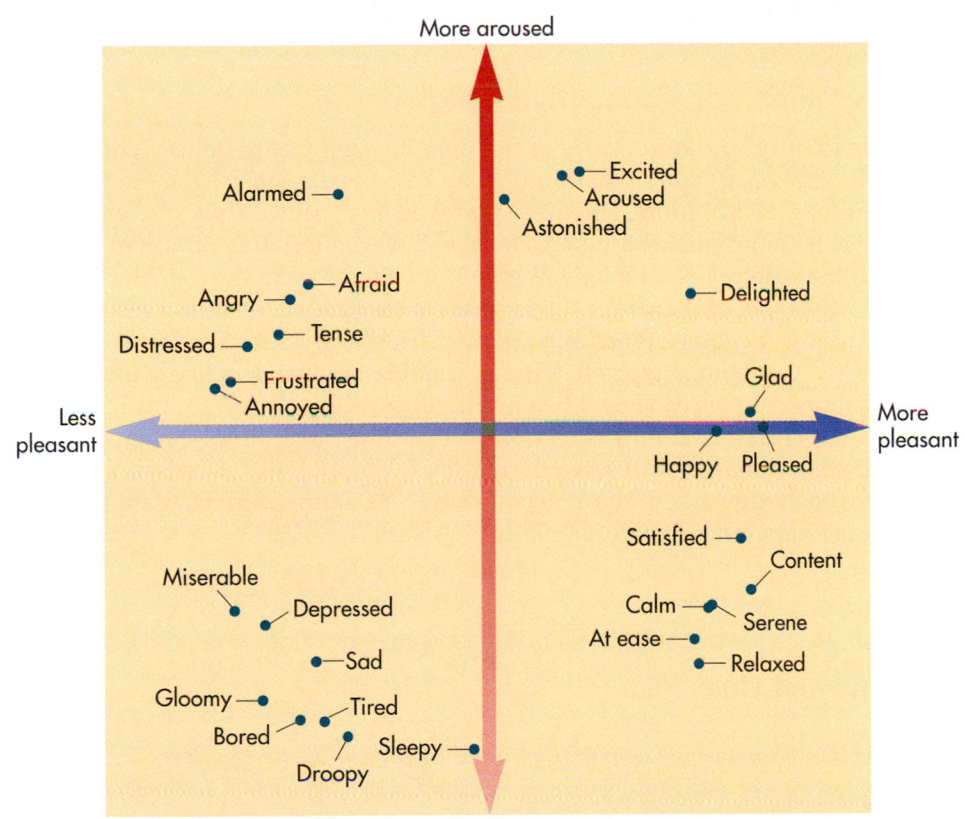

FIGURE 8.6 Comparing Emotions: The Dimensions of Emotion When emotions are compared, they can be arranged along two dimensions: how pleasant or unpleasant they are, and how much or how little arousal they involve.
(Adapted from Russell, 1980, p. 1168.)

Culture and Emotional Experience

Are such emotional dimensions universal? Psychologist James Russell compared the emotion rankings of people from several different cultures. He found that they arranged emotions in much the same way as their American counterparts (Russell & others, 1989). Other researchers have found general agreement among cultures regarding the subjective experience of different basic emotions, such as joy, anger, fear, disgust, and sadness (Scherer & Wallbott, 1994).

Researchers have also found some key differences in cultural descriptions of emotion. For example, Hazel Rose Markus and Shinobu Kitayama (1991) found that Japanese subjects added a third dimension to Americans' two basic dimensions of pleasantness and arousal. The third dimension was *interpersonal engagement*—the degree to which each emotion involved relationships with others. For example, the Japanese rated anger and shame as being about the same in terms of unpleasantness and arousal, but they rated shame as being much higher than anger in terms of interpersonal engagement.

Why would the Japanese perceive this additional emotional dimension? As Markus and Kitayama (1991) point out, social relationships are extremely important in Japan. Because Japan is a collectivistic culture, one's identity is seen as *interdependent* with those of other people, rather than *independent,* as is characteristic of the more individualistic cultures of North America and Western Europe (see Chapter 1). Thus, interpersonal engagement is an important aspect of emotional experience in Japan and other collectivistic cultures.

Individual Differences in Emotional Experience

People vary greatly in the *intensity* of the emotions they experience. That is, some people really are "more emotional" than others (Larsen & Diener, 1987; Larsen & others, 1986). Along this line, many people believe that women are "naturally" more emotional than men. Are they? We explore this notion in Culture and Human Behavior Box 8.3, "Who's More Emotional, Men or Women?"

People who experience very intense positive emotions also tend to experience very intense negative emotions (Diener & others, 1985; Diener & Emmons, 1984). When things go well, they're capable of experiencing great joy. But when things go poorly, they'll be equally miserable.

People also differ in their *expression* of emotions. Put simply, some people are more emotionally expressive than others. Emotionally expressive people tend to be better liked than people who are more inhibited in their expressions of emotions (DePaulo, 1992).

The Physiological Component of Emotion:
Hot Heads and Cold Feet

Intense emotions are accompanied by physiological changes. What physical changes are associated with different emotions? What evidence supports the idea that facial expressions of basic emotions are innate? How are facial expressions affected by cultural display rules?

The physiological, or physical, component of emotions is especially evident when you experience an intense emotion, such as anger or extreme fear. At those moments, you may become keenly aware of physical changes: your face may flush; your heart may pound; your muscles may tighten; you may get "goose bumps." In other words, you are experiencing physiological arousal.

CULTURE AND HUMAN BEHAVIOR 8.3

Who's More Emotional—Men or Women?

"You *never* talk about your feelings!" *she* said. And *he* replied, "You're *so* emotional! It's impossible to discuss anything rationally with you!"

Sound familiar? One of the most pervasive gender stereotypes is that women are "more emotional" than men. That is, women supposedly experience more intense emotions, experience intense emotions more frequently, and are less able to control their emotions than men (Grossman & Wood, 1993). In contrast, men supposedly display greater emotional control—they are emotionally cool, calm, and collected. Women are easily swayed by their emotions and by appeals to emotion; men are more rational. Women cry easily; men don't cry at all.

What evidence is there to support these stereotypes? To begin with, when men and women rate their emotions, women subjectively rate themselves as being more emotionally intense than men (Grossman & Wood, 1993; Wood & others, 1989). Women are also more likely to report that they value emotional expressiveness in themselves and others (Shields, 1987). So, in terms of self-perception, women *do* tend to see themselves as more emotional.

In terms of actual behavior, several studies have found that women more freely express emotions such as fear, sadness, happiness, and anxiety. Even as children, girls generally are more emotionally expressive than boys, and this difference seems to carry through to adulthood. In relationships, women often seem to play the role of the "emotion specialist." They tend to be more sensitive and more responsive to the emotional exchanges in a relationship (Gottman, 1994). So, in general, it seems to be true that women are more emotionally expressive and responsive than men.

There is, however, one exception to this pattern. In contrast to other emotions, *anger* is more typically associated with men than women (Shields, 1987). That is, men are thought to experience

MARVIN

Reprinted with special permission of North America Syndicate.

anger more frequently, and more intensely, than women (Grossman & Wood, 1993).

Yet several studies have failed to find sex differences in the emotional experience of anger (see Cupach & Canary, 1995). In a study where men and women kept a diary of their angry episodes, no difference was found in the amount of anger *experienced* by men and women. But differences were found in how men and women *expressed* their anger. When they are the target of another person's anger, women were more likely to feel hurt, while men were more likely to react with defiance. Women were also much more likely than men to cry when angry, often out of frustration (Averill, 1982).

Men and women also differ in where they felt comfortable displaying their anger. In *private* situations, such as the home, women express their anger in much the same way as men (Cupach & Canary, 1995). In *public* situations, men are much more likely than women to display their anger or to express anger toward a stranger (Frodi & others, 1977).

The expression of emotion is strongly influenced by cultural norms, or "rules" that tell us what is appropriate. In the United States, it's considered "unfeminine" for a woman to express anger publicly. And it's considered "unmasculine" for a man be too open in expressing emotions other than anger (Grossman & Wood, 1993). Thus, there are strong gender-role expecta-

tions concerning emotional sensitivity and emotional expressiveness. These cultural norms affect what parents teach their children about emotional expression and control, and what children see modeled by other adults.

Parents treat sons and daughters differently with regard to their emotions, even when the children are just toddlers. Mothers are more likely to pay attention to their male toddlers' angry displays and to give in to their angry demands. In contrast, mothers are more likely to either ignore their female toddlers' anger or tell them to stop. Thus, unlike little girls, little boys grow up feeling freer to express their anger and to expect that expressing anger will be rewarded (Stenberg & Campos, 1990).

With regard to other emotions, parents often insist that boys control their emotions, but tend to emphasize emotional closeness to their daughters (see Goleman, 1991a). As a result, even preschoolers learn to associate anger with males and other common emotions—such as happiness, sadness, and fear—with females (Birnbaum & others, 1980).

What can we conclude about sex differences in emotionality? At least in American culture, women do tend to be more emotionally expressive than men. However, it's impossible to say whether women are naturally "more emotional" than men or if they have simply *learned* to express their emotions more freely—with the notable exception of anger.

As you read in Chapter 2, physiological arousal involves the activation of the sympathetic division of the *autonomic nervous system*. Arousal of the *sympathetic nervous system* triggers the "fight-or-flight" response and gears you up for action. Heartbeat and blood pressure increase; breathing quickens. You perspire, your mouth becomes dry, and the hairs on your skin stand up, causing goose bumps. Blood sugar levels increase, and blood is diverted from the stomach and intestines to the brain and skeletal muscles. Activation of the sympathetic nervous system makes sense for emotions such as anger and fear, because it prepares your body to take action: to fight (an "anger" response) or to take flight (a "fear" response).

Activation of the sympathetic nervous system is also involved in other emotions, such as excitement, passionate love, or extreme joy. Watching a suspenseful movie, being reunited with a lover, and riding a roller-coaster would all involve arousal of the sympathetic nervous system. Not all emotions involve extreme physical reactions, of course. And some emotions, such as contentment, are characterized by a *lowering* of body arousal, in which certain body processes slow down (Levenson, 1992).

Several studies have found that there are distinct differences in the patterns of physiological responses for different emotions (see Levenson, 1992; Scherer & Wallbott, 1994). In one group of studies, participants were asked to simulate the distinctive facial expression for six emotions—surprise, disgust, sadness, anger, fear, and happiness. While they held the expression for 10 seconds, their heart rate, skin temperature, and other measures of autonomic arousal were measured.

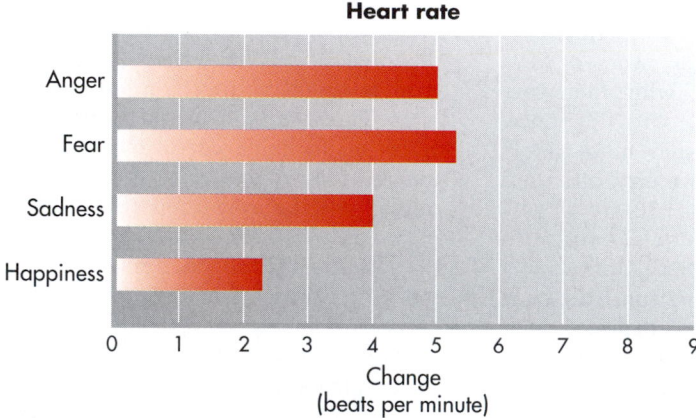

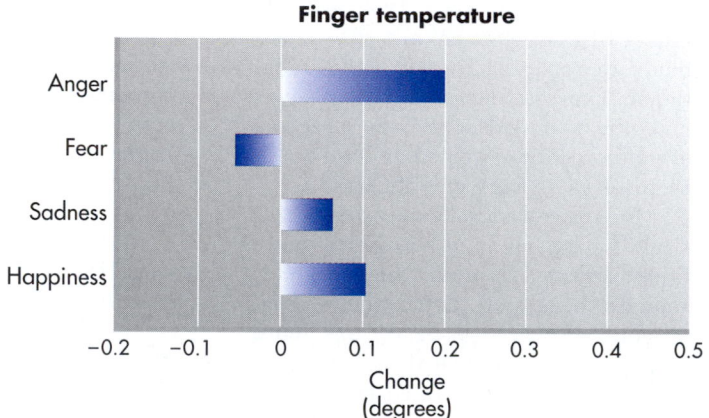

FIGURE 8.7 **Patterns of Physiological Arousal for Different Emotions** Levenson and his colleagues (1990) found that different patterns of physical arousal accompanied different emotions. Anger, fear, sadness, and happiness all involved increases in heart rate. However, the three negative emotions elevated the heart rate much more than happiness did. Anger involved a strong increase in finger temperature, while fear produced a decrease in skin temperature.
(Levenson & others, 1990, p. 369.)

The results? Different physiological patterns were found for different emotions (see Figure 8.7). Anger, fear, and sadness all involved a significantly increased heart rate. Anger produced a dramatic increase in skin temperature, while fear involved a marked decrease in skin temperature (Levenson & others, 1990). Perhaps that's why angry people sometimes say they feel "hot under the collar," and those experiencing fear speak of feeling "a chill of fear," "clammy," or getting "cold feet."

Similar patterns of physiological arousal for different emotions were found in members of a remote culture in western Sumatra, an island in Indonesia (Levenson & others, 1992). Broader surveys of many different cultures have also suggested that distinct patterns of physiological changes may well be universal, at least for basic emotions like joy, fear, anger, sadness, and disgust (Scherer & Wallbott, 1994). However, whether there are unique patterns of physiological response for *every* emotion has not been demonstrated.

The Expression of Emotion

In addition to their subjective and physiological components, emotions usually involve an *expressive,* or *behavioral,* component. When we experience an emotion, we often express it in some fashion. We talk about what we are feeling, hug another person, or slam a door. We also express our emotions by our nonverbal behavior, such as our gestures, changes in posture, and, most important, our facial expressions. Paul Ekman, a leading researcher in this area, has estimated that the human face is capable of creating over *7,000* different expressions (Ekman, 1980). This enormous flexibility allows us considerable versatility in expressing the subtleties of emotions.

How are facial expressions studied? Ekman and his colleagues have coded different facial expressions by carefully analyzing which facial muscles are involved in producing each expression (Ekman & Friesen, 1978). They've been able to precisely classify the facial expressions that characterize happiness, disgust, surprise, sadness, anger, and fear. When shown photographs of these expressions, a high percentage of subjects correctly identified the emotions depicted (Ekman, 1982).

Facial expressions for basic emotions seem to be innate or inborn rather than learned. Psychologist Carroll Izard (1989) found that the facial expressions of pain, interest, and disgust were present at birth. The social smile emerges by three or four weeks of age. By two months, sadness and anger are evident. And by six or seven months of age, infants display the facial expression indicating fear.

Which Is the "True" Smile? The human face is capable of an amazing variety of facial expressions, and people are very adept at reading them. It's relatively easy to distinguish the "true" smile (top) from the fake smile that masks negative emotions (bottom), because of subtle differences in the facial muscles, especially around the eyes and lips.

Facial Expressions Are Innate Born deaf and blind, this seven-year-old girl has never observed the facial expressions of those around her. Yet her smile and laughter are unmistakable and identical to that of other children. Facial expressions, especially for basic emotions, seem to be innate rather than learned.

Apparently, infants are not simply imitating the expressions of those around them or learning facial expressions from others. One line of evidence supporting this view comes from children who are born both blind and deaf (Goodenough, 1932; Eibl-Eibesfeldt, 1973). Despite being unable to observe facial expressions in others, these children express emotions such as joy, anger, and pleasure using the same facial expressions as other children.

Culture and Facial Expression

Are facial expressions universal across cultures? Ekman (1982) and his colleagues have found that people from many different cultures accurately recognize the emotions expressed in photographs of facial expressions. This held true even in remote, isolated villages of New Guinea where the inhabitants had not been exposed to Western culture.

In other research, people from Estonia, Germany, Greece, Hong Kong, Italy, Japan, Scotland, Sumatra, Turkey, and the United States were shown photographs of facial expressions that displayed *blends* of emotion. These expressions included combinations of disgust and contempt, fear and surprise, anger and disgust, and anger and surprise. The participants from all cultures generally agreed as to the identity of the two blended emotions and also as to the relative intensity of the two emotions shown (Ekman & others, 1987).

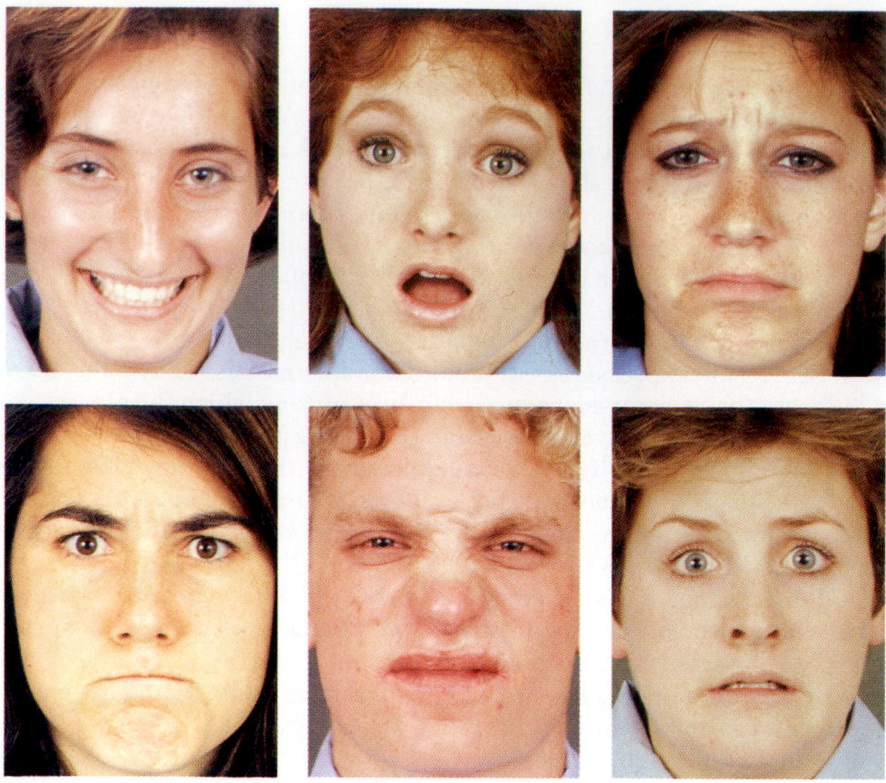

Basic Emotions and Universal Facial Expressions Paul Ekman and his colleagues have precisely calibrated the muscles used in facial expressions for basic emotions. When photographs like these are shown to people in a wide variety of cultures, they recognize the basic emotions that are being expressed: happiness, surprise, sadness (top row); and anger, disgust, and fear (bottom row).

Facial expressions for basic emotions may well be universal and, to some extent, biologically programmed. Nevertheless, people often exert control over their facial expressions. We adjust our expressions of emotion to make them appropriate to the situation. Even if deeply angered by the comments of your boss, for example, you might well smile and nod your head. Thus, social context can influence the expression of emotion.

The expression of emotion is also strongly affected by culture. Cultural differences in the management of facial expressions are called **display rules** (Ekman & others, 1987). Recall our discussion of gender and emotional expression in Box 8.3. American men who cry in public and American women who express anger in public are examples of people violating cultural display rules.

Display rules can vary greatly from one culture to another. In one experiment, Japanese and Americans watched stress-inducing films alone, unaware of a hidden camera. When alone, the Japanese and American subjects displayed virtually the same facial expressions. But when a scientist was present while the subjects watched the films, the Japanese subjects were far more likely than the American subjects to mask negative facial expressions (of disgust or fear, for example) with smiles. Why? Because, in Japanese culture, an important display rule is that you should not reveal negative emotions in the presence of an authority figure (see Ekman & others, 1987; Friesen, 1972).

Explaining Emotions: Four Key Theories

Theories about emotion tend to differ in terms of which component of emotion they emphasize. What are the James-Lange and Cannon-Bard theories of emotion? How did Cannon refute the James-Lange theory? What aspects of the two-factor theory have been supported by research? What is the cognitive-mediational theory of emotion?

Theories to explain the cause and nature of emotions have been debated throughout this century. In this section, we'll look at four of the most influential of these theories. As you'll see, the theories tend to differ in terms of which component of emotion receives the most emphasis—physical responses, expressive behavior, or subjective experience (Ellsworth, 1994).

display rules
Social and cultural rules that regulate the expression of emotions, particularly facial expressions.

James-Lange theory of emotion
The theory that emotions arise from the perception and interpretation of bodily changes.

The James-Lange Theory of Emotion:

Do You Run Because You're Afraid? Or Are You Afraid Because You Run?

Imagine that you're walking to your car alone after a night class, later than usual because you stayed after the class to ask your professor a few questions. The now-deserted parking lot was crowded when you arrived at school, so you had to park in a distant corner of the lot that is not very well lit. You're feeling just a little apprehensive because in the last few weeks there has been a rash of muggings around your campus. As you get closer to your car, a shadowy figure suddenly appears from behind a parked car. As he starts to move toward you, you walk more quickly. "Hey, what's your hurry?" he calls out. He picks up his own pace, and it's clear that he's following you.

Your heart starts pounding as you break into a run. Reaching your car, you jump in and lock the door. Your hands are trembling so badly you can hardly get the key into the ignition. Within a few moments, you zoom out of the parking lot and onto a main street. You catch a look at yourself in the rear-view mirror and notice that you look wide-eyed and pale. Still feeling shaky, you turn on the radio and try to calm down. After several minutes, you breathe a sigh of relief.

In this example, all three of the components of emotion are present. You experienced a subjective feeling that you labeled as "fear." You experienced physical arousal—pounding heart, trembling, faster breathing, and dilated pupils. And you expressed the fear, both in your facial expression and in the behavior of running. What caused the emotion of fear? What accounted for the three facets of the emotional reaction?

The common-sense view of emotion would suggest that you (1) recognized a threatening situation and (2) reacted by feeling fearful. The subjective feeling of fear triggered (3) arousal of the sympathetic nervous system and (4) fearful behavior.

In one of the first psychological theories of emotion, **William James** (1884) disagreed with this common-sense view, proposing a very different explanation of emotion. Danish psychologist Carl Lange proposed a very similar theory at about the same time (see James, 1894; Lange & James, 1922). Thus, this theory is known as the **James-Lange theory of emotion.**

Consider our example again. According to the James-Lange theory, your heart didn't pound and you didn't run because you were afraid. Rather, the James-Lange theory holds that you felt afraid *because* your heart pounded and you ran. Feedback from your physiological arousal and from the muscles involved in your behavior caused your subjective feeling of fearfulness. Thus, James believed that emotion follows this sequence: (1) we perceive a stimulus; (2) physiological and behavioral changes occur; and (3) we interpret our physiological and behavioral reaction as a particular emotion (see Figure 8.8).

The James-Lange theory stimulated a great deal of research, much of it consisting of attempts to disprove the theory. In 1927 **Walter Cannon** (1871–1945) challenged the James-Lange theory, criticizing it on several grounds. First, Cannon pointed out that body reactions are similar for many emotions, yet our subjective experience of various emotions is very different. For example, both fear and rage are accompanied by increased heart rate, but we have no difficulty distinguishing between the two emotions.

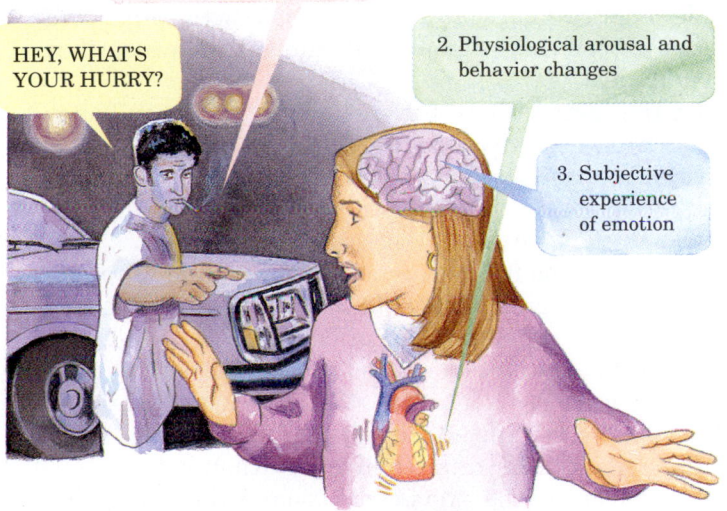

1. Stimulus: Shadowy figure of a man in a parking lot at night

HEY, WHAT'S YOUR HURRY?

2. Physiological arousal and behavior changes

3. Subjective experience of emotion

1. I see a man by that parked car.
2. I am trembling and running away.
3. I am afraid!

FIGURE 8.8 The James-Lange Theory of Emotion According to William James, we don't tremble and run because we are afraid, we are afraid because we tremble and run. James believed that body signals triggered emotional experience. These signals included physiological arousal and feedback from the muscles involved in behavior. The James-Lange theory inspired a great deal of research, but only limited aspects of the James-Lange theory have been supported by research evidence.

Common-sense says we lose our fortune, are sorry and weep; we meet a bear, are frightened and run; we are insulted by a rival, are angry and strike. The hypothesis here to be defended says that this order of sequence is incorrect, that the one mental state is not immediately induced by the other, that the bodily manifestations must first be interposed between, and that the more rational statement is that we feel sorry because we cry, angry because we strike, afraid because we tremble.

William James, 1894

facial feedback hypothesis
The view that expressing a specific emotion, especially facially, causes the subjective experience of that emotion.

Second, Cannon (1927) pointed out that our emotional reaction to a stimulus is often faster than our physiological reaction. Here's an example to illustrate this point: Not long ago, Sandy's car started to slide out of control on a wet road. She felt fear as the car began to skid, but it was only *after* the car was under control, a few moments later, that her heart began to pound and her hands started to tremble. Cannon correctly noted that it takes several seconds for the physiological changes caused by activation of the sympathetic nervous system to take effect, but the subjective experience of emotion is often virtually instantaneous.

Third, when physiological changes are artificially induced, the person does not necessarily report feeling a related emotion. Spanish psychologist Gregorio Marañon (1924) injected several subjects with epinephrine, the hormone that triggers activation of the sympathetic nervous system. When asked how they felt, the subjects did not report feeling any particular emotion. Instead, they simply reported the physical changes produced by the drug, saying, "My heart is beating very fast." Some reported feeling "as if" they should be feeling an emotion, but they said they did not feel the emotion itself: "I feel *as if* I were afraid."

James (1894) had proposed that if a person were cut off from feeling body changes, he would not experience true emotions. If he felt anything, he would experience only intellectualized, or "cold," emotions. To test this hypothesis, Cannon and his colleagues disabled the sympathetic nervous system of cats. But the cats still reacted with catlike rage when barking dogs were present: they hissed, growled, and lifted one paw to defend themselves (Cannon & others, 1927).

What about humans? The sympathetic nervous system operates via the spinal cord. Thus it made sense to James (1894) that people with spinal cord injuries would experience a decrease in emotional intensity, because they could not detect physical arousal.

Once again, however, the research has not supported the James-Lange theory. For example, Dutch psychologist Bob Bermond and his colleagues (1991) found that individuals with spinal cord injuries reported that their experience of fear, anger, grief, sentimentality, and joyfulness had either increased in intensity or was unchanged since their injury.

Similarly, Kathleen Chwalisz and her colleagues (1988) compared spinal-cord-injured subjects with a control group of people who needed to use wheelchairs but who had not suffered spinal cord injuries or loss of sensation. There was little difference between the two groups in the intensity of emotions experienced, including love, joy, sentimentality, anger, sadness, and fear. The majority of the spinal-cord-injured patients reported feeling many emotions, especially fear, *more* intensely after their injury than before.

These two studies, then, point to the same conclusion: Although physiological arousal can amplify emotional feelings, the perception of physical arousal does not seem to be *essential* to the experience of emotion. In short, these findings seemed to undermine the James-Lange theory of emotion.

Although Cannon's critique of the James-Lange theory of emotion seemed at first to have effectively demolished it, new evidence seems to support some *limited* aspects of the James-Lange theory. According to the **facial feedback hypothesis,** *expressing* a specific emotion, especially facially, causes us to *subjectively experience* that emotion. In testing this notion, researchers have asked people to manipulate their facial muscles to form a facial expression characteristic of a given emotion, such as a smile or a frown. But the researcher does not tell the subject what emotional expression the facial manipulations are supposed to represent. It's kind of like a professional photographer asking you to say "cheese" to get you to simulate a smile.

How can the facial feedback hypothesis be explained? One explanation is that feedback from the facial muscles is sent as signals to the brain, and this

Okay, Say "Cheese!" Misha obligingly demonstrates a simple test of the facial feedback hypothesis. In a study by Fritz Strack and others (1988), participants who held a pencil between their teeth (top) thought that cartoons were funnier than participants who held a pencil between their lips. How does this finding support the facial feedback hypothesis?

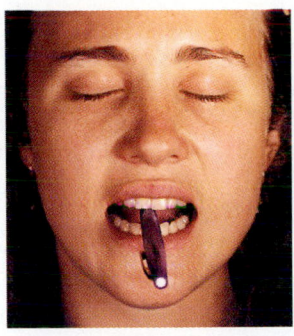 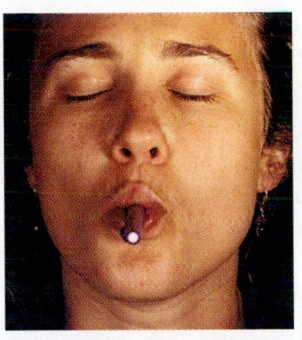

information affects our experience of the emotion (Izard, 1990b). Psychologists Paul Ekman and Richard Davidson (1993) have demonstrated that deliberately creating a "happy" smile tends to produce the same changes in some measures of brain activity as spontaneously producing a happy smile in response to a real event.

Such evidence lends limited support to one aspect of the James-Lange theory: Our body responses, including feedback from our muscles, *can* affect our subjective experience (Izard, 1990a). Keep in mind, the facial feedback hypothesis does not claim that facial expressions necessarily *cause* all emotional experiences. Rather, expressive behavior helps to activate and regulate emotional experience, intensifying or lessening emotion (Izard, 1990b).

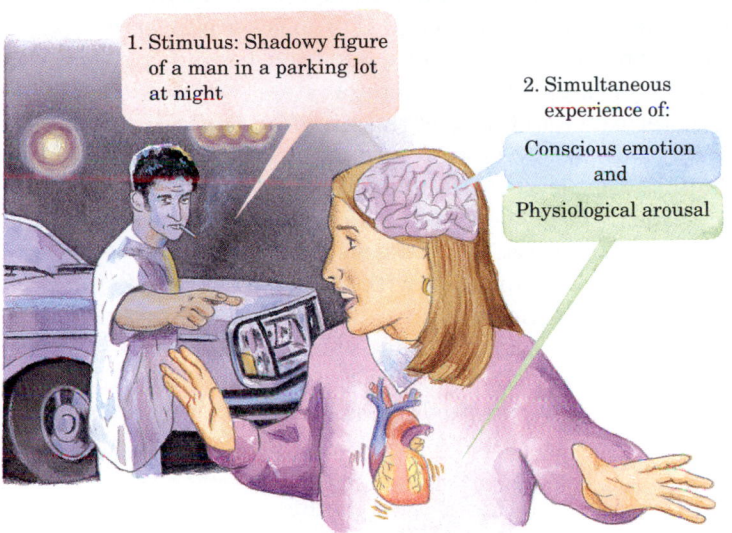

1. Stimulus: Shadowy figure of a man in a parking lot at night

2. Simultaneous experience of:

Conscious emotion and

Physiological arousal

1. I see a man by that parked car.
2. I am afraid *and* trembling!

FIGURE 8.9 The Cannon-Bard Theory of Emotion According to Walter Cannon, emotion is a two-pronged response, including both conscious experience and physiological arousal. Cannon believed that the sympathetic nervous system and the cortex in the brain were simultaneously activated. The subjective, conscious experience of emotion and physiological arousal are triggered at the same time: neither causes the other.

Cannon-Bard theory of emotion
The theory that emotions arise from the simultaneous activation of the nervous system, which causes physical arousal, and the cortex, which causes the subjective experience of emotion.

The Cannon-Bard Theory of Emotion

Along with challenging the James-Lange theory of emotion, Walter Cannon (1927) proposed his own theory. Because American physiologist Philip Bard later joined with him in endorsing this theory, it became known as the **Cannon-Bard theory of emotion.**

According to the Cannon-Bard theory of emotion, when an emotion-arousing stimulus is perceived, information is relayed *simultaneously* to the cortex in the brain and to the sympathetic nervous system (see Figure 8.9). The activation of the cortex causes the subjective experience of emotion, and the activation of the sympathetic nervous system causes the physical response, which takes a few seconds. Thus, according to Cannon and Bard, subjective experience and physiological arousal are triggered *at the same time:* neither causes the other.

The Two-Factor Theory of Emotion:
Is It Love? Or Too Much Coffee?

A third important theory of emotion was proposed by psychologists Stanley Schachter and Jerome Singer. Schachter and Singer (1962) agreed with James that physiological arousal is a central element in emotion. But they also agreed with Cannon that physiological arousal is very similar for many different emotions. Thus, Schachter and Singer argued that arousal alone is not sufficient to produce a given emotion.

Instead, Schachter and Singer added a new element to the equation of emotion. They proposed that you label physiological arousal as a given emotion on the basis of your *cognitive interpretation* of your situation. The cognition determines what emotion will be experienced. For example, you might attribute your stirred-up state to joy, anger, or fear, depending on how you interpret your situational cues and your own thoughts. If you're watching a

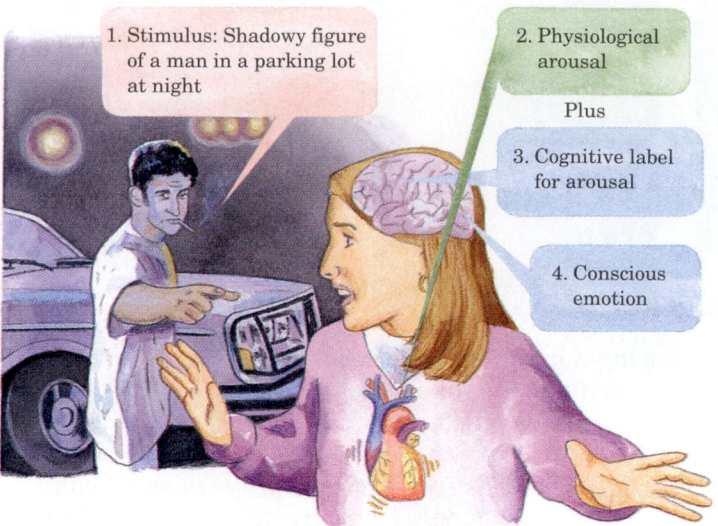

1. Stimulus: Shadowy figure of a man in a parking lot at night

2. Physiological arousal

Plus

3. Cognitive label for arousal

4. Conscious emotion

1. I see a man by that parked car.
2. I am trembling.
3. My trembling is CAUSED by fear.
4. I am afraid!

FIGURE 8.10 **The Two-Factor Theory of Emotion** According to Stanley Schachter and Jerome Singer, emotional experience requires the interaction of two separate factors: (1) physiological arousal and (2) a cognitive *label* for that arousal. *Both* factors are necessary for the subjective experience of emotion.

two-factor theory of emotion
Schachter and Singer's theory that emotion is a result of the interaction of physiological arousal and the cognitive label that we apply to explain the arousal.

scary movie on television, you'll attribute your arousal to fear. If you're standing in a long checkout line at the grocery store and someone cuts in front of you, you'll attribute it to anger. And if you're spending an evening with an attractive person, you'll attribute your arousal to sexual excitement or attraction.

According to Schachter and Singer's (1962) **two-factor theory of emotion** (also called the *cognitive arousal theory of emotion*), emotion is a result of the *interaction* of physiological arousal and the cognitive label we attach to explain the stirred-up state. If one of these factors is absent, emotion will not be experienced (see Figure 8.10). Recall that in Marañon's (1924) experiment, arousal without a cognitive label did not produce a true emotional state, but only awareness of the arousal. Marañon's subjects felt *as if* they should be afraid. Likewise, a cognitive label without physiological arousal would not produce a true emotional experience (as in, "This should make me mad, but it doesn't").

Under normal circumstances, the two factors, cognitive labeling and physiological arousal, are interrelated. The cognition (man leaping out from behind car in deserted parking lot) triggers a state of physiological arousal. The arousal is interpreted in terms of the situation or condition that triggered it (knowledge about muggings on campus and the dangers of strange men in deserted parking lots). At that point, according to Schachter and Singer, the state of arousal is labeled as an emotion—fear.

Schachter and Singer (1962) tested their theory in an ingenious experiment. Male student volunteers were injected with epinephrine, a substance that produces trembling, pounding heart, and rapid breathing—the classic symptoms of physiological arousal. Only one group of subjects was accurately told that their symptoms were the result of the injection. The other subjects were told either that the injection would produce no effects or that the injection would produce entirely different effects, such as itching and numbness of the feet.

Then each subject was exposed to one of two conditions. In the "happy" condition, a confederate of the experimenters acted euphoric and, in fact, rather goofy: shooting paper airplanes, playing with hula hoops, and so forth. In the "angry" condition, a confederate complained about the experiment, objected to items on a questionnaire, and finally ripped up the questionnaire and stomped out of the room. Afterward, the mood of the subjects was assessed.

The results? In the "happy" condition, the uninformed subjects did report feeling happier than the informed subjects. In the "angry" condition, the uninformed subjects reported feeling angrier than the informed subjects. This part of the experimental results confirmed the hypothesis. However, other aspects of the experimental results were more problematic, and did not provide support for the Schachter-Singer theory (see Beck, 1990).

The Schachter-Singer two-factor theory inspired a great deal of research on the cognitive aspects of emotion. However, after reviewing two decades of related research, German psychologist Rainer Reisenzein (1983) concluded that there was little evidence to support the Schachter-Singer two-factor theory of emotion. More specifically, Reisenzein concluded there was little evidence for (1) the claim that arousal is a necessary condition for an emotional state or (2) the idea that emotional states can result from labeling unexplained arousal.

The Cognitive-Mediational Theory of Emotion:

Is That a Mugger? Or a Friend?

Although the two-factor theory of emotion received little support from subsequent research, it did stimulate a new line of research on the importance of cognition in emotion. Let's go back to the shadowy figure lurking in your college parking lot. Suppose that as the man called out to you, "Hey, what's your hurry?" you recognized his voice as that of a good friend. Would your emotional reaction be different? Of course. This simple observation is the basis for the fourth major theory of emotion that we'll consider.

Developed by psychologist **Richard Lazarus** (b. 1922), the **cognitive-mediational theory of emotion** emphasizes that the most important aspect of an emotional experience is our cognitive interpretation, or appraisal, of the emotion-causing stimulus. All other components of emotion, including physiological arousal, follow from the initial cognitive appraisal (Lazarus, 1995).

For Lazarus, *all* emotions are the result of cognitive appraisals of the personal meaning of events and experiences. If we think that we have something to gain or lose, we experience emotion. Thus, such appraisals are closely tied to motivation. The more personally important the outcome, the more intense the emotion (Lazarus, 1991a).

In the case of the shadowy figure in the parking lot, your relief that you were not on the verge of being attacked by a mugger could turn to another emotion very quickly, depending on the personal meaning of the encounter. If it's a good friend that you hadn't seen for a while, your relief might turn to pleasure, excitement, or even joy. If it's someone you'd prefer to avoid, your relief might turn to annoyance.

Appraisal and Emotion: Basket! Lazarus believes that how the individual cognitively appraises the personal significance of any event will determine the emotion experienced. Whether the sports fan experiences elation or dismay is likely to depend upon what the event means to him personally.

Some Final Thoughts:

An Interactive Approach to Emotion

No single theory of emotion has met with general acceptance in psychology. In some ways, this is not surprising. Emotion is a complex, multifaceted phenomenon, involving three very different processes: physiological, behavioral, and cognitive. These processes vary a great deal among individuals (Cacioppo & others, 1992). Furthermore, each element of the emotion equation serves different functions and can be studied separately (Izard, 1989). What continues to be debated is which process is *most* important in causing emotional experience.

Perhaps emotion can be best conceptualized as a dynamic system in which every component is important and can influence the others (Lazarus, 1991b; Carlson & Hatfield, 1992). An *interactive approach to emotion* might acknowledge that cognitive appraisals, physiological arousal, and behavioral expression all contribute to subjective emotional experience (Averill, 1994). Viewing emotion as the result of the dynamic interaction of different processes does have some practical implications, which we discuss in the Application section.

cognitive-mediational theory of emotion
Lazarus's theory that emotions result from the cognitive appraisal of a situation's effect on personal well-being.

Identifying Key Theories of Emotion

Read the following descriptions and decide which theory of emotion is being represented: (A) Lazarus's cognitive-mediational, (B) James-Lange, (C) Cannon-Bard, or (D) Schachter-Singer two-factor theory.

_____ **1.** Tim and Kim both get a B+ grade in their statistics class. Tim is overjoyed at the news, but Kim, who plans to go to graduate school, is disappointed. Their different emotional reactions to exactly the same grade were obviously a result of their different interpretations.

_____ **2.** When Jim's car skidded on the icy road, he immediately felt fear and his heart began to pound and his hands started to sweat.

_____ **3.** Jahoudi is halfway across the swaying suspension bridge 900 feet above the canyon when he realizes that his heart is racing, his legs are shaking, and his palms are sweating. Suddenly he feels afraid.

_____ **4.** Whenever she meets Rick in class or in the hallway, Sarah's heart beats faster and she gets a trembling feeling inside. Sarah now thinks she must be in love with Rick.

APPLICATION

Bridging the Gender Gap During Emotional Conflict

As we noted earlier in the chapter, women tend to be more comfortable about expressing their emotions than men are. Beyond this basic difference, researchers have found that men and women communicate very differently, especially when they are trying to deal with problems, emotional issues, and interpersonal conflicts (Kalbfleisch & Cody, 1995; Brehm, 1992). In this Application, we will look at some of those communication differences and consider how couples can learn to overcome them.

Conflict in Intimate Relationships

Being able to handle interpersonal conflict is important in any relationship, but especially in marriage. The demands and hassles of sharing and maintaining a household make occasional conflict in marriage virtually inevitable (Stafford & Dainton, 1994). Despite what many people think, the happiest marriages are not conflict-free. Instead, as psychologist John Gottman (1994) has discovered, conflict plays a key role in marital happiness and stability.

Gottman has intensively studied hundreds of married couples over the last twenty years (Gottman & Levenson, 1992; Levenson & others, 1994). He's found that a couple's relationship grows only if the couple successfully reconciles the inevitable differences that occur. As Gottman (1994) explains, "A certain amount of conflict is needed to help couples weed out actions and ways of dealing with each other that can harm the marriage in the long run."

Gottman and his colleagues have also found that men and women react differently to conflict, particularly conflicts that involve strong emotions (Levenson & others, 1994). Men have typically learned to suppress and contain their emotions. In contrast, women tend to be more comfortable expressing their emotions. In general, women are more comfortable than men when it comes to dealing with emotional issues in intimate relationships.

According to Gottman (1994), women often become the "emotion managers" and "care-takers of intimacy" in close relationships. They tend to be more sensitive to problems that are developing in the relationship and more willing to talk about them. But when problems need to be resolved, Gottman has found, male and female patterns of reacting to and handling conflict often sabotage a couple's best efforts to resolve their differences.

What goes wrong when a couple tries to resolve their differences? First, consider the two types of responses that Gottman has found occur during emotional conflicts: flooding and stonewalling. *Flooding* means feeling overwhelmed (or "flooded") by your own emotions—feeling upset and out of control. When flooded, people experience high levels of physiological arousal. Heartbeat and blood pressure skyrocket.

As an argument or conflict heats up, both men and women can become flooded by their emotions. That said, which sex do you think is *more* likely to become flooded? Men are. In his lab, Gottman has found that during marital conflict a husband's heart rate and blood pressure increase faster, elevate higher, and stay elevated longer than his wife's (Gottman & Levenson, 1992). Not only is this high level of physiological arousal extremely unpleasant, it also makes it very difficult for a man to listen to his partner's words. Hence, because men physiologically react so strongly to conflict, they tend to be less willing to engage in it.

When flooded, what do men typically do? They go into the *stonewalling* mode—they withdraw to contain their uncomfortable emotions (Levenson & others, 1994). Women also stonewall, of course, but men are much more likely to resort to this strategy (Christensen & Heavey, 1993).

Now a vicious circle begins. Although stonewalling protects *him* from overwhelming stress and emotion, it creates enormous stress in *her*. She's accustomed to working through emotional problems. And she tends to experience his stonewalling as disapproval and rejection—and sometimes as the ultimate power play (Tannen, 1990). So how does she react to his stonewalling? Frustrated and angry, she now reacts by *flooding*.

When a woman experiences flooding, rather than withdraw she intensifies the expression of her emotions. This raises the temperature of the argument to a higher level and creates even more stress in the male, further increasing his urge to withdraw from the situation. In short, this is a very volatile scene. Each partner is exaggerating the frustration and emotional discomfort of the other.

Breaking the Vicious Circle of Flooding-Stonewalling-Flooding

In his book *Why Marriages Succeed or Fail . . . and How You Can Make Yours Last,* Gottman (1994) offers many thoughtful and concrete suggestions for handling conflicts in a healthier manner. We'll summarize four of these suggestions, which are based on extensive research by Gottman and other psychologists.

The first step in breaking the vicious circle of flooding-stonewalling-flooding is to be *aware* of the gender differences in handling emotion. To men,

stonewalling is a protective strategy. It represents an attempt to contain disturbing emotions before they become overwhelming and out of control. When women look at men's stonewalling in these terms, they're less likely to interpret it as rejection and as a refusal to try to resolve differences.

On their part, guys need to remember that women experience stonewalling as rejection, disapproval, and abandonment. Rather than abruptly stonewalling and withdrawing, men need to explain their withdrawal. The explanation can be as simple as saying, "Look, I need to be alone for a while so I can calm down and think about what you're saying. When I come back, we will keep talking." On their part, women need to accept men's need to temporarily withdraw from the situation.

Gottman (1994) advises that whenever either partner begins to feel overwhelmed or in danger of flooding, he or she should call a *time out*—a 20- to 30-minute intermission with an agreement to continue the discussion after the break. Remember, it takes at least 20 minutes for physiological arousal to subside completely. As simple as the time-out strategy is, it can promote more constructive and rational discussions, increasing the likelihood that a mutually acceptable solution to the problem will be found.

Second, it is critical that you listen to what you're saying to yourself *during* the time out. Rather than rehearsing hateful or vengeful comments, use the time out to focus on calming thoughts about the immediate situation and on

positive thoughts about your mate. For example, rather than saying to yourself, "He (she) is such a (fill in with an insult)," try saying to yourself, "Calm down and get a grip on things. This *is* basically a good relationship, and I *do* love her (him)." The important point here is to spend the time out thinking about ways to *resolve* the conflict, not about ways to mount a more effective counterattack when the battle resumes.

Third, men need to make a conscious effort to embrace, rather than avoid, the problem at hand. As Gottman (1994) writes, "The most important advice I can give to men who want their marriages to work is to try *not* to avoid conflict. Sidestepping a problem won't make it go away." In other words, guys, you need to remember that your partner *really* cares about your relationship. That's why she keeps bringing the issue up—so the two of you can resolve the problem *together*. Again, it helps if you mentally say constructive things to yourself, such as "I need to listen because it's important to her" and "She's confronting me because she wants the relationship to work."

Fourth, although women should not avoid raising issues that are in need of resolution, they should try to do it calmly, avoiding personal attacks. Gottman advises that issues be framed in the context of maintaining a loving relationship. As Gottman (1994) puts it, "It will be much easier for him to stay engaged if you let him know that talking together about what's bothering you is a way to keep the love between you alive."

Summary

Motivation and Emotion

The Study of Motivation

- *Motivation* refers to the forces that act on or within an organism to initiate and direct behavior. Three characteristics associated with motivation are activation, persistence, and intensity.

- Over the past century, psychologists tried to develop a single unified theory of motivation. Motivation theories included instinct theories, drive theories, incentive theories, and humanistic theories. Drive theories are based on the biological principle of homeostasis. Humanistic theories emphasize psychological motives, and include Maslow's hierarchy of needs.

■ Today, motivation researchers assume that the motivation of any behavior is determined by the interaction of multiple factors, including biological, behavioral, cognitive, and social components.

The Motivation to Eat

■ Psychologists have identified several internal and external signals involved in hunger and satiation. Oral sensations seem to help maintain or slow down eating behavior. Signals from sensory neurons in the stomach help to trigger feelings of satiation, as does a hormone called CCK. Increased insulin levels seem to lead to feelings of hunger. "Externals" and "nonexternals" vary in their insulin response to environmental stimuli associated with food.

■ When the ventromedial hypothalamus or the lateral hypothalamus is damaged in rats, eating behavior is affected. However, the exact role played by the hypothalamus and surrounding brain regions in eating behavior remains unclear.

■ The rate at which the body uses energy is called the basal metabolic rate (BMR). People vary greatly in their basal metabolic rate. Age, sex, genetics, and activity level all affect BMR.

■ According to set-point theory, each person's body naturally tends to have a specific set-point weight. When food intake is reduced, BMR is also reduced. Set-point theory is based on the principle of homeostasis.

■ Despite the value placed on being thin in American society, many people are obese. Obese people tend to respond differently to food cues than nonobese people and may have great difficulty maintaining weight loss.

■ Eating disorders include anorexia nervosa and bulimia nervosa. In anorexia, people do not maintain a minimal body weight, are afraid of gaining weight, and have distorted perceptions about the size of their bodies. In bulimia, people engage in uncontrolled binge eating and then purge themselves of the excessive food by self-induced vomiting, laxatives, or enemas.

Sexual Motivation and Behavior

■ In animals, sexual behavior is biologically determined and typically triggered by hormonal changes in the female. In higher animals, sexual behavior is more strongly influenced by learning and environmental factors and less influenced by biological factors.

■ Sexual orientation is not as cut and dried as many people think. More people have had some same-sex sexual experience than identify themselves as exclusively homosexual. Although psychologists do not know exactly what determines sexual orientation, genetics and differences in brain structure may be involved. Sexual orientation develops at a fairly early age and is difficult to change. In itself, homosexuality is not considered a psychological disorder.

■ The four stages of human sexual response are excitement, plateau, orgasm, and resolution. Women are capable of multiple orgasms. Men experience a refractory period following orgasm.

■ Most adults are involved in an intimate relationship by the age of thirty. Young adults today tend to have more sexual partners than previous generations. Married people tend to have the most active sex lives and are the most satisfied with their sex lives. Vaginal intercourse is the most preferred sexual activity.

Arousal Motives: Curiosity and Sensation Seeking

■ According to arousal theory, people seek to maintain an optimal level of arousal, which sometimes involves seeking out stimulation.

■ Along with increasing arousal, curiosity may be motivated by the urge to understand the environment. People differ in their tendency to approach or withdraw from novel stimuli.

■ People who prefer a high level of arousal are high in sensation seeking. Sensation seekers are drawn to new and stimulating experiences.

Competence and Achievement Motivation

■ Competence motivation refers to the drive to be capable, while achievement motivation refers to the desire to excel or outperform others. Achievement motivation can be measured by the Thematic Apperception Test (TAT). Achievement motivation is expressed differently in individualistic and collectivistic cultures.

■ Competence motivation and achievement motivation are linked to one's belief of self-efficacy. People with a high degree of self-efficacy are more likely to strive for achievement than are people who doubt their abilities.

Emotion

■ Emotions serve many different functions in human behavior and relationships, and have three basic components: subjective experience, physiological arousal, and a behavioral or expressive response.

■ Some emotion theorists believe that there is a limited number of basic emotions that are universal across cultures. Emotions can be classified in terms of two dimensions: degree of pleasantness and level of arousal. Collectivistic cultures may add a third dimension of interpersonal engagement.

■ People differ in the intensity of their emotional experience as well as in the ease with which they express their emotions.

■ Some emotions, like fear and anger, involve physiological arousal of the sympathetic nervous system. Psychologists have found specific physiological patterns that are associated with different basic emotions.

■ Facial expressions for some basic emotions seem to be universal and innate, but expression is also influenced by cultural display rules.

Explaining Emotions: Four Key Theories

■ Emotion theories differ in terms of which component of emotion is emphasized. According to the James-Lange theory of emotion, emotion results from our perceptions of physical arousal. James predicted that people who have suffered spinal cord injury would experience dampened emotions, but research does not support this prediction. The Cannon-Bard theory of emotion holds that subjective experience and physiological arousal take place simultaneously.

■ The facial feedback hypothesis holds that expressing an emotion causes us to subjectively experience that emotion. Body responses affect the subjective experience of emotion, but do not necessarily cause emotions.

■ The two-factor theory of emotion, proposed by Stanley Schachter and Jerome Singer, holds that emotion results from applying a cognitive label to physiological arousal.

■ The cognitive-mediational theory of emotion, proposed by Richard Lazarus, holds that emotion results from the cognitive appraisal of emotion-causing stimuli.

■ An interactive approach to emotion emphasizes that cognitive appraisals, physiological arousal, and behavioral expression all contribute to subjective emotional experience.

Key Terms

motivation (p. 273)

instinct theories (p. 273)

drive theories (p. 274)

homeostasis (p. 274)

drive (p. 274)

incentive theories (p. 275)

hierarchy of needs (p. 275)

self-actualization (p. 276)

cholecystokinin (CCK) (p. 278)

basal metabolic rate (BMR) (p. 280)

set-point weight (p. 281)

obese (p. 281)

anorexia nervosa (p. 282)

bulimia nervosa (p. 283)

sexual orientation (p. 287)

arousal theory (p. 293)

sensation seeking (p. 295)

competence motivation (p. 295)

achievement motivation (p. 295)

self-efficacy (p. 297)

emotion (p. 298)

display rules (p. 304)

James-Lange theory of emotion (p. 305)

facial feedback hypothesis (p. 306)

Cannon-Bard theory of emotion (p. 307)

two-factor theory of emotion (p. 308)

cognitive-mediational theory of emotion (p. 309)

Key People

Walter B. Cannon (1871–1945) American physiologist who developed an influential theory of emotion called the Cannon-Bard theory of emotion.

William James (1842–1910) American psychologist (see also Chapters 1 and 4) who developed an influential theory of emotion called the James-Lange theory of emotion.

Virginia E. Johnson (b. 1925) American behavioral scientist who, along with William H. Masters, conducted pioneering research in the field of human sexuality and sex therapy.

Richard Lazarus (b. 1922) American psychologist who promoted the cognitive perspective in the study of emotion; proposed the cognitive-mediational theory of emotion.

Abraham Maslow (1908–1970) American psychologist and a founder of humanistic psychology who developed a hierarchical model of human motivation in which basic needs must first be satisfied before people can strive for self-actualization.

William H. Masters (b. 1915) American physician who, along with Virginia E. Johnson, conducted pioneering research in the field of human sexuality and sex therapy.

CONCEPT REVIEW 8.1   Page 283

1. True
2. False
3. True
4. False
5. False
6. False

CONCEPT REVIEW 8.2   Page 293

1. False
2. False
3. False
4. False
5. False

CONCEPT REVIEW 8.3   Page 298

1. optimal arousal
2. self-efficacy
3. curiosity
4. achievement motivation
5. sensation seeking

CONCEPT REVIEW 8.4   Page 310

1. (A) Lazarus's cognitive-mediational theory
2. (C) Cannon-Bard theory
3. (B) James-Lange theory
4. (D) Schachter-Singer two-factor theory

Chapter

Lifespan Development

Prologue: Themes and Variations

"Daddy, I want to show you a magic trick!" Laura said as she bounded into my office, the cat's cradle of yarn woven into an intricate web between her fingers. "Put your hand right through there," she instructed me. Concentrating intently, she manipulated some of the strings, then proclaimed, "Abracadabra!" My hand was completely free of the web.

"Awesome," Don smiled. "Did Mom teach you that?"

"I learned it at summer camp," Laura explained. "Do you want to see it again?"

"Sure," Don replied, and Laura carefully performed the trick again, beaming with pride.

In a matter of weeks, our daughter Laura will be seven years old and beginning the second grade. And, in fact, she's been attending the same school since she was nine months old. It is a wonderfully warm, consistent, and encouraging school environment that has helped our daughter thrive, grow, and learn.

From the beginning, Laura's growth and development have been inextricably intertwined with the development of the book that you are holding in your hands. She was born in 1990 on the day after we received our contract to write our first psychology text. When Laura was a newborn, Sandy became adept at typing with one hand so she could hold Laura in her lap with the other. As an infant, Laura would nap in her baby swing next to Don's desk as he edited and rewrote countless drafts. As a preschooler, Laura would "help" us work by practicing her alphabet on scratch paper at the corner of Sandy or Don's desk. And, as a first grader, she became proficient at putting journals and books back on the bookshelves.

Many children, of course, grow up being familiar with their parents' work. In Laura's life, that's meant living in a house filled with mountains of psychology journals, research articles, books, and chapter drafts. It's also meant putting off many of the simple pleasures of childhood because her parents were trying to meet the latest deadline for completing chapters, selecting photos, or reworking art roughs. And at different times, Laura has directly participated in our work. Last summer, for example, Laura patiently endured a three-hour photo shoot to produce the pictures you'll see of her later in this chapter.

As we've experienced Laura's development from infancy to middle childhood, we've also experienced some transitions ourselves. Your authors met and married when we were in our mid-thirties. Laura was born a month after our first wedding anniversary. Thus, we were beginning our family at a relatively late age. In fact, we were the second-oldest couple in our childbirth class.

In one sense, the first eight years of our marriage have been exciting and eventful. We've learned that you never really know what life has in store for you. In our case, we never anticipated working side by side on a daily basis writing psychology textbooks. Nor did we anticipate how that goal would come to dominate our lives and our daughter's life.

In another sense, the last eight years of our lives have been incredibly "normal." Just as Laura learned to walk, talk, and ride her bicycle in a predictable fashion, we've grown and developed as parents and marital partners in a relatively predictable fashion.

Without question, virtually every life follows well-established, sometimes universal, patterns of physical, social, and mental changes. Yet at the same time, every life is distinct and different—a unique combination of the predictable and the unexpected. So although certain themes are common in the life stories of virtually every person, how those themes are played out remains highly individual. As you read this chapter, we hope you'll come to better understand some of the universal themes—and individual variations—in your life as well.

Introduction

Your Life Story

Developmental psychology is the study of how people change over the lifespan. What are the key themes in developmental psychology?

One way to look at the "big picture" of your life is to think of your life as a story (Howard, 1991). You, of course, are the main character. Your life story so far has had a distinct plot, occasional subplots, and a cast of supporting characters, including family, friends, and lovers.

Like every other person, your life story has been influenced by factors beyond your control. One such factor is the unique combination of genes you inherited from your biological mother and father. Another is the historical era during which you grew up. Your individual development has also been shaped by the cultural, social, and family contexts within which you were raised.

The patterns of your life story, and the life stories of countless other people, are the focus of **developmental psychology**—the study of how people change physically, mentally, and socially throughout the lifespan. At every age and stage of life, developmental psychologists investigate the influence of multiple factors on development, including biological, environmental, social, cultural, and behavioral factors (Bronfenbrenner, 1995, 1979).

developmental psychology
The branch of psychology that studies how people change over the lifespan.

One useful way to conceptualize the human lifespan is in terms of eight major developmental stages. Each stage is characterized by different kinds of physical, cognitive, and social changes, which we will explore in this chapter.

TABLE 9.1 **The Eight Stages of the Lifespan**

Stage	Age Range
Prenatal	Conception to birth
Infancy	0–2 years
Early childhood	2–6 years
Middle childhood	6–12 years
Adolescence	12–18 years
Young adulthood	18–40 years
Middle adulthood	40–65 years
Late adulthood	65+ years

However, the impact of these factors on individual development is greatly influenced by attitudes, perceptions, and personality characteristics. For example, the adjustment to middle school is a breeze for one child, but a nightmare for another child. So while we are influenced by the events we experience, we also shape the meaning and consequences of life events.

Along with studying common patterns of growth and change, developmental psychologists look at the ways that people *differ* in their development and life stories. As our prologue illustrated, there is considerable individual variation during adulthood in the timing of social, occupational, and interpersonal accomplishments. As we'll note several times in this chapter, the typical or "normal" pattern of development can also vary among cultures.

Continuity and Change over the Lifespan
The twin themes of continuity and change throughout the lifespan are evident in the changing nature of relationships. Childhood friendships center on sharing activities, while peer relationships in adolescence emphasize sharing thoughts and feelings. Early adulthood brings the challenge of forming intimate relationships and beginning a family. And close relationships with friends and family continue to contribute to psychological well-being in late adulthood.

Developmental psychologists often conceptualize the lifespan in terms of basic *stages* of development (see Table 9.1). Traditionally, the stages of the lifespan are defined by age, which implies that we experience relatively sudden, age-related changes as we move from one stage to the next. Indeed, some of life's transitions *are* rather abrupt, such as entering the work force, becoming a parent, or retiring. And some aspects of development, such as prenatal development and language development, are closely tied to *critical periods,* which are periods during which the child is maximally sensitive to environmental influences.

Still, most of our physical, mental, and social changes occur gradually. As we trace the typical course of human development in this chapter, the theme of *gradually unfolding changes* throughout the ages and stages of life will become more evident.

Another important theme in developmental psychology is the *interaction between heredity and environment.* Traditionally, this is called the *nature/ nurture issue* (see Chapter 1). Although we are born with a specific genetic potential that we inherit from our biological parents, our environment influences and shapes how that potential is expressed. In turn, our genetic inheritance influences the ways in which we experience and interact with the environment (Scarr, 1992; Plomin & Neiderhiser, 1992).

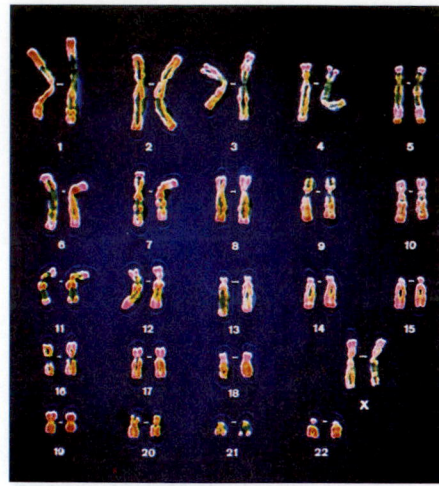

Human Chromosomes A person's unique genetic blueprint is contained in the 23 pairs of chromosomes found in every body cell. Chromosomes are numbered according to descending size. Hence, the first pair of chromosomes is the largest. The 23rd pair, which is labeled X in the above micrograph, determines a person's sex. An XX combination, which is shown, indicates a female. An XY combination indicates a male.

Genetic Contributions to Your Life Story

Your unique genetic makeup results from the pairing of one set of chromosomes from each biological parent at conception. What role does the environment play in the relationship between genotype and phenotype? How do dominant and recessive genes differ?

At the moment of your conception, you were a single cell no larger than the period at the end of this sentence. Packed in that tiny cell was the unique genetic blueprint that you inherited from your biological parents. Today, that same genetic blueprint is found in the **chromosomes** in every cell of your body. Each chromosome is a long, threadlike structure composed of twisted parallel strands of **deoxyribonucleic acid,** abbreviated **DNA.** Put simply, DNA is the chemical basis of all heredity. It contains the chemical genetic code that has directed the growth and development of many of your unique characteristics.

The DNA code carried on each chromosome is arranged in thousands of segments called genes (see Figure 9.1). Each **gene** is a unit of DNA instructions pertaining to some characteristic, such as eye or hair color, height, or handedness.

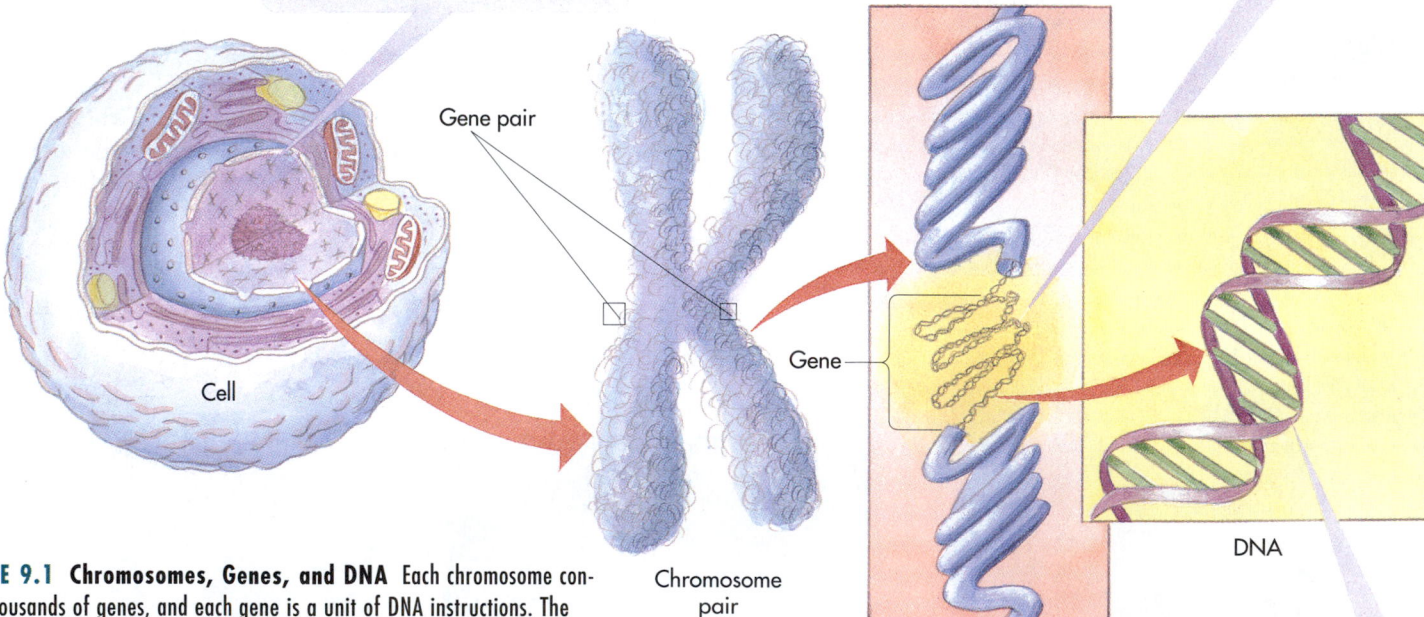

Packed in the nucleus of every cell in your body are the 23 pairs of chromosomes that represent your unique "genetic blueprint".

A gene is a segment on the chromosome that contains the genetic instructions for some aspect of development. Just as chromosomes are arranged in pairs, the gene segments are arranged in pairs.

Cell

Gene pair

Chromosome pair

Gene

DNA

Each gene is a unit of DNA—the chemical genetic code that is the basis of heredity. The twisted strands that make up the DNA molecule resemble a spiral staircase.

FIGURE 9.1 Chromosomes, Genes, and DNA Each chromosome contains thousands of genes, and each gene is a unit of DNA instructions. The twisted parallel strands of DNA contained in the genes resemble a spiral staircase, as shown on the far right. Incredibly fine, the strands of DNA in a single human cell would be over 3 inches long if unraveled. If the DNA present in one person were unraveled, it would stretch from Earth to the planet Pluto and back—*twice!*

TABLE 9.2 Dominant and Recessive Characteristics

Dominant Characteristics	Recessive Characteristics
Full lips	Thin lips
Curly hair	Straight hair
Dark hair	Light hair
Free earlobes	Attached earlobes
Normal hearing	Congenital deafness
Freckles	No freckles
Ability to make U-shape with tongue	Lack of this ability
Dimples	No dimples
Feet with normal arches	Flat feet

SOURCE: Hole, 1993.

chromosome
A long, threadlike structure composed of twisted parallel strands of DNA; found in the nucleus of the cell.

deoxyribonucleic acid (DNA)
The chemical basis of heredity; carries the genetic instructions in the cell.

gene
The basic unit of heredity that directs the development of a particular characteristic; the individual unit of DNA instructions on a chromosome.

genotype
(JEEN-oh-type) The underlying genetic makeup of a particular organism, including the genetic instructions for traits that are not actually displayed.

phenotype
(FEEN-oh-type) The observable traits or characteristics of an organism as determined by the interaction of genetics and environmental factors.

dominant gene
In a pair of genes, the gene containing genetic instructions that will be expressed whether paired with another dominant gene or with a recessive gene.

recessive gene
In a pair of genes, the gene containing genetic instructions that will not be expressed unless paired with another recessive gene.

At conception, the genes carried on the 23 chromosomes contributed by your biological mother's ovum were paired with the genes carried on the 23 chromosomes contributed by your biological father's sperm. The resulting 23 pairs of chromosomes contained an estimated 100,000 pairs of genes—your unique genetic blueprint.

Multiple gene pairs are involved in directing many complex features of development, such as brain organization, body build, and even some personality characteristics (Plomin & others, 1994). Height, for example, seems to be determined by four different pairs of genes (Hole, 1993). But some relatively simple traits are determined by the interaction of a single gene pair, such as light or dark eye color, freckles, and dimples. In the next section, we'll illustrate some basic genetic mechanisms by looking at a trait that is determined by a single gene pair: whether or not you have freckles.

Dominant and Recessive Characteristics

The term **genotype** refers to the underlying genetic makeup of a particular individual, while the term **phenotype** refers to the traits that are actually displayed. For the sake of our discussion, let's suppose that your genotype includes one gene from your mother with the genetic code for FRECKLES. This gene is paired with the gene you inherited from your father, which contains the genetic code for NO FRECKLES.

When a genotype combines such conflicting genetic information, the **dominant gene** will influence the trait you actually display. In this case, the dominant gene is the one for FRECKLES, and you'll inherit the tendency to develop freckles. Traits like freckles, dark eyes, dark hair, and dimples are referred to as *dominant characteristics* because they require *only one member of a gene pair to be dominant in order for the trait to be displayed*. If both members of the gene pair happen to be dominant, the genes will simply act in harmony. In either case, your phenotype will express the dominant characteristic.

So how do you get a phenotype displaying nondominant characteristics, like skin without freckles or dimples? *Each* gene in the gene pair must be a **recessive gene**—a gene whose instructions are not expressed if combined with a dominant gene. In other words, recessive genes are expressed only if paired with an identical recessive gene. In order to be freckle-free, you'd have to inherit a NO FRECKLES/NO FRECKLES gene combination as your genotype. Traits whose expression requires two identical recessive genes, like light hair and being dimple-free, are called *recessive characteristics*. Examples of other dominant and recessive characteristics are listed in Table 9.2.

But let's not forget the interplay between heredity and environment. What we really inherit from our biological parents is a *genetic potential that can be influenced by environmental conditions*. For example, suppose you inherited a FRECKLES/FRECKLES genotype. Because both genes are dominant, you would be genetically "programmed" to develop freckles. But would you be destined to have freckles? Not necessarily. The phenotype *expression* of that genetic programming could still be influenced by your environment. In the case of freckles, exposure to sunlight increases the phenotype expression of freckles. So, if you minimized your exposure to the sun, you might never develop freckles, despite being genetically programmed to do so.

The Sex Chromosomes and Sex-Linked Recessive Characteristics

Some recessive characteristics, such as color blindness and hemophilia (inability of the blood to clot properly), are much more common in males than

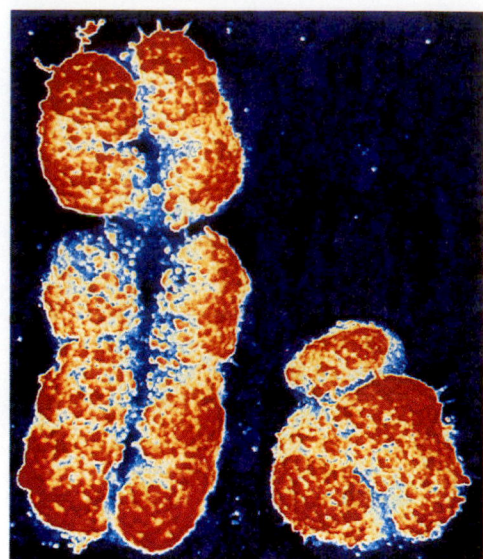

Human Sex Chromosomes The human sex chromosomes are contained in the 23rd pair of chromosomes. On the left is the large X chromosome, which carries many more genes than the smaller Y chromosome, shown on the right.

in females. Why? The answer has to do with the **sex chromosomes,** the 23rd pair of chromosomes—the ones that determine biological sex.

There are two types of sex chromosomes, the large *X chromosome* and the smaller *Y chromosome.* The large X chromosome carries more genes than the smaller Y chromosome, including genes for traits unrelated to sex. In females, the 23rd pair of chromosomes is made up of two large X chromosomes. In males, a large X chromosome and a smaller Y chromosome make up the 23rd pair.

As we've already seen, recessive characteristics normally require the presence of *two* identical recessive genes for the trait to be displayed, one on each chromosome in a particular pair. This continues to be true for females for recessive characteristics communicated on the 23rd chromosome pair. Females require the presence of *two* recessive genes, one on each X chromosome.

For males, however, the smaller Y chromosome often does *not* contain a corresponding gene segment to match the one on their X chromosome. This means that a male can display certain recessive characteristics as the result of only *one recessive gene carried on the X chromosome of his XY pair.*

Traits determined by recessive genes on the X chromosomes are referred to as **sex-linked recessive characteristics.** Red-green color blindness, congenital night blindness, hemophilia, and brown tooth enamel are examples of sex-linked recessive characteristics. Because males require only one recessive gene on their X chromosome to display the recessive trait, they are more likely than females to display these sex-linked recessive characteristics. Thus, males and females show different patterns of inheritance for recessive characteristics that are communicted on the sex chromosomes.

Beyond the special case of sex-linked recessive characteristics, other patterns of genetic influence exist. Some traits, for example, are expressed as the *average* of the genetic instructions inherited from the mother and the father. For example, skin color is usually an intermediate value between the skin color of each parent. In addition, the genetic code can *mutate,* or spontaneously change, between one generation and the next.

Prenatal Development

During the prenatal stage, the single-cell zygote develops into a full-term fetus. What are the three stages of prenatal development? What are teratogens, and what general principles seem to govern their impact on the fetus?

At conception, chromosomes from the biological mother and father combine to form a single cell—the fertilized egg, or *zygote.* Over the relatively brief span of nine months, that single cell develops to the estimated trillion cells that make up a newborn baby. This **prenatal stage** has three distinct phases: the germinal period, the embryonic period, and the fetal period.

The **germinal period,** also called the *zygotic period,* represents the first two weeks of prenatal development, or pregnancy. During this time, the zygote undergoes rapid cell division before becoming implanted on the mother's uterine wall. Some of the zygote's cells will eventually form the structures that house and protect the developing fetus and provide nourishment from the mother. By the end of the two-week germinal period, the single-celled zygote has developed into a cluster of cells called the *embryo.*

sex chromosomes
Chromosomes designated as X or Y that determine biological sex; the 23rd pair of chromosomes in humans.

sex-linked recessive characteristics
Traits determined by recessive genes located on the X chromosome; in males, these characteristics require only one recessive gene to be expressed.

prenatal stage
The state of development before birth; divided into the germinal, embryonic, and fetal periods.

germinal period
The first two weeks of prenatal development.

embryonic period
The second period of prenatal development, extending from the third week through the eighth week.

teratogens
Harmful agents or substances that can cause malformations or defects in an embryo or fetus.

fetal period
The third and longest period of prenatal development, extending from the eighth week until birth.

Prenatal Development Although it is less than an inch long, the beginnings of arms, legs, and fingers can already be distinguished in the 7-week-old embryo (left). The amniotic sac can be clearly seen in this photograph. The fetus at four months (right) now measures 6 to 10 inches long, and the mother may be able to feel the fetus's movements. Notice the well-formed umbilical cord. Near full-term (bottom photo), the 8-month-old fetus gains body fat to help it survive outside its mother's uterus.

The **embryonic period** begins with week 3 and extends through week 8. During this time of rapid growth and intensive cell differentiation, the organs and major systems of the body form. Genes on the sex chromosomes and hormonal influences also trigger the initial development of the sex organs.

Protectively housed in the fluid-filled *amniotic sac,* the embryo's lifeline is the umbilical cord. Via the *umbilical cord,* the embryo receives nutrients, oxygen, and water, and gets rid of carbon monoxide and other wastes. The umbilical cord attaches the embryo to the *placenta,* a disk-shaped tissue on the mother's uterine wall. The placenta prevents the mother's blood from mingling with that of the developing embryo, acting as a filter to prevent harmful substances that might be present in the mother's blood from reaching the embryo.

The placenta cannot, however, filter out all harmful agents from the mother's blood. Harmful agents or substances that can cause abnormal development or birth defects are called **teratogens.** Generally, the greatest vulnerability to teratogens occurs during the embryonic stage, when major body systems are forming. Known teratogens include:

- exposure to radiation
- toxic industrial chemicals, such as mercury and PCBs
- diseases, such as rubella, syphilis, genital herpes, and AIDS
- drugs taken by the mother, such as alcohol, cocaine, and heroin

By the end of the embryonic period, the embryo has grown from a cluster of a few hundred cells no bigger than the head of a pin to over an inch in length. Now weighing about an ounce, the embryo looks distinctly human even though its head accounts for about half its body size.

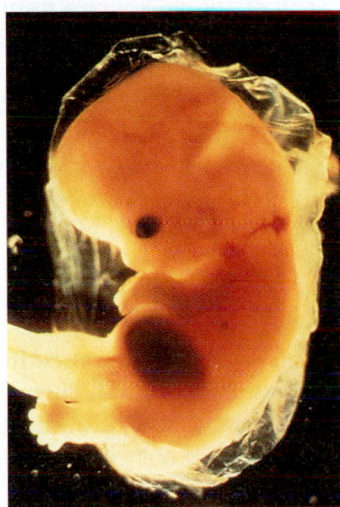

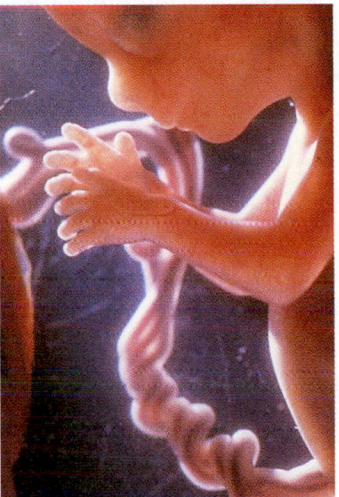

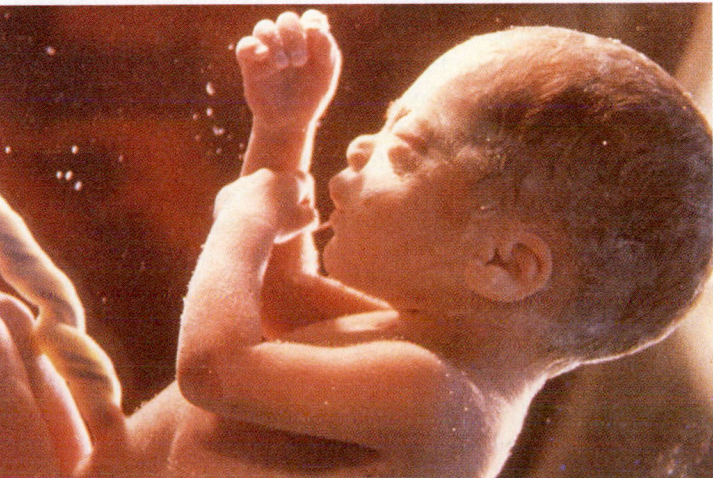

The third month heralds the beginning of the **fetal period**—the final and longest stage of prenatal development. The main task during the next seven months is for body systems to grow and reach maturity in preparation for life outside the mother's body. By the end of the third month, the *fetus* can move its arms, legs, mouth, and head. It becomes capable of reflexive responses, such as fanning its toes if the sole of the foot is stroked and squinting if its eyelids are touched. During the fourth month, the mother experiences *quickening*—she can feel the fetus moving.

By the fifth month, essentially all the brain cells the person will ever have are present, though they will continue to develop long after birth (Shatz, 1992). The fetus has distinct sleep/wake cycles and periods of activity. During the sixth month, the fetus's brain activity becomes similar to that of a newborn baby.

During the final two months, the fetus will double its weight, gaining an additional three to four pounds of body fat. This additional body fat will help the newborn adjust to changing temperatures outside the womb. It also contributes to the newborn's chubby appearance. As birth approaches, growth slows and the fetus's body systems become more active.

Development During Infancy and Childhood

While physically helpless, newborn infants are equipped with reflexes and sensory capabilities that enhance their chances for survival. How do the sensory capabilities of the newborn promote the development of relationships with caregivers? How does the brain develop after birth?

The newly born infant enters the world with an impressive array of physical and sensory capabilities. Initially, his behavior is mostly limited to reflexes that enhance his chances for survival. Touching the newborn's cheek triggers the *rooting reflex*—he turns toward the source of the touch and opens his mouth. Touching the newborn's lips evokes the *sucking reflex*. If you put a finger on each of the newborn's palms, he will display the *grasping reflex,* gripping your fingers so tightly that he can be lifted upright. As motor areas of the infant's brain develop over the first year of life, the rooting, sucking, and grasping reflexes are replaced by voluntary behaviors.

The newborn's senses—vision, hearing, smell, and touch—are keenly attuned to people, helping her quickly learn to differentiate between her mother and other humans. In a classic study, Robert Fantz (1961) demonstrated that the image of a human face holds the newborn's gaze longer than other images. Other researchers have also confirmed the newborn's visual preference for the human face. Newborns only 10 *minutes* old will turn their heads to continue gazing at the image of a human face as it passes in front of them, but they will not visually follow other images (Johnson & others, 1991).

Vision is the least developed sense at birth (Gottlieb & Krasnegor, 1985). The newborn is extremely nearsighted, meaning he can see near objects more clearly than distant objects. The optimal viewing distance for the newborn is about 6 to 12 inches, the perfect distance for a nursing baby to easily focus on his mother's face and make eye contact. Nevertheless, the infant's view of the world is pretty fuzzy for the first several months, even for objects that are within close range.

Interestingly, the interaction between adults and infants seems to naturally compensate for the newborn's poor vision. When adults interact with very young infants, they almost always position themselves so that their face is about 8 to 12 inches away from the baby's face. Adults also have a strong natural tendency to exaggerate head movements and facial expressions, such as smiles and frowns, again making it easier for the baby to see them.

The newborn also responds with increased alertness to the sound of human voices. Even at birth, he can distinguish between his mother's voice and that of another woman (DeCasper & Fifer, 1980). Especially if breast-fed,

Newborn Reflexes When this 2-week-old baby (top) is held upright with her feet touching a flat surface, she displays the *stepping reflex,* moving her legs as if she were trying to walk. Another reflex that is present at birth is the *grasping reflex* (right). The infant's grip is so strong that he can support his own weight. Thought to enhance the newborn's chances for survival, these involuntary reflexes disappear after the first few months of life.

the newborn quickly becomes sensitized to the scent of his mother's body (Makin, 1989). For her part, the mother becomes keenly attuned to her infant's characteristic appearance, smell, and skin texture (Kaitz & others, 1992).

Physical Development

By the time she begins crawling, at around seven to eight months of age, the infant's view of the world, including distant objects, will be as clear as that of her parents. The increasing maturation of the infant's visual system is a reflection of her developing brain. At birth, her brain is an impressive 25 percent of its adult weight. In contrast, her birth weight is only about 5 percent of her eventual adult weight. During infancy, her brain will grow to about 75 percent of its adult weight, while her body weight will reach only about 20 percent of her adult weight.

The newborn enters the world with essentially all the neurons his brain will ever have—an estimated 100 billion. After birth, however, the brain continues to develop rapidly. The number of *dendrites* increases dramatically during the first two years of life (Siegler, 1989). The axons of many neurons acquire *myelin*—the white, fatty covering that increases a neuron's communication speed (see Chapter 2).

One outward reflection of the infant's developing brain is the attainment of more sophisticated motor skills. Figure 9.2 illustrates the sequence and average ages of motor skill development during infancy. The basic *sequence* is universal, but the *average ages* can be a little deceptive. Infants vary a great deal in the ages at which they master each skill. While virtually all infants are walking well by fifteen months of age, some infants will walk as early as ten months. Each infant has her own genetically programmed timetable of physical maturation and developmental readiness to master different motor skills.

FIGURE 9.2 Milestones in Infant Motor Development Each bar in the graph below shows the typical range of ages for acquiring particular motor skills during infancy. Given the wide range of individual variation, can you see how simple statistical averages can be misleading?

Early Development

Answer *true* or *false* for each of the following statements. If a statement is false, write in the correct statement.

_____ **1.** Mary's genotype (Dd) includes one dominant gene (D) for DIMPLES and a recessive gene (d) for NO DIMPLES. Mary's phenotype will be to have dimples.

_____ **2.** In order for you to display a phenotype of flat feet, your genotype must be an (ff)—a flat feet/flat feet genetic combination. Hence, having flat feet must be a recessive characteristic.

_____ **3.** Sarah has an XY combination in her 23rd pair of chromosomes.

_____ **4.** Each chromosome has exactly 23 genes.

_____ **5.** The Y chromosome has twice as many genes as the X chromosome.

_____ **6.** The greatest vulnerability to teratogens usually occurs during the embryonic stage.

_____ **7.** Vision is the least well-developed sense in the human newborn.

Social and Personality Development

Temperament refers to inborn predispositions to behave and react in a particular way, while attachment refers to the emotional bond an infant forms with her primary caregivers. What temperamental patterns have been identified? What is the basic premise of attachment theory?

From birth, forming close social and emotional relationships with caregivers is essential to the infant's physical and psychological well-being. Although physically helpless, the young infant does not play a passive role in forming these relationships. As you'll see in this section, the infant's individual traits play an important role in the development of the relationship between infant and caregiver.

Temperamental Qualities: Babies Are Different!

Infants come into the world with very distinct and consistent behavioral styles. Some babies are consistently calm and easy to soothe. Other babies are fussy, irritable, and hard to comfort. Some babies are active and outgoing; others seem shy and wary of new experiences. Psychologists refer to these inborn predispositions to consistently behave and react in a certain way as an infant's **temperament** (Bates, 1989, 1994).

Interest in infant temperament was triggered by a classic longitudinal study launched in the 1950s by psychiatrists Alexander Thomas and Stella Chess. The focus of the study was on how temperamental qualities influence adjustment throughout life. Chess and Thomas rated young infants on a variety of characteristics, such as activity level, mood, regularity, and attention span. They found that about two-thirds of the babies could be classified into one of three broad temperamental patterns: *easy, difficult,* and *slow-to-warm-up.* About a third of the infants were characterized as *average* babies because they did not fit neatly into one of these three categories (Thomas & Chess, 1977).

Easy babies readily adapt to new experiences, generally display positive moods and emotions, and have regular sleeping and eating patterns. *Difficult* babies tend to be intensely emotional, are irritable and fussy, and cry a lot. They also tend to have irregular sleeping and eating patterns. *Slow-to-warm-up* babies have a low activity level, withdraw from new situations and peo-

temperament
Inborn predispositions to consistently behave and react in a certain way.

ple, and adapt to new experiences very gradually. After studying the same children from infancy through childhood, Thomas and Chess (1986) found that these broad patterns of temperamental qualities were remarkably stable.

Virtually all temperament researchers agree that individual differences in temperament have a genetic and biological basis (see Rothbart & others, 1994; Calkins & Fox, 1994). However, researchers also agree that environmental experiences can modify a child's basic temperament (Gunnar, 1994; Goldsmith & others, 1987). For example, a child with a temperamental predisposition to be shy can be encouraged to be more sociable by his parents, and may well overcome much of his tendency toward shyness in a supportive environment (Kagan & Fox, 1995). Thus, the display of temperamental qualities is yet another example of the complex interaction between heredity and environmental factors.

Attachment: Forming Emotional Bonds

During the first year of life, the emotional bond that forms between the infant and his caregivers, especially his mother, is called **attachment.** According to *attachment theory,* an infant's ability to thrive physically and psychologically depends in part on the quality of attachment (Ainsworth & others, 1978).

In all cultures, the emotional bond between infants and caregivers is an important relationship (Grossmann & Grossmann, 1990). But not surprisingly, there are cultural differences in how the attachment relationship is conceptualized and encouraged. In Culture and Human Behavior Box 9.1, "Where Does the Baby Sleep?" we describe one example of how cultural differences in child-rearing practices reflect different ideas about the appropriate relationship between infants and parents.

The Importance of Attachment Secure attachment in infancy forms the basis for emotional bonds in later childhood. At one time, attachment researchers focused only on the relationship between mothers and infants. Today, the importance of the attachment relationship between fathers and children is also recognized.

In studying attachment, psychologists have typically focused on the infant's bond with the mother, since the mother is often the infant's primary caregiver. Still, it's important to note that many fathers today are also directly involved with the basic care of their infants and children (Blair & Lichter, 1991). In homes where both parents are present, infants who are attached to one parent are also attached to the other (Fox & others, 1991). Infants tend to form attachments to both parents at about the same time (Bornstein & Lamb, 1992). An infant is also capable of forming attachments to other consistent caregivers in his life, such as relatives or workers at a day-care center (Howes & Hamilton, 1992). Thus, an infant can form *multiple* attachments (Field, 1996).

In general, when parents are consistently warm, responsive, and sensitive to their infant's needs, the infant develops a *secure attachment* to her parents (Goldsmith & Harman, 1994). The infant's expectations that her needs will be met are essential to forming a secure attachment to her parents (Thompson, 1986).

In contrast, *insecure attachment* may develop when an infant's parents are neglectful, inconsistent, or insensitive to his moods or behaviors. Insecure attachment seems to reflect an ambivalent or detached emotional relationship between an infant and his parents (Isabella & others, 1989; Ainsworth, 1979).

Psychologists assess attachment by observing the infant's behavior toward his mother. When his mother is present, the *securely attached* infant will use her as a "secure base" from which to explore the new environment, periodically returning to her side. He will show distress when his mother leaves the room and will greet her warmly when she returns. A securely attached baby is easily soothed by his mother (Lamb & others, 1985; Ainsworth & others, 1978).

attachment
The emotional bond that forms between an infant and her caregiver(s), especially her parents.

CULTURE AND HUMAN BEHAVIOR 9.1

Where Does the Baby Sleep?

In most U.S. families, infants sleep in their own bed, usually in a separate room from their parents. It may surprise you to discover that the United States is very unusual in this respect. In one survey of 100 societies, the United States was the *only* one in which babies slept in separate rooms. Another survey of 136 societies found that in two-thirds of the societies, infants slept in the same beds as their mothers (Morelli & others, 1992).

Gilda Morelli and her colleagues (1992) compared the sleeping arrangements of several middle-class U.S. families with those of Mayan families in a small town in Guatemala. They found that infants in the Mayan families slept with their mothers until they were two or three, usually until another baby was about to be born. At that point, toddlers moved to the bed of another family member, usually the father or an older sibling. Children continued to sleep with other family members throughout childhood.

Mayan mothers were shocked when the American researchers told them that infants in the United States slept alone and often in a different room from their parents. The Mayan mothers reacted with disapproval and pity for the infant. They believed that the practice was cruel and unnatural, and would have negative effects on the infant's development.

In the United States, bedtime marks the separation of the infant or small child from the family. To ease the child's transition to sleeping—and to spending long hours alone—"putting the baby to bed" often involves lengthy bedtime rituals, like stories and lullabies. Small children often take comforting items, like a favorite blanket or teddy bear, to bed with them to ease the transition to falling asleep alone. The child may also use the "security blanket" or "cuddly" to comfort himself when he wakes up in the night, as most small children do.

In contrast, the Mayan babies do not take cuddly items to bed, and no special routines marked the transition between wakefulness and sleep. Mayan parents were puzzled by the very idea. Instead, the Mayan babies simply go to bed when their parents do or fall asleep in the middle of the family's social activities.

Morelli and her colleagues found that the different sleeping customs of the U.S. and the Mayan families reflect different cultural values. Some of the U.S. babies slept in the same room as their parents when they were first born, which the parents felt helped foster feelings of closeness and emotional security in the newborns. However, most of the U.S. parents moved their babies to a separate room when they felt that the babies were ready to sleep alone, usually by three to six months of age. These parents explained their decision by saying that it was time for the baby to learn to be "independent" and "self-reliant."

In contrast, the Mayan parents felt that it was important to develop and encourage the infant's feelings of *interdependence* with other members of the family. Thus, in both Mayan and U.S. families, sleeping arrangements reflect goals for child rearing and cultural values for relations among family members (Morelli & others, 1992).

In contrast, an *insecurely attached* infant is less likely to explore the environment, even when her mother is present. Insecurely attached infants may appear either very anxious or completely indifferent. Such infants tend to ignore or avoid their mothers when they are present. Some insecurely attached infants become extremely distressed when their mothers leave the room. When insecurely attached infants are reunited with their mothers, they are hard to soothe and may resist the mother's attempts to comfort them.

The quality of attachment during infancy is associated with a variety of long-term effects (Goldsmith & Harman, 1994). Preschoolers with a history of being securely attached tend to be more prosocial, empathic, and socially competent than preschoolers with a history of insecure attachment (Suess & others, 1992; Collins & Gunnar, 1990). Adolescents who were securely attached in infancy have fewer problems, do better in school, and have more successful relationships with their peers than do adolescents who were insecurely attached in infancy (Sroufe, 1995).

Because attachment in infancy seems to be so important, psychologists have extensively investigated the impact of day care on attachment. In Critical Thinking Box 9.2, "The Effects of Child Care on Attachment and Development," we take a close look at this issue.

CRITICAL THINKING 9.2

The Effects of Child Care on Attachment and Development

The majority of infants and toddlers in the United States routinely experience care by someone other than their mother or father (Phillips, 1991). Given the importance of the emotional bond between infant and parent, should we be concerned that many young children experience daily separation from their parents?

Developmental psychologist Jay Belsky created considerable controversy when he published studies showing that infants under a year old were more likely to demonstrate insecure attachment if they experienced over 30 hours of day care per week (Belsky & Rovine, 1988; Belsky, 1986). Belsky also reviewed evidence showing that grade school children with extensive infant day-care experience were more aggressive and less compliant than children who had not been in day care. Belsky (1992) has concluded that children who entered full-time day care before their first birthday are "at risk" to be insecurely attached and to suffer later behavioral and emotional problems.

Needless to say, Belsky's conclusion sparked a heated debate over the effects of day care on infants. Does extensive experience with day care during the first year of life create insecurely attached infants and toddlers? Does it produce negative effects in later childhood? Let's look at the evidence.

High-Quality Day Care A high-quality day-care center offers a variety of age-appropriate activities and toys, and sometimes even a furry friend or two, as in this classroom. For toddlers and infants, consistency in caregivers is also extremely important.

Belsky did not claim that *all* infants in day care were likely to experience insecure attachment. Reviewing the data in Belsky's studies and others, psychologist Alison Clarke-Stewart (1989, 1992) pointed out that the actual difference in attachment was quite small when infants experiencing day care were compared to infants cared for by a parent. The proportion of insecurely attached infants in day care is only slightly higher than the proportion typically found in the general population (Lamb & others, 1992). In other words, *most* of the children who had started day care in infancy were securely attached, just like most of the children who had not experienced extensive infant day care.

So what about the long-term effects of day care? One study found that third graders with extensive infant day-care experience were more likely to demonstrate a variety of social and academic problems (Vandell & Corasaniti, 1990). However, these children were not enrolled in high-quality day care, as defined in the accompanying table. Rather, they experienced average day-care conditions in a state with relatively low standards for day-care centers. But even in this case, it's difficult to assign the cause of these problems to day care itself. Why? Because developmental problems in the third graders studied were also associated with being raised exclusively by their mothers at home.

Most psychologists today agree that the *quality* of child care is a key factor in promoting secure attachment in early childhood and preventing problems in later childhood (Scarr & Eisenberg, 1993). Many studies have found that children who experience high-quality care tend to be more sociable, better adjusted, and more academically competent than children who experience poor-quality care (Howes, 1991; Phillips & Howes, 1987). In fact, when psychologist Tiffany Field studied grade school children who had been enrolled in high-quality day care from infancy, she found *no* negative effects of their day-care experience. (Field, 1991; Field & others, 1988).

Swedish psychologist Bengt-Erik Andersson (1989, 1992) has arrived at

The Characteristics of High-Quality Day Care

- Whether care is in someone's home or in a day-care center, caregivers should be warm and responsive.

- Developmentally appropriate activities and a variety of play materials should be available.

- Caregivers should have some training and education in child development.

- Low staff turnover is essential, as consistency is especially important for infants and toddlers.

- The ratio of caregivers to children should be low. Two adults should care for no more than 8 infants, no more than 14 toddlers, or no more than 20 four- and five-year olds.

What constitutes high-quality day care? The National Association for the Education of Young Children (1990, 1989) has identified several key characteristics, which are supported by child development research.

the same conclusion. Andersson studied children who had experienced day care before one year of age in Sweden, where high-quality day care is widely available. When these children were assessed at the ages of eight and thirteen, they performed better in school and teachers rated them more highly on their social and emotional competence than children who had started day care later in childhood or who had stayed home with a parent until they entered grade school.

Clearly, day care in itself does not necessarily lead to undesirable outcomes. The quality of the care is the critical factor. High-quality day care can potentially benefit children, even when it begins in early infancy. In contrast, low-quality care can potentially contribute to social and academic problems in later childhood. Unfortunately, high-quality day care is not often readily available in the United States (Pope, 1997). High-quality day-care centers, where they exist, tend to be expensive and may have long waiting lists.

Language Development

Infants seem to be born with a biological predisposition to learn language. How is language development encouraged by caregivers? What are the stages of language development?

Probably no other accomplishment in early life is as astounding as language development. By the time a child is three years old, he will have learned approximately 3,000 words and the complex rules of his language.

According to linguist **Noam Chomsky** (b. 1928), every child is born with a biological predisposition to learn language—*any* language. In effect, each child possesses a "universal grammar"—a basic understanding of the common principles of language organization. The infant is innately equipped not only to understand language but also to easily extract grammatical rules from what she hears (Chomsky, 1965).

At birth, infants can distinguish among the speech sounds of all the world's languages, no matter what language is spoken in their homes (Werker & Desjardins, 1995). For example, adult native speakers of English cannot distinguish between two different /t/ sounds in Hindi. And adult native speakers of Japanese cannot distinguish between /l/ and /r/ sounds: *rake* and *lake* sound the same. But infants just a few months old can distinguish among all these different sounds.

Infants lose this ability by ten months of age (Kuhl & others, 1992). Instead, they can distinguish only among the speech sounds that are present in the language to which they have been exposed. Thus, during the first year of life, infants begin to master the sound structure of their native language.

Encouraging Language Development: Motherese

Just as infants seem to be biologically programmed to learn language, parents seem to be biologically programmed to encourage language development by the way they speak to infants and toddlers. People in every culture, especially parents, use a style of speech called *motherese,* or *infant-directed speech,* with babies (Kuhl & others, 1997).

Motherese is characterized by very distinct pronunciation, a simplified vocabulary, short sentences, a high pitch, and exaggerated intonation and expression. Content is restricted to topics that are familiar to the child, and "baby talk" is often used—simplified words like "go bye-bye" and "night-night." Questions are often asked, encouraging a response from the infant. Research by psychologist Ann Fernald (1985) has shown that infants prefer infant-directed speech to language spoken in an adult conversational style.

The adult use of infant-directed speech seems to be instinctive. Deaf mothers who use sign language modify their hand gestures when they communicate with infants and toddlers in a way that is very similar to the infant-directed speech of hearing mothers (Bornstein & Lamb, 1992). Furthermore, as infants mature, the speech patterns of parents change to fit the child's developing language abilities (Papoušek & others, 1985).

The Cooing and Babbling Stage of Language Development

As with many other aspects of development, the stages of language development appear to be universal. In virtually every culture, infants follow the

Deaf Babies Babble with Their Hands
Deaf babies whose parents use American Sign Language (ASL) babble with their hands, rather than their voices. Just as hearing babies repeat the same syllables over and over, deaf babies repeat the same simple hand gestures (Petitto & Marentette, 1991). The hand shapes represent basic components of ASL gestures, much like the syllables that make up the words of spoken language. Here, a baby repeats the sign for "A."

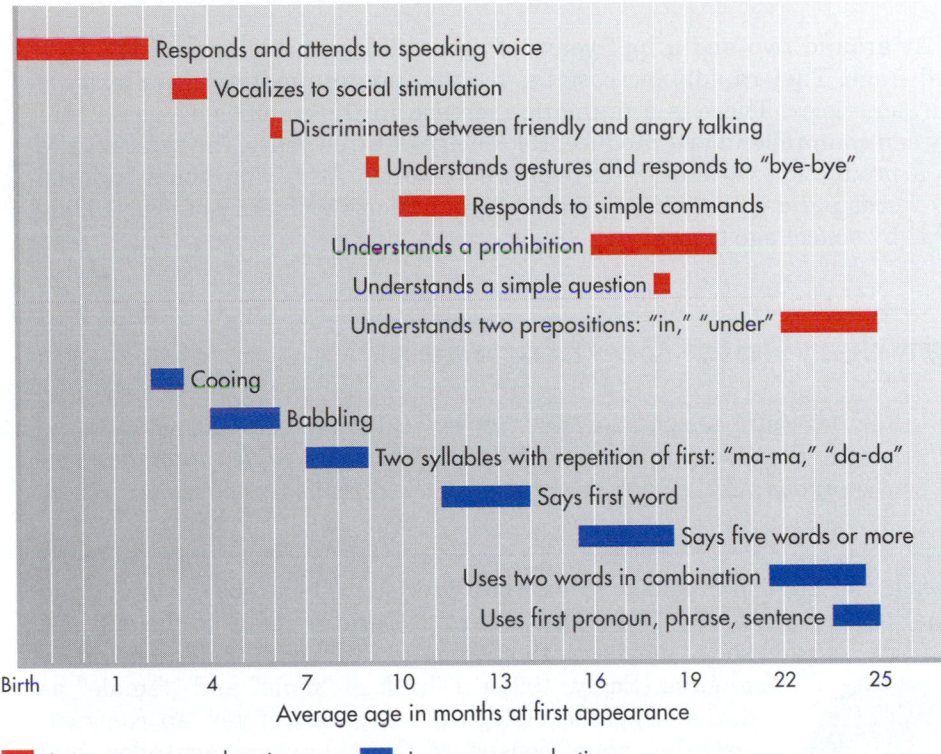

Average age in months at first appearance

- 🟥 Language comprehension
- 🟦 Language production

FIGURE 9.3 Milestones in Language Comprehension and Production
Approximate average ages for the first appearance of different stages of language development. Notice that language comprehension occurs much earlier than language production.
(Based on Bornstein & Lamb, 1992, Fig. 9.1, p. 308.)

same sequence of language development and at roughly similar ages (see Figure 9.3).

At about three months of age, the infant begins to "coo," repeating vowel sounds such as *ahhhhh* or *ooooo*, varying the pitch up or down. At about five months of age, the infant begins to *babble*. She adds consonants to the vowels and strings the sounds together in sometimes long-winded productions of babbling, such as *ba-ba-ba-ba, de-de-de-de*, or *ma-ma-ma-ma*.

When infants babble, they are not simply imitating adult speech. Infants all over the world use the *same* sounds when they babble, including sounds that do not occur in the language of their parents and other caregivers. At around nine months of age, babies begin to babble more in the sounds specific to their language (Cole & Cole, 1996). Babbling, then, seems to be a biologically programmed stage of language development.

The One-Word Stage of Language Development

Long before a baby becomes an accomplished talker, she understands much of what is said to her (Woodward & others, 1994). Before they are a year old, most infants can understand simple commands, such as "Bring Daddy the block," even though they cannot *say* the words *bring, Daddy*, or *block*. This reflects the fact that an infant's **comprehension vocabulary** (the words she understands) is much larger than her **production vocabulary** (the words she can say). Generally, infants acquire comprehension of words more than twice as fast as they learn to speak new words (Bornstein & Lamb, 1992).

Somewhere around their first birthday, infants produce their first real words. First words usually refer to concrete objects or people that are important to the child, such as *mama, daddy*, or *ba-ba* (bottle). First words are also often made up of the syllables that were used in babbling.

During the *one-word stage*, babies use a single word and vocal intonation to stand for an entire sentence. With the proper intonation and context, *ba-ba* can mean "I want my bottle!" "There's my bottle!" or "Where's my bottle?"

The Two-Word Stage of Language Development

Around their second birthday, infants begin putting words together. During the *two-word stage*, infants combine two words to construct a simple "sentence," such as "Mama go," "Where kitty?" and "No potty!" During this stage, the words used are primarily content words—nouns, verbs, and sometimes adjectives or adverbs. Articles (*a, an, the*) and prepositions (*in, under, on*) are omitted. Two-word sentences reflect the first understandings of grammar. Although these utterances include only the most essential words, they basically follow a grammatically correct sequence.

comprehension vocabulary
The words that are understood by an infant or child.

production vocabulary
The words that an infant or child understands and can speak.

gender
The cultural, social, and psychological meanings that are associated with masculinity or femininity.

gender roles
The behaviors, attitudes, and personality traits that are designated as either masculine or feminine in a given culture.

gender identity
A person's psychological sense of being either male or female.

social learning theory of gender-role development
The theory that gender roles are acquired through the basic processes of learning, including reinforcement, punishment, and modeling.

At around two and a half years of age, children move beyond the two-word stage. They rapidly increase the length and grammatical complexity of their sentences. There is a dramatic increase in the number of words that they can comprehend and produce. By the age of three years, the typical child has a production vocabulary of over 3,000 words. Acquiring about a dozen new words per day, a child may have a production vocabulary of over 10,000 words by school age (Bjorklund, 1995).

Gender-Role Development

Gender plays an important role in our culture. What gender differences develop during childhood? How do social learning theory and gender schema theory explain the development of gender roles?

Because the English language is less than precise in the arena of gender and sexuality, we need to clarify a couple of terms. **Gender** refers to the cultural and social meanings that are associated with maleness and femaleness (Eagly, 1995a). Think of "male" and "female" as designating the biological categories of sex. In contrast, **gender roles** consist of the behaviors, attitudes, and personality traits that a given culture designates as either "masculine" or "feminine" (Bailey & Zucker, 1995). Finally, **gender identity** refers to a person's psychological sense of being either male or female (Unger & Crawford, 1996).

Pink Bikes, Red Bikes Little boys and little girls clearly have a lot in common. All of these children are wearing blue jeans, and they all enjoy bicycling with their friends. Nevertheless, the girl's bike is pink with white tires, and the boy's bike is red with black tires. Why?

Roughly between the ages of two and three, children can identify themselves and other children as boys or girls, although the details are still a bit fuzzy to them (Fagot & others, 1992). Preschoolers don't yet understand that sex is determined by physical characteristics. This is not surprising, considering that the biologically defining sex characteristics—the sex organs—are hidden from view most of the time. Instead, young children identify the sexes in terms of external attributes, such as hairstyle, clothing, and activities.

From about the age of eighteen months to two years, sex differences in behavior begin to emerge. These differences become more pronounced throughout early childhood. Toddler girls play more with soft toys and dolls, and ask for help from adults more than toddler boys do. Toddler boys play more with blocks and transportation toys, such as trucks and wagons. They also play more actively than girls do (Turner & Gervai, 1995; Stern & Karraker, 1989). By the age of three, children have developed a clear preference for toys that are associated with their own sex.

Separate Worlds? In childhood, boys tend to play in groups and prefer competitive games. In contrast, girls tend to establish close relationships with one or two other girls, and cement their friendship by sharing thoughts and feelings. How might such gender differences affect intimate relationships in adolescence and adulthood?

Children also develop a strong preference for playing with members of their own sex—girls with girls and boys with boys (Thorne & Luria, 1986). It's not uncommon to hear boys refer to girls as "icky" and girls refer to boys as "mean" or "rough." And, in fact, preschool boys *do* play more roughly than girls, cover more territory, and play in larger groups (Block, 1983; Thorne, 1986). Throughout the remainder of childhood, boys and girls play primarily with members of their own sex (Powlishta, 1995a).

According to psychologist Carole Beal (1994), boys and girls almost seem to create separate "social worlds," each with its own style of interaction. They also learn particular ways of interacting that work well with other peers of the same sex. For example, boys learn to assert themselves within a group of male friends. Girls tend to establish very close bonds with one or two friends. Girls learn to maintain those close friendships through compromise, conciliation, and verbal conflict resolution.

Explaining Gender Roles: Two Contemporary Theories

Based on the principles of learning, **social learning theory** contends that gender roles are learned through *reinforcement, punishment,* and *modeling*. From a very young age, children are reinforced or rewarded when they display gender-appropriate behavior and punished when they do not. For example, psychologists Beverly Fagot and Richard Hagan (1991) observed mothers and fathers interacting with their children in their homes. They found that eighteen-month-old boys received more positive reactions from their parents for playing with male-typed toys and for exhibiting aggressive or assertive behavior. In contrast, eighteen-month-old girls received more positive responses for attempts to communicate with their parents, while boys received more negative reactions for such attempts.

To what degree do such parental behaviors influence the development of gender differences? The effect is not as great as you might think. Psychologists David Lytton and David M. Romney (1991) conducted a meta-analysis of nearly 200 studies of parents' different treatment of boys and girls. They found that the actual effects of parental socialization in many areas of gender differences are relatively small. Yes, parents *do* tend to reinforce and encourage gender-appropriate play. But for the most part, parents treat their male and female children rather similarly.

If parents have only a minimal effect, how do children acquire their understanding of gender differences? Children are exposed to many other sources of information about gender roles, including television, children's books, and observation of same-sex adult role models. Hence, children also learn gender differences through *modeling,* in which they observe and then imitate the sex-typed behavior of significant adults and older children (Beal, 1994). By observing and imitating such models—whether it's Mom cooking, Dad fixing things around

You've Come a Long Way, Baby? Children's books continue to reinforce gender stereotypes, sometimes in subtle ways. In this picture book for preschoolers, published in 1990, a little girl follows her big brother's lead. The boy is shown actively digging in the mud, happily getting dirty with his dog, bat, and ball nearby. In contrast, the little girl, dressed in pink, stays clean as she nurtures her kitten.

Who wants to sleep, anyway? Not us! We want to be busy, busy, busy!

gender schema theory
The theory that gender-role development is influenced by the formation of schemas, or mental representations, of masculinity and femininity.

the house, or a male superhero rescuing a helpless female on television—children come to understand that certain activities and attributes are considered more appropriate for one sex than the other.

In contrast to the relatively passive role played by children in social learning theory, **gender schema theory** contends that children *actively* develop mental categories (or *schemas*) for masculinity and femininity (Martin & Halverson, 1981). That is, children actively organize information about other people and appropriate behavior, activities, and attributes into gender categories. Saying that "trucks are for boys and dolls are for girls" is an example of a gender schema.

According to gender schema theory, children, like many adults, look at the world through "gender lenses" (Bem, 1987). Gender schemas influence how people pay attention to, perceive, interpret, and remember gender-relevant behavior. Gender schemas also seem to lead children to perceive members of their own sex more favorably than members of the opposite sex (Powlishta, 1995b).

Children readily assimilate new information into their existing gender schemas. In one study, four- to nine-year-olds were given boxes of gender-neutral gadgets, such as hole punches (Bradbard & others, 1986). But some gadgets were labeled as "girl toys" and some as "boy toys." The boys played more with the "boy gadgets," and the girls played more with the "girl gadgets." A week later, the children easily remembered which gadgets went with each sex, and remembered more information about the gadgets that were associated with their own sex. Simply labeling the objects as belonging to boys or to girls had powerful consequences for the children's behavior and memory—evidence of the importance of gender schemas in learning and remembering new information.

Cognitive Development

According to Piaget, children progress through four distinct cognitive stages. Each stage marks a shift in how they think and understand the world. What characterizes each stage? What are three criticisms of Piaget's theory?

When Laura was almost three, Sandy and Laura were investigating the tadpoles in the creek behind our home. "Do you know what tadpoles become when they grow up? They become frogs," Sandy explained. Laura looked very serious. After considering this new bit of information for a few moments, she asked, "Laura grow up to be a frog, too?"

The development of gender schemas is one reflection of the child's increasing sophistication in cognitive processes such as thinking, remembering, and processing information. The most influential theory of cognitive development is that of the Swiss psychologist **Jean Piaget** (1896–1980). Originally trained as a biologist, Piaget combined a boundless curiosity about the nature of the human mind with a gift for scientific observation (Brainerd, 1996).

Piaget (1952, 1972) believed that children *actively* try to make sense out of their environment rather than passively soaking up information about the world. To Piaget, many of the "cute" things children say actually reflect their sincere attempts to make sense out of their world. In fact, Piaget carefully observed his own three children in developing his theory (Fischer & Hencke, 1996).

Jean Piaget Swiss psychologist Jean Piaget (1896–1980) viewed the child as a little scientist, actively exploring his or her world. Much of Piaget's theory was based upon his careful observation of individual children, especially his own children.

This Feels Different! During the sensorimotor stage, infants and toddlers rely on sensory and motor skills to explore and make sense out of the world around them.

sensorimotor stage
In Piaget's theory, the first stage of cognitive development, from birth to about age two; the period during which the infant explores the environment and acquires knowledge through sensing and manipulating objects.

object permanence
The understanding that an object continues to exist even when it can no longer be seen.

According to Piaget, children progress through four distinct cognitive stages: the sensorimotor stage from birth to age two; the preoperational stage from age two to age seven; the concrete operational stage from seven to eleven; and the formal operational stage, which begins during adolescence and continues into adulthood. As a child advances to a new stage, his thinking is *qualitatively different* from that of the previous stage. In other words, each new stage represents a fundamental shift in *how* the child thinks and understands the world.

Piaget saw this progression of cognitive development as a continuous, gradual process. As a child develops and matures, she does not simply acquire more information. Rather, she develops new understandings of the world in each progressive stage, building on the understandings acquired in the previous stage (Siegler & Ellis, 1996). As the child assimilates new information and experiences, he eventually changes his way of thinking to accommodate new knowledge (P. H. Miller, 1993).

Piaget believed that these stages are biologically programmed to unfold at their respective ages (Flavell, 1996). He also believed that children in every culture progress through the same sequence of stages at roughly similar ages. However, Piaget also recognized that hereditary and environmental differences can influence the rate at which a given child progresses through the stages (Fischer & Hencke, 1996; Wadsworth, 1996).

For example, a "bright" child may progress through the stages faster than a child who is less intellectually capable. A child whose environment provides ample and varied opportunities to explore is likely to progress faster than the child who has limited environmental opportunities. Thus, even though the sequence of stages is universal, there can be individual variation in the rate of cognitive development.

The Sensorimotor Stage

The **sensorimotor stage** extends from birth until about two years of age. During this stage, the infant acquires knowledge about the world through actions that allow him to directly experience and manipulate objects. The infant discovers a wealth of very practical sensory knowledge, such as what objects look like and how they taste, feel, smell, and sound.

He also expands his practical knowledge about motor actions, like reaching, grasping, pushing, pulling, and pouring. In the process, the infant gains a basic understanding of the effects that his own actions can produce, such as pushing a button to turn on the television or knocking over a pile of blocks to make them crash and tumble.

At the beginning of the sensorimotor stage, the infant's motto seems to be, "Out of sight, out of mind." An object exists only if she can directly sense it. For example, if a four-month-old infant knocks a ball underneath the couch and it rolls out of sight, she will not look for it. Piaget interpreted this response to mean that, to the infant, the ball no longer exists.

However, by the end of the sensorimotor stage, the child acquires a new cognitive understanding, called object permanence. **Object permanence** is the understanding that an object continues to exist even if it can't be seen. Now, the infant will actively search for a ball that she has watched roll out of sight. Infants gradually acquire an understanding of object permanence as they gain experience with objects, as their memory abilities improve, and as they develop mental representations of the world, which Piaget called *schemas.*

FOR BETTER OR FOR WORSE

The Preoperational Stage

The **preoperational stage** lasts from roughly age two to age seven. In Piaget's theory, the word *operations* refers to logical, mental activities. Thus, the "preoperational" stage is a prelogical stage.

The hallmark of preoperational thought is the child's capacity to engage in symbolic thought. **Symbolic thought** refers to the ability to use words, images, and symbols to represent the world (DeLoache, 1995). One indication of the expanding capacity for symbolic thought is the child's impressive gains in language during this stage.

The child's increasing capacity for symbolic thought is also apparent in her use of fantasy and imagination while playing (Golomb & Galasso, 1995). A discarded box becomes a spaceship, a house, or a fort, as children imaginatively take on the roles of different characters. In doing so, a child imitates (or tries to imitate) actions she has mentally symbolized from situations she observed days, or even weeks, earlier.

Still, the child's understanding of symbols remains immature. When a two-year-old is shown a picture of a flower, for example, he may try to smell it. A young child may be puzzled by the notion that a map symbolizes an actual location—as in the cartoon above. In short, the preoperational child is still actively figuring out the relationship between symbols and the actual objects they represent (DeLoache, 1995).

preoperational stage
In Piaget's theory, the second stage of cognitive development, which lasts from about age two to age seven; characterized by increasing use of symbols and prelogical thought processes.

symbolic thought
The ability to use words, images, and symbols to represent the world.

egocentrism
In Piaget's theory, the inability to take another person's perspective or point of view.

irreversibility
In Piaget's theory, the inability to mentally reverse a sequence of events or logical operations.

centration
In Piaget's theory, the tendency to focus, or *center,* on only one aspect of a situation and ignore other important aspects of the situation.

The preoperational child's thought also often displays **egocentrism.** By *egocentrism,* Piaget did not mean selfishness or conceit. Rather, the egocentric child lacks the ability to consider events from another person's point of view. Thus, the young child genuinely thinks that Grandma would like a new Beanie Baby or a Power Ranger video for her upcoming birthday because that's what *he* wants. Egocentric thought is also operating when the child silently nods his head in answer to Grandpa's question on the telephone.

The preoperational child's thought is also characterized by irreversibility and centration. **Irreversibility** means that the child cannot mentally reverse a sequence of events or logical operations back to the starting point. For example, they don't understand that adding "3 plus 1" and adding "1 plus 3" refer to the same logical operation. **Centration** refers to the tendency to focus, or center, on only one aspect of a situation, usually a perceptual aspect. In doing so, the child ignores other relevant aspects of the situation.

The classic demonstration of both irreversibility and centration involves a task devised by Piaget. When Laura was five, we tried this task with her. First, we showed her two identical glasses, each containing exactly the same amount of liquid. Laura easily recognized the two amounts of liquid as being the same.

Then, while Laura watched intently, we poured the liquid from one of the glasses into a third container that was much taller and narrower. Which container, we asked, holds more liquid? Like any other preoperational child, Laura answered confidently, "The taller one!" Even when we repeated the procedure, reversing the steps over and over again, Laura remained convinced that the taller container held more liquid than the shorter container.

This classic demonstration illustrates the preoperational child's inability to understand conservation. The principle of **conservation** holds that two equal physical quantities remain equal even if the appearance of one is changed, as long as nothing is added or subtracted (Piaget & Inhelder, 1974). Because of *centration,* the child cannot simultaneously consider the height and the width of the liquid in the container. Instead, the child focuses on only one aspect of the situation, the height of the liquid. And because of *irreversibility,* the child cannot cognitively reverse the series of events, mentally returning the poured liquid back to its original container. Thus, she fails to understand that the two amounts of liquid are still the same.

The Concrete Operational Stage

With the beginning of the **concrete operational stage,** at around age seven, the child becomes capable of true logical thought. The child is much less egocentric in his thinking, can reverse mental operations, and can focus simultaneously on two aspects of a problem. In short, he understands the principle of conservation. When presented with two rows of pennies, each row being equally spaced, the concrete operational child now understands that the number of pennies in each row remains the same even when the spacing between the pennies in one row is increased (Wadsworth, 1996).

As the name of this stage implies, the child's thinking and use of logic tend to be limited to concrete reality—to tangible objects and events. The child in the concrete operational stage often has difficulty thinking logically about hypothetical situations or abstract ideas. For example, an eight-year-old will explain the concept of *friendship* in very tangible terms, such as saying "Friendship is when someone plays with me." In effect, the concrete operational child's ability to deal with abstract ideas and hypothetical situations is limited to his or her personal experiences and actual events.

The Formal Operational Stage

At the beginning of adolescence, the child enters the **formal operational stage.** In terms of problem solving, the formal operational adolescent is much more systematic and logical than the concrete operational child.

Formal operational thought reflects the ability to think logically even when dealing with abstract concepts or hypothetical situations (Piaget, 1972; Piaget & Inhelder, 1958). In contrast to the concrete operational child, the formal operational adolescent explains *friendship* by emphasizing more global and abstract characteristics, such as mutual trust, empathy, loyalty, consistency, and shared beliefs (Beal, 1994; Harter, 1990, 1983).

But like the development of cognitive abilities during infancy and childhood, formal operational thought emerges only gradually (Wood, 1988). Formal operational thought continues to increase in sophistication throughout adolescence and adulthood. While an adolescent may deal effectively with abstract ideas in one domain of knowledge, her thinking may not reflect the same degree of sophistication in other areas (Keating, 1990; Case, 1985).

With three-and-a-half-year-old Laura's help, Sandy opened the envelope and took out the wedding invitation. "Laura, your teacher is going to marry her boyfriend, and we're invited to her wedding! Do you know what it means to get married?" "Sure! It means that they can go to Wal-Mart," Laura replied.

conservation
In Piaget's theory, the understanding that two equal quantities remain equal even though the form or appearance is rearranged, as long as nothing is added or subtracted.

concrete operational stage
In Piaget's theory, the third stage of cognitive development, which lasts from about age seven to adolescence; characterized by the ability to think logically about concrete objects and situations.

formal operational stage
In Piaget's theory, the forth stage of cognitive development, which lasts from adolescence through adulthood; characterized by the ability to think logically about abstract principles and hypothetical situations.

Piaget (1973) acknowledged that even among many adults, formal operational thinking is often limited to areas in which they have developed expertise or a special interest.

Criticisms of Piaget's Theory

Piaget's theory has inspired hundreds of research studies (Kessen, 1996). Generally, scientific research has supported Piaget's most fundamental idea: that infants, young children, and older children use distinctly different cognitive abilities to construct their understanding of the world. However, other aspects of Piaget's theory have been criticized.

One criticism is that Piaget underestimated the cognitive abilities of infants and young children. For example, to test for object permanence, Piaget would show the infant an object, cover it with a cloth, and then observe whether the infant tried to reach under the cloth for the object. Obviously, this requires the infant to have a certain level of motor skill development. Using this procedure, Piaget found that it wasn't until around nine months of age that an infant first behaved in a way that suggested he understood that an object continued to exist after it was hidden. But even at nine months of age, Piaget maintained, the infant's understanding of object permanence was still immature and would not be fully developed for another year or so.

Today, many researchers believe that Piaget confused *motor skill limitations* with *cognitive limitations* in assessing cognitive development during infancy (Mandler, 1990). For example, psychologist Renée Baillargeon (1994, 1987) has used visual tasks, rather than manual tasks, in several studies to assess object permanence in infancy. Baillargeon has found that very young infants seem to form a mental representation of a hidden object, even though they're not capable of reaching for one (see Figure 9.4). Baillargeon's research suggests that young infants achieve object permanence at an earlier age than Piaget proposed. Other research has demonstrated that young children are less egocentric than Piaget believed (Newcombe & Huttenlocher, 1992).

Piaget's notion that his stages unfold universally has also been challenged. Researchers have found that many adults display abstract-hypothetical thinking only in limited areas of knowledge, and some adults never display formal operational thought processes. College students, for example, may not display formal operational thinking when given problems outside their major, as when an English major is presented with a physics problem (DeLisi & Staudt, 1980). Late in his life, Piaget (1972, 1973) suggested that formal operational thinking may not be a universal phenomenon, but instead the product of an individual's expertise in a specific area.

Rather than distinct stages of cognitive development, some developmental psychologists emphasize the **information-processing model of cognitive development** (Klahr, 1992; Siegler, 1991). This model focuses on the development of fundamental mental processes, like attention, memory, and problem solving (Rose & Feldman, 1995). In this approach, cognitive development is viewed as a process of continuous change over the lifespan. Through life experiences, we continue to acquire new knowledge, including more sophisticated cognitive skills and strategies. In turn, this improves our ability to process, learn, and remember information (Kail, 1991).

Another criticism is that Piaget underestimated the impact of the social and cultural environment on cognitive development (Gopnik, 1996). Other theorists have offered very different viewpoints, including the highly regarded Russian psychologist **Lev Vygotsky** (1896–1934). Vygotsky, who was born the same year as Piaget, developed his theory of cognitive development at about the same time as Piaget. Vygotsky's influence has increased dramatically in the last few decades (Wertsch & Tulviste, 1994).

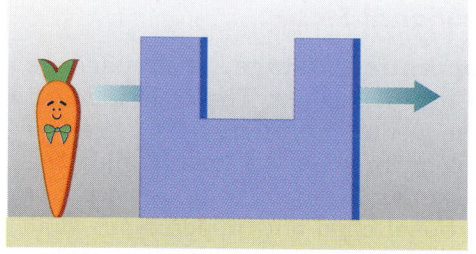

FIGURE 9.4 Testing Object Permanence in Very Young Infants
Renée Baillargeon and Julie DeVos (1991) found that three-and-a-half-month-old infants looked much longer at a surprising event in which a tall carrot passed behind a screen without being seen in the window. This suggests that the young infants mentally represented the existence, height, and path of the carrot as it moved behind the screen. Piaget believed that such cognitive abilities did not develop until infants are at least nine months old.

information-processing model of cognitive development
The model that views cognitive development as a continuous process over the lifespan and that studies the development of basic mental processes like attention, memory, and problem solving.

Lev Vygotsky Russian psychologist Lev Vygotsky was born in 1896, the same year as Piaget. He died in 1934 of tuberculosis, still a relatively young man. Recent decades have seen a resurgence of interest in Vygotsky's theoretical writings. Vygotsky emphasized the impact of social and cultural factors on cognitive development. To Vygotsky, cognitive development always takes place within a social and cultural context.

Vygotsky agreed with Piaget that children may be able to reach a particular cognitive level through their own, independent efforts. However, unlike Piaget, Vygotsky (1978, 1987) believed that cognitive development is strongly influenced by social and cultural factors, such as the support and guidance that children receive from parents, other adults, and older children. Such guidance can help "stretch" the child's cognitive abilities to new levels. Indeed, researchers have confirmed that such social interactions play a significant role in a child's cognitive development (Wertsch & Tulviste, 1992; Gopnik, 1996).

How these supportive social interactions are displayed varies from culture to culture (Rogoff & Chavajay, 1995). In middle-class American families, for example, adults often interact with children by posing questions to which the adult already knows the answer, such as asking, "How much is 2 times 2?" It's also considered culturally acceptable for children to show off their knowledge. In other cultures, however, these behaviors are not necessarily considered appropriate or acceptable (Rogoff & Morelli, 1989). Cross-cultural studies have also shown that cognitive development is strongly influenced by the skills that are valued and encouraged in a particular environment.

Despite these criticisms, Piaget's documentation of the many cognitive changes that occur during infancy and childhood ranks as one of the most outstanding contributions to developmental psychology (Beilin, 1994). With the exceptions that have been noted, Piaget's observations of the changes in children's cognitive abilities are fundamentally accurate.

CONCEPT REVIEW 9.2

Piaget's Stages of Cognitive Development

Indicate by letter which stage of cognitive development is illustrated by each of the following examples: (A) sensorimotor; (B) preoperational; (C) concrete operational; (D) formal operations.

_____ **1.** When confronted with a lawn mower that would not start, Jason approached the problem very systematically, checking and eliminating possible causes one at a time.

_____ **2.** Lynn rolls identical amounts of playdough into two balls and is quite sure they are exactly the same. However, when her Dad flattens one ball into a pancake shape, Lynn is confident that the pancake has more playdough than the ball.

_____ **3.** When Carla's mother hides her favorite toy under a cushion, Carla starts playing with another toy and acts as though her favorite toy no longer exists.

_____ **4.** Andrew is told that Michael is taller than Bridget and Bridget is taller than Patrick. When asked who is the smallest child, Andrew thinks carefully, then answers, "Patrick."

Adolescence

Adolescence is the stage that marks the transition from childhood to adulthood. What physical changes occur during adolescence? What characterizes relationships with parents and peers in adolescence? How does Erikson's theory of psychosocial development describe the process of identity formation?

adolescence
The transitional stage between late childhood and the beginning of adulthood, during which sexual maturity is reached.

Adolescence is the transitional stage between late childhood and the beginning of adulthood. Adolescence begins around age twelve and lasts until the individual assumes adult roles and responsibilities. Outwardly, the most noticeable changes that occur during adolescence are the physical changes that accompany the development of sexual maturity.

Just Friends? Interest in and affection for the opposite sex often begins in the early stages of adolescence. Because girls mature earlier than boys, they may be taller and heavier than boys of the same age.

puberty
The stage of adolescence in which an individual reaches sexual maturity and becomes physiologically capable of sexual reproduction.

primary sex characteristics
Sexual organs that are directly involved in reproduction, such as the uterus, ovaries, penis, and testicles.

secondary sex characteristics
Sexual characteristics that develop during puberty and are not directly involved in reproduction but differentiate between the sexes, such as male facial hair and female breast development.

adolescent growth spurt
The period of accelerated growth during puberty, involving rapid increases in height and weight.

menarche
A female's first menstrual period, which occurs during puberty.

Physical and Sexual Development

Nature seems to have a warped sense of humor when it comes to **puberty,** the physical process of attaining sexual maturation and reproductive capacity that begins during the early adolescent years. As you may well remember, physical development during adolescence sometimes proceeds unevenly. Feet and hands get bigger before legs and arms do. The torso typically develops last, so shirts and blouses sometimes don't fit quite right. And the left and right sides of the body can grow at different rates. The resulting lopsided effect can be quite distressing: one ear, foot, testicle, or breast may be noticeably larger than the other. Thankfully, such asymmetries tend to even out by the end of adolescence.

Although nature's game plan for physical change during adolescence may seem haphazard, puberty actually tends to follow a predictable sequence for each sex. These changes are summarized in Table 9.3. Basically, the physical changes of puberty fall into two categories.

Internally, puberty involves the development of the **primary sex characteristics,** which are the sex organs that are directly involved in reproduction. For example, the female's uterus and the male's testes enlarge in puberty. Externally, development of the **secondary sex characteristics,** which are not directly involved in reproduction, signal increasing sexual maturity. Secondary sex characteristics include changes in height, weight, and body shape, appearance of body hair, voice changes, and, in girls, breast development.

As you can see in Table 9.3, females are typically about two years ahead of males in terms of physical and sexual maturation. For example, the period of marked acceleration in weight and height gains, called the **adolescent growth spurt,** occurs about two years earlier in females than in males. Much to the chagrin of many sixth- and seventh-grade males, it's not uncommon for their female classmates to be both heavier and taller than them.

The statistical averages in Table 9.3 are informative, but—because they are only averages—they cannot convey the normal range of individual variation in the timing of pubertal events (see Brooks-Gunn & Reiter, 1990). For example, a female's first menstrual period, which is termed **menarche,** typically occurs around age twelve or thirteen, but menarche may take place as early as age nine or ten or as late as age sixteen or seventeen. For boys, the testicles typically begin enlarging around age eleven or twelve, but the

TABLE 9.3 The Typical Sequence of Puberty

Girls	Average Age
Ovaries increase production of estrogen and progesterone	9
Internal sex organs begin to grow larger	9½
Breast development begins	10
Peak height spurt	12
Peak muscle and organ growth, including widening of hips	12½
Menarche (first menstrual period)	12½
First ovulation (release of fertile egg)	13½

Boys	Average Age
Testes increase production of testosterone	10
External sex organs begin to grow larger	11
Production of sperm and first ejaculation	13
Peak height spurt	14
Peak muscle and organ growth, including broadening of shoulders	14½
Voice lowers	15
Facial hair appears	16

SOURCE: Based on data in Berger, 1995, and Brooks-Gunn & Reiter, 1990.

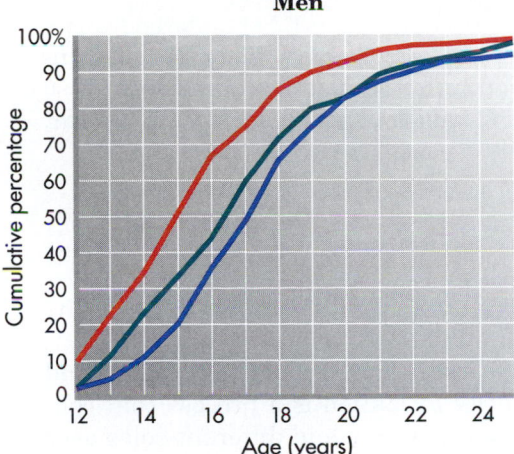

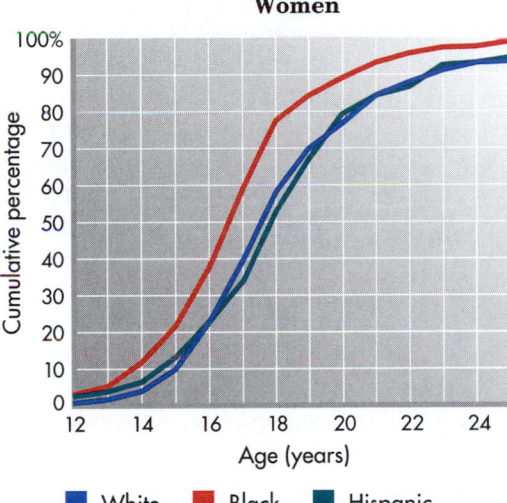

FIGURE 9.5 Cumulative Percentages of People Who Have Had Sexual Intercourse, by Gender, Race, and Age
According to data collected in a national survey of adult sexual behavior, about 90 percent of young adults have had intercourse by age 22. Notice, however, that there is some variation by gender and among racial groups.

(Michael & others, 1994, Fig. 7, p. 91.)

Peer Relationships in Adolescence Peer relationships become increasingly important in adolescence. Although parents often worry about the negative effects of peer influence, peers can also have a positive influence on one another. These teenage volunteers are helping plant trees in a public park in Austin, Texas.

process can begin before age nine or after age fourteen. Thus, it's entirely possible for some adolescents to have already completed physical and sexual maturation before their classmates have even begun puberty. Yet they would all be considered well within the normal age range for puberty.

During early and middle adolescence, the physical changes of puberty prime the adolescent's interest in sexuality. But social and cultural factors also influence when, why, and how an adolescent initiates sexual behaviors (Katchadourian, 1990; Brooks-Gunn & Furstenberg, 1989). The beginning of dating, for example, coincides more strongly with social expectations and norms, such as when friends begin to date, than with an adolescent's degree of physical maturation (Garguilo & others, 1987).

Generally, age is a good predictor of when teenagers typically begin various sexual behaviors. With increasing age, there is a corresponding increase in the number of adolescents who have engaged in such sexual activities as kissing or petting (Katchadourian, 1990; Buhrmester & Furman, 1987). As you can see in Figure 9.5, the number of adolescents who have experienced sexual intercourse also corresponds closely to age (Michael & others, 1994). Between the ages of fifteen and eighteen, there is a sharp increase in the cumulative percentages of those who have had intercourse. Although it varies somewhat by race and gender, by age nineteen approximately 70 percent of females and 80 percent of males have lost their virginity.

Social Development

Are conflicts with parents inevitable during adolescence? Contrary to what many people think, parent–adolescent relationships are usually positive. In fact, most teenagers report that they admire their parents and turn to them for advice (Steinberg, 1990). As a general rule, when parent–child relationships have been good before adolescence, they continue to be relatively smooth during adolescence (Buchanan & others, 1992).

While parents remain influential throughout adolescence, relationships with friends and peers become increasingly important. Adolescents usually encounter greater diversity among their peers as they make the transitions to middle school and high school. To a much greater degree than during childhood, the adolescent's social network, social context, and community influence his or her values, norms, and expectations (Steinberg & others, 1995).

Parents often worry that peer influences will lead to undesirable behavior. Researchers have found, however, that peer relationships tend to *reinforce* the traits and goals that parents fostered during childhood (Steinberg & others, 1995). This finding is not as surprising as it might seem. Adolescents tend to form friendships with peers who are similar in age, social class, race, and beliefs about drinking, dating, church attendance, and educational goals (Savin-Williams & Berndt, 1990).

Friends often exert pressure on one another to study, make good

identity
A person's definition or description of himself or herself, including the values, beliefs, and ideals that guide the individual's behavior.

grades, attend college, and engage in prosocial behaviors. So, while peer influence can lead to undesirable behaviors in some instances, peers can also influence one another in positive ways (Mounts & Steinberg, 1995; Berndt, 1992).

Identity Formation: Erikson's Theory of Psychosocial Development

When psychologists talk about a person's **identity,** they are referring to the values, beliefs, and ideals that guide an individual's behavior (Marcia, 1991; Erikson, 1964a). Our sense of personal identity gives us an integrated and continuing sense of self over time. Identity formation is a process that continues throughout the lifespan. As we embrace new and different roles over the course of our lives, we define ourselves in new ways (Grotevant, 1992; Erikson & others, 1986).

For the first time in the lifespan, the adolescent possesses the cognitive skills necessary to deal with identity issues in a meaningful way (Dusek, 1996). Beginning in early adolescence, self-definition shifts. Preadolescent children tend to describe themselves in very concrete social and behavioral terms. An eight-year-old might describe himself by saying, "I play with Mark and I like to ride my bike." In contrast, the adolescent uses more abstract self-descriptions that reflect personal attributes, values, beliefs, and goals (Balk, 1995; Harter, 1990). Thus, a fourteen-year-old might say, "I have strong religious beliefs, love animals, and hope to become a veterinarian."

Some aspects of personal identity involve characteristics over which the adolescent has no control, such as gender, race, ethnic background, and socioeconomic level. In effect, these identity characteristics are fixed and already internalized by the time an individual reaches the adolescent years.

Beyond such fixed characteristics, the adolescent begins to evaluate herself on several different dimensions. Social acceptance by peers, academic and athletic abilities, work abilities, personal appearance, and romantic appeal are some important aspects of self-definition. Another challenge facing the adolescent is to develop an identity that is independent of her parents while retaining a sense of connection to her family. Thus, the adolescent has not one but several self-concepts that she must integrate into a coherent and unified whole to answer the question, "Who am I?"

The adolescent's task of achieving an integrated identity is one important aspect of psychoanalyst **Erik Erikson's** (1902–1994) influential theory of psychosocial development. Briefly, Erikson (1968) proposed that each of eight stages of life is associated with a particular psychosocial conflict that can be resolved in either a positive or negative direction (see Table 9.4). Relationships with others play an important role in determining the outcome of each conflict. According to Erikson, the key psychosocial conflict facing the adolescent is *identity versus identity diffusion.*

To successfully form an identity, an adolescent not only must integrate various dimensions of his personality into a coherent whole but must also define the roles that he will adopt within the larger society upon becoming an adult (Harter, 1990). To accomplish this, adolescents grapple with a wide variety of issues, such as selecting a potential career and formulating religious, moral, and political beliefs. They must also adopt social roles involving interpersonal relationships, sexuality, and long-term commitments like marriage and parenthood.

In Erikson's (1968) theory, the adolescent's path to successful identity achievement begins with *identity diffusion,* which is characterized by little sense of commitment on any of these issues. This is followed by a *moratorium*

Psychoanalyst Erik Erikson (1902–1994)
Erikson is shown here with his wife Joan in 1988. Erikson's landmark theory of psychosocial development stressed the importance of social and cultural influences on personality throughout the stages of life.

TABLE 9.4 Erik Erikson's Psychosocial Stages of Development

Life Stage	Psychosocial Conflict	Positive Resolution	Negative Resolution
Infancy (birth to eighteen months)	Trust vs. mistrust	Reliance on consistent and warm caregivers produces a sense of predictability and trust in the environment.	Physical and psychological neglect by caregivers leads to fear, anxiety, and mistrust of the environment.
Toddlerhood (eighteen months to) three years)	Autonomy vs. doubt	Caregivers encourage independence and self-sufficiency, promoting positive self-esteem.	Overly restrictive caregiving leads to self-doubt in abilities and low self-esteem.
Early childhood (three to six years)	Initiative vs. guilt	The child learns to initiate activities and develops a sense of social responsibility concerning the rights of others. Promotes self-confidence.	Parental overcontrol stifles the child's spontaneity, sense of purpose, and social learning. Promotes guilt and fear of punishment.
Middle and late childhood (six to twelve years)	Industry vs. inferiority	Through experiences with parents and "keeping up" with peers, the child develops a sense of pride and competence in schoolwork and home and social activities.	Negative experiences with parents or failure to "keep up" with peers leads to pervasive feelings of inferiority and inadequacy.
Adolescence	Identity vs. identity diffusion	Through experimentation with different roles, the adolescent develops an integrated and stable self-definition. Forms commitments to future adult roles.	An apathetic adolescent or one who experiences pressures and demands from others may feel confusion about his or her identity and role in society.
Young adulthood	Intimacy vs. isolation	By establishing lasting and meaningful relationships, the young adult develops a sense of connectedness and intimacy with others.	Because of fear of rejection or excessive self-preoccupation, the young adult is unable to form close, meaningful relationships and becomes psychologically isolated.
Middle adulthood	Generativity vs. stagnation	Through child rearing, caring for others, productive work, and community involvement, the adult expresses unselfish concern for the welfare of the next generation.	Self-indulgence, self-absorption, and a preoccupation with one's own needs lead to a sense of stagnation, boredom, and a lack of meaningful accomplishments.
Late adulthood	Ego integrity vs. despair	In reviewing his or her life, the older adult experiences a strong sense of self-acceptance and meaningfulness in his or her accomplishments.	In looking back on his or her life, the older adult experiences regret, dissatisfaction, and disappointment about his or her life and accomplishments.

SOURCE: Adapted from Erikson, 1964a.

period, during which the adolescent experiments with different roles, values, and beliefs. Gradually, by choosing among the alternatives and making commitments, the adolescent arrives at an *integrated identity.*

Psychological research has generally supported Erikson's description of the process of identity formation (Marcia, 1991, 1980; Grotevant, 1987). However, it's important to keep in mind that identity continually changes over the entire lifespan, not just during the adolescent years (Grotevant, 1992). Adolescents and young adults seem to achieve a stable sense of identity in some areas sooner than others, such as vocational choice. Far fewer adolescents and young adults have attained a stable sense of identity in the realm of religious and political beliefs (Waterman, 1985).

So, while Erikson believed that identity formation was a critical goal for the adolescent, it appears that the process of identity formation only begins to take on serious meaning during adolescence. For most people, a stable and fully integrated identity doesn't occur until well into the adult years.

The Development of Moral Reasoning

> *Kohlberg's theory of moral development describes the stages of development in moral reasoning. What are the stages and levels of moral development? How is moral reasoning influenced by gender and culture?*

An important aspect of cognitive development during adolescence is a change in **moral reasoning**—how an individual thinks about moral decisions. The adolescent's increased capacities to think abstractly, imagine hypothetical situations, and compare ideals to the real world all influence his thinking about moral issues (Darley & Shultz, 1990; Colby & others, 1983).

The most influential theory of moral development was proposed by psychologist **Lawrence Kohlberg** (1927–1987). Kohlberg used stories like the one below to investigate moral reasoning. Read the story and then, before reading further, answer the questions at the end.

> *A woman was near death from a rare form of cancer. There was one drug that the doctors thought might save her, recently discovered by a druggist in the same town. The drug was expensive to make—about $400 for a small dose. But the druggist was charging ten times what the drug cost him to make— $4,000 for a small dose.*
>
> *The sick woman's husband, Heinz, went to everyone he knew to borrow the money, but he could only get together about $2,000, half of what the druggist was charging. He told the druggist that his wife was dying and asked him to sell it cheaper or let him pay the rest later. But the druggist refused, saying, "No, I discovered the drug and I'm going to make money from it." So Heinz gets desperate and considers breaking into the man's store to steal the drug for his wife.*
>
> *Should Heinz steal the drug? Why or why not? (Adapted from Colby & others, 1983.)*

In Kohlberg's (1984, 1976) theory, whether you think Heinz should or should not steal the drug is not the critical issue. Instead, it is the *reasoning* you use to justify your answer. Kohlberg analyzed the responses of children, adolescents, and adults to moral dilemmas like the Heinz story. He concluded that there were distinct *stages* of moral development. These stages unfold in an age-related, step-by-step fashion, much like Piaget's stages of cognitive development (Kohlberg, 1981).

Kohlberg proposed three distinct *levels* of moral reasoning: preconventional, conventional, and postconventional. Each level is based on the degree to which a person conforms to conventional standards of society. Furthermore, each level has two *stages* that represent different degrees of sophistication in moral reasoning. Table 9.5 describes the characteristics of the moral reasoning associated with each of Kohlberg's levels and stages.

Kohlberg and his colleagues found that the responses of children under the age of ten reflect *preconventional* moral reasoning based on self-interest—avoiding punishment and maximizing personal gain. Beginning in late childhood and continuing through adolescence and adulthood, responses typically reflect *conventional* moral reasoning, which emphasizes social roles, rules, and obligations. Thus, the progression from preconventional to conventional moral reasoning is closely associated with age-related cognitive abilities (Walker, 1989; Kohlberg, 1984; Colby & others, 1983).

HAGAR

moral reasoning
The aspect of cognitive development that has to do with the way an individual reasons about moral decisions.

TABLE 9.5 Kohlberg's Levels and Stages of Moral Development

I. Preconventional Level

Moral reasoning is guided by external consequences. No internalization of values or rules.

Stage 1: Punishment and Obedience

"Right" is obeying the rules simply to avoid punishment because others have power over you and can punish you.

Example:
Heinz shouldn't steal the drug because he'd go to jail if he got caught.

Stage 2: Mutual Benefit

"Right" is an even or fair exchange, so that both parties benefit. Moral reasoning guided by a sense of "fair play."

Example:
Heinz should steal the drug because the druggist is being greedy by charging so much.

II. Conventional Level

Moral reasoning is guided by conformity to social roles, rules, and expectations that the person has learned and internalized.

Stage 3: Interpersonal Expectations

"Right" is being a "good" person by conforming to social expectations, such as showing concern for others, and following rules set by others so as to win their approval. For example, behaving like a "good" child, student, citizen, spouse, friend, or employee.

Example:
Heinz should try to steal the drug because that's what a devoted husband would do.

Stage 4: Law and Order

"Right" is to help maintain social order by doing one's duty, obeying laws simply because they are laws, and showing respect for authorities simply because they are authorities.

Example:
Heinz should not steal the drug because it would be against the law and he has a duty to uphold the law.

III. Postconventional Level

Moral reasoning is guided by internalized legal and moral principles that protect the rights of all members of society.

Stage 5: Legal Principles

"Right" is to help protect the basic rights of all members of society by upholding legalistic principles that promote the values of fairness, justice, equality, and democracy.

Example:
Heinz should steal the drug because his obligation to save his wife's life must take precedence over his obligation to respect the druggist's property rights.

Stage 6: Universal Moral Principles

"Right" is determined by self-chosen ethical principles that underscore the person's profound respect for ideals such as the sanctity of human life, nonviolence, equality, and human dignity. If these moral principles conflict with democratically determined laws, the person's self-chosen moral principles would take precedence, such as the conscientious objector who refuses to be drafted because of his moral principles against war.

Example:
Even if it were a stranger and not his wife, Heinz should steal the drug because he must follow his own conscience and not let another person's desire for monetary gain outweigh the value of a human life.

SOURCES: Based on Kohlberg, 1981; Colby & others, 1983.

Do people inevitably advance from conventional to *postconventional* moral reasoning, as Kohlberg once thought? In a twenty-year longitudinal study, Kohlberg followed a group of boys from late childhood through early adulthood. Out of the 58 subjects in the study, only 8 subjects occasionally displayed stage 5 reasoning, which emphasizes respect for legal principles that protect all members of society. And *none* of the subjects showed stage 6 reasoning, which reflects self-chosen ethical principles that are universally applied (Colby & others, 1983). Kohlberg and his colleagues eventually dropped stage 6 from the theory, partly because clear-cut expressions of "universal moral principles" were so rare (Rest, 1983).

Thus, Kohlberg's original belief that the development of abstract thinking in adolescence naturally and invariably leads people to the formation of idealistic moral principles has not been supported. Only a few exceptional people display the philosophical ideals in Kohlberg's highest level of moral reasoning. The normal course of changes in moral reasoning for most people seems to be captured by Kohlberg's first four stages (Colby & Kohlberg, 1984). By adulthood, the predominant form of moral reasoning is conventional moral reasoning, reflecting the importance of social roles and rules.

Criticisms of Kohlberg's Theory

Kohlberg's theory of moral development is not without its critics (see Modgil & Modgil, 1986). For example, psychologist Carol Gilligan (1982) believes that Kohlberg's model reflects a male perspective that may not accurately depict the development of moral reasoning in women. To Gilligan, Kohlberg's model is based on an *ethic of individual rights and justice,* which is a more common perspective for males. In contrast, Gilligan has developed a model of women's moral development that is based on an *ethic of care and responsibility*. In her studies of women's moral reasoning, Gilligan found that women tended to stress the importance of maintaining interpersonal relationships and responding to the needs of others, rather than focusing primarily on individual rights (Gilligan & Attanucci, 1988).

Culture also seems to have an effect on moral reasoning (Eckensberger, 1994; Haidt & others, 1993). Some cross-cultural psychologists argue that Kohlberg's stories and scoring system reflect a Western emphasis on individual rights, harm, and justice that is not shared in many cultures (Shweder & others, 1990a).

For example, Kohlberg's moral stages do not reflect the sense of interdependence and the concern for the overall welfare of the group that is more common in collectivistic cultures. Cross-cultural psychologist Harry Triandis (1994) reports an example of a response that does not fit into Kohlberg's moral scheme. In response to the scenario, "Heinz steals the drug to save his wife's life," a man in New Guinea said, "If nobody helped him, I would say that *we* had caused the crime." Thus, there are aspects of moral reasoning in other cultures that do not seem to be reflected in Kohlberg's theory (Matsumoto, 1994; Shweder & Haidt, 1993).

CONCEPT REVIEW 9.3

Stages of Moral Reasoning

The examples below represent moral reasoning typically associated with different levels in Kohlberg's stages of moral development. Identify each one as preconventional, conventional, or postconventional.

1. Because he believed that all war is immoral, Adrian burned his draft card and refused to be inducted into the military, even though he was risking imprisonment. _____

2. While his brother was in the washroom, Jerry resisted sneaking a bit of his dessert because he was afraid his brother would punch him if he did. _____

3. When her daughter chided her about driving so slowly, Barbara replied, "I can't drive faster than the posted speed limit because responsible drivers obey the traffic laws." _____

Adult Development

Development continues throughout adulthood. What physical changes take place in adulthood? What are some general patterns of social development in adulthood? How does the transition to parenthood affect adults?

You can think of the developmental changes you experienced during infancy, childhood, and adolescence as early chapters in your life story. Those early life chapters helped set the tone and some of the themes for the primary focus of your life story—adulthood. During the half century or more that constitutes adulthood, predictable changes continue to occur. Self-definition evolves as people achieve independence and take on new roles and responsibilities. As you'll see in this section, the story of adulthood also reflects the increasing importance of individual variation. Although general patterns of aging exist, our life stories become more distinct and individualized with each passing decade of life (Schaie & Willis, 1996).

Physical Changes

Your unique genetic blueprint greatly influences the unfolding of certain physical changes during adulthood, such as when your hair begins to thin, lose its color, and turn gray. Such genetically influenced changes can vary significantly from one person to another. For example, **menopause,** the cessation of menstruation that signals the end of reproductive capacity in women, may occur anywhere from the late thirties to the early fifties.

But your destiny is not completely ruled by genetics. Your lifestyle is one key environmental factor that can influence the aging process. Staying mentally and physically active and eating a proper diet can both slow and minimize the degree of physical decline associated with aging.

Another potent environmental force is simply the passage of time. Decades of use and environmental exposure take a toll on the body. Wrinkles begin to appear as we approach the age of forty, largely due to a loss of skin elasticity combined with years of making the same facial expressions. With each decade after age twenty, the efficiency of various body organs declines. For example, lung capacity decreases, as does the amount of blood pumped by the heart.

Physical strength typically peaks in *early adulthood*, the twenties and thirties. By *middle adulthood*, roughly from the forties to mid-sixties, physical strength and endurance gradually decline. Physical and mental reaction times also begin to slow during middle adulthood. During *late adulthood*, from the mid-sixties on, physical stamina and reaction time tend to decline further and faster.

Social Development

In his theory of psychosocial development, Erik Erikson (1982) described the two fundamental themes that dominate adulthood: love and work. According to Erikson (1968, 1964b), the primary psychosocial task of early adulthood is to form a committed, mutually enhancing, intimate relationship with another person. During middle adulthood, the primary psychosocial task becomes one of *generativity*—to contribute to future generations through your children, your career, and other meaningful activities. In this section, we'll consider the themes of love and work by examining adult friendships, marriage, family life, and careers.

Friends and Lovers in Adulthood

Largely because of competing demands on their time, adults typically have fewer friends than adolescents do. The focus of adult friendships is somewhat different for men and women. Female friends tend to confide in one another about their feelings, problems, and interpersonal relationships. In contrast, male friends typically minimize discussions about relationships or personal feelings or problems. Instead, male friends tend to do things together that they find mutually interesting, such as activities related to sports or hobbies (Norris & Tindale, 1994; Winstead, 1986).

The Themes of Love and Work
Compared to the developmental milestones in earlier stages of life, the timing of the developmental tasks of adult development is characterized by a greater degree of individual variability. Nonetheless, some broad themes emerge. Establishing a career identity, forming a committed relationship, and starting a family are common developmental tasks that reflect the themes of love and work during early adulthood.

menopause
The natural cessation of menstruation and the end of reproductive capacity in women.

TABLE 9.6 Median Age at First Marriage: 1960 to 1993

Year	Men	Women
1993	26.5	24.5
1990	26.1	23.9
1985	25.5	23.3
1980	24.7	22.0
1975	23.5	21.1
1970	23.2	20.8
1965	22.8	20.6
1960	22.8	20.3

SOURCE: Saluter, 1994, p. vii.

Beyond friendship, establishing a committed, intimate relationship takes on a new urgency in adulthood. Looking for Mr. or Ms. Right, getting married, and starting a family are the traditional tasks of early adulthood. However, in contrast to their parents, today's young adults are marrying at a later average age. As Table 9.6 shows, in 1960 the median age for a first marriage was 23 for males and 20 years for females. By 1993 those averages had increased to 27 for males and 25 for females (Saluter, 1994). Many young adults postpone marriage until their late twenties or early thirties so they can finish their education and become established in a career.

Whom are we most likely to marry? As a general rule, the old adage "Birds of a feather flock together" seems to hold. We tend to be attracted to and marry people who are similar to us on a variety of dimensions, including physical attractiveness, social and educational status, ethnic background, attitudes, values, and beliefs (Brehm, 1992).

The Transition to Parenthood: Kids 'R' Us?

Although it is commonly believed that children strengthen the marital bond, marital satisfaction tends to decline after the birth of the first child (Levy-Shiff, 1994; Hackel & Ruble, 1992). For all the joy that can be derived from watching a child grow and experience the world, the first child's arrival creates a whole new set of responsibilities, pushes, and pulls on the marital relationship (Umberson & Gove, 1989).

Without question, parenthood fundamentally alters your identity as an adult. With the birth or adoption of your first child, you take on a commitment to nurture the physical, emotional, social, and intellectual well-being of the next generation. This change in your identity can be a struggle, especially if the transition to parenthood was more of a surprise than a planned event (Sandelowski & others, 1992; Mebert, 1991).

Parenthood is further complicated by the fact that children are not born speaking fluently so that you can immediately enlighten them about the constraints of adult schedules, deadlines, finances, and physical energy. Instead, you must continually strive to adapt lovingly and patiently to your child's needs while managing all the other priorities in your life.

Not all couples experience a decline in marital satisfaction after the birth of a child. The hassles and headaches of child rearing can be minimized if the marital relationship is warm and positive, and if both husband and wife share household and child-care responsibilities (Cowan & Cowan, 1992, 1988). It also helps if you're blessed with a child who is born with a good disposition and an easy temperament. When infants are irritable, cry a lot, or are otherwise "difficult," parents find it harder to adjust to their new role (van den Boom & Hoeksma, 1994; Wilkie & Ames, 1986).

That many couples are marrying at a later age and waiting until their thirties to start a family also seems to be advantageous. Becoming a parent at an older age and waiting longer after marriage to start a family helps ease the adjustment to parenthood. Why? Largely because the couple is more mature and the marital relationship is typically more stable (Cowan & Cowan, 1992; Olds, 1989).

Although marital satisfaction often declines when people first become parents, it rises again after children leave home (Norris & Tindale, 1994). Successfully launching your children into the adult world represents the attainment of the ultimate parental goal. It also means there is more time to spend in leisure activities with your spouse. Not surprisingly, then, marital satisfaction tends to increase steadily once children are out of the nest and flying on their own.

1970

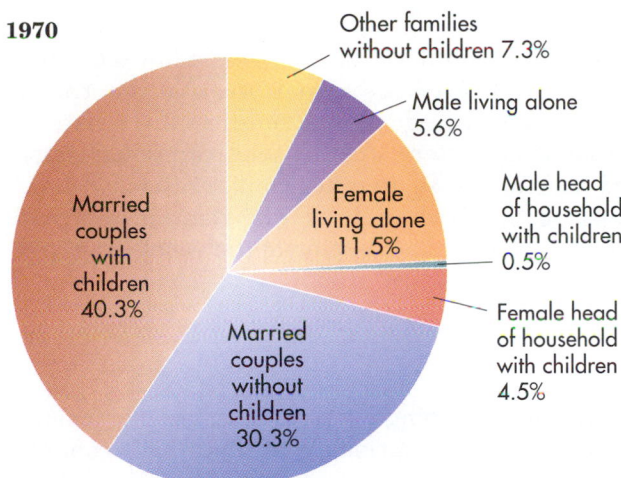

Other families without children 7.3%

Male living alone 5.6%

Married couples with children 40.3%

Female living alone 11.5%

Male head of household with children 0.5%

Female head of household with children 4.5%

Married couples without children 30.3%

1994

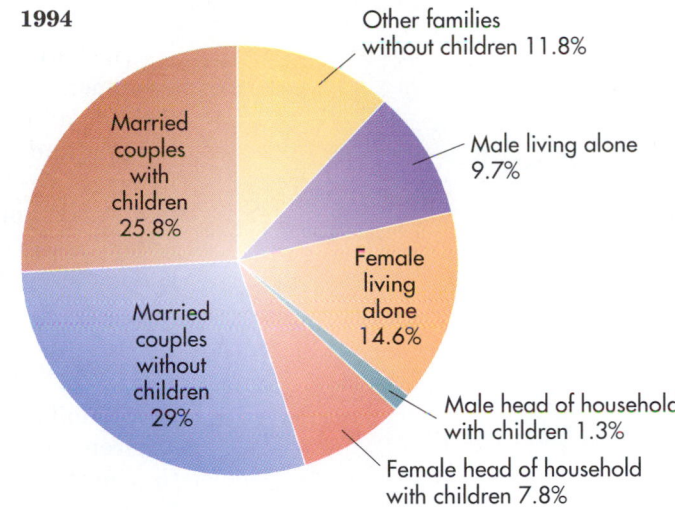

Other families without children 11.8%

Male living alone 9.7%

Married couples with children 25.8%

Female living alone 14.6%

Male head of household with children 1.3%

Female head of household with children 7.8%

Married couples without children 29%

FIGURE 9.6 **The Changing Structure of American Families and Households**
Between 1970 and 1994, the number of American households increased from 63 million to 97 million. During that same period, however, the average size of the American household decreased from 3.14 to 2.67 persons. In the two pie charts above, you can see how the structure of American households has under-gone major shifts during the last 25 years. Notice how the percentage of single-parent households has almost doubled, while the number of "traditional" families of a married couple with children has decreased dramatically.
(Rawlings & Saluter, 1995)

Single-Parent Families Today, more than thirty percent of all children are being raised by a single parent. Many single parents provide their children with a warm, stable, and loving environment. In terms of school achievement and emotional stability, children in stable single-parent households do just as well as the children with two parents living in the same home (see Berger, 1995).

Variations in the Paths of Adult Social Development

Up to this point, we've described the "traditional" track of adult social development: finding a mate, getting married, starting and raising a family. However, there is enormous diversity in how the goal of intimacy is realized during adulthood (Edwards, 1995b). The nature of intimate relationships and family structures varies widely in the United States (see Figure 9.6).

For example, the number of unmarried couples living together has increased dramatically in the last twenty years—to well over 3 million couples in the 1990s. Currently, better than 30 percent of all children are being raised by a single parent (Rawlings & Saluter, 1995). Given that more than half of all first marriages end in divorce, the phenomenon of remarrying and having a "second family" later in life is not unusual (Karney & Bradbury, 1995). As divorce has become more common, the number of single parents and stepfamilies has also risen. And among married couples, an increasing number are opting for a "child-free" life together (Macklin, 1987). There are also gay and lesbian couples who, like many married couples, are committed to a long-term, monogamous relationship with their partner (Kurdek, 1995).

A "Blended" Family Another nontraditional family structure that has become more common is the so-called blended family. Sometimes, as with the family in this photograph, the children of the first marriage are much older than the children of the second marriage.

Such diversity in adult relationships reflects the fact that adult social development does not always follow a predictable pattern. As you travel through adulthood, your life story may include many unanticipated twists in the plot and changes in the cast of characters. Just as the "traditional" family structure has its joys and heartaches, so do other configurations of intimate and family relationships. In the final analysis, *any* relationship that promotes the overall sense of happiness and well-being of the people involved is a successful one.

Careers in Adulthood

People follow a variety of routes in developing careers. Most people explore different career options, narrow down their options, and tentatively commit to a particular job in a particular field in young adulthood (Super, 1990). However, researchers have found that close to a third of people in their late twenties and early thirties do not just change jobs in a particular field, but completely switch occupational fields (Phillips & Blustein, 1994; Phillips, 1982).

Dual-career families have become increasingly common (Gilbert, 1993). However, the career tracks of men and women often differ if they have children. Although today's fathers are more actively involved in child rearing than fathers in previous generations, women still tend to have primary responsibility for child care. Thus, married women with children are much more likely than single women or childless women to interrupt their careers, leave their jobs, or switch to part-time work because of child-rearing responsibilities (Larwood & Gutek, 1987).

Do adults, particularly women, experience greater stress because of the conflicting demands of career, marriage, and family? Not necessarily. Generally, multiple roles seem to provide both men and women with a greater potential for increased feelings of self-esteem, happiness, and competence (Gilbert, 1994). The critical factor is not so much the number of roles that people take on, but the *quality* of their experiences on the job, in marriage, and as a parent (Barnett & others, 1992). When experiences in these different roles are positive and satisfying, psychological well-being is enhanced. However, when work is dissatisfying, finding high-quality child care is difficult, and making ends meet is a never-ending struggle, stress can escalate and psychological well-being can plummet—for either sex (Clay, 1995).

Establishing a Career Like this young man, a preschool teacher, many people commit to a particular career in young adulthood. However, it's common for people to change careers and even occupational fields in their late twenties and thirties.

Late Adulthood and Aging

Late adulthood does not necessarily involve a steep decline in physical or cognitive capabilities. What cognitive changes take place in late adulthood? What factors can influence social development in late adulthood?

The average life expectancy for men is about 72 years. For women, the average life expectancy is about 79 years. So the stage of late adulthood can easily last for twenty years or more. Although we experience many physical and sensory changes throughout adulthood, that's not to say that we completely fall apart when we reach our sixties, seventies, or even eighties. In fact, people in their nineties or older are sometimes healthier and more active than people twenty years younger (Perls, 1995).

Stereotypes of Aging What are your thoughts about the personalities and abilities of these two gentlemen? When American college students were shown pictures of the same man at ages 25, 52, and 74, they rated the 74-year-old as least active, intelligent, healthy, and competent (Levin, 1988). After reading this section, can you explain why these stereotypes are inaccurate?

In American culture, but certainly not all cultures, "old age" is often associated with images of poor health, inactivity, social isolation, and mental and physical incompetence. Are those images accurate? Far from it. The majority of older adults live healthy, active, and self-sufficient lives (Schaie & Willis, 1996).

In fact, the stereotypical image that most of the elderly live in nursing homes is a myth. Only about 5 percent of people over age sixty-five live in nursing homes. This percentage increases with advancing age, but not as much as you might think. Even among those aged eighty-five and older, less than 25 percent live in nursing homes. Some older adults live with relatives, but most live in their own homes (U.S. Bureau of the Census, 1992).

Although they have more chronic medical conditions, the elderly tend to see themselves as relatively healthy, partly because they have fewer acute illnesses, such as colds and the flu, than younger people (U.S. National Center for Health Statistics, 1990). Even during the final year of life, the majority of older adults enjoy relatively good health, mental alertness, and self-sufficiency (Brock & others, 1994).

The number of older adults in the United States has been gradually increasing over the past several decades. At the turn of the century, only about one American in twenty was sixty-five or older; today, one out of every eight Americans is. By the year 2030, one out of five Americans will be an older adult (Human Capital Initiative, 1993).

Culture and Images of Aging Some cultures hold the very old in great respect. Japan has a national holiday, "Respect for the Aged Day," celebrated each September. Shown here are Kin Narita and Gin Kanie, Japan's oldest twins, who recently celebrated their 104th birthday. Kin (which means "gold") and Gin (which means "silver") make regular appearances in Japanese television commercials and variety shows and have even cut a CD.

Cognitive Changes

During which decade of life do you think people reach their intellectual peak? If you answered the twenties or thirties, you may be surprised by the results of longitudinal studies done by psychologist K. Warner Schaie. Since the 1950s, Schaie and his colleagues have followed some 5,000 people as they have aged to learn what happens to intellectual abilities.

Schaie (1995b) found that general intellectual abilities gradually increase until one's early forties, then become relatively stable until about age sixty. After age sixty, a small but steadily increasing percentage of older adults experienced slight declines on tests of general intellectual abilities, such as logical reasoning, math skills, word recall, and the ability to mentally manipulate images. But even after age sixty, most older adults maintain these abilities.

When declines in mental abilities occur during old age, Schaie found, the explanation is often simply a lack of practice or experience with the kinds of tasks on mental ability tests. Even just a few hours of training on mental skills can improve test scores for most older adults (Schaie & Willis, 1986).

Is it possible to minimize declines in mental abilities in old age? In a word, yes. Schaie (1994) found that those who were better educated and engaged in physical and mental activities throughout older adulthood showed the smallest declines in mental abilities. In contrast, the greatest intellectual declines tended to occur in older adults with unstimulating lifestyles, such as people who lived alone, were dissatisfied with their lives, and engaged in few activities.

Social Development

At one time it was believed that older adults gradually "disengage," or withdraw from vocational, social, and relationship roles, as they face the prospect of their lives ending (Cumming & Henry, 1961). But consider Sandy's father, Erv, who is about to turn seventy-nine. Erv and about a dozen other retired men in their seventies belong to what they call "the Golden Agers' Club." They regularly get together to play cards, go out to lunch, forage used bookstores and flea markets, and, about once a year, go on a fishing trip.

What Erv and his buddies epitomize is the activity theory of aging. According to the **activity theory of aging,** life satisfaction in late adulthood is highest when you maintain your previous level of activity, either by continuing old activities or finding new ones (Havighurst & others, 1968).

Just like younger adults, older adults differ in the level of activity they find personally optimal. Some older adults pursue a busy lifestyle of social activities, travel, college classes, and volunteer work. Other older adults are happier with a quieter lifestyle, pursuing hobbies, reading, or simply puttering around their homes. Such individual preferences reflect lifelong temperamental and personality qualities that continue to be evident as the person ages (Costa & McCrae, 1989).

A Lifetime of Experience to Share Like many other senior adults, Ettore Buonomo of New York City derives great personal satisfaction as a volunteer helping grade-school students. Contributing to society, taking care of others, and helping people both younger and older than themselves often takes on renewed importance to senior adults.

For many older adults, caregiving responsibilities can persist well into late adulthood. Sandy's parents, Fern and Erv, for example, spend a great deal of time helping out with their young grandchildren and caring for some of their older relatives. They're not unusual in that respect. Many older adults who are healthy and active find themselves taking care of other older adults who are sick or have physical limitations (Norris & Tindale, 1994).

Even if an older adult is not very socially active, it's still important to have at least one confidant. Sometimes the confidant is simply a very close friend. For older men, the confidant is often the spouse. The social support provided by the confidant yields important psychological benefits for the

activity theory of aging
The psychosocial theory that life satisfaction in late adulthood is highest when people maintain the level of activity they displayed earlier in life.

older adult, such as higher morale, better mental health, and greater psychological well-being (Rawlins, 1992). A confidant can also provide an important buffer for the older adult in coping with stressful events, such as health problems or the deaths of friends or family members.

Along with satisfying social relationships, the prescription for psychological well-being in old age includes achieving what Erik Erikson called *ego integrity*—the feeling that one's life has been meaningful (Erikson & others, 1986). Older adults experience ego integrity when they look back on their lives and feel satisfied with their accomplishments, accepting whatever mistakes or missteps they may have made.

In contrast, those who are filled with regrets or bitterness about past mistakes, missed opportunities, or bad decisions experience *despair*—a sense of disappointment in life. Often the themes of ego integrity or despair emerge as older adults engage in a *life review,* thinking about or retelling their life story to others (Haight, 1992; Taft & Nehrke, 1990).

CONCEPT REVIEW 9.4

Adulthood and Late Adulthood

Answer *true* or *false* for each of the following statements. If a statement is false, write in the correct statement.

___ **1.** The adage "Use it or lose it" seems to apply to your brain's abilities as you grow older.

___ **2.** In general, people tend to marry others like themselves.

___ **3.** Women tend to experience much greater stress than men when faced with the demands of career, marriage, and family roles.

___ **4.** Younger parents adjust more easily to parenthood than older parents do.

___ **5.** The percentage of married couples with children has remained very consistent since 1960.

___ **6.** After the last child leaves home, parents suffer from the "empty-nest syndrome," and marital satisfaction declines significantly.

The Final Chapter: Dying and Death

> *Attitudes toward dying and death are as diverse in late adulthood as they are throughout the lifespan. How did Kübler-Ross describe the stages of dying? Does her description accurately characterize the process of dying?*

It is tempting to view death as the special province of the very old. Of course, death can occur at any point during the lifespan. It's also tempting to assume that older adults have come to a special understanding about death—that they view the prospect of dying with wisdom and serenity. In reality, attitudes toward death in old age show the same diversity that is reflected in other aspects of adult development. Not all older adults are resigned to death, even when poor health has severely restricted their activities (Kastenbaum, 1992, 1986).

As psychologist Robert Kastenbaum (1992) wrote, "Everyone lives in relationship to death at every point in the life span." In other words, long before encountering old age, each individual has a personal history of thinking about death. Some people are obsessed with issues of life and death from adolescence or early adulthood, while others, even in advanced old age, take more of a "one day at a time" approach to living.

In general, anxiety about death tends to peak in middle adulthood, then tends to *decrease* in late adulthood (Lonetto & Templer, 1986). At any age, people respond with a wide variety of emotions when faced with the prospect of imminent death, such as when they are diagnosed with a terminal illness.

Elisabeth Kübler-Ross (1969) interviewed over 200 terminally ill patients and proposed that the dying go through five stages. First, they *deny* that death is imminent, perhaps insisting that their doctors are wrong or denying the seriousness of their illness. Second, they feel and express *anger* that they are dying. Third, they *bargain*—they try to "make a deal" with doctors, relatives, or God, promising to behave in a certain way if only they may be allowed to live. Fourth, they become *depressed*. Finally, they *accept* their fate.

Although Kübler-Ross's research did much to sensitize the public and the medical community to the emotional experience of dying, it now seems clear that the dying individual does not progress through a predictable sequence of stages (Kastenbaum, 1992). Dying is as individual a process as living. People cope with the prospect of dying much as they have coped with other stresses involved in living (Schulz & Schlarb, 1987–1988).

Faced with impending death, some older adults react with passive resignation, others with bitterness and anger. Some people plunge into activity and focus their attention on external matters, such as making funeral arrangements, disposing of their property, or arranging for the care of other family members. And others turn inward, searching for the meaning of their life's story as the close of the final chapter draws near (Kastenbaum, 1992).

But even in dying, our life story doesn't just end. Each of us leaves behind a legacy of memories in the minds of those who survive us. As we live each day, we are building this legacy, through our words, our actions, and the choices we make.

Each of us began life being completely dependent upon others for our survival. Over the course of our lifespan, others come to depend upon us. It is those people whose lives we have touched in some way, whether for good or for bad, who will remember us. In this sense, the final chapter of our lives will be written not by us, but by those whose life stories have intersected with our own.

"Daddy, can I ask you a question?"

"Sure, Laura, just let me fix this typo in this sentence. Okay, shoot!"

"I have two grandpas, right?"

"That's right. Grandpa Erv in Chicago and Grandpa Ken, who died before you were born."

"Grandpa Ken was your dad, right?"

"That's right."

"Did he die because he was sick?"

"No, he just got very old and died."

"Was he nice?"

"He was a wonderful man, Laura, and even though he's not here, I know he loves you very much."

"How do you know that?"

"Trust me, my child, I know."

Raising Psychologically Healthy Children

Unfortunately, kids don't come with owner's manuals. Maybe that's why if you walk into any bookstore and head for the "Parenting" section, you'll see shelves of books offering advice on topics ranging from "how to toilet-train your toddler" to "how to talk to your teenager." We're not going to attempt to cover that range in this brief chapter Application. However, we will present some basic principles of parenting that have been shown to foster the development of children who are psychologically well-adjusted, competent, and in control of their own behavior.

Basic Parenting Styles and Their Effects on Children

Psychologist Diana Baumrind (1971, 1967) has described three basic parenting styles: authoritarian, permissive, and authoritative. These parenting styles differ in terms of (1) *parental control* and (2) *parental responsiveness* to the child's needs and wishes.

Authoritarian parents are demanding but unresponsive to their children's needs or wishes. Authoritarian parents believe that they should shape and control the child's behavior so that it corresponds to an absolute set of standards. Put simply, they expect children to obey the rules, no questions asked. Rules are made without input from the child, and they are enforced by punishment, often physical.

At the opposite extreme are two types of **permissive parents** (Maccoby & Martin, 1983). *Permissive-indulgent parents* are responsive, warm, and accepting of their children, but impose few rules and rarely punish the child. *Permissive-indifferent parents* are both unresponsive and uncontrolling. Establishing firm rules and consistently enforcing them is simply too much trouble for permissive-indifferent parents. When the lack of involvement of permissive-indifferent parenting is taken to an extreme, it can amount to child neglect.

The third parenting style is authoritative. **Authoritative parents** are warm, responsive, and involved with their children. They set clear stan-

Situation: Nine-year-old Jeff wants to stay up late to watch a special program on television.

	Low responsiveness	High responsiveness
Low control	**Permissive-Indifferent** Doesn't notice that Jeff is up late; Jeff has no regular bedtime.	**Permissive-Indulgent** Says, "Fine, if it's that important to you."
High control	**Authoritarian** Says, "You know the rules. Bedtime is nine o'clock. No exceptions!"	**Authoritative** Asks why program is so important. Offers to tape program so Jeff can watch it at a later time, or agrees that Jeff can stay up late tonight if he promises to go to bed early tomorrow.

Four Parenting Styles
Researchers have identified four basic parenting styles, based on the dimensions of parental control and parental responsiveness.

dards for mature, age-appropriate behavior and expect their children to be responsive to parental demands. However, authoritative parents also feel a *reciprocal* responsibility to consider their children's reasonable demands and points of view. Thus, there is considerable give and take between parent and child. Rules are firm and consistently enforced, but the reasons for the rules are discussed with the child (Maccoby & Martin, 1983).

How do these different parenting styles affect young children? Baumrind (1971) found that the children of authoritarian parents are likely to be moody, unhappy, fearful, withdrawn, unspontaneous, and irritable. The children of permissive parents tend to be more cheerful than the children of authoritarian parents, but they are more immature, impulsive, and aggressive. In contrast, the children of authoritative parents are likely to be cheerful, socially competent, energetic, and friendly. They show high levels of self-esteem, self-reliance, and self-control (Buri & others, 1988).

These different parenting styles also affect school performance. In a nutshell, authoritative parenting is as-

sociated with higher grades than authoritarian or permissive parenting. In one study of several hundred adolescents, this finding was consistent for virtually all adolescents, regardless of ethnic or socioeconomic background (Dornbusch & others, 1987).

Adding to the evidence, psychologist Laurence Steinberg and his colleagues (1995) conducted a three-year longitudinal study involving over 20,000 U.S. high school students. Steinberg found that authoritative parenting is associated with a broad range of beneficial effects for the adolescent, regardless of socioeconomic or ethnic background. As Steinberg summarizes, "Adolescents raised in authoritative homes are better adjusted and more competent, they are confident about their abilities, competent in areas of achievement, and less likely than their peers to get into trouble" (Steinberg & others, 1995).

Why does an authoritative parenting style provide such clear advantages over other parenting styles? First, when children perceive their parents' requests as fair and reasonable, they are more likely to comply with the requests. Second, the children are more likely to *internalize* (or accept as their own) the reasons for behaving in a certain way and thus to achieve greater self-control (Hoffman, 1994, 1977).

In contrast, authoritarian parenting promotes resentment and rebellion (Hoffman, 1988, 1977). Because compliance is based on external control and punishment, the child often learns to avoid the parent rather than independently control his or her own behavior. Finally, the child with permissive parents may never learn self-control. And, because permissive parents have low expectations, the child may well live up to those expectations by failing to strive to fulfill his or her potential (Baumrind, 1971).

How to Be an Authoritative Parent: Some Practical Suggestions

Authoritative parents are high in both responsiveness and control. How can you successfully achieve that balance? Here are several suggestions based on psychological research.

1. *Let your children know that you love them.* Attention, hugs, and other demonstrations of physical affection, coupled with a positive attitude toward your child, are some of the most important aspects of parenting, aspects that have enduring effects. Over the long haul, children who experience warm, positive relationships with their parents are more likely to become happy adults with stable marriages and good relationships with friends (Franz & others, 1991). So the question is simple: Have you hugged your kids today?

2. *Listen to your children.* Let your children express their opinions, and respect their preferences when it's reasonable to do so. In making rules and decisions, ask for their input and give it genuine consideration. Strive to be fair and flexible, especially on issues that are less than earthshaking, like which clothes they wear to school.

3. *Use induction to teach as you discipline.* The most effective form of discipline is called **induction,** because it *induces* understanding in the child. Induction combines controlling a child's behavior with *teaching* (Hoffman, 1994, 1977). Put simply, induction involves consistently explaining (a) the *reason* for prohibiting or performing certain behaviors; (b) the *consequences* of the action for the child; and (c) the *effect* of the child's behavior on others. With older children, induction can also involve describing how they can make *amends* for their misbehavior.

4. *Work with your child's temperamental qualities.* Think back to our earlier discussion of temperamental qualities. Be aware of your child's natural temperament and work with it, not against it. If your child is very active, for example, it is unrealistic to expect him to sit quietly during a four-hour plane or bus trip. Knowing that, you can increase the likelihood of positive experiences by planning ahead. Bring coloring books, picture books, or small toys to occupy the young child in a restaurant or at a family gathering. Take frequent "exercise stops" on a long car trip. If your child is unusually sensitive, shy, or "slow-to-warm-up," give

her plenty of time to make the transition to new situations, and provide lots of preparation so that she knows what to expect (Kurcinka, 1991).

5. *Understand your child's age-related cognitive abilities and limitations.* Some parents make the mistake of assuming that the child thinks in the same way as an adult. They may see a toddler or even an infant as purposely "misbehaving," "being naughty," or "rebelling" when the little one is simply doing what one-year-olds or three-year-olds do. Instead, your expectations for appropriate behavior should be geared to the child's age and developmental stage (see Barclay & Houts, 1995b). Having a thorough understanding of the information in this chapter is a good start. You might also consider taking a developmental psychology or child development class. Or go to your school library and check out some of the developmental psychology texts. By understanding your child's cognitive abilities and limitations at each stage of development, you're less likely to misinterpret his behavior or to place inappropriate demands on him.

6. *Don't expect perfection, and learn to go with the flow.* Accidents happen. Mistakes occur. Children get cranky or grumpy, especially when they're tired or hungry. Don't get too bent out of shape when your child's behavior is less than perfect. Be patient. Moments of conflict with children are a natural, inevitable, and healthy part of growing up. Look at them as part of the process by which a child achieves autonomy and a sense of self.

Finally, effective parenting is an ongoing process in which you, as the parent, should be regularly assessing your impact on your child. It's not always easy to combine responsiveness with control, or flexibility with an appropriate level of firmness. When you make a mistake, admit it not just to yourself but also to your child. In doing so, you'll teach your child how he should behave when he makes a mistake. As you'll discover, children are remarkably forgiving—and also resilient.

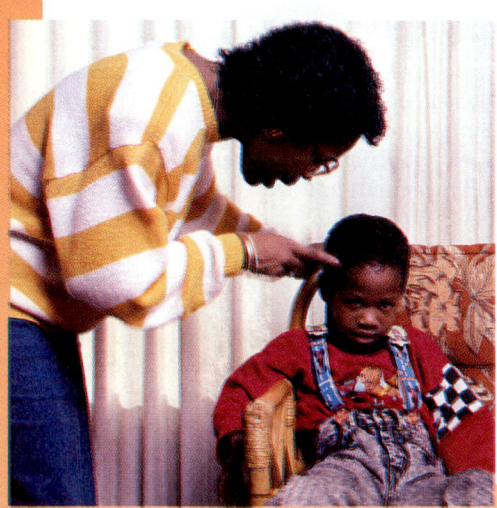

Using Induction to Teach as You Discipline
By consistently explaining why a certain behavior is not permitted and how it affects others, the child begins to understand that a parent's actions are not completely arbitrary or unfair. The child is also more likely to internalize the reasoning and apply it in new situations (Schulman & Mekler, 1985).

Summary

Lifespan Development

Your Life Story

▪ Developmental psychologists study the many ways in which people change over the lifespan. Key themes in developmental psychology include understanding the stages of lifespan development, the nature of change, and the interaction between heredity and environment.

Genetic Contributions to Your Life Story

▪ The genetic blueprint is determined at conception by the pairing of chromosomes from the biological parents. The chromosomes are made of DNA, which is arranged in thousands of segments called genes.

▪ The genotype refers to the underlying genetic makeup; the phenotype refers to the traits that are displayed. When paired with a recessive gene, a dominant gene determines the trait that will be displayed. Recessive traits are displayed only if there are two recessive genes. Environmental conditions can influence the phenotype.

▪ The 23rd pair of chromosomes determines whether male or female sexual characteristics will develop. Females have two X chromosomes, while males have an X and a Y chromosome. Females require two recessive genes for sex-linked recessive characteristics to be displayed. However, males require only one recessive gene for the same sex-linked recessive characteristic.

Prenatal Development

▪ During the nine months that make up the prenatal stage, the zygote develops into a full-term fetus. The prenatal stage includes the germinal period, the embryonic period, and the fetal period. The greatest vulnerability to teratogens occurs during the embryonic stage, when major body systems are forming.

Development During Infancy and Childhood

▪ Although physically helpless, the newborn is equipped with various reflexes and sensory capabilities that seem to enhance his chances for survival. Vision, hearing, and smell are attuned to interaction with caregivers. The brain develops rapidly after birth. The sequence of motor skill development is generally universal, although there is individual variation in the rate of development.

▪ Thomas and Chess demonstrated that infants seem to be born with different temperaments. They identified three basic temperamental patterns: easy, difficult, and slow-to-warm-up. Temperamental qualities seem to have a biological basis and persist through life, although they can be modified by environmental influences.

▪ According to attachment theory, the infant's ability to thrive is dependent on the quality of her attachment to caregivers. Secure attachment develops when parents are sensitive and responsive to the infant's needs. Insecure attachment may develop when parents are insensitive to the infant's needs.

▪ Infants seem to be biologically predisposed to learn language. At birth, infants can distinguish between the sounds that are present in any language, but soon become sensitized to the sounds of the language that is spoken in their home. Adults encourage language development in infants by using motherese.

▪ The stages of language development include cooing and babbling. Other stages of language development are the one-word stage and the two-word stage. At every stage, the infant's comprehension vocabulary is larger than her production vocabulary.

▪ Gender plays an important role in our culture. During childhood, boys and girls develop different toy preferences and play with members of their own sex.

▪ Two contemporary theories that explain gender-role development are social learning theory and gender schema theory. Social learning theory is based on the principles of learning. Through reinforcement, punishment, and modeling, children learn the appropriate behaviors for each gender.

▪ Gender schema theory is based on the idea that children actively develop mental categories for each gender. Children's gender schemas influence what they learn and remember.

▪ According to Jean Piaget's theory of cognitive development, children progress through distinct cognitive stages, each of which represents a shift in how they think and understand the world.

▪ Object permanence is acquired during the sensorimotor stage. Symbolic thought is acquired during the preoperational stage. Preoperational thought is egocentric and characterized by irreversibility and centration. Thus, the preoperational child is unable to grasp the principles of conservation. Children become capable of logical thought during the concrete operational stage, but thinking is limited to tangible objects and events. During the formal operational stage, the adolescent can engage in logical mental operations involving abstract concepts and hypothetical situations.

▪ Piaget's theory has been criticized because: Piaget underestimated the cognitive abilities of infants and children; Piaget's stages are not as universal as he believed; and Piaget underestimated the influence of social and cultural factors on cognitive development.

■ The information-processing model is an alternative description of cognitive development that emphasizes fundamental mental processes and stresses that cognitive development is a process of continuous change.

Adolescence

■ During puberty, adolescents reach sexual maturation. Puberty involves the development of primary and secondary sex characteristics, the adolescent growth spurt, and, in females, menarche. While the sequence of pubertal changes is relatively predictable, the timing of puberty varies.

■ Sexual and romantic relationships become increasingly important in adolescence. By the end of adolescence, most males and females have had sexual intercourse.

■ In general, when parent-child relationships are good before adolescence, they continue to be positive during adolescence. Relationships with peers become increasingly important. Peer influence is just as likely to be positive as negative.

■ Erik Erikson's theory of psychosocial development stresses that every stage of life is marked by a particular psychosocial conflict. Identity versus identity diffusion is the conflict associated with adolescence; however, the process of identity formation does not end in adolescence.

■ Lawrence Kohlberg described the type of reasoning used in making moral decisions. His theory of moral development includes the preconventional, conventional, and postconventional levels, with each level having two stages. Some researchers believe that moral reasoning is affected by both gender and culture.

Adult Development

■ Although there are general patterns in adult development, individual variation becomes increasingly significant in adulthood. The three phases of adulthood are early adulthood, middle adulthood, and late adulthood. Genetics, environment, and an individual's lifestyle all influence physical changes during adulthood and aging.

■ Love and work are two key themes that dominate adult development. Although friends continue to be important in adulthood, forming a committed, intimate relationship is one important task traditionally associated with early adulthood.

■ Marital satisfaction tends to decline after the first child is born and to increase after children leave home. Family structures and relationships have become increasingly diverse in the United States. Although the combination of work, marital, and family roles can be demanding, especially for women, multiple roles can lead to increased personal satisfaction when the quality of experience in each role is high.

Late Adulthood and Aging

■ Late adulthood does not necessarily involve a steep decline in physical and cognitive functioning. Mental abilities only begin to decline slightly at around age sixty, and these declines can be minimized or eliminated with an active and mentally stimulating lifestyle.

■ Many older adults do not disengage from life, but remain socially active. According to the activity theory of aging, life satisfaction in late adulthood is highest when people maintain their previous levels of activity. Older adults differ in their optimal level of activity. Erikson identified the task of ego integrity as the key psychosocial task of old age.

The Final Chapter: Dying and Death

■ Although commonly associated with old age, death can occur at any point in the lifespan. Anxiety about death tends to peak in middle adulthood and decrease in late adulthood. Elisabeth Kübler-Ross proposed a five-stage model of dying: denial, anger, bargaining, depression, and acceptance. However, individuals respond in diverse ways to impending death.

Key Terms

developmental psychology (p. 316)

chromosome (p. 318)

deoxyribonucleic acid (DNA) (p. 318)

gene (p. 318)

genotype (p. 319)

phenotype (p. 319)

dominant gene (p. 319)

recessive gene (p. 319)

sex chromosomes (p. 320)

sex-linked recessive characteristics (p. 320)

prenatal stage (p. 320)

germinal period (p. 320)

embryonic period (p. 321)

teratogens (p. 321)

fetal period (p. 321)

temperament (p. 324)

attachment (p. 325)

comprehension vocabulary (p. 329)

production vocabulary (p. 329)

gender (p. 330)

gender roles (p. 330)

gender identity (p. 330)

social learning theory of gender-role development (p. 331)

gender schema theory (p. 332)

sensorimotor stage (p. 333)

object permanence (p. 333)

preoperational stage (p. 334)

symbolic thought (p. 334)

egocentrism (p. 334)

irreversibility (p. 334)

centration (p. 334)

conservation (p. 335)

concrete operational stage (p. 335)

formal operational stage (p. 335)

information-processing model of cognitive development (p. 336)

adolescence (p. 337)

puberty (p. 338)

primary sex characteristics (p. 338)

secondary sex characteristics (p. 338)

adolescent growth spurt (p. 338)

menarche (p. 338)

identity (p. 340)

moral reasoning (p. 342)

menopause (p. 345)

activity theory of aging
(p. 350)

authoritarian parenting style
(p. 353)

permissive parenting style
(p. 353)

authoritative parenting style
(p. 353)

induction (p. 354)

Key People

Noam Chomsky (b. 1928) American linguist who proposed that people have an innate understanding of the basic principles of language, which he called a "universal grammar."

Erik Erikson (1902–1994) German-born American psychoanalyst who proposed an influential theory of psychosocial development throughout the lifespan.

Lawrence Kohlberg (1927–1987) American psychologist who proposed an influential theory of moral development.

Jean Piaget (1896–1980) Swiss child psychologist whose influential theory proposed that children progress through distinct stages of cognitive development.

Lev Vygotsky (1896–1934) Russian psychologist who stressed the importance of social and cultural influences in cognitive development.

CONCEPT REVIEW 9.1 Page 324

1. True
2. True
3. False. Females have an XX combination in the 23rd pair of chromosomes.
4. False. With the exception of the Y chromosome, each human chromosome contains thousands of genes.
5. False. The larger X chromosome contains many more genes than the small Y chromosome.
6. True
7. True

CONCEPT REVIEW 9.2 Page 337

1. D
2. B
3. A
4. C

CONCEPT REVIEW 9.3 Page 344

1. postconventional
2. preconventional
3. conventional

CONCEPT REVIEW 9.4 Page 351

1. True
2. True
3. False. Rather than gender, the critical factor for both men and women is the quality of experiences in different roles.
4. False. Older parents tend to adjust more easily to parenthood than younger parents.
5. False. The percentage has decreased significantly.
6. False. Marital satisfaction typically increases after the last child leaves home.

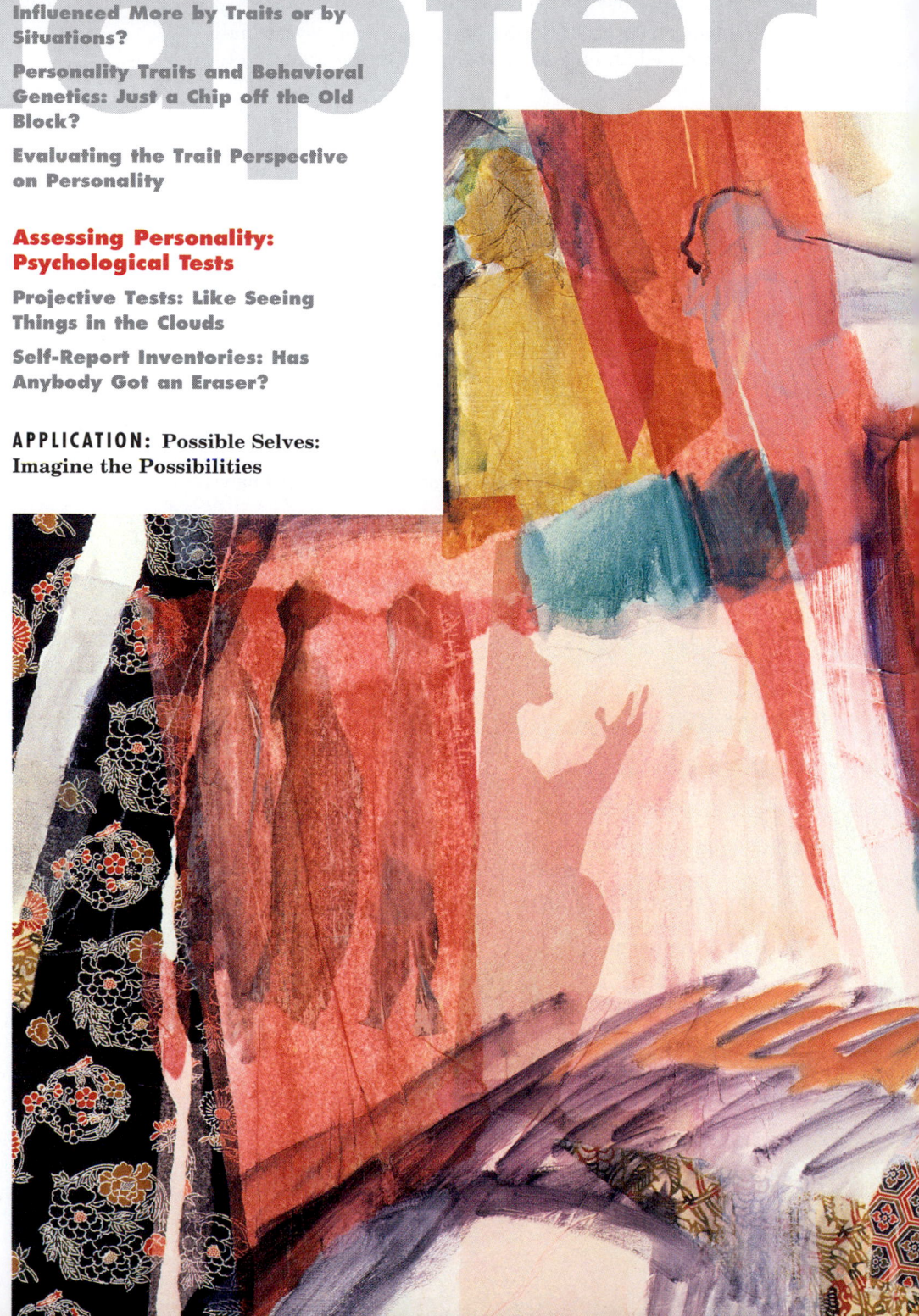

Chapter

10 Personality

Prologue: The Secret Twin

The twins, Kenneth and Julian, were born a few years after the turn of the century. At first their parents, Gertrude and Henry, thought they were identical, because the twins looked exactly alike. Both had dark hair and deep brown eyes. Kenneth's son, your author Don, would later inherit these qualities.

But Gertrude and Henry quickly learned to tell the twins apart. Kenneth was slightly larger than Julian, and even as infants, their personalities were distinctly different. In the photographs of Kenneth and Julian as children, Julian smiles broadly, almost merrily, his head cocked slightly. But Kenneth always looked straight at the camera, his expression thoughtful, serious, more intense.

We don't know much about Julian's childhood. Kenneth kept Julian's existence a closely guarded secret for more than fifty years. In fact, it was only a few years before his own death that Kenneth revealed that he had once had a twin brother named Julian.

Still, it's possible to get glimpses of Julian's early life from the letters they wrote home from summer camp in 1919 and 1920. Kenneth's letters to his mother are affectionate and respectful, telling her about their daily activities and reassuring her that he will look after his twin brother. "I reminded Julian about the boats and I will watch him <u>good</u>," Kenneth wrote in one letter. Julian's letters were equally affectionate, but shorter and filled with misspelled words. Julian's letters also reveal glimpses of his impulsive nature. He repeatedly promised his mother, "I will not go out in the boats alone again."

Julian's impulsive nature was to have a significant impact on his life. When he was twelve years old, Julian darted in front of a car and was seriously injured with a concussion. In retrospect, Kenneth believed that that was when Julian's problems began. Perhaps it was, because soon after the accident Julian first got into serious trouble: He was caught stealing money from the "poor box" at church.

Although Kenneth claimed that Julian had always been the smarter twin, Julian fell behind in high school and graduated a year later than Kenneth. After high school, Kenneth left the quiet farming community of Grinnell, Iowa, and moved to Minneapolis. He quickly became self-sufficient, taking a job managing newspaper carriers. Julian stayed in Grinnell and became apprenticed to learn typesetting. Given Julian's propensity for adventure, it's not surprising that he found typesetting monotonous. In the spring of 1928, Julian left Iowa, heading east to look for more interesting possibilities.

He found them in Tennessee. A few months after Julian left Iowa, Henry received word that Julian had been arrested for armed robbery and sentenced to fifteen years in a Tennessee state prison. Though Kenneth was only twenty-two years old, Henry gave him a large sum of money and the family car and sent him to try to get Julian released.

Kenneth's conversation with the judge in Knoxville was the first of many times that he would deal with the judicial system on someone else's behalf. After much negotiation, the judge agreed: If Julian promised to leave Tennessee and never return, and Kenneth paid the cash "fines," Julian would be released from prison.

When Julian walked through the prison gates the next morning, Kenneth stood waiting with a fresh suit of clothes. "Mother and Father want you to come back to Grinnell," he told Julian. But Julian would not hear of it, saying that instead he wanted to go to California to make his fortune.

"I can't let you do that, Julian," Kenneth said, looking hard at his twin brother.

"You can't stop me, brother," Julian responded, with a cocky smile. Reluctantly, Kenneth kept just enough money to buy himself a train ticket back to Iowa. He gave Julian the rest of the money and the family car.

Julian got as far as Phoenix, Arizona, before he met his destiny. In broad daylight, he robbed a drugstore at gunpoint. As he backed out of the store, he was spotted by a policeman. A gun battle followed, and Julian was shot twice. Somehow he managed to escape and holed up in a hotel room. Alone and untended, Julian died two days later from the bullet wounds. Once again, Kenneth was sent to retrieve his twin brother.

On a bitterly cold November morning in 1928, Julian's immediate family laid him to rest in the family plot in Grinnell. On the one hand, Kenneth felt largely responsible for Julian's misguided life. "I should have tried harder to help Julian," Kenneth later reflected. On the other hand, Julian had disgraced the family. Indeed, from the day that Julian was buried, the family never spoke of him again, not even in private.

Kenneth took it upon himself to atone for the failings of his twin brother. In the fall of 1929, Kenneth entered law school in Tennessee—the same state from which he had secured Julian's release from prison. Three years later, at the height of the Great Depression, Kenneth established himself as a lawyer in Sioux City, Iowa, where he would practice law for more than fifty years.

As an attorney, Kenneth Hockenbury was known for his integrity, his intensity in the courtroom, and his willingness to take cases regardless of the client's ability to pay. "Someone must defend the poor," he said repeatedly. In lieu of money, he often accepted labor from a working man or produce from farmers.

Sixty years after Julian's death, Kenneth died. But unlike the sparse gathering that had attended Julian's burial, scores of people came to pay their last respects to Kenneth Hockenbury. "Your father helped me so much," stranger after stranger told Don at Kenneth's funeral. Without question, Kenneth had devoted his life to helping others.

Why did Kenneth and Julian turn out so differently? Two boys, born on the same day into the same middle-class family. Kenneth the conscientious, serious one; Julian the laughing boy with mischief in his eyes. How can we explain the fundamental differences in their personalities?

No doubt your family, too, is made up of people with very different personalities. By the end of this chapter, you'll have a much greater appreciation for how those personality differences might be explained. As the chapter proceeds, we'll come back to the story of Kenneth and Julian.

The Twins Julian (left) and Kenneth (right), with their father Henry, when they were about ten years old. As boys, Kenneth and Julian were inseparable.

Introduction

What Is Personality?

Personality is defined as an individual's unique and relatively consistent patterns of thinking, feeling, and behaving. What are the four major theoretical perspectives in personality?

That you already have an intuitive understanding of the word *personality* is easy to demonstrate. Just from reading this chapter's prologue, you could easily describe different aspects of Kenneth's and Julian's personalities. Indeed, we frequently toss around the word *personality* in everyday conversations. "He's very competent, but he has an abrasive personality." "She's got such a delightful personality, you can't help liking her."

Your intuitive understanding of personality is probably very similar to the way that psychologists define the concept. **Personality** is defined as an individual's unique and relatively consistent patterns of thinking, feeling, and behaving (Pervin, 1997). A **personality theory** is an attempt to describe and explain how people are similar, how they are different, and why every individual is unique. In short, a personality theory ambitiously tries to explain the *whole person* (Pervin, 1990). At the outset, it's important to stress that no single theory can adequately explain *all* aspects of human personality. Every personality theory has its unique strengths and weaknesses.

Personality theories often reflect the work of a single individual or of a few closely associated individuals. Thus, it's not surprising that many personality theories bear the distinct personal stamp of their creators to a much greater degree than other kinds of psychological theories (Engler, 1995). Consequently, we've tried to let the personality theorists speak for themselves. Throughout this chapter, you'll encounter carefully chosen quotations from the theorists' own writings. These quotes will give you brief glimpses into the minds of some of the most influential thinkers in psychology.

There are many personality theories, but they can be roughly grouped under four basic perspectives: the psychoanalytic, humanistic, social cognitive, and trait perspectives. In a nutshell, here's what each perspective emphasizes:

- The *psychoanalytic perspective* emphasizes the importance of unconscious processes and the influence of early childhood experience.

- The *humanistic perspective* represents an optimistic look at human nature, emphasizing the self and the fulfillment of a person's unique potential.

- The *social cognitive perspective* emphasizes learning and conscious cognitive processes, including the importance of beliefs about the self, goal setting, and self-regulation.

- The *trait perspective* emphasizes the description and measurement of specific personality differences among individuals.

After looking at some of the major personality theories that reflect each perspective, we'll consider a closely related topic: how personality is measured and evaluated. And yes, we'll talk about the famous inkblots there. But for the inkblots to make sense, we need to trace the evolution of modern personality theories. We'll begin with the tale of a bearded, cigar-smoking gentleman from Vienna of whom you just may have heard—Sigmund Freud.

personality
An individual's unique and relatively consistent patterns of thinking, feeling, and behaving.

personality theory
A theory that attempts to describe and explain individual similarities and differences.

The Psychoanalytic Perspective on Personality

Sigmund Freud was the founder of psychoanalysis, which stresses the influence of the unconscious, the importance of sexual and aggressive instincts, and early childhood experience. What were some key influences on Freud's thinking?

Sigmund Freud (1856–1939) was one of the most influential figures of the twentieth century. Freud was the founder of psychoanalysis. **Psychoanalysis** is the theory of personality that stresses the influence of unconscious mental processes, the importance of sexual and aggressive instincts, and the enduring effects of early childhood experience on personality. Because so many of Freud's ideas have become part of our common culture, it is difficult to imagine just how radical a figure he appeared to his contemporaries. The following biographical sketch highlights some of the important influences that shaped Freud's ideas and theory.

The Life of Sigmund Freud

Sigmund Freud was born in 1856 in what is today Pribôr, the Czech Republic. When he was four years old, his family moved to Vienna, where he lived until the last year of his life. Sigmund was the firstborn child of Jakob and Amalia Freud. By the time he was ten years old, there were six more siblings in the household. Of the seven children, Sigmund was his mother's favorite. As Freud later wrote, "A man who has been the indisputable favorite of his mother keeps for life the feeling of being a conqueror, that confidence of success that often induces real success" (Jones, 1953).

Freud was extremely bright and intensely ambitious. He studied medicine, became a physician, and then proved himself to be an outstanding physiological researcher. Early in his career, Freud was among the first investigators of a new drug that had anesthetic and mood-altering properties—cocaine. One of Freud's colleagues, however, received credit for the discovery of the anesthetic properties of cocaine—a matter that left Freud bitter. On top of that, Freud's initial enthusiasm for the medical potential of cocaine quickly faded when he finally recognized that the drug was addictive (Fancher, 1973).

Prospects for an academic career in scientific research were very poor, especially for a Jew in Vienna. When he married Martha Bernays in 1886, Freud reluctantly gave up physiological research for a private practice in neurology. The income from private practice would be needed: Sigmund and Martha had six children (Fancher, 1973). One of Freud's daughters, Anna Freud, was later to become an important psychoanalytic theorist in her own right.

Influences in the Development of Freud's Ideas

Freud's theory evolved gradually during his first twenty years of private practice. He based his theory on observations of his patients as well as self-analysis. An early influence on Freud was Joseph Breuer, a highly respected physician. Breuer described to Freud the striking case of a young woman with an array of puzzling psychological and physical symptoms. Breuer found that if he first hypnotized this patient, then asked her to talk freely about a given symptom, forgotten memories of traumatic events would emerge. After she freely expressed the pent-up emotions associated with the event, her symptom would disappear. Breuer called this phenomenon *catharsis* (Freud, 1925).

Freud the Outsider Freud is shown here with his wife, Martha, and youngest child, Anna, in the garden of their Vienna home in 1898. Freud always considered himself to be an outsider. Along with being Jewish in a culture that was very anti-Semitic, Freud's ideas were always controversial. To some degree, Freud seemed to enjoy his role as the isolated scientist. It set him and his theory apart.

psychoanalysis
Sigmund Freud's theory of personality, which emphasizes unconscious determinants of behavior, sexual and aggressive instinctual drives, and the enduring effects of early childhood experiences on later personality development.

Freud the Leader By the early 1900s, psycho-analysis was becoming an international move-ment. In 1909, Freud and other psychoanalysts were invited to lecture at Clark University in Massachusetts. A year later, Freud founded the International Psychoanalytic Association.

Freud the Exile In the spring of 1938, Freud fled Nazi persecution for the safety of London on the eve of World War II. He is shown arriving in England, his eldest daughter, Mathilde, at his side. Four of Freud's sisters later died in Nazi extermi-nation camps.

free association
A psychoanalytic technique in which the patient spontaneously reports all thoughts, feelings, and mental images as they come to mind.

At first, Freud embraced Breuer's technique, but he found that not all of his patients could be hypnotized. Eventually, Freud dropped the use of hyp-nosis and developed his own technique of **free association** to help his pa-tients uncover forgotten memories. Freud's patients would spontaneously report their uncensored thoughts, mental images, and feelings as they came to mind. From these "free associations," the thread that led to the crucial long-forgotten memories could be unraveled. Breuer and Freud described several of their case studies in their landmark book *Studies on Hysteria*. Its publication in 1895 marked the beginning of psychoanalysis.

In 1900, Freud published what many consider to be his most important work, *The Interpretation of Dreams*. By the early 1900s, Freud had developed the basic tenets of his psychoanalytic theory and was no longer the isolated scientist. He was gaining international recognition and developing a follow-ing. For the next thirty years, Freud continued to refine his theory, publish-ing many books, articles, and lectures.

The last two decades of Freud's life were filled with many personal tragedies. The terrible devastation of World War I weighed heavily on his mind. In 1920, one of his daughters died. In the early 1920s, Freud developed cancer of the jaw, a condition for which he would ultimately undergo over thirty operations. During the late 1920s and early 1930s, the Nazis were steadily gaining power in Germany.

Given the climate of the times, it's not surprising that Freud came to focus on humanity's destructive tendencies. For years he had asserted that sexual-ity was the fundamental human motive, but now he added aggression as a sec-ond powerful human instinct. During this period, Freud wrote *Civilization and Its Discontents* (1930), in which he applied his psychoanalytic perspective to civilization as a whole. The central theme of the book is that human nature and civilization are in basic conflict—a conflict that cannot be resolved.

Freud's extreme pessimism was undoubtedly a reflection of the destruc-tion he saw all around him. By 1933, Adolf Hitler had seized power in Ger-many. Freud's books were banned and publicly burned in Berlin. Five years later, the Nazis marched into Austria.

Although Freud's life was clearly threatened, it was only after his youngest daughter, Anna, had been detained and questioned by the Gestapo that Freud reluctantly agreed to leave Vienna. Under great duress, Freud moved his family to the safety of England. A year later, Freud died at the age of eighty-three in London in 1939 (Gay, 1988).

This brief sketch cannot do justice to the richness of Freud's life and the influence of his culture and society on his ideas. Today, Freud's legacy con-tinues to influence psychology, philosophy, literature, and art.

Freud's Dynamic Theory of Personality

Psychoanalysis stresses the influence of unconscious mental proc-esses. How do we get glimpses of unconscious mental processes? What are the three basic structures of personality, and what are their functions? What role is played by the defense mechanisms?

Freud (1940) saw personality and behavior as the result of a constant inter-play between conflicting psychological forces. These psychological forces op-erate at three different levels of awareness: the conscious, the preconscious, and the unconscious. All the thoughts, feelings, and sensations that you're aware of at this particular moment represent the *conscious* level. The *pre-conscious* contains information of which you're not currently aware but which is easily capable of entering your consciousness, such as childhood memories or your social security number.

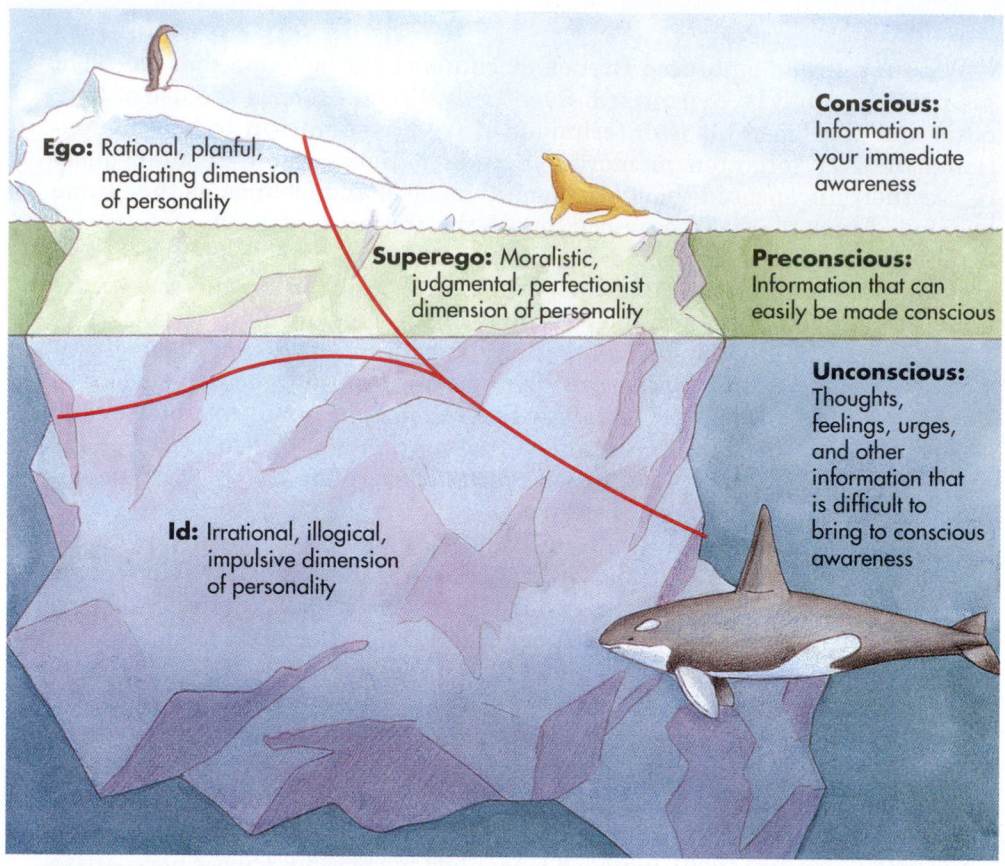

Conscious: Information in your immediate awareness

Ego: Rational, planful, mediating dimension of personality

Superego: Moralistic, judgmental, perfectionist dimension of personality

Preconscious: Information that can easily be made conscious

Unconscious: Thoughts, feelings, urges, and other information that is difficult to bring to conscious awareness

Id: Irrational, illogical, impulsive dimension of personality

FIGURE 10.1 Levels of Awareness and the Structure of Personality Freud believed personality is composed of three psychological processes that operate at different levels of awareness. If you think of personality as being like an iceberg, the bulk of this psychological iceberg is represented by the irrational, impulsive Id, which lies beneath the waterline of consciousness. Unlike the Id, the rational Ego and moralistic Superego are partially conscious.

unconscious

In Freud's theory, a term used to describe thoughts, feelings, wishes, and drives that are operating below the level of conscious awareness.

Id

Latin for *the it;* in Freud's theory, the unconscious, irrational component of personality that seeks immediate satisfaction of instinctual urges and drives.

Eros

In Freud's theory, the self-preservation or life instinct, reflected in basic biological urges that perpetuate the existence of the individual and the species.

libido

In Freud's theory, the psychological and emotional energy associated with expressions of sexuality; the sex drive.

Thanatos

In Freud's theory, the death instinct, reflected in aggressive, destructive, and self-destructive actions.

However, the conscious and preconscious are merely the visible tip of the iceberg of the mind. The bulk of this psychological iceberg is made up of the **unconscious,** which lies submerged below the waterline of the preconscious and conscious (see Figure 10.1). You're not directly aware of these submerged thoughts, feelings, wishes, and drives, but the unconscious exerts an enormous influence on your conscious thoughts and behavior.

Although it is not directly accessible, Freud (1904) believed that unconscious material often seeps through to the conscious level in distorted, disguised, or symbolic forms. Like a detective searching for clues, Freud carefully analyzed his patients' reports of dreams and free associations for evidence of unconscious wishes, fantasies, and conflicts. Dream analysis was particularly important to Freud. "The interpretation of dreams is the royal road to a knowledge of the unconscious activities of the mind," he wrote in 1900 in *The Interpretation of Dreams.* Beneath the surface images, or *manifest content,* of a dream lay its *latent content*—the true, hidden, unconscious meaning of the dream symbols (see Chapter 4).

Freud (1904, 1933) believed that the unconscious could also be revealed in unintentional actions, such as accidents, mistakes, instances of forgetting, and inadvertent slips of the tongue, which are often referred to as "Freudian slips." To Freud, seemingly accidental or unintentional actions were not accidental at all, but were determined by unconscious motives.

The Structure of Personality

According to Freud (1933), each person possesses a certain amount of psychological energy. This psychological energy evolves to form the three basic structures of personality—the Id, the Ego, and the Superego (see Figure 10.1). Understand that these are not separate identities or brain structures. Rather, they are distinct psychological processes.

The **Id,** the most primitive part of the personality, is entirely unconscious and present at birth. The Id is completely immune to logic, values, morality, danger, and the demands of the external world. It is the original source of psychological energy, parts of which will later evolve into the Ego and Superego (Freud, 1933, 1940).

The Id's reservoir of psychological energy is derived from two conflicting instinctual drives: the life instinct and the death instinct. The *life instinct,* which Freud called **Eros,** consists of biological urges that perpetuate the existence of the individual and the species—hunger, thirst, physical comfort, and, most important, sexuality. Freud (1915c) used the word **libido** to refer specifically to sexual energy or motivation. The *death instinct,* which Freud (1940) called **Thanatos,** is destructive energy that is reflected in aggressive, reckless, and life-threatening behaviors, including self-destructive actions.

Appealing to the Id How would Freud explain the appeal of a billboard like this one? In Freud's theory, the Id is ruled by the pleasure principle— the instinctual drive to increase pleasure, reduce tension, and avoid pain. Advertisements that encourage us to be hedonistic appeal to the pleasure principle.

The Id is ruled by the **pleasure principle**— the relentless drive toward immediate satisfaction of the instinctual urges, especially sexual urges (Freud, 1920). The Id strives to increase pleasure, reduce tension, and avoid pain. Equipped only with the Id, the newborn infant is completely driven by the pleasure principle. When cold, wet, hungry, or uncomfortable, the newborn wants his needs addressed immediately. As the infant gains experience with the external world, however, he learns that his caretakers can't or won't always immediately satisfy those needs.

Thus, a new dimension of personality develops from part of the Id's psychological energy: the **Ego.** Partly conscious, the Ego represents the organized, rational, and planning dimensions of personality (Freud, 1933). As the mediator between the Id's instinctual demands and the restrictions of the outer world, the Ego operates on the reality principle. The **reality principle** is the capacity to postpone gratification until the appropriate time or circumstances exist in the external world (Freud, 1940).

As the young child gains experience, she gradually learns acceptable ways to satisfy her desires and instincts, such as waiting her turn rather than pushing another child off a playground swing. Hence, the Ego is the pragmatic part of the personality that learns various compromises to reduce the tension of the Id's instinctual urges. If the Ego can't identify an acceptable compromise to satisfy an instinctual urge, such as a sexual urge, it can *repress* the impulse, or remove it from conscious awareness (Freud, 1915a).

In early childhood, the Ego must deal with external parental demands and limitations. Implicit in those demands are the parents' values and morals, their ideas of the right and wrong ways to think, act, and feel. Eventually, the child encounters other advocates of society's values, such as teachers and religious and legal authorities (Freud, 1926). Gradually, these social values move from being externally imposed demands to being *internalized* rules and values.

Establishing the Superego "Don't take something without asking" is just one of the many rules and values we learn as children from parents and other authorities. The internalization of such values is what Freud (1926) called the Superego —the inner voice that is our conscience. When we fail to live up to its moral ideals, the Superego imposes feelings of guilt, shame, and inferiority.

pleasure principle
In Freud's theory, the motive to obtain pleasure and avoid tension or discomfort; the most fundamental human motive and the guiding principle of the Id.

Ego
Latin for *I;* in Freud's theory, the partly conscious rational component of personality that regulates thoughts and behavior and is most in touch with the demands of the external world.

reality principle
In Freud's theory, the awareness of environmental demands and the capacity to accommodate them by postponing gratification until the appropriate time or circumstances exist.

CATHY

Superego
In Freud's theory, the partly conscious self-evaluative, moralistic component of personality that is formed through the internalization of parental and societal rules.

Ego defense mechanisms
In psychoanalytic theory, largely unconscious distortions of thought or perception that act to reduce anxiety.

repression
In psychoanalytic theory, the unconscious exclusion of anxiety-provoking thoughts, feelings, and memories from conscious awareness; the most fundamental Ego defense mechanism.

displacement
In psychoanalytic theory, the Ego defense mechanism that involves unconsciously shifting the target of an emotional urge to a substitute target that is less threatening or dangerous.

By about age five or six, the young child has developed the partly conscious **Superego.** As the internal representation of parental and societal values, the Superego evaluates the acceptability of behavior and thoughts, then praises or admonishes. Like your conscience, the Superego issues demands "like a strict father with a child" (Freud, 1926). It judges your behavior as right or wrong, good or bad. Should you fail to live up to these moral ideals, the Superego can be harshly punitive, imposing feeling of inferiority, guilt, shame, self-doubt, and anxiety.

The Ego Defense Mechanisms: Unconscious Self-Deceptions

The Ego has a difficult task. It must be strong, flexible, and resourceful to successfully mediate conflicts between the instinctual demands of the Id, the moral authority of the Superego, and external restrictions. According to Freud (1923), everyone experiences an ongoing daily battle between the Id and Superego. The Ego must deal with these two warring personality processes, either by giving in to one side or the other or by finding a compromise that satisfies both Id and Superego (Freud, 1926).

When Id or Superego demands threaten to overwhelm the Ego, *anxiety* results (Freud, 1915a). If instinctual Id impulses overpower the Ego, a person may act impulsively and perhaps destructively, as Julian did when he tried to rob the drugstore. In contrast, when Superego demands overwhelm the Ego, an individual may suffer from guilt, self-reproach, or even suicidal impulses for failing to live up to the Superego's moral standards (Freud, 1933, 1936). In Freudian terms, Kenneth's feelings of guilt over Julian were Superego-inspired.

If a realistic solution or compromise is not possible, the Ego may temporarily reduce anxiety by *distorting* thoughts or perceptions of reality through processes that Freud called **Ego defense mechanisms** (Freud, 1915b; A. Freud, 1946). By resorting to these largely unconscious self-deceptions, the Ego can maintain an integrated sense of self while searching for a more acceptable and realistic solution to a conflict between Id and Superego.

The most fundamental Ego defense mechanism is **repression** (Freud, 1915a, 1936). To some degree, repression occurs in every Ego defense mechanism. In simple terms, repression is unconscious forgetting. Unbeknownst to the person, anxiety-producing thoughts, feelings, or impulses are pushed out of conscious awareness into the unconscious.

Repression, however, is not an all-or-nothing psychological process. As Freud (1939) explained, "The repressed material retains its impetus to penetrate into consciousness." In other words, if you encounter a situation that is very similar to one you've repressed, bits and pieces of memories of the previous situation may begin to resurface. In such instances, the Ego may employ other defense mechanisms that allow the urge or information to remain partially conscious.

This is what occurs with the Ego defense mechanism of displacement. **Displacement** occurs when emotional impulses are redirected to a substitute

Sublimation In Freud's view, creative or productive behaviors represented the rechanneling of sexual energy or libido—an Ego defense mechanism he termed *sublimation.* Freud believed that civilization's greatest achievements were the result of the sublimation of instinctual energy into socially acceptable activities. Later personality theorists criticized Freud's refusal to consider creativity a drive in its own right.

TABLE 10.1 The Major Ego Defense Mechanisms

Defense	Description	Examples
Repression	The complete exclusion from consciousness of anxiety-producing thoughts, feelings, or impulses. Most basic defense mechanism.	Three years after being hospitalized for back surgery, the person can remember only vague details about the event.
Displacement	Emotional impulses are redirected toward a substitute person or object, usually one that is less threatening or dangerous than the original source of conflict.	Angered by a neighbor's hateful comment, a mother spanks her daughter for accidentally spilling her milk.
Sublimation	A form of displacement in which sexual urges are rechanneled into productive, nonsexual activities.	A grad student works on her thesis 14 hours a day while her husband is on an extended business trip.
Rationalization	Justifying one's actions or feelings with socially acceptable explanations rather than consciously acknowledging one's true motives or desires.	After being rejected by a large, prestigious college, a student explains that he was glad it turned out that way because he'd be happier at a smaller, less competitive college.
Projection	The attribution of one's own unacceptable urges or qualities to others.	A married women who is sexually attracted to a co-worker accuses him of flirting with her.
Reaction formation	Thinking or behaving in a way that is the extreme opposite of unacceptable urges or impulses.	Threatened by their awakening sexual attraction to girls, adolescent boys tease and torment adolescent girls.
Denial	The failure to recognize or acknowledge the existence of anxiety-provoking information.	An alcoholic fails to acknowledge that he is addicted to a drug.
Undoing	A form of unconscious repentance that involves neutralizing or atoning for an unacceptable action or thought with a second action or thought.	A woman who gets a tax refund by cheating on her taxes makes a larger than usual donation to the church collection on the following Sunday.
Regression	Retreating to a behavior pattern characteristic of an earlier stage of development.	After her parents' bitter divorce, a ten-year-old girl refuses to sleep alone in her room, crawling into bed with her mother.

object or person, usually one that is less threatening or dangerous than the original source of conflict (A. Freud, 1946). For example, the employee angered by his supervisor's unfair treatment may displace his hostility onto other drivers while driving home. He consciously experiences anger, but it is directed toward someone other than its true target, which remains unconscious.

The major defense mechanisms are summarized in Table 10.1. In Freud's view, the drawback to using any defense mechanism is that maintaining these self-deceptions requires psychological energy, energy that is needed to cope effectively with the demands of daily life.

Many psychologically healthy people temporarily use Ego defense mechanisms to deal with stressful events. Using Ego defense mechanisms is often a way of buying time while we consciously or unconsciously wrestle with more realistic solutions for whatever is troubling us. But when defense mechanisms delay or interfere with our use of more constructive coping strategies, they can be counterproductive.

Personality Development:

The Psychosexual Stages

The psychosexual stages include the oral, anal, phallic, latency, and genital stages. What are the core conflicts of the oral, anal, and phallic stages? What is the consequence of fixation? What role does the Oedipus complex play in personality development?

According to Freud (1905), people progress through five psychosexual stages of development. The foundations of adult personality are established during the first five years of life, as the child progresses through the *oral, anal,* and *phallic* psychosexual stages. The *latency stage* occurs during late childhood, while the fifth and final stage, the *genital stage,* begins in adolescence.

Each psychosexual stage represents a different focus of the Id's sexual energies. Freud (1940) contended that "sexual life does not begin only at puberty, but starts with clear manifestations after birth." This statement is often misinterpreted. Freud was *not* saying that an infant experiences sexual

psychosexual stages
In Freud's theory, age-related developmental periods in which the child's sexual urges are expressed through different body areas and the activities associated with those body areas.

Oedipus complex
In Freud's theory, a child's unconscious sexual desire for the opposite-sex parent, usually accompanied by hostile feelings toward the same-sex parent.

identification
In psychoanalytic theory, an Ego defense mechanism that involves reducing anxiety by modeling the behavior and characteristics of another person.

Competing with Mom for Dad? According to Freud, the child identifies with the same-sex parent as a way of resolving sexual attraction toward the opposite-sex parent—the Oedipus complex. He believed that imitating the same-sex parent also played an important role in the development of gender identity and, ultimately, healthy sexual maturity.

urges in the same way as an adult. Instead, Freud believed that the infant or young child expresses primitive sexual urges by seeking sensual pleasure from different body areas. Thus, the **psychosexual stages** are age-related developmental periods in which sexual impulses are focused on different body zones and are expressed through activities associated with these body areas.

Over the first five years of life, the expression of primitive sexual urges progresses from one bodily zone to another in a distinct order: the mouth, the anus, and the genitals. The first year of life is characterized as the *oral stage*. During this time the infant derives pleasure through the oral activities of sucking, chewing, and biting. During the next two years, pleasure is derived through elimination and acquiring control over elimination—the *anal stage*. In the *phallic stage*, pleasure seeking is focused on the genitals.

Fixation: Unresolved Developmental Conflicts

At each psychosexual stage, Freud (1905) believed that the infant or young child is faced with a developmental conflict that must be successfully resolved in order to move on to the next stage. The heart of this conflict is the degree to which parents either frustrate or overindulge the child's expression of pleasurable feelings. Hence, Freud (1940) believed that parental attitudes and the timing of specific child-rearing events, such as weaning or toilet training, leave a lasting influence on personality development.

If frustrated, the child will be left with feelings of unmet needs characteristic of that stage. If overindulged, the child may be reluctant to move on to the next stage. In either case, the result of an unresolved developmental conflict is *fixation* at a particular stage. The person continues to seek pleasure through behaviors that are similar to those associated with that psychosexual stage. For example, the adult who constantly chews gum, smokes, or bites her nails may have unresolved oral psychosexual conflicts.

The Oedipus Complex: A Psychosexual Drama

The most critical conflict that the child must successfully resolve for healthy personality and sexual development occurs during the phallic stage (Freud, 1923, 1940). As the child becomes more aware of pleasure derived from the genital area, Freud believed that the child develops a sexual attraction to the opposite-sex parent and hostility toward the same-sex parent. This is the famous **Oedipus complex,** named after the hero of a Greek myth. Abandoned at birth, Oedipus does not know the identity of his parents. As an adult, Oedipus unknowingly kills his father and marries his mother.

For boys, the Oedipus complex unfolds as a confrontation with the father for the affections of the mother. The little boy feels hostility and jealousy toward his father, but he realizes that his father is more physically powerful. The boy experiences *castration anxiety,* or the fear that his father will punish him by castrating him (Freud, 1933).

To resolve the Oedipus complex and these anxieties, the little boy ultimately joins forces with his former enemy by resorting to the defense mechanism of **identification.** That is, he imitates and internalizes his father's values, attitudes, and mannerisms. There is, however, one strict limitation in identifying with the father: Only the father can enjoy the sexual affections of the mother. This limitation becomes internalized as a taboo against incestuous urges in the boy's developing Superego, a taboo that is enforced by the Superego's use of guilt and societal restrictions (Freud, 1905, 1923).

Girls also ultimately resolve the Oedipus complex by identifying with the same-sex parent and developing a strong Superego taboo against incestuous urges. But the underlying sexual drama in girls follows different themes. The little girl discovers that little boys have a penis and that she does not. She feels a sense of deprivation and loss that Freud termed *penis envy*.

According to Freud (1940), the little girl blames her mother for "sending her into the world so insufficiently equipped." Thus, she develops contempt for and resentment toward her mother. However, in her attempt to take her mother's place with her father, she also *identifies* with her mother. Like the little boy, the little girl internalizes the attributes of the same-sex parent.

Freud's views on female sexuality, particularly the concept of penis envy, are among his most severely criticized ideas. Perhaps recognizing that his explanation of female psychosexual development rested on shaky ground, Freud (1924) admitted, "Our insight into these developmental processes in girls is unsatisfactory, incomplete, and vague."

The Latency and Genital Stages

Freud felt that because of the intense anxiety associated with the Oedipus complex, the sexual urges of male and female children become repressed during the *latency stage* in late childhood. Outwardly, children in the latency stage express a strong desire to associate with same-sex peers, a preference that strengthens the child's sexual identity.

The final resolution of the Oedipus complex occurs in adolescence, during the *genital stage*. As incestuous urges start to resurface, they are prohibited by the moral ideals of the Superego as well as by societal restrictions. Instead, the person directs sexual urges toward socially acceptable substitutes, who often resemble the person's opposite-sex parent (Freud, 1905).

In Freud's theory, a healthy personality and sense of sexuality result when conflicts are successfully resolved at each stage of psychosexual development. Successfully negotiating the conflicts at each psychosexual stage results in the person's capacity to love and in expressions of productive living through one's life work, child rearing, and other accomplishments.

It often happens that a young man falls in love seriously for the first time with a mature woman, or a girl with an elderly man in a position of authority; this is a clear echo of the [earlier] phase of development that we have been discussing, since these figures are able to re-animate pictures of their mother or father.

Sigmund Freud, 1905

CONCEPT REVIEW 10.1

Freud's Psychoanalytic Theory

1. The Id is guided by the _____, while the Ego is guided by the _____.
   a. manifest content; latent content
   b. reality principle; pleasure principle
   c. latent content; manifest content
   d. pleasure principle; reality principle

2. Freud developed the method of _____ to help his patients uncover forgotten memories.
   a. hypnosis   c. free association
   b. catharsis   d. Thanatos

3. The structure of personality that evaluates the morality of behavior is called the
   _____.
   a. Ego   c. libido
   b. Superego   d. repression

4. Eight-year-old Johnny wants to be a truck driver when he grows up, just like his dad. Johnny's acceptance of his father's attitudes and values indicates the process of
   _____.
   a. fixation   c. denial
   b. identification d. projection

5. Every time four-year-old Felix touches his genitals, his parents call him a "dirty little boy" and slap his hands. According to Freud, Felix's frustration may result in an unresolved developmental conflict called _____.
   a. fixation   c. sublimation
   b. identification d. denial

6. Seven-year-old Carolyn prefers to play with her girlfriends and does not like playing with boys very much. Carolyn is probably in the _____ stage of sexual development.
   a. anal   c. latency
   b. phallic   d. genital

collective unconscious
In Jung's theory, the hypothesized part of the unconscious mind that is inherited from previous generations and that contains universally shared ancestral experiences and ideas.

archetypes
In Jung's theory, the inherited mental images of universal human instincts, themes, and preoccupations that are the main components of the collective unconscious.

What we properly call instincts are physiological urges, and are perceived by the senses. But at the same time, they also manifest themselves in fantasies and often reveal their presence only by symbolic images. These manifestations are what I call the archetypes. They are without known origin; and they reproduce themselves in any time or in any part of the world.

Carl Jung, 1964

The Neo-Freudians:
Freud's Descendants and Dissenters

The neo-Freudians followed Freud in stressing the importance of the unconscious and early childhood, but they developed their own personality theories. How did the neo-Freudians generally differ from Freud? What were the key ideas of Jung, Horney, and Adler?

Freud's ideas were always controversial. But by the early 1900s he had attracted a number of followers, many of whom went to Vienna to study with him. Although these early followers developed their own personality theories, they still recognized the importance of many of Freud's basic notions, such as the influence of unconscious processes and early childhood experiences. In effect, they kept the foundations that Freud had established but offered new explanations for personality processes. Hence, these theorists are often called *neo-Freudians* (the prefix *neo* means "new"). The neo-Freudians and their theories are considered part of the psychoanalytic perspective on personality.

In general, the neo-Freudians disagreed with Freud on three key points. First, they took issue with Freud's belief that the primary motivation behind behavior was sexual urges. Second, they disagreed with Freud's contention that personality is fundamentally determined by early childhood experiences. Instead, the neo-Freudians believed that personality can also be influenced by experiences throughout the lifespan. Third, the neo-Freudian theorists departed from Freud's generally pessimistic view of human nature and society.

In Chapter 9, on lifespan development, we described the psychosocial theory of one famous neo-Freudian, Erik Erikson. In this chapter, we'll look at the basic ideas of three other important neo-Freudians: Carl Jung, Karen Horney, and Alfred Adler.

Carl Jung: Archetypes and the Collective Unconscious

Born in a small town in Switzerland, **Carl Jung** (1875–1961) was captivated by the myths, folk tales, and religions of his own and other cultures. After studying medicine, Jung was drawn to the relatively new field of psychiatry because he believed it could provide deeper insights into the human mind (Jung, 1963).

Fascinated by Freud's ideas, Jung began a correspondence with him. At their first meeting, the two men were so compatible that they talked for 13 hours nonstop. Freud called Jung his "adopted son" and his "crown prince." It would be Jung, Freud decided, who would succeed him and lead the international psychoanalytic movement. However, when Jung continued to put forth his own ideas, his close friendship with Freud ultimately ended in bitterness. Eventually, Jung developed his own theory of personality, which he called *analytic psychology*.

Jung rejected Freud's belief that human behavior was fueled by the instinctual drives of sex and aggression. Instead, Jung believed that people are motivated by a more general psychological energy that pushes them to achieve psychological growth, self-realization, and psychic wholeness and harmony. Jung (1963) also believed that personality continued to develop in significant ways throughout the lifespan.

Jung was struck by the universality of many images and themes in different cultures, which also surfaced in his patients' dreams and preoccupations. These observations led to some of Jung's most intriguing ideas, the notions of the collective unconscious and the archetypes.

The Mandala To Jung, the mandala was the archetypal symbol of the self and psychic wholeness. Mandala images are found in cultures throughout the world. Shown here are the Bhavacakra or Buddhist Wheel of Life, from Tibet (top left); a ceremonial Buffalo Robe of the Plains Indians (top right); and a rose window from Chartres Cathedral in France (bottom).

To Jung (1936), the deepest part of the individual psyche was the **collective unconscious,** which is shared by all people and reflects humanity's collective evolutionary history. He described the collective unconscious as containing "the whole spiritual heritage of mankind's evolution, born anew in the brain structure of every individual" (Jung, 1931).

Contained in the collective unconscious are the **archetypes,** the mental images of universal human instincts, themes, and preoccupations (Jung, 1964). Common archetype themes that are expressed in virtually every culture are the hero, the powerful father, the nurturing mother, the witch, the wise old man, the innocent child, and death and rebirth.

Two important archetypes that Jung (1951) described are the *anima* and the *animus*—the representations of feminine and masculine qualities. Jung believed that every man has a "feminine" side, represented by his anima, and every woman has a "masculine" side, represented by her animus. To achieve psychological harmony, Jung believed, it is important for men to recognize and accept their feminine aspects, and for women to recognize and accept the masculine side of their nature.

Not surprisingly, Jung's concepts of the collective unconscious and shared archetypes have been criticized as being unscientific or mystical. Jung's ideas make more sense if you think of the collective unconscious as reflecting shared human experiences. The archetypes, then, can be thought of as symbols that represent the common, universal themes of the human life cycle (McAdams, 1994; Stevens, 1983). These universal themes include birth, achieving a sense of self, parenthood, the spiritual search, and death.

Some of Jung's ideas have gained broad acceptance. For example, Jung (1923) was the first to describe two basic personality types: *introverts,* who focus their attention inward, and *extraverts,* who turn their attention and energy toward the outside world. Finally, Jung's emphasis on the drive toward psychological growth and self-realization anticipated some of the basic ideas of the humanistic perspective on personality, which we'll look at shortly.

Karen Horney: Basic Anxiety and "Womb Envy"

Trained as a Freudian psychoanalyst, **Karen Horney** (pronounced HORN-eye) (1885–1952) emigrated from Germany to the United States during the

Great Depression in the 1930s. Horney noticed distinct differences between her American and German patients. Whereas Freud traced psychological problems to sexual conflicts, Horney found that her American patients were much more worried about their jobs and economic problems than their sex lives. Thus, Horney came to stress the importance of cultural and social factors in personality development—matters which Freud had largely ignored (Horney, 1945).

Horney also stressed the importance of social relationships, especially the parent–child relationship, in the development of personality. She

Man, [Freud] postulated, is doomed to suffer or destroy. . . . My own belief is that man has the capacity as well as the desire to develop his potentialities and become a decent human being, and that these deteriorate if his relationship to others and hence to himself is, and continues to be, disturbed. I believe that man can change and go on changing as long as he lives.

Karen Horney, 1945

believed that disturbances in human relationships, not sexual conflicts, were the cause of psychological problems. Such problems arise from the attempt to deal with *basic anxiety,* which Horney (1945) described as "the feeling a child has of being isolated and helpless in a potentially hostile world."

Horney also sharply disagreed with Freud's interpretation of female development, especially his notion that women suffer from penis envy. What women envy in men, Horney (1926) claimed, is not their penis but their superior status in society. In fact, Horney contended that men often suffer *womb envy,* envying women's capacity to bear children. Neatly standing Freud's view of feminine psychology on its head, Horney argued that *men* compensated for their relatively minor role in reproduction by creating products and ideas through their work and other external accomplishments.

Alfred Adler: Feelings of Inferiority and Striving for Superiority

Born in Vienna, **Alfred Adler** (1870–1937) was an extremely sickly child. Through determination and effort, he overcame his physical weaknesses. After studying medicine, he became associated with Freud. But Adler placed much more emphasis on the importance of conscious thought processes and social motives. Eventually, Adler broke away from Freud to establish his own theory of personality.

To be a human being means to have inferiority feelings. One recognizes one's own powerlessness in the face of nature. One sees death as the irrefutable consequence of existence. But in the mentally healthy person this inferiority feeling acts as a motive for productivity, as a motive for attempting to overcome obstacles, to maintain oneself in life.

Alfred Adler, 1933

Adler (1933b) believed that the most fundamental human motive was *striving for superiority*—the desire to improve oneself, master challenges, and move toward self-perfection and self-realization. Striving toward superiority arises from universal *feelings of inferiority* that are experienced during infancy and childhood, when the child is helpless and dependent on others. These feelings motivate people to *compensate* for their real or imagined weaknesses by emphasizing their talents and abilities, and by working hard to improve themselves. Hence, Adler (1933a) saw the universal human feelings of inferiority as ultimately being constructive and valuable.

However, when people are unable to compensate for specific weaknesses or when their feelings of inferiority are excessive, they can develop an *inferiority complex*—a general sense of inadequacy, weakness, and helplessness. People with an inferiority complex are often unable to strive for mastery and self-improvement.

We've only been able to touch on the highlights of the work of Jung, Horney, and Adler. Like Freud, the neo-Freudians have their own followings among therapists and personality theorists.

Evaluating Freud and the Psychoanalytic Perspective on Personality

The psychoanalytic perspective has had a profound influence on Western culture and on psychology, yet it has also been criticized. What are three criticisms of Freud's theory and, more generally, the psychoanalytic perspective?

Like it or not, Sigmund Freud's ideas have had a profound and lasting impact on our culture and on our understanding of human nature. Today, opinions on Freud span the entire spectrum. Some see him as a genius who discovered

Sigmund Freud—along with Karl Marx, Charles Darwin, and Albert Einstein—is among that small handful of supreme makers of the twentieth-century mind whose works should be our prized possession.

Peter Gay, 1989

Freud's legacy, it is clear, consists chiefly of pseudoscience and cannot be defended on any grounds.

Frederick Crews, 1986

brilliant, lasting insights into human nature. Others contend that Freud was a deeply neurotic, driven man who successfully foisted his twisted personal view of human nature onto an unsuspecting public (Crews, 1996, 1986).

The truth, as you might suspect, lies somewhere in between. Although Freud has had an enormous impact on psychology and on society, there are several valid criticisms of Freud's theory and, more generally, the psychoanalytic perspective. We'll discuss three of the most important problems next.

Inadequacy of Evidence

Freud's theory relies wholly on data derived from his relatively small number of patients and from self-analysis. Most of Freud's patients were well-educated members of the middle and upper classes in turn-of-the-century Vienna. Freud (1916, 1919, 1939) also analyzed the lives of famous historical figures, such as Leonardo da Vinci, and looked to myth, religion, literature, and evolutionary prehistory for confirmation of his ideas. Any way you look at it, this is a rather small and skewed sample from which to draw sweeping generalizations about human nature.

Furthermore, it is impossible to objectively assess Freud's "data," as Freud's therapy sessions were private and he did not take notes. Was Freud imposing his own ideas onto his patients, seeing only what he expected to see? Some critics think so (e.g., Crews, 1996, 1986; P. Robinson, 1993; Masson, 1984a, 1984b).

Lack of Testability

Many psychoanalytic concepts are so vague and ambiguous that they are impossible to objectively measure or confirm (Crews, 1996). For example, how could you operationally define and measure the effects of the pleasure principle, the life instinct, or the Oedipus complex?

Psychoanalytic "proof" often has a "Heads I win, tails you lose" style to it. In other words, psychoanalytic concepts are often impossible to *dis*prove, because even seemingly contradictory information can be used to support Freud's theory. For example, if your memory of childhood doesn't jibe with Freud's description of the psychosexual stages or the Oedipus complex, well, that's because you've repressed it. Freud himself was not immune to this form of reasoning (P. Robinson, 1993). When one of Freud's patients reported a dream that didn't seem to reveal a hidden wish, Freud interpreted the dream as betraying the patient's hidden wish to disprove Freud's dream theory!

As Freud acknowledged, psychoanalysis is better at explaining *past* behavior than at predicting future behavior (Gay, 1989). Indeed, psychoanalytic interpretations are so flexible that a given behavior can be explained by any number of completely different motives. For example, a man who is extremely affectionate toward his wife might be exhibiting displacement of a repressed incestuous urge (he is displacing his repressed affection for his mother onto his wife), reaction formation (he actually hates his wife intensely, so he compensates by being overly affectionate), or fixation at the oral stage (he is overly dependent on his wife).

Nonetheless, some key psychoanalytic ideas *have* been substantiated by empirical research (Westen, 1990). Among these are the ideas that (1) much of mental life is unconscious; (2) early childhood experiences have a critical influence on interpersonal relationships and psychological adjustment in adulthood; and (3) people differ significantly in the degree to which they are able to regulate their impulses, emotions, and thoughts toward adaptive and socially acceptable ends.

Sexism

Many people feel that Freud's theories reflect a sexist view of women. According to Freud (1925), penis envy produces an innate sense of inferiority and shame in women. Freud claimed that women are more vain, masochistic, and emotional than men, and have a lesser ethical and moral sense.

In response, Horney and other female psychoanalysts pointed out that Freud's theory uses male psychology as a prototype. Women are essentially viewed as a deviation from the norm of masculinity (Horney, 1926; Thompson, 1950). Perhaps, Horney suggested, psychoanalysis would have evolved an entirely different view of women if it were not dominated by the male point of view.

The weaknesses in Freud's theory and in the psychoanalytic approach to personality are not minor problems. All the same, Freud made some extremely significant contributions to modern psychological thinking. Most important, he drew attention to the existence and importance of mental processes that occur outside of conscious awareness, an idea that continues to be actively investigated by today's psychological researchers (Kihlstrom & others, 1992; Erdelyi, 1992).

Anna Freud (1895–1982) Although Freud is criticized for his sexist views about female psychology, many women were active in the early psychoanalytic movement. Freud's youngest daughter, Anna, became his chief disciple and the founder of a psychoanalytic school in her own right. Expanding on her father's theory, she applied psychoanalysis to therapy with children. She is shown here addressing a debate on psychoanalysis at the Sorbonne University in Paris in 1950.

The Humanistic Perspective on Personality

> *The humanistic perspective emphasizes free will, self-awareness, and psychological growth. What roles do the self-concept, the actualizing tendency, and unconditional positive regard play in Rogers' personality theory? What are key strengths and weaknesses of the humanistic perspective?*

By the 1950s, the field of psychology was dominated by two completely different perspectives: Freudian psychoanalysis and B. F. Skinner's brand of behaviorism (see Chapter 5). Whereas Freud's theory of personality proposed elaborate and complex internal states, Skinner believed that psychologists should focus on observable behaviors and on the environmental factors that shape and maintain those behaviors (Rogers & Skinner, 1956). As Skinner (1971) wrote, "A person does not act upon the world, the world acts upon him."

The Emergence of the "Third Force"

Another group of psychologists had a fundamentally different view of human nature. In opposition to both psychoanalysis and behaviorism, the humanis-

humanistic psychology
The theoretical viewpoint on personality that generally emphasizes the inherent goodness of people, human potential, self-actualization, the self-concept, and healthy personality development.

actualizing tendency
In Rogers' theory, the innate drive to maintain and enhance the human organism.

tic psychologists championed a "third force" in psychology. **Humanistic psychology** is a view of personality that emphasizes human potential and such uniquely human characteristics as self-awareness and free will.

In contrast to Freud's pessimistic view of people as being motivated by unconscious sexual and destructive instincts, the humanistic psychologists saw people as being innately good. Humanistic psychologists also differed from psychoanalytic theorists by their focus on the *healthy* personality, rather than on psychologically troubled people.

In contrast to the behaviorist view that human and animal behavior is due largely to environmental reinforcement and punishment, the humanistic psychologists believed that people are motivated by the need to grow psychologically. And, rather than focusing strictly on observable behaviors, humanistic psychologists contended that the most important factor in personality is the individual's *conscious, subjective perception of his or her self.*

The two most important contributors to the humanistic perspective were Carl Rogers and Abraham Maslow. In Chapter 8, on motivation, we discussed **Abraham Maslow's** (1908–1970) famous *hierarchy of needs.* Maslow's (1970) research identified several qualities of *self-actualized* people, summarized in Figure 10.2. As you'll see in this section, Rogers also placed considerable importance on the tendency of human beings to strive to fulfill their potential and capabilities.

Maslow's Pyramid

- Self-actualization
- Esteem needs
- Belongingness and love needs
- Safety needs
- Physiological needs

Self-actualized people:
- Realistically perceive themselves, others, and external reality.
- Are spontaneous, natural, and open in their behavior.
- Easily accept themselves and others as they are.
- Focus on problems outside the self.
- Have a strong need for privacy and independence.
- Enjoy and appreciate positive aspects of everyday life.
- Tend to be creative.

FIGURE 10.2 Maslow's Characteristics of Self-Actualized People
Maslow (1970) proposed that human motives are arranged in a hierarchy of needs. Gratification of each need in the hierarchy is required before the next level of motives is activated. At the very top of the hierarchy is the need for self-actualization—the drive toward self-expression, growth, creativity, and the fulfillment of one's potential. From his investigations of psychologically healthy people, Maslow identified attributes that characterize self-actualizers, which are summarized here. Maslow also found that very few people seem to achieve self-actualization as he defined it.

Carl Rogers:

On Becoming a Person

Carl Rogers (1902–1987) grew up in a large, close-knit family in Oak Park, Illinois, a suburb of Chicago. His parents were highly religious and instilled a moral, ethical atmosphere in the home. Rogers planned to become a minister, but switched to the study of psychology. He ultimately enjoyed a long, productive, and distinguished career as a psychotherapist, researcher, writer, and university professor.

Like Freud, Rogers' personality theory developed out of his clinical experiences with his patients, whom he referred to as "clients" to emphasize their active and voluntary participation in therapy. In marked contrast to Freud, Rogers was continually impressed by his clients' drive to grow and develop their potential.

At bottom, each person is asking, "Who am I, really? How can I get in touch with this real self, underlying all my surface behavior? How can I become myself?"

Carl Rogers, 1961

These observations convinced Rogers that the most basic human motive was the **actualizing tendency**—the innate drive to maintain and enhance the human organism. According to Rogers, all other human motives, whether biological or social, were secondary. He compared the actualizing tendency to a child's drive to learn to walk, despite early frustration and falls. To get a taste of the vastly different views of Rogers and Freud, read Critical Thinking Box 10.1, "Freud Versus Rogers on Human Nature."

CRITICAL THINKING 10.1

Freud Versus Rogers on Human Nature

Freud's view of human nature was deeply pessimistic. He believed that the human aggressive instinct was innate, persistent, and pervasive. Were it not for internal Superego restraints and external societal restraints, civilization as we know it would collapse: the destructive instincts of humans would be unleashed. As Freud (1930/1961) wrote in *Civilization and Its Discontents:*

> *Men are not gentle creatures who want to be loved, and who at the most can defend themselves if they are attacked; they are, on the contrary, creatures among whose instinctual endowments is to be reckoned a powerful share of aggressiveness. As a result, their neighbor is for them not only a potential helper or sexual object, but also someone who tempts them to satisfy their aggressiveness on him, to exploit his capacity for work without compensation, to use him sexually without his consent, to seize his possessions, to humiliate him, to cause him pain, to torture and to kill him.* Man is a wolf to man. *Who, in the face of all his experience of life and of history, will have the courage to dispute this assertion?*

In Freud's view, the essence of human nature is destructive. Control of these destructive instincts is necessary; yet societal, cultural, religious, and moral restraints also make people frustrated, neurotic, and unhappy. Why? Because the strivings of the Id toward instinctual satisfaction *must* be frustrated if civilization and the human race are to survive. Hence, as the title of Freud's book emphasizes, civilization is inevitably accompanied by human "discontent."

Carl Rogers strongly disagreed. "I do not discover man to be well characterized in his basic nature by such terms as *fundamentally hostile, antisocial, destructive, evil,*" Rogers (1957a/1989) wrote. Instead, Rogers believed, people were more accurately described as *"positive, forward-moving, constructive, realistic, trustworthy."*

If this is so, how can Rogers account for the evil and cruelty in the world? Rogers didn't deny that people can behave destructively and cruelly. Yet, throughout his life, Rogers insisted that people were innately good. Rogers (1981/1989) explains the existence of evil in this way:

> *My experience leads me to believe that it is* cultural *factors which are the major factor in our evil behaviors. The rough manner of childbirth, the infant's mixed experience with the parents, the constricting, destructive influence of our educational system, the injustice of our distribution of wealth, our cultivated prejudices against individuals who are different—all these elements and many others warp the human organism in directions which are antisocial.*

In sharp contrast to Freud, Rogers (1964/1989) said we should *trust* the human organism, because the human who is truly free to choose will naturally gravitate toward behavior that serves to perpetuate the human race and improve society as a whole:

> *I dare to believe that when the human being is inwardly free to choose whatever he deeply values, he tends to value those objects, experiences, and goals that will make for his own survival, growth, and development, and for the survival and development of others. . . .*

Two great thinkers, two diametrically opposing views of human nature. What do *you* think? Do you agree with Freud that people are inherently driven by aggressive instincts? Must the destructive urges of the Id be restrained by parents, culture, religion, and society if civilization is to continue? Would an environment in which individuals were unrestrained inevitably lead to an unleashing of destructive instincts?

Or is the opposite the case, as Carl Rogers claimed? Are people naturally good? If people existed in a truly free and nurturing environment, would they invariably make constructive choices that would benefit both themselves and society as a whole?

The Self-Concept

Rogers (1959) was struck by how frequently his clients in therapy said "I'm not really sure who I am" or "I just don't feel like myself." This observation helped form the cornerstone of Rogers' personality theory: the idea of the self-concept. The **self-concept** is the set of perceptions and beliefs that you have about yourself, including your nature, your personal qualities, and your typical behavior.

According to Rogers (1980), people are highly motivated to act in accordance with their self-concept. So strong is the need to maintain a consistent self-concept that people will deny or distort experiences that contradict their self-concept.

self-concept
The set of perceptions and beliefs that you hold about yourself.

conditional positive regard
In Rogers' theory, the sense that you will be valued and loved only if you behave in a way that is acceptable to others; conditional love or acceptance.

unconditional positive regard
In Rogers' theory, the sense that you will be valued and loved even if you don't conform to the standards and expectations of others; unconditional love or acceptance.

The self-concept begins evolving early in life. Because they are motivated by the actualizing tendency, infants and young children naturally gravitate toward self-enhancing experiences. But as the child develops a greater sense of self-awareness, there is an increasing need for positive regard. *Positive regard* is the sense of being loved and valued by other people, especially one's parents.

Rogers (1959) maintained that most parents provide their children with **conditional positive regard**—the sense that the child is valued and loved only when she behaves in a way that is acceptable to others. The problem with conditional positive regard is that the child learns to deny or distort her genuine feelings. For example, if little Amy's parents scold and reject her when she expresses angry feelings, her strong need for positive regard will cause her to deny her anger, even when it's justified. Eventually, Amy's self-concept will become so distorted that genuine feelings of anger are denied, because they are inconsistent with her self-concept as "a good girl who never gets angry." Because of the fear of losing positive regard, she cuts herself off from her true feelings.

Rogers believed that feelings, memories, and experiences could be driven from consciousness by being either denied or distorted. But Rogers believed that feelings become denied or distorted not because they are threatening but because they contradict the self-concept. In this case, people are in a state of *incongruence:* their self-concept conflicts with their actual experience (Rogers, 1959). Such a person is continually defending against genuine feelings and experiences that are inconsistent with his self-concept. As this process continues over time, a person progressively becomes more "out of touch" with his true feelings and his essential self, often experiencing psychological problems as a result.

How is incongruence to be avoided? The ideal situation is one in which a child experiences a great deal of unconditional positive regard. **Unconditional positive regard** refers to the child's sense of being unconditionally loved and valued, even if she doesn't conform to the standards and expectations of others. In this way, the child's actualizing tendency is allowed its fullest expression. Rogers believed that parents should provide unconditional acceptance and love of their children, whatever their child's behavior.

Note, however, that Rogers did *not* advocate permissive parenting. He thought that parents were responsible for controlling their children's behavior and for teaching them acceptable standards of behavior. Rogers maintained that parents can discipline their child without undermining the child's sense of self-worth.

For example, parents can disapprove of a child's specific *behavior* without completely rejecting the *child himself.* In effect, the parent's message should be, "I do not value your behavior right now, but I still love and value *you.*" In this way, the child's essential sense of self-worth can remain intact.

Unconditional Positive Regard Rogers contended that healthy personality development is the result of being unconditionally valued and loved as a person. He advocated that parents and teachers should control a child's inappropriate behavior without rejecting the child himself. Such a style of discipline teaches acceptable behaviors without diminishing the child's sense of self-worth.

The Fully Functioning Person

Rogers (1957b/1989) believed that it is through consistent experiences of unconditional positive regard that one becomes a psychologically healthy, fully functioning person. The *fully functioning person* has a flexible, constantly evolving self-concept. He is realistic, open to new experiences, and capable of changing in response to new experiences.

Rather than defending against or distorting his own thoughts or feelings, the person experiences *congruence:* his sense of self is consistent with his emotions and experiences. The actualizing tendency is fully expressed, and he makes conscious choices that move him in the direction of greater growth and the fulfillment of his potential. Rogers (1957b, 1964) believed that the fully functioning person is likely to be creative and spontaneous, and to enjoy harmonious relationships with others.

Evaluating the Humanistic Perspective on Personality

The humanistic perspective has been criticized on two particular points. First, humanistic theories are hard to validate or test scientifically. Humanistic theories tend to be based on philosophical assumptions or clinical observations, rather than on empirical research. For example, concepts like the self-concept, unconditional positive regard, and the actualizing tendency are very difficult to define or measure objectively.

Second, many psychologists believe that humanistic psychology's view of human nature is *too* optimistic. For example, if the actualizing tendency is a universal human motive, why are self-actualized people so hard to find? And, critics claim, humanistic psychologists have minimized the darker, more destructive side of human nature. Can we really account for all the evil in the world by ascribing it to upbringing, society, or culture?

The influence of humanistic psychology has waned since the 1960s and early 1970s. Nevertheless, it has made lasting contributions, especially in the realms of psychotherapy, counseling, education, and parenting (Zimring & Raskin, 1992; Lietaer & others, 1990). The humanistic perspective also promoted the scientific study of such topics as the healthy personality and creativity (e.g., Harrington & others, 1987). Finally, the importance of subjective experience and the self-concept has become widely accepted by psychologists (Markus & Cross, 1990; Markus & Kitayama, 1994).

The Social Cognitive Perspective on Personality

The social cognitive perspective stresses conscious thought processes, self-regulation, and the importance of situational influences. What is the principle of reciprocal determinism? What is the role of self-efficacy beliefs in personality? What are key strengths and weaknesses of the social cognitive perspective?

Have you ever noticed how different your behavior and sense of self can be in different situations? Consider this example: You feel pretty confident as you enter your English composition class. After all, you're pulling an A, and your prof nods approvingly every time you participate in the class discussion, which you do frequently. In contrast, your college algebra class is a disaster. You're worried about passing the course, and you feel so shaky about your skills that you're afraid to even ask a question, much less participate in class. Even a casual observer would notice how differently you behave in the two different situations—speaking freely and confidently in one class, and staring at your desk in hopes that your instructor won't notice you in the other.

social cognitive theory
Bandura's theory of personality, which emphasizes the importance of observational learning, conscious cognitive processes, social experiences, self-efficacy beliefs, and reciprocal determinism.

reciprocal determinism
A model proposed by psychologist Albert Bandura that explains human functioning and personality as caused by the interaction of behavioral, cognitive, and environmental factors.

The idea that a person's conscious thought processes in different situations strongly influence his or her actions is one important characteristic of the *social cognitive perspective* on personality (Cervone, 1997). According to the social cognitive perspective, people are seen as actively processing information from their social experiences. This information influences their goals, expectations, beliefs, and behavior, as well as the specific environments that they choose.

The social cognitive perspective differs from psychoanalytic and humanistic perspectives in several ways (Meichenbaum, 1995; Pervin, 1997). First, rather than basing their approach on self-analysis or insights derived from psychotherapy, social cognitive personality theorists rely heavily on experimental findings. Second, the social cognitive perspective emphasizes conscious, self-regulated behavior rather than unconscious mental influences and instinctual drives. And third, as in our English-versus-algebra-class example, the social cognitive approach emphasizes that our sense of self can vary, depending on our thoughts, feelings, and behaviors in a given situation.

Albert Bandura and Social Cognitive Theory

People possess self-directive capabilities that enable them to exercise some control over their thoughts, feelings, and actions by the consequences they produce for themselves. Psychological function is, therefore, regulated by an interplay of self-generated and external sources of influence.

Albert Bandura, 1986

While several contemporary personality theorists have embraced the social cognitive approach to explaining personality, probably the most influential is **Albert Bandura** (b. 1925). We examined Bandura's now-classic research on observational learning in Chapter 5. In Chapter 8, we encountered Bandura's more recent research on self-efficacy. Here, you'll see how Bandura's ideas on both these topics are reflected in his personality theory called **social cognitive theory.** Social cognitive theory emphasizes the social origins of thoughts and actions, but also stresses active cognitive processes and the human capacity for *self*-regulation.

As Bandura's early research demonstrated, we learn many behaviors by observing, and then imitating, the behavior of other people. But, as Bandura (1997) points out, we don't merely observe people's actions. We also observe the *consequences* that follow people's actions, the *rules* and *standards* that apply to behavior in specific situations, and the ways in which people *regulate their own behavior.* Thus, environmental influences are important, but conscious, self-generated goals and standards also exert considerable control over thoughts, feelings, and actions.

For example, consider your own goal of getting a college education. No doubt many social and environmental factors influenced your decision. In turn, your conscious decision to attend college determines many aspects of your current behavior, thoughts, and emotions. And your goal of attending college classes determines which environment you choose.

Bandura (1997, 1986) explains human behavior and personality as being caused by the interaction of behavioral, cognitive, and environmental factors. He calls this process **reciprocal determinism** (see Figure 10.3). According to this principle, each factor both influences the other factors and is influenced by the other factors. Thus, in Bandura's view, our environment influences our thoughts and actions, our thoughts influence our actions and the environments we choose, our actions influence our thoughts and the environments we choose, and so on in a circular fashion.

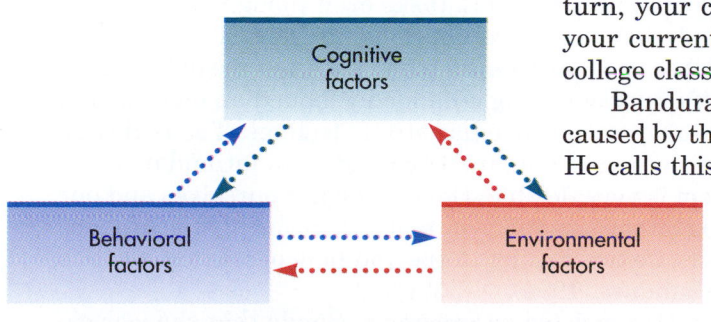

FIGURE 10.3 Reciprocal Determinism (Bandura, 1988)

Self-Efficacy We acquire a strong sense of self-efficacy by meeting challenges and mastering new skills specific to a particular situation. With her mother showing her how to ride her new bike, this three-year-old is well on her way to developing a strong sense of self-efficacy in this domain. Self-efficacy beliefs begin to develop in early childhood, but continue to evolve throughout the lifespan as we encounter new and different challenges.

Beliefs of Self-Efficacy: Anybody Here Know How to Fix a Light Switch?

Collectively, a person's cognitive skills, abilities, and attitudes represent his or her *self-system* (Bandura, 1978). According to Bandura, it is our self-system that guides how we perceive, evaluate, and control our behavior in different situations. Bandura (1997) has found that the most critical elements influencing the self-system are our beliefs of self-efficacy. **Self-efficacy** refers to the degree to which you are subjectively convinced of your own capabilities and effectiveness in meeting the demands of a particular situation.

For example, your authors, Don and Sandy, are at opposite ends of the spectrum in their beliefs of self-efficacy when it comes to repairs around the house. Don thinks he can fix anything, whether he really can or not. Sandy likes to describe herself as "mechanically challenged." When a light switch recently broke in our house, it was obvious that Sandy had very little faith in her ability to fix or replace it: she instantly hollered for help. As Don was investigating the matter, he casually asked Sandy whether *she* could replace the light switch.

"Me? You must be kidding," Sandy immediately responded. "It would never occur to me to even *try* to replace a light switch."

Bandura would be quick to point out how Sandy's weak belief of self-efficacy about electrical repairs has guided her behavior: it would prevent her from even attempting to fix a light switch on her own. When Don reassured Sandy that the directions were right on the light-switch package and that it was a very simple task, Sandy still expressed strong self-doubt about her abilities. "I'd probably blow up the house or burn it down or black out the whole neighborhood," she said.

Albert Bandura would, no doubt, smile at how readily Sandy's remark was an everyday confirmation of his research finding that our beliefs of self-efficacy help shape our imagination of future consequences (Bandura, 1997, 1992a; Ozer & Bandura, 1990). In Sandy's case, her weak belief of self-efficacy has contributed to her imagination of dire future consequences should she attempt this task.

Bandura's concept of self-efficacy makes it easier to understand why people often fail to perform optimally at certain tasks even though they possess the necessary skills. Sandy has made presentations in front of hundreds of people, knows how to slab a geode with a diamond saw, can easily navigate Chicago's rush-hour traffic, and once single-handedly landed an eight-pound northern pike. In all these situations, she has strong feelings of self-efficacy. But hand her a package containing a light switch and she's intimidated.

Hence, our self-system is very flexible. How we regard ourselves and our abilities varies depending on the situations or tasks we're facing. In turn, our beliefs influence the tasks we are willing to try and how persistent we'll be in the face of obstacles (Bandura, 1996).

With the light switch, Don insisted on proving to Sandy that she was capable of changing it. "Well, maybe if I watched you install a couple of them,

self-efficacy
The beliefs that people have about their ability to meet the demands of a specific situation; feelings of self-confidence or self-doubt.

CRITICAL THINKING 10.2

Freud Versus Bandura on Human Aggression

Freud viewed aggression as a universal, unconscious human instinct that must be controlled by the internal restraints of the Superego and the external restraints of culture, society, and morality. In Freud's eyes, aggressive instincts are part of the irrational, impulsive, and unconscious Id.

Social cognitive theorists, however, discount the importance of unconscious instincts or motives. Instead, they emphasize that behavior is driven by conscious goals and motives. Not surprisingly, Albert Bandura has taken issue with Freud's explanation of war and cruelty as being caused by the failure of the rational Ego, the Superego's restraints, and society's laws to control the Id's destructive impulses (see Box

10.1). Bandura (1986) points out that some of the most horrifying examples of human cruelty have involved conscious, *rational* behavior:

> *People frequently engage in destructive activities,* not *because of reduced self-control, but because their cognitive skills and self-control are too well enlisted through moral justification and self-exonerative devices in the service of destructive causes. The infamous extermination procedures of Nazi concentration camps were perfected in laboratories using human victims. In the Nazi value system, where the enslavement and execution of Jewish people were*

viewed as meritorious acts of patriotism, camp commandants proudly compared execution rates as if they were industrial production figures. This monstrous death industry required a methodical program of research and efficient and dedicated management. The massive threats to human welfare are generally brought about by deliberate acts of principle, rather than unrestrained acts of impulse. *[Emphasis added.]*

What do *you* think? Is violent, aggressive, and cruel behavior due to unconscious forces that are out of control? Or is it the result of conscious, deliberate motives?

I might be willing to try it," Sandy finally offered. Sandy's suggestion illustrates how we acquire new behaviors and strengthen our beliefs of self-efficacy in particular situations: through observational learning and mastery experiences (Bandura, 1997, 1990). When we perform a task successfully, our sense of self-efficacy becomes stronger. When we fail to deal effectively with a particular task or situation, our sense of self-efficacy is undermined.

From very early in life, children develop feelings of self-efficacy from their experiences in dealing with different tasks and situations, such as athletic, social, and academic activities (Bandura, 1989b). As Bandura (1992a) points out, developing self-efficacy merely begins in childhood and continues as a lifelong process. Each stage of the lifespan presents new challenges. And just for the record, Sandy *did* successfully replace the broken light switch. Now, about that dripping faucet . . .

Evaluating the Social Cognitive Perspective on Personality

A key strength of the social cognitive perspective on personality is its grounding in empirical, laboratory research. The social cognitive perspective is built on research in learning, cognitive psychology, and social psychology, rather than clinical impressions. And, unlike vague psychoanalytic and humanistic concepts, the concepts of social cognitive theory are scientifically testable—that is, they can be operationally defined and measured. For example, psychologists can study self-efficacy beliefs by comparing subjects who are low in self-efficacy in a given situation with subjects who are high in self-efficacy (e.g., Ozer & Bandura, 1990). Not surprisingly, then, the social cognitive perspective has had a major impact on the study of personality (Pervin, 1997).

Some psychologists feel that the social cognitive approach to personality applies *best* to laboratory research. In the typical laboratory study, the relationships among a limited number of very specific variables are studied. In everyday life, situations are far more complex, with multiple factors converging to affect behavior and personality. Thus, an argument can be made that clinical data, rather than laboratory data, may be more reflective of "the whole person."

The social cognitive perspective also ignores unconscious influences, emotions, or conflicts. Some psychologists argue that the social cognitive theory focuses on very limited areas of personality—learning, the effects of situations, and the effects of beliefs about the self (see Engler, 1995). Thus, it seems to lack the richness of psychoanalytic and humanistic theories, which strive to explain the *whole* person, including the unconscious, irrational, and emotional aspects of personality (Westen, 1990).

Nevertheless, by emphasizing the reciprocal interaction of mental, behavioral, and situational factors, the social cognitive perspective recognizes the complex combination of factors that influences our everyday behavior. By emphasizing the important role of learning, especially observational learning, the social cognitive perspective offers a developmental explanation of human functioning that persists throughout our lifetime. Finally, by emphasizing the self-regulation of behavior, the social cognitive perspective places most of the responsibility for our behavior, and for the consequences that we experience, squarely on our own shoulders.

CONCEPT REVIEW 10.2

Humanistic and Social-Cognitive Perspectives

Determine whether each of the following statements is true or false. If a statement is false, rewrite it to correct it.

_____ **1.** According to Carl Rogers, children's impulses are innately good, and they should never be disciplined.

_____ **2.** Carl Rogers strongly advocated the use of conditional positive regard to enhance the psychological well-being of others.

_____ **3.** The humanistic perspective on personality has been criticized for being too optimistic about human nature.

_____ **4.** According to social cognitive theory, people's behavior is determined solely by environmental influences.

_____ **5.** Self-efficacy beliefs can vary from one situation to another.

The Trait Perspective on Personality

Trait theories focus on describing individual differences. A trait is a relatively stable, enduring predisposition to behave in a certain way. How do surface and source traits differ? What are three influential trait theories? How is the expression of personality traits affected by situational demands?

Suppose we asked you to describe the personality of a close friend. How would you begin? Would you describe her personality in terms of her unconscious conflicts, the congruence of her self-concept, or her level of self-

trait

A relatively stable, enduring predisposition to consistently behave in a certain way.

trait theory

A theory of personality that focuses on identifying, describing, and measuring individual differences.

surface traits

Personality characteristics or attributes that can easily be inferred from observable behavior.

source traits

The most fundamental dimensions of personality; the broad, basic traits that are hypothesized to be universal and relatively few in number.

efficacy? Probably not. Instead, you'd probably generate a list of her personal characteristics, such as *outgoing, cheerful, confident,* and *generous.* This rather common-sense approach to personality is one that is shared by the trait theories (Funder, 1995; Funder & others, 1995).

The trait approach to personality is very different from the theories that we have encountered thus far. The psychoanalytic, humanistic, and social cognitive theories emphasize the *similarities* among people. They focus on discovering the universal processes of motivation and development that explain human personality (Revelle, 1995). While these theories do deal with individual differences, they do so only indirectly. In contrast, the trait approach to personality *focuses primarily on describing individual differences.*

Trait theorists view the person as being a unique combination of personality characteristics or attributes called *traits.* A **trait** is formally defined as a relatively stable, enduring predisposition to behave in a certain way (Pervin, 1994). A **trait theory** of personality, then, is one that focuses on identifying, describing, and measuring individual differences. Think back to our description of the twins, Kenneth and Julian, in the chapter prologue. You can probably readily identify their differing personality traits.

People possess traits to different degrees. For example, a person might be extremely shy, somewhat shy, or not shy at all. Hence, a trait is typically described in terms of a range from one extreme to its opposite. Most people fall in the middle of the range (average shyness), while fewer people fall at opposite poles (extremely shy or extremely outgoing).

Surface Traits and Source Traits

Most of the terms that we use to describe people are **surface traits**—traits that lie on "the surface" and can be easily inferred from observable behaviors. Examples of surface traits include attributes like *happy, exuberant, spacey,* and *gloomy.* The list of potential surface traits is extremely long. Personality researcher Gordon Allport combed through an English-language dictionary and discovered more than 4000 words that described specific personality traits (Allport & Odbert, 1936; John, 1990).

Source traits are thought to be more fundamental than surface traits. As the most basic dimension of personality, a source trait can potentially give rise to a vast number of surface traits (McCrae & John, 1992). Trait theorists believe that there are relatively few source traits (Goldberg, 1993). Thus, one goal of trait theorists has been to identify the most basic set of universal source traits that can be used to describe all individual differences (Pervin, 1994).

Two Representative Trait Theories:
Raymond Cattell and Hans Eysenck

How many source traits are there? Not surprisingly, trait theorists differ in their answers. For example, pioneer trait theorist **Raymond Cattell** (b. 1905) reduced Allport's list of 4,000 terms to about 171 characteristics by eliminating terms that seemed to be redundant or uncommon (see John, 1990). Cattell collected data on a large sample of people who were rated on each of the 171 terms. He then used a statistical technique called *factor analysis* to identify the traits that were most closely related to one another. After further research, Cattell eventually reduced his list to sixteen key personality factors, which are shown in Table 10.2. Cattell (1994) believes that these sixteen personality factors represent the essential source traits of human personality.

Raymond Cattell (b. 1905) Cattell was a strong advocate of the trait approach to personality. His research led to the development of the Sixteen Personality Factor Questionnaire, one of the most widely used psychological tests to assess personality.

TABLE 10.2 Cattell's Sixteen Personality Factors

1. Reserved, unsociable	⟷	Outgoing, sociable
2. Less intelligent, concrete	⟷	More intelligent, abstract
3. Affected by feelings	⟷	Emotionally stable
4. Submissive, humble	⟷	Dominant, assertive
5. Serious	⟷	Happy-go-lucky
6. Expedient	⟷	Conscientious
7. Timid	⟷	Venturesome
8. Tough-minded	⟷	Sensitive
9. Trusting	⟷	Suspicious
10. Practical	⟷	Imaginative
11. Forthright	⟷	Shrewd, calculating
12. Self-assured	⟷	Apprehensive
13. Conservative	⟷	Experimenting
14. Group-dependent	⟷	Self-sufficient
15. Undisciplined	⟷	Controlled
16. Relaxed	⟷	Tense

SOURCE: Adapted from Cattell, 1973.

Raymond Cattell believed that personality could be described in terms of 16 source traits, or basic personality factors. Each factor represents a dimension that ranges between two extremes.

An even simpler model of universal source traits was proposed by **Hans Eysenck** (1916–1997), a British psychologist. Eysenck's methods were similar to Cattell's, but his conception of personality includes just three dimensions. The first dimension is introversion–extraversion, which is the degree to which a person directs his energies outward toward the environment and other people versus inward toward his inner and self-focused experiences. A person who is high on the dimension of *introversion* might be quiet, solitary, and reserved, avoiding new experiences. A person high on the *extraversion* scale would be outgoing and sociable, enjoying new experiences and stimulating environments.

Eysenck's second major dimension is neuroticism–emotional stability. *Neuroticism* refers to a person's predisposition to become emotionally upset, while *stability* reflects a person's predisposition to be emotionally even. Surface traits associated with neuroticism are anxiety, tension, depression, and guilt. At the opposite end, emotional stability is associated with surface traits of being calm, relaxed, and even-tempered.

Eysenck believed that by combining these two dimensions people could be classified into four basic types: introverted-neurotic; introverted-stable; extraverted-neurotic; and extraverted-stable. Each basic type is associated with a different combination of surface traits, as shown in Figure 10.4.

In later research, Eysenck identified a third personality dimension, called *psychoticism* (Eysenck & Eysenck, 1975; Eysenck, 1990). A person high on this trait is antisocial, cold, hostile, and unconcerned about others. A person who is low on psychoticism is warm and caring toward others. In the chapter prologue, Julian might be described as above average on psychoticism, while Kenneth was extremely low on this trait.

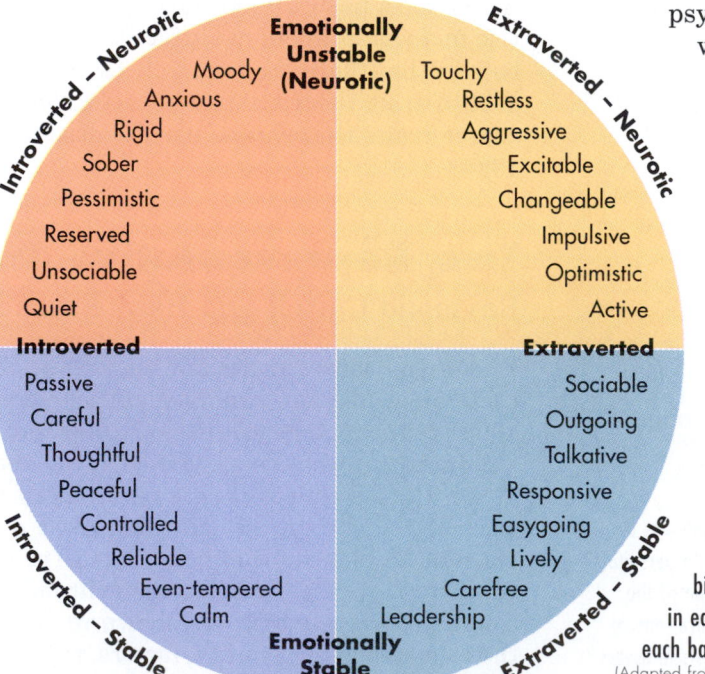

FIGURE 10.4 Eysenck's Theory of Personality Types In Hans Eysenck's representation of the four basic personality types, each type represents a combination of two basic personality dimensions: extraversion–introversion and neuroticism–emotional stability. Note the different surface traits in each quadrant that are associated with each basic personality type.
(Adapted from Eysenck, 1982, Fig. 1.3, p. 9.)

five-factor model of personality
A trait theory of personality that identifies five basic source traits (extraversion, neuroticism, agreeableness, conscientiousness, and openness to experience) as the fundamental building blocks of personality.

TABLE 10.3 The Five-Factor Model of Personality

Low ⟷ High	
Factor 1: Neuroticism	
Calm	Worrying
Even-tempered, unemotional	Temperamental, emotional
Hardy	Vulnerable
Factor 2: Extraversion	
Reserved	Affectionate
Loner	Joiner
Quiet	Talkative
Factor 3: Openness to Experience	
Down-to-earth	Imaginative
Conventional, uncreative	Original, creative
Prefer routine	Prefer variety
Factor 4: Agreeableness	
Antagonistic	Acquiescent
Ruthless	Soft-hearted
Suspicious	Trusting
Factor 5: Conscientiousness	
Lazy	Hard-working
Aimless	Ambitious
Quitting	Persevering

SOURCE: Adapted from McCrae & Costa, 1990, Table 1, p. 3.

This table shows the five major factors, or source traits, of personality, according to "Big Five" theorists Robert McCrae and Paul Costa, Jr. Each factor represents a *dimension,* or range between two extremes. Listed below each major personality dimension are surface traits that are associated with that dimension.

Eysenck (1990) believes that individual differences in personality are due to biological differences among people. For example, Eysenck has proposed that an introvert's nervous system is more easily aroused than an extravert's nervous system. Assuming that people tend to seek out an optimal level of arousal (see Chapter 8), extraverts would seek stimulation from their environment more than introverts would. And, because introverts would be more uncomfortable than extraverts in a highly stimulating environment, introverts would be much less likely to seek out stimulation.

Do introverts and extraverts actually prefer different environments? Researchers John Campbell and Charles Hawley (1982) found that extraverted students tended to study in a relatively noisy, open area of a college library, where there were ample opportunities for socializing with other students. Introverted students preferred to study in a quiet section of the library, where individual carrels and small tables were separated by tall bookshelves. As Eysenck's theory predicts, the introverts preferred study areas that minimized stimulation, while the extraverts preferred studying in an area that provided stimulation.

Sixteen Are Too Many, Three Are Too Few:
The Five-Factor Model

Many trait theorists felt that Cattell's trait model was too complex and that his sixteen personality factors could be reduced to a smaller, more basic set of traits. Yet Eysenck's three-dimensional trait theory seemed too limited, failing to capture other important dimensions of human personality (Block, 1995).

Today, the consensus among many trait researchers is that the essential building blocks of personality can be described in terms of five basic personality dimensions, which are sometimes called "the Big Five" (Goldberg, 1993; Briggs, 1992). According to the **five-factor model of personality,** these five dimensions represent the structural organization of personality traits (McCrae & Costa, 1996).

What are the Big Five? Different trait researchers describe the five basic traits somewhat differently (Johnson & Ostendorf, 1993; Zuckerman & others, 1993). However, the most commonly accepted five factors are: extraversion, neuroticism, agreeableness, conscientiousness, and openness to experience. Table 10.3 describes the Big Five traits, as defined by personality theorists Robert McCrae and Paul Costa, Jr. Note that Factor 1, neuroticism, and Factor 2, extraversion, are essentially the same as Eysenck's first two personality dimensions.

The five-factor structure of personality has been found in a variety of cultures using a variety of measures. In Canada, Finland, Poland, Germany, and other European cultures, people have been found to describe personality in much the same way, using terms that are generally consistent with the Big Five model (Paunonen & others, 1992). The same finding is seen among Filipinos, an example of the Big Five being found in a non-Western culture (Church & Katigbak, 1989).

How can we account for the seeming universality of the Big Five trait structure? Psychologist David Buss (1991) has one intriguing explanation. Buss thinks we should look at the utility of these factors from an evolutionary perspective. He believes that the Big Five traits reflect the personality dimensions that are the most important in the "social landscape" to which humans have had to adapt. Being able to identify who has social power (extraversion), who is likely to share resources (agreeableness), and who is trustworthy (conscientiousness) enhances our likelihood of survival.

The Continuity of Traits over the Lifespan
Kenneth's conscientiousness was a trait that was evident throughout his life. Because he was too old to join the military when the United States entered World War II, Kenneth volunteered his legal expertise to the American Red Cross, providing them with legal services for the western half of the United States.

The Great Debate:

Is Behavior Influenced More by Traits or by Situations?

Traits are assumed to be relatively stable, enduring aspects of an individual's personality. According to trait theorists, then, individual traits should be relatively consistent over time and in different situations.

Research has shown that traits are indeed remarkably stable over *time* (Costa & McCrae, 1994; McCrae, 1993). A young adult who is very extraverted, emotionally stable, and relatively open to new experiences is likely to grow into an older adult who could be described in much the same way (McCrae & Costa, 1990). Kenneth's conscientiousness and his willingness to help others were consistent themes throughout his long life. Likewise, Julian's lack of self-control and impulsiveness seemed to be traits that were consistent from childhood to adulthood.

Traits, then, are relatively consistent over time. But are traits consistent across different *situations*? In other words, if you know that Joan is quite extraverted, can you reliably *predict* how she will behave in different situations, such as during a classroom discussion, at a soccer game, on a date, at a family gathering, or during a job interview?

The great debate over whether people's behavior is influenced more by their traits or by the situation in which they find themselves began in the late 1960s. Social cognitive theorist Walter Mischel fired the opening shot. In a very influential book, *Personality and Assessment* (1968), he reviewed dozens of personality studies. He concluded that, at best, there was only a weak relationship between a person's traits as measured by personality tests and the person's behavior in a specific situation. Mischel claimed that behavior was much more strongly influenced by the specific external situation than by internal traits.

The trait theorists were not about to take this challenge lying down, and a heated debate ensued. Seymour Epstein helped lead the counterattack, pointing out that one shouldn't expect to find a high correlation between a personality trait and behavior on a *single* occasion (Epstein, 1979, 1983a, 1983b; Epstein & O'Brien, 1985). It would be like trying to use a student's math aptitude test score to predict the student's answer on question 5 on an algebra test next Tuesday afternoon.

Similarly, knowing that an individual scored high on neuroticism doesn't necessarily mean that she will feel tense, anxious, and depressed on a particular Friday night. Instead, Epstein argued, we must look at larger numbers of occasions. Using the same two examples, the student with a high aptitude for mathematics will, *on the average,* perform well on arithmetic tests; the person with a high neuroticism score will, *on the average,* experience more frequent bad moods than the person with a low score.

So what's the bottom line here? Is behavior more strongly influenced by a person's traits or by the situation they happen to be in? Today,

Is Behavior More Influenced by Situations or by Personality Traits? These basketball fans are jubilantly celebrating a Chicago Bulls victory. It's doubtful that they would behave the same way in church or during a psychology class. Clearly, situations can and do influence our behavior. For the most part, however, our expression of personality traits tends to be consistent across a wide range of situations.

most psychologists agree that personality traits are basically consistent in different situations. Human behavior, however, is the result of a complex *interaction* between traits and situations. People *do* respond, sometimes dramatically, to the demands of a particular situation. But the situations that people choose, and the characteristic way that they respond to similar situations, are likely to be consistent with their individual personality dispositions (Mischel & Shoda, 1995; Mischel, 1990).

Personality Traits and Behavioral Genetics:
Just a Chip off the Old Block?

> *Some theorists believe that personality traits are largely genetic in origin. To what degree are personality traits inherited? What are key strengths and weaknesses of the trait perspective?*

Do personality traits run in families? Are personality traits determined by genetics? Many trait theorists, like Raymond Cattell and Hans Eysenck, believe that traits are at least partially genetic in origin. For example, our daughter Laura has always been outgoing and sociable, traits that she shares with both her parents. But is she outgoing because she inherited that trait from us? Or is she outgoing because we modeled and reinforced outgoing behavior? How do psychologists study the relative contributions that genes and environment make to personality traits?

The field of **behavioral genetics** studies the effects of genes and heredity on behavior. Most behavioral genetics studies on humans involve measuring similarities and differences among members of a large group of people who are genetically related to different degrees. The basic research strategy is to compare the degree of difference among subjects to their degree of genetic relatedness. If a trait is genetically influenced, then the more closely two people are genetically related, the more you would expect them to be similar on that trait (see Chapter 7).

Such studies may involve comparisons between identical twins and fraternal twins, or comparisons between twins reared apart and identical twins reared together (see Box 10.3). Adoption studies, in which adopted children are compared to their biological and adoptive families, are also used in behavioral genetics.

Evidence gathered from twin studies and adoption studies shows that certain personality traits *are* substantially influenced by genetics. The evidence for genetic influence is particularly strong for extraversion and neuroticism, two of the Big Five personality traits (Plomin & others, 1994; Plomin, 1990). Twin studies have also found that openness to experience and conscientiousness, two other Big Five traits, are influenced by genetics, although to a lesser degree than extraversion and neuroticism (Bergeman & others, 1993). Thus, heredity seems to play a significant role in four of the Big Five personality traits: extraversion, neuroticism, openness to experience, and conscientiousness (Bouchard, 1994).

So is personality completely determined by genetics? Not at all. As behavioral geneticists Robert Plomin and Richard Rende (1991) explain, "The same data that point to significant genetic influence provide the best available evidence for the importance of nongenetic factors. . . . Behavioral variability is due at least as much to environment as to heredity." In other words, the influence of environmental factors on personality traits is at least equal to the influence of genetic factors. Some additional evidence that underscores this point is that identical twins are most alike in early life. As the twins grow up, leave home, and encounter different experiences and environments, their personalities become more different (McCartney & others, 1990).

behavioral genetics
An interdisciplinary field that studies the effects of genes and heredity on behavior.

IN FOCUS 10.3

Explaining Those Amazing Identical-Twin Similarities

As part of the ongoing "Minnesota Study of Twins Reared Apart" at the University of Minnesota, researchers David Lykken, Thomas Bouchard, and their colleagues (1992) have been studying a very unusual group of people: over 100 pairs of identical and fraternal twins who were separated at birth or in early childhood and raised in different homes. Shortly after the study began in 1980, the researchers were struck by some of the amazing similarities between identical twins—similarities in occupations, hobbies, personality traits, habits, and sometimes even their life histories, despite the fact that the twins had been separated for many years.

One of the most famous cases is that of the "Jim twins," who had been separated for close to forty years. Like many of the other reunited twins, the two Jims had similar heights, postures, and voice and speech patterns. More strikingly, both Jims had married and divorced women named Linda, and then married women named Betty. One Jim named his son James Allan, while the other Jim named his son James Alan. Both Jims bit their nails, chain-smoked Salems, and enjoyed working in their basement workshops. And both Jims had vacationed at the same Florida beach, driving there in the same model Chevrolet (Lykken & others, 1992).

Granted, such similarities could simply be due to coincidence (see Wyatt & others, 1984). Linda, Betty, James, and Alan are not exactly rare names in

the United States. And literally thousands of people buy the same model car every year, just as thousands of people vacation in Florida. Besides, if you look closely at any two people of the same age, sex, and culture, there are bound to be similarities. It's probably a safe bet, for example, that *you* enjoy eating pizza and often wear jeans and T-shirts.

But it's difficult to dismiss as mere coincidences all the striking similarities between identical twins in the Minnesota study. Lykken and his colleagues (1992) point out numerous quirky similarities that occurred in the identical twins they studied but did not occur in the fraternal-twin pairs.

For example, in the entire sample of twins, there were only two subjects who had been married five times; two subjects who habitually wore seven rings; and two who left love notes around the house for their wives. In each case, the two were identical twins. And only two subjects independently (and correctly) diagnosed a problem with researcher Bouchard's car—a faulty wheel bearing. Again, the two were members of an identical-twin pair.

While Lykken and his colleagues acknowledge that some identical-twin similarities are probably due to coincidence, such as the Jim twins marrying women with the same first names, others are probably genetically influenced.

So does this mean that there's a gene for getting married five times or wearing seven rings? Not exactly. While some physical characteristics and diseases are influenced by a single gene,

complex psychological characteristics, such as your personality, are influenced by a large number of genes acting in combination (Plomin, 1990). Unlike fraternal twins and regular siblings, identical twins share the same specific *configuration* of interacting genes. Lykken and his colleagues suggest that many complex psychological traits, including the strikingly similar idiosyncrasies of identical twins, may be the result of a unique configuration of interacting genes.

Lykken and his colleagues call certain traits *emergenic traits* because they appear (or *emerge*) only out of a unique configuration of many interacting genes. Although they are genetically influenced, emergenic traits do not run in families. To illustrate the idea of emergenic traits, consider the couple of average intelligence who give birth to an extraordinarily gifted child. By all predictions, this couple's offspring should have normal, average intelligence. But because of the unique configuration of the child's genes acting in combination, extraordinary giftedness emerges (Lykken & others, 1992).

Finally, it's important to point out that there were many differences, as well as similarities, between the identical twins in the Minnesota study. For example, one twin was prone to depression while the other was not; one twin was an alcoholic while the other did not drink. So, even with identical twins, it's important to remember that personality is only *partly* determined by genetics.

Evaluating the Trait Perspective on Personality

While psychologists continue to disagree on how many basic traits exist, they do generally agree that people can be described and compared in terms of basic personality traits. But like the other personality theories, the trait approach has its weaknesses (Block, 1995).

One criticism is that trait theories don't really explain human personality (Pervin, 1994). Instead, they simply label general predispositions to behave in a certain way.

TABLE 10.4 The Major Personality Perspectives

Perspective	Key Theorists	Key Themes and Ideas
Psychoanalytic	Sigmund Freud	Influence of unconscious psychological processes; importance of sexual and aggressive instincts; lasting effects of early childhood experiences
	Carl Jung	The collective unconscious, archetypes, and psychological harmony
	Karen Horney	Importance of parent–child relationship; defending against basic anxiety; womb envy
	Alfred Adler	Striving for superiority, compensating for feelings of inferiority
Humanistic	Carl Rogers	Emphasis on subjective experiences, psychological growth, free will, striving toward capabilities, and inherent goodness
	Abraham Maslow	Behavior as motivated by hierarchy of needs and striving for self-actualization; focus on psychologically healthy people
Social cognitive	Albert Bandura	Reciprocal interaction of behavioral, cognitive, and environmental factors; emphasis on conscious thoughts, self-efficacy beliefs, self-regulation, and goal setting
Trait	Raymond Cattell	Emphasis on measuring and describing individual differences; sixteen source traits of personality
	Hans Eysenck	Three basic dimensions of personality: introversion–extraversion, neuroticism–emotional stability, and psychoticism
	Robert McCrae and Paul Costa, Jr.	Five-factor model: five basic dimensions of personality: neuroticism, extraversion, openness to experience, agreeableness, conscientiousness

A second criticism is that trait theorists don't attempt to explain how or why individual differences develop. When you think about it, saying that trait differences are partly due to genetics and partly due to environmental influences isn't really saying very much.

A third criticism is that trait approaches generally fail to address other important personality issues, such as the basic motives that drive human personality, the role of unconscious mental processes, how beliefs about the self influence personality, or how psychological change and growth occur (McAdams, 1992). Conspicuously absent are the grand conclusions about the essence of human nature that characterize the psychoanalytic and humanistic theories. So, while trait theories are useful in describing individual differences and predicting behavior, there are limitations to their usefulness.

As you've seen, each of the major perspectives on personality has contributed to our understanding of human personality. The four perspectives are summarized in Table 10.4.

Our discussion of personality would not be complete without a description of how personality is formally evaluated and measured. In the next section, we'll briefly survey the two main approaches that are used in personality assessment: projective tests and self-report inventories.

Assessing Personality: Psychological Tests

Personality can be measured by projective tests and self-report inventories. How are projective tests and self-report inventories administered and scored? What are the strengths and weaknesses of projective tests and self-report inventories?

When we discussed intelligence tests in Chapter 7, we described what makes a good psychological test. Beyond intelligence tests, there are literally hundreds of **psychological tests** that can be used to assess abilities, aptitudes, interests, and personality (see Conoley & Impara, 1995; Aiken, 1994). Any psychological test is useful insofar as it achieves two basic goals: (1) it accurately and consistently reflects a person's characteristics on some dimension, and (2) it predicts a person's future psychological functioning or behavior (Kaplan & Saccuzzo, 1993).

psychological test
A test that assesses a person's abilities, aptitudes, interests, or personality, based on a systematically obtained sample of behavior.

In this section, we'll look at the very different approaches used in the two basic types of personality tests—projective tests and self-report inventories. After looking at some of the most commonly used tests in each category, we'll evaluate the strengths and weaknesses of each approach.

Projective Tests:

Like Seeing Things in the Clouds

Projective tests developed out of psychoanalytic approaches to personality. In the most commonly used projective tests, a person is presented with a vague image, such as an inkblot or an ambiguous scene, then asked to describe what he "sees" in the image. The person's response is thought to be a projection of his unconscious conflicts, motives, psychological defenses, and personality traits. Notice that this is very similar to the defense mechanism of *projection,* which was described in Table 10.1.

The first projective test was the famous **Rorschach Inkblot Test,** published by Swiss psychiatrist Hermann Rorschach in 1921 (Hertz, 1992). The Rorschach test consists of ten cards, five that show black-and-white inkblots and five that depict colored inkblots. One card at a time, the person describes whatever she sees in the inkblot. The examiner records the person's responses verbatim and also observes her behavior, gestures, and reactions.

Numerous scoring systems exist for the Rorschach. Interpretation is based on such criteria as whether the person reports seeing animate or inanimate objects, human or animal figures, and movement, and whether the person deals with the whole blot or just fragments of it (Exner, 1993).

The Rorschach Inkblot Test Because he died the year after his inkblot test was published, Hermann Rorschach (1884–1922) never knew how popular his projective test would become. The Rorschach Inkblot Test is sometimes used to "break the ice" in clinical interviews.

A more structured projective test is the **Thematic Apperception Test,** abbreviated **TAT,** which was first discussed in Chapter 8. In the TAT, the person looks at a series of cards, each depicting an ambiguous scene. The person is asked to create a story about the scene, including what the characters are feeling and how the story turns out. The stories are scored for the motives, needs, anxieties, and conflicts of the main character, and how conflicts are resolved (Bellak, 1993). As with the Rorschach, interpreting the TAT involves the subjective judgment of the examiner.

The Thematic Apperception Test Developed by psychologists Christiana Morgan and Henry Murray, the TAT involves creating a story about an ambiguous scene, like the one shown on the card this young man is holding. The person is thought to project his own motives, conflicts, and other personality characteristics into the story he creates. According to Murray (1943), "Before he knows it, he has said things about an invented character that apply to himself, things which he would have been reluctant to confess in response to a direct question."

Strengths and Weaknesses of Projective Tests

Although sometimes used in research, projective tests are mainly used to help assess emotionally disturbed individuals (see Kaplan & Saccuzzo, 1993). The primary strength of projective tests is that they provide a wealth of qualitative information about an individual's psychological functioning, information that can be explored further in psychotherapy.

However, there are several drawbacks to projective tests (see Aiken, 1994; Cronbach, 1990). First, the testing situation or the examiner's behavior can influence a person's responses. Second, the scoring of projective tests is highly subjective, requiring the examiner to make numerous judgments about the person's responses. Consequently, two examiners may test the same individual and arrive at different conclusions. Third, projective tests often fail to produce consistent results. If the same person takes a projective test on two separate occasions, very different results may be found. Finally, projective tests are poor at predicting future behavior.

projective test
A type of personality test that involves a person interpreting an ambiguous image; used to assess unconscious motives, conflicts, psychological defenses, and personality traits.

Rorschach Inkblot Test
A projective test using inkblots, developed by Swiss psychiatrist Hermann Rorschach in 1921.

Thematic Apperception Test (TAT)
A projective personality test that involves creating stories about each of a series of ambiguous scenes.

The bottom line? Despite their widespread use, hundreds of studies of projective tests seriously question their *validity* (that the tests measure what they purport to measure) and their *reliability* (the consistency of test results) (see Rorer, 1990). Nonetheless, they remain very popular, especially among clinical psychologists (Butcher & Rouse, 1996).

Self-Report Inventories:
Has Anybody Got an Eraser?

Self-report inventories typically use a paper-and-pencil format and take a direct, structured approach to assessing personality. The person answers specific questions or rates herself on various dimensions of behavior or psychological functioning. Often called *objective personality tests,* self-report inventories contain items that have been shown by previous research to differentiate between people on a particular personality characteristic. Unlike projective tests, self-report inventories are objectively scored by comparing a person's answers to standardized norms collected on large groups of people.

The most widely used self-report inventory is the **Minnesota Multiphasic Personality Inventory (MMPI)** (Butcher & Rouse, 1996). First published in the 1940s and revised in the 1980s, the current version is referred to as the *MMPI-2.* The MMPI consists of over 500 statements. The person responds to each statement with "True," "False," or "Cannot say." Topics include social, political, religious, and sexual attitudes, physical and psychological health, interpersonal relationships, and abnormal thoughts and behaviors (Graham, 1993). Sample MMPI items are shown in Table 10.5.

Designed to help in the diagnosis of psychological disorders, the MMPI is widely used by clinical psychologists and psychiatrists to assess patients. It is also used to evaluate the mental health of candidates for such occupations as police officers, doctors, nurses, and professional pilots.

What keeps people from simply answering items in a way that makes them look psychologically healthy? Like many other self-report inventories, the MMPI has special scales to detect whether a person is answering honestly and consistently (Butcher & Williams, 1992). For example, if someone responds "True" to items like "I *never* put off until tomorrow what I should do today" and "I *always* pick up after myself," it's probably a safe bet that the person is inadvertently or intentionally distorting his responses.

In contrast to the MMPI, the California Personality Inventory and the Sixteen Personality Factor Questionnaire are personality inventories that are designed to assess normal populations. Of the 462 true–false items on the **California Personality Inventory (CPI),** nearly half are drawn from the MMPI. The CPI provides measures on such characteristics as interpersonal effectiveness, self-control, independence, and empathy. Profiles generated by the CPI are used to predict such things as high school and college grades, delinquency, and job performance (Gough, 1989).

The **Sixteen Personality Factor Questionnaire (16PF®)** was originally developed by Raymond Cattell and is based on his trait theory. The 16PF uses a forced-choice format in which the person must respond to each item by choosing one of three alternatives. Just as the test's name implies, the results generate a profile on Cattell's sixteen personality factors. Each personality factor is represented as a range, with a person's score falling somewhere along the continuum between the two extremes (see Figure 10.5). The 16PF is widely used for career counseling, marital counseling, and evaluating employees and executives (Karson & O'Dell, 1989).

TABLE 10.5 Simulated MMPI-2 Items

Most people will use somewhat unfair means to gain profit or an advantage rather than lose it.

I am often very tense on the job.

The things that run through my head sometimes are horrible.

Sometimes there is a feeling like something is pressing in on my head.

Sometimes I think so fast I can't keep up.

I am worried about sex.

I believe I am being plotted against.

I wish I could do over some of the things I have done.

SOURCE: MMPI-2®.

self-report inventory
A type of psychological test in which a person's responses to standardized questions are compared to established norms.

Minnesota Multiphasic Personality Inventory (MMPI)
A self-report inventory that assesses personality characteristics and psychological disorders; used to assess both normal and disturbed populations.

California Personality Inventory (CPI)
A self-report inventory that assesses personality characteristics in normal populations.

Sixteen Personality Factor Questionnaire (16PF)
A self-report inventory developed by Raymond Cattell that generates a personality profile with ratings on sixteen trait dimensions.

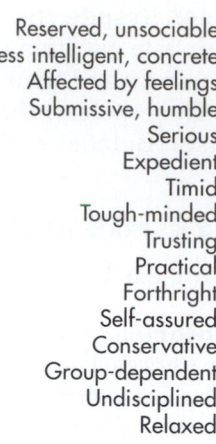

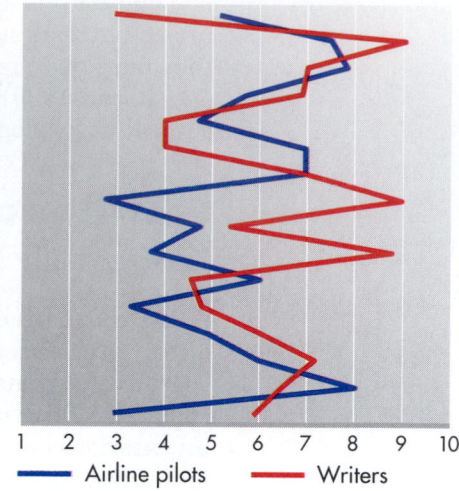

FIGURE 10.5 The 16PF: Example Questions and Profiles

The 16PF, developed by Raymond Cattell, is a self-report inventory that contains 185 items. When scored, the 16PF generates a personality profile. In the example shown, personality profiles of airline pilots and writers are compared. Cattell (1973) found that pilots are more controlled, more relaxed, more self-assured, and less sensitive than writers.

(Cattell & others, 1993.)

Strengths and Weaknesses of Self-Report Inventories

The two most important strengths of self-report inventories are *standardization* and the *use of established norms* (see Chapter 7). Each person receives the same instructions and responds to the same items. The results of self-report inventories are objectively scored and compared to norms established by previous research. In fact, the MMPI, the CPI, and the 16PF can all be scored by computer.

As a general rule, the reliability and validity of self-report inventories are far greater than those of projective tests. Literally thousands of studies have demonstrated that the MMPI, the CPI, and the 16PF provide accurate, consistent results that can be used to generally predict behavior (Anastasi, 1988).

However, self-report inventories also have their weaknesses. First, despite the inclusion of items that are designed to detect deliberate deception, there is considerable evidence that people can still successfully fake responses and answer in socially desirable ways (Anastasi, 1988). Second, some people are prone to responding in a set way, such as consistently answering "True" whether the item accurately reflects them or not. And some tests, like the MMPI and CPI, include hundreds of items. Taking these tests can become quite tedious, and people may lose interest in carefully choosing the most appropriate response.

Third, people are not always accurate judges of their own behavior, attitudes, or attributes. And some people defensively deny their true feelings, needs, and attitudes, even to themselves (Shedler & others, 1993). For example, a person might indicate that she enjoys parties, even though she actually avoids social gatherings whenever possible.

To sum up, personality tests are generally useful strategies that can provide insights about the psychological makeup of people. But no personality test, by itself, is likely to provide a definitive description of a given individual. In practice, psychologists and other professionals usually combine personality test results with behavioral observations and background information, including interviews with family members, co-workers, or other significant people.

Finally, people can and often do change over time, especially when their life circumstances undergo a significant change. Hence, projective tests and self-report inventories provide a barometer of personality and psychological functioning only at the time of the test.

SCIENCE VERSUS PSEUDOSCIENCE 10.4

Is Your Personality Written in the Stars?

Pseudoscientific explanations for personality, such as astrology, have existed long before any of the personality theories described in this chapter. In fact, the history of astrology can be traced back over 4,000 years (Dean & others, 1996). Astrology's basic premise is that the positions of the planets and stars at the time and place of your birth determine your personality and destiny. Originally, astrology was based on the theory that the earth was the center of the solar system, with the stars, the planets, and the sun revolving around the earth (Crowe, 1990). This theory was, of course, scientifically refuted in the early 1600s by Galileo, the Italian astonomer who invented the telescope.

Today, belief in astrological interpretations and predictions remains widespread. Surveys of college students have found that over 30 percent believe in astrology (Duncan & others, 1992; Clarke, 1991). Every year, about 40 million Americans seek astrological guidance from one of the approximately 200,000 practicing astrologers (Glick & others, 1989). About 1,200 North American newspapers carry astrology columns—yet another testament to astrology's widespread popularity (Kurtz & Fraknoi, 1986).

Just how valid is astrology in assessing personality? Can the claims of astrologers be scientifically tested? As it turns out, there is no shortage of scientific investigations of the abilities of astrologers to assess personality characteristics. Let's consider Shawn Carlson's (1985) carefully designed study.

Carlson's (1985) study involved 30 American and European astrologers who were considered to be among the best by their peers in the astrological community. A panel of astrological advisers was also involved in helping Carlson design his study. All the participating astrologers agreed beforehand that Carlson's study was a "fair test" of astrological claims.

In the first part of Carlson's study, the astrologers developed astrological profiles for 177 subjects based on each person's time, date, and place of birth. Each subject was later shown three astrological profiles—one that was based on their time and place of birth, and two randomly chosen astrological profiles of other subjects in the study. The question was simple: Could the subject pick out his own personality profile from the three astrological profiles? If the subjects did no better than merely guessing, you would expect them to be correct about one-third of the time.

In the second part of Carlson's study, 116 of the subjects completed the California Personality Inventory (CPI). As noted in the chapter, the CPI is one of the most widely used personality inventories and has been shown to be scientifically valid in hundreds of studies (Kramer & Conoley, 1992). All the astrologers in the study were familiar with reading CPI profiles. The astrologers were given a subject's astrological profile and three CPI profiles. All the astrologer had to do was match the person's astrological profile with the same person's CPI profile.

Carlson also presented the subjects with three CPI profiles. One was their own and two were randomly chosen. All the subjects had to do was identify which CPI profile they thought was theirs. If the astrologers or the subjects did no better than merely guessing, you would expect them to be correct only one-third of the time.

The results of Carlson's study? When presented with three astrological profiles, the subjects were correct only 33 percent of the time, meaning that they did *no better than chance* at identifying their own astrological profiles. Interestingly, the subjects were *also* unable to select their own CPI profile at a rate better than chance! In other words, Carlson's findings cast doubt on the ability of people to subjectively evaluate the accuracy of *any* kind of personality description.

How did the astrologers do when they tried to match a subject's astrological profile with his or her CPI profile? The astrologers were correct only 34 percent of the time—they performed no better than someone merely guessing. Carlson (1985) summarized the results of his study in this way:

Great pains were taken to insure that the experiment was unbiased and to make sure that astrology was given every reasonable chance to succeed. It failed. Despite the fact that we worked with some of the best astrologers in the country, recommended by the advising astrologers for their expertise in astrology and in their ability to use the CPI, despite the fact that every reasonable suggestion made by the advising astrologers was worked into the experiment, despite the fact that the astrologers approved the design and predicted 50 percent as the "minimum" effect they would expect to see, astrology failed to perform at a level better than chance.

Carlson's findings are not isolated, by any means (see Dean & others, 1996; French & others, 1991). In a thoughtful review of scientific research on astrology, University of Hawaii researcher Richard Crowe (1990) concluded: "Popular and serious astrology have absolutely no reliable basis in scientific fact. Statistically, astrology does not stand up to any valid test that can be applied."

Trait Theories and Personality Assessment

1. Trait theories focus on:
   a. individual differences.
   b. individual similarities.
   c. stages of personality development.
   d. universal processes of motivation.

2. Surface traits are to source traits as:
   a. aggression is to violent behavior.
   b. friendly is to extraversion.
   c. conscientiousness is to personality.
   d. relaxed is to tense.

3. Which of the following is one of the "Big Five"?
   a. Oklahoma State   c. conscientiousness
   b. psychoticism   d. trusting

4. Dana took the same personality test twice within three months. She obtained very different results each time. Which test did she most likely take?
   a. MMPI   c. 16PF
   b. TAT   d. CPI

5. A key strength of the MMPI and the 16PF is:
   a. They provide a wealth of qualitative information about the individual.
   b. They are unstructured.
   c. They are standardized.
   d. Scoring relies on the examiner's expertise and clinical judgment.

APPLICATION

Possible Selves: Imagine the Possibilities

Some psychologists believe that a person's self-concept is not a singular mental self-image, as Carl Rogers proposed, but a *multifaceted system* of related images and ideas (Hermans, 1996; Markus & Kunda, 1986). This collection of related images about yourself reflects your goals, values, emotions, and relationships (Markus & Cross, 1990; Markus & Wurf, 1987).

According to psychologist Hazel Markus and her colleagues, an important aspect of your self-concept has to do with the images of the selves that you *might* become—your **possible selves**. Possible selves are highly personalized, vivid, futuristic images of the self that reflect hopes, fears, and fantasies. As Markus and co-researcher Paula Nurius (1986) write, "The possible selves that are hoped for might include the successful self, the creative self, the rich self, the thin self, or the loved and admired self, whereas the dreaded possible selves could be the alone self, the depressed self, the incompetent self, the alcoholic self, the unemployed self, or the bag lady self."

The Influence of Hoped-for and Dreaded Possible Selves

Possible selves are more than just idle daydreams or wishful fantasies. In fact, possible selves influence our behavior in important ways (Markus & Nurius, 1986; Oyserman & others, 1995). We're often not aware of the possible selves that we have incorporated into our self-concepts. Nevertheless, they can serve as powerful forces that either activate or stall our efforts to reach important goals. Your incentive, drive, and motivation are greatly influenced by your possible selves, and so are your decisions and choices about future behavior.

Imagine that you harbored a hoped-for possible self of becoming a professional musician. You would probably practice with greater regularity and intensity than someone who does not hold a vivid mental picture of performing solo at Carnegie Hall or being named Performer of the Year at the American Country Music Awards.

Dreaded possible selves can also influence behavior, whether they are realistic or not. Consider Don's father, Kenneth. Although never wealthy, Kenneth was financially secure throughout his long life. Yet Kenneth had lived through the Great Depression and witnessed firsthand the financial devastation that occurred in the lives of countless people. Kenneth seems to have harbored a dreaded possible self of becoming penniless. When Kenneth died, the family found a $100 bill tucked safely under his mattress.

Conversely, a positive possible self, even if it is not very realistic, can protect an individual's self-esteem in the face of failure (Markus & Nurius, 1986). A high school girl who thinks she is unpopular with her classmates may console herself with visions of a possible self as a famous scientist who snubs her intellectually inferior classmates at her ten-year class reunion. As Hazel Markus and Paula Nurius (1986) explain:

> *Positive possible selves can be exceedingly liberating because they foster hope that the present self is not immutable. At the same time,*

negative possible selves can be powerfully imprisoning because their [emotional impact] and expectations may stifle attempts to change or develop.

Possible Selves, Self-Efficacy Beliefs, and Motivation

Self-efficacy beliefs are closely connected to the idea of possible selves. Performing virtually any task involves the construction of a possible self that is capable and competent of performing the action required (Oyserman & others, 1995; Ruvolo & Markus, 1992).

Thus, people who vividly imagine possible selves as "successful because of hard work" persist longer and expend more effort on tasks than do people who imagine themselves as "unsuccessful despite hard work" (Ruvolo & Markus, 1992). The motivation to achieve academically increases when your possible selves include a future self who is successful because of academic achievement (Oyserman & others, 1995).

Applying the Research: Assessing Your Possible Selves

How can you apply these research findings to *your* life? First, it's important to stress again that we're often unaware of how the possible selves we've mentally constructed influence our beliefs, actions, and self-evaluations. Thus, the first step is to consciously assess the role that your possible selves play in your life.

Take a few moments and jot down the "possible selves" that are active in your working self-concept. To help you in this task, write three responses to each of the following questions (Oyserman & others, 1995):

1. Next year I expect to be . . .
2. Next year I am afraid that I will be . . .
3. Next year I want to avoid becoming . . .

After focusing on the short-term future, take these same questions and extend them further to five years from now or even ten years from now. Most likely, certain themes and goals will consistently emerge. Now the critical questions:

- How are your possible selves affecting your *current* motivation, goals, feelings, and decisions?

- Are your possible selves even remotely plausible?
- Are they pessimistic and limiting?
- Are they unrealistically optimistic?

Finally, ask yourself honestly: What realistic strategies are you using to try to become like the self that you want to become? To avoid becoming the selves that you dread?

These questions should help you gain some insight into whether your possible selves are influencing your behavior in productive, constructive ways. If they are not, now is an excellent time to think about replacing or modifying the possible selves that operate most powerfully in your own self-concept. To a large extent, who we become is guided by who we *imagine* we'll become. Just imagine the possibilities of who *you* could become!

Summary · **Personality**

What Is Personality?

- *Personality* is defined as an individual's unique and relatively consistent patterns of thinking, feeling, and behaving. Personality theories attempt to explain how people are similar, why they are different, and why every individual is unique.

- The four major theoretical perspectives on personality are the psychoanalytic, humanistic, social cognitive, and trait perspectives.

The Psychoanalytic Perspective on Personality

- Psychoanalysis was founded by Sigmund Freud. It stresses the unconscious, the importance of sex and aggression, and the influence of early childhood experience. Freud's theory was extremely controversial throughout his lifetime and remains so today.

- Freud believed that behavior is strongly influenced by the unconscious. The contents of the unconscious can surface in disguised form in free associations, dreams, slips of the tongue, and seeming accidents.

- Personality consists of three psychological processes: Id, Ego, and Superego. The Id is fueled by instinctual energy and ruled by the pleasure principle. The Ego is partly conscious and is ruled by the reality principle. The Superego is partly conscious and represents internalized moral values and rules.

- Anxiety results when the demands of the Id or the Superego threaten to overwhelm the Ego. Ego defense mechanisms are used to reduce anxiety by distorting either thoughts or reality. Repression is involved in all Ego defense mechanisms.

- The psychosexual stages are age-related developmental periods in which sexual impulses are expressed through different body zones and activities associated with these body areas. The foundations of adult personality are laid down during the first five years of life by the child's progression through the oral, anal, and phallic stages. One result of the Oedipus complex is that children come to identify with the same-sex parent. Fixation at a particular stage may result if the developmental conflicts are not successfully resolved. The latency and genital stages occur during late childhood and adolescence.

- The neo-Freudians believed in the importance of the unconscious and early childhood experience, but disagreed with other aspects of Freud's theory. Carl Jung emphasized psychological growth and proposed the existence of the collective unconscious and the archetypes. Karen Horney emphasized the role of social relationships in protecting against basic anxiety and objected to Freud's views on female development, particularly his idea of penis envy. Alfred Adler believed that the fundamental human motive was to strive for superiority.

- Freud's theory has been criticized for resting on insufficient evidence, being difficult to test, and being sexist.

The Humanistic Perspective on Personality

- The humanistic perspective was championed as the "third force" in psychology. It emphasized human potential, psychological growth, self-awareness, and free will. Important humanistic theorists were Carl Rogers and Abraham Maslow.

- Rogers believed that the most basic human motive was the actualizing tendency. He viewed the self-concept as the most important aspect of personality. Conditional positive regard by parents or other caregivers causes a person to deny or distort aspects of experience, leading to a state of incongruence with regard to the self-concept. In contrast, unconditional positive regard leads to a state of congruence. The fully functioning person experiences congruence, the actualizing tendency, and psychological growth.

- The humanistic perspective on personality has been criticized for being difficult to scientifically validate or test and for being too optimistic.

The Social Cognitive Perspective on Personality

- The social cognitive perspective stresses the role of conscious thought processes, goals, and self-regulation.

- Reciprocal determinism emphasizes the interaction of behavioral, cognitive, and environmental factors in behavior and personality.

- Self-efficacy beliefs influence behavior, performance, motivation, and persistence.

- Social cognitive theories emphasize the interaction of multiple factors in determining personality and behavior. While a key strength of this perspective is its grounding in empirical research, it has been criticized for its limited view of human personality, which ignores unconscious conflicts and emotions.

The Trait Perspective on Personality

- The trait perspective focuses on measuring and describing individual differences. Surface traits can be easily inferred from observable behaviors. Source traits are thought to represent the basic, fundamental dimensions of personality.

- Raymond Cattell believed that there were sixteen basic personality factors, while Hans Eysenck proposed that there were three basic personality dimensions. Eysenck believes that the extraversion–introversion dimension may reflect physiological differences.

- According to the five-factor model, there are five basic personality dimensions: extraversion, neuroticism, agreeableness, conscientiousness, and openness to experience.

- Traits are generally stable over time and across situations, although situations do influence how and whether traits are expressed.

- Behavioral genetics research uses twin and adoption studies to measure the relative influence of genetics and environment. Extraversion, neuroticism, openness to experience, and conscientiousness seem to have a significant genetic component.

- The trait perspective is useful in describing individual differences and predicting behavior. Trait theories have been criticized for their failure to explain human personality and the development of individual differences.

Assessing Personality: Psychological Tests

- The two basic types of personality tests are projective tests and self-report inventories. Projective tests developed out of the psychoanalytic approach, and include the Rorschach Inkblot Test and the Thematic Apperception Test.

- Projective tests provide qualitative information about an individual. They have some weaknesses: Responses may be affected by the examiner or the situation; scoring is very subjective; results may be inconsistent; and they do not predict behavior well.

- Self-report inventories are objectively scored and differentiate among people on particular personality characteristics. Self-report inventories include the MMPI, CPI, and 16PF. The reliability, validity, and predictive value of self-report inventories are high. However, people do not always respond honestly or accurately to items in self-report inventories. Psychological tests provide one measure of personality at a particular point in time.

Key Terms

personality (p. 361)

personality theory (p. 361)

psychoanalysis (p. 362)

free association (p. 363)

unconscious (p. 364)

Id (p. 364)

Eros (p. 364)

libido (p. 364)

Thanatos (p. 364)

pleasure principle (p. 365)

Ego (p. 366)

reality principle (p. 365)

Superego (p. 366)

Ego defense mechanisms (p. 366)

repression (p. 366)

displacement (p. 366)

psychosexual stages (p. 368)

Oedipus complex (p. 368)

identification (p. 368)

collective unconscious (p. 371)

archetypes (p. 371)

humanistic psychology (p. 375)

actualizing tendency (p. 375)

self-concept (p. 376)

conditional positive regard (p. 377)

unconditional positive regard (p. 377)

social cognitive theory (p. 379)

reciprocal determinism (p. 379)

self-efficacy (p. 380)

trait (p. 383)

trait theory (p. 383)

surface traits (p. 383)

source traits (p. 383)

five-factor model of personality (p. 385)

behavioral genetics (p. 387)

psychological test (p. 389)

projective test (p. 390)

Rorschach Inkblot Test (p. 390)

Thematic Apperception Test (TAT) (p. 390)

self-report inventory (p. 391)

Minnesota Multiphasic Personality Inventory (MMPI) (p. 391)

California Personality Inventory (CPI) (p. 391)

Sixteen Personality Factor Questionnaire (16PF) (p. 391)

possible selves (p. 394)

Key People

Alfred Adler (1870–1937) Austrian physician who broke with Sigmund Freud and developed his own psychoanalytic theory of personality, which emphasized social factors and the motivation toward self-improvement and self-realization; key ideas included the inferiority complex.

Albert Bandura (b. 1925) Contemporary American psychologist who is best known for his research on observational learning and his social cognitive theory of personality; key ideas include self-efficacy beliefs and reciprocal determinism.

Raymond Cattell (b. 1905) British-born American psychologist who developed a trait theory that identifies sixteen essential source traits or personality factors; also developed the widely used self-report personality test, the Sixteen Personality Factor Questionnaire (16PF).

Hans Eysenck (1916–1997) German-born British psychologist who developed a trait theory of personality that identifies the three basic dimensions of personality as neuroticism, extraversion, and psychoticism.

Sigmund Freud (1856–1939) Austrian physician who founded psychoanalysis, which is both a comprehensive theory of personality and a form of psychotherapy; emphasized the role of unconscious determinants of behavior and early childhood experiences in the development of personality and psychological problems; key ideas include Id, Ego, and Superego, the psychosexual stages of development, and the Ego defense mechanisms.

Karen Horney (1885–1952) German-born American psychoanalyst who emphasized the role of social relationships and culture in personality; sharply disagreed with Freud's characterization of female psychological development, especially his notion that women suffer from penis envy; key ideas included basic anxiety.

Carl G. Jung (1875–1961) Swiss psychiatrist who broke with Sigmund Freud to develop his own psychoanalytic theory of personality, which stressed striving toward psychological harmony; key ideas included the collective unconscious and archetypes.

Abraham Maslow (1908–1970) American psychologist who was one of the founders of humanistic psychology and emphasized the study of healthy personality development; developed a hierarchical theory of motivation based on the idea that people will strive for self-actualization, the highest motive, only after more basic needs have been met; key ideas included the hierarchy of needs and self-actualization.

Carl Rogers (1902–1987) American psychologist who was one of the founders of humanistic psychology; developed a theory of personality and form of psychotherapy that emphasized the inherent worth of people, the innate tendency to strive toward one's potential, and the importance of the self-concept in personality development; key ideas included the actualizing tendency and unconditional positive regard.

CONCEPT REVIEW 10.1 Page 369

1. d
2. c
3. b
4. b
5. a
6. c

CONCEPT REVIEW 10.2 Page 382

1. False. Rogers believed it is the parents' responsibility to guide and control their children's behavior.
2. False. Rogers advocated the use of unconditional positive regard.
3. True.
4. False. Social cognitive theory holds that human behavior is determined by the interaction of environmental, cognitive, and behavioral factors.
5. True.

CONCEPT REVIEW 10.3 Page 394

1. a   4. b
2. b   5. c
3. c

Chapter

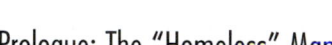

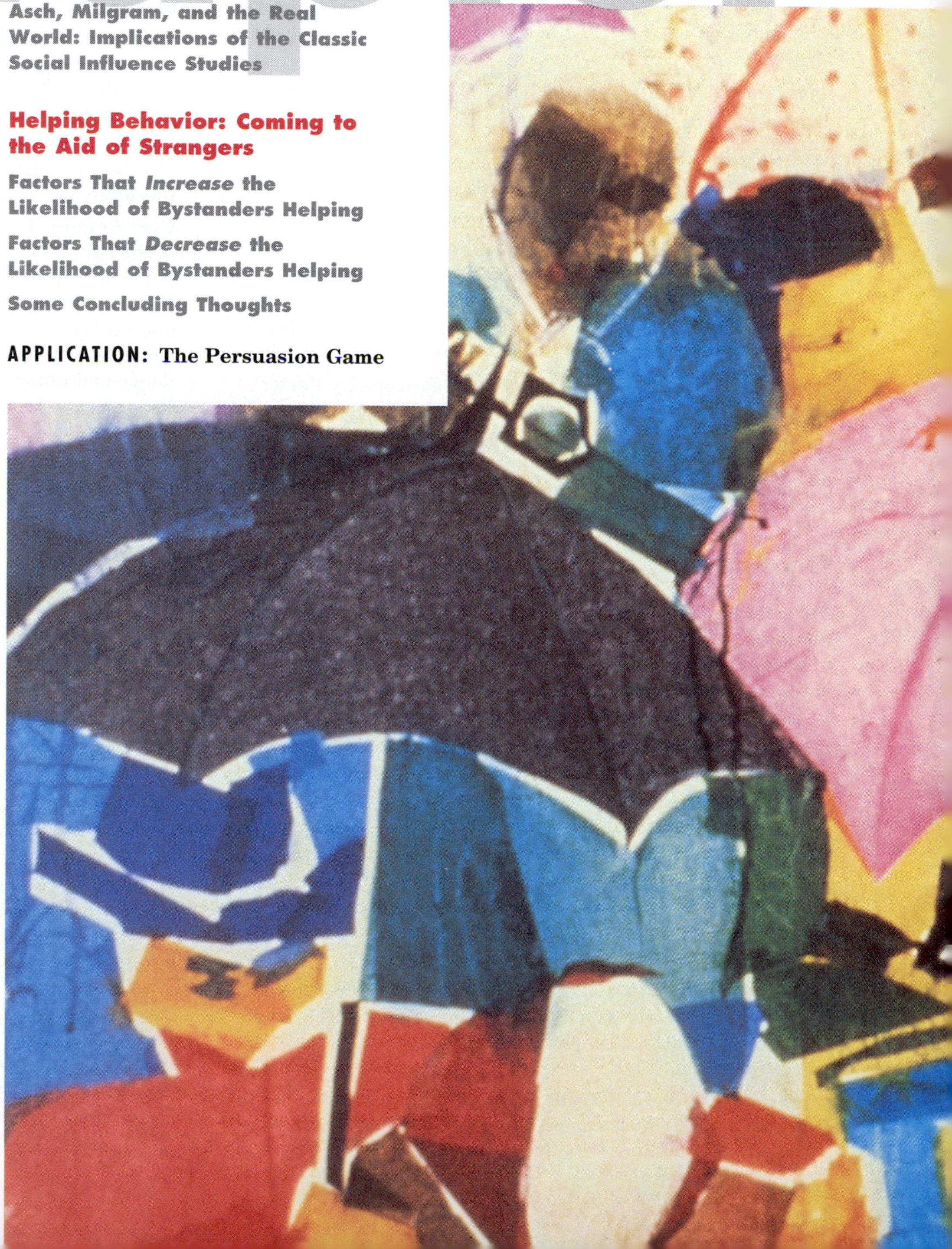

11

Social Psychology

Prologue: The "Homeless" Man

Remember Erv and Fern, Sandy's parents, from Chapter 5? A few years ago, Fern and Erv got two free plane tickets when they were "bumped" from an overbooked flight. They decided to use their free plane tickets to visit a city they had always wanted to see—San Francisco. Even though Fern was excited about the trip, she was also anxious about visiting the earthquake zone. Mostly, they both wanted to see the famous sights, eat seafood, wander through shops, and explore used bookstores, which is Erv's favorite hobby.

As it turned out, Fern and Erv were both quite taken by the beauty and charm of San Francisco. But they were also disturbed by the number of homeless people they saw on the city streets, sleeping in the doorways of expensive shops and restaurants. Especially Fern, who has a heart of gold and is known among her family and friends for her willingness to help others, even complete strangers.

On the third morning of their San Francisco visit, Erv and Fern were walking along one of the hilly San Francisco streets near the downtown area. That's when Fern saw a scruffy-looking man in faded jeans sitting on some steps, holding a cup. Surely this was one of San Francisco's less fortunate, Fern thought to herself. Without a moment's hesitation, Fern rummaged through her purse, walked over to the man, and dropped a handful of quarters in his cup.

"Hey, lady! What the hell d'ya think you're doing!?!" the man exclaimed, jumping up.

"Oh, my! Aren't you homeless!?" Fern asked, turning bright red with embarrassment.

"Lady, this *is* my home," the man snapped, motioning with his thumb to the house behind him. "I live here! And that's my cup of coffee you just ruined!"

Fortunately, the "homeless" man had a sense of humor. After fishing Fern's quarters out of his coffee, he chatted with the out-of-towners, enlightening them on the extraordinary cost of San Francisco real estate. As they parted, the not-so-homeless man recommended a couple of his favorite seafood restaurants to Erv and Fern.

Like Fern, we all try to make sense out of our social environment. We constantly make judgments about the traits, motives, and goals of other people. And, like Fern, sometimes we make mistakes! In this chapter, we will look at how we interpret our social environment, including how we form impressions of other people. We'll explore how our behavior, including our willingness to help others, is influenced by the social environment and other people. In the process, we'll come back to Erv and Fern's incident with the "homeless" man to illustrate several important concepts.

Introduction

Social Psychology

Why did Fern think the man on the steps was homeless? How did the "homeless" man initially interpret Fern's efforts to help him? And in contrast to Fern, not everyone who feels compassion toward the homeless acts in accordance with that attitude. Why did Fern do so?

These are the kinds of issues that social psychologists study. **Social psychology** is the scientific study of the way individuals think, feel, and behave in social situations. In this chapter, we're going to focus on two basic areas of social psychology. We'll begin by exploring different dimensions of social cognition. **Social cognition** refers to how we form impressions of other people, how we interpret the meaning of other people's behavior, and how our behavior is affected by our attitudes (Fiske, 1993). Later in the chapter, we'll look at **social influence,** which focuses on how our behavior is affected by situational factors and other people. The study of social influence includes such questions as why we conform to group norms, what compels us to obey an authority figure, and when people will help a stranger.

Person Perception

Person perception refers to the mental processes we use to form judgments about other people. What four principles does this process follow? How do social categories and implicit personality theories influence person perception?

social psychology
The branch of psychology that studies how people think, feel, and behave in social situations.

social cognition
The study of the mental processes people use to make sense out of their social environment.

social influence
The study of the effect that situational factors and other people have on an individual's behavior.

Consider the following scenario: You're attending a college in the middle of a big city and commute from your apartment to the campus via the subway. Today you stayed a bit later than usual on campus, so the rush hour is pretty much over. As a seasoned subway rider, you know you're safer when the subway is full of commuters. So as you step off the platform into the subway car, you're feeling just a bit anxious. The car is more than half full. If you want to sit down, you'll have to share a seat with some other passenger. You quickly survey your fellow passengers. In a matter of seconds, you must decide which stranger you'll share your ride home with, elbow to elbow, thigh to thigh. How will you decide?

Even if you've never ridden on a subway, it doesn't matter. We could just as easily use picking a seat on a bus or in a crowded movie theater. What these situations share in common is a task that each of us is confronted with almost every day: On the basis of very limited information, we must quickly draw conclusions about the nature of people who are complete strangers to us. We also have to make some rough predictions as to how these strangers are likely to behave. How do we arrive at these conclusions?

Person perception refers to the mental processes we use to form judgments and draw conclusions about the characteristics of others. Person perception is an active and subjective process that always occurs in some *interpersonal context* (E. Jones, 1990). Every interpersonal context has three key components:

- the characteristics of the individual you are attempting to size up
- your own characteristics as the perceiver
- the specific situation in which the process occurs

Each component influences the conclusions you reach about other people. As a psychological process, person perception follows some basic principles (see Jones, 1990; Fiske, 1993; Fiske & Neuberg, 1990). We'll illustrate these basic principles using the subway scenario.

Principle 1. Your reactions to others are determined by your perceptions of them, not by who or what they "really" are.
Put simply, you treat others as you perceive them to be. So, as you step inside the subway car, you quickly choose not to sit next to the big, burly-looking man with a scowl on his face. Why? Because *you* perceive Mr. Burly-Surly as potentially threatening. This guy's picture is probably on the FBI bulletin board at the post office for being an axe murderer, you think. Of course, he could just as easily be a burly florist who's surly because he's getting home late. It doesn't matter. Your behavior toward him is determined by your subjective perception of him.

Principle 2. Your goals in a particular situation determine the amount and kind of information you collect about others.
Your goal in this situation is simple: you want to share a subway seat with someone who will basically leave you alone. Hence, you focus your attention on the characteristics of other people that seem to be relevant to your goal, ignoring details that are unrelated to it (Hilton & Darley, 1991; Swann, 1984). After all, you're not looking for a date for Saturday night, a plumber, or a lab partner for your biology class. If you were, you'd focus on very different aspects of the other people in the situation.

Principle 3. In every situation, you evaluate people partly in terms of how you expect them to act in that situation.
Whether you're in a classroom, restaurant, or public restroom, your behavior is governed by **social norms**—the "rules," or expectations, for appropriate behavior in that social situation. Riding a subway is no exception to this principle (Milgram, 1992). For example, you don't sit next to someone else when empty seats are available, you don't try to borrow your seatmate's newspaper, and you tend to avoid eye contact with others.

These "subway rules" aren't posted anywhere, of course. Nevertheless, violating these social norms will draw attention from others and probably make them quite uneasy. So as you size up your fellow subway passengers, you're partly evaluating their behavior in terms of how people-riding-the-subway-at-night-in-a-big-city should behave.

person perception
The mental processes we use to form judgments and draw conclusions about the characteristics and motives of others.

social norms
The "rules," or expectations, for appropriate behavior in a particular social situation.

BIZARRO

I'D LIKE TO TALK TO YOU ABOUT THE WAY YOU'VE BEEN DRESSING AT WORK, JIM. IT DOESN'T REALLY BEFIT AN EXECUTIVE OF AN HERBAL TEA COMPANY.

Heavenly Blend HERBAL TEA

Principle 4. Your self-perception also influences how you perceive others and how you act on your perceptions. Your decision about whom to sit next to is also influenced by how you perceive your *self*. For example, if you think of yourself as looking a bit threatening (even though you're really a mild-mannered biology major), you may choose to sit next to the twenty-something guy with a briefcase rather than the anxious-looking middle-aged woman who's clutching her purse with both hands.

In combination, these four basic principles underscore that person perception is not a one-way process in which we objectively survey other people and then logically evaluate their characteristics. Instead, the context, our self-perceptions, and the perceptions we have of others all interact. Each component plays a role in the judgments we form of others (E. Jones, 1990).

Social Categorization:

Using Mental Shortcuts in Person Perception

Social categorization is the mental process of classifying people into groups on the basis of common characteristics. Much of this mental work is automatic and spontaneous, and it often occurs outside of your conscious awareness (Macrae & others, 1994; Bargh & others, 1996).

When you have limited time to form your impressions and limited information about a person, like the other passengers in the subway car, you tend to rely on very broad social categories, such as the other person's gender, race, age, and occupation (Fiske, 1993; Fiske & Neuberg, 1990). So you glance at a person and quickly categorize him as "Asian male, twenty-something, probably a college student."

Using social categories has both disadvantages and advantages. On the one hand, relegating someone to a social category on the basis of superficial information ignores that person's unique qualities. In effect, you're jumping to conclusions about a person that are based on very limited information. Sometimes, these conclusions are incorrect—as Fern was when she categorized the man with a cup in his hand as "homeless."

On the other hand, relying on social categories is a natural, adaptive cognitive process. After all, social categories provide us with considerable basic information about other people. Using social categories allows us to mentally organize and remember information about others more efficiently and effectively (Macrae & others, 1994; Fiske, 1993).

Using Social Categories We often use superficial cues like clothing and context to assign people to social categories and draw conclusions about their behavior. For example, you might characterize some people in this crowd as belonging to the category of "businessmen" because they are wearing suits and ties—and conclude that they were on their way to or from work. What other social categories are evident here?

When it's important to your goals to perceive another person as accurately as possible, you're less likely to rely on automatic categorization (Fiske & Neuberg, 1990; Fiske & Taylor, 1991). Instead, you go into mental high gear, consciously and deliberately exerting mental effort to understand the other person better and to form a more accurate impression (Fiske, 1993). You might also check the impressions that you form by seeking additional information, such as calling a job applicant's previous employers.

Implicit Personality Theories:
He's *Not* That Kind of Person!

Closely related to social categories are implicit personality theories. An **implicit personality theory** is a network of assumptions or beliefs about the relationships among various types of people, traits, and behaviors. Through previous social experiences, we form cognitive schemas about the traits and behaviors associated with different "types" of people. When we perceive someone to be a particular "type," we often assume that the person will display these traits and behaviors (Sedikides & Anderson, 1994).

Like social categories, implicit personality theories can be useful as mental shortcuts in perceiving other people. But just like social categories, implicit personality theories are not always accurate. In some instances, they can even be dangerously misleading.

"Pogo the Clown" Dressed as "Pogo the Clown," John would visit sick children in the hospital to cheer them up. He was also a successful building contractor and a local precinct captain. Given that information, what sorts of personal qualities would you expect him to display?

Consider a man named John whom Sandy met when she was a research associate at a University of Chicago research institute. John was a divorced, slightly overweight, middle-aged businessman who had built up a successful contracting and remodeling business. He lived in a quiet suburban neighborhood, where he was well-liked. Every year John threw a block party for his neighbors, and he often helped them with minor home repairs. He was involved in local politics and civic organizations. And John regularly volunteered at a nearby hospital, where he would dress up as "Pogo the Clown," perform magic tricks, and pass out candy to sick and injured children.

Sounds like the kind of person you wouldn't mind knowing, doesn't he? Sandy met John under somewhat different circumstances. When John came to see the psychiatrist for whom Sandy was a research associate, John was shackled in leg irons and handcuffs and flanked by three police officers. The psychiatrist had been appointed by the courts to evaluate John's mental condition. Outside the clinic, a squadron of police had sealed off every possible escape route from the area. Stationed on the roofs of the nearby buildings were police sharpshooters.

Why were so many police guarding a guy who dressed up as a clown and entertained sick children? Because this man was John Wayne Gacy, "the undisputed champion of American serial killers," as *Newsweek* described him (S. Holmes, 1994). Gacy was subsequently convicted of murdering 33 boys and young men, most of whom he had buried in a crawlspace under his suburban home. After years of legal appeals, Gacy was executed in 1994.

One reason Gacy had escaped detection for so many years was that he contradicted the implicit personality theory that most people have for a serial killer. Indeed, most of us find it difficult to believe that a ruthless murderer would also be well-liked by his neighbors and successful in business —or that he would compassionately visit sick children in the hospital.

Although they can lead us to inaccurate conclusions, implicit personality theories represent another important social cognition strategy in our efforts to make sense out of other people (Fiske & Neuberg, 1990). Like social categories, implicit personality theories simplify information processing about other people and provide a mental framework that helps us organize observations, memories, and beliefs about people (Macrae & others, 1994).

social categorization
The mental process of classifying people into groups (or *categories*) on the basis of their shared characteristics.

implicit personality theory
A network of assumptions or beliefs about the relationships among various types of people, traits, and behaviors.

Attribution: Explaining Behavior

Attribution refers to the process of explaining people's behavior. What are the fundamental attribution error, the actor–observer discrepancy, and the self-serving bias? How do these biases shape the attributions we make?

As you're studying in the college library, the activities of two workers catch your attention. The two men are trying to lift and move a large file cabinet. "Okay, let's lift it and tip it this way," one guy says with considerable authority. In unison, they heave and tip the file cabinet. When they do, all four file drawers come flying out, bonking the first guy on the head. As the file cabinet goes crashing to the floor, you bite your lip to keep from laughing and think to yourself, "Yeah, they're obviously a pair of 40-watt bulbs."

Why did you arrive at that conclusion? After all, it's completely possible that the workers were not dimwits. Maybe the lock on the file drawers broke. Or maybe there was some other explanation for their mishap.

Attribution is the process of inferring the cause of someone's behavior, including your own. Psychologists also use the word *attribution* to refer to the explanation you make for a particular behavior. The attributions you make have a strong influence on your thoughts and feelings about other people.

If your attribution for the file cabinet accident was that the workers were not very bright, you demonstrated a very consistent pattern that occurs in explaining the behavior of other people. *We tend to spontaneously attribute the behavior of others to internal, personal characteristics, while downplaying or underestimating the effects of external, situational factors.* This bias is so common in individualistic cultures that it's called the **fundamental attribution error** (L. Ross, 1977). Even though it's entirely possible that situational forces are behind another person's behavior, we tend to automatically assume that the cause is an internal, personal characteristic.

The fundamental attribution error plays a role in a common explanatory pattern called **blaming the victim.** The innocent victim of a crime, disaster, or serious illness is blamed for having somehow caused the misfortune or for not having taken steps to prevent it. For example, many people blame the poor for their dire straits, the sick for bringing on their illness, and battered women and rape victims for somehow "provoking" their attackers. Hindsight makes it seem as if the victim should have been able to predict and prevent what was going to happen (Carli & Leonard, 1989).

Along with committing the fundamental attribution error, people tend to blame the victim because they have a strong need to believe that the world is fair—that "we get what we deserve and deserve what we get." Social psychologist Melvin Lerner (1980) calls this the **just-world hypothesis.** Blaming the victim reflects the belief that, since the world is just, the victim must have done *something* to deserve his or her fate.

Blaming the Victim This couple's home was destroyed by a wildfire in Alaska. Why do people often "blame the victim" after natural disasters, accidents, and crimes?

attribution
The mental process of inferring the causes of people's behavior, including one's own. Also used to refer to the explanation made for a particular behavior.

fundamental attribution error
The tendency to attribute the behavior of others to internal, personal characteristics, while ignoring or underestimating the effects of external, situational factors; an attributional bias that is common in individualistic cultures.

blaming the victim
The tendency to blame an innocent victim of misfortune for having somehow caused the problem or for not having taken steps to avoid or prevent it.

just-world hypothesis
The assumption that the world is fair, and that therefore people get what they deserve and deserve what they get.

actor–observer discrepancy
The tendency to attribute one's own be-havior to external, situational causes, while attributing the behavior of others to internal, personal causes; especially likely to occur with regard to behaviors that lead to negative outcomes.

Why do we have a psychological need to believe in a just world? Well, if you believe the world is unfair, then no one—including you—is safe from tragic twists of fate and chance, no matter how virtuous, careful, or con-scientious you may be (Thornton, 1992). Hence, blaming the victim and believing the just-world hypothesis provide a way to psychologically defend yourself against the threatening thought, "It could just as easily have been me."

The Actor–Observer Discrepancy:

You're a Klutz, but *I* Slipped on Some Ice!

There is an interesting exception to the fundamental attribution error. When it comes to explaining *our own* behavior, we tend to be biased in the opposite direction: We're more likely to use an *external, situational* attribution than an *internal, personal* attribution. This common attributional bias is called the **actor–observer discrepancy** because there is a discrepancy between the attributions you make when you are the *actor* in a given situation and those you make when you are the *observer* of other people's behavior (Jones & Nisbett, 1971).

Once you become aware of the actor-observer discrepancy, it's almost embarrassing to admit how often you succumb to it. He dropped the file cabinet because he is a dimwit; you dropped the file cabinet because you didn't have room to tip it the other way. Some jerk pulled out in front of your car because she's a reckless, inconsid-erate moron; you pulled out in front of her car be-cause your view was blocked by a school bus. And so on.

How can we explain the strong tendency to com-mit the actor–observer discrepancy? One possible explanation is that we simply have more informa-tion about the potential causes of our own behavior than we do about the causes of other people's be-havior. When you observe another driver turn di-rectly into the path of your car, that's typically all the information you have on which to judge his be-havior. But when *you* pull in front of another car, you perceive your own behavior in the context of the many situational factors that influenced your ac-tion. You're aware of factors like visibility and road conditions. You also know what motivated your be-havior and how differently you have behaved in sim-ilar situations in the past. Thus, you are much more aware of the extent to which *your* behavior has been influenced by situational factors (Fiske & Taylor, 1991; E. Jones, 1990).

Not surprisingly, then, we're less susceptible to the actor–observer discrepancy with people whom we know well. Because we possess more information about the behavior of our friends and relatives in different situations, we're more aware of the possi-ble situational influences on their behavior (Aron & others, 1992; Sande & others, 1988). We're also better at seeing situations from their point of view.

TABLE 11.1 Some Common Attributional Biases

Bias	Description
Fundamental attribution error	We tend to explain the behavior of other people by attributing their behav-ior to internal, personal characteristics, while underestimating or ignoring the effects of external, situational factors.
Actor–observer discrepancy	When we are the *actor*, we tend to attribute our own behavior to external causes. When we are the *observer* of someone else's behavior, we tend to attribute their behavior to internal causes.
Blaming the victim	When we're unable to help the victims of misfortune, we tend to blame them for causing their own misfortune, or for not taking steps to prevent or avoid it. Partly due to the *just-world hypothesis.*
Self-serving bias	The tendency to take credit for our *suc-cesses* by attributing them to internal, personal causes, along with the ten-dency to distance ourselves from our *failures* by attributing them to external, situational causes. Most common in in-dividualistic cultures.
Self-effacing (or modesty) bias	The tendency to blame ourselves for our *failures*, attributing them to inter-nal, personal causes, along with the tendency to downplay our *successes* by attributing them to external, situational causes. Most common in collectivistic cultures.

self-serving bias
The tendency to attribute successful outcomes of one's own behavior to internal causes and unsuccessful outcomes to external, situational causes.

The Self-Serving Bias:
Using Explanations That Meet Our Needs

If you've ever listened to other students react to their grades on an important exam, you've seen the **self-serving bias** in action (Whitley & Frieze, 1985). When students do well on a test, they tend to congratulate themselves and to attribute their success to how hard they studied, their intelligence, and so forth—all *internal* attributions. But when a student blows a test big time, the *external* attributions fly left and right: "They were all trick questions!" "I couldn't concentrate because the guy behind me kept coughing."

In a wide range of situations, people tend to credit themselves for their success and to blame their failures on external circumstances (Schlenker & Weigold, 1992; Schlenker & others, 1990). Psychologists explain the self-serving bias as being partly due to an attempt to "save face" and protect self-esteem in the face of failure (Dunning & others, 1995; Banaji & Prentice, 1994).

Although common in many societies, the self-serving bias is far from universal, as cross-cultural psychologists have discovered. We discuss this finding in Culture and Human Behavior Box 11.1, "Attributional Biases in Collectivistic Versus Individualistic Cultures."

CULTURE AND HUMAN BEHAVIOR 11.1

Attributional Biases in Collectivistic Versus Individualistic Cultures

Although the self-serving bias is common in individualistic cultures like Australia and the United States, it is far from being universal. In collectivistic cultures, like Asian cultures, an opposite attributional bias is often demonstrated (Bond, 1994; Moghaddam & others, 1993). Called the *self-effacing bias* or *modesty bias,* it involves blaming failure on internal, personal factors, while attributing success to external, situational factors.

For example, compared to American students, Japanese and Chinese students are more likely to attribute academic failure to personal factors, such as lack of effort, instead of situational factors (Dornbusch & others, 1996). Thus, a Japanese student who does poorly on an exam is likely to say, "I didn't study hard enough." And when a Japanese or Chinese student performs poorly in school, he or she is expected to study harder and longer (Stevenson & Stigler, 1992). In contrast, Japanese or Chinese students tend to attribute academic success to situational factors, such as saying "The exam was very easy" or "There was very little competition this year" (Stevenson & others, 1986).

Psychologists Hazel Markus and Shinobu Kitayama (1991) believe that the self-effacing bias reflects the em-phasis that interdependent cultures place on fitting in with other members of the group. As the Japanese proverb goes, "The nail that sticks up gets pounded down." In collectivistic cultures, self-esteem does not rest on doing better than others in the group. Rather, standing out from the group is likely to produce psychological discomfort and tension.

Cross-cultural differences are also evident with the fundamental attribution error. In general, members of collectivistic cultures are less likely to commit the fundamental attribution error than members of individualistic cultures (M. Bond & Smith, 1996). That is, collectivists are more likely to attribute the causes of another person's behavior to external, situational factors rather than internal, personal factors—the exact *opposite* attributional bias that is demonstrated in individualistic cultures.

To test this idea in a naturally occurring context, psychologists Michael Morris and Kaiping Peng (1994) compared articles reporting the same mass murders in Chinese-language and English-language newspapers. In one case, the murderer was a Chinese graduate student attending an American university. In the other case, the murderer was an American postal worker. Re-

Haughtiness invites ruin; humility receives benefits.

Chinese proverb

gardless of whether the murderer was Chinese or American, the news accounts were fundamentally different depending on whether the *reporter* was American or Chinese.

The American reporters were more likely to explain the killings by making personal, internal attributions. For example, American reporters emphasized the murderers' personality traits, like the graduate student's "bad temper," and the postal worker's "history of being mentally unstable."

In contrast, the Chinese reporters emphasized situational factors, such as the fact that the postal worker had recently been fired from his job and the fact that the graduate student had failed to receive an academic award. The Chinese reporters also cited social pressures and problems in American society to account for the actions of the killers.

Clearly, then, the way we account for our successes and failures, as well as the way we account for the actions of others, is yet another example of how human behavior is influenced by cultural conditioning.

Person Perception and Attribution

Match each of the following concepts with one of the examples below:

a. fundamental attribution error
b. self-serving bias
c. self-effacing bias
d. implicit personality theory
e. social categorization

_____ **1.** Dr. Nobuaki, a brilliant young professor who has just joined the faculty, was asked to give a talk about her research to her new colleagues. She began her presentation by saying, "I am very poorly prepared, and my research is not very important. Thank you for being patient with me."

_____ **2.** When Fern saw the man sitting on the San Francisco steps holding a cup, she thought he was a homeless person.

_____ **3.** Your next-door neighbor is a shy, boring, and mild-mannered Latin teacher. When you sign up for a sky-diving class, you are astonished to discover that he is one of the instructors.

_____ **4.** At the very beginning of the marathon, the top three female runners collided and were all forced to drop out because of their extensive injuries. Christine, the surprise winner of the marathon, told a local sports reporter that her win was due to her hard work, running technique, and self-discipline.

_____ **5.** You're sitting in a nice restaurant looking over the menu. From behind you, you hear a loud crash as a tray full of dishes hits the floor. As you watch the waiter scrambling to clean up the mess, you think, "What a klutz!"

Attitudes and Behavior

> _An attitude is a learned tendency to evaluate some object, person, or issue in a particular way. What are the three components of an attitude? Under what conditions are attitudes most likely to determine behavior? What is cognitive dissonance, and how does it affect attitudes?_

Are the Republicans or the Democrats better at leading the United States? What's your favorite kind of music? How do you feel about gun control? abortion rights? smoking in public places? gays in the military?

On these and many other subjects, you've probably formed an attitude. Psychologists formally define an **attitude** as a learned tendency to evaluate some object, person, or issue in a particular way (Olson & Zanna, 1993; Zimbardo & Leippe, 1991). Attitudes are typically positive or negative, but they can also be _ambivalent,_ as when you have mixed feelings about an issue or person.

Attitudes can include three components (Fazio, 1990). First, an attitude may have a _cognitive component:_ your thoughts and conclusions about a given topic or object. An example might be the person who says, "In my opinion, the easy access to guns is contributing to violence in the schools." Second, an attitude may have an emotional, or _affective, component:_ "I'm really scared and upset by the number of handguns that are floating around." Finally, an attitude can have a _behavioral component,_ in which your attitude is reflected in your actions: "I've started a petition drive for stricter gun control laws in my state."

attitude
A learned tendency to evaluate some object, person, or issue in a particular way; such evaluations may be positive, negative, or ambivalent.

The Effect of Attitudes on Behavior

You may take it for granted that your attitudes tend to guide your behavior. But social psychologists have consistently found that people don't always act in accordance with their attitudes (see Eagly & Chaiken, 1993; Eagly, 1992). For example, you might disapprove of cheating, yet find yourself sneaking a peek at a classmate's exam paper when the opportunity presents itself. Or you might favor a certain political candidate, yet not vote on election day.

Under what conditions are your attitudes most likely to influence or determine your behavior? Social psychologists have found that you're most likely to behave in accordance with your attitudes when:

- *Attitudes are extreme or are frequently expressed* (Eagly & Chaiken, 1993; Bassili, 1993).

- *Attitudes have been formed through direct experience* (Fazio, 1990; Fazio & Zanna, 1981). For example, suppose you once escaped serious injury in an auto accident because you were wearing your seatbelt. You'd probably strongly favor seatbelt use, might actively support a mandatory seatbelt law in your state, and always "buckle up" whenever you get in a car.

- *You are very knowledgeable about the subject* (Wood & others, 1995; Wood, 1982).

- *You have a vested interest in the subject* (Crano, 1995; Sivacek & Crano, 1982). If you personally stand to gain or lose something on a specific issue, you're more likely to act in accordance with your attitudes.

- *You anticipate a favorable outcome or response from others* (Ajzen, 1991; Ajzen & Fishbein, 1980).

What we've summarized above meshes nicely with common sense: people tend to act in accordance with their attitudes when they feel strongly about an issue, have a personal stake in the issue, and anticipate a positive outcome in a particular situation. In short, your attitudes do influence your behavior in many instances. Now, let's consider the opposite question: Can your behavior influence your attitudes?

The Effect of Behavior on Attitudes:
Fried Grasshoppers for Lunch?!

Suppose you have volunteered to participate in a psychology experiment. When you arrive at the lab, you're asked to indicate your degree of preference for a variety of foods, including fried grasshoppers, which you rank pretty low on the list. During the experiment, the experimenter instructs you to eat some fried grasshoppers. You manage to swallow three of the crispy critters. At the end of the experiment, your attitudes toward grasshoppers as a food source are surveyed again.

After the experiment, you talk to a friend who also participated in the experiment. You mention how friendly and polite you thought the experimenter was. As it turns out, your friend had a very different experience. He thought the experimenter was an arrogant, rude jerk.

Here's the critical question: Whose attitude toward eating fried grasshoppers is more likely to change in a positive direction—yours or your friend's? Circle your answer below.

A. You, who encountered a friendly experimenter

B. Your friend, who encountered a rude experimenter

The correct answer is obvious, right? If you're like our students, you probably predicted *A* as the correct answer. Well, before you pat yourself on the back for your keen psychological insight, the correct answer is *B*!

At first glance, the correct answer seems to go against the grain of common sense. So how can we explain this outcome? To begin with, our fried grasshoppers scenario represents the basic design of a classic experiment by psychologist Philip Zimbardo and his colleagues (1965). Zimbardo's experiment and other similar ones underscore the power of cognitive dissonance (see Festinger, 1962). **Cognitive dissonance** is an unpleasant state of psychological tension (dissonance) that occurs when there's an inconsistency between two thoughts or perceptions (cognitions). This state of dissonance is so unpleasant that we are strongly motivated to reduce it (Festinger, 1957).

Cognitive dissonance commonly occurs in situations in which you become uncomfortably aware that your behavior and your attitudes are in conflict. In these situations, you are simultaneously holding two conflicting cognitions: your original attitude versus the realization that you have behaved in a way that contradicts that attitude. If you can easily rationalize your behavior to make it consistent with your attitude, then any dissonance you might experience can be quickly and easily resolved. But when your behavior *cannot* be easily justified, how can you resolve the contradiction and resolve the unpleasant state of dissonance? Since you can't go back and change the behavior, *you change your attitude to make it consistent with your behavior.*

Let's take another look at the results of the grasshopper study, this time from the perspective of cognitive dissonance theory. Your attitude toward eating grasshoppers did *not* change, because you could easily rationalize the conflict between your attitude ("Eating grasshoppers is disgusting") and your behavior (eating three grasshoppers). You probably justified your behavior by saying something like, "I ate the grasshoppers because the experimenter was such a nice guy and I wanted to help him out."

However, your friend who encountered the rude experimenter can't easily explain the contradiction between disliking grasshoppers and voluntarily eating them. Thus, he experiences an uncomfortable state of cognitive dissonance. Since he can't go back and change his behavior, he is left with only one part of the equation that can be changed—his attitude (see Figure 11.1 on page 410). "You know, eating those grasshoppers wasn't *that* bad," your friend comments. "In fact, they were kind of crunchy." Notice how his change in attitude reduces the dissonance between his previous attitude and his behavior.

Cognitive dissonance can also change the strength of an attitude so that it is consistent with some behavior we've already performed. For example, people tend to be much more favorably inclined toward a given political candidate after they have voted for him or her than just before (Regan & Kilduff, 1988; Frenkel & Doob, 1976).

A similar example of cognitive dissonance in action involves choosing between two basically equal alternatives, especially if the decision is important and difficult to undo (Festinger, 1962). Suppose you had to choose between two colleges or two jobs. Each choice has desirable and undesirable features, creating dissonance. But once you actually make the choice, you immediately bring your attitudes more closely into line with that commitment,

cognitive dissonance
An unpleasant state of psychological tension or arousal (*dissonance*) that occurs when two thoughts or perceptions (*cognitions*) are inconsistent; typically results from the awareness that attitudes and behavior are in conflict.

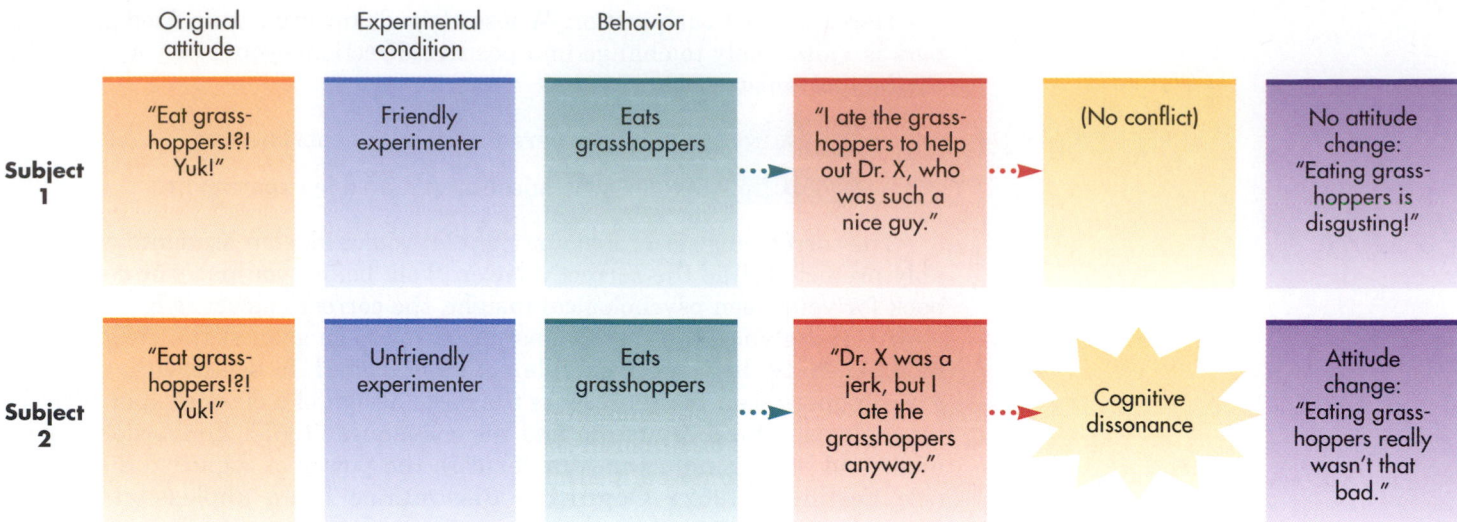

	Original attitude	Experimental condition	Behavior			
Subject 1	"Eat grasshoppers!?! Yuk!"	Friendly experimenter	Eats grasshoppers	"I ate the grasshoppers to help out Dr. X, who was such a nice guy."	(No conflict)	No attitude change: "Eating grasshoppers is disgusting!"
Subject 2	"Eat grasshoppers!?! Yuk!"	Unfriendly experimenter	Eats grasshoppers	"Dr. X was a jerk, but I ate the grasshoppers anyway."	Cognitive dissonance	Attitude change: "Eating grasshoppers really wasn't that bad."

FIGURE 11.1 Cognitive Dissonance: How It Leads to Attitude Change
When your behavior conflicts with your attitudes, an uncomfortable state of tension is produced. However, if you can rationalize or explain your behavior, the conflict (and the tension) is eliminated or avoided. If you can't easily justify your behavior, you may change your attitude so that it is in harmony with your behavior.

reducing cognitive dissonance. In other words, after you make the choice, you emphasize the negative features of the choice you've rejected, which is commonly called a "sour grapes" rationalization. You also emphasize the positive features of the choice to which you have committed yourself—a "sweet lemons" rationalization.

Understanding Prejudice

Prejudice refers to a negative attitude toward people who belong to a specific social group. What effects does in-group/out-group thinking have on our social judgments, including prejudice and stereotypes? What is ethnocentrism?

In this section, you'll see how person perception, attribution, and attitudes come together in explaining **prejudice**—a negative attitude toward people who belong to a specific social group. Prejudice is ultimately based on the exaggerated notion that members of "other" social groups are very different from members of our own social group. So as you read this discussion, it's important for you to keep two well-established points in mind. First, *racial and ethnic groups are far more alike than they are different* (J. Jones, 1991). And second, any differences that may exist *between* members of racial and ethnic groups are far smaller than differences *among* various members of the same group (Betancourt & López, 1993; Zuckerman, 1990).

Tension Between Groups Tension and mutual distrust exist among many different racial and ethnic groups in America. During the 1992 Los Angeles riots, for example, some African-Americans vented their frustrations by attacking small businesses that were run by Korean-Americans. But as the photo shows, people can take steps to reduce the distrust that exists between different ethnic groups.

From Stereotypes to Prejudice:
In-Groups and Out-Groups

As we noted earlier, using social categories to organize information about other people seems to be a natural cognitive tendency. Many social categories can be defined by relatively objective characteristics, like age, language, religion, and skin color. A specific kind of social category is a **stereotype**—a cluster of characteristics that are attributed to members of a specific social group or category. In other words, stereotypes are based on the assumption that people have certain characteristics *because* of their membership in a particular group.

Stereotypes typically include qualities that are unrelated to the objective criteria that define a given category (Taylor & Porter, 1994). For example, we can objectively sort people into different categories by age. But our stereotypes for different age groups may include many qualities that have little to do with "number of years since birth." Associating "reckless and irresponsible" with teenagers, "forgetful and incompetent" with the elderly, and "boring and stodgy" with middle-aged adults are examples of associating unrelated qualities with age groups—that is, stereotyping.

Once they are formed, stereotypes are hard to shake. One reason for this is that stereotypes are not always completely false (Ottati & Lee, 1995). Sometimes they have a kernel of truth, making them easy to confirm, especially when you only see what you expect to see (Swim, 1994; Judd & Park, 1993). However, there's a vast difference between a kernel and the cornfield. When stereotypic beliefs become expectations that are applied to *all* members of a given group, stereotypes can be very misleading and even damaging (Stangor & Lange, 1994).

Consider the stereotype that men are more assertive than women, and that women are more nurturant than men. This stereotype does have some truth to it, but only in terms of the *average* difference between men and women (see Eagly, 1995a; Swim, 1994). Thus, it would be inappropriate to automatically apply this stereotype to *every* individual male or female.

Stereotypes are closely related to another tendency in person perception. That is, people have a strong tendency to perceive others in terms of two very basic social categories: "us" and "them." More precisely, the **in-group** ("us") refers to the group or groups to which we belong, while **out-groups** ("them") refer to groups of which we are not a member. In-groups and out-groups aren't necessarily limited to racial, ethnic, or religious boundaries. Virtually any characteristic can be used to make in-group and out-group distinctions: Cubs versus White Sox fans, Northsiders versus Southsiders, math majors versus English majors, and so forth.

The Out-Group Homogeneity Effect: They All Look Alike to Me

Two important patterns characterize our views of in-groups versus out-groups. First, when we describe the members of our *in-group,* we typically see them as being quite varied, despite having enough features in common to belong to the same group. In other words, we notice the diversity within our own group.

Second, we tend to see members of the *out-group* as much more similar to one another, even in areas that have little to do with the criteria for group membership. This tendency is called the **out-group homogeneity effect.** (The word *homogeneity* means similarity or uniformity.)

For example, what qualities do you associate with the category of engineering major? If you're *not* an engineering major, you're likely to see

prejudice
A negative attitude toward people who belong to a specific social group.

stereotype
A cluster of characteristics that are associated with all members of a specific social group, often including qualities that are unrelated to the objective criteria that define the group.

in-group
A social group to which one belongs.

out-group
A social group to which one does not belong.

out-group homogeneity effect
The tendency to see members of out-groups as very similar to one another.

engineering majors as a rather similar crew: male, logical, analytical, conservative, and so forth. However, if you *are* an engineering major, you're much more likely to see your in-group as quite *heterogeneous,* or varied (Park & others, 1992). You might even come up with several subgroups, such as studious engineering majors versus party-animal engineering majors.

In-Group Bias: *We're Tactful—They're* Sneaky

In-group bias is our tendency to make favorable, positive attributions for behaviors by members of our in-group, and unfavorable, negative attributions for behaviors by members of out-groups (see Dovidio & Gaertner, 1993; Hewstone, 1990). We succeeded because we worked hard; they succeeded because they lucked out. We're thrifty; they're stingy. And so on.

One form of in-group bias is called **ethnocentrism**—the belief that one's culture or ethnic group is superior to others. You're engaging in ethnocentrism when you use your culture or ethnic group as the yardstick by which you judge other cultures or ethnic groups. Not surprisingly, ethnocentric thinking contributes to the formation of negative stereotypes about other cultures whose customs differ from our own (Triandis, 1994; E. Smith, 1993).

In combination, stereotypes and in-group/out-group bias form the *cognitive* basis for prejudicial attitudes (Hilton & von Hippel, 1996). But as with many attitudes, prejudice also has a strong *emotional* component. In this case, the emotions are intensely negative—hatred, contempt, fear, loathing. *Behaviorally,* prejudice can be displayed in the form of *discrimination*—behaviors ranging from privately sneering at another group to physically attacking members of the out-group.

HAGAR

Overcoming Prejudice

> *Psychologist Muzafer Sherif demonstrated the conditions that can foster and reduce intergroup conflict. What conditions help reduce tensions between groups? How has this finding been applied in classroom settings?*

How can prejudice be combated? A classic series of studies headed by psychologist **Muzafer Sherif** (b. 1906) helped clarify the conditions that produce intergroup conflict *and* harmony. Sherif and his colleagues (1961/1988) studied a group of eleven-year-old boys in an unlikely setting for a scientific experiment: a summer camp located at Robbers Cave State Park in Oklahoma. Pretending to be camp counselors and staff, the researchers observed the boys' behavior under carefully orchestrated conditions.

The Robbers Cave Experiment

The boys were randomly assigned to two groups. The groups arrived at camp in separate buses and were headquartered in different areas of the camp. One group of boys dubbed themselves the Eagles, the other the Rattlers. After a week of separation, the researchers arranged for the groups to meet in a series of competitive games. A fierce rivalry quickly developed, demonstrating the ease with which mutually hostile groups could be created.

in-group bias
The tendency to judge the behavior of in-group members favorably and out-group members unfavorably.

ethnocentrism
The belief that one's own culture or ethnic group is superior to all others, and the related tendency to use one's own culture as a standard by which to judge other cultures.

Creating Conflict Between Groups Psychologist Muzafer Sherif and his colleagues demonstrated how easily hostility and distrust could be created between two groups. Competitive situations, like this tug-of-war game, increased tension between the Rattlers and the Eagles.

The rivalry became increasingly bitter. The Eagles burned the Rattlers' flag. In response, the Rattlers trashed the Eagles' cabin. Somewhat alarmed, the researchers tried to diminish the hostility by bringing the two groups together under peaceful circumstances and on an equal basis—having them go to the movies together, eat in the same dining hall, and so forth. But contact alone did not mitigate the hostility. If anything, these situations only served as opportunities for the rival groups to berate and attack each other. For example, when the Rattlers and Eagles ate together in the same dining hall, a massive food fight erupted!

How could harmony between the groups be established? Sherif and his fellow researchers created a series of situations in which the two groups would need to *cooperate to achieve a common goal.* For example, the researchers secretly sabotaged the water supply. Working together, the Eagles and the Rattlers managed to fix it. On another occasion, the researchers sabotaged a truck that was to bring food to the campers. The hungry campers overcame their differences to join forces and restart the truck. After a series of such joint efforts, the rivalry diminished and the groups became good friends (Sherif, 1956; Sherif & others, 1961/1988).

Overcoming Group Conflict To decrease hostility, the researchers created situations that required the joint efforts of both groups to achieve a common goal, such as fixing the water supply. These cooperative tasks helped the boys recognize their common interests and become friends.

The Jigsaw Classroom: Promoting Cooperation

Social psychologist Elliot Aronson tried adapting the results of the Robbers Cave experiments to a very different group situation—a newly integrated elementary school. Aronson and his colleagues tried a teaching technique that stressed cooperative, rather than competitive, learning situations (see Aronson, 1990; Aronson & Bridgeman, 1979). Dubbed the *jigsaw classroom technique,* this approach brought together students in small, ethnically diverse groups to work on a mutual project. Like the pieces of a jigsaw puzzle, each student had a unique contribution to make toward the success of the group. Each student became an expert on one aspect of the overall project and had to teach it to the other members of the group. Thus, interdependence and cooperation replaced competition.

The results? Children in the jigsaw classrooms benefited. They had higher self-esteem and a greater liking for children in other ethnic groups than children in traditional classrooms. They also demonstrated a lessening of negative stereotypes and prejudice, and a reduction in intergroup hostility (see Aronson, 1995, 1987; Aronson & Bridgeman, 1979).

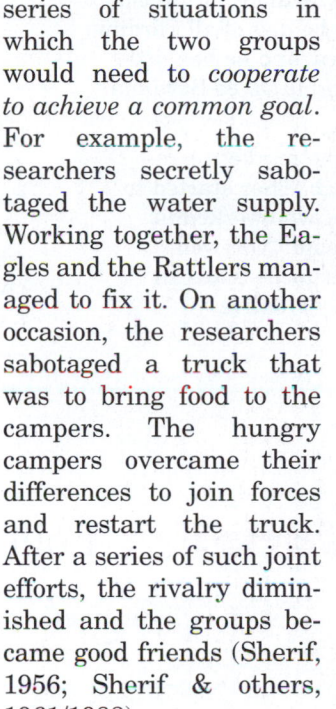

In combination, the Robbers Cave study and the jigsaw experiment illustrate how cooperative efforts between members of different groups can help promote intergroup harmony.

The Psychology of Attitudes and Prejudice

Which of the following concepts is being illustrated in each of the examples below: cognitive dissonance, stereotyping, ethnocentrism, or outgroup homogeneity?

1. Henry's classmate in college was from Sardinia, and he loved to eat sardines for lunch. Henry now believes that the diet of all Sardinians is centered on sardines, and he has little doubt about why the island is called Sardinia. _____

2. A group of employees in the marketing department went out to lunch. They started to complain about the people who worked in accounting. One of them said, "Oh, well, you know those number crunchers are all alike. They just aren't very creative." _____

CONCEPT REVIEW 11.2

3. Georgia thinks that track is a great all-around sport and desperately wants to make the track team. For the first few weeks, she trains hard every day. Gradually, however, she starts missing practice sessions, and on the day of the tryouts she oversleeps, performs poorly, and gets cut in the first round. Georgia says, "Track is so-o-o boring. I'd much rather be on the softball team." _____

4. In an introductory anthropology class, students begin to groan and laugh as they watch a film showing members of a remote tribe eating head lice, grubs, and iguanas. "How repulsive," remarked one gum-chewing student. "Those poor savages are really ignorant and uncivilized," another student agreed, as he put a pinch of chewing tobacco in his mouth. _____

Conformity: Following the Crowd

> *Social influence involves the study of how behavior is influenced by the social environment and other people. What factors influence the degree to which people will conform? Why do people conform? How does culture affect conformity?*

If you typically contribute to class discussions, you've probably felt the power of social influence in classes where no one else said a word. No doubt you found yourself feeling at least slightly uncomfortable every time you ventured a comment or question. If you changed your behavior to mesh with that of your classmates, you demonstrated conformity.

Conformity occurs when we change our behavior, attitudes, or beliefs in response to real or imagined group pressure (Kiesler & Kiesler, 1969). There's no question that all of us conform to group norms to some degree. The more critical issue is *how far* we'll go to adjust our perceptions and opinions so that they're in sync with the majority opinion—an issue that intrigued psychologist **Solomon Asch** (1907–1996). Asch (1951) posed a straightforward question: Would people still conform to the group if the group opinion was clearly wrong?

To study this question experimentally, Asch (1955) chose a simple, objective task with an obvious answer (see Figure 11.2). A group of people sat at a table and looked at a series of cards. On one side of each card was a standard line. On the other side were three comparison lines. All each person had to do was publicly indicate which comparison line was the same length as the standard line.

conformity
The tendency to adjust one's behavior, attitudes, or beliefs to group norms in response to real or imagined group pressure.

normative social influence
Behavior that is motivated by the desire to gain social acceptance and approval.

informational social influence
Behavior that is motivated by the desire to be correct.

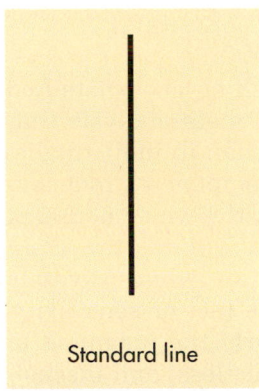 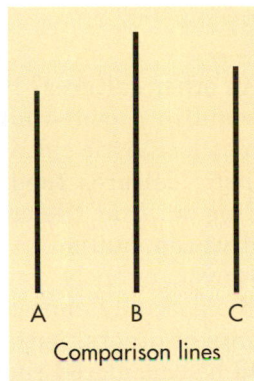

Standard line   Comparison lines

FIGURE 11.2 Sample Line Judgment Task Used in the Asch Conformity Studies
In Asch's classic studies on conformity, subjects were asked to pick the comparison line that matched the standard line.
(Asch, 1987.)

Adolescents and Conformity The adolescent uniform: T-shirts, jeans, and athletic shoes. Think back to your own adolescent years. Do you remember how important it was to you to fit in with other adolescents, especially those in your peer group? Researchers have found that conformity to group norms peaks during early adolescence (Gavin & Furman 1989; B. Brown & others, 1986).

Asch's experiment had a hidden catch: All the people sitting around the table were actually in cahoots with the experimenter, except for one—the real subject. Had you been the real subject in Asch's (1956) experiment, here's what you would have experienced: The first card is shown, and the five people ahead of you respond, one at a time, with the obvious answer: "Line B." Now it's your turn, and you respond the same. The second card is put up. Again, the answer is obvious and the group is unanimous. So far, so good.

Then the third card is shown, and the correct answer is just as obvious: line C. But the first person confidently says, "Line A." And so does everyone else, one by one. Now it's your turn. To you it's clear that the correct answer is line C. But the five people ahead of you have already publicly chosen line A. How do you respond? You hesitate. Do you go with the flow or with what you know?

The real subject was faced with the uncomfortable situation of disagreeing with a unanimous majority on twelve of eighteen trials in Asch's experiment. Notice, there was *no* direct pressure to conform—just the implicit, unspoken pressure of answering differently from the rest of the group.

Over a hundred subjects experienced Asch's experimental dilemma. Not surprisingly, participants differed in their degree of conformity. Nonetheless, the majority of Asch's subjects (76 percent) conformed with the group judgment on at least one of the critical trials. When the data for all subjects were combined, the subjects followed the majority and gave the wrong answer on *37 percent* of the critical trials (Asch, 1955, 1957). In comparison, a control group of subjects who responded alone instead of in a group accurately chose the matching line 99 percent of the time.

Although the majority opinion clearly exerted a strong influence, it's also important to stress the flip side of Asch's results. On almost two-thirds of the trials in which the majority named the wrong line, the subjects stuck to their guns and gave the correct answer, despite being in the minority (see Friend & others, 1990).

Factors Influencing Conformity

The basic model of Asch's classic experiment has been used in hundreds of studies exploring the dynamics of conformity. Why do we sometimes find ourselves conforming to the larger group? First is our desire to be liked and accepted by the group, which is referred to as **normative social influence.** If you've ever been ridiculed and rejected for going against the grain of a unanimous group, you've had firsthand experience with the pressure of normative social influence. Second is our desire to be right. When we're uncertain or doubt our own judgment, we may look to the group as a source of accurate information, which is called **informational social influence.**

Asch and other researchers identified several conditions that promote conformity, which are summarized in Table 11.2 on the next page. Asch also discovered that conformity *decreased* under certain circumstances. For example, having an ally seemed to counteract the social influence of the majority. Subjects were more likely to go against the majority view if just one other participant did so. Other researchers have found that any dissent increases resistance to the majority opinion, even if the other person's dissenting opinion is wrong (Allen & Levine, 1969).

TABLE 11.2 Factors That Promote Conformity

You're more likely to conform to group norms when:

- you are facing a unanimous majority of four or five people.
- you must give your response in front of the group.
- you have not already expressed commitment to a different idea or opinion.
- you find the task is ambiguous or difficult.
- you doubt your abilities or knowledge in the situation.
- you are strongly attracted to a group and want to be a member of it.

SOURCES: Asch, 1955; Campbell & Fairey, 1989; Deutsch & Gerard, 1955; Gerard & others, 1968; Tanford & Penrod, 1984.

Culture and Conformity

Do patterns of conformity differ in other cultures? British psychologists Rod Bond and Peter Smith (1996) found in a wide-ranging meta-analysis that conformity is generally higher in collectivistic cultures than in individualistic cultures. Because individualistic cultures tend to emphasize independence, self-expression, and standing out from the crowd, the whole notion of conformity tends to carry a negative connotation.

In collectivistic cultures, however, publicly conforming while privately disagreeing tends to be regarded as socially appropriate tact or sensitivity. Publicly challenging the judgments of others, particularly the judgment of members of one's in-group, would be considered rude, tactless, and insensitive to the feelings of others. Thus, conformity in collectivistic cultures does not seem to carry the same negative connotation that it does in individualistic cultures.

Obedience: Following Orders

Obedience refers to behaving in direct response to the orders of an authority. What was the basic design of Milgram's obedience experiments? What were the results? What conditions increase or decrease the likelihood of destructive obedience?

Though he made many contributions to social psychology, **Stanley Milgram** (1933–1984) is best known for his experimental investigations of obedience. **Obedience** is the performance of an action in response to the direct orders of an authority or a person of higher status, like a teacher or a supervisor.

Milgram was intrigued by Asch's discovery of how easily people could be swayed by group pressure. But Milgram wanted to investigate behavior that had greater personal significance than simply judging the lengths of lines on a card. Thus, Milgram posed what he saw as the most critical question: Could a person be pressured by others into committing an immoral act, some action that violated his or her own conscience, such as hurting a stranger? In his efforts to answer that question, Milgram embarked on one of the most systematic and controversial investigations in the history of psychology: how and why people obey the destructive dictates of an authority figure.

Social Psychologist Stanley Milgram (1933–1984) Milgram is best known for his obedience studies, but his creative research skills went far beyond the topic of obedience. To study social norms, for example, Milgram sent his students out into New York City to intrude into waiting lines or ask subway passengers to give up their seats. Milgram often capitalized on the "texture of everyday life" to "examine the way in which the social world impinges on individual action and experience."

Milgram's Original Obedience Experiment

Milgram was only 28 years old when he conducted his first obedience experiments. At the time, he was a new faculty member at Yale University in New Haven, Connecticut. He recruited participants through direct-mail solicitations and ads in the local paper. Collectively, Milgram's subjects represented a wide range of occupational and educational backgrounds. Postal workers, high school teachers, white-collar workers, engineers, and laborers participated in the study.

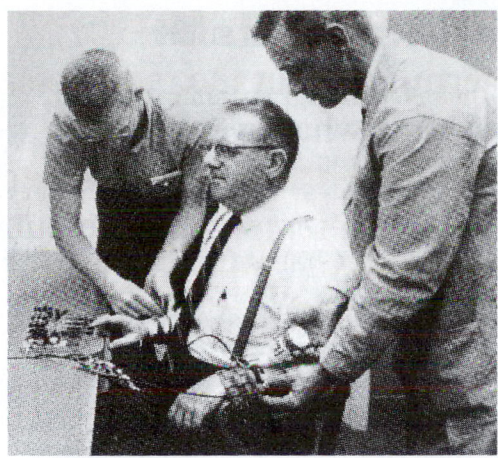

The "Electric Chair" With the help of the real subject who has been assigned the role of "teacher," the experimenter straps the "learner" into the electric chair. The experimenter told both subjects, "Although the shocks can be extremely painful, they cause no permanent tissue damage."

Outwardly, it appeared that two subjects showed up at Yale University to participate in the psychology experiment, but the second subject was actually an accomplice working with Milgram. When both subjects arrived, the experimenter greeted them and gave them a plausible explanation of the study's purpose: to examine the effects of punishment on learning.

Both subjects drew slips of paper to determine who would be "the teacher" and who "the learner." However, the drawing was rigged so that the real subject was always the teacher and the accomplice was always the learner. Assigned to the role of the teacher, the real subject would be responsible for "punishing" the learner's mistakes by administering electric shocks.

Immediately after the drawing, the teacher and learner were taken to another room, where the learner was strapped into an "electric chair." The teacher was then taken to a different room, from which he could hear but not see the learner. Speaking into a microphone, the teacher tested the learner on a simple word-pair memory task. In the other room, the learner pressed one of four switches to indicate with which alternative the word had previously been paired. The learner's response was registered in an answer box positioned on top of the "shock generator" in front of the teacher.

Just in case there was any doubt in the teacher's mind about the legitimacy of the shock generator, the *teacher* was given a sample jolt using the switch marked 45 volts. In fact, this sample shock was the only real shock given during the course of the staged experiment.

The first time the learner answered incorrectly, the teacher was to deliver an electric shock at the 15 volt level. With each subsequent error, the teacher was told to progress to the next voltage level on the shock generator. The teacher was also told to announce the voltage level to the learner before delivering the shock.

Milgram's "Shock Generator" Machine
A young Stanley Milgram sits next to his "shock generator." Milgram went to great lengths to make the shock generator as authentic as possible. Do you think you would have been fooled into believing that this was a real shock generator?

At predetermined voltage levels, the learner vocalized first his discomfort, then his pain, and, finally, agonized screams. After 330 volts, the learner's script called for him to fall silent. If the teacher protested that he wished to stop, or that he was worried about the learner's safety, the experimenter would say, "The experiment requires that you continue" or "You have no other choice, you *must* continue."

According to the script, the experiment would be halted when the teacher-subject refused to obey the experimenter's orders to continue. Alternatively, if the teacher-subject obeyed the experimenter, the experiment would be halted once the teacher had progressed all the way to the maximum shock level of 450 volts.

Either way, after the experiment the teacher was interviewed and it was explained that the learner had not actually received dangerous electric shocks. To underscore this point, a "friendly reconciliation" was arranged between the teacher and the learner, and the true purpose of the study was explained to the subject.

obedience
The performance of an action in response to the direct orders of an authority or person of higher status.

Shock Level	Switch Labels and Voltage Levels	Number of Subjects Who Refused to Administer a Higher Voltage Level
	"Slight Shock"	
1	15	
2	30	
3	45	
4	60	
	"Moderate Shock"	
5	75	
6	90	
7	105	
8	120	
	"Strong Shock"	
9	135	
10	150	
11	165	
12	180	
	"Very Strong Shock"	
13	195	
14	210	
15	225	
16	240	
	"Intense Shock"	
17	255	
18	270	
19	285	
20	300	5
	"Extreme Intensity Shock"	
21	315	4
22	330	2
23	345	1
24	360	1
	"Danger: Severe Shock"	
25	375	1
26	390	
27	405	
28	420	
	"XXX"	
29	435	
30	450	26

FIGURE 11.3 The Results of Milgram's Original Study
Contrary to what psychiatrists, college students, and middle-class adults predicted, the majority of Milgram's subjects did not refuse to obey by the 150-volt level of shocks. As this chart shows, five of Milgram's forty subjects (13 percent) refused to continue after administering 300 volts to the learner. Twenty-six of the forty subjects (65 percent) remained obedient to the end, administering the full 450 volts to the learner.
(Milgram, 1974a, p. 35.)

The Results of Milgram's Experiment

Can you predict how Milgram's subjects behaved? Milgram himself asked psychiatrists, college students, and middle-class adults to predict how subjects would behave (see Milgram, 1974a). Each group predicted that most subjects would refuse at the 150-volt level, the point at which the learner first protested. They also believed that only a few rare individuals would go as far as the 300-volt level. Finally, *none* of those surveyed thought that *any* of Milgram's subjects would go to the full 450 volts.

As it turned out, they were all wrong. *Two-thirds of Milgram's subjects—twenty-six of the forty—went to the full 450-volt level.* And of those who defied the experimenter, *not one stopped before the 300-volt level.* The results of Milgram's original obedience study are shown in Figure 11.3.

Surprised? Milgram himself was stunned by the results, never expecting that the majority of subjects would administer the maximum voltage. Were Milgram's subjects heartless, cold, and callous people? Or perhaps they saw through his elaborate experimental hoax, as some critics have suggested (Orne & Holland, 1968). Was it possible that the subjects did not believe that they were really harming the learner?

The answer seems to be no. Milgram's subjects seemed totally convinced that the situation was authentic. And they did not behave in a cold-blooded, unfeeling way. Far from it. As the experiment progressed, many subjects showed signs of extreme tension and conflict. In describing the reaction of one subject, Milgram (1963) wrote, "I observed a mature and initially poised businessman enter the laboratory smiling and confident. Within 20 minutes he was reduced to a twitching, stuttering wreck, who was rapidly approaching a point of nervous collapse."

Making Sense out of Milgram's Findings

Milgram, along with other researchers, identified several aspects of the situation that had a strong impact on the subjects (see Milgram, 1965/1992; Blass, 1991; Miller, 1986). Some of the key forces that influenced subjects to continue obeying the experimenter's orders are noted below.

> ***A previously well-established mental framework to obey.*** Having volunteered to participate in a psychology experiment, Milgram's subjects arrived at the lab with the mental expectation that they would obediently follow the directions of the person in charge—the experimenter. They also accepted compensation upon their arrival, which may have increased their sense of having made a commitment to cooperate with the experimenter.

> ***The situation, or context, in which the obedience occurred.*** The subjects were familiar with the basic nature of scientific investigation, believed that scientific research was worthwhile, and were told that the goal of the experiment was to advance the scientific understanding of learning and memory. All these factors predisposed the subjects to trust and respect the experimenter's authority (Darley, 1992).

> ***The gradual, repetitive escalation of the task.*** At the beginning of the experiment, the subject administered a very low level of shock—15 volts. Subjects could easily justify using such low levels of electric shock in the service of sci-

ence. The shocks, like the learner's protests, escalated only gradually. Each additional shock was only 15 volts stronger.

The experimenter's behavior and reassurances. Many subjects asked the experimenter who was responsible for what might happen to the learner. In every case, the teacher was reassured that the *experimenter* was responsible for the learner's well-being. Thus, the subjects could believe that they were not responsible for the consequences of their actions. They could tell themselves that their behavior must be appropriate if the experimenter approved of it.

The physical and psychological separation from the learner. Several "buffers" distanced the subject from the pain that he was inflicting on the learner. First, the learner was in a separate room and not visible. Second, punishment was depersonalized: The subject simply pushed a switch on the shock generator. Finally, the learner never appealed directly to the teacher to stop shocking him. The learner's pleas were always directed toward the *experimenter*, as in "Experimenter! Get me out of here!" Undoubtedly, this contributed to the subject's sense that the experimenter, rather than the subject, was ultimately in control of the situation.

FIGURE 11.4 Factors That Decrease Destructive Obedience
By systematically varying his basic experimental design, Milgram identified several factors that diminish the likelihood of destructive obedience. In this graph, you can see the percentage of subjects who administered the maximum shock in different experimental variations.
(Adapted from data reported in Milgram, 1974a.)

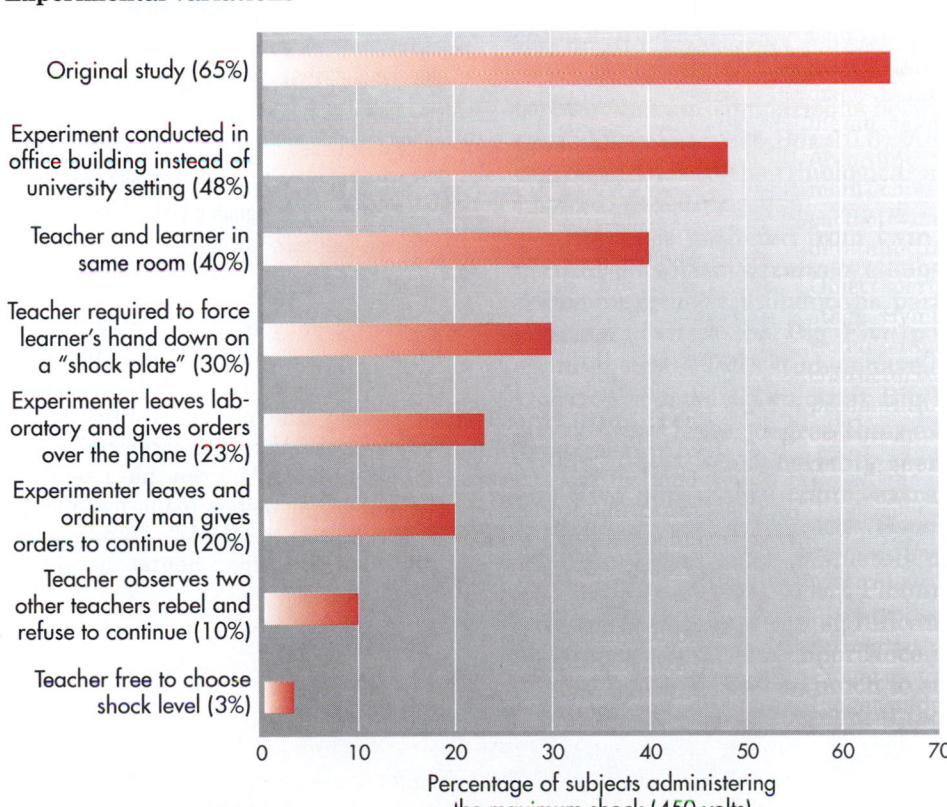

Experimental variations

Original study (65%)

Experiment conducted in office building instead of university setting (48%)

Teacher and learner in same room (40%)

Teacher required to force learner's hand down on a "shock plate" (30%)

Experimenter leaves laboratory and gives orders over the phone (23%)

Experimenter leaves and ordinary man gives orders to continue (20%)

Teacher observes two other teachers rebel and refuse to continue (10%)

Teacher free to choose shock level (3%)

0   10   20   30   40   50   60   70

Percentage of subjects administering the maximum shock (450 volts)

Conditions That Undermine Obedience

Milgram's obedience research represents one of the largest and most integrated research programs in social psychology. Approximately *1,000* subjects, each tested individually, experienced some variation of Milgram's obedience experiment. By varying his experiments, Milgram identified several conditions that decrease the likelihood of destructive obedience, which are summarized in Figure 11.4. For example, willingness to obey diminishes sharply when the buffers that separate the teacher from the learner are lessened or removed, as when both of them are put in the same room.

If Milgram's findings seem to cast an unfavorable light on human nature, there are two reasons to take heart. First, when teachers were allowed to act as their own authority and freely choose the shock level, 95 percent of them did not venture beyond 150 volts—the first point at which the learner protested. Clearly, Milgram's subjects were not responding to their own aggressive or sadistic impulses, but rather to orders from an authority figure.

Second, Milgram found that people are more likely to muster up the courage to defy an authority when they see others do so. When Milgram's subjects observed what they thought were two other subjects disobey the experimenter, the real subjects followed their lead 90 percent of the time and refused to continue. Like the subjects in Asch's experiment, we're more likely to stand by our convictions when we're not alone in expressing them.

Not surprisingly, the obedience studies were highly publicized—and extremely controversial. Many people were upset by his findings, but his methods drew fire as well. Critical Thinking Box 11.2, "The Ethics of Milgram's Obedience Experiments," describes this controversy.

CRITICAL THINKING 11.2

The Ethics of Milgram's Obedience Experiments

Less than a year after the initial publication of Milgram's obedience studies, psychologist Diana Baumrind (1964) attacked the obedience experiments for the emotional stress, tension, and loss of dignity experienced by Milgram's subjects. To Baumrind, Milgram's experiment was a violation of the trust that a naive subject is likely to place in a researcher. As Baumrind (1964) wrote:

> The subject's personal responsibility for his actions is not erased because the experimenter reveals to him the means which he used to stimulate these actions. The subject realizes that he would have hurt the victim if the current were on. The realization that he has also made a fool of himself by accepting the experimental set results in additional loss of self-esteem.

In his response to Baumrind, Milgram (1964) noted that he and other experts had assumed that few people would proceed beyond a very low level of shock. What was disturbing to people, Milgram suggested, were not so much his methods but his results:

> Is not Baumrind's criticism based as much on the unanticipated findings as on the method? The findings were that some subjects performed in what appeared to be

a shockingly immoral way. If, instead, every one of the subjects had broken off at "slight shock," or the first sign of the learner's discomfort, the results would have been pleasant, and reassuring, and who would protest?

Although Baumrind believed that the subjects were likely to experience serious aftereffects from the experiment, Milgram (1964, 1974b) pointed out that this was not the case. In a follow-up questionnaire, 84 percent of the participants in Milgram's experiment stated that they were glad to have taken part in the experiment. Only 1.3 percent said they were "sorry to have been in the experiment." An additional follow-up examination by a psychiatrist a year after the experiment found no signs of harm or traumatic reaction.

Still, the debate over Milgram's studies sensitized psychologists and other social scientists to the ethical issues involved in research with human subjects (Fisher & Fyrberg, 1994). The controversy helped lead to the establishment of ethical safeguards by the American Psychological Association and the federal government regarding experiments involving human subjects. Because of these safeguards, the last Milgram-type obedience studies conducted in the United States occurred in 1976 (Blass, 1992).

The Ethics of Deception In the experimental variation shown, the teacher was ordered to hold the learner's hand down on the shock plate. Some 30 percent of subjects were completely obedient. Was the extreme deception used in Milgram's experiments justified?

What do you think? Was the extreme deception used in Milgram's studies unethical? Did Milgram's dramatic and unexpected results justify the emotional stress experienced by his subjects? Could Milgram have reached the same conclusions using less deceptive research methods? Under what conditions is experimental deception justified?

Destructive Obedience and Prejudice
Blind obedience to authority combined with ethnic prejudice in Germany during World War II led to the slaughter of millions of Jews in concentration camps (top). When questioned after the war, Nazi officials and soldiers claimed that they were "just following orders." During the 1970s and 1980s, the followers of Pol Pot in Cambodia killed three million of their fellow Cambodians (bottom).

Asch, Milgram, and the Real World:
Implications of the Classic Social Influence Studies

The scientific study of conformity and obedience has produced some important insights. The first one is the degree to which our behavior is influenced by situational factors. Being at odds with the majority or with authority is very uncomfortable for most people—enough so that our judgment and perceptions can be distorted and we may act in ways that violate our conscience.

More important, perhaps, is the insight that each of us *does* have the capacity to resist group or authority pressure. Because the central findings of these studies are so dramatic, it's easy to overlook the fact that some subjects refused to conform or obey despite considerable social and situational pressure. Consider the response of a subject in one of Milgram's later studies. A thirty-two-year-old industrial engineer named Jan Rensaleer protested when he was commanded to continue at the 255-volt level:

> **Experimenter:** It is absolutely essential that you continue.
>
> **Mr. Rensaleer:** Well, I won't—not with the man screaming to get out.
>
> **Experimenter:** You have no other choice.
>
> **Mr. Rensaleer:** I *do* have a choice. (*Incredulous and indignant:*) Why don't I have a choice? I came here on my own free will. I thought I could help in a research project. But if I have to hurt somebody to do that, or if I was in his place, too, I wouldn't stay there. I can't continue. I'm very sorry. I think I've gone too far already, probably.

Like some other subjects in the obedience and conformity studies, Mr. Rensaleer effectively resisted the situational and social pressures pushing him in a different direction. How are such people different from those who conformed or obeyed? Unfortunately, there's no satisfying answer to that question. No specific personality trait consistently predicts conformity or obedience in experimental situations like the ones that Asch and Milgram created (see Blass, 1991; Burger, 1992, 1987). In other words, the social influences that Asch and Milgram created in their experimental situations can be compelling even to people who are normally quite independent.

Finally, we need to reemphasize that conformity and obedience are not completely bad in and of themselves. Quite the contrary: Conformity and obedience are necessary for an orderly society, which is why such behaviors were instilled in all of us as children. The critical issue is not so much whether people conform or obey, because we all do so every day of our lives. Rather, the critical issue is whether the norms we conform to, or the orders we obey, reflect values that respect the rights, well-being, and human dignity of others.

Helping Behavior: Coming to the Aid of Strangers

> *Following the murder of Kitty Genovese, social psychologists Bibb Latané and John Darley began investigating bystander intervention. What factors increase or decrease the likelihood that people will help a stranger?*

It was about 3:20 a.m. on Friday, March 13, 1964, when Kitty Genovese returned home from her job managing a bar. Like other residents in her

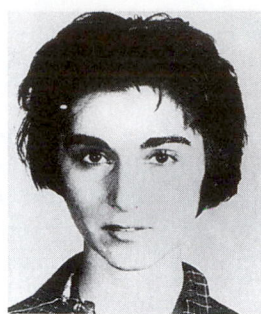

Kitty Genovese

The Murder Scene At the end of the sidewalk you can see the railroad station where Genovese parked her car. Along the sidewalk are entrances to shops as well as stairways leading to apartments above the shops. After Genovese staggered to the entrance of her apartment, her attacker returned and stabbed her to death.

middle-class New York City neighborhood, she parked her car at an adjacent railroad station. Her apartment entrance was only 100 feet away.

As she got out of her car, she noticed a man at the end of the parking lot. When the man moved in her direction, she began walking toward a nearby police callbox, which was under a street light in front of a bookstore. On the opposite side of the street was a ten-story apartment building. As she neared the street light, the man grabbed her and she screamed. Across the street, lights went on in the apartment building. "Oh, my God! He stabbed me! Please help me! Please help me!" she screamed.

"Let that girl alone!" a man yelled from one of the upper apartment windows. The attacker looked up, then walked off, leaving Kitty on the ground, bleeding. The street became quiet. Minutes passed. One by one, lights went off. Struggling to her feet, Kitty made her way toward her apartment. As she rounded the corner of the building moments later, her assailant returned, stabbing her again. "I'm dying! I'm dying!" she screamed.

Again, lights went on. Windows opened and people looked out. This time, the assailant got in his car and drove off. Fifteen minutes had passed since Kitty's first screams for help. Staggering, then crawling, Kitty moved toward the entrance of her apartment. She never made it. Her attacker returned, searching the apartment entrance doors. At the second apartment entrance, he found her, slumped at the foot of the steps. This time he stabbed her to death.

It was 3:50 a.m. when someone first called the police. The police took just two minutes to arrive at the scene. About half an hour later, an ambulance carried Kitty Genovese's body away. It was only then that people came out of their apartments to talk to the police.

Over the next two weeks, police investigators learned that a total of 38 people had witnessed Kitty's murder—a murder that involved three separate attacks over a period of 35 minutes. Why didn't anyone try to help her? Or even call the police when they first heard her screams for help?

When the *New York Times* interviewed various experts, they seemed baffled, although one expert said it was a "typical" reaction (Mohr, 1964). If there was a common theme in their explanations, it seemed to be "apathy." The occurrence was simply representative of the alienation and depersonalization of life in a big city, people said (see Rosenthal, 1964a, 1964b).

Not everyone bought this pat explanation. In the first place, it wasn't true. As social psychologists **Bibb Latané** and **John Darley** (1970) later pointed out in their landmark book *The Unresponsive Bystander: Why Doesn't He Help?*:

> People often help others, even at great personal risk to themselves. For every "apathy" story, one of outright heroism could be cited. It is a mistake to get trapped by the wave of publicity and discussion surrounding incidents in which help was not forthcoming into believing that help never comes. People sometimes help and sometimes don't. What determines when help will be given?

Factors That *Increase* the Likelihood of Bystanders Helping

Kitty Genovese's death triggered hundreds of investigations into the conditions under which people will help others (Dovidio, 1984). Those studies began in the 1960s with the pioneering efforts of Latané and Darley, who conducted a series of ingenious experiments in which people appeared to need help. Often, these studies were conducted using locations in and around New York City as a kind of open-air laboratory.

Other researchers joined the effort to understand what factors influence a person's decision to help another (see Eisenberg, 1991; Piliavin & Charng, 1990). Some of the most significant factors that have been found to increase the likelihood of helping behavior are noted below.

Bystander Intervention In the situation shown here, a bystander is coming to the aid of a stranger. What factors in this situation probably influenced the bystander's decision to help the fallen bicyclist?

The "feel good, do good" effect. People who feel good, successful, happy, or fortunate are more likely to help others (see Salovey & others, 1991; Schaller & Cialdini, 1990). Those good feelings can be due to virtually any positive event, such as receiving a gift, succeeding at a task, listening to pleasant music, finding a small amount of money, or even just enjoying a warm, sunny day.

Feeling guilty. We tend to be more helpful when we're feeling guilty. For example, after telling a lie or inadvertently causing an accident, people were more likely to help others (see Baumeister & others, 1994; Cialdini & others, 1973; Regan & others, 1972).

Seeing others who are willing to help. Whether it's donating blood, helping a stranded motorist change a flat tire, or dropping money in the Salvation Army kettle during the holiday season, we're more likely to help if we observe others do the same (Sarason & others, 1991; Bryan & Test, 1967).

Perceiving the other person as deserving help. We're more likely to help people who are in need of help through no fault of their own. For example, people are twice as likely to give some change to a stranger if they believe the stranger's wallet has been stolen than if they believe the stranger has simply spent all his money (Latané & Darley, 1970).

Knowing how to help. Research has confirmed that simply knowing what to do contributes greatly to the decision to help someone else (e.g., Huston & others, 1981; Clark & Word, 1974).

A personalized relationship. When people have any sort of personal relationship with another person, they're more likely to help that person. Even minimal social interaction with each other, such as making eye contact or engaging in small talk, increases the likelihood that one person will help the other (Solomon & others, 1981; Howard & Crano, 1974).

Factors That *Decrease* the Likelihood of Bystanders Helping

It's equally important to consider influences that decrease the likelihood of helping behavior. As we look at some of the key findings, we'll also note how these factors seemed to play a role in the murder of Kitty Genovese.

The presence of other people. People are much more likely to help when they are alone (Latané & Nida, 1981). If other people are present, helping behavior declines—a phenomenon called the **bystander effect.**

bystander effect
The phenomenon in which the greater the number of people present, the less likely each individual is to help someone in distress.

The Bystander Effect In contrast to the situation shown on p. 423, the people in this situation are walking past the man lying on the sidewalk without giving him a second glance. What factors are operating in this situation that make it much less likely that bystanders will help a stranger?

How can we account for this surprising finding? There seem to be two major reasons for the bystander effect. First, the presence of other people creates a **diffusion of responsibility.** The responsibility to intervene is *shared* (or *diffused*) among all the onlookers. Because no one person feels all the pressure to respond, each bystander becomes less likely to help (see Dovidio, 1984; Latané & Darley, 1970).

Ironically, the sheer number of bystanders seemed to be the most significant factor working against Kitty Genovese. Remember that when she first screamed, a man yelled down, "Let that girl alone!" With that, each observer instantly knew that he or she was not the only one watching the events on the street below. Hence, no single individual felt the full responsibility to help.

Second, the bystander effect seems to occur because each of us is motivated to some extent by the desire to behave in a socially acceptable way (*normative social influence*) and to appear correct (*informational social influence*). Hence, we often rely on the reactions of others to help us define the situation and guide our response. In the case of Kitty Genovese, the lack of intervention by any of the witnesses may have signaled the others that intervention was not appropriate, wanted, or needed.

Being in a big city or a very small town. Kitty Genovese was attacked late at night in one of the biggest cities in the world, New York. Are people less likely to help strangers in big cities? Researcher Nancy Steblay (1987) has confirmed that this common belief is true—but with a twist. People are less likely to help a stranger in very big cities (300,000 people or more) *or* in very small towns (5,000 people or less). Either extreme—very big or very small—seems to work against helping a stranger.

Vague or ambiguous situations. When situations are ambiguous and people are not certain that help is needed, they're less likely to offer help (Solomon & others, 1978). The ambiguity of the situation may also have worked against Kitty Genovese. The people in the apartment building saw a man and a woman struggling on the street below, but had no way of knowing whether the two were acquainted. "We thought it was a lovers' quarrel," some of the witnesses later said (Gansberg, 1964). Researchers have found that people are especially reluctant to intervene when the situation appears to be a domestic dispute or a "lovers' quarrel," because they are not certain that assistance is wanted (Shotland & Straw, 1976).

When the personal costs for helping outweigh the benefits. As a general rule, we tend to weigh the costs as well as the benefits of helping in deciding whether to act. If the potential costs outweigh the benefits, it's less likely that help will be forthcoming from you (Hedge & Yousif, 1992).

The witnesses in the Genovese case may also have felt that the benefits of helping Genovese were outweighed by the potential hassles and danger of becoming involved in the situation. Many of the witnesses said that they did not want to get involved (Gansberg, 1964).

diffusion of responsibility
The phenomenon in which the presence of other people makes it less likely that any individual will help someone in distress because the obligation to intervene is shared among all the onlookers.

Some Concluding Thoughts

On a small yet universal scale, the murder of Kitty Genovese dramatically underscores the power of situational and social influences on our behavior. Although social psychological research has provided insights about the factors that influenced the behavior of those who witnessed the Genovese murder, it should not be construed as a justification for the inaction of the bystanders. After all, Kitty Genovese's death probably could have been prevented by a single phone call. Like the topics of conformity and obedience, the research on helping behavior has important implications as we go about negotiating daily life.

We began this chapter with a prologue about Fern trying to help a stranger in a strange city. As it turned out, Fern's social perceptions of the man were inaccurate: He was not a "homeless" person living on the streets of San Francisco. As simple as this incident was, it underscored a theme that was repeatedly echoed throughout our subsequent discussions of person perception, attribution, and attitudes. Our subjective impressions, whether they are accurate or not, play a pivotal role in how we perceive and think about other people.

A different theme emerged in our later discussions of conformity, obedience, and helping behavior. Social and situational factors, especially the behavior of others in the same situation, can have powerful effects on how we act at a given moment. But like Fern, each of us has the freedom to choose how we respond in a given situation. When we're aware of the social forces that influence us, it can be easier for us to choose wisely.

In the final analysis, we are social animals who often influence one another's thoughts, perceptions, and actions, sometimes in profound ways. In the chapter Application, we'll look at some of the ways that social psychological insights have been applied by professional persuaders—and how you can counteract attempts to persuade you.

Factors That Influence Helping Behavior

In each of the following examples, first decide if help is "Likely" or "Not likely" to be forthcoming. Second, support your answer by identifying the factor or factors operating in the situation.

1. Mr. Dooley came home elated after having received a large and unexpected bonus at work earlier in the day. During dinner he receives a call from another member of his church asking if he would be willing to help on Saturday with some minor repairs around the church. Likely/Not likely _____

2. Robert is vacationing in another state. His car has broken down right beside a sign that reads "Welcome to Cedar Bluffs, Population 2,821." Likely/Not likely _____

3. Just moments after hundreds of people get off a crowded subway train on their way to work, an oddly dressed man in the crowd stumbles and falls as he is walking up the exit steps. Likely/Not likely _____

4. Three days before Christmas, the local news shows a report of a young, single, working mother whose rental house has burned down because of faulty electrical wiring. In the news report, she tearfully explains that all her possessions, including meager Christmas presents for her two children, were destroyed in the fire. Likely/Not likely _____

APPLICATION

The Persuasion Game

Persuasion is the deliberate attempt to influence the attitudes or behavior of another person in a situation where that person has some freedom of choice. In this Application, you'll see that professional persuaders often manipulate people's attitudes and behavior using techniques based on two fundamental social norms: the rule of reciprocity and the rule of commitment. Equally important, we'll give you some practical suggestions to avoid being taken in by persuasion techniques.

The Rule of Reciprocity

The *rule of reciprocity* is a simple but powerful social norm: If someone gives you something or does you a favor, you feel obligated to return the favor. That's why encyclopedia salespeople offer you a "free" dictionary for listening to their spiel and department stores that sell expensive cosmetics offer "free" makeovers. Technically, you are under "no obligation" to buy anything. Nonetheless, the tactic often creates an uncomfortable sense of obligation, so you *do* feel pressured to reciprocate by buying their product (Cialdini, 1993).

One strategy that uses the rule of reciprocity is called the *door-in-the-face technique* (see Perloff, 1993; Dillard, 1991). First, the persuader makes a large request that you're certain to refuse. For example, Joe asks to borrow $500. You figuratively "slam the door in his face" by quickly turning him down. But then Joe, apologetic, appears to back off and makes a much smaller request—to borrow $20. From your perspective, it appears that Joe has made a concession to you and is trying to be reasonable. This puts you in the position of reciprocating with a concession of your own. "Well, I can't lend you $500," you grumble, "but I guess I could lend you twenty bucks." Of course, the persuader's real goal was to persuade you to comply with the second, smaller request.

The rule of reciprocity is also operating in the *that's-not-all technique* (Zimbardo & Leippe, 1991). First, the persuader makes an offer. But before you can accept or reject it, the persuader appears to throw in something extra to make the deal even more attractive to you. So as you're standing there mulling over the price of the more expensive CD player, the salesperson says, "Listen, I'm offering you a great price but that's not all I'll do— I'll throw in some headphones at no charge." From your perspective, it appears as though the salesperson has just done you a favor by making a concession you did not ask for. This creates a sense of obligation for you to reciprocate by buying the "better" package.

The Rule of Commitment

Another powerful social norm is the *rule of commitment*: Once you make a public commitment, there is psychological and interpersonal pressure on you to behave consistently with your earlier commitment. The *foot-in-the-door technique* is one strategy that capitalizes on the rule of commitment (see Perloff, 1993; Cialdini, 1993). Here's how it works.

First, the persuader makes a small request that you're likely to agree with.

For example, she might ask you to wear a lapel pin publicizing a fundraising drive for a charity (see Pratkanis & Aronson, 1991). By agreeing to wear the lapel pin, you've made a *commitment* to the fundraising effort. At that point, she has gotten her "foot in the door." Later, the persuader asks you to comply with a second, larger request, such as donating money to the charity. Because of your earlier commitment, you feel psychologically pressured to behave consistently by now agreeing to the larger commitment (Gorassini & Olson, 1995).

The rule of commitment is also operating in the *low-ball technique*. First, the persuader gets you to make a commitment by deliberately understating the cost of the product you want. He's thrown you a "low ball," so to speak, one that is simply too good to turn down. In reality, the persuader has no intention of honoring the artificially low price.

Here's an example of the low-ball technique in action: You've negotiated an excellent price (the "low ball") on a used car and filled out the sales contract. The car salesman shakes your hand and beams, then takes your paperwork into his manager's office for approval. Ten minutes pass—enough time for you to convince yourself that you've made the right decision and solidify your commitment to it.

At that point, the salesman comes back from his manager's office looking dejected. "I'm terribly sorry," the car salesman says. "My manager won't let me sell the car at that price because we'd lose too much money on the deal. I told him I would even take a lower commission, but he won't budge."

Notice what has happened. The attractive "low-ball" price that originally prompted you to make the commitment has been pulled out from under your feet. What typically happens? Despite the loss of the original inducement to make the purchase—the low-ball price

Playing the Persuasion Game This car salesman will use a variety of persuasive techniques to try to persuade this young couple to buy a car from him. Becoming aware of common persuasion techniques can help you make decisions more objectively.

—people often feel compelled to "keep their commitment" to make the purchase even though it is at a higher price (Cialdini, 1993).

Defending Against Persuasion Techniques

How can you reduce the likelihood that you'll be manipulated into making a decision that is not in your best interest? Here are three practical suggestions.

Suggestion 1: Sleep on it. Persuasive transactions typically occur quickly. Part of this is our own doing. We've finally decided to go look at a new CD player, automobile, or whatever, so we're psychologically primed to buy the product. The persuader uses this psychological momentum to help coax you into signing on the dotted line right then and there. It's only later, of course, that

you sometimes have second thoughts. So when you think you've got the deal you want, tell the persuader that you always sleep on important decisions before making a final commitment.

The sleep-on-it rule often provides an opportunity to discover whether the persuader is deliberately trying to pressure or manipulate you. If the persuader responds to your sleep-on-it suggestion by saying something like, "This offer is good for today only," then it's likely that he or she is afraid that your commitment to the deal will crumble if you think about it too carefully or look elsewhere.

Suggestion 2: Play devil's advocate. Make a list of all the reasons why you should *not* buy the product or make a particular commitment (Pratkanis & Aronson, 1991). Arguing *against* the

decision will help activate your critical thinking skills. It's also helpful to discuss important decisions with a friend, who might be able to point out disadvantages that you have overlooked.

Suggestion 3. Pay attention to your gut feelings. Learn to trust your gut feelings when something doesn't feel quite right. If you feel like you're being psychologically pressured or cornered, you probably are. As a general rule, if you feel any sense of hesitation, lean toward the conservative side and do nothing. If you take the time to think things over, you'll probably be able to identify the source of your reluctance.

Summary Social Psychology

Social Psychology

- Social psychology is the scientific study of the way individuals think, feel, and behave in social situations. Social cognition and social influence are two important areas of research in social psychology.

Person Perception

- Person perception is an active and subjective process and occurs in an interpersonal context. The interpersonal context includes the characteristics of the individual you are judging, your own characteristics, and the situation.

- Person perception is influenced by subjective perceptions, personal goals, social norms, and self-perception.

- People often rely on social categories when they evaluate others. Social categorization may be automatic or deliberate. Using social categories is cognitively efficient, but can lead to inaccurate conclusions.

- Because we expect certain traits and behaviors to go together, we often form and rely on implicit personality theories in person perception. Implicit personality theories provide a mental framework that organizes observations, memories, and beliefs about other people.

Attribution: Explaining Behavior

- The attribution process refers to how we infer the cause of our own or another person's behavior. Attributions can strongly influence our opinions of other people, but the attribution process is susceptible to many biases.

- Three important attributional biases are the fundamental attribution error, the actor–observer discrepancy, and the self-serving bias. In some collectivistic cultures, people display the modesty or self-effacing bias and are less prone to making the fundamental attribution error than are people in individualistic cultures.

Attitudes and Behavior

- An attitude is a learned tendency to evaluate an object, person, or issue in a particular way. This evaluation is usually positive or negative, but may be ambivalent. Attitudes can have cognitive, affective, and behavioral components.

- Attitudes are likely to determine behaviors when they are extreme or expressed frequently; when they have been formed through direct experience; when people are very knowledgeable about the attitude object; when people have a vested interest in the subject of the attitude; and when people expect a favorable outcome from acting in accordance with their attitude.

■ When behavior conflicts with attitudes, cognitive dissonance may occur, and people may change their attitudes to conform to their behavior.

Understanding Prejudice

■ Prejudice refers to a negative attitude toward people who belong to a specific social group. Stereotypes are social categories about members of particular social groups. Once formed, stereotypes resist change. Relying on stereotypes can have many negative consequences. Stereotyped thinking can distort perception and cause us to inaccurately prejudge individuals.

■ Judgments of others are also influenced by whether they are members of our in-group or an out-group. We're more likely to use negative stereotypes to evaluate members of out-groups. The out-group homogeneity effect, in-group bias, and ethnocentrism are three forms of bias that can result in prejudicial thinking.

■ Stereotypes form the cognitive basis for prejudicial attitudes. Prejudice also has an emotional and behavioral component.

■ Muzafer Sherif demonstrated that intergroup conflict can be decreased when groups engage in a cooperative effort. Cooperative learning is one way of reducing prejudice in classrooms.

Conformity: Following the Crowd

■ Conformity occurs when people change their behavior, attitudes, or beliefs in response to real or imagined group pressure. Research by Solomon Asch demonstrated the degree to which people will conform to a majority view and the conditions under which conformity is most likely. Normative and informational social influence both contribute to conformity.

■ Conformity is generally higher in collectivistic cultures than in individualistic cultures. Conformity to group norms is viewed less negatively in many collectivistic cultures than it is in individualistic cultures.

Obedience: Following Orders

■ In Milgram's original obedience experiment, each subject ("the teacher") thought he was delivering ever-increasing levels of electric shock to another subject ("the learner"). In contrast to predictions, most of the subjects obeyed the experimenter and progressed to the maximum shock level.

■ Milgram identified several powerful aspects of the original experimental situation that influenced subjects to obey the experimenter and continue delivering electric shocks. In later experiments, Milgram also identified several situational factors that made people less likely to obey.

Helping Behavior: Coming to the Aid of Strangers

■ The scientific study of helping behavior was spurred by the murder of Kitty Genovese in front of 38 witnesses. Although no one intervened to save Genovese, sometimes people do help others.

■ Bibb Latané and John Darley investigated the circumstances under which people will help a stranger. Several factors have been identified that increase the likelihood of bystander intervention. Diffusion of responsibility is one important factor that explains why bystanders do not help another person.

Key Terms

social psychology (p. 400)

social cognition (p. 400)

social influence (p. 400)

person perception (p. 401)

social norms (p. 401)

social categorization (p. 402)

implicit personality theory (p. 403)

attribution (p. 404)

fundamental attribution error (p. 404)

blaming the victim (p. 404)

just-world hypothesis (p. 404)

actor–observer discrepancy (p. 405)

self-serving bias (p. 406)

attitude (p. 407)

cognitive dissonance (p. 409)

prejudice (p. 410)

stereotype (p. 411)

in-group (p. 411)

out-group (p. 411)

out-group homogeneity effect (p. 411)

in-group bias (p. 412)

ethnocentrism (p. 412)

conformity (p. 414)

normative social influence (p. 415)

informational social influence (p. 415)

obedience (p. 416)

bystander effect (p. 423)

diffusion of responsibility (p. 424)

persuasion (p. 426)

Key People

Solomon Asch (1907–1996) American social psychologist who is best known for his pioneering studies of conformity.

John M. Darley (b. 1938) Contemporary American social psychologist who, along with co-researcher Bibb Latané, is best known for his pioneering studies of bystander intervention in emergency situations.

Bibb Latané (b. 1937) Contemporary American social psychologist who, along with co-researcher John Darley, is best known for his pioneering studies of bystander intervention in emergency situations.

Stanley Milgram (1933–1984) American social psychologist who is best known for his controversial series of studies investigating destructive obedience to an authority.

Muzafer Sherif (b. 1906) American social psychologist who is best known for his "Robber's Cave" experiments to study prejudice, conflict resolution, and group processes.

CONCEPT REVIEW 11.1 Page 407

1. c
2. e
3. d
4. b
5. a

CONCEPT REVIEW 11.2 Page 414

1. stereotyping
2. out-group homogeneity
3. cognitive dissonance
4. ethnocentrism

CONCEPT REVIEW 11.3 Page 425

1. Likely. The "feel good, do good" effect.
2. Not likely. Robert is a stranger in a very small town.
3. Not likely, for five reasons: (1) diffusion of responsibility; (2) a large city; (3) no personalized relationship with the fallen man; (4) vague situation; (5) personal costs of being late to work outweigh the benefits of stopping to help a stranger.
4. Likely, for three reasons: (1) person is perceived as deserving of help through no fault of her own; (2) because the woman speaks to the viewing audience, the situation is more personalized; (3) guilt is likely to motivate helping behavior, especially in people who have much more than the person who needs help.

Chapter

Prologue: Thank God It's Friday?

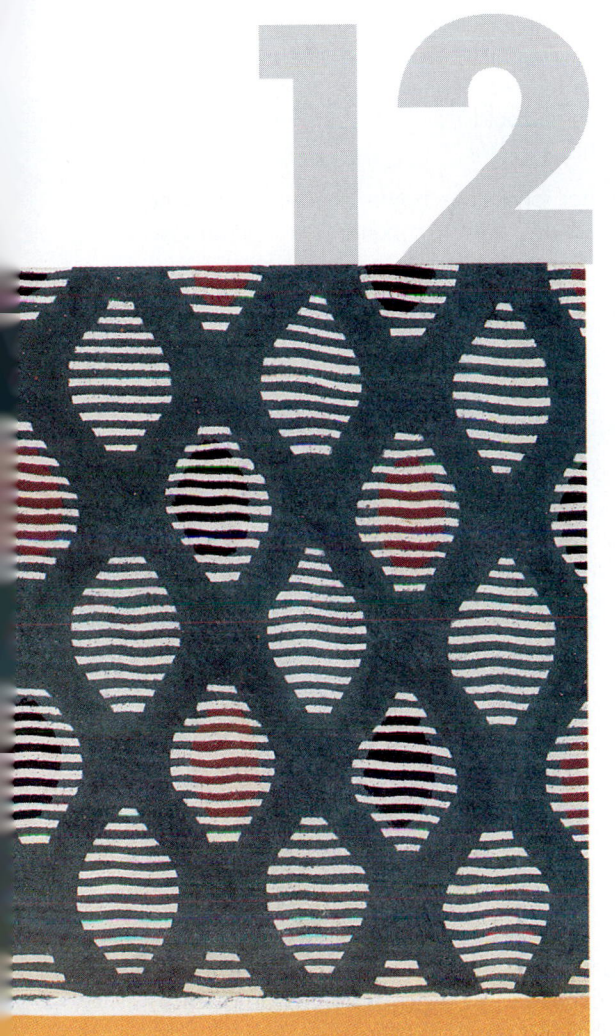

12

Stress, Health, and Coping

Prologue: Thank God It's Friday?

How do you spell *STRESS*? Our friends David and Marie joke that they spell it L-I-F-E. David and Marie are both in their mid-forties, but they have two young children. Like most parents today, they also have full-time jobs. Marie works as an accountant, and David is the computer administrator for a small firm.

Adding to their hectic lives, both Marie and David are taking evening classes at the local community college. Since Marie doesn't have an accounting degree, she's enrolled in an intensive program to prepare her to take the CPA exam. She's at school three nights a week and all day Saturday. Every spare moment when she's not at school or work, Marie immerses herself in accounting books.

David is taking classes to upgrade his computer skills. He had originally been trained as a mainframe programmer, but jobs in that field are hard to come by now. When he was laid off from his last job, it took him over a year to find a new one. On the one hand, he's glad to be employed again. On the other hand, his pay is much lower than at his old job, and he finds his new boss hard to get along with.

Like David, Marie is not completely happy with her job. The Japanese-owned company she works for recently announced that it was moving its North American headquarters from Tulsa to Mexico City. Although the managers announced that no one would be laid off, prospective tenants have twice toured the building to look over the offices. Consequently, Marie has been actively looking for a new job.

Not wanting to jeopardize her current job, Marie has been forced to devise various excuses for leaving work to go to job interviews. She doesn't have a private office, so a simple phone call to a prospective employer presents problems. "It's hard to sound cool, calm, and confident," she laughs, "when you're calling from a Kmart and the PA system is announcing a Blue Light Special in the background."

How Do You Define Stress?
From a ripped grocery bag to the threat of unemployment, stressors come in all sizes. Any event can produce stress—if you think that you don't have the resources to cope with it.

Going to an interview is even more challenging. After finding a way to duck out of her office, she has to stop somewhere to quickly change into her good suit. "I'm beginning to feel like Superwoman," Marie told us. "So far, I've changed my clothes in a bathroom at the college, two McDonalds, and a Burger King. But I draw the line at phone booths!"

Out of more than a hundred applicants, Marie and two others made the final cut for an extremely promising job. Though the company was supposed to call her within a week to tell her if she had gotten the job, they called instead to tell her that the manager who would make the decision was out of town but would *definitely* call her on Friday. Well, Friday came . . . but the call didn't. As Marie drove home from work that Friday, she felt more and more upset. "They could have at least called me and told me they hired someone else," she thought.

As Marie negotiated the rush hour traffic on her long drive home, she began making plans for the evening. David would soon be home, with two hungry children in tow. Marie mentally ticked off the contents of the refrigerator, trying to think of a quick supper she could prepare. Looks like frozen pizza again, she decided. After dinner, she would need to spend at least two hours studying for her Saturday-morning classes. David would help with the cleanup and with getting Brian and Mandy to bed, but it would still be another late night—and Marie already felt exhausted. One more time, Marie repeated her personal motto: "No one ever said life was supposed to be easy."

Without question, Marie is experiencing a great deal of stress. But we could just as easily have used a day in the life of any of our friends to illustrate the main topic of this chapter. If you're like most of our students, you probably have ample firsthand experience with the stress of juggling the demands of college, work, and family responsibilities. The simple fact is that all of us face a wide variety of obstacles, frustrations, and challenges as we negotiate daily life. Any way you look at it, stress is an unavoidable part of life.

Introduction

What Is Stress?

What exactly is stress? It's one of those words that is frequently used but is hard to define precisely. Early stress researchers, who mostly studied animals, defined stress in terms of the physiological response to harmful or threatening events (e.g., Selye, 1956). However, people are far more complex than animals in their response to potentially stressful events. Two people may respond very differently to the same stress-producing event.

Since the 1960s, psychologists have been actively studying the human response to stress, including the effect of stress on health and how people cope with stressful events. As research findings have accumulated, it has become clear that psychological and social factors, as well as biological factors, are involved in the stress experience and its effects.

Today, **stress** is widely defined as a negative emotional state occurring in response to events that are perceived as taxing or exceeding a person's resources or ability to cope (Cohen & Herbert, 1996; Lazarus, 1993). This definition emphasizes the important role that a person's perception or appraisal of events plays in the experience of stress. Whether or not we experience stress largely depends on our *cognitive appraisal* of an event and the resources that we have to deal with the event (Tomaka & others, 1993; Lazarus & Folkman, 1984).

If we think that we have adequate resources to deal with a situation, it will probably create little or no stress in our lives. But if we perceive our re-

stress
A negative emotional state occurring in response to events that are perceived as taxing or exceeding a person's resources or ability to cope.

health psychology
The branch of psychology that studies how psychological factors influence health, illness, medical treatment, and health-related behaviors.

stressors
Events or situations that are perceived as harmful, threatening, or challenging.

TABLE 12.1 Life Events and Stress: Sample Items from the Social Readjustment Rating Scale

Life Events	Life Change Units
Death of spouse	100
Divorce	73
Jail term	63
Death of close family member	63
Personal injury or illness	53
Marriage	50
Fired at work	47
Retirement	45
Pregnancy	40
Change in financial state	38
Death of close friend	37
Change to different line of work	36
Mortgage or loan for major purchase	31
Foreclosure on mortgage or loan	30
Change in responsibilities at work	29
Outstanding personal achievement	28
Begin or end school	26
Trouble with boss	23
Change in work hours or conditions	20
Change in residence	20
Change in social activities	18
Change in sleeping habits	16
Change in eating habits	15
Vacation	13
Christmas	12
Minor violations of the law	11

SOURCE: Holmes & Rahe, 1967.

The Social Readjustment Rating Scale, developed by Thomas Holmes and Richard Rahe (1967), was an early attempt to quantify the amount of stress experienced by people in a wide range of situations. Holmes and Rahe reasoned that any life event that required some sort of adaptation or change would create stress, whether the life event was pleasant or unpleasant.

Major Life Events and Stress Would a welcome pregnancy produce stress? According to the life events approach, any event that required you to change or adjust your lifestyle would produce significant stress—whether the event was positive or negative, planned or unexpected. How was the life events approach modified by later research?

sources as being inadequate to deal with a situation that we see as threatening, challenging, or even harmful, we'll experience the effects of stress. If our coping efforts are effective, stress will decrease; if ineffective, stress will increase.

The study of stress is a key topic in one of the most rapidly growing specialty areas in psychology: **health psychology.** Along with stress, health psychologists study how psychological factors influence health, illness, and treatment. They investigate issues such as how to promote health-enhancing behaviors and how people respond in the relationship between patient and health practitioner (Taylor, 1995). In looking at such issues, health psychologists are guided by the *biopsychosocial model.* According to this model, health and illness are determined by the complex interaction of biological, psychological, and social factors (Bernard, 1994).

Sources of Stress

Stressors come in all sizes. Some important sources of stress include life events, daily hassles, conflict, and social and cultural factors. What problems are associated with the life events approach? How do daily hassles and conflict contribute to stress?

Life is filled with potential **stressors**—events or situations that produce stress. In fact, virtually any event or situation can be a source of stress if you question your ability or resources to deal effectively with it (Lazarus & Folkman, 1984). In this section, we'll survey some of the most important and common sources of stress.

Life Events and Change

Early stress researchers Thomas Holmes and Richard Rahe (1967) believed that any change that required you to adjust your behavior and lifestyle would cause stress. In an attempt to measure the amount of stress people experienced, they developed the *Social Readjustment Rating Scale,* which is shown in Table 12.1. The scale includes 43 life events that are likely to require some level of adaptation. Each life event is assigned a numerical rating that estimates its relative impact in terms of *life change units.*

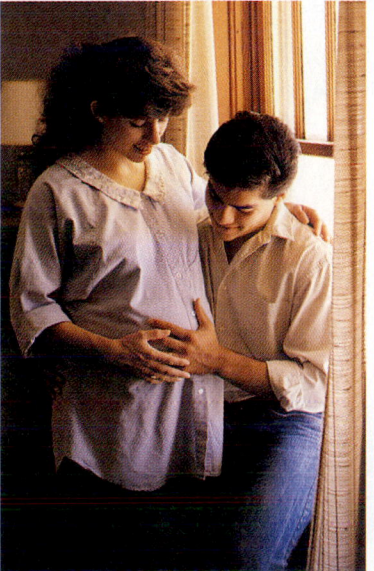

Life events ratings range from 100 life change units for the most stress-producing to 11 life change units for the least stress-producing events. Notice that many of the life events are generally considered to be positive events, such as a vacation. According to the life events approach, *any* change, whether positive or negative, is inherently stress-producing.

To measure their level of stress, people simply checked off the life events they had experienced in the past year and added up the total. Holmes and Rahe found that people who accumulated more than 150 life change units within a year had an increased rate of physical or psychological illness (Rahe, 1972; Holmes & Masuda, 1974).

Despite its initial popularity, several problems with the life events approach have been pointed out. First, the link between scores on the Social Readjustment Rating Scale and the development of physical and psychological problems is relatively weak. In general, scores on the Social Readjustment Rating Scale are *not* very good predictors of poor physical or mental health. Instead, researchers have found that most people weather major life events without developing serious physical or psychological problems (Coyne & Downey, 1991; Kessler & others, 1985).

Second, the Social Readjustment Rating Scale does not take into account a person's subjective appraisal of an event, response to that event, or ability to cope with the event (T. W. Miller, 1993; Lazarus & Folkman, 1984). Instead, the number of life change units on the scale is pre-assigned, reflecting the assumption that a given life event will have the same impact on virtually everyone. But clearly, the stress-producing potential of an event might vary widely from one person to another. For instance, if you are in a marriage that is filled with conflict, tension, and unhappiness, getting divorced (73 life change units) might be significantly less stressful than remaining married.

Third, the life events approach assumes that change in itself, whether good or bad, produces stress. However, researchers have found that negative life events have the greatest adverse effects on health, especially when they're unexpected and uncontrollable (Dohrenwend & others, 1993; Perkins, 1982). In contrast, positive or desirable events are much *less* likely to affect your health adversely (Taylor, 1995). Today, most researchers agree that undesirable events are significant sources of stress, but change in itself is not necessarily stressful.

Daily Hassles

What made you feel "stressed out" in the last week? Chances are it was not a major life event. Instead, it was probably some unexpected but minor annoyance like spilling ketchup on your new white T-shirt, losing your keys, getting stuck in a long line, or even having a bad hair day.

Stress researcher **Richard Lazarus** (b. 1922) and his colleagues suspected that such ordinary irritations in daily life might be an important source of stress. To explore this idea, they developed a scale measuring **daily hassles**—everyday occurrences that annoy and upset people (Kanner & others, 1981; DeLongis & others, 1982). The Daily Hassles Scale measures the occurrence of everyday annoyances like losing something, getting stuck in traffic, and even being inconvenienced by lousy weather.

How important are daily hassles in producing stress? The frequency of daily hassles is linked to both psychological distress and physical symptoms, like headaches and backaches (DeLongis & others, 1988; Weinberger & others, 1987). In fact, the number of daily hassles people experience is a better predictor of physical illness and symptoms than the number of major life events experienced (DeLongis & others, 1982; Burks & Martin, 1985).

Richard Lazarus Psychologist Richard Lazarus has made several influential contributions to the study of stress and coping. His definition of stress emphasizes the importance of cognitive appraisal in the stress response. He also demonstrated the importance of everyday hassles in producing stress.

Daily Hassles Life's little hassles and irritants can be a significant source of stress—especially when they pile up. Traffic jams, long lines when you're in a hurry, and misplacing your keys are just a few examples of daily hassles. What daily hassles have you experienced in the last few days?

Why do daily hassles take such a toll? One explanation is that such minor stressors are *cumulative* (Repetti, 1993). Each hassle may be relatively unimportant in itself, but after a day filled with minor hassles, the effects add up. People feel drained, grumpy, and stressed out. Daily hassles also contribute to the stress produced by major life events (Lazarus & Folkman, 1984). Any major life change, whether positive or negative, can create a ripple effect, generating a host of new daily hassles (Pillow & others, 1996).

Conflict

Another common source of stress is **conflict**—feeling pulled between two opposing desires, motives, or goals (Emmons & King, 1988; Epstein, 1982). There are three basic types of conflict, each with a different potential to be stress-producing. These conflicts are described in terms of *approach* and *avoidance*. An individual is motivated to *approach* desirable or pleasant outcomes and to *avoid* undesirable or unpleasant outcomes.

An *approach-approach conflict* represents a win-win situation—you're faced with a choice between two equally appealing outcomes. As a rule, approach-approach conflicts are usually easy to resolve and don't produce much stress. More stressful are *avoidance-avoidance conflicts*—choosing between two unappealing or undesirable outcomes. A common response is to avoid both outcomes by delaying the decision (Tversky & Shafir, 1992).

Most stressful are *approach-avoidance conflicts*. Here, a goal has both desirable and undesirable aspects. When faced with an approach-avoidance conflict, people often *vacillate,* unable to decide whether to approach or avoid the goal. From a distance, the desirable aspects of the goal can exert a strong pull. But as you move toward or approach the goal, the negative aspects loom more vividly in your mind, and you pull back (Epstein, 1982). Not surprisingly, people facing approach-avoidance conflicts often find themselves "stuck"—unable to resolve the conflict, but unable to stop thinking about it, either (Emmons & King, 1988). The result is a significant increase in feelings of stress and anxiety.

CATHY

Social and Cultural Sources of Stress

daily hassles
Everyday minor events that annoy and upset people.

conflict
A situation in which a person feels pulled between two or more opposing desires, motives, or goals.

Social conditions can also be an important source of stress. Crowding, crime, unemployment, poverty, racism, inadequate health care, and substandard housing are all associated with increased stress (Graig, 1993; Pearlin, 1993). When people live in an environment that is inherently stressful, they often experience ongoing, or *chronic,* stress (Taylor, 1995).

People in the lowest socioeconomic levels of society tend to have the highest levels of psychological distress, illness, and death (Cohen & Williamson, 1988; Lindheim & Syme, 1983). In a poverty-stricken neighborhood, people are likely to be exposed to more negative life events and to have fewer resources available to cope with those events. Daily hassles are also more common.

Stress can also result when cultures clash (Berry, 1994). For example, Marie sometimes experiences a degree of cultural stress at her job. The company is Japanese-owned, with its headquarters in Tokyo. All the firm's managers and many of its employees are Japanese. Her co-workers often speak Japanese in the office, and Marie has no idea what they're talking about.

Cultural Differences and Stress As this Sikh family crossing a busy street in Chicago has discovered, adapting to a new culture can be a stressful process. Many immigrants are faced with the challenge of learning to live in a new society where the language, style of dress, diet, and social and religious values are quite different from those of their original culture.

Marie also feels frustrated and puzzled when a manager appears to publicly agree with a suggestion she makes and then takes a completely different course of action. Such a strategy reflects the Japanese cultural style of avoiding direct social confrontation (Markus & Kitayama, 1991).

As a third-generation American, Marie is accustomed to feeling culturally "at home" in her surroundings. The feelings of being a cultural "outsider" at work are mildly stressful for her. But for refugees, immigrants, and their children, adapting to a new culture can be extremely stress-producing (Shuval, 1993). In Culture and Human Behavior Box 12.1, we describe the stress that can result from adapting to a different culture.

Defining Stress and Sources of Stress

Determine whether each of the following items is true or false. Rewrite each false statement to correct it.

_____ **1.** According to the biopsychosocial model, physical well-being is wholly determined by stress and social adjustment.

_____ **2.** In the past year, Jan has gotten divorced, changed jobs, moved three times, and lost her closest friend in an auto accident. Because of the number of stress-producing life events Jan has experienced, she is certain to develop a major illness in the next six months.

_____ **3.** The level of stress due to daily hassles is measured by the Social Readjustment Rating Scale.

CONCEPT REVIEW 12.1

_____ **4.** The amount of stress you experience depends largely on how you appraise a stressor and your ability to cope with it.

_____ **5.** Lyle can't make up his mind whether to major in cell biology or business. Business is more practical, but he finds the courses boring. He loves the field of cell biology, but he is afraid that he will not be able to find a job in the field. Because he is experiencing an approach-approach conflict, he is likely to experience a low level of stress.

_____ **6.** According to the life events approach, positive life events, such as taking a vacation or getting married, offset the stress caused by negative life events.

CULTURE AND HUMAN BEHAVIOR 12.1

The Stress of Adapting to a New Culture

Refugees and immigrants are often unprepared for the dramatically different values, language, food, customs, climate, and religions that await them in their new land. Not surprisingly, coping with a new culture can be extremely stress-producing (Johnson & others, 1995). The process of changing one's values and customs as a result of contact with another culture is referred to as *acculturation*. Thus, the term **acculturative stress** describes the stress that results from the pressure of adapting to a new culture (Williams & Berry, 1991).

Many factors can influence the degree of acculturative stress that a person experiences. For example, when the new society is one that accepts ethnic and cultural diversity, acculturative stress is reduced (Shuval, 1993). The ease of transition is also enhanced when the person has some familiarity with the new language and customs, advanced education, and social support from friends, family members, and cultural associations (Berry, 1994).

Cross-cultural psychologist John Berry has found that the person's attitudes are important in determining how much acculturative stress is experienced. When a person encounters a new cultural environment, they are faced with two fundamental questions: (1) *Should I seek positive relations with the dominant society?* (2) *Is my original cultural identity of value to me, and should I try to maintain it?*

The answers to these questions results in one of four possible patterns of acculturation: *integration, assimilation, separation,* or *marginalization* (see the diagram above). In effect, each pattern represents a different way of coping with the stress of adapting to a new culture (Berry, 1994; Williams & Berry, 1991). Let's briefly describe each pattern.

The *integrated* individual continues to value his original cultural customs, but also seeks to become part of the dominant society. Ideally, the integrated individual feels comfortable in

		Question 1: Should I seek positive relations with the dominant society?	
		Yes	**No**
Question 2: Is my original cultural identity of value to me, and should I try to maintain it?	**Yes**	Integration	Separation
	No	Assimilation	Marginalization

Patterns of Adapting to a New Culture

According to cross-cultural psychologist John Berry (1994), there are four basic patterns of adapting to a new culture. Which pattern is followed depends on how the person responds to the two key questions shown.

both his culture of origin and the culture of the dominant society, moving easily from one to the other (LaFromboise & others, 1993a). The successfully integrated individual's level of acculturative stress will be low.

The *assimilated* individual gives up her old cultural identity and tries to become part of the new society. She may adopt the new clothing, religion, and social values of her new environment and abandon her old customs and language.

Assimilation usually involves a moderate level of stress, partly because it involves a psychological loss—one's previous cultural identity. People who follow this pattern also face the possibility of being rejected either by members of the majority culture or by members of the culture of origin (LaFromboise & others, 1993a). The process of learning new behaviors and suppressing old behaviors can also be moderately stressful.

The individual who follows the pattern of *separation* maintains his cultural identity and avoids contact with the new culture. He may refuse to learn the new language, live in a neighborhood that is primarily populated by others of the same ethnic background, and socialize only with members of his own ethnic group.

In some instances, such withdrawal from the larger society is self-imposed. However, separation can also be the result of discrimination by the dominant society, as when people of a particular ethnic group are discouraged from fully participating in the dominant society. Not surprisingly, the level of acculturative stress associated with separation is likely to be very high.

Finally, the *marginalized* person is out of cultural and psychological contact with *both* her traditional cultural group and the culture of the new society. By taking the path of marginalization, she has lost the important features of her traditional culture, but has not replaced them with a new cultural identity.

The marginalized individual is likely to experience the greatest degree of acculturative stress, feeling as if she doesn't really belong anywhere. Essentially, she is stuck in an unresolved conflict between her traditional culture and her new social environment. She is also likely to experience feelings of alienation and a loss of identity (Berry & Kim, 1988).

Physical Effects of Stress:
The Mind–Body Connection

> *Stress can contribute to health problems both indirectly and directly. How did the work of Cannon and Selye contribute to the early understanding of stress? What endocrine pathways are involved in the fight-or-flight response and the general adaptation syndrome?*

From headaches to heart attacks, stress contributes to a wide range of disorders, especially when stress is long-term or chronic (see Pelletier, 1993; Kamarck & Jennings, 1991). Basically, stress appears to undermine physical well-being in two ways: indirectly and directly.

First, stress can *indirectly* affect a person's health by prompting behaviors that jeopardize physical well-being. Many studies have shown that people under chronic stress are more likely to use alcohol, coffee, and cigarettes than people under less stress (Cohen & Williamson, 1988; Baer & others, 1987). High levels of stress can also interfere with cognitive abilities, like attention, concentration, and memory (Mandler, 1993). In turn, such cognitive disruptions can increase the likelihood of accidents and injuries (Holt, 1993).

Second, stress can *directly* affect physical health by altering body functions, leading to symptoms, illness, or disease. Here's a very common example: When people are under a great deal of stress, their neck and head muscles can contract and tighten, resulting in stress-induced tension headaches. But exactly how do stressful events influence bodily processes, such as muscle contractions?

Stress and the Endocrine System

To explain the connection between stress and health, researchers have focused on how the nervous system, including the brain, interacts with two other important body systems: the endocrine and immune systems. We'll first consider the role that the endocrine system plays in our response to stressful events and then look at the connections between stress and the immune system.

Walter Cannon: Stress and the Fight-or-Flight Response

Any kind of immediate threat to your well-being is a stress-producing experience that triggers a cascade of changes in your body. As we've noted in previous chapters, this rapidly occurring chain of internal physical reactions is called the **fight-or-flight response.** Collectively, these changes prepare us either to fight or to take flight from an immediate threat.

The fight-or-flight response was first described by American physiologist **Walter Cannon** (1871–1945), one of the earliest contributors to stress research. Cannon (1932) found that the fight-or-flight response involved both the sympathetic nervous system and the endocrine system (see Chapter 2).

With the perception of a threat, the hypothalamus and lower brain structures activate the sympathetic nervous system (see left side of Figure 12.1). The sympathetic nervous system stimulates the adrenal medulla to secrete hormones called **catecholamines,** including *adrenaline* and *noradrenaline*. Circulating through the blood, catecholamines trigger the rapid and intense bodily changes associated with the fight-or-flight response. Once the threat is removed, the high level of bodily arousal subsides gradually, usually within about 20 to 60 minutes.

fight-or-flight response
A rapidly occurring chain of internal physical reactions that prepare people either to fight or take flight from an immediate threat.

catecholamines
Hormones secreted by the adrenal medulla that cause rapid physiological arousal; include adrenaline and noradrenaline.

general adaptation syndrome
Selye's term for the three-stage progression of physical changes that occur when an organism is exposed to intense and prolonged stress. The three stages are alarm, resistance, and exhaustion.

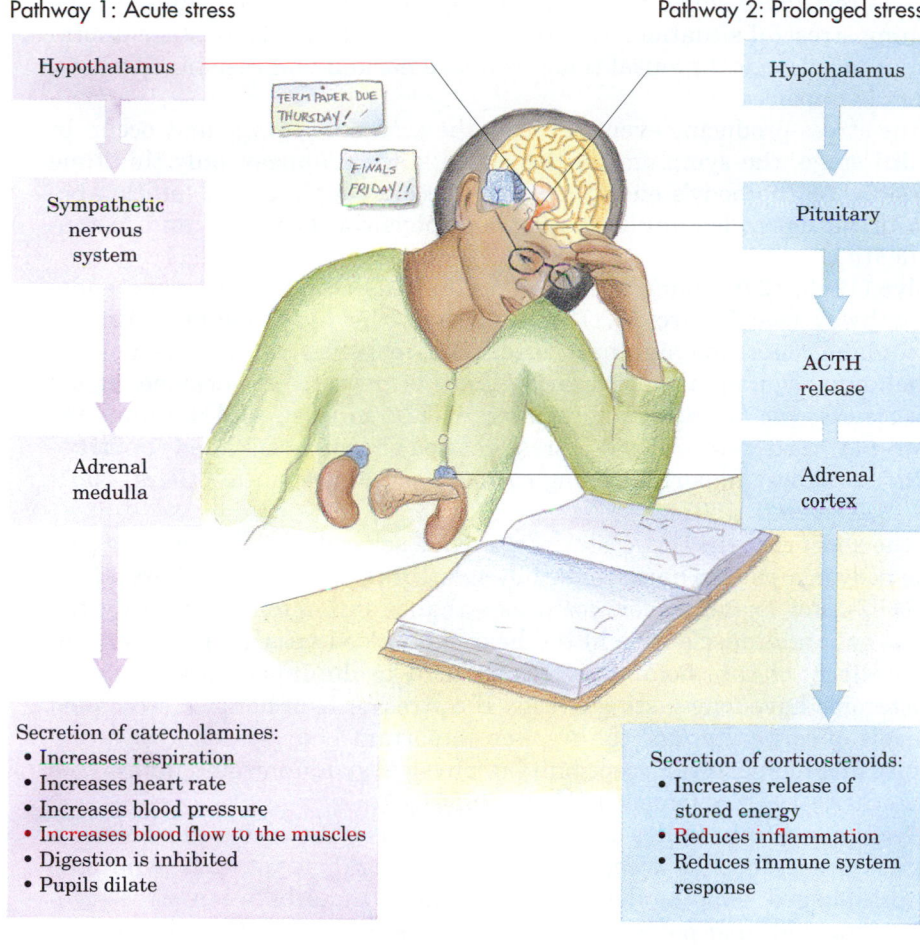

Pathway 1: Acute stress

Hypothalamus

↓

Sympathetic nervous system

↓

Adrenal medulla

↓

Secretion of catecholamines:
• Increases respiration
• Increases heart rate
• Increases blood pressure
• Increases blood flow to the muscles
• Digestion is inhibited
• Pupils dilate

Pathway 2: Prolonged stress

Hypothalamus

↓

Pituitary

↓

ACTH release

↓

Adrenal cortex

↓

Secretion of corticosteroids:
• Increases release of stored energy
• Reduces inflammation
• Reduces immune system response

TERM PAPER DUE THURSDAY!

FINALS FRIDAY!!

FIGURE 12.1 Endocrine System Pathways in Stress Two different endocrine system pathways are involved in the response to stress. Walter Cannon identified the endocrine pathway shown on the left side of this diagram; this is the pathway involved in the fight-or-flight response to immediate threats. Hans Selye identified the endocrine pathway shown on the right side. This second endocrine pathway plays an important role in dealing with prolonged or chronic stressors.

As a short-term reaction, the fight-or-flight response helps ensure survival by swiftly mobilizing internal physical resources to defensively attack or flee an immediate threat. Without question, the fight-or-flight response is very useful if you're suddenly faced with a life-threatening situation, such as a guy pointing a gun at you in a deserted parking lot. However, when exposure to an unavoidable threat is prolonged, the intense arousal of the fight-or-flight response can also become prolonged. Under these conditions, Cannon believed, the fight-or-flight response could prove harmful to physical health.

Hans Selye: Stress and the General Adaptation Syndrome

Does the man shown in the photograph below look like someone who had met and conquered stress? **Hans Selye** (1907–1982) was the Canadian endocrinologist whose pioneering scientific investigations confirmed Cannon's suggestion that prolonged stress could be physically harmful. Most of Selye's pioneering research was done with rats that were exposed to prolonged stressors, like electric shock, extreme heat or cold, or forced exercise. Regardless of the condition that Selye used to produce prolonged stress, he found the same pattern of physical changes in the rats. First, the adrenal glands became enlarged. Second, stomach ulcers and loss of weight occurred. And third, there was shrinkage of the thymus gland and lymph glands, two key components of the immune system. Selye believed that these distinct physical changes represented the essential effects of stress—the body's response to any demand placed on it.

Selye discovered that if the bodily "wear and tear" of the stress-producing event continued, the effects became evident in three progressive stages. He called these stages the **general adaptation syndrome.** During the initial *alarm stage,* intense arousal occurs as the body mobilizes internal physical resources to meet the demands of the stress-producing event. Selye (1976) found that the rapidly occurring changes during the alarm stage are the result of the release of catecholamines by the adrenal medulla, as Cannon had previously described.

A Pioneer in Stress Research With his tie off and his feet up, Canadian endocrinologist Hans Selye looks the very picture of relaxation. Selye's research at the University of Montreal documented the physical effects of exposure to prolonged stress. His popular book, *The Stress of Life* (1976), helped make stress a household word.

In the *resistance stage,* the body actively tries to resist or adjust to the continuing stressful situation. The intense arousal of the alarm stage diminishes, but physiological arousal remains above normal and resistance to new stressors is impaired.

If the stress-producing event persists, the *exhaustion stage* may occur. In this third stage, the symptoms of the alarm stage reappear, only this time irreversibly. As the body's energy reserves become depleted, adaptation begins to break down, leading to exhaustion, physical disorders, and, potentially, death.

Selye (1956, 1976) found that prolonged stress activates a second endocrine pathway (see Figure 12.1) that involves the hypothalamus, the pituitary gland, and the adrenal cortex. In response to a stressor, the hypothalamus signals the pituitary gland to secrete a hormone called *adrenocorticotropic hormone,* abbreviated *ACTH.* In turn, ACTH stimulates the adrenal cortex to release stress-related hormones called **corticosteroids,** the most important being *cortisol* (see Krishnan & others, 1991; Ritchie & Nemeroff, 1991).

In the short run, the corticosteroids provide several benefits, helping protect the body against the harm caused by stressors (see Baum & others, 1987; Gray, 1987). For example, corticosteroids reduce inflammation of body tissues and enhance muscle tone in the heart and blood vessels. However, unlike the effects of catecholamines, which tend to diminish rather quickly, corticosteroids have long-lasting effects. If a stressor is prolonged, continued high levels of corticosteroids can weaken important body systems, lowering immunity and increasing susceptibility to physical symptoms and illness (see Ader & others, 1991; Solomon & others, 1985).

Selye's pioneering studies are widely regarded as the cornerstone of modern stress research. His description of the general adaptation syndrome firmly established some of the critical biological links between stress-producing events and their potential impact on physical health. But as you'll see in the next section, the endocrine system is only part of the equation in the mind–body connection between stress and health.

Stress and the Immune System

> *Stress can undermine health by impairing the immune system. What is psychoneuroimmunology? How does the immune system interact with the nervous system? What kinds of stressors affect immune system functioning?*

Stress can diminish the effectiveness of the immune system. The **immune system** is the body's surveillance system. It detects and battles foreign invaders, such as bacteria, viruses, and tumor cells. The immune system comprises several organs, including bone marrow, the spleen, the thymus, and lymph nodes (see Figure 12.2). The most important elements of the immune system are **lymphocytes**—the specialized white blood cells that fight bacteria, viruses, and other foreign invaders. Lymphocytes are initially manufactured in the bone marrow. From the bone marrow, they migrate to other immune system organs, such as the thymus and spleen, where they develop more fully and are stored until needed (Tizard, 1992; O'Leary, 1990).

The New Field of Psychoneuroimmunology

Until the 1970s, the immune system was thought to be completely independent of other body systems, including the nervous and endocrine systems. Thus, most scientists believed that psychological processes could not influence the immune system response.

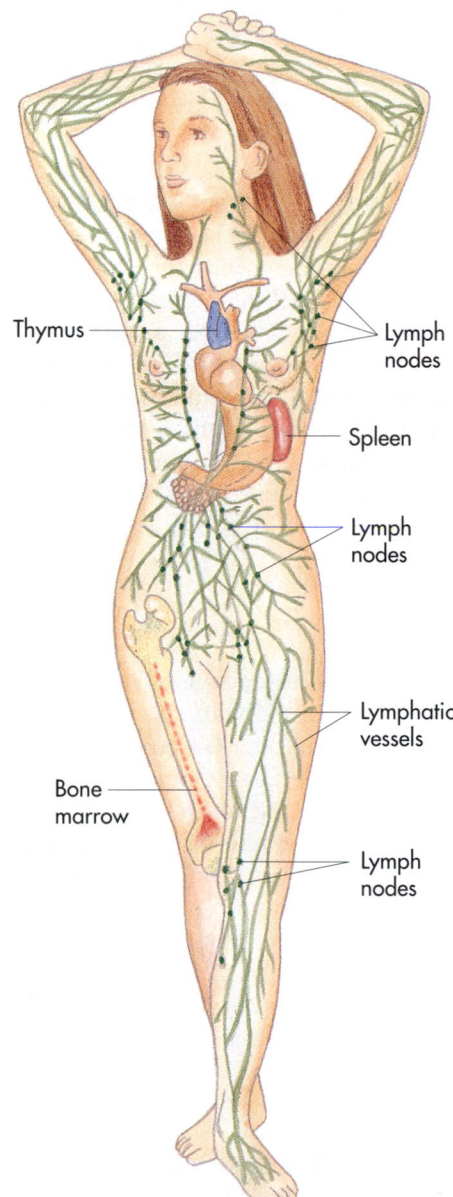

Thymus

Lymph nodes

Spleen

Lymph nodes

Lymphatic vessels

Bone marrow

Lymph nodes

FIGURE 12.2 The Immune System
Your immune system battles bacteria, viruses, and other foreign invaders that try to set up housekeeping in your body. The specialized white blood cells that fight infection are manufactured in the bone marrow and are stored in the thymus, spleen, and lymph nodes until needed.

Conditioning the Immune System Psychologist Robert Ader (right) teamed with immunologist Nicholas Cohen (left) and demonstrated that immune system responses could be classically conditioned. Ader and Cohen's groundbreaking research helped lead to the new field of psychoneuroimmunology—the study of the interconnections between psychological processes, the nervous system, and the immune system.

That notion was challenged in the mid-1970s, when psychologist **Robert Ader** (b. 1932) teamed up with immunologist Nicholas Cohen. Ader (1993b) recalls, "As a psychologist, I was not aware of the general position of immunology that there were no connections between the brain and the immune system." But Ader and Cohen showed that the immune system response in rats could be classically conditioned (see Chapter 5). After repeatedly pairing flavored water with a drug that suppressed immune system functioning, Ader and Cohen (1975) demonstrated that the flavored water *alone* suppressed the immune system.

Ader and Cohen's research helped establish a new interdisciplinary field called *psychoneuroimmunology* (Maier & others, 1994; Ader & Cohen, 1993). **Psychoneuroimmunology** is the scientific study of the interconnections among psychological processes (*psycho-*), the nervous system (*-neuro-*) and the immune system (*-immunology*).

Today, it is known that there are many interconnections among the immune system, the endocrine system, and the nervous system, including the brain (Vitkovic, 1995). First, the central nervous system and the immune system are *directly* linked via sympathetic nervous system fibers, which influence the production and functioning of lymphocytes.

Second, the surfaces of lymphocytes contain receptor sites for neurotransmitters and hormones, including catecholamines and cortisol. Thus, rather than operating independently, the activities of lymphocytes and the immune system are directly influenced by neurotransmitters, hormones, and other chemical messengers from the nervous and endocrine systems (Ader & others, 1991, 1990).

Third, psychoneuroimmunologists have discovered that lymphocytes themselves *produce* neurotransmitters and hormones. These neurotransmitters and hormones, in turn, influence the nervous and endocrine systems. In other words, there is ongoing interaction and communication among the nervous system, the endocrine system, and the immune system. Each system influences *and* is influenced by the other systems (Ader & others, 1995, 1991).

Stressors That Can Influence the Immune System

When researchers began studying how stress affects the immune system, they focused on extremely stressful events (see Kiecolt-Glaser & Glaser, 1993). For example, researchers looked at how the immune system was affected by such intense stressors as the reentry and splashdown of returning *Skylab* astronauts, being forced to stay awake for days, and going without food for over a week (Kimzey, 1975; Leach & Rambaut, 1974; Palmblad & others, 1979). Each of these highly stressful events, it turned out, was associated with reduced immune system functioning.

Could immune system functioning also be affected by more common negative life events, such as the death of a spouse, divorce, or marital separation? In a word, yes. Researchers consistently found that the stress caused by the end or disruption of important interpersonal relationships impairs immune function, putting the individuals involved at greater risk for health problems (e.g., Kiecolt-Glaser & others, 1987a; Irwin & others, 1987).

corticosteroids
Hormones released by the adrenal cortex that play a key role in the body's response to long-term stressors.

immune system
Body system that produces specialized white blood cells that protect the body from viruses, bacteria, and tumor cells.

lymphocytes
Specialized white blood cells that are responsible for immune defenses.

psychoneuroimmunology
An interdisciplinary field that studies the interconnections among psychological processes, nervous and endocrine system functions, and the immune system.

Ron Glaser & Janice Kiecolt-Glaser
Two of the leading researchers in psychoneuroimmunology are psychologist Janice Kiecolt-Glaser and her husband, immunologist Ron Glaser. Their research has shown that the effectiveness of the immune system can be lowered by many common stressors—from marital arguments to caring for sick relatives.

What about the ordinary stressors of life, such as the pressure of exams? Since 1982, psychologist **Janice Kiecolt-Glaser** (b. 1951) and her husband, immunologist Ronald Glaser, have collected immunological and psychological data from medical students. Several times each academic year, the medical students face three-day examination periods. Kiecolt-Glaser and Glaser (1993, 1991) have consistently found that even the rather commonplace stress of exams adversely affects the immune system. Interestingly, recent studies indicate that even brief exposure to a psychological stressor, such as performing a frustrating task for 30 minutes or less, can also temporarily alter immune response (Delahanty & others, 1996; Cohen & Herbert, 1996).

Taken together, the evidence strongly suggests that a wide variety of stressors are associated with diminished immune system functioning, putting us at greater risk for health problems (Cohen & others, 1993). In a carefully controlled study, psychologist Sheldon Cohen and his colleagues (1991) assessed over 400 healthy volunteers for their level of stress and health behaviors. After exposing the participants to a cold virus, the researchers noted how many of the participants developed colds. The researchers found that participants with a high level of stress were much more likely to develop colds.

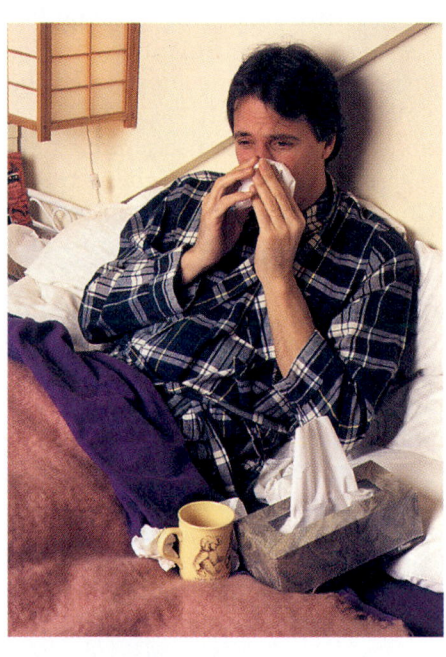

Stress and the Common Cold
Many people believe that you are more susceptible to colds and other infectious diseases when you are under stress. Is there any truth to this common sense idea?

Could it be that other factors, such as health-compromising behaviors, were underlying the stress–illness connection? Not at all. The stress–illness effect held even when the researchers took into account the participants' age, sex, smoking, alcohol consumption, exercise, diet, or quality of sleep. In other words, *none* of these factors could account for the relationship between stress and increased susceptibility to infection (Cohen & others, 1993, 1991). However, while stress-related immune system decreases may heighten our susceptibility to health problems, exposure to stressors does not automatically translate into poorer health. Your physical health is affected by the interaction of many factors, such as your unique genetic makeup, nutrition, exercise, personal habits, and access to medical care. Also required, of course, is exposure to bacteria, viruses, and other disease-causing agents.

It's also important to keep in mind that the stress-induced decreases in immune functioning that have been demonstrated experimentally are often small. As psychoneuroimmunology researchers are careful to point out, these small decreases in immune function may not translate into an added health risk for most people. As Kiecolt-Glaser and Glaser (1993) explain:

> Our best understanding at this point is that the people most likely to become ill in response to stress are probably those whose immune systems are already compromised to some extent, either by a disease like AIDS or by a natural process like aging. These people start out with poorer immunological defenses, so that small changes associated with stress could have more important consequences. But even young, generally healthy people may find themselves getting sick more often if they are subject to severe or ongoing, long-term stress.

Finally, some people are more vulnerable to the negative effects of stress than others (Adler & Matthews, 1994). Why? As you'll see in the next section, researchers have found that a wide variety of psychological factors can influence people's reactions to stressors.

The Physical Effects of Stress

1. Walking home late at night, Yvette is startled and frightened when a prankster sets off a firecracker right behind her. Walter Cannon described Yvette's physiological response as the
   a. startle-stop-stare response.
   b. fight-or-flight response.
   c. general adaptation response.
   d. learned helplessness response.

2. Shelley has just been unexpectedly told that she is going to be laid off from her job. Which phase of the general adaptation syndrome is Shelley most likely experiencing?
   a. alarm stage
   b. resistance stage
   c. exhaustion stage
   d. fight-or-flight stage

3. Daniel seems to have adjusted to the daily routine of caring for his father, who has Alzheimer's disease. Nonetheless, Daniel seems tense, and his ability to cope with new stressors is diminished. Daniel is in the _____ stage of the general adaptation syndrome.
   a. alarm **c.** exhaustion
   b. resistance **d.** fight-or-flight

4. Loraine has worked very hard, and under much pressure, for many months to complete her dissertation. According to Selye's model, Loraine's adrenal cortex has released higher than usual levels of _____ during this prolonged period of stress in her life.
   a. catecholamines **c.** teratogens
   b. lymphocytes **d.** corticosteroids

Individual Factors That Influence the Response to Stress

Researchers have identified several factors that can affect the response to stress. How do feelings of control, explanatory style, and negative emotions influence stress and health? What is Type A behavior, and what role does hostility play in its relationship to health?

People can vary a great deal in the way they respond to a distressing event, whether it's a parking ticket or a pink slip. In part, individual differences in reacting to stressors are due to how people appraise an event and to their resources for coping. However, psychologists and other researchers have identified several different factors that influence an individual's response to stressful events. In this section, we'll take a look at some of the most important psychological and social factors that seem to affect an individual's response to stress.

Psychological Factors

It's easy to demonstrate the importance of psychological factors in the response to stressors. Sit in any airport waiting room during a busy holiday and observe how differently people react to news of flight cancellations or delays. Some people take the news calmly, while others become enraged and indignant. Psychologists have confirmed what common sense suggests: Psychological processes play a key role in determining the level of stress experienced.

Uncontrollable Stressors There was nothing this family could do to protect their home from catastrophic floodwaters. Psychological research has found that stressors that are beyond our control are especially damaging to physical and mental health.

How Do You Explain Your Setbacks and Failures? Everyone experiences setbacks, rejection, and failure occasionally. The way you explain your failures has a significant impact on motivation and mental and physical health. If this jewelry store owner explained the failure of his business by blaming a temporary downturn in the economy, he might be more likely to try again in the future.

Personal Control

Who is more likely to experience more stress, a person who has some control over a stressful experience or a person who has no control? Psychological research has consistently shown that having a sense of control over a stressful situation reduces the impact of stressors and decreases feelings of anxiety and depression (e.g., Thompson & Spacapan, 1991; Taylor & others, 1991; Neufeld & Paterson, 1989). In fact, those who can control a stress-producing event often show no more psychological distress or physical arousal than people who are not exposed to the stressor (Taylor, 1989; Laudenslager & others, 1983).

Psychologists Judith Rodin and Ellen Langer (1977) demonstrated the importance of a sense of control in a series of studies with nursing home residents. One group of residents—the "high control" group—were given the opportunity to make choices about their daily activities and to exercise control over their environment. In contrast, the "low control" group had little control over their daily activities. Decisions were made for them by the nursing home staff.

Rodin and Langer found that having a sense of control over their environment had powerful effects on the nursing home residents. Eighteen months later, the high-control residents were more active, alert, sociable, and healthier than the low-control residents. The high-control group was also more likely to be alive: twice as many of the low-control residents had died (Rodin & Langer, 1977; Langer & Rodin, 1976).

How does a sense of control affect health? If you feel that you can control a stressor by taking steps to minimize or avoid it, you will experience less stress, both subjectively and physiologically (Thompson & Spacapan, 1991). Having a sense of personal control also works to our benefit by enhancing positive emotions, such as self-confidence, feelings of self-efficacy, autonomy, and self-reliance (Burger, 1992). In contrast, feeling a lack of control over events produces all the hallmarks of the stress response. Levels of catecholamines and corticosteroids increase, and the effectiveness of immune system functioning decreases (see Rodin, 1986).

Explanatory Style: Optimism Versus Pessimism

Everyone experiences defeat, rejection, or failure at some point in their lives. Yet despite repeated failures, rejections, or defeats, some people persist in their efforts. In contrast, some people give up in the face of failure and setbacks. What distinguishes between those who persist and those who give up?

According to psychologist **Martin Seligman** (1991, 1992), how people characteristically explain their failures and defeats makes the difference. People who have an **optimistic explanatory style** tend to use *external, unstable,* and *specific* explanations for negative events. In contrast, people who have a **pessimistic explanatory style** use *internal, stable,* and *global* explanations for negative events. Pessimists are also inclined to believe that no amount of personal effort will improve their situation. Not surprisingly, pessimists tend to experience more stress than optimists.

Let's look at these two explanatory styles in action. Optimistic Olive sees an attractive guy at a party and starts across the room to introduce herself and strike up a conversation. As she approaches him, the guy glances at her, then abruptly turns away. Hurt by the obvious snub, Optimistic Olive retreats to the buffet table. Munching on some fried zucchini, she mulls the matter over in her mind. At the same party, Pessimistic Pete sees an attractive female across the room and approaches her. He, too, gets a cold shoulder and retreats to the chips and clam dip. Standing at opposite ends of the buffet table, here is what each of them is thinking:

> **Optimistic Olive:** What's *his* problem? (*External* explanation: the optimist blames other people or external circumstances)
>
> **Pessimistic Pete:** I must have said the wrong thing. She probably saw me stick my elbow in the clam dip before I walked over. (*Internal* explanation: the pessimist blames self)
>
> **Optimistic Olive:** I'm really not looking my best tonight. I've just got to get more sleep. (*Unstable, temporary* explanation)
>
> **Pessimistic Pete:** Let's face it, I'm a pretty boring guy and really not very good-looking. (*Stable, permanent* explanation)
>
> **Optimistic Olive:** He looks pretty preoccupied. Maybe he's waiting for his girlfriend to arrive. Or his boyfriend! Ha! (*Specific* explanations)
>
> **Pessimistic Pete:** Women never give me a second look, probably because I dress like a nerd, and I never know what to say to them. (*Global, pervasive* explanation)
>
> **Optimistic Olive:** Whoa! Who's that hunk over there?! Okay, Olive, turn on the charm! Here goes! (*Perseverance* after a rejection)
>
> **Pessimistic Pete:** Maybe I'll just hold down this corner of the buffet table . . . or go home and soak up some TV. (*Passivity* and *withdrawal* after a rejection)

Most people, of course, are neither as completely optimistic as Olive nor as totally pessimistic as Pete. Instead, they fall somewhere along the spectrum of optimism and pessimism, and their explanatory style may vary somewhat in different situations (Peterson & Bossio, 1993). Even so, a person's characteristic explanatory style, particularly for negative events, is relatively stable across the lifespan (Burns & Seligman, 1989).

Chronic Negative Emotions: The Hazards of Being Grouchy

Everyone experiences an occasional bad mood. However, some people almost always seem to be unhappy campers—they frequently experience bad moods and negative emotions (Marshall & others, 1992; Watson & Pennebaker, 1989). Are people who are prone to chronic negative emotions more likely to suffer health problems?

Howard S. Friedman and Stephanie Booth-Kewley (1987) set out to answer this question. After systematically analyzing over 100 studies investigating the potential links between personality factors and disease, they concluded that people who are habitually anxious, depressed, angry, or hostile *are* more likely to develop a chronic disease like arthritis or heart disease.

How might chronic negative emotions predispose people to develop disease? Not surprisingly, tense, angry, and unhappy people experience more stress than happier people. They also report more frequent and more intense daily hassles than people who are generally in a positive mood (Bolger & Zuckerman, 1995; Bolger & Schilling, 1991). And they react much more intensely, and with far greater distress, to stressful events (Marco & Suls, 1993).

optimistic explanatory style
Accounting for negative events or situations with external, unstable, and specific explanations.

pessimistic explanatory style
Accounting for negative events or situations with internal, stable, and global explanations.

CALVIN AND HOBBES

Of course, everyone occasionally experiences bad moods. Are transient negative moods also associated with health risks? One series of studies investigated the relationship between daily mood and immune system functioning (Stone & others, 1994, 1987). For three months, participants recorded their mood every day. On the days that they experienced negative events and moods, the effectiveness of their immune system dipped. But their immune system improved on the days when they experienced positive events and good moods.

Type A Behavior and Hostility

The concept of Type A behavior originated about thirty years ago, when two cardiologists, Meyer Friedman and Ray Rosenman, noticed that many of their patients shared certain traits. The original formulation of the **Type A behavior pattern** included a cluster of three characteristics: (1) an exaggerated sense of time urgency, often trying to do more and more in less and less time; (2) a general sense of hostility, frequently displaying anger and irritation; and (3) intense ambition and competitiveness. In contrast, people who were more relaxed and laid back were classified as displaying the *Type B behavior pattern* (Rosenman & Chesney, 1982; Janisse & Dyck, 1988).

Friedman and Rosenman (1974) interviewed and classified more than 3,000 middle-aged, healthy men as either Type A or Type B. They tracked the health of these men for eight years and found that Type A men were twice as likely to develop heart disease as the Type B men. This held true even when the Type A men did not display other known risk factors for heart disease, such as smoking, high blood pressure, and elevated levels of cholesterol in their blood. The conclusion seemed clear: Type A behavior pattern was a significant risk factor for heart disease.

The Type A Behavior Pattern The original formulation of the Type A behavior pattern included hostility, ambition, and a sense of time urgency. Type A's always seem to be in a hurry, hate wasting time, and often try to do two or more things at once. Both the man on the far left and the frowning man on the far right would probably qualify as Type A people.

Although early results linking the Type A behavior pattern to heart disease were impressive, studies soon began to appear in which Type A behavior did *not* reliably predict the development of heart disease (see Williams, 1989). These findings led researchers to question whether the different components of the Type A behavior pattern were equally hazardous to health. After all, many people thrive on hard work, especially when they enjoy their jobs. And high achievers don't necessarily suffer from health problems (Robbins & others, 1991).

When researchers focused on the association between heart disease and the separate components of the Type A behavior pattern—time urgency, achievement striving, and hostility—an important distinction began to emerge. Feeling a sense of time urgency and being competitive or achievement-oriented did *not* seem to be associated with the development of heart disease. Instead, the critical component that emerged as the strongest predictor of cardiac disease was hostility (T. Q. Miller & others, 1996). *Hostility* refers to the tendency to feel anger, annoyance, resentment, and contempt, and to hold negative beliefs about human nature in general. Hostile people are also prone to believ-

Type A behavior pattern
A behavioral and emotional style characterized by a sense of time urgency, hostility, and competitiveness.

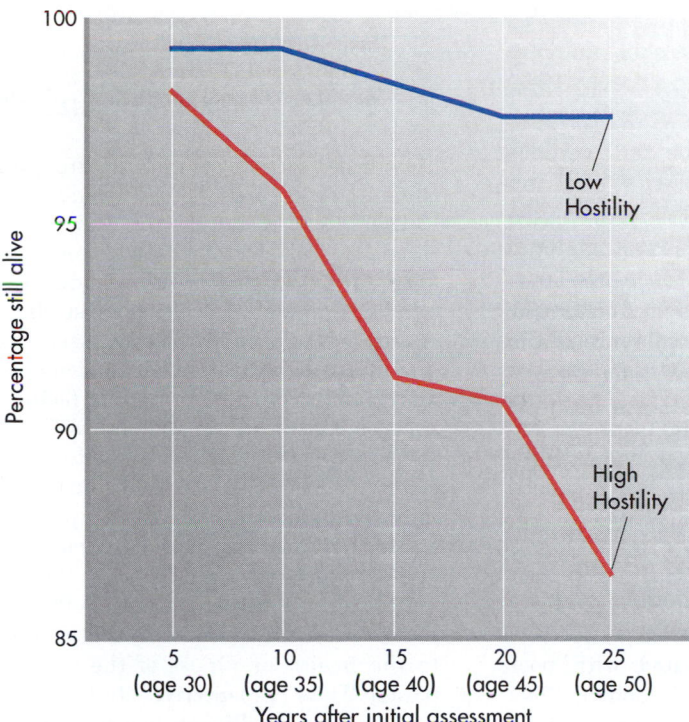

FIGURE 12.3 Hostility and Mortality
Beginning when they were in medical school, over 250 doctors were monitored for their health status for twenty-five years. In this prospective study, those who had scored high in hostility in medical school were seven times more likely to die by age fifty than were those who had scored low in hostility.

ing that the disagreeable behavior of others is intentionally directed against them. Thus, hostile people tend to be suspicious, mistrustful, cynical, and pessimistic (Barefoot, 1992).

Hostile men and women are much more likely than other people to develop heart disease. In one study that covered a twenty-five-year span, hostile men were five times as likely to develop heart disease and nearly seven times as likely to die as nonhostile men (Barefoot & others, 1983). The results of this prospective study are shown in Figure 12.3. Subsequent research has found that high hostility levels increase the likelihood of dying from *all* natural causes, including cancer (T. Q. Miller & others, 1996; Koskenvuo & others, 1988).

How does hostility predispose people to heart disease and other health problems? First, hostile Type A's tend to react more intensely to a stressor than other people do (Lyness, 1993). They experience larger increases in blood pressure, heart rate, and the production of stress-related hormones. Hostile men and women also tend to create more stress in their own lives. They experience more frequent, and more severe, negative life events and daily hassles than other people (T. Smith, 1992; Lundberg & others, 1989).

In general, the research evidence demonstrating the role of personality factors in the development of stress-related diseases is impressive. However, it's important to keep in mind that personality characteristics are just some of the risk factors involved in the overall picture of health and disease (Cohen & Herbert, 1996; Adler & Matthews, 1994). We look at this issue in more detail in Critical Thinking Box 12.2, "Do Personality Factors *Cause* Disease?"

CONCEPT REVIEW 12.3

Psychological Factors and Stress

What psychological characteristic is best illustrated by each of the examples below? Choose from the following:

A. High level of personal control
B. Optimistic explanatory style
C. Type A behavior pattern
D. Type B behavior pattern
E. Pessimistic explanatory style
F. Chronic negative emotions

_____ **1.** No matter what happens to her, Lucy is dissatisfied and grumpy. She is constantly complaining about something, and she dislikes most of the people she meets.

_____ **2.** Cheryl was despondent when she received a low grade on her algebra test. She said, "I never do well on exams because I'm not very smart. I might as well drop out of school now before I flunk out."

_____ **3.** In order to deal with the high levels of stress associated with returning to college full-time, Pat selected her courses carefully, arranged her work and study schedules to make the best use of her time, and scheduled time for daily exercise and social activities.

_____ **4.** Richard is a very competitive, ambitious stockbroker, who is easily irritated by small inconveniences. If he thinks that someone or something is wasting his time, he blows up and becomes completely enraged.

_____ **5.** Max flubbed an easy free throw in the big basketball game, but told his coach, "My game was off today because I'm still getting over the flu, and I pulled a muscle in practice yesterday. I'll do better in next week's game."

CRITICAL THINKING 12.2

Do Personality Factors *Cause* Disease?

■ You overhear a co-worker saying, "Of course he had a heart attack—the guy is a workaholic!"

■ An acquaintance casually remarks, "She's been so depressed since her divorce; no wonder she got cancer."

■ A tabloid headline hails, "New Scientific Findings: Use Your Mind to Cure Cancer!"

Statements like these make health psychologists, physicians, and psychoneuroimmunologists extremely uneasy (see Goleman & Gurin, 1993; Felten, 1993; Friedman, 1992). Why? Throughout this chapter, we've presented scientific evidence that emotional states can affect the functioning of the endocrine system and the immune system. Both systems play a significant role in the development of various physical disorders. We've also shown that personality factors, like hostility and pessimism, are associated with an increased likelihood of developing poor health. But saying that "emotions affect the immune system" is a far cry from making claims like "a positive attitude can cure cancer."

There are several reasons that psychologists and other scientists are cautious in the statements they make about the connections between personality and health. First, many studies investigating the role of psychological factors in disease are *correlational*. That is, researchers have statistical evidence that two factors happen together so often that the presence of one factor reliably predicts the occurrence of the other. However, correlation does not necessarily indicate causality—only that two factors occur together. It's completely possible that some third, unidentified factor may have caused the other two factors to occur.

Second, personality factors might indirectly lead to disease via poor health habits. Low control, pessimism, chronic negative emotions, and hostility are each associated with poor health habits (Herbert & Cohen, 1993; T. Smith, 1992; Peterson, 1988). And, in turn, poor health habits are associated with higher rates of illness. That's why psychologists who study the role of personality factors in disease are typically careful to measure and consider the possible influence of the participants' health practices.

Third, it may be that the disease influences a person's emotions, rather than the other way around. After being diagnosed with advanced cancer or heart disease, most people would probably find it difficult to feel cheerful, optimistic, or in control of their lives.

One way researchers try to disentangle the relationship between personality and health is by conducting carefully controlled prospective studies. A *prospective study* starts by assessing an initially healthy group of participants on variables thought to be risk factors, such as certain personality traits. Then the researchers track the health, personal habits, health habits, and other important dimensions of the participants' lives over a period of months, years, or decades. In analyzing the results, researchers can determine the extent to which each risk factor contributed to the health or illness of the participants. Thus, prospective studies provide more compelling evidence than do correlational studies that are based on people who are already in poor health.

People who are diagnosed with a serious disease do *not* benefit from having a sense of personal guilt added to the psychological load they are already carrying. So remember that although stress, emotions, and other psychological factors play a role in physical health, they are just some of the key factors in the complex equation of health and illness.

Social Factors

> *Social support refers to the resources provided by other people. How does social support benefit health? How can social support sometimes increase stress? What gender differences have been found in social support?*

Psychologists have become increasingly aware of the importance that close relationships play in our ability to deal with stressors and, ultimately, in our physical health. Consider the following research evidence:

● Patients with advanced breast cancer who attended weekly support group sessions survived twice as long as a matched group of patients with equally advanced cancer who did not attend support groups. Both groups of women received com-

social support
The resources provided by other people in times of need.

The Benefits of Companionship Married people and couples live longer than people who are single, divorced, or widowed (Burman & Margolin, 1992). How do close relationships benefit health?

parable medical treatment. The added survival time for those who attended support group sessions was longer than that which could have been provided by any known medical treatment (Spiegel, 1993b; Spiegel & others, 1989).

- After monitoring the health of 2,800 people for seven years, researchers found that people who had no one to talk to about their problems were three times as likely to die after being hospitalized for a heart attack than were those who had at least one person to provide such support (Berkman & others, 1992).

- The health of nearly 7,000 adults was tracked for nine years. Those individuals who had few social connections were twice as likely to die from all causes than were those who had numerous social contacts, even when risk factors such as cigarette smoking, obesity, and elevated cholesterol levels were taken into account (Berkman & Syme, 1979; Berkman, 1985).

These are just a few of the hundreds of studies conducted in the last few years exploring how interpersonal relationships influence our health and ability to tolerate stress. To investigate the role played by personal relationships in stress and health, psychologists measure the level of **social support**—the resources provided by other people in times of need (Hobfoll & Stephens, 1990). Repeatedly, researchers have found that socially isolated people have poorer health and higher death rates than people who have many social contacts or relationships (see Schwarzer & Leppin, 1992; Berkman, 1985). In fact, social isolation seems to be just as potent a health risk as smoking, high blood cholesterol, obesity, and physical inactivity (House & others, 1988).

How Social Support Benefits Health

Social support may benefit our health and improve our ability to cope with stressors in several ways (Cohen, 1988). First, the social support of friends and relatives can modify our appraisal of a stressor's significance, including the degree to which we perceive it as threatening or harmful (Cohen & McKay, 1984). Simply knowing that support and assistance are readily available may make the situation seem less threatening.

Second, the presence of supportive others seems to decrease the intensity of physical reactions to a stressor (Edens & others, 1992; Kamarck & others, 1990). Thus, when faced with a painful medical procedure or some other stressful situation, many people find the presence of a supportive friend to be calming.

Third, social support can influence our health by making us less likely to experience negative emotions (Cohen & Herbert, 1996; Cohen, 1988). Given the well-established link between chronic negative emotions and poor health, a strong social support network can promote positive moods and emotions, enhance self-esteem, and increase feelings of personal control (Rodin & Salovey, 1989). In contrast, loneliness and depression are unpleasant emotional states that increase levels of stress hormones and adversely affect immune system functioning (Herbert & Cohen, 1993; Weisse, 1992; Kennedy & others, 1990).

The Social Support of Friends Hundreds of studies have documented the beneficial effects of social support. By listening to us when we're upset, helping us move, or simply being there when we need them, friends help us handle problems and cope with stress.

Pets and Social Support Pets can be an important source of social support, especially for the elderly and people who live alone. Does the social support of pets translate into a health advantage? In one study of elderly individuals, pet owners reported feeling less stress and were also less likely to go to the doctor than people without pets (Siegel, 1990).

The flip side of the coin is that relationships with others can also be a significant *source* of stress. In fact, negative interactions with other people are often more effective at creating psychological distress than positive interactions are at improving well-being (Lepore, 1993; Rook, 1992).

Clearly, the quality of interpersonal relationships is an important determinant of whether those relationships help or hinder our ability to cope with stressful events (Feeney & Kirkpatrick, 1996). When other people are perceived as being judgmental, their presence may increase the individual's physical reaction to a stressor. In a clever study, psychologist Karen Allen and her colleagues (1991) demonstrated that the presence of a favorite dog was more effective than the presence of a friend in lowering reactivity to a stressor. Why? Perhaps because the dog was perceived as being nonjudgmental, nonevaluative, and unconditionally supportive. Unfortunately, the same is not always true of friends, family members, and spouses.

Stress may also increase when well-meaning friends or family members offer unwanted or inappropriate social support. The chapter Application offers some suggestions on how to provide helpful social support and avoid inappropriate support behaviors.

Gender Differences in the Effects of Social Support

Women may be particularly vulnerable to some of the problematic aspects of social support, for a couple of reasons. First, women are more likely than men to serve as providers of support, which can be a very stressful role (Hobfoll & Vaux, 1993; Shumaker & Hill, 1991). Consider the differences found in one study: When middle-aged male patients were discharged from the hospital after a heart attack, they went home and their wives took care of them. But when middle-aged female heart attack victims were discharged from the hospital, they went home and fell back into the routine of caring for their husbands (Coyne & others, 1990).

Second, women may be more likely to suffer from the *stress contagion effect,* becoming upset about negative life events that happen to other people that they care about (Belle, 1991). Since women tend to have larger and more intimate social networks than men, they have more opportunities to become distressed by what happens to people who are close to them. And women are more likely than men to be upset about negative events that happen to their relatives and friends. In contrast, men are more likely to be distressed only by negative events that happen to their immediate family—their wives and children (Wethington & others, 1987).

In general, men tend to rely heavily on a close relationship with their spouse, placing less importance on relationships with other people. Women, in contrast, are more likely to list close friends along with their spouse as confidants (Shumaker & Hill, 1991). Because men tend to have a much smaller network of intimate others, they may be especially vulnerable to social isolation, especially if their wife dies. Thus, it's not surprising that the

coping
Behavioral and cognitive responses used to contend with stressors; involves efforts to change circumstances, or one's interpretation of circumstances, to make them more favorable and less threatening.

health benefits of being married are more pronounced for men than for women (Belle, 1991).

In summary, it should be clear that having a strong network of social support is generally advantageous to your ability to cope with stressors and maintain health. This is especially true when you are fundamentally satisfied with both the quality and the quantity of your relationships.

Coping: How People Deal with Stress

Coping refers to the ways we try to change circumstances, or interpretations of circumstances, to make them less threatening. What are the two basic forms of coping, and when is each form typically used? What are some of the most common coping strategies? How does culture affect coping style?

Think about some of the stressful periods that have occurred in your life. What kinds of strategies did you use to deal with those distressing events? Which strategies seemed to work best? Did any of the strategies end up working against your ability to reduce the stressor? If you had to deal with the same events again today, would you do anything differently?

Two Ways of Coping:
Problem-Focused and Emotion-Focused Coping

The strategies that you used to deal with distressing events are examples of coping. **Coping** refers to the ways we try to change circumstances, or our interpretation of circumstances, to make them more favorable and less threatening (Lazarus, 1993; Folkman & Lazarus, 1991).

Coping tends to be a dynamic, ongoing process. We may switch our coping strategies as we appraise the changing demands of a stressful situation and our available resources at any given moment. We also evaluate whether our efforts have made a stressful situation better or worse, and adjust our coping strategies accordingly.

Ways of Coping
Like the stress response itself, adaptive coping is a dynamic and complex process. Imagine that you had lost your home and most of your possessions in a fire. What kinds of coping strategies might prove most helpful?

When coping is effective, we adapt to the situation and stress is reduced. Unfortunately, coping efforts do not always help us adapt (Lukoff & others, 1989; Paykel & Dowlatshahi, 1988). Maladaptive coping can involve thoughts and behaviors that intensify or prolong distress or that produce self-defeating outcomes (Bolger & Zuckerman, 1995). The rejected lover who continually dwells on her former companion, passing up opportunities to form new relationships and letting her studies slide, would be demonstrating maladaptive coping.

Adaptive coping responses serve many functions. Most important, adaptive coping involves realistically evaluating the situation and determining what can be done to minimize the impact of the stressor. But adaptive coping also involves dealing with the emotional aspects of the situation. In other words, adaptive coping often includes developing emotional tolerance for negative life events, maintaining self-esteem, and keeping emotions in balance. And third, adaptive coping efforts are directed toward preserving important relationships during stressful experiences (Lazarus, 1993; Lazarus & Folkman, 1984).

Psychologists Richard Lazarus and Susan Folkman (1984) have described two basic types of coping, each of which serves a different purpose. **Problem-focused coping** is aimed at managing or changing a threatening or harmful stressor. If we think there's nothing that can be done to alter a situation, we tend to rely on **emotion-focused coping:** we direct our efforts toward relieving or regulating the emotional impact of the stressful situation. Although emotion-focused coping doesn't change the problem, it can help you feel better about the situation.

People are flexible in the coping styles they adopt, often relying on different coping strategies for different stressors. In this section, we'll look at some common forms of problem-focused and emotion-focused coping.

Problem-Focused Coping Strategies: Changing the Stressor

Problem-focused coping strategies represent actions that have the goal of changing or eliminating the stressor. When a person uses aggressive or risky efforts to change the situation, he is engaging in *confrontive coping*. Ideally, confrontive coping is direct and assertive without being hostile. When it is hostile or aggressive, confrontive coping may well generate negative emotions in the people being confronted, damaging future relations with them (Folkman & Lazarus, 1991).

In contrast, *planful problem solving* involves efforts to rationally analyze the situation, identify potential solutions, then implement them. In effect, you take the attitude that the stressor represents a problem to be solved. Once you assume that mental stance, you follow the basic steps of problem solving (see Chapter 7).

For example, in the prologue we described Marie's efforts to deal with the possibility of being laid off from her current job. Along with looking for a new job, she went to her manager and asked for additional responsibilities, reasoning that she would be less likely to be let go if she made herself as valuable as possible. Marie's efforts to make herself indispensable to her current employer while at the same time looking for a new job represents planful problem solving in action.

Problem-Focused Coping People rely on different coping strategies at different times in dealing with the same stressor. After dealing with the emotional impact of losing their home, this California family is engaged in problem-focused coping as they help clear the site before rebuilding.

problem-focused coping
Coping efforts primarily aimed at directly changing or managing a threatening or harmful stressor.

emotion-focused coping
Coping efforts primarily aimed at relieving or regulating the emotional impact of a stressful situation.

Emotion-Focused Coping Strategies: Changing Your Reaction to the Stressor

When the stressor is one over which we can exert little or no control, we often focus on dimensions of the situation that we *can* control—the emotional impact of the stressor on us (Thompson & others, 1994). All the different forms of emotion-focused coping share the goal of reducing or regulating the emotional impact of a stressor.

When you shift your attention away from the stressor and toward other activities, you're engaging in the emotion-focused coping strategy called *escape-avoidance*. Just as the name implies, the basic goal is to escape or avoid the stressor and neutralize distressing emotions. Simple examples of using escape-avoidance to deal with a stressful situation might include escaping into fantasy (also called wishful thinking), exercising, or immersing yourself in your work, studies, or hobbies. Maladaptive forms of escape-avoidance include drug use or excessive sleeping.

IN FOCUS 12.3

Minimizing the Physical Effects of Stress

Sometimes stressful situations persist despite our best efforts to resolve them. Knowing that chronic stress can jeopardize your health, what can you do to minimize the adverse impact of stress on your physical well-being? Here are three simple suggestions that you should find helpful.

Managing Stress Everyone experiences stressful periods in their lives. How does exercise help people cope with stress?

Suggestion 1: Exercise Regularly

Regular exercise, particularly aerobic exercise like walking, swimming, or running, is one of the best ways to reduce the impact of stress. Simply walking briskly for 20 minutes four or five times a week will improve your physical health and help you cope with stress. Compared to sofa slugs, physically fit people are less physiologically reactive to stressors and produce less stress hormones (Rejeski & others, 1991, 1992). Psychologically, regular exercise reduces anxiety and depressed feelings and increases self-confidence and self-esteem (Sacks, 1993).

Suggestion 2: Avoid or Minimize Stimulants

In dealing with a stressful situation, people often turn to stimulants like coffee or tea to keep them going. Most smokers react to stress by increasing their smoking (Epstein & Jennings, 1985). However, common stimulant drugs like caffeine and nicotine actually increase the physiological effects of stress by raising heart rate and blood pressure (Lovallo & others, 1996; MacDougall & others, 1988). In effect, users of stimulant drugs are already primed to respond with greater reactivity, exaggerating the physiological consequences of stress (Dembroski, 1985).

The best advice? Avoid stimulant drugs altogether. The next best advice?

Make a conscious effort to monitor your use of stimulants, especially when you're under stress. You'll find it easier to deal with stressors when your nervous system is not already in high gear because of caffeine, nicotine, or other stimulants.

Suggestion 3: Regularly Practice a Relaxation Technique

You can significantly reduce stress-related symptoms by regularly using any one of a variety of relaxation techniques (Benson, 1993). One effective relaxation technique is *meditation,* which involves focusing your attention on an object, word, or phrase. We provided you with instructions for a simple meditation technique in Chapter 4.

Another effective technique is *progressive muscle relaxation.* This involves systematically tensing and then relaxing the major muscle groups of your body while lying down or sitting in a comfortable chair. You begin by tensing your facial and jaw muscles, paying careful attention to the feeling of muscle tightness. Then, take a deep breath, hold it for a few seconds, and exhale slowly as you relax your facial and jaw muscles as completely as possible. Notice the difference between the sensations of tension and the warm feelings of relaxation. Progressively work your way down your body, tensing and then relaxing muscle groups.

By focusing your attention on something other than the stressor, escape-avoidance tactics tend to provide emotional relief in the short run. Thus, avoidance strategies can be helpful when facing a stressor that is relatively brief and has limited consequences. But avoidance strategies like wishful thinking tend to be counterproductive when the stressor is severe or long-lasting (Stanton & Snider, 1993). Escape-avoidance strategies are also associated with increased psychological distress in facing other types of stressors, such as adjusting to college (Aspinwall & Taylor, 1992).

In the long run, escape-avoidance tactics are associated with poor adjustment and symptoms of depression and anxiety (Stanton & Snider, 1993; Folkman & others, 1986). That's not surprising if you think about it. After all, the problem *is* still there. And if the problem is one that needs to be dealt with promptly, such as a pressing medical concern, the delays caused by escape-avoidance strategies can make the stressful situation worse.

CALVIN AND HOBBES

Seeking social support is the coping strategy that involves turning to friends, relatives, or other people for emotional, tangible, or informational support. As we discussed earlier in the chapter, having a strong network of social support can help buffer the impact of stressors. Confiding in a trusted friend gives us an opportunity to vent our emotions and better understand the stressful situation (Lepore & others, 1996).

When you acknowledge the stressor but attempt to minimize or eliminate its emotional impact, you're engaging in the coping strategy called *distancing*. A relatively common example of distancing is the person who tries to change the meaning of the stressor by claiming that it's "no big deal" or "not that important." Making jokes about the stressful situation is another form of distancing (see Nezu & others, 1988; Robinson, 1983). And sometimes people emotionally distance themselves from a stressor by discussing it in a detached, depersonalized, or intellectual way.

In certain high-stress occupations, distancing can help workers cope with painful human problems. Clinical psychologists, social workers, rescue workers, police officers, and medical personnel often use distancing to some degree to help them deal with distressing situations without falling apart emotionally themselves.

In contrast to distancing, *denial* is a refusal to acknowledge that the problem even exists (Goldberger, 1983). Like escape-avoidance strategies, denial can compound problems in situations that require immediate attention.

Perhaps the most constructive emotion-focused coping strategy is *positive reappraisal*. The person who uses positive reappraisal not only tries to minimize the negative emotional aspects of the situation, but also tries to create positive meaning by focusing on personal growth (Folkman & others, 1986). People sometimes use positive reappraisal to help them make sense out of a stressful experience. This is especially true when people have experienced a tragedy, disaster, or catastrophic loss. People who can find some sense of personal meaning in the stressful event—sometimes through their religious faith—tend to cope better with loss than those who see it as senseless (Meichenbaum & Fitzpatrick, 1993; Wortman & others, 1992).

Most people use multiple coping strategies in stressful situations, often combining problem-focused and emotion-focused forms of coping (Lazarus, 1993; Dunkel-Schetter & others, 1992). Different coping strategies may be used at different stages of dealing with a stressful encounter. In the initial stages of a stressful experience, we often

Transcending Personal Tragedy Some people cope with tragedy by channeling their energies into helping others with similar problems. Elizabeth Glaser (no relation to researchers Janice Kiecolt-Glaser or Ron Glaser) became infected with the AIDS virus through a blood transfusion during childbirth. After her children tested positive for HIV, Glaser discovered that almost nothing was known about HIV in children. She co-founded the Pediatric Aids Foundation and became a national spokesperson for AIDS awareness and research. She is shown here at a press conference in 1992. Glaser herself died of AIDS in 1994.

rely on emotion-focused strategies to help us step back emotionally from a problem. Once we've regained our emotional equilibrium, we may rely more on problem-focused coping strategies to identify potential solutions to the situation.

CONCEPT REVIEW 12.4

Coping Strategies

Which of the following coping strategies is being illustrated in each of the scenarios below?

A. Confrontive coping
B. Planful problem solving
C. Escape-avoidance
D. Seeking social support
E. Distancing
F. Denial
G. Positive reappraisal

_____ **1.** In trying to contend with her stormy marriage, Bailey often seeks the advice of her best friend, Paula.

_____ **2.** Lionel was disappointed that he did not get the job, but he concluded that the knowledge he gained from the application and interview process was very beneficial.

_____ **3.** Whenever Dr. Mathau has a particularly hectic and stressful shift in the emergency room, she finds herself making jokes and facetious remarks to the other staff members.

_____ **4.** Phil's job as a public defender is filled with long days and little thanks. To take his mind off his job, Phil jogs every day.

_____ **5.** Faced with low productivity and mounting financial losses, the factory manager bluntly told all his workers, "You people had better start getting more work done in less time, or you will be looking for jobs elsewhere."

_____ **6.** Because of unavoidable personal problems, Martin did very poorly on his last two tests and was very concerned about his GPA. Martin decided to talk with his professor about the possibility of writing an extra paper or taking a makeup exam.

_____ **7.** Despite having failed five out of six quizzes, Sheila still insists that she is going to get at least a B in her economics course.

Culture and Coping Strategies

Culture seems to play an important role in the choice of coping strategies. Americans and other members of individualistic cultures tend to emphasize personal autonomy and personal responsibility in dealing with problems. Thus, they are *less* likely to seek social support in stressful situations than are members of collectivistic cultures, like Asian countries (Marsella & Dash-Scheuer, 1988). Members of collectivistic cultures tend to be more oriented toward their social group, family, or community and to seeking help with their problems.

Individualists also tend to emphasize the importance and value of exerting control over their circumstances, especially circumstances that are threatening or stressful. Thus, they favor problem-focused strategies, like confrontive coping and planful problem solving, which involve directly changing the situation to achieve a better fit with their wishes or goals (Markus & Kitayama, 1991).

In collectivistic cultures, however, a greater emphasis is placed on controlling your personal reactions to a stressful situation rather than trying to control the situation itself. This emotion-focused coping style emphasizes gaining control over inner feelings by accepting and accommodating yourself to existing realities (Thompson & others, 1994; Weisz & others, 1984).

For example, the Japanese emphasize accepting difficult situations with maturity, serenity, and flexibility (Weisz & others, 1984). Common sayings in Japan are "The true tolerance is to tolerate the intolerable" and "Flexibility can control rigidity" (Azuma, 1984). Along with controlling inner feelings, many Asian cultures also stress the goal of controlling the outward expression of emotions, however distressing the situation (Johnson & others, 1995).

These cultural differences in coping underscore the point that there is no formula for effective coping in all situations. That we use multiple coping strategies throughout almost every stressful situation reflects our efforts to identify what will work best at a given moment in time. To the extent that any coping strategy helps us identify realistic alternatives, manage our emotions, and maintain important relationships, it is adaptive and effective.

APPLICATION

Providing Effective Social Support

A close friend turns to you for help in a time of crisis or personal tragedy. What should you do or say? As we've noted in this chapter, appropriate social support can help people weather crises and significantly reduce the amount of distress that they feel. Inappropriate support, in contrast, may only make matters worse.

Researchers generally agree that there are three broad categories of social support: emotional, tangible, and informational. Each provides different beneficial functions (Taylor & Aspinwall, 1993; Peirce & others, 1996).

Emotional support includes expressions of concern, empathy, and positive regard. *Tangible support* involves direct assistance, such as providing transportation, lending money, or helping with meals, child care, or household tasks. When people offer helpful suggestions, advice, or possible resources, they are providing *informational support*.

It's possible that all three kinds of social support might be provided by the same person, such as a relative, spouse, or very close friend. More commonly, we turn to different people for different kinds of support.

Research by psychologist Stevan Hobfoll and his colleagues (1992) has identified several support behaviors that are typically perceived as helpful by people under stress. In a nutshell, you're most likely to be perceived as helpful if you:

- Are a good listener and show concern and interest.
- Ask questions that encourage the person under stress to express his or her feelings and emotions.
- Express understanding about why the person is upset.
- Express affection for the person, whether by a warm hug or simply a pat on the arm.
- Are willing to invest time and attention in helping.
- Can help the person with practical tasks, like housework, transportation, or responsibilities at work or school.

Just as important is knowing what *not* to do or say. Here are several behaviors that, however well-intentioned, are often perceived as unhelpful:

- Giving advice that the person under stress has not asked for.

- Telling the person, "I know exactly how you feel." It's a mistake to think that you have experienced the identical distress that the other person is going through.
- Talking about yourself or your problems.
- Minimizing the importance of the person's problem by saying things like, "Hey, don't make such a big deal out of it; it could be a lot worse," or "Don't worry, everything will turn out okay."
- Pretending to be cheerful.
- Offering your philosophical or religious interpretation of the stressful event by saying things like, "It's just fate," "It's God's will," or "It's your karma."

Finally, remember that while social support is helpful, it is *not* a substitute for counseling or psychotherapy. If a friend seems overwhelmed by problems or emotions, or is having serious difficulty handling the demands of everyday life, you should encourage him or her to seek professional help. Most college campuses have a counseling center or a health clinic that can provide referrals to qualified mental health workers. Sliding fee schedules, based on ability to pay, are usually available. Thus, you can assure the person that cost need not be an obstacle to getting help—or an additional source of stress!

Summary

Stress, Health, and Coping

What Is Stress?

- Stress can be defined as a negative emotional state that occurs in response to events that are appraised as taxing or exceeding a person's resources.

- Health psychologists study stress and other psychological factors that influence health, illness, and treatment. Health psychologists are guided by the biopsychosocial model.

- According to the life events approach, any event that requires adaptation produces stress. The Social Readjustment Rating Scale is one way to measure the impact of life events. The life events approach does not take into account a person's subjective appraisal of an event. It also assumes that change, whether good or bad, produces stress.

- Daily hassles are an important source of stress and also contribute to the stress produced by major life events.

- Stress can also be caused by approach-approach, avoidance-avoidance, or approach-avoidance conflicts. Approach-avoidance conflicts tend to create the most stress.

- Social factors, such as unemployment, crime, and racism, can be significant sources of stress, often producing chronic stress. Stress can also result when people encounter different cultural values. Acculturative stress results from the stress of adapting to a new culture.

Physical Effects of Stress: The Mind–Body Connection

- Stress can affect health indirectly by influencing health-related behaviors, and directly by influencing body functioning.

- Walter Cannon identified the endocrine pathway involved in the fight-or-flight response. This endocrine pathway includes the sympathetic nervous system, the adrenal medulla, and the release of catecholamines.

- In studying the physical effects of prolonged stressors, Hans Selye identified the three-stage general adaptation syndrome, which includes the alarm, resistance, and exhaustion stages. Selye found that prolonged stress involves a second endocrine pathway, which includes the hypothalamus, the pituitary gland, the adrenal cortex, and the release of corticosteroids.

- Stress affects immune system functioning. Ader and Cohen's discovery that the immune system could be classically conditioned helped launch the new field of psychoneuroimmunology. Subsequent research has discovered that the nervous, endocrine, and immune systems are directly linked and continually influence one another.

- Stressors that affect immune system functioning include both unusual and common life events, along with everyday pressures. Although stress may increase susceptibility to infection and illness, many other factors are involved in physical health.

Individual Factors That Influence the Response to Stress

- The impact of stressors is reduced when people feel a sense of control over the stressful situation. Feelings of control have both physical and psychological benefits.

- The way people explain negative events often determines whether they will persist or give up after failure. People with an optimistic explanatory style use external, unstable, and specific explanations for negative events. People with a pessimistic explanatory style use internal, stable, and global explanations for negative events. A pessimistic explanatory style contributes to stress and undermines health.

- Chronic negative emotions are related to the development of some chronic diseases. People who frequently experience negative emotions experience more stress than other people. Transient negative moods have also been shown to decrease immune system functioning.

- Type A behavior can predict the development of heart disease. The most critical health-compromising component of Type A behavior is hostility. Hostile people react more intensely to stressors and experience stress more frequently than nonhostile people.

- Social isolation contributes to poor health. Social support improves the ability to deal with stressors by modifying the appraisal of a stressor, decreasing the physical reaction to a stressor, and making people less likely to experience negative emotions. When the quality of relationships is poor, or when social support is inappropriate or unwanted, relationships may increase stress.

- Women are more likely to be the providers of social support than men and tend to be more vulnerable to the stress contagion effect. Men are less likely to be upset by negative events that happen to people outside their immediate family.

Coping: How People Deal with Stress

- Coping refers to the way that people try to change either their circumstances or their interpretations of circumstances in order to make them more favorable and less threatening. Coping may be maladaptive or adaptive.

- When people think that something can be done to change a situation, they tend to use problem-focused coping strategies, which involve changing a harmful stressor.

- When people think that a situation cannot be changed, they tend to rely on emotion-focused coping strategies, which involve changing their emotional reactions to the stressor.
- Problem-focused coping strategies include confrontive coping and planful problem solving.
- Emotion-focused coping strategies include escape-avoidance, seeking social support, distancing, denial, and positive reappraisal. People usually rely on multiple coping strategies in stressful situations.
- Culture affects the choice of coping strategies. People in individualistic cultures tend to favor problem-focused strategies. People in collectivistic cultures are more likely to seek social support, and they emphasize emotion-focused coping strategies more than do people in individualistic cultures.

Key Terms

stress (p. 432)

health psychology (p. 433)

stressors (p. 433)

daily hassles (p. 434)

conflict (p. 435)

acculturative stress (p. 437)

fight-or-flight response (p. 438)

catecholamines (p. 438)

general adaptation syndrome (p. 439)

corticosteroids (p. 440)

immune system (p. 440)

lymphocytes (p. 440)

psychoneuroimmunology (p. 441)

optimistic explanatory style (p. 444)

pessimistic explanatory style (p. 444)

Type A behavior pattern (p. 446)

social support (p. 449)

coping (p. 451)

problem-focused coping (p. 452)

emotion-focused coping (p. 452)

Key People

Robert Ader (b. 1932) American psychologist who, with immunologist Nicholas Cohen, first demonstrated that immune system responses could be classically conditioned; helped establish the new interdisciplinary field of psychoneuroimmunology.

Walter B. Cannon (1871–1945) American physiologist who made several important contributions to psychology, especially in the study of emotions. Described the fight-or-flight response, which involves the sympathetic nervous system and the endocrine system. (Also see Chapter 8.)

Janice Kiecolt-Glaser (b. 1951) American psychologist who, with immunologist Ronald Glaser, has conducted extensive research on the effects of stress on the immune system.

Richard Lazarus (b. 1922) American psychologist who helped promote the cognitive perspective in the study of emotion and stress; developed the cognitive appraisal model of stress and coping with co-researcher Susan Folkman. (Also see Chapter 8.)

Martin Seligman (b. 1942) American psychologist who conducted research on explanatory style and the role it plays in stress, health, and illness.

Hans Selye (1907–1982) Canadian endocrinologist who was a pioneer in stress research; defined stress as "the nonspecific response of the body to any demand placed on it," and described a three-stage response to prolonged stress that he termed the *general adaptation syndrome.*

CONCEPT REVIEW 12.1   *Page 436*

1. False. The biopsychosocial model holds that health and illness are determined by the interaction of biological, psychological, and social factors.
2. False. Exposure to life events is only one of many factors that influence health and illness.
3. False. The Social Readjustment Ratings Scale measures stress due to life events.
4. True
5. False. Lyle is experiencing an approach-avoidance conflict, which is likely to produce a high level of stress.
6. False. According to the life events approach, both positive and negative life events generate stress.

CONCEPT REVIEW 12.2 Page 443

1. b
2. a
3. b
4. d

CONCEPT REVIEW 12.3 Page 447

1. F
2. E
3. A
4. C
5. B

CONCEPT REVIEW 12.4 Page 455

1. D
2. G
3. E
4. C
5. A
6. B
7. F

Chapter

13 Psychological Disorders

Prologue: Behind the Steel Door

I had just turned thirteen when my dad was hospitalized. At the time, I didn't realize just how sick he was. He nearly died before a diseased kidney was removed, saving his life. As my junior high was only three blocks from the hospital, I visited him every day after school before going to my paper route. It was one of those visits that defined the course of my life.

Lost in my thoughts as I walked through the maze of dim hospital hallways, I took a wrong turn. When I got near the end of the hallway, I realized it was a dead end and started to turn around. That's when her voice pierced the silence, screaming in agony.

"*Help me!* Fire! Fire! Fire! *Please* help me!"

At first I was confused about the direction from which the voice was coming. Then I saw a panic-stricken face against the small window of a steel door. I ran to the door and tried to open it but it was locked.

"Help me, *somebody!* Fire! Fire! Fire!" she screamed again.

"I'll get help!" I yelled back to her but she didn't seem to see or hear me. My heart racing, I ran back down the dim hallway to a nurses' station.

"There's a woman who needs help! There's a fire!" I quickly explained to a nurse.

But instead of summoning help, the nurse looked at me with what can only be described as disdain. "Which hallway?" she said flatly, and I pointed the direction from which I had come. "That's the psychiatric ward down there," she explained. "Those people are crazy."

Her remark caught me off guard. I stared at her for a moment. *Crazy?* "But she needs help," I finally blurted out.

"That's why she's on the psychiatric ward," the nurse replied calmly. "Which room are you trying to find?"

I didn't answer her. Instead, I walked back down the hallway. I took a deep breath and tried to slow my heart down. As I approached the steel door, the woman was still there, screaming. Standing at the door, I watched her through the wire-reinforced glass. She was completely oblivious to my presence.

"There's fire! I *see* fire! Fire! Fire! *Fire!*"

She was probably about twenty-five years old. Her face looked gaunt, dirty, her hair stringy and unkempt. I remember the dark circles under her deep-set eyes, her pupils dilated with sheer, raw panic.

"Listen to me, there's *no* fire," I said loudly, tapping on the glass, trying to get her attention.

"Help me, *please*," she sobbed, laying her cheek against the glass.

"My name is Don," I said, tapping on the glass again. "Listen to me, there's *no* fire."

That's when the attendants came, dressed in white hospital garb. The young woman slapped at their hands as they tried to pull her away from the door. I quickly got next to the glass, trying to see what was happening. *Don't hurt her!* For just an instant I saw her face again and she looked directly into my eyes.

"It's okay, there's *no* fire!" I yelled, then she was gone.

I stood by the steel door, my mind racing. *What was wrong with her? Where did they take her? Why did she think there was a fire? Did she really see flames?*

When I finally got to my dad's hospital room, we talked the entire time about the woman. "If you'd like," my dad finally said, "I can arrange for you to talk to a psychiatrist that I know. He can probably answer your questions better than I can."

A few weeks later, I spent about 30 minutes with the psychiatrist. In very general terms, he talked to me about mental disorders and their treatment. He also explained how psychiatrists usually take a medical approach and clinical psychologists use psychotherapy in trying to help people with psychological disorders. It was at that moment that I knew I wanted to be a clinical psychologist and help people like the woman I had seen.

I never saw that young woman again, nor did I ever find out what happened to her. But I will never forget her face or the sound of her terrified voice. Since that fateful day, I've spent many years of my life working on psychiatric wards, often trying to help people who were just as confused as that young woman.

In this chapter, we'll look at the symptoms that characterize some of the most common psychological disorders, including the one that was being experienced by the young woman I saw that day. As we do, you'll come to better understand how the symptoms of a psychological disorder can seriously impair a person's ability to function. We'll also talk about what researchers have learned about some of the underlying causes of psychological disorders. As you'll see, biological, psychological, and social factors have been implicated as contributing to many psychological disorders.

Introduction

Understanding Psychological Disorders

Psychopathology refers to the scientific study of the origins, symptoms, and development of psychological disorders. What characterizes "abnormal" behavior? What is the formal definition of a psychological disorder? What is DSM-IV, and how was it developed? How prevalent are psychological disorders?

Does the *Far Side* cartoon make you smile? The cartoon is humorous, but it's actually intended to make some serious points. It reflects several common misconceptions about psychological disorders that we hope will be dispelled by this chapter.

First, there's the belief that "crazy" behavior is very different from "normal" behavior. Granted, sometimes it is, like the behavior of the young woman who was screaming "Fire!" when there was no fire. But as you'll see throughout this chapter, the line that divides "normal" and "crazy" behavior is often not as sharply defined as most people think. In many instances, the difference between normal and abnormal behavior is a matter of degree (Frances & others, 1991). For example, as you leave your apartment or house, it's normal to check or even double-check that the door is securely locked. However, if you feel compelled to go back and check the lock seventy-five times, that would be an example of abnormal behavior.

The dividing line between normal and abnormal behavior is also often determined by the social or cultural context in which a particular behavior occurs (Foulks, 1991). For example, among traditional Hindus in India, certain dietary restrictions are followed as part of the mourning process. It would be a serious breach of social norms if an Indian widow ate fish, meat, onions, garlic, or any other "hot" foods within six months of her husband's death (see Triandis, 1994; Shweder & others, 1990b). An American Catholic or Protestant widow would probably consider such dietary restrictions absurd. In a similar way, hearing "voices" or talking to disembodied "spirits" is accepted in some cultures, but evidence of serious disturbance in the United States (Mulhern, 1991).

Second, when we encounter people whose behavior strikes us as weird, unpredictable, or baffling, it's easy to simply dismiss them as "just plain nuts," as in the *Far Side* cartoon, or as "crazy," like the nurse's insensitive response in the prologue. Although convenient, such a response is too simplistic. It could also be wrong. Often, unconventional people are labeled as crazy when they're actually just creatively challenging the conventional wisdom with new ideas (Buck, 1992).

Even if a person's responses are seriously disturbed, labeling that person as "crazy" or "just plain nuts" tells us nothing meaningful. What are the person's specific symptoms? What might be the cause of the symptoms? How did they develop? How long can they be expected to last? And how might the person be helped? The area of psychology and medicine that focuses on these questions is called **psychopathology**—the scientific study of the origins, symptoms, and development of psychological disorders. In this chapter and the next, we'll look at psychological disorders and their treatment.

The *Far Side* cartoon reflects a third troubling issue. There is still a strong social stigma attached to suffering from a mental disorder (Penn & others, 1994). Partly because of this stigma, people are often reluctant to

THE FAR SIDE

psychopathology
The scientific study of the origins, symptoms, and development of psychological disorders.

seek the help of mental health professionals (Kessler & others, 1994). Understandably so. Being labeled as "crazy" carries all kinds of implications, most of which reflect negative stereotypes about people with mental problems (Räty, 1990). We discuss one significant source of negative stereotypes in Critical Thinking Box 13.1, "Media Images of Mental Illness."

CRITICAL THINKING 13.1

Media Images of Mental Illness

In analyzing U.S. television programming, researcher George Gerbner (1993) found that the typical prime-time television viewer sees an average of three characters per week who are labeled as "mentally ill." Gerbner found that people with mental disorders are portrayed in two highly negative, stereotypical ways. One stereotype is that of the mentally disturbed person who is helplessly victimized, like the woman with multiple personalities who was murdered as part of the plot in a recent made-for-TV movie. The other stereotype is that of the mentally disordered person as an evil villain who is unpredictable, dangerous, and violent.

Gerbner found that while 5 percent of "normal" television characters are murderers, 20 percent of "mentally ill" characters are killers. And while about 40 percent of normal characters are violent, 70 percent of characters labeled as mentally ill are violent.

Are people with mental disorders significantly more violent and more dangerous than other groups of people? Research has shown that people with a current, severe mental disorder in which they are hallucinating or delusional do have a *slightly* higher level of violent and illegal behavior than do "normal" people (Link & others, 1992). However, we need to put that finding in proper perspective.

According to researcher Bruce Link and his colleagues (1992), the sta-

tistical risk of violent behavior associated with mental illness is far *lower* than the risks associated with being young, a male, or being poorly educated. Each of these factors contributes much more strongly to the likelihood that a person will behave violently than does having a mental disorder.

Second, the slightly elevated rate of violent behavior by the mentally ill applies *only* to those who are actively suffering severe psychological symptoms, such as bizarre delusional ideas and hallucinated voices. The person with a mental disorder who is *not* suffering from such symptoms is no more likely than the average person to be involved in violent or illegal behavior. So what's the bottom line? The incidence of violent behavior among current or former mental patients is grossly exaggerated in media portrayals.

Just Another Media Psychopath? Anthony Hopkins won an Oscar for his chilling portrayal of "Hannibal the Cannibal," a psychopathic murderer, in *The Silence of the Lambs*. Movie thrillers and TV dramas often use the "homicidal maniac" as a plot device. Are people with psychological disorders really more dangerous than other people?

The Mentally Ill as Villains on Prime-Time Television
People with psychological disorders are the most stigmatized group on television. This graph shows eight categories of people portrayed as major characters in prime-time television shows. For each category, researchers kept track of the number of villains for every 100 heroes. As you can see, only the mentally ill were portrayed as villains more often than they were portrayed as heroes.
(Gerbner, 1993.)

Number of villains per 100 heroes

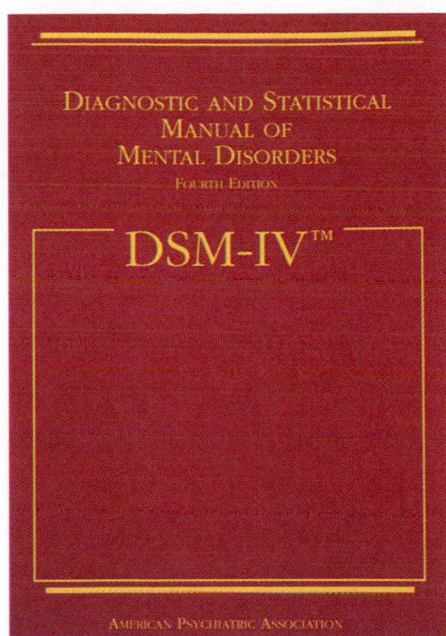

What Is a Psychological Disorder?

Up to this point we've used the terms *psychological disorder* and *mental disorder* interchangeably. And, indeed, the terms mean much the same thing. Psychologists generally prefer the term *psychological disorder,* while psychiatrists tend to prefer the term *mental disorder.* Both terms are widely used in the research literature. But what exactly are we talking about when we say that someone has a *psychological* or *mental disorder?*

A **psychological disorder** or **mental disorder** can be defined as a pattern of behavioral or psychological symptoms that causes significant personal distress, impairs the ability to function in one or more important areas of life, or both (DSM-IV, 1994). An important qualification is that the pattern of behavioral or psychological symptoms must represent a serious departure from the prevailing social and cultural norms. Hence, the behavior of a traditional Hindu woman who refuses to eat onions, garlic, or other "hot" foods following the death of her husband is perfectly normal because that norm is part of the Hindu culture (Triandis, 1994).

What determines whether a given pattern of symptoms or behaviors qualifies as a psychological disorder? Throughout this chapter, you'll notice numerous references to DSM-IV. **DSM-IV** stands for the *Diagnostic and Statistical Manual of Mental Disorders,* fourth edition, which was published by the American Psychiatric Association in 1994. DSM-IV is a book that describes approximately 250 specific psychological disorders. It includes the symptoms, the exact criteria that must be met to make a diagnosis, and the typical course for each mental disorder. An example of the diagnostic criteria for one mental disorder is shown in Figure 13.1. DSM-IV provides mental health professionals with (1) a common language to label mental disorders and (2) comprehensive guidelines to diagnose mental disorders.

It's important to understand that DSM-IV was not written by a single person or even a single organization. Rather, DSM-IV represents the *consensus* of a wide range of mental health professionals and organizations. In developing DSM-IV, teams of mental health professionals conducted extensive reviews of the research findings for each category of mental disorder. All together, more than 1,000 mental health experts, mostly psychologists and psychiatrists, participated in the development of DSM-IV. More than sixty professional organizations, including the American Psychological Association and the American Psychological Society, reviewed early drafts of DSM-IV. Despite these efforts, the *Diagnostic and Statistical Manual of Mental Disorders* has its critics (see Wilson, 1993; Kirk & Kutchins, 1992). Nevertheless, DSM-IV is the most comprehensive and authoritative set of guidelines available for diagnosing psychological disorders. Thus, we'll refer to it often in this chapter.

■ Diagnostic criteria for 300.14 Dissociative Identity Disorder

A. The presence of two or more distinct identities or personality states (each with its own relatively enduring pattern of perceiving, relating to, and thinking about the environment and self).

B. At least two of these identities or personality states recurrently take control of the person's behavior.

C. Inability to recall important personal information that is too extensive to be explained by ordinary forgetfulness.

D. The disturbance is not due to the direct physiological effects of a substance (e.g., blackouts or chaotic behavior during Alcohol Intoxication) or a general medical condition (e.g., complex partial seizures). **Note:** In children, the symptoms are not attributable to imaginary playmates or other fantasy play.

FIGURE 13.1 Sample DSM-IV Diagnostic Criteria
Each of the more than 250 psychological disorders described in DSM-IV has specific criteria that must be met in order for a person to be diagnosed with that disorder. Shown here are the DSM-IV criteria for dissociative identity disorder, which was formerly called multiple personality disorder. The number 300.14 identifies the specific disorder according to an international code developed by the World Health Organization. The code helps researchers make statistical comparisons of the prevalence of mental disorders in different countries and cultures.
(DSM-IV, 1994, p. 487.)

psychological disorder (mental disorder)
A pattern of behavioral and psychological symptoms that causes significant personal distress, impairs the ability to function in one or more important areas of daily life, or both.

How Prevalent Are Psychological Disorders? Psychological disorders are far more common than most people think. A recent survey found that 1 in 3 American adults had experienced the symptoms of a psychological disorder within the previous year. However, many people who experience such symptoms do not seek help.

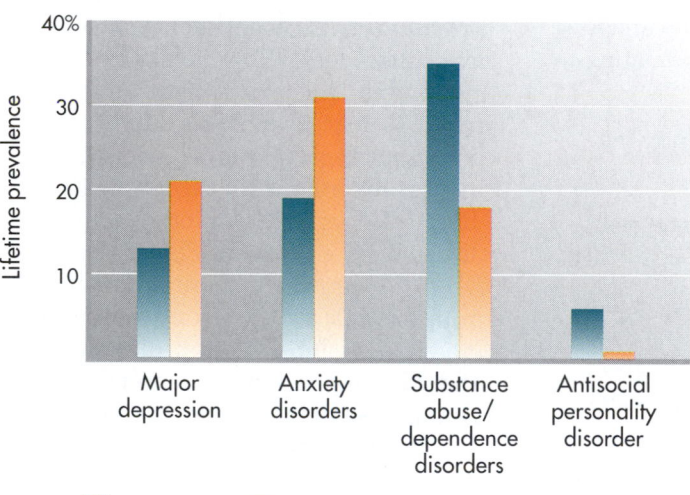

FIGURE 13.2 Gender Differences in the Lifetime Prevalence of Selected Psychological Disorders in the National Comorbidity Survey

(Adapted from Kessler & others, 1994, p. 12.)

DSM-IV
Abbreviation for the *Diagnostic and Statistical Manual of Mental Disorders,* fourth edition; the book published by the American Psychiatric Association that describes the specific symptoms and diagnostic guidelines for different psychological disorders.

The Prevalence of Psychological Disorders:
A Fifty-Fifty Chance?

Just how common are psychological disorders? In 1994 the most comprehensive survey to date on the mental health of U.S. adults was published (Kessler & others, 1994). Called the *National Comorbidity Survey* (*NCS*), it surveyed a representative sample of Americans aged fifteen to fifty-four. NCS participants were asked about the symptoms of psychological disorders that they had experienced at (1) any point in their lives and (2) within the previous 12 months.

The NCS results were surprising. First, the researchers found that the prevalence of psychological disorders was much higher than previously thought. Almost one out of two adults—48 percent—had experienced the symptoms of a psychological disorder at some point in their lifetime. The proportion of people who had experienced the symptoms of a psychological disorder in the previous 12 months was 30 percent, or roughly one in three.

Another striking finding was that 80 percent of those who had suffered from the symptoms of a mental disorder in the previous year had *not* sought any type of treatment or help for their symptoms. Although that finding may surprise you, it's consistent with previous research (Narrow & others, 1993; Manderscheid & others, 1993).

There are two ways we can look at this finding. On the one hand, it's clear that many people who could benefit from mental health treatment do not seek it. This may reflect a lack of awareness about psychological disorders or the fact that a stigma still exists when it comes to seeking treatment for psychological symptoms. It could also be that people lack access to mental health services or lack the financial resources to pay for treatment.

On the other hand, even though the incidence of mental disorders is much higher than previously believed, *most* people seem to weather the symptoms without becoming completely debilitated and without professional intervention. As NCS director Ronald Kessler (1994) explains, "Really serious conditions that demanded immediate treatment affected 3% to 5% of our sample. These people typically had developed several mental disorders over time, not just one disorder that suddenly appeared."

The NCS also found that the prevalence of certain mental disorders differed for men and women. As you can see in Figure 13.2, women had a higher prevalence of anxiety and depression, while men had a higher prevalence of substance abuse disorders (Kessler & others, 1994). The reasons for these gender differences are unknown. Among the areas being actively investigated are genetics, social roles, and degree of willingness to seek professional help and report psychological symptoms (Seeman, 1995).

For the remainder of this chapter, we'll focus on the mental disorders in four DSM-IV categories: anxiety disorders, mood disorders, dissociative disorders, and schizophrenia. The psychological disorders in these four categories are some of the most common disorders encountered by mental health professionals. They're also the ones that our students ask us about most often. Table 13.1 describes other categories of mental disorders contained in DSM-IV. Some of these disorders have been discussed in previous chapters.

TABLE 13.1 Some Key Diagnostic Categories in DSM-IV

Diagnostic Category	Core Features	Examples of Specific Disorders
Infancy, childhood, or adolescent disorders	Includes a wide range of developmental, behavioral, learning, and communication disorders that are usually first diagnosed in infancy, childhood, or adolescence. Symptoms of a particular disorder may vary depending on a child's age and development level.	**Autistic disorder:** Onset of symptoms prior to age of three. Characterized by severely impaired social and communication skills, including delayed or a complete lack of language development. Symptoms often include repetitive behaviors, such as body rocking, and abnormal interests, such as intense preoccupation with mechanical toys. **Tourette's disorder:** Onset prior to age of eighteen. Characterized by motor tics, such as recurring spasmodic movements of the head or arms, and vocal tics, such as recurring and sudden clicking, grunting, or snorting sounds. Sometimes involves uncontrollable utterances of profane or obscene words.
Substance-related disorders (see Chapter 4)	Occurrence of adverse social, behavioral, psychological, and physical effects by seeking or using substances such as alcohol, amphetamines, cocaine, marijuana, hallucinogens, and other drugs.	**Substance abuse:** A recurring pattern of impaired ability to function at work, school, or home due to repeated substance use. **Substance dependence:** A maladaptive pattern of substance use usually resulting in drug tolerance, withdrawal symptoms when the drug is discontinued, and compulsive drug-taking behavior that seriously impairs occupational and social functioning.
Somatoform disorders	Persistent, recurring complaints of bodily (or *somatic*) symptoms that have no physical or medical basis.	**Body dysmorphic disorder:** Exaggerated concern and preoccupation about minor or imagined defects in appearance. **Hypochondriasis:** Preoccupation with imagined diseases based on the person's misinterpretation of bodily symptoms or functions.
Sexual and gender identity disorders	Difficulty in the expression of normal sexuality, including confusion about gender identity, decreased sexual desire or arousal, difficulty having or in timing of orgasm, pain or discomfort during sex, or the use of inappropriate objects to produce sexual arousal.	**Fetishism:** Recurrent, intense sexually arousing fantasies, urges, or behaviors usually involving nonliving objects, such as female undergarments, shoes, boots, or other articles of clothing. **Gender identity disorder:** The strong and persistent desire to be the other sex.
Eating disorders (see Chapter 8)	Disturbances in eating behavior that involve obsessive concerns about becoming overweight, a distorted body image, and the inability to maintain a healthy body weight.	**Anorexia nervosa:** Severe restriction of eating and the failure to maintain a normal body weight due to the intense fear of gaining weight. **Bulimia nervosa:** Repeated episodes of binge eating followed by self-induced vomiting, misuse of laxatives, fasting, or excessive exercise.
Impulse-control disorders	Inability to resist an impulse, drive, or temptation to perform an act that is harmful to the self or others.	**Kleptomania:** The impulse to steal objects not needed for personal use or monetary value. **Pyromania:** The urge to set fires for pleasure, gratification, or relief of tension.
Personality disorders	An enduring, rigid pattern of thoughts, behaviors, and personality traits that produce distress and interfere with interpersonal relationships.	**Antisocial personality disorder:** A pervasive pattern of disregard for and violation of the rights of others, deceitfulness, irresponsibility, impulsiveness, and lack of remorse. **Borderline personality disorder:** A pervasive pattern of instability in interpersonal relationships, self-image, emotional control, and self-control.

SOURCE: DSM-IV, 1994.

Anxiety Disorders

The main symptom of the anxiety disorders is intense anxiety that disrupts normal functioning. How does pathological anxiety differ from normal anxiety? What characterizes generalized anxiety disorder and panic disorder? What are the phobias, and how have they been explained?

Anxiety is a familiar emotion to all of us—that feeling of tension, apprehension, and worry that often hits during personal crises and everyday conflicts. While unpleasant, anxiety is sometimes helpful. Think of anxiety as your personal, internal alarm system that tells you that something is not quite right. When it alerts you to a realistic threat, anxiety is adaptive and normal. For example, anxiety about your grades may motivate you to study harder.

Anxiety has both physical and mental effects. As your internal alarm system, anxiety puts you on *physical alert,* preparing you to defensively "fight" or "flee" potential dangers. Anxiety also puts you on *mental alert,* making you focus your attention squarely on the threatening situation. You become extremely vigilant, scanning the environment for potential threats (Barlow, 1991). When the threat has passed, your alarm system shuts off and you calm down. But even if the problem persists, you can put your anxious thoughts aside temporarily and attend to other matters.

In the **anxiety disorders,** however, the anxiety is *maladaptive.* Three features distinguish normal anxiety from pathological anxiety. First, pathological anxiety is *irrational.* The anxiety is provoked by perceived threats that are exaggerated or nonexistent, and the anxiety response is out of proportion to the actual importance of the situation. Second, pathological anxiety is *uncontrollable.* The person can't shut off the alarm reaction, even when he or she knows it's unrealistic. And third, pathological anxiety is *disruptive.* It interferes with relationships, job or academic performance, or everyday activities. In short, pathological anxiety is unreasonably intense, frequent, persistent, and disruptive.

As a symptom, anxiety occurs in many different mental disorders. In the anxiety disorders, however, anxiety is the *main* symptom. Anxiety is manifested differently in each of the anxiety disorders. To help orient you, here's a brief overview of the disorders that we'll discuss in this section:

- In *generalized anxiety disorder* and *panic disorder,* the main symptom is intense anxiety that often does not seem to be triggered by anything specific.

- In the *phobias,* severe anxiety occurs in response to a specific object or situation.

- In *posttraumatic stress disorder,* anxiety is triggered by memories of a traumatic experience.

- In *obsessive-compulsive disorder,* pathological anxiety occurs in response to uncontrollable thoughts or urges to perform certain actions.

Generalized Anxiety Disorder:
Worrying About Anything and Everything

Global, persistent, chronic, and excessive apprehension is the main feature of **generalized anxiety disorder.** People with this disorder are constantly tense and anxious, and their anxiety is pervasive. They feel anxious about a

---

anxiety
An unpleasant emotional state characterized by physical arousal and feelings of tension, apprehension, and worry.

anxiety disorders
A category of psychological disorders in which extreme anxiety is the main diagnostic feature and causes significant disruptions in the person's cognitive, behavioral, or interpersonal functioning.

generalized anxiety disorder
An anxiety disorder characterized by excessive, global, and persistent symptoms of anxiety; also called *free-floating anxiety.*

wide range of issues and life circumstances, sometimes with little or no apparent justification. The more issues about which a person worries excessively, the more likely it is that he or she suffers from generalized anxiety disorder (DSM-IV, 1994).

Normally, our anxiety quickly dissipates when a threatening situation is resolved. In generalized anxiety disorder, however, when one source of worry is removed, another quickly moves in to take its place. The anxiety can be attached to virtually any object, or none at all. Because of this, generalized anxiety disorder is sometimes referred to as *free-floating anxiety.*

Panic Attacks and Panic Disorder:
Sudden Episodes of Extreme Anxiety

A **panic attack** is a sudden episode of extreme anxiety that rapidly escalates in intensity. The most common symptoms of a panic attack are a pounding heart, rapid breathing, breathlessness, and a choking sensation. The person may also sweat, tremble, and experience light-headedness, chills, or hot flashes. Accompanying the intense, escalating surge of physical arousal are feelings of terror and the belief that one is about to die, go crazy, or completely lose control. A panic attack typically peaks within 10 minutes of onset and then gradually subsides. Nevertheless, the physical symptoms of a panic attack are so severe and frightening that it's not unusual for people to rush to an emergency room, convinced that they are having a heart attack, stroke, or seizure (Shulman & others, 1994).

When panic attacks occur *frequently* and *unexpectedly,* the person is said to be suffering from **panic disorder.** In this disorder, the frequency of panic attacks is highly variable and quite unpredictable. One person may have panic attacks several times a month. Another person may go for months without an attack, and then experience panic attacks for several days in a row. Understandably, people with panic disorder are quite apprehensive about when and where the next panic attack will hit (McNally, 1994; Barlow, 1991).

Sometimes the first panic attack occurs after a stressful experience, such as an injury or illness, or during a stressful period of life, such as while changing jobs or during a period of marital conflict (Craske & others, 1990). In other cases, however, the first panic attack seems to come from nowhere. In a recent survey of panic disorder patients, 40 percent could not identify any stressful event or negative life experience that might have precipitated the initial panic attack (Shulman & others, 1994).

Explaining Panic Disorder

Both biological and psychological causes seem to be implicated in panic disorder. On the biological side, family and twin studies have found that panic disorder tends to run in families (Goldstein & others, 1994; Torgersen, 1990). This suggests that some individuals may inherit a greater vulnerability to develop panic disorder. However, many panic disorder patients do not have relatives with the disorder (DSM-IV, 1994). So genetics alone does not provide a complete explanation.

Psychologically, people with panic disorder are unusually sensitive to the signs of physical arousal (Ehlers & Breuer, 1992; Antony & others, 1992). The fluttering heartbeat or momentary dizziness that the average person barely notices signals disaster to the panic-prone. For example, when normal subjects and panic disorder patients are given a substance, like caffeine, that triggers physiological arousal, only the panic disorder patients react with a full-blown panic attack (Margraf & Ehlers, 1989). Why?

"Normal" Panic Versus Panic Disorder
These medical workers were helping victims immediately after the bombing in Oklahoma City. When it was announced that a second bomb had been discovered, they ran from the building. Once the threat had passed, they were able to resume their rescue work. The physical arousal of a panic state helps us respond quickly when our lives are threatened. In panic disorder, however, feelings of panic seem to come from nowhere and in the absence of realistic threat.

panic attack
A sudden episode of extreme anxiety that rapidly escalates in intensity.

panic disorder
An anxiety disorder in which the person experiences frequent and unexpected panic attacks.

TABLE 13.2 Some Unusual Phobias

Amathophobia	Fear of dust
Anemophobia	Fear of wind
Aphephobia	Fear of being touched by another person
Bibliophobia	Fear of books
Catotrophobia	Fear of breaking a mirror
Ergophobia	Fear of work or responsibility
Erythrophobia	Fear of red objects
Gamophobia	Fear of marriage
Hypertrichophobia	Fear of growing excessive amounts of body hair
Levophobia	Fear of things being on the left side of one's body
Phobophobia	Fear of acquiring a phobia
Phonophobia	Fear of the sound of one's own voice
Triskaidekaphobia	Fear of the number thirteen

According to the *cognitive-behavioral theory of panic disorder,* people with panic disorder tend to misinterpret the physical signs of arousal as catastrophic and dangerous (Rapee & others, 1992; Zinbarg & others, 1992). When their heart starts to pound and their breathing escalates, they interpret their physical symptoms as frightening or dangerous. This interpretation adds to their physiological arousal and intensifies the symptoms.

After a frightening initial attack, the person becomes extremely apprehensive about suffering another panic attack. In turn, he becomes even more keenly attuned to physical changes that might signal the onset of another frightening attack. Ironically, this sensitivity simply increases the likelihood that another panic attack will occur.

The result? After a series of panic attacks, the person becomes behaviorally conditioned to respond with fear to the physical symptoms of arousal (Antony & others, 1992). Once established, such a conditioned response, combined with catastrophic thoughts, can act as a springboard for repeated panic attacks, leading to panic disorder.

The Phobias:

Fear and Loathing

A **phobia** is an intense, irrational fear that is triggered by a specific object or situation. Encountering the feared situation or object can provoke a full-fledged panic attack in some people (Craske, 1993). People with **specific phobia** are terrified of a particular object or situation and go to great lengths to avoid that object or situation, even though they know that the fear is irrational.

In the general population, *mild* phobias are extremely common. Many people are fearful of certain animals, like dogs or snakes, or mildly uncomfortable in particular situations, like flying in a plane or riding in an elevator. In comparison, the person with a phobia experiences incapacitating terror and anxiety. To be diagnosed as having a psychological disorder, a person's fear and avoidance must significantly interfere with daily life.

About 10 percent of the general population will experience a specific phobia at some point in their lives (Kessler & others, 1994). More than twice as many women as men suffer from specific phobia. Occasionally, people suffer from unusual phobias (see Table 13.2). But generally, the objects or situations that produce specific phobias tend to fall into four categories:

- *Fear of particular situations,* such as flying, driving, tunnels, bridges, elevators, crowds, or enclosed places

- *Fear of features of the natural environment,* such as heights, water, thunderstorms, or lightning

- *Fear of injury or blood,* including the fear of injections, needles, and medical or dental procedures

- *Fear of animals and insects,* such as snakes, spiders, dogs, cats, slugs, or bats

Agoraphobia: Fear of Panic Attacks in Public Places

One type of phobia deserves special mention—agoraphobia. Compared to the specific phobias, agoraphobia is both more disabling and more complex. Literally, *agoraphobia* means "fear of the marketplace." But rather than fearing public places per se, a person with **agoraphobia** fears having a panic attack in a public place from which it might be difficult to escape or get help (McNally & Louro, 1992). Consequently, people with agoraphobia avoid

phobia
An irrational fear triggered by a specific object or situation.

specific phobia
An anxiety disorder characterized by an extreme and irrational fear of a specific object or situation that interferes with the ability to function in daily life.

agoraphobia
An anxiety disorder involving the extreme and irrational fear of experiencing a panic attack in a public situation and being unable to escape or get help.

(1) situations that they think might provoke a panic attack and (2) situations in which they would be unable to escape or get help if they *did* suffer a panic attack.

What kinds of situations are we talking about? Crowds, standing in line, stores or elevators, public transportation, and traveling in a car may all be avoided because of the fear of suffering a panic attack and being unable to escape the situation. Consequently, many agoraphobics become prisoners in their own homes, unable to go beyond their front door.

Social Phobia: Fear of Social Situations

A second type of phobia also deserves additional comment—social phobia. Social phobia goes well beyond the shyness that everyone sometimes feels at social gatherings. Rather, the person with **social phobia** is paralyzed by fear of social situations, especially if the situation involves performing even routine behaviors in front of others. Eating a meal in public, making small talk at a party, or even using a public restroom can be agonizing for the person with social phobia.

The core of social phobia seems to be an irrational fear of being embarrassed, judged, or critically evaluated by others (Woody, 1996). People with social phobia recognize that their fear is excessive and unreasonable, but they still approach social situations with tremendous anxiety (J. Ross, 1993). In severe cases, they may even suffer a panic attack in social situations. When the fear of being embarrassed or failing in public significantly interferes with daily life, it qualifies as social phobia (DSM-IV, 1994).

Social Phobia Social phobia is far more debilitating than everyday shyness. This pleasant scene shows a happy bride dancing with her mother as the wedding guests look on. For those who suffer from social phobia, dancing in public would be impossible, and even attending the wedding as a guest might cause overwhelming anxiety.

Because of their avoidance of social situations, people with social phobia often have very low self-esteem, poor social skills, and few friends. Their fear of evaluation or criticism by others may lead to occupational or academic underachievement. In classroom situations, they may suffer from intense test anxiety or be afraid to ask questions or make comments (Davidson, 1993; J. Ross, 1993).

Interestingly, cultural influences can add some novel twists to social phobia. Consider the Japanese disorder called *taijin kyofusho. Taijin kyofusho* usually affects young Japanese males. It has several features in common with social phobia, including extreme social anxiety and avoidance of social situations. However, the person with *taijin kyofusho* is not worried about being embarrassed in public. Rather, reflecting the cultural emphasis of concern for others, the person with *taijin kyofusho* fears that his body's appearance or smell, facial expression, or body language will offend, insult, or embarrass other people (Russell, 1989).

Explaining Phobias

The learning principles described in Chapter 5 may be involved in the development of some phobias. If a specific phobia can be traced back to some traumatic event, *classical conditioning* may be involved. The pairing of a neutral object with a frightening or painful stimulus may result in the object becoming a *conditioned stimulus* that now automatically elicits a *conditioned response* of fear. As you may recall, this is how "Little Albert" was classically conditioned to fear a tame lab rat.

social phobia
An anxiety disorder involving the extreme and irrational fear of being embarrassed, judged, or scrutinized by others in social situations.

Operant conditioning is involved in helping to maintain the avoidance behaviors that accompany many phobias. When steps to avoid the feared object are actively taken, the avoidance behaviors are being maintained and strengthened through the process of *negative reinforcement*. *Observational learning* is involved in phobias that are the result of imitating the fearful reactions of others, such as the child who learns to fear spiders or mice from watching another family member's fearful reaction.

We also noted in Chapter 5 that humans seem *biologically prepared* to acquire fears of certain animals or situations, such as snakes or heights, that were survival threats in human evolutionary history (McNally, 1987). People also seem to be predisposed to develop phobias toward creatures that arouse disgust, like slugs, maggots, or cockroaches (Webb & Davey, 1993). Instinctively, it seems, many people find such creatures repulsive, possibly because they are associated with disease, infection, or filth. Such phobias may reflect a fear of contamination or infection that is also based on human evolutionary history (Ware & others, 1994; Davey, 1993).

Yuck! It's hard to suppress a shudder of disgust at the sight of a slug sliming its way across the sidewalk . . . or a cockroach scuttling across the kitchen floor. Are such responses instinctive? Why are people more likely to develop phobias for slugs, maggots, and cockroaches than for mosquitoes or grasshoppers?

Posttraumatic Stress Disorder:
Re-experiencing the Trauma

> *Posttraumatic stress disorder (PTSD) and obsessive-compulsive disorder both involve extreme anxiety and intrusive thoughts. What is PTSD, and what causes it? What is obsessive-compulsive disorder, and what are the most common types of obsessions and compulsions?*

Posttraumatic stress disorder, abbreviated **PTSD,** is a long-lasting anxiety disorder that develops in response to an extreme physical or psychological trauma. Extreme traumas are events that produce intense feelings of horror and helplessness, such as a serious physical injury or threat of injury to yourself or to loved ones (DSM-IV, 1994).

Originally, posttraumatic stress disorder was primarily associated with direct experiences of military combat. However, it's now known that PTSD can also develop in survivors of other sorts of extreme traumas, such as disasters, physical or sexual assault, and random shooting sprees (Sharan & others, 1996; Allodi, 1994; North & others, 1994). Children as well as adults can experience the symptoms of PTSD (Vernberg & others, 1996).

Three core symptoms characterize posttraumatic stress disorder (DSM-IV, 1994). First, the person *frequently recalls the event,* replaying it in her mind. Such recollections are often *intrusive,* meaning that they are unwanted and interfere with normal thoughts. Second, the person *avoids stimuli or situations* that tend to trigger memories of the experience and undergoes a general *numbing of emotional responsiveness.* Third, the person experiences the *increased physical arousal* associated with anxiety. He may be easily startled, experience sleep disturbances, have problems concentrating and remembering, and be prone to irritability or angry outbursts (Keane & others, 1992).

Posttraumatic stress disorder is somewhat unusual in that the source of the disorder is the traumatic event itself, rather than a cause that lies within

A Half-Century of Psychological Pain
The symptoms of posttraumatic stress disorder can apparently last a lifetime. More than fifty years after the close of World War II, thousands of veterans, now in their 70s and 80s, still suffer from nightmares, anxiety, and other PTSD symptoms (Lee & others, 1995). Some experts estimate that as many as 200,000 World War II veterans may continue to suffer from the symptoms of posttraumatic stress disorder.

posttraumatic stress disorder (PTSD)
An anxiety disorder in which chronic and persistent symptoms of anxiety develop in response to an extreme physical or psychological trauma.

obsessive-compulsive disorder
An anxiety disorder in which the symptoms of anxiety are triggered by intrusive, repetitive thoughts and urges to perform certain actions.

obsessions
Repeated, intrusive, and uncontrollable irrational thoughts or mental images that cause extreme anxiety and distress.

compulsions
Repetitive behaviors or mental acts that are performed to prevent or reduce anxiety.

the individual. Even well-adjusted and psychologically healthy people may develop PTSD when exposed to an extremely traumatic event (Sutker & others, 1994). However, it's also important to point out that no stressor, no matter how extreme, produces posttraumatic stress disorder in everyone.

So why is it that some people develop PTSD while others don't? Several factors influence the likelihood of developing posttraumatic stress disorder (Tomb, 1994). First, people with a personal or family history of psychological disorders are more likely to develop PTSD when exposed to an extreme trauma. Second, the magnitude of the trauma plays an important role. More extreme stressors are more likely to produce PTSD. Finally, when people undergo *multiple* traumas, the incidence of PTSD can be quite high.

Obsessive-Compulsive Disorder:
Checking It Again . . . and Again

When you leave your home, you probably check to make sure all the doors are locked. Sometimes, you may even double- or triple-check just to be on the safe side. But once you're confident that the door is locked, you don't think about it again.

Now imagine you've checked the door *twenty* times. Yet you're still not quite sure that the door is really locked. You know the feeling is irrational, but you feel compelled to check again and again. Imagine you've *also* had to repeatedly check that the coffeepot was unplugged, that the stove was turned off, and so forth. Finally, imagine that you only got two blocks away from home before you felt compelled to turn back and check *again*—because you still were not certain.

Sound agonizing? This is the psychological world of the person who suffers from one form of obsessive-compulsive disorder. **Obsessive-compulsive disorder** is an anxiety disorder in which a person's life is dominated by repetitive thoughts (*obsessions*) and behaviors (*compulsions*).

Obsessions are repeated, intrusive, uncontrollable thoughts or mental images that cause the person great anxiety and distress. Obsessions are not the same as everyday worries. Normal worries typically have some sort of factual basis, even if they're somewhat exaggerated (Freeston & others, 1994). In contrast, obsessions have little or no basis in reality, and are often extremely farfetched. One common obsession is an irrational fear of dirt, germs, and other forms of contamination. Another common obsession theme is pathological doubt about having accomplished a simple task, such as locking doors or shutting off appliances (Rasmussen & Eisen, 1992).

A **compulsion** is a repetitive behavior that a person feels driven to perform. Typically, compulsions are ritual behaviors that must be carried out in a certain pattern or sequence. Compulsions may be *overt physical behaviors,* such as repeatedly washing your hands, checking doors or windows, or entering and reentering a doorway until you walk through exactly in the middle. Or they may be *covert mental behaviors,* such as counting or reciting certain phrases to yourself. When the person tries to resist performing the ritual, unbearable tension, anxiety, and distress result.

Reprinted from *Health Magazine*

TABLE 13.3 The Anxiety Disorders

General Anxiety Disorder

- Persistent, chronic, unreasonable worry and anxiety
- General symptoms of anxiety, including persistent physical arousal

Panic Disorder

- Frequent and unexpected panic attacks, with no specific or identifiable trigger

Phobias

- Intense anxiety or panic attack triggered by a specific object or situation
- Persistent avoidance of feared object or situation

Posttraumatic Stress Disorder

- Anxiety triggered by memories of a traumatic experience

Obsessive-Compulsive Disorder

- Anxiety caused by uncontrollable, persistent, recurring thoughts (obsessions) and/or
- Anxiety caused by uncontrollable, persistent urges to perform certain actions (compulsions)

People may experience either obsessions or compulsions. More commonly, obsessions and compulsions are *both* present. Often, the obsessions and compulsions are linked in some way. For example, a man who was obsessed with the idea that he might have lost an important document felt compelled to pick up every scrap of paper he saw on the street, in the subway, and in other public places.

Other compulsions bear little logical relationship to the feared consequences, like the woman who believed that if she didn't get dressed according to a strict pattern, her husband would die in an automobile accident. In all cases, obsessive-compulsives feel that something terrible will happen if the compulsive action is left undone.

Interestingly, obsessions and compulsions take a similar shape in different cultures around the world. However, the *content* of the obsessions and compulsions tends to mirror the particular culture's concerns and beliefs. In the United States, compulsive washers are typically preoccupied with obsessional fears of germs and infection. But in rural Nigeria and rural India, compulsive washers are more likely to have obsessional concerns about religious purity (Rapoport, 1989).

Explaining Obsessive-Compulsive Disorder

Although researchers are far from fully understanding the causes of obsessive-compulsive disorder, biological factors seem to be involved. For example, a deficiency in the neurotransmitter serotonin has been implicated in obsessive-compulsive disorder. When treated with drugs that increase the availability of serotonin in the brain, many obsessive-compulsive patients experience a marked decrease in symptoms (Insel & Winslow, 1992; Jenike, 1992).

In addition, obsessive-compulsive disorder has been linked with dysfunction in specific brain areas, such as the frontal lobes, which play a key role in our ability to think and plan ahead. Another brain area that has been implicated is the *caudate nucleus,* which is involved in regulating movements (Schwartz & others, 1996). Dysfunctions in these brain areas might help account for the overwhelming sense of doubt and lack of control over thoughts and actions that are experienced in obsessive-compulsive disorder (Rapoport, 1991).

Brain Activity in Obsessive-Compulsive Disorder These PET scans show the change in activity in a brain area called the *caudate nucleus* before (left) and after (right) therapy for obsessive-compulsive disorder. The caudate nucleus is involved in initiating and controlling movement. In obsessive-compulsive disorder, the caudate nucleus is overactive, as indicated by the bright yellow in the left PET scan. After psychotherapy, the obsessions and compulsions cease, and the caudate nucleus becomes less active (right).

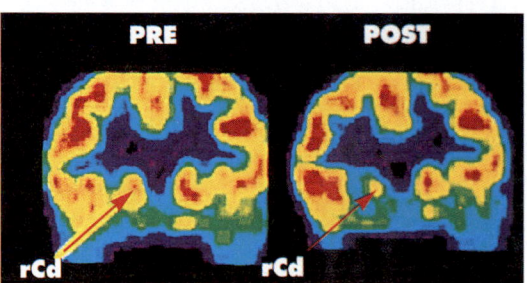

Mood Disorders: Emotions Gone Awry

In the mood disorders, disturbed emotions cause psychological distress and impair daily functioning. What are the symptoms of major depression and bipolar disorder? How prevalent are these disorders? What factors contribute to these disorders?

Let's face it, we all have our ups and downs. When things are going well, we feel cheerful and optimistic. When events take a more negative turn, our mood can sour: we feel miserable and pessimistic. Either way, the intensity and duration of our moods are usually in proportion to the events going on in our lives (Mondimore, 1993). That's completely normal.

In the mood disorders, however, emotions violate the criteria of normal moods. In quality, intensity, and duration, a person's emotional state does not seem to reflect what's going on in his or her life. A person may feel a pervasive sadness despite the best of circumstances. Or a person may be extremely energetic and overconfident with no apparent justification. These mood changes persist much longer than the normal fluctuations in moods that we all experience.

DSM-IV formally defines a **mood disorder** as a serious, persistent disturbance in a person's emotions that causes psychological discomfort, impairs the ability to function, or both. In this section, we'll look at the two most important mood disorders: major depression and bipolar disorder.

Major Depression:

"Like Some Poisonous Fogbank"

The intense psychological pain of **major depression** is hard to convey to those who have never experienced it. In his book *Darkness Visible,* bestselling author William Styron (1990) described his struggle with major depression in this way:

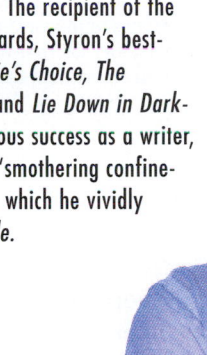

Author William Styron The recipient of the Pulitzer Prize and other awards, Styron's bestselling novels include *Sophie's Choice, The Confessions of Nat Turner,* and *Lie Down in Darkness.* Yet despite his enormous success as a writer, Styron was gripped by the "smothering confinement" of major depression, which he vividly describes in *Darkness Visible.*

All sense of hope had vanished, along with the idea of a futurity; my brain, in thrall to its outlaw hormones, had become less an organ of thought than an instrument registering, minute by minute, varying degrees of its own suffering. The mornings themselves were becoming bad now as I wandered about lethargic, following my synthetic sleep, but afternoons were still the worse, beginning at three o'clock, when I'd feel the horror, like some poisonous fogbank, roll in upon my mind, forcing me into bed. There I would lie for as long as six hours, stuporous and virtually paralyzed, gazing at the ceiling . . .

The Symptoms of Major Depression

The Styron passage gives you a feeling for how the symptoms of depression can affect the whole person. Figure 13.3 on the next page summarizes the emotional, behavioral, cognitive, and physical symptoms that are commonly seen in people experiencing major depression. To be diagnosed with major depression, a person must display most of these symptoms for two weeks or longer (DSM-IV, 1994). In some cases, a person's downward emotional spiral has been triggered by some negative event or stressful situation (Frank & others, 1994; Kendler & others, 1993a). However, in many cases, like Styron's, there doesn't seem to be any external reason for the persistent feelings of depression.

One significant negative event deserves special mention: the death of a loved one. If a family member or close friend dies, it is completely normal to feel despondent and sad for several months as part of the mourning or bereavement process (Zisook & Shuchter, 1993). Even so, most people resume attending to the routine duties of life within a few weeks. Privately, they may still feel a strong sense of loss, but they function adequately if not optimally. As a general rule, if a person's ability to function after the death of a loved one is still seriously impaired after two months, major depression is suspected (DSM-IV, 1994).

Suicide is always a potential risk in major depression. Self-esteem plummets as the person's thoughts become globally pessimistic and negative about themselves, the world, and the future (Beck & others, 1993). Often, this

mood disorders
A category of mental disorders in which significant and chronic disruption in mood is the predominant symptom, causing impaired cognitive, behavioral, and physical functioning.

major depression
A mood disorder characterized by extreme and persistent feelings of despondency, worthlessness, and hopelessness, causing impaired emotional, cognitive, behavioral, and physical functioning.

Emotional symptoms

- Feelings of sadness, hopelessness, helplessness, guilt, emptiness, or worthlessness
- Feeling emotionally disconnected from others
- Turning away from other people

Cognitive symptoms

- Difficulty thinking, concentrating, and remembering
- Global negativity and pessimism
- Suicidal thoughts or preoccupation with death

Behavioral symptoms

- Dejected facial expression
- Makes less eye contact; eyes downcast
- Smiles less often
- Slowed movements, speech, and gestures
- Tearfulness or spontaneous episodes of crying
- Loss of interest or pleasure in usual activities, including sex
- Withdrawal from social activities

Physical symptoms

- Changes in appetite resulting in significant weight loss or gain
- Insomnia, early morning awakening or oversleeping
- Vague but chronic aches and pains
- Diminished sexual interest
- Loss of physical and mental energy
- Global feelings of anxiety
- Restlessness, fidgety activity

FIGURE 13.3 The Symptoms of Depression

The experience of major depression can permeate every aspect of life. This figure shows some of the most common emotional, behavioral, cognitive, and physical symptoms of that disorder.

dysthymic disorder

A mood disorder involving chronic, low-grade feelings of depression that produce subjective discomfort but do not seriously impair the ability to function.

pervasive negativity and pessimism is manifested in suicidal thoughts or a preoccupation with death. Approximately 10 percent of those suffering major depression attempt suicide (Zweig & Hinrichsen, 1993).

Abnormal sleep patterns are another hallmark of major depression. The amount of time spent in nondreaming, deeply relaxed sleep is greatly reduced or absent (see Chapter 4). Rather than the usual 90-minute cycles of dreaming, the person experiences sporadic REM periods of varying lengths. Spontaneous awakenings occur repeatedly during the night. Very commonly, the depressed person awakens at 3:00 or 4:00 a.m., then cannot get back to sleep, despite feeling exhausted (Benca & others, 1992; Wehr, 1988). Less commonly, some depressed people sleep excessively, sometimes as much as 18 hours a day.

Dysthymic Disorder

In contrast to major depression, which significantly impairs a person's ability to function, some people experience a less severe form of depression called dysthymic disorder. Briefly, **dysthymic disorder** is chronic, low-grade depression. It's characterized by many of the symptoms of depression, but the symptoms are less intense. Usually, dysthymic disorder develops in response to some stressful event or trauma. Rather than improving over time, however, the negative mood persists indefinitely. Although the person functions adequately, she has a chronic case of "the blues" that can continue for years (Hirschfeld, 1991).

Some people with dysthymic disorder experience *double depression*. That is, they experience one or more episodes of major depression on top of their ongoing dysthymic disorder. As the person recovers from the episode of major depression, he returns to the less intense depressed symptoms of dysthymic disorder (Bower, 1994a; Lewinsohn & others, 1991b).

seasonal affective disorder (SAD)
A mood disorder in which episodes of depression typically recur during the fall and winter and remit during the spring and summer.

bipolar disorder
Often called *manic depression;* a mood disorder involving periods of incapacitating depression alternating with periods of extreme euphoria and excitement.

The Prevalence and Course of Major Depression

Major depression is often called "the common cold" of psychological disorders, and for a good reason: depression is the most common of all the psychological disorders (Gotlib, 1992). In any given year, about 12 million Americans are affected by major depression. Women are about twice as likely as men to be diagnosed with major depression, though researchers aren't completely certain why depression is more prevalent among women (Nolen-Hoeksema, 1990; Kendler & others, 1993a). If you're female, the lifetime odds are approximately 1 out of 4 that you'll experience major depression. If you're male, the lifetime odds are about 1 out of 8 (Kessler & others, 1994).

Most people who experience major depression try to cope with the symptoms without seeking professional help. Left untreated, the symptoms of major depression can easily last six months or longer. When depression is not treated, it may become a recurring mental disorder that progressively becomes more severe. Better than half of all people who have been through one episode of major depression can expect a relapse, usually within two years. With each recurrence, the symptoms tend to increase in severity and the time between major depression episodes decreases (Coryell & others, 1994b; Wells & others, 1992).

Finally, for millions of people with **seasonal affective disorder (SAD),** repeated episodes of depression are as predictable as the changing seasons, especially the onset of autumn and winter (Faedda & others, 1993). In the most common form of seasonal affective disorder, episodes of depression recur in the fall and winter months, when there is the least amount of sunlight. Seasonal affective disorder is more common among women and among people who live in the northern latitudes (Rosenthal, 1993).

Bipolar Disorder:
An Emotional Roller Coaster

It was about 6:30 a.m. when your author Don arrived for work at 2 Specialty—the hospital psychiatric ward. A few patients sat sipping their morning coffee or looking at the newspaper. As Don walked toward the nurses' station, a tall, overweight young man with black curly hair *zoomed* across the ward and intercepted him.

"Hi! My name's Kelly! What's yours?" he enthusiastically boomed, vigorously shaking hands. Before Don could respond, Kelly moved on to new topics. Within the next 90 seconds, Don heard about: (1) Kelly's plans to make millions of dollars organizing garage sales for other people; (2) several songs that Kelly had written that were all going to skyrocket to the top of the music charts; (3) Kelly's many inventions; and (4) a variety of movie stars, rock stars, and professional athletes, all of whom were Kelly's close friends.

Kelly spoke so rapidly that his words often got tangled up with each other. His arms and legs looked as if they were about to get tangled up, too—Kelly was in constant motion. His grinning, rapid-fire speech was punctuated with grand, sweeping gestures and exaggerated facial expressions. Before Don could say a word, Kelly vigorously shook his hand again, and *zoomed* to the other side of the psychiatric ward to intercept another unfamiliar face.

Patty Duke and Bipolar Disorder Actress Patty Duke was the youngest person to win an Academy Award for her performance as Helen Keller in *The Miracle Worker.* But as an adult, Duke careened from bouts of suicidal depression to episodes of manic behavior. At one point, she married a man she had known for only five hours. At another time, just moments after accepting an Emmy, she angrily rejected the award and announced she was going to become a doctor. In 1982, Patty Duke was diagnosed with bipolar disorder. Since that time, medication has stabilized her behavior.

The Symptoms of Bipolar Disorder

Kelly displayed classic symptoms of the mental disorder that used to be called *manic depression* and is today called **bipolar disorder.** In contrast to major depression, bipolar disorder almost always involves abnormal moods at *both* ends of the emotional spectrum. In most cases of bipolar disorder, the person experiences extreme mood swings. Episodes of incapacitating depression alternate with shorter periods of extreme euphoria called **manic episodes.** For most people with bipolar disorder, a manic episode immediately precedes or follows a bout with major depression. However, a small percentage of people with bipolar disorder experience only manic episodes (DSM-IV, 1994).

Manic episodes typically begin suddenly and symptoms escalate rapidly. During a manic episode, people are uncharacteristically euphoric, expansive, and excited for several days or longer. Although they sleep very little, they have boundless energy. The person's sense of self-esteem is wildly inflated. He exudes supreme self-confidence. Often, he has grandiose plans for obtaining wealth, power, and fame (Mondimore, 1993). Sometimes the grandiose ideas represent *delusional,* or false, beliefs. Kelly's belief that various celebrities were his close personal friends was delusional.

Kelly's fast-forward speech was loud and virtually impossible to interrupt. During a manic episode, words are spoken so rapidly, they're often slurred as the person tries to keep up with his own thought processes. The manic person feels as if his thoughts are racing along at Warp Factor 10. Attention is easily distracted by virtually anything, triggering a *flight of ideas*, in which thoughts rapidly and loosely shift from topic to topic.

Not surprisingly, the ability to function during a manic episode is severely impaired. Hospitalization is usually required, partly to protect people from the potential consequences of their own poor judgment and inappropriate behaviors. During manic episodes, people can run up a mountain of bills, disappear for weeks at time, become sexually promiscuous, or commit illegal acts. Very commonly, the person becomes agitated or verbally abusive when others question his grandiose claims (Hendrix, 1993).

Some people experience a milder but chronic form of bipolar disorder called **cyclothymic disorder.** In cyclothymic disorder, people experience moderate but frequent mood swings for two years or longer. These mood swings are not severe enough to qualify as either bipolar disorder or major depression. Often, people with cyclothymic disorder are perceived as being extremely moody, unpredictable, and inconsistent.

The Prevalence and Course of Bipolar Disorder

As in Kelly's case, the onset of bipolar disorder typically occurs in the person's early twenties. The extreme mood swings tend to start and stop much more abruptly than the mood changes of major depression. And whereas an episode of major depression can easily last for six months or longer, the manic and depressive episodes of bipolar disorder tend to be much shorter—lasting anywhere from a few days to a couple of months (Winokur & others, 1993).

Annually, about 2 million Americans suffer from bipolar disorder (Hendrix, 1993). Unlike major depression, there are no sex differences in the rate at which bipolar disorder occurs. For both men and women, the lifetime risk of developing bipolar disorder is about 1 percent (Leibenluft, 1996).

In the majority of cases, bipolar disorder is a recurring disorder (Gitlin & others, 1995). A small percentage of people display *rapid cycling,* experiencing four or more manic or depressive episodes every year (Maj & others, 1994). More commonly, bipolar disorder tends to recur every couple of years. Often, bipolar disorder recurs when the individual stops taking *lithium,* a medication that helps control the disorder (Keck & McElroy, 1993).

manic episode
A sudden, rapidly escalating emotional state characterized by extreme euphoria, excitement, physical energy, and rapid thoughts and speech.

cyclothymic disorder
A mood disorder characterized by moderate but frequent mood swings that are not severe enough to qualify as bipolar disorder.

Explaining Mood Disorders

Multiple factors appear to be involved in the development of the mood disorders. There is ample indirect evidence from family, twin, and adoption studies that some people inherit a *genetic predisposition,* or a greater vulnerability, to develop a mood disorder (Tsuang & Faraone, 1990). For example, researchers have consistently found that both major depression and bipolar disorder tend to run in families (Warner & others, 1992).

Twin studies have shown that if one identical twin suffers from major depression or bipolar disorder, the other twin has about a 70 percent chance of also developing the disorder (Torrey & others, 1994). The same 70 percent shared risk rate has been found in studies of identical twins who were adopted and raised apart (Klein & Wender, 1993). These findings strongly suggest that shared genetics rather than shared environmental experiences account for the high rate of similarity of mood disorders in identical twins.

There is also a great deal of indirect evidence that implicates at least two important neurotransmitters, serotonin and norepinephrine, in major depression. Since the 1960s, several medications, called *antidepressants,* have been developed to treat major depression. In one way or another, the antidepressants seem to lift the symptoms of depression by increasing the availability of norepinephrine and serotonin in the brain.

Major depression is often triggered by traumatic and stressful events (G. Brown & others, 1994). Exposure to recent stressful events is one of the best predictors of major depression episodes. This seems to be especially true for people who have experienced previous episodes of depression and who have a family history of mood disorders (Kendler & others, 1993a). There is some evidence that stressful life events also play a role in the course of bipolar disorder (Johnson & Roberts, 1995).

In summary, considerable evidence points to the role of genetic factors, biochemical factors, and stressful life events in the development of mood disorders. However, exactly how these factors interact to cause mood disorders is still being investigated.

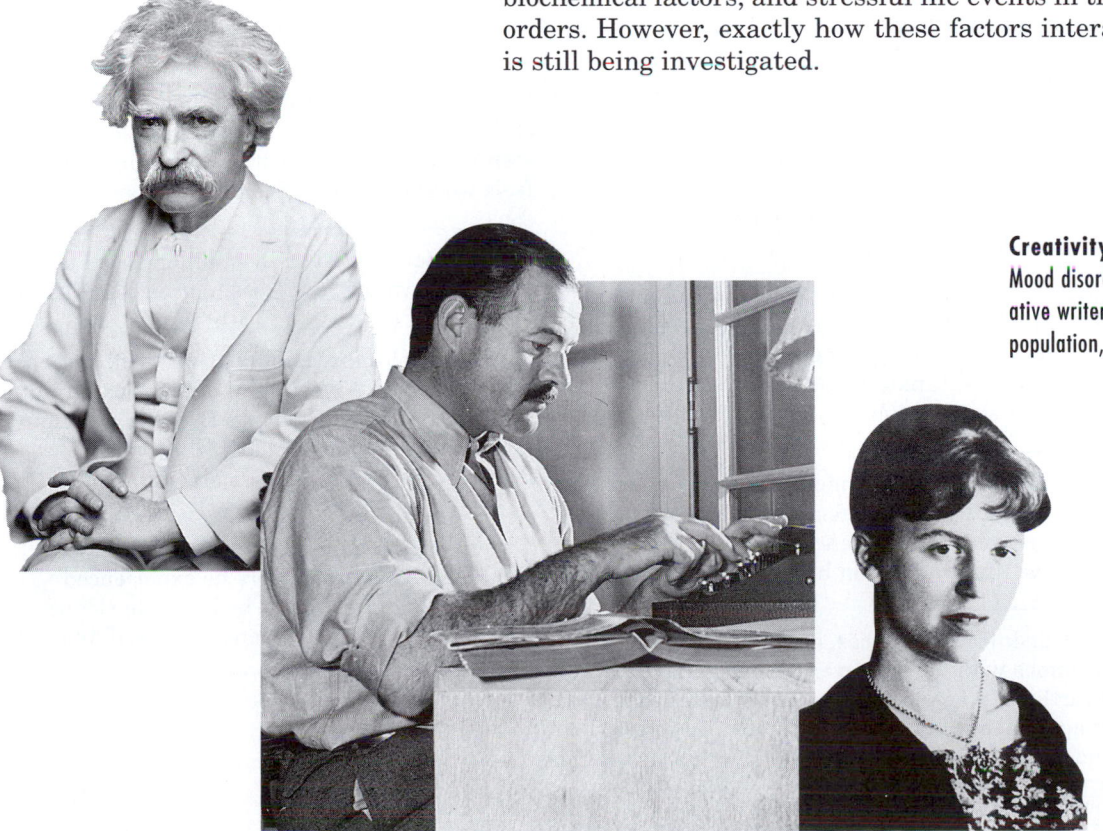

Creativity and Mood Disorders
Mood disorders occur more frequently among creative writers and artists than among the general population, leading some researchers to propose a biochemical or genetic link between mood disorders and the artistic temperament (Jamison, 1993). Writer Mark Twain, novelist Ernest Hemingway, and poet Sylvia Plath all suffered from severe bouts of depression throughout their lives. Both Plath and Hemingway committed suicide, as did Hemingway's father, brother, and sister. In 1996, Hemingway's granddaughter, actress Margaux Hemingway, also committed suicide just one day before the 35th anniversary of her famous grandfather's death.

TABLE 13.4 The Mood Disorders

Major Depression

- Loss of interest or pleasure in almost all activities
- Despondent mood, feelings of emptiness, worthlessness, or excessive guilt
- Preoccupation with death or suicidal thoughts
- Difficulty sleeping or excessive sleeping
- Diminished ability to think, concentrate, or make decisions
- Disrupted appetite and significant weight loss or gain

Dysthymic Disorder

- Chronic, low-grade depressed feelings that are not severe enough to qualify as major depression

Bipolar Disorder

- One or more manic episodes characterized by euphoria, high energy, grandiose ideas, flight of ideas, inappropriate self-confidence, and decreased need for sleep
- Usually, one or more episodes of major depression
- May alternate rapidly between symptoms of mania and major depression

Cyclothymic Disorder

- Moderate, recurring mood swings that are not severe enough to qualify as major depression or bipolar disorder

CONCEPT REVIEW 13.1

Anxiety Disorders and Mood Disorders

Match each example with one of the following: generalized anxiety disorder; panic disorder; specific phobia; posttraumatic stress disorder; obsessive-compulsive disorder; dysthymic disorder; major depression; cyclothymic disorder; bipolar disorder.

1. Alayna worries about everything and can never relax. She is very jumpy, has trouble sleeping at night, and has a poor appetite. For the last few months, her anxiety has become so extreme that she is unable to concentrate at work. _____

2. For as long as she can remember, Mary has felt negative about life. Although good things occasionally happen in Mary's life, they have little impact on her gloomy mood. _____

3. Harry disinfects his shoes, clothing, floor, and doorknobs with bleach several times a day. Nevertheless, he is tormented by worries that his apartment may be contaminated by germs from outside. _____

4. Bianca has missed almost all her college classes during the last month. She sleeps fourteen hours a day, has withdrawn from friends, feels worthless, and cries for no apparent reason. _____

5. Carl cannot bear to be in small enclosed places, such as elevators, and goes to great lengths to avoid them. _____

6. Mark is very unpredictable. One week he is a recluse, the next week he is energetic and initiating activities with others. Even though his mood swings occur regularly, they are not severe enough to qualify as bipolar disorder. _____

7. Thuan, a Vietnamese refugee, cannot stop thinking about the horrors he experienced while fleeing his country by boat. He sleeps poorly and is often awakened by terrifying nightmares. _____

The Dissociative Disorders:
Fragmentation of the Self

A dissociative experience reflects a disruption in awareness, memory, or identity. What are dissociative amnesia and dissociative fugue? What is dissociative identity disorder (DID), and what is thought to cause it? Why are some psychologists skeptical about DID?

Despite the many changes you've experienced throughout your lifetime, you have a pretty consistent sense of identity. You're aware of your surroundings and can easily recall memories from the recent and distant past. In other words, a normal personality is one in which *awareness, memory,* and *personal identity* are associated and well-integrated.

In contrast, a **dissociative experience** is one in which a person's awareness, memory, and personal identity become separated or divided. While that may sound weird, dissociative experiences are not inherently pathological. In fact, mild dissociative experiences are quite common and completely normal (Kihlstrom & others, 1994; Putnam, 1993). Here are several common examples of minor dissociative experiences, some of which have probably happened to you:

- You become so absorbed in a book or movie that you lose all track of time.

- You daydream your way through class, snapping to only when your instructor calls your name for the third time.

- You are so preoccupied with your thoughts while driving that when you get to your destination, you remember next to nothing about the trip.

- You wake up in a strange room on vacation and are momentarily unable to remember where you are or how you got there.

In each of these examples, you've experienced a temporary "break" or "separation" in your memory or awareness—a mild form of dissociation.

In some cultures, dramatic disruptions in an individual's sense of personal identity are perceived as normal and even highly valued (Mulhern, 1991). For example, *spirit possession* is common in many cultures, typically within a religious context (Krippner, 1994). The usual occupant of a human body is supposedly displaced by a "spirit" that takes control of the body. The individual often has no memory for events experienced while the spirit is in control. Another phenomenon that occurs in some cultures is a *trance state,* in which the person loses his sense of personal identity or is unaware of his surroundings (Cardeña, 1992).

If spirit possession and trance states sound like bizarre behaviors that only occur in cultures radically different from our own, think again. *Glossolalia,* or "speaking in tongues," is common in some North American Christian churches (Spanos, 1994). Speaking in tongues is another example of a dissociative possession state: the person is temporarily "possessed" by the Holy Spirit, who speaks through the individual in an unknown language. Like trance states and spirit possession, glossolalia is a highly valued experience within a specific cultural and religious context.

dissociative experience
A break or disruption in consciousness during which awareness, memory, and personal identity become separated or divided.

Dissociation and Possession A Candomble priestess in Brazil holds a woman who is "possessed" by a Christian saint during a religious ceremony. Such dissociative trance and possession states are common in religions around the world. When dissociative experiences take place within a religious ritual context, they are not considered abnormal. In fact, such experiences may be highly valued (Mulhern, 1991).

As DSM-IV points out, dissociative possession or trance states are *not* considered pathological if: (1) they occur within the context of accepted cultural or religious practices; (2) they occur voluntarily; and (3) they don't cause distress or impair functioning. In fact, people who frequently experience possession or trance states may achieve special status within their culture as spiritual leaders or healers (Mulhern, 1991).

Clearly, then, dissociative experiences are not necessarily abnormal. But in the **dissociative disorders,** the dissociative experiences are more extreme and frequent and severely disrupt everyday functioning. Awareness, or recognition of familiar surroundings, may be completely obstructed. Memories of pertinent personal information may be unavailable to consciousness. Identity may be lost, confused, or fragmented (Spiegel & Cardeña, 1991).

The category of dissociative disorders consists of three basic disorders: *dissociative amnesia, dissociative fugue,* and *dissociative identity disorder,* which was previously called multiple personality disorder. Until recently, the dissociative disorders were thought to be extremely rare. However, there is increasing evidence that dissociative symptoms and the dissociative disorders are far more common than researchers had believed (Saxe & others, 1993; C. Ross, 1991).

Dissociative Amnesia and Fugue:

Forgetting and Wandering

Dissociative amnesia refers to the partial or total inability to recall important information which is not due to a medical condition, like an illness, injury, or drug. Usually the person develops amnesia for personal events and information, rather than for general knowledge or skills. That is, the person may not be able to remember his wife's name, but does remember how to read and who Martin Luther King, Jr., was. In most cases, dissociative amnesia is a response to stress, trauma, or an extremely distressing situation, such as combat, marital problems, or physical abuse (Spiegel & Cardeña, 1991).

A closely related disorder is dissociative fugue. In **dissociative fugue,** the person outwardly appears completely normal. However, the person has

dissociative disorders
A category of psychological disorders in which extreme and frequent disruptions of awareness, memory, and personal identity impair the ability to function.

dissociative amnesia
A dissociative disorder involving the partial or total inability to recall important personal information.

dissociative fugue
A dissociative disorder involving sudden and unexpected travel away from home, extensive amnesia, and identity confusion.

extensive amnesia and is confused about his identity. While in the fugue state, he suddenly and inexplicably travels away from his home, wandering to other cities or even countries. In some cases, people in a fugue state adopt a completely new identity.

Like dissociative amnesia, dissociative fugues are associated with traumatic events or stressful periods (Loewenstein, 1993). Interestingly, when the person "awakens" from the fugue state, he may remember his past life but have amnesia for what occurred *during* the fugue state (DSM-IV, 1994).

Dissociative Identity Disorder:

Multiple Personalities

Among the dissociative disorders, none is more fascinating—or more controversial—than dissociative identity disorder, formerly known as *multiple personality disorder*. **Dissociative identity disorder,** abbreviated **DID,** involves extensive memory disruptions for personal information along with the presence of two or more distinct identities or "personalities" within a single person (DSM-IV, 1994).

Typically, each personality has its own name, and each will be experienced as if it has its own personal history and self-image. These alternate personalities, often called *alters*, may be of widely varying ages and different genders. The number of alternate personalities can range from two to over a hundred, but having ten to fifteen alters is most common (Goff & Simms, 1993; C. Ross & others, 1989).

Alters are not really separate people. Rather, they constitute a "system of mind" (Kluft, 1993; Putnam, 1991a). That is, the alters seem to embody different aspects of the individual's personality that, for some reason, cannot be integrated into the primary personality. The alternate personalities hold memories, emotions, and motives that are not admissible to the individual's conscious mind.

At different times, different alters take control of the person's experience, thoughts, and behavior (Kihlstrom, 1992). Typically, the primary personality is unaware of the existence of the alternate personalities. However, the alters may have knowledge of each other's existence and share memories (Kihlstrom & others, 1994). Sometimes the experiences of one alter are accessible to another alter but not vice versa.

Some researchers claim that there are physiological differences among the different personalities within a single individual. Differences in visual functioning, allergies, brain function, and handedness have been reported (Miller & others, 1991; Henninger, 1992). Although these accounts are intriguing, such physiological differences have yet to be convincingly demonstrated under controlled conditions (Miller & Triggiano, 1992).

Symptoms of amnesia and memory problems are present in virtually all cases of DID. There are frequent gaps in memory for both recent and childhood experiences. Commonly, the person with dissociative identity disorder "loses time" and is unable to recall her behavior or whereabouts during specific time periods. Besides memory problems, people with DID typically have numerous psychiatric and physical symptoms, along with a chaotic personal history (Putnam, 1991a, 1991b; Saxe & others, 1994). Symptoms of major depression, anxiety, posttraumatic stress disorder, substance abuse, sleep disorders, and self-destructive behavior are also very common. Often, the DID patient has been diagnosed with a variety of other psychological disorders before the DID diagnosis is made (Carlson & others, 1993; Coons & Dua, 1993).

Not all mental health professionals are convinced that dissociative identity disorder is a genuine psychological disorder. In Critical Thinking Box 13.2 on the next page, we explore this controversy.

dissociative identity disorder (DID)
Formerly called *multiple personality disorder;* a dissociative disorder involving extensive memory disruptions along with the presence of two or more distinct identities or "personalities."

CRITICAL THINKING 13.2

Is DID a Real Psychological Disorder?

Many psychologists and other mental health professionals are very skeptical about dissociative identity disorder (Hayes & Mitchell, 1994). Much of this skepticism is related to the fact that the number of reported cases of DID has risen dramatically in the last two decades (Merskey, 1992). Other psychologists point out that DID is not unique in this regard. Psychological disorders such as obsessive-compulsive disorder and PTSD have also increased in prevalance, partly because psychologists have become more aware of the symptoms (Gleaves, 1996; Davis & Breslau, 1994).

Nevertheless, some psychologists flatly claim that there is no such thing as multiple personality disorder or dissociative identity disorder. Rather, they suggest, DID patients are consciously or unconsciously "faking" the symptoms, responding to a therapist's suggestions, or mimicking the symptoms of sensational DID cases portrayed in the media. As outspoken skeptic Nicholas Spanos (1994) put it:

Patients learn to construe themselves as possessing multiple selves, learn to present themselves in terms of this construal, and learn to reorganize and elaborate on their personal biography so as to make it congruent with their understanding of what it means to be a multiple.

Although it is certainly possible that some patients may be faking DID symptoms, it seems unlikely that this is the case in all instances of dissociative identity disorder. Psychologists on the other side of this controversy point out that many of these patients experience clear-cut DID symptoms before entering treatment or learning about the disorder (Gleaves, 1996). Instead, they suggest that the increase in DID cases is due to (1) greater clinical awareness of the disorder, (2) improved diagnostic descriptions of DID symptoms, and (3) increased screening for dissociative symptoms.

For example, dissociative identity disorder was once thought to be extremely rare or nonexistent in Puerto Rico, the Netherlands, Belgium, and other countries. However, when formal screening programs for dissociative symptoms were established in these countries, cases of DID and other dissociative disorders were uncovered (Boon & Draijer, 1993; Vanderlinden & others, 1991; Martinez-Taboas, 1991). These DID patients were found to have the same core symptoms and characteristics as DID patients in the United States, including a history of childhood abuse or trauma.

What do you think? Is DID a bona fide psychological disorder? If you think so, you're not alone. Many psychologists believe it is (Gleaves, 1996). On the other hand, many psychologists remain skeptical. In any case, since DID became an official DSM diagnostic category in 1980, its clinical picture has become progressively better defined. As research on DID and other dissociative disorders continues, questions about the prevalence and nature of this diagnostic category may well be answered. For now, it remains the most controversial diagnostic category in DSM-IV.

TABLE 13.5 Dissociative Disorders

Dissociative Amnesia

- Inability to remember important personal information, too extensive to be explained by ordinary forgetfulness

Dissociative Fugue

- Sudden, unexpected travel away from home
- Amnesia
- Confusion about personal identity or assumption of new identity

Dissociative Identity Disorder

- Presence of two or more distinct identities, each with consistent patterns of personality traits and behavior
- Behavior is controlled by two or more distinct, recurring identities
- Amnesia; frequent memory gaps

Explaining Dissociative Identity Disorder

According to one explanation, dissociative identity disorder represents an extreme form of dissociative coping (Gleaves, 1996). A very high percentage of DID patients report having suffered extreme physical or sexual abuse in childhood—over 90 percent in most surveys (Coons, 1994). In order to cope with the trauma, the child "dissociates" himself or herself from it, creating alternate personalities to experience the trauma (Irwin, 1994).

Over time, alternate personalities are created to deal with the memories and emotions associated with intolerably painful experiences. Feelings of anger, rage, fear, and guilt that are too powerful for the child to consciously integrate can be dissociated into these alternate personalities (Kluft, 1991; Putnam, 1989). In effect, dissociation becomes a pathological defense mechanism that the person uses to cope with overwhelming experiences (Spiegel, 1993a).

Although widely accepted among therapists who work with dissociative identity disorder patients, the dissociative coping theory is difficult to test empirically. The main problem is that memories of childhood are notoriously

schizophrenia
A mental disorder in which the ability to function is impaired by severely distorted beliefs, perceptions, and thought processes.

positive symptoms
In schizophrenia, symptoms that reflect excesses or distortions of normal functioning, and include delusions, hallucinations, and disorganized thoughts and behavior.

negative symptoms
In schizophrenia, symptoms that reflect defects or deficits in normal functioning, and include flat affect, alogia, and avolition.

Glimpses of Schizophrenia This drawing was made by a young man hospitalized for schizophrenia. At the time the picture was drawn, he was hallucinating and extremely paranoid. The drawing provides glimpses of the distorted perceptions and thoughts that are characteristic of a schizophrenic episode. Notice the smaller face that is superimposed on the larger face, which might represent the hallucinated voices that are often heard in schizophrenic episodes.

unreliable (Loftus, 1993b). Since DID is usually diagnosed in adulthood, it is very difficult, and often impossible, to determine whether the reports of childhood abuse are real or imaginary (Frankel, 1993). Despite the difficulties of objective verification, a few researchers have confirmed memories of childhood abuse with independent evidence, such as medical records and court testimony by family members and social workers (Coons, 1994).

In the next section, we look at a mental disorder that some people mistakenly believe is the same as multiple personality disorder. As you'll see, the symptoms of *schizophrenia* are fundamentally different from those that characterize dissociative identity disorder.

Schizophrenia: A Different Reality

Schizophrenia involves severely distorted beliefs, perceptions, and thought processes. How do positive and negative symptoms differ, and what are the core symptoms of schizophrenia? What are the main subtypes of schizophrenia? What factors have been implicated in the development of schizophrenia?

Normally, you've got a pretty good grip on reality. You can easily distinguish between external reality and the different kinds of mental states that you routinely experience, such as dreams or daydreams. But as we negotiate life's many twists and turns, the ability to stay firmly anchored in reality is not a given. Rather, we're engaged in an ongoing process of verifying the accuracy of our thoughts, beliefs, and perceptions.

If any mental disorder demonstrates the potential for losing touch with reality, it's schizophrenia. **Schizophrenia** is a psychological disorder that involves severely distorted beliefs, perceptions, and thought processes. During a schizophrenic episode, people lose their grip on reality, like the woman screaming "Fire!" in the chapter prologue. They experience an entirely different inner world, one that is often characterized by mental chaos, disorientation, and frustration.

Symptoms of Schizophrenia

The characteristic symptoms of schizophrenia can be described in terms of two broad categories: positive and negative symptoms. **Positive symptoms** reflect an excess or distortion of normal functioning. Positive symptoms include: (1) *delusions,* or false beliefs; (2) *hallucinations,* or false perceptions; and (3) severely disorganized thought processes, speech, and behavior. In contrast, **negative symptoms** reflect a restriction or reduction of normal functions, such as greatly reduced motivation, emotional expressiveness, or speech.

According to DSM-IV, schizophrenia is diagnosed when two or more of these characteristic symptoms are actively present for a month or longer. Usually, schizophrenia also involves a longer personal history, typically six months or more, of odd behaviors, beliefs, perceptual experiences, and other less severe signs of mental disturbance.

In the following sections, we'll describe the positive and negative symptoms that characterize schizophrenia. While these are the core symptoms of schizophrenia, keep in mind that there is enormous individual variation in the onset, intensity, and duration of schizophrenic symptoms (Beratis & others, 1994; Keith & Matthews, 1991).

delusion
A falsely held belief that persists in spite of contradictory evidence.

hallucination
A false or distorted perception that seems vividly real to the person experiencing it.

Delusions: False Beliefs

We've all had the experience of firmly believing something that later turned out to be dead wrong. But when faced with evidence that contradicts our belief, we usually change our views, at least eventually. In contrast, a **delusion** is a falsely held belief that persists in spite of contradictory evidence or appeals to reason (Fauman, 1994; Garety, 1991).

Unlike beliefs that are simply inaccurate or unconventional, schizophrenic delusions are usually bizarre and far-fetched. The person believes that secret agents are poisoning his food, or that the next-door neighbors are actually aliens from outer space who are trying to transform him into a remote-controlled robot. Ignoring any evidence to the contrary, the delusional person clings to his erroneous belief. Even if the delusion is a frightening one, he often becomes so preoccupied with the idea that he can't stop thinking or talking about it (Spitzer, 1992; Butler & Braff, 1991). Not surprisingly, delusional beliefs typically cause great psychological distress and interfere with social or occupational functioning.

Although the content of delusions can be pretty wide-ranging, delusions are almost always centered on the person who is experiencing them. Certain themes also tend to surface consistently. For example, in *delusions of reference,* the delusional person believes that other people are constantly talking about her or that everything that happens is somehow related to her. The basic theme of *delusions of grandeur* is that the person is extremely important, powerful, or wealthy. In *delusions of persecution,* the basic theme is that others are plotting against or trying to harm the person or someone to whom the person is close.

Because people with schizophrenia find their delusions so convincing, the delusions can sometimes provoke inappropriate or bizarre behavior (Buchanan & others, 1993). In some instances, delusional thinking can lead to dangerous behaviors, such as the person who responds to his delusional ideas by hurting himself or attacking others (Martell & Dietz, 1992).

The Hallucinating Brain Researcher David Silbersweig and his colleagues (1995) used PET scans to take a "snapshot" of brain activity during schizophrenic hallucinations. The scan shown below was recorded at the exact instant a schizophrenic patient hallucinated disembodied heads yelling orders at him. The bright orange areas reveal activity in the left auditory and visual areas of his brain but not the frontal lobe, which normally is involved in organized thought processes.

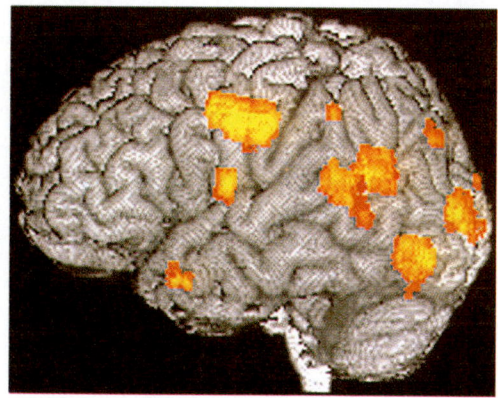

Hallucinations: False Perceptions

Among the most disturbing experiences in schizophrenia are hallucinations. **Hallucinations** are false or distorted perceptions that seem vividly real (Bentall, 1990). Schizophrenia-related hallucinations can involve any of the senses (Carter, 1992). The hallucinations of schizophrenia are often ongoing and persistent, such as hallucinated voices that continually tell the person what to do (Andreasen & Flaum, 1991).

As shown in Figure 13.4, the most common hallucinations experienced in schizophrenia are auditory, followed by visual hallucinations (Mueser & others, 1990; Bracha & others, 1989). The most frequent form of auditory hallucination is hearing a voice or voices. The content of hallucinations is often tied to the person's delusional beliefs (DSM-IV, 1994). If she harbors delusions of grandeur, hallucinated voices may reinforce her grandiose ideas by communicating instructions from God, the devil, or angels. If the person harbors delusions of persecution, hallucinated voices or im-

FIGURE 13.4 Incidence of Different Types of Hallucinations in Schizophrenia
Schizophrenia-related hallucinations can occur in any sensory modality. Auditory hallucinations, usually in the form of voices, are the most common type of hallucination that occurs in schizophrenia, followed by visual hallucinations.
[Adapted from data in Mueser & others, 1990; Bracha & others, 1989.]

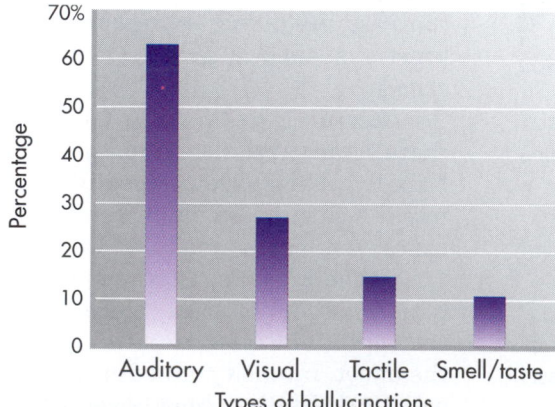

CULTURE AND HUMAN BEHAVIOR 13.3

From Cannibals to Computer Games

Around the world, schizophrenia is characterized by delusions and hallucinations. However, the *content* of delusions and hallucinations can vary from one culture to another.

One variation of culturally influenced delusional thinking is sometimes seen among the Algonquin Indians in Canada. For the Algonquin, the *Witiko,* a man-eating monster, is an important mythological figure. When the *Witiko syndrome* occurs, an Algonquin believes that he is becoming possessed by the Witiko spirit. As the syndrome progresses, he becomes convinced that he is turning into a Witiko himself. He becomes increasingly obsessed with the craving for human flesh and may become suicidal to escape the cannibalistic urges (Marano, 1985).

Like delusions, hallucinations tend to incorporate culturally relevant stimuli. As cross-cultural psychologist Richard Brislin (1993) observes:

In North America and Europe, these forces keep up to date with technology. In the 1920s, it was voices from the radio; in the 1950s, it was voices from the television; in the 1960s it could be voices from satellites in outer space; and in the 1970s and 1980s it could be spirits transmitted through people's microwave ovens.

In Third World countries, where modern technology is less common, hallucinated voices are still largely being transmitted the old-fashioned way—from demons, evil spirits, deceased relatives, and other unseen forces. But as technology and societies change, the manifestations of delusions and hallucinations also tend to change. In South America, for example, when rural Indians with schizophrenia move to the cities, delusions of radio waves and secret police replace the more traditional delusions about witchcraft, saints, and jungle spirits (Murphy, 1982).

Finally, consider the case of a woman from Zimbabwe who developed peculiar auditory hallucinations after she moved to London (Spence, 1993). Her symptoms? Persistent hallucinations of the music soundtrack from the Mario Brothers Nintendo game! Today, no doubt, some people are hearing hallucinated voices coming from cellular telephones and over the Internet via desktop computers.

---

ages may be extremely frightening, threatening, or accusing. The content of hallucinations and delusions can also be influenced by culture, as we describe in Culture and Human Behavior Box 13.3, "From Cannibals to Computer Games."

When a schizophrenic episode is severe, hallucinations can be virtually impossible to distinguish from objective reality. For example, the young woman in the prologue probably did see very vivid images of fire. But when schizophrenia symptoms are less severe, the person may recognize that the hallucination is a product of his own mind (Amador & others, 1991). As one young man confided to your author Don, "I know the voices aren't real, but I can't make them stop talking to me." As this young man got better, the hallucinated voices did eventually stop. In some cases of schizophrenia, the auditory hallucinations can last for months or even years (Krausz & Müller-Thomsen, 1993).

Disturbances in Sensation, Thinking, and Speech

People often report that during a schizophrenic episode, sights, sounds, and other sensations feel distorted. One woman described the sensory distortions in this way:

Looking around the room, I found that things had lost their emotional meaning. They were larger than life, tense, and suspenseful. They were flat, and colored as if in artificial light. I felt my body to be first giant, then minuscule. My arms seemed to be several inches longer than before and did not feel as though they belonged to me. (Anonymous, 1990)

Along with sensory distortions, the person may experience severely disorganized thinking (Braff, 1993). It can be enormously difficult to concentrate, remember, and integrate important information while ignoring irrelevant information (Chen & others, 1994). The person's mind drifts from topic to topic in an unpredictable, illogical manner.

Such disorganized thinking is also often reflected in the person's speech (Barch & Berenbaum, 1996). Ideas, words, and images are sometimes strung together in ways that seem completely nonsensical to the listener. For example, when asked, "How are you today?" a schizophrenic patient responded:

> Yes, sir, it's a good day. Full of rainbows, you know. They go along on their merry way without concern for asphyxiation or impurities. Yes, sir, like unconcerned flappers of the cosmoblue. (Reported in D. Sue & others, 1997)

This response is certainly very odd, but notice that it is not completely unintelligible. If you think carefully about this patient's words, you can see how they reflect ideas that are very loosely related to the question that triggered them. Also notice how he made up a new word—*cosmoblue*—by combining the words *cosmos* and *blue*.

Negative Symptoms: Deficits in Behavior, Emotion, and Motivation

Delusions, hallucinations, and disrupted sensations reflect positive symptoms—excesses or distortions in normal functioning. In contrast, negative symptoms reflect marked deficits or decreases in behavioral or emotional functioning.

One commonly seen negative symptom is referred to as *flat affect,* or *affective flattening.* Regardless of the situation, the person responds in an emotionally "flat" way. She consistently shows a dramatic reduction in emotional responsiveness and a lack of normal facial expressions (Raskin & others, 1993; Shtasel & others, 1992). Few expressive gestures are made, and the person's speech is slow and monotonous, lacking normal vocal inflections.

A closely related negative symptom is *alogia*—greatly reduced production of speech. In alogia, verbal responses are limited to brief, empty comments. Alogia is also referred to as *poverty of speech.*

Finally, *avolition* refers to the inability to initiate or persist in even simple forms of goal-directed behaviors, such as dressing, bathing, or engaging in social activities. Instead, the person seems to be completely apathetic, sometimes sitting for hours at a time.

Types of Schizophrenia

Figure 13.5 shows the frequency of positive and negative symptoms at the time of hospitalization for schizophrenia. These symptoms are used in diagnosing the particular subtype of schizophrenia. DSM-IV includes three basic subtypes of schizophrenia: *paranoid, catatonic,* and *disorganized* (see Table 13.6).

The *paranoid type* of schizophrenia is characterized by the presence of delu-

FIGURE 13.5 Presence of Symptoms in Schizophrenia
This graph shows how often specific positive and negative symptoms were present in a study of over 100 individuals at the time they were hospitalized for schizophrenia. Delusions were the most common positive symptom, while avolition, or apathy, was the most common negative symptom.
(Based on data reported in Andreasen & Flaum, 1991.)

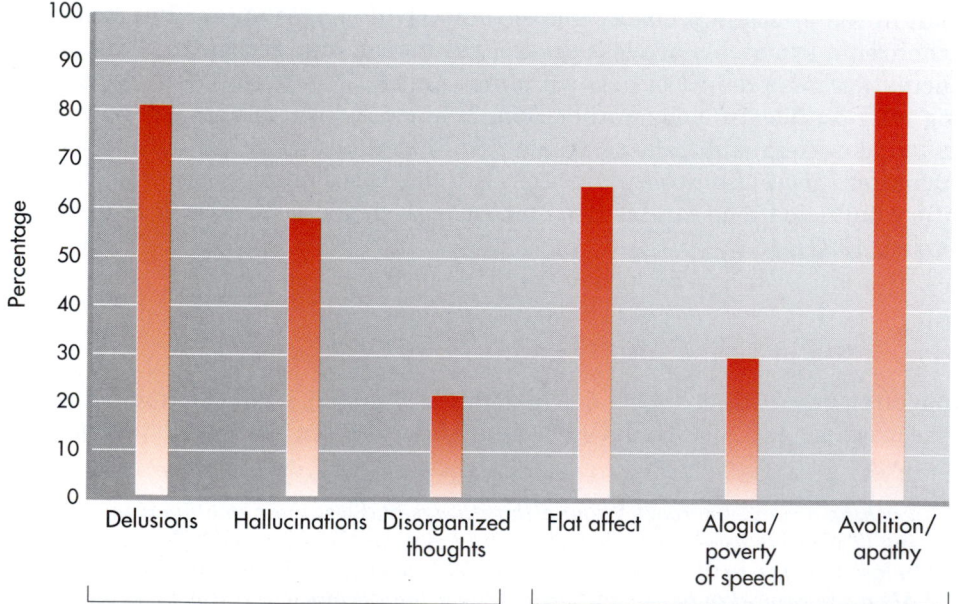

TABLE 13.6 Types of Schizophrenia

Paranoid Type

- Well-organized delusional beliefs reflecting persecutory or grandiose ideas
- Frequent auditory hallucinations, usually voices
- Little or no disorganized behavior, speech, or flat affect

Catatonic Type

- Highly disturbed movements or actions, such as extreme excitement, bizarre postures or grimaces, or being completely immobile
- Echoes words spoken by others, or imitates movements of others

Disorganized Type

- Flat or inappropriate emotional expressions
- Severely disorganized speech and behavior
- Fragmented delusional ideas and hallucinations

Undifferentiated Type

- Displays characteristic symptoms of schizophrenia but not in a way that fits the pattern for paranoid, catatonic, or disorganized type

sions, hallucinations, or both. However, the person shows virtually no cognitive impairment, disorganized behavior, or negative symptoms. Instead, well-organized delusions of persecution or grandeur are operating. Auditory hallucinations in the form of voices talking about the delusional ideas are also often evident. Convinced that others are plotting against him, the person reacts with extreme distrust of others. Or the person may assume an air of superiority, confident in the delusional belief of his "special powers." The paranoid type is the most common type of schizophrenia.

The *catatonic type* of schizophrenia is marked by highly disturbed movements or actions. These may include bizarre postures or grimaces, extremely agitated behavior, complete immobility, echoing words just spoken by another person, or imitating the movements of others. The person will resist direction from others and may also assume rigid postures to resist being moved. Catatonic schizophrenia is often characterized by another unusual symptom, called *waxy flexibility*. Like a wax figure, the person can be "molded" into any position, and she will hold that position indefinitely. The catatonic type of schizophrenia is very rare.

The prominent features of the *disorganized type* of schizophrenia are extremely disorganized behavior, disorganized speech, and flat affect. Delusions and hallucinations are sometimes present but they are not well-organized and integrated, like those that characterize paranoid schizophrenia. Instead, a person with the disorganized type experiences delusions and hallucinations that contain fragmented, shifting themes. Silliness, laughing, and giggling may occur for no apparent reason. In short, the person's behavior is very peculiar. This type of schizophrenia was formerly called *hebephrenic schizophrenia,* and that term is still sometimes used.

Finally, the label of *undifferentiated type* is used when an individual displays some combination of positive and negative symptoms that does not clearly fit the criteria for the paranoid, catatonic, or disorganized types.

The Prevalence and Course of Schizophrenia

Every year, there are about 200,000 new cases of schizophrenia in this country. The onset of schizophrenia typically occurs during young adulthood (Beratis & others, 1994). Annually, approximately 1 million Americans are treated for schizophrenia (Rosenstein & others, 1989). All told, about 1 percent of the U.S. population will experience at least one episode of schizophrenia at some point in life (Regier & others, 1993). Worldwide, no society or culture is immune to this mental disorder. Most cultures correspond very closely to the 1 percent rate of schizophrenia seen in the United States (Gottesman, 1991).

The course of schizophrenia is marked by enormous individual variability. Even so, a few global generalizations are possible (Krausz & Müller-Thomsen, 1993; Shepard & others, 1989). The good news is that about one-quarter of those who experience an episode of schizophrenia recover completely and never experience another episode. Another one-quarter experience recurrent episodes of schizophrenia, but often with only minimal impairment in the ability to function.

Now the bad news: For the rest of those who have suffered an episode of schizophrenia—one-half of the total—schizophrenia becomes a chronic mental illness, and the ability to function may be severely impaired. The people in this last category face the prospect of repeated hospitalizations and extended treatment. Thus, chronic schizophrenia places a heavy emotional, financial, and psychological burden on people with the disorder, their families, and society (Rupp & Keith, 1993; Gerace & others, 1993).

Explaining Schizophrenia

Schizophrenia is an extremely complex disorder. There is enormous individual variability in the onset, symptoms, duration, and recovery from schizophrenia. So it shouldn't come as a surprise that the causes of schizophrenia seem to be equally complex. In this section, we'll survey some of the factors that have been implicated in the development of schizophrenia.

Genetic Factors: Family, Twin, and Adoption Studies

Studies of families, twins, and adopted individuals have firmly established that genetic factors play a significant role in many cases of schizophrenia. First, family studies have consistently shown that schizophrenia tends to cluster in certain families (Prescott & Gottesman, 1993; Kendler & Diehl, 1993). Second, family and twin studies have consistently shown that the more closely related a person is to someone who has schizophrenia, the greater the risk that she will be diagnosed with schizophrenia at some point in her lifetime (see Figure 13.6). Third, adoption studies have consistently shown that if either *biological* parent of an adopted individual had schizophrenia, the adopted individual is at greater risk to develop schizophrenia (Tienari & others, 1994).

Ironically, the strongest evidence that points to genetic involvement in schizophrenia—the almost 50 percent risk rate for a person whose identical twin has schizophrenia—is the same evidence that underscores the importance of environmental factors (Torrey, 1992; Pato & others, 1989). If schizophrenia were purely a matter of inherited maladaptive genes, then you would expect a risk rate much closer to 100 percent for monozygotic twins. Obviously, nongenetic factors must play a role in explaining why half of identical twins with a schizophrenic twin do *not* develop schizophrenia.

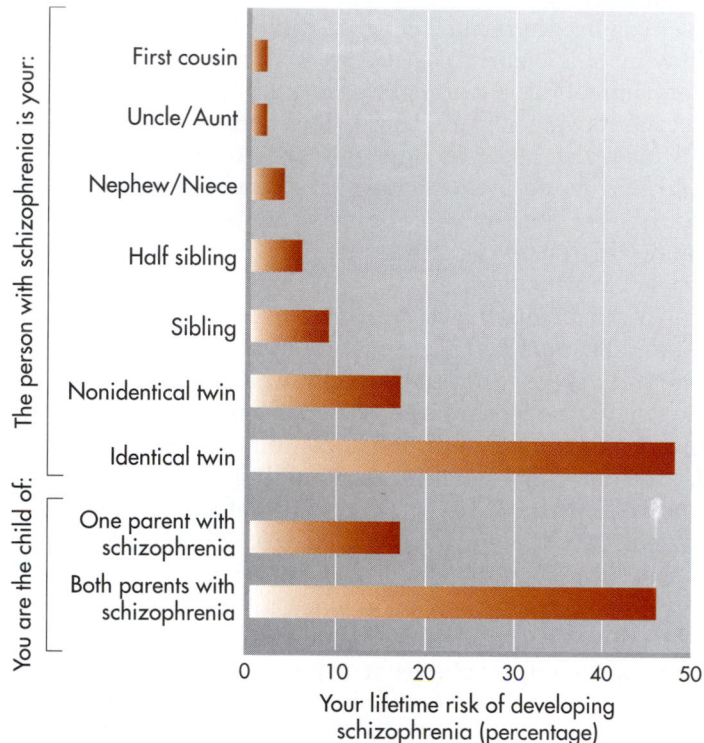

FIGURE 13.6 The Risk of Developing Schizophrenia Among Blood Relatives
The risk percentages shown here reflect the collective results of about forty studies investigating the likelihood of developing schizophrenia among blood relatives. As you can see, the greatest risk occurs if you have an identical twin who has schizophrenia (48 percent lifetime risk), or if both of your biological parents have schizophrenia (46 percent lifetime risk). However, genetics is just one of a number of factors involved in the development of schizophrenia.

(Adapted from Gottesman, 1991, p. 96.)

Abnormal Brain Chemistry: The Dopamine Hypothesis

According to the **dopamine hypothesis,** schizophrenia is related to excess activity of the neurotransmitter called dopamine in the brain (Davis & others, 1991). Two pieces of indirect evidence support this notion. First, antipsychotic drugs, such as Haldol, Thorazine, and Stelazine, *reduce or block dopamine activity in the brain* (Dykstra, 1992). These drugs reduce schizophrenic symptoms in many people. Second, drugs like amphetamines or cocaine that *enhance dopamine activity in the brain* can produce schizophrenia-like symptoms in normal adults or increase symptoms in people who already suffer from schizophrenia (Syvälahti, 1994).

Although the dopamine hypothesis is compelling, there are inconsistencies. Not all individuals who have schizophrenia experience a reduction of symptoms in response to the antipsychotic drugs that reduce dopamine activity in the brain. And for many patients, these drugs reduce some but not all schizophrenic symptoms (Heinrichs, 1993). So, while it seems likely that dopamine is somehow involved in schizophrenia, its exact role is far from clear.

dopamine hypothesis
The view that schizophrenia is related to, and may be caused by, excess activity of the neurotransmitter dopamine in the brain.

Abnormal Brain Structures and Functioning

Researchers have found that about half of the people with schizophrenia show some type of brain structure abnormality (Cannon & Marco, 1994). The most consistent finding has been the enlargement of the fluid-filled cavities

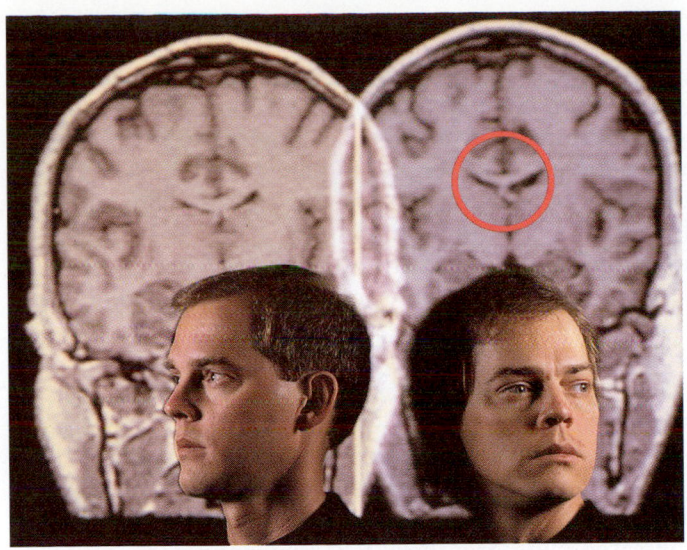

Identical Twins but Not Identical Brains
David and Steven Elmore are identical twins but they differ in one important respect—Steven (right) has schizophrenia. Behind each is a CAT scan, which reveals that Steven's brain is slightly smaller with less area devoted to the cortex at the top of the brain. Steven also has larger fluid-filled ventricles, which are circled in red on his brain scan. As researcher Daniel Weinberger (1995) comments, "The part of the cortex that Steven is missing serves as perhaps the most evolved part of the human brain. It performs complicated tasks such as thinking organized thoughts. This might help explain why paranoid delusions and hallucinations are characteristic of schizophrenia."

called *ventricles* located deep within the brain (Raz, 1994). However, researchers aren't certain how enlarged ventricles might be related to schizophrenia. Finally, PET scans have revealed differences in brain activity between schizophrenic and normal individuals.

Although these differences are intriguing, they do not prove that schizophrenia is definitely caused by brain abnormalities. First, about half of the people suffering from schizophrenia do *not* show brain structure abnormalities. Second, the evidence is correlational. Researchers are still investigating whether differences in brain structures and activity are the cause or the consequence of schizophrenia. Third, the kinds of brain abnormalities seen in schizophrenia are also seen in other mental disorders. Rather than specifically causing schizophrenia, it's quite possible that brain abnormalities might contribute to mental disorders in general.

Environmental Factors: The Viral Infection Theory

One provocative theory is that schizophrenia might be caused by exposure to an influenza virus or other viral infection during prenatal development or shortly after birth. A virus might seem an unlikely cause of a serious mental disorder, but viruses *can* spread to the brain and spinal cord by traveling along nerves. According to this theory, exposure to a viral infection during prenatal development or early infancy affects the developing brain, producing changes that make the individual more vulnerable to schizophrenia later in life (Torrey, 1991; Weinberger, 1987).

There is some evidence to support the viral infection theory. First, children whose mothers were exposed to a flu virus during the second trimester of pregnancy do show an increased rate of schizophrenia (Venables, 1996; Huttunen & others, 1994). Second, schizophrenia occurs more often in people who were born in the winter and spring months, when upper respiratory infections are most common (Torrey & others, 1993). Once again, though, the evidence is correlational. And some researchers have not found such correlations (Takei & others, 1994).

Psychological Factors: Unhealthy Families

Researchers have investigated such factors as dysfunctional parenting, disturbed family communication styles, and critical or guilt-inducing parental styles as possible contributors to schizophrenia (Miklowitz, 1994; Hahlweg & Goldstein, 1987). However, no single psychological factor seems to emerge consistently as causing schizophrenia. Rather, it seems that those who are genetically predisposed to develop schizophrenia may be more vulnerable to the effects of disturbed family environments (Fowles, 1992).

Strong support for this view comes from a landmark study being conducted by Finnish psychiatrist Pekka Tienari and his colleagues (1994, 1987). In the Finnish Adoptive Family Study of Schizophrenia, researchers are following about 150 adopted individuals whose biological mothers had schizophrenia. As part of their study, the researchers assessed the adoptive family's degree of psychological adjustment, including the mental health of the adoptive parents. The study also includes a control group of about 180 adopted individuals whose biological mothers were *not* schizophrenic.

Tienari and his colleagues (1994) found that adopted children with a schizophrenic biological mother have a much higher rate of schizophrenia than the children in the control group. However, this was true *only* when the children were raised in a psychologically disturbed adoptive home. As you can see in Figure 13.7, when children with a genetic background of

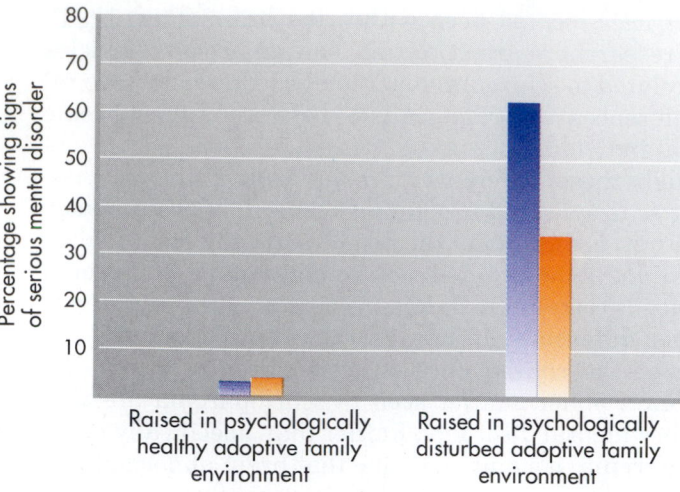

Adoptees whose biological mothers had schizophrenia

Control-group adoptees with no genetic history of schizophrenia

FIGURE 13.7 The Finnish Adoptive Family Study of Schizophrenia
In the Finnish Adoptive Family Study, researchers are following two groups of adopted individuals: one group with biological mothers who had schizophrenia and a control group whose biological mothers did not have schizophrenia. This graph shows the strong influence of the adoptive family environment on the development of serious mental disorders.
(Tienari & others, 1994; Tienari, 1991.)

schizophrenia were raised in a psychologically healthy adoptive family, they were *no more likely* to develop schizophrenia than the control-group children.

Although adopted children with no genetic history of schizophrenia were less vulnerable to the psychological stresses of a disturbed family environment, they were by no means completely immune to such influences. As Figure 13.7 shows, one-third of the control-group adoptees developed symptoms of a serious psychological disorder if they were raised in a disturbed family environment.

Tienari's study underscores the complex interaction of genetic and environmental factors. Clearly, children who were genetically at risk to develop schizophrenia benefited from being raised in a healthy psychological environment. Put simply, a healthy psychological environment may counteract a person's inherited vulnerability for schizophrenia. Conversely, a psychologically unhealthy family environment can act as a catalyst for the onset of schizophrenia, especially for those individuals with a genetic history of schizophrenia.

After more than a century of intensive research, schizophrenia remains a baffling disorder. Thus far, no single biological, psychological, or social factor has emerged as the causal agent in schizophrenia (Keefe & Harvey, 1994). Nevertheless, researchers are expressing greater confidence that the pieces of the schizophrenia puzzle are beginning to form a more coherent picture.

Even if the exact causes of schizophrenia remain elusive, there is still reason for optimism. In the last few years, new antipsychotic drugs have been developed that are much more effective in treating both the positive and negative symptoms of schizophrenia (Meltzer, 1993). In the next chapter, we'll take a detailed look at the different treatments and therapies for schizophrenia and other psychological disorders.

CONCEPT REVIEW 13.2

Dissociative Disorders and Schizophrenia

Match each example below with one of the following: dissociative amnesia; dissociative fugue; dissociative identity disorder; delusions of grandeur; delusions of reference; paranoid schizophrenia; catatonic schizophrenia; disorganized schizophrenia.

1. Jay, a high school physics teacher in New York City, disappeared three days after his wife unexpectedly left him. Six months later, he was discovered tending bar in Miami Beach. Calling himself Martin, he claimed to have no recollection of his past life. _____

2. Larry is convinced that traffic signals are symbolic communications from God directed specifically at him. _____

3. Norma has frequent memory gaps and cannot account for her whereabouts during certain periods of time. While being interviewed by a clinical psychologist, she began speaking in a childlike voice. She claimed that her name was Donna and that she was only six years old. Moments later, she seemed to revert to her adult voice and had no recollection of claiming that her name was Donna. _____

4. After getting the manager to let them into her apartment, Sylvia's parents found her standing motionless near a window and completely unresponsive to their presence. _____

5. Marian and her brother were recently involved in an automobile accident. Marian was not seriously injured, but her brother was killed. Marian is unable to recall any details from the time of the accident until four days later. _____

6. By the time the neighbors called the police, Dwight had barricaded all the doors and windows of his house because the voices had told him that aliens were coming to kidnap him. _____

Understanding and Helping Prevent Suicide

Who Commits Suicide?

About 30,000 suicides occur each year in this country (U.S. Bureau of the Census, 1995). That number is probably too low, because many suicides are misreported as accidental deaths (Phillips & Ruth, 1993).

In a given year, it's estimated that about 300,000 people will try to kill themselves (Garland & Zigler, 1993). Women outnumber men by 3 to 1 in suicide *attempts*. However, men outnumber women by 4 to 1 in suicide *deaths*, primarily because men tend to use more lethal methods, such as guns and hanging.

Over the last three decades, the suicide rate for adolescents has increased by about 200 percent, as compared to a 17 percent increase for the general population (Garland & Zigler, 1993). Still, the suicide rate of adolescents is below that of young and middle-aged adults. The highest rate of suicide consistently occurs among those aged sixty-five and above (U.S. Bureau of the Census, 1995).

Why Do People Attempt or Commit Suicide?

The suicidal person's view of life has grown progressively more pessimistic and negative. At the same time, his view of self-inflicted death as an alternative to life has become progressively more positive and permissible (Hughes & Neimeyer, 1990).

Some people choose suicide in order to escape the pain of a chronic illness or terminal disease. Others commit suicide because of feelings of depression, rejection, failure, humiliation, or shame (Van Egmond & others, 1993). The common denominator is that they see suicide as the only escape from their own painful emotions (Baumeister, 1990).

When faced with a dilemma, the average person tends to see a range of possible solutions to the problem, accepting the fact that none of the solutions may be ideal. In contrast, the suicidal person's thinking and perceptions have become *rigid and constricted*. She can see only two ways to solve her problems: a magical resolution *or* suicide. Because she cannot imagine a realistic way of solving her problems, death seems like the only logical option (Shneidman, 1985).

Helping Prevent Suicide

If someone is truly intent on taking his own life, it may be impossible to prevent him from doing so. But that does not mean that you can't try to help a friend who is expressing suicidal intentions. People often turn to their friends rather than to a mental health professional (Stillion & others, 1989). If a friend confides that he is feeling hopeless and suicidal, these guidelines may help you help your friend.

Guideline 1. Encourage the person to seek professional help. These guidelines are meant only to help you provide "psychological first aid" in a crisis situation. They do *not* qualify you as a suicide prevention expert. Your goal is to help your friend weather the immediate crisis so that he or she can be directed to a mental health professional (Stillion & others, 1989). There are any number of resources you can suggest, including suicide hot lines, local mental health agencies, the college counseling service, and the person's family doctor or religious advisor.

Guideline 2. Don't minimize the person's suicidal intentions. Brushing aside suicidal statements with platitudes like "Don't be silly, you've got everything to live for," or clichés like "Every cloud has a silver lining," is not a helpful response. This is not the time to be glib, patronizing, or superficial (Grollman, 1988).

Instead, ask your friend if she wants to talk about her feelings. Try to be matter-of-fact and confirm that she is genuinely suicidal, rather than simply exaggerating her frustration or disappointment. One sign may be talking about specific suicide plans (how, when, and where). Giving away valued possessions, taking care of legal matters, and putting her affairs in order for no apparent reason are other indications (Grosz, 1990).

Guideline 3. Let the person talk and vent her feelings. The suicidal person often feels isolated or lonely, with few sources of social support (Heikkinen & others, 1993). An understanding friend who is willing to take the time to listen patiently without passing judgment may provide just the support that the person needs to overcome the suicidal feelings.

Guideline 4. Identify other potential solutions. At this particular moment, the suicidal person is operating with psychological blinders that prevent him from seeing alternative courses of action or alternative ways of looking at his problem. How can you widen those blinders? Simply saying, "Here are some options you may not have thought about," is a good start. You might list alternative solutions to the person's problems, helping him to understand that other potential solutions do exist, even though none may be perfect (Shneidman, 1987).

Guideline 5. Ask the person to delay his decision. If the person is still intent on suicide after talking about other alternatives, ask him to delay his decision. Delaying even for a few days may give the person enough time to psychologically regroup, consider alternatives, or seek help from other sources.

Summary

Psychological Disorders

Understanding Psychological Disorders

■ Distinguishing "normal" from "abnormal" behavior involves consideration of many different factors, including cultural norms. Psychopathology refers to the scientific study of the origins, symptoms, and development of psychological disorders.

■ A psychological disorder is a pattern of behavioral or psychological symptoms that causes significant personal distress and/or impairs the ability to function. The diagnostic criteria for specific psychological disorders are described in DSM-IV.

■ The prevalence of psychological disorders is much higher than had previously been thought. According to one comprehensive survey, approximately one in two Americans will experience a psychological disorder at some point in their lifetime, while approximately one in three Americans have experienced the symptoms of a psychological disorder in the previous year.

Anxiety Disorders

■ In contrast to normal anxiety, pathological anxiety is irrational and uncontrollable, and is unreasonably intense, frequent, persistent, and disruptive.

■ Generalized anxiety disorder and panic disorder are characterized by intense anxiety that is not triggered by a specific stimulus. Generalized anxiety disorder involves a constant, persistent state of anxiety, while panic disorder involves sudden episodes of extreme, intense anxiety.

■ The phobias involve intense, irrational fear and avoidance of the feared object or situation. Important forms of phobia include specific phobia, social phobia, and agoraphobia, which is fear of having a panic attack in a public or inescapable situation. Learning theories and evolved biological predispositions have been offered as explanations of the development of phobias.

■ Posttraumatic stress disorder develops in response to an extreme psychological or physical trauma. Symptoms include frequent intrusive memories of the trauma, avoidance and emotional numbness, and increased physical arousal.

■ Obsessive-compulsive disorder is an anxiety disorder in which a person's life is dominated by repetitive thoughts (obsessions) and actions (compulsions). Biological factors that have been implicated in obsessive-compulsive disorder include serotonin deficiency and brain dysfunction.

Mood Disorders: Emotions Gone Awry

■ Mood disorders involve serious, persistent disturbances in emotions that cause psychological discomfort and/or impair the ability to function.

■ The symptoms of major depression include negative emotions, extreme pessimism, thoughts of suicide, cognitive impairment, lack of motivation, and sleep disruption for a period of two weeks or longer. Dysthymic disorder is a milder but chronic form of depression.

■ Major depression is the most common psychological disorder. Left untreated, depression may recur and become progressively more severe.

■ Bipolar disorder usually involves periods of depression alternating with manic episodes. A milder form of bipolar disorder is cyclothymic disorder. Bipolar disorder is less common than major depression.

■ Genetics, brain chemistry, and stress have all been implicated in mood disorders. Two neurotransmitters, serotonin and norepinephrine, have also been implicated in depression.

The Dissociative Disorders:
Fragmentation of the Self

■ Dissociative experiences involve a disruption in awareness, memory, and personal identity. In the dissociative disorders, however, dissociative experiences are extreme, frequent, and disruptive.

■ Dissociative amnesia refers to the inability to recall important information which is not due to a medical condition and cannot be explained by ordinary forgetfulness. Dissociative fugue involves amnesia and sudden, unexplained travel away from home.

■ Dissociative identity disorder involves memory gaps and the presence of two or more distinct identities. Some psychologists are skeptical of dissociative identity disorder. According to one theory, DID is caused by trauma in childhood, and represents an extreme form of coping through dissociation.

Schizophrenia: A Different Reality

■ Schizophrenia is a psychological disorder that involves severely distorted beliefs, perceptions, and thought processes. The positive symptoms of schizophrenia represent excesses in normal functioning, and include delusions, hallucinations, and severely disorganized thought processes, speech, and behavior.

■ Negative symptoms reflect deficits or decreases in normal functioning. The negative symptoms of schizophrenia include flat affect, alogia, and avolition.

■ Three subtypes of schizophrenia are paranoid type, catatonic type, and disorganized type, each of which is distinguished by a particular combination of symptoms. When symptoms do not match any of these three subtypes, the diagnosis of undifferentiated type is made.

■ The course of schizophrenia is highly variable. Schizophrenia becomes chronic in about one-half of people who experience a schizophrenic episode. About one-quarter recover completely, and about one-quarter experience recurrent episodes but are able to function with minimal impairment.

■ Family, twin, and adoption studies have shown that genetics contributes to the development of schizophrenia. However, studies of identical twins demonstrate that nongenetic factors play at least an equal role in the development of schizophrenia.

■ Excess dopamine and abnormalities in brain structure and function have been identified as factors that are associated with schizophrenia.

■ Environmental factors that may be involved in schizophrenia include exposure to a virus during prenatal development and a psychologically unhealthy family environment. Adopted children who were genetically at risk to develop schizophrenia were found to be less likely to develop the disorder when raised in a psychologically healthy family.

■ Given the complexity of schizophrenia, it is not surprising that no single factor has emerged as causing this psychological disorder.

CONCEPT REVIEW 13.1 Page 480

1. generalized anxiety disorder
2. dysthymic disorder
3. obsessive-compulsive disorder
4. major depression
5. specific phobia
6. cyclothymic disorder
7. posttraumatic stress disorder

CONCEPT REVIEW 13.2 Page 492

1. dissociative fugue
2. delusions of reference
3. dissociative identity disorder
4. catatonic schizophrenia
5. dissociative amnesia
6. paranoid schizophrenia

Key Terms

psychopathology (p. 463)

psychological disorder (mental disorder) (p. 465)

DSM-IV (p. 465)

anxiety (p. 468)

anxiety disorders (p. 468)

generalized anxiety disorder (p. 468)

panic attack (p. 469)

panic disorder (p. 469)

phobia (p. 470)

specific phobia (p. 470)

agoraphobia (p. 470)

social phobia (p. 471)

posttraumatic stress disorder (PTSD) (p. 472)

obsessive-compulsive disorder (p. 473)

obsessions (p. 473)

compulsions (p. 473)

mood disorders (p. 475)

major depression (p. 475)

dysthymic disorder (p. 476)

seasonal affective disorder (SAD) (p. 477)

bipolar disorder (p. 477)

manic episode (p. 478)

cyclothymic disorder (p. 478)

dissociative experience (p. 481)

dissociative disorders (p. 482)

dissociative amnesia (p. 482)

dissociative fugue (p. 482)

dissociative identity disorder (DID) (p. 483)

schizophrenia (p. 485)

positive symptoms (p. 485)

negative symptoms (p. 485)

delusion (p. 486)

hallucination (p. 486)

dopamine hypothesis (p. 490)

Chapter

14

Therapies

Prologue: "A Clear Sense of Being Heard . . ."

How would we describe Marcia? She's an extraordinarily kind, intelligent woman. Her thoughtfulness and sensitivity is tempered by a ready laugh and a good sense of humor. She's happily married, has a good job as a feature writer for a large suburban newspaper, and has two young children, who only occasionally drive her crazy. If Marcia has a flaw, it's that she tends to judge herself and her own performance much too harshly. She's too quick to blame herself when anything goes wrong.

Juggling a full-time career, marriage, and parenting is a challenge for anyone, but Marcia always makes it look easy. The last time we had dinner at Bill and Marcia's home, the meal featured home-grown vegetables, made-from-scratch bread, and fresh seasonings from the herb pots in the kitchen. Outwardly, Marcia appears to have it all. But a few years ago, she began to experience a pervasive sense of dread and unease—feelings that gradually escalated into a full-scale depression. Marcia describes the onset of her feelings in this way:

> Physically I began to feel as if I were fraying around the edges. I had a constant sense of anxiety, and a recurring sense of being a failure. My daughter Maggie was going through a rather difficult stage. Andy was still a baby. I felt worn out. I started worrying constantly about my children. Are they safe? Are they sick? What's going to happen? Are my kids going to get hurt? I knew that I really didn't have any reason to worry that much, but I did. It finally struck me that my worrying and my anxiety and my feelings of being a failure were not going to go away on their own.

Marcia decided to seek help. She made an appointment with her therapist—a psychiatrist whom she had last seen ten years before, when she had helped Marcia cope with a very difficult time in her life. Marcia explains the immediate benefits of psychotherapy in this way:

> My feelings before a therapy session may vary greatly, depending on the issue under discussion. However, I always find the sessions cathartic and I invariably feel great relief. I feel a sense of being understood by someone who knows me but who is detached from me. I have a clear sense of being heard, as though my therapist has given me a gift of listening and of allowing me to see myself as the worthwhile and capable person I am. It is as though therapy allows me to see more clearly into a mirror that my problems have obscured.

Over the course of several months, Marcia gradually began to feel better. Today, she is calmer, more confident, and feels much more in control of her emotions and her life. As Marcia's mental health improved, so did her relationships with her children and her husband. She believes that psychotherapy has had lasting, and beneficial, effects.

> Psychotherapy has helped me communicate more clearly. It has enabled me to become more resilient after some emotional conflict. It has had a preventive effect in helping me to ignore or manage situations that might under certain circumstances trigger depression, anxiety, or obsessive worry. And it makes me a better parent and marriage partner.

Marcia's experience with psychotherapy reflects many of the themes that we will touch on in this chapter. We'll look at the different forms of therapy that psychologists and other mental health professionals use to help people cope with psychological problems. Toward the end of the chapter, we'll discuss biomedical approaches to the treatment of psychological disorders. Over the course of the chapter, we'll come back to Marcia's story.

Introduction

Psychotherapy and Biomedical Therapy

> *Psychotherapy is the use of psychological techniques to treat emotional, behavioral, and interpersonal problems. What is the basic assumption common to all forms of psychotherapy? What is biomedical therapy, and how does it differ from psychotherapy?*

People seek help from mental health professionals for a variety of reasons. Like Marcia, many people seek help because they are suffering from some form of a *psychological disorder*—troubling thoughts, feelings, or behaviors that cause psychological discomfort or interfere with a person's ability to function.

Not everyone who seeks professional help is suffering from a psychological disorder. Many people seek help in dealing with troubled relationships, such as an unhappy marriage or parent–child conflicts. And sometimes people need help with life's transitions, such as coping with the death of a loved one, dissolving a marriage, or adjusting to retirement.

In this chapter, we'll look at the two broad forms of therapy that mental health professionals use to help people: *psychotherapy* and *biomedical therapy*. **Psychotherapy** refers to the use of psychological techniques to treat emo-

psychotherapy
The treatment of emotional, behavioral, and interpersonal problems through the use of psychological techniques designed to encourage understanding of problems and modify troubling feelings, behaviors, or relationships.

TABLE 14.1 Who's Who Among Mental Health Professionals

Clinical psychologist	Holds an academic doctorate (Ph.D., Psy.D., or Ed.D.) and is required to be licensed to practice. Has expertise in psychological testing, diagnosis, psychotherapy, research, and prevention of mental and emotional disorders. May work in private practice, hospitals, or community mental health centers.
Psychiatrist	Holds a medical degree (M.D. or D.O.) and is required to be licensed to practice. Has expertise in the diagnosis, treatment, and prevention of mental and emotional disorders. Often has training in psychotherapy. May prescribe medications, electroconvulsive therapy, or other medical procedures.
Psychoanalyst	Usually a psychiatrist or clinical psychologist who has received additional training in the specific techniques of psychoanalysis, the form of psychotherapy originated by Sigmund Freud.
Psychiatric social worker	Holds a master's degree in social work (M.S.W.). Training includes an internship in a social service agency or mental health center. Most states require certification or licensing. May or may not have training in psychotherapy.
Marriage and family therapist	Usually holds a master's degree with extensive supervised experience in couple or family therapy. May also have training in individual therapy. Many states require licensing.
Psychiatric nurse	Holds an R.N. degree and has selected psychiatry or mental health nursing as a specialty area. Typically works on a hospital psychiatric unit or in a community mental health center. May or may not have training in psychotherapy.

tional, behavioral, and interpersonal problems. There are hundreds of types of psychotherapy (Garfield & Bergin, 1994). Although there are many forms of psychotherapy, they all share the assumption that psychological factors play a significant role in a person's troubling feelings, behaviors, or relationships. Table 14.1 summarizes the diverse range of mental health professionals who use psychotherapy techniques to help people.

In contrast to psychotherapy, the **biomedical therapies** involve the use of medication or other medical treatments to treat the symptoms associated with psychological disorders. The biomedical therapies are based on the assumption that the symptoms of many psychological disorders involve biological factors, such as abnormal brain chemistry. As we saw in Chapter 13, the involvement of biological factors in many psychological disorders is well documented. Not surprisingly, there has been a steadily growing trend to combine biomedical therapy and psychotherapy in treating psychological disorders (Klerman & others, 1994).

Currently, only licensed physicians, such as psychiatrists, are legally allowed to prescribe the different forms of biomedical therapy. However, that tradition may be changing. In recent years, field trials have been conducted in which specially trained clinical psychologists were allowed to prescribe medications to treat psychological disorders (see Fowler, 1995; Youngstrom, 1992). Eventually, clinical psychologists may also be able to prescribe medications.

We'll begin this chapter by surveying some of the most influential approaches in psychotherapy: psychoanalytic, humanistic, behavioral, and cognitive. As you'll see, each approach is based on different assumptions about the underlying causes of psychological problems. And each approach uses different strategies to produce beneficial changes in the way a person thinks, feels, and behaves—the ultimate goal of all forms of psychotherapy.

Psychoanalytic Therapy

Psychoanalysis is a form of therapy developed by Sigmund Freud and based on his theory of personality. What techniques are used in psychoanalysis, and what is their purpose? What are short-term dynamic therapies?

biomedical therapies
The use of medications, electroconvulsive therapy, or other medical treatments to treat the symptoms associated with psychological disorders.

psychoanalysis
A type of psychotherapy originated by Sigmund Freud in which free association, dream interpretation, and analysis of resistance and transference are used to explore repressed or unconscious impulses, anxieties, and internal conflicts.

When cartoonists portray a psychotherapy session, they often draw a person lying on a couch and talking while a bearded gentleman sits in the background, passively listening. This stereotype reflects some of the key ingredients of traditional **psychoanalysis,** a form of psychotherapy originally developed by **Sigmund Freud** (1856–1939) in the early 1900s. Although psychoanalysis was developed almost a century ago, its assumptions and techniques continue to be influential today.

Sigmund Freud and Psychoanalysis

As a therapy, traditional psychoanalysis is closely interwoven with Freud's theory of personality. As you may recall from Chapter 10, on personality, Freud stressed that early childhood experiences provided the foundation for later personality development. When early experiences result in unresolved conflicts and frustrated urges, these emotionally charged memories are *repressed*, or pushed out of conscious awareness. Although unconscious, these repressed conflicts continue to influence a person's thoughts and behavior, including the dynamics of his relationships with others.

Psychoanalysis is designed to help unearth unconscious conflicts so the patient attains *insight* as to the real source of her problems. Through the intense relationship that forms between the psychoanalyst and the patient, longstanding psychological conflicts are recognized and, if the analysis is successful, ultimately resolved.

Freud's Famous Couch This photograph shows Freud's consulting room. During therapy sessions, his patients would lie on the couch. Freud usually sat by the head of the couch, out of the patient's view. He believed that this arrangement encouraged the patient's free flow of thoughts, feelings, and images. Although some traditional psychoanalysts still have the patient lie on a couch, many favor comfortable chairs in which analyst and patient are facing one another.

Freud developed several techniques to reveal clues about a patient's unconscious and to coax long-repressed memories, impulses, and conflicts to consciousness (Liff, 1992). One of Freud's most famous techniques, called **free association,** involves the patient spontaneously reporting all her thoughts, mental images, and feelings while lying on a couch. The psychoanalyst usually sits out of view, occasionally asking questions to encourage the flow of associations.

Blocks in free association, such as a sudden silence or an abrupt change of topic, were thought to be signs of resistance. **Resistance** is the patient's unconscious attempts to block the process of revealing repressed memories and conflicts. Resistance is a sign that the patient is uncomfortably close to uncovering psychologically threatening material.

Dream interpretation is another important psychoanalytic technique. Because psychological defenses are reduced during sleep, Freud believed that unconscious conflicts and repressed impulses were expressed symbolically in dream images. Often, the dream images were used to trigger free associations that might shed light on the dream's symbolic meaning.

More directly, the psychoanalyst sometimes makes carefully timed **interpretations,** explanations of the unconscious meaning of the patient's behavior, thoughts, feelings, or dreams. The timing of such interpretations is important. If an interpretation is offered before the patient is psychologically ready to confront an issue, she may reject the interpretation or respond defensively, increasing resistance (Henry & others, 1994).

One of the most important processes that occurs in the relationship between the patient and the psychoanalyst is called transference. **Transference** occurs when the patient unconsciously responds to the therapist as though the therapist were a significant person in the patient's life, often a parent. As Freud (1940) explained, "The patient sees in his analyst the return—the reincarnation—of some important figure out of his childhood or past, and consequently transfers on to him the feelings and reactions that undoubtedly applied to this model."

The psychoanalyst encourages transference by purposely remaining as neutral as possible. In other words, the psychoanalyst does not reveal personal feelings, take sides, make judgments, or actively advise the patient.

We ask the dreamer as well to free himself from the impression of the manifest dream, to switch his attention from the dream as a whole to individual parts of its content, and tell us one after another the things that occur to him in connection with these parts, what associations come into his mind when he turns his mental eye on to each of them separately.

Sigmund Freud *New Introductory Lectures on Psychoanalysis,* 1933

free association

A technique used in psychoanalysis in which the patient spontaneously reports all thoughts, feelings, and mental images as they come to mind, as a way of revealing unconscious thoughts and emotions.

resistance

In psychoanalysis, the patient's unconscious attempts to block the revelation of repressed memories and conflicts.

dream interpretation

A technique used in psychoanalysis in which the content of dreams is analyzed for disguised or symbolic wishes, meanings, and motivations.

interpretation

A technique used in psychoanalysis in which the psychoanalyst offers a carefully timed explanation of the patient's dreams, free associations, or behavior to facilitate the recognition of unconscious conflicts or motivations.

transference

In psychoanalysis, the process by which emotions and desires originally associated with a significant person in the patient's life, such as a parent, are unconsciously transferred to the psychoanalyst.

This therapeutic neutrality is designed to produce "optimal frustration" so that the patient transfers and projects unresolved conflicts onto the psychoanalyst (Eagle & Wolitzky, 1992). As these transference feelings become more intense, the patient relives unconscious emotional conflicts that have been repressed since childhood. But now, these conflicts are relived and played out in the context of the relationship between the psychoanalyst and the patient.

All these psychoanalytic techniques are designed to help the patient see how past conflicts influence her current behavior and relationships, including her relationship with the psychoanalyst. Once these kinds of insights are achieved, the psychoanalyst helps the patient work through and resolve long-standing conflicts. As resolutions occur, maladaptive behavior patterns that were previously driven by unconscious conflicts can be replaced with more adaptive emotional and behavioral patterns.

The intensive relationship between the patient and the psychoanalyst takes time to develop. On average, the traditional psychoanalyst sees the patient four or five times a week over the course of four years or longer (Garfield & Bergin, 1994). Freud's patients were on the couch six days a week (Liff, 1992). Obviously, traditional psychoanalysis is a slow, expensive process that few people can afford. For those who have the time and the money, traditional psychoanalysis is still available.

Short-Term Dynamic Therapies

Today, few psychotherapists practice traditional psychoanalysis lasting for years. Most people entering psychotherapy are not seeking the kind of major personality overhaul that traditional psychoanalysis is designed to produce. Instead, people come to therapy expecting help with specific problems. People also expect therapy to provide beneficial changes in a matter of weeks or months, not years.

Today, there are many different forms of *short-term dynamic therapies* based on traditional psychoanalytic notions (Binder & others, 1994). These short-term dynamic therapies have several features in common (Koss & Shiang, 1994). Therapeutic contact lasts for no more than a few months. The patient's problems are quickly assessed at the beginning of therapy. The therapist and patient agree on specific, concrete, and attainable goals. In the actual sessions, most psychodynamic therapists are more directive than traditional psychoanalysts, actively engaging the patient in a dialogue.

As in traditional psychoanalysis, the therapist uses interpretations to help the patient recognize hidden feelings and transferences that may be occurring in important relationships in his life (Liff, 1992). Therapy also focuses on helping the patient identify psychological resources that he can use to cope with the current difficulty as well as future problems (Koss & Shiang, 1994).

Despite the fact that traditional, lengthy psychoanalysis is seldom practiced today, it should be clear that Freud's basic assumptions and techniques continue to be influential. Although contemporary research has challenged some of Freud's original ideas, modern researchers are also studying the specific factors that seem to influence the effectiveness of basic Freudian techniques, such as interpretation and transference (Henry & others, 1994). Without question, psychoanalysis has many critics (e.g., Eysenck, 1994, 1985; Szasz, 1988). But it's equally true that the legacy of Freud's contributions to personality theory and psychotherapy have been enormous.

BIZARRO

AT THE RISK OF SOUNDING CLICHE, DOCTOR, LET ME SAY THAT I HAVE CERTAIN UN-RESOLVED ISSUES REGARDING MY PARENTS.

Humanistic Therapy

Client-centered therapy is a form of therapy that grew out of the humanistic perspective and was developed by Carl Rogers. What therapeutic conditions and techniques are important in client-centered therapy? How do client-centered therapy and psychoanalysis differ as insight therapies?

The *humanistic perspective* in psychology emphasizes human potential, self-awareness, and freedom of choice (see Chapter 10). Humanistic psychologists contend that the most important factor in personality is the individual's conscious, subjective perception of his or her self. They see people as being innately good and motivated by the need to grow psychologically. If people are raised in a genuinely accepting atmosphere and given freedom to make choices, they will develop healthy self-concepts and strive to fulfill their unique potential as human beings (Rice & Greenberg, 1992).

Carl Rogers and Client-Centered Therapy

The humanistic perspective exerted a strong influence on psychotherapy. Probably the most influential of the humanistic psychotherapies is **client-centered therapy,** also called *person-centered therapy,* developed by **Carl Rogers** (1902–1987). In naming his therapy, Rogers deliberately used the word *client* rather than *patient.* He believed that the medical term *patient* implied that people in therapy were "sick" and were seeking treatment from an all-knowing authority figure who could "heal" or "cure" them. Instead of stressing the therapist's expertise or perceptions of the patient, client-centered therapy emphasizes the *client's* subjective perception of himself and his environment (Zimring & Raskin, 1992).

Unlike Freud, Rogers believed that the therapist should be *nondirective.* That is, the therapist must not direct the client, make decisions for the client, offer solutions, or pass judgment on the client's thoughts or feelings. Instead, Rogers believed, change in therapy must be chosen and directed by the client. The therapist's role is to create the conditions that allow the client, not the therapist, to direct the focus of therapy.

What are the therapeutic conditions that promote self-awareness, psychological growth, and self-directed change? Rogers (1980) believed that three qualities of the therapist are critical: genuineness, unconditional positive regard, and empathic understanding. First, *genuineness* means that the therapist honestly and openly shares her thoughts and feelings with the client. By modeling genuineness, the therapist indirectly encourages the client to express her true feelings without defensiveness or pretension.

Second, the therapist must value, accept, and care for the client, whatever his problems or behavior. Rogers called this quality *unconditional positive regard.* Rogers believed that people develop psychological problems largely because they have consistently experienced only *conditional acceptance.* That is, parents, teachers, and others have communicated this message: "I will accept you only *if* you conform to my expectations."

The therapist who successfully creates a climate of unconditional positive regard fosters the person's natural tendency to move toward self-fulfilling de-

Carl Rogers Shown on the far right, Rogers contended that human potential would flourish in an atmosphere of genuineness, unconditional positive regard, and empathic understanding. Rogers filmed many of his therapy sessions as part of a research program to identify the most helpful aspects of client-centered therapy.

client-centered therapy
A type of psychotherapy developed by humanistic psychologist Carl Rogers in which the therapist is nondirective and reflective, and the client directs the focus of each therapy session; also called *person-centered therapy.*

cisions without fear of evaluation or rejection. Rogers (1977) described this important aspect of therapy in this way:

> Unconditional positive regard means that when the therapist is experiencing a positive, acceptant attitude toward whatever the client is at that moment, therapeutic movement or change is more likely. It involves the therapist's willingness for the client to be whatever feeling is going on at that moment—confusion, resentment, fear, anger, courage, love, or pride. . . . The therapist prizes the client in a total rather than a conditional way.

Third, the therapist must communicate *empathic understanding* by reflecting the content and personal meaning of feelings being experienced by the client. In effect, the therapist creates a psychological mirror, reflecting the client's thoughts and feelings as they exist in the client's private inner world. The goal is to help the client explore and clarify his feelings, thoughts, and perceptions. In the process, the client begins to see himself, and his problems, more clearly (Egan, 1994). Empathic understanding requires the therapist to listen *actively* for the personal meaning beneath the surface of what the client is saying.

Rogers believed that when the therapeutic atmosphere contains genuineness, unconditional positive regard, and empathic understanding, change is more likely to occur. Such conditions foster feelings of being psychologically safe, accepted, and valued. In this therapeutic atmosphere, change occurs as the person's self-concept and world view gradually become healthier and less distorted. In effect, the client is moving in the direction of *self-actualization*—the realization of his or her unique potentials and talents.

Client-Centered Therapy Rather than "interpreting" the client's thoughts and behavior, the client-centered therapist strives to create a warm, accepting climate that allows the client the freedom to explore troubling issues. The therapist engages in active listening, reflecting both the content and the personal meaning of what the client is saying. In doing so, the therapist helps the client develop a clearer perception and understanding of her own feelings and motives.

A large number of studies have generally supported Rogers' contention that it is important for the therapist to demonstrate genuineness, unconditional positive regard, and empathic understanding (Greenberg & others, 1994). Such factors promote trust and self-exploration in therapy. However, these conditions, by themselves, may not be sufficient to help clients change (Beutler & others, 1994).

The client-centered approach continues to be developed by therapists, teachers, social workers, and counselors (Lietaer & others, 1990). Along with being influential in individual psychotherapy, the client-centered approach has been applied to marital counseling, parenting, education, business, and even community and international relations (Zimring & Raskin, 1992).

TABLE 14.2 Comparing Insight-Oriented Therapies

Type of Therapy	Founder	Source of Problems	Treatment Techniques	Goals of Therapy
Psychoanalysis	Sigmund Freud	Repressed, unconscious conflicts stemming from early childhood experiences	Free association, analysis of dream content, interpretation, and transference	To recognize, work through, and resolve longstanding conflicts
Client-centered therapy	Carl Rogers	Conditional acceptance that causes the person to develop a distorted self-concept and world view	Nondirective therapist who displays unconditional positive regard, genuineness, and empathic understanding	To develop self-awareness, self-acceptance, and self-determination

behavior therapy
A type of psychotherapy that focuses on directly changing maladaptive behavior patterns by using basic learning principles and techniques; also called *behavior modification.*

Behavior Therapy

Behavior therapy uses the principles of learning theories to directly change problem behaviors. How are classical conditioning principles used to treat specific problem behaviors? How are operant conditioning principles applied to modify problem behaviors?

Psychoanalysis, client-centered therapy, and other insight-oriented therapies maintain that the road to psychologically healthier behavior is increased self-understanding of motives and conflicts. As insights are acquired through therapy, problem behaviors and feelings presumably will give way to more adaptive behaviors and emotional reactions.

However, gaining insight into the source of problems does not necessarily result in desirable changes in behavior and emotions. Even though you fully understand *why* you are behaving in counterproductive ways, your maladaptive or self-defeating behaviors may continue. For instance, an adult who is extremely anxious about public speaking may understand that he feels that way because he was raised by a critical and demanding parent. But having this insight into the underlying cause of his anxiety may do little, if anything, to reduce his anxiety or change his avoidance of such situations.

In sharp contrast to the insight-oriented therapies we discussed in the preceding section, the goal of **behavior therapy** is to modify specific problem behaviors, not to change the entire personality. And, rather than focusing on the past, behavior therapists focus on current behaviors.

Behavior therapists assume that maladaptive behaviors are *learned,* just as adaptive behaviors are. Thus, the basic strategy in behavior therapy involves unlearning maladaptive behaviors and learning more adaptive behaviors in their place. Behavior therapists employ techniques that are based on the learning principles of classical conditioning, operant conditioning, and observational learning to modify the problem behavior.

Techniques Based on Classical Conditioning

Just as Pavlov's dogs learned to salivate to a ringing bell that had become associated with food, learned associations can be at the core of some maladaptive behaviors, including strong negative emotional reactions. In the 1920s, psychologist John Watson demonstrated this in his famous "Little Albert" study. You may recall from Chapter 5 that Watson classically conditioned an infant called "Little Albert" to fear a tame lab rat by repeatedly pairing the rat with a loud clanging sound. Over time, Albert's conditioned fear generalized to other furry objects, including a fur coat, cotton, and a Santa Claus mask (Watson & Rayner, 1920).

Mary Cover Jones: The First Behavior Therapist

Watson himself never tried to eliminate Little Albert's fears. But Watson's research inspired one of his students, **Mary Cover Jones** (1896–1987), to explore ways of reversing conditioned fears. With Watson acting as a consultant, Jones (1924a) treated a three-year-old named Peter who "seemed almost to be Albert grown a bit older." Like Little Albert, Peter was fearful of various furry objects, including a tame rat, a fur coat, cotton, and wool. Because Peter was especially afraid of a tame rabbit, Jones focused on eliminating the rabbit fear. She used a procedure that has come to be known as

Mary Cover Jones This photograph, taken around 1919, shows Mary Cover Jones as a college student in her early twenties. Although Jones pioneered the use of behavioral techniques in therapy, she did not consider herself a "behaviorist," and ultimately disagreed with many of Watson's views. Fifty years after she treated Peter, Jones (1975) wrote, "Now I would be less satisfied to treat the fears of a three-year-old . . . in isolation from him as a tantalizingly complex person with unique potentials for stability and change."

counterconditioning

A behavior therapy technique based on classical conditioning that involves modifying behavior by conditioning a new response that is incompatible with a previously learned response.

systematic desensitization

A type of behavior therapy in which phobic responses are reduced by pairing relaxation with a series of mental images or real-life situations that the person finds progressively more fear-provoking; based on the principle of counterconditioning.

counterconditioning—the learning of a new conditioned response that is incompatible with a previously learned response.

Jones's procedure was very simple (Jones, 1924b; Watson, 1924). The caged rabbit was brought into Peter's view but kept far enough away to avoid eliciting fear (the original conditioned response). With the rabbit visible at a tolerable distance, Peter sat in a highchair and happily munched his favorite snack, milk and crackers. Peter's favorite food was used because, presumably, the enjoyment of eating would naturally elicit a positive response (the desired conditioned response). Such a positive response would be incompatible with the negative response of fear.

Every day for almost two months, the rabbit was inched closer and closer to Peter as he ate his milk and crackers. As Peter's tolerance for the rabbit's presence gradually increased, he was eventually able to hold the rabbit in his lap, petting it with one hand while happily eating with his other hand (Jones, 1924a, 1924b). Not only was Peter's fear of the rabbit eliminated, but he also stopped being afraid of other furry objects, including the rat, cotton, and fur coat (Watson, 1924).

Along with counterconditioning, Jones (1924a) used *observational learning* techniques to help eliminate Peter's rabbit fear. As part of the treatment, Peter observed other children petting or holding the tame rabbit. Eventually, Peter imitated the actions of the nonfearful children. For her pioneering efforts in the treatment of children's fears, Jones is widely regarded as the first behavior therapist (Gieser, 1993; Reiss, 1990).

Systematic Desensitization

On the basis of Mary Cover Jones's pioneering research, South African psychiatrist Joseph Wolpe developed a procedure called *systematic desensitization* to treat phobias and other anxiety disorders (Wolpe, 1958, 1982). **Systematic desensitization** involves learning a new conditioned response (relaxation) that is incompatible with or inhibits the old conditioned response (fear and anxiety).

Three basic steps are involved in systematic desensitization (Morris, 1991). First, the patient learns *progressive relaxation,* which involves successively relaxing one muscle group after another until a deep state of relaxation is achieved. Second, the behavior therapist helps the patient construct an *anxiety hierarchy,* which is a list of anxiety-provoking images associated with the feared situation, arranged in a hierarchy from least to most anxiety-producing (see Figure 14.1). The patient also develops an image of a relaxing *control scene,* such as walking on a secluded beach on a sunny day.

The third step involves the actual process of desensitization. While deeply relaxed, the patient imagines the least threatening scene of the anxiety hierarchy. After he can maintain complete relaxation while imagining this scene, he moves to the next. If the patient begins to feel anxiety or tension, the behavior therapist guides him back to imagining the previous scene or the control scene. If necessary, the therapist helps the patient relax again, using the progressive relaxation technique.

Degree of Fear	Imagined Scene
100	Holding mouth open, eyes closed, listening to the sound of the dental drill as a cavity is repaired
95	Holding mouth open in preparation for an oral injection
90	Lying back in dental chair, eyes closed, as dentist examines teeth
85	Lying back in dental chair, mouth open, listening to the sounds of dental equipment, as dental technician cleans teeth
80	Lying in dental chair, watching dental technician unwrap sterilized dental tools
75	Being greeted by the dental technician and walking back to dental examination chair
70	Sitting in dentist's waiting room
60	Driving to dentist's office for appointment
50	Looking at the bright yellow reminder postcard on the refrigerator and thinking about dental appointment
40	Listening to my sister talk about her last dental visit
30	Looking at television or magazine advertisements depicting people in a dentist's chair
25	Calling dentist's office to make an appointment
20	Thinking about calling dentist's office to set up an appointment
15	Driving past dentist's office on a workday
10	Driving past dentist's office on a Sunday afternoon

FIGURE 14.1 A Sample Anxiety Hierarchy

As part of systematic desensitization, the therapist helps the client develop an anxiety hierarchy. The one shown here illustrates the kinds of scenes that a person who is fearful of dental treatment might list.

Using Virtual Reality to Conquer Phobias
Virtual reality is a computer-simulated, three-dimensional environment that the viewer experiences as if it were real. The viewer wears special goggles, and if he turns his head, the computer-generated scene changes accordingly. Virtual reality is being used experimentally as a form of computer-assisted systematic desensitization in the treatment of some phobias, such as fear of heights or flying (Rothbaum & others, 1996). Rather than mental images, the person experiences computer-generated images that are "real" enough to trigger anxiety (Lamson, 1994).

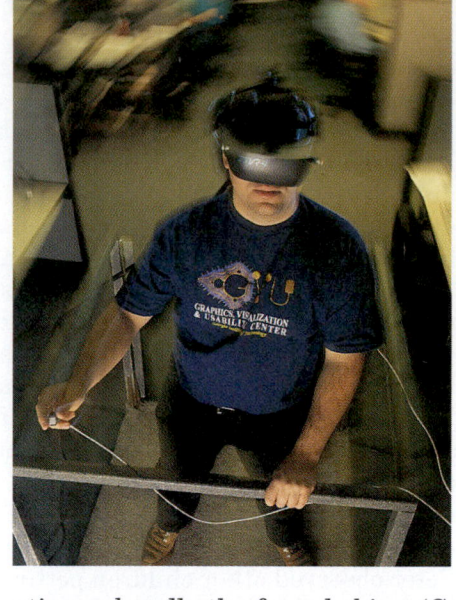

Over several sessions, the patient gradually and systematically works his way up the hierarchy, imagining each scene while maintaining complete relaxation. Very systematically, each imagined scene becomes paired with a conditioned response of relaxation rather than anxiety, and desensitization to the feared situation takes place. Once mastered with mental images, the desensitization procedure may be continued in the actual feared situation. If the technique is successful, the feared situation no longer produces a conditioned response of fear and anxiety. In practice, systematic desensitization is often combined with other behavioral techniques, such as observing people who calmly cope with the feared situation or handle the feared object (Getka & Glass, 1992).

The Bell and Pad Treatment

Another technique based on classical conditioning has been used successfully in treating persistent bedwetting in children over the age of six. Children who are bedwetters tend to be very deep sleepers (Anch & others, 1988). Behavior therapy is based on the idea that the child who wets the bed has not learned to wake up when his bladder is full. Therapy involves the **bell and pad treatment,** which uses classical conditioning to pair arousal with the sensation of a full bladder.

A special insulated pad is placed under the bottom bed sheet. When the child starts to wet the bed, a loud bell goes off, waking the child. After shutting off the alarm, the child uses the bathroom, then changes the sheet. Before going back to bed, he resets the alarm.

Over the course of a few weeks, the child becomes conditioned so that the sensation of a full bladder (the conditioned stimulus) triggers waking arousal (the desired conditioned response). In the process, the child's sleeping cycles are also modified so that the child is not such a heavy sleeper. The bell and pad procedure is effective in about 75 percent of school-aged children who have difficulties with bedwetting (Kaplan & Busner, 1993).

Aversive Conditioning

Another behavioral technique that is based on classical conditioning is called aversive conditioning. **Aversive conditioning** is used to create an unpleasant conditioned response to a harmful stimulus like cigarette smoke or alcoholic beverages. The basic procedure is to pair the harmful stimulus (like cigarettes) with an unpleasant stimulus (like a foul-tasting substance) so that the harmful stimulus comes to produce a distasteful conditioned response.

Aversive conditioning techniques have been used to treat alcohol addiction, sexual deviance, compulsive gambling, and overeating (Emmelkamp, 1994; Sandler & Steele, 1991). For example, a medication called *Antabuse* is used in aversion therapy for alcohol addiction. If a person taking Antabuse consumes any amount of alcohol, extreme nausea is induced. For some conditions, such as sexual deviance, mild electric shocks are used rather than nausea-producing drugs. In general, aversive conditioning is not very effective, and its use has been on the decline in recent years.

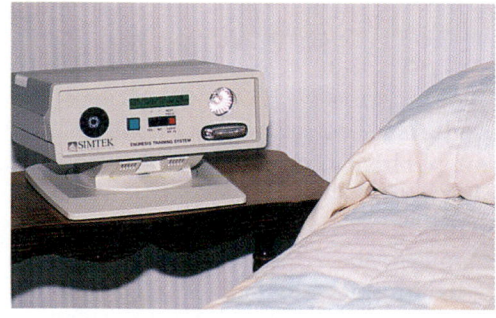

The Bell and Pad Treatment for Bedwetting On the bedside table is an electronic device that monitors a moisture-sensitive pad that is placed below the bottom sheet of the bed. If the child wets the bed, a loud buzzer and a bright light are activated, waking the child. Over the course of several weeks, the bell and pad device conditions arousal from sleep in response to the body signals of a full bladder.

bell and pad treatment
A behavior therapy technique used to treat nighttime bedwetting by conditioning arousal from sleep in response to body signals of a full bladder.

aversive conditioning
A relatively ineffective type of behavior therapy that involves repeatedly pairing an aversive stimulus with the occurrence of undesirable behaviors or thoughts.

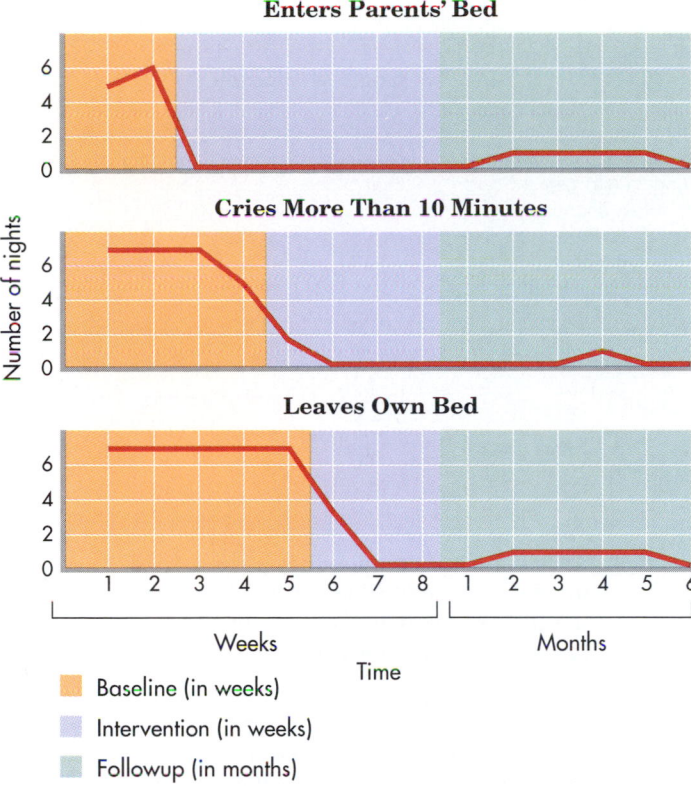

Enters Parents' Bed

Cries More Than 10 Minutes

Leaves Own Bed

Number of nights

Weeks   Months

Time

■ Baseline (in weeks)

■ Intervention (in weeks)

■ Followup (in months)

FIGURE 14.2 The Effect of Operant Conditioning Techniques
These graphs depict the changes in three specific sleep-related problem behaviors of a four-year-old girl over the course of behavioral therapy. The intervention for each problem behavior was introduced separately over several weeks. As you can see, behavior therapy produced a rapid reduction in the rate of each problem behavior. The green area shows the maintenance of desired behavior changes over a six-month followup.
(Adapted from Ronen, 1991.)

token economy
A form of behavior therapy in which the therapeutic environment is structured to reward desired behaviors with tokens or points that may eventually be exchanged for tangible rewards.

Techniques Based on Operant Conditioning

B. F. Skinner's *operant conditioning* model of learning is based on the simple principle that behavior is shaped and maintained by its consequences (see Chapter 5). Behavior therapists have devised a variety of techniques based on the principles of operant conditioning. Often, these operant techniques focus on controlling the consequences of undesired and desired behaviors. Two relatively simple operant techniques are *positive reinforcement* for desired behaviors and *extinction,* or nonreinforcement, for undesired behaviors.

Let's illustrate how operant techniques are used in therapy by describing a behavioral program to treat a four-year-old girl's sleeping problems (Ronen, 1991). The first step in the treatment program was to identify specific problem behaviors and determine their *baseline rate,* or how often each problem occurred before treatment began. After measuring the baseline rate, the therapist could target each problem behavior individually and objectively measure the child's progress. The parents next identified several very specific behavioral goals for their daughter. These goals included not crying when she was put to bed, not crying if she woke up in the night, not getting into her parents' bed, and staying in her own bed throughout the night.

The parents were taught operant techniques to decrease the undesirable behaviors and increase desirable ones. For example, to *extinguish* the girl's screaming and crying, the parents were taught to ignore the behavior rather than continue to reinforce it with parental attention. In contrast, desirable behaviors were to be *positively reinforced* with abundant praise, encouragement, social attention, and other rewards. Figure 14.2, shows the little girl's progress for three specific problem behaviors.

Operant conditioning techniques have been applied to many different kinds of psychological problems, from habit and weight control to helping autistic children learn to speak and behave more adaptively (Mazur, 1994). Techniques based on operant conditioning have also been successfully used to modify the behavior of people who are severely disabled by retardation or mental disorders (O'Leary & Wilson, 1987).

The **token economy** is an example of the use of operant conditioning techniques to modify the behavior of groups of people (Bloxham & others, 1993). A token economy is a very structured environment, a system for strengthening desired behaviors through positive reinforcement. Basically, tokens or points are awarded as positive reinforcers for desirable behaviors and withheld or taken away for undesirable behaviors. The tokens can be exchanged for other reinforcers, such as special privileges.

Token economies have been used in prisons, classrooms, juvenile correction institutes, and psychiatric hospitals (Mazur, 1994). Token economies have been shown to be effective even with severely disturbed patients who have been hospitalized for many years (Paul & Menditto, 1992). However, token economies are difficult to implement and require a great deal of staff training and cooperation to be effective. The withholding of privileges from hospital inpatients has also been challenged legally. Consequently, token economies are not in wide use today (Glynn, 1990).

TABLE 14.3 Behavior Therapy

Type of Therapy	Founder	Source of Problems	Treatment Techniques	Goals of Therapy
Behavior therapy	Based on the principles of classical conditioning, operant conditioning, and observational learning	Learned maladaptive behavior patterns	Systematic desensitization, bell and pad treatment, aversive conditioning, reinforcement and extinction, token economy, observational learning	To unlearn maladaptive behaviors, and learn adaptive behaviors in their place

Identifying Psychotherapy Techniques

Identify the general therapy approach and the specific psychotherapy technique that is illustrated in each of the following examples.

1. In a group home for mentally retarded adults, residents earn points for maintaining personal hygiene, completing assigned daily chores, and engaging in appropriate social interaction.
   Approach: _____
   Technique: _____

2. At the beginning of her therapy session, Jackie described a bizarre dream about an angry dinosaur attacking her home. Her therapist asked her to relax, close her eyes, picture the dinosaur, and tell him whatever popped into her mind.
   Approach: _____
   Technique: _____

3. Nine-year-old Ben sleeps with a special pad beneath his sheets. If he starts to wet the bed, a loud alarm goes off and wakes him up.
   Approach: _____
   Technique: _____

4. Although Dr. Freedman has purposely remained very neutral and nonjudgmental during therapy sessions, his patient, Jonathan, lashes out at him for being overly critical.
   Approach: _____
   Technique: _____

5. Janet is still ashamed of the time she was arrested for shoplifting as a teenager. But after months of therapy, she is able to discuss the episode with her therapist without fear of being rejected.
   Approach: _____
   Technique: _____

6. Alan is terrified of spiders. Alan's therapist, Dr. Burford, teaches him a relaxation technique and then helps him construct a list of spider-related images, from least to most fear-producing. Then Dr. Burford has Alan imagine each of these scenes while deeply relaxed.
   Approach: _____
   Technique: _____

Cognitive Therapies

The cognitive therapies are based on the assumption that psychological problems are due to maladaptive thinking patterns. What is rational-emotive therapy (RET)? What is Beck's cognitive therapy (CT), and how does it differ from rational-emotive therapy?

cognitive therapies
A group of psychotherapies that are based on the assumption that psychological problems are due to maladaptive patterns of thinking; treatment techniques focus on recognizing and altering these unhealthy thinking patterns.

rational-emotive therapy (RET)
A type of cognitive therapy, developed by psychologist Albert Ellis, that focuses on changing the client's irrational beliefs.

Whereas behavior therapy assumes that faulty learning is at the core of problem behaviors and emotions, the **cognitive therapies** assume that the culprit is *faulty thinking*. The key assumption of the cognitive therapies could be put like this: Most people blame their unhappiness and problems on external events and situations, but the real cause of unhappiness is the way the person *thinks* about the events, not the events themselves. Thus, cognitive therapists zero in on the faulty patterns of thinking that they believe are causing the psychological problems. Once faulty patterns of thinking have been identified, the second step is to *change* them to more adaptive, healthy patterns of thinking. In this section, we'll look at how this change is accomplished in two influential forms of cognitive therapy: Ellis's *rational-emotive therapy* (RET) and Beck's *cognitive therapy* (CT).

Albert Ellis and Rational-Emotive Therapy

There is nothing either good or bad, but thinking makes it so.

William Shakespeare Hamlet

Albert Ellis A colorful and sometimes controversial figure, Albert Ellis developed rational-emotive therapy (RET). Rational-emotive therapy promotes psychologically healthier thought processes by disputing irrational beliefs and replacing them with more rational interpretations of events.

Shakespeare said it more eloquently, but psychologist **Albert Ellis** (b. 1913) has expressed the same sentiment: "You largely feel the way you think." Ellis developed **rational-emotive therapy,** abbreviated **RET,** in the 1950s. The key premise of RET is that people's difficulties are caused by their faulty expectations and irrational beliefs. Rational-emotive therapy focuses on changing the patterns of irrational thinking that are believed to be the primary cause of the client's emotional distress and psychological problems.

Ellis points out that most people mistakenly believe that they become upset and unhappy because of external events. But Ellis (1993) would argue that it's not external events that make people miserable—it's their *interpretation* of those events. In rational-emotive therapy, psychological problems are explained by the "ABC" model, as shown in Figure 14.3. According to this model, when an *Activating event* (**A**) occurs, it is the person's *Beliefs* (**B**) about the event that cause emotional *Consequences* (**C**). Notice how this differs from the common-sense view that it is the event (A) that causes the emotional and behavioral consequences (C).

Identifying the core irrational beliefs that underlie personal distress is the first step in rational-emotive therapy. Often, irrational beliefs reflect "musts" and "shoulds" that are absolutes, such as the notion that "I should be competent at everything I do." Other common irrational beliefs are listed in Table 14.4 on the next page.

The consequences of such thinking are unhealthy negative emotions, like extreme anger, despair, resentment, and feelings of worthlessness. Not only does the person feel miserable, but she also feels that she is unable to control or cope with an upsetting situation. These kinds of irrational cognitive and emotional responses interfere with constructive attempts to change disturbing

Common-Sense View

A Activating Event	Causes →	**C** Consequence
Example: You're passed over for a promotion at work.		You're miserable and depressed.

Rational-Emotive Therapy's ABC Model

A Activating Event	Triggers →	**B** Beliefs	Causes →	**C** Consequence
Example: You're passed over for a promotion at work.		"I must be successful at everything I do or I am a complete failure. I was not successful, so I am a complete failure and a worthless human being."		You're miserable and depressed.

FIGURE 14.3 The "ABC" Model in Rational-Emotive Therapy
Common sense tells us that unhappiness and other unpleasant emotions are caused by unpleasant or disturbing events. This view is shown in the top part of the figure. But Albert Ellis (1993) points out that it is really our *beliefs* about the events, and not the events themselves, that make us miserable, as diagrammed in the bottom part of the figure.

TABLE 14.4 Irrational Beliefs

1. It is a dire necessity for you to be loved or approved by virtually everyone in your community.

2. You must be thoroughly competent, adequate, and achieving in all possible respects if you are to consider yourself worthwhile.

3. Certain people are bad, wicked, or villainous, and they should be severely blamed and punished for their villainy. You should become extremely upset over other people's wrongdoings.

4. It is awful and catastrophic when things are not the way you would very much like them to be.

5. Human unhappiness is externally caused, and you have little or no ability to control your bad feelings and emotions.

6. It is easier to avoid than to face difficulties and responsibilities. Avoiding difficulties whenever possible is more likely to lead to happiness than facing difficulties.

7. You need to rely on someone stronger than yourself.

8. Your past history is an all-important determinant of your present behavior. Because something once strongly affected your life, it should indefinitely have a similar effect.

9. You should become extremely upset over other people's problems.

10. There is a single perfect solution to all human problems, and it is catastrophic if this perfect solution is not found.

SOURCE: Based on Ellis, 1991.

According to rational-emotive therapy, unhappiness and psychological problems can often be traced to people's irrational beliefs. Becoming aware of these irrational beliefs is the first step toward replacing them with more rational alternatives. Some of the most common irrational beliefs are listed here.

Aaron Beck In Aaron Beck's cognitive therapy, called CT, clients learn to identify and change their automatic negative thoughts. Originally developed to treat depression, CT has also been applied to other psychological problems, such as anxiety disorders, phobias, and eating disorders.

situations (Ellis & Harper, 1975). According to RET, the result is self-defeating behaviors, anxiety disorders, depression, and other psychological problems.

The second step in rational-emotive therapy is for the therapist to vigorously *dispute and challenge the irrational beliefs.* In doing so, rational-emotive therapists tend to be very direct and even confrontational. Rather than trying to establish a warm, supportive atmosphere, rational-emotive therapists rely on logical persuasion and reason to push the client toward recognizing and surrendering his irrational beliefs (Hollon & Beck, 1994). According to Ellis (1991), blunt, harsh language is sometimes needed to push people into helping themselves.

From the client's perspective, rational-emotive therapy requires considerable effort. First, the person must admit her irrational beliefs and accept the fact that those beliefs are irrational and unhealthy, which is not as easy as it sounds. Old mental habits don't always yield easily. Equally challenging, the client must radically change her way of interpreting and responding to stressful events (Haaga & Davison, 1991). The long-term therapeutic goal of RET is to teach clients to recognize and dispute their own irrational beliefs in a wide range of situations.

However, responding "rationally" to unpleasant situations does not mean denying your feelings (Ellis & Bernard, 1985). Ellis believes that it is perfectly appropriate and rational to feel sad when you are rejected, or disappointed when you fail. Appropriate emotions are the consequences of rational beliefs such as "I would prefer that everyone like me, but that's not likely to happen," or "It would be nice if I never failed at anything, but it's unlikely that I will always succeed in everything I do." Such healthy mental and emotional responses encourage people to work toward constructively changing or coping with difficult situations (Ellis & Harper, 1975).

Albert Ellis is a colorful figure whose ideas have been extremely influential in psychotherapy (Haaga & Davison, 1993). Rational-emotive therapy is a popular approach in clinical practice, partly because it is straightforward and simple (Arnkoff & Glass, 1992). It has been shown to be generally effective in the treatment of depression, social phobia, and certain anxiety disorders. Rational-emotive therapy is also useful in helping people overcome self-defeating behaviors, such as excessive need for approval, extreme shyness, and chronic procrastination.

Aaron Beck and Cognitive Therapy

Aaron T. Beck (b. 1921) was initially trained as a psychoanalyst. Beck's development of **cognitive therapy,** abbreviated **CT,** grew out of his research on depression (Beck & others, 1979). Seeking to scientifically validate the psychoanalytic assumption that depressed patients "have a need to suffer,"

Beck began collecting data on the free associations and dreams of his depressed patients. What he found, however, was that his depressed patients did *not* have a need to suffer. In fact, his depressed patients often went to great lengths to avoid being rejected by others.

Instead, Beck discovered, depressed people have an extremely negative view of the past, present, and future (Beck & others, 1979). Rather than realistically evaluating their situation, depressed patients have developed a *negative cognitive bias,* consistently distorting their experiences in a negative way. Their negative perceptions of

cognitive therapy (CT)
A type of cognitive therapy, developed by psychiatrist Aaron T. Beck, that focuses on changing the client's unrealistic beliefs.

events and situations are shaped by deep-seated, self-deprecating beliefs, such as "I can't do anything right," "I'm worthless," or "I'm unlovable" (Beck, 1991). Beck's cognitive therapy essentially focuses on correcting the cognitive biases that underlie depression and other psychological disorders (see Table 14.5).

Beck's CT has much in common with Ellis's rational-emotive therapy. Like Ellis, Beck believes that what people think creates their moods and emotions. And like RET, CT involves helping clients to identify faulty thinking and to replace unhealthy patterns of thinking with healthier ones.

But in contrast with Ellis's emphasis on "irrational" thinking, Beck believes that depression and other psychological problems are caused by *distorted thinking* and *unrealistic beliefs* (Hollon & Beck, 1994; Arnkoff & Glass, 1992). Rather than logically debating the "irrationality" of a client's beliefs, the CT therapist encourages the client to *empirically test the accuracy of his or her assumptions and beliefs*. Let's look at how this process unfolds in Beck's CT.

The first step in CT is to help the client learn to recognize and monitor the automatic thoughts that occur without conscious effort or control (Beck, 1991). Whether negative or positive, automatic thoughts can control your mood and shape your emotional and behavioral reactions to events (Robins & Hayes, 1993). Because their perceptions are shaped by their negative cognitive biases, depressed people usually have automatic thoughts that reflect very negative interpretations of experiences. Not surprisingly, the result of such negative automatic thoughts is a deepened sense of depression, hopelessness, and helplessness.

In the second step of CT, the therapist helps the client learn how to *empirically test* the reality of the automatic thoughts that are so upsetting. For example, to test the belief that "I always say the wrong thing," the therapist might assign the person to initiate a conversation with three acquaintances and note how often he actually said the wrong thing.

Initially, the CT therapist acts as a model, showing the client how to evaluate the accuracy of automatic thoughts. The therapist hopes to eventually teach the client to do the same on her own. The CT therapist also strives to create a therapeutic climate of *collaboration* that encourages the client to contribute to the evaluation of the logic and accuracy of automatic thoughts (Robins & Hayes, 1993; Beck & others, 1979). This approach contrasts with the confrontational approach used by the RET therapist, who directly challenges the client's thoughts and beliefs.

TABLE 14.5 Cognitive Biases in Depression

Cognitive Bias (Error)	Description
Arbitrary inference	Drawing a negative conclusion when there is little or no evidence to support it.
Selective abstraction	Focusing on a single negative detail taken out of context, ignoring the more important aspects of the situation.
Overgeneralization	Drawing a sweeping, global conclusion based on an isolated incident and applying that conclusion to other unrelated areas of life.
Magnification and minimization	Grossly overestimating the impact of negative events and grossly underestimating the impact of positive events so that small, bad events are magnified, but good, large events are minimized.
Personalization	Taking responsibility, blaming oneself, or applying external events to oneself when there is no basis or evidence for making the connection.

SOURCE: Based on Beck & others (1979), p. 14.

According to Aaron Beck, depressed people perceive and interpret experience in very negative terms. They are prone to systematic errors in logic, or cognitive biases, which shape their negative interpretation of events. The table shows the most common cognitive biases in depression.

TABLE 14.6 Comparing Cognitive Therapies

Type of Therapy	Founder	Source of Problems	Treatment Techniques	Goals of Therapy
Rational-emotive therapy (RET)	Albert Ellis	Irrational beliefs	Very directive: Identify, logically dispute, and challenge irrational beliefs	Surrender of irrational beliefs and absolutist demands
Cognitive therapy (CT)	Aaron T. Beck	Unrealistic, distorted perceptions and interpretations of events due to cognitive biases	Directive collaboration: Teach client to monitor automatic thoughts; test accuracy of conclusions; correct distorted thinking and perception	Accurate and realistic perception of self, others, and external events

Beck's cognitive therapy has been shown to be very effective in treating depression and other psychological disorders, including anxiety disorders, eating disorders, posttraumatic stress disorder, and relationship problems (Beck, 1993; Chambless & Gillis, 1993; Klinger, 1993; Wilson & Fairburn, 1993). Beck's cognitive therapy techniques have even been adapted to help treat psychotic symptoms, such as the delusions and disorganized thought processes that often characterize schizophrenia (Alford & Correia, 1994; Chadwick & others, 1994).

Group and Family Therapy

Group therapy involves one or more therapists working with several people simultaneously. What are some key advantages of group therapy? What is family therapy, and how does it differ from individual therapy?

Individual psychotherapy offers a personal relationship between a client and a therapist, one that is focused on a single client's problems, thoughts, and emotions. But individual psychotherapy has certain limitations (Feldman & Powell, 1992). The therapist sees the client in isolation, rather than within the context of his interactions with others. Hence, the therapist must rely on the client's interpretation of reality and his description of his relationships with others.

Group Therapy

In contrast, **group therapy** involves one or more therapists working with several people simultaneously. Group therapy may be provided by a therapist in private practice or at a community mental health clinic. Often, group therapy is an important part of the treatment program for hospital inpatients (Kibel, 1993). Groups may be as small as three or four people or as large as ten or more people. Some therapy groups are made up of clients who share the same problem, but others are far more diverse.

Virtually any approach, whether psychodynamic, client-centered, behavioral, or cognitive, can be used in group therapy (Alonso & Swiller, 1993a). And just about any problem that can be handled individually can be dealt with in group therapy.

Group therapy has a number of advantages over individual psychotherapy (Dies, 1993). First, group therapy is very cost-effective: a single therapist can work simultaneously with several people. Thus, it is less expensive for the client and less time-consuming for the therapist. Second, rather than relying on a client's self-perceptions about how she relates to other people, the therapist can observe her actual interactions with others. Observing the way clients interact with others in a group may provide unique insights into their personalities and behavior patterns (Alonso & Swiller, 1993b; Porter, 1993).

Third, the support and encouragement provided by the other group members may help a person feel less alone and understand that his problems are not unique (Alonso & Swiller, 1993a). Fourth, group members may provide each other with helpful, practical advice for solving common problems and can act as models for successfully overcoming difficulties. Finally, working within a group gives people an opportunity to try out new behaviors in a safe, supportive environment (Porter, 1993). For instance, someone who is very shy and submissive can practice more assertive behaviors and receive honest feedback from other group members.

group therapy
A form of psychotherapy that involves one or more therapists working simultaneously with a small group of clients.

family therapy
A form of psychotherapy that is based on the assumption that the family is a system and that treats the family as a unit.

Group therapy is typically conducted by a mental health professional. In contrast, *self-help groups* and *support groups* are typically conducted by non-professionals. Support groups and self-help groups have become increasingly popular in the United States. Some therapists recommend self-help groups as an adjunct to traditional psychotherapy. As discussed in In Focus Box 14.1, the potential of these groups to promote mental health should not be underestimated.

Family and Couple Therapy

Most forms of psychotherapy, including most group therapies, tend to see a person's problems—and the solutions to those problems—as primarily originating within the individual himself. **Family therapy** operates on a different premise, focusing on the whole family rather than on an individual. The major goal of family therapy is to alter and improve the ongoing interactions among family members (Lebow & Gurman, 1995). Typically, family therapy involves every member of the family, even young children, and may also include important members of the extended family, such as grandparents or in-laws.

Family therapy is based on the assumption that the family is a *system,* an interdependent unit, not just a collection of separate individuals. The family is seen as a dynamic structure in which each member plays a unique role. According to this view, every family has certain unspoken "rules" of interaction and communication. Some of these tacit rules revolve around issues such as which family members exercise power and how, who makes decisions, who keeps the peace, and what kinds of alliances members have formed among themselves. As such issues are explored, unhealthy patterns of family interaction can be identified and replaced with new "rules" that promote the psychological health of the family as a unit.

Family therapy is often used to enhance the effectiveness of individual psychotherapy (Feldman & Powell, 1992). Very commonly, the therapist realizes that the individual client's problems reflect conflict and disturbance in the entire family system (Lebow & Gurman, 1995). In order for the client to make significant improvements, the family as a whole must become psychologically healthier. Family therapy is also indicated when there is conflict among family members, such as among parents and adolescent children, or when younger children are being treated for behavior problems, such as truancy or aggressive behavior (Kazdin, 1994b).

Many family therapists also provide *marital* or *couple therapy.* The term *couple therapy* is preferred today because such therapy is conducted with any couple in a committed relationship, whether they are married or unmarried, heterosexual or homosexual (Lebow & Gurman, 1995). As is the case with family therapy, there are many different approaches to couple therapy (Alexander & others, 1994). However, most couple therapies have the goal of improving communication and problem-solving skills and increasing intimacy between the pair.

A Family Therapy Session Family therapists typically work with all the members of a family at the same time, including young children. Doing so allows the family therapist to directly observe how family members interact, resolve differences, and exert control over one another. As unhealthy patterns of family interactions are identified, they can often be replaced with new patterns that promote the psychological well-being of the family as a whole.

Couple Therapy Couple therapy focuses on helping people who are in a committed relationship. Couple therapy usually emphasizes improving communication, increasing intimacy, and strengthening the relationship bond.

IN FOCUS 14.1

Self-Help Groups: Helping Yourself by Helping Others

Every month our local newspaper publishes a list of more than 300 self-help and support groups that meet in our area. These groups range from the familiar (Alcoholics Anonymous, Toughlove) to the obscure (Abused by Religion, Cult Awareness Group, Crossdressers of Green County), and from the general (Parents of Adolescents, Effective Black Parenting) to the specific (Multiple Sclerosis—Newly Diagnosed). There are groups for people with particular psychological problems, medical conditions, or problems with substance abuse. There are also groups for people dealing with life's transitions and crises, such as becoming a parent, divorce, retirement, or bereavement.

What this bewildering array of groups have in common is that all of them are organized and led by nonprofessionals. Typically, such groups are made up of members who have a common problem and meet for the purpose of exchanging psychological support (Jacobs & Goodman, 1989). Some groups are focused on psychological growth and change. Other groups have a more practical emphasis, providing information and advice (Carroll, 1993). The groups are either free or charge nominal fees to cover the cost of materials.

In the United States, the number of self-help groups is rapidly approaching 1 million. How many people belong to these groups? Estimates range from 7 million to 15 million people and growing (Christensen & Jacobson, 1994). In comparison, about 16 million people per year use professional mental health services, such as psychotherapy (Rutter, 1994). Clearly, self-help groups play an important and useful role in many people's lives.

The format of self-help groups varies enormously. Some groups are quite free-wheeling, but others are highly structured (McFadden & others, 1992). Meetings may follow a prescribed format, and there may be rules regulating contacts among group members outside the meetings. For example, our friend Marcia, whose story we told in the prologue, attends weekly meetings of a self-help group called Emotions Anonymous. In Marcia's group, each person takes a turn speaking for five minutes. Interruptions are not allowed, and other members simply listen without responding to the speaker's comments.

Many self-help groups follow a twelve-step approach, patterned after the famous twelve-step program of Alcoholics Anonymous. The twelve steps involve themes of admitting that you have a problem, seeking help from a "higher power," confessing your shortcomings, repairing your relationships with others, and helping other people who have the same problem. These twelve steps have been adapted by many different groups to fit their particular problem. Some psychologists criticize the twelve-step approach for its emphasis on the idea that people are "powerless" to cope with their problems on their own and must depend on a higher power and on other group members (Kasl, 1992).

Just how helpful are self-help groups? Research has shown that self-help groups are often just as effective as therapy provided by a mental health professional, at least for some psychological problems (Christensen & Jacobson, 1994). Given that many people cannot afford professional counseling, self-help groups may be a cost-effective alternative to psychotherapy for some people.

What is not known is *why* self-help groups are effective in helping people solve problems, change behaviors, and grow psychologically. Support and encouragement from others are undoubtedly important. So may be the "helper therapy" principle on which all self-help groups are based: people who help other people are themselves helped. But more research is needed to clarify the elements that contribute the most to a successful outcome. Research is also needed to identify the kinds of people and problems that are most likely to benefit from a self-help approach (Christensen & Jacobson, 1994).

An Alcoholics Anonymous Meeting Founded in 1935, *Alcoholics Anonymous* has more than two million members worldwide. People from all walks of life attend AA, and many credit AA for turning their lives around. Because AA group members are guaranteed anonymity, their faces cannot be shown in the photograph. Many other kinds of self-help groups are modeled on the AA program.

CONCEPT REVIEW 14.2

Types of Psychotherapy

Match each statement below with one of the following types of psychotherapy: psychoanalytic therapy, behavior therapy, humanistic therapy, cognitive therapy, family therapy.

1. Our problems are not the result of what happens to us, but instead are a function of our cognitive interpretations and irrational thinking about what happens to us. _____

2. Maladaptive behavior is learned in the same way as any other behavior. Improvement occurs when the environmental conditions are changed so that adaptive behavior is reinforced and maintained. _____

3. A client's psychological problems often reflect a disturbance or conflict in his or her family. If the client's family becomes psychologically more healthy, the client is more likely to improve. _____

4. The therapist's role is to be nondirective and to provide the client with unconditional positive regard and empathic understanding. _____

5. People can regain mental health only by developing insight into their hidden, unconscious conflicts through the techniques of free association, dream interpretation, and transference. _____

Evaluating the Effectiveness of Psychotherapy

> *In general, psychotherapy has been shown to be effective in helping people with psychological disorders. Is one form of psychotherapy superior to the others? What common factors contribute to effective psychotherapy? What is eclecticism?*

Let's start with a simple fact: Most people with psychological symptoms do *not* seek help from mental health professionals (Kessler & others, 1994). This suggests that most people eventually weather their psychological problems without professional intervention. Some people cope with psychological difficulties with the help and support of friends and family. And some people eventually improve simply with the passage of time, a phenomenon called *spontaneous remission* (see Eysenck, 1994, 1952). Does psychotherapy offer significant benefits over simply waiting for the possible "spontaneous remission" of symptoms?

The basic strategy to investigate this issue is to compare people who enter psychotherapy with a carefully selected, matched control group of people who do not receive psychotherapy (Kazdin, 1994a). During the last thirty years, hundreds of such studies have investigated the effectiveness of the major forms of psychotherapy (Seligman, 1995; Lambert & Bergin, 1994; Orlinsky & others, 1994). To combine and interpret the results of such large numbers of studies, researchers have used a statistical technique called *meta-analysis* (Lipsey & Wilson, 1993). Meta-analysis involves pooling the results of several studies into a single analysis, and essentially creates one large study that can reveal overall trends in the data.

When meta-analysis is used to summarize studies that compare people who receive psychotherapy treatment to no-treatment controls, researchers consistently arrive at the same conclusion: *Psychotherapy is significantly more effective than no treatment.* On the average, the person who completes psychotherapy treatment is better off than about 80 percent of those in the untreated control group (Lambert & Bergin, 1994; Lipsey & Wilson, 1993).

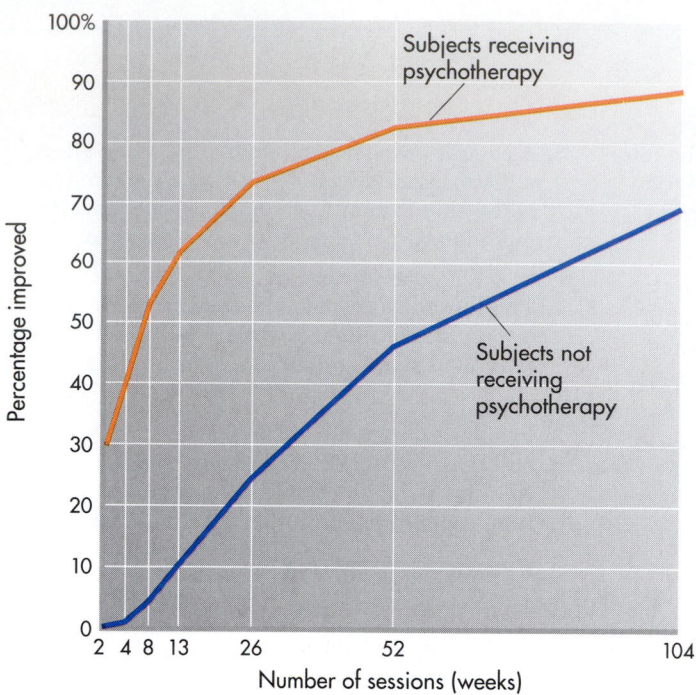

Percentage improved

Subjects receiving psychotherapy

Subjects not receiving psychotherapy

Number of sessions (weeks)

FIGURE 14.4 Psychotherapy Versus No Treatment
This graph depicts the rates of improvement for more than 2,000 people in weekly psychotherapy and for 500 people who did not receive psychotherapy. As you can see, after only eight weekly sessions, better than 50 percent of subjects receiving psychotherapy were significantly improved. After the same length of time, only 4 percent of subjects not receiving psychotherapy showed "spontaneous remission" of symptoms. Clearly, psychotherapy accelerates both the rate and degree of improvement for those experiencing psychological problems.
(Adapted from McNeilly & Howard, 1991.)

The benefits of psychotherapy are usually apparent in a relatively short period of time. As shown in Figure 14.4, approximately 50 percent of people show significant improvement by the eighth weekly session of psychotherapy. By the end of six months of weekly psychotherapy sessions, about 75 percent are significantly improved (McNeilly & Howard, 1991; Howard & others, 1986). The gains that people make as a result of psychotherapy also tend to endure long after the therapy has ended, sometimes for years (Lambert & Bergin, 1994). Even brief forms of psychotherapy tend to produce beneficial and long-lasting changes (Koss & Shiang, 1994).

Nevertheless, it's important to note that psychotherapy is not a miracle cure. While most people experience significant benefits from psychotherapy, not everyone benefits to the same degree. Some people who enter psychotherapy improve only slightly or not at all.

Is One Form of Psychotherapy Superior?

Given the very different assumptions and techniques used in the major types of psychotherapy, does one type of psychotherapy stand out as more effective than the others? In some cases, one type of psychotherapy is more effective than another in treating a particular problem. For example, cognitive and behavioral therapies tend to be more successful than insight-oriented therapies in helping people who are experiencing panic disorder, obsessive-compulsive disorder, and phobias (Hollon & Beck, 1994; Kazdin, 1994). Insight-oriented therapies are also less effective than other therapies in the treatment of disorders characterized by severe psychotic symptoms, such as schizophrenia (Mueser & Glynn, 1993).

However, when meta-analysis techniques are used to assess the collective results of treatment outcome studies, a surprising but consistent finding emerges: *In general, there is little or no difference in the effectiveness of different psychotherapies.* Despite sometimes dramatic differences in psychotherapy techniques, all of the standard psychotherapies have very similar success rates (Lambert & Bergin, 1994; Lipsey & Wilson, 1993).

What Factors Contribute to Effective Psychotherapy?

How can we explain the fact that very different forms of psychotherapy are basically equivalent in producing positive results? One possible explanation is that the factors that are crucial to producing improvement are present in *all* effective therapies. Researchers have identified a number of common factors that are related to a positive therapy outcome (Strupp, 1996; Lambert & Bergin, 1994).

First and most important is the quality of the *therapeutic relationship*. In effective psychotherapies, the therapist–client relationship is characterized

Therapeutic Sensitivity to Cultural Differences Therapist sensitivity to a client's cultural values can affect the ability to form a good working relationship and, ultimately, the success of psychotherapy. Thus, some clients prefer to see therapists who are from the same cultural background, as is the case of the Korean-American therapist and client shown. In general, therapists have become more attuned to the important role played by culture in effective psychotherapy.

by mutual respect, trust, and hope. Working in a cooperative alliance, both people are actively trying to achieve the same goals.

Second, certain *therapist characteristics* are associated with successful therapy. Effective therapists have a caring attitude and the ability to listen empathically. They are genuinely committed to their clients' welfare (Strupp, 1996). Regardless of orientation, effective therapists tend to be warm, sensitive, and responsive people, and they are perceived as sincere and genuine (Beutler & others, 1994).

Effective therapists are also sensitive to the *cultural differences* that may exist between themselves and their clients. As described in Culture and Human Behavior Box 14.2 on the next page, cultural differences can be a barrier to effective psychotherapy. Increasingly, training in cultural sensitivity and multicultural issues is being incorporated into psychological training programs in the United States (Edwards, 1995a; DeAngelis, 1994b).

Third, *client characteristics* are important. If the client is motivated, committed to therapy, and actively involved in the process, a successful outcome is much more likely. The ability to express thoughts and feelings, as well as the client's level of emotional and social maturity, also influence the likelihood of therapeutic success (Garfield, 1994; Koss & Shiang, 1994). Finally, *external circumstances,* such as a stable living situation and supportive family members, can enhance the effectiveness of therapy.

Notice that none of these factors is specific to any particular brand of psychotherapy. However, this does not mean that differences between psychotherapy techniques are completely irrelevant. Rather, it's important that there be a good "match" between the person seeking help and the specific psychotherapy techniques used. One person may be very comfortable with psychodynamic techniques, such as exploring childhood memories and free association. Another person might be more open to behavioral techniques, like systematic desensitization. For therapy to be optimally effective, the individual should feel comfortable with both the therapist and the therapist's approach to therapy.

Increasingly, such a personalized approach to therapy is being facilitated by the movement of mental health professionals toward **eclecticism**—the pragmatic and integrated use of diverse psychotherapy techniques (Garfield, 1992). Today, therapists identify themselves as eclectic more often than any other orientation (Garfield & Bergin, 1994). *Eclectic psychotherapists* carefully tailor the therapy approach to the problems and characteristics of the person seeking help. For example, an eclectic therapist might integrate insight-oriented techniques with specific behavioral techniques to help someone suffering from extreme shyness.

eclecticism
The pragmatic and integrated use of techniques from different psychotherapies.

CULTURE AND HUMAN BEHAVIOR 14.2

Cultural Values and Psychotherapy

The goals and techniques of many established approaches to psychotherapy tend to reflect European and North American cultural values. In this box, we'll look at how those cultural values can clash with the values of clients from other cultures, diminishing the effectiveness of psychotherapy.

A Focus on the Individual

In Western psychotherapy, the client is usually encouraged to become more assertive, more self-sufficient, and less dependent on others in making decisions and conducting his or her life. Problems are assumed to have an internal cause and are expected to be solved by the client alone. Therapy emphasizes meeting the client's individual needs, even if those needs conflict with the demands of significant others. In collectivistic cultures, however, the needs of the individual are much more strongly identified with the needs of the group to which he or she belongs (Triandis, 1994).

For example, traditional Native Americans are less likely than European-Americans to believe that personal problems are due to an internal cause within the individual (Sue, Zane, & Young, 1994). In some Native American cultures, personal problems are considered to be spiritual rather than "psychological" in nature. Thus, traditional Native Americans may turn to

spiritual leaders for help rather than psychologists or psychiatrists.

One person's problems may also be seen as a problem for the entire community to resolve. In traditional forms of Native American healing, family members, friends, and other members of the community may be asked to participate in the treatment or healing rituals. One type of therapy, called *network therapy*, is conducted in the person's home and can involve as many as 70 members of the individual's community or tribe (LaFromboise & others, 1993b).

Latino cultures, too, emphasize interdependence over independence. In particular, they stress the value of *familismo*—the importance of the extended family network. Because the sense of family is so central to Latino culture, psychologist Lilian Comas-Diaz (1993) recommends that members of the client's extended family, such as grandparents and in-laws, be actively involved in psychological treatment.

Like other collectivistic cultures, many Asian cultures emphasize a respect for the needs of others. The Japanese psychotherapy called *Naikan therapy* is a good example of how such cultural values affect the goals and practice of psychotherapy (Reynolds, 1990, 1989). According to Naikan therapy, being self-absorbed is the surest path to psychological suffering. Thus,

the goal of Naikan therapy is to replace the focus on the self with a sense of gratitude and obligation toward others. Rather than talking about how his own needs were not met by family members, the Naikan client is asked to meditate on how he has failed to meet the needs of others.

The Importance of Insight

Psychodynamic, humanistic, and cognitive therapies all stress the importance of insight or awareness of an individual's thoughts and feelings. But many cultures do *not* emphasize the importance of exploring painful thoughts and feelings in resolving psychological problems. For example, Asian cultures stress that mental health is enhanced by the avoidance of negative thinking. Hence, a depressed or anxious person in China and many other Asian countries would be encouraged to *avoid* focusing on upsetting thoughts. Because members of many Asian cultures believe that they can control their own mental health by exercising willpower, psychological problems are seen as shameful evidence of "weakness" (Sue, Zane, & Young, 1994).

Intimate Disclosure Between Therapist and Client

Many Western psychotherapies are based on the assumption that the clients will disclose their deepest feelings and most private thoughts to their therapist. But in many cultures, intimate details of one's personal life would never be discussed with a stranger. Asians are taught to disclose intimate details only to very close friends (Sue, Sue, & Sue, 1994). In many cultures, people are far more likely to turn to family members or friends than they are to mental health professionals. For example, among a group of Southeast Asian refugees, the majority would turn to family and friends for help with emotional or marital problems (Nishio & Bilmes, 1993).

The demand for emotional openness may also clash with cultural values. In Asian cultures, people tend to avoid the public expression of emotions and often express thoughts and feelings

Cultural Values Even after immigrating to the United States, many people maintain strong ties with their cultural heritage. Here, Arab-American children attend an Islamic school. Notice that the young female students as well as the teacher are wearing the traditional *chador,* or veil. The traditional beliefs of some cultures, such as the Islamic belief that women should be modest and obedient to their husbands, may conflict with the values inherent in Western psychotherapies.

nonverbally. Native American cultures tend to value the restraint of emotions rather than the open expression of emotions (LaFromboise & others, 1993b).

Recognizing the need for psychotherapists to become more culturally sensitive, the American Psychological Association has recommended formal training in multicultural awareness for all psychologists (Hall, 1997; Edwards, 1995a). The APA (1993) has also published a set of ethical guidelines for psychologists who provide psychological help to culturally diverse populations. The key points of the guidelines are shown in the accompanying table.

APA Ethical Guidelines for Counseling Culturally Diverse Populations

Psychologists should:

- Be aware of research and practice issues related to the specific population being served
- Be aware of how their own cultural background, experiences, values, and biases influence psychological processes, and make efforts to correct any prejudices and biases
- Incorporate an understanding of the client's ethnic and cultural background into their practice
- Help clients increase their awareness of their own cultural values
- Respect the roles of family members and community structures, hierarchies, values, and beliefs within the client's culture
- Respect clients' religious and spiritual beliefs and values

SOURCE: Excerpted from American Psychological Association, 1993.

Biomedical Therapies

Historical Treatments for Mental Illness
Left: An early treatment apparatus called the "circulating swing" involved spinning patients. Center: A "tranquilizing chair" was developed in the early 1800s to restrain and sedate unmanageable patients. Right: Found in Peru, this pre-Columbian skull shows the results of primitive surgery on the brain, called *trephining*, presumably as a treatment to allow evil spirits to leave the body.

The biomedical therapies are medical treatments for the symptoms of psychological disorders. What are the most important antipsychotic, antianxiety, and antidepressant medications, and how do they achieve their effects? What are their disadvantages? What are lithium and ECT, and how are they used?

Medical treatments for psychological disorders actually predate modern psychotherapy by hundreds of years. In past centuries, patients were whirled, soothed, drenched, restrained, and isolated—all in an attempt to alleviate symptoms of psychological disorders. Today, such "treatments" seem cruel, inhumane, and useless. Keep in mind, however, that these early treatments were based on the limited medical knowledge of the time. As you'll see in this section, some of the early efforts to treat psychological disorders did eventually evolve into treatments that are widely used today. For the most part, though, it was not until the twentieth century that effective biomedical therapies were developed to treat the symptoms of mental disorders.

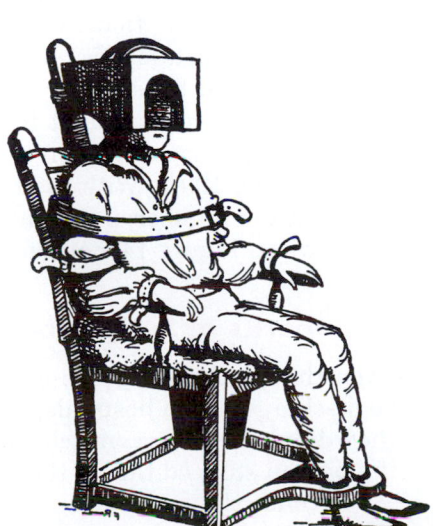

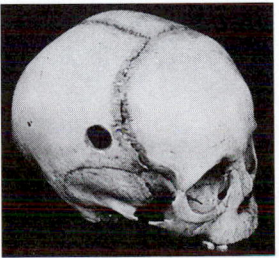

Today, the most common biomedical therapy is the use of *psychoactive medications*—prescription drugs that alter mental functions and alleviate psychological symptoms. In fact, of all medical prescriptions written today, 20 percent are for medications used to affect mental processes (Baldessarini, 1990). Although often used alone, psychoactive medications are increasingly being combined with psychotherapy.

Antipsychotic Medications

For more than 2,000 years, traditional practitioners of medicine in India used a herb derived from the snakeroot plant to diminish the psychotic symptoms commonly associated with schizophrenia: hallucinations, delusions, and disordered thought processes (Bhatara & others, 1997). The same plant was used in traditional Japanese medicine to treat anxiety and restlessness (Jilek, 1993). In the 1930s, Indian physicians developed a synthetic version of the herb's active ingredient, called *reserpine*. It was only in the 1950s that American scientists became aware of research in India demonstrating the effectiveness of reserpine in treating schizophrenia (Frankenburg, 1994).

It was also during the 1950s that French scientists began investigating the psychoactive properties of another drug, called *chlorpromazine*. Like reserpine, chlorpromazine diminished the psychotic symptoms commonly seen in schizophrenia. Hence, reserpine and chlorpromazine were dubbed **antipsychotic medications.** Because chlorpromazine had fewer side effects than reserpine, it nudged out reserpine as the preferred medication for treating schizophrenia-related symptoms. Today, chlorpromazine is better known by its trade name, *Thorazine,* and is still widely used to treat psychotic symptoms.

Reserpine and chlorpromazine act differently on the brain, but both drugs reduce levels of the neurotransmitter called *dopamine*. Since the development of these early drugs, more than thirty other antipsychotic medications have been developed (see Table 14.7). These antipsychotic medications also act on dopamine receptors in the brain (Klerman & others, 1994).

The first antipsychotics effectively reduced the so-called *positive symptoms* of schizophrenia—hallucinations, delusions, and disordered thinking (see Chapter 13). This therapeutic effect had a revolutionary impact on the number of people hospitalized for schizophrenia. Until the 1950s, patients suffering from schizophrenia were thought to be incurable. These chronic patients formed the bulk of the population on the "back wards" of psychiatric hospitals (Davison & Neale, 1994). With the introduction of the antipsychotic medications, however, the number of patients in mental hospitals decreased dramatically as shown in Figure 14.5 on the facing page.

TABLE 14.7 Commonly Prescribed Antipsychotic Drugs

	Generic Name	Trade Name
Typical Antipsychotics		
	Chlorpromazine	Thorazine
	Fluphenazine	Prolixin
	Trifluoperazine	Stelazine
	Thioridazine	Mellaril
	Thiothixene	Navane
	Haloperidol	Haldol
Atypical Antipsychotics		
	Clozapine	Clozaril
	Risperidone	Risperdal

SOURCE: Adapted from Julien, 1995, Table 11.1, p. 281.

Drawbacks of Antipsychotic Medications

Even though the early antipsychotic drugs allowed thousands of patients to be discharged from hospitals, these drugs had a number of drawbacks. First, they didn't actually *cure* schizophrenia. Psychotic symptoms often returned if a person stopped taking the medication.

Second, the early antipsychotic medications were not very effective in eliminating the *negative symptoms* of schizophrenia—social withdrawal, ap-

antipsychotic medications
Prescription drugs that are used to reduce psychotic symptoms; frequently used in the treatment of schizophrenia.

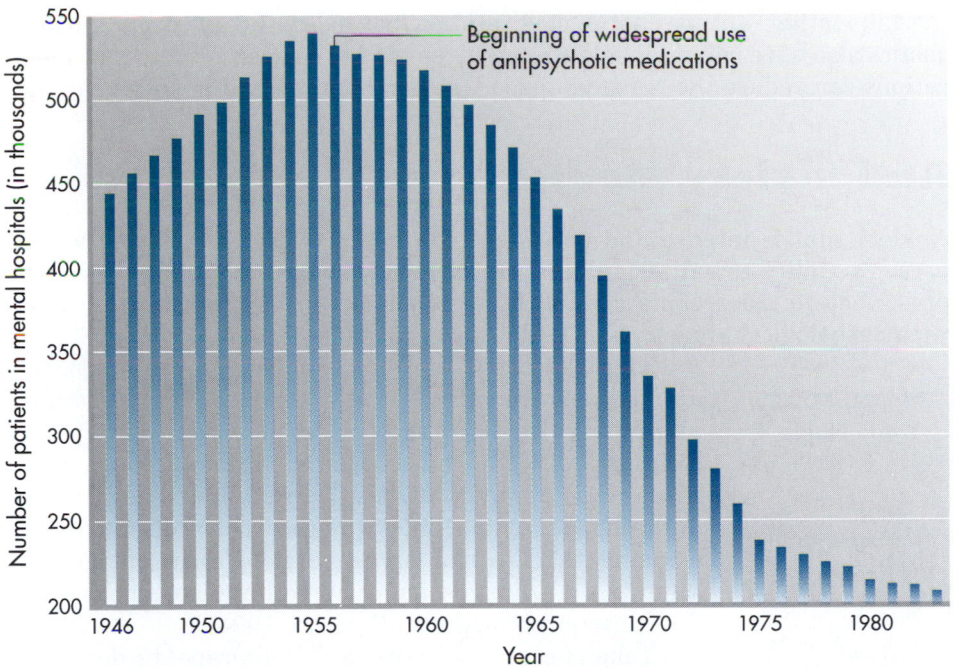

FIGURE 14.5 Change in the Number of Patients Hospitalized for Mental Disorders, 1946–1983

When the first antipsychotic drugs came into wide use in the late 1950s, the number of people hospitalized for mental disorders began to drop sharply.

(Adapted from Julien, 1995, Fig. 11.3, p. 276.)

athy, and lack of emotional expressiveness (Marder & others, 1993). In some cases, the drugs even made negative symptoms worse. Third, the antipsychotics often produced unwanted side effects, such as dry mouth, weight gain, constipation, sleepiness, and poor concentration (Gerlach & Peacock, 1994).

Fourth, the fact that the early antipsychotics *globally* altered brain levels of dopamine turned out to be a double-edged sword. Dopamine pathways in the brain are involved not only in psychotic symptoms but also in normal motor movements. Consequently, the early antipsychotic medications could produce motor-related side effects—muscle tremors, rigid movements, a shuffling gait, and a masklike facial expression (Barondes, 1993). This collection of side effects occurred so commonly that mental hospital staff members sometimes informally referred to it as the "Thorazine shuffle."

Even more disturbing, the long-term use of antipsychotic medications causes a small percentage of people to develop a potentially irreversible motor disorder called *tardive dyskinesia*. Tardive dyskinesia is characterized by severe, uncontrollable facial tics and grimaces, chewing movements, and other involuntary movements of the lips, jaw, and tongue (Marder & others, 1993).

Closely tied to the various side effects of the first antipsychotic drugs is a fifth problem: the "revolving door" pattern of hospitalization, discharge, and rehospitalization (Davison & Neale, 1994). Schizophrenic patients, once stabilized by antipsychotic medication, were released from hospitals into the community. But because of the medication's unpleasant side effects, inadequate medical followup, or both, many patients eventually stopped taking the medication. When psychotic symptoms returned, the patients were rehospitalized. Today, the majority of schizophrenic patients admitted to psychiatric facilities have been hospitalized before. Some patients have "revolved" between hospitals and the community more than forty times (Paul & Menditto, 1992).

The Atypical Antipsychotics

Recently, a new generation of antipsychotic drugs has given rise to increased optimism about the treatment of schizophrenia. Called *atypical antipsychotics,* these drugs act differently on the brain than the older antipsychotic drugs. The first atypical antipsychotics, *clozapine* and *risperidone,* affect levels of the neurotransmitter *serotonin* as well as dopamine in the brain.

Clozapine and risperidone have several advantages over the traditional antipsychotic drugs (Meltzer, 1995, 1994). Because they do not affect the area of the brain that controls movement, they are less likely to cause movement-related side effects. Instead, they act primarily on the dopamine receptors in the brain areas associated with psychotic symptoms. The atypical antipsychotics are also more effective in treating the negative symptoms of schizophrenia. Some patients who have not responded to any of the older antipsychotic drugs improve dramatically when they take clozapine or risperidone (Kane, 1994; Marder & Meibach, 1994).

antianxiety medications
Prescription drugs that are used to alleviate the symptoms of anxiety.

lithium
A naturally occurring substance that is used in the treatment of bipolar disorder.

Like other antipsychotic medications, however, the atypical antipsychotics also have potential side effects. It remains to be seen if these new medications can reduce the "revolving door" pattern of repeated hospitalization.

Antianxiety Medications

Anxiety that is intense and persistent can be disabling, interfering with a person's ability to eat, sleep, and function. **Antianxiety medications** are prescribed to help people deal with the problems and symptoms associated with pathological anxiety (see Table 14.8).

The best-known antianxiety drugs are the *benzodiazepines,* which include the trade-name drugs *Valium* and *Xanax.* These antianxiety medications calm jittery feelings, relax the muscles, and promote sleep. They take effect rapidly, usually within an hour or so. In general, the benzodiazepines produce their effects by increasing the level of *GABA,* a neurotransmitter that inhibits the transmission of nerve impulses in the brain and slows brain activity (Carlson, 1994).

TABLE 14.8 Antianxiety Drugs

	Generic Name	Trade Name
Benzodiazepines		
	Diazepam	Valium
	Chlordiazepoxide	Librium
	Lorazepam	Ativan
	Triazolam	Halcion
	Alprazolam	Xanax
Non-benzodiazepine		
	Buspirone	Buspar

SOURCE: Based on Julien, 1995, Table 4.1, p. 80.

Taken for a week or two, and in therapeutic doses, the benzodiazepines can effectively reduce anxiety levels. However, the benzodiazepines have several potentially dangerous side effects. First, they can reduce coordination, alertness, and reaction time. Second, their effects can be intensified when they are combined with alcohol and many other drugs, including over-the-counter antihistamines. Such a combination can produce severe drug intoxication, even death.

Third, the benzodiazepines are physically addictive if taken in large quantities or over a long period of time (Maxmen & Ward, 1995). If physical dependence occurs, the person must withdraw from the drug gradually, as abrupt withdrawal can produce life-threatening symptoms. Because of their addictive potential, the benzodiazepines are less widely prescribed today than they were twenty years ago.

A newer antianxiety drug with the trade name *Buspar* has fewer side effects. Exactly how Buspar works is uncertain, but it apparently relieves anxiety while maintaining normal alertness. Buspar does not cause drowsiness, sedation, or cognitive impairment, and it seems to have a very low risk of dependency and physical addiction (Julien, 1995). However, Buspar has one major drawback: it must be taken for two to three *weeks* before anxiety is reduced.

Lithium

In Chapter 13, on psychological disorders, we described *bipolar disorder,* more commonly known as *manic depression.* The medication used to treat bipolar disorder is **lithium,** a naturally occurring substance. Lithium counteracts both manic and depressive symptoms in bipolar patients (Barondes, 1993). Its effectiveness in treating bipolar disorder has been well established since the 1960s (Shou, 1993).

Lithium Water Lithium salt, a naturally occurring substance, was used in many over-the-counter medicines before it was discovered to be helpful in the treatment of mania. As this late-nineteenth-century ad shows, small amounts of lithium salt were also added to bottled water. An early version of the soft drink 7-Up included small amounts of lithium (Maxmen & Ward, 1995). Marketed as "lithium soda," the ad campaign claimed that it was the drink that took "the ouch out of the grouch!"

antidepressant medications
Prescription drugs that are used to reduce the symptoms associated with depression.

As a treatment for bipolar disorder, lithium stops acute manic episodes over the course of a week or two. Once an acute manic episode is under control, the long-term use of lithium can help prevent relapses into either mania or depression. The majority of bipolar disorder patients respond well to lithium therapy (Keck & McElroy, 1993).

Like all other medications, lithium has potential side effects. The patient's lithium blood level must be carefully monitored (Shou, 1993). If the lithium level is too low, manic symptoms persist. If it is too high, symptoms of lithium poisoning may occur, such as vomiting, muscle weakness, and reduced muscle coordination.

How lithium works is a complete mystery. Lithium's action is especially puzzling because lithium prevents mood disturbances at both ends of the emotional spectrum—mania *and* depression. Some researchers have suggested that lithium somehow regulates neurotransmission, evening out extremes in both directions (Barondes, 1993).

Recently, bipolar disorder has been treated with an anticonvulsant medicine called *Depakote,* originally used to prevent seizures in epileptics. Depakote seems to help bipolar patients who do not respond to lithium (Jefferson, 1995).

Antidepressant Medications

The **antidepressant medications** counteract the classic symptoms of depression—hopelessness, guilt, dejection, suicidal thoughts, difficulty concentrating, and disruptions in sleep, energy, appetite, and sexuality.

The first generation of antidepressant drugs consists of *tricyclics* and *MAO inhibitors.* (see Table 14.9) Tricyclics and MAO inhibitors affect multiple neurotransmitter pathways in the brain (Golden & Gilmore, 1990). Evidence suggests that these drugs alleviate depression by increasing the availability of two key brain neurotransmitters, *norepinephrine* and *serotonin.* However, even though brain levels of norepinephrine and serotonin begin to rise within *hours* of taking a tricyclic or MAO inhibitor, it can take up to six *weeks* before depressive symptoms begin to lift (Richelson, 1993).

Tricyclics and MAO inhibitors have been widely used for many years. In about 75 percent of depressed patients, they effectively eliminate depressive symptoms (Fawcett, 1994; Hornig-Rohan & Amsterdam, 1994). But these drugs can also produce numerous side effects. Tricyclic antidepressants can cause weight gain, dizziness, dry mouth and eyes, and sedation, and, because tricyclics affect the cardiovascular system, an overdose can be fatal. As for the MAO inhibitors, they can interact with a chemical found in many foods, including cheese, smoked meats, and red wine. Eating these foods while taking an MAO inhibitor can result in dangerously high blood pressure, leading to stroke or even death.

The search for antidepressants with fewer side effects led to the development of the second generation of antidepressants. Second-generation antidepressants include *trazodone* and *bupropion.* Although chemically different from the tricyclics, the second generation of antidepressants were generally no more effective than the first generation, and they turned out to have many of the same side effects (Kramer, 1993).

TABLE 14.9 Commonly Prescribed Antidepressant Drugs

	Generic Name	Trade Name
First-Generation Antidepressants		
Tricyclic antidepressants	Imipramine	Tofranil
	Desipramine	Norpramin
	Nortriptyline	Pamelor, Aventil
	Amitriptyline	Elavil
MAO inhibitors	Phenelzine	Nardil
	Tranylcypromine	Parnate
Second-Generation Antidepressants		
	Trazodone	Desyrel
	Bupropion	Wellbutrin
Selective Serotonin Reuptake Inhibitors (SSRIs)		
	Fluoxetine	Prozac
	Sertraline	Zoloft
	Paroxetine	Paxil
	Venlafaxine	Effexor

SOURCE: Based on Julien, 1995, Table 8.4, p. 198.

In 1987 the picture changed dramatically with the introduction of a third group of antidepressants, the *selective serotonin reuptake inhibitors,* abbreviated *SSRIs.* Rather than acting on multiple neurotransmitter pathways, the SSRIs primarily affect the availability of a single neurotransmitter—serotonin. Compared to the earlier antidepressants, the new antidepressants act much more selectively in targeting specific serotonin pathways in the brain. The first SSRI to be released was *fluoxetine,* which is better known by its trade name, *Prozac.* Prozac was quickly followed by its chemical cousins, *Zoloft* and *Paxil.*

Prozac was specifically designed to alleviate depressive symptoms with fewer side effects than earlier antidepressants. It achieved that goal with considerable success. Although no more effective than tricyclics or MAO inhibitors, Prozac and the other SSRI antidepressants tend to produce fewer, and milder, side effects. But remember, no medication is risk-free. Among Prozac's potential side effects are headaches, nervousness, difficulty sleeping, loss of appetite, and sexual dysfunction (Julien, 1995; Sleek, 1994).

Because of its overall effectiveness and relatively mild side-effect profile, Prozac quickly became very popular. By the early 1990s, an estimated *one million prescriptions per month* were being written for Prozac. Prozac's popularity raises some important issues: Is Prozac being overprescribed? Is it being prescribed for the wrong reasons? We tackle those issues in Critical Thinking Box 14.3, "Prozac: Better Living Through Chemistry?"

MOTHER GOOSE

Electroconvulsive Therapy

As we have just seen, millions of prescriptions are written for antidepressant medications in the United States every year. In contrast, about 40,000 patients a year receive **electroconvulsive therapy** or **ECT** as a medical treatment for severe depression (Abrams, 1992). Electroconvulsive therapy involves using a brief burst of electric current to induce a seizure in the brain, much like an epileptic seizure.

ECT is a painless, relatively quick medical procedure usually performed in a hospital (Khan & others, 1993). The patient lies on a table. Electrodes are placed on one or both of the patient's temples, and she is given a short-term, light anesthesia and muscle-relaxing drugs. To ensure adequate airflow, a breathing tube is placed in the patient's mouth.

While the patient is unconscious, a split-second burst of electricity induces a seizure. The seizure lasts for about a minute. Outwardly, the seizure typically produces mild muscle tremors. After the anesthesia wears off and the patient wakes up, he may be confused and disoriented. He may also experience temporary or permanent memory loss for the events leading up to the treatment (Devanand & others, 1994). To treat major depression, a series of six to ten ECT treatments are usually spaced over a few weeks.

ECT is a very effective treatment for severe depression, with a slightly higher overall effectiveness rate than the antidepressant drugs: about 80 percent of depressed patients improve (Maxmen & Ward, 1995). ECT relieves the symptoms of depression very quickly, typically within days. Because of its

electroconvulsive therapy (ECT)
A biomedical therapy used primarily in the treatment of depression that involves electrically inducing a brief brain seizure; also called *shock therapy* and *electric shock therapy.*

CRITICAL THINKING 14.3

Prozac: Better Living Through Chemistry?

Comic strips, comedy routines, talk shows—the buzz about the new "wonder drug" Prozac seems to be everywhere. Don't like your job? "Hey, take a Prozac," says a co-worker. The kids driving you crazy? Prozac will help. Can't seem to concentrate on your studies? Maybe Prozac is the answer. Need a confidence booster to help you get ahead in that new job? No problem—Prozac ought to do the trick.

Those are just some examples of the hype surrounding Prozac and its chemical cousins, Zoloft and Paxil. The popularity of these new antidepressants is unprecedented and undeniable. Since Prozac was introduced, over 6 million people have taken it in the United States alone—and over 20 million worldwide.

In some ways, that's good news. If anything, depression is underdiagnosed and undertreated. So if a new antidepressant comes along that effectively alleviates depressive symptoms in millions of people and has minimal side effects, that's no small accomplishment. Still, a word of caution is in order. Tinkering with the delicate balance of brain neurotransmitters is not to be taken lightly. Even though Prozac appears to be relatively safe, it hasn't been around long enough for anyone to know what its long-term effects might be (Sleek, 1994; Breggin & Breggin, 1994).

The very popularity of Prozac has drawn media attention to the antidepressant medications and has fueled misconceptions about their effects. It's simply inaccurate to label Prozac, or any other antidepressant, as a "don't-worry-be-happy pill." Prozac does *not* transform a seriously depressed person into someone who is perpetually light-hearted, confident, and on top of the world.

Instead, Prozac and other antidepressants help depressed people recover their *normal* level of psychological and physical energy, including the *normal* experience of the emotional ups and downs of everyday life. Rather than creating a supercharged, ultra-happy, carefree person, Prozac helps the seriously depressed person regain a normal level of functioning. Thus, prescribing antidepressants for depression is analogous to prescribing glasses for the nearsighted or insulin for the diabetic.

Prozac alone, of course, won't solve the problems that often contribute to major depression (Sleek, 1995). However, once a person's depressive symptoms have been alleviated, he or she may be able to cope with and resolve life problems in a healthier way.

Prozac's popularity makes many psychologists and other mental health professionals uncomfortable for another reason (Sleek, 1994). Some psychologists fear that Prozac is being overprescribed—and prescribed for the wrong reasons. According to media headlines, science now provides the opportunity to "change your personality with a pill." Prozac has raised "the prospect of nothing less than made-to-order, off-the-shelf personalities" (see Begley, 1994; Cowley, 1994). And in his best-selling book, *Listening to Prozac,* psychiatrist Peter Kramer (1993) describes how Prozac can be used to "transform your sense of self."

Prescribing Prozac to someone who is suffering from debilitating depression or some other serious psychological disorder is one matter. It's another matter altogether to prescribe Prozac or another drug to "transform" normal people and to make them more outgoing, productive, competitive, or self-confident. Or is it?

Thus far, the media claims that Prozac can enhance normal personality remain just that—anecdotal reports that have gotten a lot of play in the media. No controlled, scientific research has established that Prozac, or any other psychoactive drug, can "transform" normal personality or permanently alter basic personality traits (see Rosenhan & Seligman, 1995; Bower, 1994b).

But for the sake of argument, let's assume that Prozac could transform a normal personality into "better than well" by making a person more mellow, cheerful, self-assured, productive, optimistic, focused, thoughtful, and alive—all qualities that have been attributed to the effects of Prozac (see Begley, 1994; Kramer, 1993). Given this assumption, should Prozac be prescribed to people who are *not* clinically depressed but want to enhance their mental performance, emotional stability, and sense of psychological well-being?

Before you answer, consider the ready availability of nose jobs, facelifts, hair transplants, and tummy tucks. Our society generally approves of cosmetic surgery, especially if the surgery results in improved well-being and self-confidence. Well, if cosmetic surgery to enhance your appearance is okay, why not "cosmetic pharmacology" to chemically enhance your personality?

Here's another thought. Most cultures, including ours, have a long tradition of using psychoactive drugs to improve performance. And most of us already use all sorts of "artificial" substances to change our moods and enhance our performance (Schwartz, 1991). Caffeine, nicotine, and chocolate immediately come to mind. Even behaviors such as exercising and listening to music can be used to alter how we feel or think.

According to neuroscientist Richard Restak (1994), the development of psychoactive drugs like Prozac signals the prospect of drugs "aimed not so much at 'patients' as at people who are already functioning on a high level." Restak makes a bold claim: "For the first time in human history, we will be in a position to design our own brain." Assuming that such claims have some foundation, here's the critical issue: *Should* we be in that position? *Should* Prozac or any other psychoactive drug be used to enhance normal personality and psychological functioning? Have a cup of coffee and think it over.

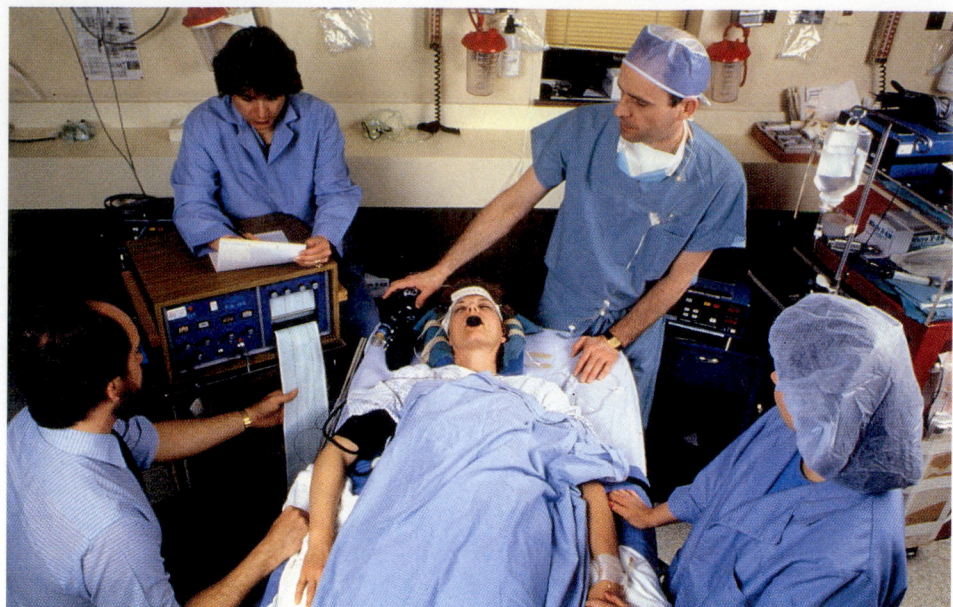

Electroconvulsive Therapy ECT is still used in the treatment of depression, especially in people who do not respond to antidepressant medication. In modern ECT, the person is given a short-acting anesthetic and muscle relaxants. A mild seizure, which lasts about a minute, is induced by a brief pulse of electricity.

rapid therapeutic effects, ECT can be a lifesaving procedure for extremely suicidal or severely depressed patients. Such patients may not survive for the several weeks it takes for antidepressant drugs to improve symptoms (Barondes, 1993).

ECT may also be considered when patients are not helped by antidepressant medications or psychotherapy, or when they cannot tolerate the side effects of medications. For some people, such as elderly individuals, ECT may be less dangerous than antidepressant drugs (Maxmen & Ward, 1995). In general, the complication rate from ECT is very low.

Nevertheless, inducing a brain seizure has potential dangers. Serious cognitive impairments can occur, such as extensive amnesia and disturbances in language and verbal abilities. However, fears that ECT might produce brain damage have not been confirmed by research (Devanand & others, 1994). ECT's biggest drawback is that its antidepressive effects can be short-lived. Relapses within four months are relatively common.

ECT is probably the single most controversial medical treatment for psychological disorders (Fink, 1991). Not everyone agrees that ECT is either safe or effective (Breggin, 1991, 1979). For example, ECT has been banned in some countries, like Japan, because of concerns about its safety.

How does ECT work? Despite more than fifty years of research, psychiatrists still have *no* idea why electrically inducing a convulsion relieves the symptoms of depression (O'Connor, 1993; Kapur & Mann, 1993).

As we've seen throughout this chapter, a wide range of therapies are available to help people who are troubled by psychological symptoms and disorders. Increasingly, people are being helped by a combination of psychotherapy and biomedical therapy, usually one of the psychoactive medications. In our chapter Application, "What to Expect in Psychotherapy," we discuss some general ground rules of psychotherapy, dispel some common misunderstandings, and describe the attitudes that should be brought to the therapeutic relationship.

CONCEPT REVIEW 14.3

Biomedical Therapies

Match each statement below with one of the following terms: atypical antipsychotic medications, antipsychotic medications, antidepressant medications, ECT, antianxiety medications, lithium.

1. The most controversial biomedical therapy. _____

2. Used in the treatment of bipolar disorder. _____

3. Drugs that globally reduce dopamine levels in the brain. _____

4. Drugs that produce their effects by increasing brain levels of GABA. _____

5. Drugs that effectively reduce both positive and negative symptoms of schizophrenia. _____

6. A category of psychoactive drugs that includes SSRIs. _____

What to Expect in Psychotherapy

The therapy relationship is different from all other close relationships. On the one hand, the therapist–client relationship is characterized by intimacy and the disclosure of very private, personal experiences. On the other hand, there are distinct boundaries to the therapist–client relationship.

The following guidelines should help you develop realistic expectations about the therapist–client relationship and the psychotherapy process.

1. Therapy Is a Collaborative Effort

Don't expect your therapist to do all the work for you. If you are going to benefit from psychotherapy, you must actively participate in the therapeutic process. Often, therapy requires effort *outside* the therapy sessions, such as keeping a diary of your thoughts and behaviors or rehearsing skills that you've learned in therapy.

2. Don't Expect Your Therapist to Make Decisions for You

Virtually all forms of therapy are designed to increase a person's sense of responsibility, confidence, and mastery in dealing with life's problems. Your therapist won't make your decisions for you, but he or she *will* help you explore your feelings about important decisions—including ambivalence or fear. If your therapist made decisions for you, it would only foster dependency and undermine your ability to be responsible for your own life.

3. Your Therapist Is Not a Substitute Friend

Unlike friendship, which is characterized by a mutual give and take, psychotherapy is focused solely on *you.* Think of your therapist as an expert consultant—someone you've hired to help you deal better with your problems. The fact that your therapist is not socially or personally involved with you allows your therapist to respond objectively and honestly.

4. Therapeutic Intimacy Does Not Include Sexual Intimacy

It's very common for clients to have strong feelings of affection, love, and even sexual attraction toward their therapist (Pope & Tabachnick, 1993). After all, the most effective therapists tend to be warm, empathic people who are genuinely caring and supportive (Beutler & others, 1994). However, *it is never ethical or appropriate for a therapist to have any form of sexual contact with a client.* There are *no* exceptions to that statement. Sexual contact between a therapist and a client violates the ethical standards of all mental health professionals.

Sexual involvement between client and therapist can be enormously damaging (Pope, 1990). Not only does it destroy the therapist's professional objectivity in the therapist–client relationship, but it also destroys the trust the client has invested in the therapist. When a therapist becomes sexually involved with a client, regardless of who initiated the sexual contact, the client is being exploited.

Rather than exploiting a client's feelings of sexual attraction, an ethical therapist will help the client understand and work through such feelings. Therapy should ultimately help you develop closer, more loving relationships with other people—but *not* with your therapist.

5. Expect Therapy to Challenge How You Think and Act

Think of therapy as a psychological magnifying glass. Therapy tends to magnify both your strengths and weaknesses. Such intense self-scrutiny is not always flattering. You may have to acknowledge your own immature, maladaptive, or destructive behavior patterns. Although it can be painful, becoming aware that changes are needed is a necessary step toward developing healthier forms of thinking and behavior.

6. Don't Confuse Insight with Change

Developing insight into the sources or nature of your psychological problems does not magically resolve them. Nor does insight automatically translate into healthier thoughts and behaviors. Instead, insight allows you to look at and understand your problems in a new light. The opportunity for change occurs when your therapist helps you use these insights to redefine past experiences, resolve psychological conflicts, and explore more adaptive forms of behavior.

7. Don't Confuse Catharsis with Change

Catharsis refers to the emotional release that people experience from the simple act of talking about their problems. Although it usually produces short-term emotional relief, catharsis in itself does not resolve the problem. However, discussing emotionally charged issues with a therapist can lessen your sense of psychological tension and urgency, and help you explore the problem more rationally and objectively.

8. Don't Expect Change to Happen Overnight

Change occurs in psychotherapy at different rates for different people. How quickly change occurs depends on many factors, such as the seriousness of your problems, the degree to which you are psychologically ready to make needed changes, and the therapist's skill in helping you implement those changes. As a general rule, most people make significant progress in a few months of weekly therapy sessions (McNeilly & Howard, 1991). You can help create the climate for change by choosing a therapist with whom you feel comfortable and by genuinely investing yourself in the therapy process.

Summary Therapies

Psychotherapy and Biomedical Therapy

■ Psychological disorders can be treated with psychotherapy or biomedical therapy. Psychotherapy is based on the assumption that psychological factors play an important role in psychological disorders and symptoms. The biomedical therapies are based on the assumption that biological factors play an important role in psychological disorders and symptoms.

Psychoanalytic Therapy

■ Psychoanalysis is a form of therapy developed by Sigmund Freud and based on his theory of personality. The goal of psychoanalysis is to unearth repressed conflicts and resolve them in therapy.

■ Psychoanalytic techniques and processes include free association, dream interpretation, resistance, interpretation, and transference. Traditional psychoanalysis involves an intensive, long-term relationship between the patient and the psychoanalyst.

■ Short-term dynamic therapies are based on psychoanalytic ideas, but are more problem-focused and shorter than traditional psychoanalysis. Therapists play a more directive role than traditional psychoanalysts, but still they use psychoanalytic techniques to help the patient resolve unconscious conflicts.

Humanistic Therapy

■ Client-centered therapy was developed by Carl Rogers. Important aspects of client-centered therapy include a client who directs the focus of therapy sessions and a therapist who is genuine, demonstrates unconditional positive regard, and communicates empathic understanding.

■ According to Rogers, clients change and grow when their self-concept becomes healthier as a result of these therapeutic conditions.

Behavior Therapy

■ Behavior therapy assumes that maladaptive behaviors are learned and uses learning principles to directly change problem behaviors.

■ Mary Cover Jones was the first behavior therapist, using the procedure of counterconditioning to extinguish phobic behavior in a child.

■ Classical conditioning principles are involved in the use of systematic desensitization to treat phobias, the bell and pad treatment to treat bedwetting, and aversive conditioning to treat harmful behaviors like smoking and alcohol addiction.

■ Operant conditioning techniques include using positive reinforcement for desired behaviors and extinction for un-

desired behaviors. The token economy represents the application of operant conditioning to modify the behavior of people in groups.

Cognitive Therapies

■ The cognitive therapies are based on the assumption that psychological problems are caused by maladaptive patterns of thinking. Treatment focuses on changing unhealthy thinking patterns to healthier ones.

■ Rational-emotive therapy (RET) was developed by Albert Ellis. RET focuses on changing the irrational thinking that is assumed to be the cause of emotional distress and psychological problems.

■ Rational-emotive therapy involves identifying core irrational beliefs; disputing and challenging irrational beliefs; and teaching clients to recognize and dispute their own irrational beliefs.

■ Cognitive therapy (CT) was developed by Aaron T. Beck. CT is based on the assumption that psychological problems are caused by unrealistic and distorted thinking.

■ Beck's cognitive therapy involves teaching the client to recognize negative automatic thoughts and biases and to empirically test the reality of the upsetting automatic thoughts.

Group and Family Therapy

■ Group therapy involves one or more therapists working with several people simultaneously. Group therapy has these advantages: it is cost-effective; therapists can observe clients interacting with other group members; clients benefit from the support, encouragement, and practical suggestions provided by other group members; and people can try out new behaviors in a safe, supportive environment.

■ Family therapy focuses on the family rather than the individual and is based on the assumption that the family is an interdependent system. Marital or couple therapy focuses on improving communication, problem-solving skills, and intimacy between members of a couple.

Evaluating the Effectiveness of Psychotherapy

■ In general, psychotherapy has been shown to be significantly more effective than no treatment. Meta-analysis has been used to combine the findings of many different studies on the effectiveness of psychotherapy.

■ Among the standard psychotherapies, no particular form of therapy is generally superior to the others. However, to treat some specific problems, one type of therapy may prove more effective than other approaches.

- Factors identified as crucial to therapy's effectiveness include: the quality of the therapeutic relationship; therapist characteristics; therapists' sensitivity to cultural differences; client characteristics; and supportive, stable external circumstances.
- Most psychotherapists today identify their orientation as eclectic, meaning that they integrate the techniques of more than one form of psychotherapy, tailoring their approach to the individual client's needs.

Biomedical Therapies

- The most common biomedical therapy is psychoactive medication, which must be prescribed by a physician.
- Antipsychotic medications include reserpine and chlorpromazine, which alter dopamine levels in the brain. While chlorpromazine and reserpine reduce positive symptoms of schizophrenia, they have little or no effect on negative symptoms. They also have potential side effects, including the development of tardive dyskinesia after long-term use.
- The new atypical antipsychotics include clozapine and risperidone, which affect both serotonin and dopamine levels in the brain. The atypical antipsychotics have fewer side effects and are more effective in treating both the positive and negative symptoms of schizophrenia.
- Antianxiety medications include the benzodiazepines. The benzodiazepines are effective in the treatment of anxiety, but are potentially addictive and have many side effects. Buspar is a newer antianxiety medication that is apparently nonaddictive.
- Lithium is effective in the treatment of bipolar disorder, although its mechanism of action is unknown. A new drug called Depakote has recently been introduced as a drug treatment for bipolar disorder.
- Antidepressant medications include the tricyclics, the MAO inhibitors, and the second-generation antidepressants. More recent antidepressants, called SSRIs, selectively inhibit the reuptake of serotonin. While their effectiveness is similar to that of older antidepressants, the SSRIs have far fewer side effects.
- Electroconvulsive therapy (ECT), which involves delivering a brief electric shock to the brain, is used in treating severe depression. There is a great deal of controversy over ECT. The therapeutic effects of ECT tend to be short-lived, lasting no more than a few months. Partly because it is controversial, ECT is used far less frequently than antidepressant medication in the treatment of depression.

Key Terms

psychotherapy (p. 498)
biomedical therapies (p. 499)
psychoanalysis (p. 499)
free association (p. 500)
resistance (p. 500)
dream interpretation (p. 500)
interpretation (p. 500)
transference (p. 500)
client-centered therapy (p. 502)
behavior therapy (p. 504)
counterconditioning (p. 505)
systematic desensitization (p. 505)
bell and pad treatment (p. 506)
aversive conditioning (p. 506)
token economy (p. 507)
cognitive therapies (p. 508)
rational-emotive therapy (RET) (p. 509)
cognitive therapy (CT) (p. 510)
group therapy (p. 512)
family therapy (p. 513)
eclecticism (p. 517)
antipsychotic medications (p. 520)
antianxiety medications (p. 522)
lithium (p. 522)
antidepressant medications (p. 523)
electroconvulsive therapy (ECT) (p. 524)

Key People

Aaron T. Beck (b. 1921) American psychiatrist who founded cognitive therapy (CT), a psychotherapy based on the assumption that depression and other psychological problems are caused by biased perceptions, distorted thinking, and inaccurate beliefs.

Albert Ellis (b. 1913) American psychologist who founded the cognitive psychotherapy called rational-emotive therapy (RET), which emphasizes recognizing and changing irrational beliefs.

Sigmund Freud (1856–1939) Austrian physician and founder of psychoanalysis who theorized that psychological symptoms are the result of unconscious and unresolved conflicts stemming from early childhood. (Also see Chapter 10.)

Mary Cover Jones (1896–1987) American psychologist who conducted the first clinical demonstrations of behavior therapy.

Carl Rogers (1902–1987) American psychologist who helped found humanistic psychology and developed client-centered therapy. (Also see Chapter 10.)

CONCEPT REVIEW 14.1 Page 508

1. Behavior therapy; token economy
2. Psychoanalytic; free association
3. Behavior therapy; bell and pad treatment
4. Psychoanalytic; transference
5. Humanistic: unconditional positive regard
6. Behavior therapy; systematic desensitization

CONCEPT REVIEW 14.2 Page 515

1. cognitive therapy
2. behavior therapy
3. family therapy
4. humanistic therapy
5. psychoanalytic therapy

CONCEPT REVIEW 14.3 Page 526

1. ECT
2. lithium
3. antipsychotic medications
4. antianxiety medications
5. atypical antipsychotic medications
6. antidepressant medications

Appendix

Marie D. Thomas
California State University, San Marcos

Statistics: Understanding Data

Prologue: The Tables Are Turned: A Psychologist Becomes a Research Subject

From December 1994 to December 1995 I participated in a research project designed to compare the effects of "traditional" and "alternative" diet, exercise, and stress-reduction programs.* Volunteers assigned randomly to the *traditional* program were taught to eat a high-fiber, low-fat diet, do regular aerobic exercise, and practice a progressive muscle relaxation technique (described in Chapter 13). Participants in the *alternative* program received instruction in yoga and in a meditation technique, and a diet based on body type and tastes. A *no-treatment* control group was monitored throughout the year for weight and general health but received no diet, exercise, or stress-reduction intervention. (I was in the control group.)

Fifteen thousand invitations to participate in this study were sent in late 1994 to members of a large medical group. Out of that initial pool, 124 volunteers were recruited, and about 40 were randomly selected for each group (*traditional, alternative,* and *no treatment,* or control). The participants included women and men between the ages of 20 and 56. A total of 88 subjects lasted the full year. The researchers were pleased that so many of us stayed with the project; it isn't easy to get people to commit to a year-long study!

*Riegel, B., Simon, D., Weaver, J., Carlson, B., Clapton, P., & Gocka, I. (1996). Ayurvedic Medicine Demonstration Project, 1 R21 RR09726-01. Report submitted to National Institutes of Health, Institute for Alternative Medicine.

Data collection began even before participants found out the group to which they had been randomly assigned. We were mailed a thick packet of questionnaires covering a wide range of topics. The questions asked about our current health status, use of prescription and over-the-counter medications, use of vitamins, and visits to both physicians and alternative health-care practitioners. Another questionnaire focused on self-perceptions of health and well-being. Here we rated our mood, energy level, physical symptoms, and health in general. A lifestyle survey requested information about diet (how often did we eat red meat? how many servings of fruits and vegetables did we consume a day?), exercise (how many times per week did we do aerobic exercise?), and behavior (such as cigarette smoking and consumption of alcoholic beverages). The lifestyle survey also assessed psychological variables such as levels of stress and happiness, and how well we felt we were coping.

At our first meeting with the researchers, we handed in the questionnaires and were told which of the three groups we had been assigned to. We returned early the next morning to have our blood pressure and weight measured and to have blood drawn for tests of our levels of cholesterol, triglycerides, and glucose. The two intervention groups also received a weekend of training in their respective programs. In addition to daily practice of the techniques they had been taught, people in the *traditional* and *alternative* groups were expected to maintain a "compliance diary"—a daily record of their exercise, diet, and relaxation/meditation activities. The purpose of this diary was to determine whether health outcomes were better for people who practiced the techniques regularly. At first I was disappointed when I was randomly chosen for the control group, because I was especially interested in learning the "alternative" techniques. However, I was relieved later, when I found out how much detailed record keeping the intervention groups had to do!

The researchers accumulated even more data over the year-long period. Every three months, our blood pressure and weight were measured. At 6 months and 12 months, the researchers performed blood tests and asked us to fill out questionnaires identical to those at the beginning of the project.

The study included many variables. The most important independent variable (the variable that the researcher *manipulates*) was group assignment: *traditional* program, *alternative* program, and *no-treatment* control. The dependent variables (variables that are not directly manipulated by the researcher but that may change in response to manipulations of the independent variable) included weight, blood pressure, cholesterol level, self-perceptions regarding health, and mood. Since the dependent variables were measured several times, researchers could study changes in them over the course of the year.

This study can help to answer important questions about the kinds of programs that tend to promote health. But the purpose of describing it here is not just to tell you whether the two intervention programs were effective and whether one worked better than the other. Instead, I use this study as a tool for explaining how researchers use statistics to help them summarize findings and draw legitimate conclusions from them. The job of assessing the legitimacy of conclusions drawn from research findings is the domain of *inferential statistics*, which I'll discuss at the end of this appendix. I begin by exploring the task of summarizing findings in ways that are brief yet meaningful and easy to understand. For this, researchers use *descriptive statistics*.

Descriptive Statistics

descriptive statistics
Statistics used to organize and summarize data in a meaningful way.

The study on programs to promote health generated a large amount of data. How did the researchers make sense of such a mass of information? How did they summarize it in meaningful ways? The answer lies in descriptive statistics. **Descriptive statistics** do just what their name suggests—they

frequency distribution

A summary of how often various scores occur in a sample of scores. Score values are arranged in order of magnitude and the number of times each score occurs is recorded.

histogram

A way of graphically representing a frequency distribution; a type of bar chart using vertical bars that touch.

describe data. There are many ways to describe information. In this appendix we examine four of the most commonly used ways: frequency distributions, measures of central tendency, measures of variability, and measures of relationships. Since I don't have access to all the data that the health-promotion researchers gathered, I'll use hypothetical numbers to illustrate these statistical concepts.

Frequency Distributions

Suppose that at the start of the health-promotion study 30 people in the *traditional* group reported getting the following number of hours of aerobic exercise each week:

2, 5, 0, 1, 2, 2, 7, 0, 6, 2, 3, 1, 4, 5, 2, 1, 1, 3, 2, 1, 0, 4, 2, 3, 0, 1, 2, 3, 4, 1

Even with only 30 cases, it is difficult to make much sense of these data. Researchers need a way to organize such *raw scores* so that the information makes sense at a glance. One way to organize the data is to determine how many participants reported exercising 0 hours per week, how many reported exercising 1 hour, and so on, until all the reported amounts are accounted for. If put into a table, the data would look like Table A.1.

This table is one way of presenting a **frequency distribution**—a summary of how often various scores occur. Categories are set up (in this case, the number of hours of aerobic exercise per week), and occurrences of each category are tallied to give the frequency of each one.

What information can be gathered from this frequency distribution table? We know immediately that most of the participants did aerobic exercise less than 3 hours per week. The number of hours per week peaked at 2 hours, and declined steadily thereafter. According to the table, the most diligent exerciser worked out about an hour per day.

Some frequency distribution tables include an extra column that shows the percentage of cases in each category. For example, what percentage of participants reported 2 hours of aerobic exercise per week? The percentage is calculated by dividing the category frequency (8) by the total number of people (30), which yields about 27 percent.

While a table is good for summarizing data, it is often useful to present a frequency distribution visually through graphs. One type of graph is the **histogram** (see Figure A.1). A histogram is like a bar chart with two special features: the bars are always vertical, and they always touch. Categories (in our example, the number of hours of aerobic exercise per week) are placed on the X (horizontal) axis, while the Y (vertical) axis shows the frequency of each category. The resulting graph looks something like a city skyline, with buildings of different heights.

TABLE A.1   A Frequency Distribution Table

Hours of Aerobic Exercise per Week	Frequency
0	4
1	7
2	8
3	4
4	3
5	2
6	1
7	1
	30

A table like this is one way of presenting a frequency distribution. It shows at a glance that most of the people in our hypothetical group of 30 were not zealous exercisers before they began their traditional health-promotion program. Nearly two-thirds of them (19 people) engaged in vigorous exercise for 2 hours or less each week.

FIGURE A.1   A Histogram

This histogram is another way of presenting the data given in Table A.1. Like the table, the histogram shows that most people do, at best, only a moderate amount of aerobic exercise (2 hours or less each week). This is immediately clear from the fact that the highest bars on the chart are on the left, where the hours of exercise are lowest.

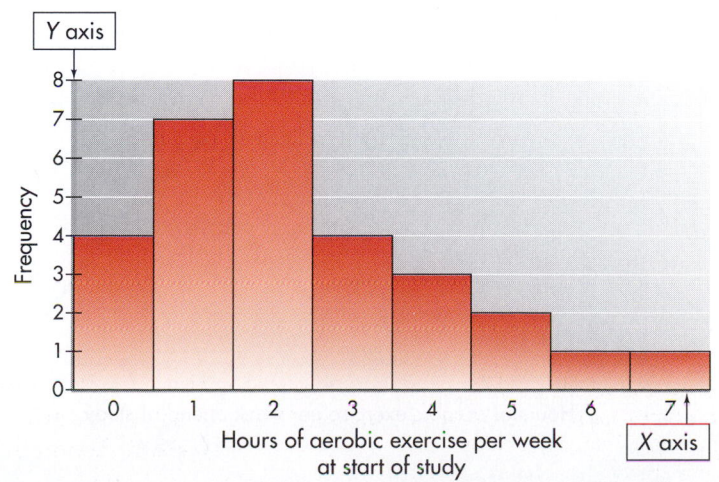

Hours of aerobic exercise per week at start of study

Another way of graphing the same data is with a **frequency polygon,** shown in Figure A.2. A mark is made above each category at the point representing its frequency. These marks are then connected by straight lines. In our example, the polygon begins before the "0" category and ends at a category of "8," even though both these categories have no cases in them. This is traditionally done so that the polygon is a closed figure.

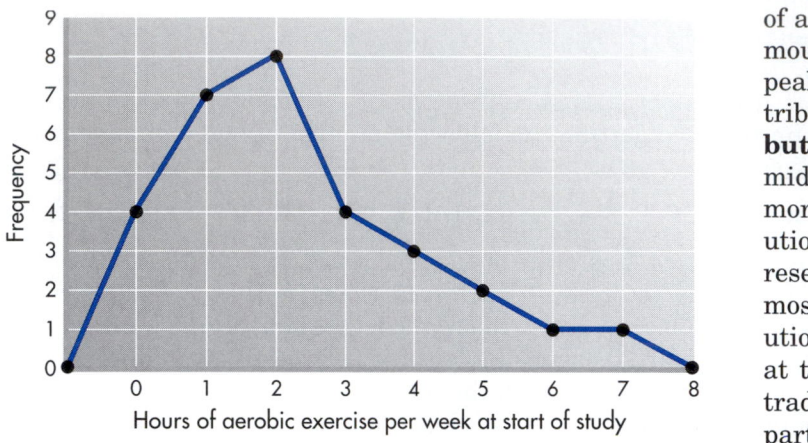

FIGURE A.2 A Frequency Polygon (Positive Skew)
Like Table A.1 and Figure A.1, this frequency polygon shows at a glance that the number of hours of aerobic exercise weekly is not great for most people. The high points come at 1 and 2 hours, which doesn't amount to much more than 10 or 15 minutes of exercise daily. An asymmetrical distribution like this one, which includes mostly low scores, is said to be positively skewed.

Frequency polygons are good for showing the shape of a distribution. The polygon in Figure A.2 looks like a mountain, rising sharply over the first two categories, peaking at 2, and slowly diminishing from there. A distribution like this is asymmetrical, or a **skewed distribution.** This means that, if we drew a line through the middle of the X axis (halfway between 3 and 4 hours), more scores would be piled up on one side of the distribution than on the other. The polygon in Figure A.2 represents a *positively skewed* distribution, indicating that most people had low scores. A *negatively skewed* distribution would have mostly high scores, with fewer scores at the low end of the distribution. For example, if the traditional diet and exercise intervention worked, the 30 participants should, as a group, be exercising more at the end of the study than they had been at the beginning. Perhaps the distribution of hours of aerobic exercise per week at the end of the study would look something like Figure A.3—a distribution with a slight negative skew.

In contrast to skewed distributions, a **symmetrical distribution** is one in which scores fall equally on both halves of the graph. A special case of a symmetrical distribution, the normal curve, is discussed in a later section.

A useful feature of frequency polygons is that more than one distribution can be graphed on the same set of axes. For example, the end-of-study hours of aerobic exercise per week for the *traditional* and *alternative* groups could be compared on a single graph. This would allow us to see at a glance whether one group was exercising more than the other after a year of their respective programs.

By the way, Figure A.3 is actually a figment of my imagination. According to the diaries kept by the traditional and alternative program participants, compliance with the exercise portion of the program decreased over time. This does not necessarily mean that these subjects were exercising *less* at the end of the study than at the beginning, but they certainly did not keep up the program as it was taught to them. Compliance with the prescribed diets was steadier than compliance with exercise; compliance by the alternative group dropped between 3 months and 6 months, and then rose steadily over time. There was, however, one major difference between the two intervention groups in terms of compliance. Participants in the alternative group were more likely to be meditating at the end of the study than their traditional-group counterparts were to be practicing progressive relaxation.

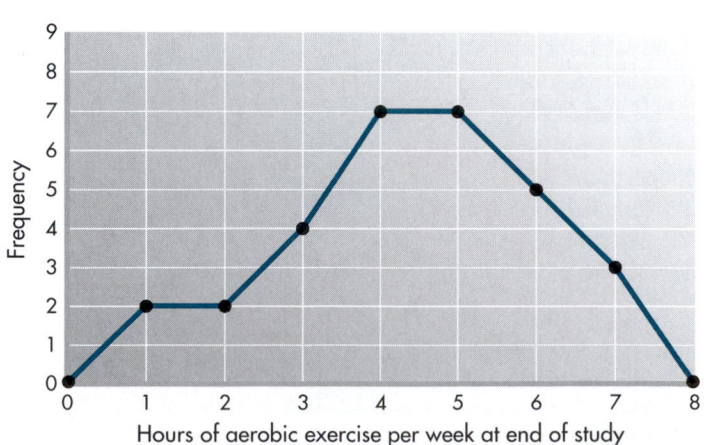

FIGURE A.3 A Frequency Polygon (Negative Skew)
When more scores fall at the high end of a distribution than at the low end, the distribution is said to be negatively skewed. We would expect a negatively skewed distribution if a health-promotion program worked and encouraged more hours of aerobic exercise. The more effective the program, the greater the skew.

Measures of Central Tendency

Frequency distributions can be used to organize a set of data and tell us how scores are generally distributed. But researchers often want to put this information into a more compact form. They want to be able to summarize a distribution with a single score that is "typical." To do this they use a **measure of central tendency.**

The Mode

The **mode** is the easiest measure of central tendency to calculate; it is simply the score or category that occurs most frequently in a set of raw scores or in a frequency distribution. The mode in the frequency distribution shown in Table A.1 is 2; more participants reported exercising 2 hours per week than any other category. In this example, the mode is an accurate representation of central tendency, but this is not always the case. In the distribution 1, 1, 1, 10, 20, 30, the mode is 1, yet half the scores are 10 and above. This type of distortion is the reason measures of central tendency other than the mode are needed.

The Median

Another way of describing central tendency is to determine the **median,** or the score that falls in the middle of a distribution. If the exercise scores are laid out from lowest to highest,

0, 0, 0, 0, 1, 1, 1, 1, 1, 1, 1, 2, 2, 2, 2, 2, 2, 2, 2, 3, 3, 3, 3, 4, 4, 4, 5, 5, 6, 7

↑

what would the middle score be? Since there are 30 scores, look for the point that divides the distribution in half, with 15 scores on each side of this point. The median can be found between the 15th and 16th scores (indicated by the arrow). In this distribution, the answer is easy: a score of 2 is the median as well as the mode.

The Mean

A problem with the mode and the median is that both measures reflect only one score in the distribution. For the mode, the score of importance is the most frequent one; for the median it is the middle score. A better measure of central tendency is usually one that reflects *all* scores. This is why the most commonly used measure of central tendency is the **mean,** or arithmetic average. You have calculated the mean many times. It is computed by summing a set of scores, and then dividing by the number of scores that went into the sum. In our example, adding together the exercise distribution scores gives a total of 70; the number of scores is 30, so 70 divided by 30 gives a mean of 2.33.

Formulas are used to express how a statistic is calculated. The formula for the mean is:

$$\overline{X} = \frac{\sum X}{N}$$

In this formula, each letter and symbol has a specific meaning:

$\overline{X}$ is the symbol for the mean.

Σ is sigma, the Greek letter for capital S, and it stands for "sum." (Taking a course in statistics is one way to learn the Greek alphabet!)

---

frequency polygon
A way of graphically representing a frequency distribution; frequency is marked above each score category on the graph's horizontal axis, and the marks are connected by straight lines.

skewed distribution
An asymmetrical distribution; more scores pile up on one side of the distribution than on the other. In a *positively* skewed distribution, most people have low scores; in a *negatively* skewed distribution, most people have high scores.

symmetrical distribution
A distribution in which scores fall equally on both sides of the graph. The normal curve is an example of a symmetrical distribution.

measure of central tendency
A single number that presents some information about the "center" of a frequency distribution.

mode
The most frequently occurring score in a distribution.

median
The score that divides a frequency distribution exactly in half, so that the same number of scores lies on each side of it.

mean
The sum of a set of scores in a distribution divided by the number of scores. The mean is usually the most representative measure of central tendency.

X represents the scores in the distribution, so the numerator of the equation says: "Sum up all the scores."

N is the total number of scores in the distribution.

Therefore, the formula says: "The mean equals the sum of all the scores divided by the total number of scores."

Although the mean is usually the most representative measure of central tendency because each score in a distribution enters into its computation, it is particularly susceptible to the effect of extreme scores. Any unusually high or low score will pull the mean in its direction. Suppose, for example, that in our frequency distribution for aerobic exercise one exercise zealot worked out 70 hours per week. The mean number of aerobic exercise hours would jump from 2.33 to 4.43. This new mean is deceptively high, given that most of the scores in the distribution are 2 and below. Because of just that one extreme score, the mean has become less representative of the distribution. Frequency tables and graphs are important tools for helping us identify extreme scores *before* we start computing statistics.

Measures of Variability

In addition to identifying the central tendency in a distribution, researchers may want to know how much the scores in that distribution differ from one another. Are they grouped closely together or widely spread out? To answer this question, we need some **measure of variability.** Figure A.4 shows two distributions with the same mean but different variability.

A simple way to measure variability is with the **range,** which is computed by subtracting the lowest score in the distribution from the highest score. Let's say that there are 15 women in the traditional diet and exercise group and that their weights at the beginning of the study varied from a low of 95 pounds to a high of 155 pounds. The range of weights in this group would be 155 − 95 = 60 pounds.

As a measure of variability, the range provides a limited amount of information, because it depends on only the two most extreme scores in a distribution (the highest and lowest scores). A more useful measure of variability would give some idea of the average amount of variation in a distribution. But variation from what? The most common way to measure variability is to determine how far scores in a distribution vary from the distribution's mean. We saw earlier that the mean is usually the best way to represent the "center" of the distribution, so the mean seems like an appropriate reference point.

What if we subtracted the mean from each score in a distribution to get a general idea of how far each score is from the center? When the mean is subtracted from a score, the result is a *deviation* from the mean. Scores that are above the mean would have positive deviations, and scores that are below the mean would have negative deviations. To get an average deviation, we would need to sum the deviations and divide by the number of deviations that went into the sum. There is a problem with this procedure, however. If

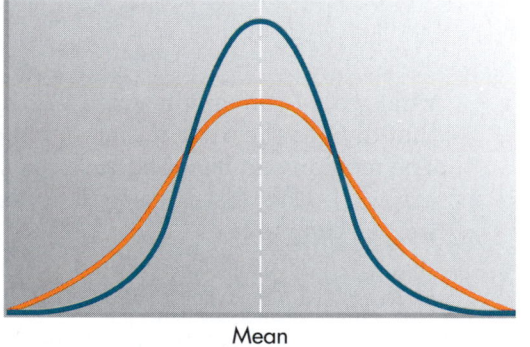

FIGURE A.4 Distributions with Different Variability
Two distributions with the same mean can have very different variability, or spread. This is shown in these two curves. Notice how one is more spread out than the other; its scores are distributed more widely.

Mean

measure of variability
A single number that presents information about the spread of scores in a distribution.

range
A measure of variability; the highest score in a distribution minus the lowest score.

TABLE A.2 Calculating the Standard Deviation

Weight X	Mean $\overline{X}$	Weight – Mean $X - \overline{X}$	(Weight – Mean) Squared $(X - \overline{X})^2$
155	124	31	961
149	124	25	625
142	124	18	324
138	124	14	196
134	124	10	100
131	124	7	49
127	124	3	9
125	124	1	1
120	124	−4	16
115	124	−9	81
112	124	−12	144
110	124	−14	196
105	124	−19	361
102	124	−22	484
95	124	−29	841

Sum (Σ) = 1,860 $\Sigma = 0$ $\Sigma = 4,388$

Mean ($\overline{X}$) = 124

$$SD = \sqrt{\frac{\Sigma(X - \overline{X})^2}{N}} = \sqrt{\frac{4,388}{15}} = 17.10$$

To calculate the standard deviation, you simply add all the scores in a distribution (the left-hand column in this example) and divide by the total number of scores to get the mean. Then you subtract the mean from each score to get a list of deviations from the mean (third column). Next you square each deviation (fourth column), add the squared deviations together, divide by the total number of cases, and take the square root.

deviations from the mean are added together, the sum will be 0, because the negative and positive deviations will cancel each other out. In fact, the real definition of the mean is "the only point in a distribution where all the scores' deviations from it add up to 0."

We need to somehow "get rid of" the negative deviations. In mathematics, such a problem is solved by squaring. If a negative number is squared, it becomes positive. So instead of simply adding up the deviations and dividing by the number of scores, we first square each of the deviations, then add together the *squared* deviations and divide by N. Finally, we need to compensate for the squaring operation. To do this, we take the square root of the number just calculated. This leaves us with the **standard deviation.** The larger the standard deviation, the more spread out are the scores in a distribution.

Let's look at an example to make this clearer. Table A.2 lists the hypothetical weights of the 15 women in the traditional group at the beginning of the study. The mean, which is the sum of the weights divided by 15, is calculated to be 124 pounds, as shown at the bottom of the left-hand column. The first step in computing the standard deviation is to subtract the mean from each score, which gives that score's deviation from the mean. These deviations are listed in the third column of the table. The next step is to square each of the deviations (done in the fourth column), then add the squared deviations ($\Sigma = 4,388$) and divide that total by the number of women ($N = 15$). Finally, we take the square root to obtain the standard deviation ($SD = 17.10$). The formula for the standard deviation (SD) incorporates these instructions:

$$SD = \sqrt{\frac{\Sigma(X - \overline{X})^2}{N}}$$

Notice that when scores have large deviations from the mean, the *standard deviation* is also large.

z Scores and the Normal Curve

The mean and the standard deviation provide useful descriptive information about an entire set of scores. But researchers can also describe the relative position of any individual score in a distribution. This is done by locating how far away from the mean the score is in terms of standard deviation units. A statistic called a **z score** gives us this information:

$$z = \frac{X - \overline{X}}{SD}$$

standard deviation
A measure of variability; expressed as the square root of the sum of the squared deviations around the mean divided by the number of scores in the distribution.

z score
A number, expressed in standard deviation units, that shows a score's deviation from the mean.

This equation says that to compute a z score, we subtract the mean from the score we are interested in (that is, we calculate its deviation from the mean) and divide this quantity by the standard deviation. A positive z score indicates that the score is above the mean, while a negative z score shows that the score is below the mean. The larger the z score, the farther away from the mean the score is.

Let's take an example from the distribution found in Table A.2. What is the z score of a weight of 149 pounds? To find out, you simply subtract the mean from 149 and divide by the standard deviation.

$$z = \frac{149 - 124}{17.10} = 1.46$$

A z score of +1.46 tells us that a person weighing 149 pounds falls about 1½ standard deviations above the mean. In contrast, a person weighing 115 pounds has a weight below the mean and would have a negative z score. If you calculate this z score you will find it is $-.53$. This means that a weight of 115 is a little more than one-half a standard deviation below the mean.

Some variables, such as height, weight, or IQ, if graphed for large numbers of people, fall into a characteristic pattern. Figure A.5 shows this pattern, which is called the **standard normal curve** or the **standard normal distribution.** The normal curve is symmetrical (that is, if a line is drawn down its center, one side of the curve is a mirror image of the other side), and the mean, median, and mode fall exactly in the middle. The X axis of Figure A.5 is marked off in standard deviation units, which, conveniently, are also z scores. Notice that most of the cases fall between -1 and $+1$ SDs, with the number of cases sharply tapering off at either end. This pattern is the reason the normal curve is often described as "bell-shaped."

The great thing about the normal curve is that we know exactly what percentage of the distribution falls between any two points on the curve. Figure A.5 shows the percentages of cases between major standard deviation units. For example, 34.13 percent of the distribution falls between 0 and +1. That means that 84.13 percent of the distribution falls *below* one standard deviation (the 34.13 percent that is between 0 and +1, plus the 50 percent that falls below 0). A person who obtains a z score of +1 on some normally distributed variable has scored better than 84 percent of the other people in the distribution. If a variable is normally distributed (that is, if it has the standard bell-shaped pattern), a person's z score can tell us exactly where that person stands relative to everyone else in the distribution.

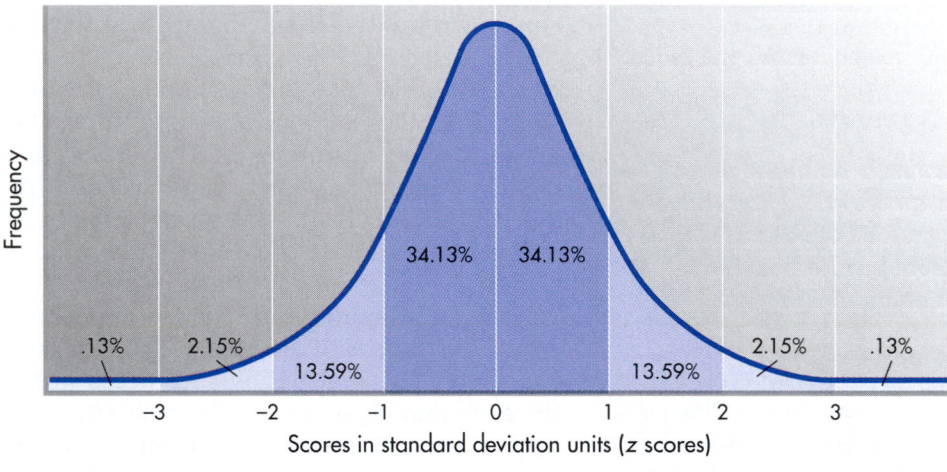

FIGURE A.5 The Standard Normal Curve
The standard normal curve has several characteristics. Most apparent is its symmetrical bell shape. On such a curve, the mean, the median, and the mode all fall at the same point. But not every curve that is shaped roughly like a bell is a standard normal curve. With a normal curve, specific percentages of the distribution fall within each standard deviation unit from the mean. These percentages are shown on the graph.

Correlation

So far, the statistical techniques we've looked at focus on one variable at a time, such as hours of aerobic exercise weekly or weight measured in pounds. Life would be simple if it were influenced by only one variable at a time! The world, however, is a far more complicated place. Accordingly, statistical techniques have been devised that allow us to look at the relationship—the

standard normal curve (standard normal distribution)
A symmetrical distribution forming a bell-shaped curve in which the mean, median, and mode are all equal and fall in the exact middle.

correlation—between two variables. This relationship is assessed by a statistic called the **correlation coefficient.**

In order to compute a correlation coefficient, we need two sets of measurements from the same individuals, or from pairs of people who are similar in some way. To take a simple example, let's determine the correlation between height (we'll call this the X variable) and weight (the Y variable). We start by obtaining height and weight measurements for each individual in a group. The idea is to combine all these measurements into one number that expresses something about the relationship between the two variables, height and weight. However, we are immediately confronted with a problem: the two variables are measured in different ways. Height is measured in inches and weight is measured in pounds. We need some way to place both variables on a single scale.

Think back to our discussion of the normal curve and z scores. What do z scores do? They take data of any form and put them into a standard scale. Remember, too, that a high score in a distribution always has a positive z score, and a low score in a distribution always has a negative z score. To compute a correlation coefficient, the data from both variables of interest can be converted to z scores. Therefore, each individual will have two z scores: one for height (the X variable) and one for weight (the Y variable).

In order to compute the correlation coefficient, each person's two z scores are multiplied together. All these "cross-products" are added up, and this sum is divided by the number of individuals. In other words, a correlation coefficient is the average (or mean) of the z-score cross-products of the two variables being studied:

$$\text{correlation coefficient} = \frac{\sum z_x z_y}{N}$$

A correlation coefficient can range anywhere from -1 to $+1$. The exact number provides two pieces of information: it tells us about the *magnitude* of the relationship being measured, and it tells us about its *direction*. The magnitude, or degree of relationship, is indicated by the size of the number. A number close to 1 (whether positive or negative) indicates a strong relationship, while a number close to zero indicates a weak relationship. The sign ($+$ or $-$) of the correlation coefficient tells us about the relationship's direction. A *positive* correlation means that as one variable increases in size, the second variable also increases. For example, height and weight are positively correlated: as height increases, weight tends to increase also. In terms of z scores, a positive correlation means that high z scores on one variable tend to be multiplied by high z scores on the other variable and that low z scores on one variable tend to be multiplied by low z scores on the other. Remember that just as two positive numbers multiplied together result in a positive number, so two negative numbers multiplied together also result in a positive number. When the cross-products are added together, the sum in both cases is positive. A *negative* correlation, in contrast, means that two variables are *inversely* related. As one variable increases in size, the other variable decreases. For example, professors like to believe that the more hours students study, the fewer errors they will make on exams. In z-score language, high z scores (which are positive) on one variable (more hours of study) tend to be multiplied by low z scores (which are negative) on the other variable (fewer errors on exams), and vice versa, making negative cross-products. When the cross-products are summed and divided by the number of cases, the result is a negative correlation coefficient.

An easy way to show different correlations is with graphs. Plotting two variables together creates a **scatter diagram** or **scatter plot,** like the ones in Figures A.6, A.7, and A.8. These figures show the relationship between

---

correlation
The relationship between two variables.

correlation coefficient
A measure of the magnitude and direction of the relationship (the correlation) between two variables. The closer the correlation coefficient is to $+1$ or -1, the stronger the relationship is. A *positive* correlation coefficient indicates that as one variable increases, the other tends to increase. A *negative* correlation coefficient indicates that as one variable increases, the other tends to decrease.

scatter diagram (scatter plot)
A graph that represents the relationship between two variables.

complying with some component of the alternative health-promotion program and some other variable related to health. Although the figures describe relationships actually found in the study, I have made up the specific correlations to illustrate key points.

Figure A.6 shows a moderately strong positive relationship between compliance with the yoga part of the alternative program and a person's energy level. You can see this just by looking at the pattern of the data points. They generally form a line running from lower left to upper right. When calculated, this particular correlation coefficient is +.59, which indicates a correlation roughly in the middle between 0 and +1. In other words, people who did more yoga tended to have higher energy levels. The "tended to" part is important. Some people who did not comply well with the yoga routine still had high energy levels, while the reverse was also true. A +1 correlation, or a *perfect* positive correlation, would indicate that frequent yoga sessions were *always* accompanied by high levels of energy, and vice versa. What would a scatter diagram of a perfect +1 correlation look like? It would be a straight diagonal line starting in the lower left-hand corner of the graph and progressing to the upper right-hand corner.

Several other positive correlations were found in this study. Compliance with the alternative diet was positively associated with increases in energy and positive health perceptions. In addition, following the high-fiber, low-fat traditional diet was associated with a higher level of coping and high vitamin intake.

The study also found some negative correlations. Figure A.7 illustrates a *negative* correlation between compliance with the meditation part of the alternative program and cigarette smoking. This correlation coefficient is −.77. Note that the data points fall in the opposite direction from those in Figure A.6, indicating that as the frequency of meditation increased, cigarette smoking decreased. The pattern of points in Figure A.7 is closer to a straight line than the pattern of points in Figure A.6. A correlation of −.77 shows a relationship of greater magnitude than does a correlation of +.59. But though −.77 is a relatively high correlation, it is not a perfect relationship. A *perfect* negative relationship would be illustrated by a straight diagonal line starting in the upper left-hand corner of the graph and ending at the lower right-hand corner.

Finally, Figure A.8 shows two variables that are not related to each other. The hypothetical correlation coefficient between compliance with the aerobic exercise part of the traditional program and a person's level of coping is +.03, barely above zero. In the scatter diagram, data points fall randomly, with no general direction to them. From a *z*-score point of view, when two variables

FIGURE A.6 Scatter Plot of a Positive Correlation

A correlation (or the lack of one) can be clearly shown on a scatter diagram. This one shows a moderately strong positive correlation between subjects' compliance with the yoga component of the alternative health-promotion program and their energy level. The positive direction of the correlation is indicated by the upward-sloping pattern of the dots: from bottom left to top right. This means that if one variable is high, the other tends to be high too, and vice versa. That the strength of the relationship is only moderate is indicated by the fact that the data points (each indicating an individual subject's score) are not all positioned along a straight diagonal line.

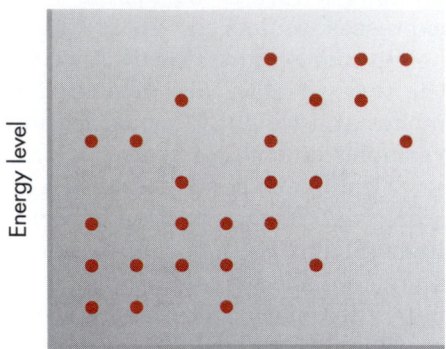

Compliance with yoga routine

FIGURE A.7 Scatter Plot of a Negative Correlation

In general, people who engage in meditation more often tend to smoke less. This negative correlation is indicated by the downward-sloping pattern of dots, from upper left to lower right. Because these dots are clustered somewhat closer together than those in Figure A.6, we can tell at a glance that the relationship here is somewhat stronger.

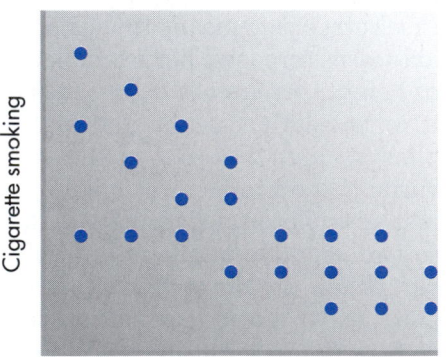

Compliance with meditation routine

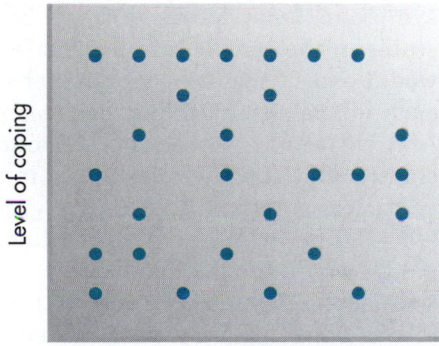

Level of coping

Compliance with
aerobic exercise program

are not related, the cross-products are mixed—that is, both positive and negative. Sometimes high z scores on one variable go with high z scores on the other, and low z scores on one variable go with low z scores on the other. In both cases, positive cross-products result. In other pairs of scores, high z scores on one variable go with low z scores on the other variable (and vice versa), producing negative cross-products. When the cross-products for the two variables are summed, the positive and negative numbers cancel each other out, resulting in a 0 (or close to 0) correlation.

In addition to describing the relationship between two variables, correlation coefficients are useful for another purpose: prediction. If we know a person's score on one of two related variables, we can predict how he or she will perform on the other variable. For example, in a recent issue of a magazine I found a quiz to rate my risk of heart disease. I assigned myself points depending on my age, HDL ("good") and total cholesterol levels, systolic blood pressure, and other risk factors, such as cigarette smoking and diabetes. My total points (-2) indicated that I had less than a 1 percent risk of developing heart disease in the next 5 years. How could such a quiz be developed? Each of the factors I rated is correlated to some degree with heart disease. The older you are, and the higher your cholesterol and blood pressure, the greater your chance of developing heart disease. Statistical techniques are used to determine the relative importance of each of these factors and to calculate the points that should be assigned to each level of a factor. Combining these factors provides a better prediction than any single factor, because none of the individual risk factors correlates perfectly with the development of heart disease.

One thing a correlation does *not* tell us is *causality*. In other words, the fact that two variables are highly correlated does not mean that one variable directly causes the other. Take the meditation and cigarette smoking correlation. This negative correlation tells us that people in the study who diligently practiced meditation tended to smoke less than those who seldom meditated. Regular meditation may have had a direct effect on the desire to smoke cigarettes, but it is also possible that one or more other variables affected both meditation and smoking. For example, perhaps participation in the study convinced some people that they needed to change their lifestyles completely. Both compliance with the meditation routine and a decreased level of cigarette smoking may have been "caused" by this change in lifestyle. The only way to determine cause and effect is to conduct an experiment, as you saw in Chapter 1. Can you think of a way to test the hypothesis that regularly practicing meditation causes a reduction in the desire to smoke cigarettes?

Inferential Statistics

Let's say that the mean number of physical symptoms (like pain) experienced by the participants in each of the three groups had been about the same at the beginning of the health-promotion study. A year later, the number of symptoms had decreased in the two intervention groups, but had remained stable in the control group. This may or may not be a meaningful result. We would expect the average number of symptoms to be somewhat different for each of the three groups, because each group consisted of different people. And we would expect some fluctuation in level over time, due simply to chance. But are the differences in number of symptoms between the intervention groups and the control group large enough *not* to be due to chance alone? If other researchers conducted the same study with different participants, would they be likely to get the same general pattern of results? To answer such questions, we turn to inferential statistics. **Inferential statistics** tell us the inferences, or conclusions, that we can legitimately draw from a set of research findings.

There are many inferential statistical techniques that can be called into service to answer questions such as the ones raised above. Each of them helps determine whether or not a set of findings can plausibly be explained merely by chance and random variation. If the results of a study are more extreme than would be expected by chance alone, we reject the idea that no *real* effect occurred, and conclude that the manipulation of the independent variable is the reason for the obtained results. In other words, we say that our results are *statistically significant*.

To see how this works, let's go back to the normal curve for a moment. Remember that we know exactly what percentage of a normal curve falls between any two z scores. If we choose one person at random out of a normal distribution, what is the chance that this person's z score is above $+2$? If you look again at Figure A.5, you will see that 2.28 percent of the curve lies above a z score (or standard deviation unit) of $+2$. Therefore, the chance, or *probability*, that the person we choose will have a z score above $+2$ is .0228 (or 2.28 chances out of 100). That's a pretty small chance. If you study the normal curve, you will see that the majority of cases fall between -2 and $+2$ SDs (95.44 percent of the cases, to be exact), so in choosing a person at random, that person is not likely to fall above a z score of $+2$.

When researchers test for statistical significance, they usually employ statistics other than z scores, and they may use distributions that differ in shape from the normal curve. The logic, however, is the same. They compute some kind of inferential statistic that they compare to the appropriate distribution. This comparison tells them the likelihood of obtaining their results if chance alone is operating.

The problem is that no test exists that will tell us for sure whether our intervention or manipulation "worked"; we always have to deal with probabilities, not certainties. Researchers have developed some conventions to guide them in their decisions about whether or not their study results are statistically significant. Generally, if the probability of obtaining a particular result if random factors alone are operating is less than .05 (5 chances out of 100), the results are considered statistically significant. Researchers who want to be even more sure set their probability value at .01 (1 chance out of 100).

Because researchers deal with probabilities, there is a small but real possibility of *erroneously* concluding that study results are significant. The results of one study, therefore, should never be completed trusted. In order to have greater confidence in a particular effect or result, the study should be repeated, or *replicated*. If the same results are obtained in different studies, then we can draw conclusions about a particular intervention or effect with greater certainty.

One final point about inferential statistics. Are the researchers interested only in the changes that might have occurred in the small groups of people participating in the health-promotion study, or do they really want to know whether the interventions would be effective for people in general?

inferential statistics
Statistical techniques that allow researchers to determine whether the outcomes in a study are likely to be more than just chance events and whether they can be legitimately generalized to a larger population.

This question focuses on the difference between a population and a sample. A **population** is a complete set of something—people, nonhuman animals, objects, or events. The researchers who designed this study wanted to know whether the interventions they developed would benefit *all* people (or, more precisely, all people between the ages of 20 and 56). Obviously, they could not conduct a study on this entire population. The best they could do is choose some portion of that population to serve as subjects; in other words, they selected a **sample.** The study was conducted on this sample. The researchers analyzed the sample results using inferential statistics to make guesses about what they would find had they studied the entire population. Inferential statistics allow researchers to take the findings they obtain from a sample and apply them to a population.

So what did the health-promotion study find? Did the interventions work? The answer is yes, sort of. The traditional and alternative groups, when combined, improved more than the no-treatment control group. At the end of the study, participants in the two intervention programs had better self-perceptions regarding health, better mood, more energy, and fewer physical symptoms. Compared with the traditional and the no-treatment groups, the alternative group showed greater improvement in health perceptions and a significant decrease in depression and the use of prescription drugs. Interestingly, participation in the treatment groups did not generally result in changes in health risk, such as lowered blood pressure or decreased weight. The researchers believe that little change occurred because the people who volunteered for the study were basically healthy individuals. The study needs to be replicated with a less-healthy sample. In sum, the intervention programs had a greater effect on health perceptions and psychological variables than on physical variables. The researchers concluded that a health-promotion regimen (either traditional or alternative) is helpful. I hope other studies will be conducted to explore these issues further!

Endnote

Although I briefly saw other study participants at each 3-month data collection point, I never spoke to anyone. The last measurement session, however, was also a celebration for our year-long participation in the project. Approximately 30 people attended my session, and participants from each of the three groups were present. After our blood was drawn and our blood pressure and weight readings were taken, we were treated to breakfast. Then one of the principal researchers *debriefed* us: She gave us some background on the study and told us what she hoped to learn. At this point, participants were given the opportunity to talk about how the study had affected their lives. It was fascinating to hear members of the intervention groups describe the changes they had made over the past year. One woman said that a year ago she could never imagine getting up early to meditate, yet now she looks forward to awakening each morning at 4:00 a.m. for her first meditation session. Other people described the modifications they had made in their diet and exercise patterns, and how much better they felt. While I did not experience either of the interventions, I know that simply being a subject in the study made me more conscious of what I ate and how much I exercised. This could have been a confounding factor—that is, it could have inadvertently changed my behavior even though I was in the control group. In fact, my weight decreased and my level of "good" cholesterol increased over the course of the year.

population
A complete set of something—people, nonhuman animals, objects, or events.

sample
A subset of a population.

We were not paid for our participation in this study, but we received small gifts as tokens of the researchers' appreciation. In addition, we were all given the option of taking any or all of the intervention training at no cost (and some courses in alternative techniques could be quite expensive). The most important thing for me was the satisfaction of participation—the fact that I had stayed with the study for an entire year and, in a small way, had made a contribution to science.

Summary

Statistics: Understanding Data

Descriptive Statistics

■ Descriptive statistics allow us to organize and summarize data in ways that are brief yet meaningful and easy to understand. One descriptive statistic is a frequency distribution, which can be presented in the form of a table, a histogram, or a frequency polygon. Some frequency distributions are positively skewed; that is, most of the scores in the distribution pile up at the low end. Distributions that are negatively skewed have mostly high scores. Symmetrical distributions have equal numbers of scores on both sides of the distribution's midpoint.

■ The mode, the median, and the mean are measures of central tendency of a distribution. The mode is the most frequent score. The median is the middle score in the distribution. The mean is the arithmetic average. To calculate the mean, scores are summed and divided by the total number of scores. The mean is usually the best overall representation of central tendency, but it is strongly influenced by extremely high or extremely low scores.

■ The range and standard deviation are measures of variability or spread of a distribution. The range is the highest score in the distribution minus the lowest score. The standard deviation is the square root of the average of the squared deviations from the mean.

■ A z score expresses a single score's deviation from the mean of a distribution in standard deviation units.

■ The standard normal curve is a symmetrical distribution forming a bell-shaped curve in which the mean, median, and mode are all equal and fall in the exact middle. The percentage of cases that fall between any two points on the normal curve is known. Over 95 percent of the cases fall between two standard deviations above the mean and two standard deviations below the mean.

■ Correlation refers to the relationship between two variables. A correlation coefficient is a number that indicates the magnitude and direction of such a relationship. A correlation coefficient may range from +1 to −1. The closer the value is to +1 or −1, the stronger the relationship is. Correlations close to 0 indicate no relationship. A positive correlation coefficient tell us that as one variable increases in size, the second variable also increases. A negative correlation coefficient indicates that as one variable increases in size, the second variable decreases. A correlation relationship may be presented visually though a scatter diagram.

■ Correlations enable us to predict the value of one variable from knowledge of another variable's value. However, a correlational relationship is not necessarily a causal relationship.

Inferential Statistics

■ Inferential statistics are used to determine whether the outcomes of a study can be legitimately generalized to a larger population. A population is a complete set of something. A sample is a subset of a population.

■ Inferential statistics provide information about the probability of a particular result if only chance or random factors are operating. If this probability is small, the findings are said to be statistically significant—that is, they are probably due to the researcher's interventions.

Key Terms

descriptive statistics (p. A-2)

frequency distribution (p. A-3)

histogram (p. A-3)

frequency polygon (p. A-4)

skewed distribution (p. A-4)

symmetrical distribution (p. A-4)

measure of central tendency (p. A-5)

mode (p. A-5)

median (p. A-5)

mean (p. A-5)

measure of variability (p. A-6)

range (p. A-6)

standard deviation (p. A-7)

z score (p. A-7)

standard normal curve (standard normal distribution) (p. A-8)

correlation (p. A-9)

correlation coefficient (p. A-9)

scatter diagram (scatter plot) (p. A-9)

inferential statistics (p. A-12)

population (p. A-13)

sample (p. A-13)

Glossary

absolute threshold The smallest possible strength of a stimulus that can be detected half the time. (p. 78)

accommodation The process by which the lens of the eye changes shape to focus incoming light so that it falls on the retina. (p. 81)

acculturative stress The stress that results from the pressure of adapting to a new culture. (p. 437)

acetylcholine (uh-seet-ull-KO-leen) Neurotransmitter that produces muscle contractions and is involved in memory functions. (p. 44)

achievement motivation Motivated behavior directed toward excelling, succeeding, or outperforming others at some task. (p. 295)

action potential A brief electrical impulse by which information is transmitted along the axon of a neuron. (p. 39)

activation-synthesis model of dreaming The theory that brain activity during sleep produces dream images (*activation*), which are combined by the brain into a dream story (*synthesis*). (p. 138)

activity theory of aging The psychosocial theory that life satisfaction in late adulthood is highest when people maintain the level of activity they displayed earlier in life. (p. 350)

actor–observer discrepancy The tendency to attribute one's own behavior to external, situational causes, while attributing the behavior of others to internal, personal causes; especially likely to occur with regard to behaviors that lead to negative outcomes. (p. 405)

actualizing tendency In Carl Rogers' theory of personality, the innate drive to maintain and enhance the human organism. (p. 375)

adaptive theory of sleep The view that the unique sleep patterns of different animals evolved over time to help promote survival and environmental adaptation. (p. 131)

adolescence The transitional stage between late childhood and the beginning of adulthood, during which sexual maturity is reached. (p. 337)

adolescent growth spurt The period of accelerated growth during puberty, involving rapid increases in height and weight. (p. 338)

afterimage A visual experience that occurs after the original source of stimulation is no longer present. (p. 86)

agoraphobia An anxiety disorder involving the extreme and irrational fear of experiencing a panic attack in a public situation and being unable to escape or get help. (p. 470)

algorithm A problem-solving strategy that involves following a specific rule, procedure, or method that inevitably produces the correct solution. (p. 239)

all-or-none law The principle that either a neuron is sufficiently stimulated and an action potential occurs or a neuron is not sufficiently stimulated and an action potential does not occur. (p. 41)

alpha brain waves Brain wave pattern associated with relaxed wakefulness and drowsiness. (p. 125)

amnesia (am-NEE-zha) Severe memory loss. (p. 225)

amphetamines (am-FET-uh-mins) A class of stimulant drugs that arouse the central nervous system and suppress appetite. (p. 149)

amplitude The intensity or amount of energy of a wave, reflected in the height of the wave; the amplitude of a sound wave determines a sound's loudness. (p. 89)

amygdala (uh-MIG-dull-uh) An almond-shaped forebrain structure that is part of the limbic system and involved in emotion and memory. (p. 62)

anorexia nervosa An eating disorder in which the individual refuses to maintain a minimally normal body weight, is extremely afraid of gaining weight or becoming fat, and has a distorted perception about the size of his or her body. (p. 282)

anterograde amnesia Loss of memory caused by the inability to store new memories. (p. 225)

antianxiety medications Prescription drugs that are used to alleviate the symptoms of anxiety. (p. 522)

antidepressant medications Prescription drugs that are used to reduce the symptoms associated with depression. (p. 523)

antipsychotic medications Prescription drugs that are used to reduce psychotic symptoms; frequently used in the treatment of schizophrenia. (p. 520)

anxiety An unpleasant emotional state characterized by physical arousal and feelings of tension, apprehension, and worry. (p. 468)

anxiety disorders A category of psychological disorders in which extreme anxiety is the main diagnostic feature and causes significant disruptions in the person's cognitive, behavioral, or interpersonal functioning. (p. 468)

aphasia (uh-FAZE-yuh) The partial or complete inability to articulate ideas or understand spoken or written language due to brain injury or damage. (p. 65)

archetypes In Jung's theory of personality, the inherited mental images of universal human instincts, themes, and preoccupations that are the main components of the collective unconscious. (p. 371)

arousal theory The view that people are motivated to maintain an optimal level of arousal that is neither too high nor too low. (p. 293)

association areas Areas of the cerebral cortex where information from different brain centers is combined and integrated. (p. 59)

attachment The emotional bond that forms between an infant and her caregiver(s), especially her parents. (p. 325)

attitude A learned tendency to evaluate some object, person, or issue in a particular way; such evaluations may be positive, negative, or ambivalent. (p. 407)

attribution The mental process of inferring the causes of people's behavior, including one's own. Also used to refer to the explanation made for a particular behavior. (p. 404)

audition The technical term for the sense of hearing. (p. 89)

authoritarian parenting style Parenting style in which parents are demanding and unresponsive toward their children's needs or wishes. (p. 353)

authoritative parenting style Parenting style in which parents set clear standards for their children's behavior, but are also responsive to the children's needs and wishes. (p. 353)

autonomic nervous system (aw-toe-NOM-ick) Subdivision of the peripheral nervous system that regulates involuntary functions. (p. 49)

availability heuristic A strategy in which the likelihood of an event is estimated on the basis of how easily other instances of the event are available in memory. (p. 243)

aversive conditioning A relatively ineffective type of behavior therapy that involves repeatedly pairing an aversive stimulus with the occurrence of undesirable behaviors or thoughts. (p. 506)

axon The long, fluid-filled tube that carries a neuron's messages to other body areas. (p. 38)

axon terminals Branches at the end of the neuron's axon that contain tiny pouches or sacs called synaptic vesicles. (p. 43)

B

barbiturates (barb-ITCH-yer-ets) A category of depressant drugs that reduce anxiety and produce sleepiness. (p. 147)

basal metabolic rate (BMR) The rate at which the body, when at rest, uses energy for vital body functions. (p. 280)

basilar membrane (BASE-uh-ler) The membrane within the cochlea of the ear that contains the hair cells. (p. 91)

behavior modification The application of learning principles to help people develop more effective or adaptive behaviors. (p. 178)

behavior therapy A type of psychotherapy that focuses on directly changing maladaptive behavior patterns by using basic learning principles and techniques; also called *behavior modification.* (p. 504)

behavioral genetics An interdisciplinary field that studies the effects of genes and heredity on behavior. (p. 387)

behavioral perspective In learning theory, a general explanation of learning that emphasizes the relationship between outwardly observable behaviors and environmental events, rather than mental processes. (p. 159)

behaviorism School of psychology and theoretical viewpoint that emphasizes the study of observable behaviors, especially as they pertain to the process of learning. (p. 6)

bell and pad treatment A behavior therapy technique used to treat nighttime bedwetting by conditioning arousal from sleep in response to body signals of a full bladder. (p. 506)

beta brain waves Brain wave pattern associated with alert wakefulness. (p. 125)

binocular cues (by-NOCK-you-ler) Distance or depth cues that require the use of both eyes. (p. 101)

biological preparedness In learning theory, the idea that an organism is innately predisposed to form associations between certain stimuli and responses. (p. 187)

biological psychology Specialized branch of psychology that studies the relationship between behavior and body processes and systems. (p. 36)

biomedical therapies The use of medications, electroconvulsive therapy, or other medical treatments to treat the symptoms associated with psychological disorders. (p. 499)

bipolar disorder Often called *manic depression;* a mood disorder involving periods of incapacitating depression alternating with periods of extreme euphoria and excitement. (p. 477)

blaming the victim bias The tendency to blame an innocent victim of misfortune for having somehow caused the problem or for not having taken steps to avoid or prevent it. (p. 404)

blind spot The point where the optic nerve leaves the eye, producing a small gap in the field of vision. (p. 84)

brainstem A region of the brain made up of the hindbrain and the midbrain. (p. 55)

brightness The perceived intensity of a color that corresponds to the amplitude of the light wave. (p. 85)

brightness constancy The perception that the brightness of an object remains the same even though the lighting conditions change. (p. 106)

bulimia nervosa An eating disorder in which a person engages in binge eating and then purges the excessive food consumption by self-induced vomiting or, less often, by taking laxatives or enemas. (p. 283)

bystander effect The phenomenon in which the greater the number of people present, the less likely each individual is to help someone in distress. (p. 423)

C

caffeine (kaff-EEN) A stimulant drug found in coffee, tea, cola drinks, chocolate, and many over-the-counter medications. (p. 149)

California Personality Inventory (CPI) A self-report inventory that assesses personality characteristics in normal populations. (p. 391)

Cannon-Bard theory of emotion The theory that emotions arise from the simultaneous activation of the nervous system, which causes physical arousal, and the cortex, which causes the subjective experience of emotion. (p. 307)

case study A highly detailed description of a single individual or event. (p. 24)

CAT scan (computerized axial tomography) An instrument that produces two-dimensional pictures of brain structures using multiple X-rays that are reassembled by a computer. (p. 52)

catecholamines Hormones secreted by the adrenal medulla that cause rapid physiological arousal; include adrenaline and noradrenaline. (p. 438)

cell body The part of a neuron that contains the nucleus. (p. 37)

central nervous system Division of the nervous system that consists of the brain and spinal cord. (p. 47)

centration In Piaget's theory, the tendency to focus, or *center,* on only one aspect of a situation and ignore other important aspects of the situation. (p. 334)

cerebellum (sare-uh-BELL-um) A large, two-sided hindbrain structure at the back of the brain responsible for muscle coordination, fine motor movements, and maintaining posture and equilibrium. (p. 57)

cerebral cortex (suh-REE-brull or SARE-uh-brull) The wrinkled outer portion of the forebrain, which contains the most sophisticated brain centers. (p. 58)

cerebral hemisphere The nearly symmetrical left and right halves of the cerebral cortex. (p. 58)

cholecystokinin (CCK) (*kole*-eh-*sist*-oh-KINE-in) A hormone that seems to play a role in signaling satiation, or fullness. (p. 278)

chromosome A long, threadlike structure composed of twisted parallel strands of DNA; found in the nucleus of the cell. (p. 318)

chunking Increasing the amount of information that can be held in short-term memory by grouping related items together into a single unit, or "chunk." (p. 201)

circadian rhythm (ser-KADE-ee-en) A cycle or rhythm that is roughly 24 hours long; refers to daily fluctuations in many biological and psychological processes. (p. 120)

classical conditioning The basic learning process that involves repeatedly pairing a neutral stimulus with a response-producing stimulus until the neutral stimulus elicits the same response. (p. 160)

client-centered therapy A type of psychotherapy developed by humanistic psychologist Carl Rogers in which the therapist is nondirective and reflective, and the client directs the focus of each therapy session; also called *person-centered therapy.* (p. 502)

clustering Organizing items into related groups during recall from long-term memory. (p. 204)

cocaine A stimulant drug derived from the coca tree. (p. 150)

cochlea (COKE-lee-uh) The coiled, fluid-filled inner-ear structure that contains the sensory receptors for sound. (p. 91)

cognition The mental activities involved in acquiring, retaining, and using knowledge. (p. 235)

cognitive dissonance An unpleasant state of psychological tension or arousal (*dissonance*) that occurs when two thoughts or perceptions (*cognitions*) are inconsistent; typically results from the awareness that attitudes and behavior are in conflict. (p. 409)

cognitive map Tolman's term to describe the mental representation of the layout of a familiar environment. (p. 181)

cognitive-mediational theory of emotion Lazarus's theory that emotions result from the cognitive appraisal of a situation's effect on personal well-being. (p. 309)

cognitive perspective In learning theory, a general approach to the study of learning that stresses the role of expectations, mental representation, and other mental processes in learning. (p. 179)

cognitive therapies A group of psychotherapies that are based on the assumption that psychological problems are due to maladaptive patterns of thinking; treatment techniques focus on recognizing and altering these unhealthy thinking patterns. (p. 508)

cognitive therapy (CT) A type of cognitive therapy, developed by psychiatrist Aaron T. Beck, that focuses on changing the client's unrealistic beliefs. (p. 510)

collective unconscious In Jung's theory of personality, the hypothesized part of the unconscious mind that is inherited from previous generations and that contains universally shared ancestral experiences and ideas. (p. 371)

collectivistic cultures Cultures that emphasize the needs and goals of the group over the needs and goals of the individual. (p. 10)

color The perceptual experience of different wavelengths of light, involving hue, saturation (purity), and brightness (intensity). (p. 85)

color blindness One of several inherited forms of color deficiency or weakness in which an individual cannot distinguish between certain colors. (p. 86)

competence motivation Motivated behavior directed toward demonstrating competence and exercising control in a situation. (p. 295)

comprehension vocabulary The words that are understood by an infant or child. (p. 329)

compulsions Repetitive behaviors or mental acts that are performed to prevent or reduce anxiety. (p. 473)

concepts The mental categories of objects or ideas based on properties that they share. (p. 237)

concrete operational stage In Piaget's theory, the third stage of cognitive development, which lasts from about age seven to adolescence; characterized by the ability to think logically about concrete objects and situations. (p. 335)

conditional positive regard In Carl Rogers' theory of personality, the sense that you will be valued and loved only if you behave in a way that is acceptable to others; conditional love or acceptance. (p. 377)

conditioned reinforcer A stimulus or event that has acquired reinforcing value by being associated with a primary reinforcer; also called a secondary reinforcer. (p. 168)

conditioned response (CR) The learned, reflexive response to a conditioned stimulus. (p. 161)

conditioned stimulus (CS) A formerly neutral stimulus that acquires the capacity to elicit a reflexive response. (p. 161)

cones The short, thick, pointed sensory receptors of the eye that detect color and are responsible for color vision and visual acuity. (p. 82)

conflict A situation in which a person feels pulled between two or more opposing desires, motives, or goals. (p. 435)

conformity The tendency to adjust one's behavior, attitudes, or beliefs to group norms in response to real or imagined group pressure. (p. 414)

consciousness Personal awareness of mental activities, internal sensations, and the external environment. (p. 118)

conservation In Piaget's theory, the understanding that two equal quantities remain equal even though the form or appearance is rearranged, as long as nothing is added or subtracted. (p. 335)

context effect The tendency to recover information more easily when the retrieval occurs in the same setting as the original learning of the information. (p. 208)

continuous reinforcement A schedule of reinforcement in which every occurrence of a particular response is reinforced. (p. 174)

control group The group of subjects who are exposed to all experimental conditions, except the independent variable. (p. 19)

coping Behavioral and cognitive responses used to contend with stressors; involves efforts to change circumstances, or one's interpretation of circumstances, to make them more favorable and less threatening. (p. 451)

cornea (CORE-nee-uh) A clear membrane covering the visible part of the eye that helps gather and direct incoming light. (p. 81)

corpus callosum A thick band of nerve fibers that connects the two cerebral hemispheres and acts as a communication link between them. (p. 58)

correlation The relationship between two variables. (p. A-8)

correlation coefficient A measure of the magnitude and direction of the relationship (the correlation) between two variables. The closer the correlation coefficient is to +1 or −1, the stronger the relationship is. A *positive* correlation coefficient indicates that as one variable increases, the other tends to increase. A *negative* correlation coefficient indicates that as one variable increases, the other tends to decrease. (p. A-9)

correlational study A research strategy that allows the precise calculation of how strongly related two factors are to one another. (p. 25)

corticosteroids Hormones released by the adrenal cortex that play a key role in the body's response to long-term stressors. (p. 440)

counterconditioning A behavior therapy technique based on classical conditioning that involves modifying behavior by conditioning a new response that is incompatible with a previously learned response. (p. 505)

creativity A group of cognitive processes used to generate useful, original, and novel ideas or solutions. (p. 266)

critical thinking The active process of trying to minimize the influence of preconceptions and biases while rationally evaluating evidence, determining what conclusions can be drawn from the evidence, and considering alternative explanations. (p. 14)

cryptomnesia (krip-tome-NEE-zha) A memory-distortion phenomenon in which a "hidden," or unremembered, memory becomes the basis for a seemingly "new" memory. (p. 213)

cued recall A test of long-term memory that involves remembering an item of information in response to a retrieval cue. (p. 207)

culture The attitudes, values, beliefs, and behaviors shared by a group of people and communicated from one generation to another. (p. 10)

cyclothymic disorder A mood disorder characterized by moderate but frequent mood swings that are not severe enough to qualify as bipolar disorder. (p. 478)

D

daily hassles Everyday minor events that annoy and upset people. (p. 434)

decay theory The view that forgetting is due to normal metabolic processes that occur in the brain over time. (p. 221)

decibel (DESS-uh-bell) The unit of measurement for loudness. (p. 89)

delusion A falsely held belief that persists in spite of contradictory evidence. (p. 486)

dendrites Multiple short fibers that extend from the neuron's cell body and receive information from other neurons or sensory receptor cells. (p. 37)

deoxyribonucleic acid (DNA) The chemical basis of heredity; carries the genetic instructions in the cell. (p. 318)

dependent variable The factor that is observed and measured for change in an experiment; thought to be influenced by the independent variable. (p. 18)

depressants A category of psychoactive drugs that depress or inhibit brain activity. (p. 146)

depth perception The use of visual cues to perceive the distance or three-dimensional characteristics of objects. (p. 100)

descriptive methods Scientific procedures that involve systematically observing behavior in order to describe the relationships among behaviors and events. (p. 23)

descriptive statistics Statistics used to organize and summarize data in a meaningful way. (p. A-2)

developmental psychology The branch of psychology that studies how people change over the lifespan. (p. 316)

difference threshold The smallest possible difference between two stimuli that can be detected half the time. Also called *just noticeable difference.* (p. 78)

diffusion of responsibility The phenomenon in which the presence of other people makes it less likely that any individual will help someone in distress because the obligation to intervene is shared among all the onlookers. (p. 424)

discriminative stimulus In operant conditioning, a specific stimulus in the presence of which a particular response is more likely to be reinforced, and in the absence of which a particular response is not reinforced. (p. 171)

displacement In psychoanalytic theory, the Ego defense mechanism that involves unconsciously shifting the target of an emotional urge to a substitute target that is less threatening or dangerous. (p. 366)

display rules Social and cultural rules that regulate the expression of emotions, particularly facial expressions. (p. 304)

dissociation The splitting of consciousness into two or more simultaneous streams of mental activity. (p. 141)

dissociative amnesia A dissociative disorder involving the partial or total inability to recall important personal information. (p. 482)

dissociative disorders A category of psychological disorders in which extreme and frequent disruptions of awareness, memory, and personal identity impair the ability to function. (p. 482)

dissociative experience A break or disruption in consciousness during which awareness, memory, and personal identity become separated or divided. (p. 481)

dissociative fugue A dissociative disorder involving sudden and unexpected travel away from home, extensive amnesia, and identity confusion. (p. 482)

dissociative identity disorder (DID) Formerly called *multiple personality disorder;* a dissociative disorder involving extensive memory disruptions along with the presence of two or more distinct identities or "personalities." (p. 483)

dominant gene In a pair of genes, the gene containing genetic instructions that will be expressed whether paired with another dominant gene or with a recessive gene. (p. 319)

dopamine (DOPE-uh-meen) Neurotransmitter that is involved in the regulation of bodily movements, thought processes, and rewarding sensations. (p. 44)

dopamine hypothesis The view that schizophrenia is related to, and may be caused by, excess activity of the neurotransmitter dopamine in the brain. (p. 490)

dream A story-like episode of unfolding mental imagery during sleep. (p. 134)

dream interpretation A technique used in psychoanalysis in which the content of dreams is analyzed for disguised or symbolic wishes, meanings, and motivations. (p. 500)

drive An impulse that activates behavior to reduce a need and restore homeostasis. (p. 274)

drive theories The view that behavior is motivated by the desire to reduce internal tension caused by unmet biological needs. (p. 274)

drug rebound effect Withdrawal symptoms that are the opposite of a physically addictive drug's action. (p. 145)

DSM-IV Abbreviation for the *Diagnostic and Statistical Manual of Mental Disorders,* fourth edition; the book published by the American Psychiatric Association that describes the specific symptoms and diagnostic guidelines for different psychological disorders. (p. 465)

dysthymic disorder A mood disorder involving chronic, low-grade feelings of depression that produce subjective discomfort but do not seriously impair the ability to function. (p. 476)

E

eardrum A tightly stretched membrane at the end of the ear canal that vibrates when sound waves hit it. (p. 90)

eclecticism The pragmatic and integrated use of techniques from different psychotherapies. (p. 517)

ecological perspective In learning theory, a general approach that emphasizes that the study of learning must consider the unique behavior patterns of different species that have evolved in relation to the species' natural environment. (p. 185)

EEG The graphic record of brain activity produced by an electroencephalograph. (p. 125)

Ego Latin for "I"; in Freud's theory of personality, the partly conscious rational component of personality that regulates thoughts and behavior and is most in touch with the demands of the external world. (p. 365)

Ego defense mechanisms In psychoanalytic theory, largely unconscious distortions of thought or perception that act to reduce anxiety. (p. 366)

egocentrism In Piaget's theory, the inability to take another person's perspective or point of view. (p. 334)

elaborative rehearsal Rehearsal that involves focusing on the meaning of information to help encode and transfer it to long-term memory. (p. 202)

electroconvulsive therapy (ECT) A biomedical therapy used primarily in the treatment of depression that involves electrically inducing a brief brain seizure; also called *shock therapy* and *electric shock therapy.* (p. 524)

electroencephalograph (electro-en-SEFF-uh-low-graph) An instrument that uses electrodes placed on the scalp to measure and record the brain's electrical activity. (pp. 52, 125)

embryonic period The second period of prenatal development, extending from the third week through the eighth week. (p. 321)

emotion A distinct psychological state that involves subjective experience, physical arousal, and a behavioral expression or response. (p. 298)

emotion-focused coping Coping efforts primarily aimed at relieving or regulating the emotional impact of a stressful situation. (p. 452)

encoding The process of transforming information into a form that can be entered into and retained by the memory system. (p. 196)

encoding failure The inability to recall specific information because of insufficient encoding for storage in long-term memory. (p. 217)

encoding specificity principle The principle that when the conditions of information retrieval are similar to the conditions of information encoding, retrieval is more likely to be successful. (p. 207)

endocrine system (EN-doe-krin) A communication system composed of glands located throughout the body that secrete hormones into the bloodstream. (p. 51)

endorphins (en-DORF-ins) Neurotransmitters that regulate pain perception. (p. 45)

episodic information Long-term memory of personally experienced events; also called *autobiographical memory.* (p. 203)

Eros In Freud's theory of personality, the self-preservation or life instinct, reflected in the expression of basic biological urges that perpetuate the existence of the individual and the species. (p. 364)

ESP or **extrasensory perception** Perception of sensory information by some means other than through the normal processes of sensation. (p. 99)

ethnocentrism The belief that one's own culture or ethnic group is superior to all others, and the related tendency to use one's own culture as a standard by which to judge other cultures. (pp. 10, 412)

expectancy effect Change in a subject's behavior produced by the subject's belief that change should happen. (p. 21)

experimental group The group of subjects who are exposed to all experimental conditions, including the independent variable. (p. 19)

experimental method A method of investigation used to demonstrate cause-and-effect relationships by purposely manipulating a factor thought to produce change in a second factor. (p. 17)

extinction In learning theory, the gradual weakening and disappearance of conditioned behavior. In classical conditioning, extinction occurs when the conditioned stimulus is repeatedly presented without the unconditioned stimulus. In operant conditioning, extinction occurs when an emitted behavior is no longer followed by a reinforcer. (pp. 163, 174)

F

facial feedback hypothesis The view that expressing a specific emotion, especially facially, causes the subjective experience of that emotion. (p. 306)

family therapy A form of psychotherapy that is based on the assumption that the family is a system and that treats the family as a unit. (p. 513)

fetal period The third and longest period of prenatal development, extending from the eighth week until birth. (p. 321)

fight-or-flight response A rapidly occurring chain of internal physical reactions that prepare people either to fight or take flight from an immediate threat. (pp. 49, 438)

figure–ground relationship A Gestalt principle of perceptual organization that states that we automatically separate the elements of a perception into the feature that clearly stands out (the figure) and its less distinct background (the ground). (p. 104)

five-factor model of personality A trait theory of personality that identifies five basic source traits (extraversion, neuroticism, agreeableness, conscientiousness, and openness to experience) as the fundamental building blocks of personality. (p. 385)

fixed-interval (FI) schedule In operant conditioning, a reinforcement schedule in which a reinforcer is delivered for the first response that occurs after a fixed time interval has elapsed. (p. 176)

fixed-ratio (FR) schedule In operant conditioning, a reinforcement schedule in which a reinforcer is delivered after a fixed number of responses has occurred. (p. 176)

flashbulb memory The recall of very specific images or details surrounding a vivid, rare, or significant personal event. (p. 209)

forebrain The largest and most complex brain region, which contains centers for complex behaviors and mental processes. (p. 58)

forgetting The inability to recall information that was previously available. (p. 215)

formal concept A mental category that is formed by learning the rules or features that define it. (p. 237)

formal operational stage In Piaget's theory, the fourth stage of cognitive development, which lasts from adolescence through adulthood; characterized by the ability to think logically about abstract principles and hypothetical situations. (p. 335)

fovea (FOH-vee-uh) A small area in the center of the retina that is composed entirely of cones, where visual information is most sharply focused. (p. 83)

free association A psychoanalytic technique in which the patient spontaneously reports all thoughts, feelings, and mental images as they come to mind. (pp. 363, 500)

frequency In hearing, the rate of vibration, or the number of sound waves per second. (p. 89)

frequency distribution A summary of how often various scores occur in a sample of scores. Score values are arranged in order of magnitude and the number of times each score occurs is recorded. (p. A-3)

frequency polygon A way of graphically representing a frequency distribution; frequency is marked above each score category on the graph's horizontal axis, and the marks are connected by straight lines. (p. A-4)

frequency theory In hearing, the view that the basilar membrane vibrates at the same frequency as the sound wave. (p. 91)

frontal lobe The largest lobe of the cerebral cortex; processes voluntary muscle movements and is involved in thinking, planning, and emotional expression and control. (p. 59)

functional fixedness The tendency to view objects as functioning only in their usual or customary way. (p. 241)

functionalism Early school of psychology that emphasized studying the purpose, or function, of behavior and mental experiences. (p. 5)

fundamental attribution error The tendency to attribute the behavior of others to internal, personal characteristics, while ignoring or underestimating the effects of external, situational factors; an attributional bias that is common in individualistic cultures. (p. 404)

G

g factor (general intelligence) The notion of a general intelligence factor that is responsible for a person's overall performance on tests of mental ability. (p. 256)

GABA (gamma-aminobutyric acid) Neurotransmitter that usually communicates an inhibitory message. (p. 45)

gate-control theory The theory that pain is a product of both physiological and psychological factors that cause spinal "gates" to open and relay patterns of intense stimulation to the brain, which perceives them as pain. (p. 96)

gender The cultural, social, and psychological meanings that are associated with masculinity or femininity. (p. 330)

gender identity A person's psychological sense of being either male or female. (p. 330)

gender roles The behaviors, attitudes, and personality traits that are designated as either masculine or feminine in a given culture. (p. 330)

gender schema theory The theory that gender-role development is influenced by the formation of schemas, or mental representations, of masculinity and femininity. (p. 332)

gene The basic unit of heredity that directs the development of a particular characteristic; the individual unit of DNA instructions on a chromosome. (p. 318)

general adaptation syndrome Selye's term for the three-stage progression of physical changes that occur when an organism is exposed to intense and prolonged stress. The three stages are alarm, resistance, and exhaustion. (p. 439)

generalized anxiety disorder An anxiety disorder characterized by excessive, global, and persistent symptoms of anxiety; also called *free-floating anxiety*. (p. 468)

genotype (JEEN-oh-type) The underlying genetic makeup of a particular organism, including the genetic instructions for traits that are not actually displayed. (p. 319)

germinal period The first two weeks of prenatal development. (p. 320)

Gestalt psychology (guess-TALT) A school of psychology founded in Germany in the early 1900s that maintained that our sensations are actively processed according to consistent perceptual rules that result in meaningful whole perceptions, or *gestalts*. (pp. 7, 99)

glial cells (GLEE-ull) Support cells that assist neurons by providing structural support, nutrition, and removal of cell wastes; also manufacture myelin. (p. 37)

group therapy A form of psychotherapy that involves one or more therapists working simultaneously with a small group of clients. (p. 512)

H

hair cells The hairlike sensory receptors for sound, found in the basilar membrane of the cochlea. (p. 91)

hallucination A false or distorted perception that seems vividly real to the person experiencing it. (p. 486)

health psychology The branch of psychology that studies how psychological factors influence health, illness, medical treatment, and health-related behaviors. (p. 433)

heritability The percentage of variation within a given population that is due to heredity. (p. 260)

heuristic A problem-solving strategy that involves following a general rule of thumb to reduce the number of possible solutions. (p. 239)

hidden observer Hilgard's term for the hidden, or dissociated, stream of mental activity during hypnosis. (p. 141)

hierarchy of needs Maslow's hierarchical division of motivation into levels that progress from basic physical needs to psychological needs to self-fulfillment needs. (pp. 275, 488)

hindbrain A region at the base of the brain that contains several structures that regulate basic life functions. (p. 56)

hippocampus A curved forebrain structure that is part of the limbic system and is involved in learning and forming new memories. (p. 62)

histogram A way of graphically representing a frequency distribution; a type of bar chart using vertical bars that touch. (p. A-3)

homeostasis (home-ee-oh-STAY-sis) The notion that the body monitors and maintains internal states, such as body temperature and energy supplies, at relatively constant levels. (p. 274)

hormones Chemical messengers secreted into the bloodstream by endocrine glands. (p. 51)

hue The property of wavelengths of light known as color, with different wavelengths corresponding to our perceptual experience of different colors. (p. 85)

humanistic psychology School of psychology and theoretical viewpoint on personality that generally emphasizes the inherent goodness of people, human potential, self-actualization, the self-concept, and healthy personality development. (pp. 8, 375)

hypermnesia (high-perm-NEES-zha) A phenomenon in which a person's memory for past events is presumably enhanced through the use of hypnotic suggestion. (p. 141)

hypnagogic hallucinations (hip-nah-GO-jick) Vivid sensory phenomena that can occur during the onset of sleep. (p. 125)

hypnosis (hip-NO-sis) A cooperative social interaction in which a person responds to suggestions with changes in perception, memory, and behavior. (p. 139)

hypothalamus (hi-poe-THAL-uh-muss) A peanut-sized forebrain structure that is part of the limbic system and regulates behaviors related to survival, such as eating, drinking, and sexual activity. (p. 62)

hypothesis (high-POTH-eh-sis) A tentative statement about the relationship between two or more variables. (p. 15)

I

Id Latin for "the it"; in Freud's theory of personality, the completely unconscious, irrational component of personality that seeks immediate satisfaction of instinctual urges and drives; ruled by the pleasure principle. (p. 364)

identification In psychoanalytic theory, an Ego defense mechanism that involves reducing anxiety by modeling the behavior and characteristics of another person. (p. 368)

identity A person's definition or description of himself or herself, including the values, beliefs, and ideals that guide the individual's behavior. (p. 340)

immune system Body system that produces specialized white blood cells that protect the body from viruses, bacteria, and tumor cells. (p. 440)

implicit personality theory A network of assumptions or beliefs about the relationships among various types of people, traits, and behaviors. (p. 403)

in-group A social group to which one belongs. (p. 411)

in-group bias The tendency to judge the behavior of in-group members favorably and out-group members unfavorably. (p. 412)

incentive theories The view that behavior is motivated by the "pull" of external goals, such as rewards. (p. 275)

independent variable The purposely manipulated factor thought to produce change in an experiment. (p. 17)

individualistic cultures Cultures that emphasize the needs and goals of the individual over the needs and goals of the group. (p. 10)

induction A discipline technique that combines parental control with explaining why a behavior is prohibited. (p. 354)

inferential statistics Statistical techniques that allow researchers to determine whether the outcomes in a study are likely to be more than just chance events and whether they can be legitimately generalized to a larger population. (p. A-12)

information-processing model of cognitive development The model that views cognitive development as a continuous process over the lifespan and that studies the development of basic mental processes like attention, memory, and problem solving. (p. 336)

informational social influence Behavior that is motivated by the desire to be correct. (p. 415)

inner ear The part of the ear where sound is transduced into neural impulses; consists of the cochlea and semicircular canals. (p. 91)

insight The sudden realization of how a problem can be solved. (p. 240)

insomnia A condition in which a person regularly experiences the inability to fall asleep, stay asleep, or feel adequately rested by sleep. (p. 132)

instinct theories The view that some motives are innate and due to genetic programming. (p. 273)

instinctive drift The tendency of an animal to revert to instinctive behaviors that can interfere with the performance of an operantly conditioned response. (p. 189)

intelligence The global capacity to think rationally, act purposefully, and deal effectively with the environment. (p. 251)

intelligence quotient (IQ) A global measure of intelligence derived by comparing an individual's score to that of others in the same age group. (p. 252)

interference theory The theory that forgetting is caused by one memory competing with or replacing another. (p. 217)

interneuron Type of neuron that communicates information from one neuron to the next. (p. 37)

interpretation A technique used in psychoanalysis in which the psychoanalyst offers a carefully timed explanation of the patient's dreams, free associations, or behavior to facilitate the recognition of unconscious conflicts or motivations. (p. 500)

intuition Coming to a conclusion or making a judgment without conscious awareness of the thought processes involved. (p. 240)

iridology (EYE-ruh-*doll*-uh-jee) A popular pseudoscience based on the unproven notion that the physical and psychological functioning of an individual is represented in the color and markings of the iris of the eye. (p. 82)

iris (EYE-riss) The colored part of the eye, which is the muscle that controls the size of the pupil. (p. 81)

irreversibility In Piaget's theory, the inability to mentally reverse a sequence of events or logical operations. (p. 334)

J

James-Lange theory of emotion The theory that emotions arise from the perception and interpretation of bodily changes. (p. 305)

just noticeable difference (jnd) The smallest possible difference between two stimuli that can be detected half the time. Also called *difference threshold*. (p. 78)

just-world hypothesis The assumption that the world is fair, and therefore that people get what they deserve and deserve what they get. (p. 404)

K

kinesthetic sense (kin-ess-THET-ick) The technical name for the sense of location and position of body parts in relation to one another. (p. 97)

L

language A system for combining arbitrary symbols to produce an infinite number of meaningful statements. (p. 246)

latent learning Tolman's term to describe learning that occurs in the absence of reinforcement but is not behaviorally demonstrated until a reinforcer becomes available. (p. 182)

learning A relatively permanent change in behavior as a result of past experience. (p. 158)

lens A transparent structure located behind the pupil that actively focuses, or bends, light as it enters the eye. (p. 81)

libido In Freud's theory of personality, the psychological and emotional energy associated with expressions of sexuality; the sex drive. (p. 364)

limbic system A group of forebrain structures, including the hypothalamus, thalamus, amygdala, and hippocampus, that form a border around the brainstem; collectively these structures are involved in emotion, motivation, learning, and memory. (p. 60)

linguistic relativity hypothesis The notion that differences among languages cause differences in the thoughts of their speakers. (p. 248)

lithium A naturally occurring substance that is used in the treatment of bipolar disorder. (p. 522)

long-term memory The stage of memory that represents the long-term storage of information. (p. 198)

loudness The intensity (or amplitude) of a sound wave, measured in decibels. (p. 89)

LSD A synthetic psychedelic drug. (p. 150)

lymphocytes Specialized white blood cells that are responsible for immune defenses. (p. 440)

M

magnetic resonance imaging scanner (MRI) An instrument that provides three-dimensional, highly detailed views of the brain using electrical signals generated by the brain in response to magnetic fields. (p. 52)

maintenance rehearsal The mental or verbal repetition of information in order to maintain it beyond the usual 30-second duration of short-term memory. (p. 200)

major depression A mood disorder characterized by extreme and persistent feelings of despondency, worthlessness, and hopelessness, causing impaired emotional, cognitive, behavioral, and physical functioning. (p. 475)

manic episode A sudden, rapidly escalating emotional state characterized by extreme euphoria, excitement, physical energy, and rapid thoughts and speech. (p. 478)

marijuana A psychoactive drug derived from the hemp plant. (p. 151)

mean The sum of a set of scores in a distribution divided by the number of scores. The mean is usually the most representative measure of central tendency. (p. A-5)

measure of central tendency A single number that presents some information about the "center" of a frequency distribution. (p. A-5)

measure of variability A single number that presents information about the spread of scores in a frequency distribution. (p. A-6)

median The score that divides a frequency distribution exactly in half, so that the same number of scores lies on each side of it. (p. A-5)

meditation Any one of a number of sustained concentration techniques that focus attention and heighten awareness. (p. 143)

medulla (meh-DULL-uh) A hindbrain structure that controls vital life functions such as breathing, circulation, and muscle tone. (p. 57)

melatonin (mel-uh-TONE-in) A hormone manufactured by the pineal gland that produces sleepiness. (p. 121)

memory The mental processes that enable us to retain and use information over time. (p. 196)

memory consolidation The gradual, physical process of converting new long-term memories into stable, enduring long-term memory codes. (p. 225)

memory trace The brain changes associated with a particular stored memory. (p. 222)

menarche A female's first menstrual period, which occurs during puberty. (p. 338)

menopause The natural cessation of menstruation and the end of reproductive capacity in women. (p. 345)

mental age A measurement of intelligence in which an individual's mental level is expressed in terms of the average abilities of a given age group. (p. 251)

mental image The mental representation of objects or events that are not physically present. (p. 235)

mental set The tendency to persist in solving problems with solutions that have worked in the past. (p. 241)

mescaline A psychedelic drug derived from the peyote cactus. (p. 150)

meta-analysis A statistical technique that involves combining and analyzing the results of many research studies on a specific topic in order to identify overall trends. (p. 16)

midbrain The smallest brain region, which helps coordinate auditory and visual sensations. (p. 57)

middle ear The part of the ear that amplifies sound waves and consists of three small bones, the hammer, the anvil, and the stirrup. (p. 90)

Minnesota Multiphasic Personality Inventory (MMPI) A self-report inventory that assesses personality characteristics and psychological disorders; used to assess both normal and disturbed populations. (p. 391)

misinformation effect A memory-distortion phenomenon in which people's existing memories can be altered by exposing them to misleading information. (p. 214)

mode The most frequently occurring score in a distribution. (p. A-5)

monocular cues (moe-NOCK-you-ler) Distance or depth cues that can be processed by either eye alone. (p. 100)

mood congruence An encoding specificity phenomenon in which a given mood tends to evoke memories that are consistent with that mood. (p. 209)

mood-dependent retrieval An encoding specificity phenomenon in which information encoded in a certain emotional state is most retrievable when the person is in the same emotional state. (p. 208)

mood disorders A category of mental disorders in which significant and chronic disruption in mood is the predominant symptom, causing impaired cognitive, behavioral, and physical functioning. (p. 475)

moon illusion A visual illusion involving the misperception that the moon is larger when it is on the horizon that when it is directly overhead. (p. 109)

moral reasoning The aspect of cognitive development that has to do with the way an individual reasons about moral decisions. (p. 342)

motivated forgetting The theory that forgetting occurs because an undesired memory is held back from awareness. (p. 218)

N

motivation The forces that act on or within an organism to initiate and direct behavior. (p. 273)

motor neuron Type of neuron that signals muscles to relax or contract. (p. 37)

Müller-Lyer illusion A famous visual illusion involving the misperception of the identical length of two lines, one with arrows pointed inward, one with arrows pointed outward. (p. 108)

myelin sheath (MY-eh-linn) A white, fatty covering wrapped around the axons of some neurons that increases their communication speed. (p. 39)

narcolepsy A sleep disorder characterized by excessive daytime sleepiness and brief lapses into sleep throughout the day. (p. 133)

natural concept A mental category that is formed as a result of everyday experience. (p. 237)

naturalistic observation The systematic observation and recording of behaviors as they occur in their natural setting. (p. 23)

negative correlation A finding that two factors vary systematically in opposite directions, one increasing as the other decreases. (p. 26)

negative reinforcement In operant conditioning, a situation in which a response results in the removal, avoidance, or escape of a punishing stimulus, increasing the likelihood of the response being repeated in similar situations. (p. 168)

negative symptoms In schizophrenia, symptoms that reflect defects or deficits in normal functioning and include greatly reduced emotional expressiveness, motivation, and/or speech. (pp. 485, 488)

nerve Bundle of neuron axons that carries information in the peripheral nervous system. (p. 47)

nervous system The primary internal communication network of the body; divided into the central nervous system and the peripheral nervous system. (p. 47)

neuron Highly specialized cell that communicates information in electrical and chemical form; a nerve cell. (p. 37)

neurotransmitter Chemical messenger manufactured by a neuron. (p. 43)

nicotine A stimulant drug found in tobacco products. (p. 149)

night terrors A sleep disturbance characterized by an episode of increased physiological arousal, intense fear and panic, frightening hallucinations, and no recall of the episode the next morning; typically occurs during stage 3 or stage 4 NREM sleep; also called *sleep terror*. (p. 132)

nightmare A frightening or unpleasant anxiety dream that occurs during REM sleep. (p. 136)

norepinephrine (nor-ep-in-EF-rin) Neurotransmitter involved in learning and memory; also a hormone manufactured by the adrenal glands. (p. 45)

normal curve (**normal distribution**) A bell-shaped distribution of individual differences in a normal population in which most scores cluster around the average score. (p. 255)

normative social influence Behavior that is motivated by the desire to gain social acceptance and approval. (p. 415)

NREM sleep Nondreaming quiet sleep, which is divided into four stages. (p. 125)

O

obedience The performance of an action in response to the direct orders of an authority or person of higher status. (p. 416)

obese Weighing 20 percent or more above one's "ideal" body weight. (p. 281)

object permanence In Piaget's theory, the understanding that an object continues to exist even when it can no longer be seen. (p. 333)

observational learning Learning that occurs through observing the actions of others. (p. 183)

obsessions Repeated, intrusive, and uncontrollable irrational thoughts or mental images that cause extreme anxiety and distress. (p. 473)

obsessive-compulsive disorder An anxiety disorder in which the symptoms of anxiety are triggered by intrusive, repetitive thoughts and urges to perform certain actions. (p. 473)

occipital lobe (ock-SIP-it-ull) An area at the back of each cerebral hemisphere that is the primary receiving area for visual information. (p. 58)

Oedipus complex In Freud's theory of personality, a child's unconscious sexual desire for the opposite-sex parent, usually accompanied by hostile feelings toward the same-sex parent. (p. 368)

olfactory bulb (ole-FACK-toe-ree) The enlarged ending of the olfactory cortex at the front of the brain where the sensation of smell is registered. (p. 93)

operant In operant conditioning, Skinner's term for an actively emitted (or voluntary) behavior that operates on the environment to produce consequences. (p. 167)

operant conditioning The basic learning process that involves changing the probability of a response being repeated by manipulating the consequences of that response. (p. 167)

operational definition A precise description of how the variables in a study will be manipulated or measured. (p. 15)

opiates (OH-pee-ets) A category of psychoactive drugs that are chemically similar to morphine and have strong pain-relieving properties. (p. 148)

opponent-process theory of color vision The theory that color vision is the product of opposing pairs of color receptors, red/green, blue/yellow, and black/white; when one member of a color pair is stimulated, the other member is inhibited. (p. 86)

optic nerve The thick nerve that exits from the back of the eye and carries visual information to the visual cortex in the brain. (p. 84)

optimistic explanatory style Accounting for negative events or situations with external, unstable, and specific explanations. (p. 444)

out-group A social group to which one does not belong. (p. 411)

out-group homogeneity effect The tendency to see members of an out-group as very similar to one another. (p. 411)

outer ear The part of the ear that collects sound waves and consists of the pinna, the ear canal, and the eardrum. (p. 90)

P

pain The unpleasant sensation of physical discomfort or suffering that can occur in varying degrees of intensity. (p. 96)

panic attack A sudden episode of extreme anxiety that rapidly escalates in intensity. (p. 469)

panic disorder An anxiety disorder in which the person experiences frequent and unexpected panic attacks. (p. 469)

parasympathetic nervous system Branch of the autonomic nervous system that maintains normal body functions and conserves the body's physical resources. (p. 50)

parietal lobe (puh-RYE-et-ull) An area on each hemisphere of the cerebral cortex located above the temporal lobe that processes somatic sensations. (p. 58)

partial reinforcement In operant conditioning, a situation in which the occurrence of a particular response is only sometimes followed by a reinforcer. (p. 174)

partial reinforcement effect In operant conditioning, the phenomenon by which behaviors that are conditioned using partial reinforcement are more resistant to extinction than behaviors that are conditioned using continuous reinforcement. (p. 175)

perception The process of integrating, organizing, and interpreting sensations. (p. 76)

perceptual constancy The tendency to perceive objects, especially familiar objects, as constant and unchanging despite changes in sensory input. (p. 106)

perceptual illusion The misperception of the true characteristics of an object or an image. (p. 108)

perceptual set The influence of prior assumptions and expectations on perceptual interpretations. (p. 107)

peripheral nervous system (per-IF-er-ull) Division of the nervous system that includes all the nerves lying outside the central nervous system. (p. 48)

permissive parenting style Parenting style in which parents are extremely tolerant and not demanding; permissive-indulgent parents are responsive to their children, while permissive-indifferent parents are not. (p. 353)

person perception The mental processes used to form judgments and draw conclusions about the characteristics and motives of others. (p. 401)

personality An individual's unique and relatively consistent patterns of thinking, feeling, and behaving. (p. 361)

personality theory A theory that attempts to describe and explain individual similarities and differences. (p. 361)

persuasion The deliberate attempt to influence the attitudes or behavior of another person in a situation in which that person has some freedom of choice. (p. 426)

pessimistic explanatory style Accounting for negative events or situations with internal, stable, and global explanations. (p. 444)

PET scan (positron emission tomography) An instrument that provides color-coded images of brain activity by measuring the amount of glucose or oxygen used in different brain regions. (p. 53)

phenotype (FEEN-oh-type) The observable traits or characteristics of an organism as determined by the interaction of genetics and environmental factors. (p. 319)

pheromones (FARE-uh-mones) Chemical signals used by animals to communicate territorial boundaries and sexual receptiveness. (p. 94)

phobia An irrational fear triggered by a specific object or situation. (p. 470)

physical dependence A condition in which a person has physically adapted to a drug so that he or she must take the drug regularly in order to avoid withdrawal symptoms. (p. 145)

pitch The relative highness or lowness of a sound, determined by the frequency of a sound wave. (p. 89)

pituitary gland (pi-TOO-ih-tare-ee) Endocrine gland attached to the base of the brain that secretes hormones that affect the function of other glands as well as hormones that act directly on physical processes. (p. 52)

place theory In hearing, the view that different frequencies cause larger vibrations at different locations along the basilar membrane. (p. 91)

placebo control group (pluh-SEE-bo) An experimental control group in which subjects are exposed to a fake independent variable. (p. 21)

pleasure principle In Freud's theory of personality, the motive to obtain pleasure and avoid tension or discomfort; the most fundamental human motive and the guiding principle of the Id. (p. 365)

pons A hindbrain structure that connects the medulla to the two sides of the cerebellum; helps coordinate and integrate movements on each side of the body. (p. 57)

population In statistics, a complete set of something—people, nonhuman animals, objects, or events. (p. A-13)

positive correlation A finding that two factors vary systematically in the same direction, increasing or decreasing together. (p. 26)

positive reinforcement In operant conditioning, a situation in which a response is followed by the addition of a reinforcing stimulus, increasing the likelihood of the response being repeated in similar situations. (p. 167)

positive symptoms In schizophrenia, symptoms that reflect excesses or distortions of normal functioning and include delusions, hallucinations, and disorganized thoughts and behavior. (p. 485)

possible selves The aspect of the self-concept that includes images of the selves that you hope, fear, or expect to become in the future. (p. 394)

posthypnotic amnesia A hypnotic suggestion that suppresses the ability to recall specific information. (p. 140)

posthypnotic suggestion A suggestion made during hypnosis that the person carry out a specific instruction following the hypnotic session. (p. 140)

posttraumatic stress disorder (PTSD) An anxiety disorder in which chronic and persistent symptoms of anxiety develop in response to an extreme physical or psychological trauma. (p. 472)

prejudice A negative attitude toward people who belong to a specific social group. (p. 410)

prenatal stage The state of development before birth; divided into the germinal, embryonic, and fetal periods. (p. 320)

preoperational stage In Piaget's theory, the second stage of cognitive development, which lasts from about age two to age seven; characterized by increasing use of symbols and prelogical thought processes. (p. 334)

primary reinforcer In learning theory, a stimulus or event that is naturally or inherently reinforcing for a given species, such as food, water, or other biological necessities. (p. 168)

primary sex characteristics Sexual organs that are directly involved in reproduction, such as the uterus, ovaries, penis, and testicles. (p. 338)

proactive interference Forgetting in which an old memory interferes with remembering a new memory. (p. 217)

problem-focused coping Coping efforts primarily aimed at directly changing or managing a threatening or harmful stressor. (p. 452)

problem solving Thinking and behavior directed toward attaining a goal that is not readily available. (p. 238)

procedural information Long-term memory of how to perform different skills, operations, and actions. (p. 203)

production vocabulary The words that an infant or child understands and can speak. (p. 329)

projective test A type of personality test that involves a person interpreting an ambiguous image; used to assess unconscious motives, conflicts, psychological defenses, and personality traits. (p. 390)

prototype The most typical instance of a particular concept. (p. 237)

pseudoscience A fake or false science that makes claims based on little or no scientific evidence. (p. 30)

psychedelic drugs A category of psychoactive drugs that create sensory and perceptual distortions, alter mood, and affect judgment. (p. 150)

psychoactive drug A drug that alters normal consciousness, perception, mood, and behavior. (p. 145)

psychoanalysis Sigmund Freud's theory of personality and form of psychotherapy; emphasizes unconscious determinants of behavior, sexual and aggressive instinctual drives, and the enduring effects of early childhood experiences on later personality development. (pp. 7, 362, 499)

psychological disorder (mental disorder) A pattern of behavioral and psychological symptoms that causes significant personal distress, impairs the ability to function in one or more important areas of daily life, or both. (p. 465)

psychological test A test that assesses a person's abilities, aptitudes, interests, or personality, based on a systematically obtained sample of behavior. (p. 389)

psychology The scientific study of behavior and mental processes. (p. 3)

psychoneuroimmunology An interdisciplinary field that studies the interconnections among psychological processes, nervous and endocrine system functions, and the immune system. (p. 441)

psychopathology The scientific study of the origins, symptoms, and development of psychological disorders. (p. 463)

psychosexual stages In Freud's theory of personality, age-related developmental periods in which the child's sexual urges are expressed through different body areas and the activities associated with those body areas. (p. 368)

psychotherapy The treatment of emotional, behavioral, and interpersonal problems through the use of psychological techniques designed to encourage understanding of problems and modify troubling feelings, behaviors, or relationships. (p. 498)

puberty The stage of adolescence in which an individual reaches sexual maturity and becomes physiologically capable of sexual reproduction. (p. 338)

punishment The presentation of a stimulus or event following a behavior that acts to decrease the likelihood of the behavior being repeated. (p. 169)

pupil In vision, the opening in the middle of the iris of the eye that changes size to let in different amounts of light. (p. 81)

R

random assignment Assigning subjects to experimental conditions in such a way that all subjects have an equal chance of being assigned to any of the conditions or groups in the study. (p. 18)

range A measure of variability; the highest score in a distribution minus the lowest score. (p. A-6)

rational-emotive therapy (RET) A type of cognitive therapy, developed by psychologist Albert Ellis, that focuses on changing the client's irrational beliefs. (p. 509)

reality principle In Freud's theory of personality, the awareness of environmental demands and the capacity to accommodate them by postponing gratification until the appropriate time or circumstances exist. (p. 365)

recall A test of long-term memory that involves retrieving information without the aid of retrieval cues. (p. 206)

recessive gene In a pair of genes, the gene containing genetic instructions that will not be expressed unless paired with another recessive gene. (p. 319)

reciprocal determinism A model proposed by psychologist Albert Bandura that explains human functioning and personality as caused by the interaction of behavioral, cognitive, and environmental factors. (p. 379)

recognition A test of long-term memory that involves identifying correct information out of several possible choices. (p. 207)

reinforcement In operant conditioning, the occurrence of a stimulus or event following a response that increases the likelihood of the response being repeated. (p. 167)

reliability The ability of a test to produce consistent results when administered on repeated occasions under similar conditions. (p. 255)

REM rebound A phenomenon in which a person who is deprived of REM sleep greatly increases the amount of time spent in REM sleep during the first opportunity to sleep uninterrupted. (p. 130)

REM sleep Type of sleep during which rapid eye movements and dreaming occur. (p. 125)

REM sleep behavior disorder A sleep disorder in which the sleeper acts out his dreams. (p. 133)

replicate To repeat or duplicate a scientific study in order to increase confidence in the validity of the original findings. (p. 16)

representative sample A selected segment that very closely parallels the larger population being studied on relevant characteristics. (p. 25)

representativeness heuristic A strategy in which the likelihood of an event is estimated by comparing how similar it is to the typical prototype of the event. (p. 244)

repression Motivated forgetting that occurs unconsciously; in psychoanalytic theory, the unconscious exclusion of anxiety-provoking thoughts, feelings, and memories from conscious awareness. (pp. 218, 366)

resistance In psychoanalysis, the patient's unconscious attempts to block the revelation of repressed memories and conflicts. (p. 500)

resting potential State in which a neuron is prepared to activate and communicate its message if it receives sufficient stimulation. (p. 39)

restorative theory of sleep The view that sleep and dreaming are essential to normal physical and mental functioning. (p. 130)

reticular formation (reh-TICK-you-ler) A network of nerve fibers located in the center of the medulla that helps regulate attention, arousal, and sleep. (p. 57)

retina (RET-in-uh) A thin, light-sensitive membrane located at the back of the eye that contains the sensory receptors for vision. (p. 82)

retrieval The process of recovering information stored in memory so that we are consciously aware of it. (pp. 196, 205)

retrieval cue A clue, prompt, or hint that helps trigger recall of a given piece of information stored in long-term memory. (p. 205)

retrieval cue failure The inability to recall long-term memories because of inadequate or missing retrieval cues. (p. 205)

retroactive interference Forgetting in which a new memory interferes with remembering an old memory. (p. 217)

retrograde amnesia Loss of memory, especially for episodic information. (p. 225)

reuptake The process by which neurotransmitter molecules detach from a postsynaptic neuron and are reabsorbed by a presynaptic neuron so they can be recycled and used again. (p. 43)

rods The long, thin, blunt sensory receptors of the eye that are highly sensitive to light but not color and are primarily responsible for peripheral vision and night vision. (p. 82)

Rorschach Inkblot Test A projective test using inkblots, developed by Swiss psychiatrist Hermann Rorschach in 1921. (p. 390)

S

sample A selected segment of the population used to represent the group that is being studied. (p. 25)

sample A subset of a population. (p. A-13)

saturation The property of color that corresponds to the purity of the light wave. (p. 85)

scatter diagram (scatter plot) A graph that represents the relationship between two variables. (p. A-9)

schedule of reinforcement In operant conditioning, the delivery of a reinforcer according to a preset pattern based on the number of responses or the elapse of a time interval. (p. 176)

schema (SKEE-muh) An organized cluster of information about a particular topic, a mental representation of an action, an object, or an event. (p. 210)

schizophrenia A mental disorder in which the ability to function is impaired by severely distorted beliefs, perceptions, and thought processes. (p. 485)

scientific method A set of assumptions, attitudes, and procedures that guide researchers in creating questions to investigate, generating evidence, and drawing conclusions. (p. 13)

seasonal affective disorder (SAD) A mood disorder in which episodes of depression typically recur during the fall and winter and remit during the spring and summer. (p. 477)

secondary sex characteristics Sexual characteristics that develop during puberty and are not directly involved in reproduction but differentiate between the sexes, such as male facial hair and female breast development. (p. 338)

self-actualization Defined by Maslow as "the full use and exploitation of talents, capacities, and potentialities." (p. 276)

self-concept The set of perceptions and beliefs that you hold about yourself. (p. 376)

self-efficacy The degree to which a person is subjectively convinced of his or her ability to effectively meet the demands of a situation; feelings of self-confidence or self-doubt. (pp. 297, 380)

self-report inventory A type of psychological test in which a person's responses to standardized questions are compared to established norms. (p. 391)

self-serving bias The tendency to attribute successful outcomes of one's own behavior to internal causes and unsuccessful outcomes to external, situational causes. (p. 406)

semantic information General knowledge of facts, names, and concepts stored in long-term memory. (p. 203)

semantic network model A model that describes units of information in long-term memory as being organized in a complex network of associations. (p. 204)

sensation The process of detecting a physical stimulus, such as light, sound, heat, or pressure. (p. 76)

sensation seeking A personality characteristic reflecting the degree to which an individual is motivated to experience high levels of arousal associated with varied and novel activities. (p. 295)

sensorimotor stage In Piaget's theory, the first stage of cognitive development, from birth to about age two; the period during which the infant explores the environment and acquires knowledge through sensing and manipulating objects. (p. 333)

sensory adaptation The decline in sensitivity to a constant stimulus. (p. 79)

sensory memory The stage of memory that registers information from the environment and holds it for a very brief period of time. (p. 197)

sensory neuron Type of neuron that conveys information to the brain from specialized receptor cells in sense organs and internal organs. (p. 37)

sensory receptors Specialized cells unique to each sense organ that respond to a particular form of sensory stimulation. (p. 77)

sensory threshold The level at which a stimulus is strong enough to be detected by activating sensory receptors. (p. 78)

serial position effect The tendency to remember items at the beginning and end of a list better than items in the middle. (p. 207)

serotonin (ser-ah-TONE-in) Neurotransmitter that is involved in sleep and emotions. (p. 45)

set-point weight The particular weight that is set and maintained by increases or decreases in basal metabolic rate. (p. 281)

sex chromosomes Chromosomes designated as X or Y that determine biological sex; the 23rd pair of chromosomes in humans. (p. 320)

sex-linked recessive characteristics Traits determined by recessive genes located on the X chromosome; in males, these characteristics require only one recessive gene to be expressed. (p. 320)

sexual orientation The direction of a person's emotional and erotic attraction, whether toward members of the opposite sex, the same sex, or both sexes. (p. 287)

shape constancy The perception of a familiar object as maintaining the same shape regardless of the image produced on the retina. (p. 107)

shaping The operant conditioning procedure of selectively reinforcing successively closer approximations of a goal behavior until the goal behavior is displayed. (p. 174)

short-term memory (working memory) The active stage of memory in which information is stored for about 30 seconds. (p. 197)

Sixteen Personality Factor Questionnaire (16PF) A self-report inventory developed by Raymond Cattell that generates a personality profile with ratings on sixteen trait dimensions. (p. 391)

size constancy The perception of an object as maintaining the same size despite changing images on the retina. (p. 106)

skewed distribution An asymmetrical distribution; more scores pile up on one side of the distribution than on the other. In a *positively* skewed distribution, most people have low scores; in a *negatively* skewed distribution, most people have high scores. (p. A-4)

Skinner box The popular name for an *operant chamber,* the experimental apparatus invented by B. F. Skinner to study the relationship between environmental events and active behaviors. (p. 173)

sleep apnea (APP-nee-uh) A sleep disorder in which the person repeatedly stops breathing during sleep. (p. 133)

sleep disorders Serious disturbances in the normal sleep pattern that interfere with daytime functioning and cause subjective distress. (p. 131)

sleep inertia Feelings of grogginess upon awakening from sleep that interfere with the ability to perform mental or physical tasks. (p. 152)

sleep spindles Short bursts of brain activity that characterize stage 2 NREM sleep. (p. 126)

sleep thinking Repetitive, bland, and uncreative ruminations about real-life events during sleep. (p. 134)

sleepwalking A sleep disturbance characterized by an episode of walking or performing other actions during stage 3 or stage 4 NREM sleep; also called *somnambulism.* (p. 132)

social categorization The mental process of classifying people into groups (or *categories*) on the basis of their shared characteristics. (p. 402)

social cognition The study of the mental processes people use to make sense out of their social environment. (p. 400)

social cognitive theory Bandura's theory of personality, which emphasizes the importance of observational learning, conscious cognitive processes, social experiences, self-efficacy beliefs, and reciprocal determinism. (p. 379)

social influence The study of the effect that situational factors and other people have on an individual's behavior. (p. 400)

social learning theory of gender-role development The theory that gender roles are acquired through the basic processes of learning, including reinforcement, punishment, and modeling. (p. 331)

social norms The "rules," or expectations, for appropriate behavior in a particular social situation. (p. 401)

social phobia An anxiety disorder involving the extreme and irrational fear of being embarrassed, judged, or scrutinized by others in social situations. (p. 471)

social psychology The branch of psychology that studies how people think, feel, and behave in social situations. (p. 400)

social support The resources provided by other people in times of need, including emotional support, tangible support, and informational support. (p. 449)

somatic nervous system Subdivision of the peripheral nervous system that communicates sensory information to the central nervous system and carries messages from the central nervous system to the muscles. (p. 48)

source confusion A memory distortion that occurs when the true source of the memory is forgotten. (p. 212)

source traits The most fundamental dimensions of personality; the broad, basic traits that are hypothesized to be universal and relatively few in number. (p. 383)

specific phobia An anxiety disorder characterized by an extreme and irrational fear of a specific object or situation that interferes with the ability to function in daily life. (p. 470)

spinal reflexes Simple, automatic behaviors that are processed in the spinal cord. (p. 47)

split-brain operation A surgical procedure that involves cutting the corpus callosum. (p. 66)

spontaneous recovery In classical conditioning, the reappearance of a previously extinguished conditioned response after a period of time without exposure to the conditioned stimulus. (p. 163)

stage model of memory A model describing memory as consisting of three distinct stages: sensory memory, short-term memory, and long-term memory. (p. 197)

standard deviation A measure of variability; expressed as the square root of the sum of the squared deviations around the mean divided by the number of scores in the distribution. (p. A-7)

standard normal curve (standard normal distribution) A symmetrical distribution forming a bell-shaped curve in which the mean, median, and mode are all equal and fall in the exact middle. (p. A-8)

standardization The administration of a test to a large, representative sample of people under uniform conditions for the purpose of establishing norms. (p. 255)

state-dependent retrieval An encoding specificity phenomenon in which information that is learned in a particular drug state is more likely to be recalled while the person is in the same drug state. (p. 208)

statistical significance A mathematical indication that research results are not very likely to have occurred by chance. (p. 16)

statistics Mathematical methods used to summarize data and draw conclusions based on the data. (p. 16)

stereotype A cluster of characteristics that are associated with all members of a specific social group, often including qualities that are unrelated to the objective criteria that define the group. (p. 411)

stimulants A category of psychoactive drugs that increase brain activity, arouse behavior, and increase mental alertness. (p. 148)

stimulus discrimination In learning theory, the occurrence of a learned response to a specific stimulus but not to other similar stimuli. (p. 163)

stimulus generalization In learning theory, the occurrence of a learned response not only to the original stimulus but to other similar stimuli as well. (p. 163)

stimulus threshold The minimum level of stimulation required to activate a particular neuron. (p. 39)

storage The process of retaining information in memory so that it can be used at a later time. (p. 196)

stress A negative emotional state occurring in response to events that are perceived as taxing or exceeding a person's resources or ability to cope. (p. 432)

stressors Events or situations that are perceived as harmful, threatening, or challenging. (p. 433)

structural plasticity A phenomenon in which brain structures physically change in response to environmental influences. (p. 69)

structuralism Early school of psychology that emphasized studying the most basic components, or structures, of conscious experiences. (p. 4)

substance P A neurotransmitter that is involved in the transmission of pain messages to the brain. (p. 96)

substantia nigra (sub-STANCE-ee-uh NEE-gruh) An area of the midbrain that is involved in motor control and contains a large concentration of dopamine-producing neurons. (p. 57)

Superego In Freud's theory of personality, the partly conscious self-evaluative, moralistic component of personality that is formed through the internalization of parental and societal rules. (p. 366)

suppression Motivated forgetting that occurs consciously. (p. 218)

suprachiasmatic nucleus (SCN) (soup-rah-kye-az-MAT-ick) A cluster of neurons in the hypothalamus in the brain that governs the timing of circadian rhythms. (p. 121)

surface traits Personality characteristics or attributes that can easily be inferred from observable behavior. (p. 383)

survey A questionnaire or interview designed to investigate the opinions, behaviors, or characteristics of a particular group. (p. 24)

symbolic thought In developmental psychology, the child's ability to use words, images, and symbols to represent the world. (p. 334)

symmetrical distribution A distribution in which scores fall equally on both sides of the graph. The normal curve is an example of a symmetrical distribution. (p. A-4)

sympathetic nervous system Branch of the autonomic nervous system that produces rapid physical arousal in response to perceived emergencies or threats. (p. 49)

synapse (SIN-aps) The point of communication between two neurons. (p. 41)

synaptic gap (sin-AP-tick) The tiny space between the axon terminal of one neuron and the dendrite of an adjoining neuron. (p. 41)

synaptic transmission (sin-AP-tick) The process in which neurotransmitters are released by one neuron, cross the synaptic gap, and affect adjoining neurons. (p. 43)

synaptic vesicles (sin-AP-tick VESS-ick-ulls) Tiny pouches or sacs in the axon terminals that contain chemicals called neurotransmitters. (p. 43)

systematic desensitization A type of behavior therapy in which phobic responses are reduced by pairing relaxation with a series of mental images or real-life situations that the person finds progressively more fear-provoking; based on the principle of counterconditioning. (p. 505)

T

taste buds The specialized sensory receptors for taste that are located on the tongue and inside the mouth and throat. (p. 95)

temperament Inborn predispositions to consistently behave and react in a certain way. (p. 324)

temporal lobe An area on each hemisphere of the cerebral cortex near the temples that is the primary receiving area for auditory information. (p. 58)

teratogens Harmful agents or substances that can cause malformations or defects in an embryo or fetus. (p. 321)

thalamus (THAL-uh-muss) A forebrain structure that processes sensory information for all senses, except smell, and relays it to the cerebral cortex. (p. 61)

Thanatos In Freud's theory of personality, the death instinct, reflected in aggressive, destructive, and self-destructive actions. (p. 364)

Thematic Apperception Test (TAT) A projective personality test that involves creating stories about each of a series of ambiguous scenes; also used to measure achievement motivation. (p. 390)

theory A tentative explanation that tries to integrate and account for the relationship among various findings and observations. (p. 17)

thinking The manipulation of mental representations of information in order to draw inferences and conclusions. (p. 235)

timbre (TAM-ber) The distinctive quality of a sound, determined by the complexity of the sound wave. (p. 89)

tip-of-the-tongue (TOT) experience A memory phenomenon that involves the sensation of knowing that specific information is stored in long-term memory but being temporarily unable to retrieve it. (p. 206)

token economy A form of behavior therapy in which the therapeutic environment is structured to reward desired behaviors with tokens or points that may eventually be exchanged for tangible rewards. (p. 507)

tolerance In drug use, a condition in which increasing amounts of a physically addictive drug are needed to produce the original, desired effect. (p. 145)

trait A relatively stable, enduring predisposition to consistently behave in a certain way. (p. 383)

trait theory A theory of personality that focuses on identifying, describing, and measuring individual differences in traits. (p. 383)

tranquilizers Depressant drugs that relieve anxiety. (p. 148)

transduction The process by which a form of physical energy is converted into a coded neural signal that can be processed by the nervous system. (p. 77)

transference In psychoanalysis, the process by which emotions and desires originally associated with a significant person in the patient's life, such as a parent, are unconsciously transferred to the psychoanalyst. (p. 500)

trial and error A problem-solving strategy that involves attempting different solutions and eliminating those that do not work. (p. 239)

triarchic theory of intelligence Sternberg's theory that there are three forms of intelligence: componential, contextual, and experiential. (p. 257)

trichromatic theory of color vision The theory that the sensation of color is due to cones in the retina that are especially sensitive to red light (long wavelengths), green light (medium wavelengths), or blue light (short wavelengths). (p. 86)

two-factor theory of emotion Schachter and Singer's theory that emotion is a result of the interaction of physiological arousal and the cognitive label that we apply to explain the arousal. (p. 308)

Type A behavior pattern A behavioral and emotional style characterized by a sense of time urgency, hostility, and competitiveness. (p. 446)

U

unconditional positive regard In Carl Rogers' theory of personality and client-centered psychotherapy, the sense that you will be valued and loved even if you don't conform to the standards and expectations of others; unconditional love or acceptance. (p. 377)

unconditioned response (UCR) In classical conditioning, the unlearned, reflexive response that is elicited by an unconditioned stimulus. (p. 161)

unconditioned stimulus (UCS) In classical conditioning, the natural stimulus that reflexively elicits a response without the necessity of prior learning. (p. 161)

unconscious In Freud's theory of personality, a term used to describe thoughts, feelings, wishes, and drives that are operating below the level of conscious awareness. (p. 364)

V

validity The ability of a test to measure what it is intended to measure. (p. 255)

variable A factor that can vary, or change, in ways that can be observed, measured, and verified. (p. 15)

variable-interval (VI) schedule In operant conditioning, a reinforcement schedule in which a reinforcer is delivered for the first response that occurs after an average time interval that varies unpredictably from trial to trial. (p. 177)

variable-ratio (VR) schedule In operant conditioning, a reinforcement schedule in which a reinforcer is delivered after an average number of responses that varies unpredictably from trial to trial. (p. 176)

vestibular sense (vess-TIB-you-ler) The technical name for the sense of balance, or equilibrium. (p. 97)

W

wavelength The distance from one wave peak to another. (p. 80)

Weber's Law A principle of sensation that holds that the size of the just noticeable difference will vary depending on its relation to the strength of the original stimulus. (p. 78)

withdrawal symptoms Unpleasant physical reactions, combined with intense drug cravings, that occur when a person abstains from a drug on which he or she is physically dependent. (p. 145)

Z

z score A number, expressed in standard deviation units, that shows a score's deviation from the mean. (p. A-7)

References

Abramov, Israel, & Gordon, James. (1994). Color appearance: On seeing red—or yellow, or green, or blue. *Annual Review of Psychology, 45,* 451–485.

Abrams, Richard. (1992). *Electroconvulsive therapy* (2nd ed.). New York: Oxford University Press.

Adams, James, L. (1979). *Conceptual blockbusting: A guide to better ideas* (2nd ed.). New York: Norton.

Ader, Robert. (1993). Conditioned responses. In Bill Moyers & Betty Sue Flowers (Eds.), *Healing and the mind.* New York: Doubleday.

Ader, Robert, & Cohen, Nicholas. (1975). Behaviorally conditioned immunosuppression. *Psychosomatic Medicine, 37,* 333–340.

Ader, Robert, & Cohen, Nicholas. (1993). Psychoneuroimmunology: Conditioning and stress. *Annual Review of Psychology, 44,* 53–85.

Ader, Robert; Cohen, Nicholas; & Felten, David. (1995, January 14). Psychoneuroimmunoloy: Interactions between the nervous system and the immune system. *Lancet, 345,* 99–112.

Ader, Robert; Felten, David; & Cohen, Nicholas. (1990). Interactions between the brain and immune system. *Annual Review of Pharmacology and Toxicology, 30,* 561–602.

Ader, Robert; Felten, David; & Cohen, Nicholas. (1991). *Psychoneuroimmunology* (2nd ed.). San Diego: Academic Press.

Adler, Alfred. (1933a/1979). Advantages and disadvantages of the inferiority feeling. In Heinz L. Anspacher & Rowena R. Ansbacher (Eds.), *Superiority and social interest: A collection of later writings.* New York: Norton.

Adler, Alfred. (1933b/1979). On the origin of the striving for superiority and of social interest. In Heinz L. Anspacher & Rowena R. Ansbacher (Eds.), *Superiority and social interest: A collection of later writings.* New York: Norton.

Adler, Nancy, & Matthews, Karen. (1994). Health psychology: Why do some people get sick and some stay well? *Annual Review of Psychology, 45,* 229–259.

Adler, Tina. (1993, November). Debate over: Qualitative, quantitative both valuable. *APA Monitor, 24* (11), 16.

Aggleton, John P. (Ed.). (1992). *The amygdala: Neurobiological aspects of emotion, memory, and mental dysfunction.* New York: Wiley–Liss.

Aghajanian, George K. (1994). Serotonin and the action of LSD in the brain. *Psychiatric Annals, 24* (3), 137–141.

Agosta, William C. (1992). *Chemical communication: The language of pheromones.* New York: Scientific American Library.

Aiken, Lewis R. (1994). *Psychological testing and assessment* (8th ed.). Boston: Allyn & Bacon.

Ainslie, George. (1975). Specious reward: A behavioral theory of impulsiveness and impulse control. *Psychological Bulletin, 82,* 463–496.

Ainsworth, Mary D. Salter; Blehar, Mary C.; Waters, Everett; & Wall, Sally. (1978). *Patterns of attachment: A psychological study of the Strange Situation.* Hillsdale, N.J.: Erlbaum.

Ajzen, Icek. (1991). The theory of planned behavior. *Organizational Behavior and Human Decision Processes, 50,* 179–211.

Ajzen, Icek, & Fishbein, M. (1980). *Understanding attitudes and predicting social behavior.* Englewood Cliffs, N.J.: Prentice Hall.

Alcock, James E. (1978–1979). Psychology and near-death experiences. *Skeptical Inquirer, 3,* 25–41.

Alcock, James E. (1981). *Parapsychology: Science or magic?* New York: Pergamon.

Alexander, Charles N.; Chandler, Howard M.; Langer, Ellen J.; Newman, Ronnie I.; & Davies, John L. (1989). Transcendental meditation, mindfulness, and longevity: An experimental study with the elderly. *Journal of Personality and Social Psychology, 57,* 950–964.

Alexander, James F.; Holtzworth-Munroe, Amy; & Jameson, Penny. (1994). The process and outcome of marital and family therapy: Research review and evaluation. In Allen E. Bergin & Sol L. Garfield (Eds.), *Handbook of psychotherapy and behavior change* (4th ed.). New York: Wiley.

Alford, Brad A., & Correia, Christopher J. (1994). Cognitive therapy of schizophrenia: Theory and empirical status. *Behavior Therapy 25,* 17–33.

Allen, Karen M.; Blascovich, Jim; Tomaka, Joe; & Kelsey, Robert M. (1991). Presence of human friends and pet dogs as moderators of autonomic responses to stress in women. *Journal of Personality and Social Psychology, 61,* 582–589.

Allen, Vernon L., & Levine, John M. (1969). Consensus and conformity. *Journal of Experimental Social Psychology, 5,* 389–399.

Allodi, Frederico A. (1994). Post-traumatic stress disorder in hostages and victims of torture. *Psychiatric Clinics of North America, 17,* 279–288.

Allport, Gordon W., & Odbert, H. S. (1936). Trait-names: A psycho-lexical study. *Psychological Monographs, 47* (211).

Alonso, Anne, & Swiller, Hillel I. (Eds.) (1993a). Group therapy in clinical practice. Washington, D.C.: American Psychiatric Press.

Alonso, Anne, & Swiller, Hillel I. (1993b). Introduction: The case for group therapy. In Anne Alonso & Hillel I. Swiller (Eds.), *Group therapy in clinical practice.* Washington, D.C.: American Psychiatric Press.

Amabile, Teresa M. (1983). *The social psychology of creativity.* New York: Springer-Verlag.

Amabile, Teresa M. (1989). *Growing up creative: Nurturing a lifetime of creativity.* New York: Crown.

Amabile, Teresa M., & Tighe, Elizabeth. (1993). Questions of creativity. In John Brockman (Ed.), *Creativity.* New York: Simon & Schuster.

Amador, Xavier F.; Strauss, David H.; Yale, Scott A.; & Gorman, Jack M. (1991). Awareness of illness in schizophrenia. *Schizophrenia Bulletin, 17,* 113–132.

American Psychiatric Association. (1994). *Diagnostic and statistical manual of mental disorders* (4th ed.). Washington, D.C.: American Psychiatric Association.

American Psychological Association (APA). (1986). *Animal Research Survey, 1985–1986.* Washington, D.C.: American Psychological Association.

American Psychological Association (APA). (1992a). *Ethical principles of psychologists and code of conduct.* Washington, D.C.: American Psychological Association.

American Psychological Association (APA). (1992b). *Guidelines for ethical conduct in the care and use of animals.* Washington, D.C.: American Psychological Assocation.

American Psychological Association (APA). (1993). Guidelines for practitioners of psychological services to ethnic, linguistic, and culturally diverse populations. *American Psychologist, 48,* 45–48.

American Psychological Association (APA). (1995). *Behavior research with animals.* Washington, D.C.: American Psychological Association.

Anand, B. K., & Brobeck, J. R. (1951). Hypothalamic control of food intake in rats and cats. *Yale Journal of Biological Medicine, 24,* 123–140.

Anastasi, Anne. (1988). *Psychological testing* (6th ed.). New York: Macmillan.

Anch, A. Michael; Browman, Carl P.; Mitler, Merrill M.; & Walsh, James K. (1988). *Sleep: A scientific perspective.* Englewood Cliffs, N.J.: Prentice Hall.

Anderson, John R. (1995). *Cognitive psychology and its implications* (4th ed.). New York: Freeman.

Andersson, Bengt-Erik. (1989). Effects of day care: A longitudinal study. *Child Development, 60,* 857–866.

Andersson, Bengt-Erik. (1992). Effects of day care on cognitive and socioemotional competence of thirteen-year-old Swedish schoolchildren. *Child Development, 63,* 20–36.

Andreasen, Nancy C., & Flaum, Michael. (1991). Schizophrenia: The characteristic symptoms. *Schizophrenia Bulletin, 17,* 27–49.

Angier, Natalie. (1995, February 14). Powerhouse of senses, smell, at last gets its due. *New York Times,* pp. C1, C6.

Anonymous. (1990). First person account: Birds of a psychic feather. *Schizophrenia Bulletin, 16,* 165–168.

Antony, Martin M.; Brown, Timothy A.; & Barlow, David H. (1992). Current perspectives on panic and panic disorder. *Current Directions in Psychological Science, 1,* 79–82.

APA Research Office. (1995). *Profile of all APA members: 1995.* Washington, D.C.: American Psychological Association.

Arkes, H. R., & Boykin, A. W. (1971). Analysis of complexity preference in Head Start and nursery school children. *Perceptual and Motor Skills, 33,* 1131–1137.

Arkin, Arthur M. (1981). *Sleep talking: Psychology and psychophysiology.* Hillsdale, N.J.: Erlbaum.

Arkin, Arthur M. (1991). Sleeptalking. In Steven J. Ellman & John S. Antrobus (Eds.), *The mind in sleep: Psychology and psychophysiology* (2nd ed.). New York: Wiley.

Arkin, Arthur M., & Antrobus, John S. (1991). The effects of external stimuli applied prior to and during sleep on sleep experience. In Steven J. Ellman & John S. Antrobus (Eds.), *The mind in sleep: Psychology and psychophysiology* (2nd ed.). New York: Wiley.

Arnkoff, Diane B., & Glass, Carol R. (1992). Cognitive therapy and psychotherapy integration. In Donald K. Freedheim (Ed.), *History of psychotherapy: A century of change.* Washington, D.C.: American Psychological Association.

Aron, Arthur; Aron, Elaine N.; & Smollan, Danny. (1992). Inclusion of Other in the Self Scale and the structure of interpersonal closeness. *Journal of Personality and Social Psychology, 63,* 596–612.

Aronson, Elliot. (1987). Teaching students what they think they already know about prejudice and desegregation. In Vivian Parker Makosky (Ed.), *G. Stanley Hall Lecture Series* (Vol. 7). Washington, D.C.: American Psychological Association.

Aronson, Elliot. (1990). Applying social psychology to desegregation and energy conservation. *Personality and Social Psychology Bulletin, 16,* 118–132.

Aronson, Elliot. (1995). *The social animal* (7th ed). New York: Freeman.

Aronson, Elliot, & Bridgeman, Diane. (1979). Jigsaw groups and the desegregated classroom: In pursuit of common goals. *Personality and Social Psychology Bulletin, 5,* 438–466.

Arvidson, K., & Friberg, U. (1980). Human taste response and taste bud number in fungiform papillae. *Science, 209,* 807–808.

Asch, Solomon E. (1951). Effects of group pressure upon the modification and distortion of judgments. In Harold S. Guetzkow (Ed.), *Groups, leadership, and men: Research in human relations. Reports on research sponsored by the Human Relations and Morale Branch of the Office of Naval Research, 1945–1950.* Pittsburgh: Carnegie Press.

Asch, Solomon E. (1955, November). Opinions and social pressure. *Scientific American, 193,* 31–35.

Asch, Solomon E. (1956). Studies of independence and conformity: A minority of one against a unanimous majority. *Psychological Monographs, 70* (9, Whole No. 416).

Asch, Solomon E. (1957). An experimental investigation of group influence. In *Symposium on preventive and social psychiatry*. Washington, D.C.: U.S. Government Printing Office, Walter Reed Army Institute of Research.

Aserinsky, Eugene, & Kleitman, Nathaniel. (1953). Regularly occurring periods of eye motility and concomitant phenomena during sleep. *Science, 118,* 273–274.

Ashcraft, Mark H. (1994). *Human memory and cognition* (2nd ed.). New York: Harper-Collins.

Ashton, Heather, & Stepney, Rob. (1983). *Smoking: Psychology and pharmacology.* New York: Tavistock.

Aspinwall, Lisa G., & Taylor, Shelley E. (1992). Modeling cognitive adaptation: A longitudinal investigation of the impact of individual differences and coping on college adjustment and performance. *Journal of Personality and Social Psychology, 63,* 989–1003.

Atkinson, Richard C., & Shiffrin, Richard M. (1968). Human memory: A proposed system and its control processes. In Kenneth W. Spence & Janet T. Spence (Eds.), *The psychology of learning and motivation: Advances in research and theory* (Vol. 2). New York: Academic Press.

Averill, James R. (1982). *Anger and aggression: An essay on emotion.* New York: Springer-Verlag.

Averill, James R. (1994). I feel, therefore I am—I think. In Paul Ekman & Richard J. Davidson (Eds.), *The nature of emotion: Fundamental questions.* New York: Oxford University Press.

Axel, Richard. (1995, October). The molecular logic of smell. *Scientific Amerian, 273,* 154–159.

Axelrod, Saul, & Apsche, Jack. (1983). *The effects of punishment on human behavior.* New York: Academic Press.

Azar, Beth. (1994a, August). Brain imaging raises, answers questions. *APA Monitor,* p. 14.

Azar, Beth. (1994b, December). Research improves lives of animals. *APA Monitor, 25* (12), 19.

Azrin, N. H., & Holz, W. C. (1966). Punishment. In W. K. Honig (Ed.), *Operant behavior: Areas of research and application.* Englewood Cliffs, N.J.: Prentice Hall.

Azuma, Hiroshi. (1984). Secondary control as a heterogeneous category. *American Psychologist, 39,* 970–971.

Babbitt, Roberta L., & Parrish, John M. (1991). Phone phobia, phact or phantasy? An operant approach to a child's disruptive behavior induced by telephone usage. *Journal of Behavior Therapy and Experimental Psychiatry, 22,* 123–129.

Baddeley, Alan D. (1990). *Human memory: Theory and practice.* Boston: Allyn & Bacon.

Baddeley, Alan D. (1995). Working memory. In Michael S. Gazzaniga (Ed.), *The cognitive neurosciences.* Cambridge, Mass.: MIT Press.

Baer, John. (1993). *Creativity and divergent thinking: A task-specific approach.* Hillsdale, N.J.: Erlbaum.

Baer, P. E.; Garmezy, L. B.; McLaughlin, R. L.; Pokorny, A. D.; & Wernick, M. J. (1987). Stress, coping, family conflict, and adolescent alcohol use. *Journal of Behavioral Medicine, 10,* 449–466.

Bahrick, Harry P., & Hall, Lynda K. (1991). Lifetime maintenance of high school mathematics content. *Journal of Experimental Psychology: General, 120,* 20–33.

Bahrick, Harry P., & Phelps, Elizabeth. (1987). Retention of Spanish vocabulary over eight years. *Journal of Experimental Psychology: Learning, Memory, and Cognition, 13,* 344–349.

Bailey, Craig H. (1992). Morphological basis of learning and memory: Invertebrates. In Larry R. Squire (Ed.), *Encyclopedia of learning and memory.* New York: Macmillan.

Bailey, J. Michael; Bobrow, David; Wolfe, Marilyn; & Mikach, Sarah. (1995). Sexual orientation of adult sons of gay fathers. *Developmental Psychology, 31,* 124–129.

Bailey, J. Michael, & Pillard, Richard C. (1991). A genetic study of male sexual orientation. *Archives of General Psychiatry, 48,* 1089–1096.

Bailey, J. Michael; Pillard, Richard C.; Neale, Michael C.; & Agyei, Yvonne. (1993). Heritable factors influence sexual orientation in women. *Archives of General Psychiatry, 50,* 217–223.

Bailey, J. Michael, & Zucker, Kenneth J. (1995). Childhood sex-typed behavior and sexual orientation: A conceptual analysis and quantitative review. *Developmental Psychology, 31,* 43–55.

Bailey, Marian Berland, & Bailey, Robert E. (1993). "Misbehavior": A case history. *American Psychologist, 48,* 1157–1158.

Baillargeon, Renée. (1987). Young infants' reasoning about the physical and spatial characteristics of a hidden object. *Cognitive Development, 2,* 179–200.

Baillargeon, Renée. (1994). How do infants learn about the physical world? *Current Directions in Psychological Science, 3,* 133–140.

Baker, Robert A. (1992). *Hidden memories: Voices and visions from within.* Buffalo, N.Y.: Prometheus Books.

Baker, Robert A. (1996). Hypnosis. In Gordon Stein (Ed.), *The encyclopedia of the paranormal.* Amherst, N.Y.: Prometheus Books.

Baldessarini, R. J. (1990). Drugs and the treatment of psychiatric disorders. In A. Goodman Gilman, T. W. Rall, A. S. Nies, & P. Taylor (Eds.), *The pharmacological basis of therapeutics* (8th ed.). Elmsford, N.Y.: Pergamon.

Balk, David E. (1995). *Adolescent development: Early through late adolescence.* Pacific Grove, Calif.: Brooks/Cole.

Banaji, Mahzarin R., & Prentice, Deborah A. (1994). The self in social contexts. *Annual Review of Psychology, 45,* 297–332.

Bandura, Albert. (1965). Influence of models' reinforcement contingencies on the acquisition of imitative behaviors. *Journal of Personality and Social Psychology, 1,* 589–595.

Bandura, Albert. (1974). Behavior theory and the models of man. *American Psychologist, 29,* 859–869.

Bandura, Albert. (1978). The self system in reciprocal determinism. *American Psychologist, 33,* 344–358.

Bandura, Albert. (1986). *Social foundations of thought and action: A social cognitive theory.* Englewood Cliffs, N.J.: Prentice Hall.

Bandura, Albert. (1988). Self-regulation of motivation and action through goal systems. In V. Hamilton, G. H. Bower, & N. H. Frijda (Eds.), *Cognitive perspectives on emotion and motivation.* Dordrecht, Netherlands: Kluwer Academic Publishers.

Bandura, Albert. (1989a). Human agency in social cognitive theory. *American Psychologist, 44,* 1175–1184.

Bandura, Albert. (1989b). Regulation of cognitive processes through perceived self-efficacy. *Developmental Psychology, 25,* 729–735.

Bandura, Albert. (1990). Conclusion: Reflections on nonability determinants of competence. In Robert J. Sternberg & John Kolligian, Jr. (Eds.), *Competence considered.* New Haven, Conn.: Yale University Press.

Bandura, Albert. (1991). Self-regulation of motivation through anticipatory and self-reactive mechanisms. In Richard Dienstbier (Ed.), *Nebraska Symposium on Motivation—1990* (Vol. 38). Lincoln: University of Nebraska Press.

Bandura, Albert. (1992). Exercise of personal agency through the self-efficacy mechanism. In Ralf Schwarzer (Ed.), *Self-efficacy: Thought control of action.* Washington, D.C.: Hemisphere.

Bandura, Albert. (1996). Failures in self-regulation: Energy depletion or selective disengagement? *Psychological Inquiry, 7,* 20–24.

Bandura, Albert. (1997). *Self-efficacy: The exercise of control.* New York: Freeman.

Bandura, Albert; Ross, Dorothea; & Ross, Sheila A. (1963). Imitation of film-mediated aggressive models. *Journal of Abnormal and Social Psychology, 66,* 3–11.

Bandura, Albert, & Wood, Robert. (1989). Impact of conceptions of ability on self-regulatory mechanisms and complex decision making. *Journal of Personality and Social Psychology, 56,* 407–415.

Barch, Deanna M., & Berenbaum, Howard. (1996). Language production and thought disorder in schizophrenia. *Journal of Abnormal Psychology, 105,* 81–88.

Barclay, Craig R. (1986). Schematization of autobiographical memory. In David Rubin (Ed.), *Autobiographical memory.* New York: Cambridge University Press.

Barclay, Deborah R., & Houts, Arthur C. (1995). Parenting skills: A review and developmental analysis of training content. In William O'Donohue & Leonard Krasner (Eds.), *Handbook of psychological skills training: Clinical techniques and applications.* Boston: Allyn & Bacon.

Barefoot, John C. (1992). Developments in the measurement of hostility. In Howard S. Friedman (Ed.), *Hostility, health, and coping.* Washington, D.C.: American Psychological Association.

Barefoot, John C.; Dahlstrom, W. Grant; & Williams, Redford B. (1983). Hostility, CHD incidence, and total mortality: A 25-year follow-up study of 255 physicians. *Psychosomatic Medicine, 45,* 59–63.

Bargh, John A.; Chen, Mark; & Burrows, Lara. (1996). Automaticity of social behavior: Direct effects of trait construct and stereotype activation on action. *Journal of Personality and Social Psychology, 71,* 230–244.

Barlow, David Harrison. (1991). Disorders of emotion. *Psychological Inquiry, 2,* 58–71.

Barnett, Rosalind C.; Marshall, Nancy L.; & Singer, Judith D. (1992). Job experiences over time, multiple roles, and women's mental health: A longitudinal study. *Journal of Personality and Social Psychology, 62,* 634–644.

Barondes, Samuel H. (1993). *Molecules and mental illness.* New York: Scientific American Library.

Barrett, Stephen. (1996). "Alternative" health practices and quackery. In Gordon Stein (Ed.), *The encyclopedia of the paranormal.* Amherst, N.Y.: Prometheus Books.

Bartecchi, Carl E.; MacKenzie, Thomas D.; & Schrier, Robert W. (1995, May). The global tobacco epidemic. *Scientific American, 272,* 44–51.

Bartoshuk, Linda M., & Beauchamp, Gary K. (1994). Chemical senses. *Annual Review of Psychology, 45,* 419–449.

Bass, Ellen, & Davis, Linda. (1994). *The courage to heal* (3rd ed.). New York: HarperPerennial.

Bassili, John N. (1993). Response latency versus certainty as indexes of the strength of voting intentions in a CATI survey. *Public Opinion Quarterly, 57,* 54–61.

Bates, John E. (1989). Concepts and measures of temperament. In G. A. Kohnstamm, John E. Bates, & Mary K. Rothbart (Eds.), *Temperament in childhood.* New York: Wiley.

Bates, John E. (1994). Introduction. In John E. Bates & Theodore D. Wachs (Eds.), *Temperament: Individual differences at the interface of biology and behavior.* Washington, D.C.: American Psychological Association.

Baudry, Michel, & Davis, Joel L. (1992). Neurotransmitter systems and memory. In Larry R. Squire (Ed.), *Encyclopedia of learning and memory.* New York: Macmillan.

Baum, Andrew; Davidson, Laura M.; Singer, Jerome E.; & Street, Stacey W. (1987). Stress as a psychophysiological process. In Andrew Baum & Jerome E. Singer (Eds.), *Handbook of psychology and health: Vol. 5. Stress.* Hillsdale, N.J.: Erlbaum.

Baum, William, & Heath, Jennifer L. (1992). Behavioral explanations and intentional explanations in psychology. *American Psychologist, 47,* 1312–1317.

Baumeister, Roy F. (1990). Suicide as escape from self. *Psychological Review, 97,* 90–113.

Baumeister, Roy F.; Stillwell, Arlene M.; & Heatherton, Todd F. (1994). Guilt: An interpersonal approach. *Psychological Bulletin, 115,* 243–267.

Baumrind, Diana. (1964). Some thoughts on ethics of research: After reading Milgram's "Behavioral Study of Obedience." *American Psychologist, 19,* 421–423.

Baumrind, Diana. (1967). Child care practices anteceding three patterns of preschool behavior. *Genetic Psychology Monographs, 75,* 43–88.

Baumrind, Diana. (1971). Current patterns of parental authority. *Developmental Psychology Monographs, 4,* 1–103.

Baumrind, Diana. (1995). Commentary on sexual orientation: Research and social policy implications. *Developmental Psychology, 31,* 130–136.

Beal, Carole R. (1994). *Boys and girls: The development of gender roles.* New York: McGraw-Hill.

Bechara, Antoine; Damasio, Hanna; Tranel, Daniel; & Damasio, Antonio R. (1997, February 23). Deciding advantageously before knowing the advantageous strategy. *Science, 275,* 1293–1295.

Beck, Aaron T. (1991). Cognitive therapy: A 30-year retrospective. *American Psychologist, 46,* 368–375.

Beck, Aaron T. (1993). Cognitive therapy: Past, present, and future. *Journal of Consulting and Clinical Psychology, 61,* 194–198.

Beck, Aaron T.; Rush, A. John; Shaw, Brian F.; & Emery, Gary. (1979). *Cognitive therapy of depression.* New York: Guilford Press.

Beck, Aaron T.; Steer, Robert A.; Beck, Judith S.; & Newman, Cory F. (1993). Hopelessness, depression, suicidal ideation, and clinical diagnosis of depression. *Suicide and Life Threatening Behavior, 23,* 139–145.

Beck, Melinda, & Borger, Gloria. (1979, August 20). The polite bandit: A priest on trial. *Newsweek,* p. 26.

Beck, Robert C. (1990). *Motivation: Theories and principles* (3rd ed.). Englewood Cliffs, N.J.: Prentice Hall.

Beecher, Michael D. (1988). Some comments on the adaptationist approach to learning. In Robert C. Bolles & Michael D. Beecher, *Evolution and learning.* Hillsdale, N.J.: Erlbaum.

Begley, Sharon. (1994, February 7). One pill makes you larger, one pill makes you small. *Newsweek,* pp. 37–40.

Beilin, Harry. (1994). Jean Piaget's enduring contribution to developmental psychology. In Ross D. Parke, Peter A. Ornstein, John J. Rieser, & Carolyn Zahn-Waxler (Eds.), *A century of developmental psychology.* Washington, D.C.: American Psychological Association.

Bell, Alan; Weinberg, Martin; & Hammersmith, Sue. (1981). *Sexual preference: Its development in men and women.* Bloomington: Indiana University Press.

Bellak, Leopold. (1993). *The Thematic Apperception Test, the Children's Apperception Test, and the Senior Apperception Technique in clinical use* (5th ed.). Boston: Allyn & Bacon.

Belle, Deborah. (1991). Gender differences in the social moderators of stress. In Alan Monat & Richard S. Lazarus (Eds.), *Stress and coping: An anthology* (3rd ed.). New York: Columbia University Press.

Belsky, Jay. (1986). Infant day care: A cause for concern. *Zero to Three, 6,* 1–7.

Belsky, Jay. (1992). Consequences of child care for children's development: A deconstructionist view. In Alan Booth (Ed.), *Child care in the 1990s: Trends and consequences.* Hillsdale, N.J.: Erlbaum.

Belsky, Jay, & Rovine, Michael J. (1988). Nonmaternal care in the first year of life and security of infant–parent attachment. *Child Development, 59,* 157–167.

Bem, Daryl J. (1994). Response to Hyman. *Psychological Bulletin, 115,* 25–27.

Bem, Daryl J., & Honorton, Charles. (1994). Does psi exist? Replicable evidence for an anomalous process of information transfer. *Psychological Bulletin, 115,* 4–18.

Bem, Sandra L. (1987). Gender schema theory and the romantic tradition. In P. Shaver & C. Hendrick (Eds.), *Sex and gender.* Beverly Hills, Calif.: Sage.

Benca, Ruth M.; Obermeyer, William H.; Thisted, Ronald A.; & Gillin, Christian. (1992). Sleep and psychiatric disorders: A meta-analysis. *Archives of General Psychiatry, 49,* 651–668.

Benderly, Beryl Lieff. (1989, September). Everyday intuition. *Psychology Today,* pp. 35–40.

Benson, Herbert. (1993). The relaxation response. In Daniel Goleman & Joel Gurin (Eds.), *Mind/body medicine: How to use your mind for better health.* Yonkers, N.Y.: Consumer Reports Books.

Bentall, R. P. (1990). The illusion of reality: A review and integration of psychological research on hallucinations. *Psychological Bulletin, 107,* 82–95.

Beratis, Stavroula; Gabriel, Joanna; & Holdas, Stavros. (1994). Age of onset in subtypes of schizophrenic disorders. *Schizophrenia Bulletin, 20,* 287–296.

Bergeman, C. S.; Chipuer, Heather M.; Plomin, Robert; Pedersen, Nancy L.; McClearn, G. E.; Nesselroade, John R.; Costa, Paul T., Jr.; & McCrae, Robert R. (1993). Genetic and environmental effects on openness to experience, agreeableness, and conscientiousness: An adoption/twin study. *Journal of Personality, 61,* 159–179.

Berger, Kathleen Stassen. (1995). *The developing person through childhood and adolescence* (4th ed.). New York: Worth Publishers.

Berkman, Lisa F. (1985). The relationship of social networks and social support to morbidity and mortality. In Sheldon Cohen & S. Leonard Syme (Eds.), *Social support and health.* New York: Academic Press.

Berkman, Lisa F.; Leo-Summers, Linda; & Horowitz, Ralph I. (1992). Emotional support and survival after myocardial infarction. *Annals of Internal Medicine, 117,* 1003–1009.

Berkman, Lisa, & Syme, S. Leonard. (1979). Social networks, host resistance, and mortality: A nine-year follow-up study of Alameda County residents. *American Journal of Epidemiology, 109,* 186–204.

Bermond, B.; Fasotti, L.; Nieuwenhuyse, B.; & Schuerman, J. (1991). Spinal cord lesions, peripheral feedback and intensities of emotional feelings. *Cognition and Emotion, 5,* 201–220.

Bernard, Larry C. (1994). *Health psychology: Biopsychosocial factors in health and illness.* Fort Worth, Tex.: Harcourt Brace.

Berndt, Thomas J. (1992). Friendship and friends' influence in adolescence. *Current Directions in Psychological Science, 1,* 156–159.

Berridge, Kent C., & Robinson, Terry E. (1995). The mind of an addicted brain: Neural sensitization of wanting versus liking. *Current Directions in Psychological Science, 4,* 71–76.

Berry, John W. (1994). Acculturative stress. In Walter J. Lonner & Roy Malpass (Eds.), *Psychology and culture.* Boston: Allyn & Bacon.

Berry, John W., & Kim, Uichol. (1988). Acculturation and mental health. In Pierre R. Dasen, John W. Berry, & Norman Sartorius (Eds.), *Health and cross-cultural psychology: Toward applications.* [Vol. 10, Cross-cultural Research and Methodology Series.] Newbury Park, Calif.: Sage.

Betancourt, Hector, & López, Steven Regeser. (1993). The study of culture, ethnicity, and race in American psychology. *American Psychologist, 48,* 629–637.

Beutler, Larry E.; Machado, Paulo P. P.; & Neufeldt, Susan Allstetter. (1994). Therapist variables. In Allen E. Bergin & Sol L. Garfield (Eds.), *Handbook of psychotherapy and behavior change* (4th ed.). New York: Wiley.

Bhatara, Vinod S.; Sharma, J. N.; Gupta, Sanjay; & Gupta, Y. K. (1997). *Rauwolfia serpentina:* The first herbal antipsychotic. *American Journal of Psychiatry, 154,* 894.

Binder, Jeffrey L.; Strupp, Hans H.; & Henry, William P. (1994). Psychodynamic therapies in practice: Time-limited dynamic psychotherapy. In Bruce Bongar & Larry E. Beutler (Eds.), *Comprehensive textbook of psychotherapy: Theory and practice.* New York: Oxford University Press.

Binet, Alfred, & Simon, Théodore. (1905). New methods for the diagnosis of the intellectual level of subnormals. *L'Année Psychologique, 11,* 191–244.

Birnbaum, D. A.; Nosanchuck, T. A.; & Croll, W. L. (1980). Children's stereotypes about sex differences in emotion. *Sex Roles, 6,* 435–443.

Bjorklund, Barbara R. (1995). Language development and cognition. In David F. Bjorklund (Ed.), *Children's thinking: Developmental function and individual differences* (2nd ed.). Pacific Grove, Calif.: Brooks/Cole.

Blackmore, Susan. (1985). Belief in the paranormal: Probability judgements, illusory control, and the chance baseline shift. *British Journal of Psychology, 76,* 459–468.

Blair, Sampson Lee, & Lichter, Daniel T. (1991). Measuring the division of household labor: Gender segregation of housework among American couples. *Journal of Family Issues, 12,* 91–113.

Blaney, P. H. (1986). Affect and memory: A review. *Psychological Bulletin, 99,* 229–246.

Blass, Thomas. (1991). Understanding behavior in the Milgram obedience experiment. *Journal of Personality and Social Psychology, 60,* 398–413.

Blass, Thomas. (1992). The social psychology of Stanley Milgram. In Mark P. Zanna (Ed.), *Advances in experimental social psychology* (Vol. 25). San Diego: Academic Press.

Bliwise, Donald L. (1997). Sleep and aging. In Mark R. Pressman & William C. Orr (Eds.), *Understanding sleep: The evaluation and treatment of sleep disorders.* Washington, D.C.: American Psychological Association.

Block, J. H. (1983). Differential premises arising from differential socialization of the sexes: Some conjectures. *Child Development, 53,* 1335–1354.

Block, Jack. (1995). A contrarian view of the five-factor approach to personality description. *Psychological Bulletin, 117,* 187–215.

Bloxham, G.; Long, C. G.; Alderman, N.; & Hollin, C. R. (1993). The behavioral treatment of self-starvation and severe self-injury in a patient with borderline personality disorder. *Journal of Behavioral Therapy and Experimental Psychiatry, 24,* 261–267.

Blumberg, Mark S., & Wasserman, Edward A. (1995). Animal mind and the argument from design. *American Psychologist, 50,* 133–144.

Boivin, Diane B.; Duffy, Jeanne F.; & Czeisler, Charles A. (1994). Sensitivity of the human circadian pacemaker to moderately bright light. *Journal of Biological Rhythms, 9* (3/4), 315–322.

Bolger, Niall, & Schilling, Elizabeth A. (1991). Personality and problems of everyday life: The role of neuroticism in exposure and reactivity to stress. *Journal of Personality, 59,* 355–386.

Bolger, Niall, & Zuckerman, Adam. (1995). A framework for studying personality in the stress process. *Journal of Personality and Social Psychology, 69,* 890–902.

Bolles, Robert C. (1972). Reinforcement, expectancy, and learning. *Psychological Review, 79,* 394–409.

Bolles, Robert C. (1985). The slaying of Goliath: What happened to reinforcement theory? In Timothy D. Johnston & Alexandra T. Pietrewicz (Eds.), *Issues in the ecological study of learning.* Hillsdale, N.J.: Erlbaum.

Bond, Michael Harris. (1986). *The psychology of the Chinese people.* New York: Oxford University Press.

Bond, Michael Harris. (1994). Continuing encounters with Hong Kong. In Walter J. Lonner & Roy Malpass (Eds.), *Psychology and culture.* Boston: Allyn & Bacon.

Bond, Michael Harris, & Smith, Peter B. (1996). Cross-cultural social and organizational psychology. *Annual Review of Psychology, 47,* 205–235.

Bond, Rod, & Smith, Peter B. (1996). Culture and conformity: A meta-analysis of studies using Asch's (1952b, 1956) line judgment task. *Psychological Bulletin, 119,* 111–137.

Bond, Susan B., & Mosher, Donald L. (1986). Guided imagery of rape: Fantasy, reality, and the willing victim myth. *Journal of Sex Research, 22,* 162–183.

Boon, Suzette, & Draijer, Nel. (1993). Multiple personality disorder in the Netherlands: A clinical investigation of 71 patients. *American Journal of Psychiatry, 150,* 489–494.

Bootzin, Richard R., & Rider, Steven P. (1997). Behavioral techniques and biofeedback for insomnia. In Mark R. Pressman & William C. Orr (Eds.), *Understanding sleep: The evaluation and treatment of sleep disorders.* Washington, D.C.: American Psychological Association.

Bornstein, Marc H., & Lamb, Michael E. (1992). *Development in infancy: An introduction* (3rd ed.). New York: McGraw-Hill.

Bouchard, Thomas J., Jr. (1994, June 17). Genes, environment, and personality. *Science, 264,* 1700–1701.

Bouchard, Thomas J., Jr.; Lykken, David T.; McGue, Matthew; Segal, Nancy L.; & Tellegen, Auke. (1990). Sources of human psychological differences: The Minnesota Study of Twins Reared Apart. *Science, 250,* 223–250.

Bouchard, Thomas J., Jr., & McGue, Matthew. (1981). Familial studies of intelligence: A review. *Science, 212,* 1055–1059.

Bovbjerg, Dana H.; Redd, William H.; Maier, Lisa A.; Holland, Jimmie C.; Lesko, Lynna M.; Niedzwiecki, Donna; Rubin, Stephen C.; & Hakes, Thomas B. (1990). Anticipatory immune suppression and nausea in women receiving cyclic chemotherapy for ovarian cancer. *Journal of Consulting and Clinical Psychology, 58,* 153–157.

Bower, Bruce. (1994a, August 20). Chronic depression: Drugs show promise. *Science News, 146,* 117–118.

Bower, Bruce. (1994b, June 4). Antidepressants may alter personality. *Science News, 145,* 359.

Bower, Gordon H. (1993). The fragmentation of psychology? *American Psychologist, 48,* 905–907.

Bowers, Kenneth S. (1976). *Hypnosis for the seriously curious.* Monterey, Calif.: Brooks/Cole.

Bowers, Kenneth S.; Regehr, Glenn; Balthazard, Claude; & Parker, Kevin. (1990). Intuition in the context of discovery. *Cognitive Psychology, 22,* 72–110.

Boynton, Robert M. (1988). Color vision. *Annual Review of Psychology, 39,* 69–100.

Bracha, H. Stefan; Wolkowitz, Owen M.; Lohr, James B.; Karson, Craig N.; & Bigelow, Llewellyn B. (1989). High prevalence of visual hallucinations in research subjects with chronic schizophrenia. *American Journal of Psychiatry, 146,* 526–528.

Bradbard, Marilyn R.; Martin, Carol L.; Endsley, Richard C.; & Halverson, Charles F. (1986). Influence of sex stereotypes on children's exploration and memory: A competence versus performance distinction. *Developmental Psychology, 22,* 481–486.

Braff, David L. (1993). Information processing and attention dysfunctions in schizophrenia. *Schizophrenia Bulletin, 19,* 233–259.

Brainerd, C. J. (1996). Piaget: A centennial celebration. *Psychological Science, 7,* 191–195.

Bransford, John D., & Stein, Barry S. (1984). *The ideal problem solver.* New York: Freeman.

Bray, George A. (1991). Weight homeostasis. *Annual Review of Medicine, 42,* 205–216.

Breedlove, S. Marc. (1994). Sexual differentiation of the human nervous system. *Annual Review of Psychology, 45,* 389–418.

Breggin, Peter R. (1979). *Electroshock: Its brain disabling effects.* New York: Springer.

Breggin, Peter R. (1991). *Toxic psychiatry.* New York: St. Martin's Press.

Breggin, Peter, & Breggin, Ginger Rose. (1994). *Talking back to Prozac.* New York: St. Martin's Press.

Bregman, Elsie O. (1934). An attempt to modify the emotional attitude of infants by the conditioned response technique. *Journal of Genetic Psychology, 45,* 169–198.

Brehm, Sharon S. (1992). *Intimate relationships* (2nd ed.). New York: McGraw-Hill.

Breland, Keller, & Breland, Marian. (1961). The misbehavior of organisms. *American Psychologist, 16,* 681–684.

Brennan, James F. (1991). *History and systems of psychology* (3rd ed.). Englewood Cliffs, N.J.: Prentice Hall.

Breuer, Josef, & Freud, Sigmund. (1895/1957). *Studies on hysteria.* (Translated and edited by James Strachey, in collaboration with Anna Freud.) New York: Basic Books.

Brewer, William F., & Treyens, James C. (1981). Role of schemata in memory for places. *Cognitive Psychology, 13,* 207–230.

Brewin, Chris R.; Andrews, Bernice; & Gotlib, Ian H. (1993). Psychopathology and early experience: A reappraisal of retrospective reports. *Psychological Bulletin, 113,* 82–98.

Briere, John, & Conte, Jon. (1993). Self-reported amnesia for abuse in adults molested as children. *Journal of Traumatic Stress, 6* (1), 21–31.

Briggs, Stephen R. (1992). Assessing the five-factor model of personality description. *Journal of Personality, 60,* 253–293.

Brislin, Richard. (1993). *Understanding culture's influence on behavior.* Fort Worth, Tex.: Harcourt Brace College Publishers.

Brock, Dwight B.; Lemke, Jon H.; & Berkman, Lisa F. (1994). Mortality and physical functioning in epidemiologic studies of three older populations. *Journal of Aging & Social Policy, 6* (3), 21–32.

Bronfenbrenner, Urie. (1979). *The ecology of human development.* Cambridge, Mass.: Harvard University Press.

Bronfenbrenner, Urie. (1995). Developmental ecology through space and time: A future perspective. In Phyllis Moen, Glen H. Elder, Jr., & Kurt Lüscher (Eds.), *Examining lives in context: Perspectives on the ecology of human development.* Washington, D.C.: American Psychological Association.

Brooks-Gunn, Jeanne, & Furstenberg, Frank F., Jr. (1989). Adolescent sexual behavior. *American Psychologist, 44,* 249–257.

Brooks-Gunn, Jeanne, & Reiter, Edward O. (1990). The role of pubertal processes. In S. Shirley Feldman & Glen R. Elliott (Eds.), *At the threshold: The developing adolescent.* Cambridge, Mass.: Harvard University Press.

Broughton, Roger J. (1990). Narcolepsy. In Michael J. Thorpy (Ed.), *Handbook of sleep disorders.* New York: Dekker.

Brown, Alan S. (1991). A review of the tip-of-the-tongue experience. *Psychological Bulletin, 109* (2), 204–223.

Brown, B. Bradford; Clasen, Donna Rae; & Eicher, Sue Ann. (1986). Perceptions of peer pressure, peer conformity dispositions, and self-reported behavior among adolescents. *Developmental Psychology, 22,* 521–530.

Brown, George William; Harris, Tirril Olivia; & Hepworth, Cathy. (1994). Life events and endogenous depression: A puzzle reexamined. *Archives of General Psychiatry, 51,* 525–534.

Brown, Gregory M. (1994). Light, melatonin, and the sleep-wake cycle. *Journal of Psychiatry and Neuroscience, 19* (5), 345–353.

Brown, Robert T. (1989). Creativity: What are we to measure? In John A. Glover, Royce R. Ronning, & Cecil R. Reynolds (Eds.), *Handbook of creativity.* New York: Plenum.

Brown, Roger, & Kulik, James. (1982). Flashbulb memories. In Ulric Neisser (Ed.), *Memory observed: Remembering in natural contexts.* San Francisco: Freeman.

Brownell, Kelly D., & Rodin, Judith. (1994). The dieting maelstrom: Is it possible and advisable to lose weight? *American Psychologist, 49,* 781–791.

Bryan, James H., & Test, Mary Ann. (1967). Models and helping: Naturalistic studies in aiding behavior. *Journal of Personality and Social Psychology, 6,* 400–407.

Buchanan, Alec; Reed, Alison; Wessely, Simon; & Garety, Philippa. (1993). Acting on delusions: The phenomenological correlates of acting on delusions. *British Journal of Psychiatry, 163,* 77–81.

Buchanan, Christy Miller; Eccles, Jacquelynne S.; & Becker, Jill B. (1992). Are adolescents the victims of raging hormones? Evidence for activational effects of hormones on moods and behavior at adolescence. *Psychological Bulletin, 111,* 62–107.

Buck, Linda B. (1996). Information coding in the vertebrate olfactory system. *Annual Review of Neuroscience, 19,* 517–544.

Buck, Linda, & Axel, Richard. (1991). A novel multigene family may encode odorant receptors: A molecular basis for odor recognition. *Cell, 65,* 175–187.

Buck, Lucien A. (1992). The myth of normality: Consequences for the diagnosis of abnormality and health. *Social Behavior and Personality, 20,* 251–262.

Buckley, Kerry W. (1982). The selling of a psychologist: John Broadus Watson and the application of behavioral techniques to advertising. *Journal of the History of the Behavioral Sciences, 18,* 207–221.

Buckley, Kerry W. (1989). *Mechanical man: John Broadus Watson and the beginnings of behaviorism.* New York: Guilford Press.

Buhrmester, D., & Furman, W. (1987). The development of companionship and intimacy. *Child Development, 50,* 1101–1115.

Bullock, Theodore H. (1993). Integrative systems research on the brain: Resurgence and new opportunities. *Annual Review of Physiology, 16,* 1–15.

Burger, Jerry M. (1987). Desire for control and conformity to a perceived norm. *Journal of Personality and Social Psychology, 53,* 355–360.

Burger, Jerry M. (1992). *Desire for control: Personality, social, and clinical perspectives.* New York: Plenum.

Burgio, Louis, D., & Sinnott, Jan. (1990). Behavioral treatments and pharmacotherapy: Acceptability ratings by elderly individuals in residential settings. *Gerontologist, 30,* 811–816.

Buri, J. R.; Louiselle, P. A.; Misukanis, T. M.; & Mueller, R. A. (1988). Effects of parental authoritarianism and authoritativeness on self-esteem. *Personality and Social Psychology Bulletin, 14,* 271–282.

Burke, Deborah M.; MacKay, Donald G.; Worthley, Joanna S.; & Wade, Elizabeth. (1991). On the tip of the tongue: What causes word finding failures in young and older adults? *Journal of Memory and Language, 30,* 542–579.

Burks, Nancy, & Martin, Barclay. (1985). Everyday problems and life change events: Ongoing versus acute sources of stress. *Journal of Human Stress, 11,* 27–35.

Burman, Bonnie, & Margolin, Gayla. (1992). Analysis of the association between marital relationships and health problems: An interactional perspective. *Psychological Bulletin, 112,* 39–63.

Burns, Melanie, & Seligman, Martin E. P. (1989). Explanatory style across the lifespan: Evidence for stability over 52 years. *Journal of Personality and Social Psychology, 56,* 471–477.

Bushman, Brad J. (1993). Human aggression while under the influence of alcohol and other drugs: An integrative research review. *Current Directions in Psychological Science, 2,* 148–152.

Buss, David M. (1991). Evolutionary personality psychology. *Annual Review of Psychology, 42,* 459–491.

Butcher, James N., & Rouse, Steven V. (1996). Personality: Individual differences and clinical assessment. *Annual Review of Psychology, 47,* 87–111.

Butcher, James N., & Williams, Carolyn L. (1992). *Essentials of MMPI-2 and MMPI-A interpretation.* Minneapolis: University of Minnesota Press.

Butler, Robert W., & Braff, David L. (1991). Delusions: A review and integration. *Schizophrenia Bulletin, 17,* 633–647.

Butters, Nelson, & Delis, Dean C. (1995). Clinical assessment of memory disorders in amnesia and dementia. *Annual Review of Psychology, 46,* 493–523.

Byne, William. (1994, May). The biological evidence challenged. *Scientific American, 270,* 50–55.

Byne, William, & Parsons, Bruce. (1993). Human sexual orientation: The biologic theories reappraised. *Archives of General Psychiatry, 50,* 228–239.

Byrd, Kevin R. (1994). The narrative reconstruction of incest survivors. *American Psychologist, 49,* 439–440.

Cacioppo, John T.; Uchino, Bert N.; Crites, Stephen L.; Snydersmith, Mary A.; Smith, Gregory; Berntson, Gary G.; & Lang, Peter J. (1992). Relationship between facial expressiveness and sympathetic activation in emotion: A critical review, with emphasis on modeling underlying mechanisms and individual differences. *Journal of Personality and Social Psychology, 62,* 110–128.

Calkins, Mary W. (1893). Statistics of dreams. *American Journal of Psychology, 5,* 311–343.

Calkins, Susan D., & Fox, Nathan A. (1994). Individual differences in the biological aspects of temperament. In John E. Bates & Theodore D. Wachs (Eds.), *Temperament: Individual differences at the interface of biology and behavior.* Washington, D.C.: American Psychological Association.

Campbell, Jennifer D., & Fairey, Patricia J. (1989). Informational and normative routes to conformity: The effect of faction size as a function of norm extremity and attention to the stimulus. *Journal of Personality and Social Psychology, 57* 457–458.

Campbell, John B., & Hawley, Charles W. (1982). Study habits and Eysenck's theory of extraversion–introversion. *Journal of Research in Personality, 16,* 139–146.

Campbell, Scott S. (1997). The basics of biological rhythms. In Mark R. Pressman & William C. Orr (Eds.), *Understanding sleep: The evaluation and treatment of sleep disorders.* Washington, D.C.: American Psychological Association.

Cannon, Tyrone D., & Marco, Elysa. (1994). Structural brain abnormalities as indicators of vulnerability to schizophrenia. *Schizophrenia Bulletin, 20,* 89–102.

Cannon, Walter B. (1927). The James-Lange theory of emotion: A critical examination and an alternative theory. *American Journal of Psychology, 39,* 106–124.

Cannon, Walter B. (1932). *The wisdom of the body.* New York: Norton.

Cannon, Walter B.; Lewis, J. T.; & Britton, S. W. (1927). The dispensability of the sympathetic division of the autonomic nervous system. *Boston Medical and Surgical Journal, 197,* 514.

Card, J. Patrick, & Moore, Robert Y. (1991). The organization of visual circuits influencing the circadian activity of the suprachiasmatic nucleus. In David C. Klein, Robert Y. Moore, & Steven M. Reppert (Eds.), *Suprachiasmatic nucleus: The mind's clock.* New York: Oxford University Press.

Cardeña, Etzel. (1992). Trance and possession as dissociative disorders. *Transcultural Psychiatric Research Review, 29,* 287–300.

Carli, Linda L., & Leonard, Jean B. (1989). The effect of hindsight on victim derogation. *Journal of Social and Clinical Psychology, 8,* 331–343.

Carlson, Eve Bernstein; Putnam, Frank W.; Ross, Colin A.; Torem, Moshe; Coons, Philip; Dill, Diana L.; Loewenstein, Richard J.; & Braun, Bennett G. (1993). Validity of the Dissociative Experiences Scale in screening for multiple personality disorder: A multicenter study. *American Journal of Psychiatry, 150,* 1030–1036.

Carlson, John G., & Hatfield, Elaine. (1992). *Psychology of emotion.* Fort Worth, Tex.: Harcourt Brace Jovanovich.

Carlson, Neil R. (1994). *Physiology of behavior* (5th ed.). Boston: Allyn & Bacon.

Carlson, Shawn. (1985, December 5). A double-blind test of astrology. *Nature, 318,* 419–425.

Carroll, Kathleen Whiteman. (1993). Family support groups for medically ill patients and their families. In Anne Alonso & Hillel I. Swiller (Eds.), *Group therapy in clinical practice.* Washington, D.C.: American Psychiatric Press.

Carter, Jerry L. (1992). Visual, somatosensory, olfactory, and gustatory hallucinations. *Psychiatric Clinics of North America, 15,* 347–358.

Case, Robbie. (1985). *Intellectual development: Birth to adulthood.* Orlando, Fla.: Academic Press.

Cattell, Raymond B. (1973, July). Personality pinned down. *Psychology Today,* pp. 40–46.

Cattell, Raymond B. (1994). A cross-validation of primary personality structure in the 16 P.F. by two parcelled factor analysis. *Multivariate Experimental Clinical Research, 10* (3), 181–191.

Cattell, Raymond B.; Cattell, A. Karen S.; & Cattell, Heather E.P. (1993). *16 PF questionnaire* (5th ed.). Champaign, Ill.: Institute for Personality and Ability Testing.

Ceci, Stephen J., & Bruck, Maggie. (1993). Suggestibility of the child witness: A historical review and synthesis. *Psychological Bulletin, 113* (3), 403–439.

Ceci, Stephen J., & Loftus, Elizabeth F. (1994). "Memory work": A royal road to false memories? Special issue: Recovery of memories of childhood sexual abuse. *Applied Cognitive Psychology, 8,* 351–364.

Cervone, Daniel. (1997). Social-cognitive mechanisms and personality coherence: Self-knowledge, situational beliefs, and cross-situational coherence in perceived self-efficacy. *Psychological Science, 8,* 43–50.

Chadwick, P. D. J.; Lowe, C. F.; Horne, P. J.; & Higson, P. J. (1994). Modifying delusions: The role of empirical testing. *Behavior Therapy, 25,* 35–49.

Chambers, Mark J. (1995). Childhood insomnia. In Charles E. Schaefer (Ed.), *Clinical handbook of sleep disorders in children.* Northvale, N.J.: Aronson.

Chambless, Dianne L., & Gillis, Martha M. (1993). Cognitive therapy of anxiety disorders. *Journal of Consulting and Clinical Psychology, 61,* 248–260.

Chase, Michael H., & Morales, Francisco R. (1990). The atonia and myoclonia of active (REM) sleep. *Annual Review of Psychology, 41,* 557–584.

Chen, E. Y. H.; Wilkins, A. J.; & McKenna, P. J. (1994). Semantic memory is both impaired and anomalous in schizophrenia. *Psychological Medicine, 24,* 193–202.

Cheney, Dorothy L., & Seyfarth, Robert M. (1990). *How monkeys see the world.* Chicago: University of Chicago Press.

Chomsky, Noam. (1965). *Aspects of a theory of syntax.* Cambridge, Mass.: MIT Press.

Christensen, Andrew, & Heavey, Christopher L. (1993). Gender differences in marital conflict: The demand/withdraw interaction pattern. In Stuart Oskamp & Mark Costanzo (Eds.), *Gender issues in contemporary society.* Newbury Park, Calif.: Sage.

Christensen, Andrew, & Jacobson, Neil S. (1994). Who (or what) can do psychotherapy: The status and challenge of nonprofessional therapies. *Psychological Science, 5,* 8–14.

Chun, Marvin M., & Cavanagh, Patrick. (1997). Seeing two as one: Linking apparent motion and repetition blindness. *Psychological Science, 8,* 74–79.

Church, A. T., & Katigbak, M. S. (1989). Internal, external, and self-report structure of personality in a non-Western culture: An investigation of cross-language and cross-cultural generalizability. *Journal of Personality and Social Psychology, 54,* 296–308.

Chwalisz, Kathleen; Diener, Ed; & Gallagher, Dennis. (1988). Autonomic arousal feedback and emotional experience: Evidence from the spinal cord injured. *Journal of Personality and Social Psychology, 54,* 820–828.

Cialdini, Robert B. (1993). *Influence: Science and practice* (3rd ed.). New York: HarperCollins.

Cialdini, Robert B.; Darby, Betty Lee; & Vincent, Joyce E. (1973). Transgression and altruism: A case for hedonism. *Journal of Experimental Social Psychology, 9,* 502–516.

Cioffi, Delia, & Holloway, James. (1993). Delayed costs of suppressed pain. *Journal of Personality and Social Psychology, 64,* 274–282.

Clark, Russell D., III, & Word, Larry E. (1972). Why don't bystanders help? Because of the ambiguity? *Journal of Personality and Social Psychology, 24,* 392–400.

Clark, Russell D., III, & Word, Larry E. (1974). Where is the apathetic bystander? Situational characteristics of the emergency. *Journal of Personality and Social Psychology, 29,* 279–287.

Clarke, Dave. (1991). Belief in the paranormal: A New Zealand survey. *Journal of the Society for Psychical Research, 57,* 412–425.

Clarke-Stewart, K. Alison. (1989). Infant day care: Maligned or malignant? *American Psychologist, 44,* 266–273.

Clarke-Stewart, K. Alison. (1992). Consequences of child care for children's development. In Alan Booth (Ed.), *Child care in the 1990s: Trends and consequences.* Hillsdale, N.J.: Erlbaum.

Clay, Rebecca A. (1995, November). Working mothers: Happy or haggard? *APA Monitor, 26* (1), 37.

Cohen, Neil J. (1984). Preserved learning capacity in amnesia: Evidence for multiple memory systems. In Larry R. Squire & Nelson Butters (Eds.), *Neuropsychology of memory.* New York: Guilford Press.

Cohen, Sheldon. (1988). Psychosocial models of the role of social support in the etiology of physical disease. *Health Psychology, 7,* 269–297.

Cohen, Sheldon, & Herbert, Tracy B. (1996). Health psychology: Psychological factors and physical disease from the perspective of human psychoneuroimmunology. *Annual Review of Psychology, 47,* 113–142.

Cohen, Sheldon, & McKay, Garth. (1984). Social support, stress, and the buffering hypothesis: A theoretical analysis. In Andrew Baum, Shelley E. Taylor, & Jerome E. Singer (Eds.), *Handbook of psychology and health: Vol. 4. Social psychological aspects of health.* Hillsdale, N.J.: Erlbaum.

Cohen, Sheldon; Tyrrell, David A. J.; & Smith, Andrew P. (1991). Psychological stress and susceptibility to the common cold. *New England Journal of Medicine, 325,* 606–612.

Cohen, Sheldon; Tyrrell, David A. J.; & Smith, Andrew P. (1993). Negative life events, perceived stress, negative affect, and susceptibility to the common cold. *Journal of Personality and Social Psychology, 64,* 131–140.

Cohen, Sheldon, & Williamson, Gail M. (1988). Perceived stress in a probability sample of the United States. In Shirlynn Spacapan & Stuart Oskamp (Eds.), *The social psychology of health: The Claremont Symposium on Applied Social Psychology* (4th ed.) Newbury Park, Calif.: Sage.

Coile, D. Caroline, & Miller, Neal E. (1984, June). How radical animal activists try to mislead humane people. *American Psychologist, 39,* 700–701.

Colby, Anne, & Kohlberg, Lawrence. (1984). Invariant sequence and internal consistency in moral judgment stages. In William M. Kurtines & Jacob L. Gewirtz (Eds.), *Morality, moral behavior, and moral development.* New York: Wiley.

Colby, Anne; Kohlberg, Lawrence; Gibbs, John; & Lieberman, Marcus. (1983). A longitudinal study of moral judgment. *Monographs of the Society for Research in Child Development, 48* (1–2), 1–123.

Cole, K. C. (1995). Innumeracy. In Russell Jacoby & Naomi Glauberman (Eds.), *The* Bell Curve *debate: History, documents, opinions.* New York: Times Books.

Cole, Michael, & Cole, Sheila R. (1993). *The development of children* (2nd ed.). New York: Freeman.

Cole, Michael, & Cole, Sheila R. (1996). *The development of children* (3rd ed.). New York: Freeman.

Collaer, Marcia J., & Hinds, Melissa. (1995). Human behavioral sex differences: A role

for gonadal hormones during early development? *Psychological Bulletin, 118,* 55–107.

Collins, A. M., & Loftus, Elizabeth F. (1975). A spreading activation theory of semantic processing. *Psychological Review, 82,* 407–428.

Collins, W. Andrew, & Gunnar, Megan. (1990). Social and personality development. *Annual Review of Psychology, 41,* 387–416.

Comas-Diaz, Lillian. (1993). Hispanic/Latino communities: Psychological implications. In Donald R. Atkinson, George Morten, & Derald Wing Sue (Eds.), *Counseling American minorities: A cross-cultural perspective* (4th ed.). Madison, Wis.: Brown & Benchmark.

Connor-Greene, Patricia A. (1993). From the laboratory to the headlines: Teaching critical evaluation of the press reports of research. *Teaching of Psychology, 20* (3), 167–169.

Conoley, Jane Close, & Impara, James C. (1995). *The 12th mental measurements yearbook.* Lincoln: University of Nebraska Press.

Coons, Philip M. (1994). Confirmation of childhood abuse in child and adolescent cases of multiple personality disorder and dissociative disorder not otherwise specified. *Journal of Nervous and Mental Disease, 182,* 461–464.

Coons, Philip M., & Dua, Vikram. (1993). Psychiatric health care costs of multiple personality disorder. *American Journal of Psychotherapy, 47,* 103–112.

Cooper, Leslie M. (1979). Hypnotic amnesia. In Erika Fromm & Ronald E. Shor (Eds.), *Hypnosis: Developments in research and new perspectives* (2nd ed.). New York: Aldine.

Cooper, Rosemary. (1994). Normal sleep. In Rosemary Cooper (Ed.), *Sleep.* New York: Chapman & Hall.

Cooper, Rosemary, & Bradbury, Sue. (1994). Techniques in sleep recording. In Rosemary Cooper (Ed.), *Sleep.* New York: Chapman & Hall.

Coren, Stanley; Ward, Lawrence M.; & Enns, James T. (1994). *Sensation and perception* (4th ed.). Fort Worth, Tex.: Harcourt Brace College Publishers.

Coryell, William; Winokur, George; Shea, Tracie; Maser, Jack D.; Endicott, Jean; & Akiskal, Hapog S. (1994b). The long-term stability of depressive subtypes. *American Journal of Psychiatry, 151,* 199–204.

Costa, Paul T., Jr., & McCrae, Robert R. (1989). Personality continuity and the changes of adult life. In Martha Storandt & Gary R. VandenBos (Eds.), *The adult years:*

Continuity and change. Washington, D.C.: American Psychological Association.

Cowan, Nelson. (1994). Mechanisms of verbal short-term memory. *Current Directions in Psychological Science, 6,* 185–189.

Cowan, Nelson; Wood, Noelle L.; & Borne, Dawn N. (1994). Reconfirmation of the short-term storage concept. *Psychological Science, 5,* 103–108.

Cowan, Philip A., & Cowan, Carolyn Pape. (1988). Changes in marriage during the transition to parenthood: Must we blame the baby? In Gerald Y. Michaels & Wendy A. Goldberg (Eds.), *The transition to parenthood: Current theory and research.* Cambridge, England: Cambridge University Press.

Cowan, Philip A., & Cowan, Carolyn Pape. (1992). *When partners become parents.* New York: Basic Books.

Cowley, Geoffrey. (1994, February 7). The culture of Prozac. *Newsweek,* pp. 41–42.

Coyne, James C., & Downey, Geraldine. (1991). Social factors and psychopathology: Stress, social support, and coping processes. *Annual Review of Psychology, 42,* 401–425.

Coyne, James C.; Ellard, John H.; & Smith, David A. F. (1990). Social support, interdependence, and the dilemmas of helping. In Barbara R. Sarason, Irwin G. Sarason, & Gregory R. Pierce (Eds.), *Social support: An interactional view.* New York: Wiley.

Craik, Fergus I. M. (1994). Memory changes in normal aging. *Current Directions in Psychological Science, 3,* 155–158.

Crano, William D. (1995). Attitude strength and vested interest. In Richard E. Petty & Jon A. Krosnick (Eds.), *Attitude strength: Antecedents and consequences.* Hillsdale, N.J.: Erlbaum.

Craske, Michelle G. (1993). Specific fears and panic attacks: A survey of clinical and nonclinical samples. *Journal of Anxiety Disorders, 7,* 1–19.

Craske, Michelle G.; Miller, Patricia P.; Rotunda, Robert; & Barlow, David H. (1990). A descriptive report of initial unexpected panic attacks in minimal and extensive avoiders. *Behaviour Research and Therapy, 28,* 395–400.

Crews, Frederick. (1984/1986). The Freudian way of knowledge. In *Skeptical engagements.* New York: Oxford University Press.

Crews, Frederick. (1996). The verdict on Freud. *Psychological Science, 7,* 63–68.

Cronbach, Lee J. (1990). *Essentials of psychological testing* (5th ed.). New York: Harper & Row.

Crowder, Robert G. (1992). Sensory memory. In Larry R. Squire (Ed.), *Encyclopedia of learning and memory*. New York: Macmillan.

Crowe, Richard A. (1990). Astrology and the scientific method. *Psychological Reports, 67*, 163–191.

Cumming, Elaine, & Henry, William. (1961). *Growing old: The process of disengagement*. New York: Basic Books.

Cupach, William R., & Canary, Daniel J. (1995). Managing conflict and anger: Investigating the sex stereotype hypothesis. In Pamela J. Kalbfleisch & Michael J. Cody (Eds.), *Gender, power, and communication in human relationships*. Hillsdale, N.J.: Erlbaum.

Cutler, W. B.; Preti, George; Krieger, A.; Huggins, G. R.; Garcia, C. R.; & Lawley, H. J. (1986). Human axillary secretions influence women's menstrual cycles: The role of donor extract from men. *Hormones and Behavior, 20*, 463–473.

Czeisler, Charles A.; Johnson, Michael P.; Duffy, Jeanne F.; Brown, E. N.; Ronda, J. M.; & Kronauer, Richard E. (1990). Exposure to bright light and darkness to treat physiologic maladaptions to night work. *New England Journal of Medicine, 322* (18), 1253–1259.

Czeisler, Charles A.; Kronauer, Richard E.; Allen, J. S.; Duffy, J. F.; Jewett, M. E.; Brown, E. N.; & Ronda, J. M. (1989, June 16). Bright light induction of strong (Type O) resetting of the human circadian pacemaker. *Science, 244*, 1328–1333.

Czeisler, Charles A.; Moore–Ede, Martin C.; & Coleman, Robert M. (1982). Rotating shift work schedules that disrupt sleep are improved by applying circadian principles. *Science, 217*, 460–463.

Damasio, Antonio R., & Damasio, Hanna. (1992, September). Brain and language. *Scientific American, 267*, 62–71.

Darley, John M. (1992). Social organization for the production of evil. Book Review Essay. *Psychological Inquiry, 3*, 199–218.

Darley, John M., & Shultz, Thomas R. (1990). Moral rules: Their content and acquisition. *Annual Review of Psychology, 41*, 525–556.

Davey, Graham C. L. (1993). Factors influencing self-rated fear to a novel animal. *Cognition and Emotion, 7*, 461–471.

Davidson, Julian M., & Myers, L. S. (1988). Endocrine factors in sexual psychophysiology. In Raymond C. Rosen & J. Gayle Beck (Eds.), *Patterns of sexual arousal: Psychophysiological processes and clinical applications*. New York: Guilford Press.

Davidson, Richard J. (1993). Parsing affective space: Perspectives from neuropsychology and psychophysiology. *Neuropsychology, 7*, 464–475.

Davis, Glenn Craig, & Breslau, Naomi. (1994). Post-traumatic stress disorder in victims of civilian and criminal violence. *Psychiatric Clinics of North America, 17*, 289–299.

Davis, Kenneth L.; Kahn, René S.; Ko, Grant; & Davidson, Michael. (1991). Dopamine in schizophrenia: A review and reconceptualization. *American Journal of Psychiatry, 148*, 1474–1486.

Davis, Mary Helen; Drogin, Eric Y.; & Wright, Jesse H. (1995). Therapist–patient sexual intimacy: A guide for the subsequent therapist. *Journal of Psychotherapy Practice and Research, 4*, 140–149.

Davis, Michael. (1992). The role of the amygdala in fear and anxiety. *Annual Review of Neuroscience, 15*, 353–375.

Davison, Gerald C., & Neale, John M. (1994). *Abnormal psychology* (6th ed.). New York: Wiley.

Dawson, Drew. (1995). Improving adaptation to simulated night shift: Timed exposure to bright light versus daytime melatonin administration. *Sleep, 18*, 11–18.

Dawson, Drew, & Campbell, Scott S. (1991). Time exposure to bright light improves sleep and alertness during simulated night shifts. *Sleep, 14*, 511–516.

Dean, Geoffrey; Mather, Arthur; & Kelly, Ivan W. (1996). Astrology. In Gordon Stein (Ed.), *The encyclopedia of the paranormal*. Buffalo, N.Y.: Prometheus Books.

DeAngelis, Tori. (1994a, February). People's drug of choice offers potent side effects. *APA Monitor, 25*, 16.

DeAngelis, Tori. (1994b, March). Massachusetts now requires multicultural training. *APA Monitor*, p. 41.

DeCasper, A., & Fifer, W. (1980). Of human bonding: Newborns prefer their mothers' voices. *Science, 208*, 1174–1176.

de Fonseca, Fernando Rodriguez; Carrera, M. Rocío A.; Navarro, Miguel; Koob, George F.; & Weiss, Friedbert. (1997, June 27). Activation of corticotropin-releasing factor in the limbic system during cannabinoid withdrawal. *Science, 276*, 2050–2054.

Delahanty, Douglas L.; Dougall, Angela Liegey; Hawken, Leanne; Trakowski, John H.; Schmitz, John B.; Jenkins, Frank J.; & Baum, Andrew. (1996). Time course of natural killer cell activity and lymphocyte proliferation in response to two acute stressors in healthy men. *Health Psychology, 15*, 48–55.

Delgado, Jose M. (1969). *Physical control of the mind*. New York: Harper & Row.

DeLisi, Richard, & Staudt, Joanne. (1980). Individual differences in college students' performance on formal operations tasks. *Journal of Applied Developmental Psychology, 1*, 163–174.

DeLoache, Judy S. (1995). Early symbol understanding and use. In Douglas L. Medin (Ed.), *The psychology of learning and motivation: Advances in research and theory* (Vol. 33). San Diego: Academic Press.

DeLongis, Anita; Coyne, James C.; Dakof, C.; Folkman, Susan; & Lazarus, Richard S. (1982). Relationship of daily hassles, uplifts, and major life events to health status. *Health Psychology, 1*, 119–136.

DeLongis, Anita; Folkman, Susan; & Lazarus, Richard S. (1988). The impact of stress on health and mood: Psychological and social resources as mediators. *Journal of Personality and Social Psychology, 54*, 486–495.

Delprato, Dennis J., & Midgley, Bryan D. (1992). Some fundamentals of B. F. Skinner's behaviorism. *American Psychologist, 47*, 1507–1520.

Dember, W. N., & Earl, R. W. (1957). Analysis of exploratory, manipulatory, and curiosity behaviors. *Psychological Review, 64*, 91–96.

Dembroski, Theodore M. (1985). Overview of classic and stress-related risk factors: Relationship to substance effects on reactivity. In Karen A. Matthews, Stephen M. Weiss, Thomas Detre, Theodore M. Dembroski, Bonita Falkner, Stephen B. Manuck, & Redford B. Williams, Jr. (Eds.), *Handbook of stress, reactivity, and cardiovascular disease*. New York: Wiley.

Dement, William C. (1978). *Some must watch while some must sleep*. New York: Norton.

Dement, William C. (1992a). The proper use of sleeping pills in the primary care setting. *Journal of Clinical Psychiatry, 53*, 50–58.

Dement, William C. (1992b). *The sleepwatchers*. Stanford, Calif.: Stanford Alumni Association in series *The Portable Stanford*.

DePaulo, Bella. (1992). Nonverbal behavior and self-presentation. *Psychological Bulletin, 111*, 203–243.

Deutsch, Morton, & Gerard, Harold B. (1955). A study of normative and informational social influence upon individual judgment. *Journal of Abnormal and Social Psychology, 51*, 629–636.

DeValois, Russell L., & DeValois, Karen K. (1975). Neural coding of color. In E. C. Carterette & M. P. Friedman (Eds.), *Handbook of perception* (Vol. 5). New York: Academic Press.

Devanand, D. P.; Dwork, Andrew J.; Hutchinson, Edward R.; Bolwig, Tom G.; & Sackeim, Harold A. (1994). Does ECT alter brain structure? *American Journal of Psychiatry, 151,* 957–970.

De Vos, George, & Wagatsuma, Hiroshi. (1967). *Japan's invisible race: Caste in culture and personality.* Berkeley and Los Angeles: University of California Press.

deWaal, Frans B. M. (1995, March). Bonobo sex and society. *Scientific American, 271,* 82–88.

Diamond, Marian Cleeves. (1988). *Enriching heredity: The impact of the environment on the anatomy of the brain.* New York: Free Press.

Diamond, Marian Cleeves. (1993). An optimistic view of the aging brain: Understanding behavior by understanding its source. *Generations: The Journal of the Western Gerontologist, 17,* 31–37.

Dickinson, Anthony. (1989). Expectancy theory in animal conditioning. In Stephen B. Klein & Robert R. Mowrer (Eds.), *Contemporary learning theories: Pavlovian conditioning and the status of traditional learning theory.* Hillsdale, N.J.: Erlbaum.

Diener, Ed, & Emmons, Robert A. (1984). The independence of positive and negative affect. *Journal of Personality and Social Psychology, 47,* 1105–1117.

Diener, Ed; Larsen, Randy J.; Levine, Steven; & Emmons, Robert A. (1985). Intensity and frequency: Dimensions underlying positive and negative affect. *Journal of Personality and Social Psychology, 48,* 1253–1265.

Dies, Robert R. (1993). Research on group psychotherapy: Overview and clinical applications. In Anne Alonso & Hillel I. Swiller (Eds.), *Group therapy in clinical practice.* Washington, D.C.: American Psychiatric Press.

Dillard, James Price. (1991). The current status of research on sequential-request compliance techniques. *Personality and Social Psychology Bulletin, 17,* 283–288.

Dillbeck, M. C., & Orme-Johnson, D. W. (1987). Physiological differences between transcendental meditation and rest. *American Psychologist, 42,* 879–881.

Dillingham, S. (1987, September 14). Inaudible messages making a noise. *Insight,* pp. 44–45.

Dinges, David F. (1989). Napping patterns and effects in human adults. In David F. Dinges & Roger J. Broughton (Eds.), *Sleep and alertness: Chronobiological, behavioral, and medical aspects of napping.* New York: Raven Press.

Dinges, David F. (1990). Are you awake? Cognitive performance and reverie during

the hypnopompic state. In Richard R. Bootzin, John F. Kihlstrom, & Daniel L. Schacter (Eds.), *Sleep and cognition.* Washington, D.C.: American Psychological Association.

Dinges, David F., & Broughton, Roger J. (1989). The significance of napping: A synthesis. In David F. Dinges & Roger J. Broughton (Eds.), *Sleep and alertness: Chronobiological, behavioral, and medical aspects of napping.* New York: Raven Press.

Dinsmoor, James A. (1992). Setting the record straight: The social views of B. F. Skinner. *American Psychologist, 47,* 1454–1463.

Dohrenwend, Bruce P.; Raphael, Karen G.; Schwartz, Sharon; Stueve, Ann; & Skodol, Andrew. (1993). The structured event probe and narrative rating method for measuring stressful life events. In Leo Goldberger & Shlomo Breznitz (Eds.), *Handbook of stress: Theoretical and clinical aspects* (2nd ed.). New York: Free Press.

Domjan, Michael, & Purdy, Jesse E. (1995). Animal research in psychology: More than meets the eye of the general psychology student. *American Psychologist, 50,* 496–503.

Dornbusch, Sanford M.; Glasgow, Kristan L.; & Lin, I-Chun. (1996). The social structure of schooling. *Annual Review of Psychology, 47,* 401–429.

Dornbusch, Sanford M.; Ritter, Philip L.; Leiderman, P. Herbert; Roberts, Donald F.; & Fraleigh, Michael J. (1987). The relation of parenting style to adolescent school performance. *Child Development, 58,* 1244–1257.

Dovidio, John F. (1984). Helping behavior and altruism: An empirical and conceptual overview. *Advances in Experimental Social Psychology, 17,* 361–427.

Dovidio, John F., & Gaertner, Samuel L. (1993). Stereotypes and evaluative intergroup bias. In Diane M. Mackie & David L. Hamilton (Eds.), *Affect, cognition, and stereotyping: Interactive processes in group perception.* San Diego: Academic Press.

DSM-IV. (1994). *Diagnostic and statistical manual of mental disorders* (4th ed.). Washington, D.C.: American Psychiatric Association.

Duncan, David F.; Donnelly, William J.; & Nicholson, Thomas. (1992). Belief in the paranormal and religious belief among American college students. *Psychological Reports, 70,* 15–18.

Duncker, Karl. (1929/1967). Induced motion. In Willis D. Ellis (Ed.), *Source book of Gestalt psychology.* New York: Humanities Press.

Duncker, Karl. (1945). On problem solving. *Psychological Monographs, 58* (Whole No. 270).

Dunkel-Schetter, Christine; Feinstein, Lawrence G.; Taylor, Shelley E.; & Falke, Roberta L. (1992). Patterns of coping with cancer. *Health Psychology, 11,* 79–87.

Dunning, David; Leuenberger, Ann; & Sherman, David A. (1995). A new look at motivated inference: Are self-serving theories of success a product of motivational forces? *Journal of Personality and Social Psychology, 69,* 58–68.

Dusek, Jerome B. (1996). *Adolescent development and behavior* (3rd ed.). Upper Saddle River, N.J.: Prentice Hall.

Dykstra, Linda. (1992). Drug action. In John Grabowski & Gary R. VanderBos (Eds.), *Master lectures in psychology: Psychopharmacology: Basic mechanisms and applied interventions.* Washington, D.C.: American Psychological Association.

Eagle, Morris N., & Wolitzky, David L. (1992). Psychoanalytic theories of psychotherapy. In Donald K. Freedheim (Ed.), *History of psychotherapy: A century of change.* Washington, D.C.: American Psychological Association.

Eagly, Alice H. (1992). Uneven progress: Social psychology and the study of attitudes. *Journal of Personality and Social Psychology, 63,* 693–710.

Eagly, Alice H. (1995). The science and politics of comparing women and men. *American Psychologist, 50,* 145–158.

Eagly, Alice H., & Chaiken, Shelly. (1993). *The psychology of attitudes.* Fort Worth, Tex.: Harcourt Brace.

Ebbinghaus, Hermann. (1885/1987). *Memory: A contribution to experimental psychology.* (Translated by Henry A. Ruger & Clara E. Bussenius.) New York: Dover Publications.

Eckensberger, Lutz H. (1994). Moral development and its measurement across cultures. In Walter J. Lonner & Roy Malpass (Eds.), *Psychology and culture.* Boston: Allyn & Bacon.

Edens, Jennifer L.; Larkin, Kenneth I.; & Abel, Jennifer L. (1992). The effects of social support and physical touch on cardiovascular reactions to mental stress. *Journal of Psychosomatic Research, 36,* 371–381.

Edwards, Randall. (1995a, February). Future demands culturally diverse education. *APA Monitor,* p. 43.

Edwards, Randall. (1995b, September). Psychologists foster the new definition of family. *APA Monitor, 26,* 38.

Egan, Gerard. (1994). *The skilled helper: A problem-management approach to helping* (5th ed.). Pacific Grove, Calif.: Brooks/Cole.

Ehlers, Anke, & Breuer, Peter. (1992). Increased cardiac awareness in panic disorder. *Journal of Abnormal Psychology, 101,* 371–382.

Eibl-Eibesfeldt, Irenäus. (1973). The expressive behavior of the deaf-and-blind-born. In M. von Cranach & I. Vine (Eds.), *Social communication and movement.* New York: Academic Press.

Eich, Eric. (1989). Theoretical issues in state-dependent memory. In Henry L. Roediger, III & Fergus I. M. Craik (Eds.), *Varieties of memory and consciousness: Essays in honour of Edel Tulving.* Hillsdale, N.J.: Erlbaum.

Eich, Eric. (1995). Searching for mood dependent memory. *Psychological Science, 6,* 67–75.

Eich, Eric; Macaulay, D.; & Ryan, L. (1994). Mood dependent memory for events of the personal past. *Journal of Experimental Psychology: General, 123,* 201–215.

Eisenberg, Nancy. (1991). Meta-analytic contributions to the literature on prosocial behavior. *Personality and Social Psychology Bulletin, 17,* 273–284.

Ekman, Paul. (1980). *The face of man.* New York: Garland Publishing.

Ekman, Paul. (1982). *Emotion in the human face* (2nd ed.). New York: Cambridge University Press.

Ekman, Paul. (1992). Are there basic emotions? *Psychological Review, 99,* 550–553.

Ekman, Paul, & Davidson, Richard J. (1993). Voluntary smiling changes regional brain activity. *Psychological Science, 4,* 342–345.

Ekman, Paul, & Davidson, Richard J. (1994). Epilogue: Affective science: A research agenda. In Paul Ekman & Richard J. Davidson (Eds.), *The nature of emotion: Fundamental questions.* New York: Oxford University Press.

Ekman, Paul, & Friesen, Wallace V. (1978). *Facial Action Coding System: A technique for the measurement of facial movement.* Palo Alto, Calif.: Consulting Psychologists Press.

Ekman, Paul; Friesen, Wallace V.; O'Sullivan, Maureen; Chan, Anthony; Diacoyanni-Tarlatzis, Irene; Heider, Karl; Krause, Rainer; LeCompte, William Ayhan; Pitcairn, Tom; Ricci-Bitti, Pio E.; Scherer, Klaus; Masatoshi, Tomita; & Tzavaras, Athanase. (1987). Universals and cultural differences in the judgments of facial expressions of emotion. *Journal of Personality & Social Psychology, 53,* 712–717.

Ellis, Albert. (1991). *Reason and emotion in psychotherapy.* New York: Carol Publishing.

Ellis, Albert. (1993). Reflections on rational-emotive therapy. *Journal of Consulting and Clinical Psychology, 61,* 199–201.

Ellis, Albert, & Bernard, Michael E. (1985). What is rational-emotive therapy (RET)? In Albert Ellis & Michael E. Bernard (Eds.), *Clinical applications of rational-emotive therapy.* New York: Plenum.

Ellis, Albert, & Harper, Robert A. (1975). *A new guide to rational living.* Hollywood, Calif.: Wilshire Book Company.

Ellis, Henry C., & Hunt, R. Reed. (1993). *Fundamentals of cognitive psychology* (5th ed.). Dubuque, Iowa: Brown & Benchmark.

Ellman, Steven J.; Spielman, Arthur J.; Luck, Dana; Steiner, Solomon S.; & Halperin, Ronnie. (1991). REM deprivation: A review. In Steven J. Ellman & John S. Antrobus (Eds.), *The mind in sleep: Psychology and psychophysiology* (2nd ed.). New York: Wiley.

Ellsworth, Phoebe C. (1994). William James and emotion: Is a century of fame worth a century of misunderstanding? *Psychological Review, 101,* 222–229.

Emmelkamp, Paul M. G. (1994). Behavior therapy with adults. In Allen E. Bergin & Sol L. Garfield (Eds.), *Handbook of psychotherapy and behavior change* (4th ed.). New York: Wiley.

Emmons, Robert, & King, Laura. (1988). Conflict among personal strivings: Immediate and long-term implications for psychological and physical well-being. *Journal of Personality and Social Psychology, 54,* 1040–1048.

Empson, Jacob. (1993). *Sleep and dreaming* (2nd ed.). New York: Harvester Wheatsheaf.

Engen, Trygg. (1991). *Odor sensation and memory.* New York: Praeger.

Engler, Barbara. (1995). *Personality theories: An introduction* (4th ed.). Boston: Houghton Mifflin.

English, Horace B. (1929). Three cases of the "conditioned fear response." *Journal of Abnormal and Social Psychology, 24,* 221–225.

Epstein, Leonard H., & Jennings, J. Richard. (1985). Smoking, stress, cardiovascular reactivity, and coronary heart disease. In Karen A. Matthews, Stephen M. Weiss, Thomas Detre, Theodore M. Dembroski, Bonita Falkner, Stephen B. Manuck, & Redford B. Williams, Jr. (Eds.), *Handbook of stress, reactivity, and cardiovascular disease.* New York: Wiley.

Epstein, Mark. (1995). *Thoughts without a thinker: Psychotherapy from a Buddhist perspective.* New York: Basic Books.

Epstein, Seymour. (1982). Conflict and stress. In Leo Goldberger & Shlomo Breznitz (Eds.), *Handbook of stress: Theoretical and clinical aspects.* New York: Free Press.

Erdelyi, Matthew Hugh. (1992). Psychodynamics and the unconscious. *American Psychologist, 47,* 784–787.

Erdelyi, Matthew Hugh. (1993). Repression: The mechanism and the defense. In Daniel M. Wegner & James W. Pennebaker (Eds.), *Handbook of mental control.* Englewood Cliffs, N.J.: Prentice Hall.

Ericsson, K. Anders, & Kintsch, Walter. (1995). Long-term working memory. *Psychological Review, 102,* 211–245.

Erikson, Erik H. (1964a). *Childhood and society* (Rev. ed.). New York: Norton.

Erikson, Erik H. (1964b). *Insight and responsibility.* New York: Norton.

Erikson, Erik H. (1968). *Identity: Youth and crisis.* New York: Norton.

Erikson, Erik H. (1982). *The life cycle completed: A review.* New York: Norton.

Erikson, Erik H.; Erikson, Joan M.; & Kivnick, Helen Q. (1986). *Vital involvement in old age: The experience of old age in our time.* New York: Norton.

Estes, W. K., & Skinner, B. F. (1941). Some quantitative properties of anxiety. *Journal of Experimental Psychology, 29,* 390–400.

Etscorn, F., & Stephens, R. (1973). Establishment of conditioned taste aversions with a 24-hour CS-US interval. *Physiological Psychology, 1,* 251–253.

Exner, John E., Jr. (1993). *The Rorschach: A comprehensive system: Vol. 1. Basic foundations* (3rd ed.). New York: Wiley.

Eysenck, Hans J. (1952). The effects of psychotherapy: An evaluation. *Journal of Consulting Psychology, 16,* 319–324.

Eysenck, Hans J. (1982). *Personality, genetics, and behavior.* New York: Praeger.

Eysenck, Hans J. (1985). *Decline and fall of the Freudian empire.* New York: Penguin.

Eysenck, Hans J. (1990). Biological dimensions of personality. In Lawrence A. Pervin (Ed.), *Handbook of personality: Theory and research.* New York: Guilford Press.

Eysenck, Hans J. (1994). The outcome problem in psychotherapy: What have we learned? *Behaviour Research and Therapy, 32,* 447–495.

Eysenck, Hans J., & Eysenck, Sybil B. G. (1975). *Psychoticism as a dimension of personality.* London: Hodder & Stoughton.

Fackelmann, Kathy A. (1994, July 2). The conscious mind: Karen Ann Quinlan case yields surprising scientific data. *Science News, 146,* 10–11.

Faedda, Gianni L.; Tondo, Leonardo; Teicher, Martin H.; Baldessarini, Ross J.; Gelbard, Harris A.; & Floris, Gianfranco F. (1993). Seasonal mood disorders: Patterns of seasonal recurrence in mania and depression. *Archives of General Psychiatry, 50,* 17–23.

Fagot, Beverly I., & Hagan, Richard. (1991). Observations of parent reactions to sex-stereotyped behaviors: Age and sex effects. *Child Development, 62,* 617–628.

Fagot, Beverly I.; Leinbach, Mary D.; & O'Boyle, Cherie. (1992). Gender labeling, gender stereotyping, and parenting behaviors. *Developmental Psychology, 28,* 225–230.

Fancher, Raymond E. (1973). *Psychoanalytic psychology: The development of Freud's thought.* New York: Norton.

Fancher, Raymond E. (1990). *Pioneers of psychology* (2nd ed.). New York: Norton.

Fancher, Rayond E. (1996). *Pioneers of psychology.* (3rd ed.). New York: Norton.

Fantz, Robert L. (1961, May). The origin of form perception. *Scientific American, 204,* 66–72.

Fantz, Robert L. (1963). Pattern vision in newborn infants. *Science, 140,* 296–297.

Fantz, Robert L. (1965). Visual perception from birth as shown by pattern selectivity. *Annals of the New York Academy of Sciences, 118,* 793–814.

Farah, Martha J. (1994). Neuropsychological inference with an interactive brain: A critique of the "locality" assumption. *Behavioral and Brain Sciences, 17,* 43–61.

Farah, Martha J. (1995). The neural bases of mental imagery. In Michael S. Gazzaniga (Ed.), *The cognitive neurosciences.* Cambridge, Mass.: MIT Press.

Farber, Ilya B., & Churchland, Patricia S. (1995). Consciousness and the neurosciences: Philosophical and theoretical issues. In Michael S. Gazzaniga (Ed.), *The cognitive neurosciences.* Cambridge, Mass.: MIT Press.

Fauman, Michael A. (1994). *Study guide to DSM-IV.* Washington, D.C.: American Psychiatric Press.

Faust, I. M.; Johnson, P. R.; & Hirsch, J. (1976). Noncompensation of adipose mass in partial lipectomized mice and rats.

American Journal of Physiology, 231, 538–544.

Faust, I. M.; Johnson, P. R.; & Hirsch, J. (1977a). Adipose tissue regeneration following lipectomy. *Science, 197,* 391–393.

Faust, I. M.; Johnson, P. R.; & Hirsch, J. (1977b). Surgical removal of adipose tissue alters feeding behavior and the development of obesity in rats. *Science, 197,* 393–396.

Fawcett, Jan. (1994). Antidepressants: Partial response in chronic depression. *British Journal of Psychiatry, 165* (Suppl. 26), 37–41.

Fazio, Russell H. (1990). Multiple processes by which attitudes guide behavior: The MODE model as an integrative framework. In Mark P. Zanna (Ed.), *Advances in experimental social psychology* (Vol. 23). San Diego: Academic Press.

Fazio, Russell H., & Zanna, Mark P. (1981). Direct experience and attitude–behavior consistency. In Leonard Berkowitz (Ed.), *Advances in experimental social psychology* (Vol. 14). San Diego: Academic Press.

Feder, H. H. (1984). Hormones and sexual behavior. *Annual Review of Psychology, 35,* 165–200.

Feeney, Brooke C., & Kirkpatrick, Lee A. (1996). Effects of adult attachment and presence of romantic partners on physiological responses to stress. *Journal of Personality and Social Psychology, 70,* 255–270.

Feldman, Larry B., & Powell, Sandra L. (1992). Integrating therapeutic modalities. In John C. Norcross & Marvin R. Goldfried (Eds.), *Handbook of psychotherapy integration.* New York: Basic Books.

Fellows, Brian J. (1990). Current theories of hypnosis: An overview. *British Journal of Experimental and Clinical Hypnosis, 7,* 81–92.

Felten, David. (1993). The brain and the immune system. In Bill Moyers (Interviewer) & Betty Sue Flowers (Ed.), *Healing and the mind.* New York: Doubleday.

Fenwick, Peter. (1987). Meditation and the EEG. In Michael A. West (Ed.), *The psychology of meditation.* New York: Oxford University Press.

Ferber, Richard. (1994). Sleep disorders in children. In Rosemary Cooper (Ed.), *Sleep.* New York: Chapman & Hall.

Ferguson, N. B. L., & Keesey, R. E. (1975). Effect of a quinine-adulterated diet upon body weight maintenance in male rats with ventromedial hypothalamic lesions. *Journal of Comparative Physiological Psychology, 89,* 478–488.

Fernald, Ann. (1985). Four-month-old infants prefer to listen to motherese. *Infant*

Behavior and Development, 8, 181–182.

Fernandez, E. (1986). A classification system of cognitive coping strategies for pain. *Pain, 26,* 141–151.

Festinger, Leon. (1957). *A theory of cognitive dissonance.* Stanford, Calif.: Stanford University Press.

Festinger, Leon. (1962). Cognitive dissonance. *Scientific American, 207,* 93–99. (Reprinted in *Contemporary psychology: Readings from Scientific American,* 1971, San Francisco: Freeman.)

Field, Tiffany. (1991). Quality infant daycare and grade school behavior and performance. *Child Development, 62,* 863–870.

Field, Tiffany. (1996). Attachment and separation in young children. *Annual Review of Psychology, 47,* 541–561.

Field, Tiffany; Masi, W.; Goldstein, D.; Perry, S.; & Parl, S. (1988). Infant day-care facilitates preschool behavior. *Early Childhood Research Quarterly, 3,* 341–359.

Field, Tiffany M.; Woodson, R.; Greenberg, R.; & Cohen, D. (1982). Discrimination and imitation of facial expressions by neonates. *Science, 218,* 179–182.

Fieldhouse, Paul. (1986). *Food & nutrition: Customs & culture.* London: Croom Helm.

Fink, Max. (1991). Impact of the antipsychiatry movement on the revival of electroconvulsive therapy in the United States. *Psychiatric Clinics of North America, 14,* 793–801.

Fischbach, Gerald D. (1992, September). Mind and brain. *Scientific American, 267,* 24–33.

Fischer, Kurt W., & Hencke, Rebecca W. (1996). Infants' construction of actions in context: Piaget's contribution to research on early development. *Psychological Science, 7,* 204–210.

Fisher, Celia B., & Fyrberg, Denise. (1994). Participant partners: College students weigh the costs and benefits of deceptive research. *American Psychologist, 49,* 417–427.

Fishman, J. A. (1960/1974). A systematization of the Whorfian hypothesis. In John W. Berry & P. R. Dasen (Eds.), *Culture and cognition: Readings in cross-cultural psychology.* London: Methuen.

Fiske, Susan T. (1993). Social cognition and perception. *Annual Review of Psychology, 44,* 155–194.

Fiske, Susan T., & Neuberg, Steven L. (1990). A continuum of impression formation, from category-based to individuating processes: Influences of information and motivation on attention and interpretation. In Mark P. Zanna (Ed.), *Advances in experimental social psychology* (Vol. 23). San Diego: Academic Press/Harcourt.

Fiske, Susan T., & Taylor, Shelley E. (1991). *Social cognition* (2nd ed.). New York: McGraw-Hill.

Flaks, David K.; Ficher, Ilda; Masterpasqua, Frank; & Joseph, Gregory. (1995). Lesbians choosing motherhood: A comparative study of lesbian and heterosexual parents and their children. *Developmental Psychology, 31,* 105–114.

Flavell, John H. (1996). Piaget's legacy. *Psychological Science, 7,* 200–203.

Flynn, James R. (1987). Massive IQ gains in 14 nations: What IQ tests really measure. *Psychological Bulletin, 101,* 171–191.

Foertsch, Julie, & Gernsbacher, Morton Ann. (1997). In search of gender neutrality: Is singular *they* a cognitively efficient substitute for generic *he*? *Psychological Science, 8,* 106–111.

Folkard, Simon; Arendt, Josephine; & Clark, Mark. (1993). Can melatonin improve shift workers' tolerance of the night shift? Some preliminary findings. *Chronobiology International, 10,* 315–320.

Folkman, Susan, & Lazarus, Richard S. (1991). Coping and emotion. In Alan Monat & Richard S. Lazarus (Eds.), *Stress and coping: An anthology* (3rd ed.). New York: Columbia University Press.

Folkman, Susan; Lazarus, Richard S.; Gruen, Rand J.; & DeLongis, Anita. (1986). Appraisal, coping, health status, and psychological symptoms. *Journal of Personality and Social Psychology, 50,* 571–579.

Foster, Russell G. (1993). Photoreceptors and circadian systems. *Current Directions in Psychological Science, 2,* 34–39.

Foulks, Edward F. (1991). Transcultural psychiatry and normal behavior. In Daniel Offer & Melvin Sabshin (Eds.), *The diversity of normal behavior: Further contributions to normatology.* New York: Basic Books.

Fowler, Raymond D. (1995, April). Should psychologists prescribe medicine? *APA Monitor, 26,* 3.

Fowles, D. C. (1992). Schizophrenia: Diathesis-stress revisited. *Annual Review of Psychology, 43,* 303–336.

Fox, Nathan A.; Kimmerly, Nancy L.; & Schafer, William D. (1991). Attachment to mother/Attachment to father: A meta-analysis. *Child Development, 62,* 210–225.

Frances, Allen J.; Widiger, Thomas A.; & Sabshin, Melvin. (1991). Psychiatric diagnosis and normality. In Daniel Offer & Melvin Sabshin (Eds.), *The diversity of normal behavior: Further contributions to normatology.* New York: Basic Books.

Frank, Barney. (1996, February 4). Quoted in Claudia Dreifus: And then there was

Frank. *The New York Times Magazine,* pp. 22–25.

Frank, Ellen; Anderson, Barbara; Reynolds, Charles F., III; Ritenour, Angela; & Kupfer, David J. (1994). Life events and the research diagnostic criteria endogenous subtype: A confirmation of the distinction using the Bedford College methods. *Archives of General Psychiatry, 51,* 519–524.

Frankel, Fred H. (1993). Adult reconstruction of childhood events in the multiple personality literature. *American Journal of Psychiatry, 150,* 954–958.

Franken, Robert E. (1994). *Human motivation* (3rd ed.). Pacific Grove, Calif.: Brooks/Cole.

Frankenburg, Frances R. (1994). History of the development of antipsychotic medication. *Psychiatric Clinics of North America, 17,* 531–540.

Franz, Carol E.; McClelland, David C.; & Weinberger, Joel. (1991). Childhood antecedents of conventional social accomplishment in midlife adults: A 36-year prospective study. *Journal of Personality and Social Psychology, 60,* 586–595.

Freeston, Mark H.; Ladouceur, Robert; Rhéaume, Josée; Letarte, Hélène; Gagnon, Fabien; & Thibodeau, Nicole. (1994). Self-report of obsessions and worry. *Behavior Research and Therapy, 32,* 29–36.

French, Christopher C.; Fowler, Mandy; McCarthy, Katy; & Peers, Debbie. (1991, Winter). Belief in astrology: A test of the Barnum effect. *Skeptical Inquirer, 15,* 166–172.

Frenkel, Oded J., & Doob, Anthony N. (1976). Post-decision dissonance at the polling booth. *Canadian Journal of Behavioural Science, 8,* 347–350.

Freud, Anna. (1946). *The ego and mechanisms of defence.* (Translated by Cecil Baines). New York: International Universities Press.

Freud, Sigmund. (1900/1974). *The interpretation of dreams.* In James Strachey (Ed.), *The standard edition of the complete psychological works of Sigmund Freud* (Vols. 4 & 5). London: Hogarth Press.

Freud, Sigmund. (1904/1965). *The psychopathology of everyday life.* (Translated by Alan Tyson and edited by James Strachey.) New York: Norton.

Freud, Sigmund. (1905/1975). *Three essays on the theory of sexuality.* (Translated by James Strachey). New York: Basic Books.

Freud, Sigmund. (1911/1989). *On dreams.* In Peter Gay (Ed.), *The Freud reader.* New York: Norton.

Freud, Sigmund. (1915a/1948). Repression. In *Collected papers: Vol. 4. Papers on meta-*

psychology and applied psychoanalysis (Translated under the supervision of Joan Riviere). London: Hogarth Press.

Freud, Sigmund. (1915b/1959). Analysis, terminable and interminable. In *Collected papers: Vol. 5. Miscellaneous papers* (2nd ed.) (Translated under the supervision of Joan Riviere). London: Hogarth Press.

Freud, Sigmund. (1915c/1959). Libido theory. In *Collected papers: Vol. 5. Miscellaneous papers* (2nd ed.) (Translated under the supervision of Joan Riviere). London: Hogarth Press.

Freud, Sigmund. (1916/1964). *Leonardo da Vinci and a memory of his childhood* (Translated by James Strachey in collaboration with Anna Freud). New York: Norton.

Freud, Sigmund. (1919/1989). *Totem and taboo: Some points of agreement between the mental lives of savages and neurotics* (Translated and edited by James Strachey, with a biographical introduction by Peter Gay). New York: Norton.

Freud, Sigmund. (1920/1961). *Beyond the pleasure principle* (Translated by James Strachey). New York: Norton.

Freud, Sigmund. (1923/1962). *The ego and the id* (Translated by Joan Riviere and edited by James Strachey). New York: Norton.

Freud, Sigmund. (1924/1948). The dissolution of the Oedipus complex. In *Collected papers: Vol. 2. Clinical papers and papers on technique* (Translated under the supervision of Joan Riviere). London: Hogarth Press.

Freud, Sigmund. (1925/1989). Some psychical consequences of the anatomical distinction between the sexes. In Peter Gay (Ed.), *The Freud reader.* New York: Norton.

Freud, Sigmund. (1926/1947). *The question of lay analysis: An introduction to psychoanalysis* (Translated by Nancy Proctor-Gregg). London: Imago Publishing.

Freud, Sigmund. (1930/1961). *Civilization and its discontents* (Translated and edited by James Strachey). New York: Norton.

Freud, Sigmund. (1933). *New introductory lectures on psychoanalysis* (Translated by W. J. H. Sprott). New York: Norton.

Freud, Sigmund. (1936). *The problem of anxiety* (Translated by Henry Alden Bunker). New York: The Psychoanalytic Quarterly Press and Norton.

Freud, Sigmund. (1939/1967). *Moses and monotheism* (Translated by Katherine Jones). New York: Vintage Books.

Freud, Sigmund. (1940/1949). *An outline of psychoanalysis* (Translated by James Strachey). New York: Norton.

Friedman, Howard S. (1992). Understanding hostility, coping, and health. In Howard S. Friedman (Ed.), *Hostility, coping, and health*. Washington, D. C.: American Psychological Association.

Friedman, Howard S., & Booth-Kewley, Stephanie. (1987). The "disease-prone personality": A meta-analytic view of the construct. *American Psychologist, 42,* 539–555.

Friedman, Meyer, & Rosenman, Ray H.. (1974). *Type A behavior and your heart.* New York: Knopf.

Friend, Ronald; Rafferty, Yvonne; & Bramel, Dana. (1990). A puzzling misinterpretation of the Asch "conformity" study. *European Journal of Social Psychology, 20,* 29–44.

Friesen, Wallace V. (1972). *Cultural differences in facial expressions in a social situation: An experimental test of the concept of display rules.* Unpublished doctoral dissertation, University of California, San Francisco.

Frijda, Nico H. (1994). Varieties of affect: Emotions and episodes, moods, and sentiments. In Paul Ekman & Richard J. Davidson (Eds.), *The nature of emotion: Fundamental questions.* New York: Oxford University Press.

Frodi, Ann; Macaulay, Jacqueline; & Thome, Pauline. (1977). Are women always less aggressive than men? A review of the literature. *Psychological Bulletin, 84,* 634–660.

Funder, David C. (1995). On the accuracy of personality judgment: A realistic approach. *Psychological Review, 102,* 652–670.

Funder, David C.; Kolar, David C.; & Blackman, Melinda C. (1995). Agreement among judges of personality: Interpersonal relations, similarity, and acquaintanceship. *Journal of Personality and Social Psychology, 69,* 656–672.

Galanter, Eugene. (1962). Contemporary psychophysics. In R. Brown, E. Galanter, E. H. Hess, & G. Mandler (Eds.), *New directions in psychology.* New York: Holt, Rinehart & Winston.

Gallo, Linda C., & Eastman, Charmane I. (1993). Circadian rhythms during gradually delaying and advancing sleep and light schedules. *Physiology and Behavior, 53,* 119–126.

Gallup Organization. (1991). *Sleep in America.* Princeton, N.J.: Gallup Organization.

Gambrill, Eileen. (1995b). Assertion skills training. In William O'Donohue & Leonard Krasner (Eds.), *Handbook of psychological skills training: Clinical techniques and applications.* Boston: Allyn & Bacon.

Gansberg, Martin. (1964, March 27). 37 who saw murder didn't call the police. *New York Times,* pp. 1, 38.

Garcia, John. (1981). Tilting at the paper mills of academe. *American Psychologist, 36,* 149–158.

Garcia, John; Ervin, Frank R.; & Koelling, Robert A. (1966). Learning with prolonged delay of reinforcement. *Psychonomic Science, 5,* 121–122.

Garcia, John, & Koelling, Robert A. (1966). Relation of cue to consequence in avoidance learning. *Psychonomic Science, 4,* 123–124.

Gardner, Howard. (1985). *Frames of mind: The theory of multiple intelligences.* New York: Basic Books.

Gardner, Howard. (1993). *Frames of mind: The theory of multiple intelligences* (2nd ed.). New York: Basic Books.

Gardner, Howard. (1995). Cracking open the IQ box. In Steven Fraser (Ed.), *The Bell Curve wars: Race, intelligence, and the future of America.* New York: Basic Books.

Garety, Philippa. (1991). Reasoning and delusions. *British Journal of Psychiatry, 159,* 14–18.

Garfield, Sol L. (1992). Eclectic psychotherapy: A common factors approach. In John C. Norcross & Marvin R. Goldfried (Eds.), *Handbook of psychotherapy integration.* New York: Basic Books.

Garfield, Sol L. (1994). Research on client variables in psychotherapy. In Allen E. Bergin & Sol L. Garfield (Eds.), *Handbook of psychotherapy and behavior change* (4th ed.). New York: Wiley.

Garfield, Sol L., & Bergin, Allen E. (1994). Introduction and historical overview. In Allen E. Bergin & Sol L. Garfield (Eds.), *Handbook of psychotherapy and behavior change* (4th ed.). New York: Wiley.

Garguilo, J.; Attie, I.; Brooks-Gunn, Jeanne; & Warren, M. P. (1987). Dating in middle school girls: Effects of social context, maturation, and grade. *Developmental Psychology, 23,* 730–737.

Garland, Ann F., & Zigler, Edward. (1993). Adolescent suicide prevention: Current research and social policy implications. *American Psychologist, 48,* 169–182.

Garry, Maryanne, & Loftus, Elizabeth F. (1994). Pseudomemories without hypnosis. *International Journal of Clinical and Experimental Hypnosis, 42* (4), 363–373.

Gastil, J. (1990). Generic pronouns and sexist language: The oxymoronic character of masculine generics. *Sex Roles, 23,* 629–642.

Gavin, Leslie A., & Furman, Wyndol. (1989). Age difference in adolescents' perceptions of their peer groups. *Developmental Psychology, 25,* 827–834.

Gay, Peter. (1988). *Freud: A life for our time.* New York: Norton.

Gay, Peter (Ed.). (1989). *The Freud reader.* New York: Norton.

Gazzaniga, Michael S. (1995). Consciousness and the cerebral hemispheres. In Michael S. Gazzaniga (Ed.), *The cognitive neurosciences.* Cambridge, Mass.: MIT Press.

Geen, Russell G. (1995). *Human motivation: A social psychological approach.* Pacific Grove, Calif.: Brooks/Cole.

Geliebter, A.; Westriech, S.; Hashim, S. A.; & Gage, D. (1987). Gastric ballon reduces food intake and body weight in obese rats. *Physiology and Behavior, 39,* 399–402.

Gerace, Laina M.; Camilleri, Dorothy; & Ayres, Lioness. (1993). Sibling perspectives on schizophrenia and the family. *Schizophrenia Bulletin, 19,* 637–647.

Gerard, Harold B.; Wilhelmy, Roland A.; & Conolley, Edward S. (1968). Conformity and group size. *Journal of Personality and Social Psychology, 8,* 79–82.

Gerbner, George. (1993). Images that hurt: Mental illness in the mass media. *The Journal of the California Alliance for the Mentally Ill, 4,* (1), 17–20.

Gerlach, Jes, & Peacock, Linda. (1994). Motor and mental side effects of clozapine. *Journal of Clinical Psychiatry, 55* (9, Suppl. B), 107–109.

Getka, Eric J., & Glass, Carol R. (1992). Behavioral and cognitive-behavioral approaches to the reduction of dental anxiety. *Behavior Therapy, 23,* 433–448.

Getzels, Jacob W., & Csikszentmihalyi, Mihaly. (1976). *The creative vision: A longitudinal study of problem finding in art.* New York: Wiley.

Gibbons, Vincent P., & Kotagal, Suresh. (1995). Narcolepsy in children. In Charles E. Schaefer (Ed.), *Clinical handbook of sleep disorders in children.* Northvale, N.J.: Aronson.

Gieser, Marlon T. (1993). The first behavior therapist as I knew her. *Journal of Behavior Therapy and Experimental Psychiatry, 24,* 321–324.

Gilbert, Lucia Albino. (1993). *Two careers/one family: The promise of gender equality.* Beverly Hills, Calif.: Sage.

Gilbert, Lucia Albino. (1994). Current perspectives on dual-career families. *Current Directions in Psychological Science, 3,* 101–105.

Gilligan, Carol. (1982). *In a different voice: Psychological theory and women's development.* Cambridge, Mass.: Harvard University Press.

Gilligan, Carol, & Attanucci, Jane. (1988). Two moral orientations. In Carol Gilligan, Janie Victoria Ward, & Jill McLean Taylor (Eds.), *Mapping the moral domain: A contribution of women's thinking to psychological theory and education.* Cambridge, Mass.: Harvard University Press.

Gilovich, Thomas. (1997, March/April). Some systematic biases of everyday judgment. *Skeptical Inquirer, 21* (2), 31–35.

Gitlin, Michael J.; Swendsen, Joel; Heller, Tracy L.; & Hammen, Constance. (1995). Relapse and impairment in bipolar disorder. *American Journal of Psychiatry, 152,* 1635–1640.

Gladue, Brian A. (1994). The biopsychology of sexual orientation. *Current Directions in Psychological Science, 3,* 150–154.

Gleaves, David H. (1996). The sociocognitive model of dissociative identity disorder: A reexamination of the evidence. *Psychological Bulletin, 120,* 42–59.

Gleitman, Henry. (1991). Edward Chace Tolman: A life of scientific and social purpose. In Gregory A. Kimble, Michael Wertheimer, & Charlotte White (Eds.), *Portraits of pioneers in psychology.* Washington, D.C., & Hillsdale, N.J.: American Psychological Association & Erlbaum.

Glick, Peter; Gottesman, Deborah; & Jolton, Jeffrey. (1989). The fault is not in the stars: Susceptibility of skeptics and believers in astrology to the Barnum effect. *Personality and Social Psychology Bulletin, 15,* 572–583.

Glynn, Shirley M. (1990). Token economy approaches for psychiatric patients: Progress and pitfalls over 25 years. *Behavior Modification, 14,* 383–407.

Godden, Duncan R., & Baddeley, Alan D. (1975). Context-dependent memory in two natural environments: On land and underwater. *British Journal of Psychology, 66,* 325–331.

Goff, Donald C., & Simms, Claudia A. (1993). Has multiple personality remained consistent over time? A comparison of past and recent cases. *Journal of Nervous and Mental Disease, 181,* 595–600.

Gökcebay, Nilgün; Cooper, Rosemary; Williams, Robert L.; Hirshkowitz, Max; & Moore, Constance A. (1994). Function of sleep. In Rosemary Cooper (Ed.), *Sleep.* New York: Chapman & Hall.

Gold, Steven N.; Hughes, Dawn; & Hohnecker, Laura. (1994). Degrees of repression of sexual abuse memories. *American Psychologist, 49,* 441–442.

Goldberg, Lewis R. (1993). The structure of phenotypic personality traits. *American Psychologist, 48,* 26–34.

Goldberger, Leo. (1983). The concept and mechanisms of denial: A selective overview. In Shlomo Breznitz (Ed.), *The denial of stress.* Madison, Conn.: International Universities Press.

Golden, Robert N., & Gilmore, John H. (1990). Serotonin and mood disorders. *Psychiatric Annals, 20,* 580–586.

Goldman-Rakic, Patricia S. (1992, September). Working memory and the mind. *Scientific American, 267,* 110–117.

Goldsmith, H. Hill; Buss, Arnold H.; Plomin, Robert; Rothbart, Mary Klevjord; Thomas, Alexander; Chess, Stella; Hinde, Robert A.; & McCall, Robert B. (1987). Roundtable: What is temperament? Four approaches. *Child Development, 58,* 505–529.

Goldsmith, H. Hill, & Harman, Catherine. (1994). Temperament and attachment; individuals and relationships. *Current Directions in Psychological Science, 3,* 53–61.

Goldstein, Avram. (1994). *Addiction: From biology to drug policy.* New York: Freeman.

Goldstein, Risë B.; Weissman, Myrna M.; Adams, Phillip B.; Horwath, Ewald; Lish, Jennifer D.; Charney, Dennis; Woods, Scott W.; Sobin, Christina; & Wickramaratne, Priya J. (1994). Psychiatric disorders in relatives of probands with panic disorder and/or major depression. *Archives of General Psychiatry, 51,* 383–394.

Goleman, Daniel. (1980, February). 1,528 little geniuses and how they grew. *Psychology Today,* pp. 28–53.

Goleman, Daniel. (1991). Sex roles reign powerful as ever in the emotions. In Daniel Goleman (Ed.), *Psychology updates: Articles on psychology from* The New York Times. New York: HarperCollins.

Goleman, Daniel. (1994, May 31). Miscoding is seen as the root of false memories. *New York Times,* pp. C-1, C-8.

Goleman, Daniel. (1995). *Emotional intelligence.* New York: Bantam.

Goleman, Daniel, & Gurin, Joel (1993). *Mind/body medicine: How to use your mind for better health.* Yonkers, N.Y.: Consumer Reports Books.

Golomb, Claire, & Galasso, Lisa. (1995). Make-believe and reality: Explorations of the imaginary realm. *Developmental Psychology, 31,* 800–810.

Golombok, Susan, & Tasker, Fiona. (1996). Do parents influence the sexual orientation of their children? Findings from a longitudinal study of lesbian families. *Developmental Psychology, 32,* 3–11.

Goodall, G. (1984). Learning due to the response–shock contingency in signalled punishment. *Quarterly Journal of Experimental Psychology, 36B,* 259–279.

Goodenough, Donald R. (1991). Dream recall: History and current status of the field. In Steven J. Ellman & John S. Antrobus (Eds.), *The mind in sleep: Psychology and psychophysiology* (2nd ed.). New York: Wiley.

Goodenough, F. (1932). The expression of emotion in a blind-deaf child. *Journal of Abnormal Social Psychology, 27,* 328–333.

Gopnik, Alison. (1996). The post-Piaget era. *Psychological Science, 7,* 221–225.

Gorassini, Donald R., & Olson, James M. (1995). Does self-perception change explain the foot-in-the-door effect? *Journal of Personality and Social Psychology, 69,* 91–105.

Gordon, T., & Doyle, J. T. (1987). Drinking and mortality: The Albany Study. *American Journal of Epidemiology, 125,* 263–270.

Gorski, Roger. (1995, February 28). Quoted in Gina Kolata. Man's world, woman's world? Brain studies point to differences. *New York Times,* pp. C1, C7.

Gotlib, Ian H. (1992). Interpersonal and cognitive aspects of depression. *Current Directions in Psychological Science, 1,* 149–154.

Gottesman, Irving I. (1991). *Schizophrenia genesis: The origins of madness.* New York: Freeman.

Gottesman, Irving I. (1997). Twins: En route to QTLs for cognition. *Science, 276,* 1522–1523.

Gottlieb, Gilbert, & Krasnegor, Norman A. (1985). *Measurement of audition and vision in the first year of postnatal life: A methodological overview.* Norwood, N.J.: Ablex Press.

Gottman, John M. (1994). *Why marriages succeed or fail: What you can learn from the breakthrough research to make your marriage last.* New York: Simon & Schuster.

Gottman, John M., & Levenson, Robert W. (1992). Marital processes predictive of later dissolution: Behavior, physiology, and health. *Journal of Personality and Social Psychology, 63,* 221–233.

Gough, Harrison G. (1989). The California Personality Inventory. In Charles S. Newmark (Ed.), *Major psychological assessment instruments* (Vol. 2). Boston: Allyn & Bacon.

Gould, James L., & Gould, Carol Grant. (1994). *The animal mind.* New York: Freeman.

Gould, Stephen Jay. (1993). *The mismeasure of man* (2nd ed.). New York: Norton.

Graham, John R. (1993). *MMPI-2: Assessing personality and psychopathology* (2nd ed.). New York: Oxford University Press.

Graig, Eric. (1993). Stress as a consequence of the urban physical environment. In Leo Goldberger & Shlomo Breznitz (Eds.), *Handbook of stress: Theoretical and clinical aspects* (2nd ed.). New York: Free Press.

Gray, D. S., & Gorzalka, B. B. (1980). Adrenal steroid interactions in female sexual behavior: A review. *Psychoneuroendocrinology, 5,* 157–175.

Gray, Jeffrey A. (1987). *The psychology of fear and stress* (2nd ed.). New York: Cambridge University Press.

Green, Celia, & McCreery, Charles. (1994). *Lucid dreaming: The paradox of consciousness during sleep.* New York: Routledge.

Greenberg, Leslie S.; Elliott, Robert K.; & Lietaer, Germain. (1994). Research on experiential psychotherapies. In Allen E. Bergin & Sol L. Garfield (Eds.), *Handbook of psychotherapy and behavior change* (4th ed.). New York: Wiley.

Greeno, Catherine G., & Wing, Rena R. (1994). Stress-induced eating. *Psychological Bulletin, 115,* 444–464.

Greenough, William T. (1992). Morphological basis of learning and memory: Vertebrates. In Larry R. Squire (Ed.), *Encyclopedia of learning and memory.* New York: Macmillan.

Greenough, William T.; Black, James E.; & Wallace, Christopher S. (1987). Experience and brain development. *Child Development, 58,* 539–559.

Greenwald, Anthony G.; Spangenberg, Eric R.; Pratkanis, Anthony R.; & Eskenazi, Jay. (1991). Double-blind tests of subliminal self-help audiotapes. *Psychological Science, 2,* 119–122.

Gregory, Richard L. (1968, November). Visual illusions. *Scientific American, 212,* 66–76.

Griffiths, Roland. (1994, February). Quoted in Tori DeAngelis, People's drug of choice offers potent side effects. *APA Monitor, 25,* 16.

Grimm, Laurence G. (1993). *Statistical applications for the behavioral sciences.* New York: Wiley.

Grollman, Earl A. (1988). *Suicide: Prevention, intervention, postvention* (2nd ed.). Boston: Beacon Press.

Grossman, Michele, & Wood, Wendy. (1993). Sex differences in intensity of emotional experience: A social role interpretation. *Journal of Personality and Social Psychology, 65,* 1010–1022.

Grossmann, K. E., & Grossmann, K. (1990). The wider concept of attachment in cross-cultural research. *Human Development, 33,* 31–47.

Grosz, Richard D. (1990). Suicide: Training the resident assistant as an interventionist. In Leighton C. Whitaker & Richard E. Slimak (Eds.), *College student suicide.* New York: Haworth Press.

Grotevant, Harold D. (1987). Toward a process model of identity formation. *Journal of Adolescent Research, 2,* 203–222.

Grotevant, Harold D. (1992). Assigned and chosen identity components: A process perspective on their integration. In Gerald R. Adams, Thomas P. Gullotta, & Raymond Montemayor (Eds.), *Adolescent identity formation.* Newbury Park, Calif.: Sage.

Gunnar, Megan R. (1994). Psychoendocrine studies of temperament and stress in early childhood: Expanding current models. In John E. Bates & Theodore D. Wachs (Eds.), *Temperament: Individual differences at the interface of biology and behavior.* Washington, D.C.: American Psychological Association.

Gustavson, Carl R.; Kelly, Daniel J.; Sweeney, Michael; & Garcia, John. (1976). Prey-lithium aversions I: Coyotes and wolves. *Behavioral Biology, 17,* 61–72.

Haaga, David A. F., & Davison, Gerald C. (1991). Cognitive change methods. In Frederick H. Kanfer & Arnold P. Goldstein (Eds.), *Helping people change: A textbook of methods* (4th ed.). New York: Pergamon.

Haaga, David F., & Davison, Gerald C. (1993). An appraisal of rational-emotive therapy. *Journal of Consulting and Clinical Psychology, 61,* 215–220.

Hackel, Lisa S., & Ruble, Diane N. (1992). Changes in the marital relationship after the first baby is born: Predicting the impact of expectancy disconfirmation. *Journal of Personality and Social Psychology, 62,* 944–957.

Hahlweg, Kurt, & Goldstein, Michael J. (Eds.). (1987). *Understanding major mental disorder: The contribution of family interaction research.* New York: Family Process Press.

Haidt, Jonathan; Koller, Silvia Helena; & Dias, Maria G. (1993). Affect, culture, and morality, or is it wrong to eat your dog? *Journal of Personality and Social Psychology, 65,* 613–628.

Haight, Barbara Kavanagh. (1992). Long-term effects of a structured life review process. *Journal of Gerontology, 47* (5), 312–315.

Hall, Calvin S., & Van de Castle, R. L. (1966). *Content analysis of dreams.* New York: Appleton-Century-Crofts.

Hall, Christine C. Iijima. (1997). Cultural malpractice: The growing obsolescence of psychology with the changing U.S. population. *American Psychologist, 52,* 642–651.

Halliday, Gordon. (1995). Treating nightmares in children. In Charles E. Schaefer (Ed.), *Clinical handbook of sleep disorders in children.* Northvale, N.J.: Aronson.

Hamilton, Mykol C. (1988). Using masculine generics: Does generic *he* increase male bias in the user's imagery? *Sex Roles, 19,* 785–799.

Hamilton, Mykol C. (1991). Masculine bias in the attribution of personhood. *Psychology of Women Quarterly, 15,* 393–402.

Hansel, C. E. M. (1991). Parapsychology re-viewed. *Contemporary Psychology, 36,* 198–200.

Harma, Mikko. (1993). Individual differences in tolerance to shiftwork: A review. *Ergonomics, 36* (1–3), 101–109.

Harrington, D. M.; Block, J. H.; & Block, J. (1987). Testing aspects of Carl Rogers' theory of creative environments: Child-rearing antecedents of creative potential in young adolescents. *Journal of Personality and Social Psychology, 52,* 851–856.

Harris, Ben. (1979). What ever happened to Little Albert? *American Psychologist, 34,* 151–160.

Harter, Susan. (1983). Developmental perspectives on the self-system. In Paul H. Mussen & E. Mavis Hetherington (Eds.), *Handbook of child psychology* (4th ed., Vol. 4). New York: Wiley.

Harter, Susan. (1990). Self and identity development. In S. Shirley Feldman & Glen R. Elliott (Eds.), *At the threshold: The developing adolescent.* Cambridge, Mass.: Harvard University Press.

Havighurst, Robert J.; Neugarten, Bernice L.; & Tobin, Sheldon S. (1968). Disengagement and patterns of aging. In Bernice L. Neugarten (Ed.), *Middle age and aging.* Chicago: University of Chicago Press.

Hawkins, John N. (1994). Issues of motivation in Asian education. In Harold F. O'Neil, Jr., & Michael Drillings (Eds.), *Motivation: Theory and research.* Hillsdale, N.J.: Erlbaum.

Hayes, Jeffrey A., & Mitchell, Jeffrey C. (1994). Mental health professionals' skepticism about multiple personality disorder. *Professional Psychology: Research and Practice, 25,* 410–415.

Hayes, John R. (1989). *The complete problem solver* (2nd ed.). Hillsdale, N.J.: Erlbaum.

Hebb, Donald O. (1955). Drives and the C. N. S. (central nervous system). *Psychological Review, 62,* 243–254.

Hedge, Alan, & Yousif, Yousif H. (1992). Effects of urban size, urgency, and cost of helpfulness: A cross-cultural comparison between the United Kingdom and the Sudan. *Journal of Cross-Cultural Psychology, 23,* 107–115.

Heider, Eleanor Rosch, & Olivier, Donald C. (1972). The structure of the color space in naming and memory for two languages. *Cognitive Psychology, 3,* 337–354.

Heikkinen, Martti; Aro, Hillevi M.; & Lonnqvist, Jouko K. (1993). Life events and social support in suicide. *Suicide and Life Threatening Behavior, 23,* 343–358.

Heinrichs, R. Walter. (1993). Schizophrenia and the brain: Conditions for a neuropsychology of madness. *American Psychologist, 48,* 221–233.

Henderson, John M. (1997). Transsaccadic memory and integration during real-world object perception. *Psychological Science, 8,* 51–55.

Hendrix, Mary Lynn. (1993). *Bipolar disorder* (NIMH Publication No. 93–3679). Rockville, Md.: National Institute of Mental Health.

Henley, Nancy M. (1989). Molehill or mountain? What we know and don't know about sex bias in language. In M. Crawford & M. Gentry (Eds.), *Gender and thought: Psychological perspectives.* New York: Springer-Verlag.

Hennessey, Beth A., & Amabile, Teresa M. (1988). The conditions of creativity. In Robert J. Sternberg (Ed.), *The nature of creativity: Contemporary psychological perspectives.* New York: Cambridge University Press.

Henninger, Polly. (1992). Conditional handedness: Handedness changes in multiple personality disordered subject reflects shift in hemispheric dominance. *Consciousness and Cognition, 1,* 265–287.

Henry, William P.; Strupp, Hans H.; Shacht, Thomas E.; & Gaston, Louise. (1994). Psychodynamic approaches. In Allen E. Bergin & Sol L. Garfield (Eds.), *Handbook of psychotherapy and behavior change* (4th ed.). New York: Wiley.

Herbert, Tracy Bennett, & Cohen, Sheldon. (1993). Depression and immunity: A meta-analytic review. *Psychological Bulletin, 113,* 472–486.

Herman, Louis M.; Kuczaj, Stan A., II; & Holder, Mark D. (1993). Responses to anomalous gestural sequences by a language-trained dolphin: Evidence for processing of semantic relations and syntactic information. *Journal of Experimental Psychology: General, 122,* 184–194.

Hermans, Hubert J. M. (1996). Voicing the self: From information processing to dialogical interchange. *Psychological Bulletin, 119,* 31–50.

Hertel, Paula T., & Rude, Stephanie S. (1991). Depressive deficits in memory: Focusing attention improves subsequent recall. *Journal of Experimental Psychology: General, 120,* 301–309.

Hertz, Marguerite R. (1992). Rorschach-bound: A 50-year memoir. *Professional Psychology: Research and Practice, 23,* 168–171.

Hetherington, A. W., & Ranson, S. W. (1940). Hypothalamic lesions and adiposity in the rat. *Anatomical Record, 78,* 149–172.

Hewstone, Miles. (1990). The "ultimate attribution error"? A review of the literature on intergroup causal attribution. *European Journal of Social Psychology, 20,* 311–335.

Hilgard, Ernest R. (1982). Hypnotic susceptibility and implications for measurement. *International Journal of Clinical and Experimental Hypnosis, 30,* 394–403.

Hilgard, Ernest R. (1986a). *Divided consciousness: Multiple controls in human thought and action.* New York: Wiley.

Hilgard, Ernest R. (1986b, January). A study in hypnosis. *Psychology Today, 20,* 23–27.

Hilgard, Ernest R. (1987). *Psychology in America: A historical survey.* New York: Harcourt Brace Jovanovich.

Hilgard, Ernest R. (1991). A neodissociation interpretation of hypnosis. In Steven J. Lynn & J. Rhue (Eds.), *Theories of hypnosis: Current models and perspectives.* New York: Guilford Press.

Hilgard, Ernest R. (1992). Divided consciousness and dissociation. *Consciousness and Cognition, 1,* 16–32.

Hilgard, Ernest R., & Hilgard, Josephine R. (1983). *Hypnosis in the relief of pain.* Los Altos, Calif.: Kaufmann.

Hilgard, Ernest R., & Marquis, D. G. (1940). *Conditioning and learning.* New York: Appleton-Century-Crofts.

Hillyard, Steven A.; Mangun, George R.; Woldorff, Marty G.; & Luck, Steven J. (1995). Neural systems mediating selective attention. In Michael S. Gazzaniga (Ed.), *The cognitive neurosciences.* Cambridge, Mass.: MIT Press.

Hilton, James L., & Darley, John M. (1991). The effects of interaction goals on person perception. In Mark P. Zanna (Ed.), *Advances in experimental social psychology* (Vol. 24). San Diego: Academic Press/Harcourt.

Hilton, James L., & von Hippel, William. (1996). Stereotypes. *Annual Review of Psychology, 47,* 237–271.

Hines, Terence. (1988). *Pseudoscience and the paranormal: A critical examination of the evidence.* Buffalo, N.Y.: Prometheus Books.

Hines, Terence. (1996). Biorhythms. In Gordon Stein (Ed.), *The encyclopedia of the paranormal.* Amherst, N.Y.: Prometheus Books.

Hirschfeld, Robert M. A. (1991). *When the blues won't go away: New approaches to dysthymic disorder and other forms of chronic low-grade depression.* New York: Macmillan.

Hirshkowitz, Max; Moore, Constance A.; & Minhoto, Gisele. (1997). The basics of sleep. In Mark R. Pressman & William C. Orr (Eds.), *Understanding sleep: The evaluation and treatment of sleep disorders.* Washington, D.C.: American Psychological Association.

Hobfoll, Stevan E.; Lilly, Roy S.; & Jackson, Anita P. (1992). Conservation of social resources and the self. In Hans O. F. Veiel & Urs Baumann (Eds.), *The meaning and measurement of social support.* New York: Hemisphere.

Hobfoll, Stevan E., & Stephens, Mary Ann Parris. (1990). Social support during extreme stress: Consequences and intervention. In Barbara R. Sarason, Irwin G. Sarason, & Gregory R. Pierce (Eds.), *Social support: An interactional view.* New York: Wiley.

Hobfoll, Stevan E., & Vaux, Alex. (1993). Social support: Resources and context. In Leo Goldberger & Shlomo Breznitz (Eds.), *Handbook of stress: Theoretical and clinical aspects* (2nd ed.). New York: Free Press.

Hobson, J. Allan. (1988). *The dreaming brain.* New York: Basic Books.

Hobson, J. Allan. (1989). *Sleep.* New York: Scientific American Library.

Hobson, J. Allan. (1990). Activation, input source, and modulation: A neurocognitive model of the state of the brain-mind. In Richard R. Bootzin, John F. Kihlstrom, & Daniel L. Schacter (Eds.), *Sleep and cognition.* Washington, D.C.: American Psychological Association.

Hobson, J. Allan, & Stickgold, Robert. (1995). The conscious state paradigm: A neurological approach to waking, sleeping, and dreaming. In Michael S. Gazzaniga (Ed.), *The cognitive neurosciences.* Cambridge, Mass.: MIT Press.

Hoffman, Martin L. (1977). Moral internalization: Current theory and research. In Leonard Berkowitz (Ed.), *Advances in experimental social psychology* (Vol. 10). New York: Academic Press.

Hoffman, Martin L. (1988). Moral development. In Marc H. Bornstein & Michael E. Lamb (Eds.), *Developmental psychology: An advanced textbook.* Hillsdale, N.J.: Erlbaum.

Hoffman, Martin L. (1994). Discipline and internalization. *Developmental Psychology, 30,* 26–28.

Holahan, Carole K., & Sears, Robert R. (1995). *The gifted group in later maturity* (in association with Lee J. Cronbach). Stanford, Calif.: Stanford University Press.

Hole, John W., Jr. (1993). *Human anatomy and physiology* (6th ed.). Dubuque, Iowa: Brown.

Holland, A. J.; Sicotte, N.; & Treasure, J. (1988). Anorexia nervosa: Evidence of a genetic basis. *Journal of Psychosomatic Research, 32,* 561–571.

Hollis, Karen L. (1997). Contemporary research on Pavlovian conditioning: A "new" functional analysis. *American Psychologist, 52,* 956–965.

Hollon, Steven D., & Beck, Aaron T. (1994). Cognitive and cognitive-behavioral therapies. In Allen E. Bergin & Sol L. Garfield (Eds.), *Handbook of psychotherapy and behavior change* (4th ed.). New York: Wiley.

Holmes, David S. (1984). Meditation and somatic arousal reduction: A review of the experimental evidence. *American Psychologist, 39,* 1–10.

Holmes, David S. (1987). The influence of meditation versus rest on physiological arousal: A second examination. In Michael A. West (Ed.), *The psychology of meditation.* New York: Oxford University Press.

Holmes, David. (1990). The evidence for repression: An examination of sixty years of research. In Jerome Singer (Ed.), *Repression and dissociation: Implications for personality theory, psychopathology, and health.* Chicago: University of Chicago Press.

Holmes, Stanley. (1994, April 25). The tortuous tale of a serial killer. *Newsweek,* p. 30.

Holmes, Thomas H., & Rahe, Richard H. (1967). The Social Readjustment Rating Scale. *Journal of Psychosomatic Research, 11,* 213–218.

Holt, Robert R. (1993). Occupational stress. In Leo Goldberger & Shlomo Breznitz (Eds.), *Handbook of stress: Theoretical and clinical aspects* (2nd ed.). New York: Free Press.

Holyoak, Keith J., & Spellman, Barbara A. (1993). Thinking. *Annual Review of Psychology, 44,* 265–315.

Hoppe, Richard B. (1988). In search of a phenomenon: Research in parapsychology. *Contemporary Psychology, 33,* 129–130.

Hoptman, Matthew J., & Davidson, Richard J. (1994). How and why do the two cerebral hemispheres interact? *Psychological Bulletin, 116,* 195–219.

Horgan, John. (1994, July). Can science explain consciousness? *Scientific American, 271,* 88–94.

Horney, Karen. (1926/1967). The flight from womanhood. In Harold Kelman (Ed.), *Feminine psychology.* New York: Norton.

Horney, Karen. (1945/1972). *Our inner conflicts: A constructive theory of neurosis.* New York: Norton.

Hornig-Rohan, Mädy, & Amsterdam, Jay D. (1994). Clinical and biological correlates of treatment-resistant depression: An overview. *Psychiatric Annals, 24,* 220–227.

Horton, David L., & Mills, Carol B. (1984). Human learning and memory. *Annual Review of Psychology, 35,* 361–394.

House, James S.; Landis, Karl R.; & Umberson, Debra. (1988). Social relationships and health. *Science, 241,* 540–545.

Howard, George S. (1991). Culture tales: A narrative approach to thinking, cross-cultural psychology, and psychotherapy. *American Psychologist, 46,* 187–197.

Howard, Kenneth I.; Kopta, Stephen M.; Krause, M. S.; & Orlinsky, D. E. (1986). The dose-effect relationship in psychotherapy. *American Psychologist, 41,* 159–164.

Howard, William, & Crano, William D. (1974). Effects of sex, conversation, location, and size of observer group on bystander intervention in a high risk situation. *Sociometry, 37,* 491–507.

Howes, Carollee. (1991). Caregiving environments and their consequences for children: The experience in the United States. In E. C. Melhuish & P. Moss (Eds.), *Daycare for young children.* London: Routledge.

Howes, Carollee, & Hamilton, Claire E. (1992). Children's relationships with caregivers: Mothers and child care teachers. *Child Development, 63,* 859–871.

Hubel, David H. (1995). *Eye, brain, and vision.* New York: Scientific American Library.

Hughes, Steven L., & Neimeyer, Robert A. (1990). A cognitive model of suicidal behavior. In David Lester (Ed.), *Current concepts of suicide.* Philadelphia: The Charles Press.

Hull, Clark L. (1943). *Principles of behavior: An introduction to behavior theory.* New York: Appleton-Century-Crofts.

Hull, Clark L. (1952). *A behavior system: An introduction to behavior theory concerning the individual organism.* New Haven, Conn.: Yale University Press.

Human Capital Initiative. (1993, December). *Human capital initiative: Vitality for life: Psychological research for productive aging: Report 2.* Special issue of the *APS Observer* published by the American Psychological Society.

Hume, K. Michelle, & Crossman, Jane. (1992). Musical reinforcement of practice behaviors among competitive swimmers. *Journal of Applied Behavior Analysis, 25,* 665–670.

Hunt, Earl, & Agnoli, Franca. (1991). The Whorfian hypothesis: A cognitive psychology perspective. *Psychological Review, 98,* 377–389.

Hurvich, Leo M. (1981). *Color vision.* Sunderland, Mass.: Sinauer.

Huston, Ted L.; Ruggiero, Mary; Conner, Ross; & Geis, Gilbert. (1981). Bystander intervention into crime: A study based on naturally-occurring episodes. *Social Psychology Quarterly, 44,* 14–23.

Huttunen, Matti O.; Machon, Ricardo A.; & Mednick, Sarnoff A. (1994). Prenatal factors in the pathogenesis of schizophrenia. *British Journal of Psychiatry, 164* (Suppl. 23), 15–19.

Hyman, Ray. (1994). Anomaly or artifact? Comments on Bem and Honorton. *Psychological Bulletin, 115,* 19–24.

Illnerová, Helena. (1991). The suprachiasmatic nucleus and rhythmic pineal melatonin production. In David C. Klein, Robert Y. Moore, & Steven M. Reppert (Eds.), *Suprachiasmatic nucleus: The mind's clock.* New York: Oxford University Press.

Insel, Thomas R., & Winslow, James T. (1992). Neurobiology of obsessive compulsive disorder. *Psychiatric Clinics of North America, 15,* 813–824.

Irving, Clive (Ed.). (1995). *In their name: Oklahoma City: The official commemorative volume.* New York: Random House.

Irwin, Harvey J. (1994). Proneness to dissociation and traumatic childhood events. *Journal of Nervous and Mental Disease, 182,* 456–460.

Irwin, M.; Daniels, M.; Smith, T. L.; Bloom, E.; & Weiner, H. (1987). Impaired natural killer cell activity during bereavement. *Brain, Behavior, and Immunity, 1,* 98–104.

Isabella, Russell A.; Belsky, Jay; & von Eye, Alexander. (1989). Origins of infant–mother attachment: An examination of interactional synchrony during the infant's first year. *Developmental Psychology, 25,* 12–21.

Ishihara, Kaneyoshi; Miyake, Susumu; Miyasita, Akio; & Miyata, Yo. (1992). Morningness-eveningness preference and sleep habits in Japanese office workers of different ages. *Chronobiologia, 19,* 9–16.

Iversen, Iver H. (1992). Skinner's early research: From reflexology to operant conditioning. *American Psychologist, 47,* 1318–1328.

Izard, Carroll E. (1989). The structure and function of emotions: Implications for cognition, motivation, and personality. In Ira S. Cohen (Ed.), *The G. Stanley Hall Lecture Series* (Vol. 9) (1988 lectures). Washington, D.C.: American Psychological Association.

Izard, Carroll E. (1990a). The substrates and functions of emotion feelings: William James and current emotion theories. *Personality and Social Psychology Bulletin, 16,* 626–635.

Izard, Carroll E. (1990b). Facial expressions and the regulation of emotions. *Journal of Personality and Social Psychology, 58,* 487–498.

Jackson, Adam J. (1993). *Iridology: A guide to iris analysis and preventive health care.* Boston: Charles E. Tuttle Co.

Jacobs, Barry L. (1987). How hallucinogenic drugs work. *American Scientist, 75* (4), 388–392.

Jacobs, Bob. (1993, April 12). Quoted in Ronald Kotulak, Mental workouts pump up brain power. *Chicago Tribune,* p. 12.

Jacobs, Bob; Schall, Matthew; & Scheibel, Arnold B. (1993). A quantitative dendritic analysis of Wernicke's area in humans. II. Gender, hemispheric, and environmental factors. *Journal of Comparative Neurology, 327,* 97–106.

Jacobs, M. K., & Goodman, G. (1989). Psychology and self-help groups: Predictions on a partnership. *American Psychologist, 44,* 536–545.

Jacobson, John W.; Mulick, James A.; & Schwartz, Allen A. (1995). A history of facilitated communication: Science, pseudoscience, and antiscience: Science working group on facilitated communication. *American Psychologist, 50,* 750–765.

Jacox, Ada; Carr, D. B.; & Payne, Richard. (1994, March 3). New clinical-practice guidelines for the management of pain in patients with cancer. *New England Journal of Medicine, 330,* 651–655.

James, William. (1884). What is an emotion? *Mind, 9,* 188–205.

James, William. (1890). *Principles of psychology.* New York: Holt.

James, William. (1892). *Principles of psychology, briefer course.* New York: Holt.

James, William. (1894). The physical basis of emotion. *Psychological Review, 1,* 516–529. (Reprinted in the 1994 Centennial Issue of *Psychological Review, 101,* 205–210)

James, William. (1899/1958). *Talks to teachers.* New York: Norton.

Jameson, Dorothea, & Hurvich, Leo M. (1989). Essay concerning color constancy. *Annual Review of Psychology, 40,* 1–22.

Jamison, Kay Redfield. (1993). *Touched with fire: Manic-depressive illness and the artistic temperament.* New York: Free Press.

Janisse, Michel Pierre, & Dyck, Dennis G. (1988). The Type A behavior pattern and coronary heart disease: Physiological and psychological dimensions. In Michel Pierre Janisse (Ed.), *Individual differences, stress, and health psychology.* New York: Springer-Verlag.

Janus, Samuel S., & Janus, Cynthia L. (1993). *The Janus report on sexual behavior.* New York: Wiley.

Jefferson, James W. (1995). Lithium: The present and the future. *Journal of Clinical Psychiatry, 56,* 41–48.

Jenike, Michael A. (1992). Pharmacologic treatment of obsessive compulsive disorders. *Psychiatric Clinics of North America, 15,* 895–920.

Jensen, Bernard, & Bodeen, Donald V. (1992). *Visions of health: Understanding iridology.* Garden City Park, N.Y.: Avery.

Jessell, Tom. (1995a). Development of the nervous system. In Eric R. Kandel, James H. Schwartz, & Thomas M. Jessell (Eds.), *Essentials of neural science and behavior.* Norwalk, Conn.: Appleton & Lange.

Jessell, Tom. (1995b). The nervous system. In Eric R. Kandel, James H. Schwartz, & Thomas M. Jessell (Eds.), *Essentials of neural science and behavior.* Norwalk, Conn.: Appleton & Lange.

Jilek, Wolfgang G. (1993). Traditional medicine relevant to psychiatry. In Norman Sartorius, Giovanni de Girolamo, Gavin Andrews, G. Allen German, & Leon Eisenberg (Eds.), *Treatment of mental disorders: A review of effectiveness.* Washington, D.C.: World Health Organization/American Psychiatric Press.

John, Oliver P. (1990). The "Big Five" factor taxonomy: Dimensions of personality in the natural language and in questionnaires. In Lawrence A. Pervin (Ed.), *Handbook of personality: Theory and research.* New York: Guilford Press.

Johnson, C. L.; Stuckey, M. K.; Lewis, L. D.; & Schwartz, D. M. (1982). Bulimia: A descriptive survey of 316 cases. *International Journal of Eating Disorders, 2,* 3–16.

Johnson, Hollyn M. (1994). Processes of successful intentional forgetting. *Psychological Bulletin, 116,* 274–292.

Johnson, John A., & Ostendorf, Fritz. (1993). Clarification of the five-factor model with the abridged Big Five dimensional circumplex. *Journal of Personality and Social Psychology, 65,* 563–576.

Johnson, Katrina W.; Anderson, Norman B.; Bastida, Elena; Kramer, B. Josea; Williams, David; & Wong, Morrison. (1995). Panel II: Macrosocial and environmental influences on minority health. *Health Psychology, 14,* 601–612. (Special issue: Behavioral and Sociocultural Perspectives on Ethnicity and Health.)

Johnson, Marcia K.; Hashtroudi, Shahin; & Lindsay, D. Stephen. (1993). Source monitoring. *Psychological Bulletin, 114,* 3–28.

Johnson, Mark H.; Dziurawiec, Suzanne; Ellis, Hadyn; & Morton, John. (1991). Newborns' preferential tracking of face-like stimuli and its subsequent decline. *Cognition, 40,* 1–19.

Johnson, Sheri L., & Roberts, John E. (1995). Life events and bipolar disorder: Implications from three biological theories. *Psychological Bulletin, 117,* 434–449.

Johnston, Daniel; Magee, Jeffrey C.; Colbert, Costa M.; & Christie, Brian R. (1996). Active properties of neuronal dendrites. *Annual Review of Neuroscience, 19,* 165–186.

Johnston, Timothy D. (1985). Introduction: Conceptual issues in the ecological study of learning. In Timothy D. Johnston & Alexandra T. Pietrewicz (Eds.), *Issues in the ecological study of learning.* Hillside, N.J.: Erlbaum.

Jones, Edward E. (1990). *Interpersonal perception.* New York: Freeman.

Jones, Edward E., & Nisbett, Richard E. (1971). *The actor and the observer: Dirvergent perceptions of the causes of behavior.* Morristown, N.J.: General Learning Press.

Jones, Ernest. (1953). *The life and work of Sigmund Freud: Vol. 1. The formative years and the great discoveries: 1856–1900.* New York: Basic Books.

Jones, Ernest. (1955). *The life and work of Sigmund Freud: Years of maturity, 1901–1919.* New York: Basic Books.

Jones, James M. (1991). Psychological models of race: What have they been and what should they be? In Jacqueline D. Goodchilds (Ed.), *Psychological perspectives on human diversity in America.* Washington, D.C.: American Psychological Association.

Jones, Mary Cover. (1924a). A laboratory study of fear: The case of Peter. *The Pedagogical Seminary and Journal of Genetic Psychology, 31,* 308–315.

Jones, Mary Cover. (1924b). The elimination of children's fears. *Journal of Experimental Psychology, 7,* 382–390.

Jones, Mary Cover. (1975). A 1924 pioneer looks at behavior therapy. *Journal of Behavior Therapy & Experimental Psychiatry, 6,* 181–187.

Jones, Warren H., & Russell, Dan W. (1980). The selective processing of belief-discrepant information. *European Journal of Social Psychology, 10,* 309–312.

Josephs, Lawrence. (1987). Dream reports of nightmares and stages of sleep. In Henry Kellerman (Ed.), *The nightmare: Psychological and biological foundations.* New York: Columbia University Press.

Judd, Charles M., & Park, Bernadette. (1993). Definition and assessment of accuracy in social stereotypes. *Psychological Review, 100,* 109–128.

Julien, Robert M. (1995). *A primer of drug action* (7th ed.). New York: Freeman.

Jung, Carl G. (1923/1976). Psychological types. In Joseph Campbell (Ed.), *The portable Jung.* New York: Penguin.

Jung, Carl G. (1931/1976). The structure of the psyche. In Joseph Campbell (Ed.), *The portable Jung.* New York: Penguin.

Jung, Carl G. (1951/1976). Aion: Phenomenology of the self. In Joseph Campbell (Ed.), *The portable Jung.* New York: Penguin.

Jung, Carl G. (1963). *Memories, dreams, reflections* (Translated by Richard and Clara Winston). New York: Random House.

Jung, Carl G. (1964). *Man and his symbols.* New York: Dell.

Kagan, Jerome, & Fox, Nathan. (1995, November). Interviewed in Beth Azar, Timidity can develop in the first days of life. *APA Monitor, 26* (11), 23.

Kahn, Edwin; Fisher, Charles; & Edwards, Adele. (1991). Night terrors and anxiety dreams. In Steven J. Ellman & John S. Antrobus (Eds.), *The mind in sleep: Psychology and psychophysiology* (2nd ed.). New York: Wiley.

Kahneman, Daniel, & Tversky, Amos. (1982). On the psychology of prediction. In Daniel Kahneman, Paul Slovic, & Amos Tversky (Eds.), *Judgment under uncertainty: Heuristics and biases.* New York: Cambridge University Press.

Kail, Robert. (1991). Developmental change in speed of processing during childhood and adolescence. *Psychological Bulletin, 109,* 490–501.

Kaitz, Marsha; Lapidot, Pnina; Bronner, Ruth; & Eidelman, Arthur I. (1992). Parturient women can recognize their infants by touch. *Developmental Psychology, 28,* 35–39.

Kalat, James W. (1985). Taste-aversion learning in ecological perspective. In Timothy D. Johnston & Alexandra T. Pietrewicz (Eds.), *Issues in the ecological study of learning.* Hillsdale, N.J.: Erlbaum.

Kalat, James W. (1995). *Biological psychology* (5th ed.). Pacific Grove, Calif.: Brooks/Cole.

Kalbfleisch, Pamela J., & Cody, Michael J. (Eds.). (1995). *Gender, power, and communication in human relationships.* Hillsdale, N.J.: Erlbaum.

Kamarck, Thomas, & Jennings, J. Richard. (1991). Biobehavioral factors in sudden cardiac death. *Psychological Bulletin, 109,* 42–75.

Kamarck, Thomas W.; Manuck, Stephen B.; & Jennings, J. Richard. (1990). Social support reduces cardiovascular reactivity to psychological challenge: A laboratory model. *Psychosomatic Medicine, 52,* 42–58.

Kamin, Leon J. (1995). The pioneers of IQ testing. In Russell Jacoby & Naomi Glauberman (Eds.), *The* Bell Curve *debate: History, documents, opinions.* New York: Times Books.

Kamps, Debra M.; Leonard, Betsy R.; Vernon, Sue; Dugan, Erin P.; & Delquadri, Joseph C. (1992). Teaching social skills to students with autism to increase peer interactions in an integrated first-grade classroom. *Journal of Applied Behavior Analysis, 25,* 281–288.

Kandel, Eric R. (1995a). Nerve cells and behavior. In Eric R. Kandel, James H. Schwartz, & Thomas M. Jessell (Eds.)., *Essentials of neural science and behavior.* Norwalk, Conn.: Appleton & Lange.

Kandel, Eric R. (1995b). Synaptic integration. In Eric R. Kandel, James H. Schwartz, & Thomas M. Jessell (Eds.), *Essentials of neural science and behavior.* Norwalk, Conn.: Appleton & Lange.

Kandel, Eric R. (1995c). Transmitter release. In Eric R. Kandel, James H. Schwartz, & Thomas M. Jessell (Eds.), *Essentials of neural science and behavior.* Norwalk, Conn.: Appleton & Lange.

Kandel, Eric R. (1995d). Cellular mechanisms of learning and memory. In Eric R. Kandel, James H. Schwartz, & Thomas M. Jessell (Eds.), *Essentials of neural science and behavior.* Norwalk, Conn.: Appleton & Lange.

Kandel, Eric R., & Hawkins, Robert D. (1993). The biological basis of learning and individuality. In *Mind and brain: Readings from Scientific American.* New York: Freeman.

Kandel, Eric R., & Kupfermann, Irving. (1995). Emotional states. In Eric R. Kandel, James H. Schwartz, & Thomas M. Jessell (Eds.), *Essentials of neural science and behavior.* Norwalk, Conn.: Appleton & Lange.

Kandel, Eric R., & Siegelbaum, Steven. (1995). An introduction to synaptic trans-mission. In Eric R. Kandel, James H. Schwartz, & Thomas M. Jessell (Eds.)., *Essentials of neural science and behavior.* Norwalk, Conn.: Appleton & Lange.

Kane, John M. (1994). Editorial: Risperidone. *American Journal of Psychiatry, 151,* 802–803.

Kanin, E. J. (1982). Female rape fantasies: A victimization study. *Victimology, 7,* 114–121.

Kanner, Allen D.; Coyne, James C.; Schaefer, Catherine; & Lazarus, Richard S. (1981). Comparison of two modes of stress management: Daily hassles and uplifts versus major life events. *Journal of Behavioral Medicine, 4,* 1–39.

Kaplan, Craig A., & Simon, Herbert A. (1990). In search of insight. *Cognitive Psychology, 22,* 374–419.

Kaplan, Robert M., & Saccuzzo, Dennis P. (1993). *Psychological testing: Principles, applications, and issues* (3rd ed.). Pacific Grove, Calif.: Brooks/Cole.

Kaplan, Steve. (1990). Capturing your creativity. In Michael G. Walraven & Hiram E. Fitzgerald (Eds.), *Annual editions: Psychology: 1990/91.* Guilford, Conn.: Dushkin.

Kaplan, Stuart L., & Busner, Joan. (1993). Treatment of nocturnal enuresis. In Thomas R. Giles (Ed.), *Handbook of effective psychotherapy.* New York: Plenum.

Kapur, Shitij, & Mann, J. John. (1993). Antidepressant action and the neurobiologic effects of ECT: Human studies. In C. Edward Coffey (Ed.), *The clinical science of electroconvulsive therapy.* Washington, D.C.: American Psychiatric Press.

Karney, Benjamin R., & Bradbury, Thomas N. (1995). The longitudinal course of marital quality and stability: A review of theory, method, and research. *Psychological Bulletin, 118* (1), 3–34.

Karni, Avi; Tanne, David; Rubenstein, Barton S.; Askenasy, Jean J. M.; & Sagi, Dov. (1994, July 29). Dependence on REM sleep of overnight improvement of a perceptual skill. *Science, 265,* 679–682.

Karson, Samuel, & O'Dell, Jerry W. (1989). The 16 PF. In Charles S. Newmark (Ed.), *Major psychological assessment instruments* (Vol. 2). Boston: Allyn & Bacon.

Kasl, Charlotte Davis. (1992). *Many roads, one journey: Moving beyond the twelve steps.* New York: HarperPerennial.

Kastenbaum, Robert. (1986). *Death, society, and the human experience.* Columbus, Ohio: Merrill.

Kastenbaum, Robert. (1992). *The psychology of death.* New York: Springer-Verlag.

Katchadourian, Herant A. (1990). Sexuality. In S. Shirley Feldman & Glen R. Elliott (Eds.), *At the threshold: The developing adolescent.* Cambridge, Mass.: Harvard University Press.

Kaufman, Alan S. (1990). *Assessing adolescent and adult intelligence.* Boston: Allyn & Bacon.

Kaufman, Lloyd, & Rock, Irvin. (1989). The moon illusion thirty years later. In Maurice Hershenson (Ed.), *The moon illusion.* Hillsdale, N.J.: Erlbaum.

Kazdin, Alan E. (1994a). Methodology, design, and evaluation in psychotherapy research. In Allen E. Bergin & Sol L. Garfield (Eds.), *Handbook of psychotherapy and behavior change* (4th ed.). New York: Wiley.

Kazdin, Alan E. (1994b). Psychotherapy for children and adolescents. In Allen E. Bergin & Sol L. Garfield (Eds.), *Handbook of psychotherapy and behavior change* (4th ed.). New York: Wiley.

Keane, T. M.; Gerardi, R. J.; Quinn, S. J.; & Litz, B. T. (1992). Behavioral treatment of post-traumatic stress disorder. In S. M. Turner, K. S. Calhoun, & H. E. Adams (Eds.), *Handbook of clinical behavior therapy* (2nd ed.). New York: Wiley.

Keating, Daniel P. (1990). Adolescent thinking. In Glen R. Elliott & S. Shirley Feldman (Eds.), *At the threshold: The developing adolescent.* Cambridge, Mass.: Harvard University Press.

Keck, Paul E., & McElroy, Susan L. (1993). Current perspectives on treatment of bipolar disorder with lithium. *Psychiatric Annals, 23,* 64–69.

Keefe, Richard S., & Harvey, Philip D. (1994). *Understanding schizophrenia: A guide to the new research on causes and treatment.* New York: Free Press.

Keesey, Richard E., & Powley, Terry L. (1986). The regulation of body weight. *Annual Review of Psychology, 37,* 109–133.

Keith, Samuel J., & Matthews, Susan M. (1991). The diagnosis of schizophrenia: A review of onset and duration issues. *Schizophrenia Bulletin, 17,* 51–67.

Kendler, Kenneth S., & Diehl, Scott R. (1993). The genetics of schizophrenia: A current genetic-epidemiologic perspective. *Schizophrenia Bulletin, 19,* 261–285.

Kendler, Kenneth S.; Kessler, Ronald C.; Neale, Michael C.; Heath, Andrew C.; & Eaves, Lindon J. (1993). The prediction of major depression in women: Toward an integrated etiologic model. *American Journal of Psychiatry, 150,* 1139–1148.

Kennedy, Susan; Kiecolt-Glaser, Janice K.; & Glaser, Ronald. (1990). Social support, stress, and the immune system. In Barbara R. Sarason, Irwin G. Sarason, & Gregory R. Pierce (Eds.), *Social support: An interactional view.* New York: Wiley.

Kessen, William. (1996). American psychology just before Piaget. *Psychological Science, 7,* 196–199.

Kessler, Ronald C. (1994, January 22). "Really serious conditions. . . ." Quoted in *Science News, 145,* 55.

Kessler, Ronald C.; McGonagle, Katherine A.; Zhao, Shanyang; Nelson, Christopher B.; Hughes, Michael; Eshleman, Suzann; Wittchen, Hans-Ulrich; & Kendler, Kenneth S. (1994). Lifetime and 12-month prevalence of *DSM-III-R* psychiatric disorders in the United States: Results from the National Comorbidity Survey (NCS). *Archives of General Psychiatry, 51,* 8–19.

Kessler, Ronald C.; Price, Richard H.; & Wortman, Camille B. (1985). Social factors in psychopathology: Stress, social support, and coping processes. *Annual Review of Psychology, 36,* 531–572.

Khan, A.; Mirolo, M. H.; Hughes, D.; & Bierut, L. (1993). Electroconvulsive therapy. *Psychiatric Clinics of North America, 16* (2), 497–513.

Kibel, Howard D. (1993). Inpatient group psychotherapy. In Anne Alonso & Hillel I. Swiller (Eds.), *Group therapy in clinical practice.* Washington, D.C.: American Psychiatric Press.

Kiecolt-Glaser, Janice K.; Fisher, Laura D.; Ogrocki, Paula.; Stout, Julie C.; Speicher, Carl E.; & Glaser, Ronald. (1987). Marital quality, marital disruption, and immune function. *Psychosomatic Medicine, 49,* 13–34.

Kiecolt-Glaser, Janice K., & Glaser, Ronald. (1991). Stress and immune function in humans. In Robert Ader, David L. Felten, & Nicholas Cohen (Eds.), *Psychoneuroimmunology.* San Diego: Academic Press.

Kiecolt-Glaser, Janice K., & Glaser, Ronald. (1993). Mind and immunity. In Daniel Goleman & Joel Gurin (Eds.), *Mind/body medicine: How to use your mind for better health.* Yonkers, N.Y.: Consumer Reports Books.

Kiesler, Charles A., & Kiesler, Sara B. (1969). *Conformity.* Reading, Mass.: Addison-Wesley.

Kihlstrom, John F. (1983). Instructed forgetting. *Journal of Experimental Psychology: General, 112,* 73–79.

Kihlstrom, John F. (1984). Conscious, subconscious, unconscious: A cognitive perspective. In Kenneth S. Bowers & Donald Meichenbaum (Eds.), *The unconscious reconsidered.* New York: Wiley.

Kihlstrom, John F. (1985). Hypnosis. *Annual Review of Psychology, 36,* 385–418.

Kihlstrom, John F. (1986). Strong inferences about hypnosis. *Behavioral and Brain Sciences, 9* (3), 474–475.

Kihlstrom, John F. (1987, September 18). The cognitive unconscious. *Science, 237,* 1445–1452.

Kihlstrom, John F. (1992). Dissociation and dissociations: A comment on consciousness and cognition. *Consciousness and Cognition, 1,* 47–53.

Kihlstrom, John F. (1995, September). On the validity of psychology experiments. *APS Observer, 8* (5), 10–11.

Kihlstrom, John F., & Barnhardt, Terrence M. (1993). The self-regulation of memory: For better and for worse, with and without hypnosis. In Daniel M. Wegner & James W. Pennebaker (Eds.), *Handbook of mental control.* Englewood Cliffs, N.J.: Prentice Hall.

Kihlstrom, John F.; Barnhardt, Terrence M.; & Tataryn, Douglas J. (1992). The psychological unconscious: Found, lost, and regained. *American Psychologist, 47,* 788–791.

Kihlstrom, John F.; Glisky, Martha L.; & Angiulo, Michael J. (1994). Dissociative tendencies and dissociative disorders. *Journal of Abnormal Psychology, 103,* 117–124.

Kimura, Doreen. (1992, September). Sex differences in the brain. *Scientific American, 267,* 80–87.

Kimzey, Stephen L. (1975). The effects of extended spaceflight on hematologic and immunologic systems. *Journal of the American Medical Women's Association, 30,* 218–232.

Kirk, Stuart A., & Kutchins, Herb. (1992). *The selling of DSM: The rhetoric of science in psychiatry.* New York: Aldine de Gruyter.

Kirsch, Irving; Silva, Christopher E.; Comey, Gail; & Reed, Steven. (1995). A spectral analysis of cognitive and personality variables in hypnosis: Empirical disconfirmation of the two-factor model of hypnotic responding. *Journal of Personality and Social Psychology, 69,* 167–175.

Kitayama, Shinobu; Markus, Hazel Rose; Matsumoto, Hisaya; & Norasakkunkit, Vinai. (1997). Individual and collective processes in the construction of the self: Self-enhancement in the United States and self-criticism in Japan. *Journal of Personality and Social Psychology, 72,* 1245–1267.

Klahr, David. (1992). Information-processing approaches. In Ross Vasta (Ed.), *Six theories of child development: Revised formulations and current issues.* London: Jessica Kingsley Publishers.

Klein, David C.; Moore, Robert Y.; & Reppert, Steven M. (Eds.). (1991). *Suprachias-*

matic nucleus: The mind's clock. New York: Oxford University Press.

Klein, Donald F., & Wender, Paul H. (1993). *Understanding depression: A complete guide to its diagnosis and treatment.* New York: Oxford University Press.

Klein, Stephen B., & Mowrer, Robert R. (1989). *Contemporary learning theories: Instrumental conditioning theory and the impact of biological constraints on learning.* Hillsdale, N.J.: Erlbaum.

Klerman, Gerald L.; Weissman, Myrna M.; Markowitz, John; Glick, Ira; Wilner, Philip J.; Mason, Barbara; & Shear, M. Katherine. (1994). Medication and psychotherapy. In Sol L. Garfield & Allen E. Bergin (Eds.), *Handbook of psychotherapy and behavior change* (4th ed.). New York: Wiley.

Klinger, Eric. (1993). Clinical approaches to mood control. In Daniel M. Wegner & James W. Pennebaker (Eds.), *Handbook of mental control.* Englewood Cliffs, N.J.: Prentice Hall.

Kluft, Richard P. (1991). Clinical presentations of multiple personality disorder. *Psychiatric Clinics of North America, 14,* 605–629.

Kluft, Richard P. (1993). Multiple personality disorders. In David Spiegel (Ed.), *Dissociative disorders: A clinical review.* Lutherville, Md.: Sidran.

Knittle, Jerome L. (1975). Endocrine and metabolic adaptations to obesity. In George A. Bray (Ed.), *Obesity in perspective* (NIH Publication No. 75–708). Bethesda, Md.: National Institutes of Health.

Koester, John. (1995a). Membrane potential. In Eric R. Kandel, James H. Schwartz, & Thomas M. Jessell (Eds.), *Essentials of neural science and behavior.* Norwalk, Conn.: Appleton & Lange.

Koester, John. (1995b). Propagated signaling: The action potential. In Eric R. Kandel, James H. Schwartz, & Thomas M. Jessell (Eds.), *Essentials of neural science and behavior.* Norwalk, Conn.: Appleton & Lange.

Koester, John, & Siegelbaum, Steven. (1995a). Ion channels. In Eric R. Kandel, James H. Schwartz, & Thomas M. Jessell (Eds.), *Essentials of neural science and behavior.* Norwalk, Conn.: Appleton & Lange.

Koester, John, & Siegelbaum, Steven. (1995b). Local signaling: Passive electrical properties of the neuron. In Eric R. Kandel, James H. Schwartz, & Thomas M. Jessell (Eds.), *Essentials of neural science and behavior.* Norwalk, Conn.: Appleton & Lange.

Koffka, Kurt. (1935). *Principles of Gestalt psychology.* New York: Harcourt, Brace.

Kohlberg, Lawrence. (1981). *The philosophy of moral development: Moral stages and the idea of justice: Vol. 1. Essays on moral development.* New York: Harper & Row.

Kohlberg, Lawrence. (1984). *The psychology of moral development.* New York: Harper & Row.

Konishi, Masakazu. (1993, April). Listening with two ears. *Scientific American, 268,* 66–73.

Koriat, Asher. (1993). How do we know that we know? The accessibility model of the feeling of knowing. *Psychological Review, 100,* 609–639.

Koskenvuo, M.; Kapiro, J.; Rose, R. J.; Kesnaiemi, A.; Sarnaa, S.; Heikkila, K.; & Langinvanio, H. (1988). Hostility as a risk factor for mortality and ischemic heart disease in men. *Psychosomatic Medicine, 50,* 330–340.

Koss, Mary P., & Shiang, Julia. (1994). Research on brief psychotherapy. In Allen E. Bergin & Sol L. Garfield (Eds.), *Handbook of psychotherapy and behavior change* (4th ed.). New York: Wiley.

Kosslyn, Stephen M. (1995). Introduction: Thought and imagery. In Michael S. Gazzaniga (Ed.), *The cognitive neurosciences.* Cambridge, Mass.: MIT Press.

Kosslyn, Stephen M.; Ball, Thomas M.; & Reiser, Brian J. (1978). Visual images preserve metric spatial information: Evidence from studies of image scanning. *Journal of Experimental Psychology: Human Perception and Performance, 4,* 47–60.

Kosslyn, Stephen M., & Sussman, Amy L. (1995). Roles of imagery in perception: Or, there is no such thing as immaculate perception. In Michael S. Gazzaniga (Ed.), *The cognitive neurosciences.* Cambridge, Mass.: MIT Press.

Kramer, Jack L., & Conoley, Jane Close (Eds.). (1992). *The eleventh mental measurements yearbook.* Lincoln: Buros Institute of Mental Measurements/University of Nebraska Press.

Kramer, Peter D. (1993). *Listening to Prozac: A psychiatrist explores antidepressant drugs and the remaking of the self.* New York: Viking.

Krausz, Michael, & Müller-Thomsen, Tomas. (1993). Schizophrenia with onset in adolescence: An 11-year followup. *Schizophrenia Bulletin, 19,* 831–841.

Krippner, Stanley. (1994). Cross-cultural treatment perspectives of dissociative disorders. In Steven Jay Lynn & Judith W. Rhue (Eds.), *Dissociation: Clinical and theoretical perspectives.* New York: Guilford Press.

Krishnan, K. Ranga Rama; Doraiswamy, P. Murali; Venkataraman, Sanjeev; Reed, Deborah A.; & Ritchie, James C. (1991).

Current concepts in hypothalamo-pituitary-adrenal axis regulation. In James A. McCubbin, Peter G. Kaufmann, & Charles B. Nemeroff (Eds.), *Stress, neuropeptides, and systemic disease.* San Diego: Academic Press.

Kronauer, Richard E. (1994). Circadian rhythms. In Rosemary Cooper (Ed.), *Sleep.* New York: Chapman & Hall.

Kübler-Ross, Elisabeth. (1969). *On death and dying.* New York: Macmillan.

Kuhl, Patricia K.; Andruski, Jean E.; Chistovich, Inna A.; Chistovich, Ludmilla A.; Kozhevnikova, Elena V.; Ryskina, Viktoria L.; Stolyarova, Elvira I.; Sundberg, Ulla; & Lacerda, Francisco. (1997, August 1). Cross-language analysis of phonetic units in language addressed to infants. *Science, 277,* 684–686.

Kuhl, Patricia K; Williams, Karen A.; Lacerda, Francisco; Stevens, Kenneth N.; & Lindblom, Bjorn. (1992, January 31). Linguistic experience alters phonetic perception in infants by 6 months of age. *Science, 255,* 606–608.

Kunoh, Hiroshi, & Takaoki, Eiji. (1994). *3-D planet: The world as seen through stereograms.* San Francisco: Cadence Books.

Kupfermann, Irving, & Kandel, Eric R. (1995). Learning and memory. In Eric R. Kandel, James H. Schwartz, & Thomas M. Jessell (Eds.), *Essentials of neural science and behavior.* Norwalk, Conn.: Appleton & Lange.

Kurcinka, Mary Sheedy. (1991). *Raising your spirited child.* New York: HarperCollins.

Kurdek, Lawrence A. (1995). Developmental changes in relationship quality in gay and lesbian cohabiting couples. *Developmental Psychology, 31,* 86–94.

Kurtz, Paul. (1994, Winter). The new skepticism. *Skeptical Inquirer, 18,* 139–147.

Kurtz, Paul, & Fraknoi, Andrew. (1986). Scientific tests of astrology do not support its claims. In Kendrick Frazier (Ed.), *Science confronts the paranormal.* Buffalo, N.Y.: Prometheus Books.

LaFromboise, Teresa; Coleman, Hardin L. K.; & Gerton, Jennifer. (1993a). Psychological impact of biculturalism: Evidence and theory. *Psychological Bulletin, 114,* 395–412.

LaFromboise, Teresa D.; Trimble, Joseph E.; & Mohatt, Gerald V. (1993b). Counseling intervention and American Indian tradition: An integrative approach. In Donald R. Atkinson, George Morten, & Derald Wing Sue (Eds.), *Counseling American minorities: A cross-cultural perspective* (4th ed.). Madison, Wis.: Brown & Benchmark.

Lamb, Michael E.; Sternberg, Kathleen J.; & Prodromidis, Margarida. (1992). Non-maternal care and the security of infant–mother attachment: A reanalysis of the data. *Infant Behavior and Development, 15,* 71–83.

Lamb, Michael E.; Thompson, Ross A.; Gardner, William; & Charnov, Eric L. (1985). *Infant–mother attachment: The origins and developmental significance of individual differences in Strange Situation behavior.* Hillsdale, N.J.: Erlbaum.

Lambert, Michael J., & Bergin, Allen E. (1994). The effectiveness of psychotherapy. In Allen E. Bergin & Sol L. Garfield (Eds.), *Handbook of psychotherapy and behavior change* (4th ed.). New York: Wiley.

Lamson, Ralph. (1994, November). Quoted in Virtural therapy. *Psychology Today, 27,* 21.

Landau, Barbara. (1994). Where's what and what's where: The language of objects in space [special issue]. *Lingua, 92,* 259–296.

Landau, Barbara, & Jackendoff, Ray. (1993). "What" and "where" in spatial language and spatial cognition. *Behavioral and Brain Sciences, 16,* 217–265.

Lange, Carl G., & James, William. (1922). *The emotions.* (Translated by I. A. Haupt). Baltimore: Williams & Wilkins.

Langer, Ellen, & Rodin, Judith. (1976). The effects of choice and enhanced personal responsibility for the aged: A field experiment in an institutional setting. *Journal of Personality and Social Psychology, 34,* 191–198.

Larsen, Randy J., & Diener, Ed. (1987). Affect intensity as an individual difference characteristic: A review. *Journal of Personality and Social Psychology, 21,* 1–39.

Larsen, Randy J.; Diener, Ed; & Emmons, Robert A. (1986). Affect intensity and reactions to daily life events. *Journal of Personality and Social Psychology, 51,* 803–814.

Larson, Jeffry H.; Crane, D. Russell; & Smith, Craig W. (1991). Morning and night couples: The effect of wake and sleep patterns on marital adjustment. *Journal of Marital and Family Therapy, 17,* 53–65.

Larwood, Laurie, & Gutek, Barbara A. (1987). Working toward a theory of women's career development. In Barbara A. Gutek & Laurie Larwood (Eds.), *Women's career development.* Newbury Park, Calif.: Sage.

Lashley, Karl. (1929). *Brain mechanisms and intelligence.* Chicago: University of Chicago Press.

Lashley, Karl. (1950). In search of the engram. In *Symposium of the Society for Experimental Biology* (Vol. 4). New York: Cambridge University Press.

Lask, Bryan. (1995). Night terrors. In Charles E. Schaefer (Ed.), *Clinical handbook of sleep disorders in children.* Northvale, N.J.: Aronson.

Latané, Bibb, & Darley, John M. (1970). *The unresponsive bystander: Why doesn't he help?* New York: Appleton-Century-Crofts.

Latané, Bibb, & Nida, Steve A. (1981). Ten years of research on group size and helping. *Psychological Bulletin, 89,* 308–324.

Laudenslager, M. C.; Ryan, S. M.; Drugan, R. C.; Hyson, R. L.; & Maier, S. F. (1983). Coping and immunosuppression: Inescapable but not escapable shock suppresses lymphocyte proliferation. *Science, 231,* 568–570.

Laumann, Edward O.; Gagnon, John H.; Michael, Robert T.; & Michaels, Stuart. (1994). *The social organization of sexuality: Sexual practices in the United States.* Chicago: University of Chicago Press.

Laurence, J. R., & Perry, C. (1983). Hypnotically created memory among highly hypnotizable subjects. *Science, 222,* 523–524.

Lavie, Peretz. (1989). To nap, perchance to sleep—ultradian aspects of napping. In David F. Dinges & Roger J. Broughton (Eds.), *Sleep and alertness: Chronobiological, behavioral, and medical aspects of napping.* New York: Raven Press.

Lawrence, D. H. (1928/1960). *Lady Chatterley's lover.* Hammondsworth, U.K.: Penguin.

Lawton, Carolyn; France, Karyn G.; & Blampied, Neville M. (1991). Treatment of infant sleep disturbance by graduated extinction. *Child and Family Behavior Therapy, 13,* 39–56.

Lazarus, Richard S. (1991a). Cognition and motivation in emotion. *American Psychologist, 46,* 352–367.

Lazarus, Richard S. (1991b). *Emotion and adaptation.* New York: Oxford University Press.

Lazarus, Richard S. (1993). From psychological stress to the emotions: A history of changing outlooks. *Annual Review of Psychology, 44,* 1–21.

Lazarus, Richard S. (1995). Vexing research problems inherent in cognitive-mediational theories of emotion—and some solutions. *Psychological Inquiry, 6,* 183–197.

Lazarus, Richard S., & Folkman, Susan. (1984). *Stress, appraisal, and coping.* New York: Springer.

Leach, C. S., & Rambaut, P. C. (1974). Biochemical responses of the *Skylab* crewmen. *Proceedings of the Skylab Life Sciences Symposium, 2,* 427–454.

Leahy, Thomas Hardy. (1992). *A history of psychology: Main currents in psychological thought.* Englewood Cliffs, N.J.: Prentice Hall.

Lebow, Jay L., & Gurman, Alan S. (1995). Research assessing couple and family therapy. *Annual Review of Psychology, 46,* 27–57.

LeDoux, Joseph E. (1994a). Memory versus emotional memory in the brain. In Paul Ekman & Richard J. Davidson (Eds.), *The nature of emotion: Fundamental questions.* New York: Oxford University Press.

LeDoux, Joseph E. (1994b, June). Emotion, memory, and the brain. *Scientific American, 270,* 50–57.

LeDoux, Joseph E . (1995). Emotion: Clues from the brain. *Annual Review of Psychology, 46,* 209–235.

Lee, Kimberly L.; Vaillant, George T.; Torrey, William C.; & Elder, Glen H. (1995). A 50-year prospective study of the psychological sequelae of World War II combat. *American Journal of Psychiatry, 152,* 516–522.

Lees, G. J. (1993). The possible contributions of microglia and macrophages to delayed neuronal death after ischemia. *Journal of the Neurological Sciences, 114,* 119–122.

Leibel, Rudolph L., & Hirsch, Jules (1984). Diminished energy requirements in reduced-obese patients. *Metabolism, 33,* 164–170.

Leibenluft, Ellen. (1996). Women with bipolar illness: Clinical and research issues. *American Journal of Psychiatry, 153,* 163–173.

Leichtman, Michelle D., & Ceci, Stephen J. (1995). The effects of stereotypes and suggestions on preschoolers' reports. *Developmental Psychology, 31* (4), 568–578.

Leitenberg, Harold, & Henning, Kris. (1995). Sexual fantasy. *Psychological Bulletin, 117* (3), 469–496.

Lepore, Stephen J. (1993). Social conflict, social support, and psychological distress: Evidence of cross-domain buffering effects. *Journal of Personality and Social Psychology, 63,* 857–867.

Lepore, Stephen J.; Silver, Roxane Cohen; Wortman, Camille B.; & Wayment, Heidi A. (1996). Social constraints, intrusive thoughts, and depressive symptoms among bereaved mothers. *Journal of Personality and Social Psychology, 70,* 271–282.

Lerner, M. R.; Gyorgyi, T. K.; Reagan, J.; Roby-Shemkovitz, A.; Rybczynski, R; & Vogt, R. (1990). Peripheral events in moth olfaction. *Chemical Senses, 15,* 191–198.

Lerner, Melvin J. (1980). *The belief in a just world: A fundamental delusion.* New York: Plenum.

Lester, David. (1990, Summer). Biorhythms and the timing of death. *Skeptical Inquirer, 14,* 410–412.

LeUnes, Arnold D., & Nation, Jack R. (1989). *Sport psychology.* Chicago: Nelson-Hall.

LeVay, Simon. (1991, August 30). A difference in hypothalamic structure between heterosexual and homosexual men. *Science, 253,* 1034–1037.

LeVay, Simon, & Hamer, Dean H. (1994, May). Evidence for a biological influence in male homosexuality. *Scientific American, 270,* 44–49.

Levenson, Michael R.; Kiehl, Kent A.; & Fitzpatrick, Cory M. (1995). Assessing psychopathic attributes in a noninstitutionalized population. *Journal of Personality and Social Psychology, 68,* 151–158.

Levenson, Robert W. (1992). Autonomic nervous system differences among emotions. *Psychological Science, 3,* 23–27.

Levenson, Robert W.; Carstensen, Laura L.; & Gottman, John M. (1994). The influence of age and gender on affect, physiology, and their interrelations: A study of long-term marriages. *Journal of Personality and Social Psychology, 67,* 56–68.

Levenson, Robert W.; Ekman, Paul; & Friesen, Wallace V. (1990). Voluntary facial action generates emotion-specific autonomic nervous system activity. *Psychophysiology, 27,* 363–384.

Levenson, Robert W.; Ekman, Paul; Heider, Karl; & Friesen, Wallace V. (1992). Emotion and autonomic nervous system activity in the Minangkabau of west Sumatra. *Journal of Personality and Social Psychology, 62,* 972–988.

Levin, William C. (1988). Age stereotyping: College student evaluations. *Research on Aging, 10,* 134–148.

Levy, Becca, & Langer, Ellen. (1994). Aging free from negative stereotypes: Successful memory in China and among the American deaf. *Journal of Personality and Social Psychology, 66,* 989–997.

Levy-Shiff, Rachel. (1994). Individual and contextual correlates of marital change across the transition to parenthood. *Developmental Psychology, 30,* 591–601.

Lewinsohn, Peter M.; Rohde, Paul; Selley, John R.; & Hops, Hyman. (1991). Comorbidity of unipolar depression: I. Major depression with dysthymia. *Journal of Abnormal Psychology, 100,* 205–213.

Lewontin, Richard. (1970, March). Race and intelligence. *Bulletin of the Atomic Scientists,* pp. 2–8.

Lewy, Alfred J., & Sack, Robert L. (1987). Phase typing and bright light therapy of chronobiological sleep and mood disorders. In Angelos Halaris (Ed.), *Chronobiology and psychiatric disorders.* New York: Elsevier.

Lewy, Alfred J.; Sack, Robert L.; & Singer, Clifford M. (1990). Bright light, melatonin, and biological rhythms in humans. In Jacques Montplaisir & Roger Godbout (Eds.), *Sleep and biological rhythms: Basic mechanisms and applications to psychiatry.* New York: Oxford University Press.

Lietaer, Germain; Rombauts, Jan; & Van Balen, Richard (Eds.). (1990). *Client-centered and experiential psychotherapy in the nineties.* Leuven, Belgium: Leuven University Press.

Liff, Zanvel A. (1992). Psychoanalysis and dynamic techniques. In Donald K. Freedheim (Ed.), *History of psychotherapy: A century of change.* Washington, D.C.: American Psychological Association.

Lilie, Jamie K., & Rosenberg, Russell P. (1990). Behavioral treatment of insomnia. In Michel Hersen, Richard M. Eisler, & Peter M. Miller (Eds.), *Progress in behavior modification* (Vol. 25). Newbury Park, Calif.: Sage.

Lindheim, R., & Syme, S. L. (1983). Environments, people, and health. *Annual Review of Public Health, 4,* 335–359.

Link, Bruce G.; Andrews, Howard; & Cullen, Francis T. (1992). The violent and illegal behavior of mental patients reconsidered. *American Sociological Review, 57,* 275–292.

Lipsey, Mark W., & Wilson, David B. (1993). The efficacy of psychological, educational, and behavioral treatment: Confirmation from meta-analysis. *American Psychologist, 48,* 1181–1209.

Little, J. D. (1993). Physiological principles in the treatment of difficulty in waking from sleep. *Australian and New Zealand Journal of Psychiatry, 27,* 502–505.

Livingstone, Margaret, & Hubel, David. (1988, May 6). Segregation of form, color, movement and depth: Anatomy, physiology, and perception. *Science, 240,* 740–749.

Lockard, R. B. (1971). Reflections on the fall of comparative psychology: Is there a message for us all? *American Psychologist, 26,* 168–179.

Lockhart, Robert S. (1992). Coding processes: Levels of processing. In Larry R. Squire (Ed.), *Encyclopedia of learning and memory.* New York: Macmillan.

Lockhart, Robert S., & Craik, Fergus I. M. (1990). Levels of processing: A retrospective commentary on a framework for memory research. *Canadian Journal of Psychology, 44* (1), 87–112.

Loewenstein, George. (1994). The psychology of curiosity: A review and reinterpretation. *Psychological Bulletin, 116,* 75–98.

Loewenstein, Richard J. (1993). Psychogenic amnesia and psychogenic fugue: A comprehensive review. In David Spiegel (Ed.), *Dissociative disorders: A clinical review.* Lutherville, Md.: Sidran.

Loftus, Elizabeth F. (1992). When a lie becomes memory's truth: Memory distortion after exposure to misinformation. *Current Directions in Psychological Science, 1,* 121–123.

Loftus, Elizabeth F. (1993). The reality of repressed memories. *American Psychologist, 48,* 518–537.

Loftus, Elizabeth F. (1997, September). Creating false memories. *Scientific American, 277,* 70–75.

Loftus, Elizabeth F.; Donders, Karen; Hoffman, Hunter G.; & Schooler, Jonathan W. (1989). Creating new memories that are quickly accessed and confidently held. *Memory and Cognition, 17,* 607–616.

Loftus, Elizabeth F.; Garry, Maryanne; Brown, Scott W.; & Rader, Marcella. (1994). Near-natal memories, past-life memories, and other memory myths. *American Journal of Clinical Hypnosis, 36,* 176–179.

Loftus, Elizabeth F., & Ketcham, Katherine. (1991). *Witness for the defense: The accused, the eyewitness, and the expert who puts memory on trial.* New York: St. Martin's Press.

Loftus, Elizabeth F., & Ketcham, Katherine. (1994). *The myth of repressed memory: False memories and allegations of sexual abuse.* New York: St. Martin's Press.

Loftus, Elizabeth F., & Palmer, J. C. (1974). Reconstruction of automobile destruction: An example of the interaction between language and memory. *Journal of Verbal Learning and Verbal Behavior, 13,* 585–589.

Logothetis, Nikos K., & Sheinberg, David L. (1996). Visual object recognition. *Annual Review of Neuroscience, 19,* 577–621.

Lonetto, Richard, & Templer, Donald I. (1986). *Death anxiety.* Washington, D.C.: Hemisphere.

Lovallo, William R.; al'Absi, Mustafa; Pincomb, Gwen A.; Everson, Susan A.; Sung, Bong Hee; Passey, Richard B.; & Wilson, Michael F. (1996). Caffeine and behavioral stress effects on blood pressure in borderline hypertensive Caucasian men. *Health Psychology, 15,* 11–17.

Lucas, F.; Bellisle, F.; & Di Maio, A. (1987). Spontaneous insulin fluctuations and the preabsorptive insulin response to food ingestion in humans. *Physiology and Behavior, 40,* 631–636.

Lugaresi, Elio, & Montagna, Pasquale. (1990). Fatal familial insomnia. In Michael J. Thorpy (Ed.), *Handbook of sleep disorders*. New York: Dekker.

Lukoff, David; Snyder, Karen; Ventura, Joseph; & Neuchterlein, Keith H. (1989). Life events, familial stress, and coping in the developmental course of schizophrenia. In Thomas W. Miller (Ed.), *Stressful life events*. Madison, Conn.: International Universities Press.

Lundberg, U.; Hedman, M.; Melin, B.; & Frankenhaeuser, M. (1989). Type A behavior in healthy males and females as related to physiological reactivity and blood lipids. *Psychosomatic Medicine, 51,* 113–122.

Lykken, David T.; McGue, Matthew; Tellegen, Auke; & Bouchard, Thomas J., Jr. (1992). Emergenesis: Genetic traits that may not run in families. *American Psychologist, 47,* 1565–1577.

Lyles, J. N.; Burish, T. G.; Krozely, M. G.; & Oldham, R. K. (1982). Efficacy of relaxation training and guided imagery in reducing the aversiveness of cancer chemotherapy. *Journal of Consulting and Clinical Psychology, 50,* 509–524.

Lynch, Gary. (1986). *Synapses, circuits, and the beginnings of memory*. Cambridge, Mass.: MIT Press.

Lyness, Scott A. (1993). Predictors of differences between Type A and B individuals in heart rate and blood pressure reactivity. *Psychological Bulletin, 114,* 266–295.

Lynn, Richard. (1987). The intelligence of the Mongoloids: A psychometric evolutionary and neurological theory. *Personality and Individual Differences, 8,* 813–844.

Lynn, Steven Jay, & Nash, Michael R. (1994). Truth in memory: Ramifications for psychotherapy and hypnotherapy. *American Journal of Clinical Hypnosis, 36,* 194–208.

Lytton, Hugh, & Romney, David M. (1991). Parents' differential socialization of boys and girls: A meta-analysis. *Psychological Bulletin, 109,* 267–296.

Maccoby, Eleanor E., & Martin, John A. (1983). Socialization in the context of the family: Parent–child interaction. In Paul H. Mussen (Ed.), *Handbook of child psychology: Vol. 4. Socialization, personality, and social development*. New York: Wiley.

MacDougall, James M.; Musante, Linda; Castillo, Sara; & Acevedo, Marcela C. (1988). Smoking, caffeine, and stress: Effects on blood pressure and heart rate in male and female college students. *Health Psychology, 7,* 461–478.

Macedonio, Michele. (1984). Regulation of energy balance. In Jean Storlie & Henry A. Jordon (Eds.), *Evaluation and treatment of obesity*. New York: Spectrum.

MacKenzie, Brian. (1984). Explaining race differences in IQ: The logic, the methodology, and the evidence. *American Psychologist, 39,* 1214–1233.

Macklin, E. D. (1987). Nontraditional family forms. In M. B. Sussman & S. K. Steinmetz (Eds.), *Handbook of marriage and the family*. New York: Plenum.

Macrae, C. Neil; Milne, Alan B.; & Bodenhausen, Galen V. (1994). Stereotypes as energy-saving devices: A peek inside the cognitive toolbox. *Journal of Personality and Social Psychology, 66,* 37–47.

Mahowald, Mark W., & Schenck, Carlos H. (1990). REM-sleep behavior disorder. In Michael J. Thorpy (Ed.), *Handbook of sleep disorders*. New York: Dekker.

Maier, Steven F.; Watkins, Linda R.; & Fleshner, Monika. (1994). Psychoneuroimmunology: The interface between behavior, brain, and immunity. *American Psychologist, 49,* 1004–1017.

Maj, Mario; Magliano, Lorena; Pirozzi, Raffaele; Marasco, Cecilia; & Guarneri, Manuela. (1994). Validity of rapid cycling as a course specifier for bipolar disorder. *American Journal of Psychiatry, 151,* 1015–1019.

Makin, Jennifer W. (1989). Attractiveness of lactating females' breast odors to neonates. *Child Development, 60,* 803–810.

Maltz, Wendy. (1991). *The sexual healing journey: A guide for survivors of sexual abuse*. New York: HarperCollins.

Manderscheid, Ronald W.; Rae, Donald S.; Narrow, William E.; Locke, Ben Z.; & Regier, Darrel A. (1993). Congruence of service utilization estimates from the Epidemiologic Catchment Area Project and other sources. *Archives of General Psychiatry, 50,* 108–115.

Mandler, George. (1993). Thought, memory, and learning: Effects of emotional stress. In Leo Goldberger & Shlomo Breznitz (Eds.), *Handbook of stress: Theoretical and clinical aspects* (2nd ed.). New York: Free Press.

Mandler, Jean. (1990). A new perspective on cognitive development in infancy. *American Scientist, 78,* 236–243.

Marano, Lou. (1985). *Windigo* psychosis: The anatomy of an Emic-Etic confusion. In Richard C. Simons & Charles C. Hughes (Eds.), *The culture-bound syndromes: Folk illnesses of psychiatric and anthropological interest*. Boston: D. Reidel Publishing.

Marañon, Gregorio. (1924). Contribution à l'etude de l'action emotive de l'adrenaline.

Revue Francaise d'Endocrinologie, 2, 301–325.

Marcia, James E. (1980). Identity in adolescence. In Joseph Adelson (Ed.), *Handbook of adolescent psychology*. New York: Wiley.

Marcia, James E. (1991). Identity and self-development. In R. M. Lerner, A. C. Petersen, & Jean Brooks-Gunn (Eds.), *Encyclopedia of adolescence* (Vol. 1). New York: Garland Publishing.

Marco, Christine A., & Suls, Jerry. (1993). Daily stress and the trajectory of mood: Spillover, response assimilation, contrast, and chronic negative affectivity. *Journal of Personality and Social Psychology, 64,* 1053–1063.

Marder, Stephen R.; Ames, Donna; Wirshing, William C.; & Van Putten, Theodore. (1993). Schizophrenia. *Psychiatric Clinics of North America, 16,* 567–587.

Marder, Stephen R., & Meibach, Richard C. (1994). Risperidone in the treatment of schizophrenia. *American Journal of Psychiatry, 151,* 825–835.

Margraf, Jürgen, & Ehlers, Anke. (1989). Etiological models of panic: a) Medical and biological aspects; b) Psychophysiological and cognitive aspects. In Roger Baker (Ed.), *Panic disorder: Theory, research and therapy*. Chichester, England: Wiley.

Markus, Hazel, & Cross, Susan. (1990). The interpersonal self. In Lawrence A. Pervin (Ed.), *Handbook of personality: Theory and research*. New York: Guilford Press.

Markus, Hazel Rose, & Kitayama, Shinobu. (1991). Culture and the self: Implications for cognition, emotion, and motivation. *Psychological Review, 98,* 224–253.

Markus, Hazel Rose, & Kitayama, Shinobu. (1994). The cultural construction of self and emotion: Implications for social behavior. In Shinobu Kitayama & Hazel Rose Markus (Eds.), *Emotion and culture: Empirical studies of mutual influence*. Washington, D.C.: American Psychological Association.

Markus, Hazel, & Kunda, Ziva. (1986). Stability and malleability of the self-concept. *Journal of Personality and Social Psychology, 51,* 858–866.

Markus, Hazel, & Nurius, Paula. (1986). Possible selves. *American Psychologist, 41,* 954–969.

Markus, Hazel, & Wurf, Elissa. (1987). The dynamic self-concept: A social psychological perspective. *Annual Review of Psychology, 38,* 299–337.

Marlatt, G. Alan; Baer, John S.; Donovan, Dennis M.; & Kivlahan, Daniel R. (1988). Addictive behaviors: Etiology and treatment. *Annual Review of Psychology, 39,* 223–252.

Marlatt, G. Alan, & Rohsenow, Damaris J. (1980). Cognitive processes in alcohol use: Expectancy and the balanced placebo design. In N. K. Mello (Ed.), *Advances in substance abuse* (Vol. 1). Greenwich, Conn.: JAI Press.

Marler, Peter. (1967). Animal communication symbols. *Science, 35,* 63–78.

Marschark, Marc. (1992). Coding processes: Imagery. In Larry R. Squire (Ed.), *Encyclopedia of learning and memory.* New York: Macmillan.

Marsella, Anthony J., & Dash-Scheuer, Alice. (1988). Coping, culture, and healthy human development: A research and conceptual overview. In Pierre R. Dasen, John W. Berry, & Norman Sartorius (Eds.), *Health and cross-cultural psychology: Toward applications.* [Vol. 10, Cross-cultural Research and Methodology Series.] Newbury Park, Calif.: Sage.

Marshall, Grant N.; Wortman, Camille B.; Kusulas, Jeffrey W.; Hervig, Linda K.; & Vickers, Ross R., Jr. (1992). Distinguishing optimism from pessimism: Relations to fundamental dimensions of mood and personality. *Journal of Personality and Social Psychology, 62,* 1067–1074.

Marshall, J. F., & Teitelbaum, P. (1974). Further analysis of sensory inattention following lateral hypothalamic damage in rats. *Journal of Comparative and Physiological Psychology, 86,* 375–395.

Martell, Daniel A., & Dietz, Park E. (1992). Mentally disordered offenders who push or attempt to push victims onto subway tracks in New York City. *Archives of General Psychiatry, 49,* 472–475.

Martens, Brian K.; Lochner, David G.; & Kelly, Susan Q. (1992). The effects of variable-interval reinforcement on academic engagement: A demonstration of matching theory. *Journal of Applied Behavior Analysis, 25,* 143–151.

Martin, Carol L., & Halverson, Charles F., Jr. (1981). A schematic processing model of sex typing and stereotyping in children. *Child Development, 52,* 1119–1134.

Martin, Jack, & Jessell, Thomas M. (1995). The sensory systems. In Eric R. Kandel, James H. Schwartz, & Thomas M. Jessell (Eds.), *Essentials of neural science and behavior.* Norwalk, Conn.: Appleton & Lange.

Martin, Laura. (1986). "Eskimo words for snow": A case study in the genesis and decay of an anthropological example. *American Anthropologist, 88,* 418–423.

Martinez-Taboas, Alfonso. (1991). Multiple personality in Puerto Rico: Analysis of fifteen cases. *Dissociation, 4,* 189–192.

Maslow, Abraham H. (1968). *Toward a psychology of being* (2nd ed.). Princeton, N.J.: Van Nostrand.

Maslow, Abraham H. (1970). *Motivation and personality* (2nd ed.) New York: Harper & Row.

Masson, Jeffrey M. (February, 1984a). Freud and the seduction theory: A challenge to the foundations of psychoanalysis. *The Atlantic, 253,* 33–60.

Masson, Jeffrey M. (1984b). *The assault on truth: Freud's suppression of the seduction theory.* New York: Farrar, Straus & Giroux.

Masters, William H., & Johnson, Virginia E. (1966). *Human sexual response.* Boston: Little, Brown.

Masters, William H.; Johnson, Virginia E.; & Kolodny, Robert C. (1995). *Human sexuality* (5th ed.). New York: HarperCollins.

Matarazzo, Joseph D. (1981). Obituary: David Wechsler (1896–1981). *American Psychologist, 36,* 1542–1543.

Mathews, Judith R.; Hodson, Gary D.; Crist, William B.; & LaRoche, G. Robert. (1992). Teaching young children to use contact lens. *Journal of Applied Behavior Analysis, 25,* 229–235.

Matlin, Margaret W. (1985). Current issues in psycholinguistics. In Theodore M. Shlechter & Michael P. Toglia (Eds.), *New directions in cognitive science.* Norwood, N.J.: Ablex.

Matlin, Margaret W. (1989). *Cognition* (2nd ed). Fort Worth, Tex.: Holt, Rinehart & Winston.

Matlin, Margaret W., & Foley, Hugh J. (1992). *Sensation and perception* (3rd ed.). Boston: Allyn & Bacon.

Matsumoto, David. (1994). *People: Psychology from a cultural perspective.* Pacific Grove, Calif.: Brooks/Cole.

Matsumoto, David; Kitayama, Shinobu; & Markus, Hazel. (1994). Culture and self: How cultures influence the way we view ourselves. In David Matsumoto (Ed.), *People: Psychology from a cultural perspective.* Pacific Grove, Calif.: Brooks-Cole.

Mavromatis, Andreas. (1987). *Hypnagogia: The unique state of consciousness between wakefulness and sleep.* New York: Routledge & Kegan Paul.

Maxmen, Jerrold S., & Ward, Nicholas G. (1995). *Essential psychopathology and its treatment* (2nd ed.). New York: Norton.

May, R. B. (1963). Stimulus selection of preschool children under conditions of free choice. *Perceptual and Motor Skills, 16,* 203–206.

Mazur, James E. (1994). *Learning and behavior* (3rd ed.). Englewood Cliffs, N.J.: Prentice Hall.

McAdams, Dan P. (1992). The five-factor model in personality: A critical appraisal. *Journal of Personality, 60,* 329–362.

McAdams, Dan P. (1994). *The person: An introduction to personality psychology* (2nd ed.). New York: Harcourt Brace Jovanovich.

McCall, Robert B. (1988). Science and the press: Like oil and water. *American Psychologist, 43,* 87–91.

McCarley, Robert W., & Hobson, J. Allan. (1977). The neurobiological origins of psychoanalytic theory. *American Journal of Psychiatry, 134,* 1211–1221.

McCartney, Kathleen; Harris, Monica J.; & Bernieri, Frank. (1990). Growing up and growing apart: A developmental meta-analysis of twin studies. *Psychological Bulletin, 107,* 226–237.

McCaul, K. D., & Malott, J. M. (1984). Distraction and coping with pain. *Psychological Bulletin, 95,* 516–533.

McClearn, Gerald E.; Johansson, Boo; Berg, Stig; Pedersen, Nancy L.; Ahern, Frank; Petrill, Stephen A.; & Plomin, Robert. (1997, June 6). Substantial genetic influence on cognitive abilities in twins 80 or more years old. *Science, 276,* 1560–1563.

McClelland, David C. (1984). *Motives, personality, and society: Selected papers.* New York: Praeger.

McClelland, David C. (1985). *Human motivation.* Glenview, Ill.: Scott, Foresman, & Co.

McClelland, David C.; Atkinson, John W.; Clark, Russell A.; & Lowell, Edgar L. (1953). *The achievement motive.* New York: Appleton-Century-Crofts.

McClintock, Martha K. (1971). Menstrual synchrony and suppression. *Nature, 229,* 244–245.

McClintock, Martha K. (1992, October). Quoted in John Easton, Sex, rats, and videotapes: From the outside in. *The University of Chicago Magazine, 85* (1), 32–36.

McConnell, James V. (1989). Reinvention of subliminal perception. *Skeptical Inquirer, 13,* 427–428.

McCrae, Robert R., & Costa, Paul T., Jr. (1990). *Personality in adulthood.* New York: Guilford Press.

McCrae, Robert R., & Costa, Paul T., Jr. (1996). Toward a new generation of personality theories: Theoretical contexts for the five-factor model. In Jerry S. Wiggins (Ed.), *The five-factor model of personality: Theoretical perspectives.* New York: Guilford Press.

McCrae, Robert R., & John, Oliver P. (1992). An introduction to the five-factor model and its applications. *Journal of Personality, 60,* 175–215.

McFadden, Lisa; Seidman, Edward; & Rappaport, Julian. (1992). A comparison of espoused theories of self- and mutual help: Implications for mental health professionals. *Professional Psychology: Research and Practice, 23,* 515–520.

McHugh, P. R., & Moran, T. H. (1985). The stomach: A conception of its dynamic role in satiety. *Progress in Psychobiology and Physiological Psychology, 11,* 197–232.

McKellar, Peter. (1972). Imagery from the standpoint of introspection. In Peter W. Sheehan (Ed.), *The function and nature of imagery.* New York: Academic Press.

McNally, Richard J. (1987). Preparedness and phobias: A review. *Psychological Bulletin, 101,* 283–303.

McNally, Richard J. (1994). Cognitive bias in panic disorder. *Current Directions in Psychological Science, 3,* 129–132.

McNally, Richard J., & Louro, Christine E. (1992). Fear of flying in agoraphobia and simple phobia: Distinguishing features. *Journal of Anxiety Disorders, 6,* 319–324.

McNeilly, Cheryl L., & Howard, Kenneth I. (1991). The effects of psychotherapy: A reevaluation based on dosage. *Psychotherapy Research, 1,* 74–78.

Mebert, C. J. (1991). Variability in the transition to parenthood experience. In Karl Pillemer & Kathleen McCartney (Eds.), *Parent–child relations throughout life.* Hillsdale, N.J.: Erlbaum.

Meichenbaum, Donald H. (1995). Cognitive-behavioral therapy in historical perspective. In Bruce Bongar & Larry E. Beutler (Eds.), *Comprehensive textbook of psychotherapy: Theory and practice.* New York: Oxford University Press.

Meichenbaum, Donald, & Fitzpatrick, Deborah. (1993). A constructivist narrative perspective on stress and coping: Stress inoculation applications. In Leo Goldberger & Shlomo Breznitz (Eds.), *Handbook of stress: Theoretical and clinical aspects* (2nd ed.). New York: Free Press.

Mellinger, G. D.; Balter, M. B.; & Uhlenhuth, E. H. (1985). Insomnia and its treatment: Prevalence and correlates. *Archives of General Psychiatry, 42,* 225–232.

Melton, Gary B. (1989). Public policy and private prejudice: Psychology and law on gay rights. *American Psychologist, 44,* 933–940.

Meltzer, Herbert Y. (1993). New drugs for the treatment of schizophrenia. *Psychiatric Clinics of North America, 16,* 365–386.

Meltzer, Herbert Y. (1994). Clozapine and other atypical neuroleptics: Efficacy, side effects, optimal utilization. *Journal of Clinical Psychiatry Monograph 12* (2), 38–42.

Meltzer, Herbert Y. (1995). The role of serotonin in schizophrenia and the place of serotonin-dopamine antagonist antipsychotics. *Journal of Clinical Psychopharmacology, 15,* (Suppl. 1), 2S-3S.

Meltzoff, Andrew N., & Moore, M. Keith. (1977). Imitation of facial and manual gestures by human neonates. *Science, 198,* 75–78.

Meltzoff, Andrew N., & Moore, M. Keith. (1983). Newborn infants imitate adult facial gestures. *Child Development, 54,* 702–709.

Melzack, Ronald, & Wall, Patrick D. (1965). Pain mechanisms: A new theory. *Science, 150,* 971–980.

Melzack, Ronald, & Wall, Patrick D. (1983). *The challenge of pain.* New York: Basic Books.

Merckelbach, Harald; Arntz, Arnoud; Arrindell, Willem A.; & De Jong, Peter J. (1992). Pathways to spider phobia. *Behaviour Research and Therapy, 30,* 543–546.

Merikle, P. M. (1988). Subliminal auditory messages: An evaluation. *Psychology and Marketing, 5,* 297–316.

Merskey, H. (1992). The manufacture of personalities: The production of multiple personality disorder. *British Journal of Psychiatry, 160,* 327–340.

Mervis, Carolyn B., and Rosch, Eleanor. (1981). Categorization of natural objects. *Annual Review of Psychology, 32,* 89–115.

Michael, Robert T.; Gagnon, John H.; Laumann, Edward O.; & Kolata, Gina. (1994). *Sex in America: A definitive survey.* New York: Warner Books.

Miklowitz, David J. (1994). Family risk indicators in schizophrenia. *Schizophrenia Bulletin, 20,* 137–149.

Milewski, A. (1976). Infants' discrimination of internal and external pattern elements. *Journal of Experimental Child Psychology, 22,* 229–246.

Milgram, Stanley. (1963). Behavioral study of obedience. *Journal of Abnormal Psychology, 67,* 371–378.

Milgram, Stanley. (1964). Issues in the study of obedience: A reply to Baumrind. *American Psychologist, 19,* 848–852.

Milgram, Stanley. (1965/1992). Some conditions of obedience and disobedience to authority. In John Sabini & Maury Silver (Eds.), Stanley Milgram, *The individual in a social world: Essays and experiments* (2nd ed.). New York: McGraw-Hill.

Milgram, Stanley. (1974a). *Obedience to authority: An experimental view.* New York: Harper & Row.

Milgram, Stanley. (1974b, June). Interview by Carol Tavris: The frozen world of the familiar stranger: An interview with Stanley Milgram. *Psychology Today,* pp. 71–80.

Milgram, Stanley. (1992). On maintaining social norms: A field experiment in the subway. In John Sabini & Maury Silver (Eds.), Stanley Milgram, *The individual in a social world: Essays and experiments* (2nd ed.). New York: McGraw-Hill.

Miller, Arthur G. (1986). *The obedience experiments: A case study of controversy in social science.* New York: Praeger.

Miller, George A. (1956/1994). The magical number seven, plus or minus two: Some limits on our capacity for processing information. *Psychological Review, 101,* 343–352.

Miller, Neal E. (1985, April). The value of behavioral research on animals. *American Psychologist, 40,* 423–440.

Miller, Patricia H. (1993). *Theories of developmental psychology* (3rd ed.). New York: Freeman.

Miller, Scott D.; Blackburn, Terrell; Scholes, Gary; White, George L.; & Mamalis, Nick. (1991). Optical differences in multiple personality disorder: A second look. *Journal of Nervous and Mental Disease, 179,* 132–135.

Miller, Thomas W. (1993). The assessment of stressful life events. In Leo Goldberger & Shlomo Breznitz (Eds.), *Handbook of stress: Theoretical and clinical aspects* (2nd ed.). New York: Free Press.

Miller, Todd Q.; Smith, Timothy W.; Turner, Charles W.; Guijarro, Margarita L.; & Hallet, Amanda J. (1996). A meta-analytic review of research on hostility and physical health. *Psychological Bulletin, 119,* 322–348.

Miller-Jones, Dalton. (1989). Culture and testing. *American Psychologist 44,* 360–366.

Milner, Brenda. (1965). Memory disturbance after bilateral hippocampal lesions. In Peter M. Milner & Steven E. Glickman (Eds.), *Cognitive processes and the brain: An enduring problem in psychology: Selected readings.* Princeton, N.J.: Van Nostrand.

Milner, Brenda. (1970). Memory and the medial temporal regions of the brain. In Karl H. Pribram & Donald E. Broadbent (Eds.), *Biology of memory.* New York: Academic Press.

Mindell, J. A. (1993). Sleep disorders in children. *Health Psychology, 12,* 152–163.

Mindell, Jodi A. (1997). Children and sleep. In Mark R. Pressman & William C. Orr (Eds.), *Understanding sleep: The evaluation and treatment of sleep disorders*. Washington, D.C.: American Psychological Association.

Mischel, Walter. (1966). Theory and research on the antecedents of self-imposed delay of reward. *Progress in Experimental Personality Research, 3,* 85–132.

Mischel, Walter. (1981). Objective and subjective rules for delay of gratification. In G. d'Ydewalle & W. Lens (Eds.), *Cognition in human motivation and learning*. Hillsdale, N.J.: Erlbaum.

Mischel, Walter. (1983). Delay of gratification as process and as person variable in development. In David Magnusson & Vernon L. Allen (Eds.), *Human development*. New York: Academic Press.

Mischel, Walter. (1990). Personality dispositions revisited and revised: A view after three decades. In Lawrence Pervin (Ed.), *Handbook of personality: Theory and research*. New York: Guilford Press.

Mischel, Walter, & Shoda, Yuichi. (1995). A cognitive-affective system theory of personality: Reconceptualizing situations, dispositions, dynamics, and invariance in personality structure. *Psychological Review, 102,* 246–268.

Mitler, Merrill M. (1994). Sleep and catastrophes. In Rosemary Cooper (Ed.), *Sleep*. New York: Chapman & Hall.

Modgil, Sohan, & Modgil, Celia (Eds.). (1986). *Lawrence Kohlberg: Consensus and controversy*. Philadelphia: Falmer Press.

Moghaddam, Fathali M.; Taylor, Donald M.; & Wright, Stephen C. (1993). *Social psychology in cross-cultural perspective*. New York: Freeman.

Mohr, Charles. (1964, March 28). Apathy is puzzle in Queens killing: Behavioral specialists hard put to explain witnesses' failure to call police. *New York Times*, pp. 21, 40.

Mondimore, Francis Mark. (1993). *Depression: The mood disease* (Rev. ed.). Baltimore: Johns Hopkins University Press.

Monk, Timothy H. (1997). Shift work. In Mark R. Pressman & William C. Orr (Eds.), *Understanding sleep: The evaluation and treatment of sleep disorders*. Washington, D.C.: American Psychological Association.

Mook, Douglas G. (1996). *Motivation: The organization of action* (2nd ed.). New York: Norton.

Moore-Ede, Martin C. (1993). *The twenty-four hour society: Understanding human limits in a world that never stops*. Reading, Mass.: Addison-Wesley.

Morelli, Gilda A.; Rogoff, Barbara; Oppenheim, David; & Goldsmith, Denise. (1992). Cultural variation in infants' sleeping arrangements: Questions of independence. *Developmental Psychology, 28,* 604–613.

Morgan, Christiana, & Murray, Henry A. (1935). A method of investigating fantasies: The Thematic Apperception Test. *Archives of Neurology and Psychiatry, 4,* 310–329.

Morin, Charles M. (1993). *Insomnia: Psychological assessment and management*. New York: Guilford Press.

Morokoff, Patricia J. (1994, Summer). Issues in adult treatment of childhood sexual abuse. *The Health Psychologist, 16,* 6–7, 10.

Morris, Michael W., & Peng, Kaiping. (1994). Culture and cause: American and Chinese attributions for social and physical events. *Journal of Personality and Social Psychology, 67,* 949–971.

Morris, Richard J. (1991). Fear reduction methods. In Frederick H. Kanfer & Arnold P. Goldstein (Eds.), *Helping people change: A textbook of methods* (4th ed.). New York: Pergamon.

Mounts, Nina S., & Steinberg, Laurence. (1995). An ecological analysis of peer influence on adolescent grade point average and drug use. *Developmental Psychology, 31,* 915–922.

Mueser, Kim T.; Bellack, Alan S.; & Brady, E. U. (1990). Hallucinations in schizophrenia. *Acta Psychiatrica Scandinavica, 82,* 26–29.

Mueser, Kim T., & Glynn, Shirley M. (1993). Efficacy of psychotherapy for schizophrenia. In Thomas R. Giles (Ed.), *Handbook of effective psychotherapy*. New York: Plenum.

Mukerjee, Madhusree. (1997, February). Trends in animal research. *Scientific American, 276*(2), 86–93.

Mulhern, Sherrill. (1991). Embodied alternative identities: Bearing witness to a world that might have been. *Psychiatric Clinics of North America, 14,* 769–786.

Murphy, H. B. M. (1982). Culture and schizophrenia. In Ihsan Al-Issa (Ed.), *Culture and psychopathology*. Baltimore: University Park Press.

Murray, Henry A. (1938). *Explorations in personality*. New York: Oxford University Press.

Murray, Henry A. (1943). *Thematic Apperception Test Manual*. Cambridge, Mass.: Harvard University Press.

Musto, David F. (1991, July). Opium, cocaine and marijuana in American history. *Scientific American, 265,* 40–47.

Muth, Denise K.; Glynn, Shawn M.; Britton, Bruce K.; & Graves, Michael F. (1988). Thinking out loud while studying text: Rehearsing key ideas. *Journal of Educational Psychology, 80,* 315–318.

Nader, Karim; Bechara, Antoine; van der Kooy, Derek. (1997). Neurobiological constraints of behavioral models of motivation. *Annual Review of Psychology, 48,* 85–114.

Nadon, Robert; Hoyt, Irene P.; Register, Patricia A.; & Kihlstrom, John F. (1991). Absorption and hypnotizability: Context effects reexamined. *Journal of Personality and Social Psychology, 60,* 144–153.

Naeye, Robert. (1994, July). The brain at work. *Discover*, pp. 30–31.

Narrow, William E.; Regier, Darrel A.; Rae, Donald S.; Manderscheid, Ronald W.; & Locke, Ben Z. (1993). Use of services by persons with mental and addictive disorders: Findings from the National Institute of Mental Health Epidemiologic Catchment Area Program. *Archives of General Psychiatry, 50,* 95–107.

Nash, Michael. (1987). What, if anything, is regressed about hypnotic age regression? A review of the empirical literature. *Psychological Bulletin, 102* (1), 42–52.

National Association for the Education of Young Children. (1989). *Quality child care*. Washington, D.C.: National Association for the Education of Young Children.

National Association for the Education of Young Children. (1990). *How to choose a good early childhood program*. Washington, D.C.: National Association for the Education of Young Children.

Neher, A. (1991). Maslow's theory of motivation: A critique. *Journal of Humanistic Psychology, 31,* 89–112.

Neisser, Ulric (Chair); Boodoo, Gwyneth; Bouchard, Thomas J., Jr.; Boykin, A. Wade; Brody, Nathan; Ceci, Stephen J.; Halpern, Diane F.; Loehlin, John C.; Perloff, Robert; Sternberg, Robert J.; & Urbina, Susana. (1996). Intelligence: Knowns and unknowns. *American Psychologist, 51,* 77–101.

Neisser, Ulric, & Harsch, Nicole. (1992). Phantom flashbulbs: False recollections of hearing the news about *Challenger*. In Eugene Winograd & Ulric Neisser (Eds.), *Affect and accuracy in recall: Studies of "flashbulb" memories*. New York: Cambridge University Press.

Nelson, Anna. (1995, November/December). Quoted in Cybershrink. *Psychology Today, 28,* 20–21.

Nelson, Katherine. (1993). The psychological and social origins of autobiographical memory. *Psychological Science, 4,* 7–14.

Neufeld, Richard W. J., & Paterson, Randolph J. (1989). Issues concerning control and its implementation. In Richard W. J. Neufeld (Ed.), *Advances in the investigation of psychological stress.* New York: Wiley.

Nevid, Jeffrey S.; Fichner-Rathus, Lois; & Rathus, Spencer A. (1995). *Human sexuality in a world of diversity* (2nd ed.). Boston: Allyn & Bacon.

Newcombe, Nora, & Huttenlocher, Janellen. (1992). Children's early ability to solve perspective-taking problems. *Developmental Psychology, 28,* 635–643.

New prairie dog vacuum catching on in Southwest. (1992, January 24). *Tulsa World,* p. C-7.

Nezu, Arthur M.; Nezu, Christine M.; & Blissett, Sonia E. (1988). Sense of humor as a moderator of the relation between stressful events and psychological distress: A prospective analysis. *Journal of Personality and Social Psychology, 54,* 520–525.

Nichelli, Paolo; Grafman, Jordan; Pietrini, Pietro; Alway, David; Carton, John C.; & Miletich, Robert. (1994, May 19). Brain activity in chess playing. *Nature, 369,* 191.

Nickerson, Raymond S., & Adams, Marilyn J. (1982). Long–term memory for a common object. In Ulric Neisser (Ed.), *Memory observed: Remembering in natural contexts.* San Francisco: Freeman.

Nisbett, Richard. (1995). Race, IQ, and scientism. In Steven Fraser (Ed.), *The Bell Curve wars: Race, intelligence, and the future of America.* New York: Basic Books.

Nishio, Kazumi, & Bilmes, Murray. (1993). Psychotherapy with Southeast Asian American clients. In Donald R. Atkinson, George Morten, & Derald Wing Sue (Eds.), *Counseling American minorities: A cross-cultural perspective* (4th ed.). Madison, Wis.: Brown & Benchmark.

Nolen-Hoeksema, Susan. (1990). *Sex differences in depression.* Stanford, Calif.: Stanford University Press.

Norris, Joan E., & Tindale, Joseph A. (1994). *Among generations: The cycle of adult relationships.* New York: Freeman.

North, C.; Gowers, S.; & Byram, V. (1995). Family functioning in adolescent anorexia nervosa. *British Journal of Psychiatry, 167,* 673–678.

North, Carol S.; Smith, Elizabeth M.; & Spitznagel, Edward L. (1994). Posttraumatic stress disorder in survivors of a mass shooting. *American Journal of Psychiatry, 151,* 82–88.

Oakley, B. (1986). Basic taste physiology: Human perspectives. In H. L. Meiselman & R. S. Rivlin (Eds.), *Clinical measurement of taste and smell.* New York: Macmillan.

Ochse, R. (1990). *Before the gates of excellence: The determinants of creative genius.* New York: Cambridge University Press.

Ochsner, Kevin N., & Kosslyn, Stephen M. (1994). Mental imagery. In V. S. Ramachandran (Ed.), *Encyclopedia of human behavior.* San Diego: Academic Press.

O'Connor, M. Kevin. (1993). Hypotheses regarding the mechanism of action of electroconvulsive therapy, past and present. *Psychiatric Annals, 23,* 15–18.

Ofshe, Richard, & Watters, Ethan. (1994). *Making monsters: False memories, psychotherapy, and sexual hysteria.* New York: Scribner's.

Ogbu, John U. (1986). The consequences of the American caste system. In Ulric Neisser (Ed.), *The school achievement of minority children: New perspectives.* Hillsdale, N.J.: Erlbaum.

Ogden, Jenni A., & Corkin, Suzanne. (1991). Memories of H.M. In Wickliffe C. Abraham, Michael Corballis, & K. Geoffrey White (Eds.), *Memory mechanisms: A tribute to G. V. Goddard.* Hillsdale, N.J.: Erlbaum.

Olds, James. (1958). Self-stimulation of the brain. *Science, 127,* 315–324.

Olds, James. (1962). Hypothalamic substrates of reward. *Physiological Reviews, 42,* 554–604.

Olds, M. E., & Fobes, J. L. (1981). The central basis of motivation: Intracranial self-stimulation studies. *Annual Review of Psychology, 32,* 523–574.

Olds, Sally Wendkos. (1989). *The working parents' survival guide.* Rocklin, Calif.: Prima Publishing.

O'Leary, Ann. (1990). Stress, emotions, and human immune function. *Psychological Bulletin, 108,* 363–382.

O'Leary, K. Daniel, & Wilson, G. Terence. (1987). *Behavior therapy: Application and outcome* (2nd ed.). Englewood Cliffs, N.J.: Prentice Hall.

Olivardia, Roberto; Pope, Harrison G.; Mangweth, Barbara; & Hudson, James I. (1995). Eating disorders in college men. *American Journal of Psychiatry, 152,* 1279–1285.

Olson, James M., & Zanna, Mark P. (1993). Attitudes and attitude change. *Annual Review of Psychology, 44,* 117–154.

Olton, David S. (1992). Tolman's cognitive analysis: Predecessors of current approaches in psychology. *Journal of Experimental Psychology: General, 121,* 427–428.

Orlinsky, David E.; Grawe, Klaus; & Parks, Barbara K. (1994). Process and outcome in

psychotherapy—*noch einmal.* In Allen E. Bergin & Sol L. Garfield (Eds.), *Handbook of psychotherapy and behavior change* (4th ed.). New York: Wiley.

Orne, Martin T., & Holland, Charles H. (1968). On the ecological validity of laboratory deceptions. *International Journal of Psychiatry, 6,* 282–293.

Orr, William C. (1997). Obstructive sleep apnea: Natural history and varieties of the clinical presentation. In Mark R. Pressman & William C. Orr (Eds.), *Understanding sleep: The evaluation and treatment of sleep disorders.* Washington, D.C.: American Psychological Association.

Ortony, Andrew, & Turner, Terence J. (1990). What's basic about basic emotions? *Psychological Review, 97,* 315–331.

Ottati, Victor, & Lee, Yueh-Ting. (1995). Accuracy: A neglected component of stereotype research. In Yueh-Ting Lee, Lee J. Jussim, & Clark R. McCauley (Eds.), *Stereotype accuracy: Toward appreciating group differences.* Washington, D.C.: American Psychological Association.

Oyserman, Daphna; Grant, Larry; & Ager, Joel. (1995). A socially contextualized model of African American identity: Possible selves and school persistence. *Journal of Personality and Social Psychology, 69,* 1216–1232.

Ozbayrak, Kaan R., & Berlin, Richard M. (1995). Sleepwalking in children and adolescents. In Charles E. Schaefer (Ed.), *Clinical handbook of sleep disorders in children.* Northvale, N.J.: Aronson.

Ozer, Elizabeth M., & Bandura, Albert. (1990). Mechanisms governing empowerment effects: A self-efficacy analysis. *Journal of Personality and Social Psychology, 58,* 472–486.

Paivio, Allan. (1986). *Mental representations: A dual coding approach.* New York: Oxford University Press.

Palmblad, J.; Petrini, B.; Wasserman, J.; & Akerstedt, T. (1979). Lymphocyte and granulocyte reactions during sleep deprivation. *Psychosomatic Medicine, 41,* 273–278.

Papoušek, Mechthild; Papoušek, Hanus; & Bornstein, Marc H. (1985). The naturalistic vocal environment of young infants: On the significance of homogeneity and variability in parental speech. In Tiffany M. Field & N. Fox (Eds.), *Social perception in infants.* Norwood, N.J.: Ablex.

Park, Bernadette; Ryan, Carey S.; & Judd, Charles M. (1992). Role of meaningful subgroups in explaining differences in perceived variability for in-groups and out-groups. *Journal of Personality and Social Psychology, 63* (4), 553–567.

Pato, Carlos N.; Lander, Eric S.; & Schultz, S. Charles. (1989). Prospects for the genetic analysis of schizophrenia. *Schizophrenia Bulletin, 15,* 365–372.

Patterson, Charlotte J. (1992). Children of lesbian and gay parents. *Child Development, 63,* 1025–1042.

Patterson, Charlotte J. (1995a). Sexual orientation and human development: An overview. *Developmental Psychology, 31,* 3–11.

Patterson, Charlotte J. (1995b). Families of the lesbian baby boom: Parents' division of labor and children's adjustment. *Developmental Psychology, 31,* 115–123.

Patterson, Charlotte J. (1995c). Lesbian mothers, gay fathers, and their children. In Anthony R. D'Augelli & Charlotte J. Patterson (Eds.), *Lesbian, gay and bisexual identities across the lifespan: Psychological perspectives.* New York: Oxford University Press.

Paul, Diane B., & Blumenthal, Arthur L. (1989). On the trail of Little Albert. *The Psychological Record, 39,* 547–553.

Paul, Gordon L., & Menditto, Anthony A. (1992). Effectiveness of inpatient treatment programs for mentally ill adults in public psychiatric facilities. *Applied and Preventive Psychology, 1,* 41–63.

Paunonen, Sampo V.; Jackson, Douglas N.; Trzebinski, Jerry; & Fosterling, Friedrich. (1992). Personality structure across cultures: A multimethod evaluation. *Journal of Personality and Social Psychology, 62,* 447–456.

Pavlov, Ivan. (1904/1965). On conditioned reflexes. In Richard J. Herrnstein & Edwin G. Boring (Eds.), *A source book in the history of psychology.* Cambridge, Mass.: Harvard University Press.

Pavlov, Ivan. (1927/1960). *Conditioned reflexes: An investigation of the physiological activity of the cerebral cortex* (Translated by G. V. Anrep). New York: Dover Books.

Pavlov, Ivan. (1928). *Lectures on conditioned reflexes.* New York: International Publishers.

Paykel, Eugene S., & Dowlatshahi, D. (1988). Life events and mental disorder. In Shirley Fisher & James Reason (Eds.), *Handbook of life stress, cognition, and health.* New York: Wiley.

Payne, John W.; Bettman, James R.; & Johnson, Eric J. (1993). *The adaptive decision maker.* Cambridge, England: Cambridge University Press.

Payton, Jack R. (1992, May 16). The sad legacy of Japan's outcasts. *Chicago Tribune,* Section 1, p. 21.

Pearlin, Leonard I. (1993). The social contexts of stress. In Leo Goldberger & Shlomo Breznitz (Eds.), *Handbook of stress: Theoretical and clinical aspects* (2nd ed.). New York: Free Press.

Peirce, Robert S.; Frone, Michael R.; Russell, Marcia; & Cooper, M. Lynne (1996). Financial stress, social support, and alcohol involvement: A longitudinal test of the buffering hypothesis in a general population study. *Health Psychology, 15,* 38–47.

Pekala, Ronald J. (1987). The phenomenology of meditation. In Michael A. West (Ed.), *The psychology of meditation.* New York: Oxford University Press.

Pelletier, Kenneth R. (1993). Between mind and body: Stress, emotions, and health. In Daniel Goleman & Joel Gurin (Eds.), *Mind/body medicine: How to use your mind for better health.* Yonkers, N.Y.: Consumer Reports Books.

Pendergrast, Mark. (1995). *Victims of memory: Incest accusations and shattered lives.* Hinesburg, Vt.: Upper Access.

Penfield, Wilder, & Perot, Phanor. (1963). The brain's record of auditory and visual experience: A final summary and discussion. *Brain, 86,* 595–696.

Penn, David L.; Guynan, Kim; Daily, Tamara; Spaulding, William D.; Garbin, Calvin P.; & Sullivan, Mary. (1994). Dispelling the stigma of schizophrenia: What sort of information is best? *Schizophrenia Bulletin, 20,* 567–577.

Pennisi, Elizabeth. (1994, November 26). Gut counts calories even when we do not. *Science News, 146,* 359.

Pepler, Debra J., & Craig, Wendy M. (1995). A peek behind the fence: Naturalistic observations of aggressive children with remote audiovisual recording. *Developmental Psychology, 31* (4), 548–553.

Pepperberg, Irene. (1993). Cognition and communication in an African gray parrot (*Psittacus erithacus*): Studies on a nonhuman, nonprimate, nonmammalian subject. In Herbert L. Roitblat, Louis M. Herman, & Paul E. Nachtigall (Eds.), *Language and communication: Comparative perspectives.* Hillsdale, N.J.: Erlbaum.

Perkins, D. V. (1982). The assessment of stress using life events scales. In Leo Goldberger & Shlomo Breznitz (Eds.), *Handbook of stress: Theoretical and clinical aspects.* New York: Free Press.

Perloff, Richard M. (1993). *The dynamics of persuasion.* Hillsdale, N.J.: Erlbaum.

Perls, Thomas T. (1995, January). The oldest old. *Scientific American, 272,* 70–75.

Pervin, Lawrence A. (1990). A brief history of modern personality theory. In Lawrence

A. Pervin (Ed.), *Handbook of personality: Theory and research.* New York: Guilford Press.

Pervin, Lawrence A. (1994). A critical analysis of current trait theory. *Psychological Inquiry, 5,* 103–113.

Pervin, Lawrence A. (1997). *Personality: Theory and research* (7th ed.). New York: Wiley.

Peters, Roger, & McGee, Rob. (1982). Cigarette smoking and state-dependent memory. *Psychopharmacology, 76* (3), 232–235.

Peterson, Christopher. (1988). Explanatory style as a risk factor for illness. *Cognitive Therapy and Research, 12,* 117–130.

Peterson, Christopher, & Bossio, Lisa M. (1993). Healthy attitudes: Optimism, hope, and control. In Daniel Goleman & Joel Gurin (Eds.), *Mind/body medicine: How to use your mind for better health.* Yonkers, N.Y.: Consumer Reports Books.

Petitto, Laura Ann, & Marentette, Paula F. (1991, March 31). Babbling in the manual mode: Evidence for the ontogeny of language. *Science, 251,* 1493–1496.

Petri, Herbert L. (1996). *Motivation: Theory, research, and applications* (4th ed.). Pacific Grove, Calif.: Brooks/Cole.

Phillips, D. P., & Brugge, J. F. (1985). Progress in neurophysiology of sound localization. *Annual Review of Psychology, 36,* 245–274.

Phillips, David P., & Ruth, Todd E. (1993). Adequacy of official suicide statistics for scientific research and public policy. *Suicide and Life Threatening Behavior, 23,* 307–319.

Phillips, Deborah. (1991). Day care for young children in the United States. In E. C. Melhuish & Peter Moss (Eds.), *Day care for young children.* London: Routledge.

Phillips, Deborah A., & Howes, Carollee. (1987). Indicators of quality in child care: Review of research. In Deborah A. Phillips (Ed.), *Quality in child care: What does research tell us? Research Monograph of the National Association for the Education of Young Children* (Vol. 1). Washington, D.C.: National Association for the Education of Young Children.

Phillips, Susan D. (1982). Career exploration in adulthood. *Journal of Vocational Behavior, 20,* 129–140.

Phillips, Susan D., & Blustein, David L. (1994). Readiness for career choices: Planning, exploring, and deciding. *The Career Development Quarterly, 43,* 63–75.

Piaget, Jean. (1952). *The origins of intelligence in children* (Translated by Margaret Cook). New York: International Universities Press.

Piaget, Jean. (1972). Intellectual evolution from adolescence to adulthood. *Human Development, 15,* 1–12.

Piaget, Jean. (1973). The stages of cognitive development: Interview with Richard I. Evans. In Richard I. Evans (Ed.), *Jean Piaget: The man and his ideas.* New York: Dutton.

Piaget, Jean, & Inhelder, Bärbel. (1958). *The growth of logical thinking from childhood to adolescence: An essay on the construction of formal operational structures* (Translated by Anne Parsons and Stanley Milgram). New York: Basic Books.

Piaget, Jean, & Inhelder, Bärbel. (1974). *The child's construction of quantities: Conservation and atomism.* London: Routledge and Kegan Paul.

Piliavin, Jane Allyn, & Charng, Hong-Wen. (1990). Altruism: A review of recent theory and research. *Annual Review of Sociology, 16,* 27–65.

Pillow, David R.; Zautra, Alex J.; & Sandler, Irwin. (1996). Major life events and minor stressors: Identifying mediational links in the stress process. *Journal of Personality and Social Psychology, 70,* 381–394.

Pinker, Steven. (1994). *The language instinct: How the mind creates language.* New York: Morrow.

Pinker, Steven. (1995). Introduction: Language. In Michael S. Gazzaniga (Ed.), *The cognitive neurosciences.* Cambridge, Mass.: MIT Press.

Plomin, Robert. (1990). The role of inheritance in behavior. *Science, 248,* 183–188.

Plomin, Robert; DeFries, John C.; McClearn, Gerald E.; & Rutter, Michael. (1997). *Behavioral genetics* (3rd ed.). New York: Freeman.

Plomin, Robert, & Neiderhiser, Jenae. (1992). Genetics and experience. *Current Directions in Psychological Science, 1,* 160–163.

Plomin, Robert; Owen, Michael J.; & McGuffin, Peter. (1994, June 17). The genetic basis of complex human behaviors. *Science, 264,* 1733–1739.

Plomin, Robert, & Rende, Richard. (1991). Human behavioral genetics. *Annual Review of Psychology, 42,* 161–190.

Plutchik, Robert. (1984). Emotions: A general psychoevolutionary theory. In Klaus R. Scherer & Paul Ekman (Eds.), *Approaches to emotion.* Hillsdale, N.J.: Erlbaum.

Polk, Thad A., & Newell, Allen. (1995). Deduction as verbal reasoning. *Psychological Review, 102,* 533–566.

Pope, Kenneth S. (1990). Therapist–patient sexual involvement: A review of the research. *Clinical Psychology Review, 10,* 477–490.

Pope, Kenneth S., & Tabachnick, Barbara G. (1993). Therapists' anger, hate, fear, and sexual feelings: National survey of therapist responses, client characteristics, critical events, formal complaints, and training. *Professional Psychology: Research and Practice, 24,* 142–152.

Pope, Victoria. (1997, August 4). Day-care dangers. *U.S. News & World Report, 123,* 30–37.

Porter, Kenneth. (1993). Combined individual and group psychotherapy. In Anne Alonso & Hillel I. Swiller (Eds.), *Group therapy in clinical practice.* Washington, D.C.: American Psychiatric Press.

Povinelli, Daniel J. (1993). Reconstructing the evolution of mind. *American Psychologist, 48,* 493–509.

Powlishta, Kimberly K. (1995a). Intergroup processes in childhood: Social categorization and sex role development. *Developmental Psychology, 31,* 781–788.

Powlishta, Kimberly K. (1995b). Gender bias in children's perceptions of personality traits. *Sex Roles, 32,* 223–240.

Pratkanis, Anthony R., & Aronson, Elliot. (1991). *Age of propaganda: The everyday use and abuse of persuasion.* New York: Freeman.

Prescott, Carol A., & Gottesman, Irving I. (1993). Genetically mediated vulnerability to schizophrenia. *Psychiatric Clinics of North America, 16,* 245–268.

Preti, George; Cutler, W. B.; Garcia, C. R.; Huggins, G. R.; & Lawley, H. J. (1986). Human axillary secretions influence women's menstrual cycles: The role of donor extract of females. *Hormones and Behavior, 20,* 474–482.

Prinzmetal, William. (1995). Visual feature integration in a world of objects. *Current Directions in Psychological Science, 4,* 90–94.

Pullum, Geoffrey K. (1991). *The great Eskimo vocabulary hoax and other irreverent essays on the study of language.* Chicago: University of Chicago Press.

Putnam, Frank W. (1989). *Diagnosis and treatment of multiple personality disorder.* New York: Guilford Press.

Putnam, Frank W. (1991a). Recent research on multiple personality disorder. *Psychiatric Clinics of North America, 14,* 489–502.

Putnam, Frank W. (1991b). Dissociative disorders in children and adolescents: A de-velopmental perspective. *Psychiatric Clinics of North America, 14,* 519–531.

Putnam, Frank W. (1993). Dissociative phenomena. In David Spiegel (Ed.), *Dissociative disorders: A clinical review.* Lutherville, Md.: Sidran.

Rabinowitz, D. (1970). Some endocrine and metabolic aspects of obesity. *Annual Review of Medicine, 21,* 241–258.

Rachlin, Howard. (1974). Self-control. *Behaviorism, 2,* 94–107.

Rakic, Pasko. (1995). Corticogenesis in human and nonhuman primates. In Michael S. Gazzaniga (Ed.), *The cognitive neurosciences.* Cambridge, Mass.: MIT Press.

Ramachandran, Vilayanur S. (1992a, May). Blind spots. *Scientific American, 266,* 86–91.

Ramachandran, Vilayanur S. (1992b). Filling in gaps in perception: Part 1. *Current Directions in Psychological Science, 1,* 199–205.

Randi, James. (1980). *Flim-flam!* New York: Lippincott & Crowell.

Randi, James. (1982). *The truth about Uri Geller.* Buffalo, N.Y.: Prometheus Books.

Rapee, Ronald M.; Brown, Timothy A.; Antony, Martin M.; & Barlow, David H. (1992). Response to hyperventilation and inhalation of 5.5% carbon dioxide-enriched air across the *DSM-III-R* anxiety disorders. *Journal of Abnormal Psychology, 101,* 538–552.

Rapoport, Judith L. (1989). *The boy who couldn't stop washing: The experience and treatment of obsessive-compulsive disorder.* New York: Dutton.

Rapoport, Judith L. (1991). Basal ganglia dysfunction as a proposed cause of obsessive-compulsive disorder. In Bernard J. Carroll & James E. Barrett (Eds.), *Psychopathology and the brain.* New York: Raven Press.

Raskin, Allen; Pelchat, Rodney; Sood, Ramn; Alphs, Larry D.; & Levine, Jerome. (1993). Negative symptom assessment of chronic schizophrenia patients. *Schizophrenia Bulletin, 19,* 627–635.

Rasmussen, Steven A., & Eisen, Jane L. (1992). The epidemiology and clinical features of obsessive-compulsive disorder. *Psychiatric Clinics of North America, 15,* 743–758.

Ratcliff, Roger, & McKoon, Gail. (1994). Retrieving information from memory: Spreading-activation theories versus compound-cue theories. *Psychological Review, 101,* 177–184.

Räty, Hannu. (1990). A world without mental illness: Concepts of mental health and mental illness among a student group. *Social Behaviour, 5,* 315–326.

Rawlings, Steve W., & Saluter, Arlene F. (1995). *Household and family characteristics: March 1994* (U.S. Bureau of the Census, Current Population Reports, Series P20-483). Washington, D.C.: U.S. Government Printing Office.

Rawlins, William K. (1992). *Friendship matters: Communication, dialectics, and the life course.* Hawthorne, N.Y.: Aldine de Gruyter.

Raz, Sarah. (1994). Gross brain morphology in schizophrenia: A regional analysis of traditional diagnostic subtypes. *Journal of Consulting and Clinical Psychology, 62,* 640–644.

Reed, Stephen K. (1996). *Cognition: Theory and applications* (4th ed.). Pacific Grove, Calif.: Brooks/Cole.

Reese, Ellen. (1986). Learning about teaching from teaching about learning: Presenting behavioral analysis in an introductory survey course. In Vivian Parker Makosky (Ed.), *The G. Stanley Hall Lecture Series* (Vol. 6). Washington, D.C.: American Psychological Association.

Regan, Dennis T., & Kilduff, Martin. (1988). Optimism about elections: Dissonance reduction at the ballot box. *Political Psychology, 9,* 101–107.

Regan, Dennis T.; Williams, Margo; & Sparling, Sondra. (1972). Voluntary expiation of guilt: A field experiment. *Journal of Personality and Social Psychology, 24,* 42–45.

Regier, Darrel A.; Narrow, William E.; Rae, Donald S.; Manderscheid, Ronald W.; Locke, Ben Z.; & Goodwin, Fredrick K. (1993). The de facto U.S. mental and addictive disorders service system: Epidemiologic catchment area prospective one-year prevalence rates of disorders and services. *Archives of General Psychiatry, 50,* 85–94.

Reisberg, Daniel, & Chambers, Deborah. (1991). Neither pictures nor propositions: What can we learn from a mental image? *Canadian Journal of Psychology, 45,* 336–348.

Reisenzein, Rainer. (1983). The Schachter theory of emotion: Two decades later. *Psychological Bulletin, 94,* 239–264.

Reiss, B. K. (1990). *A biography of Mary Cover Jones.* Berkeley, Calif.: Wright Institute.

Rejeski, W. Jack; Gregg, Edward; Thompson, Amy; & Berry, Michael. (1991). The effects of varying doses of acute aerobic exercise on psychophysiological stress responses in highly trained cyclists. *Journal of Sport and Exercise Psychology, 13,* 188–199.

Rejeski, W. Jack; Thompson, Amy; Brubaker, Peter H.; & Miller, Henry S. (1992). Acute exercise: Buffering psychosocial responses in women. *Health Psychology, 11,* 355–362.

Renzulli, Joseph S. (1986). The three-ring conception of giftedness: A developmental model for creative productivity. In Robert J. Sternberg & Janet E. Davidson (Eds.), *Conceptions of giftedness.* New York: Cambridge University Press.

Repetti, Rena L. (1993). Short-term effects of occupational stressors on daily mood and health complaints. *Health Psychology, 12,* 125–131.

Rescorla, Robert A. (1980). *Pavlovian second-order conditioning: Studies in associative learning.* Hillsdale, N.J.: Erlbaum.

Rescorla, Robert A. (1988). Pavlovian conditioning: It's not what you think it is. *American Psychologist, 43,* 151–160.

Rest, James R. (1983). Morality. In Paul H. Mussen, John H. Flavell, & Ellen M. Markman (Eds.), *Handbook of child psychology* (4th ed.), Vol. 3. New York: Wiley.

Restak, Richard M. (1994). *Receptors.* New York: Bantam.

Revelle, William. (1995). Personality processes. *Annual Review of Psychology, 46,* 295–328.

Reynolds, David K. (1989). *Pools of lodging for the moon: Strategy for a positive lifestyle.* New York: Morrow.

Reynolds, David K. (1990). *A thousand waves: A sensible life-style for sensitive people.* New York: Morrow.

Riccio, David C.; Rabinowitz, Vita C.; & Axelrod, Shari. (1994). Memory: When less is more. *American Psychologist, 49,* 917–926.

Rice, Laura N., & Greenberg, Leslie S. (1992). Humanistic approaches to psychotherapy. In Donald K. Freedheim (Ed.), *History of psychotherapy: A century of change.* Washington, D.C.: American Psychological Association.

Richelson, Elliott. (1993). Treatment of acute depression. *Psychiatric Clinics of North America, 16,* 461–478.

Rimm, Eric B.; Giovannucci, Edward L.; Willett, Walter C.; Colditz, Graham A.; Ascherio, Alberto; Rosner, Bernard; & Stampfer, Meir J. (1991, August 24). Prospective study of alcohol consumption and risk of coronary disease in men. *Lancet, 338,* 464–468.

Rissman, Emilie F. (1995). An alternative animal model for the study of female sexual behavior. *Current Directions in Psychological Science, 4,* 6–10.

Ritchie, James C., & Nemeroff, Charles B. (1991). Stress, the hypothalamic-pituitary-adrenal axis, and depression. In James A. McCubbin, Peter G. Kaufmann, & Charles B. Nemeroff (Eds.), *Stress, neuropeptides, and systemic disease.* San Diego: Academic Press.

Robbins, Ann S.; Spence, Janet T.; & Clark, Heather. (1991). Psychological determinants of health and performance: The tangled web of desirable and undesirable characteristics. *Journal of Personality and Social Psychology, 61,* 755–765.

Robins, Clive J., & Hayes, Adele M. (1993). An appraisal of cognitive therapy. *Journal of Consulting and Clinical Psychology, 61,* 205–214.

Robinson, Daniel N. (1993). Is there a Jamesian tradition in psychology? *American Psychologist, 48,* 638–643.

Robinson, Paul. (1993). *Freud and his critics.* Berkeley: University of California Press.

Robinson, Vera M. (1983). Humor and health. In Paul E. McGhee & Jeffrey H. Goldstein (Eds.), *Handbook of humor research: Vol. 2. Applied studies.* New York: Springer-Verlag.

Roche, Suzanne M., & McConkey, Kevin M. (1990). Absorption: Nature, assessment, and correlates. *Journal of Personality and Social Psychology, 59,* 91–101.

Rock, Irvin. (1995). *Perception.* New York: Scientific American Library.

Rodin, Judith. (1981). Current status of the internal-external hypothesis for obesity: What went wrong? *American Psychologist, 36,* 361–372.

Rodin, Judith. (1982). Obesity: Why the losing battle? In Benjamin B. Wolman (Ed.), *Psychological aspects of obesity: A handbook.* New York: Van Nostrand-Reinhold.

Rodin, Judith. (1985). Insulin levels, hunger, and food intake: An example of feedback loops in body weight reduction. *Health Psychology, 4* (1), 1–24.

Rodin, Judith. (1986, September 19). Aging and health: Effects of the sense of control. *Science, 233,* 1271–1275.

Rodin, Judith, & Langer, Ellen. (1977). Long-term effects of a control-relevant intervention with the institutionalized aged. *Journal of Personality and Social Psychology, 35,* 897–902.

Rodin, Judith, & Salovey, Peter. (1989). Health psychology. *Annual Review of Psychology, 40,* 533–579.

Roediger, Henry L., III. (1992). Retrieval processes in memory. In Larry R. Squire (Ed.), *Encyclopedia of learning and memory*. New York: Macmillan.

Roemer, Lizabeth, & Borkovec, Thomas D. (1993). Worry: Unwanted cognitive activity that controls unwanted somatic experience. In Daniel M. Wegner & James W. Pennebaker (Eds.), *Handbook of mental control*. Englewood Cliffs, N.J.: Prentice Hall.

Rogers, Carl. (1957a/1989). A note on "The Nature of Man." In Howard Kirschenbaum & Valerie Land Henderson (Eds.), *The Carl Rogers reader*. Boston: Houghton Mifflin.

Rogers, Carl. (1957b/1989). A therapist's view of the good life: The fully functioning person. In Howard Kirschenbaum & Valerie Land Henderson (Eds.), *The Carl Rogers reader*. Boston: Houghton Mifflin.

Rogers, Carl. (1959). A theory of therapy, personality, and interpersonal relationships, as developed in the client-centered framework. In S. Koch (Ed.), *Psychology: A study of a science: Vol. 3. Formulations of the person and the social context*. New York: McGraw-Hill.

Rogers, Carl. (1961). *On becoming a person*. Boston: Houghton Mifflin.

Rogers, Carl. (1964/1989). Toward a modern approach to values: The valuing process in the mature person. In Howard Kirschenbaum & Valerie Land Henderson (Eds.), *The Carl Rogers reader*. Boston: Houghton Mifflin.

Rogers, Carl. (1977). *Carl Rogers on personal power: Inner strength and its revolutionary impact*. New York: Delacorte Press.

Rogers, Carl R. (1980). *A way of being*. Boston: Houghton Mifflin.

Rogers, Carl. (1981/1989). Notes on Rollo May. In Howard Kirschenbaum & Valerie Land Henderson (Eds.), *Carl Rogers: Dialogues*. Boston: Houghton Mifflin.

Rogers, Carl, & Skinner, B. F. (1956, November 30). Some issues concerning the control of human behavior: A symposium. *Science, 124,* 1057–1066.

Rogers, T. B.; Kuiper, N. A.; & Kirker, W. S. (1977). Self–reference and the encoding of personal information. *Journal of Personality and Social Psychology, 35,* 677–688.

Rogo, D. Scott. (1985). *The search for yesterday: A critical examination of the evidence for reincarnation*. Englewood Cliffs, N.J.: Prentice Hall.

Rogoff, Barbara, & Chavajay, Pablo. (1995). What's become of research on the cultural basis of cognitive development? *American Psychologist, 50,* 859–877.

Rogoff, Barbara, & Morelli, Gilda. (1989). Perspectives on children's development from cultural psychology. *American Psychologist, 44,* 343–348.

Ronen, Tammie. (1991). Intervention package for treating sleep disorders in a four-year-old girl. *Journal of Behavior Therapy and Experimental Psychiatry, 22,* 141–148.

Rook, Karen S. (1992). Detrimental aspects of social relationships: Taking stock of an emerging literature. In Hans O. F. Veiel & Urs Baumann (Eds.), *The meaning and measurement of social support*. New York: Hemisphere.

Rorer, Leonard G. (1990). Personality assessment: A conceptual survey. In Lawrence A. Pervin (Ed.), *Handbook of personality: Theory and research*. New York: Guilford Press.

Rosch, Eleanor H. (1973). Natural categories. *Cognitive Psychology, 4,* 328–350.

Rosch, Eleanor H. (1978). Principles of categorization. In Eleanor H. Rosch & Barbara B. Lloyd (Eds.), *Cognition and categorization*. Hillsdale, N.J.: Erlbaum.

Rosch, Eleanor H. (1987). Linguistic relativity. *Et Cetera, 44,* 254–279.

Rosch, Eleanor H., & Mervis, Carolyn B. (1975). Family resemblances: Studies in the internal structure of categories. *Cognitive Psychology, 7,* 573–605.

Rose, G. A., & Williams, R. T. (1961). Metabolic studies on large and small eaters. *British Journal of Nutrition, 15,* 1–9.

Rose, Kenneth Jon. (1988). *The body in time*. New York: Wiley.

Rose, Richard J. (1995). Genes and human behavior. *Annual Review of Psychology, 46,* 625–654.

Rose, Steven. (1993). *The making of memory: From molecules to mind*. New York: Doubleday.

Rosenberg, Harold. (1993). Prediction of controlled drinking by alcoholics and problem drinkers. *Psychological Bulletin, 113,* 129–139.

Rosenhan, David L., & Seligman, Martin E. P. (1995). *Abnormal psychology* (5th ed.). New York: Norton.

Rosenman, Ray H., & Chesney, Margaret A. (1982). Stress, Type A behavior, and coronary disease. In Leo Goldberger & Shlomo Breznitz (Eds.), *Handbook of stress: Theoretical and clinical aspects*. New York: Free Press.

Rosenstein, Marilyn J.; Milazzo-Sayre, Laura J.; & Manderscheid, Ronald W. (1989). Care of persons with schizophrenia: A statistical profile. *Schizophrenia Bulletin, 15,* 45–58.

Rosenthal, Abraham M. (1964a, May 3). Study of the sickness called apathy. *The New York Times Magazine,* Section VI, pp. 24, 66, 69–72.

Rosenthal, Abraham M. (1964b). *Thirty-eight witnesses*. New York: McGraw-Hill.

Rosenthal, Norman E. (1993). *Winter blues: Seasonal affective disorder: What it is and how to overcome it* (Rev. ed.). New York: Guilford Press.

Rosenthal, Robert. (1994). Science and ethics in conducting, analyzing, and reporting psychological research. *Psychological Science, 5* (3), 127–134.

Rosenzweig, Mark R. (1996). Aspects of the search for neural mechanisms of memory. *Annual Review of Psychology, 47,* 1–32.

Ross, Barbara. (1991). William James: Spoiled child of American psychology. In Gregory A. Kimble, Michael Wertheimer, & Charlotte White (Eds.), *Portraits of pioneers in psychology*. Washington, D.C.: American Psychological Association.

Ross, Colin A. (1991). Epidemiology of multiple personality disorder and dissociation. *Psychiatric Clinics of North America, 14,* 503–517.

Ross, Colin A.; Norton, R.; & Wozney, K. (1989). Multiple personality disorder: An analysis of 236 cases. *Canadian Journal of Psychiatry, 34,* 414–418.

Ross, Jerilyn. (1993). Social phobia: The consumer's perspective. *Journal of Clinical Psychiatry, 54* (12, Suppl.), 5–9.

Ross, Lee. (1977). The intuitive psychologist and his shortcomings: Distortions in the attribution process. In Leonard Berkowitz (Ed.), *Advances in experimental social psychology* (Vol. 10). New York: Academic Press.

Ross, Lee, & Anderson, Craig A. (1982). Shortcomings in the attribution process: On the origins and maintenance of erroneous social assessments. In Daniel Kahneman, Paul Slovic, & Amos Tversky (Eds.), *Judgment under uncertainty: Heuristics and biases*. New York: Cambridge University Press.

Rossman, Martin L. (1993). Imagery: Learning to use the mind's eye. In Daniel Goleman & Joel Gurin (Eds.), *Mind/body medicine: How to use your mind for better health*. Yonkers, N.Y.: Consumer Reports Books.

Rothbart, Mary K.; Derryberry, Douglas; & Posner, Michael I. (1994). A psychobiological approach to the development of temperament. In John E. Bates & Theodore D. Wachs (Eds.), *Temperament: Individual differences at the interface of biology and behavior*. Washington, D.C.: American Psychological Association.

Rothbaum, Barbara Olasov; Hodges, Larry F.; Opdyke, Dan; Williford, James S.; & North, Max. (1996). Virtual reality exposure therapy in the treatment of fear of flying: A case report. *Behaviour Research and Therapy, 34,* 477–486.

Rothenberg, Saul A. (1997). Introduction to sleep disorders. In Mark R. Pressman & William C. Orr (Eds.), *Understanding sleep: The evaluation and treatment of sleep disorders.* Washington, D.C.: American Psychological Association.

Rowan, Andrew N. (1997, February). The benefits and ethics of animal research. *Scientific American, 276* (2), 79.

Rupp, Agnes, & Keith, Samuel J. (1993). The costs of schizophrenia: Assessing the burden. *Psychiatric Clinics of North America, 16,* 413–423.

Russell, James A. (1980). A circumplex model of affect. *Journal of Personality and Social Psychology, 39,* 1161–1178.

Russell, James A.; Lewicka, Maria; & Niit, Toomas. (1989). A cross-cultural study of a circumplex model of affect. *Journal of Personality and Social Psychology, 57,* 848–856.

Russell, John G. (1989). Anxiety disorders in Japan: A review of the Japanese literature on *shinkeishitsu* and *taijinkyofusho*. *Culture, Medicine, and Psychiatry, 13,* 391–403.

Russell, Tanya G.; Rowe, Wayne; & Smouse, Albert E. (1991). Subliminal self-help tapes and academic achievement: An evaluation. *Journal of Counseling and Development, 69,* 359–362.

Rutter, Michael L. (1997). Nature-Nurture integration: The example of antisocial behavior. *American Psychologist, 52,* 390–398.

Rutter, Virginia. (1994, April). Oops! A very embarrassing story. *Psychology Today,* pp. 12–13, 95.

Ruvolo, Ann Patrice, & Markus, Hazel Rose. (1992). Possible selves and performance: The power of self-relevant imagery. *Social Cognition, 10,* 95–124.

Sacks, Michael H. (1993). Exercise for stress control. In Daniel Goleman & Joel Gurin (Eds.), *Mind/body medicine: How to use your mind for better health.* Yonkers, N.Y.: Consumer Reports Books.

Sakheim, David K., & Devine, Susan E. (Eds.). (1992). *Out of darkness: Exploring Satanism and ritual abuse.* New York: Lexington Books.

Salens, Lester B. (1984). *Obesity and energy metabolism* (NIH Publication No. 86–1805). Bethesda, Md.: National Institutes of Health.

Salovey, Peter; Mayer, John D.; & Rosenhan, David L. (1991). Mood and helping: Mood as a motivator of helping and helping as a regulator of mood. In Margaret S. Clark (Ed.), *Prosocial behavior: Vol. 12. Review of personality and social psychology.* Newbury Park, Calif.: Sage.

Salthouse, Timothy. (1993). Speed mediation of adult age differences in cognition. *Developmental Psychology, 29,* 722–738.

Saluter, Arlene F. (1994). *Marital status and living arrangements: March 1993* (U.S. Bureau of the Census, Current Population Reports, Series P20-478). Washington, D.C.: U.S. Government Printing Office.

Sande, Gerald N.; Goethals, George R.; & Radloff, Christine E. (1988). Perceiving one's own traits and others': The multifaceted self. *Journal of Personality and Social Psychology, 54,* 13–20.

Sandelowski, M.; Holditch-Davis, D.; & Harris, B. G. (1992). Using qualitative and quantitative methods: The transition to parenthood among infertile couples. In Jane F. Gilgun, Kerry Daly, & Gerald Handel (Eds.), *Qualitative methods in family research.* Newbury Park, Calif.: Sage.

Sandler, Jack, & Steele, Holly Villareal. (1991). Aversion methods. In Frederick H. Kanfer & Arnold P. Goldstein (Eds.), *Helping people change: A textbook of methods* (4th ed.). New York: Pergamon.

Sarafino, Edward P. (1994). *Health psychology: Biopsychosocial interactions* (2nd ed.) New York: Wiley.

Sarason, Irwin G.; Sarason, Barbara R.; Pierce, Gregory R.; Shearin, Edward N.; & Sayers, Merlin H. (1991). A social learning approach to increasing blood donations. *Journal of Applied Social Psychology, 21,* 896–918.

Saskin, Paul. (1997). Obstructive sleep apnea: Treatment options, efficacy, and effects. In Mark R. Pressman & William C. Orr (Eds.), *Understanding sleep: The evaluation and treatment of sleep disorders.* Washington, D.C.: American Psychological Association.

Saufley, W. H.; Otaka, S. R.; & Bavaresco, J. L. (1985). Context effects: Classroom tests and context independence. *Memory and Cognition, 13,* 522–528.

Savage-Rumbaugh, E. Sue. (1993). Language learnability in man, ape, and dolphin. In Herbert L. Roitblat, Louis M. Herman, & Paul E. Nachtigall (Eds.), *Language and communication: Comparative perspectives.* Hillsdale, N.J.: Erlbaum.

Savage-Rumbaugh, E. Sue, & Lewin, Roger. (1994, September). Ape at the brink. *Discover, 15,* 91–98.

Savin-Williams, Ritch C.; & Berndt, Thomas J. (1990). Friendship and peer relations. In S. Shirley Feldman & Glen R. Elliott (Eds.), *At the threshold: The developing adolescent.* Cambridge, Mass.: Harvard University Press.

Saxe, Glenn N.; Chinman, Gary; Berkowitz, Robert; Hall, Kathryn; Lieberg, Gabriele; Schwartz, Jane; & van der Kolk, Bessel A. (1994). Somatization in patients with dissociative disorders. *American Journal of Psychiatry, 151,* 1329–1334.

Saxe, Glenn N.; van der Kolk, Bessel A.; Berkowitz, Robert; Chinman, Gary; Hall, Kathryn; Lieberg, Gabriele; & Schwartz, Jane. (1993). Dissociative disorders in psychiatric inpatients. *American Journal of Psychiatry, 150,* 1037–1042.

Scarr, Sandra. (1992). Developmental theories for the 1990s: Development and individual differences. *Child Development, 63,* 1–19.

Scarr, Sandra (1997). Rules of evidence: A larger context for the statistical debate. *Psychological Science, 8,* 16–17.

Scarr, Sandra, & Eisenberg, Marlene. (1993). Child care research: Issues, perspectives, and results. *Annual Review of Psychology, 44,* 613–644.

Scarr, Sandra, & Weinberg, Richard A. (1976). IQ test performance of black children adopted by white families. *American Psychologist, 31,* 726–739.

Schachter, Stanley. (1971a). *Emotion, obesity, and crime.* New York: Academic Press.

Schachter, Stanley. (1971b). Some extraordinary facts about obese humans and rats. *American Psychologist, 26,* 129–144.

Schachter, Stanley, & Singer, Jerome E. (1962). Cognitive, social, and physiological determinants of emotional state. *Psychological Review, 69,* 379–399.

Schacter, Daniel L. (1995a). Consciousness: Introduction. In Michael S. Gazzaniga (Ed.), *The cognitive neurosciences.* Cambridge, Mass.: MIT Press.

Schacter, Daniel L. (1995b, April). Memory wars. *Scientific American, 272,* 135–139.

Schaie, K. Warner. (1994). The course of adult intellectual development. *American Psychologist, 49,* 304–313.

Schaie, K. Warner. (1995a). Brain-astics: Mind exercises to keep you sharp. *New Choices in Retirement Living, 35,* 22–28.

Schaie, K. Warner. (1995b). *Intellectual development in adulthood: The Seattle Longitudinal Study.* New York: Cambridge University Press.

Schaie, K. Warner, & Willis, Sherry L. (1986). Can decline in adult intellectual functioning be reversed? *Developmental Psychology, 22,* 223–232.

Schaie, K. Warner, & Willis, Sherry L. (1996). *Adult development and aging* (4th ed.). New York: HarperCollins.

Schaller, Mark, & Cialdini, Robert B. (1990). Happiness, sadness, and helping: A motivational integration. In Richard M. Sorrentino & E. Tory Higgins (Eds.), *Handbook of motivation and cognition: Vol. 2. Foundations of social behavior.* New York: Guilford Press.

Schattschneider, Doris. (1990). *Visions of symmetry: Notebooks, periodic drawings, and related work of M. C. Escher.* New York: Freeman (p. 169. Notes on p. 301).

Schatzman, Morton, & Fenwick, Peter. (1994). Dreams and dreaming. In Rosemary Cooper (Ed.), *Sleep.* New York: Chapman & Hall.

Scheibel, Arnold B. (1994, July). Quoted in Daniel Golden, Building a better brain. *Life,* p. 66.

Scherer, Klaus R., & Wallbott, Harald G. (1994). Evidence for universality and cultural variation of differential emotion response patterning. *Journal of Personality and Social Psychology, 66,* 310–328.

Schlenker, Barry R., & Weigold, Michael F. (1992). Interpersonal processes involving impression regulation and management. *Annual Review of Psychology, 43,* 133–168.

Schlenker, Barry R.; Weigold, Michael F.; & Hallam, J. R. (1990). Self-serving attributions in social context: Effects of self-esteem and social pressure. *Journal of Personality and Social Psychology, 58,* 855–863.

Schmidt, Frank L. (1992). What do data really mean? Research findings, meta-analysis, and cumulative knowledge in psychology. *American Psychologist, 47,* 1173–1181.

Schneider, David J. (1993). Mental control: Lessons from our past. In Daniel M. Wegner & James W. Pennebaker (Eds.), *Handbook of mental control.* Englewood Cliffs, N.J.: Prentice Hall.

Schooler, Jonathan W.; Ohlsson, Stellan; & Brooks, Kevin. (1993). Thoughts beyond words: When language overshadows insight. *Journal of Experimental Psychology: General, 122,* 166–183.

Schulman, Michael, & Mekler, Eva. (1985). *Bringing up a moral child: A new approach for teaching your child to be kind, just, and responsible.* Reading, Mass.: Addison-Wesley.

Schultz, Wolfram; Dayan, Peter; & Montague, P. Read. (1997, March 14). A neural substrate of prediction and reward. *Science, 275,* 1593–1599.

Schulz, R., & Schlarb, J. (1987–1988). Two decades of research on dying: What do we

know about the patient? *Omega, 18,* 299–317.

Schwartz, James H. (1995a). Neurotransmitters. In Eric R. Kandel, James H. Schwartz, & Thomas M. Jessell (Eds.), *Essentials of neural science and behavior.* Norwalk, Conn.: Appleton & Lange.

Schwartz, James H. (1995b). The neuron. In Eric R. Kandel, James H. Schwartz, & Thomas M. Jessell (Eds.), *Essentials of neural science and behavior.* Norwalk, Conn.: Appleton & Lange.

Schwartz, Jeffrey M.; Stoessel, Paula W.; & Phelps, Michael E. (1996). Systematic changes in cerebral glucose metabolic rate after successful behavior modification treatment of obsessive-compulsive disorder. *Archives of General Psychiatry, 53,* 109–117.

Schwartz, Richard S. (1991). Mood brighteners, affect tolerance, and the blues. *Psychiatry, 54,* 397–403.

Schwarzer, Rolf, & Leppin, Anja. (1992). Possible impact of social ties and support on morbidity and mortality. In Hans O. F. Veiel & Urs Baumann (Eds.), *The meaning and measurement of social support.* New York: Hemisphere.

Scott, Allene J. (1994). Chronobiological considerations in shiftworker sleep and performance and shiftwork scheduling. *Human Performance, 7* (3), 207-233.

Sedikides, Constantine, & Anderson, Craig A. (1994). Causal perceptions of intertrait relations: The glue that holds person types together. *Personality and Social Psychology Bulletin, 20,* 294–302.

Seeman, Mary V. (Ed.). (1995). *Gender and psychopathology.* Washington, D.C.: American Psychiatric Press.

Segall, Marshall H. (1994). A cross-cultural research contribution to unraveling the nativist/empiricist controversy. In Walter J. Lonner & Roy Malpass (Eds.), *Psychology and culture.* Boston: Allyn & Bacon.

Segall, Marshall H.; Campbell, Donald T.; & Herskovits, Melville J. (1963). Cultural differences in the perception of geometric illusions. *Science, 193,* 769–771.

Segall, Marshall H.; Campbell, Donald T.; & Herskovits, Melville J. (1966). *The influence of culture on visual perception.* Indianapolis, Ind.: Bobbs-Merrill

Seidman, Stuart N., & Rieder, Ronald O. (1994). A review of sexual behavior in the United States. *American Journal of Psychiatry, 151,* 330–341.

Seligman, Martin E. P. (1970). On the generality of the laws of learning. *Psychological Review, 77,* 406–418.

Seligman, Martin E. P. (1971). Phobias and preparedness. *Behavior Therapy, 2,* 307–320.

Seligman, Martin E. P. (1990). *Learned optimism.* New York: Knopf.

Seligman, Martin E. P. (1992). *Helplessness: On development, depression, and death.* New York: Freeman.

Seligman, Martin E. P. (1995). The effectiveness of psychotherapy: The *Consumer Reports* study. *American Psychologist, 50,* 965–974.

Selye, Hans. (1956). *The stress of life.* New York: McGraw-Hill.

Selye, Hans. (1976). *The stress of life* (Rev. ed.). New York: McGraw-Hill.

Shadid, Anthony. (1997, June 28). They bellydance their way to fat. *The Times of India.* <http://www.timesofindia.com/280697/worl9.htm> (1997, August 18).

Shanahan, T. L., & Czeisler, Charles A. (1991). Light exposure induces equivalent phase shifts of the endogenous circadian rhythms of circulating plasma melatonin and core body temperature in men. *The Journal of Clinical Endocrinology and Metabolism, 73* (2), 227–234.

Shapiro, K. L. (1991, July). Use morality as basis for animal treatment. *APA Monitor,* p. 5.

Sharan, Pratap; Chaudhary, Geeta; Kavathekar, Surabhi A.; & Saxena, Shekhar. (1996). Preliminary report of psychiatric disorders in survivors of a severe earthquake. *American Journal of Psychiatry, 153,* 556–558.

Shatz, Carla J. (1992, September). The developing brain. *Scientific American, 267,* 34–41.

Shaywitz, Bennett A.; Shaywitz, Sally E.; & Gore, J. C. (1995, February 16). Sex differences in the functional organization of the brain for language. *Nature, 373,* 607–615.

Shedler, Jonathan; Mayman, Martin; & Manis, Melvin. (1993). The *illusion* of mental health. *American Psychologist, 48,* 1117–1131.

Shepard, Michael; Watt, David; Falloon, Ian; & Smeeton, Nigel. (1989). The natural history of schizophrenia: A five-year follow-up study of outcome and prediction in a representative sample of schizophrenics. *Psychological Medicine, 19* (Monograph Suppl. 15), 1–46.

Sherif, Muzafer. (1956, November). Experiments in group conflict. *Scientific American, 195,* 33–47.

Sherif, Muzafer; Harvey, O. J.; White, B. Jack; Hood, William R.; & Sherif, Carolyn W. (1961/1988). *The Robbers Cave experiment: Intergroup conflict and cooperation.* Middletown, Conn.: Wesleyan University Press.

Shields, Stephanie A. (1987). Women, men, and the dilemma of emotion. In Phillip Shaver & Clyde Hendrick (Eds.), *Sex and gender: Review of personality and social psychology*. Newbury Park, Calif.: Sage Publications.

Shiffrin, Richard M., & Nosofsky, Robert M. (1994). Seven plus or minus two: A commentary on capacity limitations. *Psychological Review, 101*, 357–361.

Shneidman, Edwin. (1985). *Definition of suicide*. New York: Wiley.

Shneidman, Edwin S. (1987). A psychological approach to suicide. In Gary R. VanderBos & Brenda K. Bryant (Eds.), *Cataclysms, crises, and catastrophes: Psychology in action*. Washington, D.C.: American Psychological Association.

Shotland, R. Lance, & Straw, Margret K. (1976). Bystander response to an assault: When a man attacks a woman. *Journal of Personality and Social Psychology, 34*, 990–999.

Shou, Mogens. (1993). *Lithium treatment of manic-depressive illness: A practical guide*. (5th ed.). Basel, Switzerland: Karger.

Shtasel, Derri L.; Gur, Raquel E.; Gallacher, Fiona; Heimberg, Carolyn; Cannon, Tyrone; & Gur, Ruben C. (1992). Phenomenology and functioning in first-episode schizophrenia. *Schizophrenia Bulletin, 18*, 449–462.

Shulman, Ian D.; Cox, Brian J.; Swinson, Richard P.; Kuch, Klaus; & Reichman, Jaak T. (1994). Precipitating events, locations and reactions associated with initial unexpected panic attacks. *Behaviour Research and Therapy, 32*, 17–20.

Shumaker, Sally A., & Hill, D. Robin. (1991). Gender differences in social support and physical health. *Health Psychology, 10*, 102–111.

Shuval, Judith T. (1993). Migration and stress. In Leo Goldberger & Shlomo Breznitz (Eds.), *Handbook of stress: Theoretical and clinical aspects* (2nd ed.). New York: Free Press.

Shweder, Richard A., & Haidt, Jonathan. (1993). The future of moral psychology: Truth, intuition, and the pluralist way. *Psychological Science, 4*, 360–365.

Shweder, Richard A.; Mahapatra, Manamohan; & Miller, Joan G. (1990a). Culture and moral development. In James W. Stigler, Richard A. Shweder, & Gilbert Herdt (Eds.), *Cultural Psychology*. New York: Cambridge University Press.

Shweder, Richard A.; Mahapatra, Manamohan; & Miller, Joan G. (1990b). Culture and moral development. In Jerome Kagan & Sharon Lamb (Eds.), *The emergence of morality in young children*. Chicago: University of Chicago Press.

Siegel, Judith M. (1990). Stressful life events and use of physician services among the elderly. *Journal of Personality and Social Psychology, 58*, 1081–1086.

Siegler, Robert S. (1989). Mechanisms of cognitive development. *Annual Review of Psychology, 40*, 353–379.

Siegler, Robert S. (1991). *Children's thinking* (2nd ed.). Englewood Cliffs, N.J.: Prentice Hall.

Siegler, Robert S. (1992). The other Alfred Binet. *Developmental Psychology, 28*, 179–190.

Siegler, Robert S., & Ellis, Shari. (1996). Piaget on childhood. *Psychological Science, 7*, 211–215.

Silbersweig, David A.; Stern, Emily; & Frackowaik, R. S. J. (1995, November 9). A functional neuroanatomy of hallucinations in schizophrenia. *Nature, 387*, 176–184.

Silva, Christopher E., & Kirsch, Irving. (1992). Interpretive sets, expectancy, fantasy proneness, and dissociation as predictors of hypnotic response. *Journal of Personality and Social Psychology, 63*, 847–856.

Simon, Allie; Worthen, David M.; & Mitas, John A. (1979). An evaluation of iridology. JAMA, *Journal of the American Medical Association, 242* (13), 1385–1389.

Simon, Bernd; Pantaleo, Giuseppe; & Mummendey, Amelie. (1995). Unique individual or interchangeable group member? The accentuation of intragroup differences versus similarities as an indicator of the individual self versus the collective self. *Journal of Personality and Social Psychology, 69*, 106–119.

Sivacek, John, & Crano, William D. (1982). Vested interest as a moderator of attitude–behavior consistency. *Journal of Personality and Social Psychology, 43*, 210–221.

Skinner, B. F. (1935). Two types of conditioned reflex and a pseudo type. *Journal of General Psychology, 12*, 66–77.

Skinner, B. F. (1938). *The behavior of organisms: An experimental analysis*. New York: Appleton-Century-Crofts.

Skinner, B. F. (1948). *Walden two*. New York: Macmillan.

Skinner, B. F. (1948/1992). Superstition in the pigeon. *Journal of Experimental Psychology: General, 121*, 273–274.

Skinner, B. F. (1953). *Science and human behavior*. New York: Macmillan.

Skinner, B. F. (1956). A case history in scientific method. *American Psychologist, 11*, 221–233.

Skinner, B. F. (1961, November). Teaching machines. *Scientific American, 205*, 90–102.

Skinner, B. F. (1967). B. F. Skinner . . . An autobiography. In E. G. Boring & G. Lindzey (Eds.), *A history of psychology in autobiography* (Vol. 5). New York: Appleton-Century-Crofts.

Skinner, B. F. (1971). *Beyond freedom and dignity*. New York: Bantam.

Skinner, B. F. (1974). *About behaviorism*. New York: Knopf.

Skinner, B. F. (1987). Whatever happened to psychology as the science of behavior? *American Psychologist, 42*, 780–786.

Slamecka, Norman J. (1992). Forgetting. In Larry R. Squire (Ed.), *Encyclopedia of learning and memory*. New York: Macmillan.

Sleek, Scott. (1994, April). Could Prozac replace demand for therapy? *APA Monitor*, p. 28.

Sleek, Scott. (1995, February). Prozac under new scrutiny by researchers, practitioners. *APA Monitor*, p. 31.

Sloane, Martin C. (1981). A comparison of hypnosis vs. waking state and visual vs. nonvisual recall instructions for witnesses/victims memory retrieval in actual major crimes. Florida State University Ph.D. thesis. *Dissertation Abstracts International, 42*, 6, 2551-B. (University Microfilms No. 8125873.)

Smith, Carlyle, & Lapp, Lorelei. (1991). Increases in numbers of REMs and REM density in humans following an intensive learning period. *Sleep, 14* (4), 325–330.

Smith, David E., & Seymour, Richard B. (1994). LSD: History and toxicity. *Psychiatric Annals, 24*, 145–147.

Smith, Eliot R. (1993). Social identity and social emotions: Toward new conceptualizations of prejudice. In Diane M. Mackie & David L. Hamilton (Eds.), *Affect, cognition, and stereotyping: Interactive processes in group perception*. San Diego: Academic Press.

Smith, Marilyn C. (1983). Hypnotic memory enhancement of witnesses: Does it work? *Psychological Bulletin, 94* (3), 387–407.

Smith, S. M.; Glenberg, A. M.; & Bjork, R. A. (1978). Environmental context and human memory. *Memory and Cognition, 6*, 342–355.

Smith, Timothy W. (1992). Hostility and health: Current status of a psychosomatic hypothesis. *Health Psychology, 11*, 139–150.

Snyder, Solomon H. (1986). *Drugs and the brain*. New York: Scientific American Books.

Snyder, Solomon H. (1990, August 9). Planning for serendipity. *Nature, 346,* 508.

Snyderman, Mark, & Rothman, Stanley. (1987). Survey of expert opinion on intelligence and aptitude testing. *American Psychologist, 42,* 137–144.

Snyderman, Mark, & Rothman, Stanley. (1988). *The IQ controversy, the media, and public policy.* New Brunswick, N.J.: Transaction Books.

Solomon, George F.; Amkraut, Alfred A.; & Rubin, Robert T. (1985). Stress, hormones, neuroregulation, and immunity. In Susan R. Birchfield (Ed.), *Stress: Psychological and physiological interactions.* Washington, D.C.: Hemisphere.

Solomon, Henry; Solomon, Linda Zener; Arnone, Maria M.; Maur, Bonnie J.; Reda, Rosina M.; & Roth, Esther O. (1981). Anonymity and helping. *Journal of Social Psychology, 113,* 37–43.

Solomon, Linda Zener; Solomon, Henry; & Stone, Ronald. (1978). Helping as a function of number of bystanders and ambiguity of emergency. *Personality and Social Psychology Bulletin, 4,* 318–321.

Solso, Robert L. (1991). *Cognitive psychology* (3rd ed.). Boston: Allyn & Bacon.

Spangler, William D. (1992). Validity of questionnaire and TAT measures of need for achievement: Two meta-analyses. *Psychological Bulletin, 112,* 140–154.

Spanos, Nicholas P. (1986). Hypnotic behavior: A social-psychological interpretation of amnesia, analgesia, and "trance logic." *The Behavioral and Brain Sciences, 9,* 449–502.

Spanos, Nicholas P. (1987–1988, Winter). Past-life hypnotic regression: A critical view. *Skeptical Inquirer, 12,* 174–180.

Spanos, Nicholas P. (1989). Hypnosis, demonic possession, and multiple personality: Strategic enactments and disavowals of responsibility for actions. In Colleen A. Ward (Ed.), *Altered states of consciousness and mental health: A cross-cultural perspective.* Newbury Park, Calif.: Sage.

Spanos, Nicholas P. (1994). Multiple identity enactments and multiple personality disorder: A sociocognitive perspective. *Psychological Bulletin, 116,* 143–165.

Spanos, Nicholas P.; Brett, P. J.; Menary, E. P.; & Cross, W. P. (1987). A measure of attitudes toward hypnosis: Relationships with absorption and hypnotic susceptibility. *American Journal of Clinical Hypnosis, 30,* 139–150.

Spanos, Nicholas P.; Burnley, Caroline E.; & Cross, Patricia A. (1993). Response expectancies and interpretations as determinants of hypnotic responding. *Journal of*

Personality and Social Psychology, 65, 1237–1242.

Spearman, Charles E. (1904). "General intelligence" objectively determined and measured. *American Journal of Psychology, 15,* 201–293.

Spence, Sean A. (1993). Nintendo hallucinations: A new phenomenological entity. *Irish Journal of Psychological Medicine, 10,* 98–99.

Sperling, George. (1960). The information available in brief visual presentations. *Psychological Monographs, 74* (Whole No. 48).

Sperry, Roger W. (1982). Some effects of disconnecting the cerebral hemispheres. *Science, 217,* 1223–1226.

Spiegel, David. (1993a). Dissociation and trauma. In David Spiegel (Ed.), *Dissociative disorders: A clinical review.* Lutherville, Md.: Sidran.

Spiegel, David. (1993b). Social support: How friends, family, and groups can help. In Daniel Goleman & Joel Gurin (Eds.), *Mind/body medicine: How to use your mind for better health.* Yonkers, N.Y.: Consumer Reports Books.

Spiegel, David; Bloom, J. R.; Kraemer, H. C.; & Gottheil, E. (1989). Effect of psychosocial treatment on survival of patients with metastatic breast cancer. *Lancet, 2,* 888–891.

Spiegel, David, & Cardeña, Etzel. (1991). Disintegrated experience: The dissociative disorders revisited. *Journal of Abnormal Psychology, 100,* 366–378.

Spielberger, Charles D., & Starr, Laura M. (1994). Curiosity and exploratory behavior. In Harold F. O'Neil, Jr., & Michael Drillings (Eds.), *Motivation: Theory and research.* Hillsdale, N.J.: Erlbaum.

Spielman, Arthur J., & Glovinsky, Paul B. (1991). Psychology and sleep: The interdependence of sleep and waking states. In Michael J. Thorpy & Jan Yager (Eds.), *The encyclopedia of sleep and sleep disorders.* New York: Facts on File.

Spiro, Rand J. (1980). Accommodative reconstruction in prose recall. *Journal of Verbal Learning and Verbal Behavior, 19,* 84–95.

Spitzer, Manfred. (1992). The phenomenology of delusions. *Psychiatric Annals, 22,* 252–259.

Springer, Sally P., & Deutsch, Georg. (1993). *Left brain, right brain* (4th ed.). New York: Freeman.

Squire, Larry R. (1987). *Memory and the brain.* New York: Oxford University Press.

Squire, Larry R., & Butters, Nelson. (1992). *Neuropsychology of memory.* New York: Guilford Press.

Squire, Larry R., & Knowlton, Barbara J. (1995). Memory, hippocampus, and brain systems. In Michael S. Gazzaniga (Ed.), *The cognitive neurosciences.* Cambridge, Mass.: MIT Press.

Squire, Larry R.; Knowlton, Barbara J.; & Musen, G. (1993). The structure and organization of memory. *Annual Review of Psychology, 44,* 453–495.

Squire, Larry R.; Ojemann, J. G.; Miezin, F. M.; Petersen, S. E.; Videen, T. O.; & Raichle, Marcus E. (1992). Activation of the hippocampus in normal humans: A functional anatomical study of memory. *Proceedings of the National Academy of Sciences, USA, 89,* 1837–1841.

Sroufe, Alan. (1995, September). Quoted in Beth Azar, The bond between mother and child. *APA Monitor, 26* (9), 28.

Stacy, Alan W.; Widaman, Keith F.; & Marlatt, G. Alan. (1990). Expectancy models of alcohol use. *Journal of Personality and Social Psychology, 58,* 918–928.

Staddon, J. E. R. (1988). Learning as inference. In Robert C. Bolles & Michael D. Beecher (Eds.), *Evolution and learning.* Hillsdale, N.J.: Erlbaum.

Stafford, Laura, & Dainton, Marianne. (1994). The dark side of "normal" family interaction. In William R. Cupach & Brian H. Spitzberg (Eds.), *The dark side of interpersonal communication.* Hillside, N.J.: Erlbaum.

Stangor, Charles, & Lange, James E. (1994). Mental representations of social groups: Advances in understanding stereotypes and stereotyping. In Mark P. Zanna (Ed.), *Advances in experimental social psychology* (Vol. 26). San Diego: Academic Press.

Stanton, Annette L., & Snider, Pamela R. (1993). Coping with a breast cancer diagnosis: A prospective study. *Health Psychology, 12,* 16–23.

Stanton, H. E. (1989). Using rapid change techniques to improve sporting performance. *Australian Journal of Clinical & Experimental Hypnosis, 17* (2), 153–161.

Steblay, Nancy Mehrkens. (1987). Helping behavior in urban and rural environments: A meta-analysis. *Psychological Bulletin, 102,* 346–356.

Steele, Claude M. (1986, January). What happens when you drink too much? *Psychology Today, 20,* 48–52.

Steele, Claude M. (1997). A threat in the air: How stereotypes shape intellectual identity and performance. *American Psychologist, 52,* 613–629.

Steele, Claude M., & Aronson, Joshua. (1995). Stereotype threat and the intellectual performance of African Americans.

Journal of Personality and Social Psychology, 69, 797–811.

Steele, Claude M., & Josephs, Robert A. (1990). Alcohol myopia: Its prized and dangerous effects. *American Psychologist, 45,* 921–933.

Stein, Marvin, & Miller, Andrew H. (1993). Stress, the immune system, and health and illness. In Leo Goldberger & Shlomo Breznitz (Eds.), *Handbook of stress: Theoretical and clinical aspects.* New York: Free Press.

Steinberg, Laurence. (1990). Autonomy, conflict, and harmony in the family relationship. In S. Shirley Feldman & Glen R. Elliott (Eds.), *At the threshold: The developing adolescent.* Cambridge, Mass.: Harvard University Press.

Steinberg, Laurence; Darling, Nancy E.; Fletcher, Anne C; Brown, Bradford B.; & Dornbusch, Sanford M. (1995). Authoritative parenting and adolescent adjustment: An ecological journey. In Phyllis Moen, Glen H. Elder, Jr., & Kurt Luscher (Eds.), *Examining lives in context: Perspectives on the ecology of human development.* Washington, D.C.: American Psychological Association.

Steinhausen, Hans-Christoph. (1994). Anorexia and bulimia nervosa. In Michael Rutter, Eric Taylor, & Lionel Hersov (Eds.), *Child and adolescent psychiatry: Modern approaches.* Boston: Blackwell Scientific Publications.

Steinhausen, Hans-Christoph, & Seidel, R. (1993). Correspondence between the clinical assessment of eating-disordered patients and findings derived from questionnaires at follow-up. *International Journal of Eating Disorders, 14,* 367–379.

Steinhausen, Hans-Christoph, & Vollrath, M. (1993). The self-image of adolescent patients with eating disorders. *International Journal of Eating Disorders, 13,* 221–229.

Stenberg, C. R., & Campos, J. J. (1990). The development of anger expressions in infancy. In Nancy Stein, Bennett Leventhal, & Tom Trabasso (Eds.), *Psychological and biological approaches to emotion.* Hillsdale, N.J.: Erlbaum.

Stern, Marilyn, & Karraker, Katherine Hildebrandt. (1989). Sex stereotyping of infants: A review of gender labelling studies. *Sex Roles, 20,* 501–522.

Sternberg, Robert J. (1982). Lies we live by: Misapplication of tests in identifying the gifted. *Gifted Child Quarterly, 26,* 157–161.

Sternberg, Robert J. (1985). *Beyond IQ: A triarchic theory of human intelligence.* New York: Cambridge University Press.

Sternberg, Robert J. (1986). *Intelligence applied: Understanding and increasing your intellectual skills.* San Diego: Harcourt Brace Jovanovich.

Sternberg, Robert J. (1988). *The triarchic mind: A new theory of human intelligence.* New York: Viking.

Sternberg, Robert J. (1990). *Metaphors of mind: Conceptions of the nature of intelligence.* New York: Cambridge University Press.

Sternberg, Robert J. (1991). Theory-based testing of intellectual abilities: Rationale for the Triarchic Abilities Test. In Helga A. H. Rowe (Ed.), *Intelligence: Reconceptualization and measurement.* Hillsdale, N.J.: Erlbaum.

Sternberg, Robert J. (1995). For whom the bell curve tolls: A review of *The Bell Curve. Psychological Science, 6,* 257–261.

Sternberg, Robert J. (1997). What does it mean to be smart? *Educational Leadership, 54,* 20–24.

Stevens, A. (1983). *Archetypes.* New York: Quill.

Stevens, Gwendolyn, & Gardner, Sheldon. (1982). *The women of psychology: Vol. 1. Pioneers and innovators.* Cambridge, Mass.: Schenkman.

Stevenson, Harold W., & Lee, Shin-Ying. (1990). Contexts of achievement: A study of American, Chinese, and Japanese children. *Monographs of the Society for Research in Child Development, 55* (Serial No. 221, Nos. 1–2).

Stevenson, Harold W.; Lee, Shin-Ying; & Stigler, James W. (1986). Mathematics achievements of Chinese, Japanese, and American children. *Science, 236,* 693–698.

Stevenson, Harold L., & Stigler, James. (1992). *The learning gap: Why our schools are failing and what we can learn from Japanese and Chinese education.* New York: Summit Books.

Stewart, V. M. (1973). Tests of the "carpentered world" hypothesis by race and environment in America and Zambia. *International Journal of Psychology, 8,* 83–94.

Stillings, Neil A.; Feinstein, Mark H.; Garfield, Jay L.; Rissland, Edwina L.; Rosenbaum, David A.; Weisler, Steven E.; and Baker-Ward, Lynne. (1987). *Cognitive science: An introduction.* Cambridge, Mass.: MIT Press.

Stillion, Judith M.; McDowell, Eugene E.; & May, Jacque H. (1989). *Suicide across the life span: Premature exits.* New York: Hemisphere.

Stone, Arthur A.; Cox, Donald S.; Valdimarsdottir, Heiddis; Jandorf, Lina; & Neale, John M. (1987). Evidence that secretory IgA antibody is associated with daily mood. *Journal of Personality and Social Psychology, 52,* 988–993.

Stone, Arthur A.; Neale, John M.; Cox, Donald S.; Napoli, Anthony; Valdimarsdottir, Heiddis; & Kennedy-Moore, Eileen. (1994). Daily events are associated with a secretory immune response to an oral antigen in men. *Health Psychology, 13,* 440–446.

Strack, Fritz; Martin, Leonard L.; & Stepper, Sabine. (1988). Inhibiting and facilitating conditions of the human smile: A non-obtrusive test of the facial-feedback hypothesis. *Journal of Personality and Social Psychology, 54,* 768–777.

Street, Warren R. (1994). *A chronology of noteworthy events in American psychology.* Washington, D.C.: American Psychological Association.

Strickland, Bonnie R. (1995). Research on sexual orientation and human development: A commentary. *Developmental Psychology, 31,* 137–140.

Stromswold, Karin. (1995). The cognitive and neural bases of language acquisition. In Michael S. Gazzaniga (Ed.), *The cognitive neurosciences.* Cambridge, Mass.: MIT Press.

Strupp, Hans H. (1996). The tripartite model and the *Consumer Reports* study. *American Psychologist, 51,* 1017–1024.

Stuart, Richard B., & Davis, Barbara. (1972). *Slim chance in a fat world.* Champaign, Ill.: Research Press.

Stunkard, A. J.; Sorensen, T. I. A.; Hanis, C.; Teasdale, T. W.; Chakraborty, R.; Skull, W. J.; & Schulsinger, F. (1986). An adoption study of human obesity. *New England Journal of Medicine, 314,* 193–198.

Styron, William. (1990). *Darkness visible: A memoir of madness.* New York: Vintage.

Sue, David; Sue, Derald; & Sue, Stanley. (1994). *Understanding abnormal behavior* (4th ed.). Boston: Houghton Mifflin.

Sue, David; Sue, Derald; & Sue, Stanley. (1997). *Understanding abnormal behavior* (5th ed.). Boston: Houghton Mifflin.

Sue, Stanley; Zane, Nolan; & Young, Kathleen. (1994). Research on psychotherapy with culturally diverse populations. In Allen E. Bergin & Sol L. Garfield (Eds.), *Handbook of psychotherapy and behavior change* (4th ed.). New York: Wiley.

Suess, G. J.; Grossmann, K. E.; & Sroufe, L. Alan. (1992). Effects of infant attachment to mother and father on quality of adaptation in preschool: From dyadic to individual organisation of self. *International Journal of Behavioral Development, 15* (1), 43–65.

Sumerlin, J. R., & Norman, R. L. (1992). Self-actualization and homeless men: A known-groups examination of Maslow's hierarchy of needs. *Journal of Social Behavior and Personality, 7,* 469–481.

Super, Donald E. (1990). Career and life development. In Duane Brown, Linda Brooks, & Associates (Eds.), *Career choice and development: Applying contemporary theories to practice.* San Francisco: Jossey-Bass.

Sutker, Patricia B.; Uddo, Madeline; Brailey, Kevin; Vasterling, Jennifer J.; & Errara, Paul. (1994). Psychopathology in war-zone deployed and nondeployed Operation Desert Storm troops assigned graves registration duties. *Journal of Abnormal Psychology, 103,* 383–390.

Swann, William B. (1984). Quest for accuracy in person perception: A matter of pragmatics. *Psychological Review, 91,* 457–477.

Swim, Janet K. (1994). Perceived versus meta-analytic effect sizes: An assessment of the accuracy of gender stereotypes. *Journal of Personality and Social Psychology, 66,* 21–36.

Syvälahti, E. K. G. (1994). Biological factors in schizophrenia: Structural and functional aspects. *British Journal of Psychiatry, 164* (Suppl. 23), 9–14.

Szasz, Thomas. (1988). *The myth of psychotherapy: Mental healing as religion, rhetoric, and repression.* Syracuse, N.Y.: Syracuse University Press.

Taft, Lois B., & Nehrke, Milton F. (1990). Reminiscence, life review, and ego integrity in nursing home residents. *International Journal of Aging and Human Development, 30,* 189–196.

Takei, Noriyoshi; Sham, Pak; O'Callaghan, Eadbhard; Murray, Graham K.; Glover, Gyles; & Murray, Robin M. (1994). Prenatal exposure to influenza and the development of schizophrenia: Is the effect confined to females? *American Journal of Psychiatry, 151,* 117–119.

Takeuchi, Tomoka; Miyasita, A.; Sasaki, Y.; & Inugami, M. (1992). Isolated sleep paralysis elicited by sleep interruption. *Sleep, 15,* 217–225.

Tanford, Sarah, & Penrod, Steven. (1984). Social influence model: A formal integration of research on majority and minority influence processes. *Psychological Bulletin, 95,* 189–225.

Tannen, Deborah. (1990). *You just don't understand: Women and men in conversation.* New York: Ballantine.

Tart, Charles T. (1979). Measuring the depth of an altered state of consciousness, with particular reference to self-report scales of hypnotic depth. In Erika Fromm & Ronald E. Shor (Eds.), *Hypnosis: Developments in research and new perspectives* (2nd ed.). New York: Aldine.

Tart, Charles T. (Ed.). (1990). *Altered states of consciousness* (3rd ed.). San Francisco: HarperCollins.

Tart, Charles T. (1994). *Living the mindful life: A handbook for living in the present moment.* Boston: Shambhala.

Taylor, Donald M., & Porter, Lana E. (1994). A multicultural view of stereotyping. In Walter J. Lonner & Roy Malpass (Eds.), *Psychology and culture.* Boston: Allyn & Bacon.

Taylor, Shelley. (1989). *Positive illusions: Creative self-deceptions and the healthy mind.* New York: Basic Books.

Taylor, Shelley E. (1995). *Health psychology* (3rd ed.). New York: McGraw-Hill.

Taylor, Shelley, & Aspinwall, Lisa G. (1993). Coping with chronic illness. In Leo Goldberger & Shlomo Breznitz (Eds.), *Handbook of stress: Theoretical and clinical aspects* (2nd ed.). New York: Free Press.

Taylor, Shelley E.; Helgeson, Vicki S.; Reed, Geoffrey M.; & Skokan, Laurie A. (1991). Self-generated feelings of control and adjustment to physical illness. *Journal of Social Issues, 47,* 91–109.

Terman, Lewis M. (1916). *Measurement of intelligence.* Boston: Houghton Mifflin.

Terman, Lewis M. (1926). *Genetic studies of genius: Vol. I. Mental and physical traits of a thousand gifted children* (2nd ed.). Stanford, Calif.: Stanford University Press.

Terman, Lewis M., & Oden, Melita H. (1947). *Genetic studies of genius: Vol. 4. The gifted child grows up: Twenty-five years' follow-up of a superior group.* Stanford, Calif.: Stanford University Press.

Terman, Lewis M., & Oden, Melita H. (1959). *Genetic studies of genius: Vol. 5. The gifted at mid-life: Thirty-five years' follow-up of the superior child.* Stanford, Calif.: Stanford University Press.

Thomas, Alexander, & Chess, Stella. (1977). *Temperament and development.* New York: Brunner/Mazel.

Thomas, Alexander, & Chess, Stella. (1980). *The dynamics of psychological development.* New York: Brunner/Mazel.

Thomas, Alexander, & Chess, Stella. (1986). The New York Longitudinal Study: From infancy to early adult life. In Robert Plomin & Judith Dunn (Eds.), *The study of temperament: Changes, continuities, and challenges.* Hillsdale, N.J.: Erlbaum.

Thompson, Clara. (1950/1973). Some effects of the derogatory attitude toward female sexuality. In Jean Baker Miller (Ed.), *Psychoanalysis and women.* Baltimore: Penguin Books.

Thompson, Richard F. (1993). *The brain: A neuroscience primer* (2nd ed.). New York: Freeman.

Thompson, Richard F. (1994). Behaviorism and neuroscience. *Psychological Review, 101,* 259–265.

Thompson, Ross A. (1986). Temperament, emotionality, and infant social cognition. In Jacqueline V. Lerner & Richard M. Lerner (Eds.), *Temperament and social interaction in infants and children.* New Directions for Child Development, No. 31. San Francisco: Jossey-Bass.

Thompson, Suzanne C.; Nanni, Christopher; & Levine, Alexandra. (1994). Primary versus secondary and central versus consequence-related control in HIV-positive men. *Journal of Personality and Social Psychology, 67,* 540–547.

Thompson, Suzanne C., & Spacapan, Shirlynn. (1991). Perceptions of control in vulnerable populations. *Journal of Social Issues, 47,* 1–21.

Thorndike, Edward L. (1898). Animal intelligence: An experimental study of the associative processes in animals. *Psychological Review Monograph Supplement, 2* (Serial No. 8).

Thorndike, Edward L. (1911). *Animal intelligence.* New York: Macmillan.

Thorne, Barrie. (1986). Girls and boys together, but mostly apart. In Willard W. Hartup & Zick Rubin (Eds.), *Relationships and development.* Hillsdale, N.J.: Erlbaum.

Thorne, Barrie, & Luria, Zella. (1986). Sexuality and gender in children's daily worlds. *Social Problems, 33,* 176–190.

Thornton, Bill. (1992). Repression and its mediating influence on the defensive attribution of responsibility. *Journal of Research in Personality, 26,* 44–57.

Thorpy, Michael J. (1991). History of sleep and man. In Michael J. Thorpy & Jan Yager (Eds.), *The encyclopedia of sleep and sleep disorders.* New York: Facts on File.

Thorpy, Michael J., & Yager, Jan (Eds.). (1991). *The encyclopedia of sleep and sleep disorders.* New York: Facts on File.

Thurgood, Delores H., & Clarke, Julie E. (1995). *Summary report 1993: Doctoral recipients from United States universities.* Washington, D.C.: National Academy Press, National Research Council Office of Scientific and Engineering Personnel.

Thurstone, Louis L. (1937). *Primary mental abilities.* Chicago: University of Chicago Press.

Tienari, Pekka. (1991). Interaction between genetic vulnerability and family environment: The Finnish Adoptive Family

Study of Schizophrenia. *Acta Psychiatrica Scandinavica, 84,* 460–465.

Tienari, Pekka; Sorri, Anneli; Lahti, Ilpo; Naarala, Mikko; Wahlberg, Karl-Erik; Moring, Juha; Pohjola, Jukka; & Wynne, Lyman C. (1987). Genetic and psychosocial factors in schizophrenia: The Finnish Adoptive Family Study. *Schizophrenia Bulletin, 13,* 477–484.

Tienari, Pekka; Wynne, Lyman C.; Moring, Juha; Lahti, Ilpo; Naarala, Mikko; Sorri, Anneli; Wahlberg, Karl-Erik; Saarento, Outi; Seitamaa, Markku; Kaleva, Merja; & Läksy, Kristian. (1994). The Finnish Adoptive Family Study of Schizophrenia: Implications for family research. *British Journal of Psychiatry, 164* (Suppl.), 20–26.

Tizard, Ian. (1992). *Immunology: An introduction* (3rd ed). Philadelphia: Saunders.

Todd, James T., & Morris, Edward K. (1992). Case histories in the great power of steady misrepresentation. *American Psychologist, 47,* 1441–1453.

Todes, Daniel P. (1997). From the machine to the ghost within: Pavlov's transition from digestive physiology to conditional reflexes. *American Psychologist, 52,* 947–955.

Tolman, Edward C. (1932). *Purposive behavior in animals and men.* New York: Appleton-Century-Crofts.

Tolman, Edward C. (1948). Cognitive maps in rats and men. *Psychological Review, 55,* 189–208.

Tolman, Edward C., & Honzik, C. H. (1930a). "Insight" in rats. *University of California Publications in Psychology, 4,* 215–232.

Tolman, Edward C., & Honzik, C. H. (1930b). Introduction and removal of reward, and maze performance in rats. *University of California Publications in Psychology, 4,* 257–275.

Tolman, Edward C.; Ritchie, B. F.; & Kalish, D. (1946/1992). Studies in spatial learning. I. Orientation and the short-cut. *Journal of Experimental Psychology: General, 121,* 429–434.

Tomaka, Joe; Blascovich, Jim; Kelsey, Robert M.; & Leitten, Christopher L. (1993). Subjective, physiological, and behavioral effects of threat and challenge appraisal. *Journal of Personality and Social Psychology, 65,* 248–260.

Tomb, David A. (1994). The phenomenology of post-traumatic stress disorder. *Psychiatric Clinics of North America, 17,* 237–250.

Torgersen, S. (1990). Genetics of anxiety and its clinical implications. In Graham D. Burrows, Martin Roth, & Russell Noyes, Jr. (Eds.), *Handbook of anxiety: Vol. 3.*

The neurobiology of anxiety. Amsterdam: Elsevier.

Torrey, E. Fuller. (1991). A viral-anatomical explanation of schizophrenia. *Schizophrenia Bulletin, 17,* 15–18.

Torrey, E. Fuller. (1992). Are we overestimating the genetic contribution to schizophrenia? *Schizophrenia Bulletin, 18,* 159–170.

Torrey, E. Fuller; Bowler, Ann E.; Rawlings, Robert; & Terrazas, Alejandro. (1993). Seasonality of schizophrenia and stillbirths. *Schizophrenia Bulletin, 19,* 557–562.

Torrey, E. Fuller; Bowler, Ann E.; Taylor, Edward H.; & Gottesman, Irving I. (1994). *Schizophrenia and manic-depressive disorder: The biological roots of mental illness as revealed by the landmark study of identical twins.* New York: Basic Books.

Triandis, Harry C. (1994). *Culture and social behavior.* New York: McGraw-Hill.

Triandis, Harry C. (1996). The psychological measurement of cultural syndromes. *American Psychologist, 51,* 407–415.

Trimble, Joseph E. (1994). Cultural variations in the use of alcohol and drugs. In Walter J. Lonner & Roy Malpass (Eds.), *Psychology and culture.* Boston: Allyn & Bacon.

Tsuang, Ming T., & Faraone, Stephen V. (1990). *The genetics of mood disorders.* Baltimore: Johns Hopkins University Press.

Tulving, Endel. (1983). *Elements of episodic memory.* Oxford: Clarendon Press/Oxford University Press.

Tulving, Endel. (1985). How many memory systems are there? *American Psychologist, 40,* 385–398.

Tulving, Endel. (1995). Organization of memory: *Quo vadis?* In Michael S. Gazzaniga (Ed.), *The cognitive neurosciences.* Cambridge, Mass.: MIT Press.

Turk, Dennis C. (1994, April). Perspectives on chronic pain: The role of psychological factors. *Current Directions in Psychological Science, 3* (2), 45–48.

Turk, Dennis C.; Meichenbaum, Donald; & Genest, Myles. (1983). *Pain and behavioral medicine: A cognitive-behavioral perspective.* New York: Guilford Press.

Turk, Dennis C., & Nash, Justin M. (1993). Chronic pain: New ways to cope. In Daniel Goleman & Joel Gurin (Eds.), *Mind/body medicine: How to use your mind for better health.* Yonkers, N.Y.: Consumer Reports Books.

Turk, Dennis C., & Rudy, Thomas E. (1992). Cognitive factors and persistent pain: A glimpse into Pandora's box. *Cognitive Therapy and Research, 16* (2), 99–122.

Turner, Patricia J., & Gervai, Judit. (1995). A multidimensional study of gender typing in preschool children and their parents: Personality, attitudes, preferences, behavior, and cultural differences. *Developmental Psychology, 31,* 759–772.

Turner, Terence J., & Ortony, Andrew. (1992). Basic emotions: Can conflicting criteria converge? *Psychological Review, 99,* 566–571.

Tversky, Amos. (1972). Elimination by aspects: A theory of choice. *Psychological Review, 80,* 281–299.

Tversky, Amos, & Kahneman, Daniel. (1982). Judgment under uncertainty: Heuristics and biases. In Daniel Kahneman, Paul Slovic, & Amos Tversky (Eds.), *Judgment under uncertainty: Heuristics and biases.* New York: Cambridge University Press.

Tversky, Amos, & Shafir, Eldar. (1992). Choice under conflict: The dynamics of deferred decision. *Psychological Science, 3,* 358–361.

Umberson, Debra; & Gove, Walter R. (1989). Parenthood and psychological well-being: Theory, measurement, and stage in the family life course. *Journal of Family Issues, 10,* 440–462.

Underwood, Geoffrey (Ed.). (1996). *Implicit cognition.* New York: Oxford University Press.

Unger, Rhoda K., & Crawford, Mary. (1996). *Women and gender: A feminist psychology* (2nd ed.). New York: McGraw-Hill.

U.S. Bureau of the Census. (1992). *Sixty-five plus in America* (Current Population Reports, Special Studies, Series P-23, No. 178). Washington, D.C.: U. S. Government Printing Office.

U. S. Bureau of the Census. (1995). *Statistical abstract of the United States: 1995* (115th ed.). Washington, D.C.: U. S. Government Printing Office.

U.S. National Center for Health Statistics. (1990). *Vital and health statistics* (Series 10). Washington, D.C.: U.S. Government Printing Office.

Uttal, William R. (1981). *A taxonomy of visual processes.* Hillsdale, N.J.: Erlbaum.

Vandell, Deborah Lowe, & Corasaniti, Mary Ann. (1990). Child care and the family: Complex contributors to child development. In Kathleen McCartney (Ed.), *Child care and maternal employment: A social ecology approach* (New Directions for Child Development, No. 49). San Francisco: Jossey-Bass.

van den Boom, Dymphna C., & Hoeksma, Jan B. (1994). The effect of infant irritability on mother–infant interaction: A growth-curve analysis. *Developmental Psychology, 30,* 581–590.

Vanderlinden, Johan; Van Dyck, Richard; Vandereycken, Walter; & Vertommen, Hans. (1991). Dissociative experiences in the general population in the Netherlands and Belgium: A study with the Dissociative Questionnaire (DIS-Q). *Dissociation, 4,* 180–184.

Van Egmond, Marjan; Garnefski, Nadia; Jonker, Daan; & Kerkhof, Ad. (1993). The relationship between sexual abuse and female suicidal behavior. *Crisis, 14,* 129–139.

Venables, Peter H. (1996). Schizotypy and maternal exposure to influenza and to cold temperature: The Mauritius study. *Journal of Abnormal Psychology, 105,* 53–60.

Vernberg, Eric M.; La Greca, Annette M.; Silverman, Wendy K.; & Prinstein, Mitchell J. (1996). Prediction of posttraumatic stress symptoms in children after Hurricane Andrew. *Journal of Abnormal Psychology, 105,* 237–248.

Vitkovic, Ljubisa. (1995). Neuroimmunology and neurovirology. In Stephen H. Koslow (Ed.), *The neuroscience of mental health II: A report on neuroscience research: Status and potential for mental health and mental illness* (NIMH Publication No. 95–4000). Rockville, Md.: National Institute of Mental Health.

Volkow, N. D.; Wang, G. J.; Fischman, M. W.; Foltin, R. W.; Fowler, J. S.; Abumrad, N. N.; Vitkun, S.; Logan, J.; Gatley, S. J.; Pappas, N.; Hitzemann, R.; & Shea, C. E. (1997, April 24). Relationship between subjective effects of cocaine and dopamine transporter occupancy. *Nature, 386,* 827–830.

Vygotsky, Lev S. (1978). *Mind in society: The development of higher psychological processes.* Edited by Michael Cole, Vera John-Steiner, Sylvia Scribner, & Ellen Souberman. Cambridge, Mass.: Harvard University Press.

Vygotsky, Lev S. (1987). *Thinking and speech* (Translated by Norris Minick). New York: Plenum.

Wadsworth, Barry J. (1996). *Piaget's theory of cognitive and affective development: Foundations of constructivism* (5th ed.). White Plains, N.Y.: Longman.

Wagner, Shlomo; Castel, Mona; Gainer, Harold; & Yarom, Yosef. (1997, June 5). GABA in the mammalian suprachiasmatic nucleus and its role in diurnal rhythmicity. *Nature, 387,* 598–603.

Wald, George. (1964). The receptors of human color vision. *Science, 145,* 1007–1017.

Waldman, Irwin D.; Weinberg, Richard A.; & Scarr, Sandra. (1994). Racial group differences in IQ in the Minnesota Transracial Adoption Study: A reply to Levin and Lynn. *Intelligence, 18,* 29–44.

Walker, Lawrence J. (1989). A longitudinal study of moral reasoning. *Child Development, 60,* 157–166.

Wallace, B., & Persanyi, M. W. (1989). Hypnotic susceptibility and familial handedness. *Journal of General Psychology, 116* (4), 345–350.

Wallace, R. K. (1987). *The Maharishi technology of the unified field: The neurophysiology of enlightenment.* Fairfield, Iowa: MIU Press.

Wallach, Hans. (1987). Perceiving a stable environment when one moves. *Annual Review of Psychology, 38,* 1–27.

Wangensteen, O., & Carlson, A. (1931). Hunger sensation after total gastrectomy. *Proceedings of the Society for Experimental Biology, 28,* 545–547.

Ware, Jacqueline; Jain, Kumud; Burgess, Ian; & Davey, Graham C. L. (1994). Disease-avoidance model: Factor analysis of common animal fears. *Behaviour Research and Therapy, 32,* 57–63.

Warner, Virginia; Weissman, Myrna M.; Fendrich, Michael; Wickramaratne, Priya; & Moreau, Donna. (1992). The course of major depression in the offspring of depressed patients: Incidence, recurrence, and recovery. *Archives of General Psychiatry, 49,* 795–801.

Wasserman, Edward A. (1993). Comparative cognition: Beginning the second century of the study of animal intelligence. *Psychological Bulletin, 113,* 211–228.

Waterman, Alan S. (1985, December). Identity in the context of adolescent psychology. In Alan S. Waterman (Ed.), *Identity in adolescence: Processes and contents* (New Directions in Child Research Series, No. 30). San Francisco: Jossey-Bass.

Watson, David, & Clark, Lee Anna. (1994). Emotions, moods, traits, and temperaments: Conceptual distinctions and empirical findings. In Paul Ekman & Richard J. Davidson (Eds.), *The nature of emotion: Fundamental questions.* New York: Oxford University Press.

Watson, David, & Pennebaker, James W. (1989). Health complaints, stress, and distress: Exploring the central role of negative affectivity. *Psychological Review, 96,* 234–254.

Watson, D. L., & Tharp, R. G. (1985). Self-directed behavior: *Self-modification for per-sonal adjustment* (4th ed.). Monterey, Calif.: Brooks/Cole.

Watson, John B. (1913). Psychology as the behaviorist views it. *Psychological Review, 20,* 158–177.

Watson, John B. (1924). *Behaviorism.* New York: Norton.

Watson, John B. (1924/1970). *Behaviorism.* New York: Norton.

Watson, John B. (1930). *Behaviorism* (Rev. ed.). Chicago: University of Chicago Press.

Watson, John B., & Rayner, Rosalie. (1920). Conditioned emotional reactions. *Journal of Experimental Psychology, 3,* 1–14.

Watson, Robert I., & Evans, Rand B. (1991). *The great psychologists: A history of psychological thought.* New York: HarperCollins.

Weaver, Charles A., III. (1993). Do you need a "flash" to form a flashbulb memory? *Journal of Experimental Psychology: General, 122,* 39–46.

Webb, K., & Davey, Graham C. L. (1993). Disgust sensitivity and fear of animals: Effect of exposure to violent or revulsive material. *Anxiety, Coping and Stress, 5,* 329–335.

Webb, Wilse B. (1975). *Sleep: The gentle tyrant.* Englewood Cliffs, N.J.: Prentice Hall.

Webb, Wilse B. (1994). Sleep as a biological rhythm: A historical review. *Sleep, 17,* 188–194.

Wechsler, David. (1944). *The measurement of adult intelligence* (3rd ed.). Baltimore: Williams & Wilkins.

Wechsler, David. (1974). *Manual for the Wechsler Intelligence Scale for Children* (Rev.). New York: Psychological Corporation.

Wegner, Daniel M. (1989). *White bears and other unwanted thoughts: Suppression, obsession, and the psychology of mental control.* New York: Viking.

Wehr, Thomas A. (1988). Sleep and biological rhythms in affective illness. In David J. Kupler, Timothy H. Monk, & Jack D. Barchas (Eds.), *Biological rhythms and mental disorders.* New York: Guilford Press.

Weinberg, Richard A. (1989). Intelligence and IQ: Landmark issues and great debates. *American Psychologist, 44,* 98–104.

Weinberg, Richard A.; Scarr, Sandra; & Waldman, Irwin D. (1992). The Minnesota Transracial Adoption Study: A follow-up of IQ test performance at adolescence. *Intelligence, 16,* 117–135.

Weinberger, Daniel R. (1987). Implications of normal brain development for the pathogenesis of schizophrenia. *Archives of General Psychiatry, 44,* 660–669.

Weinberger, Daniel. (1995, June). Quoted in Joel L. Swerdlow, "Quiet miracles of the brain." *National Geographic, 187,* 2–41.

Weinberger, M.; Hiner, S. L.; & Tierney, W. M. (1987). In support of hassles as a measure of stress in predicting health outcomes. *Journal of Behavioral Medicine, 10,* 19–31.

Weinstein, Lissa N.; Schwartz, David G.; & Arkin, Arthur M. (1991). Qualitative aspects of sleep mentation. In Steven J. Ellman & John S. Antrobus (Eds.), *The mind in sleep: Psychology and psychophysiology* (2nd ed.). New York: Wiley.

Weisberg, Robert W. (1988). Problem solving and creativity. In Robert J. Sternberg (Ed.), *The nature of creativity.* New York: Cambridge University Press.

Weisberg, Robert W. (1993). *Creativity: Beyond the myth of genius.* New York: Freeman.

Weisse, Carol Silvia. (1992). Depression and immunocompetence: A review of the literature. *Psychological Bulletin, 111,* 475–489.

Weisz, John R.; Rothbaum, Fred M.; & Blackburn, Thomas C. (1984). Standing out and standing in: The psychology of control in Japan and America. *American Psychologist, 39,* 955–969.

Wells, Gary L. (1993). What do we know about eyewitness identification? *American Psychologist, 48,* 553–571.

Wells, Kenneth B.; Burnam, M. Audrey; Rogers, Williams; Hayes, Ron; & Camp, Patti. (1992). The course of depression in adult outpatients: Results from the Medical Outcomes Study. *Archives of General Psychiatry, 49,* 788–794.

Wenar, Charles. (1994). *Developmental psychopathology: From infancy through adolescence* (3rd ed.). New York: McGraw-Hill.

Werker, Janet, & Desjardins, Renee. (1995). Listening to speech in the 1st year of life: Experiential influences on phoneme production. *Current Directions in Psychological Science, 4,* 76–81.

Wertheimer, Max. (1912/1965). Experimentelle Studien über das Sehen von Bewegung. *Zeitschrift für Psychologie, 61,* 162–163, 221–227. Portions of original publication translated and reprinted in Richard J. Herrnstein & Edwin G. Boring (Eds.), *A source book in the history of psychology* (Translated by Don Cantor). Cambridge, Mass.: Harvard University Press.

Wertsch, James V., & Tulviste, Peeter. (1992). L. S. Vygotsky and contemporary developmental psychology. *Developmental Psychology, 28,* 548–557.

Wertsch, James V., & Tulviste, Peeter. (1994). Lev Semyonovich Vygotsky and contemporary developmental psychology. In Ross D. Parke, Peter A. Ornstein, John J. Rieser, & Carolyn Zahn-Waxler (Eds.), *A century of developmental psychology.* Washington, D.C.: American Psychological Association.

West, Michael A. (1987). Traditional and psychological perspectives on meditation. In Michael A. West (Ed.), *The psychology of meditation.* New York: Oxford University Press.

Westen, Drew. (1990). Psychoanalytic approaches to personality. In Lawrence A. Pervin (Ed.), *Handbook of personality: Theory and research.* New York: Guilford Press.

Wethington, Elaine; McLeod, Jane D.; & Kessler, Ronald C. (1987). The importance of life events for explaining sex differences in psychological distress. In Rosalind C. Barnett, Lois Biener, & Grace K. Baruch (Eds.), *Gender and stress.* New York: Free Press.

Wheeler, Anthony. (1990, Fall). Biological cycles and rhythms vs. biorhythms. *Skeptical Inquirer, 15,* 75–82.

White, Francis J. (1996). Synaptic regulation of mesocorticolimbic dopamine neurons. *Annual Review of Neuroscience, 19,* 405–436.

White, Robert W. (1959). Motivation reconsidered: The concepts of competence. *Psychological Review, 66,* 297–333.

Whitley, Bernard E., & Frieze, Irene H. (1985). Children's causal attributions for success and failure in achievement settings: A meta-analysis. *Journal of Educational Psychology, 77,* 608–616.

Whorf, Benjamin L. (1956). Science and linguistics. In J. B. Carroll (Ed.), *Language, thought, and reality: Selected papers of Benjamin Lee Whorf.* Cambridge, Mass.: MIT Press.

Whyte, Jamie, & Schaefer, Charles E. (1995). Introduction to sleep and its disorders. In Charles E. Schaefer (Ed.), *Clinical handbook of sleep disorders in children.* Northvale, N.J.: Aronson.

Wiedemann, Carl F. (1987). REM and non-REM sleep and its relation to nightmares and night terrors. In Henry Kellerman (Ed.), *The nightmare: Psychological and biological foundations.* New York: Columbia University Press.

Wilcoxon, Hardy C.; Dragoin, W. B.; & Kral, P. A. (1971). Illness-induced aversions in rat and quail: Relative salience of visual and gustatory cues. *Science, 171,* 826–828.

Wilkie, C. F., & Ames, E. W. (1986). The relationship of infant crying to parental stress in the transition to parenthood. *Journal of Marriage and the Family, 48,* 545–550.

Wilkinson, T. R. (1992). How fast should the night shift rotate? *Erogonomics, 35,* 1425–1446.

Williams, C. L., & Berry, John W. (1991). Primary prevention of acculturative stress among refugees. *American Psychologist, 46,* 632–641.

Williams, Martin H. (1992). Exploitation and inference: Mapping the damage from therapist–patient sexual involvement. *American Psychologist, 47,* 412–421.

Williams, Redford B. (1989). *The trusting heart: Great news about Type A behavior.* New York: Times Books/Random House.

Williams, Robert L.; Gökcebay, Nilgün; Hirshkowitz, Max; & Moore, Constance A. (1994). Ontogeny of sleep. In Rosemary Cooper (Ed.), *Sleep.* New York: Chapman & Hall.

Wilson, G. Terence, & Fairburn, Christopher G. (1993). Cognitive treatments for eating disorders. *Journal of Consulting and Clinical Psychology, 61,* 261–269.

Wilson, Mitchell. (1993). DSM-III and the transformation of American psychiatry: A history. *American Journal of Psychiatry, 150,* 399–410.

Windholz, George. (1990). Pavlov and the Pavlovians in the laboratory. *Journal of the History of the Behavioral Sciences, 26,* 64–73.

Windholz, George. (1997). Ivan P. Pavlov: An overview of his life and psychological work. *American Psychologist, 52,* 941–946.

Winokur, George; Coryell, William; Endicott, Jean; & Akiskal, Hapog. (1993). Further distinctions between manic-depressive illness (bipolar disorder) and primary depressive disorder (unipolar depression). *American Journal of Psychiatry, 150,* 1176–1181.

Winstead, Barbara A. (1986). Sex differences in same-sex friendships. In Valerian J. Derlega & Barbara A. Winstead (Eds.), *Friendship and social interaction.* New York: Springer-Verlag.

Wise, R. A. (1996). Addictive drugs and brain stimulation reward. *Annual Review of Neuroscience, 19,* 319–340.

Wolpe, Joseph. (1958). *Psychotherapy by reciprocal inhibition.* Stanford, Calif.: Stanford University Press.

Wolpe, Joseph. (1982). *The practice of behavior therapy.* New York: Pergamon.

Wolpe, Joseph & Plaud, Joseph J. (1997). Pavlov's contributions to behavior therapy: The obvious and the not so obvious. *American Psychologist, 52,* 966–972.

Wood, David. (1988). *How children think and learn.* New York: Blackwell.

Wood, James M., & Bootzin, Richard R. (1990). The prevalence of nightmares and their independence from anxiety. *Journal of Abnormal Psychology, 99* (1), 64–68.

Wood, Robert, & Bandura, Albert. (1991). Social cognitive theory of organizational management. In Richard M. Steers & Lyman W. Porter (Eds.), *Motivation and work behavior.* New York: McGraw-Hill.

Wood, Wendy. (1982). The retrieval of attitude-relevant information from memory: Effects on susceptibility to persuasion and on intrinsic motivation. *Journal of Personality and Social Psychology, 42,* 798–810.

Wood, Wendy; Rhodes, Nancy; & Biek, Michael. (1995). Working knowledge and attitude strength: An information-processing analysis. In Richard E. Petty & Jon A. Krosnick (Eds.), *Attitude strength: Antecedents and consequences.* Hillsdale, N.J.: Erlbaum.

Wood, Wendy; Rhodes, Nancy; & Whelan, Melanie. (1989). Sex differences in positive well-being: A consideration of emotional style and marital status. *Psychological Bulletin, 106,* 249–264.

Woodward, Amanda L.; Markman, Ellen M.; & Fitzsimmons, Colleen M. (1994). Rapid word learning in 13- and 18-month-olds. *Developmental Psychology, 30,* 553–566.

Woodworth, Robert S. (1958). *Dynamics of behavior.* New York: Holt.

Woody, Shelia R. (1996). Effects of focus of attention on anxiety levels and social performance of individuals with social phobia. *Journal of Abnormal Psychology, 105,* 61–69.

Worrall, Russell S. (1986). Iridology: Diagnosis or delusion? In Kendrick Frazier (Ed.), *Science confronts the paranormal.* Buffalo, N.Y.: Prometheus Books.

Wortman, Camille B.; Sheedy, Collette; Gluhoski, Vicki; & Kessler, Ron. (1992). Stress, coping, and health: Conceptual issues and directions for future research. In Howard S. Friedman (Ed.), *Hostility, coping, and health.* Washington, D.C.: American Psychological Association.

Wundt, Wilhelm. (1874). *Grundzüge der physiologischen Psychologie* (Principles of physiological psychology) (5th ed.). Leipzig, Germany: Engelmann. (English version published by Macmillan, New York, 1904.)

Wyatt, J. W.; Posey, A.; Welker, W.; & Seamonds, C. (1984). Natural levels of similarities between identical twins and between unrelated people. *Skeptical Inquirer, 9,* 62–66.

Yapko, Michael D. (1994a). Suggestibility and repressed memories of abuse: A survey of psychotherapists' beliefs. *American Journal of Clinical Hypnosis, 36,* 163–171.

Yapko, Michael D. (1994b). *Suggestions of abuse: True and false memories of childhood sexual trauma.* New York: Simon & Schuster.

Yarnell, Phillip R., & Lynch, Steve. (1970, April 25). Retrograde memory immediately after concussion. *Lancet, 1,* 863–865.

Youdim, Moussa B. H., & Riederer, Peter. (1997, January). Understanding Parkinson's disease. *Scientific American, 276,* 52–59.

Youngstrom, Nina. (1992, October). Training brings psychologists closer to prescribing drugs. *APA Monitor, 23,* 31.

Yu, Bolin; Zhang, W.; Jing, Qicheng; Peng, R.; Zhang, G.; & Simon, Herbert A. (1985). STM capacity for Chinese and English language materials. *Memory and Cognition, 13,* 202–207.

Zammit, Gary K. (1997). Delayed sleep phase syndrome and related conditions. In Mark R. Pressman & William C. Orr (Eds.), *Understanding sleep: The evaluation and treatment of sleep disorders.* Washington, D.C.: American Psychological Association.

Zgourides, George. (1996). *Human sexuality: Contemporary perspectives.* New York: HarperCollins.

Zhang, D.-M.; Bula, W.; & Stellar, E. (1986). Brain cholecystokinin as a satiety peptide. *Physiology and Behavior, 36,* 1183–1186.

Zimbardo, Philip G., & Leippe, Michael R. (1991). *The psychology of attitude change and social influence.* New York: McGraw-Hill.

Zimbardo, Philip G.; Weisenberg, Matisyohu; Firestone, Ira; & Levy, Burton. (1965). Communicator effectiveness in producing public conformity and private attitude change. *Journal of Personality, 33,* 233–256.

Zimring, Fred M., & Raskin, Nathaniel J. (1992). Carl Rogers and client/person-centered therapy. In Donald K. Freedheim (Ed.), *History of psychotherapy: A century of change.* Washington, D.C.: American Psychological Association.

Zinbarg, Richard E.; Barlow, David H.; Brown, Timothy; & Hertz, Robert M. (1992). Cognitive-behavioral approaches to the nature and treatment of anxiety disorders. *Annual Review of Psychology, 43,* 235–267.

Zisook, Sidney, & Shuchter, Stephen R. (1993). Uncomplicated bereavement. *Journal of Clinical Psychiatry, 54,* 365–372.

Zola-Morgan, Stuart, & Squire, Larry R. (1993). Neuroanatomy of memory. *Annual Review of Neuroscience, 16,* 547–563.

Zoltoski, Rebecca K., & Gillin, J. Christian. (1994). The neurochemistry of sleep. In Rosemary Cooper (Ed.), *Sleep.* New York: Chapman & Hall.

Zuckerman, Marvin. (1983). *Biological bases of sensation seeking, impulsivity, and anxiety.* Hillsdale, N.J.: Erlbaum.

Zuckerman, Marvin. (1990). Some dubious premises in research and theory on racial differences. *American Psychologist, 45,* 1297–1303.

Zuckerman, Marvin. (1994). *Behavioral expressions and biosocial bases of sensation seeking.* New York: Cambridge University Press.

Zuckerman, Marvin; Kuhlman, D. Michael; Joireman, Jeffrey; Teta, Paul; & Kraft, Michael. (1993) A comparison of three structural models for personality: The Big Three, the Big Five, and the Alternative Five. *Journal of Personality and Social Psychology, 65,* 757–768.

Zusne, Leonard; & Jones, Warren H. (1989). *Anomalistic psychology: A study of magical thinking* (2nd ed.). Hillsdale, N.J.: Erlbaum.

Zweig, Richard A., & Hinrichsen, Gregory A. (1993). Factors associated with suicide attempts by depressed older adults: A prospective study. *American Journal of Psychiatry, 150,* 1687–1692.

Illustration Credits

p. ii Howard Bingham

CHAPTER OPENERS

Phoebe Beasley is the artist who created the art used in the chapter openers.

Chapter 1: *Repeat Again, I Do Believe,* collage on acrylic, 16 × 40" (detail); **Chapter 2:** *Temporary Shelter,* collage on acrylic, 36 × 48" (detail); **Chapter 3:** *105 Countdown #2,* collage on acrylic, 30 × 40" (detail); **Chapter 4:** *Shaded Lives,* collage, 30 × 40" (detail); **Chapter 5:** *We're More Alike,* collage, 36 × 36"; **Chapter 6:** *His Grandmother's Quilt,* collage, 30 × 40", flopped; **Chapter 7:** *Yellow Legal Pad #2,* collage, 36 × 24" (detail); **Chapter 8:** *Love Lesson for All Seasons,* collage, 40 × 30" (detail); **Chapter 9:** *Fine China,* original hand-pulled serigraph, 26 × 31"; **Chapter 10:** *Two Generations,* collage, 30 × 40"; **Chapter 11:** *Precipitation,* collage, 30 × 40", collection of Louise Grantham (detail); **Chapter 12:** *In Resignation,* collage, 36 × 24", flopped; **Chapter 13:** *Absolution,* collage, 24 × 36" (detail), flopped; **Chapter 14:** *Training Ground #2,* collage, 48 × 24" (detail).

CHAPTER 1

p. 2 *(top)* Lana Tyree/Gamma-Liaison Network; *(left)* Steve Goch/The Daily Oklahoman/Saba; **p. 3** A. Glauberman/Photo Researchers, Inc.; **p. 4** Corbis-Bettmann; **p. 5** *(top)* and *(bottom)* Corbis-Bettmann; **p. 6** *(top)* Wellesley College Archives; *(left)* Culver Pictures; *(center)* Corbis-Bettmann; *(right)* Archives of the History of American Psychology, University of Akron; **p. 7** Stock Montage; **p. 8** *(top)* Courtesy Carl Rogers Memorial Library; *(bottom)* Courtesy of Brandeis University; **p. 10** Figaro Magahn/Photo Researchers, Inc.; **p. 12** Ralf-Finn Hestoff/Saba Press Images; **p. 15** Wayne Hoy/The Picture Cube; **Fig. 1.4** Leichtman, Michelle, & Ceci, Stephen J. (1995). "The Effects of Stereotypes and Suggestions on Preschoolers' Reports." *Developmental Psychology,* 31(4), 568–578. Copyright © 1995 by the American Psychological Association. Adapted with permission; **p. 23** Baron Hugo Van Lawick/National Geographic Society Image Collection; **p. 29** Beate Rettberg-Beck.

CHAPTER 2

p. 36 Ted Kawalerski/The Image Bank; **p. 41** Courtesy Tim Murphy and Gil Wier, The University of British Columbia; **p. 52** Dan McCoy/Rainbow; **p. 53** *(top)* Scott Camazine/Science Source/Photo Researchers, Inc.; *(right)* Hank Morgan/Science Source/Photo Researchers, Inc.; *(bottom)* Beringer-Dratch/The Picture Cube; *(a)* and *(b)* Courtesy Jordan Grafman, National Institute of Neurological Disorders & Stroke; **p. 55** Nestle/Petit Format/Science Source/Photo Researchers, Inc.; **p. 59** Martin M. Rotker; **p. 62** AP/Wide World Photos; **p. 63** © 1995, Newsweek, Inc. All Rights Reserved. Reprinted with permission. Photo by Douglas Levere.; **p. 66** Courtesy California Institute of Technology; **p. 67** Dan McCoy/Rainbow; **p. 69** Courtesy T. A. Jones and W. T. Greenough; **p. 70** Barlettani-Sestini/Gamma-Liaison Network.

CHAPTER 3

p. 77 Paul Conklin/Monkmeyer Press Photos; **p. 80** John Downer/Planet Earth Pictures; p. 82 From *Visions of Health—Understanding Iridology* by Bernard Jensen and Dr. Donald V. Bodeen. Avery Publishing Group; **p. 83** Lennart Nilsson/Bonnier Alba AB, *Behold Man;* Little, Brown & Co.; **p. 85** Jerome Wexler/Photo Researchers, Inc.; **p. 86** *(left)* and *(right)* Bob Daemmrich/Stock, Boston; **p. 90** Lennart Nilsson/Bonnier Alba AB, *Behold Man;* Little, Brown & Co.; **p. 93** Lennart Nilsson/Bonnier Alba AB, *Behold Man;* Little, Brown & Co.; **p. 95** Science Source/Photo Researchers, Inc.; **p. 96** W. Hill, Jr./The Image Works; **p. 97** Bruce Curtis/© 1996 The Walt Disney Co. Reprinted with permission of *Discover Magazine;* **p. 98** *(both)* Courtesy of the authors; **p. 100** Mike Caldwell/Tony Stone Images; **p. 101** *(top)* Superstock; *(center)* Steve McGurry/Magnum Photos; *(bottom)*

© Hiroshi Kunoh. This image was originally published in *3-D Planet* by Cadence Books, San Francisco; **p. 103** Globus Bros. Studios/The Stock Market; **Fig. 3.11** Barbara Landan and Ray Jackendoff (1993). "'What and where' in spatial languages and spatial cognition." *Behavioral and Brain Sciences, 16,* 217–265. Reprinted with the permission of Cambridge University Press; **p. 105** *(center)* Matlin, M. W. & Foley, H. J. (1992) *Sensation & Perception,* 3rd ed. Boston: Allyn & Bacon. Reprinted with permission.; **p. 105** *(a–d)* Photodisc; **p. 107** *(top)* Joel Meyerowitz; *(bottom)* Dick Ruhl; **p. 108** *(top)* and *(bottom)* Sol Mednick; **p. 109** *(left)* Esbin-Anderson/The Image Works; *(right)* Grantpix/Monkmeyer Press Photos.

CHAPTER 4

p. 119 Colin Molyneux/The Image Bank; **p. 122** PhotoDisc; **Box 4.1 figure** Terence Hines, "Biorhythms" in *The Encyclopedia of the Paranormal,* edited by Gordon Stein (Amherst, NY: Prometheus Books, 1996). © Gordon Stein, p. 126; **p. 124** Hank Morgan/Rainbow; **Figs. 4.1, 4.2, and 4.3** From: *Sleep* by J. Allan Hobson. Copyright © 1989 by J. Allan Hobson. Used with permission of W.H. Freeman and Company; **p. 127** *(all)* Estate of Ted Spagna; **p. 129** Lennart Nilsson/Bonnier Alba AB, *A Child Is Born,* Dell Publishing Company; **p. 131** *(right)* Michio Hoshino/Minden Pictures; *(left)* Stan Osolinski/Oxford Scientific Films/Animals Animals; **p. 133** The Granger Collection; **p. 140** News and Publications Service, Stanford University; **p. 141** Paul Avis/Gamma-Liaison Network; **p. 143** *(top)* John Giannini/Zuma Press; *(bottom)* Steve Satushek/The Image Bank; **p. 147** New York Newsday; **p. 148** Corbis-Bettmann; **Table 4.5** From: *A Primer of Drug Action 7/e* by Robert M. Julien. Copyright © 1995 by W. H. Freeman and Company. Used with permission; **p. 149** Greg Meadors/Stock, Boston; **p. 150** *(top)* The Granger Collection; *(bottom)* Kal Muller/Woodfin Camp & Associates.

CHAPTER 5

p. 159 Archives of the History of American Psychology, University of Akron; **p. 160** Stock Montage; **p. 164** Archives of the History of American Psychology, University of Akron; **p. 165** *(left)* Gaslight Advertising Archives; *(right)* Duke University, Special Collections Library; **p. 166** Yvonne Hemsey/Gamma-Liaison Network; **p. 168** *(top)* David Rae Morris/Impact Visuals; *(bottom)* Ed Malitsky/Gamma-Liaison Network; **p. 172** © 1996 Washington Post Writers Group; **p. 173** Nina Leen, LIFE magazine © Time Warner, Inc.; **p. 174** Peter Vandermark/Stock, Boston; **p. 175** UPI/Corbis-Bettmann; **Figs. 5.6 and 5.7** Adapted from "Teaching Machines" by B. F. Skinner. Copyright © 1961 by Scientific American, Inc. All rights reserved; **p. 178** L. Marescot/Gamma-Liaison Network; **p. 181** Archives of the History of American Psychology, University of Akron; **pp. 183 and 184** Courtesy Albert Bandura, Stanford University; **p. 186** *(top)* Courtesy John Garcia; *(bottom)* James Balog; **p. 187** Rick Strange/The Picture Cube.

CHAPTER 6

p. 198 Wernher Krutein/Gamma-Liaison Network; **p. 200** Larry Mayer/Gamma-Liaison Network; **p. 203** Carol Halebeian/Gamma-Liaison Network; **p. 208** Bob Schatz/Gamma-Liaison Network; **p. 209** Don Jurick Studio; **p. 211** Brewer, W. F. & Treyens, J. C. (1981). "Role of schemata in memory for place." *Cognitive Psychology, 13,* Figure 1, pp. 207–230; **p. 212** *(top)* and *(bottom)* UPI/Corbis-Bettmann; **p. 214** Robbie McClaran; **p. 215** Sylvie Chappaz/Vandystadt/Allsport; **p. 220** *(all)* Treë; **p. 223** *(top)* Squire, Larry R., Ojemann, J. G., Miezin, F. M., Petersen, S. E., Videen, T. O., & Raichle, Marcus E. (1992). "Activation of the hippocampus in normal humans: A functional anatomical study of memory." *Proceedings of the National Academy of Sciences, 89,* 1837–1841; *(bottom)* Jonathan Levine; **p. 225** Jonathan Daniel/Allsport.

CHAPTER 7

p. 235 Skjold/The Image Works; **Fig. 7.1** Kosslyn, Stephen M., Reiser, Brian J., Ball, Thomas M. (1978). "Visual images preserve metric spatial information: Evidence from studies of image scanning." *Journal of Experimental Psychology: Perception and Performance, 4* (1), 47–60. Copyright © 1978 by the American Psychological Association. Adapted with permission; **Table 7.1** Rosch, Eleanor H., and Mervis, Carolyn B. (1975). "Family resemblances: Studies in the internal structure of categories." *Cognitive Psychology, 7,* 573–605. Copyright © Academic Press; **p. 238** *(left)* Flip Nicklin/Minden Pictures; *(center)* Merlin D. Tuttle/Photo Researchers, Inc.; *(right)* Dale Spartas/Gamma-Liaison Network; **Fig. 7.3** Problem 1: Ashcraft, Mark H. (1994). *Human Memory and Cognition, 2nd ed.* New York: HarperCollins. Reprinted by permission of Addison-Wesley Educational Publishers, Inc.; Problem 2: Excerpt from *Intelligence Applied: Understanding and Increasing Your Intellectual Skills* by Robert J. Sternberg, Copyright © 1986 by Harcourt, Brace & Company, reprinted by permission of the publisher; **p. 243** UPI/Corbis-Bettmann; **p. 246** Michael Newman/Photo Edit; **p. 249** Frans Lanting/Minden Pictures; **p. 250** *(top)* Courtesy of Language Research Center, Georgia State University, photo Anne Clopet; *(bottom)* Michael Goldman; **p. 251** Archives of the History of American Psychology, University of Akron; **p. 252** Archives of the History of American Psychology, University of Akron; **p. 253** News Service, Stanford University; **p. 254** *(top)* Archives of the History of American Psychology, University of Akron; *(bottom)* Laura Dwight/Photo Edit; **p. 257** *(top)* John Blaustein/Gamma-Liaison Network; *(center)* Andy Freeberg/Gamma-Liaison Network; *(bottom)* Ira Wyman/Sygma; **p. 259** Mary Kate Denny/Photo Edit; **p. 261** Robert A. Isaacs/Photo Researchers, Inc.; **p. 263** Tom Wagner/Saba Press Images; **p. 264** Alexandra Avakian/Contact Press Images; **p. 267** Jerry Cleveland/Denver Post.

CHAPTER 8

p. 273 Lawrence Migdale/Stock, Boston; **p. 277** Nouvelle China/Gamma-Liaison Network; **p. 278** Don Mason/The Stock Market; **p. 279** Courtesy Neal E. Miller, Yale University; **Fig. 8.2** © Richard B. Stuart, Department of Psychiatry, University of Washington; **p. 282** Norberd Schiller/AP/Wide World Photo; **p. 283** Jill Greenberg © 1996 The Walt Disney Co. Reprinted with permission of *Discover Magazine;* **p. 284** Frans Lanting/Minden Pictures; **p. 285** John Chiasson/Gamma-Liaison Network; **p. 288** Burke Uzzle; **p. 289** Deborah Davis/Photo Edit; **Fig. 8.5** From *Sex in America* by Michael et al. Copyright © 1994 by CGS Enterprises, Inc., Edward O. Laumann, Robert T. Michael, and Gina Kolata. By permission of Little, Brown & Co.; **p. 290** Sotographs/Gamma-Liaison Network; **p. 291** Jonathan Novak/Photo Edit; **p. 292** *(both)* Treë; **p. 294** *(top)* Courtesy of the authors; *(bottom)* A. Ramey/Photo Edit; **p. 295** Tom Sanders/Adventure Photo & Film; **p. 296** Doug Pensinger/Allsport; **p. 298** Tony Freeman/Photo Edit; **p. 303** *(top)* and *(center)* From Ekman, P., Friesen, W. V., and O'Sullivan. M. (1988). "Smiles when lying." *Journal of Personality and Social Psychology, 54,* 414–420. Photos courtesy of Paul Ekman; *(bottom)* Eibl-Eibesfeldt, I. (1970). *Ethology: The Biology of Behavior.* New York: Holt Photo Courtesy I. Eibl-Eibesfeldt; **p. 304** *(all photos)* From Matsumoto, D. and Ekman, P. (1989) Japanese and Caucasian Facial Expressions of Emotion. JACFEE. Photographs courtesy of Paul Ekman; **p. 306** Corbis-Bettmann; **p. 307** *(both)* Treë; **p. 309** Nancy Richmond/The Image Works.

CHAPTER 9

p. 317 *(top)* Nancy Sheehan/Photo Edit; *(bottom left)* Merrill Vincent/Photo Edit; *(bottom center)* M. Ferguson/Photo Edit; *(bottom right)* D. Young-Wolff/Photo Edit; **p. 318** CNRI/Science Photo Library/Photo Researchers, Inc.; **p. 320** Biophoto Associates/Photo Researchers, Inc.; **p. 321** *(all photos)* Petit Format/Nestle/Science Source/Photo Researchers, Inc.; **p. 322** *(top)* Elizabeth Crews/The Image Bank;

(bottom) Petit Format/Science Source/Photo Researchers, Inc.; **p. 325** John Lei/Stock, Boston; **p. 327** Stephen Agricola/The Image Works; **p. 328** Romilly Lockyer/The Image Bank; **Fig. 9.3** Marc H. Bornstein and Michael E. Lamb, *Development in Infancy, 3rd ed.* Copyright © 1992 McGraw-Hill. Reproduced with permission of McGraw-Hill, Inc.; **p. 330** *(top)* and *(bottom)* Mryleen Ferguson/Photo Edit; **p. 331** *(left)* Tony Freeman/Photo Edit; *(right)* Myrleen Ferguson/Photo Edit; *(bottom)* From *Good Night, Sleep Tight! Shh . . .* by Gyo Fujikawa. Copyright © 1990 by Gyo Fujikawa. Reprinted by permission of Random House, Inc.; **p. 333** *(top)* Bill Anderson/Monkmeyer Press Photos; *(bottom)* Elizabeth Crews/The Image Bank; **p. 334** *(bottom)* Laura Dwight; **p. 335** *(all photos)* Bill Armstrong; **Fig. 9.4** Baillargeon, Renee & DeVos, Julie (1991). "Object Permanence in Young Infants: Further Evidence." *Child Development, 62,* 1227–1246. Reprinted with permission of the Society for Research in Child Development; **p. 337** Sovfoto/Eastfoto; **p. 338** Jerry Koontz/The Picture Cube; **Fig. 9.5** From *Sex in America* by Michael et al. Copyright © 1994 by CGS Enterprises, Inc., Edward O. Laumann, Robert T. Michael, and Gina Kolata. By permission of Little, Brown & Co.; **p. 339** Bob Daemmrich/Stock, Boston; **p. 340** Sarah Putman/The Picture Cube; **Table 9.4** From *Childhood and Society* by Erik H. Erikson. Copyright 1950, © 1963 by W. W. Norton & Company, Inc., renewed © 1978, 1991 by Erik H. Erikson. Reprinted by permission of W. W. Norton & Company, Inc.; **p. 345** Myrleen Ferguson/Photo Edit; **p. 347** *(left)* Michael Newman/Photo Edit; Michelle Bridwell/Photo Edit; **p. 348** Robert Rathe/Stock, Boston; **p. 349** *(right)* Jonathan Novrok/Photo Edit; *(left)* K. Kurita/Gamma-Liaison Network; **p. 350** Joel Gordon; **p. 354** Lew Merrim/Monkmeyer Press Photos.

CHAPTER 10

p. 360 Courtesy of the authors; **p. 362** Mary Evans/Sigmund Freud Copyrights/Photo Researchers, Inc.; **p. 363** *(top)* Culver Pictures; *(bottom)* Corbis-Bettmann; **p. 365** *(top)* Tony Freeman/Photo Edit; *(center)* Michael Newman/Photo Edit; **p. 366** Eric Futran/Gamma-Liaison Network; **p. 368** Paul Gish/Monkmeyer Press Photos; **p. 370** Karsh/Woodfin Camp & Associates; **p. 371** *(top)* Transparency #3416 (2). Courtesy Dept. of Library Services, American Museum of Natural History, Photo P. Hollembeak; *(center)* Courtesy Dharma Publishing; *(right)* UPI/Corbis-Bettmann; *(bottom)* Scala/Art Resource, NY; **p. 372** UPI/Corbis-Bettmann; **p. 374** Corbis-Bettmann; **p. 375** Courtesy Carl Rogers Memorial Library; **Fig. 10.2** From *Motivation and Personality, 2nd ed.* by Abraham H. Maslow. Copyright 1954 by Harper & Row Publishers, Inc. Copyright © 1970 by Abraham H. Maslow. Reprinted by permission of Addison-Wesley Educational Publishers Inc.; **Box 10.1** First quotation from *Civilization and Its Discontents* by Sigmund Freud, translated by James Strachey. Translation copyright © 1961 by James Strachey, renewed 1989 by Alix Strachey. Reprinted by permission of W. W. Norton & Company, Inc.; Second quotation from *Carl Rogers: Dialogues,* edited by Kirschenbaum and Henderson. Copyright © 1989 by Howard Kirschenbaum and Valerie Land Henderson. Reprinted by permission of Houghton Mifflin Company. All rights reserved; Third quotation from *The Carl Rogers Reader,* edited by Kirschenbaum and Henderson. Copyright © 1989 by Howard Kirschenbaum. Reprinted by permission of Houghton Mifflin Company. All rights reserved; **p. 377** Russell D. Curtis/Photo Researchers, Inc.; **Fig. 10.3** *Social Foundations of Thought & Action* by Bandura, © 1986. Adapted by permission of Prentice-Hall, Inc., Upper Saddle River, NJ; **p. 379** Courtesy Albert Bandura, Stanford University; **p. 380** Jean Hangarter/The Picture Cube; **p. 383** Courtesy Mary Cattell; **Table 10.2** Cattell, Raymond B. (1973) "Personality pinned down." *Psychology Today.* Reprinted with permission from *Psychology Today Magazine,* Copyright © 1973 (Sussex Publishers, Inc.); **Fig. 10.4** *Personality, Genetics and Behavior* by H. J. Eysenck. Copyright © 1982. Reproduced with permission of Greenwood Publishing Group, Inc., Westport, CT. Reprinted with permission; **p. 386** *(top)* Courtesy of the authors; *(bottom)* Michael Springer/Gamma-Liaison Network; **p. 390** *(top)* and *(bottom)* Lew

Merrim/Monkmeyer Press Photos; **Table 10.5** Minnesota Multiphasic Personality Inventory (MMPI-2). Copyright © 1942, 1943 (renewed 1970), 1989 by the Regents of the University of Minnesota. Reproduced by permission of the publisher. "MMPI-2" and "Minnesota Multiphasic Personality Inventory-2" are trademarks owned by the University of Minnesota; **Fig. 10.5** Examples from instruction pages 3 and 14 of the 1993 5th edition of the 16PF®, © Institute for Personality and Ability Testing, P.O. Box 188, Champaign, IL 61820; Figure from Cattell, Raymond B. (1973) "Personality pinned down." *Psychology Today.* Reprinted with permission from Psychology Today Magazine, Copyright © 1973 (Sussex Publishers, Inc.).

CHAPTER 11

p. 401 Tony Freeman/Photo Edit; **p. 402** Alan Carey/The Image Works; **p. 404** Anchorage Daily News/Gamma-Liaison Network; **p. 410** Allan Tannenbaum/Sygma; **p. 413** *(top)* and *(bottom)* From Sherif, Muzafer, Harvey, O.J., White, B. Jack, Hood, William R., & Sherif, Carolyn W. (1961/1988). *The Robbers Cave Experiment: Intergroup Conflict and Cooperation.* Middletown, CT: Wesleyan University Press; **Fig. 11.2** Asch, Solomon E. (1987). *Social Psychology.* Reprinted by permission of Oxford University Press; **p. 415** David Young-Wolff/Photo Edit; **p. 416** Courtesy of CUNY Graduate School and University Center; **p. 417** *(left)* From the film "Obedience," distributed by The New York University Film Library; *(right)* Courtesy Alexandra Milgram; **Figs. 11.3 and 11.4** From *Obedience to Authority* by Stanley Milgram. Copyright © 1974 by Stanley Milgram. Reprinted by permission of HarperCollins Publishers, Inc.; **p. 420** From the film "Obedience" distributed by the New York University Film Library; **p. 421** *(top)* Corbis-Bettmann; *(bottom)* Les Stone/Sygma; **p. 422** *(top)* New York Times Pictures; *(bottom)* Edward Hausner/New York Times Pictures; **p. 423** Tony Freeman/Photo Edit; **p. 424** Freida Leinwand/Monkmeyer Press Photos; **p. 426** Mark Richards/Photo Edit.

CHAPTER 12

p. 432 Myrleen Ferguson/Photo Edit; **Table 12.1** Reprinted by permission of the publisher from Holmes, T. H. & Rahe, R. H. (1967), "The Social Readjustment Ratings Scale," *Journal of Psychosomatic Research, 11,* 213–218. Copyright 1967 by Elsevier Science Inc.; **p. 433** Tony Freeman/Photo Edit; **p. 434** *(left)* Courtesy Richard S. Lazarus, University of California, Berkeley; *(right)* Billy E. Barnes/Stock, Boston; **p. 436** Steve Liss/Gamma-Liaison Network; **p. 439** John Olson, LIFE Magazine © Time Inc.; **p. 441** *(right)* Courtesy Robert Ader, photo by James Montanus, University of Rochester; **p. 441** *(left)* Courtesy Nicholas Cohen, University of Rochester; **p. 442** *(top)* Courtesy Janice Kiecolt-Glaser, Ohio State University College of Medicine; *(bottom)* D. Ogust/The Image Works; **p. 444** *(top)* Mike Okoniewski/The Image Works; *(bottom)* Rob Crandall/Stock, Boston; **p. 446** *(bottom)* Robert Brenner/Photo Edit; **p. 449** *(top)* Frank Siteman/Monkmeyer Press Photos; *(bottom)* Jim Vecchione/Gamma-Liaison Network; **p. 450** Joe Carini/The Image Works; **p. 451** Tony Freeman/Photo Edit; **p. 452** Lester Sloan/Gamma-Liaison Network; **p. 453** Joel Gordon; **p. 456** Piers Cavendish/Zuma.

CHAPTER 13

p. 464 Photofest; **Fig. 13.1** Reprinted with permission from the *Diagnostic and Statistical Manual of Mental Disorders, Fourth Edition.* Copyright 1994 American Psychiatric Association; **p. 465** Treë; **p. 466** Alan Carey/The Image Works; **p. 469** David J. Phillip/AP/Wide World Photos; **p. 471** Bernard Wolf/Monkmeyer Press Photos; **p. 472** *(top)* John Kaprielian/Photo Researchers, Inc.; *(right)* Gilbert S. Grant/Photo Researchers, Inc.; *(bottom)* Seth Resnick; **p. 473** Frank Gotham: Reprinted from *Health* Magazine.; **p. 474** © 1996 American Medical Association, from *Archives of General Psychiatry,*

February 1996, Vol. 53. Courtesy of Jeffrey M. Schwartz; **p. 475** Excerpt from *Darkness Visible: A Memoir of Madness* by William Styron. Copyright © 1990 William Styron. Reprinted by permission of Random House, Inc.; **p. 475** Eric Feinblatt/Sygma; **p. 477** Jonathan Exley/Gamma-Liaison Network; **p. 479** *(left)* and *(right)* Corbis-Bettmann; **p. 479** *(center)* Robet Capa/Magnum Photos; **p. 482** K. McGlynn/The Image Works; **p. 485** Courtesy Mental Health Clinical Research Center, University of Iowa; **p. 486** Courtesy David Silbersweig, M.D.: Emily Stern, M. D. Cornell Medical Center; **Fig. 13.4** Bracha, H. S., Wolkowitz, O. M., Lohr, J. B., Karson, C. N., and Bigelow, L. B. (1989). "High prevalence of visual hallucinations in research subjects with chronic schizophrenia." *American Journal of Psychiatry, 146,* 526–528. Copyright 1989, the American Psychiatric Association. Reprinted by permission; Kim T. Mueser, Ph.D., New Hampshire-Dartmouth Psychiatric Research Center; **Fig. 13.6** From: *Schizophrenia Genesis* by Gottesman. Copyright © 1991 by Irving I. Gottesman. Used with permission of W.H. Freeman and Company; **p. 491** Joe McNally/National Geographic Society Image Collection.

CHAPTER 14

p. 500 Edmund Engelman; **p. 502** Michael Rougier, LIFE Magazine © 1966 Time Warner, Inc.; **p. 503** Dratch/The Image Works; **p. 504**

Larson/Watson Papers, Archives of the History of American Psychology, University of Akron; **p. 506** *(top)* Kevin Horan; *(left)* Courtesy Wayne Simpson, Simtek, Inc.; **Fig. 14.2** Reprinted from Tammie Ronen, "Intervention package for treating sleep disorders in a four-year-old girl," *Journal of Behavior Therapy and Experimental Psychiatry,* pp. 141–148. Copyright 1991 with kind permission from Elsevier Science Ltd., The Boulevard, Langford Lane, Kidlington OX5 1GB, UK; **p. 509** Courtesy of Albert Ellis; **p. 510** Courtesy of Aaron T. Beck, University of Pennsylvania Medical Center; **p. 513** *(top)* F. Pedrick/The Image Works; *(bottom)* Michael Newman/Photo Edit; **p. 514** Hank Morgan/Science Source/Photo Researchers, Inc.; **p. 517** Michael Newman/Photo Edit; **p. 518** Steve Liss/Gamma-Liaison Network; **p. 519** *(right)* The Granger Collection; *(center)* Corbis-Bettman; *(left)* Culver Pictures; **Fig. 14.5** From: *A Primer of Drug Action, 7/e* by Julien. Copyright © 1995 by W.H. Freeman and Company. Used with permission; **p. 522** Corbis-Bettmann; **p. 525** Paul S. Howell/Gamma-Liaison Network; **p. 526** James Wilson/Woodfin Camp & Associates.

Name Index

Subject Index